___ 31. Circumcision makes it more difficult for a male to control ejaculation.

___ 32. Nocturnal emissions, or "wet dreams," often are a sign of sexual problems.

___ 33. Brain damage can be one of the results of untreated syphilis.

___ 34. Certain foods have been shown to be aphrodisiacs (sexual stimulants).

___ 35. Transvestites are individuals who receive sexual pleasure from dressing in the clothes of the opposite sex.

___ 36. Young married couples who have an active sex life are more likely to maintain regular sexual activity in their old age than are less sexually active couples.

___ 37. Relatively few cases of frigidity are caused by biological problems.

___ 38. Women generally enjoy rape although they are unlikely to admit it.

___ 39. It is possible to get "crabs" without having sex with anyone.

___ 40. The condom (rubber) is the most reliable birth-control method.

___ 41. A woman can get pregnant again while she is breast-feeding her baby.

___ 42. A woman's desire for sexual activity usually shows a great decrease after the first three months of pregnancy.

___ 43. Males are capable of experiencing multiple orgasms during sexual intercourse.

___ 44. The vaginal walls secrete most of the fluid that lubricates the vagina during sexual arousal.

___ 45. There are no medical reasons why a woman cannot engage in sexual intercourse during her menstrual period.

___ 46. A female can become pregnant the first time she has sexual intercourse.

___ 47. A female does not have to experience orgasm in order to become pregnant.

___ 48. Friction along the walls of the vagina causes orgasm in most females.

___ 49. Large breasts are more sensitive to sexual stimulation than are small breasts.

___ 50. Large amounts of alcohol inhibit sexual performance.

___ 51. Sexual intercourse during pregnancy is the most frequent cause of twins.

___ 52. In studies on sexual arousal, women report being aroused by sexual material almost as frequently as do men.

___ 53. Males who expose themselves in public (exhibitionists) are seldom dangerous.

___ 54. Castration of an adult male will cause his voice to change.

___ 55. The larger the penis, the more the vagina is stimulated in sexual intercourse.

___ 56. A diaphragm should remain in place for at least six hours following sexual intercourse if it is to be effective in preventing conception.

___ 57. Douching solutions sold in stores are more effective as a contraceptive than is regular water.

___ 58. AIDS is caused by one or more viruses.

___ 59. Most cases of gonorrhea ("clap") take several years to disappear even with medical treatment.

___ 60. A mother with syphilis can transmit the disease to her unborn child.

# STUDY SMARTER

*With a little help from this specially designed study aid, you can prepare easily and effectively for tests to get the best grade possible.*

## STUDY GUIDE (0-669-33338-7) includes:

- Overviews of all the textbook chapters plus study objectives to help you review the material in the text.

- Multiple-choice, fill-ins, and matching exercises, plus an answer key to reinforce what you have read.

- Short-answer essay questions and critical thinking activities to help you clarify your own personal values and beliefs about sexuality.

## LOOK FOR THIS SUPPLEMENT IN YOUR BOOKSTORE.

If you don't find it, check with your bookstore manager or call
D. C. Heath toll free at 1-800-334-3284. In Canada,
call toll free at 1-800-268-2472.
Shipping, handling, and state tax may be added where applicable
(tell the operator you are placing a #1-PREFER order).

# Sexual
## Interactions

# Sexual
# Interactions

## FOURTH EDITION

## Albert Richard Allgeier
Allgeier and Associates, Bowling Green, Ohio

## Elizabeth Rice Allgeier
Bowling Green State University

D. C. Heath and Company
Lexington, Massachusetts   Toronto

*Address editorial correspondence to*:

D. C. Heath and Company
125 Spring Street
Lexington, MA 02173

Acquisitions Editor: Randall Adams
Developmental Editor: Elisa Adams
Production Editor: Carolyn Ingalls
Designer: Jan Shapiro
Photo Researcher: Mary Lang
Art Editor: Jim Roberts
Production Coordinator: Dick Tonachel
Permissions Editor: Margaret Roll

Cover: "Cupid and Psyche" by Antonio Canova (detail), marble/Louvre/Archiv fur Kunst und Geschichte

International Standard Book Number: 0-669-33337-9

Library of Congress Catalog Number: 94-75587

10 9 8 7 6 5 4 3 2 1

*We dedicate this book with much love*
*to our parents, children, and grandchildren,*
*Forrest, Laurel, Larkin, Maya, and Max.*

# About the Authors

Albert Richard Allgeier earned his B.A. from Gannon University in 1967, his M.A. from the American University of Beirut in Lebanon in 1969, and his Ph.D. from Purdue University in 1974. He has been Clinical Director at both the Northwest Center for Human Resources in Lima, Ohio, and the Wood County Mental Health Center in Bowling Green, Ohio. He has served on the faculty of Alma College, the State University of New York at Fredonia, and Bowling Green State University. Currently, he is in private practice in Bowling Green. He has conducted research on interpersonal attraction and sexual knowledge, and has participated with his wife, Elizabeth Rice Allgeier, in a series of studies on attitudes about abortion. He is also interested in the implications of evolutionary theory for the study of human sexuality.

Elizabeth Rice Allgeier earned her B.A. from the University of Oregon in 1969, her M.S. from the State University of New York at Oswego in 1973, and her Ph.D. from Purdue University in 1976. Currently Professor of Psychology at Bowling Green State University, she has won numerous teaching awards, including the BGSU Alumni Association's Master Teacher Award in 1988, and the BGSU Outstanding Contributor to Graduate Education in 1992. In 1986, she was named the American Psychological Association's G. Stanley Hall Lecturer on Sexuality. She has taught human sexuality at Eastern Michigan University and at the State University of New York at Fredonia. Dr. Allgeier's interest in studying human sexual behavior began while she was living with the So, a preliterate, polygynous tribe in Uganda. Her study of this tribe resulted in a two-volume ethnography that she coauthored. Her current research interests include the societal regulation of sexual behavior, sexual coercion, and the relationship between gender-role norms and sexual interaction. On the last-named subject, she edited, with Naomi McCormick, *Changing Boundaries: Gender Roles and Sexual Behavior* (1983). Actively involved in The Society for the Scientific Study of Sex, she has served as national secretary and as president for that organization, and in 1991 was awarded its Distinguished Service Award. In 1994, she was also awarded the Alfred C. Kinsey Award for Outstanding Contributions to Sexual Science by the Midcontinent Region of The Society for the Scientific Study of Sex. She sits on the editorial board of four scholarly journals that publish sex research and currently is editor of *The Journal of Sex Research*.

The Allgeiers have four children ranging in age from 16 to 31, and five grandchildren. They enjoy traveling, reading novels, and watching college athletics.

# Preface

In the short time since we completed the third edition of *Sexual Interactions,*many developments have arises in the field of human sexuality. Controversies over sex education, sexual orientation, abortion, birth control, the effects of erotic materials, appropriate treatments for those who reject their gender, sexual coercion, child-adult sexual contacts, and other sexual issues continue to rage, fueling a fire storm of rhetoric and, to a lesser extent, important empirical research on these topics. The specter of Acquired Immuno-deficiency Syndrome (AIDS) has darkened the sexual landscape and will undoubtedly continue to affect sexual feelings and behavior until a vaccine or cure is found. In this fourth edition, we hope to convey the challenges, complexities, and wonder of human sexuality while retaining the multidisciplinary approach we employed in the first three editions.

## An Integrative Approach to an Emerging Discipline

Consistent with the goals of the earlier editions, we had two primary objectives in this revision. First, we chose to integrate religion and ethics, cross-cultural comparisons, and the regulation of sexual behavior with the specific topics described in each chapter. For example, in the chapter on sexual orientation (Chapter 15), we consider cross-cultural attitudes about homosexuality, religious views, and laws and norms regulating partner choice. We employed a similar integrative approach in discussing sexually transmitted diseases (Chapter 17), describing not only the causes and treatments of the diseases themselves, but also societal attitudes, psychological reactions, legislative actions, and methods of communicating with potential partners to reduce the risk of contracting HIV/AIDS and other STDs. We believe that it is important to acknowledge

that sexual attitudes and behavior cannot be understood in terms of biological/physiological factors, or emotional factors, or cultural, religious, or legal factors alone. Rather, each person's experience with sexuality is the result of complex interactions of these influences, always in the context of his or her unique life history and circumstances. Thus we treat the topics in each of the 20 chapters in this edition from multiple perspectives.

Our second objective was to demonstrate, without undue solemnity, that human sexuality is a subject of serious intellectual inquiry. This goal has become easier to achieve in this edition owing to the continued development of both theoretical foundations and methodologies for investigating sexual decisions and behaviors.

## A Research-Based Approach with Practical Applications

Throughout the book, we have relied heavily on the accumulated wisdom from history and literature and on contemporary research findings in anthropology, biology, health education, medicine, sociology, and psychology to provide accurate information about the diverse topics that make up the study of human sexuality. We have included practical information aimed at helping students to make informed decisions about a wide variety of sexual issues. Assuming no prior course work in physiology, we have presented a thorough treatment of the biological aspects. We have aimed for an unbiased treatment of the sensitive issues related to sexuality, and, in keeping with our integrative approach, have offered a research-based perspective on love and sex and realistic advice on ways to experience mature, loving sexual interactions.

Because the scientific study of sexuality is young, many questions remain unanswered. For that reason, we have focused heavily on ways of evaluating new information as it emerges. We hope that our readers will become both competent and cautious in assessing conclusions from the newly published studies frequently profiled in the mass media.

## Overview of the Contents of *Sexual Interactions*, Fourth Edition

For those familiar with the earlier editions of *Sexual Interactions*, an overview of the major differences between the earlier editions and the current edition may be helpful. Chapter 1, "Perspectives on Sexuality," provides a broad historical and cross-cultural perspective to help readers reexamine their probable assumptions that their own attitudes and beliefs about sexuality are "natural" or reflect a "correct" view. Thus the chapter retains the third edition's topical (rather than chronological) review of variations in sexual attitudes and behaviors. The range of topics is not exhaustive, of course, but the subjects were selected to demonstrate the enormous diversity in the behavior, beliefs, and regulation of sexual issues during different historical periods and by different societies.

In Chapter 2, "Research on Sexuality," we retained descriptions of the personal costs paid by such pioneers in the study of sexuality as the Kinsey group, William Masters and Virginia Johnson, and Vern Bullough, as they tried to gather reliable data. This edition contains new material on the problems besetting contemporary researchers' attempts to collect scientific data on various sexual behaviors. For example, the initial federal approval and subsequent congressional blockage of two major national studies, both aimed at obtaining information to help people to alter sexual behavior to reduce their risk of contracting AIDS, is described in considerable detail. To demonstrate that such erotophobic behavior is not peculiar to the United States, we also describe the former Ceaușescu regime's response to AIDS in Romania. The section that describes the sex-research process continues to emphasize developing competency in evaluating research conclusions.

In Chapter 3, "Contemporary Explanations of Human Sexuality," we have retained coverage of the four major theoretical perspectives: evolutionary, psychoanalytic, social learning, and sociological. We discuss kinship and jealousy, power and gender, and possible influence of ideological positions on beliefs about what constitutes normal sexuality. We have also incorporated new research on the criteria used in mate selection.

Chapter 4, "Development and Sexual Differentiation," contains material on atypical physical differentiation both before and after birth. The section on transsexuality has been moved to Chapter 19. Chapter 5 covers anatomy, hormones, and the nervous system. We present some new material on the Gräfenberg spot, although research on the topic has been minimal since the initial flurry of work in the early 1980s.

In Chapter 5, "Sexual Anatomy and Physiology," we have incorporated coverage of the cancers and diabetes from Chapter 14, as well as new information on those topics. In response to recommendations of instructors using the text, Chapter 6, "Arousal and Communication," in the current edition continues to focus heavily on communication. Communication issues are also discussed in other relevant chapters, because we believe that repetition and reinforcement of this essential topic is crucial for students.

Aside from updated references, Chapter 7, "Sexual Behavior," retains the same general organization as before and continues to emphasize the importance of using safer-sex practices, given the data linking some forms of sexual pleasure with the potential transmission of AIDS. Chapter 8, "Sexual Dysfunctions and Therapy," continues the basic framework of the third edition and presents the most recent research.

Chapter 9 contains updated material on the events involved in pregnancy and birth. The latest data on substances dangerous to the mother and fetus are discussed in this chapter, and the current controversy regarding circumcision is examined.

Chapter 10, "Contraception," updates information on contraceptive behavior, particularly among adolescents, and reviews existing birth control methods. We also discuss cross-cultural studies on the relationship between the provision of contraceptive education and devices. The research illustrates that countries providing more intensive sexual and contraceptive education have lower rates of unwanted pregnancies and abortions than characterize the United States.

Chapter 11, "Resolving Unwanted Pregnancy," features updated coverage of unwanted pregnancy and the correlates of unplanned parenthood for the baby, the single mother, and/or the couple. The often confusing and contradictory laws regulating abortion have been streamlined into a new box in this chapter.

In Chapters 12 and 13, we examine sexual development over the life span. Chapter 12, "Gender and Sexuality in Childhood and Adolescence," covers gender differences and similarities in sexual socialization from toddlerhood on and describes the latest research on the initial sexual experimentation and relationship formation that occur during adolescence. We have moved the material on sexual and reproductive maturation to Chapter 4 because of its biological emphasis and added a major new section comparing abstinence-only versus postponement-and-protection approaches to sex education. Evaluation studies clearly illustrate the effectiveness of the latter over the abstinence-only curricula for increasing the likelihood that young people will postpone intercourse, and that those who do decide to become sexually active will use contraceptives. In Chapter 13, "Gender and Sexuality in Adulthood," we retain the same structure as in the third edition. In addition to updating, we have included recent studies suggesting an increase in monogamy among married couples and cohabiting gay or heterosexual couples.

In Chapter 14, "Enhancing Sexual Health," we have added and updated material on infertility formerly presented in Chapter 9. The research on aphrodisiacs and anaphrodisiacs also has been updated. We also discuss body image and eating disorders and their relationship to sexual behavior. We conclude Chapter 14 with a discussion of epilepsy, a disorder formerly thought to interfere with sexual desire and response. Research has shown that particular treatments, rather than the disability itself, appear to be responsible for decrements in sexual capacity, and we point out that this may also be the case for a number of other diseases and disabilities traditionally thought to interfere with sexual response.

Although variations in sexual orientation are considered throughout the text, Chapter 15, "Sexual Orientation," focuses on what is known about similarities and differences in the history and life experiences of people who have heterosexual, bisexual, and homosexual relationships. Attempts to understand various facets of sexual orientation continue to receive a good deal of attention by researchers, so we have updated this chapter extensively, including research by LeVay (1993) on brain differences between gay and heterosexual men, and Hamer et al.'s (1993) report of a region of the X chromosome that contains genetic material for homosexual orientation. We have retained and updated the material on adjustment, antigay prejudice, and bisexuality (which continues to receive relatively little attention by researchers).

Chapter 16, "Sex for Profit," considers the use of sex in advertising, erotic media, and prostitution. We cover the soft-core and hard-core erotica industry, the relationship between fantasies and exposure to erotica, and legal stances toward the availability of erotica. In a major section on public policy and the "effects" of erotica we critically evaluate research on this topic. We examine the issue of X-rated versus R-rated movies and the portrayal of violence and gender-role inequality in each. The final section discusses prostitution and the numerous controversies surrounding this form of sexual interaction. A full-color picture essay explores the history of sexual themes in advertising and in popular entertainment.

In Chapter 17, "Sexually Transmitted Diseases" (STDs), we review the major STDs and discuss how societal attitudes may impede efforts to reduce them. A great deal more has become known about AIDS since we published the last edition in 1991, and this heavily revised chapter reflects the explosion of information. We have included a self-test box so that students can probe the accuracy of their knowledge about AIDS before they read about it. We have devoted considerable space to describing those particular sexual behaviors that increase one's risk for AIDS, emphasizing that sexual orientation per se is irrelevant; and we present new research on the stigma faced by AIDS patients. We stress that one contracts AIDS from contact with blood or body fluids containing the human immunodeficiency virus (HIV). The chapter ends with practical advice on negotiating sexual relationships and on giving and receiving informed consent about past sexual behaviors. We use the word *safer* to describe these sex practices, agreeing with those who have pointed out that the modifier *safe* is misleading. There are no 100% guarantees, but through knowledge and honest communication with potential sex partners, one can reduce the risk of negative or undesired consequences of sexual intimacy.

Chapter 18, "Sexual Coercion," covers sexual assault, sexual harassment, and child sexual abuse. Research on these topics has been very active, requiring considerable updating for this edition. The material on rape focuses heavily on acquaintance assault because studies have revealed that females and males alike are at far greater risk of assault by acquaintances than by strangers. We have retained and updated the treatment of hypotheses about the causes and the psychological and legal sequelae of sexual assault, and we have included material on communication and other methods of reducing vulnerability to sexual coercion. The second half of the chapter explores sexual harassment in occupational, educational, and therapeutic settings. Recent research on sexual relationships between children and adults indicates that the short- and long-term correlates of such sexual experiences on youngsters vary considerably, depending on the extent of force, the context, and the reactions of significant others to the sexual contact.

In updated Chapter 19, "Atypical Sexual Activity," we distinguish between those activities that are noninvasive (for example, fetishes and transvestism) and those that are invasive of others' rights (for example, voyeurism and pedophilia). Our description of transsexuality (in Chapter 4 in the third edition) has been moved to the section on noninvasive conditions here. We have added material on the effect of cognitive-behavior therapies in reducing recidivism rates for the invasive paraphilias.

Although a few instructors have questioned our decision to make "Loving Sexual Interactions" the final chapter (20), others have expressed appreciation for the optimistic tone and the rounding-off of the text that this concluding chapter provides. We have retained and updated material from the third edition, including Sternberg's model of love. A.R.A. has found this triadic model of love involving passion, intimacy, and decision/commitment useful in his clinical practice, and E.R.A. has observed considerable enthusiasm among her students as they examine their own current relationships in light of Sternberg's conceptualization of the variety of forms that love can take.

## Supplementary Materials

*Sexual Interactions*, Fourth Edition, has an unusually complete and high-quality supplementary program:

- A greatly expanded and improved *Instructor's Guide with Test Item File*, written by Deborah McDonald Winters and Elizabeth R. Allgeier, containing E.R.A.'s lecture notes and other classroom demonstrations, projects, and exercises, and a wealth of multiple-choice and essay items. The test items are also available in a computerized testing program for both the Macintosh and the IBM.

- A *Study Guide*, rewritten by Jan Campbell, providing students with a brief overview and outline of the contents of each chapter and detailed learning objectives. It also features numerous samples of multiple-choice, sentence-completion, and short-answer essay questions, as well as exercises asking students to analyze recent newspaper reports dealing with issues in human sexuality. There are also diagrams of the male and female sexual anatomy and questions asking students to identify various bodily structures.

- Media Policy, a variety of films and videos to help enliven classes, available to adopters. Instructors should contact their local D. C. Heath sales representatives for further information about these materials.

- A set of transparencies for projection in the classroom.

- A newsletter, *The Allgeier Update*, issued periodically to all adopters. We review the latest research findings that affect the substance of our discussion and pass along suggestions for teaching, including interesting tips from our adopters, making the newsletter a lively as well as informative forum. To become a newsletter subscriber, contact your sales representative or call D. C. Heath directly at 1-800-235-3565.

## Acknowledgments

One of the most pleasant tasks associated with publishing a book is to acknowledge the help and advice we have received from many people. When we began the first edition of this book 17 years ago, we had the luxury of choosing from a number of companies to publish our text. We selected D. C. Heath because its staff shared our commitment to producing a mainstream introductory survey of human sexuality. Many of the contributions of the editors, designers, artists, and reviewers of the first three editions have been retained in the fourth edition.

In preparing subsequent editions, we naively assumed that revising would be relatively easy compared to writing the first edition. We have been wrong in this assumption; but, on the other hand, it has been exciting to witness and pass on the ever-accumulating knowledge about human sexuality. We have been unusually blessed with our editors: Nancy Osman in the first edition, James Miller in the second edition, Sylvia Mallory in the third edition, and Randall Adams in the current edition. As I (E.R.A.) sit here typing this, I am smiling at the opportunity to express our good fortune in having the help of these four editors, each of whom has improved the quality of *Sexual Interactions*.

We also wish to express our appreciation to the other D. C. Heath staff members who helped with the fourth edition. Our production editor, Carolyn Ingalls, has been wonderfully clear and thorough. We are particularly pleased with the new illustrations that photo editor Mary Lang obtained for this edition. We thank designers Henry Rachlin and Jan Shapiro for their beautiful and accessible design; permissions editor Margaret Roll, who secured all the necessary text permissions; and production coordinator Dick Tonachel. Editorial associate Heather Monahan was a very pleasant liaison and very helpful in preparing the text for production, particularly the art manuscript. Our copyeditor, Sarah Doyle, did an excellent job of clarifying our prose. We also thank Karen Silverio, our product manager for the previous edition, and Corinne Castano, our product manager for this edition. Both of them have brought great energy, enthusiasm, and insight to the job of helping us reach our audience for the previous and the current edition.

Although space does not permit us to acknowledge all the reviewers of the first three editions, many contributors' suggestions are reflected in the current edition. We thank M. Betsy Bergen, Kansas State University; Katherine Bruce, University of North Carolina, Wilmington; Robert Brush, Purdue University; Vern Bullough, State University of New York–Buffalo; T. Jean Byrne, Kent State University; Sandra Cole, University of Michigan Medical Center; Eva Conrad, San Bernardino Valley College; William W. Darrow, Centers for Disease Control; Clive M. Davis, Syracuse University; John DeLamater, University of Wisconsin; Lewis Diana, Virginia Commonwealth University; Joan Fimbel DiGiovanni, Western New England College; Beverley Drinnen, Des Moines Area Community College; Robert Embree, Westmar College; Gene Ezell, University of Tennessee, Chattanooga; Randy D. Fisher, University of Central Florida; William A. Fisher, University of Western Ontario; Greer Litton Fox, Wayne State University; Robert Friar, Ferris State University; Frederick P. Gault, Western Michigan University; Donald Granberg, University of Missouri at Columbia; Shelley Green, East Carolina University; Pat House, University of Illinois, Urbana-Champaign; Betty Hubbard, University of Central Arkansas; Louis Janda, Old Dominion University; James D. Johnson, University of North Carolina, Wilmington; Anthony P. Jurich, Kansas State University; Lois Kessler, San Diego State University; Douglas Kimmel, City University of New York; Vera Konig, Nassau Community College; Eugene Levitt, Indiana University School of Medicine; James Lochner, Weber State University; Patricia MacCorquodale, University of Arizona; Elinor MacDonald, Quinebaug Valley Community College; Jay Mancini, Virginia Polytechnic Institute; David McAllister, Borough of Manhattan Community College; Naomi McCormick, State University of New York at Plattsburgh; Norma L. McCoy, San Francisco State

University; Deborah McDonald, New Mexico State University; Lee Meserve, Bowling Green State University; Marilyn Myerson, University of South Florida; Judith Nevin, University of Arizona; Patty Reagan, University of Utah; Lauralee Rockwell, University of Iowa; Laurna Rubinson, University of Illinois, Urbana-Champaign; Herb Samuels, La Guardia Community College; Donald Schaffer, Broward Community College; Jane Smith, University of New Mexico; Wendy Stock, Texas A & M University; Deborah Stone, University of Southern Maine; Michael Storms, University of Kansas; Gail Thoen, University of Minnesota; Kenrick S. Thompson, Northern Michigan University; Gay Thrower, Arizona Western College; T. Nicholas Tormey, Drake University; Jane L. Veith, Washington State University; Donald Wagner, University of Cincinnati Medical Center; John Wattendorf, U.S. Military Academy; James D. Weinrich, University of California, San Diego; Joel Wells, University of Northern Iowa; Beverly Whipple, Jefferson Medical College; and Sarah Murnen, Diane Phillis, and George Scheuch, all at Bowling Green State University at the time that they provided reviews.

Reviewers and others who provided valuable resources for the fourth edition include Veanne N. Anderson, Indiana State University; Thomas E. Billimek, San Antonio College; Toni M. Blake, University of Nebraska–Lincoln; Martha Wingerd Bristor, Michigan State University; T. Jean Byrne, Kent State University; James F. Calhoun, University of Georgia; James Dedic, Cypress College; William W. Darrow, Centers for Disease Control; Saul Feinman, University of Wyoming and Navajo Community College; Nicholas E. Heyneman, Idaho State University; Peggy J. Kleinplatz, University of Ottawa; Sydney Langdon, Arizona State University; Roger N. Moss, California State University–Northridge; Mary Davis Nickerson, Andover College; Robert H. Pollack, University of Georgia; Galdino F.

Pranzarone, Roanoke College; Harry M. Robinson, Jr., Bryant College; Kathy Shepherd Stolley, Old Dominion University; Kenrick S. Thompson, Northern Michigan University; Mary Ann Watson, Metropolitan State College of Denver; and Deborah McDonald Winters, New Mexico State University. In addition to helpful comments made by many of our undergraduate students, a number of E.R.A.'s current graduate students have made suggestions and provided astute observations that have found their way into the current edition. These colleagues include Sherral Austin, Jennifer C. Lamping, Lucia F. O'Sullivan, Christine C. Sensibaugh, Ronald R. Ross, and last but definitely not least, Michael W. Wiederman. Finally, many improvements in the fourth edition are the result of letters and phone calls from instructors who used earlier editions, and we thank them for their praise as well as their constructive suggestions.

One of us (E.R.A.) is fortunate to be affiliated with the Department of Psychology at Bowling Green State University. Two successive chairpersons of my department, Bob Conner and Joe Cranny, provided extremely important, though relatively indirect, support. Beyond telling me not to work so hard, they helped me when I was frantic over broken external disk drives or pressing deadlines; and they, along with a number of other members of my department, consistently contribute to a wonderful work environment.

Finally, we thank our immediate and extended family for the fourth time for accepting our preoccupation with this book. Our four offspring, Beth, Sarah, Kate, and Don, have generally handled our alternating states of frustration and euphoria with remarkable aplomb. All four of them have offered insights that have found their way into this book.

ALBERT RICHARD ALLGEIER

ELIZABETH RICE ALLGEIER

# Contents

## 3  *Contemporary Explanations of Human Sexuality*  65

## 4  *Development and Sexual Differentiation*  91

## 5   Sexual Anatomy and Physiology   123

## 6   Arousal and Communication   161

## 7  *Sexual Behavior*

## 8  *Sexual Dysfunctions and Therapy*

## 9  *Pregnancy and Birth*   263

# 10 *Contraception*

# 11 *Resolving Unwanted Pregnancy*

## 12 *Gender and Sexuality in Childhood and Adolescence* 371

## 13 *Gender and Sexuality in Adulthood* 415

## 14  *Enhancing Sexual Health*

## 15  *Sexual Orientation*

## 16  *Sex for Profit*

# ✳ 17  *Sexually Transmitted Diseases*                    **553**

# ✳ 18  *Sexual Coercion*                    **591**

*19 Atypical Sexual Activity*  637

# 20 *Loving Sexual Interactions*

# Introduction

The classroom atmosphere on the first day in a human sexuality course is usually charged with tension, and laughter is frequent—perhaps indicating anxiety. A study was conducted indicating that people who feel guilty (therefore anxious) about sex remember less information from a lecture about birth control than do those with less guilt (Schwartz, 1973). This is supported by Robert Hatfield's (1987) finding that students in human sexuality classes taking an exam in which half the multiple-choice items contain a choice evoking humor score significantly better than do students who are given an exam in which none of the answers are intended to be humorous. Even students who are highly anxious when taking tests got a higher grade on the humorous version than on the nonhumorous version of the exam.

Many students enroll in the course with personal concerns and trepidations not associated with enrolling in other classes. Some have even been asked by parents or roommates to justify taking the class. The queries have ranged from "Why would you want to take a dirty class like that?" to "How can it take a whole semester just to study sex?" One woman dropped our class after her fiancé saw it listed on her schedule. She told us apologetically, "He won't let me take it. He said he'll teach me anything I need to know about sex after we get married."

When we first began teaching human sexuality, we were struck by the qualities in the students who enrolled. They seemed to be more sexually active and knowledgeable than were students enrolled in other courses offered at a comparable level. We tested our impression on the first day of class by surveying sexual attitudes, behaviors, and knowledge among students in a sexuality course and among those in several other courses. The knowledge of students in the sexuality course was typically more accurate than that of students enrolled in other classes, and their attitudes tended to be more tolerant.

You might take a few minutes to respond to an updated version of the Sexual Knowledge Survey (Allgeier, 1978a,b). In addition to letting you know how accurate your knowledge is before you read this book, it will also give you an idea of the range of topics to be covered.

## The Sexual Knowledge Survey

**Instructions:** This is a survey of the accuracy of your knowledge about human sexual behavior. Each of the following statements can be answered true or false. Answers appear in Appendix A on page A1.

____ 1. A female can become pregnant during sexual intercourse without the male's having an orgasm.

____ 2. The imbalance of sexual hormones is the most frequent cause of homosexuality.

____ 3. Women can become sexually aroused when breast-feeding an infant.

____ 4. Direct contact between the penis and clitoris is necessary to produce female orgasm during sexual intercourse.

____ 5. There are no biological differences in orgasms attained through sexual intercourse, masturbation, or any other technique.

____ 6. Males are not able to have an erection until they reach puberty (adolescence).

____ 7. Women are biologically more capable of multiple orgasms than are men.

___ 8. A hysterectomy (removal of the uterus) causes the loss of sexual desire in women.

___ 9. There are two different types of biological orgasms in women: clitoral and vaginal.

___ 10. The area most sensitive to sexual stimulation in most women is the clitoris.

___ 11. Erection of the nipples is often a sign of sexual arousal in the male.

___ 12. Homosexual behavior, masturbation, and rape occur among other species of animals besides humans.

___ 13. Rapists have an above-average sex drive.

___ 14. In this culture, some homosexual behavior is often a normal part of growing up.

___ 15. A male is not able to have an orgasm until he reaches puberty (adolescence).

___ 16. Sexual intercourse after the first six months of pregnancy is usually dangerous to the health of the mother or the fetus.

___ 17. Sex criminals use pornographic material more often in their youth than does the average person in this culture.

___ 18. Most prostitutes are nymphomaniacs.

___ 19. The majority of cases of impotency are caused by psychological problems.

___ 20. The rhythm method is just as effective as the birth control pill in preventing pregnancy.

___ 21. Masturbation by a married person is almost always related to marriage problems.

___ 22. The castration of an adult male always results in a loss of his sexual desire.

___ 23. Almost all homosexuals can be identified by their physical characteristics.

___ 24. Sexual satisfaction associated with the infliction of pain is called sadism.

___ 25. If a female does not have a hymen (maidenhead, "cherry"), she is not a virgin.

___ 26. Sexual stimulation often causes erection of the nipples of the female breasts.

___ 27. A majority of the sexual crimes committed against children are committed by adults who are friends or relatives of the victim.

___ 28. For a short period following orgasm, men usually are not able to respond to further stimulation.

___ 29. Frequent masturbation is one of the most common causes of premature ejaculation.

___ 30. During lovemaking, it usually takes the female less time to become sexually aroused and reach climax than it does the male.

___ 31. Circumcision makes it more difficult for a male to control ejaculation.

___ 32. Nocturnal emissions, or "wet dreams," often are a sign of sexual problems.

___ 33. Brain damage can be one of the results of untreated syphilis.

___ 34. Certain foods have been shown to be aphrodisiacs (sexual stimulants).

___ 35. Transvestites are individuals who receive sexual pleasure from dressing in the clothes of the opposite sex.

___ 36. Young married couples who have an active sex life are more likely to maintain regular sexual activity in their old age than are less sexually active couples.

___ 37. Relatively few cases of frigidity are caused by biological problems.

___ 38. Women generally enjoy rape although they are unlikely to admit it.

___ 39. It is possible to get "crabs" without having sex with anyone.

___ 40. The condom (rubber) is the most reliable birth-control method.

___ 41. A woman can get pregnant again while she is breast-feeding her baby.

___ 42. A woman's desire for sexual activity usually shows a great decrease after the first three months of pregnancy.

___ 43. Males are capable of experiencing multiple orgasms during sexual intercourse.

___ 44. The vaginal walls secrete most of the fluid that lubricates the vagina during sexual arousal.

___ 45. There are no medical reasons why a woman cannot engage in sexual intercourse during her menstrual period.

___ 46. A female can become pregnant the first time she has sexual intercourse.

___ 47. A female does not have to experience orgasm in order to become pregnant.

___ 48. Friction along the walls of the vagina causes orgasm in most females.

___ 49. Large breasts are more sensitive to sexual stimulation than are small breasts.

___ 50. Large amounts of alcohol inhibit sexual performance.

___ 51. Sexual intercourse during pregnancy is the most frequent cause of twins.

___ 52. In studies on sexual arousal, women report being aroused by sexual material almost as frequently as do men.

___ 53. Males who expose themselves in public (exhibitionists) are seldom dangerous.

___ 54. Castration of an adult male will cause his voice to change.

___ 55. The larger the penis, the more the vagina is stimulated in sexual intercourse.

___ 56. A diaphragm should remain in place for at least six hours following sexual intercourse if it is to be effective in preventing conception.

___ 57. Douching solutions sold in stores are more effective as a contraceptive than is regular water.

___ 58. AIDS is caused by one or more viruses.

___ 59. Most cases of gonorrhea ("clap") take several years to disappear even with medical treatment.

___ 60. A mother with syphilis can transmit the disease to her unborn child.

## Sexual Interactions: Goals, Focus, and Values

The scientific study of sexuality is very new. With the loosening of sexual taboos in the past few decades, a great deal of research has been devoted to human sexuality. This research activity produces both frustration and a great deal of excitement among scholars in the area. No sooner is a book about sexuality published than new research emerges that questions the "facts" published in the book. It is quite possible, therefore, that a few of the "correct" answers to the sex knowledge survey will be modified by the results of future research.

The first three chapters in this book reflect two general convictions regarding sexual values. First, it is important to know something about the past in order to understand and form opinions about contemporary issues such as perceptions of differences in the sexuality of women and men, the healthiness of homosexuality, the morality of masturbation, and, at the broadest level, the purpose of sex. Second, beyond gaining some historical perspective and some understanding of the current explanations of sexuality, it is also extremely important to develop evaluative skills to cope with the barrage of information that

emerges from the popular press. Some of the information, based on careful and systematic research by trained scientists, is very solid. Other claims, however, stem from people's strongly held but unsupported beliefs. We examine, for example, the evidence regarding conservative Phyllis Schlafly's assertions that only nonvirtuous women are victims of sexual harassment.

Without some understanding of how to evaluate research, it is very difficult to determine the accuracy or usefulness of emerging information as we try to make decisions. Some of these decisions are personal: How can I protect myself against contracting AIDS? Is a particular contraceptive method safe for me? Will masturbation hurt me? Others are social decisions: Is premarital sex undesirable? Do women "ask for" sexual assault? We are also faced with political decisions: Should I support sex and contraceptive education in the public schools? Should abortion be banned? Should AIDS victims be isolated from the rest of the population? Many of these questions involve values, of course.

Insofar as our beliefs and values influence the way we vote, the stands we take on community issues, and the way we treat others around us, it is important to determine whether the assumptions underlying our values are accurate. For instance, if one votes to deny homosexuals equal opportunity for employment in public schools in the belief that homosexuals seduce young children, then one is limiting the freedom of others on the basis of an inaccurate belief.

Having raised the issue of values and biases, it is only fair that we, the authors, acknowledge our own. We believe that the capacity of human beings for sexual feeling and fantasy is one of life's great rewards. Sexual intimacy between people can be the source of a deep sense of connection and communion. It can also be a great deal of fun.

All societies have regulated sexual expression. When such regulation is aimed at protecting people from force or exploitation by others, we support it. We reject the use of law, however, to control noncoercive sexual interaction just because that behavior does not conform to the norms of the majority. Sexual minorities have been persecuted to varying degrees throughout history. Although we have witnessed a great deal of progress in our civilization with regard to re-

ligious and political freedoms, our society has not yet reached the point at which we are equally tolerant in permitting people to love or to be sexually intimate with whom they choose.

With any freedom, of course, come certain responsibilities. Our society emphasizes the importance of providing young people with the education needed for responsible citizenship. But ironically, although the majority of North Americans now support sex education, many public school boards still shy away from teaching the information needed for safer, responsible sexuality. Sex is exploited by the mass media to sell products, yet adults expect young people to express their sexuality in nonexploitative and responsible ways. Little knowledge and few opportunities for discussion are provided to children and adolescents to help them achieve sexual maturity. We believe that in our roles as citizens, lovers, and parents, it is important to examine what is known about sexuality and to be aware of our own sexual values in order to develop sexual responsibility and integrity. We hope that this book can provide some help with these tasks.

# Sexual
## **Inter**actions

# Historical and Cross-Cultural Perspectives on Sexuality

$\mathscr{F}$ROM the fact that our species has thrived, we can assume that *Homo sapiens* has been engaging in sexual intercourse for at least 50,000 years, and our *hominid* ancestors for several million years before that. Until recently, however, we knew little about the meaning, quality, or context of human sexual activity.

In this chapter, we describe some of the ways in which various aspects of sexuality have been viewed across different cultures and historical periods. There are two important reasons for looking at the sexual beliefs and behaviors of members of other cultures and of our ancestors. First, it will put our own beliefs in perspective. Those who know only our own culture and time may assume that what we do sexually is the "natural" and "correct" way to express our sexual capacities. We may also believe that those people within our own culture who deviate from the norm are, by definition, sinful or sick. Some aspects of the sexual mores of non-Western cultures have been similar to those of Western societies, for example, the practice of sexual *asceticism* throughout Asian history. However, the celebration of sexuality as a central life force has been more apparent in some non-Western cultures

**Homo sapiens**—the modern human being.
**hominid**—humanlike creature.
**asceticism** (uh-SET-ih-SIH-zum)—the practice of extreme self-denial, especially for religious reasons.

than in cultures based on the Judeo-Christian tradition. Beliefs about sexual contact, including beliefs about its very purpose, have varied enormously throughout history and are diverse also in present-day cultures.

Second, we will see which contemporary beliefs about sexuality are based more on the traditions and mythology developed by our ancestors than on current factual knowledge. Our sexual feelings and experiences can be the source of ecstatic pleasure and intense intimacy. But we can also feel deprivation, rejection by a loved one, inability to respond to a partner in the way we wish, and guilt about what we may view as our own inappropriate or immoral sexual responses. These feelings can be painful, and some of this pain is caused by simple ignorance. Given the pervasive role that sexuality plays in our lives, it is important to try to free ourselves of as many misconceptions about it as possible. To quote the philosopher George Santayana, "Those who ignore history are doomed to repeat it." To take his idea a step further, those who are sexually ignorant may experience more pain than pleasure in the sexual aspects of their relationships—a notion aptly, if crudely, expressed in the common saying, "The screwing you get ain't worth the screwing you take."

As you will see throughout this book, people's beliefs and attitudes about sex determine the extent to which they enjoy sexual feelings. Before reading further, you might want to write down your responses to the following questions or discuss them with a classmate or friend so that you can compare your beliefs with those held by members of other cultures and time periods.

How are the sexual intentions and reactions of females similar to and different from those of males?

What are the purposes of sex?

Why are children circumcised?

Why do some people try to avoid conception or parenthood at a particular time in their lives, or permanently?

Is your general health influenced by how frequently you experience orgasm or ejaculation?

What are the causes of same-gender sexual relations?

Is love necessary for pleasurable sexual relations or for a successful marriage?

Is the marriage of one man to several women normal?

Before we look at historical and cross-cultural answers to these and other questions, let us consider the limits on our ability to interpret information gleaned from our ancestors and from other cultures.

The earliest written records of Western civilization, which document life in cities of the Near East about 5,000 years ago, were created and kept by (almost exclusively male) authors, poets, historians, medical authorities, and healers. It is from these records and from artwork and other material remnants unearthed by archaeologists that we have some idea of ancient sexual behaviors and attitudes. The problem with such sources is that they provide a glimpse of how only a few men in these groups perceived the sexual norms and laws of their time. They do not necessarily reveal what the women (who typically did not receive enough education to create written records) or the vast majority of ordinary men thought about sexuality or how they expressed their sexual feelings.

The gathering of information about sexuality in other cultures and historical periods has been further hindered by the suppression or destruction of documents that those in authority thought threatening or dangerous. Rulers have a vested interest in suppressing any descriptions of their culture that may undermine the mythologies that justify their own ruling status. In addition, they may wish to avoid disclosure of behaviors not in accord with the norms of their society. Thus some documents may be vehicles for distorting rather than clarifying descriptions of sexual norms and behavior.

Even when accurate records are available, understanding other people's sexuality can be hindered by ethnocentrism—the tendency to read the values of one's own culture into these accounts. Descriptions of sexual behavior in other cultures may be influenced by the beliefs and assumptions of anthropologists about the appropriate role of sexuality in human life. The sexual practices of people in other cultures or in the past may look like contemporary sexual behaviors, and some people assume that the reasons for their behaviors are the same as our own. As you will see, sexual relations can have extraordinarily different meanings to people in cultures or times different from our own. Therefore, in evaluating the sexual practices of people in other places and times, we need to understand their perceptions of the purposes of their behaviors.

## Beliefs About the Nature of Female and Male Sexuality

In contemporary North American culture, it is commonly believed that males are more sexual than females—that males have stronger and more readily stimulated sexual appetites and that they enjoy sex more than females do. Earlier in this century, it was believed that females were passive and uninterested in sex, but during the latter half of the century, females have come to be perceived as willing to engage in sexual relations under certain conditions and—given a considerate partner—able to enjoy sexual stimulation. The general belief about differences in male and female sexuality is reflected in the old phrase, ''Men give love to get sex; women give sex to get love.''

To understand many contemporary controversies surrounding sexuality, it is crucial to examine historical beliefs about the nature of female and male sexuality. Present-day Western assumptions about female sexuality represent a relatively atypical view when seen in historical perspective. The biblical story of Eve's disastrous influence on Adam in the Garden of Eden (see Figure 1.1) represents a belief about the nature of female and male sexuality that has been more prevalent throughout history than is the current stereotype of men as being more sexually driven than women are. Although males have consistently held the reins of economic, political, and social power over females in the *patriarchies* characteristic of Western civilization, the dominant view has long been that females are insatiably seductive and powerful sexual temptresses

**patriarchy** (PAY-tree-ar-kee)—a society in which men have supremacy over women, who are legally and socially dependent on them.

**FIGURE 1.1**
**Dürer's Adam and Eve (1504)**
This painting reflects a common theme in Western civilization: woman as a seductive and powerful sexual temptress.

who pose danger to males. For centuries, the common perception has been that males need to protect themselves from females' sexual powers or else face dire physical and moral consequences.

This view of women's sexual power as a source of peril to men is apparent in the earliest records of Western civilization. It is a theme that was frequently repeated until a couple of centuries ago, and remnants of it persist in a number of contemporary beliefs about female sexuality. Two of these include the myth that the vagina has teeth—called *vagina dentata*—that will injure the penis, and that the vagina can capture the penis—called *penis captivus*. These myths appear all over the world and are reflected in certain contemporary Western fashion photography, jokes, novels, and movies (Beit-Hallahmi, 1985). Jack

Nicholson, playing a man consumed with sexual conquests in the movie *Carnal Knowledge*, expressed his ambivalence about female genitals: "When you think what a man has to dip into, he's got the right to turn soft every once in a while." Further, you may have heard stories about couples who claimed that they had been caught in compromising positions because the man's penis got "locked" in the woman's vagina, a variation of the *penis captivus* myth (Beit-Hallahmi, 1985). Although this is rare among humans, it is not uncommon among dogs, who may complete copulation in seconds but remain "locked" to each other for up to half an hour. To understand the simultaneous approach-and-avoidance that men have had toward women, we will return to the beginnings of recorded history.

## Early Mediterranean Cultures

Among the earliest important population centers in Western civilization were cities in Mesopotamia (now Iraq) and Egypt. Mesopotamian culture, which flourished from about 3000 B.C. to 300 B.C., included such peoples as the Sumerians, Babylonians, and Assyrians. Most of the gods worshipped during this period were divine representations of aspects of the natural world. They symbolized the belief that life was dependent on fertility and thus on sex. The original Sumerian signs for female and male were simple drawings of the sexual parts. The sexual act represented fertility, and in the New Year festival, a priest and a priestess had sex to insure general fertility for the state (Bullough, 1980).

In Mesopotamian culture, men had conflicting attitudes toward women. Although women were low-status creatures owned by men, they had a power that men did not possess: they could bring life into the world. These attitudes were vividly expressed in the cults that worshipped the Great Mother (see Figure 1.2). Throughout the ancient Mediterranean world, the earth was likened to a mother who contained and produced life. She was a fertile cradle receiving seeds into her womb, where they developed into new life. But this process was a mystery; often the earth's bounty failed and people starved. Thus the Great Mother was feared as well as worshipped; and

**FIGURE 1.2**
**The Great Mother**
In ancient times, small stone carvings such as this frequently were deposited in planted fields, reflecting the association of women and fertility. This terracotta figure from North Syria is now in the Louvre in Paris.

women, with their ability to conceive and nourish new life, were feared as well as revered.

In contrast, in ancient Egypt, which enjoyed considerable agricultural prosperity because of the predictable flooding of the Nile and the resulting fertility of the earth, women had relatively high status. Although they were not considered to be men's equals, Egyptian women could own property, initiate lawsuits, and pay taxes (Bullough, Shelton, & Slavin, 1988). In Egypt, as in Mesopotamia, however, the male was dominant.

A thousand years before the Greek and Roman civilizations emerged, various groups worshipped the fertility goddess under different names: Cybele, Aphrodite, Ishtar, Isis. Temples built to honor the Great Mother provided the setting for sexual rituals performed to ensure the fertility of individuals, groups, livestock, and crops. These ceremonies in honor of the Great Mother featured both heterosexual (sexual relations between a male and a female) and homosexual (sexual relations between two people of the same gender) intercourse. It may appear to us that these practices provided the population with a paradise for the celebration of sensual pleasures. The tales that survived this era, however, reflect a *phobic* attitude toward women. As bearers of offspring, women were reputed to have the power to sexually entice, maim, and destroy men.

Among the ancient Hebrews, who flourished after about 1000 B.C., women were also portrayed as more sexual than men, and their status was inferior. Sexual expression was supposed to be confined to one's spouse, but transgressions by females were dealt with more severely than those by males because women were considered to be men's property (Bullough, 1980). The Jewish law of that period defined *adultery*, which was punishable by death, differently from the way we do today. Among the Hebrews, adultery referred only to a married woman's sexual intercourse with a man other than her husband. A man who had intercourse with a woman who was married to someone else was charged merely with the violation of the husband's property rights. Although the punishment for this violation was severe, the man was not condemned to death (Murstein, 1974).

Some Hebrew sexual laws may have derived from competition between the Jews' god Jehovah and the Great Mother. The Hebrews strongly disapproved of the ritual sex associated with the Great Mother's worship; for example, many of her admirers *castrated* themselves to glorify her. Vidal (1979) suggested that

> many Jews in Babylon were attracted, if not to the goddess' worship, to the sexual games

> that went on in her temples. Therefore, the authors of Leviticus . . . made it clear that any Jew who went with a male or female temple prostitute was guilty of an idolatrous or abominable act in the eyes of the Great God Jehovah—a notoriously jealous God by his own admission. As a result, the abominations in Leviticus refer not to sexual acts as such but to sexual acts associated with the cult of the Great Goddess. (p. 345)

## The Rise of Christianity

In the 4th century A.D. the Christian church (at the time Rome's official religion) insisted that women were temptresses who threatened men's spirituality. As late as the 9th century, serious debate arose over whether women had souls. Early medieval clergy blamed such ailments as impotence and loss of memory on the devil and his allies, female witches, an attitude that is still widespread among preliterate and preindustrial societies throughout the world. In medieval Europe, it was believed that witches had sex with the devil. The demons could take the form of either a male (incubus) or a female (succubus) for the purpose of sexual intercourse. Given the belief that the devil was the agent responsible for disease, it was quite logical for clergymen to involve themselves in the diagnosis and treatment of disease.

In 1486 Sprenger and Krämer, two German theologians, published *Malleus Maleficarum* ("The Witches' Hammer"), a handbook describing the procedures for diagnosing witchcraft. Many church leaders thereafter considered it heresy to question the existence of witches. This manual illustrated the prevailing prejudices against women, who were presumed to be susceptible to evil influences because all witchcraft came from carnal (sexual) lust, supposedly insatiable in women. See Box 1.1 for a sampling of the beliefs expressed in *Malleus Maleficarum* about the dangers arising from females' sexual appetites and moral depravity.

In the 15th and 16th centuries, negative attitudes toward women's sexuality took their most malicious form in witch hunts—the prosecution

---

phobic—irrationally fearful.

adultery—in contemporary Western legal terms, a married person's having sexual relations with someone other than the spouse.

castration—the surgical removal of the testes or ovaries.

### Box 1.1

## The Diagnosis of Witchcraft

In *Malleus Maleficarum* ("The Witches' Hammer," 1486), Sprenger and Krämer put forth the rationale for women's greater susceptibility to demonic influence to become witches.

*Therefore, let us now chiefly consider women; and first, why this kind of perfidy [witchcraft] is found more in So fragile a sex than in men. . . .*

*Now the wickedness of women is spoken of in Ecclesiasticus xxv: "There is no head above the head of a serpent, and there is no wrath above the wrath of a woman. . . . All wickedness is but little to the wickedness of a woman." What else is woman but a foe to friendship, an unescapable punishment, a necessary evil, a natural temptation, a desirable calamity, a domestic danger, a delectable detriment, an evil of nature, appointed with fair colours! . . . When a woman thinks alone, she thinks evil. . . .*

*Others again have propounded other reasons why there are more superstitious women found than men. And the first is, that they are more credulous; and since the chief aim of the devil is to corrupt faith, therefore he rather attacks them. . . . The second reason is that women are naturally more impressionable, and more ready to receive the influence of a disembodied spirit. . . .*

*The third is that they have slippery tongues, and are unable to conceal from their fellow women those things which by evil arts they know;*

*and, since they are weak, they find an easy and secret manner of vindicating themselves by witchcraft. . . .*

*For it is true that in the Old Testament the Scriptures have much that is evil to say about women, and this because of the first temptress, Eve, and her imitators. . . .*

*But the natural reason is that she is more carnal than a man, as is clear from her many carnal abominations. And it should be noted that there was a defect in the formation of the first woman, since she was formed from a bent rib, that is, a rib of the breast, which is bent as it were in a contrary direction to a man. And since through this defect she is an imperfect animal, she always deceives. . . .*

*To conclude. All witchcraft comes from carnal lust, which is in women insatiable. See Proverbs xxx: "Wherefore for the sake of fulfilling their lusts they consort even with devils." More such reasons could be brought forward, but to the understanding it is sufficiently clear that there are more women than men found infected with the heresy of witchcraft. . . . And blessed be the Highest Who has So far preserved the male sex from So great a crime: for since He was willing to be born and to suffer for us, therefore He has granted to men this privilege.*

---

and execution of alleged witches (see Figure 1.3). Although witch hunts were justified on religious and sexual grounds, they also may have been motivated by the clergy's and the medical profession's desire to eliminate competition from village healers, usually women, who for centuries had supplied herbs and potions to the populace as cures for various afflictions. These women served as scapegoats, taking the blame for such social crises as wars, epidemics, and famines. Recurrent periods of frenzied witch hunts claimed

thousands of victims before the hysteria ran its course.

Only in the late 17th and early 18th centuries, with the spread among the elite of religious skepticism and of more modern scientific views, did the legal prosecution of witches cease. The last executions for witchcraft in Europe took place in 1782 in Switzerland. The final such occurrence in the American colonies involved the execution of 19 witches in 1692 in Salem, Massachusetts. But there is evidence that some Americans still be-

**FIGURE 1.3**
**The Burning of Witches**
After being convicted of witch-craft, people—primarily women—were burned at the stake, as shown in this German drawing of the Inquisition.

lieve in and fear witches as a source of evil (see Box 1.2).

The perceived need to control women's sexuality, which underlay the fear of witches, was also reflected in the widespread use of chastity belts in the 15th century (Bullough, 1980). These girdles of *chastity* were designed to prevent

**chastity**—sexual abstinence.

---

 **Box 1.2**

## Modern Witches

The witch continues to hold the imagination of certain groups in our culture even in recent times, as this story reveals (*Dayton Journal Herald*, March 17, 1981, p. 1).

### Church Teens Burn "Demon" Books, Records

*Blue Springs, NE (AP)*

*Books and records have been burned by members of an independent church.*

*They said they were destroying the work of witches, demons and druids. The burning was organized by teenagers.*

*"In rock and roll, the drumbeat hypnotizes the listener, and the words are a coded spell," said Dave Kruse, one of the teenagers.*

*"The record production companies have witches write songs, and the companies have old druid manuscripts containing melodies and drumbeats. They hire top musicians. . . ."*

*About 30 members of the Gospel Fellowship Church gathered Saturday in the backyard of Doc Barton, the church leader, to burn several dozen albums and single records and about a dozen books.*

Contemporary beliefs in witches are not confined to Western cultures. In one district in India, about 200 women are killed annually by mobs of fellow villagers who have branded them as witches (Gandhy, 1988).

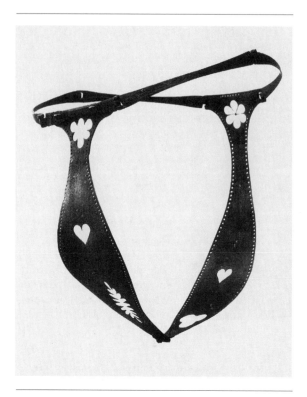

**FIGURE 1.4**
**Chastity Belt**
During the Middle Ages, girdles like this were designed to assure the chastity of the women in a man's household when he was away.

wives' infidelity and daughters' premature loss of virginity (see Figure 1.4). The master of a household who had his women wear a chastity belt could rest assured of their faithfulness when he was away from home. Some chastity belts are displayed in the Cluny Museum in Paris. One such device has two iron plates joined at their narrowest point. The plates are attached to two jointed iron bands that pass around the wearer's hips. One of the plates bears a design showing Adam and Eve in the Garden of Eden.

## The Industrial Revolution

In the 19th century, when the Industrial Revolution created an expanded middle class, male and female roles became increasingly differentiated. The dominant sexual ideology of this time, commonly referred to as Victorianism, was in full flower well before 1837, when Victoria, for whom the period is named, became queen of England. During this era, men were expected to be aggressive manipulators, supplying the energy of the Industrial Revolution, generating capital, making money, and building the new order. Women were expected to be passive and emotional and to concern themselves only with their "proper" domain, the home.

Whereas in the Middle Ages women were viewed as sexual creatures who lured men to sin, in the 19th century sexual anxieties were quieted by putting the blame for lust directly on men. Nineteenth-century convention portrayed females as *asexual*, as frail, delicate, refined creatures who had to be protected from the crude and lustful desires that besieged the male. In Victorian society, a woman's task was to domesticate her husband, and women's judgment in matters of morality, taste, and feelings was thought to be more developed than that of men.

Proper Victorian men and women maintained a facade of public morality, but pornography, prostitution, and extramarital sex flourished behind the scenes. Although officially the prostitute was considered the worst of all women and a social outcast, society tolerated her because she provided an outlet through which the proper Victorian husband could satisfy his burdensome passion (see Figure 1.5). It has been estimated that 80,000 prostitutes plied their trade in London during some periods in the 19th century (Trudgill, 1976).

In North America, as in England, Victorian morality was the public norm. A recently discovered study raises some doubt, however, as to whether the private lives of Victorian women corresponded to their public image. Historian Carl Degler (1980) discovered in the Stanford University Archives a study of 45 women, most of whom had been born before 1870 and thus grew up, married, and had children in the 19th century. The study had been conducted via questionnaire by Dr. Clelia Mosher (1863–1940), a physician who devoted her life to destroying myths about the inferiority of women. She provided the earliest systematic study of the sexual attitudes and behaviors of U.S. women. She did

asexual—without sexual feelings or qualities.

**FIGURE 1.5**
**Victorian Propriety and Prostitution**
Despite her plunging neckline, the woman on the left was a proper Victorian lady
of the 1870s. On the right, prostitutes display themselves to a potential aristocratic
customer.

not have a representative sample (that is, a sample that could be generalized to all U.S. women), but she found that at least some women defied the Victorian stereotype of the passionless female. Most of these women reported engaging in sex with neither reluctance nor distaste. Most expressed a desire for sexual intercourse and used some form of birth control. Although the majority of the women believed that the primary purpose of sex was reproduction, more than half also felt that mutual pleasure was a worthy purpose in itself. Consistent with Mosher's findings, the historian Peter Gay (1984) also maintained that pleasurable sexual experience was the norm

rather than the exception during the 19th century.

The legacy of the Victorian era was so influential that until recently many women attempted to hide their sexual interest and worried about being considered "animalistic" if they felt "horny." Meanwhile, during the first half of the 20th century, men commonly believed that it took enormous effort to persuade a woman to have sex, and even more work to get her aroused and orgasmic. A shift away from these extreme views was inspired partially by the research reports of the Kinsey group (1948, 1953) and Masters and Johnson (1966). Today, at least in some circles, females are seen as sexual, and a few people even argue that females are more capable of sexual responsiveness than are males. For example, Masters and Johnson suggested that women's sexual capacity may surpass that of men because of women's potential for multiple orgasm (see Chapter 7).

Still, we have not totally escaped the influence of the time when women were feared to have magical powers and thought to be a source of danger to men because of their seductive capacities. For example, the phrase "woman's intuition" suggests that women's powers of perception exceed those of men. And the idea that women provoke rape by tempting men beyond their ability to control themselves—a belief that degrades both men and women—is accepted by many contemporary North Americans (see Chapter 18). Although it is popularly assumed that many of these beliefs and attitudes developed within our Judeo-Christian culture, these ideas were in fact passed on to the early Hebrews and Christians from Mesopotamian culture.

## Beliefs About Sexual Intercourse

Many ancient cultures, apparently unaware of the male's role in conception, believed that pregnancy resulted from the entrance of ancestral spirits into a woman's body. Nonetheless, men and women still engaged in sex—the activity necessary for the continuation of their group into successive generations—and created other justifications for it.

Most 20th-century North Americans understand that *coitus* is necessary for conception. In fact, some believe that conception is the only justification for sexual relations, an idea in line with the longstanding official position of the Roman Catholic church. This notion that procreation is the sole justification for having sexual relations, known as *reproductive bias*, has a lengthy history in Western cultures. Beliefs about the purposes of

**coitus**—penetration of the vagina by the penis, also called sexual intercourse.

**reproductive bias**—the belief that procreation is the sole purpose for sexual contact.

sex are intimately tied to the religious and ideological perspectives of cultures throughout human history. In general, the early Greeks and Egyptians appear to have been relatively tolerant of most sexual activities as long as they did not interfere with the stability of the family. Sexual norms among the ancient Hebrews and the Mesopotamians before them, however, were straightforward: procreation was the primary purpose of sex (Bullough, 1980).

In reaction to what they saw as pagan excesses in Greek culture, early Christian writers such as St. Augustine (354–430) and St. Thomas Aquinas (1225–1274) developed a tradition of sexual austerity that was refined and elaborated over the following centuries. They condemned any sexual activity that did not have reproduction as its main purpose. These early Christian writers regarded sex as a necessary evil, sometimes giving the impression that they would have been relieved if reproduction could have been accomplished without sexual contact.

Although Jesus is reported to have said relatively little about sex, the Gospel of Matthew attributed to Jesus one pronouncement that has had far-reaching ramifications: "Whosoever looketh upon a woman to lust after her hath committed adultery with her already in his heart." This statement highlights a crucial difference between Christianity and other religions of the time. Christianity would not accept mere behavioral conformity; inner thoughts also had to be pure. Rules and prohibitions should be fully internalized and made part of the conscience, and fantasies or emotional transgressions should produce feelings of guilt. The power of this idea even in contemporary times is revealed in former president Jimmy Carter's revelations of his own inner lust in a 1976 interview: "I try not to commit a deliberate sin. I recognize that I am going to do it anyhow, because I'm human and I'm tempted, and Christ set some impossible standards for us. I've looked on a lot of women with lust. I've committed adultery in my heart many times. This is something that God recognized I will do and I have done it and God forgives me for it" (*Playboy*, 1976, pp. 63–86).

Early Christians generally attempted to attain spiritual perfection by suppressing their physical needs. Whereas they considered the body to be matter and therefore subject to decay, they believed that the soul was eternal and therefore far more important. The path to perfection lay in conquering the flesh, particularly its sexual impulses. The hostile attitudes of early Christian writers toward sex reflected earlier Hebrew tradition.

Many early Christian writers reported an intense personal struggle over what they perceived as temptations of the flesh. St. Paul was one of the most influential of the early Church authorities to write about sex. After devoting much of his early life to the persecution of Christians, Paul experienced a vision, followed by three days of blindness. As a result of his experience, Paul switched from a fanatical hatred of Christians to a zealous devotion to their faith and became a Christian leader (see Figure 1.6). Convinced that the world was about to end, Paul preached that humans must keep themselves pure in preparation for that event. On Christ's rather vague and brief sexual code, Paul built a system that viewed *celibacy* as the ideal. For those who could not manage celibacy, marriage was better than burning with lust. He reported great internal conflict:

> For I know that nothing good dwells within me that is in my flesh. I can will what is right, but I cannot do it. For I delight in the law of God, in my inmost self, but I see in my members another law at war with the law of my mind and making me captive to the law of sin which dwells in my members. (Romans, 7.18, 7.22, 7.23)

St. Jerome, after spending years in the desert fasting and wearing sackcloth in an attempt to banish his visions of dancing girls, further refined Paul's pronouncements. He declared that if a man loved even his wife too ardently, he was guilty of adultery, a view that Pope John Paul II echoed in a series of sermons on sex delivered in St. Peter's Square. On October 8, 1980, the pope asserted:

> Adultery in the heart is committed not only because a man looks in a certain way at a woman who is not his wife . . . but precisely because he is looking at a woman that way. Even if he were to look that way at his wife, he would be committing adultery.

celibacy—abstention from sexual intercourse.

**FIGURE 1.6**
**St. Paul**

Although the Vatican maintained that the pope simply meant that marriage does not permit a man to use a woman solely for his own pleasure, the statements provoked powerful controversy and reinforced the idea that the papal view of marital love was so idealistic that only saints could have sex without sin.

St. Augustine, who helped to solidify many of the antisexual attitudes of the early Church leaders, struggled most of his life with the conflict between his father's pagan beliefs and his mother's saintly adherence to Christian principles. The first part of his life was marked by conflict between sexuality and spirituality. For eleven years, he was a member of a non-Christian religious movement, Manichaeanism (now extinct), that considered procreation to be an evil act. Augustine, who had taken a lover when he was fairly young and had a son by her, had great difficulty adhering to this group's belief about sex. That he was ambivalent about his inability to control his sexual feelings is demonstrated in the prayer attributed to him: "Give me chastity and continence, but do not give it yet."

Eventually, Augustine sent his lover and son away. But while waiting to marry another woman, of whom his mother approved, he experienced a crisis of conscience that resulted in his conversion to Christianity. From then on, Augustine believed that we are all born as a result of lust and are therefore conceived in sin. To atone for that original sin, he maintained, we must learn to control our impulses through willpower. He saw sexual intercourse as animal lust to be tolerated only for the purpose of reproduction; sexual activity for any other purpose was a sin. Although Augustine reported having "contaminated" his own male friendships with lust, he condemned homosexual behavior as a sin against nature (Boswell, 1980). He eventually adopted a celibate lifestyle, and his ideas became part of Church doctrine.

St. Thomas Aquinas systematized and expanded Augustine's thinking. His work, which became official Church dogma by papal decree in 1563, dominated thinking on sexual matters until the end of the Middle Ages. Aquinas defined lust as any sexual behavior, inside or outside marriage, that was engaged in solely for pleasure and excluded procreation. Because lust constituted a sin against nature and because the laws of nature were derived from God, lust was exceeded in seriousness only by bestiality (sex with animals), homosexuality, coitus in "unnatural" positions, and masturbation.

## Cross-Cultural Research

Like historical research, cross-cultural research provides information about differences and similarities among groups and can help us to gain perspective on our own culture's sexual beliefs and practices. Some cultures believe that sexual intercourse is important for promoting the growth of children. For example, among the Tiwi people of Melville Island, off the northern coast of Australia, girls go at the age of seven to live with their future husbands, who are already adults. Within a year the girls begin to have sexual intercourse because the Tiwi believe that intercourse stimulates the onset of puberty (Goodall, 1971). Members of Tiwi society believe that young girls are incapable of developing breasts, pubic hair, and broadened hips and of beginning to menstruate unless they experience intercourse. The Sambia of New Guinea hold a somewhat similar view, except that they think that boys, rather than girls, need sexual stimulation. Specifically, they believe that young boys need to swallow semen to achieve manhood (Herdt, 1981).

In contrast to the Tiwi and the Sambia, the Mehinaku of central Brazil believe that the sexual stimulation of children is dangerous. Although tolerant of sexual games between young boys and girls, the Mehinaku believe that as boys approach puberty, they need to practice sexual abstinence (Gregor, 1985). When a boy is 11 or 12, his father builds a palmwood seclusion barrier behind which the youth remains for most of the next three years, taking growth-producing medicines and following strict dietary rules. Although the Mehinaku idea that contact between boys and sexually mature women is dangerous resembles contemporary Western attitudes, it has a different rationale. The Mehinaku believe that women's menstrual blood and vaginal secretions can poison the growth medicines that boys are given and can even cause a fatal paralysis in boys. Girls are also secluded for a period of time following their first menstrual period so that they will not "contaminate" the village boys.

The Mehinaku think of fathering children through sexual intercourse as a collective project by the males. The number of ejaculations into a woman's vagina contributed by multiple partners is considered important in conception. The Mehinaku believe that one sexual act is insufficient to conceive a child, for the semen of a woman's husband forms only a portion of the infant. Yet at the same time, moderation is important: a woman who produces a larger-than-normal child or who bears twins has had too many lovers. Such offspring are immediately buried alive.

Beliefs and feelings about sexual activity can also vary within a society. Among the So of northeastern Uganda, described in Box 1.3, women have sex solely for the purpose of reproduction and experience painful rather than pleasurable intercourse. When asked about having sex during pregnancy, their response was, "Why would you do that? There is already someone in there." Although So men also see the purpose of sex as procreation, they relish the feelings that accompany ejaculation (Allgeier, 1992; Laughlin & Allgeier, 1979).

## Beliefs About the Role of Circumcision

The problems that can arise from applying contemporary values to the practices of peoples in other cultures and time periods become evident when we consider the issue of *circumcision*, the surgical removal of the foreskin from the penis of a male or the hood from the clitoris of a female.

circumcision—the surgical removal of parts of the genitals, including the foreskin from the penis of a male or the hood from the clitoris of a female. In some cultures, the labia and/or clitoris are removed.

A look at the customs of our ancestors and of members of other cultures shows that, although circumcision has long been a common practice, the reasons for it have varied widely. The tradition of performing genital surgery on both males and females appears to have existed long before Christianity and Islam. The practice apparently was related to beliefs about the development of gender roles during puberty. Removal of genital tissues (see Figure 1.7) from boys and girls signified their passage into sexual maturity and adulthood (*Isis*, 1976).

According to Meinardus (1967), certain gods in ancient Egypt were believed to be bisexual, and humans were also thought to have both masculine and feminine "souls." It was believed that these "souls" revealed their physiological characteristics in the genitals, with femininity in males appearing in the foreskin of the penis (akin to the labia?), and masculinity in females appearing in the clitoris (a small penis?). Thus, as a prerequisite for boys' acceptance into the ranks of male adulthood, their feminine characteristics had to be eliminated by removal of the foreskin. Similarly, girls were released from the influence of masculine traits by removal of the clitoris, and sometimes the labia. These surgical procedures were perceived as eliminating any barriers to having adult male or female sexual lives.

Clearly, these beliefs about the reason for circumcision differ markedly from those held by

---

### Box 1.3

## A Polygynous African Tribe

In 1969–1970 the anthropologist Charles Laughlin and I spent a year living with the So tribe in the semiarid mountains of northeastern Uganda in Africa (Allgeier, 1992; Laughlin & Allgeier, 1979). In this polygynous tribe, the number of cows and goats owned by a man is a measure of his wealth, and it is in cows and goats that he pays for his wives.

We spent several months informally observing the So, learning their language, and taking a census. I then conducted a series of interviews with a random sample of the tribal members to attempt to understand their sexual attitudes and behavior. Did the women feel jealous of their co-wives? What coital positions did So couples use? Who initiated intercourse? What stimulation techniques did the people use? Were masturbation, homosexuality, bestiality, and adultery practiced? What was the purpose of sexual intercourse? I also wanted to learn their attitudes and behavior regarding contraception, procreation, sterility, gender roles, intercourse during menstruation and pregnancy, and other aspects of sexuality.

Following a general principle for studying sensitive topics, in the first interview I asked relatively innocuous questions to give the informant and me some time to become acquainted and feel at ease. In constructing the most intimate questions, I tried to avoid wording that would imply any value judgment.

There were some topics for which there were no So words. For instance, there was no term for *masturbation*, and although I was able to get the idea across to males through appropriate gesturing, the practice seemed to be totally unimaginable to females. Although adolescent males occasionally masturbated, it was taboo for married adult males to masturbate, because doing so constituted a "wasting of seed."

*Love* was another word for which no So term existed. There was *apudori* (sexual intercourse), and there were words for friendship, but no word for *love* per se. The So did not practice homosexuality, which fell into a category of behaviors (including adult masturbation, intercourse during menstruation, and bestiality) that they considered evidence of witchcraft. In addition, contraception was totally unknown to the So. My question, "What can you do if you don't want to have any more children?" was greeted with the same sort of astonishment that you might express if someone asked, "What can you do if you no longer want your legs?"

The attitudes and experiences of men and women regarding intercourse differed strikingly. For men, intercourse was positive, both because they valued procreation highly and because they enjoyed the activity itself. Those men who were married to more than one woman spent an equal amount of time with each wife, but they avoided a particular wife when she was menstruating. During intercourse they did not engage in any foreplay. Female breasts, which So women left exposed, had no erotic significance. And except for the incidental contact that occurs during vaginal penetration, to touch any portion of the vulva was forbidden.

In the absence of precoital stimulation, the negative attitude of So women toward sexual intercourse was not particularly surprising. I still have a vivid memory of one very beautiful middle-aged woman, with clenched teeth and hands, describing her first experience with intercourse. She said that it hurt badly—it burned—but that she got through it by telling herself repeatedly that she had to do this to get a baby and that she had to have a baby to get cows. When asked how she felt about sex now, she said that she wished her husband had enough cows to take a "little wife" but that it did not hurt as much now as it had at first. In no instance did a woman indicate ever having an orgasm; in fact, the So viewed orgasm as synonymous with ejaculation and as exclusively a male phenomenon. In exploring the total absence of female orgasm, I attempted to find out if So women were aware of having a clitoris. I described it and drew pictures of vulvas, but to no avail.

Over the years, I have considered at length these gender differences in sexual attitudes, attempting to find explanations. Perhaps the tribe's survival depended to some extent on these attitudes. In the face of disease and constant warfare with neighboring tribes, the tribe was in danger of extinction. Because females outnumbered males, the population could be maintained as long as women gave birth to as many children as possible. If women enjoyed sex, they might not want to share their husbands with other women. As it was, however, co-wives tended to have rather close relationships with one another. They did not compete for men; rather, they shared the responsibilities of raising their husband's children and providing him with food from their gardens. Were wives to value sexual intercourse other than for reproduction, they might resent the time their husbands spent with the others—three weeks out of four in the case of a man with four wives.

Source: E.R.A.

**FIGURE 1.7**

**Circumcision in Ancient Egypt**

This depiction of Egyptian surgeons performing circumcision with a stone or a shaped flint dates to about 3000 B.C.

contemporary North Americans. Many people today see possession of both masculine and feminine personality characteristics, called *androgyny,* as preferable to rigid adherence to stereotypic behaviors expected of people as a function of their biological sex. Only one in seven males worldwide is circumcised, but in the United States, more than 1 million circumcisions are performed each year (Robson & Leung, 1992). Why? Some parents choose to do so because of adherence to religious beliefs that prescribe circumcision—for example, Orthodox Jews. Other parents commonly give such reasons as preventing infection or cancer, and so that their son's penis will not look different from those of other males. Some people erroneously believe that the circumcision of male infants is legally required.

Since 1989, the American Academy of Pediatrics (AAP) has maintained that the circumcision of newborn boys has potential benefits and risks. Although the AAP did not support routine circumcision, it did advise that "the decision not to circumcise a male infant must be accompanied by a lifetime commitment to genital hygiene to minimize the risk of penile cancer developing" (Schoen et al., 1989, p. 389). (Of course, both men and women should regularly cleanse their genitals while taking showers or baths to reduce the risks of infections and diseases.) The task force did not recommend routine circumcision, because many studies of the correlates of having or not having a foreskin were marred by methodological problems such as variations in hygienic practices and general health in different cultures. Also in 1989, a review of research on the relationship between circumcision and contracting AIDS and other sexually transmitted diseases indicated that uncircumcised African men may be five to eight times more likely than circumcised men to get AIDS during heterosexual intercourse (Marx, 1989). In contrast, data collected in New York City found no relationship between circumcision and AIDS in three studies of patients at clinics for treatment of sexually transmitted diseases (Chiasson et al., 1989). Despite the inconclusiveness of these various studies, the parents of newborn baby boys should seek the most current information available on the risks and benefits of circumcision to inform their decision-making. (See Chapter 9 for further details.)

## Beliefs About Female Circumcision

Most North Americans consider the circumcision of male infants normal, but view female circumcision as barbaric. However, this practice, also described as female sexual mutilation, is performed on millions of females today in about 40 nations, most of them in Africa. One reason for this practice among Islamic practitioners is to reduce women's sexual desire. The smaller the opening for urination and menstruation following the surgery, the greater the honor to the woman's family (Gallo & Viviani, 1992; Lightfoot-Klein, 1989) (see Box 1.4). Historically, it has been suggested that female circumcision arose among pastoral groups in Somalia because it rendered women "odorless." Women who tended herds of small animals, such as sheep and goats, were less likely to attract predators or disquiet their herds through sexually linked female odors (Gallo & Viviani, 1992). The World Health Organization and the United Nations Children's

**Box 1.4**

## Female Circumcision

In the Sudan, a procedure known as Pharaonic circumcision involves removal not only of the entire clitoris but also of the inner and all except the outer layers of the vaginal lips. The remaining skin is then sewn together, leaving a vaginal opening that is the circumference of a matchstick. Following surgery, females must pass urine and menstrual discharge through this small opening.

Lightfoot-Klein (1989) observed and conducted interviews with Sudanese women, doctors, historians, midwives, and religious leaders in an attempt to understand the contemporary rationale for and effects of this practice. More than 90% of the 300 women in her sample had been Pharaonically circumcised. The exceptions were from upper-class, educated families.

Female circumcisions are generally performed by trained midwives in cities or towns and by untrained women in villages, on girls between four and eight years old. Of the women interviewed by Lightfoot-Klein, more than half had been circumcised without any form of anesthesia. Immediate complications included infection, hemorrhage, shock, septicemia (bloodstream infection), tetanus (acute bacterial infection causing spasmodic muscle contractions), urine retention, trauma to adjacent tissues, and emotional trauma. No count of fatalities from the procedure could be obtained, but some Sudanese doctors estimated that in regions where antibiotics are unavailable, a third of the females who are circumcised die from the procedure. Nearly all of the women reported urinary and menstrual problems until their labia were "opened" at marriage. Pharaonically circumcised virgins described taking an average of 10 to 15 minutes to urinate, with urine emerging drop by drop, and some women in Lightfoot-Klein's sample reported needing 2 hours to empty their bladders. As would be expected, urinary-tract and kidney infections were common. In addition, the small opening often blocked menstrual flow almost completely, producing a buildup of clotted blood that often could be removed only by surgery.

When a Pharaonically circumcised woman marries, her husband is expected to open the sewn-up entrance, which is usually difficult to do. The scars are often so extensive and hardened that even surgical scissors cannot cut through the tissue. The women reported going through extreme suffering during a process of gradual penetration that lasted an average of two and a half months. Tearing of surrounding tissues, hemorrhage, infections, and psychic trauma were common. Of the women Lightfoot-Klein interviewed, 15% reported that penetration was impossible. Other women had had midwives cut their labia with knives, but they did so secretly because of the belief that the necessity for this surgery demonstrated a husband's lack of potency. In addition, almost all Sudanese women who became pregnant required surgery during labor to permit their infant to be born because the circumcision scar prevents normal dilation. Following childbirth, almost all women had their labia sewn together again.

In view of this account, you might find it surprising that 90% of the women Lightfoot-Klein interviewed said that they had experienced orgasm during sexual relations. Her findings call into question the emphasis placed on the central role of the clitoris by Western experts (see Chapter 7). Despite the formidable obstacles, including removal of the clitoris and cultural prohibitions against female enjoyment of sexuality, most Sudanese women apparently retain their ability to have pleasure and orgasm during sexual relations.

In 1946 British rulers of the Sudan passed a law that made all forms of female sexual mutilation illegal. In reaction to this colonial interference, many Sudanese promptly Pharaonized their daughters. In the mid-1970s, the Sudanese passed a law against surgically altering the labia, but removal of the clitoris remains legal.

Fund support the view that all forms of female genital circumcision should be abolished.

## Beliefs About the Use of Birth Control

In many contemporary cultures and across most historical periods in Western cultures, deliberate attempts to avoid conception have not been officially sanctioned. Throughout most of recorded history, however, people have used a variety of methods to avoid conception (Riddle, Estes, & Russell, 1994). The availability of birth-control methods, despite explicit "official" pronouncements against them, illustrates that sometimes what people say about the purposes of sex may not be reflected in their behavior.

The Egyptians, who tolerated nonprocreative sex, relied on a number of contraceptive practices, including insertion of crocodile or elephant dung into the vagina (Bullough, 1980). They also used tampons fashioned from honey and the resinous gums of acacia shrubs. These tampons may have been effective to some extent because honey reduces sperm motility and acacia gum produces lactic acid, which kills sperm. In addition, Egyptian women ingested various drinks to avoid pregnancy, but these were probably ineffective.

McLaren (1981) traced attitudes toward birth control and abortion in England from the 17th century on. Large numbers of herbal abortives were available in preindustrial England. At that time, neither medical nor legal authorities could determine the presence of fetal life in the first few months of pregnancy; thus women were essentially free to end a pregnancy if they wished. The English believed that until quickening (the first movements of the fetus felt by the mother) occurred about 14 weeks after conception, ensoulment had not taken place (even the Catholic church employed the term *ensouled fetus* until 1869). There was no specific word for the use of abortive drugs before quickening. In fact, the very books that condemned abortion contained information on using drugs to bring on menstruation. Thus women who took such drugs prior to quickening could legitimately describe their actions as attempts to "restore the menses." Not

until 1803 was abortion (after quickening) made a statutory offense in England.

In the United States, contraception was illegal until the middle of the 20th century. The fact that it is still a controversial issue reveals conflicting social beliefs about the purpose of sexual relations (see Chapters 10 and 11).

### Infanticide

In a darker vein, many species have engaged in *infanticide* to limit their number of offspring (Fisher, 1992; Hrdy, 1981). Male langur monkeys attempt to kill an infant sired by another male because the mother then becomes sexually receptive again and the male can impregnate her.

Humans practice infanticide, too. Throughout history, infants have been left exposed to winter's ravages, drowned, and neglected in attempts to limit family size. This fate has generally fallen on baby girls because they were not considered as valuable as boys. This is not just an ancient custom. Recent reports from India indicate that female infanticide, although now illegal, is still common (Freed & Freed, 1989; Gandhy, 1988; Prasad, 1993). Despite the fact that more females than males are born in most populations, the ratio of male to female infants in India is 1,000 : 935, a decrease from 1,000 : 970 at the beginning of the 20th century. Part of this unbalanced sex ratio stems from prenatal genetic testing permitting knowledge of the sex of the fetus (see Chapter 9). According to a study cited by Gandhy (1988), of 8,000 abortions performed in India following sex determination, 7,999 were of female fetuses. However, infanticide also contributes to India's unusually unbalanced sex ratio. Female infants are seen as a financial burden, because a dowry is to be paid for their marriage. Videotaped interviews about infanticide were conducted with 1,250 women in 100 randomly selected villages in India, and 111 of the women admitted to killing at least one infant. Further, 547 reported that infanticide had occurred in their families, and 837 women in the sample indicated that infanticide was common in their villages (Prasad, 1993).

infanticide—killing of a baby.

## Beliefs About the Relationship Between Sexual Stimulation and Health

The notion that sexual excesses could cause ill health was long a popular belief. In the United States in the 19th century, Sylvester Graham (1794–1851) found his calling as a prophet of the temperance movement, which was dedicated to encouraging abstinence from alcoholic beverages (Bullough & Bullough, 1992). Graham, acclaimed as a lecturer on health and disease, maintained that health depended on avoiding all stimulants such as alcohol, tobacco, coffee, tea, vinegar, pepper, salt, spices, and rich gravies. In his view, sexual passion also constituted an excess of stimulation that led to debility and disease; even in marriage, too many orgasms were dangerous. Graham recommended eating homemade breads to reduce stimulation and promote good health, and he developed the graham cracker as an aid for those who wished to reduce their susceptibility to sexual passion. (Presumably, the innovation of adding cinnamon to graham crackers would have deeply offended Graham!) Similarly, John Harvey Kellogg (1852–1943) invented his corn flakes as an antimasturbation food to reduce sexual desire and foster good health, as shown in Figure 1.8 (Money, 1991). Indeed, the general view that avoidance of sexual stimulation is important for good health has been popular throughout much of recorded history.

Whereas Graham saw sexual intercourse as having a negative effect on health, the historian Lawrence Stone (1977), looking at the relationship between health and sexuality from a different perspective, sees good health as having a positive effect on sexual intercourse. Stone reported that in England just 300 years ago, only a small proportion of adults were both healthy and attractive. English people endured

> periods of crippling illness which incapacitated them for months or years. Even when relatively well, they often suffered from disorders which made sex painful to them or unpleasant to their partners. Women suffered from a whole series of gynecological disorders, particularly leukorrhea [vaginal infections involving smelly discharge; see Chapter

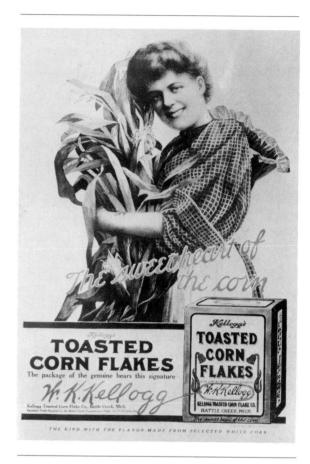

**FIGURE 1.8**
**Kellogg's Corn Flakes**
Kellogg's Corn Flakes were marketed as an aid for reducing sexual desire and maintaining purity. This advertisement appeared in 1907.

> 17], but also vaginal ulcers, tumors, inflammations, and hemorrhages which often made sexual intercourse disagreeable, painful, or impossible. (1977, pp. 486–487)

Stone suggested that many people in those days probably also had bad breath from inadequate dentistry and oral hygiene. Stomachaches, running sores, ulcers, scabs, and other unpleasant skin diseases were extremely common, and these maladies and disorders often lasted for years. Such health problems are likely to reduce not only a person's sexual appetite but also the individual's sexual appeal to others.

In their book *Healthy Pleasures* (1989), Robert Ornstein and David Sobel maintain that pleasurable activities are linked to human health and well-being. Ornstein, a psychologist, and Sobel, a physician, have studied particularly healthy and robust people. These individuals tend to ignore standard advice about exercise and diet but have a sense of optimism and an orientation toward pleasure. Ornstein and Sobel emphasize the importance to good health of engaging in enjoyable pursuits such as sex, good food, and playful behavior. They note that 20 minutes of sexual activity is not only fun but can burn 110 calories! This is the equivalent of about 3 miles of jogging.

**FIGURE 1.9**
**Greek Mentor-Lover Relationships**
Among the ancient Greeks, a young male and his older male mentor might develop a relationship involving sexual as well as emotional and intellectual bonds.

## Beliefs About Same-Gender Sexual Relationships

Beliefs about the causes and meanings of sexual relationships between individuals of the same gender have varied considerably across time and culture. The ancient Hebrews prohibited homosexual relationships.

In contrast, the Greeks, at least from about 650 B.C. to 150 B.C., idealized male beauty, and male homosexuality was not objectionable as long as it did not interfere with a man's obligation to marry and have offspring (Bullough, 1980). Greek men viewed women as useful for having children, but inferior to men for purposes of companionship. Men, as citizen-warriors and the most important members of the Greek city-states, seemed to have found their most profound intellectual, emotional, and erotic relationships with adolescent boys (Greenberg, 1988). In its pure form, this relationship involved a transfer of learning about manliness from older men to the young (see Figure 1.9). *Pederasty* was an important part of the relationship; many ancient Greeks believed that manliness could be symbolically transferred to boys through the adult male's penis and semen. The typical homosexual partnership, therefore, involved an adult and an adolescent male in a teacher-student relationship (Greenberg, 1988). For a short period in his life, a young man was allowed to play the passive role in a homosexual relationship. As he approached adulthood, the young man abandoned the passive role, going on to fulfill society's expectation that he marry and have children. Later in life, he might take a younger male lover; thus the roles of youthful beloved and older lover could be played by the same person at different stages in his life.

Little information is available regarding sexual relationships between women in ancient times. In the 6th century B.C., however, the Greek poet Sappho wrote erotic poetry describing sexual relations between women. The term *lesbian* comes from Lesbos, the name of the island where Sappho lived.

In contrast to the Greeks, the ancient Hebrews believed that a man who rejected women, thereby neglecting his obligation to marry and perpetuate the family, was a threat to the status quo. Therefore, male homosexuality was condemned and punished. Lesbianism, however, was not illegal. Women's sexual or emotional relationships with other women were of little concern, because such attachments (unlike adultery) did not threaten a man's property rights. A woman was incapable of owning property and

**pederasty** (PEH-dur-AS-tee)—sex between an adult and a child, usually an adult male and child.

thus incapable of "stealing" property (another woman) from a man.

The Romans generally disapproved of and punished homosexuality. Unlike the Greeks, the Romans did not perceive homosexual relations between an adult and a child as a source of education for boys. Mothers were responsible for the education of young children. When professional teachers became more common, these instructors' roles were to act as fathers rather than as lovers to the children they taught (Bullough, 1980).

In tracing the history of homosexuality from the beginning of the early Christian era to the 14th century, John Boswell (1980) found a range of attitudes about sexual orientation. After several hundred years of repression during the early Middle Ages, homosexual relationships emerged into the open in the 11th and 12th centuries in Europe. The flowering of courtly romance in the Middle Ages extended to passionate love among monks, archbishops, and saints and was expressed in openly homosexual erotic poetry, as quoted by Boswell (1980, p. 374):

> Beautiful boy, flower fair,
> Glittering jewel, if only you knew
> That the loveliness of your face
> Was the touch of my life.

When the European social order crumbled in the 13th and 14th centuries, the vehemently antihomosexual opinions of the early Christians gained power, reinforced by the teachings of Thomas Aquinas. Sexual tolerance decreased as political stability declined. Homosexuals faced widespread social and moral disapproval and were again culturally repressed for nearly 600 years (Boswell, 1980).

Toward the end of the 17th century, the religious domination of sexual morality weakened. During this time, Europeans began to question traditional views of sexuality. Legal and literary sources suggest that sexual variations of all kinds became more common. Still, a negative official view of homosexuality prevailed. In Britain and France, the penalty for homosexual acts was death. The Swedish penal code of 1734 favored decapitation followed by exposure or burning of the body—a penalty more severe than that for murder or treason (Karlen, 1971).

## Another Culture

Beliefs and attitudes regarding homosexual relations have also varied widely across cultures. A modern counterpart of early Greek beliefs and practices may be seen among the Sambia of the New Guinea highlands. While studying these people from 1974 to 1976, the anthropologist Gilbert Herdt (1981, 1990) learned of secret homosexual practices among adolescent men and boys. At age seven or eight, Sambian boys are taken from their mothers for initiation. They are told that semen is a source of life and growth, like mother's milk. The Sambians believe that to grow and mature, youngsters must consume semen by having oral sex with older boys. In addition, the ingestion of sperm is thought to strengthen the boys, ultimately allowing them to produce their own sperm and impregnate a wife. At about 15 years of age, the boys' roles change: they provide semen to a new generation of children. Initially, the older boys are anxious because they fear that loss of semen is potentially dangerous, but after instruction in how to replace it "magically" by consuming tree sap, the boys accept and enjoy this form of homosexual relations. The next phase of male sexuality, a bisexual one, begins with betrothal to a preadolescent girl. When the girl matures, the couple is married. At this time the husband gives up his homosexual contacts and devotes himself exclusively to heterosexual activities. Herdt estimated that only about 5% of the men retain a preference for homosexual behavior. Thus in Sambian society, as in ancient Greece, homosexual relations for males constitute a normal part of the sexual life cycle.

As you know, contemporary Westerners hold very different attitudes toward homosexuality. However, scholars continue to debate the sources and meanings of homosexual feelings and behavior (see Chapter 15).

## Beliefs About the Relationships Among Love, Sex, and Marriage

If you are looking for a special person with whom to share your life, what criteria do you use for judging potential mates? If you have already formed a strong commitment, on what basis did you make the choice?

The notion that romantic love per se can and should be the basis for an enduring bond or marriage is a relatively modern one that simply did not exist in most Western cultures until the last few centuries. Before that, parents generally arranged their children's marriages to cement economic relationships. Some married couples did come to love one another, but love was not seen as a prerequisite to marriage or as a necessity within marriage.

The records that survive from Mesopotamian culture contain few references to romantic relationships between men and women. Men appear to have sought close friendships with other men rather than with women. Among the early Romans, marriages were arranged to strengthen economic and political alliances. The legal age for marriage was 14 for boys and 12 for girls, but parents could establish betrothals when their children were very young (Bullough, 1990). (Remember that the Romans' life expectancy was considerably shorter than ours.) Although love might develop between husband and wife during the course of a marriage, it was seldom a prelude to marriage (Boswell, 1980).

The Church was even more liberal toward early marriage than the Romans had been. The early medieval Church considered youth a period of irrepressible sexual desire. Marriage, therefore, was seen as an antidote to uninhibited lust. Church law regarded the minimum age for matrimony as $11\frac{1}{2}$ for girls and $13\frac{1}{2}$ for boys unless "malice replace age"; that is, if a 10-year-old boy could ejaculate or "deflower" a virgin, or if a girl that age could "tolerate the company of a man," the individual could be legally married (Flandrin, 1977).

## Courtly Love

In addition to ushering in a greater tolerance for homosexuality, the 12th century saw the emergence among the European upper classes of what is called *courtly love*. Courtly love between no-

**courtly love**—a form of intense love not to be contaminated by lust or coitus.

blemen and their ladies was governed by a set of elaborate conventions. The literature on chivalry described love as an emotion produced by the man's unrestrained adoration of his lady. Love was associated with knighthood and nobility and was celebrated in songs and poems by artists of the time. In theory, courtly love was not to be consummated by sexual intercourse (Bullough, 1980). Lust was evidence of animal impulses, and to express lust toward a beloved defiled that person. Pure love referred to the joining of the hearts and minds of lovers, who experienced everything together except physical sexuality. Only in nonmarital relationships between young people was pure love thought to be possible. The elderly were excluded because such passion was considered too overwhelming for them, and marriage relationships were excluded because they involved contracts, which precluded free choice. In practice, of course, adulterous sexual relationships probably occurred despite these literary and social conventions.

Many historians view courtly love as a forerunner of the romanticism typical of the 19th and 20th centuries. Some have suggested that the popularity of courtly love reflected a wish for more freedom in heterosexual relations, which had been hampered by a rigid class system and arranged marriages (Murstein, 1974). The same force may also have influenced the spread in the cult of the Virgin Mary, who was particularly revered by celibate monks and was exalted as an ideal for all women.

## The Middle Ages

Over the course of the 13th century, the Catholic church's attitude toward sexuality and marriage changed: marriage was no longer viewed largely as a cure for lust. Moreover, early Church leaders had considered marriage a relatively private issue for the bride and groom and their respective families, even though the Church had encouraged a priest's attendance at the wedding rite as a mark of spirituality. By the 14th century, however, the bride and groom no longer married themselves but were united by a priest, and marriage came under the dominion of the Church.

In the 16th century, challenges to the Catholic church by two theologians, Martin Luther (1483–

1546) and John Calvin (1509–1564), led to the formation of Protestant denominations with new attitudes toward sexuality and marriage. Luther advocated marriage for the clergy in part to protect women from clerical lust. In addition, he challenged the Church's jurisdiction over marriage. Calvin was also critical of the monasticism of Catholic priests; he advocated marriages of modesty and moderation for the clergy. He linked sex with love in the marital relationship but at the same time advocated a doctrine of avoiding worldly pleasures and the temptations of leisure. His "puritanism" arose from his belief that God had predestined some individuals for salvation. Although no one could be sure of being counted among the "elect"—the people whom God had saved—those who had experienced religious conversion were expected to live frugal, industrious, and sexually unblemished lives.

In the 17th and 18th centuries, as the average age at marriage rose, young people faced a period of about 10 years of sexual maturity during which they were expected to repress their sexual feelings. This gap still exists in most Western countries.

## Victorian Views

The 19th century saw a romanticizing of the marital relationship, reminiscent of the earlier ideal of courtly love. Purity and prudery became the keynote of Victorian sexuality. The Victorian period, however, was hardly a time of sexual malaise. Conflict simmered between a keen interest in sex and a reluctance to admit the interest, a situation that bred much hypocrisy. For example, although they avoided exposing their legs and ankles at all costs, Victorian women apparently felt no qualms about wearing dresses with plunging necklines. The scholar Havelock Ellis claimed that the Victorian model of womanhood led to society's simultaneously treating a woman as an angel and an idiot (Grosskurth, 1980).

Considering the conflict that raged at that time, our historical knowledge of Victorian sexuality may reflect what the moral authorities then wanted to believe rather than what actually took place (Gay, 1984). Just as the conservative "Moral Majority" of the 1980s and 1990s did not represent the sexual views of all Americans, so the Victorian moralists probably did not capture the essential sexual values of the Victorian era. It

would be interesting to know whether our present sexual diversity will be obscured by some catch-all word such as *Victorianism* two centuries from now. Presumably, we have established enough sources of information in our society today that the richness of our complex sexual views and practices will be expressed and will not fall victim to a history that, in the words of the philosopher Voltaire, "plays tricks on the dead."

## Other Cultures

In many cultures, families commonly arrange the marriage of their offspring to obtain economic or political benefits. Among the So of northeastern Uganda, there is no stigma attached to pregnancy before marriage; in fact, evidence that a woman is fertile enhances her value in the negotiations between her father and her prospective father-in-law. The greater her value, the greater the number of cows and goats her father's clan can demand for her betrothal. The relationship among sex, marriage, and economic relations was aptly demonstrated by the So woman who remarked that, while enduring painful intercourse, she told herself over and over: "I must do this to have babies; I must have babies to get cows."

Among the Mehinaku of central Brazil, the notion of romantic love is considered absurd (Gregor, 1985). Although all romantic love is suspect, romance between spouses borders on bad taste. The Mehinaku believe that spouses should respect each other and retain a degree of separateness. Each represents a set of in-laws to whom the other owes work, gifts, and deference. Whatever potential there is for romantic attachment is diluted by living closely with many kinsmen and by an elaborate network of extramarital affairs. New couples are permitted only small expressions of affection. According to Gregor, despite the absence of romance, some spouses take an enduring pleasure in each other's company, bathing together each day and going off to their garden to have sex and converse.

Although many 20th-century Westerners may find it difficult to believe there are groups for whom romantic love is either inherently unimportant or unimportant as a factor in decisions about marriage, history paints a different picture. Religion and economics have been tied to marriage more than the bonds of romantic love.

## Variations in Marital and Family Forms

For contemporary North Americans, when a partner is sexually intimate with someone else, the experience of jealousy can be so intense and arise so automatically that it may seem a natural or innate reaction. Some of us experience pain at the idea that our mate is interested in or aroused by someone else, even if he or she does not act on those feelings. The available evidence suggests that the value individuals place on sexual exclusivity may be related to the extent to which they enjoy sexual contact and the meaning and interpretation of such contacts. The degree to which different groups experience jealousy is tied to their beliefs about acceptable relationship forms. Contemporary laws and norms in North America support the belief that marital partners should be monogamous, that is, have sexual relations only with each other.

Within Western civilization, most groups have practiced *monogamy*. For example, the Egyptians were generally monogamous, and sexual expression outside marriage was unaccept-

**monogamy** (muh-NAW-guh-mee)—a marital form in which a person mates with just one other person.

able among the ancient Hebrews (Bullough, 1980). For an individual reared in a culture in which monogamy is the accepted pattern, it is easy to assume that this form of male-female relationship is natural and other forms immoral. The characteristic pattern of modern American relationships is *serial monogamy*; that is, although people are expected to confine themselves to only one partner at a time, they may have a number of sexual partners over their lifetime. If the definition of natural or moral is determined by what the majority of cultures have practiced, then it should be noted that *polygamy*—a marital form that allows a person to have more than one lover or spouse at a time—has been normative in more cultures than has monogamy (Figure 1.10). Usually this takes the form of *polygyny*, the marriage of one man to more than one woman. Roughly 80% of primate species are polygynous, a figure close to the esti-

**serial monogamy**—a marital form in which a person mates with just one other person at a time but may end that relationship and form another.

**polygamy** (puh-LIH-guh-mee)—a marital form that allows a person to have more than one lover or spouse at a time; may take the form of polygyny or polyandry.

**polygyny** (pah-LIH-jih-nee)—the marriage of one man to more than one woman.

**FIGURE 1.10**
**Polygamy**
This former Utah policeman is pictured with his two wives and six children after being fired from his job for being a polygamist.

mates of the practice among human groups in hunter-gatherer societies (Buss, 1994). *Polyandry*—a marital form in which a woman may have more than one lover or spouse but a man is expected to have only one partner—is rare but has been documented in several cultures. Polygyny is strongly correlated with a *patrilineal* social organization (that is, lineage and inheritance are traced through the father) and with agricultural economies (Reiss, 1986). Monogamy is characteristic of industrialized and complex societies. In some cultures, all three patterns of relationship are still practiced. The historical origins and frequency of these three patterns will probably never be completely known.

Cultures have also varied in their prohibitions against sex among relatives; that is, incest is defined differently in different cultures. In some, a relationship is considered incestuous only if an individual has sex with a member of his or her immediate family (a parent, sibling, or offspring). In others, members are barred from sexual relations with relatives with whom there is any genetic relationship, as well as with members of their clan with whom they may share no traceable genetic relationship. Although several groups, including the early Egyptians, Hawaiians, and Peruvians, have accepted marriage between brothers and sisters (at least among the ruling families), Bixler (1982) has argued that marriage between siblings probably did not involve sexual intercourse. Cleopatra is probably the most famous sibling-spouse.

In another variation in beliefs about appropriate partners for sex and marriage, relatives in some groups inherit the spouses of their siblings. More than two-thirds of nonindustrialized cultures, for example, practice the *levirate*; that is, when a woman's husband dies, his younger brother (her brother-in-law) may marry her. The levirate was required by ancient Hebrew law. The corresponding practice of the marriage of a widowed man to his former wife's sister—the practice of *sororate*—is much less common (Reiss, 1986). Among the Tiwi people of Melville Island,

who have the levirate, a woman typically first marries a man who is much older than she. She may sequentially marry and then be widowed by several of his brothers, ending up with a husband who is younger than she. Female power in this culture comes not from having many mates, however, but from the fact that the culture is *matrilocal*; that is, couples reside near the wife's mother, and the husband is considered to be indebted to his mother-in-law. Because their descent group consists of female offspring of the mother's line, the Tiwi are also basically a *matrilineal* group. Males, however, through their male kin, control the land, and thus can improve their economic status by arranging advantageous marriages for these male kin. The Tiwi system serves as an example of the ways in which the definition of kinship can affect the balance of power between males and females.

In patrilineal societies, biological and social inheritance are traced through paternal links; that is, all children of a married couple belong to the father's social group. In most patrilineal societies, women must leave their own relatives at marriage and spend the major part of their lives in the company of their husbands' relatives. Patrilineal societies are usually dominated by males, and in some cases women are strictly segregated from public life. Patrilineal communities often have been associated with the rise of agriculture. With the spread of intensive cultivation techniques, women dropped out of the mainstream of production for the first time in the history of cultural evolution. Rigid division of labor by gender developed, in which production of goods for consumption was distinguished from work connected with the home. This division of labor had the effect of isolating men and women from one another and of separating women from public life. Indeed, many agricultural societies placed a high value on restricting women to the home. This pattern is the normative one in Islamic groups, where the segregation of women, known as *purdah*, is often a sign of wealth and status (Figure 1.11).

Some patrilineal cultures also practice the levirate system. Among the So of northeastern Uganda, if a woman's husband dies, one of his

**polyandry** (PAH-lee-AN-dree)—a marital form in which a woman may have more than one lover or spouse but a man is expected to have only one partner.

**purdah**—the practice of secluding women from men.

**FIGURE 1.11**
**Purdah**
The segregation of women is often a sign of wealth and status in some Islamic societies. The two women in the upper left follow the traditional pattern of covering their faces when in public.

brothers may marry and impregnate her. Because of the strong reproductive bias of the So, however, a woman whose husband dies after she has gone through menopause and is no longer able to have children will not be wed to her husband's brother. In view of the value that many of us place on having a partner throughout life, and our sympathy for the lonely widow or widower, we might feel sorry for the So woman who is postmenopausal. But to understand her feelings, we need to remember the potential mistake of letting our own cultural experiences bias our interpretations of the experiences of people in other historical periods or in other cultures. For So women, menopause provides a relief from the burden of engaging in sex for procreation and allows them to devote themselves to their relationships with their co-wives, sisters, and other women in their clan with whom they are closely bonded.

There are few sexual behaviors that have not been perceived as good or appropriate in some historical time or place, and bad or inappropriate in others. If history serves as any guide to the future, there is little reason to believe that the norms, values, and perceptions that prevail in 20th-century North America will be the same 300 years from now, or that people will interact sexually in the future as they do now. Economic and political factors such as overpopulation and war and sexually transmitted diseases such as AIDS will shape sexual values and behaviors.

In this chapter, we have highlighted the historical and cross-cultural diversity of human sexual expression in hopes of increasing your appreciation for the relationship of our society's beliefs and behaviors to those of other times and places. We hope that after reading this chapter, you will be more cautious about evaluating variations in sexual behaviors and values.

## Summary of Major Points

1. **Evaluating cross-cultural and historical sexual behaviors.**

Sexual behaviors approved of or rejected by contemporary North Americans may have been perceived differently in other times and places. The application of one's cultural values to many of these behaviors can be inappropriate and misleading.

2. **Beliefs about the nature of female and male sexuality.**

Beliefs about the nature of female sexuality have both reflected and determined attitudes toward women, and women's treatment, throughout history. Most cultures and time periods have experienced conflict between the idealization of women because of their child-bearing capacities and the belief that women tempt and entrap men and endanger their health and morality. Less commonly, women have been seen as sexually passive, as in our own culture beginning around the time of the Industrial Revolution. In contrast, male sexuality has been perceived quite consistently as involving relatively involuntary behavior.

3. Beliefs about sexual intercourse.

The idea that the sole purpose of sexual intimacy is procreation has dominated most, but not all, Western cultures. This belief has led to the punishment or persecution of people who engage in nonprocreative acts. Within our own culture in some historical periods, avoidance of sexual "excess" even within marriage has been seen as crucial for good health, morality, and longevity. Although reproductive bias is also seen in a number of groups cross-culturally, some societies view frequent sexual activity and skill in pleasing partners as factors in increasing status, and these societies look upon sex as pleasurable recreation.

4. Beliefs about same-gender sexual relationships.

There have been enormous variations in values and beliefs regarding homosexual relationships. In some cultures and time periods, societies have seen such relationships as the highest form of emotional bond and a vehicle for transmitting knowledge to adolescents. Other groups have severely punished or put to death people who engage in same-gender sex. The majority of contemporary North Americans disapprove of homosexual contacts. Some even believe that gay people are emotionally disturbed, although scientific data do not support that belief.

5. Beliefs about the relationships among love, sex, and marriage.

The belief among North Americans that love is a prerequisite for marriage developed relatively recently, and many other cultures do not share this view. In most cultures and time periods, the purpose of marriage has been procreation and the cementing of economic, political, and social bonds. Many groups either do not have a concept of romantic love or else perceive it as an experience that one has with someone other than a spouse. Similarly, love has been seen as quite independent of sexual activity in many cultures.

## Review of Key Concepts*

1. The perception that females are sexually insatiable and dangerously seductive is: a) common to all cultures; b) true mainly of Western culture up to relatively recent times;

---

*Answering these questions correctly will help you to verify your understanding of what you have read. Many more questions, as well as other helpful study aids, are available in the Study Guide.

c) characteristic of the So of Uganda; d) supported by modern research. (pp. 5–9)

2. The Christian tradition has: a) emphasized that one may incur personal guilt for having "lustful" thoughts; b) been comparable to the Hindu tradition in its repressive attitudes toward sexuality; c) been deeply influenced by Greek attitudes toward sexuality; d) none of the above. (p. 9)

3. Prostitution: a) was officially tolerated by 19th-century church officials; b) flourished in Victorian times as an outlet for male passion; c) was closely linked to the persecution of witches in medieval Europe; d) first emerged in the 20th century. (p. 10)

4. Male circumcision is: a) almost universal in modern industrial societies; b) generally a medically recommended procedure; c) legally required in many places in North America; d) a practice rooted in ancient cultural traditions. (p. 17)

5. Birth control: a) has been practiced only in the 20th century; b) was attempted through the use of contraceptives as early as ancient Egypt; c) by means of abortion was strictly illegal under Anglo-American law until the 20th century; d) was tolerated by the medieval Catholic church as a concession to "lust." (p. 19)

6. Most cultures and past societies have generally regarded marriage as: a) the culmination of the lovers' sexual attraction to each other; b) primarily a social and economic relationship out of which love and affection may develop; c) an institution that can be adapted to the couple's chosen lifestyle; d) a religious ceremony. (p. 25)

7. Romantic love: a) is strongly rooted in Western cultural traditions, although it became the preferred basis of marriage only in relatively recent times; b) was characteristic of ancient Greek and Roman society but was later condemned by the Christian church; c) is considered to be the cornerstone of marital relations among the Mehinaku of Brazil; d) none of the above. (p. 23)

8. Evidence suggests that: a) jealousy is a universal emotion; b) the extent to which different groups experience jealousy is tied to their beliefs about acceptable sexual-relationship forms; c) people in monogamous cultures seem particularly prone to feeling jealousy; d) both b and c. (p. 25)

9. Monogamy: a) has been normative in more cultures than polygamy; b) has been normative in fewer cultures than polygamy; c) is related to the practice of tracing inheritance through the mother's line; d) is associated primarily with agricultural societies. (p. 26)

10. To what extent do you feel that the social and economic status of women has reflected men's sexual attitudes toward them? What historical and cultural evidence can you cite in support of your answer?

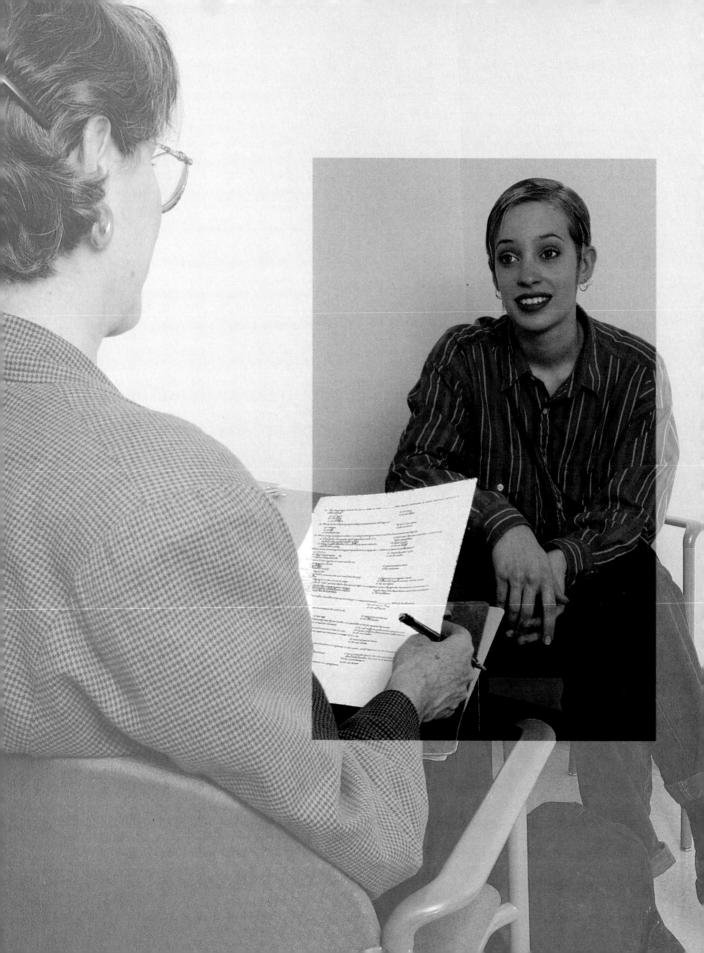

# Research on Sexuality

*W*HEN we make decisions that affect our lives, it is helpful to have information about the potential consequences of the choices available to us. In deciding which college major or career to pursue, we want to know the costs and benefits associated with our alternatives. Sexual decisions can also have major consequences in terms of costs and benefits, but in this area many of us make decisions in the dark, so to speak. With relatively little knowledge, we must make judgments as voters for or against sex education, as parents giving advice about nonmarital sex, or as consumers of contraceptives or products to promote fertility.

One of the goals of sex researchers is to increase knowledge about the causes, correlates, and consequences of sexual attitudes and behaviors. In this chapter, we will first look at the movement away from religious doctrines and toward empirical research as bases for reaching conclusions about various sexual issues. Next we will consider contemporary political and social barriers to sex research and the risks taken by several pioneering 20th-century sex researchers. We will discuss a number of ethical considerations that arise in conducting research on sexual and nonsexual topics. In the second half of the chapter, we will turn to the process of sex research in a discussion that should help you evaluate the findings of sex researchers as you make sexual decisions in the coming years.

## The Rise of Science

For several centuries prior to 1900, religious influence and interpretations were on the decline in intellectual circles as scientific explanations of the world and human behavior became increasingly influential. In their response to sexuality, however, scientists were not much more tolerant than clergymen had been. As the devil and his disciples were held less accountable for the world's misfortunes, a new scapegoat had to be found. Insanity was the choice, and its alleged cause was not a pact with the devil, but masturbation. From the 18th century until the end of the 19th century, this new "illness" was known as masturbatory insanity (Szasz, 1990) (see Figure 2.1).

In 1758 Simon André Tissot (1728–1797), a prominent Swiss physician, published *Onania, or a Treatise upon the Disorders Produced by Masturbation*. This book gave medical backing to the supposed role of self-stimulation as a cause of madness. The idea of a connection between masturbation and insanity soon spread across Europe, and medical authorities warned of the dire consequences of what some called the secret sin. In the United States, the father of American psychiatry, Dr. Benjamin Rush (1745–1813), claimed that masturbation produced pulmonary consumption, dimness of sight, vertigo, epilepsy, hypochondriasis, and loss of memory (Szasz, 1990).

Treatments for disorders believed to be rooted in masturbation included castration of males, removal of the clitoris of females, circumcision, and other rather grotesque and painful medical procedures. An 18th-century English physician, J. L. Milton, recommended that young men wear locked chastity belts by day and spiked or toothed rings at night. The spiked ring would awaken a boy if he had an erection. He was to bathe his penis in cold water until the erection subsided, and then put the ring back on his penis and return to bed (see Figure 2.2).

The assumption that masturbation caused various maladies continued well into the 20th century. This belief represented a transformation of the religious equation of sexual pleasure with sin into the medical idea that losing sperm is dis-

**FIGURE 2.1**
**Supposed Effects of Masturbation**
This 19th-century picture shows the supposed fate of a masturbator. In addition to insanity, masturbation was thought to cause a variety of physical disorders, among them epilepsy, poor eyesight, and loss of memory.

ease-producing. Perhaps the most influential medical proponent of these ideas was Richard von Krafft-Ebing.

## Richard von Krafft-Ebing

Krafft-Ebing (1840–1902), considered during his lifetime to be one of the world's leading psychiatrists, is an appropriate symbol for Victorian sexual attitudes. His major work, *Psychopathia Sexualis* (1882), reflected the dominant theme of the time—sex as disease. It catalogued many types of sexual variations, illustrated with more than 200 case histories. Krafft-Ebing emphasized bizarre cases of sexual expression, and the thread running through all the variations he documented was masturbation and hereditary degeneracy.

Krafft-Ebing's work reflected the concern of the times about "deviant" sexuality, which in-

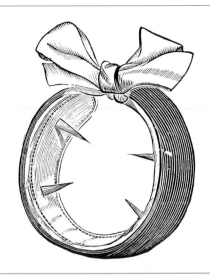

**FIGURE 2.2**
**A Penile Ring**
Some 18th-century boys wore spiked rings around the penis at night. If the wearer experienced a nocturnal erection, the spikes in the ring would cause pain that would awaken him, deterring him from the temptation of masturbation.

cluded all sexual acts that did not have reproduction as their goal. He helped to spread the fear of most forms of eroticism by lending a scientific cast to these beliefs. Krafft-Ebing was a leading figure in the pseudoscientific linking of nonreproductive sexual activity with disease.

Ironically, two other people who were also contemporaries of the Victorian era transformed the way we think about sex in the 20th century: Henry Havelock Ellis and Sigmund Freud. Both were born in the middle of the 19th century, and both died in 1939. Their work transcended the Victorian era and set the stage for the scientific study of human sexuality.

## Henry Havelock Ellis
## and Sigmund Freud

Henry Havelock Ellis (1859–1939) was perhaps the central figure in the emergence of the modern study of sexuality (see Figure 2.3). The historian Paul Robinson (1976) contended that Ellis was to modern sexual theory what Albert Einstein was

to modern physics, because Ellis established a framework that has influenced all recent theories about sexuality. The first six volumes of Ellis's *Studies in the Psychology of Sex* were published between 1897 and 1910. His initial volume, *Sexual Inversion*, was an attempt to broaden the spectrum of normal sexual behavior to include homosexuality. He argued that homosexuality was congenital (that is, existing at or before birth) and thus was not a vice or a moral choice. Homosexuality was simply a variation from a statistical norm, heterosexuality.

In his second volume, *Auto-Eroticism*, Ellis attacked the 19th-century theories that linked masturbation to insanity. His work transformed masturbation from "a malignant vice into a benign inevitability" (Robinson, 1976, p. 13). Elsewhere, Ellis argued that most of the major forms of sexual deviation are congenital and related to some aspect of normal sexual life. Ellis fostered an acceptance of sexual variation that stood in marked contrast to the Victorian atmosphere of his lifetime.

In contrast to Ellis, who focused his work exclusively on sexuality, Sigmund Freud (1856–

**FIGURE 2.3**
**Henry Havelock Ellis**
Ellis was a key figure in the modern study of sexuality. His writings on sexual deviance contradicted prevailing Victorian views.

### Box 2.1

## Vaginal-Clitoral Orgasm and Psychological Circumcision

In his theory of female sexuality (1905), Freud described young girls' source of sexual pleasure as masculine because they obtain pleasure from stimulation of the clitoris, just as young boys do from stimulation of the penis. Freud claimed that as women become healthy adults, the source of pleasure and orgasm shifts from the clitoris to the vagina.

Some psychoanalytic writers took this idea at face value and asserted that orgasm from clitoral stimulation is an expression of immaturity, neuroticism, masculinity, and frigidity. In *The Power of Sexual Surrender* (1959), Marie Robinson claimed that the truly mature woman always experiences vaginal orgasms; the woman who has only clitoral orgasms is suffering from a form of frigidity. Interestingly, Robinson acknowledged that scores of women find clitoral stimulation and orgasm so gratifying that they are not motivated to achieve what was thought of as sexual maturity.

Many psychoanalytic writers disagreed with the position that healthy adult women should experience pleasure from stimulation of the vagina rather than from the clitoris (Benedek, 1959; Horney, 1933; Marmor, 1954), but they were not as influential as the doctrinaire Freudians. Their lack of influence probably can be attributed to the predominant cultural belief that the sole purpose of sexuality is reproduction.

In Chapter 1, we described ancient and modern views of female circumcision in North Africa. We discussed the notion that removing the clitoris allows a female to shed the "masculine" part of herself as well as to reduce her sexual desire. Freudian theorists followed similar reasoning, although they took a less drastic approach. They advocated what could be called "psychological circumcision"; that is, they called the woman who did not reject clitoral stimulation immature, masculine, and/or neurotic. Thus, many women who experienced sexual pleasure and orgasm through clitoral stimulation but did not have vaginal orgasms were left with doubts, guilt, and feelings of inadequacy about their sexuality. Rather than physically obliterating a source of sexual pleasure, then, Freudian ideas psychologically blocked many women's enjoyment of clitoral stimulation. As you will see in Chapter 7, there is no evidence to indicate that women who receive pleasure and orgasm from clitoral stimulation are immature or emotionally disturbed. Nonetheless, because of the Freudians' theories, many women sought therapy for a source of pleasure that they were led to believe was a problem. Ideas change slowly, and it is humbling to ponder how many of our current beliefs about sexuality will be shown to have as little substance as the Freudian view on clitoral versus vaginal orgasms.

---

1939) developed a comprehensive theory of human behavior that encompassed many different fields. He emphasized sex as the central aspect of human development. Most intellectuals at the time derided his *Three Contributions to the Theory of Sex* (1905). But Freud and other representatives of the school of thought he founded, psychoanalysis, persevered through the early torrent of criticism, and psychoanalysis gradually became one of the most influential theoretical frame-

works of the time. Freud's theories will be discussed in Chapter 3.

Although Freud contributed enormously to our understanding of human sexuality, his theories also led to some major misunderstandings, particularly regarding the nature of female sexuality. As Box 2.1 shows, these inaccuracies had a major impact on women's feelings about themselves and their sexual capacities. Ellis and Freud opened up the subject of sexuality to serious research and tore down barriers of prudery that had blocked public and scientific discussion, but many societal barriers remain.

## The Impact of Societal Beliefs, Political Attitudes, and Ethical Issues on Research

The questions researchers ask about sexuality and the methods they use to try to obtain answers are intimately related to societal values and beliefs and ethical considerations. Sometimes it is hard to see the difference between these influences. For example, it has been difficult to obtain information about childhood sexual experience. Sex research with children is contrary to the ethical values held by the scientific community because it violates the principle of *informed consent*; that is, a young child is not considered mature enough to consent to participate in sex research. Such research also violates the societal belief that sex research with children is immoral. In this instance then, ethical values and societal beliefs are in agreement regarding the moral inappropriateness of conducting such research. Here we will separate the discussion of these influences on research, however, because sometimes societal beliefs conflict with ethical views of appropriate topics for sex research.

## Political and Societal Barriers to Research

*Backlash by society*

Until the mid-20th century, most of our knowledge of sexual behavior was based on observations of animal sex, native sex, or crazy sex, as Byrne (1977) put it—that is, it was more acceptable to study the behavior of animals, non-Western nonindustrialized populations, or people who were considered psychologically disturbed than it was to study what the typical adult in Western populations thought or did sexually.

informed consent—the ethical principle of informing potential research participants, before they consent to participate, of any aspects of the research that might be embarrassing or damaging.

Most of Freud's theorizing was based on the experiences of emotionally disturbed patients.

When a few 19th-century physicians attempted to institute training or research procedures related to sexuality, they suffered dire consequences. In the mid-19th century, for example, Dr. James Platt White allowed 20 medical students to do vaginal examinations of a consenting pregnant woman prior to and during childbirth as part of a teaching technique that he called demonstrative midwifery. Responding to the objections of other physicians, who believed that it was improper for a doctor to see women's genitals even while delivering babies, the American Medical Association expelled White in 1851 and passed a resolution against demonstrative midwifery. A similar response by the medical community greeted Dr. Emo Nograph's presentation of research on sexually transmitted diseases. He was booed after his presentation to the newly founded American Gynecological Society in 1875, and an invitation to present a paper the following year was withdrawn. An 1885 graduate of Jefferson Medical College reported that he had received his M.D. without ever having seen a maternity case, although he later specialized in the area (Bullough, 1983).

You might assume that extreme reactions of this kind are relics of the 19th century, but even scientists who studied sexual behavior in the mid-20th century paid a price for doing so, both professionally and personally. To illustrate the risks taken by sex-research pioneers, we will focus on the work of Alfred C. Kinsey, William Masters, and Vern Bullough, who were all advised by their teachers to develop firm reputations in other scientific areas before they ventured into the relatively taboo world of sexuality. Thus biologist Alfred Kinsey published work on the gall wasp, obstetrician-gynecologist William Masters studied ovulatory patterns in rabbits, and Vern Bullough developed his reputation by writing about nonsexual aspects of history. After establishing their scholarly credibility, these researchers turned to the study of human sexuality.

### The Kinsey Group

In the mid-1930s, Alfred Kinsey and some other Indiana University faculty members were asked

**FIGURE 2.4**
**Kinsey and His Colleagues**
In a meeting at the Institute for Sex Research in Bloomington, Indiana, Kinsey and his colleagues discuss some of their statistical analyses. From left to right are Alfred C. Kinsey, Clyde E. Martin, Paul H. Gebhard, and Wardell B. Pomeroy.

to teach a marriage-and-family course. In preparing for the course, Kinsey discovered that there was little scientific information about the sexual aspects of marriage, so he decided to do his own research. Initially, he administered questionnaires to his students about their sexual experiences. By 1938 he had established a research group at Indiana, and they began the first of their interviews with thousands of Americans about their sexual experiences and behaviors. Kinsey and his colleagues, Wardell Pomeroy, Clyde Martin, and Paul Gebhard (see Figure 2.4), undertook the task of describing the sexual behavior of typical Americans throughout the life span by using a combination of intensive interviews and questionnaires.

Kinsey and his colleagues described some of the difficulties they encountered as they interviewed volunteers about their sexual behavior. For the first several years of this project, they were repeatedly warned about the dangers involved in collecting sex histories, and they experienced some organized opposition, "chiefly from a particular medical group" (1948, p. 11). The medical association in one city tried to sue

them on the grounds that they were practicing medicine without a license. The police interfered with their work in several cities, and a sheriff investigated them in one rural area. Threats of legal action and political investigation hounded them, as did criticism from some scientific colleagues. The harassment was not limited to the scientists on the project; a high-school teacher who helped the Kinsey group find volunteers outside the school but in the same city was dismissed by his school board. In addition, there were attempts to persuade Indiana University to stop the study, censor or prevent publication of the results, and fire Kinsey. But the university's administration defended the Kinsey group's right to do scientific research. By the time the group published *Sexual Behavior in the Human Male* (1948) and its sequel, *Sexual Behavior in the Human Female* (1953), however, the United States was going through the McCarthy era, years of intense political repression. Under pressure from a congressional committee, the Rockefeller Foundation withdrew its financial support of the project. Kinsey died three years later, and his colleagues continued their studies of human sexuality separately.

The Kinsey group's findings have benefited the general public in providing a basis for social comparison that previously had not existed. For instance, we now know that the majority of people report masturbating at various times, a fact unknown before the publication of the Kinsey group's two major books. Presumably, people who realize that masturbation or other sexual behavior is typical of most people in our culture do not suffer the pangs of remorse and guilt that previous generations endured—or that still afflict those people who are unaware that most people masturbate.

Kinsey and his associates also helped pave the way for subsequent researchers to investigate sexual attitudes and behavior.* "Without their

---

*In fact, we recommend that students who are writing a paper or research proposal on some aspect of sexuality begin by checking their topic in the indexes of the Kinsey group's (1948, 1953) volumes. Students may then consult Frayser and Whitby's *Studies in Human Sexuality: A Selected Guide* (1987), which reviews books and monographs on sexuality from 1970 to about 1985 and provides a good basis for reviewing the research relevant to their topic.

**FIGURE 2.5**
**William Masters and Virginia Johnson**
Masters and Johnson are pioneering researchers on physiological aspects of human sexual response.

original foot in the door," said William Masters, "we would never have been allowed to work. . . . These people broke the ice. When I went to the powers that be at Washington University in 1953, the [Kinsey] male book was out and the female book was just being published. I asked for permission to work in human sexuality. Well, obviously, there was a precedent set" (quoted in Allgeier, 1984).

*William Masters and Virginia Johnson*

In 1966 William Masters and Virginia Johnson (see Figure 2.5) published their first major book on sexuality, *Human Sexual Response,* describing the results of their observations of human sexual

response in laboratory settings. Instead of interviewing people about what they did sexually, as the Kinsey group had done, Masters and Johnson directly observed sexual stimulation in a laboratory. They studied volunteers through one-way glass as they masturbated, had oral sex, or engaged in coitus. They measured sexual responsiveness with the use of devices that fit around the penis or were inserted into the vagina. Their work is responsible for the popularization of the finding that—contrary to Freud (refer to Box 2.1)—the clitoris is involved in most women's sexual responsiveness.

In 1983 William Masters recounted some of the difficulties that he and Virginia Johnson experienced as they developed what is now known as the Masters and Johnson Institute in St. Louis. Despite the Kinsey group's precedent-setting work, when Masters asked the Washington University authorities for permission to do sex research, "they were terrified . . . but had they known what we were going to do, they'd have been even more so." In 1954 Masters finally obtained approval from the university's board of trustees to begin his work. But he ran into problems right away because his interest in the basic physiology of human sexual functioning was taking him into uncharted waters. At the outset, he could rely for previous research on only one book—Dickinson's *Atlas of Human Sexual Anatomy*—and the library would not let Masters have the book! (Only full professors could check it out, and Masters held the rank of associate professor at the time.) His department's chairperson checked it out for him, but it had little information relevant to his topic. Undaunted, Masters spent a year working with a group who might know something about the physiology of sexual response: prostitutes. But when he sought permission from the chancellor of his university to set up a laboratory, "the man turned deathly pale." Masters did ultimately obtain permission, however, and his work was supervised by a review board headed by the chancellor, a newspaper publisher, the chief of police, and a member of the clergy (Allgeier, 1984).

One prostitute with whom Masters worked ("a most attractive prostitute who had a Ph.D. in sociology and had hit upon a uniquely tax-free method of enhancing her university salary") told him that to understand the subjective aspects of female sexual functioning, he would need a female colleague. After interviewing many candidates, he found Virginia Johnson. "She met the following criteria," he later explained: "(a) good with people, because I'm not; (b) had to work; (c) married and divorced, and at least one child . . . ; (d) intelligent; and (e) no post-graduate degree." Masters included the last criterion because he did not want the responsibility of exposing a woman to the risk of losing her degree (women with advanced degrees were rare in the mid-1950s), although he was well aware that he himself "had a good chance of losing an M.D." (Allgeier, 1984).

Masters and Johnson began working in their laboratory in 1957 with two different populations: one group that was observed in the research laboratory (to gain information about normal sexual response), and one group that was studied in a clinical setting (to gain information about—and treat—sexual and reproductive problems). In the late 1950s, the team experienced sabotage. Parts of their equipment disappeared, and personal attacks followed. "What we didn't expect was how they were done: They were fundamentally carried out against our children, [who] were socially ostracized [and] bitterly attacked as being sex-mongers. I had to move my daughter from St. Louis and send her to prep school." After publication of *Human Sexual Response* (1966), "the hate mail was unbelievable. . . . The drop dead category was about 90–95% of the mail." Despite this early harassment, Masters and Johnson persevered, and we know of no books dealing with human sexual response that do not reference Masters and Johnson's work—a testament to their important contributions to the field.

### Vern Bullough

Historian Vern Bullough also endured his share of professional difficulties resulting from his work on sexuality. Bullough obtained his Ph.D. in history from the University of Chicago in 1954 and began his career with historical analyses of nonsexual topics. In 1957 the Wolfenden Report—a study of prostitution and homosexuality in Britain—was published, and Bullough wrote a review of it. Repeatedly invited by a publisher to write a book on either of these topics, Bullough

eventually consented to examine the history of prostitution: "I did not consent to write about homosexuality because, at that time, I was very concerned about being labeled a homosexual. I didn't mind being labeled a prostitute. I also took great care to publish research on a number of other topics so that I would not be labeled as a sexologist" (Bullough, 1983).

Bullough has described himself (personal communication, June 6, 1986) as a historian of science and medicine, not a sexologist, but he has not completely succeeded in avoiding that label. In introducing Bullough's presentation on medieval universities and professionalism at the American Historical Association, the session's moderator described him as a "historian who specializes in whores, queers, and perverts, but who occasionally could do some real research if he put his mind to it." In fact, of the 40 books that he has written, half of which were coauthored with his wife, Dr. Bonnie Bullough (see Figure 2.6), less than half have focused on sexual topics.

Bullough learned in the 1970s that the FBI was investigating him. In 1976, under the provisions of the Freedom of Information Act, Bullough requested his FBI file. It took him almost a year to get the file, which exceeded 100 pages, and its contents "shocked and horrified" him. He learned that the FBI had classified him as a security risk, meaning that he could be imprisoned in the event of a national crisis. He earned this classification during the years that J. Edgar Hoover, the longtime director of the FBI, was in office. Ironically, rumors had long circulated that Hoover was gay and occasionally dressed in women's attire. His "tough cop" image may have been, at least in part, an attempt to counteract the rumors of his homosexuality (Gentry, 1991). In the late 1960s, when Bullough received a Fulbright scholarship (one of the nation's most prestigious awards) to do research in Egypt, overseas agencies of the United States were alerted to keep watch on him and his family because they were regarded as "dangerous subversives." It is not clear how or why a dangerous subversive would receive a Fulbright, but as Bullough put it, "Sometimes, one wing of the government doesn't know what the other wing does."

In this section we have considered some of the barriers and risks faced by pioneering sex re-

**FIGURE 2.6**
**Vern and Bonnie Bullough**
This husband and wife team lean on some of the books they have written individually and in collaboration with one another. Fewer than half of their books have focused on sexuality. Nonetheless, known for his historical analyses of sexual attitudes and behavior, Vern Bullough was once classified as a dangerous subversive by the FBI, presumably because of his sex research.

searchers, but as the Kinsey group wrote in 1953, sex researchers are not alone in experiencing such barriers:

> There was a day when the organization of the universe, and the place of the earth, the sun, the moon, and the stars in it, were considered of such theologic import that the scientific investigation of these matters was bitterly opposed by the ruling forces of the day. The scientists who first attempted to explore the nature of matter, and the physical laws af-

fecting the relationships of matter were similarly condemned. . . . There is an honesty in science which refused to accept the idea that there are aspects of the material universe that are better not investigated, or better not known, or the knowledge of which should not be made available to the common men. . . . We do not believe that the happiness of individual men, and the good of the total social organization, is ever furthered by the perpetuation of ignorance. (1953, p. 10)

The historian Paul Robinson concluded a review (1976) of the Kinsey group's work by suggesting that those of us who believe that sexual ignorance and prejudice create high levels of anxiety about sex may appreciate the group's research for providing information to reduce our anxieties and, perhaps, to increase our happiness. On the other hand, those who believe that the scientific study of sexuality trivializes sex, and that "in eliminating the anxiety we have also eliminated the ecstasy, then Kinsey, while not to be despised, must be regretted. . . . My historical sense, however, is that we are still some way from such jadedness" (Robinson, 1976, p. 119). We agree with Robinson's judgment. As the rest of our book demonstrates, we believe that researchers are still some distance from understanding many aspects of human sexuality, despite the knowledge contributed by 20th-century sex researchers.

Having read this review of the harassment experienced by several sex-research pioneers, you may be left with the mistaken impression that hostility to sex research is behind us. In fact, contemporary efforts to gather data, even those buttressed with the justification of reducing the spread of AIDS, still face uphill battles. For example, a clear association exists between government support and advocacy for sex education throughout the school years and the relatively low rates of sexuality-related problems in some countries, among them Sweden (Allgeier, 1993; Jones et al., 1986). However, such evidence has had little impact on the conservative politicians who have consistently blocked funds for research on human sexuality (see Box 2.2). Other associated problems have been described by Fisher (1989), who noted that in this field, many laypersons consider themselves experts on a topic

**Box 2.2**

## Contemporary Political and Social Barriers to Sex Research

One of the most tragic consequences of sexual contact in our time is the AIDS epidemic. Because researchers have concluded that a cure for AIDS is unlikely to be available within the next few years, right now the only major way of slowing or stopping the spread of AIDS is to convince people to alter their sexual practices. To do so, we need to understand the factors involved in the development of sexual attitudes and behaviors.

Accordingly, both the World Health Organization (WHO) (Carballo, Cleland, Carael, & Albrecht, 1989) and the U.S. National Institutes of Health (NIH) (Booth, 1989) drafted requests for research proposals to obtain information on sexual attitudes and behavior. The WHO secured the cooperation of governments in Europe, Africa, and Asia to administer its surveys, but the NIH experienced much more difficulty in being able to support large-scale studies of sexual behavior.

In 1987–1988, two requests for proposals were released by the NIH seeking research on adult and adolescent sexual behavior. After reviews by panels of scientists, two contracts were granted. In October 1987, the adult contract was awarded to the Survey of Health and AIDS Risk Prevalance (SHARP). The adolescent contract was awarded in May 1991 to the American Teenage Study (ATS). Each study involved a large national sample and each was funded for almost $20 million (Udry, 1993). Although the cost of the research may seem prohibitive, it pales in comparison with cost projections of long-term treatment of AIDS patients.

### The Survey of Health and AIDS Risk Prevalence (SHARP)

The SHARP study was designed by Drs. Edward Laumann of the University of Chicago, Robert Michael of the National Opinion Research Center (NORC), and John Gagnon of the State University of New York at Stony Brook. The SHARP group would have been the first to question a nationally representative sample of adults about their numbers of sexual partners, their sexual behaviors, and their attitudes toward their behaviors. Pilot work for the study included questioning 2,000 Americans, and funding for the pilot research was awarded in July 1988. After revisions based on the pilot study, interviews were planned with about 20,000 Americans. Proponents of the SHARP study, including a blue-ribbon panel of social scientists advising the National Research Council, pointed out that "information on sexual practices is vital for predicting and mitigating the spread of AIDS and other sexually transmitted diseases in the United States" (Booth, 1989, p. 419).

### The American Teenage Study (ATS)

The ATS, created by Drs. Ronald Rindfuss and J. Richard Udry of the Carolina Population Center at the University of North Carolina at Chapel Hill, was to be based on a nationally representative sample of 20,000 adolescents aged 12–17. Their intent was to study adolescent development comprehensively,

*with special emphasis on the influence of the family, the school, the peer group, religious institutions, and the community. . . . Sexual behavior was studied not as a collision of bodies but as a significant part of the developing relationships of the teenager. (Udry, 1993, p. 106)*

They planned two waves of interviews with the adolescents and their parents.

### Retraction of the SHARP and ATS Funds

After the SHARP and ATS proposals had been favorably reviewed by scientists and approved for funding by the NIH, political forces intervened. In 1989, James Mason, the U.S. Assistant Secretary of Health and Human Services (HHS), sought a copy of the ATS project while simultaneously reviewing the question naire for the SHARP study (Udry, 1993). Mason was asked by then HHS secretary Louis Sullivan to review the SHARP study—*after* it had already been approved for funding (Laumann, Gagnon, & Michael, 1993). Mason reviewed the ATS survey following the intervention of William Dannemeyer, a U.S. Congressional Representative from California. In an editorial published in *USA Today* under the headline, "We don't need this pornographic research," Dannemeyer acknowledged the threat of AIDS but stated that tax dollars are better spent on studies that measure the extent of AIDS infection than on research that might shed light on how to prevent further transmission. He asserted that the government should "leave this sort of sex 'study' to the porno industry" ("We Don't Need This Pornographic Research," *USA Today*, April 20, 1989, p. 8A).

Then secretary of HHS Louis Sullivan pondered what to do about SHARP. While he pondered, in April 1989, Kay James, HHS assistant secretary for public affairs, imposed

*a gag rule prohibiting the members of the research team to make public statements in behalf of the survey. She was the public affairs director for the National Right to Life Committee from 1985 to 1988. The effect of this was to eliminate our participation in the public debate over the feasibility and utility of such a study for the next three years. (Laumann et al., 1993)*

Thus, the investigators were held up and ultimately blocked from conducting research that had already been approved and funded, and they could not even talk about it!

Dannemeyer was joined in his opposition by U.S. Senator Jesse Helms from North Carolina. Speaking before the U.S. Senate, Helms claimed that

*The real purpose . . . is not to stop the spread of AIDS. . . . These sex surveys have not—have not—been concerned with legitimate scientific inquiry as much as they have been concerned with a blatant attempt to sway public attitudes in order to liberalize opinions and laws regarding homo sexuality, pedophilia, anal and oral sex, sex edu-*

*cation, teenage pregnancy and all down the line.* (Congressional Record, *September 12, 1991, pp. S12861–S12862*).

Helms's attitude is an excellent example of some government officials' ignorance of scientific methodology. Ironically, Bernadine Healy, the head of NIH, had read the ATS and praised it publicly. After sitting on the ATS study for nearly two years, Mason cleared it and released it back to NIH for action, and it was funded in May 1991. However, then HHS secretary Louis Sullivan

*was asked on a Christian Network talk show in July 1991 why he was funding the ATS. He obviously did not know about it and was blindsided. Within days he announced he was canceling the study. His announced reason was that the study might undermine the administration's message to teenagers that they should not engage in sex. (Udry, 1993)*

Efforts by Representative Dannemeyer to block funding for any government support for research on sexuality were voted down by a strong majority in Congress. However, neither SHARP nor ATS survived the political forces; their federal funding was not reinstated.

Lest you think that the United States has the corner on accurate reporting and the blocking of needed research, consider the following series of events described by *Newsweek* (February 19, 1990, p. 63) on the handling of AIDS in Romania under the former dictator Nicolae Ceauşescu. Before the Romanian revolution in December 1989 that ultimately led to his death by firing squad, Ceauşescu claimed that AIDS existed only in "decadent" countries, not in Romania. In conflict with his position, out of about 2,000 Romanian children sampled, 700 tested positive for the AIDS virus. In 1987 his regime had ordered hospitals to reuse needles to save money. What did Ceauşescu do when physicians, in the summer of 1989, reported the widespread infection of babies with HIV? He banned all further tests for AIDS infection and threatened those physicians reporting the infection with imprisonment.

under scrutiny by a given sex researcher—a phenomenon that researchers in such areas as physics, chemistry, or demography do not experience. For example, a colleague dismissed Fisher's research on the effect of varying levels of alcohol on female orgasm with the comment that Shakespeare had understood the effect of alcohol on sex 400 years ago, so why had Fisher bothered to study it?

## Ethical Issues

In addition to the limitations that societal attitudes and beliefs impose on the kinds of questions that can be investigated, scientists must also be concerned with the rights, safety, and well-being of those who participate in their research. Over the years, several principles have been developed to safeguard the rights of volunteers for research, and federal guidelines mandate that any institution or organization that receives federal funds must ensure that research carried on in its institution is reviewed by an ethics board prior to any data collection. In evaluating the ethical acceptability of research procedures, ethics boards generally rely on four major principles: informed consent, freedom from coercion, protection from physical or psychological harm, and the risk-benefit principle.

### Informed Consent

Research on sexual attitudes and behavior occasionally involves exposure to erotic material that some individuals would prefer to avoid. In addition, volunteers for research may be asked to provide highly personal information about their sexual experiences and preferences. The principle of *informed consent* stipulates that participants be informed of any aspects of a study that might be embarrassing or damaging to them, including all the procedures they will undergo, before they consent to participate. Prisoners, psychiatric patients, developmentally disabled adults, and children are not considered capable of giving informed consent. When children are the population of interest for a particular study, researchers must obtain the informed consent of their parents or school personnel.

### Freedom from Coercion

The principle of *freedom from coercion* requires that potential volunteers be free of undue pressure to participate in research. In the past, prison inmates have been induced by offers of shortened sentences to participate in drug research, and college students have been required to "volunteer" for research or accept an incomplete grade in particular courses. Such practices are now viewed as coercive.

### Protection from Physical or Psychological Harm

The principle of *protection from physical or psychological harm* deals with a particularly thorny ethical problem. If we knew all the potential effects of a sex-therapy treatment, medical procedure, or contraceptive drug, there would be no reason to conduct research to determine these effects. But not knowing what the effects may be, researchers run a real risk of negatively affecting the physical or psychological health of research participants. The ethical principle of protection from physical or psychological harm requires that researchers be aware of this danger and design their study to minimize it. Specifically, volunteers should encounter no more risk to their physical or psychological health during the course of a research project than they would in their normal daily lives.

To test the hypothesis that being questioned about their sexual behavior may encourage adolescents to increase their level of sexual activity, Halpern, Udry, & Suchindran (1994) compared students who were questioned twice with those

freedom from coercion—an ethical principle requiring that potential volunteers be free to accept or decline participation in research without penalty.

protection from physical or psychological harm—the ethical principle requiring that volunteers be able to participate in research with no more risk to their psychological or physical health than would be encountered in their normal daily lives. Under this principle, volunteers are usually guaranteed anonymity and confidentiality.

who were questioned a number of times about their age at first intercourse, number of sexual partners, and so forth. At the end of the study, the two groups did not differ in their age at first intercourse, frequency of sexual activity, or number of partners. Thus, it does not appear that being questioned about their sexual behavior per se alters the sexual behavior of respondents.

Protecting the anonymity of volunteers and the confidentiality of their responses is an important part of the research principle of protecting participants from harm. If, for example, we were interested in the relationship between women's responses to first intercourse and the duration of involvement with their current partner, the partner's behavior during the experience, or the amount of prior experience with necking and petting with other partners, we would need to ask a number of sensitive questions. Some women in the sample might not wish to share this information with their parents or current partners; thus their participation in the study and their responses would need to be held confidential. In keeping with the principle of protection from physical or psychological harm, most informed-consent statements explicitly indicate that anonymity and confidentiality will be maintained.

### The Risk-Benefit Principle

Research on some subjects—for example, the use of specific therapeutic approaches to alter atypical sexual behavior, the effectiveness of contraceptives, and the side effects of drugs that lengthen the lives of AIDS patients—poses dilemmas that cannot be adequately resolved by reference to the principle of protection from physical or psychological harm. We evaluate testing in these and similar areas on the basis of the *risk-benefit principle*.

For example, after the birth-control pill had been developed and tested with animals, it could not be marketed until its effects on humans had

been measured (Reed, 1983). Because the researchers were trying to determine whether the pill produced serious side effects, they obviously could not give unconditional guarantees of protection from harm to volunteers for the testing program. Pregnancy itself poses a health risk, however, and the mortality rates for women and babies were known to be higher when pregnancies occurred less than two years apart than when they occurred at longer intervals. Thus development of a highly reliable contraceptive appeared to offer great potential benefits when testing began in the 1950s. In support of the application of the risk-benefit principle to this case, it is clear today that the maternal mortality rate from pregnancy and childbirth is higher than that from any form of contraception or early abortion. Therefore, when the potential benefit of the results far outweighs the potential risks of research, research is considered permissible, provided the principle of informed consent is maintained.

The goals of scientific research are to increase our understanding of how variables are related, and ultimately to augment our general well-being. The need to prepare proposals for review by ethics boards adds an extra step to the research process, and a study is sometimes blocked or slowed down even when it adheres to the four ethical principles just described. Nonetheless, some research procedures used in past studies demonstrate the critical importance of adhering to ethical guidelines in conducting scientific studies. A case in point is the Tuskegee study, which James Jones (1981) documented in the book *Bad Blood* (see Box 2.3).

After an ethics review board approves a research proposal, scientists can begin their study. The results of their research may be presented at professional meetings and published in scholarly journals (see Appendix B) and subsequently reported in the popular press. At that point, you may become aware of the research and wonder to what extent you should make personal decisions on the basis of it (see Figure 2.7). The remainder of this chapter is aimed at providing you with sufficient evaluative skills to make an educated judgment regarding the applicability of research findings to you as an individual, (potential) parent, or voter.

**risk-benefit principle**—an ethical principle requiring that the potential benefits of research outweigh the risks to participants in that research.

**Box 2.3**

## Ethical Principles and the Tuskegee Study

In 1932 the U.S. Public Health Service sponsored a research program in Tuskegee, Alabama, to study the long-term effects of untreated syphilis—a research project that exemplifies the violation of all four ethical principles of research. Syphilis, a sexually transmitted disease (see Chapter 17), is now easily cured in its early stages, but it can lead to mental and physical disability and death if left untreated.

In the 1930s mercury and two arsenic compounds were known to be effective in killing the bacterium that causes syphilis. Unfortunately, these drugs were also highly toxic, and patients experienced serious, and occasionally fatal, reactions to the drugs. When the study began, therefore, the treatments may have been worse than the disease, at least in the short term. The Tuskegee study, however, involved no treatment; its goal was to examine the long-term effects of untreated syphilis in blacks.

To obtain research participants, the Public Health Service held meetings at black schools and churches in Macon County, Alabama, at which it was announced that "government doctors" were giving free blood tests. As residents of one of the poorest counties in the South, most of the citizens had never even seen a doctor, much less been treated by one. The response to the announcement was overwhelmingly positive, and thus began one of the most tragic human studies of the 20th century. Between 1932 and 1972, approximately 625 black males in the county who were identified as having syphilis received blood tests and underwent physical examinations to determine the progression of the disease. This study may have had some ethical justification during the 1930s, when the treatment for syphilis was dangerous. But the withholding of treatment after 1943, the year in which it was discovered that penicillin could kill the bacterium without killing the victim, represented a serious violation of the risk-benefit principle.

The lack of ethical principles of the researchers became clear when the men visited local clinics for checkups for other disorders. The Public Health Service informed the attending physicians that the men were not to be treated for syphilis because they were part of an experiment; World War II military authorities dealing with draftees got similar instructions. The denial of effective treatment not only endangered the lives of the men being studied without their informed consent, but also resulted in the transmission of syphilis to their wives, and of congenital syphilis to their children. The principle of informed consent was also seriously violated because the men did not even realize that effective treatment for syphilis was being withheld from them. They were told that they had "bad blood" and that they were being studied by the government. "After commenting that he and his friends had been used as 'guinea pigs,' one survivor said, 'I don't know what that means. . . . I don't know what they used us for. . . . I ain't never understood the study'" (Jones, 1981, p. 219). This man was one of only 120 in the group known to be still alive in 1974. Most of the remaining 500 or so syphilis victims could not be located and were presumed dead.

In sum, the Tuskegee-study volunteers did not give informed consent because they were never given the opportunity to do so. The risks to these men far outweighed any potential benefits to society gained from knowledge of the long-term effects of untreated syphilis, particularly after 1943, when penicillin became available. It is to be hoped that the training scientists now receive in the moral, ethical, and legal importance of protecting the rights of research volunteers, as well as the scrutiny by ethical review boards that is now required for research proposals, makes the kind of abuse rampant in the Tuskegee study unlikely today.

**FIGURE 2.7**
**Opposing Views Toward RU-486**
Members of prochoice and antiabortion groups express opposing views on the importation of the abortion drug, RU-486, outside the French Embassy in Washington, D.C., in June 1993. The drug is expected to be available in the United States in 1995.

## Understanding the Sex Research Process

Attempting to understand the research process for the first time is a bit like making bread or making love for the first time. It is one thing to read about evaluating research in a textbook, kneading dough in a cookbook, or caressing genitals in a sex manual, but quite another to engage in these processes. Initially, you are likely to feel unsure of yourself (see Box 2.4). Exactly how do you knead dough, anyway? Are you supposed to push it or squeeze it? How hard are you supposed to knead it and for how long? Similarly, how do you caress genitals? In understanding research, what are the relevant questions, and how do you get the answers?

## Definition of Research Terms

Many of us have spent enjoyable, if at times frustrating, hours engaged in arguments with friends about various sexual topics. For instance, in heated discussions about the effect of pornography, one person may maintain that erotic material provides information, a second person may suggest that it helps drain off sexual energy in a harmless fashion, and a third may claim that it encourages rape.

Rather than endlessly arguing, scientists attempt to resolve disputes by following procedures to gather evidence that supports or refutes a contention. Modern sex research rests on these scientific procedures. When researchers seek scientific evidence relevant to issues in any discipline or field, they generally begin by stating their question as a *hypothesis*. A hypothesis is a statement of a specific relationship between two or more variables. Put another way, a hypothesis is an educated guess stated in such a way that it can be accepted or rejected on the basis of research results. A *variable* is anything that can vary or change. For instance, our levels of hunger, happiness, sexual arousal, and time spent studying can all change, so these can all be defined as variables.

To formulate a testable or researchable hypothesis, a scientist must operationally define the variables. An *operational definition* involves describing each variable so that (a) it can be measured or counted, and (b) people can agree on the definition. Given these criteria, some variables cannot be operationally defined. For example, consider the classic question, ''How many angels can dance on the head of a pin?'' Although we

**hypothesis** (hy-PAW-theh-sis)—statement of a specific relationship between two or more variables.
**variable**—any situation or behavior capable of change or variation.
**operational definition**—description of a variable in such a way that it can be measured.

**Box 2.4**

## Research Phobia

When I first enrolled in college, research was a mysterious, incomprehensible process that apparently occupied the lives of a few (male) scientific geniuses with long, wispy white hair. My career goal was to help people, so I took a number of psychology courses. However, I was afraid to major in that area, because I knew that psychology majors had to do research. In my mind, research had little to do with helping people.

Later, when I entered graduate school, it was clear that I could not obtain the credentials to help people unless I did some research. I still hadn't a clear idea of what that meant, but I signed up for courses in research design, statistics, and so forth. I studied inefficiently, anxious that I couldn't possibly master the information; that I had overreached my capabilities; and that my final grade would expose my stupidity to my teachers, classmates, and family.

At this point, I look back on my feelings about research with some sadness. My assumption that I couldn't possibly grasp it led me to put a lot more energy into avoiding it

than would have been needed to understand it. And, of course, the assumption that "research" had little to do with "helping people" was also dead wrong. In fact, I am a bit embarrassed at my naiveté: I had the nerve to plan on intervening in people's lives without knowing what researchers had found to be effective intervention.

Imagine that you are a therapist and a couple tells you that they are having sexual problems. The man claims that the woman is "frigid," and the woman claims that the man "comes" too soon. What would you do? For some reason, I had imagined that I could magically help them—perhaps with platitudes such as "All you need is love"—without knowing anything about the research on sexual dysfunction or about how to evaluate the results of those studies. As it happens, learning to evaluate research conclusions is a matter of learning to ask some relatively simple questions, as you will see in reading this chapter.

Source: E. R. A.

could probably agree on what we mean by "head of a pin" and "dance," we might hit a snag with the term *angel.* Counting or measuring the angels is even more difficult. If we cannot operationally define a variable, we cannot study it.

### Kinds of Variables

There are three kinds of variables: independent, dependent, and control. *Independent variables* are those that can be manipulated or varied by an experimenter. For instance, to investigate the

effect of nudity on arousal, we might vary the degree of nudity (the independent variable) in a series of photos, such as those in Figure 2.8.

*Dependent variables* are variables that are measured. Changes in dependent variables are assumed to depend on variations in the independent variable. For instance, after exposure to one of the photos in Figure 2.8, volunteers could be asked to indicate their level of arousal (see Figure 2.9). Their response—their reported level of arousal—would then be the dependent variable. Independent variables are sometimes called

**independent variable**—a variable that is manipulated or varied by the experimenter.

**dependent variable**—a variable that is measured or observed.

**FIGURE 2.8**

**Degree of Nudity as an Independent Variable**

Although the degree of nudity varies in these photos, other factors vary as well. Thus responses to the photos may differ not only because of the degree of nudity but also because of the extent of body contact.

*stimulus* variables, and dependent variables can also be called response variables.

*Control variables* are factors that could vary but that are controlled or held constant. Because in our example we are interested in the effect of nudity on arousal, it is important to try to hold all other variables constant. A number of variables were controlled by using the same couple in all three photos in Figure 2.8. Otherwise, differences in reported arousal might be confounded—that is, unintentionally influenced—

**stimulus** (STIM-u-lus)—any objectively describable situation or event that produces a response in an organism.

**control variable**—a variable that is held constant or controlled to reduce its influence on the dependent variable.

by responses to variations in the age, attractiveness, race, and so forth of each couple rather than to the degree of nudity per se.

Other variables, however, were not controlled. The set of photos in Figure 2.8 demonstrates a significant problem for researchers: the mixture of variables that are accidentally varied with those that are intentionally varied may confound interpretations of results. Specifically, the degree of nudity in Figure 2.8 does systematically vary from completely clothed to completely nude. In the second photo the woman is totally nude, whereas the man is partially clothed. Thus it is important to control (hold constant, not allow to vary) those factors that are not under investigation so that the results clearly indicate the effect of the manipulation of particular variables on responses, in this case, the effect of the degree of nudity on self-reported arousal.

**FIGURE 2.9**

**Extent of Arousal as a Dependent Variable**

In our fictitious experiment, a person responds to one of the photos in Figure 2.8 by indicating her level of arousal, the dependent variable.

## Obtaining Research Participants: Problems in Sampling

The last time a lab technician pricked your finger to draw some blood, you were participating in a *sampling* process. When physicians order a blood sample, of course, they are not particularly interested in the properties of the small amount of blood that is drawn. Rather, they assume that the properties of that sample are the same as those of the person's entire blood supply.

**sampling**—the process of selecting a representative part of a population.

Scientists conducting sex research would be delighted if they could place as much confidence in their sampling procedures as the lab technician can in blood-sampling procedures. Obtaining accurate results in sampling most aspects of human sexuality, however, is considerably more difficult. Most characteristics of sexual behavior are not evenly distributed throughout whatever population we might wish to sample. Further, because all potential sources of *bias* have not been identified, it is difficult to obtain a representative sample. Among the most persistent sources of sampling bias that have been identified are volunteer bias and self-report bias.

### Volunteer Bias

*Volunteer bias* refers to the differences that exist between those who volunteer and those who refuse to participate in research. After a sample has been selected, ethical considerations require that the researcher obtain the informed consent of participants. For example, in conducting research on the relationship between sexual responses to erotic movies and recommendations that such material be censored, researchers would have to tell participants ahead of time that the research involves exposure to erotic materials. Presumably, those people who would be most offended by erotica would be unwilling to give their consent. With the loss of those participants, the sample would no longer accurately represent the population from which it was drawn.

The degree to which representativeness is lost depends on the extent to which there are systematic, or nonrandom, differences between volunteers and nonvolunteers. The mere fact that some members of a sample do not participate is not necessarily a problem. As long as participation is unrelated to the variables being studied, there is probably no systematic volunteer bias.

**bias**—an attitude for or against a particular theory or hypothesis that influences one's judgment.

**volunteer bias**—bias introduced into the results of a study stemming from systematic differences between those who volunteer for research and those who avoid participation.

Assume, however, that we want to determine the extent of support for installing condom vending machines in campus dorms. We try to select a sample that represents the entire student population on campus by sending a questionnaire to every tenth dorm resident. We get a 50% return rate, and the responses indicate overwhelming support for the machines. If those who thought that students ought to take the responsibility for obtaining their own condoms off campus tore up the questionnaire in disgust, however, while those who supported the project enthusiastically completed it, we would no longer have a sample that represents the attitudes of all students on campus. Thus, although we could conclude that the majority of the respondents approve of the condom vending machines, we could not conclude that the majority of students on campus feel that way.

A review of studies of volunteer bias indicated that, although volunteers for sex research do not differ from nonvolunteers in general personality characteristics or in level of psychopathology, systematic differences do appear in their attitudes toward sexuality and in their experience with various sexual activities (Morokoff, 1986). Specifically, compared to nonvolunteers, volunteers are more sexually liberal, more permissive, more sexually curious, more positive toward erotic material, and more supportive of sex research. Generally, volunteers are more sexually experienced and report having had a greater number of sexual partners than do nonvolunteers. Males are more likely than females to volunteer for research on sexuality and other "unusual" topics. Among females, volunteers date more frequently and masturbate more frequently than do nonvolunteers.

At this point, you may be wondering how volunteers can be compared to nonvolunteers. In one study designed to assess differences between volunteers and nonvolunteers for sex research, 748 male and female college students responded to a questionnaire regarding their past sexual experiences and their sexual attitudes. At the end of the questionnaire, there was an invitation to participate in a study involving exposure to "erotic movies depicting explicit sexual scenes" (Wolchik, Braver, & Jensen, 1985, p. 98). The researchers then compared the sexual attitudes and experiences of those who volunteered to see the erotic movies with those who declined to participate. The team obtained results consistent with those reported by Morokoff in her review of studies of volunteer bias.

### Limiting Volunteer Bias

To reduce the likelihood of volunteer bias, many researchers use broad descriptive terms in their ads or sign-up sheets to solicit volunteers. For example, in our own research on various aspects of sexuality, we describe projects as involving ratings of photographs or interpersonal relations when in fact we are studying responses to erotic photos, flirtation, sexual coercion, and the like. When participants arrive at the designated time, we tell them that they have earned their experimental credit or money simply by showing up. Then we provide complete oral and written informed-consent information regarding the nature of the research. Under these conditions few people decline to participate, and data obtained by Saunders, Fisher, Hewitt, and Clayton (1985) indicated that 98% of their participants believed that the informed-consent document they received prior to that study gave them enough information to decide whether they wanted to participate. Such procedures protect the rights of individuals who choose freely whether to participate in research, while reducing the extent to which volunteer bias limits the ability of researchers to generalize their findings. For example, a random sample of men and women were called in Toledo, Ohio, and asked a number of questions. Embedded within the questions—many of which dealt with nonsensitive topics—were a set of questions involving respondents' involvement in extramarital sex. Half of the sample received a justification for asking these personal questions. Specifically, they were told that concerns about AIDS led the researchers to inquire about their extramarital sexual behavior. The other half did not receive that preface. The likelihood of men responding was unaffected by the presence of the preface, but women were more likely to answer the questions when they received the preface than when they did not (Wiederman, Weis, & Allgeier, 1994).

## Self-Report Bias

After volunteers have been obtained for sex research, another kind of bias can restrict generalizability—*self-report bias*. Self-report bias can result from a reluctance to provide honest answers or from an inability to give accurate answers. Fearing that they will appear deviant in their sexual feelings and behavior, volunteers may either fail to report or underreport (or in some cases overreport) their behavior. They may respond with what they believe is the socially desirable behavior rather than reporting their actual behavior (Wiederman, 1993).

Even when volunteers want to report accurately, they may have difficulty recalling some past events. For example, you can probably remember quite accurately the first time you kissed someone erotically. But can you give as accurate an account if you are asked how many times you have kissed someone, or how many different people you have kissed?

These two problems—volunteer bias and self-report bias—affect the interpretation of information from studies that depend on self-reports for their conclusions. Some studies have relied on direct observation in an attempt to eliminate self-report bias. Volunteers were observed during sexual interaction in Masters and Johnson's (1966) laboratory, for example, so they did not need to remember their past behavior, nor could they distort their reports. Nonetheless, the issue of volunteer bias may arise when we try to generalize Masters and Johnson's findings to people who would not volunteer to be observed during sexual stimulation.

These sources of bias do not eliminate the usefulness of sex research, nor are they unique to sex research. They simply limit the extent to which we can assume that all people feel or behave precisely the way research volunteers do. With these potential limitations in mind, let us turn to the two major methods used to gather information about sexual attitudes and behavior.

**self-report bias**—bias introduced into the results of a study stemming either from participants' desire to appear "normal" or from memory lapses.

## Research Methods

In gathering evidence relevant to the testing of a hypothesis, researchers generally rely on one of two methods: the *correlational method* and the *experimental method*. With both methods, researchers pay close attention to the bases for selection of samples of the organisms under study, whether they are people, monkeys, rats, sperm cells, or egg cells.

As we went to press in 1994, a variety of experimental drugs, for example AZT (azidothymidine), were being tested that appeared to slow the onset of the infections associated with AIDS, thus prolonging the lives of AIDS patients. Research with these drugs provides another example of the use of the risk-benefit principle. Although scientists do not know the long-term side effects of these drugs, research has been permitted on the grounds that the effects of AIDS are generally lethal. Thus the risks of experiencing potentially negative long-term effects may be outweighed by the potential benefits of slowing the course of the disease in the hope that an AIDS cure may be found. Research on these drugs may also be used as an example of correlational versus experimental methods.

## Correlational Methods

To use the correlational approach, we might enlist the cooperation of people who have tested positive for the AIDS virus and who have taken varying levels of AZT. We could examine the relationship between dosage levels and extent of AIDS symptoms. If those with higher AZT doses have fewer AIDS-related symptoms (a negative correlation), this would provide evidence suggesting that the use of higher doses may be justified. If, on the other hand, dose level were unrelated to symptoms but associated with more

**correlational methods**—research methods involving the measurement of two or more variables to determine the extent of their relationship.

**experimental methods**—research methods involving the manipulation of one or more independent variables to determine their influence on dependent variables.

severe side effects (a positive correlation), this finding would support a reduction in AZT dosage levels.

Note that such hypothetical correlations would not allow us to infer a cause-and-effect relationship between AZT doses and greater or lesser levels of health. Observed relationships in correlational research sometimes stem from other variables. For example, assume that those people taking high AZT doses have only mild AIDS symptoms, or assume that poor people, among whom AIDS is most prevalent, would be less able to afford high doses of AZT and more likely to have other untreated health problems, rendering them more susceptible to infections than more affluent people with AIDS. We see from these examples that the hypothetical correlation between high doses of AZT and fewer symptoms might be due to a number of uncontrolled factors rather than to dosage level alone. We cannot assume cause-and-effect (causal) relationships when using correlational methods.* All we can say is that two or more variables are related.

### Experimental Methods

We could test the hypothesis that AZT use reduces the impact of the AIDS virus through an experimental approach. To do so, we would assemble a large group of people who tested positively for the AIDS virus, and randomly assign these people to one of four groups receiving (a) high drug doses, (b) medium drug doses, (c) no treatment, or (d) a *placebo*. The reason for administering a placebo is to control for the potential impact of expectations on the measured outcome—severity of symptoms, in this case.

The purpose of random assignment of AIDS patients to the various groups is to control for the influence of some of the other variables, such as income and general health. Through random assignment, it is assumed that equal numbers of people having particular characteristics will end up in the different treatment groups. Manipulation of the treatment (two drug dose levels, no treatment, placebo) allows researchers to control drug effects and eliminates dependence on the memory of volunteers regarding dosage and how long they have taken the drug.

### Differences Between Correlational and Experimental Methods

Both methods also involve careful and consistent measurement of the relevant variables. The two methods vary in the following ways: (a) control of variables, (b) artificiality, (c) generalizability, and (d) conclusions that may be drawn. Correlational and experimental methods differ in the extent to which the variables of interest are controlled. With the correlational method, researchers simply measure the level of variables (in our example, AZT level and severity of symptoms). With the experimental method, the independent variable (AZT) is manipulated or varied, and the dependent variables (symptoms) are measured. Researchers thus have much more control over the amount and frequency of the independent variable in the experimental than in the correlational method.

A second difference between the two approaches is the extent of *artificiality*. In general, correlational methods involve more natural settings and processes than do experimental methods. Experimental methods can produce what is known as *reactivity*; that is, volunteers may react to the knowledge that they are being studied. This circumstance may make their responses somewhat less spontaneous and natural than if they did not know that they would be asked to report their behavior.

**placebo** (pluh-SEE-boh)—an inert substance used in place of an active drug; usually given to the control group in an experiment.

**artificiality**—the extent to which a research setting differs from one's normal living environment.

**reactivity**—the tendency of a measurement instrument (or observer) to influence the behavior under observation.

---

*There are exceptions to this statement, but these involve sophisticated causal modeling techniques of a sort rarely used in sex research.

Third, partly because of the artificiality typically involved in the experimental method, the results obtained sometimes have less *generalizability*. Thus, although it is probably safe to assume that other groups of volunteers who might participate in the same experimental procedures would behave in about the same way, we do not know the extent to which the knowledge that they are taking part in an experiment alters their normal behavior.

The issues of artificiality, reactivity, and generalizability would probably not be a problem in our example of research on AZT with AIDS patients but can pose difficulties in studies involving psychological or behavioral variables. You perhaps volunteered for an experiment while taking an introductory psychology course. If so, you may have had a number of motives for responding in ways other than the way you would respond normally. To begin with, most people prefer to be evaluated positively rather than negatively. Thus they attempt to figure out the researcher's hypothesis. Once they have an idea, they may choose one of three alternatives instead of reporting their actual responses. First, they may respond in a way that will put them in a favorable light, creating what is known as social-desirability bias. Second, they may try to help confirm what they believe to be the experimental hypothesis. This is referred to as complying with the demand characteristics of an experiment (or, informally, as the ''help the experimenter'' effect). Third, volunteers may be irritated at feeling forced to participate in research as part of a course requirement and may respond inaccurately in an attempt to refute what they believe to be the hypothesis (known informally as the ''screw you!'' effect). These kinds of influences limit the extent to which we can generalize findings from experiments to the real world.

The two methods also differ regarding the conclusions that can be drawn. With correlational methods, finding an association between two variables does not permit the conclusion that there is a cause-and-effect relationship. A causal

connection can be established through the use of experimental methods, however, by controlling nonrelevant variables—through random assignment of volunteers to groups, as in our AZT example—or by holding other variables constant. If there is a systematic difference in the level of the dependent variable between the two groups, then there is support for the hypothesis that variations in the independent variable have caused the change in response—the dependent variable.

To sum up, there are advantages and disadvantages to the correlational and experimental methods. Therefore, it is desirable to use both methods in trying to answer a particular question. If the findings from both correlational and experimental methods yield the same results, we can have greater confidence in the conclusions.

### Other Methodological Variations

Beyond using correlational and experimental methods, researchers also select the location of research and the length of time needed to collect information. Research may be conducted in a laboratory or in a field setting. By the terms *lab* and *field* we do not mean that the researcher takes the participants either to a gleaming white sterile laboratory or to the middle of a grassy sunlit meadow. *Lab* refers to a specific location of the researcher's choice in which to observe participants' behavior. *Field* generally means the participants' own environment—wherever they normally live. Field research, then, can refer to studies that are conducted in people's homes, to observations of baboons in their natural environment, or to observations of flirting in singles' bars.

Research on a particular topic sometimes begins in lab settings and then moves into field settings so that the researcher can see whether results from the lab are consistent with those from the field. In other cases, initial studies are begun in field settings and then repeated in lab settings. For example, observations of flirting behavior in singles' bars led Perper (1985) and Moore (1985) to question the stereotype that it is always the active male who selects the female as a potential romantic partner, and that females must passively await male interest, hoping that they will be approached by a male who is appealing to

**generalizability**—the extent to which the results of a study conducted with a particular sample represent the population from which the sample was drawn.

**FIGURE 2.10**
**Field Research in Singles' Bars**
Observations and interviews in singles' bar settings have demonstrated that it is usually women rather than men who select partners, by engaging in various signals and displays to indicate their interest. After this woman had signaled the man, he approached her and asked whether she would like to have a drink. Her continued interest in him is reflected in her direct gaze and smile.

them rather than one who is unappealing. Their observations (described in more detail in Chapter 6) led them to conclude that it is women rather than men who select potential partners and initiate interaction (see Figure 2.10).

Rather than using the observation-in-bars approach, Gaulier, Travis, and Allgeier (1986) tested this hypothesis in several ways, in a more artificial setting. First, they asked volunteers to indicate, by responding to open-ended questions, what they did when they wanted to initiate and develop a romantic/sexual relationship. Gaulier et al. then took the common responses and asked a second sample of men and women to report which behaviors they used when they were interested in getting to know a potential romantic partner. Consistent with research by Moore (1985) and Perper (1985), Gaulier et al. found women were more likely than men to endorse the items indicating initial signaling of interest in a potential partner. When findings from two different settings, using different methods (in the case of research on courtship strategies, field and then lab, direct observation and then question-

naires) provide the same general findings, we can have more confidence in the results, in this case, that women are more likely than men to take an active role in selecting potential partners.

### Cross-Sectional and Longitudinal Research

Research also varies in terms of whether it is cross-sectional or longitudinal. Imagine that we are interested in determining the effects of oral contraceptives on fertility. Using a *cross-sectional* approach, we might try to find a large group of women who used the pill for five years and then stopped two years ago in an attempt to become pregnant. We could then compare the pregnancy rate of this group with that of another group of women who were as similar as possible to the first group in every respect except that they relied on a contraceptive method not involving hormones, such as the diaphragm or the contra-

**cross-sectional research**—comparisons of distinct but similar groups over the same time period.

ceptive sponge. Although it might take some time to locate two equivalent groups of women, the comparison in fertility rates could be made at one point in time.

A *longitudinal* approach may also be used to examine the relationship between oral-contraceptive use and later fertility. In a longitudinal design, researchers study the same group over a period of time. An example is research involving 17,000 women in Britain (Vessey et al., 1976, 1985). These women, who were using a range of contraceptive methods, have been monitored closely for more than 15 years so that the researchers can compare the women's fertility rates after they stop using the various contraceptive methods. Relatively few researchers rely on longitudinal approaches because they are time-consuming and therefore more expensive than cross-sectional research. Further, a relatively high proportion of the initial volunteers in a longitudinal study may be lost through relocation, death, or decisions that automatically remove them from the sample. For instance, among the Vessey team's original sample, some of those who had been trying to conceive changed their minds for various reasons, including divorce and financial problems.

Nonetheless, longitudinal studies offer some distinct advantages over cross-sectional approaches. Instead of relying on participants' memories of past events—such as the date they began using a particular contraceptive, exact ingredients and dosage levels, how long they used the contraceptive, and how long it took to conceive after they stopped using the contraceptive—researchers can ask that each of these events be reported at the time it occurs, and that feature provides greater accuracy.

Just as experimental or correlational methods may be used in laboratory or field settings, either method may be applied in conducting cross-sectional or longitudinal research. The Vessey study, for example, involves longitudinal research that relies on correlational measures in a field setting.

**longitudinal research**—comparisons of the same group over different time periods.

## Measurement in Sex Research

Sex researchers have exposed volunteers to a wide range of stimuli, including questionnaires, tests, photos, slides, films, erotic literary passages, line drawings, silhouettes, double entendres, music, and other people. Experimenters have even asked volunteers to create their own stimuli by imagining sexual acts. Methods of measuring responses include self-administered measures, interviews, direct observation, physiological and biochemical measures, and case studies (Beere, 1990; Davis, Yarber, & Davis, 1988).

### Self-Administered Questionnaires, Surveys, and Scales

Hundreds of self-administered measures have been developed to record attitudinal and behavioral responses to various aspects of sexuality. The formats of these measures vary in the degree to which the responses are structured. At one extreme, the measuring instrument may contain such open-ended questions as, "How do you feel about premarital sex?" followed by blank spaces in which the respondents write their answers with as much or as little detail as they choose. At the other extreme, the response format may be highly structured, as in the Sexual Knowledge Survey (see Introduction), in which participants indicate true or false in response to a statement. Alternatively, volunteers may be asked to indicate the extent of their agreement with a statement by checking one of several alternatives (refer to Figure 2.9).

By comparing responses to these measures across samples from different populations, the researcher can get an idea of how different groups of people (for example, men versus women, adolescents versus adults, sexually experienced versus sexually inexperienced people) differ in their attitudes, knowledge, and behavior regarding such matters as contraception, abortion, homosexuality, and rape. By comparing the survey responses from samples of the same population across different time periods, we can get an idea of what changes over time.

When someone is designing or choosing research measures, it is important to determine their *reliability* and *validity*. If a measure is reliable, then individuals will get about the same score when they take it several times over a period of weeks or months. For example, if you were interested in determining whether the Sexual Knowledge Survey (SKS) is a reliable measure of sexual knowledge, you would look at the scores of individual participants on repeated administrations of the SKS. A person completing the SKS for the second time should receive about the same score as he or she did several weeks earlier, assuming that no sex education occurred between the first and second administrations of the SKS. If the two scores are very similar, then the measure is assumed to be reliable.

A measure is valid to the extent that scores on it accurately reflect the variable in question. If, for example, you created a self-report measure of sexual arousal in response to erotic stimuli, you might test its validity by using it in conjunction with physiological measures of arousal (for example, erection and vaginal lubrication). If physiological measures reflect greater levels of arousal as self-reported ratings of arousal increase, then confidence in the validity of the self-report measure increases. If, on the other hand, high arousal ratings are reported in the absence of erection or vaginal lubrication, and low arousal ratings are reported in the presence of firm erections and copious lubrication, the self-report measure of arousal is obviously not valid.

*Interviews*

Researchers also obtain information about sexual attitudes and behavior by interviewing people. This method is usually more expensive and time-consuming than pencil-and-paper measures are, but it can allow for greater flexibility in acquiring in-depth information.

Although Alfred Kinsey and his colleagues conducted the classic interview studies of the sexual behavior of American males (Kinsey et al.,

reliability—the extent to which a measure elicits the same response at different times.
validity—the extent to which a measure measures what it is designed to measure.

1948) and females (Kinsey et al., 1953) almost half a century ago, the Kinsey-group research is still the largest study of sexual behavior ever done in North America. They interviewed more than 10,000 people and amassed an incredible amount of information. Both the quantity and the quality of the interviews earned the group a great deal of respect.

Changes in the proportion of people engaging in certain sexual behaviors (Billy, Tanfer, Grady, & Klepinger, 1993; DeLamater & MacCorquodale, 1979; Smith, 1991) limit the applicability of the results of the Kinsey studies to contemporary American behavior. First, Kinsey and his colleagues did not attempt to select a random or representative sample of the U.S. population. Instead, they selected various organizations and tried to interview all the members. This strategy produced a sample in which the responses of middle-class, relatively well-educated whites were overrepresented. For example, about 75% of the females who responded had attended college. On the other hand, given the paucity of information at the time on what normal or typical Americans did, and the difficulty of getting agreement from a representative sample of people to participate in sex research, the Kinsey group did obtain valuable data by sampling groups that were likely to represent diverse patterns of sexual behavior.

Second, there is the problem of the accuracy of participants' reports of their behavior. The Kinsey group attempted to assess the accuracy of these reports in a number of ways. They interviewed some of the volunteers a second time 18 months after the first interview. This procedure, similar to a test-retest check for reliability, is known as a take-retake interview. They also compared the reports of husbands and wives on questions about which they should have had the same answers, such as their frequency of marital sex. Correlations for the take-retake and husband-wife comparisons were generally high on such items as extent of education, number of children, and occupation of the father, but they were much lower for frequencies of sexual activity. Memory errors probably account for much of this variability, but Kinsey did not take this factor into account statistically. He gave as much weight to reports based on memories of events that took place many years earlier as he did to reports of current activities.

Third, demographic and personality differences among interviewers can influence the responses of volunteers and thus also constitute a potential source of bias. However, checks on the reliability of responses to one interviewer versus another interviewer in the Kinsey studies indicated few differences.

Although there are obvious limits to the extent to which the Kinsey results were generalizable to all Americans at that time, most sex researchers remain impressed with the broad and thorough description of *normative* sexual behavior contributed by the Kinsey group.

### Direct Observation

Direct observation involves exactly what its name implies: the behavior of interest is directly observed. For example, researchers have directly observed such sexual behaviors as flirtation in bars (Moore, 1985; Perper, 1985) and sexual activity of heterosexual and homosexual couples (Masters & Johnson, 1966, 1979). This approach is also useful with nonhuman species, since they cannot respond to questionnaires or interviews.

In her study of the social structure, gender roles, and sexual interaction of one of our close relatives, the baboon, Shirley Strum (1975) spent more than a year in Kenya observing a troop in their natural environment. Her study illustrates some of the issues involved in the use of this method (see Figure 2.11).

It is impossible to observe everything, so the researcher must therefore be selective. Specific behaviors are generally selected in advance, and the presence, absence, and duration of these behaviors are recorded. Strum recorded the behavior of each baboon for 15 minutes. Because the troop contained 65 baboons, it took her about 20 days to complete each cycle of observations. In selecting which behaviors to record, researchers can be influenced by their own biases and assumptions. In fact, part of Strum's reason for con-

normative—the average response of members of a sample.

**FIGURE 2.11**
**Shirley Strum's Field Research**
In her field research with baboons in Kenya, anthropologist Shirley Strum faced the difficult task of becoming an accepted part of the baboons' environment without influencing the behavior she was attempting to observe.

ducting the study was to test the hypothesis that biases of some previous researchers had influenced their conclusions about the relationship between gender and dominance in baboons' sexual relations.

Another problem with direct observation is that the presence of an observer may alter the behavior of the organisms being observed—the problem of reactivity, discussed earlier. Many of us have experienced this phenomenon while under observation when we were learning to drive or type. Strum faced some special problems in dealing with the baboons. Because the baboons avoided humans, close observation of the baboon troop was impossible initially; in fact, it took several months for the baboons to tolerate Strum's presence.

The problem of potential bias introduced by the presence of observers may be magnified when humans are the object of study. You might ask 10 of your sexually experienced friends how willingly they would volunteer for a sexual-behavior study requiring: a) responding to a questionnaire, b) participating in an interview, or c) being observed during sexual activity. More of them would probably be willing to participate in the first two alternatives than in the last. Volunteer bias, then, may be a greater problem when researchers use direct observation than when they rely on self-reported behavior for information about sexuality.

One way in which a researcher may reduce volunteer bias in direct observation is to participate in the behavior being studied. This method is known as *participant observation*. For example, Marilyn Story (1993) has described the benefits of being a social nudist and conducting research on the attitudes and behaviors of social nudists compared to people who did not engage in social nudism. Also, openly gay anthropologist Walter Williams (1993) has conducted cross-cultural research on sexual orientation, and he believes that acknowledging his gay orientation has allowed him to get more reliable and complete data from gays than he would if he were heterosexual.

### Physiological Response Measures

Freud began a continuing controversy when he distinguished clitoral from vaginal orgasms, described earlier in Box 2.1. How would we go about testing the hypothesis that there is a difference in orgasms resulting from stimulation of the clitoris versus the vagina? To test it via self-administered surveys, interviews, or direct observation would be difficult, for several reasons. For one thing, it is hard for a volunteer to give precise self-reports, whether on a survey or to an interviewer, about the exact location or boundaries of the contractions associated with orgasm. Direct observation of the process is also problematic, because the relevant areas are not easily

**participant observation**—conducting research while simultaneously engaging in the behavior with the group being studied.

seen, and during heterosexual intercourse they tend to be completely obscured by the body of the woman's partner.

Masters and Johnson (1966) found a solution to some of these difficulties. They gave their female volunteers a clear plastic "penis" containing a small camera that could take color pictures of physiological responses. In this way, they could record the changes that occurred during sexual response, whether the stimulation was directed to the clitoris or occurred from the thrusting of the penis into the vagina. Through these internal pictures and other measures to be described in Chapter 7, Masters and Johnson concluded that there was no physiological difference between orgasms from clitoral versus vaginal stimulation.

Some other approaches that are used to record changes resulting from sexual arousal range from measures of general responses, such as heart rate and dilation of the pupils, to measures of genital responses. The general measures do provide information about arousal; however, these measures do not indicate whether sexual or nonsexual stimulation is the source of the observed arousal. For example, when Hoon, Wincze, and Hoon (1976) showed videotapes containing neutral material, erotic material, or Nazi war atrocities, the participants' arousal, as measured by heart rate and other general measures of bodily arousal, did not differ according to whether they were watching the erotic tape or the one depicting war atrocities. Genital responses, however, did vary according to the content of the films.

Among the devices for measuring male genital response are the penile plethysmograph, the mercury-in-rubber strain gauge, and the metal-band gauge (see Figure 2.12). All three of these devices fit partially or totally around the penis and are designed to measure changes in its circumference.

The devices that are currently being used to measure female genital response are the vaginal myograph and the rectal myograph (see Figure 2.13). Both of these devices monitor the muscular activity of the pelvic floor.

Although these genital measures have advantages over more general measures, their use

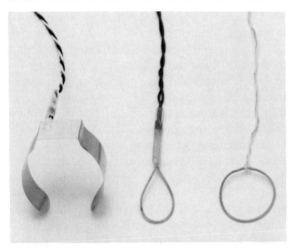

**FIGURE 2.12**
**Devices for Measuring Male Response**
The three gauges (top photo) measure the extent of tumescence. A gauge is placed on the cylinder (bottom photo) to determine the specific measurement of tumescence.

reflects an unintended bias: that sexual response is primarily a genital rather than a total body-and-mind process.

*Biochemical Response Measures*

One of Sigmund Freud's fundamental ideas was his insistence that sexual energy, or libido, is central to all human activity, whether it was overt or disguised (sublimated). But objectively, what is libido, and how can we measure it? One way that contemporary researchers have tried to deal with this question is by measuring a biochemical response—that is, by examining the influence of sex hormones on behavior.

Masculinizing hormones—those that produce typically masculine physical characteristics—are known as androgens. Both men's and

women's bodies manufacture them, but men secrete larger amounts than do women. Estrogens are feminizing hormones, which are secreted in greater volume by women than by men. Of the sex hormones, testosterone appears to be the most involved in sexual desire. One obvious way to measure the effects of testosterone on behavior would be to deprive a male of the hormone and then observe the changes that occurred. Doses of the hormones could be given later to see whether the effects observed during deprivation were reversed. Because males produce most of their testosterone in their testes, testosterone production is sharply reduced if the testes are surgically removed.

There are, however, some difficulties in drawing conclusions about the relationship between testosterone and sexual behavior in men who have been castrated for legal or medical reasons. First, many other variables besides testosterone influence human sexual behavior. Second, castrated men still produce some testosterone in their adrenal glands.

**FIGURE 2.13**
**Devices for Measuring Female Response**
This photograph shows the current models of the vaginal and the rectal myographs that monitor the muscular activity of the pelvic floor.

A more exact method of measuring testosterone levels is to analyze blood samples. Procedures such as radioimmunoassay and gas chromatography do permit more precise measurement of testosterone and several other sex hormones.

*Case Studies and Focus-Group Research*

When a researcher studies a single person, family, or small group without the intention of comparing that person, family, or group with others in the same study, the approach is known as the case study or focus group research. With the case study, a single individual is studied extensively via one or more of the methods described above (e.g., scales, interviews, biochemical measures). This approach does not permit cause-and-effect inferences, nor can the responses from a single person be generalized beyond that person. On the other hand, the case study of one individual can disprove an always or never assertion, for example, that women never ejaculate or men always ejaculate.

Researchers using focus groups select people who share some common characteristics and interview the participants in groups. For example, Offir, Fisher, Williams, and Fisher (1993) were interested in studying inconsistencies in the use of safer-sex practices by gay men. Their work indicated that although most of the men in their samples had modified their sexual behaviors in an effort to reduce the risk of HIV transmission, the men reported that there were circumstances in which they engaged in unsafe sex.

One purpose of focus groups is to permit group members to generate their own questions and issues. When researchers select questions without giving volunteers the opportunity to indicate the issues relevant to a particular topic that they consider important, the researchers may miss important variables that potentially influence sexual decisions. For example, if you were asked on a questionnaire whether you had asked a potential partner to discuss contraception with you, or to tell you his or her number of previous partners, you might indicate that you had asked neither of these questions. The researcher might then conclude that in making sexual decisions, you were unconcerned about contraception or

about the potential risk of contracting a sexually transmitted disease from a partner who had had many sexual partners in the recent past. In the context of a focus-group discussion, however, you might say that, although you did not explicitly ask these questions or discuss these issues aloud, your (potential) partner had placed a packet of condoms on the coffee table while you were necking, and that you had checked with friends who knew a lot about your potential partner before agreeing to date him or her. Thus an advantage of this approach is that it can allow participants to express information that the researchers who designed the questions overlooked. The understanding that can emerge from such focus groups can help health care professionals to target educational programs to try to increase people's willingness to engage in healthier sexual behaviors.

As with case studies of individuals, focus-group research with groups of people is aimed at hypothesis generation rather than hypothesis testing. The hypotheses that develop from case studies and focus groups can then be tested with larger samples using correlational or experimental designs.

## Comparing Methods of Measurement

Six ways to obtain information about sexuality have been described, including pencil-and-paper measures, interviews, direct observation, physiological measures, biochemical assays, and case studies and focus groups. Pencil-and-paper tests, interviews, and case studies/focus groups may be regarded as relatively subjective in that they rely on volunteers' self-reports. Direct observation, physiological measures, and biochemical measures are more objective because they assess the response directly rather than relying on volunteers to report their responses.

Because self-report measures are the easiest to use, researchers have tried to see whether responses obtained via self-report are consistent with those obtained from physiological measures. To compare self-reports with results from physiological measures, Heiman (1977) exposed college students to a series of erotic audiotapes. Physiological arousal was assessed by using the mercury-in-rubber strain gauge for males and the photoplethysmograph for females. The great majority of participants reported arousal and responded physiologically to the erotic tapes. In general, there was a strong relationship between the physiological and the self-report measures of arousal for both males and females; that is, when the physiological records of their responses suggested that they were sexually excited, they also reported that they were aroused. This relationship, however, was considerably stronger for males than for females. As Heiman put it in describing male responses, "Exactly zero percent were able to ignore an erection—the male approximation of genital blood volume change" (1975, p. 94).

Females reported arousal when the physiological measure of vaginal pressure pulse suggested that they were highly aroused, but they were less likely to report any arousal when the photoplethysmograph recorded moderate levels of arousal. It is probable that biological and sociological factors are jointly responsible for this difference between males and females. In any event, the fact that females appear to make more "errors" in their subjective recognition of physiological arousal does discourage reliance solely on self-reports of sexual excitement, at least in work with female volunteers.

## Evaluating Results of Studies of Sexuality

In the desire to improve our lives and relationships and to reduce discomforts, we tend to be receptive to new information. In making decisions about whether to act on new information, it is wise to keep several questions in mind. At the least, such factors as generalizability, potential side effects, temporary and lasting effects, and *replication* of the results should be considered before one embraces a new discovery.

**replication**—the practice of repeating a study with a different group of research participants to determine whether the results of previous research are reliable.

## Generalizability and Potential Side Effects

In evaluating a treatment, whether it involves a drug, psychotherapy, or other kinds of intervention, we should ask whether it applies to everyone under all conditions. It is also important to determine possible side effects, particularly those that may not appear right away. For example, millions of women adopted the pill within the first decade after it was marketed. The developers had tested it for potential short-term side effects prior to making it widely available and found that the immediate side effects were relatively minor and temporary. Unfortunately, it took far longer to discover that the pill could have more serious long-term effects for a small percentage of women, primarily those women who were already at risk for cardiovascular illness (see Chapter 10). Thus in making a decision about the use of a treatment, consumers should attempt to determine what is known about its short- and long-term risks.

Another important issue is the extent to which we can generalize the results of research on animals to human populations. Researchers commonly test new drugs on nonhuman species such as rats and monkeys. Although many drugs have similar effects on humans and nonhumans, occasionally a drug will have a different effect on humans than it does on animals, as researchers working on a new rubella vaccine discovered. If a woman is exposed to rubella (German measles) during the first three months of pregnancy, her fetus is likely to die or to be born with serious defects. Therefore, researchers attempted to develop a rubella vaccine that could be given to pregnant women. They thought they had found such a vaccine when initial testing with animals indicated that the serum did not pass through the placenta to the fetus. When the serum was tested with women who were planning to abort their fetuses, however, it did pass through the placenta, damaging the fetus. If the researchers had not first tested humans before marketing their serum, the result might have been as disastrous as the outcome of thalidomide use by pregnant women, in which about 8,000 European babies (now young adults) were born with missing or stunted limbs.* The sale of thalidomide in the United States was blocked by the Food and Drug Administration.

We must also consider whether variations in the way in which a treatment is administered make a difference. For example, during the 1940s, DES (diethylstilbestrol), a powerful estrogen, was administered to pregnant women from about the 6th to the 35th week of pregnancy to prevent miscarriage. Would DES have been effective if taken at conception by women who had a history of miscarriages? Just as amphetamines have different effects depending on the age and the weight of the person taking them, DES also has varying effects: taken within 72 hours of conception (as the "morning-after pill"), it acts to prevent implantation of the fertilized egg. Taken later in a pregnancy, it acts to prevent spontaneous abortion. Obviously, it is important to know the limits of a treatment to get the desired effect. Developed in 1938, DES was widely used until 1971, when it was linked to a higher risk of cancer in women who had taken it and in their daughters (Colton et al., 1993; Herbst et al., 1977; Saunders, 1988).

Not all side effects of a specific treatment are as tragic, or even as undesirable, as those of thalidomide and DES. Some small-breasted women are pleased when their breasts become a bit fuller as a side effect of taking oral contraceptives. The point is that we need to have as much information as possible about all potential side effects of a new treatment.

---

*The detective work involved in the discovery of the link between the birth defects and thalidomide use by women early in their pregnancies is described in a fascinating book, *Suffer the Children: The Story of Thalidomide* (Knightly, Evans, Potter, & Wallace, 1979).

## Temporary Versus Lasting Effects

Will a treatment that appears to solve a particular problem continue to be effective, or are there other factors responsible for a "quick fix" that may disappear in time? Central to this question are two phenomena: the effect of placebos and the effect of novelty.

In a variety of situations, a belief that something will help appears to contribute to a cure, known as the placebo effect. For example, when a couple spend time and money to avail themselves of a sex therapist to improve their sexual relationship, it is possible that making a joint decision and setting aside time to focus on their relationship is responsible for much of the benefit the couple experiences. If the couple's mutual commitment to their relationship is the cause of the high cure rate reported by sex therapists, thousands of dollars could be saved, at least by some clients.

Novelty may also produce temporary effects. A person who has had various problems in his or her relationship may decide that the appropriate "treatment" is to find a new partner. In the new relationship, the person may describe the success of this solution. "Oh, he (she) is so warm, and so much more capable of intimacy than so-and-so. I didn't realize how great a relationship could be...." The "treatment" (leaving the former partner and entering a new relationship) appears to be effective. Sometimes a conversation with this person six months later indicates, however, that the problems that riddled the previous relationship have emerged in the present one. The "treatment" had only a temporary effect. Before investing in a new treatment, then, it is important to determine whether its effect is likely to be temporary or long lasting.

## Summary of Major Points _____

1. **Scholars of sexuality before the 20th century.**

The writings of most pre-20th-century scholars reflect a continuation of traditional religious beliefs that all forms of nonreproductive sexual expression are linked with mental illness. Henry Havelock Ellis's contention that masturbation, homosexuality, and other sexual variations are normal was an exception to most of his contemporaries' beliefs.

| | |
|---|---|
| 2. The emergence of the scientific study of sexuality. | During the first half of the 20th century, scientists began to conduct empirical research on sexual attitudes and behaviors. Their pioneering efforts were met with considerable opposition and harassment from those who believed that research on sexuality was immoral or unnecessary. Their courageous work laid the groundwork for what is now an active field of research. |
| 3. Ethical issues in research. | In an attempt to eliminate abusive practices in the conduct of research on sexual and nonsexual topics, the scientific community has made adherence to specific ethical principles an indispensable part of research procedures. These principles include informed consent, freedom from coercion, protection from physical or psychological harm, and risk-benefit considerations. |
| 4. The research process. | Research involves gathering information about some phenomenon. In its most precise application, research requires testing hypotheses about the relationship between operationally defined variables. A population is sampled, and members of the sample volunteer for research in which stimuli are manipulated or measured. The volunteers' responses are obtained and analyzed. |
| 5. Research methods. | In testing hypotheses about sexuality, researchers rely on one or more of the following approaches: surveys, interviews, direct observation, physiological measures, biochemical analysis, and case histories and focus groups. Each method has its advantages and disadvantages. More confidence may be placed in research results if the same findings are obtained using more than one of these measures. |
| 6. Making inferences about research results. | When experimental research involves the manipulation of the variables of interest and adequate control of other variables, it is appropriate to infer a cause-and-effect relationship between variables. When stimuli are measured but not manipulated, as in correlational research, information about the extent to which two or more variables are related may be obtained, but causal inferences cannot be made. |
| 7. Evaluation of sex research. | In making decisions based on research results, investigators must determine the situations and populations to which results can be generalized. They must also be concerned with the duration of effects and possible side effects. Before research results can be considered valid, they should be replicated with a variety of samples, locations, situations, and researchers. |

## Review of Key Concepts

1. The connection between masturbation and various physical maladies: a) was once widely supported by physicians; b) is well known in many primitive societies; c) was popularized by medieval Church authorities; d) is the subject of current scientific research. (p. 32)

2. The increasing acceptance of sexual variations in post-Victorian society owed much

to the scientific work of: a) Richard von Krafft-Ebing; b) Henry Havelock Ellis; c) Robert Hatfield; d) none of the above. (p. 33)

3. As a sex researcher, Alfred Kinsey was: a) fully supported by his professional colleagues; b) criticized by many for using too small a sample size; c) generally ignored and unknown in his day; d) subjected to political harassment by McCarthy-era government zealots. (pp. 35–36)

4. William Masters and Virginia Johnson: a) exemplify 19th-century research methods on sexuality; b) were criticized for publishing "sensationalist" findings in the popular press; c) verified Freud's theories on human sexuality; d) refuted Freud's theory of adult female sexual response. (pp. 37–38)

5. Scientists doing funded research on human sexuality: a) are subject to political harassment even today; b) must demonstrate that their research is relevant to the solution of a societal problem; c) are free to use whatever procedures they choose; d) both a and b. (pp. 40–41)

6. Research on the effects of birth-control pills on humans must be conducted subject to the principle of: a) risk-benefit; b) informed consent; c) diminishing returns; d) both a and b. (p. 43)

7. A crucial step in doing experimental research on sexual behavior is: a) holding constant those factors that are not under investigation; b) holding constant the dependent variables; c) eliminating the invariables; d) refuting the hypothesis. (pp. 46–47)

8. In a research project, sampling involves: a) separating volunteers from nonvolunteers; b) obtaining complete data from every possible source; c) measuring the presence of self-report bias; d) none of the above. (pp. 48–49)

9. Research on flirting in singles' bars has been conducted using: a) the experimental method; b) field research; c) longitudinal studies; d) all of the above. (pp. 52–53)

10. Which of the following is not essential to establishing valid research conclusions? a) replication; b) reliability; c) direct observation; d) accurate sampling. (pp. 51–53)

11. Devices to measure physiological response to sexual stimulation have been used in: a) the experimental method; b) the research of Masters and Johnson; c) research on the effects of pornography; d) all of the above. (pp. 57–58)

12. "The findings of Kinsey, Masters and Johnson, and other researchers show only that most people lie when asked about their sex lives." Discuss.

# Contemporary Explanations of Human Sexuality

WHAT is sex? The amount of time spent physically engaging in it—even for the most sexually active people—is minuscule compared to the amount of time spent eating, bathing, sleeping, working, studying, and commuting.

*. . . if we take the generally accepted duration of intercourse in Western societies at a little over five minutes and the rate of copulation at a little less than 2.5 times per week, . . . a couple spend some 15 minutes per week actually copulating, which would amount to 99.9% of their time doing something else. . . . If you up-rate the performance to a twice nightly half-hour session, the percentage of time spent in non-copulatory activities still does not fall below 95%! (Ford, 1980, p. 49)*

Yet nonsexual activities do not generally feature the mysterious, obsessive, exhilarating, and anxiety-producing qualities that most people associate with sexual thoughts and events. Although most of us do not spend more than a tiny part of our waking lives directly engaging in sexual stimulation, we spend enormous amounts of time on quasi-sexual activities. We bathe, dress carefully, comb our hair, and put cologne or shaving lotion on our skin to make ourselves

**copulation** (kop-you-LAY-shun)—sexual intercourse involving insertion of the penis into the vagina.

more sexually appealing. We notice attractive strangers and flirt with colleagues and classmates. And we think about sex. We indulge in elaborate fantasies and mental rehearsals of potential interactions. We visualize running into someone in whom we are interested and then engaging in conversation and in physical contact at increasingly intimate levels. Sometimes the fantasy does not go the way we want it to, so we return to an earlier point in the fantasy to alter the script to our liking.

Part of this activity—the thoughts and fantasies—is an attempt to understand and explain sexual events to ourselves. We continue this process at the most personal and practical level as we try to make sexual decisions:

Will she think I'm not a man if I don't try to make love to her?

Will she think I'm only interested in sex if I do try to make love to her?

Will he lose interest if I don't go to bed with him?

Will he think I'm too ''easy'' if I do have sex with him?

We also try to understand and explain various aspects of sexuality at a more global level:

What effect would sex education beginning in kindergarten have on young children?

Why does someone feel attraction toward another person?

What are the behavioral effects of viewing erotic materials?

We develop informal theories or explanations to try to answer some of these questions for ourselves. For example, regarding the issue of early sex education, some people believe that sex is so powerful that young children should be shielded from it until puberty or even marriage. Others maintain that part of the power of sexuality comes from people's attempt to hide it and to repress children's interest in it.

Theorists also try to understand and explain various aspects of sexuality. A theory is essentially a model of how something—in this case, sexuality—works. It is a tentative explanation that may have received some empirical testing but is not yet accepted as fact. Ideally, a theory leads to research questions that can be tested to see whether the evidence supports or refutes the theory.

Theories can become part of the belief systems of individuals and cultures. For example, as noted earlier, the theory that women are dangerous sexual temptresses and inferior to men has dominated much of the history of Western civilization. In the 20th century, Freud's theory about female sexuality has had a profound effect on the sex lives of millions of women and men. Accordingly, it is important to test theories whenever possible. Theories and the research that evolves from them provide us with the only reliable way of advancing knowledge about ourselves and our world.

In this chapter we examine four theoretical explanations of the function of sexuality in our lives. We look first at evolutionary explanations of sexual behaviors and *gender* differences in sexual strategies. Next we examine psychoanalytic explanations, which emphasize early childhood sexual experience as a determinant of adult behavior. A third model, social-learning theory, focuses on the mechanisms and impact of learning and societal training. Finally, we consider a sociological theory that describes how various social structures account for the differences and similarities among the sexual lifestyles found throughout the world.

All these approaches have strengths and weaknesses. They will undoubtedly continue to be refined and altered as we learn more about sexuality. At present, however, they provide us with the most useful and provocative vantage points available from which to attempt to understand human sexuality.

## Evolutionary Approaches

The origins of modern evolutionary theory can be traced back to the work of Gregor Mendel and Charles Darwin (see Figure 3.1). Mendel discovered that biological inheritance is based on the transfer of genetic material. The genetic material remains relatively unchanged, although it is

**gender** (JEN-der)—the characteristics associated with being a male or a female in a particular culture.

heredity, transmitted to future generations. However, according to evolutionary theorists, the effect of the sheer number of offspring is moderated by the characteristics of those offspring. Offspring inherit characteristics from their parents that may be more or less adaptive, or useful, in the particular environmental conditions in which they live. Some of these characteristics—for example, hunting prowess, ability to forage and store food, and skill in attracting mates—increase the likelihood that the offspring will go on to produce children of their own. Thus adaptive characteristics are "selected" for continuation, producing *reproductive success*, a crucial concept in the theory of natural selection (see Figure 3.2).

**FIGURE 3.1**
**Charles Darwin**
The contemporary theory of evolution is based on Darwin's theory of natural selection combined with modern genetics.

shuffled and reshuffled over the course of successive generations.

Darwin proposed that living organisms evolved from one or more simple forms of life through a process called *natural selection*. Obviously, individuals in a population differ in the number and the characteristics of offspring they produce during their lifetimes. Individuals who produce a relatively large number of children are more likely to have their *genes*, the basic units of

**natural selection**—the process whereby species evolve genetically as a result of variations in the reproductive success of their ancestors.

**genes**—complex molecules found in chromosomes of cells that are responsible for the transmission of hereditary material from parents to offspring.

**FIGURE 3.2**
**Reproductive Success?**
According to evolutionary theory, characteristics of the more reproductively successful organisms of a species are passed on to the next generation.

**reproductive success**—the extent to which organisms are able to produce offspring who survive long enough to pass on their genes to successive generations.

Evolutionary theorists describe the period of time during which humans have existed on earth as very recent history. The past 5,000 years constitute a minutely thin slice of time compared to the vast stretches of the past from which humans have emerged. Give or take a billion years, the universe is about 15 billion years old. About 65 million years elapsed between the appearance of the first creatures with grasping hands, eyes at the front of their heads, and the ability to hold their bodies upright, and the appearance of a humanlike creature. It took about 5 million more years for the first identifiable hominid to appear. Viewed from our tiny niche of time and space, this is an immense period of time, but many scientists have been perplexed by how swiftly the longevity and intelligence of our species increased—a mere several million years from our prehominid beginnings.

Whatever the explanation of our rapid development, an evolutionary perspective gives us a far more panoramic view of sexuality than do most other theoretical frameworks. This perspective prompted an interesting statement from sociologist Alice Rossi (1978):

> *Modern society is a mere second in our evolutionary history, and it is naive to assume that our audacious little experiments in communal living, birth control, sexual liberation and sex-role equality can overturn in a century, let alone a decade, millennia of custom and adaptation. (p. 72)*

Most contemporary evolutionists assume that the particular characteristics of an organism exist because of their past usefulness in perpetuating the reproductive success of his or her ancestors. Those organisms having greater reproductive success are considered to have greater *fitness*. Natural selection can favor us not only through our own reproductive success in transmitting our genes, but also through the fitness of other people who share our genes such as our brothers and sisters. Natural selection, therefore,

operates for the maximization of *inclusive fitness*. Inclusive fitness involves both an individual's reproductive contribution to the gene pool of the next generation and that person's contribution in aiding the survival of kin, who pass on their shared genes (see Figure 3.3).

This view of natural selection has interesting ramifications for the study of current social and sexual behavior (Buss, 1994; Symons, 1979; Tooby & Cosmides, 1992; Wilson, 1978). Evolutionary theorists are interested in inherited psychological mechanisms underlying adaptive behaviors.

## Proximate Versus Ultimate Causes of Behavior

Evolutionary theorists suggest that we can ask two kinds of questions about the causes of behavior. Contemporary questions concern how a particular behavior came to exist; that is, they seek the *proximate cause* of a behavior. These questions involve analysis of the genetic, biological, or psychological causes of a particular behavior.

In addition, evolutionary theorists are interested in why a behavior exists; that is, they seek the *ultimate cause* of a behavior. As Symons (1979) put it, "Answers to questions about ultimate causation will be that the behavior functions in specific ways to maximize the animal's inclusive fitness." However, a problem arises:

> *Questions about the ultimate causes of behavior thus consider primarily the species' history, and, for this reason, are difficult to answer. . . . The ancestral populations in which the behavior evolved are gone and cannot be studied. (Symons, 1979, p. 8)*

**fitness**—a measure of one's success in transmitting genes to the next generation (reproductive success).

**inclusive fitness**—a measure of the total contribution of genes to the next generation by oneself and those with whom one shares genes, such as siblings and cousins.

**proximate cause**—explanations of behavior that focus on the immediate sources (how a particular behavior came to exist).

**ultimate cause**—explanations of behavior that focus on why a particular behavior increased reproductive success during the process of evolution.

**FIGURE 3.3**
**Families and Inclusive Fitness**
This Zuni family group illustrates one aspect of inclusive fitness—the bonds that relatives develop for their mutual well-being.

Evolutionary theorists assume that sexual behaviors exist and are maintained because, in the past, they served the ultimate cause of reproduction. According to this perspective, many of our current sexual activities can be traced back to reproductive behaviors that are believed to have existed in early hunting and gathering groups. Scientists have used evolutionary theoretical analyses to try to explain a variety of human sexual behaviors. Three of the most interesting hypotheses that have emerged from this analytical framework concern gender differences in sexuality, courtship strategies, and mate selection preferences.

## Gender Differences in Sexuality

In a major analysis of the findings from 239 samples of a total of almost 130,000 men and women studied regarding the relationship of gender to 21 sexual attitudes and behaviors, Oliver and Hyde (1993) found a number of gender differences. One of the most pronounced differences between men and women emerged in attitudes toward casual sex. Compared to women, men held considerably more permissive attitudes regarding coitus between people in a casual relationship or in a dating relationship that did not involve commitment. This finding is quite consistent with evolutionary predictions, because during the time our species was evolving, women who conceived with uncommitted partners (i.e., single mothers) would usually have been less able to provide for their offspring from infancy to adulthood than would women who were impregnated by men who were committed to a long-term relationship with the woman and their children. In contrast, the survival of men's genes in successive generations would have been less endangered by the absence of commitment to a woman. What men might have lost in the survival of some of their offspring would have been compensated for by the large numbers of offspring that they sired. We will return to this issue in more detail in the section on parental investment.

Focusing explicitly on the self-reported roles taken by men and women in sexual activity, psychologist Naomi McCormick examined contemporary sexual behaviors among college students (McCormick, 1979, 1994). In one study, aptly titled "Come-Ons and Put-Offs" (McCormick,

1979), men reported using more strategies to initiate sexual activity than did women; conversely, women reported employing more strategies to avoid or limit sexual activity than did men.

What do you think accounts for observed gender differences in this area? To answer this question, you might want to collect some empirical data. You could, for example, ask a few sexually intimate couples whom you know to tell you who took the active role in initiating the first a) date, b) kiss, c) necking, d) petting, and e) sexual stimulation to orgasm and/or ejaculation. Assuming that your survey, like those of other researchers, shows men taking the active role in initiating sexual activity and women playing the limit-setting role, how would you explain the gender difference?

## Parental-Investment Theory

In response to this question, the evolutionary perspective has yielded an intriguing model called parental-investment theory. Specifically, Trivers (1972) proposed that gender differences in the sexual behavior of a particular species are determined by fathers' versus mothers' amount of resources, time, and energy invested in their offspring.

Your mother and father committed various resources in rearing you. Who committed more? If your parents are typical of most in our culture, your mother invested a lot more than did your father (see Figure 3.4). After conception, she carried you for about nine months in her uterus. After giving birth to you, she fed you when you were too helpless to feed yourself. As you grew up, she took care of you to a greater extent than your father did. This pattern of greater investment in offspring by females than by males is still characteristic of humans and, in fact, of most species. This does not mean that human males are lacking in the capability for parental investment. During the evolutionary period in which we evolved, males incurred significant risks in hunting for meat and fighting off predators to protect their mates and offspring. But among most humans today, parental investment by women is greater than that by men.

According to Trivers, the average parental investment in a species influences sexual behavior in at least three ways. Among species such as

our own, in which the female invests more, Trivers predicted that a) male-male competition for female mates will be greater than female-female competition for male mates, b) there will be a greater variation in reproductive success among males than among females, and c) selective pressure will be greater on males than on females because of the competition among males and because some succeed in mating and some do not. This selective pressure on males should produce larger body size, greater strength, and other attributes that help some males compete successfully for mates against other males who do not have these attributes or who have them to a lesser extent. Selective pressure should also result in greater variation in hair and skin color and more aggressiveness, insofar as those male traits help males to attract females.

To put all this simply, among species in which females invest more as parents and thus control reproductive success, males are at a disadvantage. Males, therefore, must try harder to succeed in passing on their genes. Whatever strategies and attributes males have that help them to succeed will be passed on. Characteristics that may render males less successful in competing against other males in attracting females, such as passivity and physical limitations, will tend to drop out of the gene pool. In species in which females have greater parental investment, there is less selective pressure on females because they control reproductive success.

## Courtship Strategies

At first glance, the foregoing argument might suggest that gender is destiny in determining courtship strategies. However, in a few species, the males, who are bearers of a multitude of tiny sperm, have greater parental investment than do females, who contribute a few large eggs. According to Trivers, there should be greater selective pressure on females than on males in these species, and the females in these species should demonstrate greater competitiveness, body size, and sexual aggressiveness. Observations of pipefish, sea horses, and some bird species support this theory: it is the females in these species who aggressively court males, and females are willing to mate with any male (Williams, 1966). In contrast, males in these species are more cautious

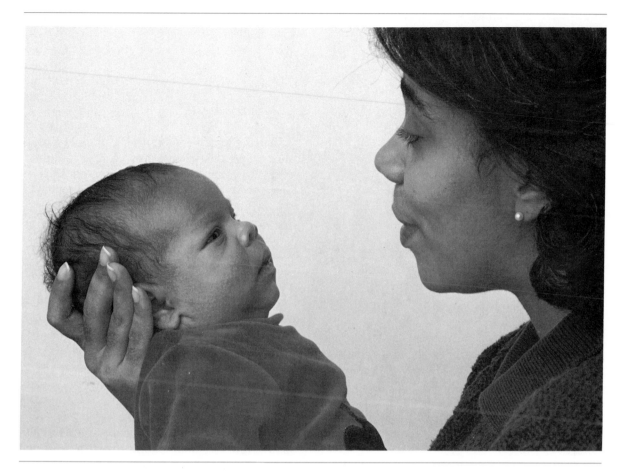

**FIGURE 3.4**
**Parental Investment**
From conception into adolescence, mothers typically invest more resources in their offspring than do fathers.

and more selective about choosing a sexual partner. Symons (1979) pointed out that among those species of birds in which there is female-female competition to mate with males, the females are larger and more aggressive than the males. Evolutionary theorists, then, view male and female sex differences as the result of different reproductive strategies.

In response to those who accuse evolutionary theorists of sexism, Williams (1966) wrote, "The evidence strongly supports the conclusion that promiscuity, active courtship, and belligerence toward rivals are *not* inherent aspects of maleness" (p. 186, emphasis added). Williams based his argument, however, on cross-species comparisons. In the case of a particular species, such as

humans, the impression remains that the male sexual behaviors Williams described are linked to the lesser parental investment by human males compared to females. Despite these observations, male versus female sexual behaviors among contemporary humans appear to be more strongly related to sexual socialization than to genetic influences, as we will see in later chapters.

The assumption that each species, including humans, evolves to enhance its reproductive success seems strange to most people. Even though some members of a particular species may choose not to reproduce, findings based on evolutionary predictions are consistent with data gathered since Darwin's time (Barkow, Cosmides, & Tooby, 1992; Buss, 1994; Symons, 1979).

## Box 3.1

## What Do You Look for in a Partner?

Indicate the importance to you of the following mate-selection characteristics by putting the number that best reflects your feelings in front of each attribute:

Irrelevant or unimportant →0—1—2—→3 Indispensable

_____ 1. Dependable

_____ 2. Chaste (no previous sexual intercourse)

_____ 3. High in financial prospects

_____ 4. Intelligent

_____ 5. Good looking (physical attractiveness)

_____ 6. Sociable

_____ 7. Ambitious and industrious

_____ 8. In love with the person

_____ 9. Gets along with your family

_____10. Considerate

After you have rated the importance of these characteristics in terms of what is important to you in selecting a partner, consider what the average man versus the average woman might rank as most important. You may want to check your hypotheses by asking 10 men and 10 women to respond anonymously to these characteristics to see how they differ in their relative rankings in the importance of each of the traits. NOTE: _Check with your instructor before doing so: your class might want to carry out this project by asking a large number of people to rate these characteristics, and your instructor will probably need to obtain your university's ethical review board approval._

## Mate Selection

Given the central importance of reproductive success in evolutionary theory, it is not surprising that a great deal of attention has been applied to how we select potential mates. Before reading further, please respond to the questionnaire in Box 3.1.

Assume that you and your classmates were able to gather responses from other people to the questionnaire in Box 3.1. If your hypotheses were guided by evolutionary theory, you probably assumed that, compared to women, men would give higher ratings to physical attractiveness as indications of reproductive fitness. In contrast, you may have hypothesized that women, compared to men, would give higher ratings to a potential partner's ability to be a good provider, as shown by high ratings for financial prospects and for ambitiousness and industriousness.

In a study of staggering proportions designed to test these hypotheses, David Buss (1989) studied more than 10,000 respondents. He obtained samples from 37 cultures in Africa,

Asia, Eastern and Western Europe, Canada, Australia, New Zealand, South America, and the United States. The measures were translated into the language spoken by each particular group and were administered by members of the culture from which the samples were obtained. The measures consisted of 18 characteristics, including the following target items: physical attractiveness, good financial prospects, and ambition and industriousness.

In support of Buss's hypotheses, women placed higher value on the financial prospects of potential partners than men did: significant differences occurred in 36 of the 37 samples. In 29 of the 37 samples, women rated a potential partner's ambition and industriousness more highly than men did, providing moderate support for that expectation.

If you also conducted the project, you can probably guess the results of Buss's study regarding the importance to men versus women of the physical attractiveness of a potential partner. In 34 of the 37 samples, men rated this characteristic as more important in selecting a mate than did women. In the remaining three samples (India, Poland, and Sweden), the differences were not significant, but they were in the same direction as in the other 34 samples. Thus this hypothesis received strong support.*

We wondered if contemporary college students still showed these gender differences in what is considered important in selecting a potential mate, so we conducted a similar project with more than 1,000 college students (Wiederman & Allgeier, 1992). Our findings were consistent with the results from the Buss (1989) study and with predictions based on evolutionary theory. Specifically, the characteristics that were most important in differentiating men's from women's ratings were financial prospects, ambition and industriousness, and physical attractiveness. The first two were rated as more important by women than by men in selecting a partner, whereas the physical attractiveness of a potential partner was rated more highly by men than by women.

Evolutionary analyses have been applied to a number of other human behaviors relevant to sexual behavior and gender differences. As you are undoubtedly aware if you have ever owned a dog or cat who was "in heat," the fertile period of most female mammals is readily apparent to male mammals of their species, not to mention humans in the neighborhood who are trying to sleep! In contrast, human females have what is known as concealed ovulation, so men cannot tell when a woman is fertile. Evolutionary theorists have tried to explain the possible advantages for our species of such concealed female fertility (Fisher, 1992; Symons, 1979). One explanation is that a female is continuously attractive to a male seeking to mate if the male cannot tell when she is fertile.

Evolutionary theorists have also attempted to explain the reasons for such diverse behaviors as homicide among family members (Daly & Wil-

son, 1989), incest (Welham, 1990), social status (Ellis, 1991), and jealousy (Buss, Larsen, Western, & Semmelroth, 1992; Wiederman & Allgeier, 1993a).

Evolutionary theorists have come under attack for attempting to reduce complex social behavior to a genetic drama—*reductionism*. They are accused of painting a picture of humans as automatons driven by genetic codes. Evolutionary theorists, however, consider humans to be a species with an evolutionary history who are also influenced by current circumstances. They emphasize the psychological mechanisms arising from evolution that underlie human emotion, learning, and behavior (Allgeier, A.R., 1994; Buss, 1994; Tooby & Cosmides, 1992). In addition to sparking controversy over the accuracy of evolutionary explanations of gender differences in courtship strategies, mate selection, and other sexual behaviors, evolutionary approaches have generated a great deal of debate on political and moral grounds (e.g., Fairchild, 1991), a topic to which we return at the end of this chapter.

Evolutionary theorists, as we have seen, are concerned with how and why the early history of entire species determines what characteristics are transmitted through reproduction. Psychoanalytic theorists take a different perspective, however, emphasizing the influence of an individual's early experience on his or her subsequent development.

## Psychoanalytic Approaches

The creator of psychoanalytic theory, Sigmund Freud (Figure 3.5; Box 3.2), utterly transformed beliefs about the influence of sexuality early in the life span. Freud argued that sexual experiences during infancy influence the development

---

*If you are intrigued by the study and are searching for research ideas to test, you should read the Buss (1989) article; look for the complete reference in the back of this text. If you do carry out projects designed to test some of his hypotheses, we welcome your reports for inclusion in future editions of *Sexual Interactions*.

**reductionism**—explaining complex processes in terms of basic physical/chemical activities (for example, explaining human sexual desire just in terms of hormonal activity without reference to the particular characteristics of a desired partner or the situations in which the desire occurs).

### Box 3.2

## Freud

Freud (see Figure 3.5) was born in the small town of Freiberg, Moravia (now in the Czech Republic). His father, a merchant, had been widowed, and Freud was the first child of his father's second wife. His mother was only 21 years old when Freud was born, and he was the apple of her eye. When Freud was about five, his family moved to Vienna, Austria, where he entered school and rose to the top of his grammar-school class. When he was 17, he entered the University of Vienna. He received his Doctor of Medicine degree eight years later, after conducting various studies, one of which involved trying to locate the gonads, or sex organs, of the eel. Although Freud wanted to become a researcher, his poor financial situation and the problems arising from laboratory politics led him into the practice of medicine. From these beginnings, the founder of psychoanalysis launched his intellectual career.

For most of his 83 years, Freud lived and worked in Vienna. The year before his death, he was forced to leave after the Nazis entered Austria, because of his Jewish heritage. He emigrated to England, where, on September 23, 1939, he died after a 20-year battle with cancer of the mouth and jaw.

**FIGURE 3.5**
**Sigmund Freud**
Freud, creator of psychoanalysis, emphasized the role of sexuality in personality development.

of adult personality. His assertions challenged the prevailing view that the child was pure and asexual. His theory of infantile sexuality was a revolutionary idea that described sexuality as a prime factor in human development. His ideas still shock and offend some people (see Box 3.2).

In Freud's view, sexuality is interwoven with all aspects of personality. Sexual energy, or *libido*, is the source of all human endeavors. Because social prohibitions prevent humans from acting freely on their sexual impulses, this energy is then sublimated, or diverted into other activities. Religion, art, and culture itself result from displaced sexual energy (Gay, 1988).

Although Freud's theories were often depicted as the product of an obscene mind, the man himself was a conservative moralist. He believed that society must restrict and channel libido. Just as theologians had argued that all humans were tainted with original sin, Freud bestowed on them original lust. Society—and, more specifically, parents—had to bring this lust under control. Freud's major complaint against Victorian society, however, was that it too severely suppressed childhood sexuality.

**libido** (lih-BEE-doe)—psychoanalytic term for sexual energy or drive.

## Freud's Theory of Personality Development

Freud developed his theory in the process of treating disturbed patients and in conducting his own self-analysis. His perceptions of sexuality were, to some extent, limited by the Victorian times in which he lived. Freud read works from an extensive range of disciplines, including anthropology, sociology, psychology, medicine, and literature. Out of these influences, he fashioned a theory of personality development that revolved around sexuality.

Freud believed that all human beings have two kinds of *instincts*. One kind—*eros*, the life instinct—operates to preserve or enhance the individual and species. The other kind—*thanatos*, the death instinct—motivates the organism to return to its original state of inorganic matter, and is expressed in aggressive and destructive behavior. Freud assumed that each of the instincts had an accompanying energy source, pushing for release or expression. As part of the life instinct, he proposed a sexual instinct, and he named its accompanying energy source the libido. This instinct interested Freud the most. Unlike the need for food and water, the instinctive need for love and sex, according to Freud, can be repressed by the society or the individual. However, its energy source, the libido, remains. Freud spun his theory of personality development around the fate of the libido.

### The Id, Ego, and Superego

Freud believed that the influence of libido on an individual's personality and behavior is determined by three subsystems in the mind: the id, ego, and superego. The *id* contains such instincts as hunger and sex. It is also the energy source for the entire personality, providing both sexual and aggressive power for behavior. According to Freud, the id is present at birth and is not controlled by knowledge of reality or morality. It seeks only to gratify instinctual drives and to enjoy the pleasure that results when tension aroused by instinctual needs is discharged. The id seeks immediate gratification without regard for moral or practical consequences. This instinctual need, according to Freud, is not necessarily carried out behaviorally; sometimes people simply have fantasies or dreams in which they focus on mental images of the desired object or behavior. The attempt to satisfy instinctual demands by producing a mental image is called wish fulfillment.

When we feel sexual tension or desire, we may for hours on end imagine an encounter with a partner, but wishing does not provide one. To satisfy our sexual tensions, thirst, or hunger, we must be able to perceive and solve problems, organize and store knowledge, and initiate acts to achieve these goals. In short, we need to be able to carry out transactions with the real world. According to Freud, a second subsystem of the personality, the *ego*, develops out of the id to perform these functions.

The ego is shaped by conscious perceptions and contacts with the external world. It seeks to satisfy the demands of the id in light of the constraints of the real world. In working out a realistic strategy to fulfill our needs, the ego must try to satisfy three masters. It must deal with the id, which wants satisfaction of needs. It must take into account the demands of external reality, which prohibit many selfish behaviors. Finally, it must satisfy the last subsystem of personality to emerge, the *superego*.

The superego develops initially from the learning of societal values, as taught by parents and other caretakers. As a child matures, the superego is also influenced by the child's own critical examination of different values. The superego includes what is called the conscience, which is concerned with whether a thought or behavior is good or bad, right or wrong.

In Freud's model, aspects of the ego and the superego can be conscious, preconscious, or

**instinct**—as Freud used this term, biological excitation that leads to mental activity.

**id**—in psychoanalysis, the source of psychic energy derived from instinctive drives.

**ego**—in psychoanalysis, the rational level of personality.

**superego**—in psychoanalysis, the level of personality corresponding to the conscience.

**TABLE 3.1 Freud's Psychosexual Stages**

| Age | Psychosexual Stage | Erogenous Zone | Activities | Psychoanalytic Expectations |
|---|---|---|---|---|
| 0–1 yr. | Oral | Mouth | Sucking, biting, "taking things in" | Dependency on caretaker |
| 2–3 yrs. | Anal | Anus | Expulsion and retention of feces | Clash of wills between child and parent; delay of gratification |
| 4–5 yrs. | Phallic | Genitals | Playing with genitals | Oedipal complex, Electra complex, gender identity |
| 6–12 yrs. | Latency | Genitals | Preference for same-gender playmates | Sublimation and repression of libido |
| 13–20 yrs. | Puberty | Genitals | Dating, "practicing" for eventual mate selection | Flare-up of Oedipal conflict, usually reflected in a "crush" on older person |
| 21–? yrs. | Genital | Genitals | Sexual intercourse | Mate selection, propagation of the species |

unconscious. Consciousness refers to thoughts and feelings of which we are presently aware. The preconscious comprises mental content of which we are currently unaware but which, with effort, we can remember—for example, old addresses or childhood friends. The unconscious contains all those thoughts and feelings that are outside our awareness. We can have access to our unconscious thoughts, intentions, and desires only through indirect means such as dreams and slips of the tongue. Freud placed great emphasis on the unconscious and believed that all our thoughts originate there. Whether these thoughts eventually come into consciousness or remain outside our awareness depends on the degree of resistance they meet. Sexual memories, images, or ideas that we find objectionable may not emerge into awareness because of their threatening nature.

## Psychosexual Stages

As should be clear by now, the unfolding of sexual energies from infancy on forms a central part of Freud's theory of personality development. In dealing with his patients, Freud listened to many accounts of childhood memories of sexual episodes, some of which involved parents or siblings. At one point he accepted these accounts; later he thought that his patients' memories were rooted in their own desires and fantasies. We now know, of course, that many children do experience sexual approaches by family members, friends of the family, and peers (see Chapter 18). In any event, Freud concluded that whether his patients' memories of sexual experiences were real or imagined, his patients were definitely concerned with sexual issues in childhood. He believed that early in life, libido is channeled into certain body zones, which then become the center of eroticism (see Table 3.1). Each stage of development poses demands that must be met and conflicts that must be resolved. If conflicts are not resolved, fixation occurs, in which some libido remains invested in that stage, to be reflected in adult behavior. For instance, Freudians see smokers as partially fixated at the oral stage. Freud believed that much of adult personality was influenced by what went on in these early developmental stages.

Of particular interest to Freud was the so-called Oedipus complex. Freud maintained that

**FIGURE 3.6**
**Daughter-Father Affection**
During early childhood, most daughters are very affectionate toward their fathers. Freud attributed the attachment to the Electra complex—a daughter's desire to take the place of her mother in gaining her father's attention.

we go through a period of sexual attraction toward, and conflict with, our parents that is exemplified by the ancient Greek myth of Oedipus. According to Freud, boys and girls develop love and jealousy relationships with their parents. Children initially identify with their mothers. However, boys must shift their identification to their fathers. Around the ages of three to five, the young boy develops a sexual desire for his mother. Simultaneously, he fears that his father will punish him and cut off his penis. At this age, according to Freud, the penis is the center of a boy's sexual energy, and it is where the boy feels most vulnerable.

This castration anxiety leads the boy to repress his desire for his mother and to begin to identify with his father. By identifying with his father, he strives to become as strong and invulnerable as his father appears, and to be able to possess a woman just as his father does. Boys thereby resolve the Oedipus complex at about six

years of age by developing an intense identification with their fathers' values and behaviors.

The female Oedipal complex, which some of Freud's students called the Electra complex, refers to the desire of a young girl for her father (see Figure 3.6). Penis envy plays basically the same role in the development of girls that castration anxiety does in the development of boys. The girl, having no penis, assumes that she has been castrated. Blaming her mother for this loss, she shifts her love to her father. It does not take long, however, for her to find that she cannot compete with her mother for her father's affection, so she continues to identify with her mother and develops a feminine identity. Eventually, she finds an appropriate love object in an adult male.

Freud's theories were primarily masculine in orientation, reflecting his Victorian upbringing. For him, women were essentially inferior males, burdened by an envy of the male penis. This masculine bias was roundly attacked and revised by some later psychoanalysts, among them Karen Horney and Clara Thompson. Horney, in particular, did not think much of Freud's concept of penis envy. She claimed that envy of the penis could be explained by looking at the dominant role of men in Western societies, which created a subservient role for women. The "envy" that women feel arises from the desire for the autonomy and freedom that men have rather than from the wish for a penis specifically.

Critics have also attacked Freud for placing too much emphasis on the role of sex in human behavior, for being unduly pessimistic about human nature, for paying minimal attention to female personality, and for neglecting to supply adequate scientific evidence for many of his assumptions. As Box 2.1 (highlighted in the previous chapter) showed, researchers have also heavily criticized the Freudian assumption that women who have orgasms primarily from clitoral stimulation are fixated at an immature phallic stage of development.

Whatever the weaknesses or inaccuracies in psychoanalytic theory, some of its major hypotheses—for example, the concept of developmental stages and their importance for adult behavior, and the concept of the unconscious—have been incorporated in one form or another into most current theories of personality.

## Recent Psychoanalytic Developments

Psychoanalytic theorists have taken many new directions since Freud did his original work. Some of these theorists, Wilhelm Reich, Herbert Marcuse, and Geza Roheim among them, have stressed the importance of sex in human affairs to an even greater extent than Freud did. Reich, for example, took libido theory to the ultimate extreme by claiming that almost all maladaptive behavior was tied to dammed-up sexual energy. For Reich, the extent of orgasmic release became a measure of health. The unhealthy person was one who was unable to experience a full orgasm and the release of sexual energy.

In contrast to Reich's approach, most refinements of psychoanalytic theory, some of which are called object-relations theory, have stressed the adaptiveness of the ego, and how we interact with others. Margaret Mahler, W. R. D. Fairbairn, Heinz Kohut, Nancy Chodorow, and Erik Erikson are a few of the major names in these relatively recent developments.

For example, Chodorow (1978) pointed out that because infants—both boys and girls—generally have the most contact with their mothers, they initially identify and form intense relationships with their mothers. For girls, this identification is never completely severed, but boys must relinquish their identification with their mothers as they take on masculine roles. Chodorow maintained that this differing experience produced distinct coping strategies for males and females in dealing with the world. Specifically, women emphasize relationships *with* others, whereas men focus on their own individualism and independence *from* others.

Actually, in agreement with Carol Gilligan (1982), who wrote an insightful and very readable book called *In a Different Voice*, we believe that an exclusive focus on either way of dealing with the world may restrict both men and women. The woman (or, for that matter, man) who views herself only in relationship to others (wife, mother, but not an individual in her own right) may limit her own independent development. The man (or woman) who views himself only in terms of his own achievements and independence (boss, owner, director, sole author) may handicap his capacity for intimate connection with others.

Erikson (1968a, 1968b) accepted Freud's idea that sexual impulses and experiences have their onset in infancy. He also adopted Freud's notion that much of the child's developing personality is influenced by biological drives focused first on the mouth, then on the anus and genitals.

Erikson departed from Freud, however, in a number of important ways. Although he agreed that early experiences are extremely influential in personality development, he gave far more weight to the power of experiences throughout life to modify positive and negative early events. Erikson thought that the development of a trusting nature was extremely important for a one-year-old, but he also suggested that positive experiences later in life could offset a less-than-desirable set of early-life circumstances. Similarly, optimal experiences during infancy could be overshadowed by the impact of negative events later in life.

Perhaps Erikson's needs were consistently and affectionately met during his first year of life. In any event, he is one of the most optimistic of personality theorists. He was also well ahead of his time in being concerned with the interaction of biological, psychological, and environmental factors in the development of the individual. We cover his assumptions in more detail in the chapters on life-span development.

## Learning Approaches

The evolutionary and psychoanalytic theories that we have just described emphasize biological explanations of human sexual behavior. We turn now to an approach that focuses on the relationship of learning to our sexual behavior. The research presented throughout the text demonstrates that much of our sexual behavior—what we do; with whom we do it; when, where, and how we do it—is influenced by learning processes.

Learning theorists assume that most behavior, including sexual behavior, is strongly affected by learning processes. Many of the processes or "laws" of learning were formulated in the first half of the 20th century, when a brand of psychology called *behaviorism* was developing. The early behaviorists, among them John Watson (1878–1958), maintained that to be scientific, researchers must focus only on what is observable and thus measurable. Behavior is observable; thoughts and fantasies are not. Thus the early behaviorists studied overt behavior and disregarded mental events—thoughts, ideas, beliefs, and attitudes.

Watson studied sexual response by connecting measuring instruments to himself and his partner while they had sexual intercourse. He collected several boxes of data before his wife discovered the reason for her husband's long hours in the laboratory. He not only was forced to resign from his university position but also was divorced by his wife. During his divorce trial, the judge called him an expert in *mis*behavior (Magoun, 1981).

Despite his misbehavior, Watson was instrumental in initiating a school of research that has yielded several important principles that have become part of most contemporary theories of learning. Behavioral research has been conducted on both common behavior (that related to heterosexual attraction, for instance) and uncommon behavior (that related to shoe fetishes, for example). Two basic principles central to learning theory are classical conditioning and operant conditioning.

## Conditioning

Most students who have taken an introductory psychology course have learned about the concept of classical conditioning developed by the Russian physiologist Ivan Pavlov (1849–1936). In the classic experiment, Pavlov presented dogs with food, an *unconditioned stimulus (UCS)* that caused them to salivate, salivation being an *unconditioned response (UCR)* to food. Pavlov

sounded a buzzer at the same time that he gave the dogs the food; he repeated the conditioning until eventually the dogs would salivate at the sound of the buzzer alone. In terms of classical conditioning, the buzzer was a *conditioned stimulus (CS)*, and the salivation in response to it was a *conditioned response (CR)*. The dogs learned to salivate in response to a stimulus that previously had not elicited this response.

Researchers have employed classical conditioning to explain how people can come to be sexually aroused by a wide range of stimuli. The way in which a neutral object can acquire sexual significance was suggested by a study involving three male graduate students (Rachman, 1966). The students were asked to judge a series of photos of nude females. The photographs they judged to be sexually stimulating were then paired with slides of women's high black boots. The students were repeatedly shown slides of women's high black boots followed by the photos of the nude women they had rated as sexually stimulating. After repeated pairings of the nudes and the boots, the students were shown the boots alone, to which the males responded with sexual arousal, as measured by changes in penile blood volume. Gradually, arousal was produced in response to other types of women's shoes as well. In short, the pairing of previously neutral stimuli with sexual stimuli led to the neutral stimuli acquiring erotic significance.*

You have undoubtedly experienced some classical conditioning of your own sexual arousal without fully recognizing it at the time. Have you

**conditioned stimulus (CS)**—in classical conditioning, a stimulus that is paired with an unconditioned stimulus until it evokes a response that was previously associated with the unconditioned stimulus.

**conditioned response (CR)**—an acquired response to a stimulus that did not originally evoke such a response.

**behaviorism**—a theoretical approach that emphasizes the importance of studying observable activity.

**unconditioned stimulus (UCS)**—a stimulus that evokes a response that is not dependent on prior learning.

**unconditioned response (UCR)**—a stimulus-evoked response that is not dependent on experience or learning.

---

*Subsequent attempts to replicate Rachman's study of the classical conditioning of atypical sexual arousal have not been successful; however, Rachman's study does provide an example of how we may learn to find particular objects erotic.

ever felt arousal when smelling a particular cologne or perfume? If you have an erotic interest in someone who wears a specific brand, you may have noticed that the smell arouses you; that is, you shake, you feel short of breath, your pulse races, and your heart beats faster when you smell a scent that you associate with the person who attracts you.

Similarly, you may respond with arousal to a particular jacket or hairstyle, for example, only to discover at closer range that it was a case of mistaken identity. As we document in Chapter 16, the advertising industry has made extensive use of humans' tendency to associate arousal from and attraction to one stimulus (for instance, a "sexy" woman) with another (for example, a car).

## Operant Conditioning

Besides learning to respond to one stimulus because of its association with another stimulus to which we already have an unconditioned response, humans also learn to behave in particular ways as a function of whether their behaviors are rewarded, ignored, or punished. This form of learning is called operant conditioning, or instrumental conditioning. Its principles were first described by E. L. Thorndike and developed into an influential theory by B. F. Skinner. In its most general form, this theory maintains that behavior is influenced by its consequences. Behavior followed by pleasurable consequences (positive reinforcement) is likely to recur and increase in frequency. Behavior associated with the removal of an aversive (unpleasant) stimulus is also likely to recur and increase in frequency (negative reinforcement). Conversely, behavior that is not rewarded or is associated with an aversive stimulus (punishment) occurs at a diminished frequency or not at all. Upon removal of the aversive stimulus, the behavior may reappear or increase in frequency.

We appear to learn many kinds of behavior through being rewarded, ignored, or punished for them. If an experience with another person—a conversation, a date, or sexual intimacy—is pleasurable, we are likely to try to repeat the experience. Positive sexual experiences are certainly rewarding, but in both laboratory and field experiments other, less obviously rewarding experiences have been shown to provide pleasure or reinforcement and to influence attraction (Byrne & Schulte, 1990). We are more likely to feel attraction to and to want contact with people who praise and compliment us, who demonstrate attitudes similar to ours, and whom we perceive as physically appealing. That is, we are attracted toward those who reward us in some way. In contrast, we are less likely to feel attracted toward those who put us down (but see Chapter 6 for exceptions to this generalization), who hold very different attitudes from ours, or toward whom we are not physically attracted.

We are less likely to repeat experiences that are not particularly pleasant or are punishing. Punishment tends to work best when it is immediate, intense, and unavoidable. In the short run, mild punishments have mild effects. And in the long run, people adapt to punishment if its intensity is gradually increased, so ultimately it loses its power to change behavior.

Although research has demonstrated that punishment reduces the frequency of undesirable sexual behavior, it has also shown that harmful side effects may occur. The child or adolescent who is yelled at, scolded, or physically punished may cry, cringe, or feel suppressed anger. These responses are incompatible with the punished behavior and thus replace it for the moment. The child or adolescent may engage in the punished behavior again, but he or she will feel guilty while doing it.

In general, punishment may produce aggressive behavior by the person who is punished, thus undermining the impact of the attempt to alter the person's behavior (Catania, 1992). Punishment can be useful when the immediate suppression of behavior is necessary, such as when a child runs into the street. However, it is difficult to think of any sexual behavior for which the positive effects of punishment would be worth the cost of the negative effects. Even in the case of rape, punishment has not been particularly effective in eliminating a rapist's tendency to assault others. In fact, it may increase the aggression and anger that most contemporary scholars believe is part of the motivation of some rapists, as we shall see in Chapter 18.

Other techniques—such as removing rewards in cases of undesirable behavior, and rewarding responses that are incompatible with undesirable behavior—are more effective. In the case of children playing with their genitals, for example, parents can encourage a son or daughter to engage in that pleasurable activity in the privacy of the bedroom, or at least not in the presence of people who might object, such as grandparents or neighbors. Interestingly, the work of many learning theorists supports some religious teachings stressing that acts of love (positive reinforcement) influence behavior more than does punishment.

Learning theorists are probably correct in saying that some of our sexual behaviors are acquired through classical and operant conditioning. Most sexual behavior is difficult to understand without taking into account a person's history of social processes and mental events. In many studies, little is said about the social context in which people were punished or what the punished people thought about it. Many students of sexual behavior consider these factors to be as important as conditioning principles. Concern with the influence of social and *cognitive* factors has led to extensions and revisions of the basic learning theories outlined above.

## Social Learning Theory

We learn most of our behavior in the context of our interactions with others. People need other people from the beginning of life to the end of it. Most of us can look at our own histories and see the central place of our interactions with particular people, and the importance of our thoughts about them. In their early fervor to be scientific and to isolate behavior in the laboratory, behaviorists overlooked the significance of such social interactions and thoughts. Gradually, some behavioral scientists, known as social learning theorists, began to examine the influence of other people and of cognitions—observations, perceptions, ideas, beliefs, and attitudes—on sexual behavior.

Albert Bandura is one of the most influential of the social learning theorists. He argued that sex-related behavior can be learned, without the learner receiving any direct reinforcement, by ob-

serving other people and events. This process is called *modeling*. Bandura (1986) would suggest, for example, that if we observed someone being rewarded or reinforced for engaging in premarital sex, we would be more likely to engage in this behavior. Similarly, if we observed someone being punished for practicing premarital sex, we would be less likely to have sex before marriage. In support of this hypothesis, Christopher, Johnson, and Roosa (1993) found that perceived peer sexual behavior was a strong predictor of early sexual involvement.

The principles of social learning theory have been applied to the widespread problem of sexual assault. A common concern among those who conduct research on eroticized film and magazine depictions of sexual aggression against females is that victimized females are portrayed as ultimately enjoying violations of their bodies. During exposure to such depictions, viewers may be incorrectly "learning" that women are sexually aroused by sexually assaultive approaches (see Chapter 16).

Social learning approaches, in short, tend to underline the importance of such factors as past experiences, parental influences, social norms, biological events, and current sexual experiences in shaping how we think and behave sexually. Most significant is the emphasis placed on cognitions (Bandura, 1989). Many current investigators of sexuality are guided by the general philosophy of social learning theory: that some combination of learning and cognitive principles will best explain sexual behavior. In attempting to explain sexual attitudes and behaviors in terms of cognition and complex social events, contemporary learning theorists have taken an approach similar to that of sex researchers trained in the discipline of sociology.

## Sociological Approaches

In contrast to those scientists who take the evolutionary and psychoanalytic approaches, most

---

**cognitive** (KOG-nih-tive)—related to the act or process of engaging in mental activity.

**modeling**—learning through the observation of others.

sociologists concerned with sexuality believe that human sexual behavior is more readily understood by examining *socialization* processes and cultural beliefs and norms rather than by studying biological development. According to Gagnon and Simon (1973), without the complex psychosocial process of development experienced by humans, the physical acts involved in sexual activity would not be possible:

> *This combination of various periods of development into the articulate behavioral sequence that leads to orgasm is not fated or ordained at any level; it is neither fixed by nature or by the organs themselves. The very experience of excitement that seems to originate from hidden internal sources is in fact a learned process, and it is only our insistence on the myth of naturalness that hides these social components from us. (p. 9)*

The sociological perspective is similar to that taken by social learning theorists. The foci of the two are somewhat different, however. Social learning theorists tend to examine the socialization and conditioning of the individual; in contrast, sociologists take a broader view, looking at the relationship between beliefs and norms shared by members of a society to understand the sexual interactions of members of that group.

In addition, sociologists maintain that these individual learning experiences do not allow an adequate explanation for why people in one society differ so much in their sexual lifestyles from people in another society. For example, Ira Reiss (see Figure 3.7) examined research from a number of sources, including descriptions of 186 nonindustrialized cultures. From his review of studies of these societies, Reiss (1986) concluded that, although biological and psychological factors are crucial in comparing individuals, they are not of major importance in comparing societies.

For example, although all human females are capable biologically of experiencing great pleasure during sexual interaction, whether in fact they do enjoy sexual relations varies from one culture to another and is related to the culture's

**FIGURE 3.7**
**Sociologist Ira Reiss**
Reiss is well known for his research on changes in premarital sexual standards during the 1950s and 1960s. He subsequently devoted more than a decade developing a theory of the ways in which society influences our sexual attitudes and behavior.

perception of the importance of female sexual pleasure, and of the purpose of sex. As discussed in Chapter 1, the So women of Uganda do not enjoy sex but endure it because they want to conceive. In their culture, genital touching is taboo, and orgasm is assumed to occur only in males (Allgeier, 1992). In contrast, the Mangaian people of Polynesia are encouraged from childhood on to learn as much as they can about how to give and receive sexual pleasure. Mangaian girls learn that women should be sexually active and responsive and should experience sexual relations with a number of men to find a spouse with whom they enjoy sex. Marshall (1971) estimates

---

**socialization**—the process of developing the skills needed to interact with others in one's culture.

that women in this culture have three times as many orgasms as men. Thus, although we can assume that both So and Mangaian women are equally capable biologically of experiencing intense sexual pleasure, their actual experiences differ markedly.

Reiss (1986) hypothesized that in almost all societies (the So are an exception), genital response usually leads to physical pleasure and self-disclosure. No matter how permissive they are about sexuality, most societies place importance on the potential for developing an interpersonal bond through the pleasure and disclosure characteristics of sexuality. Interpersonal bonding is universally emphasized because it is the basis of stable social relationships, the structural foundation of societies.

> Societies organize the bonding power of sexuality so as to enhance socially desired relationships and avoid socially undesired relationships. To illustrate: sexual bonding is encouraged in marital relations that tie together individuals from different social groups, whereas sexual bonding is discouraged in parent-child relationships to avoid role conflict and jealousy and also to encourage young people to seek mates from other groups and thereby build alliances that can be helpful. (Reiss, 1986, p. 210)

## Scripts

To develop social stability, groups attempt to define what is proper behavior for a specific situation. Members of a particular society then have a set of social guidelines, or *scripts*, that they can adopt or alter to suit their purposes. On the individual level, scripts are cognitive plans that enable us to behave in an organized and predictable fashion.

The concept of scripts allows us to discuss sexual orientation—or any other sexual behavior—in terms of public labeling and the attendant roles and scripts associated with a label. Those theorists who interpret behavior using the con-

**scripts**—largely unconscious, culturally determined mental plans that individuals use to organize and guide their behavior.

cept of scripts believe that neither sexual orientation nor any other aspect of sexual identity involves permanent traits or genetic influences within the individual. Instead, sexual orientation is based on a loosely defined set of behaviors that a person employs in dealing with others. Thus, similar to some homosexuals who pass for heterosexuals in the "straight" world, one may play the homosexual role in certain situations and the "straight" role in others.

These roles come from scripts that are part of the cultural expectations about interactions between people (see Figure 3.8). Just as actors have their scripts to guide them through a play, we have our own scripts to guide us through various interactions. Just as actors learn their parts so thoroughly that they perform their roles without being conscious of the script, so do we perform much of our own scripted behavior as if it were second nature.

Gagnon (1990) described three levels of sexual scripts. In addition to the societal scripts or cultural scenarios just mentioned, we can also examine interpersonal scripts and intrapsychic scripts. Interpersonal scripts refer to our social interactions with others. The expectations that we perceive others to have of us may influence the way in which we behave or act out our role. The patient-doctor relationship illustrates the power of interpersonal scripts. There is no other circumstance under which we would allow, and in fact pay, a relative stranger to probe intimate parts of our bodies, occasionally inflicting some discomfort in the process. Further, most people do not perceive a gynecological or urological exam as sexual, even when the exam includes manual penetration of the vagina and anus and breast or testicle "fondling" to check for lumps. Variations in context can make huge differences in the probability of a person perceiving a situation as sexual.

Intrapsychic scripts refer to those ideas, images, and plans we think about in the privacy of our minds. Thus, we can rehearse various scenarios using our imagination before deciding on a plan of action, or deciding not to act at all. It is in this sphere that we attempt to integrate cultural scripts and interpersonal scripts. For example, think of times when you have mentally rehearsed the sequence of events as you hoped

**FIGURE 3.8**
**Scripting Romantic Behavior**
Organized dances are one way that young people learn scripts about how to behave romantically.

they might happen during an upcoming date. Your fantasies about what you might or might not do will be influenced by cultural scripts regarding what is "appropriate" dating behavior and how much you adhere personally to these scripts. You might allow yourself a range of fantasies of what could happen, but decide not to act on any of them.

Research has indicated that college students' views of sexual interactions are very scripted, with certain sexual behaviors occurring in a particular sequence. When asked to arrange a series of 25 statements about activities ranging from kissing to orgasm in the order in which they would be most likely to occur, men and women described very similar sequences (Jemail & Geer, 1977).

Abelson (1981) contended that three conditions are necessary for scripted behavior to occur:

1. A stable cognitive representation of the script
2. An evoking context for the script
3. A willingness to enter the script

How does a man come to be a customer, for example, in a visit-the-prostitute script? First, he must know something about prostitute-customer roles, such as how to identify a prostitute and how to behave as a customer. Second, a situation must be present that calls for a visit to a prostitute, such as the unavailability of another partner or a wish for sexual novelty. Third, the man must make the decision to approach a prostitute rather than to reject or ignore the idea.

Abelson (1981) suggested that we have a tendency to fill in the gaps of incomplete scripts. This gap-filling phenomenon can lead to difficulty in ambiguous situations. You may have experienced a situation in which you were following a friendship script, having coffee or a sandwich with a person, only to discover that your friend's script did not match yours. Your friend, who had been following a romantic script, had filled the gaps by attributing to you sexual feelings and intentions that you did not have. Relating to each other may have been somewhat awkward until you resolved the differences between your scripts.

From the standpoint of script theory, then, there is little sexual interaction (or other behavior) that can truly be called spontaneous. Members of each culture share learned patterns that facilitate their sexual interaction. Inherent in script theory is the notion that scripts allow a sexual encounter to take place by providing the participants with a program for action. The script defines the situation, names the actors, and plots the sequence of events in a sexual interaction.

On the societal level, sexual scripts are beliefs that people in a particular group share about what are good and bad sexual thoughts, feelings, and behaviors. These sexual scripts function as guideposts, describing the proper social circumstances in which sexual responses may occur. In a large and complex society such as our own, sexual scripts vary somewhat depending on social class and age group, but there is still much similarity in the sexual scripts across these groups. Reiss (1986) maintained that "human sexuality in all societies consists of those scripts shared by a group that are supposed to lead to erotic arousal and in turn to produce genital response" (p. 20).

Scripts are subject to change. As societal changes occur, people edit their scripts over the years. The rapid increase in the percentage of North American adolescents engaging in premarital sexual relations during the decade from 1965 to 1975 is an example of script alteration.

The centrality of heterosexuality in the sexual scripts of human societies stems from its connection with *kinship* and gender roles. Acceptable sexual behavior (what is "natural," according to the society) is basically that which is compatible with the basic kinship and gender conceptions of

**kinship**—a social relationship defined either by descent ties, such as those to parents, children, and siblings, or by ties to in-laws via marriage.

a society. According to Reiss, one outcome of the development of sexual bonds was the linking of sexuality in marriage to jealousy and power. The greater the sexual power of men, the more able they are to organize gender roles in ways that stabilize their power in important institutions.

## Kinship and Jealousy

Reiss (1986) claimed that all societies value stable social relationships—particularly, stable heterosexual relationships that provide a context for the nurturance of offspring—and view sexuality as the basis for these relationships. Because the bonding properties of sexual relationships are seen as the basis for husband-wife and parent-child roles, societies set boundaries on sexual relationships, particularly marital relationships. These boundaries are designed to minimize conflict between kin and friends.

Jealousy is a major boundary-setting mechanism for what society considers an important relationship, marriage. When the boundaries of this relationship are flouted, jealousy occurs, with the attendant hurt and anger that develops when a basic norm is violated. In support of this theory of the role of jealousy, Hupka (1981) found that the greater the emphasis placed on the importance of marriage, the greater the jealousy response in the 92 cultures that he examined. Reiss concluded that all societies have jealousy norms about marital sexuality concerning the ways, if any, to negotiate extramarital sexual access without disturbing the existing marriage relationships.

## Power and Gender

According to Reiss (1986), power is the ability to influence others and achieve one's objectives despite the opposition of others. Powerful people seek to maximize their control over the valuable elements in their society. Insofar as sexuality is considered a valuable resource, powerful people seek to gain control of it. As described in Chapter 1, males generally have had more power than females have had in almost all cultures. So according to Reiss's theory, powerful males seek not only to obtain sexual satisfaction for themselves but also to control sexual access to those who are important to them, such as wives, daughters, and sisters. In his view, differences between the roles of men and women stem not from innate differences but from the degree of male control of key societal institutions.

## Ideologies and Normality

Underlying and reinforcing the scripts that protect a society's valued institutions is an ideology. An ideology consists of a society's assumptions about human nature. Because ideologies determine what is expected of people, they define what a particular group judges to be normal attitudes and behavior.

Reiss (1986) argued that use of the terms *abnormal, dysfunctional,* and *pathological* to refer to certain types of sexual behavior is improper because it does not take into account the diversity in ideologies across cultures. For example, premature ejaculation—ejaculation shortly after insertion of the penis into the vagina—is considered a sexual dysfunction in our culture. In some cultures, however, ejaculation within 15 to 30 seconds after vaginal entry is the norm. Reiss suggested that the only problem with premature ejaculation is one of conformity in our culture. Whereas a male experiencing this "problem" is not conforming to our own societal norms, he would be displaying normative behavior in another culture, such as that of East Bay in Melanesia (Davenport, 1978).

In Reiss's view, a premature ejaculator is a nonconformist rather than dysfunctional or abnormal. Reiss reserved the term *abnormal* for those personal traits or behaviors that disable an individual from functioning in *all* societies. If there is any group or society in which a particular behavior would not be a problem, Reiss would call a person engaging in that behavior a nonconformist rather than assign a more negative label such as *dysfunctional* or *abnormal.*

We have described and discussed four major theoretical approaches to understanding human sexual behavior: evolutionary, psychoanalytic, learning, and sociological approaches. Most research is conducted to test hypotheses derived from one or more of these theories, and thus we refer to them throughout the text. We end this chapter with a discussion of how political and moral reactions to particular theories can sometimes impede scientific understanding of human sexual behavior.

## Theories, Politics, and Morality

Confusion about the purpose of a theory is common among laypersons and not unknown among scientists. The goal of a theory is to present a tentative model of the causes of human behavior. A theory is not intended to be a blueprint or set of directions for how we should behave, but rather a picture of why we do behave in particular ways. When Freud theorized that humans are capable of sexual feelings and motives from infancy on, the public and many of Freud's scientific colleagues were deeply offended. Some of their reactions resulted from a confusion between theory and advocacy. Freud was not advocating sexual experience for infants and children; instead, he was trying to understand factors that influence personality development, and he theorized that sexual energy was one of these factors that was present from birth onward.

Subsequent research (see Chapter 12) has supported some of Freud's hypotheses and refuted others. For example, findings that preschool children masturbate and demonstrate interest in sexuality supports Freud's theory. On the other hand, research by the Goldmans (1982) and others does not support Freud's hypothesis that, fearing castration by their fathers, little boys repress sexual interest in their mothers and enter a period of "latency" from age five or six to the onset of puberty, during which they show no interest in sexual matters. The point is that Freud was not advocating childhood masturbation or, for that matter, subsequent repression of all interest in sexuality. He was simply trying to understand human psychosexual development.

This same confusion of theory and advocacy is apparent today in the passionate controversy surrounding evolutionary theory (Fairchild, 1991; Oyama, 1991). Questions of free will versus determinism (do we freely choose our behavior, or are we genetically programmed to respond in particular ways?), racial and gender discrimination, and religion are among the issues that have been raised by those who reject evolutionary approaches. Again, those scientists who propose evolutionary theories to try to explain human sexual behavior are not advocating superiority of males over females, or of one racial group over another. Instead, they are trying to understand how a widespread phenomenon—for example, that men generally *do* dominate women in most cultures—could have developed. Evolutionary theorists also are not suggesting that humans are forced by ''inherited'' characteristics to behave like robots responding to genetic programs. Evolutionary approaches explicitly recognize the ability to learn as an adaptive capacity. It is what enables us to evaluate the likely consequences of our behavioral choices.

People with political motives use bits and pieces of a theory to justify their beliefs and prejudices, just as they may select one biblical passage and reject another when they want to support a particular argument. But in doing so, they are merely displaying their ignorance of the purpose of theory, which is to try to understand human behavior rather than to advocate particular policies. The validity and usefulness of theories should be determined on the basis of research results that support or refute their tenets, not on the basis of anyone's beliefs.

Some of the criticisms of learning theory and sociological approaches also stem from a misunderstanding of the nature of a theory. The issue, again, is one of free will versus determinism. Most of us prefer to believe that we freely choose our behaviors. We may, by gaining knowledge, increase our ability to enhance our freedom of choice. But the research described throughout this book also demonstrates that our individual experiences and our cultural beliefs are quite predictive of how we behave. In subscribing to learning theories and sociological theories, researchers are not suggesting that we *should* be influenced by our individual reinforcement histories or by

societal norms and beliefs, only that most of us *are* so influenced.

Another problem that has confronted scientists is opposition from those who see scientific theories as conflicting with religious morality. Most views of ultimate causation presume a divine creator of life and source of morality. Theorists who attribute the behavior of humans to natural selection, socialization, and cultural norms are often perceived by these critics as usurping some Supreme Being(s) as the director of human behavior, and thus destroying the basis of morality. In fact, that concern fuels the evolutionist-creationist debate that continues to plague our educational and court systems.

Religious and moral thinking is quite different, however, from scientific reasoning. Modern science is not a set of absolute truths; it is a method of inquiry—of hypothesizing and theory-building on the basis of data collected and verified according to standard procedures. Scientific theories are always tentative and subject to modification or rejection if they do not fit observable data. Religions, on the other hand, consist of absolute beliefs, which are not subject to empirical tests in scientific terms. As such, science and religion operate in different spheres of human experience.

Rather than judging theories in terms of politics, morality, or even the elusive quality of accuracy, scientists judge on the basis of usefulness. All four theories that we have reviewed, as well as the findings of research conducted to test them, have contributed to our understanding of human sexual behavior. We are all affected by our ancestral history (evolutionary theory), our childhood experiences (psychoanalytic theories), our socialization and conditioning (social learning theories), and our cultural expectations and beliefs (sociological theories). Rather than competing with one another, the four theories generally complement one another. The questions that arise from each theory demand analysis at different levels of abstraction. At present, it appears that the factors emphasized by each of the theoretical approaches combine to produce the complexities that are involved in our sexual interactions.

## Summary of Major Points

1. The role of theory in understanding sexual behavior.

Sexual theories are explanatory models of the causes and/or consequences of various facets of sexual attitudes and behaviors. Theories lead to predictions about particular responses under specific conditions. Such predictions can then be tested by research. Research findings may support a theory or, if they do not, can lead to modification of the theory in an attempt to increase its accuracy.

2. Evolutionary approaches.

Evolutionary approaches trace the causes of much of contemporary sexual behavior back thousands of years to our distant ancestors. According to this view, modern sexual behaviors exist because they served the cause of reproductive success in the past. The characteristics of contemporary men and women, as well as their courtship patterns and sexual proclivities, evolved because they all led to the reproductive success of their ancestors.

3. Psychoanalytic approaches.

To explain sexual behavior, the creator of psychoanalytic theory, Sigmund Freud, examined the history of the individual rather than the history of our species. Psychoanalytic theory has undergone many revisions and changes since Freud's day, but it still places heavy emphasis on early experience as a determinant of adult sexuality and personality.

4. Learning approaches.

Social learning theories, as the name implies, assume that most, if not all, sexual behavior is learned. Learning theorists have applied the principles of learning to the conditioning, maintenance, and elimination of sexual behaviors. By manipulating the reinforcements for a particular sexual act, learning theorists have been able to increase, reduce, or eliminate the performance of that act.

5. Sociological approaches.

Sociologists have attempted to explain how social institutions affect our sexual behavior. First, because kinship, particularly marriage, is important in preserving the social relationships valued by society, violation of the sexual norms associated with marriage is discouraged by jealousy responses. Second, because sexuality is a potent resource, the power structure of a society determines how male and female gender roles are defined. Underlying the scripts that protect a society's institutions is an ideology that reflects the group's assumptions about what is normal behavior. Inherent in the sociological approach is the idea that we must learn a complicated sequence of behaviors before a sexual or nonsexual interaction takes place. Thus sexual interaction is not spontaneous but rather is the result of scripts that we learn so thoroughly that often we do not have to think about them.

6. The role of theories in society.

Confusion over the purpose of theory is common. A theory represents an attempt to build a model or picture of what we do and why we do it. A theory of some aspect of sexual behavior is not a recommendation that we engage in or avoid that behavior. Nor is a theory an attempt to promote or advocate any particular moral or political stance.

If research supports a theoretical prediction, members of a society may wish to make personal or public decisions based on that information. Each of the four theoretical perspectives in this chapter is useful because each provides hypotheses about human sexual behavior that can be tested by researchers. People may argue about whether evolutionary, psychoanalytic, learning, or sociological theories are more accurate, but such arguments will probably never be resolved because each type of theory attempts to explain human sexual behavior from a different level of abstraction. In the real world, the multiple factors considered by multiple theories all appear to interact in their impact on our sexual attitudes and behaviors.

## Review of Key Concepts

1. A theory is: a) a statement that has been proven; b) a model of how one or more variables is related to particular outcomes; c) a meaningless generalization; d) none of the above. (p. 66)

2. Evolutionary theory: a) generally focuses on the development of sexual behaviors over long spans of time; b) investigates the connection between biological factors and sexual behavior; c) developed from the evolutionary theories of Darwin and Mendel; d) all of the above. (pp. 66–68)

3. Parental investment theory has been used by evolutionary theorists to explain: a) females' fears of being aggressive; b) males' fears of nurturance; c) gender differences in sexual behavior; d) all of the above. (p. 70)

4. Sigmund Freud: a) argued that sexuality was interwoven with all aspects of personality; b) insisted that children be shielded against sexuality in all forms; c) encouraged adults to act openly on their sexual desires; d) located the id, ego, and superego in the human brain. (pp. 73–75)

5. Freud considered which subsystem of personality to be guided by constraints of the real world? a) the id; b) libido; c) the ego; d) the superego. (p. 75)

6. Sexual arousal by a wide range of stimuli has been scientifically investigated using: a) evolutionary theory; b) contemporary psychoanalytic techniques; c) classical conditioning; d) both b and c. (p. 79)

7. Operant conditioning is associated primarily with learning through: a) being rewarded for particular behaviors; b) being punished for particular behaviors; c) recall of pleasant or unpleasant childhood experiences; d) both a and b. (p. 80)

8. In contrast to classical and operant conditioning, social learning theory holds that sex-related behavior can be acquired by: a) heredity; b) observing how other people act and are rewarded or punished; c) being rewarded or punished for one's own behavior; d) experimenting freely. (p. 81)

9. The hypothesis that guilt over engaging in extramarital sex can be explained by the values of one's social class best exemplifies: a) a psychoanalytical approach; b) a social learning approach; c) an evolutionary approach; d) a sociological approach. (p. 82)

10. According to script theory, sexual interactions result from: a) naturally occurring biological processes; b) an innate drive to reproduce; c) cognitive plans that enable people to behave in organized and predictable ways; d) spontaneously occurring opportunities present in the environment. (p. 83)

11. In his analysis of different cultures, Ira Reiss concluded that: a) all societies have jealousy norms about marital sexuality; b) differences between the status of men and women are innate; c) premature ejaculation is considered dysfunctional in all cultures; d) both b and c. (pp. 85–86)

12. Why is it important to realize that a theory in the social sciences can never be proven?

# Development and Sexual Differentiation

*How* are babies made?

*The father mixes the seed in the cocoa one night and she swallows it.*

*I'm not sure, but they go to a hospital and ask can they put their things together and start off a baby.*

*The baby just grows from the food Mother eats. Father warms her tummy in bed and it grows.*

These are responses of children aged five and older to the question "How are babies made?" This question was asked by the Goldmans in their study of children's thinking about sexuality and reproduction (1982, pp. 220, 227). In this chapter, we describe the process of fertilization and the intricacies of genetic inheritance. We examine conception and prenatal development and then conclude the chapter with an overview of sexual differentiation.

## Fertilization

Although the origins of life on earth are still shrouded in mystery, we know a great deal about how individual humans begin life. Much of this knowledge is quite recent. As late as the 18th century, the scientific community was engaged in vigorous debate about whether a female's ovaries contained tiny embryos that were activated by

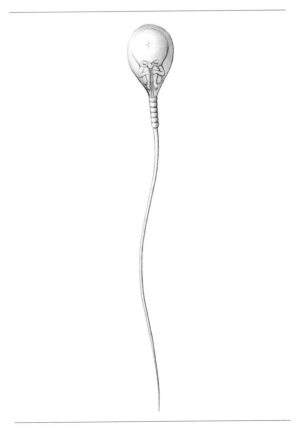

**FIGURE 4.1**

**An Early Theory of Conception**

This drawing is from a 17th-century representation of a little man (homunculus) in the head of a sperm. At that time, some people believed that small, preformed humans were ejaculated from the penis into the womb, where they were housed and nourished until birth.

male sperm, or whether sperm contained preformed miniature human beings that began to grow after they were deposited in a fertile womb (see Figure 4.1). Many historians think that the latter idea, which had circulated for centuries, was at least partially responsible for the Catholic church's condemnation of masturbation, because a logical corollary was that masturbation amounted to sending tiny humans to certain death in a hostile environment (Bullough, 1976).

Even in this century, certain groups remain ignorant about the reproductive process. Some Australian aborigine groups, for example, do not consider sexual intercourse to be particularly important in producing pregnancy. Rather, inter-

course is seen as an act of preparation for the reception of a spirit baby (Montagu, 1969). The Mehinaku of Brazil believe that pregnancy develops through repeated acts of intercourse that accumulate enough semen to form a baby (Gregor, 1985).

In 1677 Anton van Leeuwenhoek reported his observation of live sperm cells to the Royal Society of London. About five years earlier, Reanier de Graaf had viewed embryonic cells removed from the reproductive tubes of a female rabbit. The contemporaries of these two men did not fully appreciate the significance of their discoveries. Gradually, however, this information about the nature of sperm and egg cells became part of our general knowledge.

## Meeting of Sperm and Egg

We now know that one of a woman's two ovaries releases an egg (ovum) about halfway through her monthly reproductive cycle in the process known as *ovulation*. The egg, about one-fourth the size of this dot (.), is the human body's largest type of cell. After its release, the egg usually makes its way to the funnel-shaped end of the nearer fallopian tube.

Sperm are among the smallest cells in the body: each sperm is only 1/600th of an inch from its head to its tail. Before reaching the upper third of the fallopian tube, where fertilization usually occurs (see Figure 4.2), sperm must make a lengthy journey, and most of them die en route. During emission and ejaculation, rhythmic contractions expel the sperm from the testes through the vas deferens to the urethra, where they are ejected from the penis through the urethral opening.

The semen of fertile men who have not ejaculated in the previous 24 hours or so contains between 100 million and 500 million sperm. Because only one sperm normally penetrates an egg, such enormous numbers may seem rather wasteful. However, only 50% to 60% of the average man's sperm are *motile*, and some of these may be destroyed by the normally acidic secre-

**ovulation**—release of an egg by the ovary.

**motile**—exhibiting or demonstrating the power of motion.

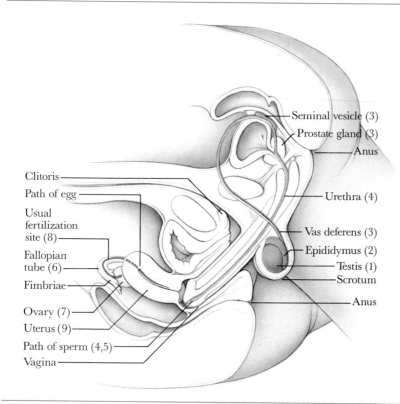

**Sperm:**

1. produced in the seminiferous tubules of the testes.
2. stored in epididymis.
3. during sexual arousal, travel through the vas and mix with seminal fluid from seminal vesicles and prostate.
4. released through urethra of penis during ejaculation.
5. deposited in the seminal pool of vagina, near cervix.
6. pass through cervix into uterus and fallopian tubes.

**Egg:**

7. produced by one of the ovaries.
8. fertilization site in upper third of fallopian tube.
9. site of implantation for developing zygote around 6th day.

Labels on the figure:
Seminal vesicle (3)
Prostate gland (3)
Anus
Urethra (4)
Vas deferens (3)
Epididymus (2)
Testis (1)
Scrotum
Anus
Clitoris
Path of egg
Usual fertilization site (8)
Fallopian tube (6)
Fimbriae
Ovary (7)
Uterus (9)
Path of sperm (4,5)
Vagina

**FIGURE 4.2**

**Fertilization**

This drawing illustrates the journey of egg and sperm toward fertilization, which generally occurs in the upper third of the fallopian tube.

tions of the vagina. Others fail to get through the cervical mucus to enter the uterus. Of those entering the uterus, some head toward the fallopian tube that contains no egg. Each of these factors reduces the number of sperm that meet the egg.

After the remaining sperm (about 2,000) have reached the egg, they attach themselves to the membrane surrounding it (see Figure 4.3). While affixed to the membrane, the sperm release enzymes that eliminate the extracellular material on the outside of the egg. As soon as one sperm has entered the egg, penetration by other sperm is generally impossible, but the mechanism that protects the egg from the entrance of more than one sperm is not yet fully understood.

For fertilization to take place, the meeting of the egg and sperm generally must occur between 2 and 48 hours after sexual intercourse. Although it has been suggested that the fertile life of a sperm may be as long as five days (Overstreet, 1986), most sperm do not live longer than 48 hours after ejaculation, about the same length of time the egg is fertilizable.

The fertilized ovum contains in its genes all the information needed to produce the estimated 100 trillion cells of an adult human. But to understand what happens after fertilization, we must first know something about the cellular structure of the human body.

## Cell Division

The human body is composed of two structurally and functionally different types of cells. The

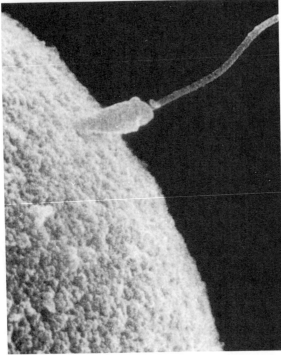

**FIGURE 4.3**

**Sperm Penetrates Egg**

Although numerous sperm surround an egg, only one sperm is able to penetrate it. The bottom photo shows a sperm just touching the surface of an ovum. At this point, the egg is impenetrable to other sperm.

sperm and ova are gametes, or *germ cells*. All other cells are somatic cells, or *body cells*. Germ cells and body cells differ not only in function but also in the way they divide, and in the number of *chromosomes* they contain.

Chromosomes—literally, "colored bodies"—are complex, threadlike bodies made up of two kinds of chemical material: deoxyribonucleic acid (DNA) and protein. They are found in the nucleus of every cell. All organisms possess chromosomes, which contain the genetic material that is passed on from generation to generation. Chromosomes were discovered in 1842, but the exact number contained in human cells was not clarified until 1956, when Tijo and Levan reported finding 46 chromosomes in embryonic cells.

The human body develops and repairs itself through a complex process of cell division. Division of the somatic, or body, cells occurs through *mitosis*, a process that creates two new, identical cells. The replication process leads to two new cells that are exactly like the original parent cell and are called daughter cells. Mitosis is the process responsible for the development of the single cell that is the fertilized ovum into the trillions of cells that make up every adult human.

The gametes, or germ cells, divide by a different process, called *meiosis*. Meiosis results in the production of sperm in males and ova in females. In each case, however, the process produces daughter cells having half the number of chromosomes contained in the parent cell. That is, in the testes and ovaries, a body cell with 46 chromosomes—23 pairs—divides in such a way

**germ cells**—sperm or egg cells.

**body cells**—all the cells in the body except germ cells.

**chromosomes**—the strands of deoxyribonucleic acid (DNA) and protein in the nucleus of each cell. They contain the genes that provide information vital for the duplication of cells and the transmission of inherited characteristics.

**mitosis** (my-TOE-sis)—a form of cell division in which the nucleus divides into two daughter cells, each of which receives one nucleus and is an exact duplicate of the parent cell.

**meiosis** (my-OH-sis)—cell division leading to the formation of gametes, in which the number of chromosomes is reduced by half.

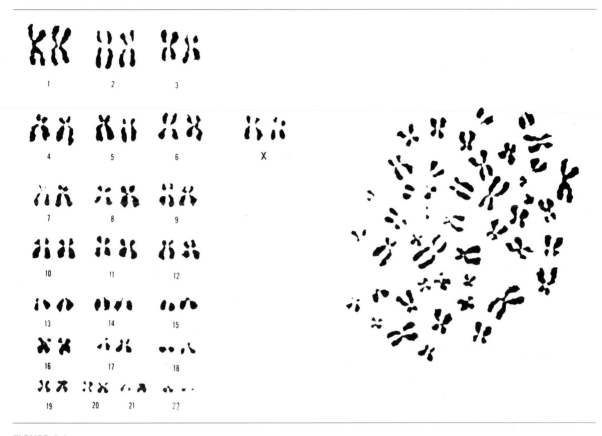

**FIGURE 4.4**

**Human Female Chromosomes**

These chromosomes from body cells were specially prepared to arrest division and obtain maximum spreading out of the 46 chromosomes. On the left is a photograph of the 23 pairs of chromosomes in descending order of size. On the right are the chromosomes as they appear when taken from a specially prepared cell.

that each daughter cell includes only one member of each pair of chromosomes. Thus mature egg and sperm cells contain only 23 single chromosomes rather than 23 chromosome pairs. When a sperm and an egg cell unite, the resulting *zygote* contains 46 chromosomes, arranged in two sets of 23, one set from the mother and the other set from the father (see Figure 4.4). This procedure ensures that the amount of genetic material will not double with each generation, producing zygotes whose cell division becomes logistically impossible.

**zygote** (ZYE-goat)—the developing organism from fertilization to implantation.

## Chromosomes and Genetic Inheritance

Chromosomes carry the information that determines a person's inherited characteristics. Strung along the length of each chromosome like beads are thousands of segments called *genes*. These genes are the basic units of hereditary transmission. Genes are made up of the complex chemical *deoxyribonucleic acid (DNA)*, which is

**genes**—part of DNA molecules, found in chromosomes of cells, that are responsible for the transmission of hereditary material from parents to offspring.

**deoxyribonucleic acid (DNA)** (dee-OX-see-RYE-boh-new-KLAY-ik)—a chemically complex nucleic acid that is a principal element of genes.

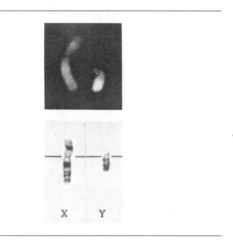

**FIGURE 4.5**
**The X and Y Chromosomes**
The Y chromosome can be detected by its fluorescence when it is stained, as the top picture shows.

the information-containing molecule that forms part of every organism (with the exception of certain viruses). DNA acts as a blueprint for all cellular activity. It determines the makeup of every cell in our bodies, each of which contains an estimated 100,000 genes that determine our inherited characteristics.

Through a microscope, chromosomes can be distinguished as either *sex chromosomes* (chromosomes that determine whether an individual is female or male) or *autosomes* (chromosomes that do not determine a person's genetic sex). The 22 pairs of autosomes, which are similar in structure but of variable size, are responsible for the differentiation of cells that results in various characteristics of the body.

## Sex Chromosomes and Genetic Sex

The 23rd pair of chromosomes in each cell of the human body is composed of the sex chromosomes, X and Y (see Figure 4.5). The X chromosome is about five times longer than the Y chro-

**sex chromosomes**—the pair of chromosomes that determines whether an individual is female or male.
**autosomes**—the 22 pairs of chromosomes that are involved in general body development in humans.

mosome and contains at least 100 genes. A female has two X chromosomes in each body cell; a male has an X and a Y chromosome in each body cell. Eggs, therefore, all carry X chromosomes, whereas a sperm may carry either an X or a Y. If a sperm with an X chromosome fertilizes an egg, the offspring will be female (XX). If a sperm with a Y chromosome fertilizes an egg, the offspring will be male (XY). The genetic sex of a child is thus determined by the father.

A female can apparently live with only one viable X chromosome, as males do, but there is no known case of a human being having no X chromosomes. Obviously humans can thrive in the absence of the Y chromosome, for females have none. If an embryo has more than two X chromosomes and lacks a Y, then female development takes place. If, however, an embryo has both more than one X chromosome and a Y chromosome, in a combination such as XXY, XXXY, or XXXXY, development includes some male characteristics despite the presence of multiple female chromosomes. Gene sequence that determines male sexual differentiation exists on the Y chromosome (Lukusa, Fryns, & van den Berghe, 1992).

Our understanding of the genetic sex of an individual was given a major boost in 1949 when Murray L. Barr and E. G. Bertram reported that a well-defined mass of *chromatin*, the substance from which chromosomes form, is absent from the body cells of males but can be observed in the nuclei of female body cells at a certain phase in cell division. Through a microscope, the chromatin body appears as a dense clump of heavily stained material. It is called a *Barr body* in honor of the scientist who discovered it.

The Barr body does not appear in cells with only one X chromosome, for there is always one less Barr body than there are X chromosomes. Thus the cells of normal males, who have only

**chromatin** (CROW-mah-tin)—the substance in the nucleus of a cell from which chromosomes form during mitosis.
**Barr body**—condensed, inactive X chromosome that distinguishes female cells from male cells. It appears as a dense clump when stained and examined under a microscope.

one X chromosome, lack the Barr body, and the cells of normal females, who have two X chromosomes, have one Barr body. Apparently, each X chromosome in excess of one becomes condensed and appears as a Barr body. Because the presence or absence of the Barr body is an indication of the genetic status of XX or XY, respectively, it has been used to establish the genetic sex of athletes in the Olympics: cells are scraped from the lining of the cheek inside the mouth and examined with a microscope.

Part of the Y chromosome, when stained, appears as a small, brightly fluorescent body in the nuclei of male cells. This portion of the Y chromosome, called the Y-body, can also be used to determine genetic sex.

### Dominance and Recessiveness

In addition to carrying the genes that determine genetic sex and sex characteristics, the X and Y chromosomes carry a variety of other genes. All the genes located on these sex chromosomes are called sex-linked genes because inheritance of these genes is connected to inheritance of the sex of the individual. Studies of patterns of inheritance are based on this concept of *sex linkage*— that a person who inherits a chromosome also inherits the genes it carries. Thus males, who always inherit a Y chromosome, inherit other Y-linked characteristics, such as testes formation. Males also inherit an X chromosome, however, and they inherit with it characteristics that are X-linked, some of which are not related to sex characteristics.

Because we inherit a set of genes from each parent, our two sets of genes do not contain identical genetic information. One gene in each set is usually dominant over the other, in which case the dominant gene determines the person's inherited characteristic. For recessive genes to determine a person's characteristics, he or she must have either two recessive genes—one from each parent—or one recessive gene without a corre-

sponding dominant gene. For example, brown eyes are dominant over blue eyes and dark hair is dominant over blond hair. So for recessive genes to produce blue eyes, a person must have two recessive genes for blue eyes, or one recessive gene for blue eyes without a corresponding dominant gene for brown eyes.

The latter condition usually occurs only in males because only when a person's sex chromosomes are X and Y (as in a male) does a chromosome normally lack an identical paired chromosome. In females, both X chromosomes must carry a recessive gene before the characteristic controlled by the recessive gene is displayed. Because males can inherit recessive X-linked traits with only one recessive gene, they have more recessive X-linked traits. Thus males are more susceptible than females to a number of disorders carried by recessive genes, such as hemophilia and color blindness, even though the transmitters of such disorders are always females.

There is evidence for more than 150 X-linked traits in humans, many of them disease-related and recessive (McKusick & Amberger, 1993). Y-linked traits are comparatively few. The only one we know about comes from a gene that produces hairy ears, and there is some doubt as to whether it is in fact a Y-linked trait.

Because of the difference in the size of the X and Y chromosomes, the female technically has more genetic material than does the male. Generally, an excess or deficit in the chromosomal material of autosomes results in deformities, both physical and mental. This generalization does not appear to hold for the sex chromosomes, however, because females suffer no adverse effects from their more abundant genetic material.

To account for the apparent difference between the autosomes and the sex chromosomes, Lyon (1962) hypothesized that only one X chromosome is active in any cell, with the other X chromosome becoming genetically inactive. According to Lyon, the genetically inactive X chromosome becomes compressed and appears as the Barr body. It is probably a matter of chance whether it is the X chromosome contributed by the mother or the one contributed by the father that becomes inactive in a genetic female. The process of deactivation is believed to begin early in the development of the embryo, the sixth or

---

**sex linkage**—the connection between the sex chromosomes and the genes one inherits. When a person inherits a sex chromosome, he or she also inherits the genes it carries.

ZYGOTE
CONCEPTION → 2 WEEKS

EMBryo
2 – 9TH WEEK

FETUS
9 – birTH

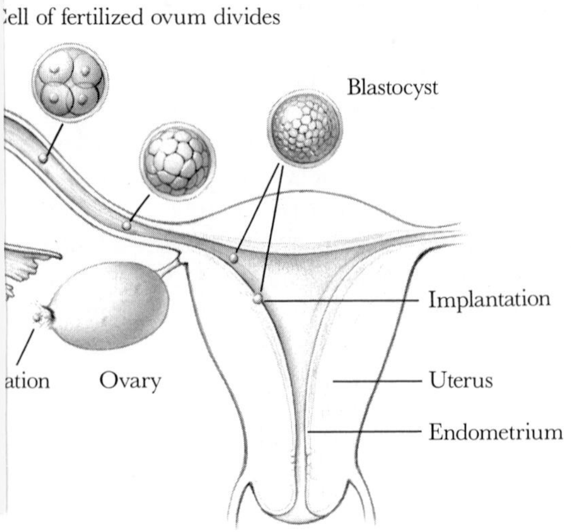

Cell of fertilized ovum divides

Blastocyst

Implantation

Ovary

Uterus

Endometrium

**FIGURE 4.6**
**Fertilization and Migration**
The ovum is fertilized typically in the upper third of the fallopian tube, and numerous cell divisions take place before it implants in the uterine wall approximately five days later.

seventh day after fertilization. We now consider the remarkable process of prenatal development following conception.

## Prenatal Development

The nine months of pregnancy, called *gestation*, are conventionally described in terms of three trimesters. The first trimester includes the first through the third month, the second spans the fourth through the sixth month, and the third extends from the seventh through the ninth month.

### First Trimester

After fertilization has occurred but before a woman knows that she is pregnant, the zygote begins a period of rapid cell division. It has en-

tered the germinal stage, a period of time encompassing the first two weeks following conception. Within 30 hours of conception, the zygote divides into two cells. Within three days, continuing cell division produces a solid ball of cells. Meanwhile, the zygote has been moving down the fallopian tube toward the uterus, and enters it at approximately this time (see Figure 4.6).

On about the fourth day, after entering the uterine cavity, the mass of cells separates into two parts. The outer cell mass develops into the major part of the *placenta*. On roughly the sixth day, the entire cell mass attaches itself to the uterine wall, and by the end of the first week, it is loosely implanted in the upper part of the uterus. After implantation, the developing inner cell mass is called an *embryo*, and by the end of the second week, the embryo is usually firmly im-

gestation—the entire period of prenatal development from conception to birth.

placenta—the organ formed by the joining of the tissue of the uterine wall with that of the developing fetus; a major source of hormones during pregnancy.
embryo—the unborn organism from the second to about the eighth week of pregnancy.

planted in the uterus. The outer layer of the embryo, called the ectoderm, will become the skin, sense organs, and nervous system. The middle layer, the mesoderm, will develop into the heart, blood vessels, muscles, and skeleton. The inner layer, the endoderm, will form the respiratory system, the digestive system, and such related organs as the liver, pancreas, and salivary glands.

Meanwhile, the outer mass is developing into structures to nurture and protect the organism during its stay in the uterus. These include the placenta, the umbilical cord, and the amniotic sac. The placenta, which initially surrounds the fetus, subsequently moves to the side, but the placenta and the embryo remain connected by the *umbilical cord*. Through this passageway, the placenta absorbs oxygen and nourishment from the mother's bloodstream, and delivers body wastes from the embryo and transfers them to the mother. The placenta protects the embryo from microbes by filtration, although small viruses such as rubella (responsible for German measles) can pass through to the embryo. The placenta produces the hormones that support pregnancy and that later assist in preparation of the mother's breasts for lactation, the manufacture and secretion of milk. The *amniotic sac* is a fluid-filled space bounded by the amniotic membrane that encases the developing organism, cushioning it, giving it room to move, and ensuring that it does not permanently adhere to the uterine wall. The embryo's kidneys are the source of the fluid in the amniotic sac.

Although a woman is generally unaware of this burst of life within her, her body is responding to the pregnancy. Her uterus accepts the developing embryo into its thickened wall, the dense network of maternal blood vessels that has developed since ovulation merges with the placenta, and maternal blood flows around the embryonic blood vessels. The end of the germinal stage is marked by the time when a woman would normally expect her menstrual period.

A critical embryonic stage begins with full implantation of the cell mass at the beginning of

the second week of pregnancy and lasts until the end of the eighth week. It is a period of remarkable growth, during which the embryo develops its major organs, among them the eyes, which begin to form by 21 days.

At the sixth or seventh week, about 100 embryonic cells become the material from which sperm or ova are produced 10 to 15 years later. This process is called sexual differentiation, and we return to it later in this chapter.

At eight weeks, the embryo is about an inch long. It has a recognizable brain and a heart that pumps blood through tiny arteries and veins. It has a stomach that produces digestive juices, and a liver that manufactures blood cells. Its kidneys have already begun to function, and it has an endocrine system. The embryo now has limbs and a disproportionately large head with eyes, nose, ears, and mouth, although its eyelids have not yet formed.

Development during this period illustrates a rule from evolutionary theory that *ontogeny* repeats the major stages of *phylogeny*: the idea that during prenatal development, we briefly display characteristics of our species' evolutionary past. The embryo passes through a stage wherein it has gill slits like those of our fish ancestors. These gill slits develop into the chin, cheek, jaw, and outer ear. We also have tails at one point during prenatal development (see Figure 4.7). The tail ends up as a small triangular bone—the coccyx, or tailbone—at the base of the spine.

At about the beginning of the ninth week of pregnancy, bone cells appear, and the embryo enters the fetal stage. The embryo is called a *fetus* from this point until birth. These bone cells gradually begin to replace the cartilage cells that formed the initial embryonic skeleton, although cartilage continues to make up the soft parts of the nose and ears of an adult.

Only a few new structures appear during the fetal period. Development primarily involves the growth and maturation of tissues and organs that

---

umbilical cord—the connection of the fetus to the placenta, through which the fetus is nourished.

amniotic sac—the pouch containing a watery fluid that envelops a developing fetus in the uterus.

ontogeny (on-TOJ-en-ee)—the history of the development of an individual organism.

phylogeny (fy-LOJ-en-ee)—the evolutionary history of a species or group.

fetus—the unborn organism from the ninth week up until birth.

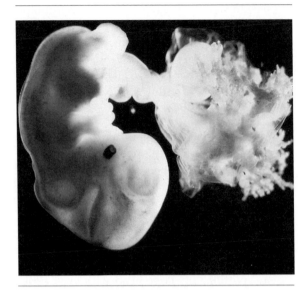

**FIGURE 4.7**
**A 28-Day-Old Embryo**
This embryo has a characteristic C-shape, a tail, and four bronchial arches with gill slits. The bud of the arm and the heart may be seen.

began to form during the embryonic stage. This delicate growth continues as the fetus moves month by month toward the point of birth.

The fetus is protected from the outside world by the fluid-filled amniotic sac. The amniotic liquid provides a stable, buffered environment, and the fetus floats in a state of relative weightlessness.

At the end of the eighth week, the head constitutes about half the length of the fetus (see Figure 4.8). The fetus has fingernails, toenails, lips, vocal cords, and a prominent nose. The arms have almost reached their final relative lengths, but the legs are not well developed. By the end of the 12th week, the external genitals of the fetus are distinguishable. At this point, the fetus has also developed basic reflexes. If an aborted 12-week-old fetus has its lips stroked, it responds with a sucking reflex; if its eyelids are stroked, it squints. If its palm is touched, the fetus makes a partial fist.

## Second Trimester

The fourth month begins a period characterized by rapid body growth. The umbilical cord is as

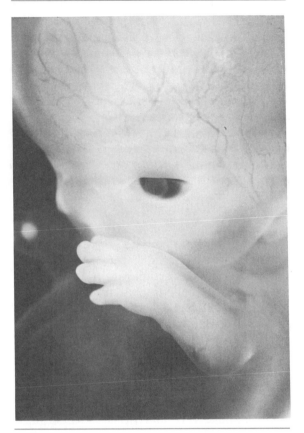

**FIGURE 4.8**
**An Eight-Week-Old Embryo**
At eight weeks, the embryo has the beginnings of both internal and external genitals. Fingernails, toenails, lips, nose, and ears have also begun to develop.

long as the fetus and continues to grow with it. Skeletal bones are hardening; X-rays (taken only for diagnostic reasons) clearly show skeletal bones by the beginning of the 16th week. The legs are well developed, and the ears stand out from the head. A fetus at this age can suck its thumb.

By the time a fetus is five months old, it appears in many ways to be a fully developed human being. If it were to be taken from its protective environment, however, the fetus would not survive. Only about 10 inches long and weighing about half a pound, it has lungs that are well formed but not yet ready to function, and its digestive system cannot yet process food (see Figure 4.9).

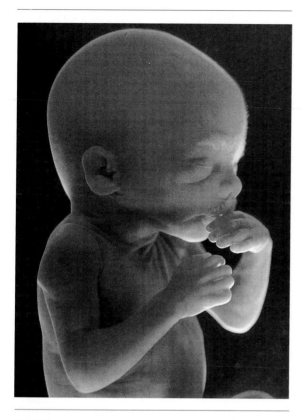

**FIGURE 4.9**
**A Five-Month-Old Fetus**
Weighing only about half a pound, this fetus could not survive outside the uterine environment.

By this time, the fetal skin is covered by a greasy substance, the *vernix caseosa*, which protects it from abrasions and chapping as a result of being enveloped in the amniotic fluid. Twenty-week-old fetuses are usually covered with a fine, downy hair called *lanugo*, which may, among other things, help to hold the vernix on the skin. The fetus has now found its favorite position in the uterus and is stretching, squirming, and hiccuping.

At six months, the fetus has begun to develop a padding of fat beneath its skin. Its skin is somewhat wrinkled and is pink-to-red in color because blood in the capillaries has become visible. It can cry and make a fist with a strong grip. Fin-

**vernix caseosa** (VUR-nix kah-see-OH-sah)—a greasy substance that protects the skin of the fetus.

**lanugo** (lah-NEW-goh)—fine hair that appears on the developing fetus during the fifth or sixth month.

gernails are present, and all organs are fairly well developed. The fetus that is born prematurely at this point, however, often dies within a few days because of the functional immaturity of its respiratory system.

## Third Trimester

At seven months the fetus could live if it were born prematurely. Its potential for survival, however, is still low because of the continuing likelihood of respiratory difficulties. A premature infant weighing at least $3\frac{1}{2}$ pounds has a fairly good chance of survival if intensive medical care is provided. A fetus born at this point would probably have to live in an incubator until its weight increased to five pounds.

Lanugo may disappear around this time, or it may remain until shortly before birth. The skin is slightly wrinkled, but the fetus is "filling out," as fat forms under the skin. The fetal nervous system has developed to the point at which the fetus can sustain rhythmic breathing movements and control its body temperature. Eyes are open, and eyelashes are present. From this point on, the fetus is aware of events outside its mother's body. It responds to loud sounds as well as to the reaction of its mother's heart to such sounds (Sontag, 1966).

At eight months, layers of fat continue to develop and smooth out the skin. The fat helps the fetus adjust to temperature variations that it will experience after leaving the uterus. Toenails are now present. The fetus is 18 to 20 inches long, and it weighs between five and seven pounds.

At nine months, most fetuses are plump and crowd the uterus. The reddish color of the skin is fading. The chest is prominent, and the mammary glands protrude in both males and females because they are affected by the hormones that are preparing the mother's breasts to secrete milk. In males, the testes have usually descended from the abdominal cavity to the scrotum.

During the ninth month, the fetus usually acquires some antibodies from its mother's bloodstream. These provide the fetus with temporary immunity against whatever agents (bacteria and viruses, for example) from which its mother is protected. This is important because the newborn's immune system is not yet fully functional. It is now ready for birth, but we will save the

**TABLE 4.1 Chronology of Sexual Differentiation**

*Prenatal Development*

| Characteristic | Source | Male Development | Female Development |
|---|---|---|---|
| Gonadal | Y chromosome | Testes | Ovaries |
| Internal Sex Organs | Androgens and Müllerian-inhibiting substance | Wolffian structures develop into ejaculatory duct and other reproductive structures; Müllerian structures degenerate | Wolffian structures degenerate; Müllerian structures develop into uterus, fallopian tubes, and other reproductive structures |
| External Sex Organs | Androgens | Scrotal sacs and penis | Labia and clitoris |
| Brain | Androgens | Masculine organization | Feminine organization |

*Pubescent Development*

| Characteristic | Source | Male Development | Female Development |
|---|---|---|---|
| Breasts | Pituitary growth hormone; estrogens, progestins | | Growth of breasts (8–13 years old) |
| Genitals | Pituitary growth hormone, testosterone | Growth of testes, scrotal sac (10–14 years); penis (11–15 years) | |
| Pubic hair | Testosterone in males; adrenal androgens in females | Growth of pubic hair (10–15 years) | Growth of pubic hair (8–14 years) |
| Menarche | Gonadotropin-releasing hormone, FSH, LH, estrogens, progestins | | Onset of menstrual cycle (10–17 years) |
| Voice change | Testosterone | Growth of larynx, deepening of voice (11–15 years) | |
| Body hair | Testosterone in males; adrenal androgens in females | Growth of underarm and facial hair (12–17 years) | Growth of underarm hair (10–16 years) |
| Oil and sweat glands | Testosterone in males; adrenal androgens in females | Development of oil- and sweat-producing glands; acne (12–17 years) | Development of oil- and sweat-producing glands; acne when glands blocked (10–16 years) |

description of that remarkable event until Chapter 9. Here, we return to a point halfway through the first trimester—the sixth or seventh week of gestation—to consider the process by which humans differentiate into males or females.

## Sexual Differentiation

The process by which we differentiate into either males or females occurs in a series of stages during the development of the embryo and fetus, and then again during puberty (see Table 4.1). Although the steps are usually predictable, errors occasionally occur. We look first at the normal processes.

## Normal Sexual Differentiation

As described earlier, your genital sex was determined at conception as a result of whether the sperm that your father contributed contained an X or a Y chromosome. If someone with "X-ray vision" had peered at you in your mother's womb six weeks after you were conceived, they could have seen your eyes and your major organs, but they would have been unable to tell whether you were a male or a female. Shortly after the 6th week, however, the process of sexual differentiation begins, and it continues until about the 12th or 13th week of gestation.

### Gonadal Sex

At eight weeks the embryo, whether it is genetically male (XY) or female (XX), has a pair of gonads (which will become testes or ovaries) and the beginnings of external genitals. It also contains tissue that may eventually form female structures such as the fallopian tubes, the uterus, and the upper part of the vagina called the *Müllerian-duct system*. The lower two-thirds of the vagina forms from the same tissue that gives rise to the urinary bladder and urethra. It also contains tissue that may form male structures such as the epididymis, vas deferens, seminal vesicles, and ejaculatory duct called the *Wolffian-duct system* (see Figure 4.10).

The location of the genes for the testes-determining factor is on the short arm of the Y chromosome (Lukusa et al., 1992). If no Y chromosome is present to issue these instructions, the embryo continues to grow for another few weeks before the outer part of the primitive gonads develops into ovaries packed with immature egg cells.

### Hormonal Sex

The early development of the testes appears to be related to another embryonic phenomenon that provides a clue to how the process of sexual differentiation works. If the gonads are removed during the critical embryonic period, the embryo develops as a female, even if it is genetically (XY) male. Therefore, as Money and Ehrhardt (1972, p. 7) put it, "Nature's rule is, it would appear, that to masculinize, something must be added." This extra something consists of *testosterone* and *Müllerian-inhibiting substance (MIS)*. When the primitive gonads differentiate as testes in the male, they begin to manufacture these two substances.

Testosterone promotes the development of the Wolffian ducts into the internal male reproductive structures. MIS is responsible for curbing the growth of the Müllerian-duct system. Both of these substances must be present if normal development of the internal reproductive structures of the male is to occur. In normal male anatomical development, then, only one of the duct systems expands and develops. The development of the other system regresses, so that only traces of it remain in the body.

Because of the popular definition of *androgens* as male hormones and *estrogens* as female hormones, many people mistakenly assume that we produce one or the other, depending on whether we are male or female. In fact, both males and females secrete the same three kinds of sex hormones. In males, the testes synthesize

---

**Müllerian-duct system**—fetal tissue that develops into the internal female reproductive structures if the fetus is genetically female.

**Wolffian-duct system**—fetal tissue that develops into the internal male reproductive structures if the fetus is genetically male.

**testosterone**—the major natural androgen.

**Müllerian-inhibiting substance (MIS)**—a hormone secreted by the fetal testes that inhibits the growth and development of the Müllerian-duct system.

**androgens**—generic term for hormones that promote development and functioning of the male reproductive system.

**estrogens**—generic term for hormones that stimulate maturation and functioning of the female reproductive system.

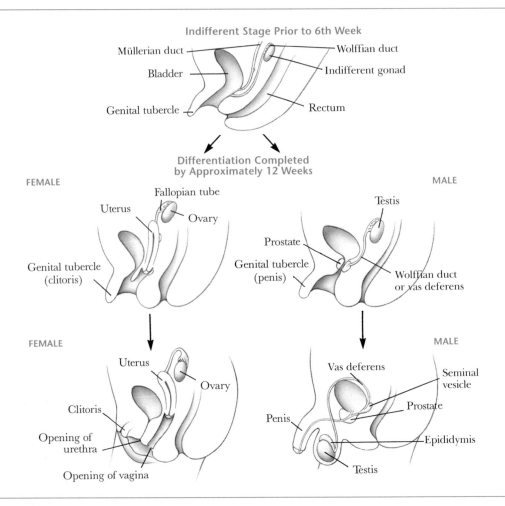

**FIGURE 4.10**

**Internal Gender Differentiation**

This diagram shows differentiation of the internal sexual structures in a male or female direction. This gender differentiation occurs during the latter part of the first trimester of pregnancy.

progesterone, one of a general class of feminizing hormones called *progestins*; testosterone (an androgen); and *estradiol* (an estrogen). Similarly, in females, the ovaries secrete progesterone, androgens, and estrogen. Both males and females also secrete small amounts of all these hormones from the outer portion (cortex) of their adrenal glands.

**progestins**—generic term for hormones that prepare the female reproductive system for pregnancy.

**estradiol**—the major natural estrogen, secreted by the ovaries, testes, and placenta.

Sexual differentiation depends on the relative amounts of these hormones in much the same way that the products of baking depend on the amounts of flour, sugar, salt, leavening, shortening, eggs, and liquid. Just as a cake is generally made with larger proportions of sugar and shortening, and bread results from higher proportions of flour and salt, the development of sexual anatomy is influenced by the relative proportions of androgens and estrogens secreted, as well as the numbers of cells that are responsive to these hormones. The proportion of androgens and estrogens varies somewhat among individuals, but as

**Box 4.1**

# Hormones and the Brain

During the fetal and early postnatal development of mammals, the brain is quite vulnerable to environmental stimuli. Among these influences on the developing brain are the sex hormones. Just as sex hormones produce changes in the reproductive organs, they also cause structural changes during critical periods in the development of the brain. Increasing evidence indicates that males and females differ in how some areas of their brains respond to sex hormones (see Hoyenga & Hoyenga, 1993a). John Money and Anke Ehrhardt (1972) proposed that, at the neural level, nature has programmed everyone for female development, and that the addition of androgens at certain critical periods of fetal development dramatically alters this plan. It has been found that, between the fourth and seventh month of fetal life, the concentration of testosterone in the *amniotic fluid* of human infants is higher in males than in females.

We are still not sure what implications these differences in brain structure may have for human behavior. Much of what is known about differences in the brain structures and behavior of males and females comes from research on laboratory animals. In the majority of species studied, the hormones produced by the gonads are of fundamental importance in the development of sex differences in the function and structure of the *central nervous system (CNS)*. If the action of these hormones is inhibited, sexual differentiation of the CNS is impaired. When a radioactive masculinizing hormone was given to female animals during a critical period of development and then traced through the CNS, it was observed that the cells of the *hypothalamus* became masculinized. As a result, they never released their chemical messages to the pituitary to activate the typical female cycle (Gorski, 1987).

Critical periods for the sexual differentiation of the CNS have been established for rats, gerbils, guinea pigs, hamsters, and primates (Hoyenga & Hoyenga, 1993b; Ulibarri & Yahr, 1993). The available evidence suggests that the beginning of the critical period may follow differentiation of the testicular cells and the onset of testosterone secretion. Many of the effects of testosterone result from its conversion by the neural tissue of the brain of androgen into estrogen to produce sexual differentiation in the nervous system, a process called *aromatization* (Hoyenga & Hoyenga, 1993b; MacLusky & Naftolin, 1981).

In the rat, specific areas of the hypothalamus involved in male-versus-female behavior have been shown to be sensitive to the influence of estrogen, androgen, and progestin at critical periods. During these stages, the structure of the hypothalamus is affected by hormonal levels. Such structural alterations underlie some sexual behaviors. A similar area in the human hypothalamus has been reported to be larger in males than in females and, overall, the structures that connect the two halves of the brain (see Chapter 5) are often larger in females (Hoyenga & Hoyenga, 1993a). It is not yet known, however, what implications, if any, these differences might have for human behavior because of the much greater sophistication in communication and socialization in humans than in other species.

Although activities in the human brain are obviously important in sexual arousal and interaction, the extent to which the brain's contribution to human sexuality results from structural differences between male and female brains is not yet understood. Any contributions that may be attributable to differences in brain structure can clearly be diminished or exaggerated by the environment and culture in which the infant finds itself after leaving the womb.

**amniotic fluid**—the watery liquid that surrounds a developing fetus in the uterus.

**central nervous system (CNS)**—the brain and the spinal cord.

**hypothalamus**—a marble-sized structure at the base of the brain that regulates body temperature, eating and drinking, sexual behavior, sexual cycles, sleep, and emotional and motivational aspects of behavior.

long as this variation falls within normal limits, it does not seem to affect the individual's gender identity or sexual functioning. The effects of differences in the levels of masculinizing and feminizing hormones on the developing brain are a subject of controversy (see Box 4.1).

To get a rough idea of the importance of the hormonal mix for sexual differentiation, consider that the testosterone level in male fetuses between the critical 12th and 17th weeks of pregnancy is about 10 times the level found in female fetuses, and about equal to the level found in adult males (Lev-Ran, 1977). The level of testosterone begins to decline after about the 17th week. Testosterone concentrations in male fetuses are identical to those in female fetuses by the seventh month and remain so until puberty (Vermeulen, 1986).

### Genital Sex

Several weeks after the internal structures of the embryo have differentiated, with one set of potential reproductive organs beginning to develop and the other set beginning to atrophy, the external genitals start to differentiate (see Figure 4.11). Our external genitals are created from a small protruding bud of tissue called a *genital tubercle*, an opening with a small swelling called the *labioscrotal swelling*, and folds or strips of skin called the *urogenital folds* on each side of the tubercle. If testes are developing, testosterone begins circulating in the bloodstream. As we have seen, testosterone acts directly on the Wolffian ducts to cause differentiation of the vas deferens, epididymis, and seminal vesicles. For the development of the external male genitals, however,

genital tubercle—a small protruding bud of fetal tissue that develops into either a penis or a clitoris.

labioscrotal swelling—the fetal tissue that develops into either the scrotum in a male or the two outer vaginal lips in a female.

urogenital folds—folds or strips of skin on each side of the genital tubercle of the fetus that fuse to form the urethral tube in a male or the inner vaginal lips in a female.

*dihydrotestosterone (DHT)* is produced by the metabolism of testosterone in cells within and outside the testes. DHT causes the elongation of the genital tubercle into the *phallus*. As the phallus grows, it pulls the urogenital folds forward, and they fuse with each other on the underside of the penis to form a urethral tube. The urethra connects to the bladder, prostate gland, and vas deferens. The two labioscrotal swellings fuse together to form a scrotum, which houses the testes when they eventually descend from the abdominal cavity, about eight months after conception.

The development of female external genitals needs no hormonal prompting; it occurs in the absence of androgens. In females, the genital tubercle remains relatively small and becomes a clitoris. Instead of fusing, the urogenital folds of skin remain distinct and form the two inner vaginal lips and the clitoral hood. The two labioscrotal swellings also remain separate, forming the two outer vaginal lips. The opening develops a dividing wall of tissue that separates the vaginal entrance to the uterus from the urethra, which connects to the bladder.

## Secondary Sexual Characteristics

Sexual differentiation remains relatively quiescent until around the age of 9 or 10, when the first signs of puberty occur—the growth of pubic hair and the formation of breast buds. The age at which puberty begins varies from one person to the next. Menstruation starts for some girls at the age of 10 or 11 but does not begin for others until they are 15 or 16. Similarly, although the onset of sexual maturation occurs on the average a couple of years later in boys than it does in girls, boys vary considerably in the age at which the process of sexual maturation begins.

Puberty represents another major biological event in our development as a male or a female. At puberty both males and females begin to grow

dihydrotestosterone (DHT)—a hormone produced from testosterone that is responsible for the development of the external genitals of the male fetus.

phallus—the penis.

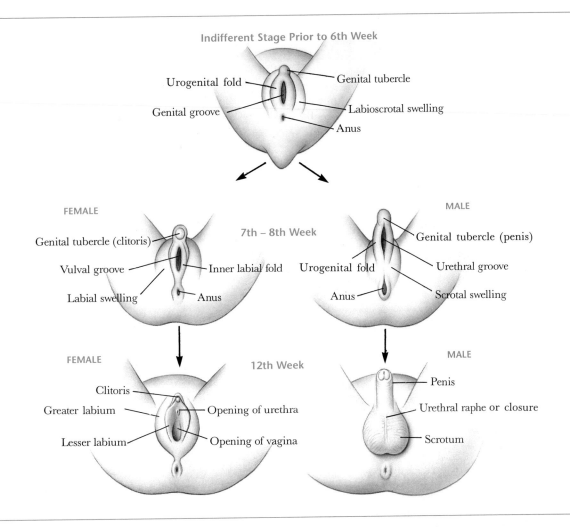

**FIGURE 4.11**
**Differentiation of External Genitals**
After the internal reproductive structures of the fetus have differentiated, the external genitals differentiate in a male or female direction, as this figure shows.

hair around their genitals and, somewhat later, under the arms. Both discover that their developing sweat glands emit relatively strong odors. For the first time, both become capable of releasing mature germ cells (eggs or sperm). And both discover themselves suddenly, and involuntarily, emitting fluid from their bodies—menstrual flow in the case of females, and semen in the case of males.

Offsetting these developmental similarities are a number of differences. First, whereas males are totally unaware of the reproductive processes

of sperm production and maturation taking place in their bodies, females are dramatically reminded of their reproductive capacity through the regular appearance of their menstrual periods.

Second, the role of hormones in the reproductive capacities is different for males and females. Prior to the onset of puberty, equal levels of estrogen (secreted by the adrenal glands) are found in the urine of boys and girls. One of the first indicators of puberty in females is an increase in the production of estrogen. Although both genders manufacture the same three major hormones—estrogens, progestins, and androgens—after they have reached puberty, the average female produces more of the first two, and the average male manufactures more of the third. Thus the reproductive capacities of women are influenced by the interactions and fluctuations of these major hormones, which, together with other hormones secreted by the brain and the adrenal glands, produce the characteristic monthly cycle. In contrast, the reproductive capacity of males is relatively acyclic (stable). The extent to which men experience cycles is a matter of debate, but any cycles that males may experience are less obvious and dramatic than are the cycles of females.

### Female Maturation

Between the ages of 8 and 14, the ovaries begin to secrete estrogen, and the follicles in the ovaries grow. At the same time, the uterus enlarges. The formerly convoluted fallopian tubes mature and increase in both length and width, becoming straighter in the process. The vagina and clitoris also grow, and the fine downy hair on the vulva is gradually replaced with a few coarse little hairs. At about the same time, the breasts start to protrude a bit, mainly right around the nipples. The areola and labia also increase in size. Estrogen plays an extremely important role in most of these specific changes, as well as in the spurt of general body growth and the widening of the pelvic girdle. Many other hormones, either in interaction with estrogen or on their own, also stimulate the differentiation and growth of the pubescent female. (Refer to Box 5.2 on page 138 for the influences of various hormones.)

Several years after the onset of these initial, relatively subtle signs of puberty, menarche—the first menstrual period—occurs. Adolescent girls tend to be shy about this event, often using euphemisms for menstruation: ''My Aunt Flo(w) is coming from Redfield, PA'' (Emster, 1975). Although the average age of menarche is 12.5, the point at which the first menstruation begins ranges widely from about 9 to 17 years. Biologically, puberty is considered to be precocious (unusually early) if its presence is detected before age 8 in females, and is considered to be delayed

if no breast growth has occurred by age 14, or if no skeletal growth spurt has appeared by age 15.

Menstruation can be quite erratic after the first period. Within a few years, however, the interval tends to become fairly regular, with menstruation appearing every 23 to 32 days or so. Over the course of their approximately 35 years of reproductive capacity, women will menstruate about 420 times, minus 9 or 10 menstrual periods per birth. Such a repetitive event becomes routine for most women, and they take menstrual periods in stride.

### Male Maturation

For males, the onset of puberty arrives later on average than for females (Hoyenga & Hoyenga, 1993b). Male puberty is considered to be precocious if it occurs before age 10; it is considered to be delayed if it has not begun by age 15. The pituitary gland and the hypothalamus begin secreting FSH and LH (sometimes called interstitial-cell stimulating hormone—ICSH) just as they do in females. The LH stimulates the interstitial cells in the testicles to manufacture increased levels of testosterone. FSH elicits the production of sperm cells in the seminiferous tubules and causes the various other sexual structures to increase in size.

Externally, the testes and penis begin to grow, pubic hair gradually replaces the softer body hair around the genitals, and height and muscular strength increase. Several years later, hair grows under the arms and on the face, although the coarse hair that characterizes the adult beard does not appear until several years after soft, downy hair first appears on the upper lip. Although a young man may take pleasure in these effects of testosterone, he does not welcome another common symptom of male pubescence, acne. These skin eruptions are partially the result of the influence of testosterone. Secretion of that hormone elicits a dramatic increase in the production of oil-releasing glands in the skin. Sebum, the oil manufactured by these glands, acts as a lubricant and can irritate and block the hair follicles, causing redness and blackheads. Because acne is primarily due to the pubescent rise in adrenal androgens, it is less common in females, who secrete lower levels of these androgens. Testosterone also stimulates the growth of the larynx; the adolescent boy's voice begins to break unpredictably at about 13 or 14, becoming the reliably deeper voice of an adult male at about 15 or 16. The areolae double in diameter, and marked breast enlargement occurs in the majority of boys, diminishing within a year or so.

Just as pubescent girls begin to menstruate, pubescent boys start to experience *nocturnal emissions*; that is, while asleep they expel semen containing sperm. Although they are capable of orgasm from birth on, the ability to ejaculate semen does not develop until the testes enlarge at puberty. The onset of sperm emission has been labeled *spermarche* (Hirsch et al., 1985). In a study of a large sample of Belgian males, investigators found that the average age at first ejaculation was 13 years and 2 months (Carlier & Steeno, 1985). In another study, researchers discovered that 69% of the males had begun producing sperm by the age of 13 (Hirsch et al., 1985).

We have been discussing normal development and sexual differentiation. However, much of our understanding of those normal processes has been produced by studies of atypical development, the topic to which we turn now.

## Atypical Sexual Differentiation

Errors in the process of sexual differentiation can occur at any stage of development. Conceptualizing fetal sexual development as a two-stage process—an organizing phase and an activating phase—is a somewhat simplistic description, in that sexual differentiation includes a number of other complicated steps as well. Nonetheless, the two-stage distinction is useful for understanding some of the complexities of sexual differentiation.

The earlier, organizing phase primarily involves the anatomical differentiation of the male

nocturnal emission—ejaculation of semen during sleep.

spermarche—the beginning of sperm emission in adolescent boys.

and female. In the later, activating phase, sexual behavior that is influenced by the brain and hormones comes into play. Alterations during either of these phases of development can result in a mismatching of anatomic development and later sexual functioning. Abnormalities can be caused by defects in chromosomes, environmental threats to fetal development, inheritance of atypical sex chromosomes, abnormal differentiation of gonads, or alterations in the secretion or metabolism of sex hormones. We first examine autosomal defects.

## Autosomal Abnormalities

Estimates vary as to the number of conceptions that are spontaneously aborted (miscarried), but perhaps half of all conceptions do not culminate in birth. Many miscarriages occur before a woman is even aware she is pregnant. Some result from errors in cell division, causing changes in the amount or arrangement of chromosomal material. Chromosomal defects may be inherited, or they may be produced through accidents during development. Chromosomal defects tend to result in spontaneous abortion or serious abnormality. Chromosomal abnormalities are present in about 50% of all spontaneous abortions (Verma, 1990), and a visible chromosome-related abnormality is present in more than 8 out of every 1,000 live births, a number that has remained relatively constant since the United States began recording these data in the 1960s.

Down's syndrome is the most common chromosomal defect, affecting about 1 in every 1,000 live births. About 95% of Down's syndrome cases are caused by the acquisition of an extra chromosome from either the egg or the sperm. The fetus then has three copies of the number 21 chromosome instead of the normal two, so the total number of chromosomes in the fertilized egg is 47 instead of 46. The extra genetic material in this chromosome is responsible for the physical and mental abnormalities associated with the syndrome.

The mortality rate for Down's syndrome babies is high, with about one in six dying within the first year. Those who survive are mentally retarded, with IQs ranging from under 25 up to 74. Many have additional physical defects such

**TABLE 4.2 Common Sex Chromosome Abnormalities**

| Syndrome | Makeup of Chromosomes | Incidence per Live Births | Characteristics | Treatment |
|---|---|---|---|---|
| Klinefelter's syndrome | XXY; in rare cases an extra X occurs (XXXY). | 1 in 1,000 | Shrunken testes, breast development (gynecomastia) in about one-half of all cases, disproportionate arms and legs, elevated urinary gonadotropins, infertility in most cases, low levels of testosterone sometimes, increased likelihood of mental retardation | Administration of testosterone during adolescence often produces more masculine body contours and sexual characteristics in addition to increasing sexual drive. |
| XYY syndrome | XYY | 1 in 1,000 | Genital irregularities, decreased fertility, increased likelihood of mental retardation | None |
| Turner's syndrome | XO | 1 in 5,000* | Short stature (4 to 5 ft.), loose or weblike skin around the neck, a broad and "shieldlike" chest with the nipples widely spaced, nonfunctional ovaries, no menstruation or development of adult breasts, infertility in almost all cases | Administration of estrogen and progesterone can induce menstruation and development of the breasts, external genitals, and pubic hair. Androgen administered during puberty can help the child attain a greater adult height. |
| Triple-X syndrome | XXX | 1 in 1,000 | Most of these women show no major abnormalities, though they are likely to be less fertile than XX females; higher incidence of mental disturbance than among XX females | None |

*This figure is not an accurate indicator of the incidence of the condition. About one-tenth of all pregnancies that end in spontaneous abortion are XO—although this is a conservative estimate because many embryos with Turner's syndrome and other atypical chromosomal patterns are spontaneously aborted, at times before the woman is even aware she is pregnant.

as cardiac abnormalities, and their average life expectancy is 16.2 years (Levitan, 1988).

Because a disproportionate number of children with Down's syndrome are born to women older than 34, it was once assumed that the extra chromosome came from the mother. The reasoning was that a woman's germ cells are as old as she is because she is born with all the egg cells she will ever have, whereas men produce new sperm daily. However, as many as 20% to 25% of all babies born with Down's syndrome are conceived from a faulty sperm fertilizing an egg (Verma, 1990).

Down's syndrome and a number of other birth defects can be detected through tests for genetic abnormalities (see Chapter 9). Such testing is wise if a woman is over 35 or if there is a history of birth defects in the family. Analysis of the fetal chromosomes can detect all known chromosomal defects, as well as the gender of the fetus. The most straightforward form of analysis is to identify and count the chromosomes, noting any abnormalities in appearance or number. Such analysis reveals any defects caused by aberrations in the number of chromosomes, such as Down's syndrome. In addition, biochemical tests of the cultured fetal cells can be used to detect many problems owing to genetic abnormalities that cause no visible changes in chromosomes.

## Sex Chromosome Abnormalities

So far, more than 70 irregularities of the sex chromosomes have been identified (Levitan, 1988). Many of these result from abnormal combinations of sex chromosomes that cause a person to be neither an XX female nor an XY male. Some of the more common sex chromosome abnormalities are presented in Table 4.2.

The X chromosome appears to be crucial for survival. The genes on the Y chromosome are coded for "maleness" and little else. The presence of a single Y chromosome generally results in an individual having a male appearance, no matter how many X chromosomes that person has in his chromosomal makeup. Female development can occur without the presence of a second X, as in Turner's syndrome. But the absence of the second X reduces the likelihood of ovarian development and fertility.

In general, extra X chromosomes do not enhance feminine characteristics in females, but they may make males more like females. An extra Y chromosome, however, may increase height (see Box 4.2). In addition, the presence of extra X and Y chromosomes appears to be related to below-normal intelligence, although the intelligence of individuals with an extra Y chromosome

is not as limited as that of persons with extra X chromosomes (Hoyenga & Hoyenga, 1993).

## Inconsistencies in Prenatal Sexual Differentiation

In addition to atypical sex chromosome patterns, another cause of atypical sexual differentiation is an error in the differentiation process during prenatal development. A discrepancy may occur between genetic sex and gonadal, hormonal, or genital sex. An inconsistency in the process of prenatal sexual differentiation results in a condition known as intersexuality or *hermaphroditism*. The cause of hermaphroditism is still not understood.

The word *hermaphrodite* comes from the names of the Greek god and goddess of love, Hermes and Aphrodite. Their union was thought to have produced a god having characteristics of both males and females. The term is used to refer to an infant born with abnormal anatomical development.

True hermaphrodites, possessing an ovary on one side (usually the left) and a testis on the other, are exceedingly rare (Mittwoch, 1990). In some cases, ovotestes appear. *Ovotestes* are undifferentiated gonads—that is, gonads that did not develop into either testes or ovaries.

Hermaphrodites are usually genetic females, despite the presence of testes or other male anatomical features. In almost all cases, a uterus is present, but the external genitals can vary considerably. Because the phallus is generally enlarged, two-thirds of true hermaphrodites are raised as males (Lev-Ran, 1977). Complications arise when a true hermaphrodite, assigned as a male at birth, begins at puberty to develop breasts and to menstruate as a result of the secretion of estrogens from the previously undetected ovaries.

Most forms of atypical gender differentiation fall in the category of pseudohermaphroditism.

**hermaphroditism**—condition in which a person is born with both male and female characteristics, such as an ovary on one side and a testis on the other.

**ovotestes**—gonads that do not develop into ovaries or testes.

### Box 4.2

## Aggression and the XYY Syndrome

The XYY syndrome was discovered more than three decades ago. As in most cases in which there is an extra sex chromosome, genital irregularities appear relatively often, but major physical abnormalities do not occur regularly in XYY men, probably because the Y chromosome carries so little genetic material. Overall, XYY men tend to be less fertile than normal males, but many have fathered normal sons or daughters.

The XYY syndrome has received more publicity than any other sex-chromosome abnormality because of early research in a Scottish security institution, revealing that the number of XYY men among a group of mentally retarded male patients with violent or criminal potential was greater than would be dictated by chance (Jacobs et al., 1965). The mass media played up this finding, popularizing the notion that the single Y chromosome found in most men contributes to male aggression, and that the extra Y chromosome heightens aggression and possible criminal tendencies. The idea was appealing because it accounted for male aggression in a simple, straightforward way. Male aggression appears to derive from more complex factors, however, than possession of one or more Y chromosomes.

Since Jacobs's original report, research has concentrated on the link between criminality and the XYY syndrome. One of the most comprehensive studies was undertaken in Copen-

hagen, Denmark (Witkin et al., 1976). To increase the chances that their sample would include enough XYY males, who tend to be taller than XY males, the Witkin team chose to study only men in the top 15.9% of the population with respect to height.

Of the 4,139 men studied, 120 were found to exhibit the XYY syndrome. These men were compared with the normal males. The XYY men did have a higher rate of criminal convictions than did the XY males. The crimes committed by men in both groups, though, were more often crimes against property than crimes of aggression against other people. The XYY men were found to be no more likely to engage in violent crimes than were the XY men. Therefore, the image of XYY men as violent, assaultive individuals does not appear valid.

An alternative explanation of the original research finding of the disproportionately high incidence of XYY men in security institutions is suggested by an examination of the intelligence of XYY men. The fact that these individuals tend to be mentally dull, with IQs ranging between 80 and 95 (Levitan, 1988), may mean that those XYY men who break the law are more likely to be caught than are brighter criminals. The history of research on the XYY syndrome is a cautionary tale about jumping to sweeping conclusions on the basis of a single study.

---

In male pseudohermaphrodites, external genitals fail to develop as expected for normal males. Similarly, in female pseudohermaphrodites, external genitals fail to develop as expected for normal females.

### Sexual Differentiation in Genetic Males

We now briefly examine some of the conditions that can lead to problems in sexual differentiation in males. As we have seen, hormones are impor-

tant in the determination of early sexual differentiation. Thus it may be reasonable to assume that atypical patterns of exposure to sex hormones might lead to atypical sexual differentiation. Numerous researchers have investigated this hypothesis.

**Prenatal Hormone Exposure**   Exposure of genetic males to excessive levels of androgen appears to have no effect on the development of their internal or external genitals, but it may affect behavior. Ehrhardt (1975) compared nine boys who were prenatally exposed to higher-than-normal levels of androgens with their unaffected siblings. The androgen-exposed boys differed from their brothers only in their greater interest in sports and rough outdoor activities.

Prenatal exposure to elevated levels of estrogen and progesterone does not affect anatomical development and has little effect on the gender-related behavior of human males (Ehrhardt et al., 1984; Reinisch, Ziemba-Davis, & Sanders, 1991). Nonetheless, in experiments with mammals, this exposure does seem to result in the demasculinization of the genitals and more "feminine" behavior (Ehrhardt & Meyer-Bahlburg, 1981). These studies, in which both males and females who experienced increased prenatal exposure to estrogen were compared with others in appropriate control groups, indicate that such exposure might be related to somewhat more stereotypic feminine behaviors.

**Androgen Insensitivity Syndrome** Some XY people have a condition known as androgen insensitivity syndrome (AIS, sometimes called testicular feminization). The body secretes normal amounts of androgen, but the normal target cells are unresponsive to androgen. They do not have a normal androgen receptor gene on the X chromosome (Hoyenga & Hoyenga, 1993b).

The Wolffian structures of an AIS fetus fail to develop into normal internal male structures (prostate, seminal vesicles, and vas deferens) because they are insensitive to androgen. The Müllerian-inhibiting substance, however, is usually produced, so the Müllerian structures do not develop, either. Thus the fetus is born without a complete set of either male or female internal genital organs.

AIS individuals develop a normal clitoris and a short vagina. The vagina generally does not lead to a functional uterus, but occasionally a small structure regarded as a rudimentary uterus is present. Testes do not usually descend; if they do, they appear only as small lumps near the labia. (These small lumps are often misdiagnosed as hernias.) The undescended gonads (testes) do not produce viable sperm. Because people with this syndrome respond to the presence of female hormones, breast development and female pelvic changes occur at the onset of puberty. Menstru-

ation does not occur, and the person with AIS cannot reproduce.

Sexual activity and orgasm can occur in individuals afflicted with AIS. Because their genitals appear to be female, they are typically reared as females from birth, and they develop feminine identities. Minor surgery is sometimes needed to lengthen the upper vagina for satisfactory sexual intercourse. If testes are discovered, they are generally surgically removed during childhood or adolescence because leaving the testes in place increases the risk of cancer. These individuals then take estrogen supplements to replace the estrogen formerly secreted by the testes.

John Money and his colleagues studied 14 people with AIS who were reared as females. In attitude and behavior, they resembled traditional females, exhibiting well-developed maternal desires. The research group described them as excellent adoptive mothers (Money & Ehrhardt, 1972; Money, Ehrhardt, & Masica, 1968). Because they were socialized as females, of course, it is difficult to separate the effects of their insensitivity to androgen from the effects of their being brought up as females.

Occasionally, an individual with AIS has a phallus large enough to cause him to be identified as a male at birth. When he reaches puberty, however, he begins to develop breasts and lacks masculine body traits (see Figure 4.12). His penis may not have the ability to become erect, and his prostate gland may not produce ejaculatory fluid. Surgery can complete the fusion of his scrotum and bring his sterile testes down into it, but it cannot make his penis grow. His pubescent breasts can be surgically removed, but masculine secondary sexual characteristics cannot be created. Giving him extra doses of testosterone is useless: he is producing all that he needs, but his body cells cannot use it. People with AIS tend to have bodies that appear female, and they have difficult sex lives.

**Borderline Androgen Insensitivity Syndrome** Individuals with a condition known as borderline androgen insensitivity syndrome can make partial use of testosterone. The infant is born with a "penis" only slightly larger than a clitoris, and a urethra located in the peritoneal area rather than in the penis. His scrotum is partially unfused, and the testes can be felt as lumps in the

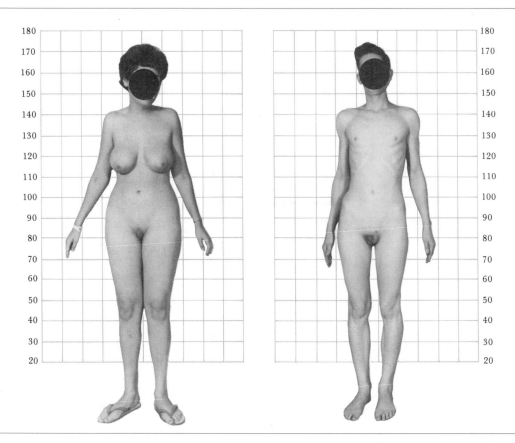

**FIGURE 4.12**

**Androgen Insensitivity Syndrome**
The development of genetic males with this abnormality is influenced solely by the secretion of estrogen during both the prenatal period and at puberty, since their cells are unresponsive to the testosterone that they secrete. The individual in the photograph on the right has had his breasts and testes surgically removed. His penis remains very small despite surgery, and erection is impossible for him.

groin. The usual solution is for this child to be reared as a female. Surgery can reduce the size of the penis and separate the scrotum to open and deepen the vagina. Female hormones (estrogen) can be administered to produce the development of breasts and other feminine characteristics. For the individual with AIS, then, the possession of an XY chromosome pattern and testes does not always mean being "male."

**Dihydrotestosterone (DHT)-Deficiency Syndrome**    DHT-deficiency syndrome is a genetic

disorder that prevents the prenatal conversion of testosterone into DHT. Males with DHT-deficiency syndrome lack an enzyme (5-alpha reductase) that is necessary for this conversion. As described earlier, DHT stimulates the development of the external male genitals. Thus at birth males with DHT-deficiency syndrome do not have identifiably male genitals.

Researchers studied 33 genetically male inhabitants of an isolated village in the Dominican Republic who had the enzyme deficiency (Imperato-McGinley et al., 1974, 1982). At birth these males had genitals that either were ambiguous or resembled those of females. At puberty, however, they experienced an increase in muscle mass, growth of the phallus and scrotum, and deepening of the voice. Nineteen of the males studied by the researchers had been brought up as females to the age of puberty. Of these, adequate information could be obtained on 18. Of the 18, 16 gradually adopted a masculine gender identity and erotic interest in women.

Imperato-McGinley and her colleagues hypothesized that the increase in testosterone at puberty masculinized not only the body, but also the mind, including the sex drive. Thus nature seems to have triumphed over nurture among these boys. As you might expect, however, this explanation is oversimplified and underestimates some important psychosocial factors. Although these males lived as girls, they had been stigmatized as freaks. At age 12, they were called *quevodoces*, which translates literally as "eggs" (balls). They were also known as *machihembra*, which translates roughly to "macho miss," with the implication that they were half-girl, half-boy freaks. In their traditional Hispanic village culture, there was no possibility of their becoming wives or mothers, nor was there any other feminine role for them that would not make them an economic liability to their families. The only real alternative was to adapt as best they could to being males.

Further implicating the role of psychosocial variables in DHT-deficiency syndrome, Herdt and Davidson (1988) described five males in New Guinea who were reared as females until puberty, at which point they changed to a male role. The researchers reported that these individuals suffered considerable social trauma in making the gender switch. Because they live in a male-dominant society, however, their gender-switching was a practical adaptation in that it potentially elevated their status.

The foregoing discussion of DHT-deficiency syndrome illustrates that gender identity and sexual orientation cannot be ascribed to any one nature or nurture variable. The "females" would not have changed to "males" if their bodies had not failed them at puberty. After their bodies no longer supported a feminine identity, cultural expectations and social conditions helped to create their gender-identity change.

## Sexual Differentiation in Genetic Females

Prenatal exposure to excess androgen has the effect of masculinizing genetic females. Research has identified three sources of such masculinization: 1) malfunction of fetal adrenal glands, 2) administration of hormones to pregnant women, and 3) ovarian tumors during pregnancy.

**Congenital Adrenal Hyperplasia (CAH)**    Congenital adrenal hyperplasia is a genetically transmitted malfunction of the adrenal glands. The fetus with this condition secretes too much adrenal androgen. Normally, the adrenal glands secrete both cortisol and androgens (cortisol is related to androgen levels in the body). The adrenal glands of CAH females, however, fail to synthesize cortisol and instead secrete excess androgens (Money, 1988).*

The release of extra androgens during the critical period for differentiation of the external genitals (about three months after conception) leads to masculinization of the external genitals. The vagina may not be open and the clitoris is often enlarged. The surge in androgen comes too late in development to affect the internal organs, so the ovaries, fallopian tubes, and uterus are normal (Hoyenga & Hoyenga, 1993b). If it is realized at birth that the masculinized baby is really a female, her external genitals can be surgically altered shortly after birth. In addition, she can be given cortisone to reduce the output of androgens from the adrenal glands. Under these conditions, the child will be relatively well adjusted and undergo the typical sexual differentiation associated with puberty (Hurtig & Rosenthal, 1987). If the problem is not corrected by cortisone injections from infancy onward, however, the excessive androgen secretion continues to masculinize the child after birth and at puberty (see Figure 4.13).

**Changes in Maternal Hormone Levels**    Masculinization of the external genitals of genetic females may also result from the mother receiving hormones called progestins during pregnancy

---

*Males also can inherit CAH, but it probably would not be detected were it not for illnesses that some males experience from malfunctioning of the adrenal glands.

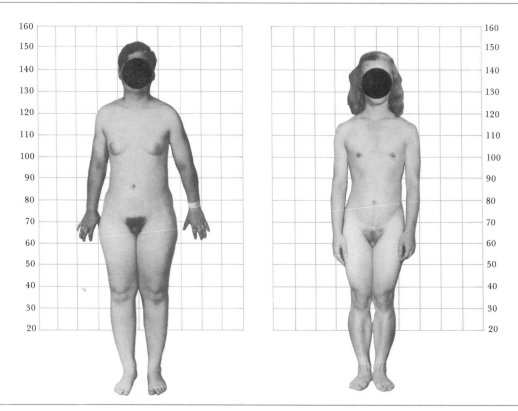

**FIGURE 4.13**
**Congenital Adrenal Hyperplasia (CAH)**
The 13-year-old on the left was reared as a boy. His penis needed no surgery, but
he received masculinizing hormones. The photo on the right shows a 12-year-old
genetic female who was reared as a girl. Her genitals were later surgically feminized,
and she was given feminizing hormones.

(Money & Ehrhardt, 1972). Progestins were at one time given to women who were at risk of miscarriage to help them maintain their pregnancies. Progestins, whether natural or synthetic, are biochemically similar to androgens and act on the body in similar ways. Follow-up studies of baby girls born to women who took progestins during their pregnancies have shown that the masculinizing effects of the hormones were limited to the prenatal period. After the babies were born, the masculinizing influence ended.

At birth the appearance of babies affected by progestins varied, depending on the strength of the masculinizing hormone. Some looked female, some looked male, and some looked ambiguous.

Their internal reproductive organs, however, developed normally. Thus babies recognized as females and given adequate surgical and hormonal treatment developed normally and were capable of reproduction.

The fate of genetic females with progestin-induced masculinized external genitals provides an example of the interaction of biological, psychological, and social factors in the formation of gender identity. When the effect of the progestin is pronounced, females may be born with a clitoris the size of a penis and with labia that have fused and give the appearance of a scrotum. The "penis" may even contain the urethral tube. Under these circumstances, the pronouncement at birth that it's a boy is quite understandable. The fact that the newborn's "scrotum" is empty would not necessarily raise questions because in 2% of all males the testes do not descend into the scrotum until after birth. At puberty, however, the child's ovaries secrete normal amounts of estrogen, which elicits menarche (first menstruation) and the beginnings of female body contours. By this time, of course, the genetic female has lived a dozen or more years under the assumption that she is a male, and the discovery of her internal femininity, not to mention the enlargement of breasts, can be a shock. After passing so many years with a male gender identity, the person may choose to have the female internal organs (ovaries and uterus) removed surgically. At the same time, administration of androgen helps to masculinize the body, and artificial testes can be inserted into the scrotum, although no sperm will be produced.

**Assigned Sex Versus Genetic Sex**    Money and Ehrhardt (1972) made an intriguing comparison among genetic females with 1) progestin-induced masculinization, 2) congenital adrenal hyperplasia (CAH), and 3) normal sexual differentiation. Individuals in all three groups were perceived as female at birth and were reared with no ambiguity regarding their gender. The 10 girls in the first group were exposed to progestin prenatally but to no masculinizing agents after birth. The 15 girls in the second group were immediately recognized as having CAH and placed on cortisone therapy to correct the condition.

Comparisons of the childhood behavior of the girls in the first two groups with that of the 25 normal girls in the third group indicated that the prenatally masculinized girls were more likely to display a number of stereotypically male interests and behaviors while developing a female gender identity. They liked strenuous physical activity and were not concerned about "feminine" attire. They tended to join boys in rough games such as football. Girls in the first two groups were more likely to be described as tomboys throughout their childhood. Although some of the girls in the normal control group also engaged in episodes of tomboyish behavior—a stage that is typical for most girls in our culture—the consistency of the behavior in the first two

groups led Money and Ehrhardt to speculate that the masculine childhood behavior was linked to the presence of progestin or androgen during prenatal development. The behavioral differences between the CAH girls and the normal girls could derive from genetic factors or from some alteration in the uterine environment other than the excess androgen. The girls who were prenatally masculinized by the artificial progestins, however, showed many of the same masculine childhood behaviors.

The dosage level appears to be a crucial factor in the effect of progestin. With the use of lower doses of progestin, the masculinizing effect seen by Money and Ehrhardt does not appear (Freund, 1985). Ehrhardt et al. (1984) reported that young girls who had been exposed to progestin prenatally exhibited slightly more female-stereotyped behavior than did normal girls.

In experiments with monkeys, testosterone has been observed to have a masculinizing effect. The period of gestation, or prenatal development, for a rhesus monkey is 168 days. Injection of testosterone into the pregnant mother between days 40 and 134 of pregnancy partially masculinized the genitals of XX monkeys (Goy & Phoenix, 1971). The genetically female monkeys usually developed a small but well-formed penis with a urethral opening at its tip, and a well-developed but empty scrotum. These monkeys nonetheless retained their internal female structures, which developed because there was no Müllerian-inhibiting substance to block them.

Although they did not attain the activity level of normal males, the testosterone-treated infant female monkeys engaged in more physical activity—wrestling, chasing, and threatening or aggressive behaviors—than did normal females. This difference may have stemmed from differential treatment that they received from other monkeys as a result of their masculine appearance rather than from fetal testosterone exposure. However, we know that testes are not necessary for normal male social play during the first two years because males who are castrated at birth are indistinguishable from normal males in their social-play behavior until the end of their second year. Similarly, removing the ovaries from otherwise normal female rhesus monkeys does not alter their social play. Presumably, then, this

difference stemmed from the presence of testosterone during the fetal period. With the addition
of testosterone, the brain is biased in the male
direction, even if that brain belongs to a genetic
female.

The effects of excess estrogen on human genetic females are not clear. There appear to be no
effects on sexual differentiation of the genitals.
There also seems to be little or no effect on gender-role behavior (Ehrhardt & Meyer-Bahlburg,
1981; Lish et al., 1992).

## Sexual Differentiation and Gender Identity

The preceding overview of the disorders associated with atypical hormone exposure suggests
two important conclusions. First, the sex hormones, particularly the androgens, have an enormous influence on anatomical differentiation in
a male or a female direction during prenatal
development.

Given the dramatic effects of the presence or
absence of androgens on the internal and external
genitals, the second conclusion is even more remarkable: that gender assignment and socialization—that is, being reared as a boy or a girl—
often have a greater impact on gender identity—the psychological sense of being male or
female—than does one's genetic (XX or XY) sex.
Thus when an anatomical error is discovered in
infancy and is corrected, gender identity will be
consistent with genetic sex. When an error is not
discovered until puberty or later, however, gender identity is often more important for self-concept than is genetic sex. In these cases, surgical
and hormonal treatments are generally more successful when their goal is to make anatomical
(genital) sex consistent with gender identity
rather than with genetic sex (Money, 1988). Research on atypical sexual differentiation has contributed to our understanding of normal anatomical and physiological functioning, the topic to
which we turn in the next chapter.

## Summary of Major Points

| | |
|---|---|
| 1. Fertilization. | Fertilization depends on the depositing of a large number of viable sperm in the vagina around the time of ovulation. Many sperm are lost in the journey from the vagina to the fallopian tube containing the mature egg (ovum). For fertilization to occur, a large number of sperm must attach themselves to the egg, where they secrete an enzyme that helps to dissolve the cellular material on the outside of the ovum, permitting one sperm to penetrate it. |
| 2. The fertilization process and genetic sex. | Fertilization of an egg by a sperm creates a zygote. The genetic sex of the fetus is determined immediately upon fertilization. The egg contains 22 autosomes (chromosomes that determine body characteristics) and one X chromosome. The sperm contains 22 autosomes and either one X chromosome or one Y chromosome. The combination of the X chromosome from the egg and an X chromosome from the sperm results in a genetic female (XX); the combination of the X chromosome from the egg and a Y chromosome from the sperm results in a genetic male (XY). |
| 3. Development during the germinal phase. | During the first week of gestation, the fertilized cell mass undergoes rapid cell division as it migrates from the fallopian tube to the upper part of the uterus, where it firmly implants itself. |
| 4. Development during the embryonic stage. | From the second week to the second month of gestation, the embryo develops its major organs, including the brain and heart, but it is still only about an inch long by the end of this stage. Because of the early development of major body systems during this period, the embryo is particularly vulnerable to damaging influences. Up to half of all embryos do not survive this phase. |
| 5. Development during the fetal stage. | The developing human is called a fetus when its bone cells, replacing cartilage cells, begin to appear, approximately two months after conception. From this point on, development consists primarily of the growth and maturation of organs and structures that appeared during the embryonic stage. |
| 6. Sexual differentiation. | Genetic sex is determined by the combination of sex chromosomes (XX or XY), which occurs at fertilization. Sexual differentiation of the male fetus begins about two months after conception, at the onset of the fetal stage. If the fetus carries a Y chromosome, this chromosome signals the development of gonads into testes rather than into ovaries. The testes then secrete testosterone, which masculinizes first the internal and then the external genital organs. The testes also secrete Müllerian-inhibiting substance (MIS), which inhibits the development of female sexual and reproductive structures. In the absence of testosterone or MIS, the fetus differentiates in a female direction, regardless of genetic gender. This finding suggests that the basic human form is female and that substances must be added in order to produce a male. |

7. Sexual and reproductive maturation.

As young people move into their second decade, hormonal processes within their bodies stimulate the changes associated with puberty. Females generally enter puberty at an earlier age than do males. The most obvious physical sign of girls' maturation is menarche, and of boys' maturation, nocturnal emission.

8. Atypical sexual differentiation.

Observations of individuals who have experienced atypical sexual differentiation have enhanced our understanding of fetal differentiation into a male or a female. Possession of at least one X chromosome appears to be crucial for survival, whereas possession of the Y chromosome seems to be important for maleness but not for life. Regardless of genetic sex, exposure to androgens during the early fetal period masculinizes a fetus. In the absence of androgens, or if the fetus is unable to respond to them, it differentiates in a feminine direction. The effects of atypical masculinization or feminization can be surgically and hormonally corrected under some conditions if the error is recognized during the first few years after birth, before the person has developed gender identity.

# Review of Key Concepts

1. Sperm are: a) miniature, preformed human beings that need to be united with an egg (ovum) to survive and develop; b) among the largest cells in the human body; c) produced by the endometrium; d) among the smallest cells in the human body. (p. 92)

2. By the process known as mitosis: a) the zygote is formed; b) it is determined whether an embryo is male or female; c) body cells divide, creating two new, identical cells; d) genes are arranged in place on chromosomes. (p. 94)

3. Dominant genes are those that: a) are located on the male Y chromosome; b) are located on the female Y chromosome; c) survive the perilous journey down the fallopian tubes; d) none of the above. (p. 97)

4. The ovum: a) is fertilized by the sperm in the vagina; b) becomes implanted in the uterine wall within 24 hours after it is fertilized; c) is the largest cell in the human body; d) all of the above. (pp. 92–93)

5. From the least to the most developed, which is the correct order? a) zygote, embryo, fetus; b) fetus, embryo, zygote; c) embryo, fetus, zygote; d) fetus, zygote, embryo. (pp. 98–99)

6. Chromosomal sex: a) is not understood by modern science; b) begins in the second trimester of pregnancy; c) is established at conception; d) is linked to the inheritance of a dominant gene. (p. 97)

7. The external male and female genitals begin to differentiate: a) at the moment of fertilization; b) after the internal structures of the embryo have differentiated; c) at birth; d) none of the above. (p. 106)

8. Describe the physical changes that mark the onset of puberty for males and for females. (pp. 108–109)

9. Research on the XYY syndrome: a) suggests that aggressive males also tend to have higher IQs; b) has established that an extra Y chromosome causes increased aggression; c) has called into question older theories of sexual differentiation; d) demonstrates the dangers of jumping to conclusions on the basis of a single study. (p. 112)

10. Prenatal exposure to excess androgen has the effect of masculinizing genetic females. This can occur through: a) malfunction of fetal adrenal glands; b) administration of hormones to pregnant women; c) ovarian tumors during pregnancy; d) all of the above. (p. 116)

11. Nature's rule is, it would appear, that to masculinize, something must be added. What evidence supports this statement? (p. 103)

# Sexual Anatomy and Physiology

EXUAL arousal involves the body in a concert of responses that usually culminates in a coordinated climax far more intricate than that achieved by the conductor and members of an orchestra. Sexual response is influenced by the interactions of the sexual organs, the endocrine system, the brain and the nervous system, childhood socialization processes, previous sexual experience, and the immediate situation. In this chapter we will focus on the first three variables: the sexual organs, the endocrine system, and the nervous system. We will also explore the effects of certain illnesses on sexual functioning.

## Sexual Anatomy

The entire body participates in sexual response. In this section, we describe the anatomy of the genitals—those parts of the body most closely identified with sexual response.

### The Male Sexual System

The male sexual system consists of a pair of testes, which produce sperm and sex hormones; a network of ducts that transport sperm from the testes to the outside world; a number of glands that produce seminal fluid; and the penis, which delivers the semen (see Figure 5.1).

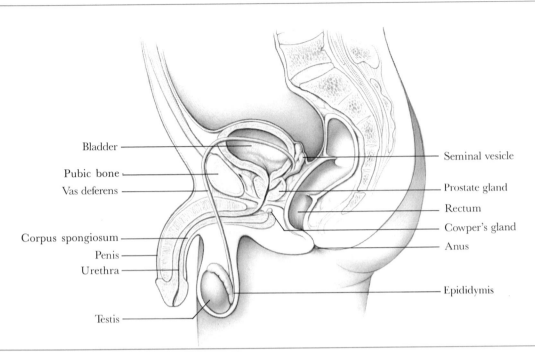

Bladder

Pubic bone

Vas deferens

Corpus spongiosum

Penis

Urethra

Testis

Seminal vesicle

Prostate gland

Rectum

Cowper's gland

Anus

Epididymis

**FIGURE 5.1**
**The Male Genital System**

## The Testes

The word *testes* (singular, *testis*) comes from the Latin word for "to testify" or "to witness." Instead of placing their hands on a Bible, as is customary today, the early Romans placed their hands over their testes when taking an oath. The fact that women do not have testes did not pose a problem because Roman women were not considered important enough to take oaths.

A popular slang term for the testes, *balls*, suggests that they are round in shape. Actually they are oval, or egg-shaped, organs, located in a sac-like structure called the *scrotum*. The scrotum helps to maintain the temperature necessary for the production of viable sperm. Normal scrotal temperature is about $5\frac{1}{2}°$F lower than normal core body temperature. Within the scrotum, each tes-

tis is suspended at the end of a cord called the *spermatic cord*. The cord may be located by placing the fingers at the top of the testis and moving the scrotal skin back and forth gently. The spermatic cord contains blood vessels, nerves, a sperm duct called the vas deferens, and the thin *cremaster muscle*, which encircles each testis and raises it closer to the body in response to cold, fear, anger, or sexual arousal.

Each testis contains seminiferous tubules and interstitial cells (also called Leydig cells). Sperm are produced within the *seminiferous* ("seed-bearing") *tubules*. Hundreds of these tubules lie

---

**testes** (TES-tees)—two small, oval organs, located in the scrotum, that produce mature sperm and sex hormones.

**scrotum** (SCROH-tum)—the sac that contains the testes.

**spermatic cord** (spur-MAH-tik)—the cord that suspends the testes and contains the vas deferens, blood vessels, nerves, and the cremaster muscle.

**cremaster muscle** (CRE-mah-ster)—the muscle that runs from the testes into the spermatic cord and controls the proximity of the testes to the body.

**seminiferous tubules** (se-me-NIF-er-us)—long, thin, tightly coiled tubes, located in the testes, that produce sperm.

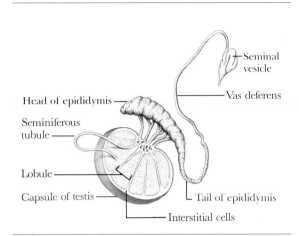

Seminal vesicle

Vas deferens

Head of epididymis

Seminiferous tubule

Lobule

Capsule of testis

Tail of epididymis

Interstitial cells

**FIGURE 5.2**
**Cross-Section of the Internal Structure of a Testis**

tightly coiled within each testis, and each tubule is between one and three feet long (see Figure 5.2). The *interstitial cells*, which are located in the connective tissue between the seminiferous tubules, synthesize and secrete sex hormones. About 95% of the testosterone manufactured by the body comes from testicular interstitial cells; the remainder comes from the adrenal glands. Interstitial cells also produce small amounts of estrogen, a feminizing hormone. In addition, each testis produces *inhibin*, a hormone involved in regulating sperm production. When sperm count rises, inhibin signals the brain to inhibit further production of sperm. When sperm count decreases, inhibin secretion decreases and sperm production begins again.

Sperm pass out of the seminiferous tubules and into the *epididymis*, which lies adjacent to the back portion of each testis. It is in the tightly coiled tubules that make up the epididymis that sperm become functionally mature and then are stored until they are ejaculated from the body. The smooth muscle of the wall of the epididymal

interstitial cells—cells in the spaces between the seminiferous tubules that secrete hormones; also known as Leydig cells.

inhibin —a hormone produced by the testes that regulates sperm production by reducing the pituitary gland's secretion of FSH.

epididymis (ep-i-DIH-dih-mis)—tightly coiled tubules, located at the top of the testes, in which sperm are stored.

tubules contracts when a male ejaculates. These contractions move the sperm out of the epididymis and into the vas deferens for transport to the urethra.

## The Male Genital Ducts

The ducts of the male genital organs include the vasa deferentia, the ejaculatory ducts, and the urethra. The *vasa deferentia* (singular, *vas deferens*) consist of two slender ducts or tubes, one from each epididymis. These run from the epididymis into the abdominal cavity and join with the duct from the seminal vesicles at the back of the urinary bladder to form the ejaculatory ducts. Sperm travel through each vas deferens to the ejaculatory duct, where they receive fluid from the seminal vesicles.

The *ejaculatory ducts* enter the *prostate gland*, where fluid from the prostate and the seminal vesicles combines with sperm to produce the semen that enters the urethra. The *urethra* has two functions in the male: it conveys both urine and semen.

## Glands Producing Seminal Fluid

Despite the presence of 200 million to 400 million sperm in the average ejaculate, sperm account for only about 1% of the total volume of *semen*. Secretions from the epididymis contribute a small amount of fluid, but most of the teaspoonful of semen in the average ejaculate comes from the seminal vesicles, the prostate gland, and the Cowper's glands.

vas deferens (vas-DEH-fur-renz)—the slender duct through which sperm are transported from each testis to the ejaculatory duct at the base of the urethra.

ejaculatory duct (ee-JAK-u-la-TOR-ee)—the tubelike passageway that carries semen from the prostate gland to the urethra.

prostate gland—gland located at the base of the male urinary bladder that supplies most of the seminal fluid.

urethra (ur-REE-thrah)—the duct or tube through which urine and ejaculate leave the body.

semen (SEE-men)—the milky-white alkaline fluid containing sperm; a product of fluids from the epididymis, seminal vesicles, prostate, and Cowper's glands, combined with sperm cells from the testes.

The *seminal vesicles* are two saclike structures on either side of the bladder. At their base are two straight, narrow ducts that enter into the ejaculatory duct. The seminal vesicles secrete a fluid that not only provides sperm with energy in the form of fructose (a sugar) but also neutralizes the acidity of the female's vagina. The normal acidity of the vagina provides some protection against infection, but the acidity can also be fatal to sperm. Thus the neutralizing elements in semen increase the likelihood that sperm survive to penetrate the egg.

The prostate gland, which surrounds the urethra at the base of the urinary bladder, is about the size of a large walnut. At the moment of ejaculation, it expels its alkaline fluid into the urethra just below the urinary bladder. During ejaculation the nervous system coordinates the closing of sphincter muscles where the urethra leaves the urinary bladder, preventing urine from entering the urethra. Thus semen can pass through the urethra without mixing with urine.

The *Cowper's glands*, each about the size of a pea, flank the urethra and empty into it through tiny ducts. During sexual arousal, these glands secrete a clear, slippery fluid, a drop of which usually appears at the tip of the penis prior to ejaculation. This alkaline fluid may help to neutralize the acidic effects of urine in the urethra, making the urethra more hospitable to the passage of sperm. The fluid sometimes contains small numbers of sperm, particularly when a couple engages in coitus a second time without the male's having urinated. In such a case, any sperm remaining in the urethra from the previous ejaculation are likely to be carried out of the penis in the fluid secreted from the Cowper's glands during sexual arousal. People who have been practicing withdrawal to avoid conception may be surprised to learn that sperm can be carried into the vagina by this fluid before ejaculation, sometimes causing pregnancy to occur even if the man avoids ejaculating into the woman's vagina. Clearly, withdrawal is better than nothing, but a couple wishing to avoid pregnancy is advised to employ a more reliable method of contraception.

Individuals vary in their attitudes toward coming into contact with semen during the process of oral-genital stimulation. Although there is no evidence that healthy semen harms the mouth or digestive system,* some people find the idea of having semen in their mouths distasteful and thus are not enthusiastic about oral sex. As one of our students wrote:

*I like to have oral sex with him because I know he really likes it. But one time, he came before he meant to, and getting his semen in my mouth made me kind of sick. I got right up and went to the bathroom to spit it out and rinse my mouth with mouthwash. Since then, I've always been kind of nervous when we're having oral sex.*

Some may fear getting semen in the mouth because of their association of the genitals with the products of elimination. Other people, however, respond positively to ejaculation during oral sex. Another student reported:

*His semen tastes extremely clean, with the flavor a little different from one time to the next. Sometimes, it is very sweet, and almost tasteless. Other times, it has a stronger flavor. When we're kissing each other and I'm holding his penis in my hand, I can feel the pulsing at the bottom of his penis just before he comes. That makes me more excited, and then his semen spurts into my mouth and that pushes me into orgasm and it feels like I'm him and he's me, and we're coming everywhere.*

---

**seminal vesicles** (SEM-in-al VES-i-kelz)—two saclike organs, lying on either side of the prostate, that deposit fluid into the ejaculatory ducts to contribute to semen.

**Cowper's glands** (COW-perz)—two small glands that secrete a clear, alkaline fluid into the urethra during sexual arousal.

---

*Note that we are discussing healthy semen. Partners should not have oral sex or any other sexual activity involving the exchange of body fluids unless both partners are free of AIDS or any other sexually transmitted disease.

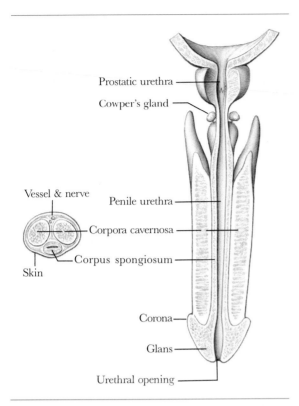

Prostatic urethra

Cowper's gland

Vessel & nerve

Penile urethra

Corpora cavernosa

Corpus spongiosum

Skin

Corona

Glans

Urethral opening

**FIGURE 5.3**
**The Internal Structure of the Circumcised Penis**
A cross-section and a longitudinal section are shown.

## The Penis

The male sexual organ, the *penis*, seems to have evolved when organisms developed reproductive strategies leading to internal rather than external fertilization. Internal fertilization has the advantage of placing sperm deep inside a female's body. External fertilization is not as economical because many sperm are lost before they reach their destination. External fertilization is exhibited by most species of fish, which release eggs and sperm into the water, where they may become fertilized. The males of many mammalian species have a bone that runs the length of the penis. Humans and whales are two exceptions: their penises do not contain bones.

The human penis consists of three parallel cylinders of spongy tissue that provide the penis

**penis** (PEE-nis)—the male sexual organ.

with its capacity to become erect (see Figure 5.3). Two of these cylinders are called the cavernous bodies, or *corpora cavernosa*. If the penis is held straight out, the third cylinder, the *corpus spongiosum*, can be felt on the underside of the penis. It surrounds the penile urethra.

Each of these cylinders contains tissue with irregular cavities, or spaces. These spaces do not have much blood in them when the penis is flaccid, or soft. When a male becomes sexually aroused, however, the blood vessels that carry blood into the penis dilate, and the cavities become engorged with blood. This engorgement produces the rigidity and stiffness of an erection, known in slang as a "hard-on."

The end of the corpus spongiosum enters the *glans* at the tip of the penis. The glans is more sensitive to stimulation than the rest of the penis because it contains abundant sense receptors to pressure and touch. The most sensitive parts of the glans are the *corona*, or rim, and the *frenulum*, a strip of skin on the underside where the glans meets the body of the penis. At the time of birth, the penis has a fold of skin called the foreskin, or prepuce. Many North American males have their foreskins surgically removed by circumcision within a few days after birth.

When flaccid, the average penis is about 9 cm (3.5 in.) in length and about 9.5 cm (3.75 in.) in circumference. An erect penis (see Figure 5.4) is about 16 cm (6.3 in.) in length and about 12 cm (4.85 in.) in circumference (Jamison & Gebhard, 1988; Masters & Johnson, 1966). Kinsey's colleague Wardell Pomeroy (1972) reported that the largest penis he and his associates encountered

**corpora cavernosa** (COR-por-ah kah-ver-NOH-sa)—two columns within the penis that contain small cavities capable of filling with blood to produce an erection.

**corpus spongiosum** (COR-puhs spun-gee-OH-sum)—a column of spongy tissue within the penis that surrounds the urethra and is capable of blood engorgement during sexual arousal.

**glans** (glanz)—the sensitive tip of the penis or clitoris.

**corona** (cor-OH-nah)—the sensitive rim of the glans.

**frenulum** (FREN-you-lum)—a small piece of skin on the underside of the male glans where the glans meets the body of the penis.

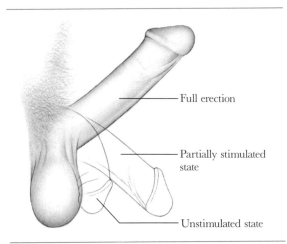

**FIGURE 5.4**
**Penile Response**
The penis changes in circumference, length, and position as a function of stimulation.

in their research was 10 in. long when erect. The smallest erect penis was 1 in. long. Medical literature contains reports of men whose penises do not exceed 1 cm when erect. This condition, sometimes called micropenis, usually results from inadequate levels of masculinizing hormones during early development.

Penis size tends to be of great concern to many people because size is commonly equated with sexual prowess. Among adolescent women, rumors circulate that you can tell the length of a man's penis by his height or by the length of his foot, nose, or thumb. Research has not demonstrated a relationship between penis length and the proportions of any other part of a man's body. In addition, smaller flaccid penises undergo greater increases in size during erection than do larger flaccid penises (Jamison & Gebhard, 1988).

As far as the issue of sexual prowess is concerned, it is important to realize that various characteristics of female sexual anatomy make penis length irrelevant to the physiological arousal of most women. For many women, stimulation of the vagina is less effective for sexual arousal than is stimulation of the clitoris. Further, the vagina is an extraordinarily elastic organ. Although it expands to accommodate the passage of babies, which are far larger than the biggest penis, it is quite small in its nonaroused state.

Some people have speculated that long penises may be more psychologically arousing than shorter penises. So far, only one study has examined the influence of penis length on erotic arousal (Fisher, Branscombe, & Lemery, 1983). Although volunteers were clearly aroused by the erotic stories they were given to read, their arousal did not vary as a function of the length of the penises described in the stories. The answer to the question posed by the researchers in the title of their study, ''The Bigger the Better?'' seems to be no.

## The Female Sexual System

The female sexual system consists of a pair of ovaries, a pair of fallopian tubes, a uterus (or womb), vagina, clitoris, and vulva (see Figure 5.5). The female has at least two areas of intense erotic sensation. One area is the clitoris, which is located externally at the top of the vulva, where the inner lips meet. The inner lips and the entrance to the vagina are also sensitive in some women, as are the breasts and nipples. A second area, known as the Gräfenberg spot, located internally on the front (anterior) wall of the vagina, is still a matter of some controversy among sex researchers. We return to the Gräfenberg spot later in this chapter.

### The Ovaries

The *ovaries* are flattened, egg-shaped organs located in the pelvic cavity. They lie nestled in the curve of the fallopian tubes. The ovaries are similar to the testes: both develop from similar tissue within a few months after conception, both produce reproductive cells (eggs or sperm), and both secrete hormones. The principal hormones secreted by the ovaries are the feminizing estrogens and progesterone. The ovaries also secrete smaller amounts of masculinizing hormones, one of which is testosterone.

The ova (singular, *ovum*), or eggs, are found near the surface of the ovary. Each ovum is encircled by clusters of nutrients and hormone-

---

**ovaries** (OH-vah-rees)—two small organs that produce eggs and hormones; located above and to each side of the uterus.

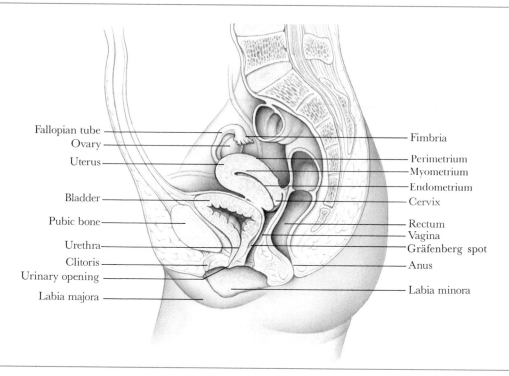

**FIGURE 5.5**
**The Female Genital System**

secreting cells. These bundles (ovum, nutrients, and hormone-secreting cells) are called ovarian *follicles*. The number of ovarian follicles present in both ovaries at birth ranges from 400,000 to 500,000. During a woman's lifetime, however, no more than 400 to 500 ova are released through ovulation. Generally, one ovum is discharged from its follicle every month from puberty until menopause, except during pregnancy or in some women while they are breast-feeding.

*The Fallopian Tubes*

Each *fallopian tube* is about four inches long. The end of the fallopian tube nearest the ovary is not

**follicle** (FAHL-lih-kul)—in the ovary, the sac of estrogen-secreting cells that contains an egg.
**fallopian tubes** (fah-LOW-pee-un)—the tubes through which eggs, or ova, are transported from the ovaries to the uterus; fertilization normally takes place within these tubes.

directly connected to the ovary but opens into the abdominal cavity. The other end of each tube is connected to the uterus.

When an ovum is released from an ovary, it is propelled into the near fallopian tube by thin, hairlike structures (called *fimbriae,* from the Latin word for "fringe") that line the opening of the fallopian tube. After the ovum is in the fallopian tube, tiny hairlike structures called *cilia* help transport it toward the uterus. The cilia sweep in the direction of the uterus, acting as tiny fingers that aid the ovum in its movement. Contractions of the fallopian tube itself also help to propel the ovum. The upper third of the fallopian tube is typically the site of the union between egg and sperm if fertilization occurs.

*The Uterus*

Some young girls receive their first information about their internal sexual organs when their mothers draw a picture of an upside-down pear to represent the uterus during discussions about

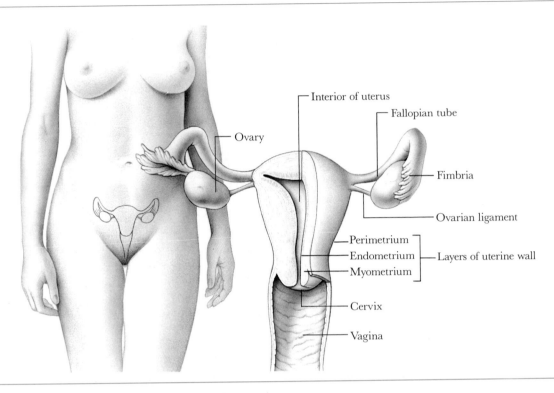

**FIGURE 5.6**
**Internal Female Reproductive System**
Parts of the uterus and vagina are cut away in this illustration.

menstruation. The *uterus*, or womb, does resemble an upside-down pear (see Figure 5.6). In contrast to the thin-skinned pear, however, the uterus has thick, muscular walls. It is suspended in the pelvic cavity by a collection of ligaments, which allow it to shift and contract in response to sexual tension, pregnancy, and the filling of the urinary bladder or rectum. The uterine walls are composed of three layers of tissue. The most internal layer—the one that lines the uterine cavity—is the *endometrium*. The inner two-thirds of

the endometrium are shed during menstruation. The middle layer of the uterine wall is the *myometrium*, a thick layer of smooth muscle. The myometrium is responsible for the contractions of the uterus that occur during sexual tension, orgasm, childbirth, and menstruation. The external surface of the uterus is covered by a thin membrane, the *perimetrium*.

The lower end of the uterus extends into the vagina. This portion of the uterus, which is called the *cervix* (neck), contains glands that secrete

**uterus**—the site of implantation of the fertilized cell mass, where the fetus develops during gestation; also called the womb.

**endometrium** (en-do-MEE-tree-um)—the lining of the uterus, part of which is shed during menstruation.

**myometrium** (my-o-MEE-tree-um)—the smooth muscle layer of the uterine wall.

**perimetrium** (peh-rih-MEE-tree-um)—the thin connective-tissue membrane covering the outside of the uterus.

**cervix**—the lower end of the uterus, that opens into the vagina.

varying amounts of mucus. The presence of this mucus, which plugs the opening into the uterus, may explain why males evolved with their ejaculate containing many millions of sperm. Despite the action of enzymes in the semen that digest the cervical mucus, it still creates a formidable barrier, which is more likely to be penetrated when the number of sperm is great and the mucus is thin. Cervical mucus is thin when estrogen is high, just prior to and at the time of ovulation. The mucus thickens as progesterone rises after ovulation.

### The Vagina

The *vagina* is a thin-walled muscular tube that extends from the uterus to the external opening in the vulva. The vagina is a passageway that increases in length and width during sexual arousal and childbirth. The vaginal walls contain many small blood vessels that become engorged with blood during sexual excitement, in a process similar to that leading to erection in the male. The pressure from this congestion causes small droplets of the colorless, fluid portion of the blood to ooze through the vaginal walls. These droplets appear as beads on the internal surface of the vaginal walls, and they coalesce into a layer of shiny *lubricant* that coats the walls.

The concern of some males with penis size, noted earlier, is probably based on the false assumption that intercourse is the primary sexual event for females as well as males. Because this process provides the male with intense stimulation to the organ that is most erotically sensitive—his penis—he may assume that the organ into which he places his penis during heterosexual intercourse—the vagina—is equally sensitive. In general, it is not. Because the vagina also functions as the passageway through which babies emerge, such sexual sensitivity in the vaginal

walls would make childbirth more painful than it is. In fact, the walls of the vagina, particularly the inner two-thirds, contain few touch and pressure receptors.

### The Gräfenberg Spot

The *Gräfenberg spot*, or G spot, provides the exception to the general rule that the vagina is erotically insensitive. The researchers who identified the area, Perry and Whipple (1981), called it the Gräfenberg spot in honor of Ernest Gräfenberg, the physician who in 1950 first described it. The Gräfenberg spot is accessed through the anterior wall (the upper wall nearest the urethra) of the vagina, about halfway between the pubic bone and the cervix (see Figure 5.7). It varies from about the size of a dime to that of a half-dollar. Coital positions in which the penis hits the spot, such as woman-above or rear-entry, as well as stimulation of the spot with the fingers, may produce intense erotic pleasure (see Box 5.1).

Perry and Whipple (1982) trained physicians to locate the Gräfenberg spot during vaginal examinations. In their initial work, 250 women were examined by four collaborating physicians. The spot was located in every woman, without exception. Stimulation of the spot can produce orgasmic contractions of the upper vagina (near the cervix) and of the uterus. Of the women examined by Perry and Whipple, about 10% ejaculated a fluid from the urethra upon stimulation of the Gräfenberg spot. It is hypothesized that the source of the ejaculate is a rudimentary female prostate gland (the Skene's gland) located at the base of the urinary bladder, just as it is in males (Belzer, Whipple, & Moger, 1984; Zaviacic & Whipple, 1993).

There is conflicting evidence on the location of the Gräfenberg spot. As we shall see in Chapter 7, some researchers maintain that the entire front wall of the vagina, not just a single spot, is erotically sensitive.

---

**vagina** (vah-JYE-nah)—the portion of the female sexual system that extends from the uterus to the vulva; a muscular tube that can accommodate the penis during intercourse, and through which menstrual blood from the uterus is passed and babies are born.

**lubricant**—a shiny, slippery fluid secreted through the walls of the vagina during sexual arousal.

**Gräfenberg spot** (GRAY-fen-berg)—also known as G spot; an area of sensitivity accessed through the upper wall of the vagina, usually within two inches of the vaginal entrance.

**Box 5.1**

## How to Find the Gräfenberg Spot

Beverly Whipple has written a set of explicit directions for those women interested in locating the Gräfenberg spot.

*Women have reported that they have difficulty locating and stimulating the Gräfenberg spot by themselves (except with a dildo or similar device) but they have no difficulty identifying the erotic sensation when the spot is stimulated by a partner.*

*The problem with trying to locate the Gräfenberg spot by yourself is that you need long fingers and/or a short vagina to reach the spot while lying on your back. The spot does not lie on the vaginal wall itself, but can be felt through it. It is usually about halfway between the back of the pubic bone and the cervix and feels like a small lump that swells as it is stimulated. When it is first touched, many women report that it feels like they need to urinate, even if the bladder has just been emptied. However, within 2 to 20 seconds of massage, the initial reaction is replaced in some*

*women by a strong and distinctive feeling of sexual pleasure. In fact, some women have actually experienced their first orgasm by stimulation of the G spot.*

*Some women report an orgasm from stimulation of this area, and some also report an expulsion of fluid from the urethra when they experience this type of orgasm. The fluid expelled looks like watered-down fat-free milk.*

*A few women have reported that they are able to locate the Gräfenberg spot by themselves while seated on a toilet. After emptying their bladder, they explore along the anterior (upper front) wall of the vagina with a firm pressure pushing up toward the navel. Some women find it helpful to apply a downward pressure on the abdomen, with their other hand, just above the pubic bone or top of the pubic hair line. As the Gräfenberg spot is stimulated and begins to swell, it can often be felt between the two sets of fingers.*

*It often feels like a small bean and in some women swells to the size of a half dollar. Experi-*

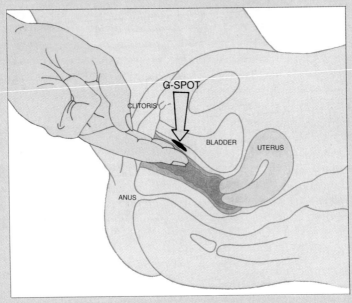

**FIGURE 5.7**
The Gräfenberg Spot

*ment with the Gräfenberg spot. You will probably need to use a heavier pressure than you do on the clitoris, and you may feel the sensations deeper inside than you do with clitoral stimulation.*

*After you have explored your Gräfenberg spot, you may want to share the experience with a partner. The Gräfenberg spot can be stimulated by the partner's fingers, with a dildo, or with a penis. The position most likely to lead to stimulation with a penis is the female on top. Some women report multiple orgasms from this type of stimulation, and some report experiencing an orgasmic expulsion of fluid. The orgasm that results from this type of stimulation is often reported as feeling deeper inside. The fluid that is sometimes expelled does not smell or taste like urine, and its chemical composition is different from urine.*

*By sharing this information with you, we do not want to create a new goal for women to* achieve. *However, we want you to be aware of the variety of orgasmic experiences available. We want to help those women who enjoy this type of stimulation and the resulting orgasms with or without the ejaculation of fluid to feel good about themselves and what they are experiencing. Many women have reported that they felt abnormal because they liked this type of stimulation or because they expelled fluid at orgasm. In fact, many women in the past learned to hold back the fluid and also learned to hold back and not have an orgasm, to avoid the embarrassment of being what they considered abnormal.*

Source: Whipple, 1981.

## The Vulva

The *vulva*, which includes all the external genitals of the female, is shown in Figure 5.8. Terms for the various parts of the vulva reflect the historical attitudes toward women and sex that we traced in Chapter 1. Another term for the vulva, *pudendum*, comes from the Latin word *pudere*, "to be ashamed." The major external female genitals are the mons pubis, the outer and inner lips, the clitoris, and the vaginal opening.

The *mons pubis, or mons veneris* ("mound of Venus"), is essentially a cushion of fatty tissue that is covered by pubic hair. The mons has more touch receptors than does the clitoris, but fewer pressure receptors. Stimulation of the mons can produce intense sexual excitement and can even trigger orgasm in some women.

The *outer lips (labia majora)* are the outermost, hair-covered folds of skin that envelop the external genitals. They merge with the other body skin in the back, near the anus. In the front, they come together a small distance above the clitoris. The outer lips are similar to the skin of the scrotum in the male. They have fewer touch and pressure receptors than does the mons. During sexual stimulation, the outer lips flatten and expose the inner lips as well as the vaginal opening.

The *inner lips (labia minora)* are the second, inner covering of the vaginal opening. The minor (inner) lips are thinner than the major (outer) lips and are hairless. During sexual stimulation, these layers of skin become engorged with blood and turn from their customary pink to a dark red. The concentration of sensory receptors is lower than

**vulva** (VULL-vah)—the external female genitals, including the mons pubis, the outer and inner lips, the clitoris, and the vaginal opening.

**mons pubis**—in the adult female, a cushion of fatty tissue above the labia that is covered by pubic hair.

**outer lips or labia majora** (LAY-bee-ah ma-JOR-ah)—the hair-covered lips that enfold the inner lips, the clitoris, and the vaginal entrance.

**inner lips or labia minora** (LAY-bee-ah mih-NOR-ah)—the hairless lips between the outer lips that enclose the clitoris and the vaginal opening.

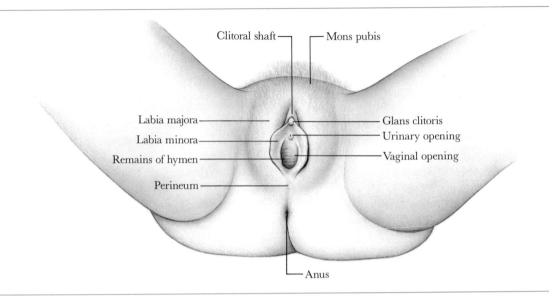

**FIGURE 5.8**
**The Vulva**
The external genitals of the female, collectively referred to as the vulva, are shown.

in the mons or clitoris. The minor lips enclose both the vaginal and urethral openings, as well as the ducts of the Bartholin's glands.

At one time, the Bartholin's glands were thought to be vital for vaginal lubrication. Masters and Johnson (1966) found, however, that the few drops of secretion they produce are not the source of vaginal lubrication. The Bartholin's glands correspond to the Cowper's glands in the male, but their function is not yet known.

The *clitoris* is the only part of the human external sexual anatomy that appears to have purely a sexual function; all of the other structures also have reproductive functions. At the top of the vulva, the inner lips come together to form the clitoral hood, also known as the prepuce or foreskin of the clitoris. Anatomically, the hood is similar to the foreskin of the penis. The minor lips, which closely surround the vagina, are

stretched back and forth during intercourse as the penis thrusts in and out. The minor lips, in turn, tug on the clitoral hood, providing stimulation that may elicit orgasm. Alternatively, the clitoris may be stimulated manually or orally.

The clitoris develops out of tissue similar to that which forms the penis in the male. Like the penis, the clitoris contains two corpora cavernosa. Unlike the penis, the clitoris is physically separated from the urethra and does not contain the corpus spongiosum. It does, however, have a swelling at its tip—the glans—similar to the male penile glans. During sexual excitement, the clitoris becomes engorged with blood, increasing in diameter and remaining enlarged during sexual stimulation. The clitoris is permeated with sensory receptors and has more pressure receptors than the penis (Levin, 1992).

Most newborn girls have a ring or fold of connective tissue at the vaginal opening. This tissue is the *hymen*, commonly called the "cherry"

**clitoris** (CLIH-tor-is)—the small, highly sensitive, erectile tissue located just below the point where the minor lips converge at the top of the vulva; its only known function is to provide female sexual pleasure.

**hymen** (HYE-men)—a layer of tissue that partially covers the vaginal entrance of most females at birth.

in slang. The hymen varies in size, shape, and in the extent to which it blocks the vaginal opening. Some females are born without hymens. Contrary to popular belief, the presence or absence of the hymen is not a reliable indicator of whether a woman has had sexual intercourse. The hymen may be ruptured during bicycle or horseback riding, vigorous exercise, or insertion of menstrual tampons. On the other hand, the hymens of some sexually active women remain intact until they go through childbirth.

Another common belief is that first intercourse for a woman is painful because of the rupture of the hymen. This may be the case for a woman with a particularly thick hymen that blocks most of the vaginal entrance. Other women, however, experience first intercourse and the rupturing of the hymen, if it is intact, without any pain. The example of one of our students is rather typical.

*After he came, the man I had sex with for the first time accused me of lying about being a virgin. He said that if I were a virgin, it would have hurt and there would have been some bleeding when my cherry was broken. Actually, I didn't feel much of anything physically—no pain, and no particular pleasure. What I did feel was disappointment that sex wasn't any big deal, and anger over his accusation.*

Because of the myth that an intact hymen indicates virginity, many men have attached a lot of importance to the tissue, and many women have expended a lot of energy to demonstrate its existence. To this day, physicians are asked to sew in hymens for women without them. Some of these women are hymenless virgins, whereas others are sexually experienced women who wish to convince a future partner that they are inexperienced. Despite all the concern about this little piece of tissue, its purpose or function is not yet known.

Although the pelvic muscle, breasts, and lips are not part of the female genitals, all are important in sexual arousal. We shall therefore turn to a description of their sexual functions.

### The Pelvic Muscles

A ring of muscles surrounds the vaginal opening. One of these muscles, the *pubococcygeus muscle (PC muscle)*, is especially important in female orgasmic response. The PC muscle is a slinglike band of muscle fibers that forms part of the floor of the pelvic cavity and partially supports the uterus, part of the vagina, the urinary bladder, the urethra, and the rectum. If this muscle is not taut, the uterus and vagina can sag, allowing leaking of urine from the urethra (that is, urinary incontinence). Some time ago, Kegel (1952) suggested that sexual responsiveness could be increased through exercise of this muscle (see Chapter 14 for directions). Exercising these muscle fibers can produce pleasurable sensations for women in and of itself, as well as with (and for) their partners during sexual intercourse. Tension in the PC muscle, along with a lack of lubrication because of inadequate sexual stimulation (or inability to receive the stimulation), probably accounts for many cases of discomfort during a woman's first experiences with intercourse.

### The Breasts

The breasts are fatty appendages that play an important role in sexual arousal for many women and men. A few women have orgasm solely through stimulation of their nipples and breasts, and some can experience arousal while breast-feeding.

Embedded in the fatty breast tissue are secreting glands that have the potential to produce milk. The nipples contain erectile tissue and can become erect through sexual stimulation or in response to cool temperatures. The sensitivity of the nerve fibers in the breasts is associated with hormonal levels that fluctuate with pregnancy and the menstrual cycle. Both women and men should carefully examine their breasts on a monthly basis for lumps that may be cancerous.

Just as men experience concern over penis size, many women worry about the shape and

**pubococcygeus muscle (PC muscle)** (pew-bow-cawk-SEE-gee-us)—the muscle that surrounds the vaginal entrance and walls.

size of their breasts. The fact that the number of nerve endings does not vary with breast size suggests that small-breasted women would be more erotically stimulated by the fondling of a particular amount of breast tissue than would large-breasted women. However, responsiveness to the stimulation of breasts—by both the receiver and the giver—is generally related far more to learning than to the size or shape of the breasts.

### The Lips

The interaction of cultural training and sexual responsiveness is demonstrated by a consideration of the erotic meaning of the lips. Pressing the lips against a partner's lips, inserting the tongue into a partner's mouth, and nibbling or sucking a partner's lips are important aspects of sexual intimacy and arousal in our culture.

The practice of touching mouths together for erotic pleasure is far from universal, however. Leonore Tiefer's (1978) fascinating review of the topic indicates that kissing—particularly deep kissing (in slang, "French," or "soul," kissing), which involves insertion of the tongue into another's mouth—is relatively rare cross-culturally. Tiefer concluded that the practice of deep kissing appears to be unrelated to the degree of sexual inhibition or repression in a specific culture. Some sexually permissive societies encourage their young people to practice sexual activity with a number of partners before selecting a mate, but exclude kissing from their repertoire of arousing activities, regarding the practice as dangerous, unhealthful, or disgusting.

Among Westerners who rely on kissing for erotic arousal, there are also many nonsexual reasons for the pressing together of lips. For instance, we kiss to greet and say good-bye to people toward whom we feel no erotic attachment or interest. We also kiss dice for luck, kiss children's injuries to comfort them, and kiss to seal bargains.

Almost all the parts of the sexual anatomy that we have been describing are strongly affected by the hormonal secretions of the endocrine system, to which we now turn.

## Hormones and the Endocrine System

The body has two kinds of glands: *endocrine*, or ductless, *glands* that secrete hormones directly into the bloodstream, and exocrine glands. Exocrine glands secrete substances into ducts that empty into body cavities and other body surfaces. Sweat glands, salivary glands, mammary glands, and digestive glands are examples of exocrine glands.

### The Endocrine Glands

The term *hormone* derives from the Greek word meaning "to set in motion" or "to activate." Hormones are carried by the blood throughout the entire body. The internal organs, glands, and the central nervous system can be affected by any hormones for which they have receptors. Six endocrine glands are directly involved in sexual functioning: the adrenal glands; the pituitary gland; the hypothalamus; the testes; the ovaries; and, when pregnancy occurs, the placenta (see Figure 5.9).

### The Adrenal Glands

The adrenal glands lie on top of the kidneys and are composed of two sections, the outer cortex and the inner medulla. The outer cortex secretes androgens (masculinizing hormones) and estrogens (feminizing hormones), along with other steroid hormones that are only indirectly related to sexual function. The inner medulla secretes epinephrine.

### The Pituitary Gland

The pituitary is a pea-size gland attached to the base of the brain and functionally connected to

**endocrine gland** (EN-doe-crin)—a ductless gland that discharges its products directly into the bloodstream.

**hormones** (HOR-mohnz)—the internal secretions of the endocrine glands that are distributed via the bloodstream.

changers"), stimulate the gonads (ovaries and testes). One of the gonadotropins is *follicle-stimulating hormone (FSH)*, which induces the ovarian follicles to mature. In the male, FSH stimulates sperm production in the testes beginning at puberty. The other gonadotropin is *luteinizing hormone (LH)*, which stimulates the female to ovulate and the male to secrete androgen from his testes.

Prolactin and oxytocin are two other hormones that come from the pituitary gland. Both are important in the production of breast milk. Prolactin stimulates the mammary glands in the breasts to manufacture milk, and oxytocin causes the release of milk from the glands so that it is available to the sucking infant. Oxytocin secretion also induces contraction of the uterus at birth and during nursing, an action that is helpful in getting a new mother's uterine muscles back into shape after she gives birth.

Oxytocin is also released by males and females during the orgasmic phase of sexual response (Carmichael, Walburton, Dixen, & Davidson, 1994). It may play a role in sperm transport in males as it contracts smooth muscles. In females it stimulates uterine contractions that may facilitate sperm transport (Carter, 1992).

### The Hypothalamus

As noted earlier, the functioning of the pituitary gland is under the direct control of the central nervous system through a network of blood vessels that links the pituitary with the hypothalamus. Some of the cells of the hypothalamus secrete substances that directly control the synthesis and storage of pituitary hormones. For example, cells of the hypothalamus secrete gonadotropin-releasing hormone (GnRH) through the system of blood vessels, prompting the pituitary to release gonadotropins, which in turn

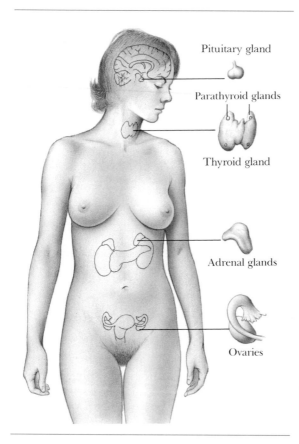

**FIGURE 5.9**
**The Endocrine Glands**
This figure shows the location of the adrenal glands, the pituitary gland, the ovaries, the thyroid gland, and the parathyroid glands.

the hypothalamus by a system of blood vessels and nerve fibers. The pituitary gland is largely controlled by the hypothalamus (see below). It secretes many different hormones, some of which stimulate the other endocrine glands to produce their hormones.

One of the pituitary hormones, growth hormone, stimulates the development and maturation of various body tissues. Two other pituitary hormones, *gonadotropins* (which means "gonad

**follicle-stimulating hormone (FSH)**—a gonadotropin that induces the maturation of the ovarian follicles in females and sperm production in males.

**luteinizing hormone (LH)**—a gonadotropin that stimulates female ovulation and male androgen secretion.

**gonadotropins** (goh-NAH-doe-TROE-pinz)—chemicals produced by the pituitary gland that stimulate the gonads.

### Box 5.2

## The Major Sex Hormones

**Androgens**   The general name for masculinizing sex hormones; the two most common are testosterone and androstetenedione. In males, most of the androgen is produced in the testes; a small portion (about 5%) is produced by the adrenal glands. In females, the ovaries and adrenal glands manufacture small amounts of androgen. Testosterone is considered to be the major biological determinant of sexual desire in men and women.

**Estrogens**   The general name for feminizing hormones that are secreted in the ovaries, testes, and placenta. Of the three major estrogens in humans, the most potent and abundant is estradiol. In both males and females, estradiol is metabolized within the body from progesterone of which the source is the steroidal substance cholesterol, from which the body derives all of its steroidal hormones. In females estrogens are important in maintaining the elasticity of the vagina and the texture and function of the breasts. They also contribute to the production of vaginal lubricant. In males the function of estrogens is unknown. Too much estrogen in males can result in diminished sexual desire, enlargement of the breasts, and difficulties with erection.

**Progestins**   The general name for hormones that prepare the reproductive organs for pregnancy. The most abundant of the progestins, progesterone, is produced by the corpus luteum of an ovary. Generally, progestins are active only in females because their effect is dependent on the previous action of estrogen. Males who receive estrogen and progesterone sequentially develop male mammary glands. Progesterone inhibits the flow of cervical mucus that occurs during ovulation, and it diminishes the thickness of the vaginal lining.

**Follicle-Stimulating Hormone (FSH)**   One of the gonadotropins (gonad-changers) secreted by the pituitary. Beginning at puberty, FSH stimulates the production of sperm cells in the testes in males and prepares the ovary for ovulation in females.

**Luteinizing Hormone (LH)**   Another gonadotropin that is produced by the pituitary. In females LH triggers ovulation, release of an egg from the ovary. In males it is sometimes referred to as interstitial cell stimulating hormone (ICSH) because it stimulates the interstitial (Leydig) cells of the testes to manufacture testosterone.

**Prolactin**   A hormone produced by the pituitary gland that stimulates the production of milk in the breasts.

**Oxytocin**   A pituitary hormone that causes milk to flow from the glandular tissue of the breast to the nipple in response to a baby's sucking and induces strong contractions during childbirth. It is also released by males and females during the orgasmic phase of sexual response.

**Vasoactive intestinal polypeptide (VIP)**   A peptide hormone involved in erection of the penis and vaginal blood flow during sexual arousal.

**Gonadotropin-Releasing Hormone (GnRH)**   A hormone produced by the hypothalamus that regulates the secretion of both follicle-stimulating hormone (FSH) and luteinizing hormone (LH) by the pituitary. GnRH is also called luteinizing hormone-releasing factor (LHRF).

**Inhibin**   A hormone produced by the testes that regulates sperm production by reducing the pituitary gland's secretion of FSH.

affect the activities of the gonads and their discharge of sex hormones. GnRH is also known as luteinizing hormone-releasing factor (LH-RF).

Two of the other endocrine glands directly involved in sexual functioning, the ovaries and the testes, were discussed earlier in this chapter.

Both the ovaries and the testes reach maturity during puberty through the action of the sex hormones. For a review of the known effects of these hormones, see Box 5.2.

Finally, there are more than a dozen neuropeptides that may be involved in sexual arousal (Levin, 1992). Peptide hormones are constructed of the same components of which proteins are made and function as *neurotransmitters*. Of these, vasoactive intestinal polypeptide (VIP), first isolated from the small intestine, has received the most empirical support for its role in the arousal of the sexual organs. VIP is involved in erection of the penis and in vaginal blood flow. The highest concentrations of VIP in the genital tracts are in the vagina and penis.

## The Effects of Hormones

The hypothalamus, pituitary, and gonads operate in continuous feedback loops, in which specific glands monitor levels of hormones and secrete substances that regulate the release of hormones from other glands. For example, the hypothalamus is sensitive to varying levels of circulating sex hormones. It monitors the levels of various hormones in the body and responds by either increasing or decreasing the rate of secretion of hormones or releasing factors. If the level of a particular hormone becomes too low, gonadotropins are discharged by the pituitary until the gonads produce enough sex hormone to signal a stop to gonadotropin secretion. Thus the brain, pituitary, and gonads interact continuously. Changes in one system lead to alterations in the other systems.

Hormones also affect the sex centers of the brain. In most female mammals, estrogen influences sexual attraction and receptivity, but in human females the estrogen level, if within the normal range, does not appear to affect sexual desire. Excessive estrogen, on the other hand, seems to reduce sexual desire in both men and women. Testosterone is evidently the hormone that plays the major role in the sexual desire by both males and females: when it is not present, there is little

sexual desire. However, research indicates that GnRH may enhance sexual desire in the absence of testosterone or in cases where testosterone is ineffective (Dornan & Malsbury, 1989).

The major difference between male and female sex-hormone secretion lies in the pattern of secretion. Females secrete estrogen in a cyclic pattern, resulting in the monthly rhythm of the menstrual cycle. Males secrete testosterone in a daily cycle with the highest levels typically occurring at night (Dabbs, 1990). These daily cycles are related to the time of year. Testosterone reaches a peak between July and November in males living in the northern hemisphere (Hoyenga & Hoyenga, 1993b).

Experiments have shown that these patterns are not controlled by a single gland. When female pituitaries are transplanted into male animals, the rate of the males' secretion of hormones is not affected. Similarly, transplanting a male pituitary into a female animal does not alter the characteristic cyclic pattern of female hormone secretion. The difference in the secretion of hormones, therefore, seems to reflect sex differences in the brain as a whole and does not appear to be a specific function of the pituitary (Gorski, 1987).

Most of the time, we go about our lives unaware of the efficient performance of our endocrine glands and of the effects of the hormones they secrete. One of the most dramatic demonstrations of the complex relationships between the activities of these glands, however, appears with the onset of the menstrual cycle in females. Most women can describe where they were and what they were doing at *menarche*. For a description of the particularly happy experience of one 13-year-old, see Box 5.3. The memories of many young women are unfortunately considerably less joyful, for the menarche is often an event shrouded in ignorance or negative expectations.

## The Menstrual Cycle

The menstrual cycle involves a highly intricate set of interactions of physiological processes, some of the details of which are beyond the scope of this book. The menstrual cycle can be conceptualized as a series of five overlapping processes:

---

**neurotransmitter**—one of many different body chemicals released by brain and nerve cells that carry messages between cells.

**menarche** (MEN-ark)—the first menstrual period.

**Box 5.3**

# Menarche and Maturity

The feelings I had the day I got my first period are clear to me. When I saw the blood on my underpants while in the bathroom at school, I felt scared. Then a surge of warmth ran all through me, and I caught myself smiling alone in the bathroom stall. I went to find my best friend. She went with me to the nurse's office. The nurse's scratchy voice seemed extra loud that day when she asked me if I wore tampons or napkins. I said quietly, "I don't know, this is my first time." She got me a belted napkin and went on explaining how to use it for what seemed like an eternity while I turned crimson. After that, I called my mom and said, "Guess what? I got my period!"

She shared and even increased my enthusiasm as she congratulated me and said,

"We'll have to celebrate tonight!" When my family was all seated around the dinner table that night, mom brought out a bottle of champagne and toasted me, saying, "You're a woman. Congratulations!" I felt a little embarrassed and I'm sure I blushed, but more than that I felt special, as if in that day I had matured years. I am especially thankful for my mother's response of delight and enthusiasm, which made my coming into womanhood as special and wonderful as it should be.

Source: Authors' files.

the *follicular phase*, *ovulation*, the *luteal phase*, the *premenstrual phase*, and *menstruation*. The complete cycle generally ranges from 21 to 35 days in length. A cycle longer than 35 days or shorter than 21 days is considered irregular. Each phase of the cycle is controlled by fluctuations in the kind and amount of hormones secreted into the bloodstream from the ovaries, the pituitary, and the brain (see Figure 5.10).

**follicular phase**—menstrual-cycle stage during which FSH stimulates the growth of the ovarian follicles.

**ovulation**—the release of a mature egg from an ovary.

**luteal phase**—menstrual-cycle stage following ovulation during which growth of the uterine lining is stimulated by the secretion of progesterone from the corpus luteum.

**premenstrual phase**—the six days prior to menstruation when the corpus luteum begins to disintegrate if the egg has not been fertilized.

**menstruation**—the sloughing of the uterus's endometrial lining, which is discharged through the vaginal opening.

The fact that a woman produces only about two tablespoons of estrogen and progesterone over her entire life span reveals the potency of the sex hormones. These hormones are primarily responsible for the development of the uterine lining, which nurtures an egg in the event that it is fertilized; if the egg is not fertilized, the subsequent drop in the levels of these hormones results in the disintegration and discharge of the uterine lining (menstruation). FSH stimulates the growth of the follicle that contains the ovum; the cells of this follicle secrete estrogen as they grow. LH then triggers the release of the ovum (ovulation) from the follicle, the conversion of the ruptured follicle into a corpus luteum, and the secretion of progesterone.

### The Follicular Phase

The follicular phase lasts from 7 to 19 days, and it is controlled by sensitivity of the ovary to FSH. At about the time menstruation (uterine discharge) begins, the production of estrogen and progesterone drops. The low levels of these hormones bring about an increase in ovarian

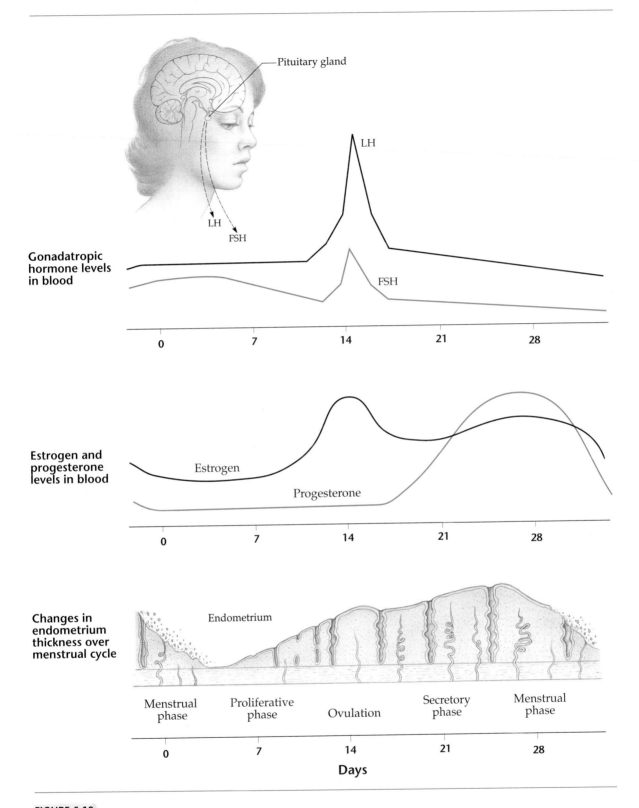

**Gonadatropic hormone levels in blood**

Pituitary gland

LH

FSH

LH

FSH

0    7    14    21    28

**Estrogen and progesterone levels in blood**

Estrogen

Progesterone

0    7    14    21    28

**Changes in endometrium thickness over menstrual cycle**

Endometrium

| Menstrual phase | Proliferative phase | Ovulation | Secretory phase | Menstrual phase |

0    7    14    21    28

**Days**

**FIGURE 5.10**

**The Menstrual Cycle and Hormonal Fluctuations**

This figure shows the cyclical secretion of LH, FSH, estrogen, and progesterone during the menstrual cycle. Changes in the endometrial thickness are also shown.

sensitivity to FSH. FSH causes 6 to 12 follicles to start growing within the ovaries—the phenomenon from which the follicular phase gets its name. Normally, only one of these follicles reaches the mature stage.

As the follicle grows, its cells secrete estrogen. After several days, the estrogen level in the blood reaches the point of creating a relative insensitivity of the ovary to FSH. The high levels of estrogen prompt the hypothalamus to release Gn-RH, which stimulates the LH surge shown earlier in Figure 5.10.

By way of analogy, just as a decrease in temperature signals a thermostat to turn on the heat in your house, a drop in the level of estrogen in a woman's system at the time of uterine bleeding signals the hypothalamus to secrete Gn-RH. In turn, Gn-RH prompts the pituitary to secrete FSH and LH. The FSH then brings about the growth of the follicle, and the LH signals the follicle to produce estrogen and secrete it into the bloodstream. The rise in the estrogen level in the bloodstream directs the pituitary to stop releasing FSH, just as an increase in the temperature in a home signals a thermostat to turn off the furnace.

### Ovulation

About 18 hours after the LH surge, the mature follicle in the ovary ruptures and releases the developing ovum. This process is called ovulation. The ovum enters the fallopian tube, where it may be fertilized by a sperm. Some women are able to feel the rupturing of the follicle releasing the ovum from the ovary: a sharp twinge known as *mittelschmerz* (German, "middle pain"). But most women must rely on other methods to determine the date of ovulation (see Chapter 9).

### The Luteal Phase

The luteal phase lasts from 8 to 10 days. Following ovulation, the ruptured follicle, known in its empty state as the *corpus luteum* ("yellow

body"), secretes progesterone, starting the luteal phase. Progesterone stimulates the growth of the endometrium (the uterine lining) in preparation for the egg if it is fertilized.

### The Premenstrual Phase

Women vary in their awareness of the premenstrual phase, which lasts approximately from four to six days. Some experience a sense of heaviness or aching in the pelvic area and at times some depression. In the absence of fertilization, the corpus luteum begins to disintegrate, producing a decrease in the levels of both progesterone and estrogen.

### Menstruation

Menstruation—the disintegration and discharge of part of the endometrium—goes on for about three to seven days. This part of the menstrual cycle results from a decrease in progesterone and estrogen. The lining of the uterus, containing blood, nutrients, and mucus, is discharged through the cervix and vagina to the vaginal opening.

In describing the menstrual cycle, we started with the follicular phase, as if the menstrual cycle proceeded in a linear fashion, with the follicular phase representing the first phase and menstruation representing the last phase. The menstrual cycle is continuous, however, and thus is more accurately represented by a set of overlapping circles than by a line with a beginning and an end point. For instance, before the end of the premenstrual phase, the follicular phase begins again, with prompting of the growth of follicles in the ovary opposite the one that released a follicle the previous month.

Although the menstrual cycle does not really begin with any one phase, the first day on which menstrual blood appears is counted as day one of the cycle simply because this is the easiest way to keep track of the phases. Monitoring the menstrual cycle is useful for purposes of becoming pregnant, avoiding pregnancy, or determining whether one's cycle has suddenly changed (a circumstance that might indicate either pregnancy or disease).

---

**corpus luteum** (COR-pus LOO-tee-um)—the cell mass that remains after a follicle has released an egg; it secretes progesterone and estrogen.

The complex relationship between the sexual organs and the endocrine system cannot be fully understood without considering the nervous system. It coordinates the menstrual cycle as well as other sexual and reproductive events.

## The Nervous System

As you read this text, you are probably not paying much attention to such life-sustaining activities as breathing, the pumping of blood by your heart, and the activity of your digestive system. Although you can deliberately affect these and a number of other bodily activities, most of the time they go on without any conscious choices on your part. Such bodily functions are controlled by nerves that extend to every organ in the body.

We can divide the nervous system into a number of different components. The peripheral nervous system and the central nervous system are the two major components. The *central nervous system* includes the brain and spinal cord. The *peripheral nervous system* includes the nerves and ganglia (clusters of cell bodies) that provide input to and output from the sense organs, muscles, glands, and internal organs in communication with the central nervous system.

Many bodily functions are directed by the autonomic portion of the peripheral nervous system. The word *autonomic* means "autonomous," or independent. The *autonomic nervous system* derives its name from its independent control of involuntary functions. Its network of nerves extends to various internal parts of the body and exercises control over glands, smooth muscles, and the heart. It also regulates urination and def-

ecation. We learn to control our elimination processes during the second or third year of life, but these functions would still be carried out if we did not learn to control them.

## The Sympathetic and Parasympathetic Components of the Autonomic Nervous System

Sexual functioning is intricately tied to the subdivisions of the autonomic nervous system: the sympathetic and parasympathetic systems. These two systems differ from one another in both structure and function. Although they affect many of the same organs, they usually act in an antagonistic manner.

The *sympathetic nervous system* prepares the body to deal with emergency situations. It prepares us for "fight or flight." The system speeds up the heart, sends blood to the muscles, and releases sugar from the liver for quick energy. It can be activated by threat or by sexual arousal.

In contrast, the *parasympathetic nervous system* predominates when we are relaxed and inactive or when an emergency has passed. The parasympathetic system carries out a variety of maintenance needs. It promotes digestion, provides for the elimination of wastes, directs tissue repair, and generally restores the supply of body energy.

In sexual arousal, the two systems take turns in influencing sexual response. The initial arousal and penile erection of an erotically stimulated male primarily result from the firing of the parasympathetic nerves, which causes the arteries in the penis to dilate so that blood can rush in. The system primarily involved in periods of relaxation is also responsible for initial sexual arousal. The sympathetic nervous system, which figures in intense arousal, then becomes dominant. It

---

**central nervous system**—the part of the nervous system that consists of the brain and spinal cord.

**peripheral nervous system**—the part of the nervous system outside the brain and spinal cord.

**autonomic nervous system**—the system of nerve cells and fibers that regulates involuntary actions such as smooth-muscle and glandular activity.

**sympathetic nervous system**—the part of the autonomic nervous system that is active in emotional or physical excitement and stress.

**parasympathetic nervous system**—the part of the autonomic nervous system that is active in relaxed or quiescent states of the body.

appears likely that parasympathetic stimulation causes the sympathetic nerve fibers to close off valves in the penis, thus reducing the flow of blood out of the penis (Batra & Lue, 1990).

Ejaculation is carried out primarily by the sympathetic nervous system, with some help from nerve fibers that are partially under voluntary control. Ejaculation of semen consists of two phases: emission and expulsion. During the emission phase, seminal fluid and the glandular secretions of the prostate are moved by muscular contractions from the epididymis through the vas deferens to the base of the penis. This movement is under the control of the sympathetic nervous system. After emission, nerves more responsive to voluntary control produce the muscular contractions that propel semen out of the penis. This event, known as the expulsion phase, also involves movements of the pelvic muscles and other portions of the body. Shortly after ejaculation, the penis begins to become flaccid. The action of the sympathetic nerves accompanying ejaculation constricts the arteries in the penis. The accumulated blood then flows out of the penis through veins.

Both processes—emission and expulsion—take far longer to read about than to experience. Emission occurs just before ejaculation. For a man who is about to ejaculate, emission is experienced as the point of no return, or, more formally, the sense of ejaculatory inevitability. Research by Bohlen, Held, and Sanderson (1980) indicated, however, that a man's awareness of the onset of orgasm can occur as long as seven seconds before orgasmic contractions begin.

We have used male sexual arousal and response to describe the interactions of the sympathetic and parasympathetic nervous systems, partially because little research has centered on the working of these two parts of the autonomic nervous system in female sexual arousal. It has been assumed that the swelling of various parts of the female vulva and vagina and subsequent lubrication lie primarily under the control of the parasympathetic nervous system. The sympathetic nervous system becomes dominant at orgasm (Levin, 1992).

The fact that anxiety or fear is common to most sexual dysfunctions can be explained in terms of the different roles of the sympathetic and parasympathetic nervous systems. Anxiety or fear activates the sympathetic nervous system, which can interfere with the functioning of the parasympathetic nervous system by blocking the relaxation needed for initial sexual arousal (erection, lubrication).

## The Central Nervous System

The central nervous system (CNS) coordinates all bodily functions and behavior. The CNS consists of the spinal cord and its enlarged ending, the brain. The CNS generates, transmits, and receives impulses from other nerves. It is the processing unit for all components of the nervous system.

Networks of nerves within the CNS are organized into hierarchical schemes to serve certain functions; that is, higher centers exert control over lower ones. Such human sexual responses as ejaculation, erection, and vaginal lubrication are influenced by reflex centers located in the lower centers. Anatomically, these functions are controlled by nerves located toward the lower end of the spinal column. These reflex centers control the same processes in our primate vertebrate ancestors (animals with segmented spinal columns). As the human brain evolved, these reflex centers were influenced and modified by higher centers located in the brain. Some of our reflexes—for example, ejaculation and orgasm—can be influenced by our thought processes and can therefore be brought under some degree of voluntary control.

Other reflexes operate on an involuntary basis. For instance, we usually cannot decide to produce an erection of the nipples or penis. We cannot simply choose to make our genitals fill with blood (vasocongestion) to produce erection or vaginal lubrication. Many factors do affect the lower reflex centers, however, and thus can influence sexual response, whether the particular response is voluntary or involuntary.

Among these factors are various thought processes in the brain. Although we cannot directly command our genitals to respond sexually, we can think about, or discuss with a partner, erotic situations that may, in turn, produce erection or lubrication. Alternatively, sexual response can be inhibited by thoughts of pregnancy, punishment, or interruption. In fact, one of the strat-

sensations are actually felt, and down the cord to muscles and other organs, where actions are carried out. The brain and spinal cord thus work together as an integrated unit.

The spinal cord is divided into segments and numbered relative to the spinal vertebrae (see Figure 5.11). Different segments are associated with specific functions. For instance, when a man's genitals are touched erotically, spinal cord segments S2, S3, and S4 (the S stands for sacral segment) produce a reflexive response mediated by the parasympathetic nervous system.

A second penile erection center is located higher in the spinal cord, in segments T11 through L2 (T stands for thoracic, and L stands for lumbar), which are part of the sympathetic nervous system. This center is affected by brain activity such as thinking or fantasizing about sex.

Responses involved in ejaculation also have dual locations on the spinal cord. The first phase of ejaculation, seminal emission, is triggered by the sympathetic segment of the spinal cord (segments T11 through L2). The second phase of ejaculation, expulsion, is triggered by segments S2 through S4 and can be voluntarily controlled. Individuals whose spinal cords have been severed may be able to respond to stimulation of the penis with ejaculation, although they feel no genital sensation when it occurs; that is, ejaculation can occur without erection, just as erection can occur without ejaculation.

In the erotic response of males, two nerves running from the genitals to segments S2 through S4 of the spinal cord appear to be important. One of these, the *pudendal nerve*, transmits sensations arising from stimulation of the surface of the penis. The other, the *pelvic nerve*, relays sensations of sexual tension from within the corpora cavernosa and corpus spongiosum inside the penis. Because a reflex center higher up in the spinal cord mediates these sexual responses and transmits them to the brain, these involuntary reflexes

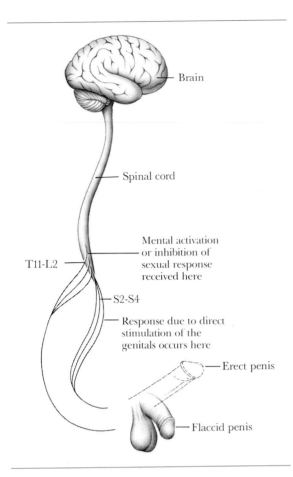

**FIGURE 5.11**
**The Spinal Cord and Sexual Response**
The spinal cord is intimately involved in sexual response. Different portions of the spine transmit sensory and mental stimulation.

egies that is used by some men who ejaculate sooner than they want to is to focus on non-erotic thoughts or tasks (for example, mental arithmetic or unpleasant situations) to try to forestall ejaculation.

*The Spinal Cord*

The spinal cord is crucial in sexual response. It is a thick cable of nerves that extends through the interior of the bony spinal column to and from the brain. The spinal cord carries nerve fibers in both directions—up the cord to the brain, where

**pudendal nerve**—the nerve that passes from the external genitals through spinal cord segments S2 through S4, transmitting sensations from the genitals.
**pelvic nerve**—the parasympathetic nerve involved in involuntary sexual responses of the genital organs.

may be modified by specific learned experiences or emotional states.

### The Brain

The enlarged mass at the top of the spinal cord—the brain—is the culmination of our evolutionary development. It is one of nature's most complex structures, and the extent of its development sets humans apart from all other species. Most of our knowledge about brain function comes from research with animals, however, because ethical-review boards generally prohibit experimental research involving surgery on the human brain.

Most brain structures play some role in our sexual functioning. We focus here on those shown to have the most direct effects on sexual behavior. The major portions of the brain are the hindbrain, the midbrain, and the forebrain (see Figure 5.12).

The hindbrain is believed to be the earliest part of the brain to have evolved because it is found in even the most primitive vertebrates. In humans, it is located at the base of the skull where the spinal cord emerges from the spinal column, and it forms the lower part of the brain.

The medulla, which is the part of the hindbrain nearest the spinal cord, contains cell bodies that control breathing, heart rate, and blood pressure. The medulla also acts as a relay and routing station for various nerve fibers. Animal experiments suggest that this area plays a role in sexual receptivity. When progesterone is implanted in the medulla of female rats, they lift their tails and squat down as they normally do when they come into heat.

The midbrain, as the name implies, lies between the base of the brain and the top of the brain (forebrain). It contains cell bodies that either trigger immediate responses or relay information to more complex parts of the brain.

The forebrain contains a number of structures that are important for sexual functioning, including the thalamus, the hypothalamus, and the cerebrum. The *thalamus* acts as a relay sta-

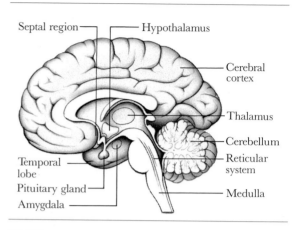

**FIGURE 5.12**
**Side View of the Human Brain**
Most of the structures and processes affecting sexual behavior are centered in the forebrain. The medulla is part of the hindbrain, and the reticular activating system extends from the hindbrain through the midbrain and into the forebrain. The remaining structures shown here are part of the forebrain.

tion for incoming messages from the sense organs to the outer layer of the cerebrum. The nerve pathways involved in transmitting and relaying tactile information to the forebrain are also involved in ejaculation. Stimulation of certain areas in the thalamus and along a nerve tract that enters the thalamus produces ejaculation.

The *amygdala* is a complex collection of cell groups adjacent to the temporal lobe. It was named in the 19th century for a supposed resemblance to an almond (Latin: *amygdelum*). The amygdala is thought to play an important role in the regulation of a number of primary emotional states, including sexual arousal. Among its roles, it appears that the amygdala interprets sensory information for its emotional significance. Is the stimulus aversive or rewarding? Damage to the amygdala is associated with hyposexuality which results from the inability to appreciate the significance of sensory stimuli (LeVay, 1993).

thalamus—the major brain center involved in the transmission of sensory impulses to the cerebral cortex.

amygdala—brain center involved in the regulation of sexual motivation.

The hypothalamus, although only about the size of a marble, contains cells that regulate body temperature, eating, drinking, and sexual behavior. Parts of the hypothalamus are important in the control of milk production and the reproductive cycles in females and can affect the manufacture of masculinizing hormones. As noted earlier, the hypothalamus is connected to the pituitary gland, which is involved in the production of sex hormones. The hypothalamus also plays a role in erection and in orgasmic response. The fact that damage to the hypothalamic regions of the human brain can produce either extreme sexual desire or loss of interest in sex suggests the existence of a region that regulates sexual behavior.

A group of neurons in the anterior hypothalamus has been reported to be on average twice as large in heterosexual men as in either women or homosexual men (LeVay, 1991; 1993). Although much more research needs to be done, this finding suggests that the hypothalamus may be involved in sexual orientation.

Electrical stimulation of centers in the hypothalamus regulating sexual behavior has brought about dramatic changes in the sexual activity of animals. Moreover, a few scattered reports based on observations of human neurological patients indicate that similar stimulation of the human brain can produce sexual feelings and thoughts. These patients had wire electrodes implanted in specific regions of the brain as part of therapy for various medical or mental problems. Low levels of electric current were passed through the electrodes to stimulate the small bit of brain tissue surrounding the electrode tip, with patients fully conscious and able to report their sensations. Only one study that we are aware of has reported electrical stimulation to orgasm by electrodes in men, and they were suffering from mental disorders (Sem-Jacobsen, 1968). Because participants in this research did not include "normal" men or women, it is not known whether the findings would apply to the general population.

The hypothalamus contains both pleasure and pain centers that are probably intimately connected with sexual response. Experiments with the pleasure centers in the brain were first described by J. Olds and P. M. Milner in 1954. Rats were given access to a lever that could deliver a brief pulse of electric current to a thin wire electrode implanted in the brain. If the electrode tip was in one of the so-called pleasure centers of the brain, the rats repeatedly pressed the lever. They chose to stimulate their brains in preference to eating, drinking, and other activities. One rat pressed the lever as often as 5,000 times an hour.

Research has indicated that the cells of the pleasure center respond to endorphins, a special class of molecules manufactured by brain cells. These molecules act on brain cells in much the same way as do morphine and other opiates, producing euphoria and alleviating pain.

Close to these pleasure centers are systems that, if stimulated, produce unpleasant feelings. These pain centers are crucial to our survival, and it makes evolutionary sense that they take priority over areas associated with pleasure. Attending to sexual desire rather than to a threat would leave us vulnerable. Thus the pain centers of the brain inhibit sexual desire when we experience physical harm, anticipate danger, or undergo severe stress (Dornan & Malsbury, 1989).

The most recently evolved and physically prominent part of the human brain is the *cerebrum*, which balloons out over the rest of the brain. The surface layer of the cerebrum is called the cerebral cortex. The cerebrum is divided into two nearly symmetrical halves, called the cerebral hemispheres. Each of the cerebral hemispheres is, in turn, divided into four sections, or lobes.

The cerebral cortex is at the top of the hierarchical scheme of the nervous system and is involved in the complex functions of perception, learning, thinking, and language. Thus it can facilitate or inhibit the sexual response systems found lower in the CNS. Erotic fantasies, daydreams, and memories of pleasant sexual experiences are processed by the cortex and can produce arousal. Penfield (1975) reported an area in the frontal lobes (near the forehead) that seems to have some influence over the genitals. Generally, however, the entire cortex is concerned with the control and integration of sexual behavior.

cerebrum—the surface layer of cell bodies that constitutes the bulk of the brain in humans.

For simplicity in describing the brain's physical structure, we have divided this remarkable organ into the hindbrain, midbrain, and forebrain. These classifications are only of limited use, however, in describing brain functioning because some systems within the brain are not limited to one area of the brain. One such system is called the *reticular activating system (RAS)*, which is the arousal center of the brain. Beginning in the hindbrain, the RAS extends through the midbrain and sends its fibers up to the forebrain. When it is stimulated, a person seems to become receptive to sexual stimulation. People have reported experiencing relatively long periods of sexual stimulation under the influence of drugs such as cocaine and amphetamines, which affect the RAS (Rosen, 1991).

The *limbic system* is another example of a functional entity within the brain that is not confined to just one area. It consists of a ring of structures in the center of each cerebral hemisphere. The limbic system includes the amygdala, hypothalamus, part of the thalamus, and several other forebrain structures that lie inside the cortex. The limbic system also contains nerve fibers that connect it to the hindbrain. Stimulation of parts of the limbic system in male animals produces erection, mounting, and grooming behavior; pleasure centers have been found near these sites. Stimulation of other parts of the limbic system provokes aggressive behavior.

Destruction of portions of the limbic system causes nonaggressive, trusting, and highly erotic behavior in monkeys—a set of behaviors called the Klüver-Bucy syndrome, after the scientists who described it. Half a century ago, Heinrich Klüver and Paul Bucy of the University of Chicago reported striking alterations in the behavior of rhesus monkeys following extensive damage to the lower portion of the limbic ring. The monkeys tried to mount a variety of inappropriate sexual partners, including the experimenters who were studying them. The monkeys also became quite gentle, an unusual characteristic for these creatures unless they are tamed when young. In a film of the monkeys' postoperative behavior, one was shown sitting on Dr. Klüver's shoulder and then shifting to a position at the back of his neck, where it engaged in pelvic thrusts. Destruction of parts of the limbic system in the temporal lobes, as well as the amygdala, produces the Klüver-Bucy syndrome in other species. In one case, a male cat was observed attempting to copulate with a dog, a chicken, and a small monkey (Valenstein, 1973).

The limbic system is also involved in the sense of smell in most species, including humans. The close relationship between arousal and smell in some animals reinforces the idea that the limbic system is connected to sexual response. When dogs or cats are in heat, they secrete substances called *pheromones* that sexually stimulate members of the other sex of their species when they are detected through the sense of smell. Researchers have proposed that humans also secrete pheromones. So far, the only evidence for any impact of pheromones on humans is that the menstrual cycles of women living in close proximity become synchronized (McClintock, 1971; Haynes, 1994). The mechanism producing this synchrony is unknown, but when women in one study were exposed to the underarm odor of a female stranger, their menstrual cycles became synchronized with that of the stranger (Preti et al., 1986), a development suggesting that pheromones secreted by glands under the arms may be partially responsible.

The intricate physiology of sexual response goes unnoticed by most of us in our day-to-day lives. When these processes are disturbed by illness, we become aware of functions that we no longer take for granted. In the next section, we describe several illnesses that affect sexual functioning.

**reticular activating system (RAS)**—the system of nerve paths within the brain that is involved in arousal.

**limbic system**—the set of structures around the midbrain involved in regulating emotional and motivational behaviors.

**pheromones** (FARE-oh-mohnz)—externally secreted chemical substances to which other members of a common species respond.

## Illness and Disease

Cancer, heart disease, and diabetes can deal a devastating blow to the morale—and to the life expectancy—of the millions of North Americans who become affected by these conditions each year. Healthy people sometimes avoid individuals who have these diseases because dealing with illnesses or handicaps makes them uneasy. The fact that cancer, heart disease, and diabetes patients remain sexual beings with the capacity for love, intimacy, and sexual response does not occur to some observers. Diseases and disabilities that threaten an individual's ability to remain sexually active can occur at any stage of life, although the likelihood of their onset rises with age.

## Cancer

Cancers of the breast in women and of the prostate gland in men are among the most common forms of cancer in adults. In this section we examine the impact on sexuality of these cancers as well as uterine, cervical, and testicular cancers.

### Breast Cancer

There is perhaps no more profound demonstration of the value we attach to breasts as symbolic of female attractiveness than the reaction of many women to the diagnosis of breast cancer. The discovery of any cancerous condition is frightening, and the source of terror is typically the fear of impending death. With breast cancer, however, fear of breast loss and mutilation often outweighs fear of remaining malignancy and death. As one writer observed, "It is an outrage to have one's breast turn cancerous. The change in breast tissue from life-giving to life-threatening is a betrayal, a form of somatic treason" (Gates, 1988, p. 148). For a poignant account of one woman's reaction to the diagnosis of breast cancer, see Betty Rollin's book *First You Cry* (1976).

Mildred Witkin (1975), a sex therapist, wrote some specific suggestions to help breast cancer patients and their partners through the adjustment period following mastectomy and the re-

sumption of sexual intimacy. A few of these are presented in Box 5.4. Because each partner may fear a negative response from the other, it is important that they communicate their positive and negative feelings about the cancer before, during, and after surgery (Schultz et al., 1992).

One in eight U.S. women get breast cancer by the time they are 85, and 183,000 new cases were estimated for 1993, with 1,000 of these expected in men. Killing 46,000 women (and 300 men) in 1993, breast cancer is the second leading cause of cancer deaths among women (Bowen, Urban, Carrell, & Kinne, 1993). With early detection and treatment, 93% of women with localized breast cancer survive for at least five years after treatment (American Cancer Society, 1993). If the cancer is noninvasive, the survival rate is almost 100%, and even when the cancer is invasive and has spread, the survival rate is 71%.

Breast cancer is rare among women under the age of 25, but the incidence climbs steadily from that age on. The spread of breast cancer may be accelerated by increased hormone secretion during pregnancy. The use of oral contraceptives, however, is not associated with the development of breast cancer. Breast cancer is more common among women from families with a history of breast cancer, early menstruators, and those who go through late menopause. First childbirth after the age of 30, childlessness, and obesity are also associated with developing breast cancer.

**Detection and Diagnosis**   At age 20, women should begin engaging in monthly breast self-examinations (BSEs). BSEs increase the likelihood that women will detect cancerous lumps before they have spread beyond the readily treatable stage (see Box 5.5), but 80% of breast lumps are nonmalignant. The rate of monthly BSEs is higher among women who have benign breast disease (49%) than among those with prior breast cancer (34%) and a control group of women (32%). Among women with a family history of breast cancer, the increased practice of monthly BSEs was associated only with a woman's having had breast cancer herself (Hill & Shugg, 1989).

Early detection of a lump through monthly BSEs improves one's chance of survival. Because

**Box 5.4**

## Sexual Intimacy After Mastectomy

Mildred Witkin, a sex therapist who underwent two mastectomies 20 years apart, has described her experience in an article we recommend for women with breast cancer and for their families. She wrote that because the emotional trauma of mastectomy is worse than the physical trauma, the woman's recovery is strongly affected by the reactions of her husband or lover. Witkin's first mastectomy was followed by the near collapse of her marriage. Her husband had been advised to treat the operation, and her, matter-of-factly. Displays of concern or special care were to be avoided, because these behaviors might encourage dependency and fears that the prognosis for survival was gloomy. Witkin says that she interpreted her husband's behavior as coldness and rejection of her because of the surgery. She described her second mastectomy, in contrast, as a victorious experience that deepened and intensified the relationship she had with her husband. She reported that a mastectomized woman is

*left with a feeling of numbness that extends from the breast area around to the back. The area is not totally devoid of sensation but [there is] an unpleasant feeling of "wrongness" when stroked or contacted with too much pressure. It takes from 6 months to a year or more for the pain and unpleasantness to be relieved, and with some women, the unpleasant feeling never really disappears. Very light kisses by the husband on the area of the missing breast may not be felt by the wife physically, but will be experienced by her as a sign of great love. (1975, p. 297)*

Witkin recommends the resumption of sexual relations within a week after the surgery or as soon as the woman feels physically able. Witkin describes several coital positions that permit lovemaking without straining the surgical wound. She discourages the use of a prosthesis (false breast) during intercourse because it allows the couple to delay confronting and dealing with the mastectomy. Finally, Witkin advises sex-therapy exercises, including body imagery and sensate focus, to ease the couple's confrontation and acceptance of the mastectomy.

most breast lumps are painless, some time may elapse before a woman detects a lump unless she performs BSEs routinely. More than 90% of all breast cancers are self-diagnosed.

When they reach age 40, women are advised to obtain a baseline mammogram, which involves an X-ray technique called *mammography*. In their 40s, women should have a mammogram every other year unless they are in one of the high-risk groups, in which case a mammogram

**mammography** (mam-MAW-graf-ee)—a technique for X-raying the breasts to detect the presence or absence of a tumor.

should be obtained each year. Beginning at age 50, an annual mammogram is recommended (American Cancer Society, 1993).

Some women avoid mammograms because they believe that the procedure is painful. The mammogram involves placing the breast on a clear plastic surface; another sheet of plastic is then placed on top of the breast, which is then X-rayed. The breast is then positioned between two vertical plastic surfaces and again X-rayed (see Figure 5.13). The pressure on the breast is sometimes a bit uncomfortable for the several seconds needed to take the diagnostic photograph, but the discomfort—if any—disappears immediately when the plastic surfaces are removed. If cancer is present, early detection allows for far less

## Box 5.5

## Breast Self-Examination

### 1. Before a Mirror

Facing the mirror, inspect your breasts with arms at your sides. Next, raise your arms high overhead. Look for changes in the contour of each breast: a swelling, dimpling of skin, or changes in the nipple. Left and right breast will not exactly match: few women's breasts do. Then rest your palms on your hips and press down firmly to flex your chest muscles. Again, look for changes and irregularities. Regular inspection reveals what is normal for you and will give you confidence in your examination.

breast. Check for any lump, hard ~~ot, or thickening.

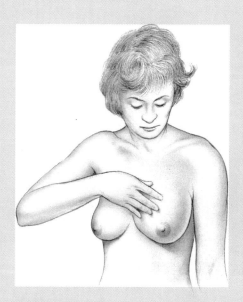

### 3. Lying Down

To examine your right breast, put a pillow or folded towel under your right shoulder. Place your right hand behind your back; adopting this position distributes breast tissue more evenly on the chest. With the left hand, fingers flat, press gently in small circular motions around an imaginary clock face. Begin at the outermost top of your right breast for twelve o'clock, then move to one o'clock and so on around the circle back to twelve. (A ridge of firm tissue in the lower curve of each breast is normal.) Then move 1 inch inward, toward the nipple. Keep circling to examine every part of your breast, including the nipple. A thorough inspection will require at least three more circles. Now slowly repeat the procedure on your left breast with a pillow under your left shoulder and your left hand behind your head. Notice how your breast structure feels. Finally, squeeze the nipple of each breast gently

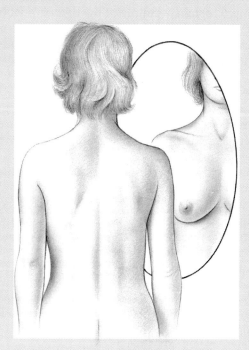

### 2. In the Shower

Examine your breasts during your bath or shower, because your hands will glide more easily over wet than dry skin. Hold your fingers flat and move them gently over every part of each breast. Use the right hand to examine the left breast and the left hand for the right

between the thumb and index finger. Immediately report any discharge, clear or bloody, to your doctor.

Periodic self-examination of the breasts is recommended for men as well as for women. Most lumps are benign, but if one is discovered, it is best to see a physician for a more thorough examination.

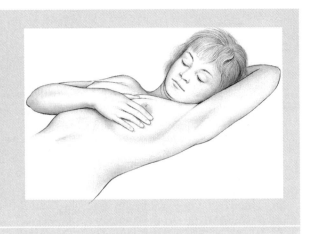

Source: American Cancer Society.

**FIGURE 5.13**
**Mammography**
Although women should perform a breast self-examination (BSE) monthly, they should obtain a baseline mammogram by age 40. Mammograms permit detection of tumors that are too small to be felt during a BSE.

invasive (and less painful) treatment than if the cancer spreads beyond the early stages.

If a breast lump is discovered, the person should immediately see a physician. Often the presence or absence of cancer can be determined simply by insertion of a hollow needle into the lump to obtain a sample of the tissue for laboratory analysis. Or the physician may *biopsy* a suspicious lump—that is, remove it from the breast in a surgical operation requiring anesthesia.

**Treatment**   If a biopsy reveals signs of a *malignancy*, treatment almost always involves surgery to remove the affected area. The traditional treatment for breast cancer has been radical *mastectomy*. This procedure involves the surgical removal of the entire breast, the underlying tissue and muscle, and the lymph nodes under the arms. But this extreme surgical approach is no longer the preferred treatment for breast cancer, except in rare cases. The most common contemporary treatment is the modified radical mastectomy, which does not involve removing all of the underlying muscles or all of the lymph nodes. *Radiation* therapy, *chemotherapy*, or hormone therapy (or some combination of these) may also be recommended.

**biopsy**—surgical removal of tissue for diagnostic purposes.

**malignancy**—a cancerous growth.

**mastectomy**—surgery involving removal of a breast.

**radiation**—treatment of an illness by directing X-rays at a malignancy to kill cancer cells.

**chemotherapy**—treatment of an illness through the use of chemicals.

If there is no evidence that the cancer has spread beyond the tumor, a *lumpectomy* may be performed. In this procedure, the breast is left intact, and the surgery is confined to the removal of the malignant tumor and some surrounding tissue.

In considering whether to have a mastectomy or the less invasive lumpectomy, the patient should seek the opinions of more than one physician. In recognition of the appropriateness of obtaining a second opinion, many insurance policies now cover this additional expense. Comparative studies of mastectomy and lumpectomy treatments found that the less invasive method was associated with fewer adverse effects on body image, fewer fears of disfigurement, and a less-impaired sense of femininity (Schultz et al., 1992).

Regardless of the type of treatment, two-thirds of women with breast cancer are able to master the crisis and resume sexual activity. Psychological factors are assumed to play a major role for those who do not adjust sexually (Schultz et al., 1992).

Recent developments in breast reconstruction have increased the choices for women who have been treated for breast cancer. Researchers have found that the sooner after treatment that breast cancer reconstruction begins, the less psychological distress and sexual dissatisfaction (Schultz et al., 1992).

### Gynecological Cancers

In 1993 it was estimated that 44,500 cases of uterine cancer would be diagnosed, with 10,000 deaths expected from the disease. Of the uterine-cancer diagnoses, cancer of the endometrium—the lining of the uterus—was expected to account for 31,000 cases; cancer of the cervix, for the remaining 13,500. An estimated 5,700 deaths from endometrial cancer and 4,400 from cervical cancer were expected in 1993 (American Cancer Society, 1993).

Cervical cancer is most readily treated in its early stages. To improve the chances of early detection, women should get a Papanicolaou smear (PAP test) done at least once a year beginning in their late teens or at the point when they become sexually active. The PAP test screens for cervical cancer and other cervical infections. The procedure involves the removal of cervical mucus with a small wooden spatula. The mucus is then placed on a glass plate, stained, and examined under a microscope for the presence of cancerous and precancerous cells. Overall, the death rate for uterine cancer has decreased more than 70% in the past 40 years. This dramatic decline is attributable to early detection through the PAP test and regular checkups (American Cancer Society, 1993).

Cervical cancer occurs most frequently in women who begin having sexual intercourse at a young age, who have a large number of sexual partners, and who have particular sexually transmitted diseases. The reason for the relationship among cervical cancer, age, and number of partners is not known, but it is possible that the more partners a woman has, the greater her risk of exposure to various infections that irritate the cervix and vagina. Although the genital-herpes virus has been a prime suspect in cervical cancer, recent research has implicated the papilloma virus as a causative agent. This virus, which causes genital warts (see Chapter 17), has been present in 90% of cervical-cancer samples that have been studied (Koutsky et al., 1992). Most investigators believe that if the papilloma virus is the culprit, it does not act alone. Cervical cancer is also more common among women who smoke, who are obese, and who were exposed prenatally to DES (see Chapter 2). Research is under way to identify other factors that contribute to the risk of cervical cancer.

For women diagnosed with cervical cancer, the five-year survival rate is 66%. If cervical cancer is diagnosed and treated early, before it has spread beyond the cervix, the five-year survival rate is 89%, and if it is noninvasive, the rate is almost 100% (American Cancer Society, 1993). Treatment depends on the stage at which the cancer is discovered. It may involve hysterectomy followed by radiation, or, if the disease is detected early, destruction of the cancerous cells

---

**lumpectomy**—surgical procedure in which a malignant breast tumor and surrounding tissue are removed while the rest of the breast is left intact.

through extreme cold (cryotherapy) or extreme heat (electrocoagulation).

Endometrial cancer may also be detected by the PAP test and primarily afflicts women beyond the age of 50. As with cervical cancer, treatment involves a hysterectomy and radiation. The five-year survival rate after treatment is about 83% overall, and 94% when it is detected at an early stage (American Cancer Society, 1993). Regardless of the type of cancer and treatment, almost 70% of women are able to have a satisfactory sexual life (Schultz et al., 1992).

### The Hysterectomy: Biology and Society

Cervical cancer patients are not the only women who undergo hysterectomies. About half of American women have their uteruses surgically removed by the time they are 65.

Beliefs about the effects of a *hysterectomy* on sexual response provide a good example of the way in which societal and scientific thinking may affect an individual's interpretation of his or her own experience. Whereas biological explanations dominated many early attempts to account for variations in sexual behavior, the prevailing view is that most aspects of our sexuality are not biologically determined but are instead learned and relatively adaptable. Although this point of view has helped to eliminate some outmoded and simplistic explanations of sexuality as merely the sum of biological drives, it has oversimplified the complex interaction among biological, psychological, and social systems in eliciting sexual responses. Thus an overreliance on psychological and social variables to explain sexual behavior has some potentially damaging implications.

A once-popular myth, probably based on the notion that the sole purpose of sexuality is reproduction, held that a hysterectomy meant the end of a woman's sex life. In reaction to this myth, a great deal of publicity has been given to the idea that a woman's sexual feelings and desires are primarily affected by her *emotional* reaction to the loss of her uterus rather than to the surgical removal itself. Although it is true that a woman may continue to have intercourse and orgasm af-

ter a hysterectomy, denying that a hysterectomy has any physical influence on sexuality is potentially harmful, as Morgan (1982) pointed out. Convinced that any alteration she experiences is in her head, a woman may blame herself for shifts in her sexual experience.

As long as the ovaries remain intact following a hysterectomy, a woman's hormone levels are not affected. However, because the uterus is involved in sexual response, the sensations attending sexual interaction can be markedly altered after a hysterectomy, in the following ways. First, during the excitement phase, the blood flow to the entire pelvic area increases, and this vasocongestion is experienced as arousal. In the absence of the uterus, there is less tissue to receive the blood. Second, also during excitement, the typical elevation of the uterus cannot occur. Third, the fact that the scar tissue replacing the cervix is inelastic prevents full ballooning of the vagina, which formerly increased in diameter by as much as three inches and in length by as much as one inch. Fourth, the plateau phase involves further elevation and enlargement of the uterus, which can expand to as much as twice its nonaroused size. This additional sexual tension is not felt by a woman after a hysterectomy. Fifth, orgasm usually involves uterine contractions, with the intensity of orgasm linked to the strength of these contractions. After a hysterectomy, orgasms may not reach their previous level of intensity. Finally, in the resolution phase, some women have additional orgasms if they maintain plateau-level sexual tension. After a hysterectomy, however, reduced vasocongestion makes multiple orgasms less probable.

Thus, a number of *physical* changes can affect sexuality after a hysterectomy. This knowledge may eliminate the tendency of some women to attribute changes in their sexual experience following a hysterectomy to psychological problems or conflicts. The problem may *not* be just in their heads.

More severe changes may result if the ovaries are also removed during a hysterectomy; hormone-replacement therapy (see Chapter 14) can reduce the impact of many of these changes (Bellerose & Binik, 1993). The complexity of the relationship among hysterectomy, life circumstances, and sexual experience was shown in

**hysterectomy**—surgical removal of the uterus.

research by Darling and McKoy-Smith (1993). They randomly sampled members of a national association of college-educated women between the ages of 45 and 60 to examine the relationship between having had a hysterectomy (or not) and several sources of stress, sexual satisfaction, and quality of life. Among the 346 women who responded to the questionnaire, those with hysterectomies reported greater sexual satisfaction than did women who had not had hysterectomies! In this well-educated group, hysterectomies may have eliminated problems that interfered with sexual desire or functioning, but clearly, as the authors pointed out, further research with groups across socioeconomic levels is needed to clarify the relationship between hysterectomies and sexual satisfaction.

*Prostate Cancer*

The majority of men beyond their mid-40s experience enlargement of the prostate, the walnut-sized gland that produces most of the liquid in which sperm cells swim. The condition is usually benign, although it can cause urination problems insofar as the enlarged prostate partially blocks the urethra. It is generally treated through chemotherapy or minor surgery.

Prostate cancer, which develops in some of these cases, was expected to result in 165,000 new cases in 1993, with 35,000 deaths expected, a rate making it the second leading cause of cancer deaths in men (American Cancer Society, 1993). By the time they are 85, about 1 in 10 men have developed prostate cancer. Black American men have the highest rate incidence of prostate cancer in the world, and a 40% higher risk than do White American men, but it is not known whether this incidence stems from genetic or environmental influences. It is unusual for males to get prostate cancer before the age of 50. In fact, 80% of all prostate cancers are diagnosed in men who are age 65 or older (American Cancer Society, 1993). Herpes-II has been implicated as a factor that increases the likelihood of developing prostate cancer. Fortunately, prostate cancer tends to grow slowly and spreads to other organs in only a small proportion of cases.

Frequent urination, particularly at night, is a common symptom of prostate enlargement. This may also lead to difficulty in urinating and in emptying the bladder, because the enlargement sometimes partly blocks the urethra. During the initial stages of prostate cancer, men may experience an increase in sexual interest and frequency of erection, but later there is a reduction in sexual functioning.

Prostate cancer may be detected through laboratory tests and rectal exams involving palpation (examination through touching) of the prostate. Transrectal ultrasound, a newly developed technique that uses sound waves to reflect the prostate on a video console, can reveal cancers too small to be detected through palpation. The prostate-specific antigen test (PSA) can detect elevations in a blood substance which are associated with diseases of the prostate, including cancer. The PSA reportedly has been able to detect 79% of prostate cancers and is twice as effective as the digital rectal exam.

Men over 40 are advised to have prostate examinations annually (American Cancer Society, 1993). Prostate cancer may be treated with estrogen, which retards its growth. Because androgens tend to accelerate the growth of the cancer, treatment may also include castration of the testes to eliminate the major source of androgen. The cancerous prostate may also be surgically removed. Of all prostate cancers, 58% are diagnosed while still localized, and the five-year survival rate for these men is 91%. For all stages combined, the survival rate has increased steadily in the past three decades from 50% to 76% (American Cancer Society, 1993).

Radical surgery called prostatectomy frequently results in the loss of erectile capacity. Learning that he has prostate cancer can be very unsettling for a man, partially because of the equation of masculinity with the capacity to have erections. Of patients treated with more recent surgical techniques, however, 65% have been reported to have had erections sufficient for vaginal penetration within nine months after surgery (Graber, 1993).

*Testicular Cancer*

Cancer of the testes strikes at a younger age than do most other cancers, usually afflicting men between the ages of 20 and 35. The American

**Box 5.6**

## Testes Self-Examination

Cancer of the testes, which afflicts approximately 4 out of every 100,000 males, is highly curable if discovered early. Early detection is possible if a man examines his testes about once a month. In this procedure, each testis is rolled between the thumb, which is placed on the top of the testis, and the index and middle fingers, which are positioned on the underside of the testis. Any hard lump should be examined immediately by a physician. Although a lump may simply be a boil or a cyst, all testicular lumps should be checked for cancer.

**Self-Examination of Testes**

Cancer Society estimated that 6,600 new cases of testicular cancer would develop in 1993, but expected only 350 deaths. Risk of developing this cancer increases to 11% to 15% in men whose testes either do not descend or descend after the age of six.

Because self-examination can be helpful in detecting testicular cancer, men should examine themselves monthly (see Box 5.6). If they discover a hard lump, they should see a doctor immediately, even though the lump may not be cancerous. With early detection and treatment, testicular cancer is highly curable. Delayed treatment, however, increases the risk of the cancer's spreading to other parts of the body. Treatment generally involves removal of the diseased testis. Sexual functioning and fertility usually remain unimpaired because the other testis can manufacture enough androgen and sperm to compensate for the missing testis. Following surgical castration, an implant resembling the lost testis can be placed inside the scrotum.

### Cardiovascular Illness

The cancers of the sexual organs have a direct impact on our sexual functioning and sexual feelings. Other illnesses can affect us sexually but in a less direct way. Anything that makes us feel differently about ourselves can influence our sexual functioning. We now consider one of the physical conditions that has been found to be related to sexual arousal and response to a greater or lesser extent: cardiovascular illness.

One in 10 Americans experience heart and blood-vessel ailments at some point during their lifetime. Heart-attack and stroke patients sometimes fear sexual activity because the process increases blood pressure and heart rate, stressing the cardiovascular system. After a heart attack in particular, many people report reduced levels of sexual activity. A common reason they give is the fear of dying during sexual activity. Such anxiety may be exaggerated by fiction writers and filmmakers. An early scene in the movie *Private Benjamin*, for example, depicted a husband dying of a heart attack after having an orgasm on his wedding night. The likelihood that a person would actually experience a heart attack under such conditions is very slight.

Masters and Johnson (1966) reported relatively large surges in blood pressure and heart rate during sexual activity in a laboratory setting. Is it possible, however, that performing in the laboratory setting elicited high levels of arousal or anxiety, inflating these figures? To investigate this possibility, Hellerstein and Friedman (1970) used portable monitors to study the heart rates of patients carrying out various everyday activities at home. For those patients who engaged in sexual activity, the resulting changes in heart rate were compared to the changes brought on by other activities. In contrast to Masters and Johnson, Hellerstein and Friedman reported only modest changes in heart rate. The mean maximum heart rate during orgasm was 117.4 beats per minute, as compared to Masters and Johnson's finding of rates of up to 170 and 180 beats per minute. Thus it does not appear that sexual activity is particularly stressful on the cardiovascular system when compared with other physical activities, unless the sexual activity takes place in a laboratory.

For heart-attack and stroke patients, the severity of the damage to the cardiovascular system determines the limits of exertion during sexual activity and the speed with which they may return to their normal modes of sexual expression. In most cases, cardiovascular illnesses do not impose a permanent ban on sexual interaction. Individuals experiencing hypertension (high blood pressure) and/or recovering from heart attacks are usually encouraged to keep their level of exertion to a minimum when resuming sexual stimulation, and to rest after sexual activity. Counseling and physical-conditioning programs can aid cardiovascular patients. Patients in physical-conditioning programs describe a higher quality and quantity of sexual activity than do patients not enrolled in these programs (Papadopoulos, 1989).

## Diabetes Mellitus

A susceptibility to diabetes may be transmitted as a recessive genetic trait and is present in about 20% of the U.S. population. About 5% of these people go on to develop diabetes, a disease characterized by either an insufficient supply of insulin or deficient responsiveness to insulin.

Insulin is a hormone that regulates carbohydrate metabolism by controlling blood glucose levels. Type-I diabetes involves insulin dependency (the need to inject insulin because too little is secreted) and has its onset in childhood or adolescence. Type-II diabetes begins in adulthood and can often be managed through dietary restrictions and with orally administered medication (Schover & Jensen, 1988).

People with diabetes are vulnerable to a range of impairments to their sexual functioning. For example, many diabetic men eventually develop erectile difficulties. This dysfunction is more prevalent in older men with diabetes than in younger men, although there is no direct correlation with age of onset (Turner et al., 1990). It appears that vascular and neurological impairment and psychological factors are involved in most cases.

Women with insulin-dependent diabetes report relatively little effect on their sexuality, whereas those who have the noninsulin-dependent form encounter problems with sexual desire, vaginal lubrication, orgasm, and sexual satisfaction (Schreiner-Engel et al., 1987). Interestingly, Type-I women show lower physiological sexual arousal to erotic stimuli than "normal" women but no differences in subjective ratings of their own sexual arousal (Wincze, Albert, & Bansal, 1993). Women's sexual responsivity may be less influenced by physiological factors than men's, whose physiological arousal is observable (erection).

Chapters 4 and 5 have emphasized the biological bases of sexual development and function. Although our biological capacities are crucial for human sexual activity, it is interwoven with the texture of human experience. We turn to this experience in Chapter 6 as we explore the many ways in which humans assign meaning to their sexuality and communicate their feelings.

## Summary of Major Points

1. **The structural similarity of males and females.**

Both males and females have gonads (ovaries or testes) that secrete sex hormones and produce reproductive cells (eggs or sperm). The hormones are released into the bloodstream, and the reproductive cells are transported through a system of ducts: the fallopian tubes in the female or the vasa deferentia in the male. For females, stimulation of the clitoris and of the Gräfenberg spot produces intense arousal. For males, penile stimulation triggers the most intense sexual arousal.

2. **Hormones and sexuality.**

The hormone-secreting endocrine glands also influence sexual behavior. These glands—the adrenals, pituitary, ovaries, and testes—secrete hormones into the bloodstream. The hormones, in turn, affect the nervous system and influence the secretion of other endocrine glands. Hormone secretion in females of reproductive age fluctuates in a monthly cycle. Testosterone levels fluctuate daily in males and also vary by time of year.

3. **The menstrual cycle.**

One effect of the cyclical pattern of hormone secretion in females is the menstrual cycle. This cycle consists of a continuous series of overlapping processes. During the follicular phase, ovarian follicles ripen and mature. At ovulation, a follicle ruptures from the ovary and an egg is released from the follicle. The ruptured follicle, known in its empty state as the corpus luteum, secretes the progesterone that stimulates the growth of the uterine lining during the luteal phase. In the absence of fertilization, the egg fails to implant in the uterine lining, which then begins to disintegrate during the premenstrual phase. The uterine lining is discharged from the body during menstruation.

4. **Sexual response and the nervous system.**

The responsiveness of the genitals to sexual stimulation is mediated by the nervous system. The parasympathetic nervous system is predominant in initial arousal: erection in males and vaginal lubrication in females. The sympathetic nervous system is more active during emission in males and during orgasm in females. Psychological responses such as fear, anxiety, stress, and fatigue can inhibit nervous system responses and thus inhibit sexual feelings and processes.

5. **The contribution of the brain and spinal cord to sexual response.**

Some people have been taught that sexual response involves animalistic drives. All levels of the brain, however, from the lower centers that we share with our animal ancestors to the distinctly human portions, are involved in human sexual behavior. Supplementing the roles played by the thalamus, hypothalamus, and limbic system, the cerebrum can aid sexual response through erotic fantasies and pleasant memories or can inhibit it through negative learning and painful memories. Arousal can occur through genital stimulation and is transmitted via the spinal cord to the brain. Conversely, erotic or painful mental events processed by the brain can result in the transmission through the spinal cord of messages that either enhance or inhibit genital response.

6. **Sexuality, illness, and disease.**

Major conditions, including cancers of the sexual organs, cardiovascular ailments, and diabetes, also have widely varying effects on human sexual responsiveness. Some people with these illnesses are able to maintain or restore satisfying sexual lives; others find their sexual expression reduced or impaired by their medical situations. Research on the relationship of various medical conditions—and on the drugs used for treatment—to sexual response is badly needed, to increase the likelihood that people experiencing a disruption in their lives by illness may resume satisfying sexual interactions.

## Review of Key Concepts

1. Penis length is a factor of primary importance to: a) the extent of female sexual arousal; b) the intensity of vaginal stimulation; c) male sexual performance; d) none of the above. (p. 128)

2. Intense sexual sensitivity in females is concentrated in the: a) cervix; b) clitoris; c) vagina; d) both a and c. (p. 134)

3. The Gräfenberg spot is: a) located on the cervix; b) a center of female sexual sensitivity; c) a possible but controversial center of male sexual sensitivity; d) now established to be nonexistent. (pp. 131–132)

4. Anatomically, the clitoris is most akin to the: a) lips; b) tongue; c) penis; d) prostate. (p. 128)

5. Menarche is: a) one of the female sex hormones; b) the phase of the menstrual cycle in which the ovum (egg) can be fertilized; c) the first menstrual period; d) the diminishing of the menstrual flow, around the time of menopause. (pp. 140–142)

6. Ovulation is the phase of the menstrual cycle in which the ovum (egg) is: a) produced; b) released from the ovary into the fallopian tube; c) expelled from the uterus; d) none of the above. (p. 142)

7. Discuss the ways in which human ovaries and testes are similar.

8. What are pheromones? Discuss current evidence for the possible impact of pheromones on humans.

9. What proportion of breast lumps is nonmalignant? a) 20%; b) 40%; c) 60%; d) 80%. (p. 149)

10. The most invasive treatment for breast cancer is: a) radical mastectomy; b) modified mastectomy; c) lumpectomy; d) These procedures are equally invasive. (pp. 152–153)

11. Orgasm generally becomes impossible after a hysterectomy. True or false? (p. 154)

12. There is perhaps no more profound demonstration of the value we attach to the breasts as symbolic of female attractiveness than the reaction of many women to the diagnosis of breast cancer. Discuss. (p. 149)

# Arousal and Communication

*Maybe I'll see him at the party Friday night and be able to talk to him. . . . Maybe I'll ask him what his summer was like. . . . No, that's dumb. . . . Let's see, maybe we'll be at the party and a snowstorm will close everything down, and we'll be marooned. Well, no, there will be a lot of people there. . . . We'll get into a good conversation, get hungry for pizza and decide to go pick up some, and then get stuck and have to leave the car. And then we'll walk back to my apartment. He'll come in and take off his coat, and I'll put some music on. He'll say, "Do you want to dance?"—I wonder if he likes to dance. We'll start dancing, and he'll nuzzle my neck. We'll kiss, and then sit down on the couch. He'll start to play with my breasts slowly and gently, and. . . . No, let's see, I'll put some music on, but I'll say I'm really freezing and want to take a nice warm bath. So I'll go turn on the water, and then when I come out, he'll ask me if I want to dance. He'll start nuzzling my neck, and we'll kiss, and then I'll say I have to turn off the water. When I come back, he'll be sitting on the couch, so I'll sit down, too, and we'll start kissing again. He'll start to take my clothes off and ask me if I want him to wash my back, and I'll ask him if he wants to take a bath, too, and . . .*

In the previous two chapters, we examined the process by which humans differentiate into males or females. We develop male or female anatomies, and we secrete masculinizing and feminizing hormones at some point around the beginning of our second decade of life. We then typically have sexual *fantasies* and feel sexual arousal. We mentally construct sequences of events leading to romantic and sexual interaction, such as the fantasy in the vignette above, and we experience sexual arousal in connection with our fantasies. Before we can decide whether to express some of our fantasies and feelings with a potential partner, we first need to be able to communicate, both verbally and nonverbally, with other people.

In this chapter we describe the process by which we learn to feel sexually aroused and the purposes of sexual arousal. The impact of our senses and our thoughts on sexual arousal are examined. We then turn to the interpersonal communication of arousal and consider individual differences in reactions to arousal. For example, some people respond to feelings of arousal with happiness and pleasure, whereas others feel embarrassment and guilt. Finally, we discuss the importance of being able to communicate clearly with one another if we are to have satisfying relationships, and we consider some practical issues relevant to the management of fantasy and arousal.

## Learning to Be Aroused

The capacities for language and sexual arousal are both innate; however, just as the specific language that we speak is learned, the specific objects and acts that we find sexually arousing appear to be—for the most part—conditioned by our culture and our own experiences. For example, if a man or woman with a nickel-size hole in the lower lip, out of which tobacco juice and saliva were dribbling, walked up to you enticingly, would you feel sexual attraction (see Figure 6.1)? You might if you had been reared among the So of northeastern Uganda. In contrast, a member of

**fantasy**—usually a pleasant mental image unrestrained by the realities of the external world.

**FIGURE 6.1**
**What Is Attractive?**
Ideas about beauty differ from culture to culture. The So of northeastern Uganda consider neck rings and a hole in the lip to be attractive.

that tribe who fit the stereotype of the attractive, late-adolescent woman in our culture (high, firm breasts; small waist; long legs; relatively narrow hips; slightly protruding buttocks) would not be considered particularly attractive to the So. And within a culture, the specific stimuli that are paired with arousal vary from one time period to the next. For example, sometimes big breasts are fashionable, whereas at other times in the same culture, people may respond erotically to small, delicately formed breasts.

If you watch a 10-year-old movie on late-night television, you might remember wearing styles similar to those of the actors and considering those fashions attractive at the time. The hairstyles and hem lengths probably look silly now, however, because we have learned to find current styles attractive. Although we may at first have a negative reaction to new styles, within mere months, the repeated pairing of a particular style with the concept of sex appeal begins to affect our perception of what is attractive (see Figure 6.2).

Both of these examples demonstrate culturally shared ideas about what is arousing. When everyone around us seems to share the same gen-

# Beauty and Sexuality

Through the Ages and Across Cultures

Conceptions of beauty and sexual appeal have been closely linked throughout human history. But can there be absolute standards of what constitutes beauty, or what arouses us sexually? Perceptions of glamour and sexual magnetism are based on subjective individual judgments, strongly influenced by social custom, cultural conditioning, and traditions that vary from one society (and one time period) to another. We arrive at our interpretations of what is beautiful and desirable through a complex interaction of biology, learning, and cultural conditions.

Western society has had relatively consistent ideas of what constitutes human beauty. Yet what seemed beautiful to our ancestors sometimes seems less than desirable to us. The deeper *meaning* of beauty, too, has always been elusive, although philosophers and religious thinkers have pondered it deeply. Do we find particular human characteristics beautiful because they convey some spiritual purpose, recalling some high ideal?

Consider this bust of the ancient Egyptian queen Nefertiti, dated before 1400 B.C. Does her beauty appeal to us almost 3,500 years later because this is a true portrait, not a symbolic representation of a ruler or goddess (as was the custom in most other Egyptian art)? Does her image somehow connect with a traditional beauty that we have later come to admire?

The ancient Greeks made a cult of youthful beauty, and Greek philosophers tried to define the mystery of beauty and sexual attractiveness. In an art form called the *kouros* (Greek, "young man"), represented here by the marble statue c. 540–515 B.C., ancient Greek sculptors depicted gods and youthful athletes as broad-shouldered, narrow-waisted, powerfully muscled figures, in keeping with the contemporary ideal. The century after this work was created, Plato was declaring homosexual attraction to be inspired by beauty and in turn a desire for the Good; the love two people felt for each other was only the starting point of a journey to an understanding and sharing of divine, eternal Truth.

**Nefertiti**

**Greek *kouros***

Top, **Michelangelo's** *Creation of Adam*

Bottom, **Renoir's** *Bather Drying Her Leg*

Top right, **Charles V**

Bottom right,
**Rossetti's** *Proserpine* (detail)

The Greek view of beauty as divinely inspired and of human love as the steppingstone to the love of God was latent in medieval Christianity. It was powerfully revived in the Renaissance, as exemplified in Michelangelo's famous painting in the Sistine Chapel of the creation of Adam, which conveys sexual energy as well as calm beauty and spirituality. Like their Greek predecessors, such Renaissance images continue to influence definitions of beauty and sexual appeal. Our idea of beauty is also connected with clothing, jewelry, and other adornments. The portrait of sixteenth-century emperor Charles V shows him wearing a prominent codpiece, which was high fashion as well as an advertisement of sexual prowess. The French impressionist Pierre Auguste Renoir's *Bather Drying Her Leg* is an indication that slimness was not always considered desirable. The English artist Dante Gabriel Rossetti's *Proserpine* (1874) recalled the Renaissance world of Charles V and its romantic ambience; the painter lovingly adorned his subject in softly flowing robes and captured her in a mood of seductive languor.

In our own time, the media—television, films, and mass-circulation magazines—constantly bombard us with visions of glamour and sex appeal. The particular image—hem length, body type, hairstyle, and so on—varies from one fashion season to another, each time subtly, or not so subtly, conditioning us to perceive these "looks" as attractive. Consciously or unconsciously, many of us compare ourselves and our lovers or potential lovers to these ideals. After Clark Gable stripped off his shirt to reveal his bare chest in a 1930s movie, sales of men's undershirts reportedly plummeted. Postwar America was fascinated by Marilyn Monroe, a voluptuous beauty idolized by men and imitated by women. Although she was an emotionally unstable woman who died of alleged suicide, her beauty remains legendary decades later. Contemporary Americans emphasize physical fitness, and a major model, Cindy Crawford, is shown working out at the beach.

Top, **Clark Gable**
Bottom, **Marilyn Monroe**

**Cindy Crawford**

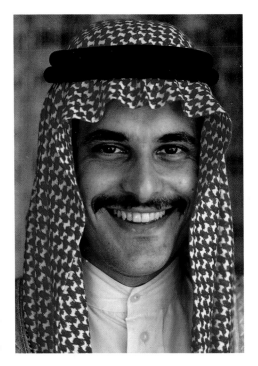

Right, **Modern Saudi man**

Far right, **Burmese woman of today**

Right, **Sharon Stone**

Far right, **Tom Cruise**

Thanks to global media coverage, the speed and ease of international travel, and widespread interest in foreign ways, contemporary conceptions of beauty and sexuality are ever expanding. Most of us would agree that this Saudi man, though garbed in traditional native attire, is darkly handsome. What is your reaction to him, and to the picture of a modern Burmese woman? American film stars Sharon Stone and Tom Cruise are known to audiences worldwide. Will *their* looks, or those of the Saudi man or Burmese woman, one day become the standards of beauty in other nations?

**FIGURE 6.2**
**Changing Perceptions of Attractiveness**
Hair styles, which change over time, can acquire "sex appeal" by being associated
with attractive models.

eral perceptions about what is attractive, it is easy to assume that there is something natural about being attracted to particular types. Our own unique experiences, however, can lead us to respond sexually to certain types that do not have any erotic significance for our friends.

What would happen if you showed the drawing in Figure 6.3 to friends, parents, grandparents, and members of the clergy and asked them for their reactions? It is likely that their responses would vary, and that the variations would be a function of their age, gender, and moral beliefs. The picture would probably be meaningless to a two-year-old or three-year-old child. A child that age would be unlikely to perceive the picture as either erotic or disgusting. (We are *not* suggesting that you show this picture to young children. You might be accused of corrupting their morals, even though the picture would have little meaning to them.) The point is that we *learn* to interpret certain pictures, objects, and parts of people's bodies as sexually arousing. We go through a long period of training during childhood and adolescence. Depending on our generation, culture, socioeconomic status, unique experiences, and momentary feelings, we learn to feel aroused, unaffected, or disgusted by particular body types, pictures, objects, sensations, and situations (see the color insert, Beauty and Sexuality).

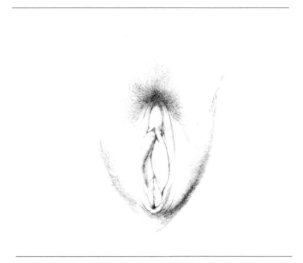

**FIGURE 6.3**

**What Is Your Response?**

Most of our erotic responses are learned. Depending on their training, adults might respond to this drawing with arousal, indifference, or disgust, but it would be meaningless to a three-year-old.

## Models of Arousal

If you have ever felt intense erotic attraction toward someone, the experience probably defied easy explanation. You might say that you simply "fell in love." The language that we use in describing our intense arousal often places responsibility for our feelings outside ourselves. This tendency to attribute our feelings to some force beyond our control is so thoroughly ingrained in our culture that it is difficult to imagine thinking otherwise. Carried to its extreme, this tendency can result in blaming rape or harassment on the appearance or behavior of the victim rather than on the motivations of the person committing the act. In fact, however, sexual arousal is a complex set of responses by an individual. Even something that is commonly assumed to evoke unconditioned (that is, unlearned or involuntary) responses—such as having our genitals stroked—does not necessarily elicit sexual arousal.

In attempting to explain intense, erotic arousal, scientists have relied on three models: classical conditioning, operant conditioning, and a two-stage model of emotions. We examined the first two of these models in Chapter 3. Classical conditioning involves the pairing of a previously neutral stimulus with a stimulus that can produce sexual arousal, resulting in the neutral stimulus acquiring erotic significance. Operant conditioning involves the shaping of sexual arousal by reward, punishment, or lack of attention. For example, we are generally more attracted to those who reward us.

Looking back on your own experiences, you may recall feeling arousal and attraction toward people who rewarded you (operant conditioning) and toward stimuli associated with those people (classical conditioning). You may have had other experiences, however, that do not fit neatly into the classical- and/or operant-conditioning models. What about the situation in which you feel respect and admiration for one person who is good to you, and yet your sexual arousal and attraction are directed toward someone not nearly so kind or admirable? In fact, you may be most aware of your arousal and desire for this person at times when you are feeling jealousy, an emotion that is not pleasant or rewarding. How does this kind of feeling develop?

## The Two-Stage Model of Sexual Arousal

Noting that people feel attracted to and aroused by others who apparently provide them with more pain than pleasure, Berscheid and Walster (1974) proposed that simple conditioning models may not be adequate to explain all instances of intense attraction. They argued that the experience of love (perhaps *lust* would be a more accurate word) may result from a two-stage process. First, we feel physiological arousal and the responses that accompany it, such as a racing heart and pulse, sweating palms, and heavy breathing. Second, in our desire to understand the source of the arousal, we search for an explanation—a label—for the arousal.

Berscheid and Walster (1974) proposed that under some conditions, we may experience physiological arousal and conclude that we are feeling love or sexual attraction. If the arousal occurs in the context of sexual intimacy with an appropriate object of our love, this conclusion seems logical. However, Berscheid and Walster suggested that *any* source of arousal can, under certain conditions, increase the likelihood of labeling our feelings as love or attraction. This hypothesis was tested by Dutton and Aron (1974) in a somewhat unusual setting—two bridges overlooking the Capilano River in British Columbia, Canada. One of the bridges was 5 feet wide, 450 feet long, and made out of wooden boards attached to wire cables. As the researchers put it (p. 511),

> The bridge has many arousal-inducing features such as 1) a tendency to tilt, sway, and wobble, creating the impression that one is about to fall over the side; 2) very low handrails of wire cable which contribute to this impression; and 3) a 230-ft. drop to rocks and shallow rapids below the bridge. The "control" bridge was a solid wood bridge farther upriver. Constructed of heavy cedar, this bridge was wider and firmer than the experimental bridge, was only 10 ft. above a small, shallow rivulet which ran into the main river, had high handrails, and did not tilt or sway.

After walking over either the arousal-inducing bridge or the control bridge, men were approached by either a male or a female interviewer and asked to respond to a short questionnaire, then to write a short story based on a picture of a young woman covering her face with one hand and reaching with the other. Two measures were used to assess the volunteers' sexual arousal. First, the volunteers' stories were examined for sexual content. When the interviewers were female, the stories from volunteers who were on the arousing bridge contained significantly more sexual content than did those from volunteers on the control bridge. When the interviewer was male, sexual content did not vary according to which bridge the volunteers were on. Second, after the volunteers had completed the questionnaire, they were offered the interviewer's name and phone number in case they wanted to have the experiment explained in more detail. The researchers hypothesized that volunteers on the arousing bridge would be more likely to call the female interviewer than would volunteers on the control bridge. As Table 6.1 shows, 50% of the males from the arousing bridge did call the female interviewer; this percentage is higher

**TABLE 6.1 Attraction and Sexuality on Anxiety-Arousing Bridge and on Safe Bridge**

| | Percentage of Subjects Telephoning Interviewer |
|---|---|
| *Female interviewer* | |
| Safe bridge | 12.5 |
| Anxiety-arousing bridge | 50.0 |
| *Male interviewer* | |
| Safe bridge | 16.7 |
| Anxiety-arousing bridge | 28.6 |

Source: Adapted from Dutton and Aron, 1974 (Table 7–3), p. 516.

than both the percentage from the control bridge who called the female interviewer and the percentage from either bridge who called the male interviewer.

Other research has also provided evidence that misattribution of arousal may affect romantic attraction. For example, in another laboratory study, White and Kight (1984) asked males to run for 15 seconds (low physiological arousal) or for 2 minutes (high physiological arousal). Regardless of whether they ran for 15 seconds or 2 minutes, the importance of the physical activity in the experiment was either minimized or emphasized. The men were then shown a videotape of a female college sophomore in "appealing, form-fitting clothes talking energetically about a variety of topics including . . . favorite dating activities. . . . She also mentioned that she was looking forward to meeting people in general and the subject if possible and that she had no current boyfriend" (p. 58). Some of the men were told that they would meet the woman, whereas others were told that they would not meet one another. The men were more attracted to the woman when they were more physiologically aroused, when they expected to meet her, and when the importance of the source of initial arousal was minimized.

In general, then, the less able we are to identify the source of our physiological feelings of

**FIGURE 6.4**
**Intensity in a New Relationship**
This couple's behavior reflects the consuming connection that often accompanies the beginning of a relationship.

arousal and the more likely we are to have the chance to interact with a person, the more romantically attracted we feel toward the person. Strictly speaking, this finding only applies to the romantic attraction of a man to a woman, because these studies of arousal have used only heterosexual males. Although it may seem reasonable to assume that females and homosexuals respond similarly, research with women and with gay people is needed to determine whether these findings generalize beyond heterosexual men.

On the basis of experiments examining the influences of arousal on attraction, Berscheid and Walster (1974) concluded that under the appropriate circumstances, arousal—regardless of its source—increases the likelihood that one person will be attracted to another. Their analysis may help to explain why someone is attracted to another person when, to outside observers, there seems to be no logical reason for the attraction.

A related point, which we discuss in more detail in Chapter 20, is the importance of distinguishing between anxiety-related arousal and lasting attraction. During the initial stages of a relationship, the arousal from sexual attraction is likely to be laced heavily with anxiety, which increases the level of *epinephrine* in our bodies (see Figure 6.4). We wonder: How interested is she in me for myself? Is she just being nice, or does she really care about me? Do I look attractive to her? If the relationship blossoms and endures, there is usually a decrease in arousal, associated with the lessening of anxiety. A couple may interpret this change as a diminishing of love if they have defined love as intense arousal. Labeling feelings of sexual attraction, euphoria, and anxiety as *love* may evoke disappointment when these sources of physiological arousal subside. Arousal associated with anxiety is reduced by trust, mutual understanding, and the sense that your partner loves you enough to accept your imperfections.

**epinephrine**—secreted by the adrenal gland, a hormone that is involved in emotional excitement; sometimes called adrenaline.

Thus it is important to differentiate between the roller-coaster feelings that accompany the early stages of a relationship and the feelings associated with the kind of love that develops over a long time.

## The Purposes of Sexual Arousal

Cultural beliefs about the goodness or badness of sexual feelings affect individuals' responses to sexual stimulation. From childhood on, some people are taught that sexual arousal is bad or sinful and should be avoided or controlled except for purposes of reproduction. Others learn that their capacity for sexual arousal and expression is an enjoyable, healthy, and positive aspect of being alive. Still other people receive mixed messages about sexuality, leading to confusion and doubts about their own sexual experiences and desires. In this section we discuss both cultural and individual variations in beliefs about sex.

Beliefs regarding the purposes of sexual arousal are strongly related to our religious, moral, and legal codes. One of the most common beliefs—that arousal serves to ensure survival of the species—is less straightforward than it sounds. Some people interpret this belief to mean that the sole purpose of sexual arousal and intercourse is to conceive. In fact, one of the most influential contemporary religious leaders, Pope John Paul II of the Roman Catholic Church, maintains that it is sinful to use birth-control devices other than natural family planning (see Chapter 10) to avoid conception while having sexual intercourse.

Comparing our species with others helps us to understand the functions of human sexual arousal. If the only purpose of sexual arousal is to reproduce, it would make more sense for human females to be uninterested in sexual interaction except when they are fertile. In fact, the females of most species are receptive to sexual interaction only when they are fertile. In contrast, human females, though fertile only one-seventh of the time, are continuously capable of strong sexual interest and arousal. Peaks in sexual arousal may occur when a woman is most fertile (at ovulation), when she is least fertile (just prior to menstruation), or at any other time in her cycle (Meuwissen & Over, 1992). Indeed, most human females report sexual arousal and behavior long after they cease menstruating and are no longer able to reproduce.

Another interesting difference between human and nonhuman species is in the timing of the female's secretion of blood. In the females of many nonhuman species, the appearance of blood signals a time of fertility referred to as *estrus*. Yet, among human females, the discharge of blood from the uterus occurs at a time of minimal fertility, two weeks after the release of an egg.

In many species, then, female sexual interest is clearly tied to the capacity for impregnation. But in more complex species, sexuality has both reproductive and nonreproductive functions. The fact that human females eagerly engage in sexual intimacy at times when they are not fertile leads to an enhancement and lengthening of the period of sexual attraction. This was an evolutionary adaptation that made sense for the survival of our early ancestors' offspring. Human infants take nine months to mature in the uterus and many more years to develop to the point of self-sufficiency and reproductive maturity. Presumably, until recently in our evolution, it would have been difficult for a single parent to rear offspring to the point of reproductive maturity; forming a strong bond with a companion who would help to provide sustenance and support for the offspring would improve the child's chances of survival. The offspring of those early humans who felt continuing attraction toward one another may therefore have been more likely to survive than those whose parents were less sexually attached to one another.

Sexual arousal, then, can form the basis of a continuing bond. It can also be disruptive of bonding, however, when it promotes attraction to persons outside the bond. Sexual arousal can lead to short-term, pleasure-oriented encounters or to nothing at all. The many purposes of sexual arousal depend on how the individual has learned to interpret and perceive his or her arousal.

**estrus**—in many nonhuman species, a peaking of the sexual cycle that signals ovulation, or being "in heat."

## Sources of Arousal

Our senses are an intimate part of our sexuality. Touch, smell, sight, and hearing can all be sources of erotic arousal as a wide variety of sensory stimuli come to be associated with the pleasure of sexual experience. Kissing, which involves most or all of our senses, and fantasies, which can be stimulated by sensory input as well as by our thoughts, also can play a major role in human sexual excitement. Songs, perfumes, and advertisements are but a few of the other stimuli that may evoke sexual arousal. In this section we examine the role of the senses and these other factors in arousal.

### Touch

Our tactile capacities (that is, our ability to receive sensory stimulation from touch and pressure receptors) are intricately involved in sexual arousal. Our bodies—particularly our genitals—are richly endowed with receptors for touch and pressure. Because these receptors are distributed unevenly, some parts of the body are more sensitive than others. The most erotically sensitive areas are called *erogenous zones*. Many areas besides the genitals can be erotically sensitive to touch: the mouth, ears, buttocks, palms of the hands, fingers, abdomen, inner thighs, soles of the feet, and toes, for example.

Touch is the only type of stimulation that can elicit a reflexive response that is independent of higher brain centers. Men with spinal-cord injuries that prevent impulses from reaching the brain but leave the sexual centers in the lower spinal cord intact are able to respond with an erection when their genitals or inner thighs are touched.

The erotic aspects of touching must be understood in the broader context of the fundamental human need for bodily contact, a need that is apparent from infancy. Of all our senses, neural pathways underlying skin sensation and responses to body stimulation are the first to de-

---

**erogenous zones**—areas of the body that are erotically sensitive to tactile stimulation.

---

velop. Touch is crucial in the fulfillment of the basic needs for affection, security, and love and in the development of our capacity to give affection (Hatfield, 1994). The detrimental effects of depriving infants of adequate sensory stimulation by withholding touching, caressing, and cuddling are examined in Chapters 12 and 20.

### Smell

As you read in Chapter 5, many species rely heavily on chemical attractants in their sexual interactions. Such attractants are loosely categorized as pheromones. There are numerous examples of the importance of pheromones in regulating the behavior of nonhuman organisms. Among insects, for instance, pheromones seem to have an irresistible and predictable effect on behavior. Female moths have special abdominal glands that manufacture pheromones capable of attracting mates from far away. The automatic response to pheromones shown by male insects does not appear to characterize species closer to humans on the evolutionary scale.

This does not mean that pheromones do not function as sex attractants as well as territorial markers and orientation signals in a number of higher species, but merely that these species appear to be less impelled to respond to the chemical substances. If you have a male dog, you have probably noticed him marking territory by urinating on the boundaries. Primates signal sexual availability to potential mates through both the release of odors and the use of such visual signals as swollen, reddish genitals.

Interest in searching for human pheromones has grown since it was discovered that female rhesus monkeys secrete fatty acids called copulins, which seem to have an aphrodisiac effect on males. Consistent with the finding that the influence of biological factors decreases among species closer to humans, however, a monkey's response to copulins is not necessarily as automatic and irresistible as that of certain insects. It appears too that human females vaginally secrete copulins, which may have some effect on sexual desire. Smelling copulins may stimulate the desire for sexual activity among some couples, although for other couples, sexual desire seems to be unaffected by copulins (Morris & Udry, 1978).

It is interesting, in this regard, that most people in our culture believe that the secretory odors of bodily areas as diverse as the mouth, underarms, genitals, and feet are unpleasant or downright disgusting. Adolescents use the comment "He sniffs bicycle seats" as an insult, implying that someone who would deliberately expose himself to such an odor is perverted. You too may think that an aversion to the odor of bodily secretions is natural. The deodorant industry spends millions of dollars attempting to convince us so. Television commercials and magazine advertisements display women in gauzy dresses running eagerly toward unseen lovers, only to hesitate in concern over potentially offensive vaginal odors. The ads assure us that if we buy underarm and vaginal deodorants, we will be free of worries about these unpleasant and embarrassing smells. Many vaginal deodorants on the market are harmful to the delicate genital tissues. Further, they are unnecessary; regular bathing with soap and water is sufficient to eliminate old bacteria that produce strong odors. Young children do not appear to be troubled by the smell of bodily secretions, and cross-cultural data suggest that not all adults characterize bodily odors as offensive. Thus in all likelihood our response to such smells is learned rather than innate.

## Sight

As with the sense of smell, the extent to which our sexual responses are affected by inborn versus learned reactions to what we see is not clear. We do know that what we consider visually attractive is heavily influenced by our training. What we do not know is whether humans, as a species, have any innate preferences for specific visual sights as erotic stimuli.

You may have noticed the swollen red buttocks of some female primates at the zoo. Their genitals are most brightly colored when they are sexually receptive. This pattern of swollen red skin may signal the females' fertility and sexual receptivity to males, who typically approach from the rear to mate.

Evolutionary theorists have suggested that human males are inherently attracted by females' complexions, which are seen as windows into their general health and reproductive fitness. In contrast, females may place more importance on males' physical stamina, which might serve as an indication that a male may be a good provider. In their examination of what college students rate as important in judging male and female physical attractiveness, Franzoi and Herzog (1987) found generally that men stressed those parts of women's bodies directly related to sexuality, and women emphasized men's physical condition or endurance. Franzoi and Herzog suggested that men are "socialized to perceive women as sexual providers, whereas women may be taught to perceive men as material providers" (1987, p. 29). As we pointed out in Chapter 3, Buss (1989) found that, across cultures, men placed more stress on a potential mate's physical attractiveness than did women, whereas women rated financial prospects, ambitiousness, and industriousness as more central in their choice of a mate than did men. Thus sight seems to play a more central role in evaluating attractiveness for men than for women.

## Hearing

Touch, smell, and sight are the senses most strongly implicated in sexual arousal, but hearing can also come into play. The sensuous rhythms associated with certain types of music and poetry can raise our level of sexual arousal and thus are often used to enhance sexual excitement. We may also learn to respond sexually to the tone and rhythm of a person's voice or to the kind of language used by a partner. The particular terms or phrases that arouse us vary from one person to another. For example, some individuals are turned on by explicit sexual words, whereas others are excited by gentle romantic whispers of endearment.

Generating sounds during sexual interaction is widespread among primates and humans but little attention has been paid to its significance. Groans, moans, sighs, and screams and logical, directive vocalizations can provide information about pleasure, reactions to sexual stimulation, and orgasm (Wiederman, Allgeier, & Weiner, 1992). Many of these sounds can be highly arousing to men and women and may facilitate orgasm. In addition, commercial telephone sex produced mainly for the male market relies exclusively on sounds and vocalization to arouse the listener sexually.

## Fantasy and Sexual Arousal

One of the most intriguing aspects of being human is the ability to fantasize. In our minds we can recall and refashion past experiences, anticipate and rehearse future events, and create unique scenes that are neither likely nor desired in reality. People may imagine receiving recognition for scholastic or athletic achievements, or appreciation for their acts of generosity. They may imagine failing, perhaps on tests or in job interviews.

Similarly, sexual fantasies may involve either pleasant events such as sexual or romantic interest from a person toward whom we are attracted, or unpleasant occurrences such as rejection by a desired partner. Fantasies can arouse us more than do external erotic stimuli. In a study conducted about a quarter of a century ago, imagining each of 19 erotic themes led to much greater arousal among 42 married couples than did actual exposure to either erotic pictures or sexually stimulating stories, especially for women (Byrne & Lamberth, 1971).

Erotic fantasies can give both intensity and direction to sexual goals, and they may be a major influence on sexual identity and orientation. Many scholars believe that early adolescence is a critical period in the formation of sexual attitudes and behavior (Byrne, 1977; Money, 1991; Storms, 1980, 1981). Surveys on adolescent sexual fantasies indicate that they begin shortly after the onset of sexual arousal. For males, this is around 11.5 years and for females about one to two years later (Gold & Gold, 1991; Knoth, Boyd, & Singer, 1988). At first, these fantasies tend to be about familiar persons or situations such as a teacher, an older acquaintance, or dates. By late adolescence, most people have developed fantasies with well-defined, specific, erotic scripts that often involve daring, unconventional themes such as engaging in group sex, being caught or observed having sex, and having sex with strangers.

Gender differences are present from the beginning of sexual fantasy life. In general, males' fantasies contain visual images, physical characteristics, active and explicit sexual behavior, and interchangeable partners. Compared to males, females' fantasies are more concerned with emotional involvement, romance, committed partners in a caring relationship, and touching. Females' fantasies are also more complex and vivid (Alfonso, Allison, & Dunn, 1992; Chick & Gold, 1987–1988; Ellis & Symons, 1990; Gold & Gold, 1991). Males tend to report more frequent sexual fantasies than do females. These gender differences in sexual fantasy are consistent with traditional societal definitions of gender roles.

Most people fantasize when they are engaged in nonsexual activities such as washing dishes, and the majority of individuals report employing sexual fantasies while they are masturbating or involved in sexual interactions with others (Cado & Leitenberg, 1990; Lunde et al., 1991; Pelletier & Herold, 1988). For both men and women, sexual fantasies decrease but do not disappear as they advance from adolescence to old age (Halderman & Zelhart, 1985; Purifoy, Grodsky, & Giambra, 1992).

### Fantasies: Healthy or Deviant?

Sigmund Freud theorized that sexual fantasies represented wishes or unfilled needs. Basically, he believed that sexual fantasies were the products of unhappy, sexually frustrated people. Wilhelm Reich (1942) carried this idea even further, theorizing that people used fantasies to avoid giving themselves up to the full power and release of orgasm. Freud and Reich both thought that sexual fantasies were signs of emotional immaturity. In the beginning of the 20th century, their thinking was reflected in the beliefs of many clinicians and psychoanalytic theorists.

More recently, clinicians have emphasized the positive contributions of fantasy to sexual interaction (Heiman & LoPiccolo, 1988; Leiblum, Pervin, & Campbell, 1989). This change may be welcome news to the majority of North Americans who fantasize during masturbation and coitus but who may experience guilt over their thoughts (Cado & Leitenberg, 1990; Davidson & Hoffman, 1986).

Guilt reactions to fantasies, particularly when they occur during intercourse, are related to beliefs that such fantasies are deviant and negatively related to sexual adjustment. In fact, Cado and Leitenberg (1990) found that those people who reported feeling most guilty about having fantasies during intercourse were more sexually dissatisfied and had more frequent sexual problems than those individuals who felt less guilty.

Perhaps the reason that sexual fantasies have been regarded historically with fear and guilt lies in the Christian belief that thinking about something is the same as doing it, in which case thinking about having sex with someone other than a marital partner is as much a sin as having sex with the person (see Chapter 1). This lack of distinction between thought and behavior continues to color opinion about sexual fantasy. Much of the contemporary concern over pornography is based on the assumption that fantasies derived from erotic material are eventually put into action. Such a progression from thinking to behavior among those who view erotic material has not yet been demonstrated (see Chapter 16).

In any case, it is important to recognize the difference between fantasy and reality. Fantasizing about socially unacceptable behavior is not the same as engaging in it. We may have numerous fantasies in the course of a day that we never act out. Although relatively little research is available on the various functions that fantasy can fulfill, some of the more common of these functions can be identified.

### The Functions of Fantasy

At different times and at different stages in a relationship, the same person can have fantasies for different reasons. Many of us have felt attraction to someone with whom we have been casually acquainted. In the desire to change the relationship from a platonic friendship to a romance, one or both people may imagine conversations and interactions leading to increasingly intimate emotional and physical contact. An example of such an extended fantasy appeared at the beginning of this chapter. These imaginary encounters permit us to rehearse ways of approaching the other person, to consider his or her likely responses, and even to make ourselves aware of the long-term consequences of the various behaviors that we envision ourselves trying. The utility of such rehearsal fantasies is that we can select the one that feels most comfortable and that seems most likely to lead to the outcome we desire.

Fantasies and daydreams can be a source of entertainment, transporting us to exciting places

and allowing us to mingle with celebrities and embark on exciting erotic adventures. Such fantasies can relieve the monotony of driving on a tedious stretch of road or sitting in a boring class or meeting. Sexual reveries also permit us to indulge in thinking about behavior that we would not consider doing in reality, and to imagine having partners who are unavailable to us. Alternatively, our fantasies can be built around the memories of previously rewarding sexual experiences.

Some fantasies involve imagined events that the person has no desire to experience in reality, such as sadomasochistic activities or rape. Such fantasies may be either solitary or shared with a partner. It is particularly important to realize that this kind of fantasy does not in and of itself indicate that the fantasizer actually desires to be the helpless victim of an aggressor. For example, Gold, Balzano, and Stamey (1991) asked college women to report their sexual fantasies and to describe their feelings following the fantasy. Those women who reported fantasies involving force, compared to those who did not, reported more fear, guilt, and disgust, and less happiness and less likelihood to act on their fantasy. Women with childhood sexual abuse experiences are also likely to report more fantasies containing images of force (Gold, 1991).

As noted earlier, males and females in our culture are socialized to play different roles in their sexual interactions. Just as women are traditionally expected to play a passive sexual role, men are trained to take the initiative sexually. As the traditional active partner, however, the man not only has responsibility for selecting and carrying out a sexual script, but also regularly risks rejection. Moreover, the initiator of sexual interactions misses the pleasure of being pursued.

Accordingly, some women may have difficulty allowing themselves to be sexually desirous and responsive unless they imagine themselves as unable to control a partner's advances. This fantasy is reflected in such common expressions as "He swept me off my feet" and "He hypnotized me with his eyes" (Cassell, 1984). Fantasies about being raped, tied down, or made love to while sleeping may also have the effect of releasing the fantasizer from responsibility for her (or his) own arousal.

Finally, individuals may use fantasy either to enhance or to intensify sexual intimacy in a relationship of long duration. For example, in numerous studies, a majority of the women reported having fantasies during sexual intercourse with their husbands or partners (Crepault et al., 1977; Hariton & Singer, 1974; Lunde et al., 1991; Pelletier & Herold, 1988). They often employed these fantasies to enhance their sexual arousal and to help to trigger orgasm (Davidson & Hoffman, 1986; Lunde et al., 1991; Talbot, Beech, & Vaughan, 1980). The use of fantasies for this purpose appears to be positively related to orgasmic capacity and sexual satisfaction for women, but this relationship is less clear in men (Alfonso, Allison, & Dunn, 1992; Arndt, Foehl, & Good, 1985; Davidson & Hoffman, 1986; Purifoy et al., 1992). In other words, fantasies are not necessarily compensations for an unrewarding sexual existence. Such fantasies may be enjoyed without the knowledge of the other partner, or they may be shared and enacted with a partner, as described in Barbach and Levine's book, *Shared Intimacies* (1980, pp. 85–86):

*Once we were traveling out of the country and we decided to act out a fantasy of mine. I went down to the hotel bookstore and Murray came down and acted as if we were strangers and picked me up. We just started talking, asking each other our names and where we were from. Then he invited me back to the room and it was as if we hardly knew each other and were having sex for the first time.*

*Kate and I wanted to go to a porno drive-in but we got there late and were unable to get in. On the way home, we decided to act out our own fantasy, to make up our own film, so to speak. . . . It was weird because when we walked in the door, we felt like these other people. We sat on the couch and talked, and I don't remember if we had much of a dialogue. I don't think we did. I think it was mostly expressions, visual eye contact and that sort of thing. And we went to bed and put on our pajamas, which we don't wear ordinarily. We crawled into bed and we lay there for a long time with no conversation and found ourselves getting closer and closer and then touching. I put my arm around her*

*and we lay like that for a long time, feeling very, very close. Then it became obvious to both of us, these two new people, that there was an interest and a desire to continue from that point on. We undressed each other and explored each other's bodies and the whole time it was nonverbal. . . . We made love to each other, I don't remember the specific events, but we kissed and held each other and got into oral-genital sex and held each other afterward. Then we just went to sleep. The next morning, we were back to ourselves.*

These two fantasies, the first by a 35-year-old woman and her husband, and the second by a 34-year-old woman and her female lover, show how sharing fantasies can provide both partners with pleasure. But a word of caution is in order. When two people know each other well, are secure in their relationship, and have agreed that the sharing of fantasies is fun and a source of pleasure, mutual disclosures can enrich a relationship. However, the disclosure of fantasies under other conditions can evoke pain in a mate, who may conclude that the partner finds him or her unsatisfying or who may come to feel inadequate in the face of a lover's desires that he or she can never fulfill. In deciding whether to share fantasies with a loved partner, it is appropriate to consider one's reasons as well as the potential effect of doing so.

## Communication About Sexuality

In the preceding section, we considered the communication of fantasies with a loved one. In this section, we broaden the discussion to include the development of communication skills relating to sexuality. Communicating sexual feelings to a potential or actual partner requires care and practice. For people who have learned to associate their sexual feelings with shame or sin, sharing sexual feelings can also take courage. We discuss socialization practices that increase or reduce the likelihood that we can communicate our sexual feelings effectively. Traditionally, males and females are given different messages about discussing their feelings, and we examine how that may relate to heterosexual communication. Finally, we focus on methods of enhancing interpersonal communication, especially relating to sexual issues.

## Socialization for Communicating About Sex

We are constantly bombarded with the message that sexiness is an attractive quality; indeed, our media stars get a great deal of money and adulation for projecting "sexy" images. But just like the rest of us, stars such as Madonna, Tom Cruise, and Kim Basinger have private lives in which they need to communicate and negotiate their desires with their partners. Unfortunately, many of us—private citizens and media stars alike—are given little training in communication skills.

During infancy, we do not possess fine discriminations for our feelings. Our parents and caretakers learn to distinguish between when we are feeling hungry versus when we want to be held. When we become verbal as toddlers, they provide us with labels to help us express our wants. We learn to communicate that we desire food, have tummyaches, or crave attention. Few members of our culture, however, are given labels for sexual feelings during infancy, childhood, or adolescence. Further, if we fondled our genitals during infancy and childhood, most of us not only learned no label for that activity but also may have been punished for our behavior.

Although students enrolled in a human sexuality course tend to be more liberal and knowledgeable about sex—even when they begin the class—than those enrolled in other classes at the same academic level, these well-informed students typically received little of their information from their parents. For example, only 14% of students enrolled in our sexuality course in 1994 had heard the word *clitoris* from their mothers, and only 3% (all males) had heard the word from their fathers. The word *penis* had been used by 20% of the students' mothers and 55% of their fathers.

We have also asked our students to indicate their most accurate source of information regarding the reproductive and passionate aspects of sexuality. Opponents of public-school sex edu-

cation assert that children should receive information about sexuality from their families rather than from teachers. As Table 6.2 shows, however, students clearly perceived their parents as providing little information about the reproductive aspects of sex and even less about its passionate aspects. These findings about our own students are consistent with other research (Allgeier, 1983; Gebhard, 1977a).

The discrepancy described above in the likelihood of hearing the word *clitoris* versus the word *penis* from parents might be explained partially by the fact that the penis can be seen more easily than the clitoris. The word *vagina*, however, which also refers to an organ not easily seen, was used by 52% of our students' mothers and 14% of their fathers. Why, then, is the term *clitoris* so neglected by parents, and why is discussion of that organ so often omitted from sex-education materials?

One possible explanation is that every other organ of the body can be described as having some separate, societally approved function. The nose is for breathing and smelling, the mouth is for eating and talking, the penis is for expelling urine and depositing sperm in the woman's uterus, the rectum is for eliminating feces, and the vagina is the passage for menstrual discharge and for a baby during childbirth. To describe clitoral function, however, parents or teachers must introduce the concept of sexual arousal and pleasure. All those other parts of the body (nose, mouth, penis, rectum, vagina) may also be associated with sexual pleasure, but parents can provide an explanation of what those organs do without ever mentioning sexual pleasure. Parental reluctance to acknowledge the pleasurable sensations that many children experience may explain the failure to discuss the clitoris when describing sexual anatomy to children.

For young girls, ignorance of the clitoris and its function presents a severe disadvantage in sexual self-stimulation. Either they do not acquire important knowledge about the erotic capacities of their own bodies, or, if they do, the unexplained and unacknowledged experience may lead them to associate pleasure with guilt.

Not only do we often ignore the function of the clitoris, but we have few ways of referring to it. Although we have many slang terms for the

**TABLE 6.2  Sources of Sex Information**

In 1994, we asked our sexuality course students to indicate their most accurate source of information regarding the reproductive aspects of sexuality, such as fertilization, pregnancy, and the passionate aspects, such as arousal, lubrication, erection, and orgasm. Their responses are presented in this table.

| Source | Reproductive Aspects (%) | Passionate Aspects (%) |
|---|---|---|
| Mother | 22 | 0 |
| Father | 1 | 0 |
| Sibling | 1 | 5 |
| Friends | 7 | 25 |
| Boyfriend/girlfriend | 0 | 22 |
| Books/magazines | 11 | 32 |
| School | 47 | 11 |
| Doctor | 3 | 0 |
| Church | 0 | 0 |
| Other | 3 | 0 |

penis (*prick, bone, dick, tool, rod, peter, womper,* and *thing,* to name several), there are few slang terms for the clitoris beyond the shortened form *clit.* In our informal search among students, friends, and colleagues, we have encountered only three other slang terms for the clitoris—*joy button, magic button,* and (ironically, given that the clitoris is part of the female anatomy) *little man in a boat.* There is a similar discrepancy in the number of slang terms for male ejaculate and vaginal lubrication. How many expressions have you heard for each?

Thus both the biological differences in the obviousness of the penis and the clitoris and societal attitudes about sexual pleasure may conspire to produce an interesting developmental paradox. During prenatal as well as pubescent development, females mature earlier than males—physiologically, intellectually, and socially—but in the development of interest in sex and self-stimulation, they mature later. That is, a larger proportion of boys than girls report masturbating in early adolescence, and males experience orgasm with more consistency than do females through-

out the life span. This difference in the development of the capacity for sexual enjoyment may be magnified by socialization experiences that emphasize males as sexual and females as asexual (see Chapter 12).

When punishment and an absence of labels for touching genitals characterize our initial experience with expressing sexual curiosity and feelings, then discussing our feelings about sexual arousal with our parents as we enter adolescence is difficult. We have already learned that sexual topics are not acceptable for dinner-table talks or even private discussions with family members. Many of us are left to muddle through our feelings without guidance from our parents.

What if our parents did, however, acknowledge that we have sexual feelings and that there are words—labels—for these feelings: *arousal, irritation, interest, curiosity*? We might then be given permission to talk freely about our own sexual feelings. But that parental acknowledgment rarely occurs in our society. So we enter adolescence with an inadequate vocabulary, and, in many cases, without an environment conducive to open discussions with our parents. Thus the people who presumably care about us the most at that point in our lives avoid giving us the opportunity to "rehearse" later discussion of sexual feelings.

Those parents who avoid discussion of sexual topics may do so because of fears that such conversations encourage their offspring to engage in early sexual exploration. To examine the relationship of parental attitudes, extent of family communication, and adolescent sexual activity, Terri Fisher conducted a series of studies in which data were gathered from adolescents and their parents (Fisher, 1987, 1988, 1989a, 1989b, 1990; Fisher & Hall, 1988). She found that among parents with relatively permissive attitudes, family discussions of sex were related to a greater likelihood of females engaging in premarital sexual behavior. One could argue that permissive families produce more sexually active adolescents. It is also plausible, however, that sexually active young women find it easier to discuss their sexual experiences and feelings with relatively permissive parents than do sexually active women with more restrictive parents. Fisher also found that males who had discussed sex with their parents, and males with sexually liberal parents, had more accurate sexual information and that they were more likely to be using effective contraceptive methods.

However, in a comparison of nine measures of family communication with 363 college students and their parents, Fisher (1993) found no relationship among responses to measures of parent-child communication and the sexual activity and contraceptive use of the students. To some extent, Fisher's finding of no relationship between parent-child communication and offspring's sexual and contraceptive behavior may stem from differing perceptions of parents and offspring. Specifically, other studies have demonstrated that parents and their offspring do not always agree on the extent of communication that has taken place (Gecas & Schwalbe, 1986; Tims & Masland, 1985). Fisher (1989a) suggested that adolescents' reports probably should be given more weight than those of parents because it probably matters "less how much discussion actually took place than how much discussion the student perceives to have taken place" (p. 639).

## Male-Female Differences in the Communication of Feelings

Despite overall societal restrictions on parent-child communication about sex, there are differences in the extent to which it is acceptable for males versus females to talk about feelings versus sex. In most families, it is more acceptable for girls than boys to talk about their positive or depressed emotions (the so-called "tender" feelings), and more acceptable for boys than girls to talk about hostile feelings such as anger and aggression, and sexual interests. To understand this distinction, consider these situations.

1a. Mary, a ninth grader, comes home from school and tells her mother that she has had a really bad day. She likes Tom and thought that he liked her, but he seems to be a lot more interested in her best friend, Becky. While Mary was talking to Rick, Becky's boyfriend, about the school play, Tom walked Becky to math class and offered to help Becky with her assignment. Mary is feeling ignored by Tom and resentful toward Becky—who knows that Mary is interested in Tom—for encouraging Tom's attention. Mary cries because she feels as if she is losing not only Tom but also her best friend. Her mother holds her to comfort her.

1b. Tom, who is in the ninth grade, returns from school and yells at the family dog. His father asks what is wrong, and Tom says that he would like to punch Rick out because he is coming on to Mary.

Now, let's reverse these scenarios:

2a. Tom, a ninth grader, comes home from school and tells his mother that he has had a really bad day. He likes Mary and thought that she liked him, but she seems to be a lot more interested in his best friend, Rick. While Tom was talking to Becky, Rick's girlfriend, about the school play, Rick walked Mary to math class and offered to help Mary with her assignment. Tom is feeling ignored by Mary and resentful toward Rick—who knows that Tom is interested in Mary—for encouraging Mary's attention. Tom cries because he feels as if he is losing not only Mary but also his best friend. His mother holds him to comfort him.

2b. Mary, who is in the ninth grade, comes home from school and yells at the family dog. Her father asks what is wrong, and she says that she would like to punch Becky out because she is coming on to Tom.

You may find the first set of scenarios familiar from your own days in high school, but given differences in gender-role expectations in our society, the second set probably sounds ludicrous. Most girls do not talk about punching out their girlfriends, and most ninth-grade boys do not cry on their mother's shoulders or give their parents detailed descriptions of their feelings. We are not suggesting that these differences in communication styles are inherent aspects of being male or female. Instead, the tendency in our culture for males to ignore their feelings or to give only minimal information about their emotions, and for females to provide more detail than males about their fears and hopes, presumably stems from the differences in training that boys and girls receive about acceptable ways to express their feelings. When people subsequently attempt to establish heterosexual relationships, these gender differences in the content and style of communication of feelings may magnify the difficulty of resolving the inevitable problems that emerge in ongoing relationships.

When the focus is on sexual feelings per se, the gender-role expectations are reversed. A stereotypic part of being masculine in our culture involves intense interest in obtaining sexual experience, for example, "scoring." In contrast, many adolescent women fear that communicating about their sexual desires in general, or their preferences for specific kinds of stimulation in particular, indicates to their partners that they are immoral, dirty, or "experienced." Another concern that women may have is that sexual requests may threaten their partners' feelings of prowess. Regardless of its source, such reluctance to communicate may result in sexual dysfunctions and/or date rape (see Chapters 8 and 12).

Negative attitudes about sexuality may also interfere with clear communication and thus may be associated with difficulties in relationships in both the sexual and the nonsexual realms. Several different measures have been developed to assess attitudes about sexuality, including the Sexual Opinion Survey and the Sex Guilt Scale.

## Erotophilia and Erotophobia

To measure emotional responses to sexuality, Byrne and his colleagues (Byrne et al., 1974) developed the 21-item Sexual Opinion Survey (SOS). Responses to the survey can range from primarily negative (when a respondent is *erotophobic*) to primarily positive (when a respondent is *erotophilic*). Items in the survey include the following: "Swimming in the nude with a member of the opposite sex would be an exciting experience" (positive); "If people knew that I was interested in oral sex, I would be embarrassed" (negative); "Thoughts that I may have homosexual tendencies would not worry me at all" (positive). Erotophilia-erotophobia is thought to be learned in childhood and adolescence through experiences associating sexual cues with positive or negative emotional states.

SOS scores are predictive of a wide range of sexual attitudes and behaviors among North American students, as well as among university graduates from India and Hong Kong. In most studies, females have tended to be more erotophobic than are males. This gender difference may stem from females' greater exposure than males to negative messages about sexuality. As might be expected, erotophobic students reported more parental strictness about sex than did erotophilic students. Compared to erotophilic parents, erotophobic parents reported having given their children less information about sex. And the college students' early experiences appear to be related to differences in their sexual and contraceptive behaviors. Erotophilic college students reported more past sexual experience, more frequent masturbation, and more sexual partners than did erotophobic students. Further, use of contraception was both more common and more consistent among erotophilic students than

---

**erotophobic**—having a negative emotional response to sexual feelings and experiences.

**erotophilic**—having a positive emotional response to sexual feelings and experiences.

**Box 6.1**

## Do You Feel Guilty About Your Sexual Feelings?

*Nice bias [underlined] of course I am going to be like all healthy people [handwritten]*

The following statements are a sample of items from Mosher's (1988) revised measure of sex guilt. Respondents are instructed to rate each item on a 7-point scale from 0 (not at all true) to 6 (extremely true).

*Horrible questionnaire [handwritten]*

**Masturbation . . .**

1. is wrong and will ruin you
2. helps one feel eased and relaxed

**Sex relations before marriage . . .**

3. should be permitted
4. are wrong and immoral

**When I have sexual desires . . .** ✓

5. I enjoy it like all healthy human beings
6. I fight them for I must have complete control of my body

**As a child, sex play . . .**

7. is immature and ridiculous
8. was indulged in

**Unusual sex practices . . .**

9. are awful and unthinkable
10. are all right if both partners agree

---

among their erotophobic peers. A number of other behaviors are associated with erotophilia-erotophobia. Erotophilic people, compared to those who are erotophobic, have more positive reactions to erotic material, think about sex more often, draw more explicit and more detailed nude figures, and create more explicit and positively toned erotic fantasies (Byrne & Schulte, 1990; Fisher, Byrne, White, & Kelley, 1988).

*Sex Guilt*

Among the emotions that can become associated with sexual arousal is guilt. *Sex guilt* is defined as a generalized expectancy for self-mediated punishment in response to violating or anticipating the violation of one's standards of proper sexual conduct (Mosher, 1966, 1988). Psychologist Donald Mosher constructed a measure of sex guilt in 1966 that was revised in 1988. The measure has been widely used in the investigation of various sexual issues. For a sample of the items in the revised Mosher Guilt Inventory, see Box

**sex guilt**—sense of guilt resulting from the violation of personal standards of proper sexual behavior.

6.1. Mosher assumed that individuals who feel guilty about their sexual responses were scolded and punished during their childhood for interest in sexual matters to a greater extent than were people who respond to their sexual feelings with acceptance and enjoyment (see Figure 6.5).

For example, imagine a three-year-old girl playing idly with her vulva while watching "Sesame Street" on television. Her parents might scold her, slap her hand, or order her to stop. Alternatively, they might talk to her about the enjoyment of touching one's genitals but point out that it is more appropriate to masturbate ("rub yourself") in private. Yet even this latter message can have inhibiting consequences for the little girl when she grows up because she is being told that the activity of fondling her vulva is a solitary one. Years later, she might be uncomfortable with self-stimulation in the context of sexual interaction with her partner. It is probably advisable, however, to let her know that most people in our culture react negatively to the sight of someone casually masturbating in the presence of others.

One such isolated incident would probably have little effect on the extent to which the child will associate guilt and anxiety with sexuality in

**FIGURE 6.5**
**Parental Responses to Self-Exploration**
Although many parents take a dim view of their toddlers' self-exploration and genital stimulation, this mother grins while watching her son playing with his genitals.

her adulthood. The parent who spanks a 3-year-old for casually playing with herself, however, is probably also likely to punish the girl for other activities that the parent interprets as sexual, for example, playing doctor, asking questions about genitals, or telling sexual jokes. Over time, the child absorbs the message that sex is bad, dirty, and sinful, and the person who shows too much curiosity or interest about sexuality is equally bad, dirty, and sinful.

To protect their children from the unwanted consequences of sexual intimacy, such as unintended pregnancy and sexually transmitted diseases, parents may discourage children from having anything to do with sex. The problem with such discouragement is that associating sex with anxiety and guilt over long periods of time is linked to the development of certain undesirable characteristics. Indeed, several studies have

found that people high in sex guilt operate at lower levels of moral reasoning than do people with less sex guilt. For example, Gerrard and Gibbons (1982) studied the relationship among sexual experience (not necessarily intercourse), sex guilt, and sexual moral reasoning. Their findings indicated that experience is important in the development of sexual morality, and that people high in sex guilt tend to avoid sexual experience, thus hindering their development of sexual morality. Based on her research with female college students, Gerrard (1987) concluded that, although sex guilt did not necessarily keep women from having sexual intercourse, it did appear to inhibit the use of effective contraceptives.

Extensive research on sex guilt after childhood demonstrates the influence of conditioned or learned responses on our capacity for sexual arousal and pleasure. Cannon (1987) summarized the research on the relationship of sex guilt to other variables. Based on these studies, he characterized a "sexually guilty" person as

> an individual who is devout and constant in religious beliefs, who subscribes to higher authority, believes in myths about sex, may use denial in dealing with feelings about sex, is less sexually active, is more offended and disgusted by explicit sexual material, less tolerant of variations in others' sexual behavior, at a lower level in Kohlberg's stages of moral reasoning, and who holds traditional views of what males' and females' sexual roles should be. (p. 9)

Rather than rearing offspring to feel guilty about sex, parents might emphasize effective communication skills and the importance of open discussion about sexual functions and feelings. Building children's sexual knowledge and confidence will more adequately prepare them for dealing with their emerging sexual feelings in a healthy manner than will instilling guilt.

## Gender Differences and Similarities in Arousal

Studies of sex guilt have consistently yielded this finding: females score higher on measures of sex guilt than do males. Is there something in the biology of females that makes them more susceptible than males to anxiety and guilt over sexuality? Probably not. The explanation probably lies in the fact that daughters, not sons, can become pregnant, and so parents may be more restrictive in training their daughters than in training their sons. As we will see in Chapters 12 and 13, females are less likely to engage in self-stimulation than are their male counterparts, and they generally respond more slowly during sexual interaction. An examination of research on the conditions under which males and females respond to erotic material suggests that different cultural expectations for men and women contribute heavily to the observed gender differences.

A great deal of survey research has supported the assumption that men are more interested in, and more responsive to, sexual cues than are women. However, experimental studies conducted during the past decade have indicated that men and women respond similarly to erotic stimuli such as sexually explicit stories and pictures, and X-rated films. Why does survey research find gender differences that experimental research does not?

In the survey method, men and women are asked to report their past and present levels of arousal to erotic material, how often they purchase or seek such material, and so forth. In our culture interest in sex is considered more appropriate for men than for women.* Thus, in responding to surveys, men may accurately estimate, or even overestimate, their interest in erotica, whereas women may underestimate theirs in an attempt to present themselves in a socially desirable light.

How have the experimental studies differed from the survey methods? Volunteers for experimental research on erotica are exposed to sexual stimuli. Their responses are then measured through self-reports, physiological recordings of their genital responses, or both. These physiological measures generally demonstrate little or no difference in arousal between men and women when they are exposed to erotica. As Fisher (1983) pointed out, compared with men, women have been trained over a long period of time to avoid erotic material and to show less interest in sex. But when men and women are exposed to sexual stimuli, women are as capable of arousal as are men.

The differences produced by the two research approaches are exemplified by Heiman's (1975) study of responses to erotic audiotapes. She found that males and females did not differ when their arousal was assessed by physiologic measures. When self-reports of arousal were compared, however, several male-female differences emerged. First, on average, males reported greater arousal than did females. Second, whereas the arousal reported by males matched

---

*We observe this attitude in the students who take our human sexuality classes. When we ask them for the term referring to a woman who has an insatiable desire for sex, they readily answer "nymphomaniac." When we ask for the corresponding term for a man (satyr), the silence is invariably broken by a male voice saying "normal!"

the arousal indicated by their physiologic recordings, females' reports did not always reflect the physiologically measured arousal. In fact, in about half the cases, females reported either no arousal at all or less arousal than was indicated by the devices attached to their bodies.

We might attribute the discrepancies between the reported and measured arousal of women in this study solely to cultural training that discourages women from being frank about sexual feelings. This explanation seems unlikely, though, given the way in which Heiman obtained the sample of women who participated in her study. These women answered a newspaper ad seeking volunteers for a study of responses to erotic stimulation. The volunteers were not virgins, and before they agreed to participate in the study, they were told that participation would involve the insertion of devices into their vaginas to measure the extent of their arousal. Presumably, relatively modest females would have been unlikely to answer the ad in the first place.

If modesty is not responsible, why did many of the women in Heiman's study fail to perceive their own arousal? When we first read her study, that question intrigued us, so we asked students in our human-sexuality classes to recall the first time they could remember having the kind of feeling that they would now label as sexual arousal. We asked them to write down, anonymously, their thoughts on the reasons for their physical responses at that time.

In general, the men attributed their erections, pre-ejaculatory emissions, and so forth, to having been aroused either by their thoughts about, or their interaction with, another person. About half the women drew similar conclusions about their vaginal lubrication and "tingling" genital feelings. But the other half of the women gave various other explanations. Many thought the vaginal lubrication had been just another variation in their menstrual cycle that they had not noticed before. Several women attributed the lubrication to a "clear period," and a sizable number reported that they thought they might have had a vaginal infection. One woman wrote that she had asked her mother whether she should see a doctor or get some medicine.

Biological differences in the extent to which physical changes associated with sexual arousal are readily observable may also account for some of these gender differences. Although arousal produces vasocongestion (blood engorgement) in both men and women, women are sometimes unaware of the lubrication of their vaginas, whereas erect penises call attention to themselves.

This biological difference in the effects of vasocongestion, in turn, is enhanced by cultural expectations. Men are encouraged to be sexually active, whereas women are generally discouraged from seeking sexual stimulation and satisfaction. Men are trained to be sexual responders, and women learn to be sexual stimuli. In summary, anatomical differences and learned psychological differences between males and females may interact to produce differences in the tendencies of men and women to report arousal. When physiological arousal is directly measured, however, the gender differences are reduced or eliminated (Heiman, 1977). Some stereotypes about gender differences in sexual behavior may be less accurate than is commonly believed.

We now turn to a discussion of the role of communication in the development of sexual relationships.

## Interpersonal Communication and Sexual Intimacy

Have you ever tried to matchmake—that is, to set up a relationship between two friends of yours who did not know one another? Have you ever watched a female friend attempt to develop a relationship with a man to whom she is attracted? If so, some of the findings that we are about to report will probably be less surprising to you than if you have accepted the stereotypic belief that it is men who control the selection of partners, who "come on" to women, and who determine whether a relationship will develop.

Based on 900 hours of observations in bar settings, Perper (1985) concluded that it is often women, not men, who determine the outcome of a casual contact in a singles' bar. Perper observed a fairly standard sequence of events between couples in their initial interaction: approach, talk, turn, touch, and synchronization of body movements and posture. Initially, synchronization involves only arm and head movements, but it progresses to such complex, simultaneous movements as drinking in unison, and it can end in full-body synchronization. Either person in a potential courtship can escalate the situation by making an overture that, if accepted, raises the level of intimacy between the two people. If the overture is not accepted or responded to, the interaction de-escalates—for example, one person may look away while the other is talking.

Perper observed that more than half the time, the woman initiated the courtship sequence by signaling or approaching the man. Women, Perper found, have a much clearer understanding of courtship strategies than do men; he estimated that 90% of men cannot coherently describe the courtship sequence, even though most of them can enact it with a female initiator. A female's ability to initiate and escalate a sexual interaction is called *proceptivity*. In proceptive behavior, a woman must first choose a man in whom she is interested. If a man responds with arousal to a woman's proceptive behavior, a "power transition" may occur, in which he initiates overt sexual behavior. Perper hypothesized that couples pass through a transition state that begins proceptively and ends with both people's being sexually aroused; the man then initiates sexual foreplay.

There is further evidence that women take an active role in courtship (Moore, 1985; McCormick & Jones, 1989; O'Sullivan & Byers, 1992). Moore observed more than 200 women in diverse settings and coded their nonverbal behaviors. (As you read this, you might try to recall whether you saw these patterns the last time that you were in a college bar or singles' bar.) For example, Moore described different kinds of glances that she observed women using. With the room-encompassing glance, a woman scans an entire room in not more than five or ten seconds without making eye contact with anyone. With the short darting glance, a woman gazes at a man but looks away within three seconds. With the gaze fixate, a woman makes eye contact for more than three seconds; sometimes her glance is returned. Moore also frequently witnessed such behaviors

as smiling and laughing, and tossing, touching, or twisting the hair; but she observed coy smiles and giggles less commonly. A woman's signaling gestures included hiking her skirt slightly, and touching various parts of her own body or the potential partner's body. Two behaviors involved whole-body movement: parade and approach. In parade, a woman walks across the room with an exaggerated swing of her hips, her stomach held in, her head held high, and her back arched, so that her breasts are pushed out. In approach behavior, a woman positions herself within two feet of a man, after which the two usually talk.

The women whom Moore (1985) studied were discriminating in terms of the circumstances under which they displayed these behaviors. She observed women in four different settings: a singles' bar, a university snack bar, the university library, and a women's meeting. Women were most likely to perform these displays and solicitations in a bar; such displays were not so common in a snack bar and even less frequent in a library, and least frequent in the women's meeting. Moore found a strong correlation (.89) between the number of solicitations or displays that women gave to men and the likelihood of men approaching the women. Moore concluded that women are able to determine when and where they interact with potential partners by exhibiting or withholding displays and solicitations. She theorized that because women can successfully elicit numerous male approaches, they can choose from a variety of available men. Moore also noted that sometimes it took several solicitation behaviors by a particular woman before a man would approach, and that a man was generally reluctant to approach if he had not been signaled that the woman would accept his advances.

More recently, Moore (1993) observed junior-high-school girls' signaling. They displayed a smaller number of signals to junior high school boys, but the signals they employed were more exaggerated than those employed by adult women. For example, the hair toss was considerably more dramatic than that displayed by women. In addition, they appeared to mimic the signaling behavior of the dominant girls in their group. Interestingly, the boys were far less likely

---

**proceptivity**—the initiation and escalation of a sexual interaction with another person.

to approach these girls than were men to approach women who engaged in the more subtle but wider range of signals. Perhaps these displays by the girls were rehearsals for later behaviors that will be more effective in eliciting male interest.

In summary, then, recent research bears out what many women may already know: women use a wide repertoire of signals and displays to attract men. If a man responds to a woman's initiations, the dance of courtship begins. If both partners respond to each other, there follows an escalation of intimacy and eventually a power transition, in which the man assumes responsibility for initiating sexual intimacy.

We have considered situations in which two people respond to one another's initiations. Courtship does not always proceed so smoothly, however; two problems may arise. First, at any point in the sequence, one person may reject the other's advances. Second, one person may misinterpret the other's signals. We will have more to say about these possible misinterpretations of courtship behaviors in Chapters 18 and 19.

## Enhancing Interpersonal Communication

During infancy and early childhood, we are provided with labels to help us to distinguish and to communicate our desires for hunger versus holding. Many of us, however, are not given labels to help us distinguish, as we advance into adolescence and adulthood, between desire for cuddling and desire for coitus or for *cunnilingus* or *fellatio* (oral stimulation). Negative cultural connotations associated with desire for various forms of sexual stimulation, or the fear that specific sexual requests will upset a partner, can make it difficult for us to say to a mate, "You know, what I'd really enjoy right now is to give (or receive) oral sex," or to say, "Right now, I'm feeling very tense about my final exams, and I'd just like for you to cuddle me."

How can we improve interpersonal communication about our personal and/or sexual feelings? What can we do to increase the likelihood of honestly relating our feelings to potential or actual partners? At the outset, as noted earlier,

we need a vocabulary to use, and permission to use it from those whom we admire: our parents, teachers, peers, and partners. Assuming that we have a sexual vocabulary and feel free to use it, we need to communicate—verbally and nonverbally—what we want from potential or actual sexual partners.

In a widely cited and widely misinterpreted study, Abbey (1982) asked heterosexual men and women who were previously unknown to one another to engage in a brief dialogue. Observers watched each man and woman through a one-way mirror. Using three separate 7-point scales, the observers indicated the extent to which they perceived each man and woman first as flirtatious, then as seductive, and finally as promiscuous. Abbey found that female observers were less likely to perceive the woman in the couple as engaging in these behaviors than were male observers, and from this she concluded that men sometimes misinterpret women's friendly behavior as a sign of sexual intent.

Abbey's conclusion would be warranted except for the fact that both male and female observers gave low ratings of sexual intent to the men and women whom they were watching. That is, on the three 7-point scales, with 7 indicating seductiveness, promiscuity, and flirtatiousness, and 1 indicating the absence of these traits, both male and female observers gave ratings well below the midpoint (1, 2, or 3) to the woman, which showed a perceived absence of these behaviors. Abbey's (1982) findings have been replicated in subsequent research by Gaulier and Allgeier (1988) and Saal, Johnson, and Weber (1989). As with Abbey's findings, ratings of women on the dimensions of seductive, flirtatious, and promiscuous were below the midpoint; thus neither males nor females perceived women to be signaling sexual intent in a casual conversation.

On the other hand, in an actual interaction, it may sometimes be difficult for a man to interpret a woman's signals, and vice versa. Men's difficulties in evaluating a woman's desire may be magnified by the fact that in our society, it is still considered the man's prerogative to initiate sexual intimacy, whereas women are expected to be the "gatekeepers"—that is, to take responsibility for setting the limits on the extent of sexual intimacy. In several surveys of students' misperceptions in natural settings, 72% of women and 60% of men reported having had their friendliness misperceived as a sexual invitation (Abbey, 1987). Misperceptions were most common by casual friends (35%) or acquaintances (24%) and less common by strangers (21%) or close friends (14%). When students in Abbey's surveys were also asked to describe their experiences with misperceiving the intentions of potential partners, men and women were equally likely to report having misperceived someone else's friendliness as indicating sexual interest (40%). For example, one woman wrote, "We had a very good conversation (at a party)." Another said, "Since I liked him I took everything he did as a hint, and he was very attentive and nice to me. However, the next day he acted as though he had never seen me before in my life" (pp. 189–90).

We noted earlier that women appear to select men and to signal their interest in getting to know them better. A signaling of interest is simply that; it does not necessarily mean that a woman is ready to have sex with the man. Women appear to be signaling a desire to get to know the man better and then deciding whether they want to develop a relationship with him; that is, women may perceive the process as involving a series of steps, with each decision dependent on previous interactions (see Allgeier & Royster, 1990). Let us examine a possible scenario from a woman's standpoint.

1. Hmm . . . that guy looks interesting. I wonder who he is and what he's like. [Woman then tries to attract his attention—for example, a trip to the bathroom or bar—parading, glancing, and smiling at him, then returns to her "home" spot.]

2. Ah, here he comes; he looks really neat. [Man approaches and asks woman about further interaction; for example, would she like to dance? Would she like a drink? They begin talking for a little while, and the woman decides either that she is interested in further interaction or that, on closer inspection, the man is really not interesting to her. One of the following interactions may result.]

3a. Oh, I'm at the university, too. What's your major? Yes, I'd like to dance (or drink), or . . .

3b. [Thinking that he is not someone with whom she would like to pursue a relationship] Oh, I'm at the university, too. Thanks for the invitation, but I'm waiting for a friend, so I guess I'll see you later.

In the event of 3a, they may dance or have a drink together and talk further. If the man is interested in the woman, he may suggest that they leave their location for his or her place, or that they get together for a date. If the woman is interested, she may agree to leave the location or to meet at a future time. But interest does not necessarily mean a desire for sexual intimacy in the immediate future. Misperceptions may occur because the behaviors that are misperceived can have ambiguous meanings. As Abbey noted (1987, p. 193), "Smiling may be used to convey friendliness or sexual attraction. . . . Agreeing to go to someone's apartment may be done in order to talk quietly or to signal willingness to have sex."

Thus difficulties may arise in an individual's interpretations of others' intentions and behavior. In light of women's socialization in our culture, and perhaps because of the gender differences in mate-selection strategies discussed earlier, most women want to spend some time getting to know a man before deciding whether to become sexually intimate. Even if a woman desires intimacy fairly early in the relationship, she risks the stereotype that a woman who does so is "easy" or has "rocking-chair heels" (that is, if a man pushes her slightly, she will immediately lie down for him).

If she is interested in further interaction with the man, therefore, a woman is confronted with a dilemma. She needs to communicate interest but probably wants to avoid giving him the impression that she is sexually available to anyone who approaches her. The man with whom she is interacting faces the problem of deciphering her intentions, assuming that he is interested in pursuing the relationship.

The man's difficulties in trying to infer the woman's intentions are also increased by the woman's use of what is known as the token no. If they leave the location where they have met for a more private place, such as his or her apartment, and become involved in kissing and petting, he may press for further intimacy to the point of intercourse. He sometimes may do so even when he is not ready to become more intimate because of his culturally based perceptions that he is supposed to press for sex to demonstrate his masculinity. In fact, Muehlenhard and Cook (1988) found that more men (63%) than women (46%) reported engaging in sexual intercourse when they did not wish to do so. Most of the unwanted sex reported by both men and women could have been avoided. However, the people having unwanted sex indicated that they did so because of feelings of pressure from their partner or peers, or their own internalized standards. In the men's cases, one of the internalized standards centered on the idea that "real" men do not refuse opportunities for sex.

Regardless of a woman's feelings, she may engage in the token no, that is, say no to sex when she really wants to become sexually intimate (Muehlenhard, 1988). For example, in Muehlenhard and Hollabaugh's (1988) study, almost 40% of the women reported refusing sexual intercourse when they wanted to have coitus. About a third of the women had used the token no only once, almost half of them had used it two to five times, and the remaining fifth had used it more frequently.

Their explanations for saying no when they really meant yes are instructive. Muehlenhard and Hollabaugh (1988) isolated three major categories of reasons for the use of the token no. The first involved "practical reasons," which included the fear of appearing promiscuous, the belief that sex was inappropriate in the relationship (because he was a boss or co-worker, or because she or the man was involved in another relationship), uncertainty about the potential partner's feelings for her, fear of getting pregnant or contracting a sexually transmitted disease, and inappropriateness of the physical setting for a sexual interaction. Of the women who used the token no, 98% indicated that such practical reasons were at least somewhat important in their decision. The second category was labeled

"inhibition-related reasons" and included emotional, religious, and moral reasons, the woman's fear of physical discomfort, and self-consciousness or embarrassment about her body. A large proportion of women (88%) indicated that these reasons were also at least somewhat important in their communication of the token no. The third category, "manipulative reasons," included game playing, anger with partner, and the desire to be in control. Again, a large majority (87%) endorsed this category as at least somewhat important in saying no when they wanted to become sexually intimate.

Individual differences among the women were also related to the probability of their use of the token no. Those who say no when they want to say yes to sex are at intermediate levels of traditionalism in their sexual attitudes. They are more likely to believe that token resistance is a common behavior among women, that male-female relationships are adversarial, that it is acceptable for men to use physical force in obtaining sex, and that women enjoy it more when men resort to force in sexual relationships.

These findings do not sit well with those who endorse egalitarian relationships between men and women (or between sexual partners of the same gender, for that matter), but use of the token no does exist. For example, in a study by Travis (cited by Allgeier, 1989), one woman described her last experience of sexual intercourse with a partner for the first time as involving force. In her narrative description of the occasion, she wrote:

> My boyfriend and I were alone at his house during the day last winter ... when we didn't have school because of a snow day. I went to his house to watch movies. Previously, before this day, we had had foreplay but not intercourse. We were on his bed watching TV when we began to kiss romantically. One thing led to another. I didn't want to have intercourse with him yet, but my body was saying yes. He kept trying and I kept saying no. Finally, he just sort of forced it in. I was a little mad but we continued to have sex. I did not stop him once we began. We've had sex ever since. We've been going out for over a year. During our first experi-

*ence, I loved him very much. I would have had sex earlier with him but I wanted to make sure it was right. I have to be in love with a guy. I could never have a one-nighter. Although I felt as if I wasn't ready, I now believe I was. The situation was awkward, but I think I was just afraid to admit that I did want to have sex so I rationalized by saying no to him.*

When asked if she had made a prior decision to have sex with that partner, she replied,

*Yes. I had decided to have sex with him earlier, but I wanted to wait awhile and play hard to get. I feel guys like a challenge, they want what they can't have. I've always wanted "sex" from my boyfriend but I said no so he'd respect me.*

When asked about her feelings now, she wrote: "Now my boyfriend and I laugh at it because he stated that it was an extremely mild form of date rape."

When asked to compare that experience with other sexual encounters, the woman replied, "Although I have more fun with my present boyfriend sexually, my ex-boyfriend [of] three years was extremely loving, understanding, and fun. My ex-boyfriend would have *never* forced himself on me! But, weirdly enough, I liked that forcefulness from my [present] boyfriend because I knew it was out of love." One might easily criticize this woman's reasoning, but it is important to remember the different cultural pressures on men (to have sex if possible) and women (to say no even when they want to have sex) before making such a judgment.

Harmonious relationships are further hindered by the fact that men believe they are being given a token no to a greater extent than women report saying no when they mean yes (Muehlenhard, 1988; Muehlenhard & Felts, 1987). For example, men were asked to respond to two vignettes describing a dating couple. In the first vignette, the woman behaved in a manner that would suggest a lack of sexual interest. She was dressed in a blouse with a prim bow, drank iced tea, and did not voluntarily kiss the man. Although she said no three times to the man's sexual advances and tried to move away, male re-

spondents thought that she was somewhat interested in having sex (a mean response of 4.5 on a 1 to 9 scale, with a 1 indicating no interest). In the second vignette, the woman wore a miniskirt, drank alcohol with the man, and voluntarily kissed him. As in the first vignette, the woman then verbally refused three times to have sex with the man, and moved away from him, but the mean response on the 1 to 9 scale was 7, indicating that respondents believed that she did want to have sex. Thus men may use *non*verbal cues to try to interpret the woman's intentions regarding sex.

## Informed Consent and Sexual Intimacy

Clearly, men and women have difficulty communicating their sexual intentions to one another, in part because of their fear of what their potential partners will think about them (for example, a man's worries that he will not be seen as masculine if he refuses an opportunity for sex, or a woman's apprehensions that she will be perceived as easy if she agrees to have sex too readily). In this section, we propose what should not be a radical model of communication but is, given contemporary stereotypes about sexual communication. In this model, we recommend that people be direct with one another about what they want. This directness should apply equally to the initial phases of courtship, and to specific acts and timing after two people have become sexually involved. In Chapter 2 we introduced the concept of informed consent in the context of research. We believe that the concept of informed consent is also useful for couples who are negotiating their sexual relationships.

The process of obtaining informed consent for sexual intimacy involves several steps. Until you have tried the technique, you may react to what follows with reactions of "Aargh—this will ruin the spontaneity and turn off my partner." Nothing could be further from the truth. Regardless of your ultimate decision to have or to avoid sex with a potential partner, the *process* of engaging in informed consent is arousing and fun. One of us (ERA) demonstrates the process with the dean of the College of Health and Human Services in a class on AIDS (see Box 6.2 for the

### Box 6.2

### Negotiating a Sexual Relationship

To demonstrate techniques for talking about sex before deciding whether to become intimate with someone, another professor and I (ERA, or "Betsy," below) engage in the following role-play in front of the class. We ask the students to assume that we no longer teach at the same university and that we have run into each other accidentally at a hotel registration desk at the beginning of a national convention.

BETSY: Clyde, it's good to see you, it's been ages! How long has it been since you left BG (Bowling Green State University)?

CLYDE: It's great to see you, too, Betsy. I guess we moved to Virginia about three years ago. When did you get in?

BETSY: Just a few minutes ago. I don't have any sessions until tomorrow, but I like to get registered and settled before the meetings begin.

CLYDE: Me, too. Do you have plans for the evening? I'm free, and there are a couple of movies I'm interested in seeing.

BETSY: That sounds good. What did you have in mind?

[Clyde suggests two contemporary movies, one of which Betsy has already seen, but they agree that they would both like to see the other one.]

CLYDE: Well, why don't we get registered, and I'll check the paper to see when it's showing and call you in your room. Depending on what time the movie is showing, we might try to get dinner before or after the movie.

BETSY: I ate on the plane on the way in, so unless the movie is very late, I'd prefer to have dinner after the movie.

[Later, after the movie, they negotiate where to have dinner. During dinner, they share information about their careers, spouses, and offspring and have a good time. They then go back to the hotel together.]

CLYDE: How about a nightcap? I have a bottle of scotch in my room.

BETSY: Ah, you remember my taste in liquor. I'd love a nightcap, but can we have it at one of the bars in the hotel? I'll treat.

[He agrees, and they go to the bar and order a drink.]

CLYDE: You know [taking Betsy's hand and smiling at her], it is really good to see you again. I thought about you from time to time after we moved, but never got around to writing.

BETSY: I thought about you, too [leaving her hand in his, and smiling]. I was always attracted to you—which made me a bit standoffish at times because I have a policy not to get too close to people where I work.

CLYDE: Yeah, things get too complicated that way. What about with people who don't work in the same place?

BETSY: Well, that depends. I'm not looking for a replacement for Rick or a long-term affair . . . my husband *does* understand me. Also, I don't want to get pregnant or catch an STD, so it just depends.

CLYDE: It sounds as if we're on the same wavelength. I'm also very satisfied with Judy, but I'd really like to spend more time with you at the convention. I had a vasectomy years ago, so I can't get anyone pregnant. As for STDs, I get myself screened during my annual medical check-up. What about you?

BETSY: I also get screened annually when I get my PAP test, and so far, so good. Even so, I think using condoms is a good idea. Have you heard of Rough Riders?

CLYDE: No, what are they?

BETSY: Well, they are condoms that have little knobby things on them, and you can put on one right-side out and one inside out for double protection! I haven't used them, but I happen to have some in my suitcase from a conference on contraception that I attended last month. Oh, goodness—I'm getting pretty direct; this scotch is good, and you look wonderful.

CLYDE: So do you. The prices for this scotch are pretty hefty! I still have that bottle in my room. Would you like to join me?

BETSY: I'd love to, but [smiling ruefully] we *have* been drinking, and I'd rather make a decision tomorrow about joining you in your room, and whatever else, with a clear head.

CLYDE: Well, how long will you be at the conference? I'm here for the whole four days.

BETSY: So am I. I have meetings tomorrow until about five. Do you want to give me a call in my room sometime between five and six, and we can talk about what we want to do?

CLYDE: Yes, that would work out fine with my schedule. I hope that we'll be able to do some rough riding together!

The essential feature of this role-play is to demonstrate the importance of potential sexual partners' discussing issues relevant to their emotional and physical well-being, negotiating in public settings, and avoiding decisions while drinking. The hypothetical outcome of the telephone conversation the next evening is left up to the students' imaginations.

—Source: E.R.A.

dialogue). Students in the class have responded positively to the role-play. Although they laugh uproariously at these two "old" people negotiating sex, they acknowledge that if we can role-play such an encounter in front of a class, then they will be able to talk to potential partners about sex.

In essence, the concept of informed consent reflects Western democratic ideas, and specifically the notion that humans have the right to make decisions based on knowledge about the potential outcomes of those decisions. If you enter into a verbal contract with other students to split up the reading of materials in a course that has a large reading list, you want assurance that the other students will extract the essential points from the articles that they have agreed to read. You promise to do your part in providing the main points for them from the articles that are your responsibility.

Obtaining informed consent for sexual intimacy is much more enjoyable than is reaching agreement about who will read which articles. In many cases involving interpersonal intimacy, the stakes are higher than the grade on a test for which you and others have agreed to cooperate in your studying. Here are some of the issues that

one must consider in seeking to obtain informed consent for sexual intimacy.

1. What are the conditions under which you and your partner are comfortable with increased sexual intimacy? How well do you believe you should know one another? What level of relationship is needed before you become sexually intimate—mutual attraction? dating each other exclusively? engagement? marriage? Two partners may view one another as an "S.O.," but "S.O." may stand for "significant other" to one and "sex object" to the other. This is not to suggest that sex is appropriate only under conditions of strong commitment. Instead, it is important that each person understand his or her own motivations for the sexual interaction.

2. Assuming that you do not wish to conceive a child, and considering that no contraceptive is 100% effective, how will you reduce the likelihood of conception? What will you do in the event that pregnancy occurs?

3. How will you reduce the risk of contracting or transmitting a sexually transmitted disease (STD)? If one or both of you have had multiple sexual partners in the past, have you been

screened to confirm that you do not currently have an STD? Testing is important because STDs do not necessarily have symptoms in their early, most treatable stages; one of you may have an STD without being aware of it.

4. What are your beliefs about sexual exclusivity? A couple may assume that if they become sexually intimate with each other, they will not engage in sex with others until or unless the current relationship ends. Based on responses from our students, many do not even discuss the issue. If both assume that they will be sexually exclusive with one another, fine. But if that is not the case, then both people need to be aware of their potential differences in beliefs about exclusivity before making a decision to become intimate.

Several other issues come into play in the process of obtaining informed consent, and these are discussed throughout the text. The main point is that it is important to discuss your intentions, feelings, and motives with a partner, preferably before becoming physically intimate. Such discussions will reduce the likelihood of disappointment and feelings of degradation or abuse.

In a couple's discussions either prior to or after sexual intimacy, a general format taught in communication-skills classes can be helpful in clarifying feelings, resolving problems, and preventing arguments. The format centers on taking responsibility for your own feelings and behavior and realizing that neither you nor your partner can read minds. At the practical level, people who are skilled in this method of communicating use what are called "I feel" messages and then describe the other person's behavior while avoiding the attribution of motives or intentions to the other person.

For example, assume that Doug and Chris are lovers but have not discussed the issue of sexual exclusivity. Doug is upset with Chris because he has discovered that she is having sexual relations with someone else, while Doug assumed that he and Chris would have sex only with each other. In the attempt to resolve the issue, Doug has the following discussion with Chris.

DOUG: "Chris, I'm feeling really hurt that you had sex with Ron. I thought that when we got in-

volved, you wouldn't be intimate with anyone else." [Note that Doug avoids words like *cheating* and makes no attributions about Chris's motives: for example, "You don't love me."]

CHRIS: "Oh, Doug, I'm sorry that you're feeling hurt. Because we never discussed it, I didn't realize that you assumed we'd see only each other. I guess we'd better talk about this; I really care about you." [Note that Chris does not put Doug down or accuse him of trying to control her or tie her down.]

DOUG: "I really care about you, too, and I want us to give our relationship a chance to see where it goes. If you want to see other people, that's your right, but I want us to date just each other." [Note that while Doug acknowledges Chris's freedom to make her own choices, he also places value on his own desires.]

Chris may have assumed all along that Doug was also seeing other people. She may in fact be quite happy to agree to a monogamous relationship with him. Alternatively, she may not want to confine herself to one person at this point in her life. In any event, if each partner can communicate using "I feel . . . about your behavior, and I want . . ." without making attributions about the other's motives, the couple is more likely to be able to resolve differences or, conversely, to discover that their desires are so different that they perhaps should not continue their intimate relationship.

## The Management of Sexual Feelings and Behavior

Regardless of whether we are single or involved in an ongoing, committed relationship, most of us feel sexually attracted to different people throughout our lives. Attraction and sexual arousal are feelings, and as such they do not necessarily require any action or guilt. If we decide not to act on them, we can simply enjoy them. These feelings can be intense, however, and if we are moved to express them, it is important to rely on rationality in our decision making.

As noted earlier, women, to a greater extent than men, have been socialized to be sexual gatekeepers. Societal expectations may be such a source of emotional conflict that a woman will justify an affair with the claim that she could not resist her feelings of attraction to a particular person. For those who have had that experience, we recommend Carol Cassell's book *Swept Away* (1984), which includes descriptions of how women may rationalize (rather than deal rationally with) their feelings of sexual attraction. The tendency to attribute one's behavior to a force greater than one's will—"I just couldn't help myself"— is not unique to women. Both men and women indulge in rationalizations of helplessness in a sexual encounter, such as "I got carried away," "I was drunk," "I thought I was in love," "I thought she/he loved me." The fact is that humans generally *are* capable of controlling their behavior. People who truly cannot help acting on irresistible impulses tend to end up in institutions—jails or mental hospitals.

Most of us believe that there are certain conditions under which it is appropriate to become sexually intimate with another person. The first step in directing our own behavior so that we avoid causing chaos and pain for others and for ourselves is to identify the specific conditions under which we think that a sexual relationship is acceptable. These conditions vary for different people, of course. Some believe that sexual relations are acceptable only with one other human being and only after marriage. Others in our culture, however, believe that sexual relations between two people who feel affection for one another are acceptable, provided that neither is involved with anyone else. For both men and women, in the days after the development of 98% effective contraceptives and before awareness of the incurability of such sexually transmitted diseases as genital herpes and AIDS (see Chapter 17), the main risks associated with impulsive sexual choices were guilt, disappointment with the relationship, and, depending on how public the relationship was, loss of reputation. These days, of course, the risk of contracting a sexually transmitted disease can be added to the others. For people already in a committed relationship, an additional risk is the potential loss of their primary relationship.

In the next section we focus on people who are committed to a primary relationship but feel attraction to someone outside the relationship. In our sexuality classes, we have found that students equate engagement and marriage with sexual exclusivity—that is, monogamy. More research is needed on the extent to which engaged couples and newlyweds discuss how they will handle extramarital relationships, but anecdotal evidence suggests that most people assume that they and their partner will be sexually involved only with each other for the rest of their lives. The statistics on the incidence of extramarital sexual relationships, however, indicate that many married people are sexually intimate with individuals other than their spouses at some point in the relationship (see Chapter 13). Therefore it is wise for people who feel commitment to a primary relationship—marital or otherwise—to reach agreements on how they will handle the (inevitable) attraction to people who are outside the relationship.

There are different models for handling such "extra-relationship" attractions, including total monogamy; relative monogamy, with occasional extra-relationship involvements that may or may not be disclosed to the primary partner; and open marriage. There is also, of course, old-fashioned adultery, in which a couple promise to be monogamous but one or both spouses break that commitment. Our focus here, however, is on arriving at an agreement and then devising practical ways to honor that agreement or renegotiate it. Keep in mind that there is no guarantee that either partner will be able to live up to any agreement.

## Honoring Agreements

Regardless of what agreements you and your partner make, there will be times when you feel intense sexual arousal toward someone outside your primary relationship. Let us assume that the feelings you experience are ones that you believe you should not actualize (express behaviorally) with the other person. The trick is to give yourself time to think about the strong attraction you feel and what you are comfortable doing and not doing about it. That is not always easy; a chance meeting, a long-term friendship, or an effective working relationship with a classmate or with a colleague can suddenly (sometimes it seems as if it takes only a few seconds) turn into a potential romance. There you are, minding your own business, having a conversation with a person whom we will call Tracy. All of a sudden, you see Tracy differently. You may start shaking or perspiring, and you may wonder what is wrong. The situation can be particularly difficult if the shift in feelings is reciprocal, that is, if Tracy also sees you in a new light. What do you do?

First, get away from Tracy as quickly as you can to give yourself time to think. Then try to decide whether increased involvement with Tracy is consistent with, or a violation of, your agreement with your primary partner. If an affair with Tracy would be accepted in the context of your agreements with your partner, then consider the potential ramifications of intimacy for everyone else involved in the situation—Tracy's partner, for example. And what if Tracy wants more of an investment than you, who are already committed to someone else, can give? You should also examine your own motives. Clearly, one person cannot satisfy all our needs, be interested in all facets of our personality, and share all our interests.

Part of your attraction to Tracy may stem from the fact that he/she has qualities or characteristics that your partner does not. If you find yourself thinking about replacing your partner with Tracy, then it is probably not advisable to involve yourself further with Tracy. Your attraction to Tracy may be a signal that there are some serious problems with your primary relationship that need attention. Perhaps you and your primary partner should go off for a get-away weekend to try to clarify sources of dissatisfaction; a few sessions with a counselor who conducts relationship therapy can also be helpful. If, on the other hand, you feel comfortable with your partner and see Tracy as primarily a supplement rather than as a potential replacement, then—provided that you and Tracy discuss these issues so that you are each aware of the other's motives and goals—an affair might then be mutually satisfying.

If you decide that you are not going to get involved in an affair with Tracy, with whom you already have an ongoing friendship, what do you do about your feelings of sexual arousal? You can enjoy the feelings and fantasies, but your behavior must be consistent with your decision rather than with your fantasies. From a practical standpoint, here are three guidelines that you might apply to your situation with Tracy.

1. *Avoid any location (your apartments, a hotel room, a classroom) where only the two of you will be present.* If you have been in the habit of spending time alone with Tracy studying or attending conferences, you may want to let Tracy know that, because you are experiencing a lot of attraction that you do not want to act on, you are going to avoid being alone with him/her for the next few weeks or so. (Surprisingly, heightened sexual arousal can sometimes fade almost as quickly as it develops.) In this way you can let Tracy know that what you are rejecting is another kind of relationship, not Tracy or your friendship.

2. *Avoid drinking alcohol or using other intoxicants when you are with Tracy.* A beer or a glass of wine at a party probably will not hurt, but if you become tipsy, you may find yourself acting on fantasies rather than decisions. Inhibitions drop quickly in the presence of intoxicants.

3. *Learn from your feelings and fantasies.* Are there some aspects of your relationship with Tracy that you could infuse into your primary relationship? Revitalizing your primary relationship may reduce the intensity of your attraction to Tracy so that you can resume the pleasure of your friendship without fear that you will violate your decisions about sexual intimacy.

In this chapter, we have examined sexual fantasies, arousal, and communication, and their roles in sexual intimacy. In the next chapter, we explore the variety of sexual behaviors that intimate partners enjoy.

## Summary of Major Points _____

1. **The conditioning of arousal.**

Our capacity for sexual arousal is part of our biological heritage, but the specific objects, acts, situations, and people that we find arousing are influenced by societal norms and by our own unique experiences. We learn to respond sexually to particular external stimuli through association of those stimuli with arousal (classical conditioning) and through sexually rewarding or punishing experiences involving those stimuli (operant conditioning). Some evidence supports the hypothesis that any source of arousal, whether positive or negative, can lead to heightened attraction to a person who is associated with that arousal.

2. **Sexual arousal and our sensory capabilities.**

Almost all of our senses come into play when we are sexually stimulated. Touch, smell, and sight are all important in sexual arousal. We learn to consider particular kinds or locations of tactile contact, particular smells, and certain sights to be erotic. Because these associations are unique to each individual, the specific touches, sights, smells, and sounds that arouse one person do not necessarily arouse another.

3. **Variations in response to sexual arousal.**

Just as we learn to associate sexual responses with different stimuli, we learn different attitudes toward the process of sexual arousal. Some of us are taught that sexual arousal is a healthy, normal, enjoyable process, whereas others learn to feel guilty about feeling sexy. These attitudes are instilled over a long time, from an early age, and are consistently related to our capacity to respond sexually in a variety of situations. Females are more frequently taught to view their sexuality more negatively than are males, and the average female feels guiltier about sexual feelings and behavior than does the average male. This pattern of socialization probably explains male-female differences in seeking out, and reporting enjoyment of, erotic material. When their responses are physiologically measured, however, males and females do not differ in their arousal by erotic material.

4. **Fantasy and sexual arousal.**

Just as learned attitudes toward sexual arousal vary, so do reactions to the capacity to have fantasies. Fantasies provide us with a way to rehearse future events and to try out different alternatives in our minds. They can also embellish our own experiences, enhance our relationships, and entertain us. Traditional Christianity's emphasis on the importance of purity in thoughts and motives as well as in actions may be responsible for the negative reactions that some people have toward their fantasies. Imagination and reality are not the same thing, and it is only when an individual confuses them, or uses fantasy as a substitute for relations with others, that any problem with fantasy arises. Fantasies of arousal can be acted out with a willing partner under certain conditions. When we experience sexual arousal that we would rather not act on, we must take practical steps to manage our behavior.

5. Communication and sexual feelings.

In making wise decisions about whether to act on sexual feelings, it is important that we are aware of, and discuss, our sexual policies with potential partners. Open communication enhances the likelihood that our interactions with others will be pleasurable and satisfying.

## Review of Key Concepts ⎯⎯⎯⎯⎯⎯⎯⎯⎯⎯⎯⎯⎯⎯⎯⎯⎯⎯

1. The capacity for sexual arousal is: a) inborn; b) learned from peers; c) acquired by experience; d) acquired from one's specific culture. (pp. 162–163)

2. Erotic attraction to specific stimuli is: a) culturally conditioned; b) learned from peers; c) an example of classical and operant conditioning; d) all of the above. (pp. 164–166)

3. The two-stage model of sexual arousal involves: a) the pairing of a previously neutral stimulus with a stimulus that can evoke sexual arousal; b) feeling sexual arousal, followed by reward, punishment, or lack of attention; c) the awareness of physiological arousal, followed by the search for a cognitive label; d) none of the above. (pp. 164–167)

4. The conclusion to be drawn from experiments testing the two-stage model of sexual arousal is that: a) arousal regardless of its source increases the likelihood that the aroused person will be attracted to another person; b) arousal is purely a matter of chance; c) males are more likely to seek out their female interviewers than are females to seek out their male interviewers; d) swaying bridges are more arousing to females than to males. (pp. 164–167)

5. Which of the following statements about our sense of touch is true? a) Touch is the only type of stimulation that can produce a reflexive response that is independent of higher brain centers. b) Receptors for touch and pressure are evenly distributed throughout the body. c) Adequate human development can occur even in the absence of touching and cuddling during infancy. d) The areas where touch receptors are most highly concentrated are called the pheromonic zones. (p. 168)

6. Evidence suggests that human evaluation of bodily odors as pleasant or unpleasant is: a) innate; b) learned; c) similar to that of animals; d) an instinctive defense against harmful substances. (pp. 168–169)

7. Estrus is: a) a dangerous drug sometimes used as an aphrodisiac; b) in females of nonhuman species, the period of fertility signaled by the discharge of blood; c) universal in all female mammals, including humans; d) a learned response to sexual stimulation through fantasies. (p. 167)

8. Research on the conditions under which males and females respond to erotic materials suggests that: a) there are no significant differences in male and female sexual responses to erotic stimuli; b) observed gender differences in response to erotic materials reflect basic biological gender differences; c) females are rarely aroused by such materials; d) differing cultural expectations for men and women contribute heavily to the observed gender differences. (p. 179)

9. Sadomasochistic fantasizing is: a) strongly indicative of an underlying desire to act out such behavior; b) evidence substantiating Freud's theory that fantasies are symptoms

of immaturity; c) always harmless; d) none of the above. (pp. 171–172)

10. "Attraction and sexual arousal are feelings, and as such they do not necessarily require any action or guilt." Comment on this statement. (p. 171)

11. Discuss the consequences of women's traditional role in Western sexual culture as "gate-keepers" who set limits on the extent of sexual intimacy. What social, cultural, religious, and biological factors might account for this role, and what conditions might change it? (pp. 175–176)

12. When disagreements arise between you and your partner, your best course of action is to: a) confront your partner directly, describing his or her motivations for the behavior; b) describe your partner's behavior and your feelings about it; c) do the same thing to your partner that he or she did to offend you; d) see your family physician. (pp. 185–187)

# Sexual Behavior

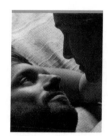

*ᴮᴇᴄᴀᵁsᴇ we can't live to-gether right now and are often sepa-rated, we masturbate together by talk-ing on the telephone, which is just out of sight! We talk to each other late in the evening because both of us are very busy during the day and sometimes we'll be on the phone almost all night talking each other into coming, . . . and then we become more intimate and feel closer.*

*It's not like masturbating alone; that's a whole different thing, but it's sort of like shar-ing something very intimate with someone that you care about. It's not as good as the real thing, but it's pretty damn good.*

*To me, good sex means being able to give and also being able to take. When I'm with a man who doesn't like to take, who's unwilling to just lie back and let me give to him, a man who needs to be in charge all the time, I lose interest.*

*The most important breakthrough in my sex life was when I learned it was all right for me to touch my own clitoris during in-tercourse. Since I've started doing that, I al-most always have orgasms, and I have come to believe that this is just the way I am and that there's nothing wrong with it. Because I believe that, my partners have accepted it without any difficulty.*

*The relationship is what has always mattered to me. I never went to bed just to be going to bed or because he was "Joe Blow." It had to be with a person who had some depth and warmth. I didn't have to be in love necessarily, but we had to be able to communicate well. For me, good sex comes from good communication.*

As the foregoing quotations of different individuals from Barbach and Levine's book *Shared Intimacies* (1980, pp. 11, 91–92) illustrate, there is a great deal of diversity in what people find sexually pleasurable. In our culture, however, the popular perception is that in heterosexual intercourse the woman lies on her back and the man lies on top of her. After they have engaged in enough foreplay to elicit vaginal lubrication, he inserts his erect penis into her vagina and moves it in and out until he is stimulated to ejaculation. She may or may not have an orgasm. This method works well for purposes of procreation, but it represents a rather rigid, stereotyped view of sexual intimacy, and the extent to which it provides sexual pleasure varies from one person to the next and, for some individuals, from one sexual encounter to the next.

In this chapter we consider what humans do sexually to stimulate themselves and others. Effective sexual stimulation evokes a relatively predictable pattern of bodily responses, which we review. We also examine researchers' varying views on what actually happens in the human sexual response cycle, and we examine the similarities and differences in male and female orgasmic patterns. Finally, we explore the debate over whether women experience ejaculation.

---

## Sources of Sexual Pleasure

Our focus in examining what humans do to produce sexual sensation and response is behaviorally oriented. Remember, however, as we emphasized in the last chapter, that our sexual actions and responses are strongly associated with our thoughts, feelings, and fantasies.

## Nocturnal Orgasm

*Nocturnal orgasm* refers to sexual arousal and response that occur while a person is sleeping. It is experienced by both males and females and is often accompanied by erotic dreams—thus the popular term *wet dream* for ejaculation during sleep. Almost all the men and 70% of the women who participated in the Kinsey et al. (1948, 1953) studies reported having sexual dreams. Nocturnal orgasms were reported by 90% of the men but by less than 40% of the women. This gender difference may stem from differences in anatomy. The extension of the male penis allows for the possibility of more stimulation by movement against sheets or a mattress than does the less exposed clitoris of the female. In addition, evidence of male orgasm with ejaculation is available upon awakening, whereas confirmation of nocturnal orgasm is far less detectable among females. Alternatively, men may simply be more likely than women to experience nocturnal orgasm.

The Kinsey group (1948, 1953) found that males reported the highest frequency of nocturnal orgasm during their late adolescence and early 20s. In contrast, females reported the highest frequency of nocturnal orgasm during their 40s. Among women who experienced nocturnal orgasm, the frequency was about three or four per year, whereas men reported having three to eleven nocturnal orgasms per year. About 5% of men and 1% of women averaged one nocturnal orgasm per week.

Wells (1986) found evidence that the percentage of young women reporting nocturnal orgasms may be increasing. She reported that 37% of the 245 undergraduate and graduate women whom she surveyed had experienced nocturnal orgasms. In contrast, only 8% of the women in the Kinsey group sample (1953) had experienced nocturnal orgasm by the time they were 20 years old. Liberal sexual attitudes, as well as positive feelings about and knowledge of nocturnal orgasm, were strongly associated with experiencing orgasm in one's sleep (Wells, 1986).

**nocturnal orgasm**—orgasm that occurs when a person is asleep.

Why do people have orgasms while they sleep? One common belief is that nocturnal orgasm fulfills a compensatory function; that is, if sexually mature adults have a decrease in sexual outlets during their waking hours, they will experience a corresponding increase in nocturnal orgasms. This hypothesis has not been supported, however; the available research has found no relationship between the frequency of sexual release while people were awake and the frequency of nocturnal orgasm (Burg, 1988; Kinsey et al., 1948). Whatever the function of nocturnal orgasms, they should be enjoyed as much as other sexual activities because for most of us they are few and far between.

## Masturbation

*Masturbation* appears to be the most frequent form of sexual outlet for the majority of North Americans (Breakwell & Fife-Schaw, 1992; Clement, 1990; Kinsey et al., 1948, 1953; Leitenberg, Detzer, & Srebnik, 1993) (see Table 7.1). Clement, Schmidt, and Kruse (1984) found masturbation to be the first sexual experience among the majority of a sample of German students (66% of women and 90% of men). More males masturbate than do females, and of those who do, males masturbate more frequently than do females (Oliver & Hyde, 1993). In one study of U.S. university students, nearly twice as many men as women reported ever having masturbated. Of those who masturbated, men reported doing so almost three times more frequently than did women (Leitenberg et al., 1993).

Masturbation is sometimes called autoeroticism, or the seeking of pleasure with oneself. In this section we focus on solitary masturbation—stimulation of the genitals when no one else is present. One also may engage in self-stimulation in the presence of a partner; or a couple may masturbate each other.

Throughout history attitudes toward this pleasurable practice have been riddled with misconceptions, guilt, and fear. We briefly examined

**masturbation**—self-stimulation of the genitals.

### TABLE 7.1  Popularity of Self Stimulation

Results of surveys by the Kinsey group, Hunt, and research conducted by Janus and Janus (1993) show that the proportion of people who report engaging in masturbation has remained about the same for males and females, with slight variations that probably stem from methodological differences.*

|         | Kinsey group 1938–1949 | Hunt 1972 | Janus & Janus 1988–1992 |
|---------|------------------------|-----------|-------------------------|
| Males   | 92%                    | 94%       | 81%                     |
| Females | 62%                    | 63%       | 72%*                    |

*Women's masturbatory experiences are dramatically related to changes in their culture. For example, Asayama (1976) found that self-reported masturbation increased from 6% to 24% for Japanese women from 1952 to 1974.

some of the historical attitudes toward self-stimulation in Chapter 1. As you will see, these traditional biases continue to have an impact on many people.

In the 18th century, Simon André Tissot (1728–1797) theorized that semen was important for healthy bodily functioning and that wasting it through sexual activity would weaken the body and produce illness. This "vital liquid" was supposed to be carefully monitored, and semen was to be "spent" only when there was a reasonable chance of conception. Building on this theory, 19th-century physicians developed a catalogue of illnesses that they traced to the waste of semen through unprofitable sexual activity, including masturbation. Fear of masturbation and of its supposed harmful effects was rampant in the 19th century, creating some extreme "treatments" for this practice, although some individuals did not take these ideas seriously (see Box 7.1). According to the physician W. H. Walling (1904, p. 37), the effects of masturbation included the following:

> . . . *loss of memory and intelligence, morose and unequal disposition, aversion, or indifference to legitimate pleasures and sports, mental abstractions, stupid solidity, etc.*

**Box 7.1**

## Mark Twain on Masturbation

Mark Twain delivered the following musings at a private club in Paris in 1879. The material was considered so scandalous that it was not published until many years later.

*Homer in the second book of the* Iliad, *says with fine enthusiasm, "Give me masturbation or give me death!" Caesar, in his* Commentaries, *says, "To the lonely it is company; to the forsaken it is a friend; to the aged and to the impotent it is a benefactor; they that are penniless are yet rich, in that they still have this majestic diversion." In another place this experienced observer has said, "There are times when I prefer it to sodomy."*

*Robinson Crusoe says, "I cannot describe what I owe to this gentle art." Queen Elizabeth said, "It is the bulwark of Virginity." Cetewayo, the Zulu hero, remarked, "A jerk in the hand is worth two in the bush." The immortal Franklin has said, "Masturbation is the mother of invention." He also said, "Masturbation is the best policy." Michelangelo and all the other old masters—Old Masters, I will remark, is an abbreviation, a contraction—have used similar language. Michelangelo said to Pope Julius II, "Self-negation is noble, self-culture is beneficial, self-possession is manly, but to the truly grand and inspiring soul they are poor and tame compared to self-abuse."*

Additionally, Walling cited the observations of a distinguished German physician that

> the masturbator gradually loses his moral faculties, he acquires a dull, silly, listless, embarrassed, sad, effeminate exterior. He becomes indolent; averse to and incapable of all intellectual exertion; all presence of mind deserts him; he is discountenanced, troubled, inquiet whenever he finds himself in company; he is taken by surprise and even alarmed if required simply to reply to a child's question; . . . previously acquired knowledge is forgotten; the most exquisite intelligence becomes naught, and no longer bears fruit. (pp. 37–38)

Some 19th-century commentators considered people who masturbated dangerous to society and believed that their lives were shortened by the practice. Moreover, these catastrophic consequences of self-stimulation could not, according to Shannon (1913), be avoided by having someone else stimulate the genitals. He wrote that married couples who manually brought one another to orgasm risked all these same physical and mental afflictions and thereby, of course,

shortened their lives. Presumably, these physicians would be terribly concerned about the threat to our species if they could see such contemporary books as Betty Dodson's *Sex for One: The Joys of Selfloving* (1987) and Lonnie Barbach's *For Yourself* (1976), which encourage self-stimulation as part of healthy sexuality. Further, masturbation training has become part of the therapeutic techniques used in treating certain sexual dysfunctions.

Beginning in the 20th century, the connection between masturbation and illness became more difficult to defend. Concern shifted to particular aspects of masturbation. One controversy centered on the definition of "excessive" masturbation. While grudgingly accepting the possibility that occasional indulgence in the "secret sin" or "self-abuse" did not lead directly to the deathbed or insane asylum, many physicians and health educators still preached that masturbating too often was harmful to character development. Unfortunately for the masturbator, these "authorities" never concretely defined what was too much, normal, or too little. Leitenberg et al. (1993) found that the university men in their sample reported masturbating once a week and the women reported doing so once a month. In addition, conventional religious doctrine has denounced the practice of masturbation throughout the 20th century. Barraged by such pronouncements from secular and religious authorities, a person who masturbated could easily conclude that he or she was on the road to weak character development from a medical point of view or on the road to hell from a religious point of view. The Roman Catholic church still condemns masturbation as a mortal sin, although many Catholics ignore this dictum.

Contemporary parental views on masturbation were investigated by Gagnon (1985). A majority (86%) of a sample of 1,482 parents thought that their preadolescent children masturbated. About 60% of the parents felt that masturbation was acceptable, but only about one-third wanted their children to have a positive attitude toward masturbation. The latter finding is puzzling; one would think that parents would wish their adolescents to see masturbation as a positive alternative to engaging in sexual activity with others, which would expose the youths to the risks of pregnancy and sexually transmitted diseases. Perhaps many parents simply prefer that their children remain asexual for as long as possible. Alternatively, parents may fear possible social embarrassment if their children, particularly younger offspring, publicly express positive attitudes toward masturbation. Maybe it is acceptable to the parents as long as masturbation is practiced privately and not talked about openly. Whatever their motivation, parents can rest assured because early masturbation experience appears to be unrelated to sexual adjustment in young adulthood (Leitenberg et al., 1993).

The conditions under which masturbation occurs also affect attitudes about self-stimulation. For example, masturbation may be condoned in cases in which a person has no partner, but considered inappropriate if a person has a spouse or regular partner. Even though more than two-thirds of young husbands and wives masturbate at least once a month, these beliefs persist (Hunt, 1974). Perhaps they are maintained by our culture's view that a person's sexuality belongs to his or her sexual partner. From this perspective, to masturbate when an appropriate partner is available is a violation of that partner's property rights. Or perhaps people assume that something is lacking in a couple's sexual relationship if one or both engage in solitary masturbation. In one study of married women, however, those who reported having masturbated to orgasm had higher self-esteem, more orgasms, greater sexual desire, and greater marital and sexual satisfaction than married women who did not masturbate to orgasm (Hurlbert & Whittaker, 1991).

The age at which humans discover that playing with particular parts of the body produces strong pleasure varies from one person to another. Some young people accidentally stumble on sexual arousal and orgasm in the course of engaging in some other physical activity. The result can be surprising, and sometimes distressing, if the child or adolescent has received no prior information. Other youngsters purposefully stimulate themselves, goaded by curiosity after getting suggestions or advice from friends. These initial explorations can be both clumsy and ineffective. We have a friend, for example, who told us that when he was 12 years old, he associated with a group of older boys who frequently discussed masturbation as something that "grown" boys did. These discussions never dealt with the specifics of self-stimulation; that is, no one explained exactly how to do it. Our friend, who was less interested in masturbating than he was in being accepted as a full member of the group, tried to masturbate but experienced no success. He finally gave up in despair, convinced either that he was not old enough or that something was wrong with him. About six months later he woke up with an erection and began to move up and down against his sheet, finally experiencing orgasm. He said that he realized only then that an erection was necessary, his previous attempts having been made when his penis was flaccid.

Self-stimulation can fulfill at least three important purposes. First, it feels good. By masturbating you can reward yourself for spending hours on a chore or for doing well on an exam. You can give yourself solace after a bad day by being good to yourself physically. Second, self-stimulation can provide sexual release when a partner is unavailable, or when you are feeling

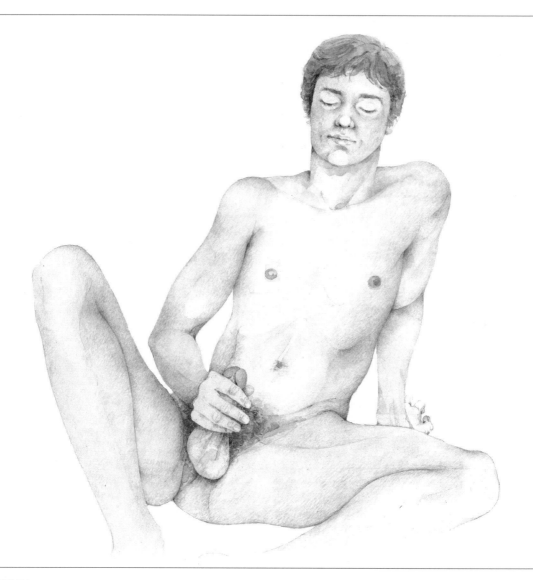

**FIGURE 7.1**
**Male Masturbation**
Although we are all unique in what pleases us sexually, there are some general differences between the self-stimulation methods used by males and those used by females.

intensely aroused by someone with whom greater sexual intimacy is impossible or inappropriate. Third, knowing how to make yourself feel good gives you self-knowledge—information that you can share with another person.

### Male Methods

When masturbating, men tend to focus on stimulation of the penis. It may be rubbed against the body with one or both hands, or it may be rolled between the palms of the hands as they move up and down the shaft of the penis. Some men reach orgasm by lying on a pillow and thrusting against it. However, the majority of the 312 men who masturbated while being observed by Masters and Johnson (1966) moved their hands up and down the shaft of their penises (see Figure 7.1). Stroking of the penis can vary from a light touch to a strong grip, as well as from a leisurely

**FIGURE 7.2**
**Female Masturbation**

speed to a more rapid movement. As males approach ejaculation, they tend to increase the speed of stimulation to the penis. When they begin to ejaculate, however, most men decrease or stop penile stimulation abruptly, reporting that continued intense stimulation of the glans is unpleasant (Masters & Johnson, 1966).

Aside from a minute amount of fluid, produced by the Cowper's glands, that appears at the opening of the urethra, there is no natural lubrication of the external skin of the penis. Therefore, some men use saliva, oil, cream, or soap (during a shower or bath) to allow the hand to glide smoothly over their penises. A vibrator may also be used to stimulate the penis. Some men stimulate their nipples or anus with one hand while rubbing their penis with the other hand.

Many males are completely oriented toward orgasm in their masturbatory techniques. The average man reported to the Kinsey group (1948) that he ejaculated after stimulating himself for two or three minutes. Some men reported a more leisurely pattern of self-stimulation; a few men reported ejaculating within 30 seconds of the on-set of masturbation. This efficiency is useful if one has an appointment to keep, but it may be poor preparation for shared sex; racing through the sexual response cycle is not generally conducive to mutual pleasure.

*Female Methods*

In contrast to males, females vary considerably in the methods they use to stimulate themselves. Masters and Johnson (1966) found that no two of their female research volunteers masturbated in quite the same way. Stimulation of the clitoral shaft, clitoral area, and mons with a hand or an object is the method that women most commonly employ (see Figure 7.2 on page 201). For direct stimulation, making a circular motion around the clitoral shaft and glans and rubbing up and down one side of the clitoris are popular methods. Pull-ing on the inner lips causes the loose skin cov-ering the clitoral glans to slide back and forth, creating a sensation that can be quite sexually arousing. Clitoral stimulation can also be accom-panied by moving the fingers in and out of the vagina. Vaginal penetration alone, however, is not frequently used by women as a masturbatory technique. Masters and Johnson (1966) reported that most women in their research preferred to stimulate the entire mons area rather than con-centrate exclusively on the clitoris. The clitoral glans is sensitive, and direct stimulation for an extended period of time can be irritating.

Other masturbatory techniques that women use include pelvic thrusting, squeezing and con-tracting the thigh muscles, inserting objects into the vagina, stimulating the breasts, and fantasiz-ing. Pelvic thrusting of the genitals against a bed, pillow, clothing, or other objects produces direct stimulation of the vulval area as well as increas-ing muscular tension through contraction of the thigh and gluteal muscles. This technique spreads stimulation over a wide area. For some women, pressing the thigh muscles together, usually with their legs crossed, applies steady, rhythmic pressure on the genitals.

Some women also masturbate by using a vi-brator. Vibrators, which may be purchased in a variety of sizes and shapes (see Figure 7.3), are usually battery-operated or electric. Some vibra-tor kits have a number of different accessories

and provide a choice of several vibration speeds. Vibrators should not be loaned to other people because of the potential for passing on infections and sexually transmitted diseases.

A small percentage of women report that they can reach orgasm through breast and/or nipple stimulation alone (Kinsey et al., 1953; Masters & Johnson, 1966). Usually, however, women who stimulate their breasts during mas-turbation (about one in ten of Kinsey's respon-dents) do so in combination with stimulation of the clitoral area. About 2% of Kinsey's respon-dents claimed that they could reach orgasm through erotic fantasy with no direct stimulation of the genitals—a real tribute to the powers of the mind. This phenomenon has been measured by self-report and physiological indices in lab set-tings where seven out of ten women had orgasm relying only on fantasy (Whipple, Ogden, & Komisaruk, 1992). Breast stimulation or fantasy alone is rarely used by women, however, and even less commonly by men.

Masters and Johnson (1966) observed an in-teresting gender difference in the process of self-stimulation. Most women prefer continued stim-ulation of the clitoral shaft or mons area during orgasm. In contrast, men typically slow down or stop manual stimulation during orgasm. This gender difference appears to be true of coital or-gasm as well and thus has implications for sexual interaction.

Female sexual response is not much slower than male response during masturbation: a little less than 4 minutes after beginning self-stimula-tion (Kinsey et al., 1953). Some women have an orgasm in less than 30 seconds. The relatively small difference between male and female pat-terns of response becomes larger during stimu-lation through sexual intercourse. It takes the av-erage woman longer than the average man to have orgasm during coitus because there is usu-ally not as much direct stimulation of the clitoral area as there is during masturbation.

## Mutual Masturbation

Mutual caressing of the breasts and genitals is widely practiced in our culture. More than 90% of men and women report manually stimulating the genitals of their sexual partners (Breakwell & Fife-Schaw, 1992; Kinsey et al., 1948, 1953). Man-

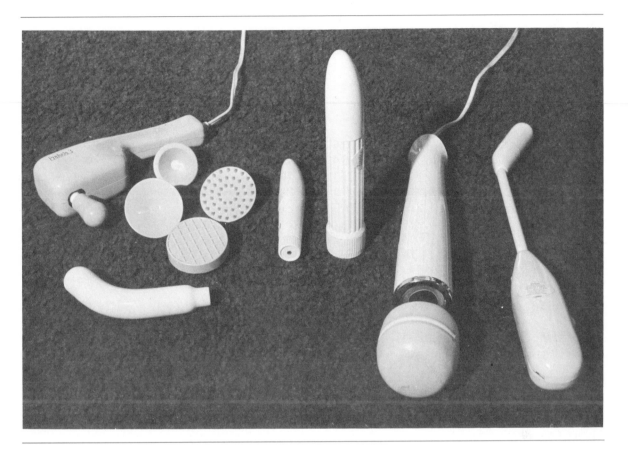

**FIGURE 7.3**
**Examples of the Various Vibrators Available**

ual stimulation of a partner's genitals can serve as a prelude to oral sex or sexual intercourse, or it can be the means of achieving orgasm for one or both partners. Couples who have considerable experience with solitary masturbation can give each other information and guidance about what techniques are most pleasing.

Mutual masturbation provides a satisfying and pleasurable form of sexual intimacy and release for many couples. If birth control is unavailable and a heterosexual couple wants to have sex, it offers one of several enjoyable alternatives to sexual intercourse. Mutual masturbation is also one of the most common techniques that gay couples use during sexual intimacy. The two women shown in Figure 7.4 are stroking one another's bodies in an episode that may proceed to such mutual masturbation.

## Oral Sex

Kissing—mouth-to-mouth contact—is usually the first step in sexual interactions in Western cultures. Among other cultures and species, however, deep kissing for the purpose of erotic arousal is relatively rare. Although all human cultures use some form of mouth or nose contact to indicate greeting and affection, in many societies people do not include kissing in their erotic interactions. Traditional Chinese did not kiss for any reason. Until about three decades ago, there was no word for *kiss* in Japanese. In their survey of a variety of cultures, Ford and Beach (1951) found that kissing was mentioned in only 21 cultures and accompanied sexual intercourse in only 13 cultures. Around the world the deep kiss is less often a part of sexual intimacy than are other

**FIGURE 7.4**
**Mutual Caressing**

forms of mouth or nose contact. The Tinguians place their lips near their partner's face and suddenly inhale. Balinese lovers bring their faces close enough to sense each other's perfume and skin (Tiefer, 1978).

Human kisses are probably related to the olfactory investigations that mammals make upon greeting. Most mammals rely on their sense of smell to recognize friends or enemies and to determine each other's state of sexual arousal. The popularity of the kiss in many cultures may be traced back to the infant-mother bond. Infants are lavishly touched, cuddled, and kissed all over their bodies, not only by their mothers, but also by relatives and friends. Because the mouth conveys positive feelings between infant and adult, the infant may learn that touching something soft with the mouth is a calming and pleasurable sensation.

The pleasure that lovers obtain from kissing may be partially due to the fact that all the senses can be stimulated during that activity. The lips, mouth, and tongue are among the most exquisitely sensitive parts of the body. Sensitivity to pressure is only one aspect of the mouth's capabilities. Because of the neural connections from the lips, tongue, cheek, and nose to the brain, a kiss also permits participants to detect temperature, taste, smell, and movement. Indeed, five of the twelve cranial nerves that affect brain functions are involved in a kiss. Kissing also involves our senses of hearing and sight. We may be aroused by the associated sounds of sucking and licking, and we may be affected by the sight of a partner's lips and tongue.

### Oral-Genital Sex

Although deep kissing is relatively uncommon across cultures, kissing or licking of other parts of the body—including the genitals—is widely documented in many societies.

Historically, North Americans have held negative attitudes toward oral-genital sex. It has been, and remains, illegal in a number of states (see Box 7.2). Current views of oral sex vary widely. Some people see it as a way of expressing deeply intimate feelings; others react with disgust to the mere idea of oral-genital contact. Negative feelings about the odor, texture, and appearance of the genitals may inhibit some people from participation in oral sex. Because urination and defecation are associated with the genitals, some may feel that oral contact with the genitals will expose them to excrement and germs. In addition, some people may not like the idea of taking semen or vaginal secretions into their mouths or may dislike the taste. And some perceive oral sex as less intimate than sexual intercourse because it precludes extensive body-to-body and face-to-face contact. Others, feeling that oral sex is more personal than sexual intercourse, believe only couples within a committed relationship should engage in it.

Attitudes toward oral-genital sex have changed rapidly in this century (Breakwell & Fife-Schaw, 1992). Acceptance of oral sex has increased significantly among married couples and for many is a favored means to orgasm (Hurlbert & Whittaker, 1991) (see Table 7.2). In one study, 18% of women and 10% of men indicated that oral sex was their preferred way to experience orgasm (Janus & Janus, 1993). The incidence of oral sex is also rising among adolescents, particularly among those with coital experience, partly because it eliminates worries about birth control for heterosexuals (Billy, Tanfer, Grady, & Klepinger, 1993; Gagnon & Simon, 1987; Whitley, 1989).

There appear to be ethnic differences, at least among men, in giving and receiving oral sex. In a nationally representative sample of men aged 20 to 39 in the United States, White men performed (79%) and received (81%) oral sex more than did Black men, 43% and 62% respectively (Billy et al., 1993). White Hispanics were less likely than other Whites to have performed or received oral sex. In addition, oral sex is more common among middle-class people than among lower-class individuals (Billy et al., 1993; Clement, 1990).

There are many ways of having oral sex. A couple may stimulate each other's genitals with

### TABLE 7.2 Popularity of Oral Sex

The proportion of married people who reported engaging in oral sex increased from the 1930s to the 1990s.

|  | Kinsey group 1938–1949 | Hunt 1972 | Billy et al.* 1991 |
|---|---|---|---|
| *Fellatio* | | | |
| Males | 59–61% | 54–61% | 75% |
| Females | 46–52% | 52–72% | |
| *Cunnilingus* | | | |
| Males | 16–51% | 55–66% | 79% |
| Females | 50–58% | 58–72% | |

*Only males were studied.

their mouths before sexual intercourse or orally caress one another to mutual orgasm. Depending on preference, a person can swallow the semen or stop orally stimulating the penis just before ejaculation and move slightly away.

Partners can perform *cunnilingus* and *fellatio* using a variety of positions. Some couples like to take turns, bringing one another to orgasm in sequence. Others prefer to stimulate each other orally at the same time (see Figure 7.5). Simultaneous oral stimulation is known popularly as 69 or *soixante-neuf*. Many couples enjoy having other parts of their bodies kissed and licked during sexual intimacy. For some partners, the sexual repertoire includes *analingus*, the oral stimulation of the sensitive tissue around the anus. It

**cunnilingus** (KUN-nih-LING-gus)—oral stimulation of the female genitals.

**fellatio** (fell-LAY-shee-oh)—oral stimulation of the male genitals.

**soixante-neuf** (SWAH-sahnt-nuff) (French, sixty-nine)—simultaneous oral stimulation by both partners of one another's genitals.

**analingus** (A-nul-LING-gus)—oral stimulation of the anus.

**FIGURE 7.5**
**Mutual Oral-Genital Stimulation**

is important for both heterosexual and homosexual couples to realize, however, that the AIDS virus can be transmitted during oral stimulation of the genitals (see Chapter 17). Small fissures in the gums, genitals, or anus may permit transmission of the virus from an infected person to the bloodstream of a noninfected person. Thus, unless a couple is monogamous, partners should make sure that they are both free of the AIDS virus before engaging in oral sex or analingus.

In cunnilingus, a woman's partner can caress and separate her vaginal lips with the hands or tongue. The clitoris can be licked, sucked, or gently nibbled, although too much direct stimulation may be uncomfortable because the clitoris is extremely sensitive. Having the side of the clitoral shaft massaged or rapidly flicked by the tongue is generally quite pleasurable for women.

Oral stimulation of a man's genitals can also provide deep pleasure. The most sensitive parts of the penis are the glans, or tip, and the frenulum on the underside of the glans. Having these areas licked or sucked is quite pleasurable. The testes can also be taken gently into the mouth and sucked or licked. The head and shaft of the penis

can be sucked slowly or rapidly while the penis is held and the scrotum is caressed.

These are some of the more common means of oral stimulation. As with other forms of sexual intimacy, people need to be sensitive to the likes and dislikes of their partners when giving and receiving oral stimulation.

## "Foreplay" and Coitus

The term *foreplay* usually refers to activities like kissing, manual caressing of the genitals, and oral sex that are seen as a prelude to intercourse. The term reflects the long-ingrained bias in our culture that "having sex" is an experience that must culminate in coitus and male orgasm, or else it isn't really sex. Rather than being viewed as pleasures and ends in themselves, mutual caressing, kissing, and oral sex are often seen as necessary tasks on the way to achieving coital orgasm.

Given this belief, how much time do couples spend in stimulating each other before and during sexual intercourse? The average duration of foreplay appears to be about 12 to 15 minutes

**Box 7.2**

## The Law and Sexual Relations

Almost all states have had laws prohibiting sodomy, or "crimes against nature." These laws forbid "unnatural" sexual acts such as anal intercourse, oral-genital sex, pederasty (sex with children), bestiality (sex with animals), and necrophilia (sex with corpses). Sodomy laws vary from state to state in terms of the acts prohibited and the severity of the penalties.

Over the past 60 years, the U.S. Supreme Court has expanded the rights of individuals to protection against encroachment by the state. A movement to decriminalize sodomy began in 1961, and by 1993, the majority of

**FIGURE 7.6**

**Protesting Contemporary Sodomy Laws**

Gay protesters demonstrate against sodomy laws in this Atlanta march of January 1990. They are carrying a bed containing dolls simulating the act of sodomy. The sign of the protester at the right compares current anti-sodomy laws to the persecution of witches.

states no longer considered it a crime (see Figure 7.6 on page 207). Although sodomy laws are out of step with what most Americans believe, the trend toward their elimination may have ended in the summer of 1986. In a 5–4 decision, the Supreme Court upheld a Georgia law that makes it a felony, punishable by 20 years in prison, for consenting adults to commit sodomy—that is, oral or anal sexual relations. The Gallup Organization conducted a poll of a nationally representative sample of U.S. adults shortly after the Supreme Court decision. Of those surveyed, 57% thought that

states should not prohibit private homosexual practices between consenting adults, and 74% said that states should not prohibit noncoital (that is, oral or anal) heterosexual activity (*Newsweek*, July 14, 1986). In Canada, buggery, or sodomy, is an offense only if a participant is under age 21 and the act is carried out publicly or involves an animal (*Pocket Criminal Code*, 1987).

Sodomy laws are seldom enforced against heterosexuals. They are used almost exclusively against homosexuals, as was true in the Georgia case (see Chapter 15).

(Fisher, 1973; Hunt, 1974). In more recent research, women indicated that they preferred an average of about 17 minutes of foreplay prior to penile penetration (Darling, Davidson, & Cox, 1991). Thus there may be a discrepancy of 2 to 5 minutes between what women desire and what they get.

After penile insertion, women seem to require an average of about 8 minutes to experience orgasm, although the preferred length of intercourse after penile insertion was about 11 minutes (Darling et al., 1991; Fisher, 1973). It should be noted that there was a wide range in the length of time women needed to experience orgasm, with some requiring just 1 minute and others needing about 30 minutes.

For men, the average time from insertion to orgasm was about 10 to 11 minutes (Darling et al., 1991; Hunt, 1974). This longer duration to orgasm for men than for women is interesting in that women in the Fisher study estimated that it took them 40% to 80% more time to attain orgasm than it did their partners. Some of this discrepancy is undoubtedly due to different sampling and methodological techniques used in these studies. However, women who experienced orgasm after their partner reported less sexual satisfaction than did women who had orgasm before or simultaneously with their partner (Darling et al., 1991). Although women prefer more time spent in sexual foreplay and in sexual intercourse, research on men's preferences is lacking.

Having reported these data on time spent in "foreplay" and intercourse, we want to caution readers not to focus too heavily on timing as an index of sexual pleasure. We know one couple who ended up in therapy because the husband was experiencing difficulty getting an erection. It turned out that his wife—a very busy woman—was in the habit of keeping a stopwatch by their bed to time how long it took him to reach orgasm!

## Coitus and Coital Positions

Nonhuman species rely almost entirely on rear entry as their main position during sexual interaction, although porpoises use a face-to-face position while swimming. In contrast, humans employ a wide range of positions during sexual activity, and the popularity of various positions differs from one culture to another. The typical coital position used in a particular culture appears to be correlated with the social status of females (Beigel, 1953). For example, among several American Indian tribes and among groups in the South Pacific, where females enjoy high status, the woman-above position is most popular, and sexual satisfaction is considered at least as important for women as it is for men. The cross-cultural association between female status and coital position is especially interesting in light of two studies in our own culture. Although Masters and Johnson (1966) found that the woman's sexual response develops more rapidly and with greater intensity in the face-to-face, woman-

## TABLE 7.3 Popularity of Coital Positions

The Kinsey and Hunt surveys showed the following trends among married people.

| Coital Positions | Percentages of Respondents Practicing | |
| --- | --- | --- |
| | Kinsey Study (1938–1949) | Hunt Study (1972) |
| Female-above | 33% | 75% |
| Side-by-side | 25% | 50% |
| Rear-entry (vaginally) | 10% | 40% |
| Sitting | 8% | 25% |

above position than in any other coital position, the Kinsey group (1948, p. 578) concluded that

*nearly all coitus in our English-American culture occurs with the partners lying face to face, with the male above the female. There may be as much as 70% of the population which has never attempted to use any other position in intercourse.*

This man-above position remains quite popular, but many couples now vary the positions they use during sexual intercourse (see Table 7.3). Although different coital positions can produce different physical sensations, any position in which the penis penetrates the vagina can result in conception, so couples who do not want to conceive should use a reliable contraceptive when they have coitus of any kind.

### Face-to-Face, Man-Above

In the face-to-face, man-above position, a woman usually lies on her back with her legs apart and her knees slightly bent (see Figure 7.7). A man lies on top of her with his legs between hers, and he supports most of his weight with his elbows and knees.

Because the partners are face to face, they can communicate their feelings by continued erotic kissing, eye contact, and facial expressions. The penis can be inserted into the vagina as the couple move their bodies together, or it can be di-

rected by hand. After insertion of the penis, the man has more control of body movement than does the woman, whose pelvic movements are restricted by the pressure of his weight. Such limitation of the woman's pelvic movement can be a drawback of this position. When a man is considerably heavier than a woman, another coital position may permit greater participation from the woman. In the man-above position, however, a woman can enhance her capacity to move in pleasurable ways by pulling her legs up toward her shoulders or by placing them on the man's shoulders. She can also entwine her legs around his back and lock her feet together. These actions can be supplemented by placing a pillow under her lower back, which increases the contact between a woman's clitoris and her partner's body. By changing the position of her legs, a woman can then more easily coordinate the movement of her pelvis with the man's coital thrusts, as well as maintain the kind of stimulation to her clitoral area that will result in orgasm.

A disadvantage of the face-to-face, man-above position is that a man's hands are not free to stimulate his partner. For couples who desire this pleasure, the coital position that follows is recommended.

### Face-to-Face, Woman-Above

In the face-to-face, woman-above position, a man lies on his back with a woman kneeling over him, her knees positioned on either side of his body. She can lean her upper body forward and guide his penis into her vagina as she moves down on it. She can then either sit upright or lie down on top of her partner, depending on how much body contact she wants (see Figure 7.8). If she remains sitting or kneeling over the man, he can readily caress her breasts and face.

The advantages of this position for women are similar to the advantages of the man-above position for men. Positioned above her partner, a woman has better control over coital movement and depth of penetration, and either she or her partner can manually stimulate her clitoris. Men often experience less sexual intensity in this position, and this may be desirable if the woman is typically slower to respond than the man, or if the man ejaculates more quickly than he wishes. Furthermore, when a man wants to prolong the

**FIGURE 7.7**
**Face-to-Face, Man-Above Coital Position**

pleasure of arousal, leisurely lovemaking may be easier for him in this position than in the man-above position, in which he is likely to reach orgasm faster.

The woman-above position is not desirable on those occasions when a man wants to take primary responsibility for sexual movement. In addition, the position may put some men in a passive or subordinate role that makes them psychologically uncomfortable. Similarly, women who hold traditional gender-role attitudes may feel somewhat threatened by this position or may worry about a partner's reaction to the suggestion that the two of them take turns being on top. In research using slides depicting a couple in the woman-above position and the man-above position, women rated the same couple as more moral, more normal, and more clean when they were in the man-above than in the woman-above position. In contrast, men gave equally high ratings to the couple regardless of their coital position (Allgeier & Fogel, 1978). This finding suggests that a person who wishes to try the woman-above or any other coital position

should ask his or her partner's feelings about it rather than simply assuming that the partner has the same desires.

### Face-to-Face, Side-by-Side

The side-by-side variation of the face-to-face position offers both partners the opportunity to control their own body movements during coitus (see Figure 7.9 on page 212). The couple can lie in several different positions, all of which eliminate weight on either partner. These positions allow a lot of body contact and free the hands for caressing and touching. The side-by-side positions are particularly useful for overweight individuals and during the latter stage of pregnancy, when man-above and woman-above positions may both be uncomfortable because of the woman's enlarged abdomen.

Couples may begin in the man-above position and then roll onto their sides with the penis inserted in the vagina. In this position penetration tends to be shallow, and movements may be somewhat restricted or less vigorous. Depending

**FIGURE 7.8**
**Face-to-Face, Woman-Above Coital Position**

on a couple's preferences at a particular time, the more gentle movement can be either an advantage or a disadvantage. They might choose this position, for example, when they want to prolong playful and intimate sexual relations before orgasm.

*Rear-Entry Positions*

This approach involves vaginal intercourse in which the male positions himself behind the woman. Rear-entry coitus does not mean anal sex, with which it is sometimes confused. Because rear entry is the most prevalent coital position among nonhuman species, some people believe that the position is degrading or animalistic. This idea is unfortunate because there are advantages to rear-entry positions. For example, they allow a man more access to a woman's body. If

both of them are lying on their sides, the man can caress the woman's breasts, most of her upper body, and her abdomen, clitoris, buttocks, and back. In fact, stimulation of the clitoris is easier in rear-entry than in any other coital position. In addition, stimulation of the Gräfenberg spot by thrusting the penis against the anterior wall of the vagina is more likely in rear-entry than in the face-to-face positions.

Rear entry can be accomplished with a woman lying on her stomach or kneeling. The man faces her back and inserts his penis into her vagina. Alternatively, the woman can sit on the man's lap, facing away, or the man can enter the woman while both are standing up, although it may be necessary for the woman to stand on a stool if the man is considerably taller than she is.

A variation of this position, known as the scissors position, permits a woman to vary her

**FIGURE 7.9**
**Face-to-Face, Side-by-Side Coital Position**

pelvic thrusting with more ease while allowing a man greater ejaculatory control. To use the scissors position, a couple may begin with both the woman and the man lying on their left sides, with the woman's back to the man. She then rolls partially onto her back, putting her right leg over the man's legs so that his penis can enter her vagina. For ease of entry, their heads and upper bodies should be at some distance from each other so that their bodies resemble a pair of open scissors. This position allows the man to caress the woman's genitals or breasts easily. The ease with which the couple may caress and look at each other contributes to the intimacy of this position.

Rear-entry positions can be less physically demanding than other positions. They can be used during the third trimester of pregnancy or during illnesses that limit physical activity.

## Anal Sex

Anal sex involves the stimulation of the anus by a partner. The stimulation may involve fingers, the tongue, a penis, or an object. The anus is rich in nerve endings and is involved in sexual response regardless of whether it is directly or indirectly stimulated. The anus does not produce much lubrication, but lubrication can be supplied through the use of a sterile, water-soluble product such as K-Y jelly. Vaseline and other petroleum-based lubricants should not be used in the anus or the vagina because they tend to accumulate and are not as easily discharged as are water-soluble lubricants.

The anal sphincter muscle responds to initial penetration with a contraction that may be uncomfortable. The spasm usually relaxes within 15

**TABLE 7.4  Popularity of Anal Intercourse**

These studies are difficult to compare because the researchers asked questions in different ways, and the Billy et al. group included only males.

| Kinsey group 1938–1949 | Hunt 1972 | Billy et al. 1991 |
|---|---|---|
| Never tried: 89% | Under age 25: 25% | Experienced at ages 20–39: 20% |
| Tried unsuccessfully: 3% | At ages 25–34: 25% | |
| Have experienced: 8% | At ages 35–44: 14% | |

to 30 seconds in a person who is familiar with anal intercourse (Masters & Johnson, 1979). In a tense, inexperienced person, the spasm may last for a minute or longer, but the discomfort usually disappears. Masters and Johnson (1979) reported that in 11 of 14 episodes that they observed, women experienced orgasm during anal penetration. Orgasm occurred in 2 of 10 episodes involving anal penetration of males, but in both cases the penetrated male was also masturbating.

Like masturbation, oral stimulation, and coital position variations, anal sex apparently became more prevalent in the past 50 years. Research reviewed by Voeller (1991) indicates that 25% of American women occasionally engage in receptive anal intercourse, and 10% do so regularly for pleasure. Most women report experience with anal sex only after repeated personal interviews with a trusted interviewer. Even with the advent of AIDS and the urgent need for safer-sex practices, there has not been a marked decline in anal sex in the United States, as can be seen in Table 7.4. (See Chapter 17 regarding AIDS and ways to reduce the risks associated with sexual activity.)

As with oral sex, there appear to be ethnic differences in the likelihood of people engaging in anal sex (Billy et al., 1993). White males (21%) are more likely to report engaging in anal intercourse than are Black males (14%), and more Hispanics (24%) do so than non-Hispanics (20%).

If couples choose to engage in anal sex despite the risk of AIDS, a lubricated condom should be worn, and penile penetration of the anus should be carried out gradually and gently. The penis should never be inserted into the vagina or mouth after anal penetration unless it has been washed. The anus contains bacteria that can cause infection.

## Frequency of Coitus and Number of Sexual Partners

Concern about what is a "normal" or average number of sexual contacts often surfaces in our sexuality classes. Most of these questions involve sexual intercourse. In addition to frequency, the number of sexual partners people have has become a mounting concern with the threat of AIDS as well as other sexually transmitted diseases.

The average American couple has coitus about one to three times a week in their early 20s, with the frequency declining to about once a week or less for those age 45 and older (Blumstein & Schwartz, 1983; Hunt, 1974; Kinsey et al., 1948, 1953). The coital frequency for several more recent national surveys is presented in Table 7.5. These figures give us rough estimates for the total sample but do not give us a true notion of the variability in sexual activity among Americans. For example, 22% of Smith's (1991) national sample reported total abstinence in the past year, whereas Billy et al. (1993) found a few men in their national sample who reported having vaginal intercourse more than 22 times a week! Thus there is no "gold standard" against which we can measure the "appropriate" frequency of sexual activity. There is simply a great deal of

| TABLE 7.5  Sexual Intercourse: Frequency per Week | | |

Comparisons across studies are difficult because of the different measures employed.

|        | Donnelly 1987–1988 | Smith 1988–1989 | Billy et al. 1991 |
|--------|------------------|----------------|------------------|
|        | *Mean*           | *Mean*         | *Median\**        |
| Female | 1.67             | .98            |                  |
| Male   | 1.60             | 1.27           | .92              |

*The median is the middlemost response reported by members of a sample.

variability among couples and for a given couple over different time periods. As we discuss in the next chapter, however, lack of, or very little, sexual activity is associated with relationships characterized by friction and strain and other problems (Blumstein & Schwartz, 1983; Donnelly, 1993).

Regarding the number of sexual partners, Smith (1991) found an average of 7 partners since age 18, although men reported considerably more partners (12) than did women (3), which he believed stems from men overreporting and women underreporting. When the 12 to 18 months prior to data collection were considered, the number of partners was a little over 1. As might be expected from the decrease in frequency of sexual activity with age, the number of sexual partners also declined with age. As with frequency of sexual activity, there is a great deal of variability among individuals in their reported number of sexual partners. In the Billy et al. (1993) study, 23% of the men had 20 or more coital partners, and a few men reported more than 900 lifetime coital sex partners. The median (middlemost) number of partners reported by men since age 20 was 7, and in the past year and a half, 1. No consistent ethnic differences emerged in self-reported numbers of sexual partners (Billy et al., 1993; Smith, 1991).

Smith (1991) estimated that a little less than 7% of his sample was involved in risky sexual

behavior, such as having multiple or unfamiliar partners or being gay or bisexual—although, as discussed in Chapter 17, it is *particular sexual behaviors* rather than sexual orientation or number of partners that is most closely associated with contracting the AIDS virus and other sexually transmitted diseases. Overall, 48% of married adults reported no sexual partners other than their spouse (Smith, 1991).

## Sexual Satisfaction and Enjoyment

The preceding descriptions of the various types of sexual stimulation are by no means exhaustive. The possibilities are limited only by imagination, body build, energy level, and agility. Some couples may find a particular position or stimulation technique so satisfying that they have little interest in exploring others. If they do not find their pattern monotonous, there is no compelling reason why they should experiment. On the other hand, partners who feel that their sexual interaction has become automatic may be able to add zest and intensity to their lovemaking by trying alternative ways of giving pleasure to each other.

It is important to keep in mind that the physical expression of our sexuality takes place in the context of daily life. Sexual intimacy can provide a break from a demanding schedule in the form of experiences ranging from simple physical release to the communication of intensely felt affection and connection. Perhaps the ultimate measure of sexual satisfaction is the quality of the period of time following orgasm. At its best, it is a time of mutual relaxation and shared intimacy, a time when we may be more open than usual to new ideas and suggestions. Mosher (1980) hypothesized that an engrossing sexual interaction, and the time immediately following it, are similar to a hypnotic trance in that the individuals involved tend to be more accessible than usual to each other's influence. This aftermath can provide an opportunity to talk about and reflect on matters not directly related to mundane daily tasks. At other times, they may feel energized by sexual interaction, ready to return to work or other activities with renewed vigor.

Sexual intimacy, then, can have different purposes. Release from tension, the sense of intense union, or the expression of affection can be part of any sexual contact that is more than just momentary. Sometimes a source of ecstasy, sometimes mediocre or rather disappointing, the experience of sexual contact can fluctuate a great deal. If we accept these variations and do not focus on any one episode as the main determinant of the quality of our sexuality, we can enjoy the diversity.

## Simultaneous Orgasm: A Note

In the section on masturbation, we pointed out that most men slow down or stop manual stimulation of the penis during orgasm. In contrast, women generally prefer continued stimulation of the clitoris or mons during orgasm. This difference is consistent with the observation that most men attempt deep vaginal penetration with little further thrusting at the onset of ejaculation during coitus, whereas the typical woman prefers continued male thrusting during her orgasm (Masters & Johnson, 1966). Because of this difference in the typical response styles of men and women, simultaneous orgasm can be difficult to obtain. In a study of female nurses, only 17% of the sample experienced orgasm at about the same time as their partner (Darling et al., 1991). Because women can continue coitus indefinitely before and/or after orgasm, whereas men's erections generally subside after ejaculation, an approach to orgasm that emphasizes "ladies first" may be most satisfying for many couples. For example, if a woman finds it easier to have an orgasm in the woman-above position, a couple can employ this position until the woman has orgasm. At that point, the couple can move into whatever position the man finds most stimulating. Preoccupation with the attempt to achieve simultaneous orgasm can mar what might otherwise be a pleasurable experience. An exception to this generalization is when a couple is "swept away" with the emotional intensity of their interaction, a typical situation in the early stages of a sexual relationship or during the periodic renewal of intensely passionate feelings that can occur in long-term relationships. These conditions can lead to simultaneous orgasm that has little to do with sexual technique.

Another kind of satisfying experience may provide a useful model for many couples: a massage. Having your body massaged allows another person to give you pleasure while you simply relax and let your feelings emerge. It can also be rewarding to take the active role, arousing great pleasure in your partner. Regardless of what positions and techniques couples use in their sexual interaction, their bodies tend to respond in one of just a few relatively predictable patterns of physical response.

## The Sexual Response Cycle

William Masters and Virginia Johnson were the first researchers to study human sexual response through systematic observation in a laboratory setting. Out of their work came a model for describing human sexual response, called the sexual response cycle (SRC). Later we describe an alternative model of sexual response developed by Helen Singer Kaplan. One reason for the development and testing of these models is that precise descriptions of the sequence of behaviors in normal sexual responding can help therapists to pinpoint sources of sexual dysfunctions and provide treatment (see Chapter 8). Masters and Johnson (1966) focused primarily on the physiological and behavioral aspects of sexual responses. Aside from our awareness of excitement and orgasm, most of us do not distinguish our sexual responses. For convenience in describing the biological processes involved during sexual response, Masters and Johnson identified four successive phases: excitement, plateau, orgasm, and resolution.

Prior to Masters and Johnson's work, men and women were believed to be different in their sexual responses. Common "wisdom" held that men had easily triggered sexual drives, whereas women's responses needed careful nurturing through long periods of courtship and foreplay. In addition, men were thought to reach orgasm readily and quickly. In contrast, orgasm for women was perceived by those who believed in its existence as a highly elusive response. Furthermore, it was thought that men could ejaculate and that women could not. The extent to which these perceived differences resulted from

**Box 7.3**

## Physical Reactions of the Male During the Sexual Response Cycle

### Excitement

Increase in length and diameter of penis

Elevation of testes

Possible erection of the nipples

Appearance in 50% to 60% of males of a "sex flush," a rosy, measleslike rash over the chest, neck, face, shoulders, arms, and thighs

Increase in heart rate and blood pressure

Increase in muscle tension

### Plateau

Slight increase in the area of the glans penis and sometimes a color change

Secretion of a drop or two of fluid from the Cowper's glands

Continued elevation of the testes in the scrotal sac until they are up against the body

Increase of as much as 50% in size of testes

Rotation of testes by approximately 30%

Rapid spread of sex flush

Further increases in heart rate and blood pressure

Increase in respiration

Increase in muscular tension

### Orgasm

Contractions beginning as far back as the testes and continuing through the epididymis, vas deferens, seminal vesicles, prostate gland, urethra, and penis itself

Occurrence of three or four powerful ejaculatory contractions at 0.8-second intervals, followed by two to four slower contractions of the anal sphincter

Testes at their maximum elevation

Sex flush at its peak

Heart and respiratory rates at a maximum

General loss of voluntary muscle or motor control

Vocalizations (in some instances)

### Resolution

Gradual return of penis to its unstimulated size

Descent of testes and return of testes to normal size

Loss of nipple erection

Disappearance of sex flush

Return of heart rate, respiration, and blood pressure to pre-excitement levels

General relaxation of muscles

Sweating reaction in 30% to 40% of males

---

differences in cultural training rather than (or in addition to) differences in physiology was seldom considered.

In their focus on biological capacities, Masters and Johnson emphasized the similarities rather than the differences in the sexual responses of men and women. They found that most of the bodily changes that occurred in the sexual response cycles of both men and women were attributable to two major alterations in the genital organs: vasocongestion and myotonia.

*Vasocongestion*, or blood engorgement, is the process by which various parts of the genitals

**vasocongestion** (VAY-soh-con-JES-tion)—the process that results in an increase of blood in the genital organs of either males or females or in breasts of females during sexual arousal.

become filled with blood during sexual excitement. *Myotonia*, or muscle tension, refers to contractions of muscles during sexual response. Masters and Johnson's physiological recordings of the contractions of orgasm showed that one occurred every eight-tenths of a second in males—precisely the same interval as was recorded between the orgasmic contractions in females.

Masters and Johnson concluded that there were only two major differences between the sexual responses of men and women. First, they believed that men could ejaculate and that women could not. Second, they believed that women were capable of having a series of orgasms within a short period of time and that men were not. More recent research has suggested that even these differences may not be absolute. As you will see later, some men are capable of multiple orgasms, and some women appear to ejaculate a fluid at orgasm (Davidson, Darling, & Conway-Welch, 1989; Dunn & Trost, 1989; Zaviacic & Whipple, 1993).

## The Sexual Response Cycle (SRC) in the Male

A summary of male responses during the SRC is presented in Box 7.3. In the excitement phase, the penis begins to become erect. This swelling is due entirely to vasocongestion—the filling of the three spongy columns of the penis (the two corpora cavernosa and the corpus spongiosum) with blood. Arteries carrying blood into the penis dilate, allowing blood to engorge the spongy tissues.

During the plateau phase, the erection of the penis becomes more stable; that is, a man is less likely to lose his erection in the face of such distractions as ringing phones and nonerotic thoughts. This stability may be related to a further engorgement of the penis with blood, which has the effect of constricting the three veins that carry blood out of the penis.

In addition to swelling the penis, vasocongestion affects the testes, increasing their size by about 50%. Because of the tightness of the capsule surrounding each testis, most men can feel the sensations associated with this swelling. Contraction of the muscles surrounding the vas deferens pulls the testes up during excitement so that they press against the body. When men become sexually aroused but do not ejaculate, the swollen testes can become painful, a condition popularly known as "blue balls" or "lover's nuts." There are women (see Chapter 18) who have consented to unwanted intercourse to relieve their partners of such pain (O'Sullivan & Allgeier, 1994). No one has ever died of swollen testes, however, and if a woman does not want to engage in further sexual activity, a man can readily reduce the swelling in his testes by masturbating.

The orgasm phase actually occurs in two stages, both of which involve myotonia—contractions of the muscles associated with the internal sex organs. The first stage, *emission*, takes two or three seconds (see Figure 7.10). During emission, sperm and fluid are expelled from the vas deferens, seminal vesicles, and prostate gland into the base of the urethra near the prostate. As seminal fluid collects there and the urethra expands, men have the feeling that they are about to ejaculate ("ejaculatory inevitability"), but semen is not yet expelled from the urethra.

The second stage, *ejaculation*, involves expulsion of the semen by means of muscle contractions. There is also a contraction of the neck of the bladder, which prevents semen from flowing into the bladder. The semen is propelled by the muscular contractions of orgasm into the portion of the urethra within the penis and then expelled from the urethral opening in the glans (see Figure 7.11). These orgasmic contractions occur four or five times, at intervals of eight-tenths of a second. Simultaneously, muscles within the anus contract because both sets of muscles share a common nerve supply.

---

**myotonia** (MY-oh-TONE-ee-ah)—involuntary contractions of the muscles during the sexual response cycle.

**emission**—propulsion of sperm and fluid to the base of the urethra during orgasm.

**ejaculation**—expulsion of seminal fluid out of the urethra during orgasm.

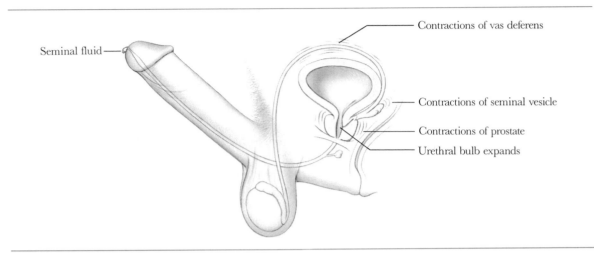

**FIGURE 7.10**
**Emission Stage of Orgasm**

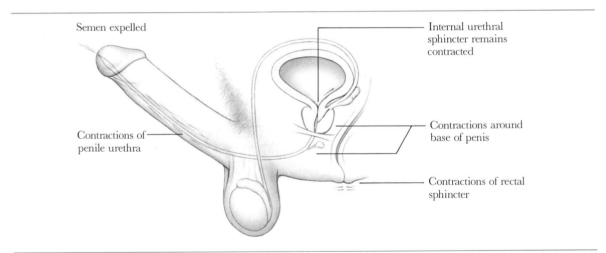

**FIGURE 7.11**
**Ejaculation Stage of Orgasm**

After ejaculation, the resolution phase begins. This process restores the genital organs and tissues to their pre-excitement phase as the blood that filled the penis flows back into the veins. After this phase, most men experience a *refractory period*—that is, a period of time during which

**refractory period**—the period immediately following ejaculation, during which further arousal is not possible; not present in the female's sexual response cycle.

nerves cannot respond to further stimulation. Most of us have experienced refractory periods in other contexts. For example, when a flash bulb is used to take our picture, most of us are momentarily blinded because the nerves in our eyes are temporarily unable to respond to the stimulation of light. Similarly, for many men, further erotic stimulation for a period of time following ejaculation provokes no response and may even be unpleasant. Masters and Johnson described the male refractory period as lasting between 30

**Box 7.4**

# Physical Reactions of the Female During the Sexual Response Cycle

## Excitement

Onset of vaginal lubrication

Lengthening and expansion of inner two-thirds of the vaginal barrel

Engorgement of vaginal walls with blood

Increase in diameter of clitoral shaft

Slight swelling of glans clitoris

Engorgement of inner lips with blood

Flattening of outer lips and their retraction from the vaginal entrance

Erection of nipples

Size increase in breasts

Sex flush

Increase in muscle tension

## Plateau

Further engorgement of outer third of the vagina and inner lips with blood, forming the orgasmic platform

Retraction of the clitoris until it is completely covered by the tissue of the clitoral hood and decreases about 50% in length

Further engorgement of nipples

Possible spread of sex flush to the stomach, thighs, and back

Marked increase in heart rate, respiration, and blood pressure

Increase in muscle tension

## Orgasm

Beginning of strong muscle contractions in outer third of the vaginal barrel

First contractions may last for 2 to 4 seconds, with later contractions lasting from 3 to 15 seconds. These occur at 0.8-second intervals, just as in the male.

Slight expansion of inner two-thirds of the vagina

Contraction of uterus

Peak intensity and distribution of sex flush

Frequently strong muscular contractions in many parts of the body

Possible doubling of respiratory rate and heart rate

Blood-pressure elevation to as much as a third above normal

Vocalizations (in some instances)

## Resolution

Quick dispersion of blood in outer third of the vaginal walls

Gradual return of coloring and size of the inner two-thirds of vagina to prestimulation levels

Return of inner lips to their normal color, and accompanying decrease in size

Closing of outer lips toward the vaginal entrance

Return of clitoris from under the clitoral hood to its usual exposed condition

Disappearance of sex flush, fading first in the areas where it appeared last

Gradual decrease of nipples and breasts in size

Return of breathing, heart rate, and blood pressure to normal

Sweating reaction in 30% to 40% of females

Relaxation of body muscles

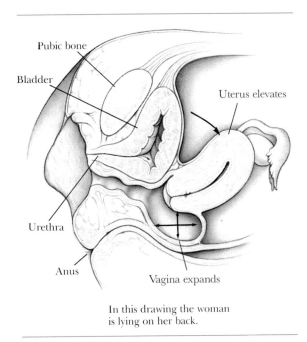

Pubic bone

Bladder

Uterus elevates

Urethra

Anus

Vagina expands

In this drawing the woman
is lying on her back.

**FIGURE 7.12**
**Muscular Contractions of Orgasm**

and 90 minutes. As you will see later, however, some men are not able to become erect again for a considerably longer interval. Other men can have multiple orgasms; that is, they do not experience the typical refractory period.

## The Sexual Response Cycle (SRC) in the Female

A summary of female responses during the SRC appears in Box 7.4, page 219. Erotic excitement produces vasocongestion in the female genitals, as in the male genitals. Whereas engorgement of the penis results in erection, engorgement of the inner lips, clitoris, and vaginal walls with blood produces a slippery, clear fluid—vaginal lubrication—on the vaginal walls. As the vaginal walls swell with blood, the inner two-thirds of the vagina widens and lengthens, in what is called the tenting effect (see Figure 7.12). The clitoris becomes congested with blood and increases in diameter. It remains enlarged during the plateau and orgasm phases. The outer lips, which touch when the woman is not aroused,

now flatten and move apart to leave the swollen inner lips, clitoris, and vaginal entrance exposed.

The enlarged clitoris retracts beneath the clitoral hood during the plateau phase and cannot be seen again until after orgasm. However, it can continue to receive stimulation through manual or oral movements on the clitoral hood. Thrusting of the penis in the vagina can also stimulate the clitoris, as pressure of the penis on the inner lips pulls the clitoral hood back and forth.

The outer third of the vagina becomes constricted through blood engorgement. This constriction forms a narrow tube, called the "orgasmic platform" by Masters and Johnson (1966). The muscular contractions associated with orgasm occur in the vagina, uterus, and fallopian tubes (refer to Figure 7.12). Most women, however, subjectively experience the contractions in the outer third of the vagina—the orgasmic platform—as the most intense. Muscular contractions often occur in many other parts of the body as well.

During the resolution phase, the genitals return to their pre-excitement state. Masters and Johnson found that with continued stimulation, however, women could have additional orgasms with little intervening time; that is, they concluded that females did not have the refractory period characteristic of males.

## Patterns of Sexual Response

Major differences in the patterns of sexual response among males mainly involve the length of various phases rather than the intensity of response. In contrast, among females, Masters and Johnson (1966) concluded that there is a wide range of intensity. Also, a particular woman may respond with different patterns at various times, depending on her past experiences and the effectiveness of stimulation.

Masters and Johnson observed three typical patterns of sexual response in their female volunteers. In pattern A, a female proceeds through the entire response cycle into one or more orgasms without interruption. This pattern is the typical multiple-orgasm response, with orgasms occurring far enough apart that they are distinguishable from one another. In pattern B, there is a gradual increase in arousal and a fluctuating

**Box 7.5**

# Whose Is It?

Some of the following descriptions of excitement and orgasm were written by women, and some by men (Vance & Wagner, 1976). Can you tell the gender of the author of each description? For the answers, see page 223.

*1. I think that there are a variety of orgasms that I experience. I have noted a shallow "orgasm" which consists of a brief period that is characterized by an urge to thrust but which passes quickly. On the other hand, I have also experienced what I call a hard climax, characterized by a mounting, building tension and strong thrusting movements which increase in strength and frequency until the tension is relieved.*

*2. It is a very pleasurable sensation. All my tensions have really built to a peak and are suddenly released. It feels like a great upheaval; like all of the organs in the stomach area have turned over. It is extremely pleasurable.*

*3. Tension builds to an extremely high level—muscles are tense, etc. There is a sudden expanding feeling in the pelvis and muscle spasms throughout the body followed by release of tension. Muscles relax and consciousness returns.*

*4. Orgasm gives me a feeling of unobstructed intensity of satisfaction. Accompanied with the emotional feeling and love one has for another, the reality of the sex drive, and our culturally conditioned status on sex, an orgasm is the only experience that sends my whole body and mind into a state of beautiful oblivion.*

*5. Physical tension and excitement climaxing and then a feeling of sighing, a release of tension-like feelings.*

*6. An orgasm is a very quick release of sexual tension which results in a kind of flash of pleasure.*

plateau phase with small surges toward orgasm, followed by a relatively slow return to the physiological state of pre-arousal. This pattern seems to occur in young or sexually inexperienced women, who may not be sure that they have experienced orgasm. In pattern C, there is a single orgasm of extreme intensity with little time spent in the plateau phase. Women report feelings of great release and gratification with this pattern.

Despite gender differences at the physiological level, the subjective feelings of men and women during intense sexual response may be similar (see Box 7.5).

## Normal Variations

In examining the patterns of sexual response, it is important to remember that they represent the typical patterns that Masters and Johnson found in their volunteers. Some people are tempted to

measure themselves against such patterns. If their own responses do not generally match one of these patterns, they may conclude that there is something wrong with them, ignoring the fact that there are variations from one person to the next, and from one sexual episode to the next. There are two reasons why we may be tempted to place undue importance on such patterns in evaluating our own sexual responses.

First, until recently, little research on sexual response was conducted. We had no authorities to provide us with information or bases for comparing our own feelings and responses to those of other people. Second, although we are encouraged to ask parents, friends, and teachers about a variety of matters, including facts pertaining to reproduction, a cultural taboo has prevailed against "comparing notes" or seeking information about sexual pleasure, a circumstance that may make us overly receptive to recent research

| TABLE 7.6 The Sexual Response Cycle: Masters and Johnson Versus Kaplan | | | | | |
|---|---|---|---|---|---|
| *Kaplan:* | Desire | Excitement | — | Orgasm | — |
| *Masters & Johnson:* | — | Excitement | Plateau | Orgasm | Resolution |

and information on the topic.* It is fascinating, for instance, that each of the volumes by Masters and Johnson (1966, 1970) has sold well, even though the writing is quite technical and thus difficult for the average person to understand.

These two factors—the absence of research on sexual response until recently, and the taboo against sharing information with our relatives and friends—have conspired to make us overly vulnerable and insecure about our own sexual feelings and responses. In our eating habits, we do not generally worry that we sometimes enjoy wolfing down a hamburger but at other times love the ritual of a seven-course meal. Nor are we upset when we have no appetite for either potato chips or chateaubriand. We realize that what is important is whether we feel good while having a particular meal, not whether we conform to the average American's typical pattern of eating an average of 700 calories per meal in an average of 17.3 minutes. Yet we may become overly concerned about going from the sexual-excitement phase through plateau to orgasm in the space of 5 minutes or less, or, on the other hand, responding slowly during sexual intimacy, lingering over each phase. At times like this, we should remember that the measure of sexual health is not the

extent to which we conform to some average pattern, but whether the process feels good and is satisfying to us and to our partners.

This brings us to the work of Helen Singer Kaplan. Whereas Masters and Johnson stressed the behavioral and physiological aspects of sexual response, Kaplan placed more emphasis on the psychological experience of sexuality—our thoughts and emotions during sexual interaction.

### Kaplan's Three Phases of Human Sexual Response

Kaplan proposed a framework (1974, 1979) for understanding human sexual response that, in terms of the subjective experience of sexual response, makes better sense than Masters and Johnson's framework. She divided sexual functioning into three phases: sexual desire, excitement, and orgasm. Table 7.6 shows her modification of Masters and Johnson's sexual response cycle, in which the resolution phase is omitted because that phase actually represents the lack of sexual response.

Kaplan believes that all three phases of the sexual response system are governed by interconnected but separate biological systems. Her framework is appealing from both a subjective and a psychological point of view. Most of us can distinguish among desire, excitement, and orgasm. Few of us, however, can differentiate between excitement and plateau as described by Masters and Johnson.

Distinguishing sexual desire as a separate phase in the sexual cycle has important implications for sexual dysfunctions and their treatment, discussed in Chapter 8. For now, we will simply let Kaplan (1979, p. 10) describe the desire phase of sexual response:

---

*For example, as I was working on this chapter, a student enrolled in my sexuality class appeared at my office door and asked shyly if she could talk to me. After closing the door and telling me how embarrassed she felt, she said that she thought she had ejaculated the night before with her boyfriend. We talked for about 15 minutes, and she mentioned that her roommate, who had been enrolled in the class last term, had told her about the research on female ejaculation. "But I just didn't feel as if I should tell her about last night, and I didn't know who else to talk to."—E.R.A.

*Sexual desire or libido is experienced as specific sensations which move the individual to seek out, or become receptive to, sexual experiences. These sensations are produced by the physical activation of a specific neural system in the brain. When this system is active a person is "horny"; he may feel genital sensations or he may feel vaguely sexy, interested in sex, open to sex, or even just restless. These sensations cease after sexual gratification, i.e., orgasm.*

Regardless of the framework, orgasm consistently draws more attention, rightly or wrongly, than any other sexual response, both by the public and the sex-research community. In the following section, we present some of the current research on this human phenomenon.

## Varieties of Orgasm

Females show greater variability in their sexual response patterns than do males. It appears, however, that the personal or subjective experience of orgasm does not differ between men and women. Earlier, we presented some descriptions of orgasm written by men and women who participated in Vance and Wagner's (1976) study. These researchers obtained 48 such descriptions. After removing obvious gender cues, they presented these descriptions to physicians, psychologists, and medical students and asked them to judge whether each had been written by a male or a female. The fact that these professionals could not accurately judge the samples suggests that the experience of orgasm is quite similar for females and males. How did you do? The first three quotes in Box 7.5 were written by women, and the last three by men.

### Female Orgasm: Different Types?

The inquiry into different types of orgasms in the female is unique to the study of humans. With all other species, the question is whether female orgasm occurs at all. Box 7.6 presents an overview of this controversy.

For decades, psychoanalysts believed that adult women should respond orgasmically to pe-

nile thrusting in the vagina. They described women who obtained orgasm primarily from clitoral stimulation as being fixated at the phallic stage of childhood, as suffering from penis envy, and as having failed to develop "normal" adult female patterns of sexual response. It was in an atmosphere of general acceptance of that point of view that Masters and Johnson (1966) published one of their most influential findings. Specifically, they reported that, for a woman, the site of effective stimulation for orgasm is the clitoris, with orgasmic contractions then occurring in the vagina. Their conclusion helped deal the death blow to the idea that there was a clitoral orgasm which was distinct from a vaginal orgasm. Their physiological recordings of responses at the outer portion of the vagina indicated that the same orgasmic response occurred regardless of the site of stimulation.

Masters and Johnson did not focus on psychological reactions to orgasms or compare orgasms produced during coitus with those produced by clitoral stimulation alone. Other studies, however, have indicated that women do make subjective distinctions between masturbatory and coital orgasms (Bentler & Peeler, 1979; Butler, 1976; Singer & Singer, 1978). For example, among Butler's volunteers, 42% of those aged 29 and under reported that they experienced vaginally induced orgasms differently from clitorally stimulated orgasms, and 57% of those over the age of 30 made the same distinction. They described vaginally induced orgasms as "more internal," "deeper," "fuller, but not stronger," and "more subtle" than orgasms resulting from clitoral stimulation.

Perhaps the most well-developed criticism of Masters and Johnson's work on orgasm came from Singer and Singer (1978). The latter took issue with the conclusion that all orgasms are physiologically the same regardless of the type or site of stimulation. The Singers favor a broader definition of orgasm that includes emotional satisfaction as well as physiological changes. Accordingly, they have described three types of female orgasm.

The first type is the vulval orgasm, which can be induced by coital or noncoital stimulation and does not have a refractory period following it. This orgasm is the type measured by Masters and

**Box 7.6**

## Evolution and Female Orgasm

Intense debate rages over whether female orgasm exists in nonhuman species. At one end of the continuum are those scientists who argue that female orgasm is unique to humans. Essentially, they maintain that female orgasm is a human adaptation that strengthens the male-female emotional bond and enhances monogamous family life.

At the other end of the continuum are those who maintain that orgasm is not uncommon among female mammals, and that the absence or infrequency of orgasm in human females indicates some repressive force at work. Sherfey (1972), a radical advocate of this position, maintained that women were sexually insatiable in our evolutionary past. Her argument relied heavily on Masters and Johnson's research indicating that females do not experience a refractory period following orgasm and that some females may have multiple orgasms with further stimulation. Sherfey argued that primitive women's sexual drives had to be repressed to fit the demands of family life. Thus monogamy was ruthlessly imposed on the female by male-dominated societies. The age-old theme of the female as the unsatisfied sexual temptress who must be brought under the rational control of men is evident in Sherfey's argument.

What is the evidence for or against these conflicting views? Our knowledge of orgasm in nonhuman females is vague because of differences in definitions of orgasm and because we cannot talk with other species. C. A. Fox (1977) suggested four criteria for orgasm: 1) changes in blood pressure, respiratory pattern, and heart rate; 2) changes in muscular tension, including vaginal and uterine contractions; 3) hormonal changes; and 4) vocalizations. Although these criteria have been observed to varying extents among other mammals, most students of mammalian behavior are not convinced that orgasm among nonhuman mammals is anything but an extremely rare occurrence.

In his review of the literature on mammalian orgasm, Symons (1979) concluded that evidence for nonhuman primate orgasm has been obtained only among captive animals, and even then the occurrence was highly variable. When orgasm did occur, there had been direct and prolonged stimulation of the clitoral area. Thus it is likely that in the wild, female mammals would rarely experience sufficient stimulation to reach orgasm. Although there are some exceptions, most mammals mate quickly because it is reproductively advantageous for males to ejaculate as soon as possible after penetration (Ford & Beach, 1951); the position that is taken by the male during copulation leaves him open to attacks by potential predators.

What are the implications of the research for theories about the evolution of orgasm? Symons (1979, p. 94) pointed out that there is no compelling evidence for either view: "Sexually insatiable females and people who pair-bond like gibbons* appear to exist in substantial numbers only in the human imagination." Whereas orgasm in human males appears to be a continuation of mechanisms in lower species, the human female seems to be unique in her ability to reach orgasm easily.

---

*Slender, long-armed apes native to tropical Asia; they are monogamous.

Johnson (1966). It is characterized by involuntary rhythmic contractions of the orgasmic platform. In contrast, a uterine orgasm is characterized by a gasping type of breathing that culminates in involuntary breath-holding. The breath is explosively exhaled at orgasm, and the orgasm is followed by a feeling of relaxation and sexual satiation. This response seems to occur upon repeated deep stimulation involving penis-cervix contact that displaces the uterus and causes stimulation of the membrane lining the abdominal cavity (peritoneum). This type of orgasm is followed by a refractory period. The third type of orgasm, which combines elements of the other two types, is called a blended orgasm. It is felt as being deeper than a vulval orgasm and is characterized by both breath-holding and contractions of the orgasmic platform.

It is possible that orgasm resulting from clitoral stimulation corresponds to what Singer and Singer (1978) call vulval orgasm. The uterine orgasm described by the Singers may correspond to orgasm produced by vaginal-wall stimulation. Finally, the blended orgasm they describe may result from simultaneous stimulation of the clitoris and the vaginal wall. Researchers continue to study possible variations in female orgasm as well as the physical-response systems associated with them. In addition to watching for the results of their findings, you may want to note interpretations of the significance of different kinds of orgasms. We hope that there will be no return to the practice of attributing moral and emotional superiority to any particular orgasmic pattern.

## Research on Female Ejaculation

References to women's expelling a fluid at orgasm have appeared in such fictional works as *Lady Chatterley's Lover* (Lawrence, 1930), in marriage manuals (van de Velde, 1930), and in the professional literature. Ernest Gräfenberg (1950, p. 147) observed:

> *This convulsory expulsion of fluids occurs always at the acme of the orgasm and simultaneously with it. If there is the opportunity to observe the orgasm of such women, one can see that large quantities of a clear, transparent fluid are expelled not from the vulva, but out of the urethra in gushes.*

Some have interpreted women's ejaculation of fluid as a normal, if atypical, response to sexual stimulation. Others have assumed that women who experienced ejaculation were simply suffering from incontinence—the inability to control urination—and developed a number of surgical, chemical, and electrical procedures to correct what they believed was a pathological condition.

In 1982, however, a book that dealt with female ejaculation and the Gräfenberg spot (*The G Spot*, Ladas, Whipple, & Perry) was published, followed by scores of reviews and articles. More information about the phenomenon should be forthcoming in the future, but we will summarize the results of the research published so far.

Some women have reported that stimulation of the anterior wall of the vagina produces enlargement of the Gräfenberg spot at the base of the bladder (see Chapter 5). A number of these women report ejaculating a clear to milky-white fluid from the urethra when they reach orgasm (Belzer, 1981). A number of researchers have conducted chemical comparisons of urine with samples of this fluid (Zaviacic & Whipple, 1993). The ejaculate differed from urine in a number of respects, the most notable of which was that the ejaculate was high in *prostatic acid phosphatase (PAP)*, a chemical believed to be secreted only by the male prostate gland. However, other analyses of the fluid expelled from the urethra by women at the height of sexual excitement indicated no differences between this fluid and urine for some of the women in the sample (Zaviacic & Whipple, 1993). At present, it appears that some women expel a fluid similar to urine from the urethra during sexual release, others expel a urethral fluid different from urine, and still others expel no fluid from the urethra at all during orgasm.

On the basis of their work with volunteers, Perry and Whipple (1982) concluded that perhaps 10% of women ejaculate. In a study of professional women, almost 40% reported experiencing ejaculation at the moment of orgasm (Davidson et al., 1989). But those women who believe themselves to be ejaculators would be more

---

**prostatic acid phosphatase (PAP)**—a fluid secreted by the prostate gland.

likely to participate in lab research, and to complete questionnaires, than would those women who do not believe themselves to be ejaculators or who believe that research on sexual response is immoral. At this time, then, we have no basis for accurately estimating the incidence of female ejaculation. Nor do we know the source of the ejaculate, although some researchers have suggested the presence of a rudimentary prostate gland at the base of the urethra (Sevely & Bennett, 1978; Zaviacic & Whipple, 1993). Considerably more investigation is needed before researchers can reach firm conclusions about the function of female ejaculation.

## The Consistency of Female Orgasm

Although most women are capable of experiencing orgasm, some women do so inconsistently, and others do not have orgasms at all. Kinsey et al. (1953) reported that 10% of married American women and 30% of sexually active unmarried women had never experienced orgasm. More recent studies indicate that 4% to 10% of adult women have never experienced orgasm (Davidson & Darling, 1989; Hunt, 1974; Klassen & Wilsnack, 1986). However, women in general are orgasmic about 40% to 80% of the time regardless of the method of stimulation.

Fewer than half of the 8,000 women interviewed by the Kinsey group (1953) consistently had orgasms during intercourse. Interestingly, these researchers found that women who had experienced orgasm before marriage by any means, whether with a partner or through self-stimulation, were more likely to do so after marriage than were women who had not experienced premarital orgasm. This suggests a "practice" effect. Premarital orgasmic experience increases the likelihood of marital orgasmic responsiveness. It should be noted that some women who do not experience orgasm nevertheless report their sexual activity as quite pleasurable. However, many women who do not experience orgasm consistently may feel pressured to meet their partner's and society's expectations that people should have at least one orgasm during each sexual encounter. Some pretend to have orgasms in their desire to please their partners. In a sample of 805 professional nurses, 58% reported that they had pretended at some point to have orgasm during sexual intercourse (Darling & Davidson, 1986). Although these women may have attempted to soothe the egos of their partners, they actually provided misleading feedback and disrupted sexual communication with their partners. This sexual deception could lead the partner into thinking everything is going well in the couple's lovemaking rather than looking for other approaches that might be more satisfying to the woman.

## The Consistency of Male Orgasm

The Kinsey group (1948) did not present detailed data on the consistency of male orgasm because they assumed that married men had orgasms almost 100% of the time. However, of the men in Hunt's (1974) study who were 45 or older, 8% did not have orgasm anywhere from occasionally to most of the time. Of the men between the ages of 25 and 44, 7% did not have orgasm at least a quarter of the time. Of the married men who were under age 25, 15% did not have orgasm about a quarter of the time or more often. Hunt speculated that these young husbands did not have orgasms because of anxiety, awkwardness, or inexperience. Men as well as women can fake orgasm, although there has been no systematic research on men faking orgasm.

## Multiple Orgasms in Females

One of the most frequently quoted findings of Masters and Johnson (1966) is their report of multiorgasmic responses among some of their female volunteers. Terman (1938) described the existence of multiple orgasms in women, and the Kinsey group (1953) estimated that 13% of women have multiple orgasms. More recently, the Darling, Davidson, and Jennings (1991) survey of nurses indicated that almost 43% usually experienced multiple orgasms during some form of sexual activity. However, it was Masters and Johnson's (1966) report of physiological recordings of multiple orgasm in women that prompted contemporary interest in the phenomenon. Their research indicates that most women are capable of having multiple orgasms if they are adequately stimulated.

Some writers have interpreted women's capacity for multiple orgasm as an indication that women are "more sexual" than men (Sherfey, 1972). Others have assumed that multiorgasmic women are sexually superior to women who have one orgasm or who do not have orgasms at all. Most of this reasoning could be dismissed as downright silly if it did not adversely affect the sexual lives of many women and men. The multiple orgasm response is not the zenith of sexual activity. Many women who are able to have multiple orgasms often prefer to experience just one intense uterine orgasm (Singer & Singer, 1978). Some women enjoy alternating their sexual patterns so that they experience multiple orgasms some of the time and one orgasm at other times. Sometimes they may experience no orgasm at all during lovemaking.

In one study of college women (Clifford, 1978), no clear preference for multiple or single orgasms appeared. Most of the women who experienced multiple orgasms found them no more satisfying than single ones. Thus it appears that the quality of sexual interaction is more important than the quantity.

## Multiple Orgasms in Males

Masters and Johnson (1966) found a few men below age 30 who experienced repeated orgasm and ejaculation without the refractory period that is characteristic of most men. These individuals were called multiejaculatory because the repeated orgasms were each accompanied by ejaculation.

More recently, there is evidence that some men can experience two or more orgasms before or following ejaculation (Dunn & Trost, 1989; Robbins & Jensen, 1978). These men reported having an average of 2 to 16 orgasms per sexual encounter, and one of the individuals in Robbins and Jensen's study reported as many as 30 orgasms in a one-hour period (confirmed by physiological measures). After an orgasm, the degree of penile engorgement decreased, but his penis remained fully erect, and the resolution phase did not occur.

Some of the men in the Dunn and Trost (1989) study thought that they had always been multiorgasmic and that their experience was "natural," whereas others reported learning to inhibit or control ejaculation until the final orgasm. It is widely believed that men are capable of only a single orgasm and ejaculation. As men become more aware of the possibility of multiple orgasm, it will be interesting to see whether the percentage of men experiencing it, which is presumably small, increases. For those who are interested, Hartman and Fithian's (1984) book *Any Man Can* provides detailed instructions for learning how to have multiple orgasms.

The techniques that elicit sexual responses obviously do not develop in a social vacuum. Our personal histories and the social situations in which we interact are strongly related to our patterns of sexual arousal. In Chapter 8 we examine some ways in which learning and feelings, as well as medical problems, may interfere with sexual arousal and response.

## Summary of Major Points _____

1. Autoeroticism and sexual learning.

Self-stimulation can provide useful training for sexual interaction with a partner, as well as being pleasurable in its own right. Women show more variety in the kinds of stimulation they use during masturbation than do men. Women tend to prefer continued self-stimulation during orgasm, whereas men usually stop stimulation or move their hands more slowly as they begin to have an orgasm.

2. Mutual sexual stimulation.

Almost any part of the body can be employed in stimulating another person, but the hands, mouth, genitals, and, to a lesser extent, the anus generally are used most often during sexual interaction. A couple can engage in coitus in a variety of positions, each of which provides somewhat different possibilities for stimulation. The choice of positions and stimulation techniques during sexual interaction should be guided by personal preference and pleasure; no one way is necessarily superior or inferior to any other.

3. Response of the body during sexual stimulation.

In their description of what goes on in the body during sexual stimulation, Masters and Johnson focused on physiological changes. The first stage in their four-stage sexual response cycle is excitement, during which erection and lubrication take place. This stage is followed by plateau, orgasm, and resolution. Kaplan proposed a model that corresponds more closely to our conscious awareness of sexual pleasure, including desire, excitement, and orgasm.

4. Varieties of orgasmic experience in women.

Recent evidence indicates that women are capable of having a diversity of orgasmic experiences, depending on the site of stimulation. Both clitoral stimulation and deep pressure on the vaginal walls can produce intense pleasure for women. Preliminary data suggest that some women ejaculate fluid from the urethra. The range of responses to sexual stimulation from one woman to the next is quite large, and individual women respond differently from one sexual encounter to the next. Some women rarely have an orgasm, others have a series of orgasms during sexual stimulation, and still others experience a single, intense orgasmic release.

5. Varieties of orgasmic experience in men.

Compared with women, men appear to show fewer individual differences in response to sexual stimulation. In general, sexual contact leads quite reliably to a single orgasm, followed by a refractory period during which the nerves do not respond to further stimulation. A few men, however, have trained themselves to have multiple orgasms by preventing full ejaculation until the final time they have orgasm in a particular sexual encounter.

## Review of Key Concepts

1. During the period from puberty to old age, the most common form of sexual outlet for most Americans apparently is: a) vaginal intercourse; b) nocturnal emission; c) masturbation; d) coitus. (p. 197)

2. Oral sex: a) decreased substantially in the past 50 years; b) is against the law in many American states; c) is practiced only by humans; d) all of the above. (p. 205)

3. Studies of sexual behavior have established that most couples: a) find it difficult to have simultaneous orgasm; b) find the quest for simultaneous orgasm deeply satisfying even if they rarely achieve it; c) achieve simultaneous orgasm with increasing frequency as their relationship develops; d) have simultaneous orgasm with decreasing frequency as a result of aging. (p. 215)

4. Masters and Johnson: a) established that women have easily triggered sexual drives, whereas men's responses have to be carefully developed; b) supported the long-standing belief that men normally have orgasm easily, whereas in women orgasm is highly unpredictable; c) emphasized the similarities rather than differences in male and female sexual responses; d) reached no conclusions about the nature of female versus male sexual response. (pp. 216–217)

5. During the excitement phase: a) women vaginally lubricate and men ejaculate; b) the clitoris expands in diameter and the penis increases in length and diameter; c) the respiratory rate and heart rate may double in both genders; d) muscular tension increases in men and decreases in women. (p. 219)

6. Kaplan modified Masters and Johnson's view of the sexual response cycle by: a) emphasizing sexual desire as a distinct phase of the cycle; b) combining the excitement and plateau phases into a single phase; c) eliminating the resolution phase; d) all of the above. (p. 222)

7. Which of the following is most likely true? a) Males show greater variability in sexual response than do females. b) The personal or subjective experience of orgasm does not differ between men and women. c) Neither is true. d) Both are true. (pp. 215–221)

8. Research by Masters and Johnson established that: a) stimulation of the clitoris is the most effective for orgasm in females; b) the physiological responses during orgasm produced by vaginal stimulation do not differ from those produced by clitoral stimulation; c) primate females do not experience orgasm; d) vaginal stimulation is the most effective way of triggering female orgasm; e) both a and b. (pp. 220–221)

9. Multiple orgasm is apparently: a) possible for both men and women; b) impossible for men but possible for women; c) generally regarded as the peak of sexual experience for all women capable of experiencing it; d) a myth. (pp. 220–221)

10. Regarding oral-genital sex, what changes in attitudes and behavior have occurred since the time of the original studies conducted by the Kinsey group? (pp. 204–206)

11. What risk factors are associated with anal sex? What precautions should be taken by those who practice this kind of sexual interaction? (pp. 212–213)

12. List some reasons why simultaneous orgasm may be less satisfying to partners than their taking turns at pleasuring one another. (p. 215)

# Sexual Dysfunctions and Therapy

Bob and Elaine have been cuddling on the couch, drinking wine, and watching the late movie on television. Elaine starts fondling Bob's penis, but it does not get erect, although Bob wants to have intercourse. Across town, Sally and Don returned from the ball game more than an hour ago and immediately took off their clothes and went to bed. They have been kissing and caressing pretty much steadily since then, but Sally's vagina has remained dry. Meanwhile, next door, their neighbors, Mary and Lisa, are both excited and wet, and Mary has come several times. Lisa wants badly to have an orgasm, too, but no matter what she and Mary do, she cannot quite come.

Does Bob have erectile dysfunction? Is Sally the victim of inhibited sexual excitement? What about Lisa—does she have orgasmic dysfunction? Yes, all three are sexually dysfunctional for the moment; that is, they are not responding sexually in the way that they want. Whether they would be diagnosed as having sexual dysfunctions would depend on the frequency of their inability to respond sexually.

The diagnoses also depend greatly on the beliefs of the particular clinicians whom they saw if they decided to seek help. Professionals do not always agree with one another on the sources of, and solutions to, sexual problems, as you will see. In this chapter we examine common dysfunctions and some factors associated with them. We also look at various therapeutic approaches

**Box 8.1**

## Kaplan's Categories of Disorders, Diseases, and Other Factors Affecting Sexual Functioning in Males and Females

*Neurogenic* **disorders** affect the sex centers of the brain and the spinal cord structures that serve the genital reflexes. Head injuries, strokes, psychomotor epilepsy, and multiple sclerosis are examples of such disorders.

*Vascular* **disorders** affect the circulatory system. Diseases of the blood vessels, cardiac disease, leukemia, and sickle-cell disease are some vascular disorders that can impair sexual functioning.

**Endocrine disorders** affect the body's hormonal balance. Any problem that results in

neurogenic—caused by a problem in the nervous system.
vascular—pertaining to the vessels that transport body liquids such as blood and lymph.

lowered testosterone levels may affect sexual response. Diabetes and kidney disease are examples of endocrine disorders that can affect sexual functioning.

**Debilitating diseases** refer to such conditions as advanced stages of cancer, lung disease, degenerative diseases, and genital infections that produce general ill health and affect sexual responsiveness.

**Drugs** such as tranquilizers, antipsychotics, and antidepressants used to treat emotional problems can cause sexual dysfunction. Alcohol, heroin, and barbiturate abuse can have the same result. Drugs that are frequently prescribed for the treatment of hypertensive conditions (high blood pressure) may periodically cause sexual dysfunction.

---

and controversies regarding their use. Finally, we consider the issue of sexual interaction between therapist and client, the use of surrogate sexual partners, and some other sources of controversy among therapists who treat sexual dysfunction.

## Sexual Dysfunction: Contributing Factors

Although there is little systematic survey information on the frequency of sexual dysfunction in this country or in any other, most experts believe that sexual distress is common (Spector & Carey, 1990). One study (Frank et al., 1978) of 100 couples, most of whom were well educated, middle-class, and White, offers some support for this idea. No couples in the study were in sex therapy, and 80% claimed to find their sexual relations satisfying. However, 40% of the men had experienced problems with erection and ejaculation, and 63% of the women had encountered diffi-

culty in becoming sexually aroused or reaching orgasm. One conclusion that we can draw from this study is that, at the least, occasional difficulties with sexual functioning may be widespread.

Most factors that impair sexual functioning are classified as either biological or psychosocial in origin. Although we make use of this convenient division, it does not reflect the complex interactions of biological, psychological, and social factors that produce sexual dysfunctions—a fact that we discuss further at the end of this section.

### Biological Factors

In general, any disease or surgery that affects the reflex centers in the spinal cord and the nerves that serve them can result in sexual impairment. Many of the drugs used to treat particular mental and physical conditions also reduce responsiveness. Kaplan (1974, 1979) has described a variety of medical conditions that can influence sexual functioning. She grouped the conditions into five general categories (see Box 8.1).

### Box 8.2

## Incest and Anesthesia

When I was in my early teens, my mother left one night to visit relatives. I made dinner for my stepfather, but was very nervous about it because he was always so critical. He had several drinks and was very complimentary about dinner. In fact, he'd never been so warm and friendly toward me.

After dinner, we watched TV for a while and then he told me that his father had taught his sister about sex and it was time for him to teach me. I was flattered, confused, and afraid to say no. He was very gentle and played with me for a long time. I didn't feel much of anything except pleasure that he was paying attention to me. I was amazed to see his erection because I had wondered how men and women had intercourse. I did everything he told me—until he wanted to put his penis in my vagina. For some reason, I got the courage to say I didn't want to do that until I got married. That was OK with him and we went to sleep.

I woke up in the morning feeling very happy because I thought my stepfather finally loved me. When he left for work, though, he told me very sternly not to tell anyone about last night. He was cold and very distant, the way he always was except for the night before, and I felt dirty and ashamed.

Years later, after I got married, the only way I could come—and then, not very often—was when my husband was inside me. When he would touch my clitoris with his hand, I didn't feel anything. Eventually, I went to a psychotherapist, and he said that maybe I was making myself numb whenever my husband did anything my stepfather had done. After a while, I stopped feeling guilty about my stepfather and I also began to have feeling in my clitoris.

Source: Woman in her 20s.

## Psychosocial Factors

It is generally assumed that the majority of sexual difficulties result from psychosocial factors, but there is little consensus on the nature of these factors. Those professionals influenced by psychoanalytic theory look to critical childhood experiences to explain sexual dysfunction. The underlying assumption is that specific incidents in one's childhood exert a subconscious influence on one's adult behavior. In contrast, other therapists and researchers assume that the causes of sexual problems can be found in a couple's immediate situation. Communication difficulties, sexual misinformation, destructive relationships, and faulty learning are some of the immediate factors seen as crucial in the development of dysfunctions.

Sexual dysfunctions can be related to both recent experiences *and* childhood events. Although we categorize factors related to dysfunction as either past or current, keep in mind that recent and remote factors often interact to produce sexual difficulties.

### Past Experiences and Sexual Dysfunctions

Our experiences with our bodies and with sexuality begin in infancy. Deprivation of physical contact and love can blunt our emotional growth and our potential for sexual expression (Hatfield, 1994). Although most of our early experiences take place within a family, the nature and quality of those experiences can also depend on the larger social context that encompasses a family. For example, some cultures are extremely restrictive about eroticism; others are relatively permissive. The restrictiveness of a culture is linked to the incidence of difficulties in a man's getting or maintaining an erection. In an examination of 30 preindustrial and industrializing countries, Welch and Kartub (1978) found that the more restrictive a society was regarding such behaviors as premarital, marital, and extramarital sex, the greater the number of reported problems with erectile functioning.

Within North America, the restrictiveness of attitudes toward eroticism varies according to one's particular religious and moral beliefs. In general, people whose religions condemn sexual activity occurring outside of marriage and including acts other than procreative coitus are at greatest risk for sexual dysfunction. People who are taught to repress or despise sexual desire and bodily sensations have difficulty being comfortable even with marital sex.

In addition to the sexual restrictiveness of a specific culture and family background, traumatic childhood events have also been implicated in sexual dysfunction (Beitchman et al., 1992). Rape, parental discovery of sexual activity, and incestuous experiences are examples of events that can bring about a sexual dysfunction. Box 8.2 illustrates how a childhood sexual experience can contribute to later sexual problems.

Many sexual problems originate in myths and misinformation that individuals are exposed to at a fairly young age. These mistaken ideas can lead to misguided or ineffective attempts at sexual interaction that leave the individual feeling depressed and incompetent. Several botched sexual experiences can result in the avoidance of future sexual contact.

The differences between the backgrounds of people with healthy sexual responses and those of people with sexual dysfunctions should not lead you to believe that being brought up in a sexually restrictive environment is sufficient by itself to cause sexual dysfunction. Many people with adequate sexual functioning have family and cultural backgrounds that are similar to those of people with sexual dysfunctions (Heiman et al., 1986). Factors such as the ones described below are also related to developing dysfunctions and may interact with the more remote factors that we have just discussed.

### Current Sources of Sexual Dysfunction

The most frequent contributors to current sources of dysfunction are: a) anxiety, perhaps over sexual performance, and ideas that interfere with sexual arousal; b) inadequate information about sexuality that leads to ineffective sexual behavior; c) failures in communication; and d) stress (Cran-

ston-Cuebas & Barlow, 1990; Kaplan, 1974; Masters & Johnson, 1970; Morokoff & Gillilland, 1993). Anxiety and thoughts about sex can interact in complex ways (see Box 8.3).

**Anxiety.**   Kaplan (1974) and Masters and Johnson (1970) concluded that anxiety about sexual performance is the most important immediate cause of sexual dysfunction. Concerns about performance consist of an emotional component (performance anxiety) and a cognitive component (a person's evaluation of his or her sexual performance). Anxiety over sexual performance usually involves the fear of failure. After a person has experienced the inability to have or maintain an erection or vaginal lubrication, he or she may become obsessed with failing again. This fear of failure can start a vicious cycle in which the person does fail again because of fear.

*Spectating** refers to inspecting and monitoring one's own sexual activity rather than becoming immersed in the sexual experience. The person becomes a spectator rather than a participant, monitoring his or her own behavior and the partner's response. A man may worry: "Is my erection firm enough?" "Is my thrusting adequate?" "Is my partner being satisfied?" A woman may engage in the same sort of judgmental viewing: "Am I wet enough for him?" "Is my partner getting tired of rubbing my clitoris?" "Should I change the rhythm of my movement?" "Will I come?" People who become absorbed in such self-questioning cannot suspend distracting thoughts and lose themselves in the erotic experience. Interrupting the unfolding of sexual feeling and autonomic functioning leads to problems with arousal and/or orgasm. Not paying attention to one's own sexual feelings and responses is a foolproof method for obtaining minimal sexual gratification.

The relationship between anxiety and sexual dysfunction is not simple, however. Anxiety, in

spectating—evaluating and observing one's sexual activity rather than becoming immersed in the sexual experience.

---

*The concept of spectating was originated by Masters and Johnson (1970), who called it *spectatoring*.

**Box 8.3**

## Excessive Sexual Desire

The client was a 26-year-old male who was referred for therapy by his parole officer. He was living in a halfway house after having been released from prison following conviction for automobile theft. While in prison he had been raped many times and was involved in several stabbing incidents, one of which led to another inmate's death.

Although the client was in therapy to attempt to develop some control over a tendency for aggressive outbursts, it soon became apparent that his sexual behavior was problematic. Staff at the halfway house reported that he often masturbated in public and had been accused of exhibitionism at a modeling school.

He was short (5 ft., 3 in.) and slender and had several scars running across his face. During the first therapy session, his voice cracked several times and he cried as he discussed his prison experiences. The homosexual rapes had traumatized him, and he felt his sexual behavior had changed drastically. He had had several sexual experiences with different women

since he was released from prison and was steadily dating a woman 15 years older than he was. All his sexual episodes involved rather long bouts of intercourse in which he had orgasm 10 or 15 times. He reported that the women all commented positively on his sexual prowess.

Closer questioning revealed that the client experienced little relief or relaxation after orgasm. He also claimed that he masturbated from 8 to 20 times a day. Whenever he began to feel tense, he would "jack off." The client had an obsessive-compulsive reaction. His short stature and the prison rapes led to obsessive fears that he was not masculine and possibly gay. This fear created anxiety that he could reduce temporarily by compulsive sexual behavior, which reassured him. Without the ritual of sex, his anxieties would overwhelm him and drive him "crazy."

Source: Authors' files.

some circumstances, appears to facilitate sexual response. In a series of carefully designed experiments, Barlow and his colleagues (summarized in Cranston-Cuebas & Barlow, 1990) compared men who were functioning well sexually ("functional") to men who had sexual difficulties—in particular, inability to develop and maintain an erection ("dysfunctional"). They found that these two groups responded very differently while watching erotic films.

Anxiety produced by the threat of being given a painful electric shock often *increased* sexual response of functional men but *decreased* the sexual response of dysfunctional men. Performance demands—telling the men that if they do not have an erection, they will be given a shock—increased the arousal of functional men and decreased the arousal of dysfunctional men. Heightened arousal, produced by whatever

means, accentuated this pattern. Distraction (being asked to listen to a nonerotic cue while watching an erotic stimulus) reduced the sexual response in functional men but made little difference or even increased the sexual response in dysfunctional men. The explanation for this may be that the dysfunctional men were already attending to nonerotic cues that were even more nonerotic than the distracting one. Finally, when self-reports of sexual arousal were compared to physiological measures of arousal (penile strain gauge), functional men were fairly accurate in their reporting of physical arousal whereas dysfunctional men tended to report lower levels of arousal than the physiological measures had indicated.

To summarize, functional men and dysfunctional men react differently to their motivational states and use different cognitive processes to understand them. Dysfunctional men perceive a performance demand in sexual situations, which causes them to feel anxiety. This then leads to cognitive interference, and they focus their attention on nonerotic thoughts, for example, "Am I losing my erection?" These thoughts increase arousal of the autonomic nervous system, which produces a negative emotional state (anxiety), whereas functional men perceive their increased arousal as sexual arousal.

This analysis of sexual dysfunction is promising, but it has been done primarily with men. It also does not tell us how these men developed different ways of perceiving emotional states, nor why they interpreted their arousal in different ways.

**Misinformation**    Some couples who seek help for sexual dysfunctions reveal a lack of knowledge about their bodies and sexual functioning that leads to ineffective sexual behavior. They may not know where the clitoris is or may not be aware of its erotic potential. If ignorant of a woman's sexual response, a man may not engage in sufficient stimulation to arouse his partner. Because of her own socialization, the woman may be too naive or embarrassed to tell him what feels good. Thus she may be inadequately lubricated for intercourse and consequently experiences it as painful.

The abundance of sexual misinformation in our culture also can contribute to sexual problems. Men may succumb to the myth that they should always be ready to engage in genital sex with regularity, enthusiasm, and efficiency, regardless of their mood and the situation. When they experience temporary fluctuations in desire or when their sexual response is diminished by fatigue, they may react with great alarm and subsequently become obsessed with "failing" again. Women may succumb to the myth that they should be interested in sex only when their partners are, or that they should reach orgasm only through stimulation of the vagina in intercourse—and then they wonder why they experience difficulties with orgasm.

**Communication**    A substantial number of sexual problems could be resolved if people felt free to communicate with their sexual partners or

**FIGURE 8.1**
**Communication and Sexuality**
Couples may avoid sexual problems by sharing information about their sexual feelings.

friends about their sexual feelings, as noted in Chapter 6. The notion that sex is something people do not and should not talk about is directly associated with sexual problems. This attitude assumes that we are mind readers and should know each other's sexual feelings. At their first therapy session, one or both members of a sexually troubled couple often make such statements as, "Gee, I never knew you felt that way" or "I never tried to do that because I thought you wouldn't like it" (see Figure 8.1). Some of these couples might have saved themselves time and money if they had learned to communicate effectively by giving information about their sexual feelings and asking about their partner's feelings. Many people have difficulty telling their sex partner directly about their feelings and responses, but they must learn to do so if the other person is to find out whether or not he or she is providing pleasure. Talking about sex involves revealing our innermost private feelings, but taking this risk can lead to more intimate and satisfying sexual relationships.

Trust is central to any personal relationship, particularly one that involves sexuality. A couple's progression into intimate behavior can be a complicated ritual as each person tries to determine the other's intentions and trustworthiness (see Figure 8.2). Traditionally, the complications have often revolved around women's feelings of being used as sexual objects. However, being used is a concern for men as well. Uncertainty about commitment to a relationship, whether heterosexual or homosexual, can lead to mixed sexual feelings and behavior that fosters sexual problems. Fear of sexually transmitted diseases and concerns about birth control and pregnancy also can inhibit pleasurable sexual relations.

Sexual dysfunctions are often related to nonsexual problems that are not discussed openly in a relationship. Money worries, conflicts involving dominance, decision-making controversies, or problems in expressing affection are a few of the difficulties that can manifest as sexual problems. For instance, women who feel that their partners are not affectionate except when making love may express their resentment by not becoming aroused or orgasmic. Their partners then cannot have the satisfaction of bringing them sexual pleasure.

The problem of inadequate communication can increase a couple's difficulties in resolving some of the problems associated with sexual dysfunction. Overall sexual satisfaction for these partners is likely to improve if their communication about the frequency and nature of sexual activities improves. Such openness presumably increases a couple's abilities to deal constructively with the inevitable differences in opinions and feelings that occur in any relationship, and to avoid using sex as a weapon.

Many romantic relationships are as much about power and control as they are about love and sex. Some people feel that one partner dominates the relationship and makes most of the important decisions. Their resentment toward the partner may result in an inability to release themselves to the pleasure of sex because doing so would be seen as another sign of dependency. Similarly, they may make themselves sexually unavailable to demonstrate that they have the power to control sexual activity in the relationship. Thus the bed can become a battleground on which combatants vie for the upper hand in a relationship.

**FIGURE 8.2**
**The Importance of Trust**
The development of intimacy in a relationship depends on mutual trust. In the absence of trust and understanding of each other's intentions, one or both partners may have difficulty experiencing sexual desire, arousal, or orgasmic response.

Until clinically sophisticated techniques were developed for distinguishing between the relative contributions of biological and psychosocial factors to sexual dysfunction, it was generally assumed that most cases of sexual dysfunction were the result of psychological factors. These estimates were usually based on erectile dysfunction in males. Most of the advances in diagnosis of sexual dysfunction have involved the male, probably because our culture places a high value on men's sexual performance and because most researchers are men. Other studies, however—of older men at a medical clinic (Slag et al., 1983) and of men referred to a sex therapist by general practitioners (Legros et al., 1978)—showed that fewer than 20% of the men had erectile dysfunctions that were thought to be only psychological in nature. In the face of such disparate reports, it is probably reasonable to assume that the truth lies somewhere between these extremes. Some of the discrepancy may stem from differences in the training of the persons who provide the diagnoses. A physician may be more likely to look for medical difficulties, whereas a psychologist may emphasize the contributions of socialization and psychological variables to dysfunction.

**Stress**    The diagnosis of causes of sexual dysfunction as biological *or* psychosocial obscures the complex interactions between our minds and our bodies. Sexual dysfunctions are almost always the result of *stress* originating from biological and psychosocial sources (see Figure 8.3). Whatever the cause(s), stress can disrupt sexual functioning, decrease testosterone and luteinizing hormone levels, and lower sexual drive (Morokoff & Gillilland, 1993).

Some diseases or psychological factors may be severe enough to disrupt sexual functioning directly. In other cases, a physical illness may make an individual vulnerable to psychological factors, such as depression and anxiety, that result in sexual dysfunction. For example, although diabetes leads to erectile dysfunction in a substantial number of men with the disease, it would be careless to assume that a diabetic with erectile dysfunction simply had a biological problem. Abel and his coworkers (1982) found that approximately 30% of diabetics claiming erectile dysfunction appeared to suffer from psychological factors. Schumacher and Lloyd (1981, p. 49) postulated the following relationship between stress and sexual dysfunction:

> In the hierarchy of systems of the body, sexual function has a low status since it does not appear essential for the individual's life or health. Therefore when the body is under threat from physical and/or psychological stress, sexual functions may be sacrificed to foster the systems that are more important for survival or health.

stress—physical, emotional, or mental strain or tension.

**FIGURE 8.3**
**Stress, Sensuality, and Sexuality**
Stress can interfere with partners' feelings of sexual desire for one another. Giving each other a sensual back rub—whether it leads to sexual interaction at the time—may help to maintain a couple's feelings of intimacy and connection.

One example of the relationship between stress and sexual dysfunction comes from a study by Wabrek and Burchell (1980). They reported that of 131 male patients hospitalized for an acute myocardial infarction (heart attack), two-thirds reported having had a significant sexual problem before the attack. Among the sexually dysfunctional group, 64% reported erectile difficulties, 28% reported more than a 50% decrease in frequency of sexual activity, and 87% reported premature ejaculation. Wabrek and Burchell suggested that sexual problems are often associated with stress, which is in turn associated with myocardial infarction. One wife in this study reported how her husband had reacted, before his heart attack, when he could not get an erection:

> *He got very upset, swore, stamped around the room, got red in the face, beat his fist on the furniture, and once or twice broke vases.* (p. 70)

The man's frustration is understandable, but other, less violent ways of expressing it are preferable, particularly for coronary heart patients. Heart patients can be caught in a vicious cycle. Their cardiovascular disorder probably contributes to sexual dysfunction. The dysfunction in turn produces psychological frustration, which puts the body under even more stress, which may contribute to further deterioration of the heart.

A severe emotional state such as clinical depression brought about by a psychosocial factor (rejection, or loss of a job or partner, for example) can impair sexual functioning by affecting the nervous and endocrine systems (Morokoff & Gillilland, 1993). Thus biology and psychology are delicately intertwined, influencing each other in many ways. To arrive at a complete understanding of a sexual dysfunction, we must attempt to understand the relative contribution of these factors to the different types of sexual dysfunctions.

## Types of Sexual Dysfunction

There is ongoing debate over the definition and classification of various sexual dysfunctions. The first two editions of the American Psychiatric Association's *Diagnostic and Statistical Manual (DSM)*, a handbook used by almost all mental health professionals, omitted sexual dysfunctions in its list of sexual disorders. The sexual disorders included were limited to those that society disapproved of at the time (for example, homosexuality) and those involving coercion or violation of others' freedom (for example, pedophilia). Psychosexual disorders were listed for the first time in 1980, in the third edition of the manual, known as the *DSM-III*.

One negative effect of the increasing medicalization of sexual problems is that it allows individuals to avoid examining their own attitudes

and experiences that could have contributed to their dysfunction. If the source of the problem is "medical," then individuals do not see the need to take responsibility for their problems. If the problem is a lack of desire, the medical diagnosis can be used as a rationale to continue to avoid sexual activity.

In fact, many individuals do not fit neatly into any of the diagnostic categories we are about to describe. In one study, almost half the patients seeking treatment had a sexual problem in more than one area. Thus in many cases problems with desire, arousal, and orgasm overlap (Segraves & Segraves, 1991). In this section we discuss these disorders as well as other difficulties experienced by individuals and couples in their sexual interactions. As you read about these disorders, remember that describing or naming them does not explain them.

## Sexual Desire Disorders

Deciding whether a given response should be considered a dysfunction is particularly problematic in the case of desire disorders, where the variable is the amount of sexual interest. What is a "normal" level of sexual desire? In our culture men are expected to want sex more frequently than are women. Thus gender-role expectations are related to our beliefs about what constitutes "normal" levels of sexual desire.

### Hypoactive Sexual Desire and Sexual Aversion

The *DSM-IV* divides desire disorders into two categories: hypoactive sexual desire disorders and sexual aversion disorders. The first of these, *hypoactive sexual desire disorder*, is defined as deficient or absent sexual fantasies and desire for sexual activity. The judgment of deficiency or absence is made by the clinician, taking into account factors that affect sexual functioning such as age, sex, and the context of the person's life. The deficiency may be selective: a person may experience erection or lubrication and orgasm but derive little pleasure from the physical feelings. In other cases, the individual's desire is at such a

**hypoactive sexual desire disorder**—lack of interest in sexual expression with anyone.

low ebb that he or she has no interest in self-stimulation or in participating in sexual interaction that might lead to arousal. For example, a young man whom we know told us about his strong romantic attraction to another man, but said that he felt inhibited about trying to develop the relationship because, although his feelings of love had previously been directed toward men rather than women, he experienced very little desire for sexual interaction. In other instances, a person may avoid a romantic relationship or marriage because he or she feels that lack of sexual desire should serve as a deterrent from forming such attachments. Some individuals can be described as asexual; that is, they do not experience desire for any kind of sexual activity. This is not considered a dysfunction if the individual is satisfied with not engaging in sexual activity.

The sources of sexual desire disorders have not been well clarified. In fact, until the publication of Kaplan's (1979) model, most investigators did not distinguish between desire and excitement disorders. Most current knowledge of the causes of low sexual desire is based on clients who are seen in therapy and thus must be viewed with caution until more objective research has been conducted, using nonclinical samples. With that caveat in mind, low sexual desire has been associated with such factors as anxiety, religious orthodoxy, depression, *habituation* to a sexual partner, fear of loss of control over sexual urges, sexual assault, medication side effects, marital conflict, and fear of closeness (Letourneau & O'Donohue, 1993; LoPiccolo & Friedman, 1988).

A comparison of married women experiencing inhibited sexual desire with married women expressing normal sexual desire revealed no differences in psychological adjustment or hormonal levels (Stuart, Hammond, & Pett, 1987). In this study, however, women with inhibited sexual desire did report significantly greater dissatisfaction with their marital relationship than did

the control group. Other research has produced no evidence of a hormonal basis for hypoactive sexual desire (Letourneau & O'Donohue, 1993). Depression may play a crucial role in hypoactive sexual desire; women with inhibited sexual desire report twice as many depressive episodes as reported by women with normal sexual desire (Schreiner-Engel & Schiavi, 1986). In the latter study, the initial episode of the depressive disorder almost always coincided with or preceded the onset of lack of sexual desire. Additional research is needed, however, to determine whether depression leads to low sexual desire, low desire produces depression, or other factors mediate this relationship.

Reports from a number of clinics that treat sexual dysfunction indicate that problems with desire have become one of the most common complaints that clients describe when they seek therapy (LoPiccolo & Friedman, 1988; Spector & Carey, 1990). In the early 1980s, the proportion of couples seeking help for desire disorders reached 55% in clinical samples, with more men than women presenting this complaint.

The suppression of sexual desire is, of course, not dysfunctional in and of itself. Most of us learn scripts to suppress sexual desire for inappropriate partners, such as parents, close relatives, and children, and in inappropriate situations. Before they learn to suppress their sexual feelings in public situations, some young men experience quite a bit of discomfort and embarrassment. Trying to hide an erection when one is asked to come to the front of a classroom can be difficult. Researchers have demonstrated that men can suppress their erections in the presence of erotic stimuli (Adams, Motsinger, McAnulty, & Moore, 1992; Cranston-Cuebas & Barlow, 1990). They accomplished this by concentrating on nonsexual thoughts, such as arithmetic computations. Women have the advantage in this case, because their signs of arousal are less externally observable. Many people also learn scripts to suppress sexual desire for individuals of a certain gender. Persons with a strong heterosexual identity may have learned to suppress sexual desire for people of the same gender. Those with a strong homosexual identity may use the same mechanism to keep their desires channeled only toward people

**habituation**—responding to something out of habit rather than because of current feeling.

of the same gender and to suppress sexual desire for individuals of the other gender. People who feel sexual desire for both men and women (bisexuals) have apparently not learned to suppress desire toward either gender.

Alcohol and marijuana may act to release suppressed sexual desire, but this release is usually only temporary. A person who experiences an intense sexual desire for someone after drinking alcohol or smoking marijuana may not feel the same way after the drug wears off—a situation colloquially called "beer goggles." Awakening in the morning with their inhibitions back, some people who have acted on the desires unleashed while they were "high" then wonder how they ever found the person lying next to them sexually desirable.

*Sexual aversion disorder* is a persistent aversion to almost all genital sexual contact with a partner. Whereas individuals displaying hypoactive sexual desire are often indifferent about sexual interaction, sexual aversion reflects fear, disgust, or anxiety about sexual contact with a partner. An individual with sexual aversion disorder may still engage in autosexual behaviors such as masturbation and fantasy while avoiding interpersonal sexual behavior.

People with sexual aversion disorder tend to experience anxiety and sometimes hostility toward their partners. When they anticipate sex with their partners, their feelings of anxiety or hostility suppress any initial stirrings of erotic sensation. Eventually, they block sexual arousal at its earliest stage and avoid the anxiety associated with sexual expression. Childhood sexual abuse and adult rape have also been found to be significantly related to sexual aversion (Gold & Gold, 1993).

*Excessive Sexual Desire*

Excessive sexual desire, which has also been called hyperactive desire, sexual compulsion, or sexual addiction (see Chapter 19), has received

considerable publicity in the popular media. Despite this attention, clinicians and therapists seldom encounter individuals with excessive sexual desire (Leiblum & Rosen, 1988). Although people with enormous sexual appetites are fairly common in erotic literature and films, *nymphomania* in women and *satyriasis* in men appear to be rarities in real life (Allgeier, 1994a). Symons (1979, p. 92) suggested that the "sexually insatiable woman is to be found primarily, if not exclusively, in the ideology of feminism, the hopes of boys and the fears of men."

Excessive sexual desire is often associated with paraphilias (see Chapter 19) and/or with an *obsessive-compulsive reaction*, such as the one described earlier in Box 8.3. In obsessive-compulsive states, the individual becomes preoccupied with sexuality. Masturbation and/or sexual interaction with a partner may occur 5 or 10 times a day. The sexual activity is used to reduce anxiety and tension resulting from obsessive thoughts about sex or other aspects of the person's life.

## Sexual Arousal Disorders

Some individuals feel deep sexual desire and want to make love with their partners but experience little or no physical response (erection or vaginal lubrication and swelling) to sexual stimulation. *Sexual arousal disorders* are diagnosed when there is recurrent or persistent) failure by a woman to attain or maintain the lubrication and swelling response, or, in a man, absence of erection during sexual activity. Such a diagnosis is made only when the clinician is sure that the dif-

---

**sexual aversion disorder**—a dysfunction characterized by extreme dislike and avoidance of genital contact with a partner.

**nymphomania**—excessive and uncontrollable sexual desire in women.

**satyriasis** (SAH-ter-RYE-uh-sis)—excessive and uncontrollable sexual desire in men.

**obsessive-compulsive reaction**—a condition in which a person engages in compulsive behaviors in reaction to persistent or obsessive thoughts.

**sexual arousal disorder**—failure to obtain or maintain erection or vaginal lubrication and swelling, despite adequate stimulation.

ficulty does not stem from physical disorders or medication, and when the amount of sexual stimulation provided should be adequate to produce vasocongestion. Sometimes failure to respond results from insufficient stimulation rather than from inhibition of excitement.

Sexual arousal disorders were formerly called frigidity in women and impotency in men. Both terms are degrading and sound more like complaints than like clinical disorders. They suggest rigid and distant women and ineffectual and helpless men. We have known men who employ the term *frigid* to describe any woman who refuses to have sex with them. In contrast, the phrase *sexual arousal disorder* is descriptive without being demeaning.

Sexual arousal disorders may be either primary or secondary. An individual who has never experienced sexual excitement with any partner under any circumstances is considered to have the primary form, which is quite rare. Secondary arousal disorder is diagnosed when a person has experienced sexual excitement in the past but is not presently responsive.

It is important to realize that occasional nonresponsiveness during sexual interaction is common. Many men have experienced sexual arousal and a desire for interaction when they have had too much to drink, only to find that, although the mind was willing, the genitals were unresponsive. Women who smoke marijuana may also notice a diminishing of vaginal lubrication (along with a sense of dryness in the mouth and nose). Similarly, fatigue, stress, and minor irritations with one's partner can temporarily interfere with sexual response. Such occasional nonresponsiveness can become problematic if people fear that they may not be able to respond sexually in the future. This fear of failure can create anxiety about sexual performance, which can lead in turn to future problems in responding. If the individual instead accepts the fact that occasional inability to respond sexually is normal, dysfunctions are less likely to arise.

Women's reactions to an inability to respond to erotic stimulation show a much greater variation than do men's. Most men react to erectile dysfunction as if it were a disaster, whereas women's responses range from anxiety or distress to casual acceptance of the dysfunction. To

some extent, cultural expectations are responsible for these differences. In most cultures, men are expected to be sexually active and to perform satisfactorily. Women are not generally subjected to the same performance pressures and in some cultures are not expected to be sexually responsive. In addition, differences in anatomy and physiology make it more difficult for men to cover up and compensate for a dysfunction. A limp penis is difficult to hide and to use in a sexual interaction, whereas a dry vagina is more easily hidden and, with the aid of a lubricant, can even accommodate sexual intercourse.

The inability to attain or maintain an erection—*erectile dysfunction*—is generally the most common complaint among men who seek sex therapy. Community-based research, however, indicates that less than 10% of men experience erectile dysfunction (Spector & Carey, 1990). Some men with erectile dysfunction never have more than a partial erection during sexual activity. Others become erect, only to lose firmness when they attempt to have intercourse. Some men have erection problems with one partner but not with another.

Ruling out medical difficulties as a major cause is easier with erectile dysfunction than with most other dysfunctions. During an average night, a male will have three to five erections during the stage of sleep called rapid eye movement (REM) sleep, which is highly correlated with dreaming. If a procedure called the nocturnal penile tumescence (NPT) test in a sophisticated sleep laboratory reveals that a male does not have these erections or that they are impaired, the source of his problem is likely to be physical. This procedure is not foolproof, however. Normally functioning males sometimes have few erections over several nights of sleep, particularly on nights when the REM phase of sleep is absent (LoPiccolo & Stock, 1986). This and other problems result in a diagnostic accuracy of NPT evaluations of 80% (Rosen & Beck, 1988). On the other hand, simply asking men whether they have early-morning erections—the so-called "piss hard-on"—is just as predictive of biological im-

**erectile dysfunction**—recurrent and persistent inability to attain or maintain a firm erection, despite adequate stimulation.

pairment as are the fairly sophisticated and expensive biological measures. Men who report that they do not have morning erections usually have biological or medical problems (Segraves, Segraves, & Schoenberg, 1987).

Most men who experience problems with erection after a period of normal responsiveness respond well to treatment. The prognosis is not so good for men who have never been able to attain or maintain an erection with a partner (Hawton, 1992).

A rare condition that seems to be the opposite condition of erectile dysfunction is *priapism*. It involves persistent and painful erection of the penis, without sexual desire. Priapism can result from damage to the valves in the corpus cavernosa that regulate the flow of blood, as well as from infection, tumors, cocaine and heroin use, and some medications. Untreated, it can lead to destruction of the spongy tissue of the penis from the coagulation of blood, resulting in permanent erectile dysfunction.

For women experiencing sexual arousal disorders, Masters and Johnson (1970) lumped excitement and orgasm dysfunctions under the general term *frigidity*. As noted earlier, this term does not accurately describe either problem; further, some women experience intense excitement with copious amounts of vaginal lubrication but have difficulty progressing to orgasm. Nonclinical studies suggest that arousal phase disorder occurs in 11% to 48% of the general population of women (Spector & Carey, 1990). Often the problem stems from the combination of widespread ignorance in our culture regarding women's sexual anatomy, and from the socialization of women to attend more to others' needs than to their own. We consider the issue of women's difficulties with orgasm in the next section.

## Orgasm Disorders

Some people have orgasms within minutes of sexual interaction. Others engage in sexual stimulation for an hour or more before having or-

gasm. And some people do not have orgasm at all. Nowhere is the problem of defining sexual dysfunction more evident. In fact, except in extreme cases involving orgasm within seconds or no orgasm at all, the main difficulty is a difference in the speed of the partners' responsiveness rather than any dysfunction.

People vary enormously in the amount of stimulation they enjoy before having an orgasm. The fact that one person responds quickly and his or her partner responds more slowly does not necessarily imply that either is dysfunctional. As noted in Chapter 7, orgasm need not and generally does not occur simultaneously for a couple. In fact, using simultaneity as a standard can lead to an inappropriate exchange of labels. That is, a woman whose partner comes before she does may be labeled as frigid or as afflicted with orgasmic dysfunction. He, in turn, may be branded a premature ejaculator. And the man whose partner climaxes before he does may be described as a retarded ejaculator. This does not imply that there is no such thing as an orgasmic dysfunction or ejaculation problem, but that differences between two people are not necessarily problematic or indicative of sexual dysfunction.

### Premature Ejaculation

The variety of ways in which experts have defined *premature ejaculation* should instill a healthy skepticism regarding the diagnostic process. Among the vague criteria that have been used to determine and define premature ejaculation are the following:

1. the number of times a man thrusts his penis into his partner before ejaculating;

2. the amount of time between penetration and ejaculation;

3. whether the man ejaculates before his partner has orgasm at least half the time.

The last definition is an improvement over the first two in that it takes into account a couple's relationship. It has its own built-in limitations,

---

**priapism** (PRE-uh-PIZ-um)—prolonged erection that is not linked to sexual arousal.

**premature ejaculation**—unintentional ejaculation prior to or shortly following insertion of the penis in the vagina.

however. First, it falsely assumes that one person's speed of response should match another person's, but as we have seen, simultaneous orgasm is not necessary for intimate and satisfying sexual interaction. Second, and more problematic, it can have the effect of applying a diagnostic label to a man on the basis of his partner's responses. Using this definition, we might describe a man whose partner does not reach orgasm as a premature ejaculator even though he has learned to control his ejaculatory response for long periods of time with that partner. Alternatively, the man might be diagnosed as a premature ejaculator in one relationship but a retarded ejaculator (see below) in a relationship with a partner who experiences orgasm relatively quickly.

Perhaps the most useful definition of premature ejaculation is ejaculation before the man wants it to occur. Speed of ejaculation is associated with such factors as age (older men have fewer problems with ejaculatory control than do younger men, particularly adolescents), inexperience with intercourse, and novelty of the sexual partner.

The diagnosis of premature ejaculation is not appropriate unless the speed of a man's ejaculation becomes a regular, unwanted aspect of a couple's sexual activity. Ejaculation is a reflex that is difficult to control once it has been activated. The key to learning control is to recognize those signals that occur just before ejaculation—an awareness that can be difficult for young, inexperienced men. Roughly one-third of men report that they ejaculate more rapidly than they would like, and premature ejaculation is the initial problem in sexual dysfunction clinics for 15% to 46% of those men treated (Spector & Carey, 1990). Some men who continue to have problems with premature ejaculation after they have become sexually experienced may be hypersensitive to penile arousal and predisposed to early ejaculation (Strassberg et al., 1990).

Cultural factors play an important role in determining whether rapid ejaculation is perceived as a problem. In a society where sexual pleasure for women is not valued, such as among the So people described in Chapter 1, rapid ejaculation may be desirable because it shortens the time spent on an activity that women do not enjoy. In contrast, within cultures that value sexual interaction for its role in strengthening emotional intimacy, the expression of loving feelings, and the sharing of intense pleasure, rapid ejaculation would be less desirable.

### Inhibited Male Orgasm

In clinical studies, inhibited male orgasm (also known as retarded ejaculation or ejaculatory incompetence) accounts for about 3% to 8% of men seeking treatment, and this rarer form of sexual dysfunction has been found to occur in about 1% to 10% of men in community samples (Spector & Carey, 1990). The inhibition or orgasm may include delayed ejaculation or a total inability to ejaculate despite adequate periods of sexual excitement. As with the other dysfunctions, a diagnosis of inhibited male orgasm is not made when the problem stems from medication or some physical disorder.

*Inhibited orgasm* can be primary or secondary. An individual who has been unable to ejaculate during coitus from the time of the first coital experience is considered to have the primary form. Many men with a primary dysfunction are nevertheless able to ejaculate through masturbation or during oral-genital sex. Secondary inhibited orgasm is diagnosed when inhibition occurs after a period of effective sexual functioning.

Interestingly, many men diagnosed as having inhibited ejaculation sustain erections far beyond the ordinary range during coitus, and their wives are often multiorgasmic (Apfelbaum, 1989). Many of these men say that they prefer masturbation over intercourse, even though they continue to produce an erect penis for coitus with their partner. It also appears that some men may condition themselves to patterns of stimulation and ejaculation that are different from the stimulation provided by coitus. Mann (1977) reported examples of masturbation techniques that include stroking the urethral opening with a throat

---

**inhibited orgasm**—persistent difficulty in having orgasm or inability to have orgasm, despite adequate stimulation; in males, also called ejaculatory incompetence or retarded ejaculation.

swab and striking the shaft of the penis forcefully with the heel of the hand. It is understandable that men accustomed to such stimulation might not be able to have orgasm during coitus.

Clinicians have identified various factors that may contribute to inhibited orgasm. Religious orthodoxy, fear of creating a pregnancy, negative feelings toward the sexual partner, maternal dominance, hostility, aggression, fears of abandonment, and tendencies toward holding back have been implicated in the development of this condition (Dekker, 1993). Individuals who have lost the capacity to ejaculate after a period of normal functioning often report that a stressful event preceded the problem.

In another physical condition known as *retrograde ejaculation*, the usual expulsion of ejaculate through the urethra is reversed. The neck of the bladder does not contract, allowing the semen to flow into the bladder rather than out through the urethral opening in the penis. The condition usually results from surgery involving the genitourinary system or can be a side effect of some medications.

### Inhibited Female Orgasm

Some women suffer from inhibited orgasm, a condition that prevents them from having orgasm despite adequate sexual stimulation. Difficulty with orgasm is one of the most common sexual complaints among women who seek treatment at sex therapy clinics, and community-based research indicates that 5% to 10% of women experience orgasmic difficulty (Spector & Carey, 1990).

Women with this dysfunction may look forward to sex, and many experience high levels of sexual excitement with vaginal swelling and lubrication, but they are usually unable to have orgasm. Sexual arousal causes congestion of the pelvic blood vessels, and without orgasm, the congested blood remains for a while (analogous

retrograde ejaculation—a condition in which the neck of the bladder does not contract during ejaculation, resulting in semen discharging into the man's bladder.

to the congestion in the testes associated with the absence of orgasmic release in highly aroused men). Consistent arousal in women without orgasmic release can result in cramps, backache, irritation, and chafing.

The immediate problem in inhibited female orgasm is the involuntary inhibition of the orgasmic reflex. This inhibition may arise from guilt-producing thoughts. Kelly, Strassberg, and Kircher (1990) compared the sexual activities reported by orgasmic women with the sexual experiences of women who seldom had orgasms. The relatively nonorgasmic women described more negative attitudes toward masturbation, greater sex guilt and endorsement of sex myths, and more discomfort over communicating with their partners about sexual activities involving direct clitoral stimulation than did the women who experienced orgasm more consistently.

Problems with orgasm are usually divided into the categories of primary and secondary, or situational. Primary orgasmic dysfunction occurs in women who have never had an orgasm; secondary orgasmic dysfunction occurs in women who have difficulty in having orgasm even after considerable stimulation. Secondary (situational) orgasmic problems are encountered more frequently by clinicians than are primary orgasmic dysfunctions (Stock, 1993).

In keeping with the view that sexual dysfunction is a problem only when it persistently interferes with personal satisfaction, only those woman who wish to have orgasm during coitus but cannot do so should seek treatment. It is debatable whether a dysfunction exists when a woman does not have orgasm during coitus but does climax during other kinds of stimulation—oral or manual stimulation, for example. Calling this pattern a sexual dysfunction and assuming that it requires sex therapy would dictate treatment for a large number of women, given that fewer than 50% of women consistently have orgasm during coitus, as discussed in Chapter 7. Darling, Davidson, and Cox (1991) found that the most frequently used sexual technique to have orgasm among the more than 700 nurses they studied involved simultaneous stimulation of the clitoris and vagina, and/or stimulation of the clitoris without sexual intercourse. Darling et al.

asked their respondents to report the factors they believed inhibited them from having orgasm during coitus, and the women's responses are shown in Table 8.1. Many therapists no longer consider a woman dysfunctional unless she suffers from primary orgasmic dysfunction and then only if she perceives it as a problem.

## Sexual Pain Disorders

Sexual pain disorders include dyspareunia, which can be experienced by males and females, and vaginismus, which is exclusively a female complaint.

### Dyspareunia (Painful Intercourse)

*Dyspareunia* is the technical term for recurrent and persistent genital pain in either a male or female before, during, or after sexual intercourse. In women, repeated dyspareunia is likely to result in vaginismus (see below). The pain may be experienced as repeated, intense discomfort; momentary sharp sensations of varying intensity; or intermittent twinges and/or aching sensations. Dyspareunia rates in community-based research range from 8% to 23% (Spector & Carey, 1990). Dyspareunia in men appears to be much less common than painful intercourse in women (Quevillon, 1993). In these cases, men may experience pain in the testes and/or the glans after ejaculation.

A wide variety of diseases and disorders of the external and internal sex organs and their surrounding structures can make intercourse painful for men and women. When physical disorders have been ruled out, psychological factors are assumed to be the cause. Lazarus (1989) reviewed 20 cases of female dyspareunia that he had treated and noted that almost half these women reported they were involved in unhappy relationships. Lazarus speculated that, after ruling out biological factors, it would not surprise him if "about half the women who suffer from dyspareunia are simply having sexual intercourse with the wrong man!" (1989, p. 91).

**dyspareunia** (DIS-par-OO-nee-ah)—painful intercourse.

### TABLE 8.1 Factors Inhibiting Women's Orgasm During Coitus

| Factors | Percent |
| --- | --- |
| Lack of foreplay | 63.8 |
| Fatigue | 53.6 |
| Preoccupation with nonsexual thoughts | 45.5 |
| Ejaculation too soon after intromission* | 43.1 |
| Conflicts between partners unrelated to intromission | 34.6 |
| Lack of interest or foreplay by partner | 24.3 |
| Lack of adequate vaginal lubrication | 23.7 |
| Lack of tenderness by partner | 22.7 |
| Lack of privacy for intromission | 20.3 |
| Overindulgence in alcohol | 16.3 |
| Desire to perform well after intromission | 14.9 |
| Difficulty with sexual arousal with partner | 14.3 |
| Painful sexual intercourse | 12.0 |
| Overeating | 10.3 |

*Insertion of the penis into the vagina.

Source: Adapted from Darling et al.'s (1991) study of more than 700 nurses, p. 11.

### Vaginismus

*Vaginismus* refers to the involuntary spasm of the pelvic musculature surrounding the outer third of the vagina. Women who experience these spasms of the pubococcygeus (PC) and related muscles cannot have intercourse but may be quite capable of becoming sexually aroused, lubricating, and experiencing orgasm (Beck, 1993). The partner of a woman with this dysfunction who tries to have intercourse with her may have the sensation that his penis is hitting a rigid wall

**vaginismus** (VAH-jih-NIS-mus)—involuntary spasms of the pelvic musculature surrounding the outer third of the vagina.

about an inch inside of the vagina. Vaginismus rates have ranged from 12% to 17% of the women treated at sex therapy clinics (Spector & Carey, 1990).

The vaginismus spasm can be triggered by anticipated penetration of the vagina. Vaginismus can be a source of dyspareunia, just as recurrent dyspareunia can precede vaginismus. One study of 80 women who were diagnosed as having vaginismus indicated that half these women developed the condition after a history of dyspareunia. A third of the women had never been able to have intercourse (married women in this category are technically virgin wives), and 14% developed vaginismus after a period of pleasurable intercourse (Lamont, 1977). At the time these women were seen, the majority of them had complete vaginismus—that is, their PC muscles contracted in response to attempts to insert anything (finger, speculum, tampon) into the vagina. About 20% of the women, however, experienced situational vaginismus; that is, the vaginal spasms occurred only when they attempted to have intercourse. Some of the women also reported severe vaginismus except when they had consumed alcohol.

Among the events triggering vaginismus are rape, abortion, painful gynecological exams, pelvic inflammatory disease, and accidents producing vaginal injury. Other factors in women's histories related to vaginismus included vaginal surgery, problems stemming from episiotomies (surgical incision of the vagina in preparation for childbirth, see Chapter 9), vaginal infections, constipation, and pelvic congestion (Beck, 1993). Imagined rapes and general fears about men and vaginal penetration are also associated with vaginismus in some women.

Regardless of the source of the difficulty, the contractions of vaginismus cannot be controlled by the woman. Attempts at vaginal penetration produce pain and anxiety, and the woman may try to avoid the possibility of such pain by avoiding sexual encounters. Treatment ranges from the medical correction of physical problems to the use of psychotherapy, although it is sometimes difficult to determine the precise source(s) of the vaginismus.

Treatment appears to be highly effective in eliminating this dysfunction (Beck, 1993; Hawton, 1992). Relaxation training and gradual insertion of successively bigger dilators into the vagina appear to be very effective in curing vaginismus. It is very important, however, that the woman (rather than a therapist or her partner) control the pace of treatment and the size of the dilator (LoPiccolo & Stock, 1986).

From the foregoing review of sexual dysfunctions, it should be clear that whatever the original source (biological and/or psychosocial) of a person's inability to respond as he or she wishes, the problem may be aggravated by the development of fear of failure in future sexual contacts. Such fear can produce self-fulfilling prophecies; that is, an intense focus on whether a person will respond adequately can reduce the likelihood that healthy sexual feelings and responses will unfold. No matter what particular treatment procedures they use, sex therapists should also identify and attempt to eliminate both clients' fears of sexual inadequacy and their tendency to engage in distracting and maladaptive thoughts during sexual intimacy.

## Sex Therapy

Until the 1960s the predominant approach to the treatment of sexual dysfunction was psychoanalysis. Sexual problems were viewed as symptoms of emotional conflict originating in childhood. The sexual difficulties or symptoms would persist, the analysts claimed, unless the conflict could be resolved and the personality of the individual restructured. The trouble with this approach is that the sexual difficulties may persist even after the client understands or gains insight into the origin of the problem. In addition, psychoanalytic therapy can be time-consuming and expensive.

Behavioral psychologists have long taken issue with the psychoanalytic approach. They believe that a person can be emotionally healthy and still have sexual difficulties. Maladaptive sexual functioning is learned, they believe, and it can be unlearned without probing extensively into a client's past. Behavioral approaches deal directly with sexual dysfunction by using conditioning techniques designed to overcome anxiety and to lessen sensitivity to anxiety-provoking stimuli. Behavioral therapies were first applied to sexual problems in the 1950s. Joseph Wolpe (1958) was one of the first to employ anxiety-relieving techniques to treat sexual difficulties. The behavioral approach was later popularized by Masters and Johnson (1970), although they did not use conditioning in a formal way. The various tasks they assigned to clients were similar to the techniques that Wolpe employed. Although sexual dysfunctions have also been treated by a wide array of different psychotherapies, including cognitive-behavioral, object-relations, and family systems, in this section we concentrate on the most commonly used techniques in sex therapy.

## Masters and Johnson's Approach

The treatment program developed by Masters and Johnson is a two-week process. It is conducted by a man and a woman, one of whom is a physician. Each partner in the couple seeking treatment is given a thorough medical examination and is interviewed by the therapist of the same gender. This interview is followed by an interview with the other therapist. All four people (the couple and the two therapists) then discuss treatment goals.

Masters and Johnson recommended the use of both a male and a female therapist to provide a "friend-in-court" for the client of the same gender. They stressed the treatment of specific symptoms rather than extensive psychotherapy aimed at determining potential underlying, unconscious sources of difficulty.

## How Successful Is Sex Therapy?

One of the most impressive aspects of Masters and Johnson's (1970) therapeutic approach with more than 500 couples and individuals without partners was the overall "failure rate" of 18.9%. Put another way, they reported success in treating more than 80% of their clients who experienced various types of sexual dysfunction (Kolodny, 1981). Of the successful clients who could be found five years later (313 couples), only 5.1% reported recurrence of the dysfunctions for

which they had obtained treatment. The therapeutic community was quite impressed with the success of Masters and Johnson's approach, and for years other therapists used modified versions of many of their methods.

Gradually, however, outcome statistics reported from clinical practice revealed overall improvement in only about two-thirds of cases. The improvements obtained from controlled treatment studies have all been more modest than the proportions reported by Masters and Johnson (Hawton, 1992). Other studies revealed relapse rates as high as 54% (Zilbergeld & Evans, 1980). Do these findings indicate that the only reliable source of sex therapy is Masters and Johnson? Probably not. Instead, differences between the failure rates reported by Masters and Johnson and those reported by other sex therapists and researchers are probably due to a combination of factors other than Masters and Johnson's skill as therapists. Among these factors are methodological problems, increasing sexual knowledge among members of the population, and changing characteristics of clients.

Zilbergeld and Evans (1980) noted that Masters and Johnson's research methodology was quite vague, and that they may have been lenient in their judgments of what constitutes a successful outcome. Another problem with Masters and Johnson's methodology was that they did not employ a "no treatment" group. Yet Kolodny (1981) reported that a sizable group of Masters and Johnson's clients had to wait three to six months before their therapy began, and few of these clients reported significant improvement in their sexual functioning while on the waiting list.

One factor in Masters and Johnson's reported success rates may have been that 90% of their clients traveled to St. Louis from other parts of the country. Having left behind the routine and cares of their daily lives and made the commitment of time and money to improve their relationships, these couples were likely candidates for rekindling sexual interest and changing their sexual attitudes and behavior.

Another factor may have been cultural attitudes toward information about sexuality. Many of the problems experienced by Masters and Johnson's clients stemmed from misinformation and ignorance; people in the 1950s and 1960s did

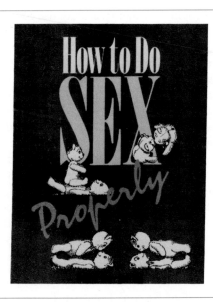

**FIGURE 8.4**
**Sex Manuals**
The flood of sex manuals on the market has led to satires such as this book, entitled *How to Do Sex Properly*. Nonetheless, sex manuals have been helpful in building general knowledge and expertise and in eliminating the need for sex therapy among people who simply lack accurate information about sexual response.

not have the easy access to information about sexuality that we have today. In fact, the seemingly endless stream of sex manuals being published has provoked countless satires (see Figure 8.4). Clients who simply lack information today may be "curing" themselves instead of seeking professional treatment. The caseloads of sex therapists today may include a greater proportion of clients with sexual difficulties resulting from deeply rooted emotional problems or from conflicts within their relationships. These kinds of sexual problems are often difficult to treat. This factor would, of course, result in lower success rates and higher relapse rates.

Support for this idea comes from research suggesting that people seeking sex therapy often have difficulties beyond the sexual symptoms for which they seek treatment (Hawton, 1992). In one series of studies (Derogatis & Meyer, 1979; Derogatis, 1981), sexually dysfunctional people had disproportionate levels of psychological stress as measured by psychological tests. One-third of the men and half the women were diagnosed as having significant psychiatric problems. The researchers also compared the psychological characteristics of 47 men and 40 women with sexual dysfunctions to 200 heterosexual "normals." As might be expected, the first group showed higher levels of psychological distress, more negative emotional states, and less sexual knowledge than did the control group. Dysfunctional males also reported lower sex drive, less sexual experience, and lower scores on a measure of masculinity than did the "normal" men.

Similarly, 92 couples who requested sex therapy in West Germany were found to differ from "normals" on psychological tests (Clement & Friedemann, 1980). The couples in therapy showed low self-confidence and were easily irritated and depressed. They thought of themselves as unattractive and described themselves as obstinate and uncooperative. When the couples were retested a year after treatment, a reduction in their *neuroticism* and a general increase in their emotional stability were observed.

Another question that must be addressed in evaluating any sex therapy is whether the treatment yields sustained change over the years. There is very little available research on this subject. Summarizing what is known, Hawton (1992) reported that the successful short-term results of sex therapy for erectile dysfunction were maintained in the long term (one to six years), whereas those for premature ejaculation were less permanent. Men with low sexual desire had a fairly poor response to treatment in the short and long term. Sex therapy for vaginismus is highly effective in the short and long term, whereas the long-term results of treatment for low sexual desire in women are fairly poor. Interestingly, there was improvement in the way clients *felt* about their sexuality, despite the fact that some had returned to pretreatment dysfunctions in sexual behavior. If these clients had received occasional clinical "booster" sessions over the years, their posttreatment improvement would perhaps have been

neuroticism—an emotional disturbance in which the individual is unable to cope with his or her anxieties and conflicts.

**FIGURE 8.5**
**Helen Singer Kaplan**
This sex therapist has described a pattern of sexual desire, arousal, and response that is probably closer to the sequence of feelings that most of us experience than that described by Masters and Johnson on the basis of their physiological recordings of sexual responding.

maintained through relapse prevention (McCarthy, 1993).

## Kaplan's Approach

Helen Singer Kaplan (see Figure 8.5) has developed an approach to sex therapy that combines some of the insights and techniques of psychoanalysis with behavioral methods. Her approach begins at the "surface" level or behavioral level, and probes more deeply into emotional conflicts only if necessary.

Many sexual difficulties stem from superficial causes. If a sexual difficulty is rooted in a lack of knowledge, for example, information and instruction may be all that is needed to treat it. If the trouble is of recent origin, a series of guided sexual tasks may be enough to change patterns of response. If deep-seated emotional problems

exist, however, the therapist may use more analytic approaches to help clients obtain insight into the less conscious aspects of their personality. This last approach has been designated as psychosexual therapy to distinguish it from sex therapy.

Kaplan has questioned Masters and Johnson's use of two therapists. Recent research, too, has suggested that the effectiveness of a treatment is not enhanced by assigning two therapists instead of one, or by employing a therapist who is of the same gender as the dysfunctional member of the couple being treated (Hawton, 1992; LoPiccolo et al., 1985). The involvement of two trained professionals is, of course, also twice as expensive as the use of one.

## Treatment of Sexual Dysfunctions

In this section we consider some of the more common treatments used in sex therapy. See Box 8.4 for an atypical method.

Caird and Wincze (1977) have suggested that most behavioral treatment programs include three general components:

*Education:* The client and/or partner receives instruction in communication skills, sexual techniques, and the anatomy and physiology of sexual functioning.

*Redirection of sexual behavior:* The client's focus of attention is redirected from self-monitoring to giving pleasure to the partner.

*Graded sexual exposure:* Anxiety about sexual performance is reduced through gradual exposure to the anxiety-evoking situation. Exposure may be brought about through a series of relaxation exercises or through homework exercises with a partner.

When problems are based on marital conflicts or serious individual disturbances, behavioral approaches may not be effective, because they require both partners' active cooperation. Marital conflicts and/or individual disturbances, therefore, are more likely to be resolved by marriage counseling, individual psychotherapy, and/or communication skills training than by the following techniques.

**Box 8.4**

# An Unusual Treatment Approach to Inhibited Ejaculation

Jay Mann (1977) reported an unusual innovation in treating a man who had never experienced ejaculation except in his sleep. The man and his wife had gone through a series of therapeutic exercises without the man becoming able to ejaculate. In the next to last session, the couple revealed how badly they wanted to have a child, a fact that they had not stressed initially. Mann reported:

*Immediately after the session, I telephoned a colleague who had done male fertility research with rhesus monkeys and asked her advice. She assured me that viable sperm could be drawn from Williams' epididymis with a hypodermic syringe and could be used to inseminate his wife. Without double-checking the validity of the method, I telephoned the good tidings to Williams. He sounded*

*pleased, but I also noted a moment of silence after I mentioned the hypodermic needle.*

*Between the time of my call to him and the final session, he succeeded in masturbating to ejaculation three times in three trials. He said that it felt as though a weight had rolled off his shoulders when he learned that he would be able to father a child. He also confessed to some apprehension about the syringe. (pp. 203–04)*

Williams was able to generalize his newfound ejaculatory skill to coitus with his wife, and they conceived within a month. Thus separating the act of procreation from the act of ejaculation (not to mention Williams's desire to avoid the hypodermic syringe) seemed to reverse his dysfunction.

## Systematic Desensitization

*Systematic desensitization* involves learning a series of muscle-relaxation exercises. The client and therapist construct a set of anxiety-provoking scenes arranged in order from the least to the most anxiety-producing. The goal of treatment is to replace the anxiety-laden response to each scene with a relaxation response. The client starts by imagining the least anxiety-laden scene. If the client feels anxiety, he or she is told to stop imagining and to employ relaxation procedures. This exercise is repeated until the person can imagine the scene without feeling anxiety. The client then imagines the next scene, practicing relaxation techniques if necessary. This process is continued until the last scene can be imagined without anxiety. The process can take from a few sessions to

15 or more. Box 8.5 provides an abbreviated example of a systematic desensitization hierarchy for inhibited ejaculation.

A problem with the use of systematic desensitization lies in its lack of generalizability to real-life situations. For example, if a man experiencing inhibited orgasm is successful in completing the hierarchy in Box 8.5, he can now imagine ejaculating into his partner's vagina without anxiety. But the fact that he can *imagine* a behavior does not necessarily mean that he can *engage* in the behavior with his partner. To overcome this problem, some clinicians use *in vivo* desensitization, which involves actual sexual experiences rather than imaginary ones. For example, if a person learns that it is acceptable to tell his or her partner about feelings of nervousness and does so, the partner can pull back from sexual activity while the tense person relaxes. The procedure gives the nervous partner a sense of personal control and may also encourage both partners to communicate their feelings more openly.

**systematic desensitization**—a behavior therapy in which deep relaxation is used to reduce anxiety associated with certain situations.

**Box 8.5**

# Systematic Densensitization Hierarchy for Inhibited Ejaculation

1. You and your wife have turned out the lights and are lying in bed talking before going to sleep.

2. You feel close to her at this moment as you begin to kiss her.

3. You feel your penis becoming erect as you continue kissing and begin to fondle her breasts.

4. She responds warmly to your caresses by rubbing your inner thigh.

5. You now feel your penis becoming hard and elongated as you manually stimulate her genitals.

6. You reach to the bedside table and take out the electric vibrator you know gives her pleasure and begin to stimulate her genitals as she massages your penis.

7. She moves her body to you and presses your penis against her stomach while whispering how much she wants you.

8. You remove her gown and position yourself between her legs.

9. As your penis penetrates your wife's vagina, you experience very pleasurable sexual sensations.

10. You both begin thrusting, gradually at first, enjoying the sensations of intercourse.

11. As you continue thrusting, you notice your wife increasing the tempo of thrusting as she nears orgasm.

12. As you meet the tempo of your wife's thrusting, she reaches orgasm while holding you tightly.

13. You feel your muscles tensing as you continue thrusting while your wife verbally encourages you toward ejaculation.

14. Your muscles tighten and you feel a wave of sensations radiating through your body as you ejaculate into your wife's vagina.

Source: Abridged from Tollison and Adams (1979) p. 133.

---

### Nondemand Pleasuring and Sensate Focus

In exercises involving nondemand sensate focus, the clients initially avoid sexual intercourse. In fact, couples are forbidden to engage in any sexual activity until the therapist instructs them to do so. Over the course of treatment, they receive homework assignments that gradually increase their range of sexual behaviors. Initially, only kissing, hugging, and body massage may be allowed.

The partners are instructed to take turns in the roles of giver and receiver as they touch and caress each other's body. When playing the role of giver, the person explores, touches, and caresses the receiver's body. In applying this technique, called nondemand pleasuring, the giver does *not* attempt to arouse the receiver sexually.

In an exercise called *sensate focus*, the receiver concentrates on the sensations evoked by the giver's touch on various parts of the body. In these exercises, the giver's responsibility is to provide pleasure and to be aware of his or her own pleasure in touching. The receiver's role is to prevent or end any stimulation that is uncomfortable or irritating by either telling or showing the partner his or her feelings.

Women with sexual excitement difficulties may find that taking a turn as the receiver helps to counteract any guilt they have learned about receiving sexual attention. Because they are not

**sensate focus**—an exercise involving concentration on sensations produced by touching.

**FIGURE 8.6**
**Nondemand Pleasuring**
This position, which allows easy access to the breasts and vulva, is often used in
exercises designed to relieve sexual problems.

expected to do anything but receive the pleasure and give feedback when appropriate, the exercise may help them focus on their own erotic sensations. Similarly, such exercises may be helpful to men with erectile difficulties, because intercourse is forbidden and they are under no pressure to produce an erection.

The next step is engaging in nondemand breast and genital caressing while avoiding orgasm-oriented stimulation. Masters and Johnson (1970) recommend the position shown in Figure 8.6 for this phase, because it allows easy ac-

cess to the breasts and vulva when the woman is in the receiving role. It also allows the receiver to place his or her hand over the partner's hand to provide guidance to the kind of stimulation that is most pleasurable. If the partner of the person who is experiencing sexual difficulty becomes highly aroused during this exercise, that partner may be brought to orgasm orally or manually *after* completion of the exercise.

Other sexual behaviors are gradually added to the clients' homework. Successive assignments may include nongenital body massage, breast

## Box 8.6

# A Treatment Program for Orgasmically Inhibited Women

The psychologist Joseph LoPiccolo and his colleagues (Heiman & LoPiccolo, 1988; LoPiccolo & Lobitz, 1972) developed a treatment program for orgasmically inhibited women that involves four major components.

1. Masturbation Training

   a. The woman is instructed to take a warm bath and examine her genitals with a mirror. Diagrams are used to aid her in identifying her muscles and genital organs. Pubococcygeal muscle exercises are begun.

   b. The client is instructed to explore her genitals by touch.

   c. The client continues tactile and visual exploration in an effort to locate pleasure-sensitive areas.

   d. The woman manually stimulates the pleasure-producing areas while using a sterile lubricant.

   e. If orgasm has not occurred, the client is instructed to stimulate herself for longer periods of time while engaging in erotic fantasies and viewing sexual material such as photographs. Some clients who have very negative attitudes about masturbation must be desensitized or re-educated through films, books, and discussion.

   f. If orgasm has not occurred by this time, the client is instructed to purchase a vibrator and use it to reach orgasm, placing it on her mons pubis near her clitoris.

2. Skill Training for the Male Partner

   a. The man observes the woman's masturbation to learn what is pleasurable for her. Various aspects of sensate focus exercises are begun.

   b. The husband masturbates his wife to orgasm.

   c. Manual stimulation is combined with intercourse.

3. Disinhibition of Arousal: Some women may not be able to reach orgasm with their partner because they are embarrassed about showing intense arousal or fear losing self-control. These women are asked to role-play a grossly exaggerated orgasm, with violent convulsions, screaming, and other extreme behavior. Repeated performances in the company of the partner usually result in amusement and eventually boredom.

4. Practice of Orgasmic Behaviors: The client is instructed to engage in certain behaviors that may facilitate orgasm. These actions, such as pelvic thrusting, pointing the toes, tensing the thigh muscles, holding the breath, pushing down with the diaphragm, and throwing back the head to displace the glottis, often occur involuntarily during intense orgasm. If the woman practices these behaviors voluntarily when she is experiencing sexual arousal, they may trigger orgasm.

and genital touching, simultaneous masturbation, penile insertion with no movement, mutual genital manipulation to orgasm, and finally intercourse.

After the couple reach a sufficient level of arousal through sensate focus and nondemand pleasuring, they proceed to nondemand coitus. If the woman has had problems involving either excitement or orgasm, she is instructed to initiate sexual intercourse when she feels ready. Masters and Johnson (1970) recommended the woman-above position because it gives the woman more control over both insertion of the penis and intensity and frequency of thrusting. Her partner is

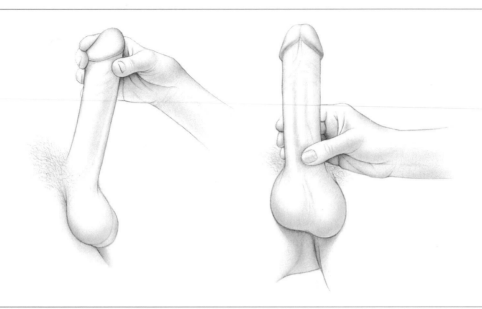

**FIGURE 8.7**
**The Squeeze Technique**
The squeeze technique, which can be applied either at the corona (left) or at the base of the penis (right), is useful for the treatment of premature ejaculation.

typically advised to thrust slowly rather than forcefully. Usually the couple is counseled to disengage several times during coitus and to perform the nondemand-genital-stimulation exercises. Throughout these exercises, the woman is encouraged to remain relaxed and to indulge in arousing fantasies. The couple can thus learn to enjoy sexual pleasure without worrying about performing later.

*Masturbation Training*

Most treatment programs for orgasmically inhibited women include training in masturbation, particularly if the woman has never had an orgasm. A treatment program is available for such women, which is presented in Box 8.6. This approach, which is used mainly in cases of primary orgasmic dysfunction, encourages women to learn about their bodies and relax to the point where they can experience orgasm.

Women with secondary orgasmic dysfunction usually do not require such an extensive and involved approach. Nondemand sensate focus

exercises combined with techniques to heighten arousal are often effective in treating secondary inhibited orgasm. Kaplan (1974) claimed that sexual arousal can be enhanced by having a man penetrate his partner slowly and then withdraw after a brief period, engaging in sexual foreplay before reentering with slow, teasing thrusts. Kegel exercises to strengthen the PC muscles may also be helpful for women who experience difficulty having orgasm (see Chapter 14.).

*The Squeeze Technique*

The approach most commonly employed for premature ejaculation is the *squeeze technique* (Masters & Johnson, 1970). The partner circles the tip of the penis with her hand, as shown in Figure 8.7. The thumb is placed against the frenulum on the underside of the penis, while the fingers are

**squeeze technique**—a treatment for premature ejaculation in which a man signals his partner to apply manual pressure to his penis to avert ejaculation.

placed on either side of the corona ridge on the upper side of the penis. When the man signals that he is approaching ejaculation, his partner applies fairly strong pressure for 3 to 5 seconds and then stops with a sudden release. She stimulates his penis again after the sensations of impending ejaculation diminish, usually within 20 to 30 seconds. Typically, the man is told that he should not try to control his ejaculation but should rely instead on the squeeze technique. The entire process is usually carried out three to four times per session before ejaculation is allowed.

Some couples prefer to apply the squeeze technique at the base of the penis rather than the tip. This variation has the advantage of being easier to do during intercourse, but for some couples it does not work. In this procedure, the penis must be grasped as close as possible to its base.

The next step is to apply a lubricant such as K-Y jelly or another water-soluble lubricant to the penis to approximate more closely the sensations experienced during vaginal intercourse. The squeeze technique is then applied again. If this step is successfully completed, the couple then proceeds to intercourse using the woman-above position. The woman guides the penis into her vagina while remaining motionless. If the man does not feel close to orgasm, the woman can start to lift her body slowly on and off her partner's body. The man can place his hands on her hips to guide the pace of intercourse. When he signals that he feels the sensations of impending orgasm, his partner withdraws from contact and applies the squeeze technique. The process is repeated after the urge to ejaculate diminishes. The man is usually not permitted to ejaculate until the squeeze technique has been applied three or four times or until the woman experiences orgasm.

If the couple is successful with this position, they most often proceed to side-by-side intercourse, employing the squeeze technique as needed. The final step is to have coitus in the man-above position. After the couple have attained satisfactory intercourse with the man on top, the choice of sexual positions and techniques is left up to them. Having tried the side-by-side position, couples treated by Masters and Johnson (1970) continued to use it 75% of the time, even after having achieved success with the man-above position.

## Group Therapy and Hypnosis

Numerous other therapy formats and techniques are sometimes used in conjunction with the foregoing approaches to treatment of sexual dysfunctions. For example, for women who have primary or secondary orgasmic dysfunction, group therapy is effective and less expensive than individual therapy (LoPiccolo & Stock, 1986; McCabe & Delany, 1992).

Although we know of no systematic research on the effectiveness of hypnosis in treating sexual dysfunctions, many therapists use hypnosis in their treatment (Araoz, 1985; Dekker, 1993). Attaining a hypnotic trance requires learning relaxation techniques, which presumably reduce the extent to which clients engage in fearful or distracting thoughts about their sexual responses.

## Sexual Surrogates

Most sexual therapies include homework assignments that require a cooperative partner. In attempting to meet the needs of the dysfunctional client who has no steady partner, some therapists have used "body-work therapy," in which the client and a *sexual surrogate*, with the direction of a therapist, may engage in private sexual activity as part of the treatment (Apfelbaum, 1980).

Most professionals view sexual contact between clients and therapists as unethical. Masters and Johnson (1970) attempted to solve this problem by employing sexual surrogates. They reported that the participation of a cooperative and skilled surrogate who had no prior association with the client was as effective as the participation of marital partners in the treatment of sexual difficulties. But Masters and Johnson discontinued the controversial practice, as have many other therapists.

Critics have contended that the use of surrogates is thinly disguised prostitution, with potentially damaging consequences. Defenders of the practice claim that surrogates are carefully screened and taught to be sensitive to the thera-

---

**sexual surrogate**—a member of a sex therapy team whose role is to have sexual interactions with a client as part of the therapy.

peutic nature of their task. That is, they are trained to help the client learn skills that he or she can use with a regular partner.

In an ideal world, the employment of sexual surrogates would depend on their effectiveness in attaining treatment goals. A comparison of the progress of clients treated by therapists employing surrogates with that of clients treated without surrogates would aid in determining their usefulness. But in the world in which we live, no such study has been conducted or is likely to be done in the near future, because of legal and ethical concerns. In most clinics that treat sexual dysfunctions, the use of sexual surrogates has been largely abandoned (Leiblum & Rosen, 1989).

### Other Treatment Approaches

Various approaches involving surgery, hormones, and drugs have been used in the attempt to treat sexual dysfunctions. The fact that most of these treatments have been developed for male sexual difficulties probably reflects our culture's emphasis on male sexual performance. In general, before permitting these kinds of treatments, the client should make sure that no other type of treatment is effective for him and obtain a second opinion.

Surgical procedures, including implants, have been used in the treatment of erectile dysfunction. Early bone implants resulted in a state of constant or semirigid erection, which could be an embarrassing nuisance in some situations. Plastic or silicone implants were a definite improvement. There are two basic types of plastic or silicone implants. One is a semirigid rod that keeps the penis in a constant state of erection but can be bent for concealment under clothing. The other type of silicone or plastic (polyurethane) implant, an inflatable device (see Figure 8.8), is implanted under the skin of the penis, and erection is achieved by pressing a pump implanted in the scrotum. The pump forces fluid from a reservoir put under the abdominal muscles into the cylinders implanted in the penis. Complications of this method include infection and mechanical failure. Follow-up studies of *prosthesis* recipients

prosthesis—artificial replacement for a body part.

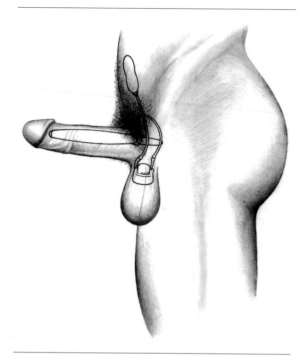

**FIGURE 8.8**
**Inflatable Penile Prosthesis**
This drawing shows an inflatable penile prosthesis. With most inflatable penile prostheses, a reservoir of fluid is implanted under the abdominal muscles, and an attached pump is embedded in either the abdominal cavity or the scrotum. A man presses the pump to force fluid into cylinders in his prosthesis when he wishes to have an erection. A release valve allows the fluid to return to the abdominal reservoir.

and their partners have indicated that they were generally satisfied with the choice to have the surgery (Graber, 1993). No differences in satisfaction have been reported between men who received the inflatable or the semirigid prostheses (Tiefer & Melman, 1989).

From 90% to 95% of men with penile implants are able to have satisfactory sexual relations after the implant is functioning effectively, and most would recommend this surgery to others with erectile dysfunction (Krane, 1986; McCarthy & McMillan, 1990). Most men who have implants can still experience ejaculation and orgasm unless there has been previous neurological damage.

A diversity of surgical techniques, including microsurgery, has been developed to increase blood flow to the penises of men with erectile dysfunction. The surgery is similar in principle to bypass surgery for heart patients with blocked arteries. Blocked arteries are bypassed through grafts that allow for a greater blood supply to the penis. This procedure appears promising, but results so far have been quite variable and the procedure appears suited for only a small percentage of men who have erectile dysfunction (Graber, 1993; Tiefer & Melman, 1989).

Hormones have also been used for years to treat erectile dysfunction. If the problem is not due to hormone deficiency, however, hormones can increase sexual arousability without improving performance, which can result in further deterioration of the client's condition. Current research indicates that androgen replacement therapy can increase libido in men with an abnormally low level of this hormone, but there is little evidence that it is effective for men within the normal hormonal range who experience sexual difficulties (Rosen & Ashton, 1993; Segraves, 1988a). Hormone treatment also increases the risk of coronary thrombosis, atherosclerosis, and cancer of the prostate.

Drugs are sometimes used to alleviate some of the symptoms associated with the dysfunctions. As noted earlier, anxiety plays a large role in the development of sexual dysfunction in both women and men. Physicians may attempt to treat some dysfunctions through the prescription of minor tranquilizers, such as Librium or Valium, that reduce anxiety. Some individuals with a sexual dysfunction have reported improvement after treatment with an antidepressant medication (Crenshaw, Goldberg, & Stein, 1987). Although their frequency of sexual behavior did not increase significantly, their satisfaction with their own sexuality did.

A number of drugs can create pharmacological erection (Wagner & Kaplan, 1993). One of them, papavarine, when injected relaxes the smooth muscle of the corpora cavernosa. It appears to be most useful for men with irreversible biological erectile dysfunction. The client can be taught to inject the drug himself. There is some risk with this treatment, for it can cause permanent penile scarring, priapism, cardiac irregularities, and changes in the liver with long-term use.

Self-help groups offer support to individuals affected by erectile dysfunction. Bruce MacKensie, who received an inflatable penile implant in 1981, and his wife, Eileen, were cofounders of Impotents Anonymous in 1983. As of 1994, the organization had approximately 100 chapters in 45 states. There are also groups for partners of men with erectile dysfunctions (see Appendix C). We have tried to locate corresponding self-help groups for nonorgasmic women, but to the best of our knowledge no such nationwide groups exist.

## Qualifications and Ethics of Therapists

One of the challenges faced by individuals experiencing sexual problems is finding a qualified therapist. The field of sex therapy is quite young, and qualifications for practitioners are still being determined. There are a considerable number of people who call themselves sex therapists, but they have little training or competence.

How can you find out whether a therapist is qualified? Most qualified sex therapists make themselves and their credentials known to other professionals in the community. Family physicians, gynecologists, and urologists can provide the names of sex therapists. There is no legislative control of the title "sex therapist" in many states, and so the appearance of the title in the phone book does not testify to an individual's skills. In all states, however, licensing laws control who can be listed as a psychologist or physician. Many states also restrict the listings of social workers and marriage counselors. When you call professionals, it is important to ask about their qualifications, experience, and fees.

There are certain practices that we believe are not appropriate in sex therapy regardless of the therapist's qualifications. Unless a therapist is a licensed physician who recommends a physical examination, he or she should not ask clients to take off their clothes. And even though the conversation, material, and assignments are explicitly sexual, overt sexual activities should *not* occur in the therapist's presence. Not all therapists share our sentiments on this subject. From 2% to 7% of psychologists report sexual contact with their clients (Pope, Sonne, & Holroyd, 1993; Stake & Oliver, 1991). A few therapists even advocate therapist-client sexual intimacy as part of sex therapy. However, sexual contact between client and therapist is generally considered unethical and destructive to the therapeutic relationship. One study indicated that 90% of the clients who had been sexually intimate with their therapists reported some negative effects, such as feeling guilty or exploited (Bouhoutsos, 1981).

Our opposition to therapist-client sexual intimacy is based on the ethical and emotional problems inherent in the practice. First, the purpose of therapy is to aid individuals who are distressed about some aspect of sexual functioning. These people seek professional help for problems they have been unable to resolve themselves. Therapists and their clients are not equal; therapists, as professionals, are in a position of greater power stemming from their expertise in the area, and clients are vulnerable to exploitation because of their position of need. A therapist-client sexual relationship ultimately exploits (and potentially harms) rather than aids the client.

Second, the purpose of seeing a therapist is to receive help in identifying feelings and resolving conflicts *without* having another person's desires imposed on oneself. In cases in which the therapist believes that sexual interaction during treatment is necessary or useful but the client has no partner, the use of a surrogate minimizes the likelihood that a conflict of interest will develop between the therapist and client, although its controversial nature raises problems of its own.

Third, as we have emphasized, sexual difficulties often include conflicts about relationships and anxiety about sex rather than simple problems of technique. The problems typical of persons seeking sex therapy are thus not likely to be solved through sexual relations with a therapist and may, in fact, be worsened.

More adequate therapist training aimed at preventing therapist-client sexual interaction might avert the problems that can arise when therapists and clients become sexually intimate. It is not uncommon for therapists to experience attraction toward clients. In one study of more than 500 psychologists, 95% of the men and 76% of the women reported sexual attraction toward some of their clients (Pope, Keith-Spiegel, & Tabachnick, 1986). Only 9% felt that they had received sufficient training for dealing with potential attraction toward clients. Many student therapists refrained from discussing this issue with their supervisors for fear of being perceived as having "problems." Clearly, graduate school and medical school courses must give greater attention to the management of therapists' sexual feelings toward clients. Just as people must develop ways to manage their sexual feelings and behavior in social situations, prospective therapists need training to deal with these emotions in the clinical environment (Yarris & Allgeier, 1988).

## Summary of Major Points

| | |
|---|---|
| 1. Stress and sexual dysfunctions. | Problems in sexual response are associated with a variety of physical and psychological stresses, including long- or short-term medical conditions, fatigue or illness, anxiety, a disproportionately heavy focus on performance evaluation, ignorance about sexuality, and relationships dominated by conflict or inadequate communication. |
| 2. Specific types of sexual dysfunction. | Levels of desire and responsiveness normally vary from one individual to the next and for a single individual from one time to the next. Such variations do not, in and of themselves, indicate that a person is sexually dysfunctional or in need of treatment. When an individual is bothered by consistent failure to respond in the way he or she wishes, however, it may be appropriate to seek professional help. A person can experience difficulty during any phase of a sexual interaction. The individual may feel little or no desire for sexual relations or may be obsessed with the desire for sexual stimulation. If a person's level of desire is consistently different from that of his or her partner, |

therapy can be used to resolve the discrepancy. Alternatively, an individual may feel deep desire for sexual relations but have difficulty becoming excited or aroused. Finally, an individual may respond quickly or slowly to sexual stimulation. When a person's pattern of desires is consistently different from that of his or her partner and from the way the person wishes to respond, sex therapy may help the couple.

3. Major approaches to sex therapy.

Masters and Johnson's approach, which stresses the learned nature of many sexual responses, focuses on developing more satisfying patterns of response. Kaplan includes a similar approach in her therapeutic treatment but distinguishes between specific maladaptive sexual responses and more general sources of difficulty, including personal conflicts and unresolved problems between a couple, which may require more prolonged and in-depth treatment.

4. Effectiveness of sex therapy.

Masters and Johnson reported higher success rates than many contemporary sex therapists typically experience. Although it is possible that they employed superior techniques, it is likely that several other factors explain this difference, including an increase in sexual knowledge in the population as a whole since the 1950s and 1960s, when Masters and Johnson's pioneering work was done. This increase may have eliminated potential clients whose main difficulty was ignorance, leaving a population of clients with more problematic sources of sexual dysfunction.

5. Treatment of sexual dysfunctions.

Sex therapists use various techniques to help people have more satisfying sexual experiences. These include systematic desensitization, nondemand pleasuring, sensate focus, masturbation training, and the squeeze technique, in addition to psychotherapy.

6. Controversies surrounding sex therapy.

The use of client-therapist sexual contact, the employment of sexual surrogates, and the basis for providing sex therapists with credentials to practice are among the issues currently debated by therapists. Sexual contact between therapist and client is unethical and usually has negative effects on the client. There is no evidence regarding the effectiveness of sexual surrogates in treating sexual dysfunction, and few therapists employ them because of the additional expense. Most sex therapists have licenses to practice as psychologists, physicians, social workers, or counselors.

# Review of Key Concepts _____

1. In general, any disease or surgery that affects the reflex centers in the spinal cord and the nerves that serve them can result in sexual impairment. True or false? (p. 232)

2. According to recent research, which of the following statements is most likely to be true? a) Most sexual dysfunctions result from psychological factors alone. b) Freud's theory that critical childhood experiences explain sexual dysfunctions has now been supported. c) Most sexual difficulties have biological causes. d) Anxiety about sex and performance is probably the most important immediate cause of sexual dysfunctions. (pp. 232–237)

3. Excessive sexual desire is the most common male dysfunction. True or false? (p. 241)

4. Sexual desire disorders and sexual arousal disorders are interchangeable designations for the same dysfunction. True or false? (p. 240)

5. Vaginismus is: a) a condition involving the involuntary contraction of the pubococcygeus (PC) muscle surrounding the outer third of the vagina; b) correlated with such factors as rape, abortion, painful gynecological exams, pelvic inflammatory disease, accidents, and general fears about men and/or rape; c) often readily cured by therapy; d) all of the above. (pp. 246–247)

6. The overall success rate of sex therapy may well have decreased over the past two decades. True or false, and why? (pp. 248–249)

7. Systematic desensitization is a procedure used in treating sexual dysfunctions that involves: a) removing the physical causes of vaginal pain and involuntary contraction; b) deep relaxation to reduce anxiety associated with certain situations; c) undergoing psychotherapy to uncover the source of sexual inhibitions or fears; d) none of the above. (p. 251)

8. Nondemand pleasuring is a therapeutic approach involving: a) sexual intercourse in a relaxed, low-anxiety environment; b) mutual masturbation; c) the giver's deliberate avoidance of attempts to arouse the receiver sexually; d) use of the squeeze technique. (p. 252)

9. The use of implants to correct male erectile dysfunctions is: a) completely impractical and unsafe; b) painful; c) almost always a failure; d) now generally effective, and should be used only if all other approaches have failed. (p. 257)

10. Evaluate Kaplan's and Masters and Johnson's assertion that anxiety about sexual performance—the fear of failing—is the most important immediate cause of sexual dysfunction. What factors can generate this fear of failure? What can be done about it?

11. "It is important to realize that occasional nonresponsiveness during sexual interaction is common." Comment on this statement, citing circumstances that may be related to such nonresponsiveness in both men and women.

12. Do you believe that a sexual relationship between a therapist and a client can be ethically acceptable? Why or why not?

# Pregnancy and Birth

*To impregnate and to become pregnant signify to the individual a kind of categorical maturity as human beings; the natural consequence of sexual intercourse fixes more permanently and obviously the private experience of love-making and the status of adulthood, of being grown up. (Rainwater & Weinstein, 1960, pp. 81–82)*

In this chapter we first consider ways of increasing the chances of pregnancy and then present the processes of pregnancy and birth. Sexual intercourse during pregnancy, preparation for childbirth, normal birth, and some of the controversies regarding medical and hospital childbirth policies are reviewed. We discuss such *postpartum* issues as depression, breast-feeding, circumcision, and sexual intimacy between the new parents. Although most babies are born without problems, complications occasionally arise, and we consider a few of the more common of these toward the end of the chapter.

## Increasing the Chances of Conception

We have a friend who claims that she gets pregnant every time her husband looks at her. In

**postpartum** (post-PAR-tum)—relating to the time immediately following birth.

reality, however, women are capable of conception only during a few days each month, when they ovulate. Further, human sperm are capable of fertilizing an egg for only a few days after they have been ejaculated into the vagina. These facts and other information about conditions affecting conception can be helpful to couples trying to conceive. It can also be useful to those wishing to choose the gender of their baby and the month of the birth.

To maximize the chances of conception, a couple should have coitus when the man has a high sperm count and when the woman is ovulating. They should use the face-to-face, man-above coital position, with deep penetration of the penis into the vagina during ejaculation, and the woman should remain on her back for about 20 minutes after the man has ejaculated into her vagina. Each of these procedures increases the likelihood that sperm reach and swim through the cervical opening into the uterus. If the woman is on top or if she gets up immediately after the man ejaculates, some semen seeps out of her vagina, reducing the number of sperm that reach the fallopian tubes. These procedures should not be used in reverse, to avoid conception, because even women with intact hymens who have never been vaginally penetrated have become pregnant as a result of ejaculation outside the vagina.

## Gender Selection

Most parents-to-be leave the selection of their baby's gender to chance. However, for those who have produced an unbroken sequence of boys in their attempts to have a girl, and vice versa, gender-selection methods can be useful.

### Methods of Gender Selection

Although folk methods for trying to determine gender have long existed, little scientific work on reliable methods with humans was available until Shettles and his colleagues began to publish the results of their research on the subject in the late 1960s. Their gender-selection techniques were based on the observation of differences between sperm carrying X chromosomes and those carrying Y chromosomes. Y-bearing sperm tend to have greater motility, but they are less resistant to hostile environments and die more quickly than do X-bearing sperm.

Based on these observations, Shettles (1972; see also Rorvik & Shettles, 1977) developed the *timing-plus-douche* method, a gender-selection procedure relying on differences between X- and Y-bearing sperm. Shettles suggested that couples wanting to improve their chances of conceiving a female could handicap the Y-bearing sperm by having coitus several days *before* ovulation because a higher proportion of Y-bearing than of X-bearing sperm die before the egg enters the fallopian tube.* Further, prospective parents create an additional obstacle for Y-bearing sperm when the woman uses a vinegar-and-water douche. The increased acidity of the vagina injures the Y-bearing sperm more easily than the X-bearing sperm. Therefore, a couple wishing to conceive a female should have coitus a few days before ovulation *and* use the acidic douche.

Alternatively, to increase the chances of having a boy, couples should have intercourse on the day of ovulation, after a woman has used an *alkaline* (baking-soda-and-water) douche. Although the alkaline environment increases the chances of survival for both X- and Y-bearing sperm, the Y-bearing sperm generally swim faster and thus may reach the newly released egg first. It should be noted that the 80% success rate claimed for Shettles's techniques has been questioned (Simcock, 1985; Williamson, 1978).

Another way of enhancing the chances of conceiving a boy is the *sperm-separation method*, in which various laboratory procedures are used to separate the Y-bearing sperm from the X-bear-

**timing-plus-douche**—a method of gender selection relying on the acidity or alkalinity of the vaginal environment and the timing of intercourse and ovulation.

**alkaline**—having the power to neutralize acids.

**sperm-separation method**—a method of gender selection in which X-bearing and Y-bearing sperm are separated and the woman is artificially inseminated with Y-bearing sperm.

---

*For methods of determining the date of ovulation, see Chapter 10.

ing sperm. One separation procedure involves placing semen on top of a dense fluid. The woman is then artificially inseminated with those sperm that reach the bottom first—predominantly the faster-swimming Y-bearing sperm (Glass & Ericsson, 1982). Sperm-separation methods are useful only for couples desiring boys, however.

Finally, it is possible to determine the gender of the fetus through the prenatal diagnostic procedures of chorionic villi sampling or amniocentesis (see pp. 271-272), and to elect abortion if the baby is not of the desired gender (see Chapter 1).

### The Pros and Cons of Gender Selection

The sperm-separation methods require a number of steps, some of which may be perceived as invasive. First, the man must provide semen samples. The semen is processed to separate the X- and Y-bearing sperm, and the woman is then artificially inseminated with the Y-bearing sperm. Although about 1% of the U.S. population has been produced through artificial insemination, most couples resort to it only if they have infertility problems (see Chapter 14). It seems unlikely that many North Americans would go through this tedious process to produce a child of a specific gender.

Another method—the use of prenatal diagnostic techniques and the subsequent abortion of undesired fetuses—can present both medical and moral problems. Prenatal diagnostic procedures carry some risk of accidentally aborting a desired fetus.

Steinbacher (1980) objected to the very notion of gender selection. She expressed concern about the gender ratio (the proportion of males to females) in the population. According to numerous studies conducted prior to 1980, an overwhelming majority of couples indicated a preference for a boy if they could have only one child. Couples who wanted two children preferred to have a male first. In general, first-born children tend to dominate subsequent children. Thus Steinbacher suggested that the use of reliable gender selection techniques might result in a surplus of males, a shortage of females, increased male homosexuality, and polyandry (the mating of a woman with two or more men).

The traditional preference for males may rest upon a belief that girls are less likely than boys to become sources of pride to their families through achievement or economic success. The status of women has risen dramatically over the past few decades, and the preference for sons over daughters has been declining (Steinbacher & Gilroy, 1990).

Despite the problems associated with gender selection, the U.S. trend toward more positive attitudes about the process suggests a widespread belief that women and men should have the greater control over their reproductive lives offered by gender-selection methods. Further, contemporary evidence does not appear to support the earlier concern that such methods would result in an unbalanced gender ratio.

## Pregnancy

Even though millions of women give birth each year, there is a tendency for women, particularly with their first pregnancies, to feel that they are doing something uniquely remarkable, and indeed they are.

### Early Symptoms of Pregnancy

A few women—especially those who have been pregnant before and those who are actively trying to conceive—suspect pregnancy within 10 days or so of conceiving. They may recognize heaviness in the abdomen and breasts, and the nipples may feel a bit irritated. For most women, the first real indication of pregnancy is the absence of menstruation about two weeks after conception.

As soon as a woman believes that she is pregnant, she should obtain a pregnancy test. Early diagnosis of pregnancy is important for a number of reasons. First, pregnant women should avoid most drugs and exposure to certain diseases (see Table 9.1 and Figure 9.1). Second, some potentially dangerous medical conditions, if identified early on, can be corrected, drastically improving the chances of a positive outcome for both woman and baby. Third, occasionally a woman

## TABLE 9.1 Factors That May Affect the Fetus

### Drugs

| | |
|---|---|
| *Alcohol* | Small head size, defective joints, congenital heart defects, mental retardation |
| *Nicotine* | Spontaneous abortion, prematurity, low birth weight, stillbirth, nicotine dependency at birth |
| *Vitamin A (excessive doses)* | Cleft palate, neural tube defects |
| *Aspirin (moderate use)* | Relatively safe until third trimester; use then may prolong labor and lengthen clotting time for both mother and baby, increasing the risk of hemorrhage |
| *Tetracycline* | Bone and tooth damage, discolored teeth |
| *Heroin* | Spontaneous abortion, low birth weight, fetal addiction and withdrawal, respiratory depression |
| *Methadone* | Low birth weight, respiratory depression, mild degrees of mental retardation |
| *Marijuana* | Reduced fetal growth rate; overall risk of congenital malformations, limb deficiencies |
| *Cocaine* | Neonatal intoxication |

### Diseases or Medical Conditions

| | |
|---|---|
| *Rubella virus* | Infant deafness, blindness, cataracts, heart malformations |
| *Diabetes* | Spontaneous abortion, maternal toxemia, stillbirths, abnormally large fetus, respiratory difficulties |
| *Syphilis* | Spontaneous abortion, prematurity, stillbirth, syphilitic infant |
| *Herpes, type II* | Spontaneous abortion, prematurity, stillbirth, neonatal herpes infection, congenital abnormalities |
| *AIDS* | Postnatal death from opportunistic infections |
| *Radiation* | Microcephaly, mental retardation, skeletal malformations |

### Hormones

| | |
|---|---|
| *Androgens* | Female offspring: masculinization of internal and/or external genitals |
| *Estrogens* | Female offspring: clitoral enlargement, labial fusion, congenital anomalies |
| *Progestins* | Cardiovascular anomalies |
| *DES* | Male offspring: semen and testicular abnormalities, reduced fertility; female offspring: abnormal vaginal or cervical growth, masculinization, reproductive organ cancers |
| *Oral contraceptives* | Suspected but unconfirmed reports of physiological difficulties, among them anal, cardiac, kidney, and limb abnormalities |

Sources: K. L. Moore (1989); Mattson and Smith (1993).

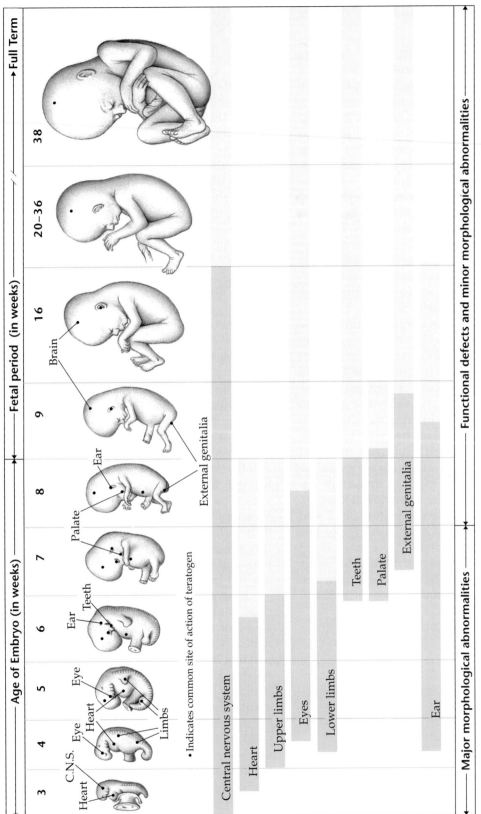

## FIGURE 9.1

### Effects of Teratogens on the Developing Fetus

The effects of teratogens (conditions or substances that induce malformations), and the particular organs they affect, vary according to when the teratogens come into play. In the two weeks from conception to the first missed menstrual period, the zygote (fertilized egg) is at little risk because the umbilical cord is not yet developed and functional. The greatest risk occurs from the second week of pregnancy to the end of the first trimester. During this period, the major organs are developing and are especially susceptible to teratogenic influences. Above, darkly shaded areas indicate highly sensitive periods.

can have symptoms of pregnancy, including *amenorrhea* (absence of expected menstrual bleeding), abdominal swelling, or nausea, even though she is not pregnant. Early examination can help detect the sources of such nonpregnancy-related bodily changes, and the problems are more readily treated and cured with early detection. Possible causes include tumors and cysts, which may be benign or malignant.

Most pregnancy tests are based on detecting *human chorionic gonadotropin (HCG)* in a woman's blood or urine. After conception, the *placenta*, which connects the uterus to the developing fetus, begins to produce HCG at rapidly increasing levels. HCG secretion reaches its maximum level about nine weeks after conception and then declines (Hatcher et al., 1994). The presence of HCG in a woman's bloodstream may be detected in a blood sample within a week after conception. Analysis of urine for the presence of HCG is highly accurate as early as the first day of the expected (but missed) menstrual period. Contemporary at-home pregnancy-test kits also work by detecting HCG in urine and are highly reliable if a woman adheres precisely to the directions for their administration. They are useful for early screening if a woman suspects that she is pregnant and cannot obtain an immediate appointment with a health care provider. However, such test kits should always be followed by a visit to a health care provider if the result is positive (indicating that the woman is pregnant). If the result is negative, but the conditions that led a woman to believe that she was pregnant persist for the next week, she should also see a health care provider.

## Stages of Pregnancy

Pregnancy has an enormous impact on a woman's body and emotions. In many cases, the emotions of an expectant father are also strongly affected. Impending parenthood alters both women's and men's definitions of themselves and of their relationships. It changes their status among their relatives and in society as a whole, as the quote at the beginning of this chapter conveys.

Paralleling the stages in fetal development and growth described in Chapter 4 is a series of remarkable physiological and psychological changes that women undergo during the nine months of pregnancy. Each stage of the pregnancy brings characteristic alterations in the woman's body and in her feelings about herself and her role as a mother. For the first-time mother, each sensation is a new experience.

The gestation period lasts approximately 266 days from conception to birth, but the expected delivery date is normally calculated by subtracting three months from the first day of the last menstrual period and then adding 53 weeks to that figure. This method is not foolproof, because some women continue to menstruate for a month or more after becoming pregnant. A friend of ours was undergoing a final check before going into surgery for a tumor when it was discovered that the "tumor" was a four-month-old fetus. She had not suspected that she was pregnant because she continued to have normal menstrual periods. Five months later, she gave birth to a healthy baby girl. Most women stop menstruating when they are pregnant, however, and most babies are born within a week of the date calculated by the method just described.

Pregnancy is conventionally divided into three trimesters. It is important that couples be aware of the physical, emotional, social, and financial challenges imposed by pregnancy, impending birth, and the responsibilities of parenthood. If a couple have been experiencing serious marital problems, it is a good idea to consider marital counseling to try to resolve their conflicts before the child is born. As Reamy and White (1987, p. 178) pointed out, "The idea that a child will bring harmony and intimacy into a dysfunctional marriage is erroneous, if not ludicrous." Difficulties in a couple's relationship that existed prior to pregnancy usually remain or intensify, and new problems may emerge. Among couples who have a stable and mutually satisfying relationship, the decision to have a baby and the

---

**amenorrhea** (a-MEN-or-REE-ah)—absence of menstruation.

**human chorionic gonadotropin (HCG)** (CORE-ee-ON-ik goh-NAH-doe-TROE-pin)—a hormone produced by the placenta.

**placenta**—the organ formed by joining of the uterine wall tissue with that of the developing fetus; a major source of hormones during pregnancy.

sharing of feelings about the pregnancy may add to their sense of commitment and intimacy—two factors that are important for the experience of love (see Chapter 20).

### First Trimester

Most women do not realize that they are pregnant for several weeks or even a month or more following conception. Although women should record the dates of their periods on a calendar, not all do. Those who do not are sometimes unaware that they have skipped a period.

In addition to ceasing menstruation, many women experience swelling in their breasts. Their nipples may become temporarily sensitive, so that manual stimulation or contact with clothing is uncomfortable. In a first pregnancy, the *areolas* of some women darken early in the first trimester. During pregnancy, estrogens aid in the development of the milk ducts, and progesterone stimulates the completion of the development of these ducts and *alveoli*.

About six weeks after conception, noticeable changes occur in a woman's cervix. Normally, the cervix has a hardness and resiliency similar to that of the end of the nose or the top of the ear. About a month after the first missed menstrual period, however, the cervix feels relatively soft and malleable, a difference that can be detected by a woman who is familiar with the feeling of her cervix as well as by a health care provider during manual inspection.

During the first trimester, about half of all pregnant women have periodic bouts of nausea as a result of elevated levels of HCG and changed carbohydrate metabolism (Olds, London, & Ladewig, 1992). This condition is called "morning sickness" because it is usually most severe in the morning. For some women, the nausea is relatively mild and can be controlled by eating dry crackers before getting up in the morning, eating small frequent meals, and avoiding spicy foods. For other women, the nausea is considerably

more severe and is accompanied by vomiting. A few women must be hospitalized to control the potential dehydration from constant vomiting. Many women, however, do not experience any of these unpleasant side effects of pregnancy.

Increased fatigue and sleepiness are common during the first trimester. Many women also report feeling more irritable, vulnerable, and dependent than they did prior to conception. The changes in the shapes of their bodies depress some women. At this stage they are not yet "showing" the pregnancy enough to justify wearing maternity clothes, but they may have trouble buttoning slacks or skirts toward the end of the first trimester.

Pregnancy is commonly depicted as a time of calm and radiance, but women often feel ambivalent in the first trimester. Even in a planned pregnancy, a woman is frequently surprised that conception has actually occurred. Women who need to make changes in career plans and commitments or who feel financially stressed are most likely to feel ambivalence. Some women also express fears about pregnancy, labor, and delivery. Such worries are likely to be the most intense when the pregnancy is unwanted or unplanned.

During the first trimester some women seriously consider the possibility of an abortion. Those whose religious convictions prohibit abortion may experience guilt over having such thoughts. Other women, especially those who had difficulty conceiving, may worry about possible miscarriage (spontaneous abortion). This concern is realistic, in that the majority of miscarriages occur during the first trimester.

A pregnant woman tends to look for physical signs to prove to herself that she is truly pregnant. She becomes conscious of small changes in her body. She watches for thickening of her waist, weight gain, and breast development (see Figure 9.2). Even morning sickness, however unpleasant, is confirmation that she is in fact pregnant. Usually by the end of the first trimester she has resolved any ambivalence and has accepted the developing fetus as a temporary part of herself.

Like the expectant mother, the father also needs to adjust to the pregnancy and to the coming changes in his life. Most men feel pride that conception has occurred; at the same time, however, many express ambivalence. The extent of

**alveoli** (AL-vee-OH-lee)—milk-secreting cells in the breast.

**areola** (AIR-ee-OH-lah)—the darkened skin surrounding the nipples, containing oil-secreting glands.

**FIGURE 9.2**

**Physical Changes During the First Trimester of Pregnancy**

The first trimester of pregnancy does not produce major physical changes in most women. Compare this figure with the changes illustrated in Figures 9.4 and 9.7

the father's ambivalence is related to a variety of factors, such as his relationship with the mother, his age, their financial status, and whether the pregnancy was planned.

After the initial excitement and announcement of the pregnancy, many fathers feel left out. Attention becomes focused on the mother, who may act differently than she did prior to her pregnancy. Her mood changes and fatigue may confuse the expectant father. He may also experience her obsession with herself as a kind of rejection. Many men worry about their ability to be a good father and spend much time thinking about their own fathers.

Some men develop symptoms, such as fatigue, sleeping difficulties, backaches, and nausea, similar to those of pregnant women. The term *couvade* refers to men developing symptoms similar to those of their pregnant partners. Perhaps these symptoms provide a way for a man

to identify with his partner and to participate in the pregnancy.

### Second Trimester

For most women, the second trimester is characterized by a sense of well-being and pleasure. The symptoms of the first trimester diminish or disappear entirely, and the threat of miscarriage has diminished. Because they may take better care of themselves during pregnancy, some women report having more energy and feeling healthier in their second trimester than they did before they became pregnant. Some acknowledge the pregnancy by wearing maternity clothes, even if such clothes are not yet necessary. Small amounts of *colostrum*, a thin, yellowish fluid high in proteins and antibodies, may be expelled from the nipples during the second trimester. Colostrum production continues throughout pregnancy. The abdomen increases in fullness, particularly in women who have been pregnant before. The pressure of the enlarging uterus on the bladder interferes with women's activities, as well as their sleep, by increasing the frequency of their need to urinate.

Most health care providers schedule monthly prenatal checkups for women who have reached the beginning of the second trimester. During these visits, the woman's weight, blood pressure, and urine are checked. Some appointments also include a pelvic examination to determine the position and development of the fetus. Genetic testing or ultrasonography may be ordered for pregnant women over age 35 with family histories of genetic disorders, or for those susceptible to any other potential difficulties (see Box 9.1 and Figure 9.3).

Expectant parents generally are very excited by two events that occur around the middle of the second trimester. One is *quickening*, when the woman first becomes aware of fetal movement.

---

**colostrum** (cuh-LAWS-trum)—a thin, yellowish fluid, high in proteins and antibodies, secreted from the nipples before and around the time of birth.

**quickening**—the first fetal movements felt by the mother.

**Box 9.1**

## Tests for Identifying Fetal Abnormalities

*Ultrasonography*, developed in the 1950s, is a procedure for examination of the internal portions of the body. It is used in conjunction with amniocentesis or CVS to locate the fetus so that the needle can be positioned to avoid the fetus. Sound waves are directed at the uterus, and then, through computer translation, the echoes are bounced back into a visual picture of the fetus (a sonogram or ultrasound scan). Ultrasonography helps resolve questions about the due date by determining fetal size and development. It can also detect fetal abnormalities, twins, ectopic pregnancies, or tumors.

Ultrasonography is in widespread use. In 1984, however, the National Institutes of Health recommended that it not be routinely used on all pregnant women because its long-term effects are not fully known. This recommendation is controversial because some doctors use ultrasonography with all their pregnant clients, and it has identified unsuspected problems in 10% to 15% of women who have undergone it. It is expected that routine ultrasound exams will be in place by 1995 (Olds et al., 1992).

Three major methods are used in checking the fetus for the presence of genetic disorders: amniocentesis, chorionic villi sampling, and alpha-feto protein screening. *Amniocentesis* is the traditional method for identifying fetal chromosomal defects. It is done on an outpatient basis but needs to be performed near a birthing center in case fetal distress is encountered. First, ultrasonography is used to determine the position of the fetus. Next, a narrow, hollow needle is inserted into the woman's abdomen until it penetrates the uterus. A small

**ultrasonography**—a procedure in which sound waves and a computer are used to create a visual representation of the fetus.

**amniocentesis**—a diagnostic procedure in which amniotic fluid is extracted from the uterus and fetal cells are analyzed for chromosome defects.

amount of amniotic fluid surrounding the fetus is then removed through the needle (see Figure 9.3). Cells from the fluid are cultured (grown) for several weeks, at which point photographs of the chromosomes are examined for abnormalities. Amniocentesis is useful for diagnoses only after the first trimester.

Analysis of the fetal chromosomes can detect chromosomal defects such as Down's syndrome, as well as the gender of the fetus. In addition, biochemical tests of the cultured fetal cells can detect many problems from genetic abnormalities that cause no visible changes in chromosomes, such as spina bifida (opening in the spine) and cleft palate.

For some parents, the decision to undergo amniocentesis implies that the pregnancy will be terminated if defects are found. Abortion during the second trimester can be psychologically difficult and poses some physical risk to the mother. But when amniocentesis shows that the fetus has an ultimately fatal condition or massive disabilities that will require extensive and prolonged institutional care, parents may choose abortion.

Yet, decisions about many defects are not so straightforward. If a genetic disorder detected through amniocentesis will not manifest itself until later in life, or if the extent of disability is not predictable, the expectant parents are faced with a difficult decision and little time in which to consider all the implications. Those who choose to have their babies then encounter more daunting problems; for example, finding the personal and financial resources to provide for the child and later informing the child of the condition and its genetic implications.

Antiabortion groups oppose genetic testing on the grounds that women who learn of a defective embryo will abort it. These procedures uncover no defects in 95% of cases, however, and less than 1% of abortions are performed because of defective embryos. Further, early detection of defects increases the possibility that newly developed surgical techniques such as genetic repair and laser surgery can be performed before permanent damage is done.

Amniocentesis poses relatively little risk for the mother or the fetus. Some women experience temporary abdominal cramps and vaginal bleeding after amniocentesis, but this generally does not affect the fetus. The risk of loss of the fetus following the procedure ranges from 0.5% to 1% (Andolsek, 1990).

Another genetic test, *chorionic villi sampling (CVS)*, involves insertion of a thin tube through the cervix into the placenta (the location of which is determined by ultrasonography) to obtain a sample of chorionic villi. The chorion is a layer of tissue that surrounds the embryo and develops into the placenta, and villi are fingerlike projections of tissue that transfer oxygen, nutrients, and waste between mother and embryo. The villi are composed of the same cells as the fetus.

**chorionic villi sampling (CVS)**—a procedure in which embryonic cells are removed from the tissue surrounding the embryo and then analyzed for evidence of genetic defects.

The advantages of CVS over amniocentesis are that it can be performed at about the eighth week of pregnancy, it is a less invasive procedure, and results are available within 24 hours. The risk of fetal loss following CVS is only slightly higher than with amniocentesis (Andolsek, 1990). Some of this increased risk, however, may be due to the greater risk of miscarriage during the first trimester that occurs regardless of whether prenatal diagnostic tests are performed. Further, if a woman elects to terminate the pregnancy based on the results of CVS analysis, she faces relatively low risk because she is still in her first trimester. Like amniocentesis, CVS can help to detect Down's syndrome, Tay-Sachs disease, sickle-cell anemia, hemophilia, and about 90 other genetic diseases.

Alpha-feto protein (AFP) screening involves drawing blood from the mother at about the 16th week of pregnancy. It reveals defects of the central nervous system (Olds et al., 1992). If the results are positive, other tests such as amniocentesis are performed to confirm the results of the AFP screening. Like amniocentesis, the results of AFP screening are not available until about the 20th week of pregnancy, producing the same drawbacks associated with second-trimester abortion.

The other is detection of the fetal heartbeat, amplified with a device known as a Doppler. Some health care providers invite women to bring their partners with them to their next checkup after the heartbeat is detected, so that both expectant parents can hear the fetal heartbeat.

By the middle of the second trimester, women usually have to replace most of their regular clothing with loose slacks, smocks, and dresses to allow for the expansion of the uterus. Having adjusted to the changes in her appearance, the woman usually takes pleasure in the sensations of pregnancy and begins to picture the fetus as a real person. Quickening gives a woman a sense of "knowing" the baby. Many women are

eager to learn about childbirth and child care during this time. Most spend time thinking about being a mother, and many experience a new bond with their own mothers (see Figure 9.4).

The changes of early pregnancy also prompt a woman to think about her relationship with her partner and her status as a new mother. Many women feel anxiety about their partners, especially if their mates respond to the pregnancy by withdrawing. Like the mother, an expectant father needs to resolve any ambivalence he feels about the pregnancy. His involvement in preparing for the baby, hearing the baby's heartbeat, and feeling fetal movements usually help him adjust to his new situation.

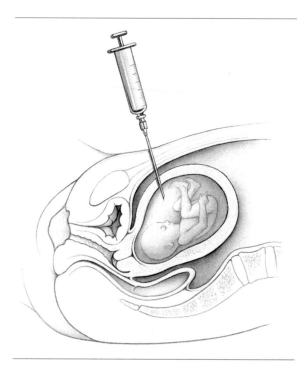

**FIGURE 9.3**
**Amniocentesis**
In this procedure, fluid and loose fetal cells are withdrawn from the amniotic sac. The cells are then cultured and examined for abnormalities.

An expectant father may also feel ambivalent about his partner's changing appearance; some men experience a diminished interest in sex, although others have the opposite reaction (see Figure 9.5). An expectant father may resent his partner's demands and need for attention, or he may willingly give her the extra time and interest she typically wants. Some men feel aloof during this time and withdraw, focusing on an outside interest or hobby. This behavior can in turn cause problems in the couple's relationship. Although a man may be confused by his partner's behavior—which characteristically includes mood swings, oversensitivity, and internal focus—it is important that he not withdraw, because she requires his attention, support, and understanding. Knowing that these psychological responses are a normal part of pregnancy often helps a couple to deal with the changes in their relationship. The second trimester is an important time for them to communicate and recognize each other's feelings.

### Third Trimester

During the last three months of pregnancy, most women have an awkward gait and feel rather blimplike. The average weight for a full-term baby is 7.5 pounds, but the average woman gains 25 to 30 pounds during pregnancy. Increased fluid retention and fat are responsible for much of the gain, as Figure 9.6 shows.

The baby's kicking and movement—initially a source of great pleasure and interest—may become downright irritating in the third trimester, particularly during the mother's attempts to sleep. Occasionally the fetus gets hiccups, and the regular spasms can be as distracting as a slowly dripping faucet. An expectant father may feel the kicking and movement readily with his hands or occasionally in the small of his back when the woman snuggles against him in bed. Many women have difficulty finding a comfortable position in which to sleep. The need for frequent urination returns, requiring several trips to the bathroom at night to release the small amount of

**FIGURE 9.4**
**Physical Changes During the Second Trimester of Pregnancy**
Compare this figure with Figures 9.2 and 9.7.

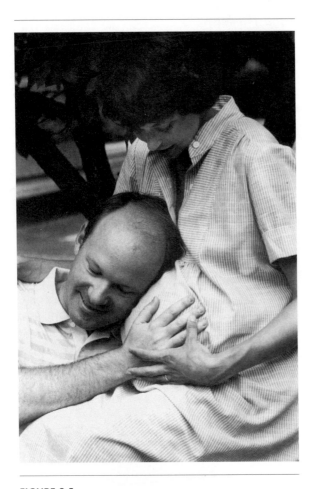

**FIGURE 9.5**
**Expectant Father's Connection**
This expectant father is obviously enjoying listening to and feeling his baby in his partner's uterus.

urine under pressure in the bladder, which is being crowded by the growing fetus.

During the third trimester a pregnant woman generally feels a sense of pride combined with anxiety about the future. Many women simultaneously experience an intense desire for the pregnancy to be over and anxiety about labor and birth. Fears about the baby's health and possible birth defects tend to surface in the last trimester. With her increased girth, the woman may need help with some tasks (see Figure 9.7). For example, if she is somewhat short, she may find that she has to move the driver's seat of her car so far back to accommodate her swollen abdomen that she can no longer reach the pedals to drive. Toward the end of this period, the woman usually experiences a burst of energy and a need to prepare a "nest" for the baby. She makes final arrangements for the baby's needs and plans for the first few months after the birth.

If the couple have communicated effectively and resolved their problems, the third trimester is likely to be the most peaceful one. The father usually has adjusted to the pregnancy and is ready to become involved in preparing for the baby. He may participate in prepared-childbirth classes and become increasingly supportive of the mother (see Figure 9.8).

If the father has remained detached, however, his early anxieties about the pregnancy may recur. For example, he may worry about family finances, or he may be concerned about his ability to be a good father. Even a detached father-to-be may feel an increased sense of responsibility as the birth approaches.

### Sex During Pregnancy

Sexual expression during pregnancy varies widely across cultures and among couples. Depending on the culture, pregnancy provides a rationale either for or against sexual intercourse. In some cultures sexual intercourse ceases for most couples as soon as a woman knows that she is pregnant. When asked about intercourse during pregnancy, the So of northeastern Uganda asked, "Why would you want to do that? There is already someone in there." Among the Mehinaku of Brazil, however, repeated intercourse is perceived as necessary for the growth of the developing fetus (Gregor, 1985).

In North America, two patterns appear to be common. In one pattern, the frequency of sexual intercourse declines with each trimester of pregnancy. The other pattern involves a decrease in sexual activity during the first trimester, followed by an increase in sexual interest and frequency during the second trimester. Regardless of which pattern is followed during the first two trimesters, either a sharp decrease or a cessation of sexual intercourse is typical of the third trimester, particularly in the final month of pregnancy (Olds et al., 1992).

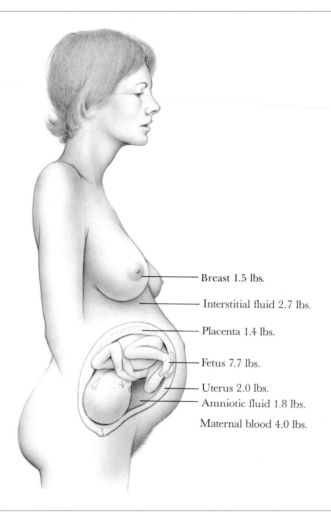

Breast 1.5 lbs.

Interstitial fluid 2.7 lbs.

Placenta 1.4 lbs.

Fetus 7.7 lbs.

Uterus 2.0 lbs.
Amniotic fluid 1.8 lbs.

Maternal blood 4.0 lbs.

**FIGURE 9.6**
**Weight Gain in Pregnancy**
The weight of the full-term baby contributes only about a third of the weight
gained by the average woman during pregnancy.

Coital positions and sites of sexual stimulation generally shift during pregnancy. After the first part of pregnancy, use of the man-above coital position tends to be replaced with a preference for positions that place less pressure on the woman's abdomen (see Figure 9.9 on p. 278).

The reasons for a declining frequency of coitus in the final trimester of pregnancy vary from woman to woman, but physical discomfort is probably the most frequent. Other reasons cited by expectant mothers include fear of injuring the

baby, lack of interest, feelings of awkwardness or unattractiveness, and health care providers' recommendations (Mattson & Smith, 1993).

Couples' fears notwithstanding, in a healthy pregnancy there is no reason to limit sexual activity (Olds et al., 1992). If a woman in her third trimester is uncomfortable with coitus for whatever reason, she and her partner can engage in such noncoital forms of sexual intimacy as manual and oral stimulation of the genitals. A study of pregnant Israeli women found that although

**FIGURE 9.7**
**Physical Changes During the Last Trimester of Pregnancy**
Compare this figure with Figures 9.2 and 9.4.

they reported a decline in coital frequency, the frequency of oral and anal sex and masturbation remained unchanged throughout pregnancy (Hart, Cohen, Gingold, & Homburg, 1991). Cuddling, kissing, and holding each other can often meet the needs of a pregnant woman and her partner. However, in a study of 14,000 women, Read and Klebanoff (1993) found that women who reported having engaged in coitus one to four times a week during weeks 23 to 26 (end of second and beginning of third trimesters) were about a third less likely to have a premature birth than were women who had coitus less frequently. As the authors noted, this finding certainly does not indicate that frequent coitus causes full-term delivery, but it does suggest that coitus is unlikely to produce premature delivery.

Two sexual practices should be avoided during pregnancy. One of these is blowing air into the vagina during cunnilingus: 14 fetal and 13 maternal deaths from air embolisms caused by this practice have been reported (Fyke, Kazmier, & Harms, 1985). In addition, pregnant women

should avoid sexual contact with a partner who has a sexually transmitted disease. If a woman becomes infected, the disease may also be transmitted to her baby during the pregnancy or vaginal delivery.

## Labor and Birth

As the end of pregnancy draws near, a woman may be reluctant to make appointments or to start new projects because the birth process may begin at any moment. This waiting game, with its persistent phone calls from relatives and friends, can get tedious, and expectant parents become increasingly eager to see their baby. In addition to preparing the household for the baby, many parents spend the last weeks of pregnancy

**FIGURE 9.8**
**The Waiting Game**
After waiting nine months, this couple is pleased that the contractions of labor are now frequent enough to be timed.

**Box 9.2**

## A Personal Account of Childbirth

Pregnant women generally receive a great deal of advice and information from other women who have experienced childbirth. Here is mine. —E.R.A.

*I have given birth in a hospital and at home, with and without anesthesia, with and without the help of my husband, with and without the benefit of prepared-childbirth instruction. In my experience, the ideal birth takes place at home, without anesthesia, and with the assistance of the expectant father, who has also participated in prepared-childbirth classes. The most important of these four conditions are the help of a mate and the classes. I would avoid anesthesia unless it is really needed, both for the baby's well-being and for the quality of the birth process. Because an unusually prolonged or complicated labor will mar the experience for the mother, however, anesthesia should be used when necessary.*

*Second-stage labor has been compared to a particularly prolonged bowel movement and*

*to orgasm, but neither approaches the intensity of childbirth. Given my druthers on a Sunday afternoon, I'd prefer orgasm to childbirth. However, the exhaustion produced by the labor of childbirth is followed by exhilaration at birth and a period of euphoria following birth that is unique in my experience.*

*My advice to expectant parents is to get as much information about pregnancy and birth as possible. The more they know about it, the more fascinating the process. Prepared-childbirth classes and diligent practice of childbirth exercises are invaluable.*

*Amidst the rhetoric regarding women's and men's liberation, childbirth provides an extraordinarily liberating opportunity for a woman. It presents her with the opportunity to experience the union of her voluntary and involuntary processes in an event that wholly claims her—the expression of life force through her with her utter cooperation.*

---

actively preparing for childbirth. In giving birth, the average woman puts in about 15 hours of increasingly strenuous work—hence the term *labor* for the stages directly leading to the birth.

## Preparation for Childbirth

Until the last three decades in Western countries, preparing for childbirth meant packing a suitcase with clothes for the hospital stay of the mother and newborn baby. Few expectant parents actually prepared for childbirth, and most women received little education about labor and giving birth (see Box 9.2). After admission to a hospital,

**labor**—the process of childbirth, consisting of contractions, thinning out and expansion of the cervix, delivery of the baby, and expulsion of the placenta.

they went through labor and birth in a sort of solitary confinement, attended only by hospital personnel who administered enemas, shaved pubic hair, gave pelvic exams, and checked vital signs. Despite having contributed half the genetic heritage of the baby, the father rarely participated in the delivery, much less witnessed the emergence of his child into the outside world.

In contrast, most health care providers and hospitals now encourage expectant parents to enroll in prepared-childbirth classes and to work as a team during labor and childbirth. Expectant parents usually enroll in these classes at the beginning of the third trimester. Instructors typically provide information about pregnancy and the stages of childbirth, dispelling fears and myths about birth. The course also generally includes a tour of the hospital's birthing center or maternity ward, unless the couple plans to give birth at home with the help of a midwife. Finally,

**FIGURE 9.9**
**Sex During Late Pregnancy**
During the third trimester, a couple often shifts to coital positions that place less pressure on the woman's abdomen.

expectant parents learn exercises and procedures designed to facilitate childbirth. Expectant fathers master massage techniques to help relieve the lower back pain that sometimes accompanies labor contractions. Expectant mothers learn procedures to help them relax and work with contractions instead of bracing against them. They also are taught breathing techniques that are useful during different stages of labor. Participants in these courses have reported that this preparation reduced their anxieties.

Although enrollment in a prepared-childbirth course is now a routine part of the process of pregnancy and birth, the idea of active participation by both the mother and the father became popular only in the late 1960s, partly stemming from changing attitudes toward the use of anesthesia. Anesthesia was not used for childbirth un-

**FIGURE 9.10**
**Childbirth Preparation**
A regular program of exercise during pregnancy is effective preparation for the strenuous work of labor and delivery.

til 1847, at least in part because the Bible held that "children should be brought forth in pain and sorrow." After anesthesia was introduced, however, it quickly became routine in hospital deliveries.

In his book *Childbirth Without Fear* (1932), the English physician Grantley Dick-Read questioned the use of anesthetics during labor. His objections were based on the potential danger to the baby and mother. He maintained that the pain stemming from labor contractions could be eliminated or reduced through the kind of education and training for relaxation that is now a routine part of prepared-childbirth classes.

The French obstetrician Bernard Lamaze also contributed to our contemporary approach to birth. After observing women in Russia undergoing labor with little pain, he began to train pregnant women and their husbands (or other "coaches") in muscle-relaxation and breathing techniques that used more systematic methods than those recommended by Dick-Read. One

technique introduced by Lamaze, called *effleurage*, consists of light circular stroking of the abdomen with the fingertips to help a woman relax. Lamaze students today also are strongly encouraged to be in top physical condition for labor (see Figure 9.10). Exercises to strengthen the leg muscles are taught, because the legs undergo considerable strain during childbirth.

The assistance of a familiar, supportive person is of great benefit to a woman giving birth. During labor and delivery, a woman's "coach" not only times her contractions (see Figure 9.11), but also supports and encourages her in relaxation and proper breathing. Following these techniques is associated with fewer birth complications, less use of anesthesia, and shorter labor than is typical with more traditional approaches to childbirth. Mothers using prepared childbirth also have more positive attitudes following birth, higher self-esteem, and a greater sense of self-control (Felton & Segelman, 1978; Olds et al., 1992; Zax et al., 1975).

The repertoire of techniques used in prepared childbirth is similar to that employed in hypnosis. For example, a woman is told to concentrate on an object—a bead in a necklace, for example, or a picture on a wall—to aid her in relaxing during labor. She learns to control her breathing and is reassured that she can manage the stress of childbirth.

## Labor for Childbirth

Although childbirth may be the most concentrated physical effort that a woman experiences in her life, women who have carried a growing baby for nine months are generally eager for labor to begin. Sometimes they experience *Braxton-Hicks contractions* for weeks prior to the onset of labor. Some women also undergo false

**effleurage**—a Lamaze massage technique involving light circular stroking of the abdomen with the fingertips.

**Braxton-Hicks contractions**—irregular contractions of the uterus that are often mistaken for the onset of labor.

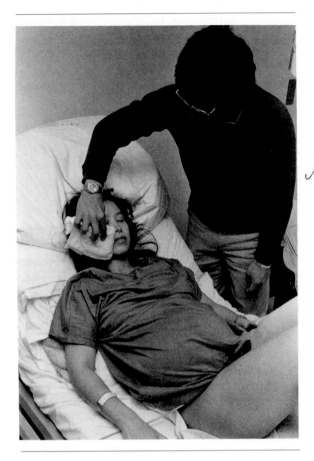

**FIGURE 9.11**
**Labor Partner**
The participation of a partner who provides encouragement, times contractions, and gives lower-back massages can be very helpful to a woman in labor.

labor—periodic contractions that seem to signal the beginning of labor but stop rather than increase in frequency and intensity.

### The Onset of Labor

As the due date approaches, pregnant women begin watching for signs of the onset of labor. It is thought that labor begins when the fetus's adrenal glands produce hormones that are secreted into the placenta and uterus. These secretions stimulate the release of prostaglandins that induce contractions in the uterus (Mattson & Smith, 1993). The gradual awareness of these contractions is the first symptom of labor for many women. Initially, the contractions may be so mild and infrequent (30 minutes or more apart) that women are unsure that they are actually experiencing them. The contractions gradually increase in frequency, duration, and intensity. Most women are instructed to call their doctors or midwives when the contractions occur at five-minute intervals.

Other symptoms of impending labor that can occur either before or after the onset of contractions include a pinkish discharge from the vagina and/or varying amounts of a watery discharge ("breaking waters") from the vagina. The pinkish vaginal discharge results from the release of the mucus plug in the cervix. The watery discharge comes from the rupture of the amniotic sac. During pregnancy the fetus is protected by a cushion of almost two pounds of amniotic fluid. With the onset of labor, the fluid is generally released in varying amounts from a trickle to a gush. After the release of the amniotic fluid, contractions usually increase in frequency and intensity, although some women go through most of labor or even childbirth without the amniotic sac breaking. An Irish myth suggests that a baby born "in a caul"—that is, in the unruptured amniotic sac—is lucky. Such a baby, somewhat protected from the contractions of labor, may experience a relatively easy time during birth.

### Location of Labor and Birth

In 1900 more than 95% of American women delivered their babies at home rather than in hospitals. At this point, the figures are reversed, with only a small percentage of women giving birth at home. Some of these home deliveries are unplanned, but many families choose to deliver at home with the aid of a physician or *midwife*. Today's midwives can be nurses who can be certi-

**midwife**—a person who has received special training as a birth attendant.

fied as nurse-midwives in most states or laypersons who are trained by experienced midwives.

The advantages of home birth are the greater familiarity and comfort of the environment to the mother, the greater accessibility of family and friends who wish to be present at the birth, and the reduced expense. The most obvious disadvantage of home birth is the reduced access to equipment and trained personnel in the event that an emergency develops during labor or delivery.

Although home birth is gaining in popularity, most couples in North America go to a hospital or birthing center for childbirth. Birthing centers—health care facilities usually affiliated with hospitals but physically separated from them—generally allow a woman and her family more control over the experience of childbirth than they are likely to have in a hospital. Birthing centers are typically less expensive than are hospitals, and are designed for early discharge from the center, generally within a day of the birth (Olds et al., 1992). Birthing centers are supplied with emergency equipment for medical problems and have advance arrangements for transferring a woman to a hospital if an emergency occurs. Rooks et al. (1989) reported that such transfers to hospitals occurred in 16% of a sample of almost 12,000 women at birthing centers, but no maternal deaths resulted. Other research indicates that delivery at birthing centers is associated with a low Cesarean section rate and low or no neonatal mortality (Eakins, 1989). Nurses and nurse-midwives usually staff the facilities. Physicians often attend the deliveries, but some centers are staffed entirely by nurses affiliated with a particular hospital.

Labor is divided into three stages. During first-stage labor, the cervix gradually opens enough to permit passage of the baby. Birth occurs during second-stage labor. The placenta, or afterbirth, is expelled during third-stage labor.

### First-Stage Labor

At the beginning of first-stage labor, a woman is given a checkup and a pelvic exam. The checkup usually includes measuring her blood pressure and obtaining blood and urine samples. These samples are analyzed for any signs of abnormality that might affect the process or outcome of birth.

The position of the fetus is checked to see whether *engagement* has occurred. With engagement the fetus drops several inches lower in the abdominal cavity, and when the head has gone past the mother's pelvic bone structure, it is said to be engaged. Engagement may happen at any time from a week before birth to several hours after the onset of labor.

During the pelvic exam, some labor contractions are monitored. The uterus becomes very firm, almost rigid, during each uterine contraction. This firmness can be felt by placing a hand on the abdomen; the characteristic hardness is absent during a false labor contraction. The extent of *effacement* and *dilation* (thinning out and opening up of the cervix) is also checked. If one or more of these signs indicates that the woman is in labor or if the amniotic sac has ruptured and released some amniotic fluid, the woman is prepared ("prepped") for childbirth.

At this point, many women, particularly those with a first pregnancy, experience one of the two most frustrating events associated with normal childbirth.* They are sent home! They may have been having regular contractions five or fewer minutes apart, only to have the contractions come to an abrupt halt after they reach the hospital or birthing center. In recognition of this phenomenon, many hospitals do not admit maternity patients until after the initial checkup and

**engagement**—movement of the fetus into a lower position in the mother's abdominal cavity, with its head past her pelvic bone structure.

**effacement**—flattening and thinning of the cervix that occurs before and during childbirth.

**dilation**—expansion or opening up of the cervix prior to birth.

---

*The other source of frustration for a woman is learning that her cervix has dilated only a few centimeters after she has been in labor for several hours and is sure that delivery is near.

pelvic exam. If the amniotic sac has not ruptured and if the cervix is completely undilated, hours or even a few days may elapse before effective labor begins. In this event, it makes no sense to keep a woman in the hospital or birthing center. Nonetheless, after notifying relatives that the baby's birth is imminent, a woman who must return home, still pregnant, can be disappointed to tears.

When effective labor is in progress, however, women are prepared for childbirth. The vulva, thighs, and stomach are washed with an antiseptic solution to reduce the chances of transmitting infection to the baby during birth. Traditionally, women were given enemas and had all their pubic hair shaved, but some researchers have questioned the necessity of both practices.

Shaving the pubic hair was done to facilitate sterilization of the area. In contemporary obstetric practice, shaving is recommended only if an *episiotomy* is planned. Otherwise, shaving of the pubic hair is unnecessary, and the irritation of the vulva that women feel as the hair grows back adds to their postpartum discomfort. Further, shaving may slightly increase the likelihood of maternal infection (Andolsek, 1990).

The rationale for the enema was twofold: the bowels should be empty so that feces are not pushed out during birth, and the enema might speed labor. Because women are given no solids after labor begins, however, any food that they have eaten previously has been digested and expelled unless labor is very rapid, in which case the enema does not eliminate the food further up in the intestines. Enemas are currently recommended only if the woman has a large amount of hard stool in the rectum.

After the preliminary pelvic exam and checkup, the woman is taken to a labor room or birthing room—accompanied by the expectant father or another birth coach—where her contractions prepare her body to expel the baby. The contractions of early first-stage labor feel like a tightening of the abdomen and are generally not uncomfortable. As labor progresses, the tight feeling is accompanied by a sense of pressure, sometimes in the lower back and sometimes inside the abdomen just above the line of the pubic hair. The feelings grow in intensity, particularly after the release of amniotic fluid, but there are "resting" periods of a minute or two between each contraction. The breathing exercises taught in prepared-childbirth classes help a woman to avoid tensing her muscles in opposition to the work of the contractions. Fear and tension may create or heighten the pain of a contraction.

After the cervix has dilated 5 or 6 cm (about 2 in. or 3 "fingers"), the hormone oxytocin is secreted by the pituitary, and the frequency and intensity of the contractions increase considerably. The end of first-stage labor is signaled by a relatively short period of intense and seemingly incessant contractions known as *transition*. The transitional contractions complete the dilation of the cervix to 10 cm (4 in.) so that the baby's head can pass through it.

After the baby's head appears in the vagina, doctors often perform the minor surgical procedure known as an episiotomy—a surgical cut from the bottom of the entrance to the vagina down toward the anus. The supposed purpose of the episiotomy is to decrease the likelihood of vaginal tearing when the baby's head and shoulders pass out of the woman's body. The surgery is performed in more than 60% of U.S. deliveries (Olds et al., 1992). However, except in cases in which a woman is delivering an exceptionally large baby or has an exceptionally small vaginal opening, the episiotomy is unnecessary. Further, there is no reduction in rates of tearing among women given episiotomies compared to those who deliver without the surgery (Thacker & Banta, 1983). Even if some slight tearing does occur, the wound tends to mend quite readily without any postpartum stitching, whereas a surgical cut requires stitches, although they usually dissolve within a few days.

---

**episiotomy** (eh-PEE-zee-AW-tuh-mee)—an incision made from the bottom of the entrance to the vagina down toward the anus to prevent vaginal and anal tissues from injury during childbirth.

**transition**—a short period of intense and very frequent contractions that complete dilation of the cervix to 10 cm.

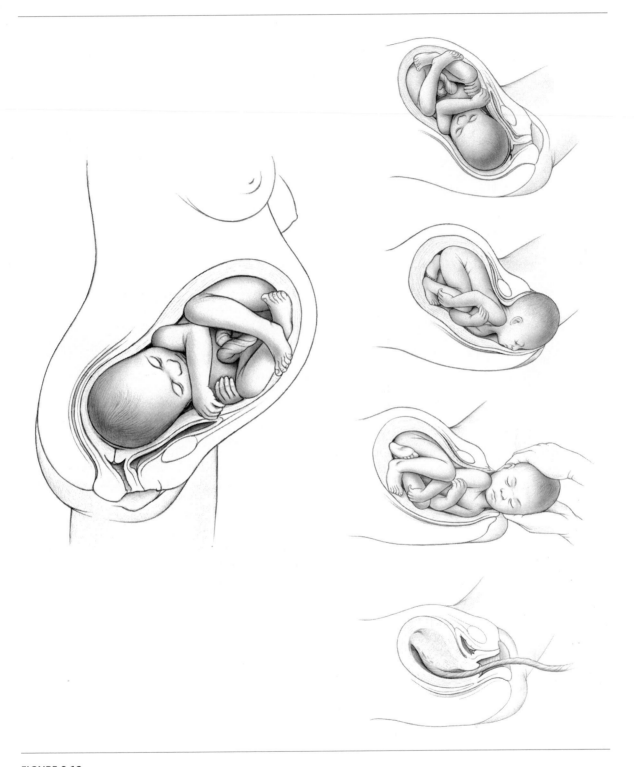

**FIGURE 9.12**
**Movement of the Baby**
Labor contractions help to move the baby from the uterus to the outside world.

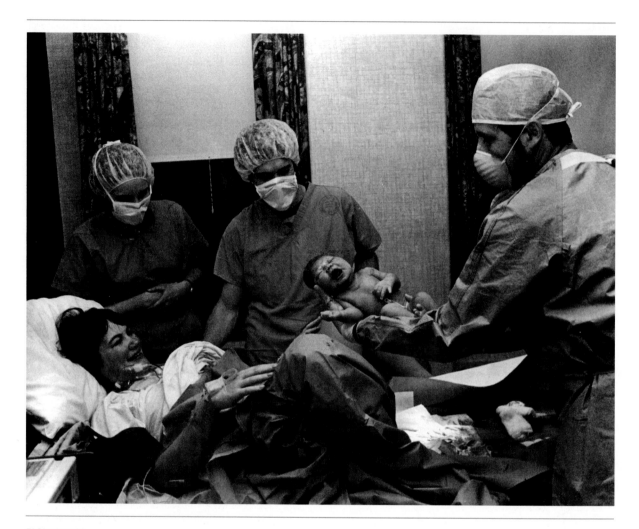

**FIGURE 9.13**
**Birth**
This woman expresses her joy following the birth of her baby.

### Second-Stage Labor

In the second stage of labor, the intense and constant contractions of transition are replaced by an extremely strong urge to "bear down"—that is, to push the baby out—with each contraction. Contractions at this stage are strong but, compared to the contractions of transition, they are not particularly uncomfortable, and they are less frequent. Any discomfort is relieved when the woman does push, but depending on the position of the baby, the woman may need to control the urge to bear down so that the baby's position may be altered by the doctor or midwife to decrease the likelihood of tearing the cervical or vaginal opening. The rapid panting learned in prepared-childbirth classes can be helpful at this time. When the baby is positioned correctly (see Figure 9.12 on page 283), a woman is told that she may bear down at the next contraction.

Within a period of time that varies from a few minutes to more than an hour, the woman succeeds in pushing the baby out (see Figure 9.13). After the baby's head has emerged, a woman may feel a wonderful combination of relief, exhaustion, and exhilaration. Controlling the urge to bear down at this point is considerably easier. When the baby's shoulders have emerged, the rest of the baby's body usually pops out readily. Thus ends second-stage labor.

After a normal birth and a quick inspection of the baby's genitals, the midwife or doctor proclaims "It's a girl!" or "Its a boy!" Depending on the policies of the doctor and hospital and the wishes of the mother, the baby may be given to her immediately to hold and nurse.

When it is clear that the baby is able to rely on its own lungs to obtain oxygen and the umbilical cord has ceased pulsating, the cord is clamped in two places and cut. This procedure is painless for both mother and baby. If the woman has had an episiotomy, the health care provider stitches up the incision.

### Third-Stage Labor and Recovery

After the baby is born, a woman continues to have a few contractions, usually quite mild, that aid her in expelling the placenta, or so-called afterbirth. Third-stage labor ends with the expulsion of the placenta. It is this process that poses the greatest risk for the mother. As the placenta is expelled, the blood vessels formerly attaching the placenta to the uterus generally close off. If they do not, hemorrhage and shock are possible. To avoid this danger, the woman's vital signs are monitored for an hour or so to ensure that blood vessels close properly.

The baby is bathed, and an antibiotic solution is placed in its eyes to minimize the chances of infection. Having abstained from solid food for 10 hours or more, many women are ravenous and are given a meal. New mothers are generally encouraged to get up and walk around, use the bathroom, or go to the windows of the nursery to peer at their babies as soon as they feel comfortable doing so.

Some hospitals and birthing centers provide the option of "rooming in" for the mother. Rooming in means that the baby is housed in a bassinet right next to the mother's bed. This option is particularly convenient for the mother who wishes to breast-feed her baby because she can respond much more quickly to the baby's cry or restlessness than can nursery-room staff.

Within a day or so, if all is well with the mother and baby, they are released from the hospital or birthing center to go home. The lives of couples who are parents for the first time enter a different stage, with a host of new joys and responsibilities.

## Postpartum Events and Decisions

Within hours of their child's birth, the mother and father turn their attention to the innumerable decisions they have considered over the course of the pregnancy. Two of these are the method of feeding and, if the infant is a male, the question of circumcision.

### Feeding

All mammals, including humans, have the capacity to suckle their offspring. Throughout most of our history, human mothers have breast-fed their babies. During the earlier part of the 20th century, the popularity of breast-feeding declined throughout the world in favor of the use of bottled milk, or formula. Breast-feeding was perceived as "lower class," and bottled formula was thought to be antiseptic and scientific.

Just prior to birth, the woman's estrogen and progesterone levels fall. This hormonal decline stimulates the pituitary to secrete prolactin, a hormone that aids in milk production and stimulates the alveoli to secrete milk. The release of oxytocin, another pituitary hormone, is activated by the baby's sucking (Huff & Bucci, 1990). Just as oxytocin stimulates contractions of the smooth muscles of the uterus during birth, it stimulates contractions of the cells that surround the alveoli, and these contractions eject the milk into the ducts so that the baby can easily obtain the milk by sucking. Colostrum provides the newborn with its first liquid food. The colostrum is replaced by milk about 48 hours after birth.

Numerous studies have compared the benefits of bottle- and breast-feeding. Breast-fed babies acquire *passive immunity* from their mothers. Because breast milk contains antibodies from the mother's immune system, breast-fed babies are temporarily immune to a variety of diseases including viruses and respiratory and gastrointestinal infections (Olds et al., 1992).

Breast milk is usually better than cow's milk or commercial formulas for the infant's physical well-being for several other reasons. First, babies can digest human milk more easily than they can other animals' milk or vegetable-based formulas such as those made from soybeans. Second, although human milk contains less protein and iron than cow's milk, human infants can use most of the protein and absorb more iron from their mother's milk than from cow's milk (Campbell, Waller, Andolsek, Huff, & Bucci, 1990). Third, breast-fed babies are less likely to suffer from diarrhea or constipation than are bottle-fed babies. Fourth, breast-fed babies tend to have healthier teeth and are less likely to be obese or to get premature atherosclerosis (formation of fatty deposits on the walls of arteries). Because of these benefits, the American Pediatric Society has concluded that breast milk is superior to bottled formula for infants and recommends breast milk as the optimal food for the first four to six months of life (Olds et al., 1992). For women who cannot or do not wish to breast-feed their babies but who want them to have the nutritional advantages of human milk, milk banks are now operating in many large metropolitan areas.

Breast-feeding is particularly pleasant when the baby gets older and becomes active and playful (see Figure 9.14). The average baby takes in approximately 1,000 calories per day from its mother's breast milk, a circumstance that benefits a woman who gained more weight than she wished during pregnancy. A woman can generally shed pounds steadily without denying herself food if she nurses for six months or so. The oxytocin secretion stimulated by the baby's sucking also stimulates the smooth muscles of the

uterus, providing another major benefit to a nursing mother. The resulting involuntary ''exercise'' of the uterus helps it to return to its normal size more quickly than it would if the woman did not breast-feed. The introduction of solid foods to supplement breast milk should be implemented by the fourth to the sixth month (Campbell et al., 1990).

Some mothers find the sucking of their nipples sexually arousing, and a few experience orgasm during breast-feeding (Reamy & White, 1987). Depending on a woman's sexual attitudes, such arousal can be either extremely disconcerting or an additional pleasure associated with breast-feeding. Some women begin to breast-feed but terminate the process within a few days because of tender nipples and the engorgement of their breasts with milk, characteristics of the early weeks of breast-feeding. The duration and frequency of breast-feeding appear to be related to nipple discomfort. For those women who experience nipple tenderness from breast-feeding, the discomfort is slight to moderate, and it usually peaks at the third day and then decreases rapidly thereafter (de Carvalho, Robertson, & Klaus, 1984). Nipple tenderness can be reduced or eliminated by allowing the breast milk to dry on the nipples. Breast engorgement can be reduced by nursing the baby and by taking a warm shower to release some of the milk.

Just as some drugs and medications taken by a pregnant woman can transfer through the placenta to the fetus, so may they also be received by a baby through breast milk. A nursing mother should check with her health care provider before taking any medications.

## Circumcision

Throughout history, diverse operations have been performed on the sex organs of infants, as well as children and young adults (see Chapter 1). Males have had their foreskins removed (circumcision) and slits made in the entire length of their penises (subincision). Females have had their clitorises, their clitoral hoods, and their labia removed. Some women have had their labia sewn together. These operations have been performed in compliance with religious, ritual, hygienic, or sexual beliefs in various cultures. At

---

**passive immunity**—a kind of immunity to certain diseases or conditions acquired by a baby when it receives its mother's antibodies through her breast milk.

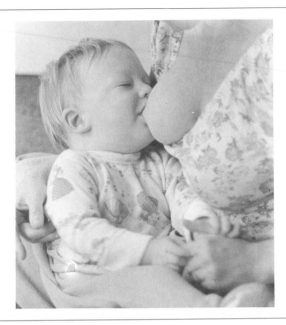

**FIGURE 9.14**
**Breast-Feeding: Food and Fun**
This year-old baby nurses to obtain nutrition, but breast-feeding also provides the baby and mother with an opportunity to cuddle and play. Notice the hand-holding in both photos.

present, these practices remain common only in some parts of the Middle East, Africa, and Australia, as well as in the United States. More than 1 million male babies are circumcised each year in the United States, and circumcision is the most common surgery performed on children (Robson & Leung, 1992).

Many contemporary American parents support circumcision, either because their religion prescribes it, because they mistakenly think that it is legally required, or because they believe that the presence of the foreskin causes cancer later in life. On the latter point, researchers indeed once believed that cancer of the penis and cancer of the cervix in the sexual partners of uncircumcised men were linked to intact foreskins. These beliefs were based on some early, poorly controlled studies that found an association between circumcision and decreased risk of cancer (Wolbarst, 1932). More recent research indicates that circumcision is associated with a reduced risk of penile cancer (Robson & Leung, 1992). Since 1930, about 60,000 men have been diagnosed with this rare form of cancer. Almost all were uncircumcised. The average age of occurrence is 67 years with a median survival time of 7.5 years. Although the incidence of penile cancer is believed to be related to personal hygiene, there are no data to support the idea that good hygiene is as effective as circumcision in reducing the risk of penile cancer. Evidence linking cervical cancer to sexual intercourse with uncircumcised men is inconclusive (Robson & Leung, 1992). A task force of the American Academy of Pediatrics (AAP) reviewed the available data and concluded that the evidence on the risks and benefits of circumcision is contradictory. The AAP task force concluded its report with the following recommendation:

*Newborn circumcision has potential medical benefits and advantages as well as disadvantages and risks. When circumcision is being considered, the benefits and risks should be explained to the parents and informed consent obtained. (Schoen, Anderson, Bohen et al., 1989, p. 390)*

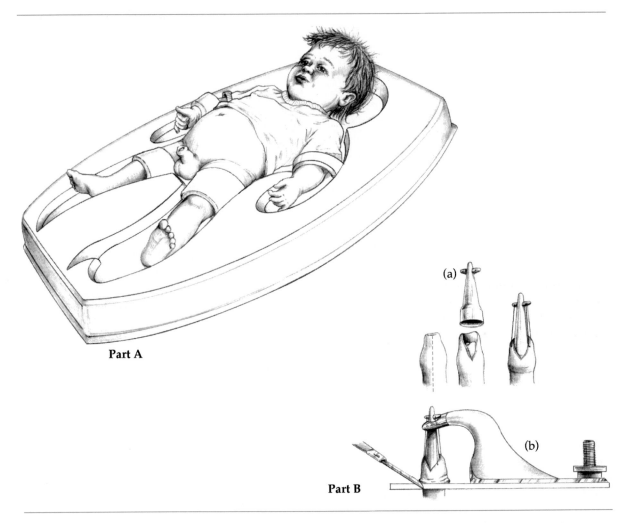

**FIGURE 9.15**
**Male Circumcision**
Part A: this shows the proper positioning of the infant on a circumcision board.
Part B: To circumcise an infant, his foreskin is drawn over the cone (a), and a clamp
is applied (b). Pressure is maintained for three to five minutes, and then the excess
foreskin is cut away.

Another common belief is that circumcision affects sexual arousal. Some have argued that the removal of the foreskin reduces sensitivity because constant contact with clothing toughens the glans. In earlier times, this assumed reduction in sensitivity was considered an advantage in curbing masturbation. More recently, the assumed decrease in sensitivity was believed to delay orgasm in men, thereby enhancing their desirability as sexual partners because women tend to become aroused more slowly than do men. These long-held ideas notwithstanding, the presence or absence of the foreskin is not related to sexual sensitivity, the tendency to masturbate, or the speed of orgasm. As K. E. Paige (1978, p. 45) put it, "Sexual sensitivity appears to be in the mind of a man, not in his foreskin."

Circumcision is usually done with an analgesic and/or anesthesia (Olds et al., 1992). A variety of techniques are used (see Figure 9.15), and the complication rate is about 4%, which translates into more than 50,000 complicated circumcisions each year. Hemorrhage, mutilation, infection, and surgical trauma are the most serious complications (Olds et al., 1992). Further, evidence suggests that for a short time after the operation, circumcised babies not only have increased heart rates and hormone-release patterns but also manifest greater levels of irritability than do uncircumcised babies (Schoen et al., 1989).

A growing number of insurance companies and state Medicare agencies in the United States refuse to cover the cost of circumcision unless it is medically indicated. For example, in rare cases of phimosis (a condition in which the foreskin is so tight that it cannot be retracted from the glans), circumcision is considered medically appropriate. The proportion of newborn U.S. boys who are circumcised has been dropping. In Canada, after an examination of research on the effects of circumcision to determine if the government should continue to pay for the procedure, Cadman, Gafini, and McNamee (1984) concluded that the operation constitutes cosmetic surgery, and thus should be paid for by those parents desiring it for their sons.

## Postpartum Adjustment

Because giving birth involves both physiological and psychological adjustment, the six weeks following childbirth are inherently stressful. First, the new mother experiences a rapid decline in estrogen and progesterone levels. As we will see in Chapter 14, high levels of estrogen during the menstrual cycle are associated with a general sense of well-being, whereas the low levels that precede the onset of menstruation are often accompanied by unwanted premenstrual symptoms. The decrease in estrogen associated with birth might also be expected to be related to such symptoms as fatigue, depressed mood, and edginess.

Second, both parents may get little sleep because most infants awaken frequently at night. The resulting fatigue can be particularly taxing for the mother, who may still be tired from lack of sleep in the final weeks of pregnancy and from the strenuous activity of giving birth. In addition, the deep sleep phase is reduced in women prior to delivery and typically does not return to normal until the second week following birth (Hostetter & Andolsek, 1990).

Third, for first-time parents, the loss of freedom and the number of tasks involved in caring for a helpless infant can be overwhelming. For couples who were accustomed to accepting last-minute invitations to parties or requests to work overtime, the realization that they cannot act as spontaneously as before can lead to a sense of being trapped, even when the pregnancy was planned. The opportunity for uninterrupted conversation or lovemaking may be sharply curtailed for months after the birth, leaving the mother and/or father feeling neglected, jealous, or resentful of the baby. Some new parents suspect that their seemingly helpless infants are considerably more aware of the surrounding environment than is commonly thought. As one young father put it, "That damn kid has ESP. . . . Every time I get his mother alone for a few minutes, he wakes up and starts wailing!"

Although women are generally expected to be elated, even if exhausted, by the arrival of the "blessed event," as many as 50% to 80% of new mothers experience what is known as "postpartum blues" within a few days of delivery (Mattson & Smith, 1993). These blues, which involve spells of crying for no apparent reason, mood swings, irritability, and various other symptoms, may last for a few days to several weeks. Considering the factors described above—changes in hormone levels, loss of sleep, and reduced freedom—it is surprising that postpartum blues are not universal.

When these symptoms continue beyond a few weeks, a woman may be diagnosed as experiencing *postpartum depression*, including

**postpartum depression**—sadness or general letdown experienced by some women following childbirth.

prolonged dysphoria (absence of enjoyment of life), and loss of concentration and self-esteem. Severe and lengthy symptoms of depression affect only about 1 or 2 women per 1,000 births (Olds et al., 1992).

## Postpartum Sexual Expression

Many physicians have routinely banned coitus for six weeks following birth. This ban may be linked more to societal or religious taboos based on beliefs about women's "uncleanliness" during menstruation and the immediate postpartum period than to empirical data indicating medical risks (Reamy & White, 1987). Yet, for the first few weeks after giving birth, coitus may be the furthest thing from a new mother's mind. Tenderness in the vaginal area (particularly after an episiotomy), general fatigue, diminished levels of estrogen, and the vaginal discharge that occurs in the days following birth all may contribute to temporarily diminished sexual desire. Gradually, these symptoms decline. The original discharge is replaced by *lochia*, a discharge consisting of a smaller amount of red or brown blood that may continue for two to four weeks or more following birth. This discharge need not interfere with intercourse, however, if the woman begins to feel the familiar stirrings of desire.

If a woman has not had an episiotomy, or if the episiotomy has healed quickly, there are generally no medical contraindications to resuming coitus within three weeks after birth (Pritchard, MacDonald, & Gant, 1985). For women who experience a lengthier period of discomfort during the healing of an episiotomy, the couple can engage in cuddling, mutual manual stimulation, or masturbation until the woman feels ready for vaginal penetration. For most women, first postpartum coitus occurs between the first and second month following birth, with the fifth week being the most common time for resumption of coitus (Reamy & White, 1987).

It is normal for women to feel apprehensive when resuming coital relations; many fear a renewal of the vaginal discomfort that they experienced during childbirth and recovery. But new mothers have other concerns as well. Worries are common about resumption of coitus because of concerns about birth control, vaginal tenderness, harming internal organs, contracting infections, waking the baby, and decreased vaginal lubrication (Olds et al., 1992).

The issues of effective contraception and waking the baby can be handled readily, with some preplanning. However, if a woman is experiencing perineal tenderness from the birth or from an episiotomy, the couple should postpone coitus until she is more comfortable. A temporary reduction in vaginal lubrication for a short time following childbirth is normal, but water-soluble lubricants can be used until the woman begins to secrete adequate amounts of vaginal lubrication.

Some new mothers also worry about their sexual attractiveness. Stretch marks left over from the pregnancy, extra weight, and loose skin in their abdomens may contribute to their self-doubt. But the stretch marks lose their reddish color and become less noticeable with time, and weight reduction and the firming of abdominal skin and muscles can be accomplished with appropriate diet and exercise. Of additional concern to some women are the shape, size, and tone of the vagina after birth. One of the remarkable features of the vagina, however, is its elasticity. Although it stretches to permit the birth of a baby, the vaginal muscles tighten again fairly soon after birth. The new mother can speed the process by which these muscles regain their tone and strength by doing Kegel exercises (see Chapter 14). Henderson (1983) instructed a group of new mothers to perform these exercises and found that they had greater muscle tone at their first postpartum checkup than did a control group of women.

Although the physical changes following childbirth temporarily require substantial adjustment, psychological and social changes may pose greater challenges for both parents. First-time parents may find that it takes time to learn to integrate their new roles as parents with their former roles as companions and lovers (see Figure 9.16). A candlelit dinner away from home, a walk in the woods—any activity that gives a couple time away from the baby—may help to speed that integration.

**lochia** (LOH-kee-ah)—dark-colored vaginal discharge that follows childbirth for several weeks.

**FIGURE 9.16**
**Parents as Lovers**
New parents may take a while to adjust to their roles and to the demands of caring for their offspring. It is important that they set aside time for themselves as individuals and as friends and lovers.

## Reproductive Problems

Although many couples have no major problems with conception, pregnancy, and birth, some face obstacles with one or more of the processes needed to produce a healthy baby. Infertility problems and their solutions are described in Chapter 14. The remainder of this chapter focuses on threats to fetal life and development and to the expectant mother during pregnancy and birth.

## Threats to Fetal Development

Maternal exposure to environmental factors such as diseases and chemicals can threaten fetal development. These factors generally have their most devastating effect early in pregnancy, when the embryo is undergoing primary development. Almost all developmental birth defects, such as blindness, deafness, and missing limbs, occur within the first trimester of pregnancy. Exposure of either parent to certain substances (for example, marijuana and alcohol) shortly before conception is also associated with embryonic defects (refer back to Table 9.1 on p. 266 for a listing of common threats).

### Use of Drugs

Almost all drugs ingested by a pregnant woman cross the placenta and enter the fetus's bloodstream. In view of what we know about the effects of drugs on embryos, it is a good idea for pregnant women to avoid exposure to any substances that might possibly be *teratogenic* (causing birth defects; literally, "monster-producing"). Showing a causal relationship between a particular drug and a birth defect is difficult. For example, more than 10,000 babies were born with stunted or absent limbs and other deformities before the tranquilizer thalidomide was finally isolated as the cause of the problem. Therefore, a pregnant woman should avoid drugs that are under suspicion until they are conclusively eliminated as the source of any difficulties.

It is essential that a pregnant woman consider dosage levels when deciding whether to ingest drugs; a proper dose for a woman of, say, 125 pounds may be a large overdose for a 1- or 2-pound fetus. The livers of newborn mammals, including humans, do not begin functioning until a week after the infants are born, and full functioning of the liver does not occur for several more months. When the fetus is exposed to drugs taken by the mother, its liver is incapable of breaking them down as efficiently as an adult's liver would.

Heavy alcohol ingestion during pregnancy is the leading environmental cause of mental retardation in infants. Whereas the prevalence of retardation is 1 or 2 per 1,000 births in the general population, 40% of chronically alcoholic women produce an infant with symptoms of *fetal alcohol syndrome (FAS)*. Chronic use is defined as the daily consumption of more than 4 ounces of whiskey or other hard liquor or 32 ounces of beer. Daily consumption of up to 4 ounces of whiskey or 16 ounces of beer is defined as moderate use, and 11% of the offspring of women who drink moderately have fetal alcohol effects (Andolsek, 1990).

Symptoms of FAS in humans include a short upturned nose, small and underdeveloped midface, short eyeslits, and missing or minimal ridges between the nose and the mouth. Mental retardation, poor motor development, and retarded physical growth also occur. There are no reports of pregnant women who drank less than 2 ounces of alcohol a day giving birth to babies with FAS characteristics (Andolsek, 1990). No absolutely safe levels have been established, however, and most health care providers now advise their patients to abstain from alcohol during pregnancy.

### Maternal Infections

Fetal health is seriously jeopardized when the mother is infected with a sexually transmitted disease. Chlamydia is a sexually transmitted bacterial infection (see Chapter 17) that can be passed from mother to fetus during pregnancy or to the baby during vaginal delivery. Although it is readily treated, many women are asymptomatic (without symptoms) and thus do not seek treatment. Women who have chlamydia during the first trimester of pregnancy have a greater incidence of premature births. All pregnant women should be tested and treated for chlamydia rather

---

**teratogenic**—causing birth defects.

**fetal alcohol syndrome (FAS)** —a disorder found in the offspring of problem drinkers (women who drink daily or get drunk during pregnancy). FAS causes a group of specific symptoms, including mental retardation.

than waiting for their babies to get sick with con-junctivitis (which occurs in up to 50% of exposed babies) and pneumonia (which is seen in up to 15% of exposed babies) (Hatcher et al., 1994).

Another major sexually transmitted infection that cannot yet be treated is genital herpes (see Chapter 17). A women infected with an initial case of genital herpes during the first 20 weeks of gestation is more likely to have a spontaneous abortion, a stillbirth, or a fetus born with congenital abnormalities. Recurrent episodes of herpes are less threatening to the fetus unless the woman has an active outbreak at the time of delivery. In that case, a Cesarean section should be performed to protect the baby from potential contact with the virus during a vaginal delivery. Of those babies who do become infected, 25% to 50% die, and the survivors have a 25% to 50% risk of blindness and neurological complications (Olds et al., 1992). Finally, there is an increase in the number of babies being born with human immunodeficiency virus, or HIV, the retrovirus that causes AIDS. Transmission is usually through the placenta, breast-feeding, and/or infusion of contaminated blood (Hatcher et al., 1994).

## Threats to Pregnant Women

In the first trimester, the principal threat to the life of a pregnant woman is ectopic pregnancy. In the third trimester, the greatest dangers are pre-eclampsia (toxemia) and eclampsia. Spontaneous abortion late in pregnancy can also threaten a woman's life.

### Ectopic Pregnancy

In an *ectopic pregnancy*, the fertilized egg implants itself outside the uterus, either in the fallopian tube or on an ovary or other internal organ (see Figure 9.17). In one documented case a

woman gave birth to a healthy baby that developed in her abdomen, but ectopic pregnancies generally result in the death of the embryo and sometimes of the pregnant woman as well. From 1970 to 1989, the rate of ectopic pregnancies increased from 5 to 20 per 1,000 live births (Olds et al., 1992).

In 96% of ectopic pregnancies, the fertilized egg implants itself in the fallopian tube, in what is known as a *tubal pregnancy*. A tubal pregnancy can occur when a woman has scar tissue in her fallopian tubes from untreated gonorrhea, endometriosis, pelvic inflammatory disease, or other infections. A woman with a tubal pregnancy may stop menstruating or may have intercycle bleeding and abdominal pain. Tubal pregnancies are often aborted spontaneously, but when they are not, they may threaten the life of the expectant mother. As the fertilized egg continues to develop, it expands beyond the ability of the tube to hold it, and the tube may rupture about six weeks after conception. If a woman with a ruptured tube does not receive medical treatment for the internal bleeding within 30 minutes, she may die.

When an ectopic pregnancy is diagnosed, a small incision is made near the navel, into which a laparoscope (a long instrument with a light and magnifying glass) is inserted. The physician inspects the abdominal cavity and fallopian tubes for the fertilized egg. If the egg is lodged in the fallopian tube, a second incision is made just above the line of the pubic hair, through which both the egg and the tube are removed.

As long as the other tube is intact, the woman can become pregnant again, although her chances of having another tubal pregnancy are about 25%. This high risk probably results from the fact that whatever caused the blockage or the scar tissue in the removed tube may have also affected the remaining tube. Nonetheless, pregnancy has occurred in women with only one tube and one ovary, even when the tube and ovary were on opposite sides.

**ectopic pregnancy**—a pregnancy that occurs when a fertilized egg implants itself somewhere outside the uterus. In most cases, the site of implantation is a fallopian tube, in which case the condition is known as tubal pregnancy.

**tubal pregnancy**—an ectopic pregnancy in which the embryo is implanted in the woman's fallopian tube.

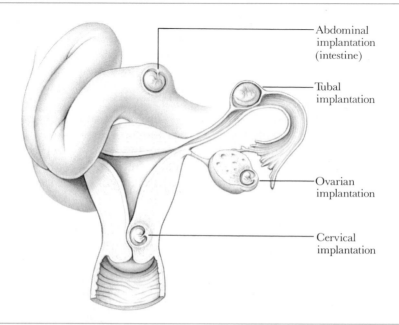

Abdominal
implantation
(intestine)

Tubal
implantation

Ovarian
implantation

Cervical
implantation

**FIGURE 9.17**
**Ectopic Pregnancy**
In most ectopic pregnancies, the fertilized egg implants itself in a fallopian tube,
but cervical, ovarian, and abdominal implantation can also occur.

*Spontaneous Abortion (Miscarriage)*

Spontaneous abortion can occur at any point in pregnancy. The later it occurs, the more dangerous it is for the mother. The specific cause of the abortion is not known in most cases, but it can result from the genetic or chromosomal conditions described in Chapter 4 or from some of the drugs or diseases listed in Table 9.1.

Signs of impending miscarriage include vaginal bleeding, abdominal cramping, and lower backache. Women experiencing these symptoms should contact a health care provider. Sometimes a miscarriage and the expulsion of the fetus can be relatively painless and physically nontraumatic. Still, both the woman and the fetal remains should be examined by a doctor. Tissue left in the uterus can be a source of maternal infection, so if the aborted fetus does not appear to be intact, the physician should check for and remove any remaining fetal tissue to reduce the risk of later infections or difficulties.

*Pre-Eclampsia and Eclampsia*

Up to 10% of American women develop *pre-eclampsia* (also called toxemia) during pregnancy. Symptoms include retention of toxic body wastes, high blood pressure, protein in the urine, swelling, and fluid retention. Pre-eclampsia generally develops in the third trimester. It is more common during first pregnancies than during subsequent pregnancies (Andolsek, 1990). It is also associated with excessive weight gain, which is one of the reasons pregnant women are advised to avoid gaining more than 30 to 35 pounds during pregnancy. The condition may result from an abnormal response to hormone changes

**pre-eclampsia**—a maternal condition that may occur in the last trimester of pregnancy; symptoms include swelling, high blood pressure, and retention of toxic body wastes (hence the more general term *toxemia*).

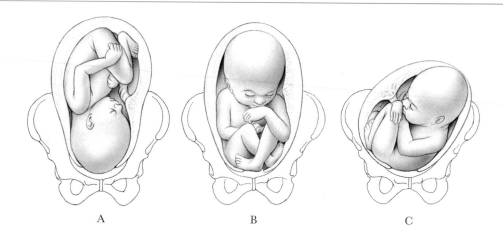

A                    B                    C

**FIGURE 9.18**
**Birth Presentations**
Most babies are born headfirst (left), but a few present their buttocks first, in a breech presentation (center). With transverse presentation (right), an attempt must be made to change the baby's position prior to birth.

during pregnancy, or from an abnormal immune reaction to the fetus.

About 5% of toxemic women suffer from *eclampsia*, a condition that brings on convulsions and coma. The mortality rate for women who develop eclampsia is about 15%. The only real "cure" is the termination of pregnancy, so if the symptoms reach dangerous levels, preterm delivery may be recommended as soon as tests indicate that the fetus is mature enough to have a good chance of surviving. Treatment includes various measures to control the symptoms, including a diet designed to control weight gain, fluid retention, and blood pressure.

## Childbirth Complications

In almost 1% of full-term births, the baby is born dead (stillborn). In addition, a small percentage of babies born alive die during their first year,

sometimes for reasons associated with the birth process.

The advent of electronic methods of monitoring fetal heart rate has made possible the detection of early signs of fetal distress. Comparisons of the use of these highly sensitive electronic monitoring devices with the use of a stethoscope indicate no greater risk of infant mortality or morbidity from the electronic devices (Olds et al., 1992). In the following sections we consider factors that can elevate the risk of infant mortality.

### Birth Position

Birth position is one source of childbirth complications that can endanger the baby's or the mother's life. Most babies spend the first two trimesters of pregnancy upright in the mother's uterus. During the third trimester, the fetus generally reverses its position so that its head is near the cervix and its buttocks and feet are at the top of the uterus. Approximately 90% of babies are born headfirst. This position is the safest and easiest one for birth.

A small number (4%) of babies, however, do not reverse their direction before the onset of labor. Instead, they may present the buttocks first

eclampsia—a severe state of toxemia that can occur in late pregnancy, leading to convulsions and coma in the pregnant woman.

(breech presentation) or a shoulder or side first (transverse presentation) (see Figure 9.18). In many cases, the doctor or midwife is able to alter the position so that the baby emerges headfirst. If attempts at such repositioning are unsuccessful and if the mother is very small or the baby is very large, a Cesarean section may be necessary.

### Cesarean Section (C-Section)

Each year about 25% of U.S. babies are delivered by Cesarean section (C-section) rather than through the vagina (MMWR, 1993). In a C-section, the woman is given general or local anesthesia, and an incision is made through the abdomen and uterus so that the baby can be removed. Because a C-section is a surgical procedure requiring anesthesia, women tend to be more uncomfortable following this kind of delivery than after a vaginal delivery. Typically, women who have a C-section remain hospitalized for 4 or 5 days. They may resume coitus within the usual length of time. Women undergoing a C-section because of problems with the baby's presentation or size, lengthy labor, or other medical emergencies can usually deliver subsequent babies vaginally. But if small pelvic size is the reason for the C-section, then future births may also require this method, unless the subsequent babies are small.

Under some conditions, a C-section is invaluable in saving the lives of both the mother and the baby. The risk of infant mortality and postpartum infection is four times higher for C-section (Marieskind, 1989), however, than it is for vaginal delivery (1 to 2 deaths per 1,000 C-sections compared to .06 deaths per 1,000 vaginal births). Critics have expressed concern that some physicians may be performing the procedure for their own convenience, for profit, or to avoid malpractice suits rather than as a response to genuine medical emergencies that occur during birth (Marieskind, 1989). From 1965 to 1987, the number of Cesarean sections shot up 442%. Marieskind suggested that one reason for the spurt is the rise in the average age of pregnant women, which doctors may perceive as creating greater risk. The belief on a doctor's part that the use of C-sections reduces the likelihood of malpractice suits may also contribute to increased reliance on the procedure. In fact, however, the malpractice suit is brought typically as a result of *doing* rather than *not* doing a C-section (Marieskind, 1989).

### Multiple Births

Twins are born once in every 90 pregnancies, and triplets occur once in about 8,100 pregnancies. Multiple conceptions result from the splitting of a single fertilized egg (identical twins) or from the fertilization of two or more eggs released during the ovulatory cycle (fraternal twins).

The splitting of a zygote produces monozygotic twins, triplets, quadruplets, and so forth. Monozygotic twins, accounting for about one-third of all twins, carry the same genetic information and thus are sometimes called identical twins (Moore, 1989). Dizygotic twins are the result of the release of several eggs in a single month, each of which is fertilized by a separate sperm. The release of multiple eggs may occur naturally or may be stimulated by the administration of fertility treatments (see Chapter 14). In addition, a woman may be simultaneously pregnant with both monozygotic twins and a dizygotic sibling, resulting in triplets (Moore, 1989).

Multiple births usually occur after a shorter gestation period and the infants typically weigh significantly less than single-birth children. These two factors result in a mortality rate for twins that is two to three times higher than that for children born one at a time, and the mortality rate increases with each additional baby in a multiple birth. Multiple-birth babies also tend to lag behind in motor and intellectual development for a year or two, after which they catch up to their peers (Krall et al., 1980).

### Variations in Length of Gestation

The chances of a baby surviving birth and infancy are reduced by premature birth, low birth weight, and delayed birth.

---

**breech presentation**—a birth position in which the baby's buttocks appear first.

**transverse presentation**—a birth position in which the baby's side appears first.

*Prematurity*

Babies are considered premature when they are born before they are due—that is, sooner than 266 days after conception—and when they weigh less than $5\frac{1}{2}$ pounds. In general, a baby has less than a 50% chance of survival if it is born before the end of the seventh month. Only a minority of infants delivered at 22-25 weeks of gestation survive for 6 months, and most of these infants have severe cranial abnormalities (Allen, Donohue, & Dusman, 1993). In their study of 14,000 pregnant women, Read and Klebanoff (1993) found that more than 11% of the mothers delivered their babies prematurely.

Factors associated with premature birth include complications during pregnancy, the ingestion of drugs, maternal malnutrition, inadequate prenatal care, multiple pregnancies, emotional disturbances, and some infectious and noninfectious illnesses. Women having a first baby after age 40 and those having a series of babies during adolescence are more likely to have premature babies than are women giving birth during their 20s and 30s. Premature birth is also more common with first babies than with subsequent babies.

Babies born from about the 28th to the 34th week tend to have less fat, more wrinkles, and proportionately larger heads than do full-term babies. Depending on how early they are born, they may need a number of interventions to survive. These include an incubator to help control body temperature and exposure to infection, intravenous feeding if their sucking and swallowing skills are inadequately developed, and a respirator to help them breathe (see Figure 9.19). Premature babies tend to develop somewhat slowly at first, but if they are given adequate treatment, they generally show normal physical development by the time they are three years old.

*Low Birth Weight*

A baby weighing less than 5 or $5\frac{1}{2}$ pounds at full term has different and potentially more serious problems than a low-birth-weight baby born early. When birth to a small woman is the cause of low birth weight, the infant is unlikely to be intellectually or physically impaired; however,

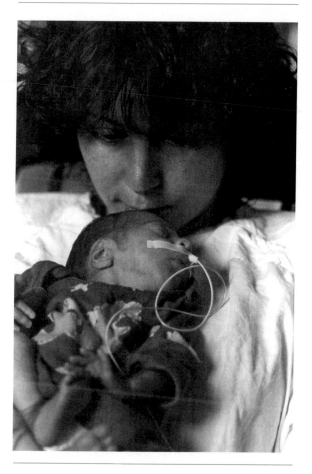

**FIGURE 9.19**
**Mother and Premature Baby**
This first-time mother holds her premature baby, who has just come from the neonatal intensive-care unit. Even an infant this small will respond to parental care.

other causes of low birth weight are likely to be associated with significant difficulties.

Causes of low birth weight in full-term babies include problems within the baby (congenital abnormalities or genetic diseases) and problems within the mother (disease or malnutrition). An inadequate diet during pregnancy is particularly dangerous for the developing fetus. In addition to lower birth weights, malnutrition is associated with increased mortality and permanent retardation, both intellectual and behavioral (Mattson & Smith, 1993).

*Delayed Birth*

About 12% of babies are born two weeks after they were expected, and 4% are born at least three weeks late. Late babies have a mortality rate three times that of babies born when expected. Causes of death include cerebral hemorrhage and suffocation. Although some late babies are heavier than average, others may be underweight because the placenta stopped functioning after the due date.

When the symptoms of labor have not appeared several weeks after the due date or when medical problems indicate that birth should be accomplished as quickly as possible, a woman may be given synthetic oxytocin in the form of the drug pitocin to speed the labor. Oxytocin is the hormone associated with the intense contractions of transition. Labor-inducing drugs should be used only when the risks of prolonged labor outweigh the risks of administering the drug. A somewhat safer method that sometimes hastens labor is to use an instrument to rupture the amniotic sac.

Reading about potential difficulties that can occur during pregnancy and childbirth can be alarming, particularly for the couple expecting their first child. With effective prenatal care and a nutritionally balanced maternal diet, however, most couples have little need to worry about their expected baby. About 94% of U.S. babies are born healthy and normal (Olds et al., 1992).

Such healthy births are more likely for couples who carefully plan the timing of their pregnancies through the use of contraceptives. Couples who use birth control except when they wish to conceive can postpone pregnancy and birth until they are emotionally, financially, and physically ready to take on the responsibilities of parenthood. In the next chapter we describe the benefits and risks of contemporary contraceptive methods.

## Summary of Major Points _____

1. **Conception and gender selection.**

   Conception occurs most readily in the man-above, woman-below coital position, with deep penetration. Various procedures can be used to increase the likelihood of conceiving a girl or a boy. Although earlier studies indicated that such gender-selection measures might create unbalanced gender ratios in favor of males, recent research shows that the preference for male over female babies has decreased.

2. **Symptoms of pregnancy.**

   A missed menstrual period is generally, but not always, the first indication that a woman is pregnant. Most lab tests for pregnancy are based on the detection of the hormone HCG in a blood or urine sample. Reliable test results can be obtained as early as a week after conception. Home pregnancy-test kits administered as early as the first day of the expected menstrual period are also highly reliable when done correctly. Although these home tests may be a convenient preliminary indicator of pregnancy, they should not be used as a substitute for a lab test, because conditions other than pregnancy can affect test results.

3. **The experience of pregnancy.**

   Although each pregnancy is unique, women commonly experience some fatigue and occasional nausea during the first trimester and lose some interest in sexual interaction. Many women feel ambivalent and vulnerable during the early stages of pregnancy. In contrast, during the second trimester, most women feel very healthy and energetic, and many describe this period as a time of enhanced sexual interest and pleasure. During the third trimester, pregnant women tend to feel increasingly bulky as the fetus gains in weight and size, and fatigue and discomfort are common. For healthy women who desire it, sexual interaction appears to have no negative effects on the fetus during the third trimester. Fathers also experience pregnancy in stages, with responses ranging from ambivalence to a heightened sense of responsibility.

4. **The onset of labor.**

   Various events signal the onset of labor, including uterine contractions and release of the cervical mucus plug and amniotic fluid. The extent of "prepping" a woman undergoes depends on the policies of the physician or midwife and the hospital or birthing center.

5. **The process of labor.**

   During first-stage labor, increasingly frequent and intense contractions efface and dilate the cervix to widen it for the baby's passage. The most frequent and intense contractions occur during transition at the end of first-stage labor. During second-stage labor, a woman bears down at the height of the birth contractions to help push the baby out of the uterus and vagina. During third-stage labor, the placenta and the umbilical cord are delivered.

6. **Postpartum parental decisions.**

   One issue that must be decided shortly after the birth of a baby is whether to breast-feed. Breast milk is nutritionally superior to bottled milk or formula. Another decision that new parents must make is whether to circumcise a baby boy. The practice of removing the fore-skins of infant boys (circumcision) is currently the source of considerable controversy.

**7. Postpartum adjustment.**

New parents, and particularly new mothers, normally experience fatigue and bouts of depression from a combination of abrupt hormonal changes, loss of sleep, and loss of freedom brought on by the responsibility of caring for a helpless new human. Not all new parents experience these problems, however, and those who do can reduce the severity of their reactions considerably by reserving some time for their own needs as individuals and as a couple. Although emotional intimacy can be maintained throughout childbirth and the postpartum period, sexual intercourse is generally not resumed for three to six weeks following birth. For new parents, the weeks following the birth of a first baby are devoted to adding the new role of coparents to their former roles as lovers and spouses, and this process has both its stresses and its joys.

**8. Pregnancy problems.**

Although a pregnant woman can avoid many problems through effective prenatal care, certain inherited and environmental conditions can disrupt fetal development and/or maternal health. Environmental threats such as maternal abuse of alcohol, nicotine, and various other substances are related to spontaneous abortions, birth defects, stillbirths, and physical or mental disorders. The first trimester is the period of highest risk for the fetus because major organs and systems are developing. In contrast, the last trimester poses the greatest risk for the mother from such threats as pre-eclampsia (toxemia) and eclampsia.

**9. Variations in labor and birth.**

Although a headfirst presentation is most common, babies vary in their birth positions, with some presenting their buttocks or sides first. If the baby does not present its head first during labor, a Cesarean section (C-section) is sometimes necessary to avoid prolonged labor and risk to the baby. C-sections are also performed when the baby is too large or when the mother's pelvis is too small for the baby. C-sections and labor-inducing drugs are very beneficial when needed.

**10. Childbirth problems.**

Although the risks associated with premature and delayed delivery have been greatly reduced thanks to recent medical advances, both premature and delayed delivery are associated with an above-average risk of physical and mental damage to the infant. Problems with delivery, as well as low birth weight, whether from premature delivery or from other factors, may require a longer hospital stay for the infant.

## Review of Key Concepts

1. Conception is most likely when coitus occurs: a) within a day or two of ovulation; b) just before menstruation; c) just after menstruation; d) a week after ovulation. (p. 264)

2. Recent research has substantiated the long-accepted observation that pregnancy and birth can aid a couple in restoring harmony to a troubled marriage. True or false? (p. 268)

3. The cause of the nausea ("morning sickness") associated with pregnancy in some women is still not known. True or false? (p. 269)

4. In North America, sexual intercourse during the last trimester of pregnancy is: a) often less frequent than in the earlier trimesters; b) often more frequent than in the earlier trimesters; c) forbidden by medical authorities; d) generally recommended in order to increase the couple's sense of intimacy. (pp. 274–275)

5. The first, second, and third stages of labor correspond to: a) the gradual opening of the cervix, birth, and the expulsion of the placenta; b) initial sensation of contractions, the gradual intensification and increasing frequency of contractions, and the culmination of contractions just before birth; c) the opening of the cervix, the onset of contractions, and birth; d) the onset of contractions, the opening of the cervix, and birth. (pp. 268–273)

6. Ectopic pregnancies: a) generally involve the implantation of the fertilized egg in a fallopian tube rather than the uterus; b) can pose a serious risk to the mother's life as well as to the fetus; c) often result in spontaneous abortions; d) all of the above. (p. 293)

7. In general, a baby has less than a 50% chance of survival if it is born before the end of the: a) fifth month; b) sixth month; c) seventh month; d) eighth month. (p. 293)

8. During the past two decades, there has been a heightened emphasis on prospective parents' involvement in an impending birth through childbirth classes, the father's presence in the delivery room, and the like. Comment on the consequences of this development for a couple's emotional and sexual relationship.

9. Discuss the reasons for and the impact of difficulties in postpartum psychological and sexual adjustment for both parents.

10. Assess the environmental risks to the fetus, including maternal infections and the mother's use of alcohol and other drugs.

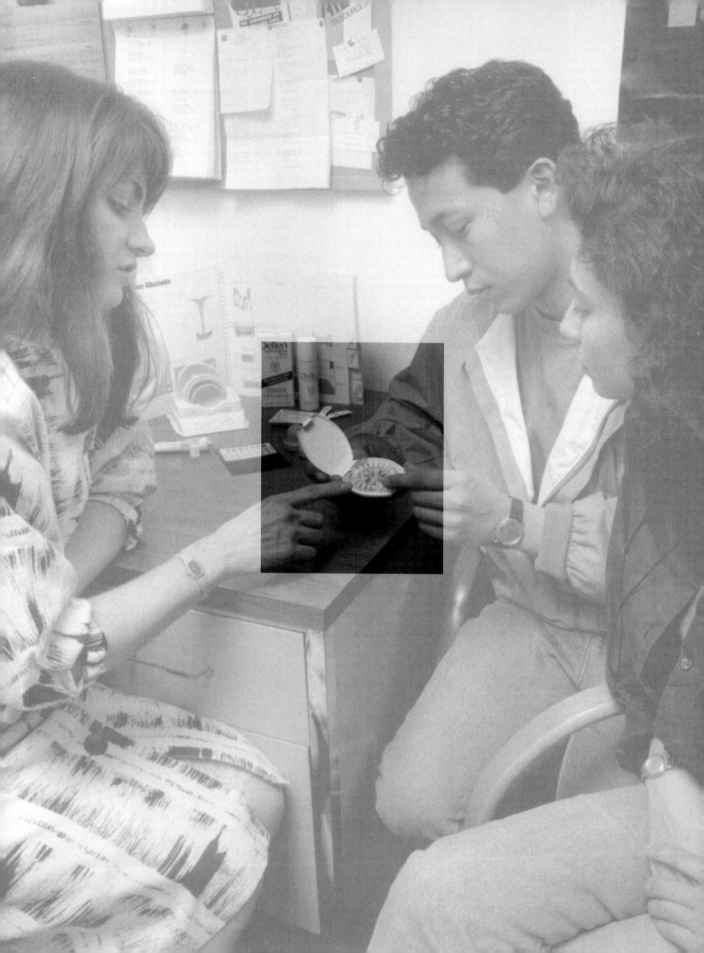

# $\mathcal{C}$ontraception

*$\mathcal{W}$HAT do people do if they don't
want to start a baby?
If you don't want to start one, you don't
get married. There's no other way.
(Goldman & Goldman, 1982, p. 275)*

This was the conclusion of one seven-year-old American girl who participated in the Goldmans' research on children's sexual knowledge. The majority of the children in the Goldman's study, however, became aware by about age nine that couples can take other steps to avoid conception during intercourse.

In this chapter we describe *contraceptives* and the major political and social factors that influenced their development and legal acceptance. We also examine some of the reasons why people engage in unprotected intercourse. The vast majority of married couples use reliable contraceptives to prevent or space pregnancies, but many unmarried teenagers do not use any form of *birth control* when they first become sexually active. Finally, we consider the advantages and disadvantages of each of the temporary and permanent methods of contraception currently available, along with some that are now being developed.

**contraceptive**—any technique, drug, or device that prevents conception.
**birth control**—the regulation of conception, pregnancy, or birth by preventive devices or methods.

## The Development and Use of Modern Contraceptives

Despite the age-old belief that *the* purpose of sexual interaction is to reproduce, people have attempted to practice birth control for thousands of years (see Chapter 1). In Europe, large segments of the population began to use birth control in the latter part of the 18th century. They employed such methods as withdrawal, absorbents placed in the vagina, postcoital douching, abortion, and even infanticide (the killing of newborns). With the obvious exception of the last two, these methods were not highly reliable, but they did lower the birthrate. During the 19th century, the widespread desire for more effective methods of birth control resulted in the development of the forerunners of modern diaphragms, spermicidal agents, cervical caps, condoms, and methods of female sterilization. The early 20th century witnessed the development of the IUD, modern methods of male sterilization, and new techniques for abortion. The latest of the widely available methods of birth control—oral contraception, or "the pill"—was first marketed in 1960. These advances have occurred in spite of numerous controversies surrounding the morality, marketing, and medical risks and benefits of contraceptives.

### Political and Social Issues

Control of the growth of the earth's population is one of the most fundamental problems facing our species. The world's population now surpasses 5 billion, and it is expected to reach 6 billion by the time we reach the year 2000 and possibly climb to 70 billion by the year 2150 if current sexual practices do not change (Haub, 1992). In the *minute* that it takes you to read this paragraph, more than 175 babies will have been added to our population! Many are unplanned or unwanted, and our planet's air, land, and water resources are being overwhelmed by population growth.

The notion that individuals should have the right to control the number of children they produce, independent of the frequency of their sexual intimacy, continues to be a source of

**FIGURE 10.1**
**Margaret Sanger**
Margaret Sanger (1883–1966) was a pioneer in the birth control movement.

controversy. When the reproductive-rights pioneer Margaret Sanger (see Figure 10.1) devoted much of her life to facilitating the development and distribution of reliable methods of birth control, she did so as a staunch advocate of women's right to control their own reproductive capacity. In her career as a nurse, Margaret Sanger, who was one of 11 children, personally saw the problems associated with uncontrolled fertility, illegal abortions, and unwanted children. After her husband's death, she used her personal and financial resources to provide support for research on female contraceptives. She founded The National Birth Control League in the United States in 1914, published the magazines *Birth Control Review* and *Woman Rebel*, and opened a birth control clinic in Brooklyn that police closed after a mere two weeks. Despite jail sentences and a 2-year exile from the United States to escape a 45-year prison term (later overturned), she continued to support the birth control movement, providing financial backing for various scientists, including the so-called father of the pill, Gregory Pincus (Reed, 1983).

In 1965, the U.S. Supreme Court overturned state laws prohibiting the dissemination of contraceptive information and devices. Such laws were judged to be unconstitutional because they interfered with a couple's right to privacy. With the marketing of the pill and the IUD in the 1960s and the Supreme Court's removal in 1973 of any legal barriers to a woman's decision to obtain an abortion during the first three months of pregnancy, Margaret Sanger's goals were realized.

These achievements made an important contribution to the reproductive freedom of women. Women, however, continue to bear the major burden of contraception. Although the only contraceptive for men—the condom—does not have side effects, all recently developed contraceptive methods are for women, and the most effective of them—the pill, the IUD, and Norplant—have negative side effects for some women. The fact that some women want contraceptive control over their bodies during certain periods of their fertile years does not mean that all women want total responsibility for contraception throughout their entire reproductive life span.

Research is in progress on several male contraceptives (described later in this chapter), but the financial and scientific investment in developing female methods has been far greater, probably because women are fertile for only a few days a month; men are always fertile, so an effective male contraceptive would have to inhibit sperm production continuously. Also, because women rather than men become pregnant, it is assumed that women are more motivated than men to use contraception.

Another major contraception-related controversy centers on the marketing and advertising of contraceptives. Although North Americans are exposed to thousands of sexual scenes on television each year, in daytime soap operas and prime-time programming alike, the major television networks have banned advertisements for contraceptives. This ban obviously has not been applied to vaginal douches, hemorrhoid medication, and the like, but it has prevented the promotion of contraceptives on the major television networks. In 1994, the ban on one contraceptive, the condom, was limited when the U.S. government sponsored a relatively explicit advertising campaign for television and radio media aimed at young Americans. The message: Use condoms or abstain from sex; above all, protect yourself from AIDS. The use of condoms for contraceptive protection was not mentioned.

## Technological and Medical Issues

One of the most important considerations in the selection of a birth control method is its effectiveness. The term *effective* was used several times in the previous section; let us now consider what it means and how we measure effectiveness.

We often think of a word such as *effective* in an absolute sense: either something works or it does not. In the realm of birth control, such certainty is impossible. On rare occasions, babies have even been born following attempted abortions or sterilizations. Birth control methods are therefore evaluated in terms of their probability of failure. This probability is calculated by determining the number of sexually active women out of 100 who become pregnant in the course of a year while relying on a particular method. For instance, the failure rate for the diaphragm indicates that out of 100 women, from 2 to 18 become pregnant each year, despite use of the diaphragm and spermicide (see Table 10.1).

Contraceptive effectiveness is measured in terms of both the theoretical and the actual failure rate. The *theoretical failure rate* is the number of failures that occur when the method is used correctly. In those cases conception results from the failure of the method itself: the pill fails to inhibit ovulation for some reason, the condom breaks, the foam or suppository does not keep all sperm from entering the cervix, or the diaphragm shifts during vigorous intercourse.

The *actual failure rate* is the total number of pregnancies that occur as a result of either failure of the method or failure to use a method correctly. This category would include, for example, a pregnancy experienced by a couple who generally rely on the diaphragm with spermicide for

**theoretical failure rate**—the failure rate of a contraceptive method when it is used correctly.

**actual failure rate**—the failure rate of a contraceptive method that takes into account both failure of the method and human failure to use it correctly.

### TABLE 10.1 Yearly Failure Rates of Birth Control Methods

| Method | Lowest Expected or Observed Failure Rate[a] | Failure Rate Among Typical Users[b] |
|---|---|---|
| Tubal ligation | 0.4 | 0.4 |
| Vasectomy | 0.10 | 0.15 |
| Injectable progestin (Depo-Provera) | 0.3 | 0.30 |
| Combined birth control pills | 0.1 | |
| Progestin-only pill | 0.5 | |
| Norplant (6 capsules) | 0.09 | 0.09 |
| IUD | 1.5 | 2.0 |
| Condom | 3.0 | 12.0 |
| Diaphragm | 6.0 | 18.0 |
| Contraceptive sponge | 9.0 | 36.0 |
| Cervical cap | 9.0 | 36.0 |
| Foam, creams, jellies, and vaginal suppositories | 6.0 | 21.0 |
| Withdrawal | 4.0 | 19.0 |
| Sympto-thermal | 2.0 | |
| Chance (no method of birth control) | 85.0 | 85.0 |

[a]Designed to complete the sentence: "Of 100 women who start out the year using a given method, and who use it correctly and consistently, the lowest observed failure rate has been . . ."

[b]Designed to complete the sentence: "Of 100 typical users who start out the year employing a given method, the number who will be pregnant by the end of the year will be . . . "

Sources: Hatcher et al. (1994); Klitsch (1988); Trussell, Strickler, & Vaughn (1993).

contraception but who had unprotected coitus (that is, coitus without contraceptive protection) because the woman thought she was not fertile or the man planned to withdraw before ejaculation. In such a case, the cause of conception is failure to employ the method consistently. The actual failure rate varies widely from one study to the next because the number of pregnancies observed may vary for reasons unrelated to the method being tested. For example, women who do not want any more children tend to have a smaller actual failure rate than women who want to postpone their next pregnancy (Grady, Hayward, & Yagi, 1986).

In choosing a birth control method, consider both the advantages and the disadvantages. The advantages include relative effectiveness and convenience. Possible disadvantages include health risks, other undesirable side effects, or the potential need to interrupt lovemaking (for example, to use the condom or diaphragm). Unfortunately, some people, particularly adolescents, avoid obtaining contraceptives because of the highly publicized risks associated with some of them, such as the pill. Yet more women die each year from a variety of other life risks including complications of pregnancy and childbirth—the likely consequences of unprotected intercourse—than from the side effects of any method of birth control (see Table 10.2).* Further, among the half-million females under the age of 15 who engage

---

*The one exception is women over 40 who take the pill. For this group, the mortality rate from use of the pill is higher than that associated with pregnancy and childbirth complications.

| TABLE 10.2 Risks Associated with Life and Fertility | |
| --- | --- |
| **Risk** | **Chance of Death in a Year (U.S.)** |
| Smoking | 1 in 200 |
| Motorcycling | 1 in 1,000 |
| Automobile driving | 1 in 6,000 |
| Power boating | 1 in 6,000 |
| Rock climbing | 1 in 7,500 |
| Playing football | 1 in 25,000 |
| Canoeing | 1 in 100,000 |
| *Preventing pregnancy:* | |
| Oral contraceptive, nonsmoker | 1 in 63,000 |
| Oral contraceptive, smoker | 1 in 16,000 |
| IUD | 1 in 100,000 |
| Barrier methods | None |
| Natural methods | None |
| *Undergoing sterilization:* | |
| Laparoscopic tubal ligation | 1 in 67,000 |
| Hysterectomy | 1 in 1,600 |
| Vasectomy | 1 in 300,000 |
| *Deciding about pregnancy:* | |
| Continuing pregnancy | 1 in 11,000 |
| Terminating pregnancy | |
|   Illegal abortion | 1 in 3,000 |
|   Legal abortion | |
|     Before 9 weeks | 1 in 260,000 |
|     9–12 weeks | 1 in 100,000 |
|     13–15 weeks | 1 in 34,000 |
|     After 15 weeks | 1 in 10,200 |

Source: Adapted from Hatcher et al. *Contraceptive Technology*. New York: Irvington Publishers, 1994.

in intercourse, the mortality rate for conception, pregnancy, and childbirth is higher than it is for women as a whole.

## Adolescents and Contraceptive Use

As the number of adolescent pregnancies climbed during the last quarter century, researchers strove to find out why sexually active teenagers were not using contraceptives. The follow-ing statistics give some idea of the magnitude of the problem.

1. The majority of Americans become sexually active before age 20 (see Figure 10.2). The data below give the percentages of American females who have engaged in premarital intercourse by the time they have reached each of the following birthdays (Dawson, 1986; Hatcher et al., 1994):

**FIGURE 10.2**

**Sexual Intimacy Among Adolescents**

Before the time of their senior proms, the majority of American teenagers have already engaged in sexual intercourse. Unfortunately, most do so without using contraception, and thus more than 1 million unintended teenage pregnancies occur each year.

14th birthday: 5%
15th birthday: 12%
16th birthday: 23%
17th birthday: 38%
18th birthday: 53%
19th birthday: 64%
20th birthday: 71%

2. Of those teenagers who began premarital sex at age 16 or younger, fewer than half had received sexual and contraceptive education in school, and only 35% of those who became sexually active by age 18 had received course instruction on where to obtain contraceptives (Marsiglio & Mott, 1986). Thus it should not be particularly surprising that the majority of adolescents do not use effective contraceptives for quite some time after they become sexually active, or that nearly one-third of sexually active adolescent females have at least one premarital pregnancy (Dawson, 1986).

3. More than 1 million teenagers become pregnant each year; the majority of these pregnancies are unplanned (see Figure 10.3). Just under half a million teenage girls obtain abortions each year, a little less than the number who give birth (Henshaw, 1993; Henshaw & Van Vort, 1989).

4. More than half a million girls age 14 and under are sexually active, and about 30,000 of these

**FIGURE 10.3**

**Unplanned Adolescent Pregnancy**

Of the more than 1 million U.S. teenagers who become pregnant annually, about half maintain the pregnancy and give birth. These young women, often unmarried mothers, generally lack the financial, social, and emotional support they need.

**Box 10.1**

## The Relationship Between the Provision of Sex and Contraceptive Education and Unwanted Pregnancies in Western Nations

The quality of sex and contraceptive education and the timing of its provision vary dramatically among Western nations. Elise Jones and her colleagues (1986, 1988) examined teenage pregnancy rates in 37 developed countries to isolate variables that might explain why teenage pregnancy rates are so much higher in the United States than in other Western nations (see the accompanying figure). Despite the soaring U.S. teen pregnancy statistics, the authors not only found the United States far less open about sex than most of the other countries, but also described the United States as having "an ambivalent, sometimes puritanical attitude about sex" (Jones et al., 1986, p. 230).

To measure the degree of openness about sex in the nations they were studying, Jones et al. developed an index that included condom ads on television, in other media, and on billboards; complete female nudity in mass circulation media; sale of sexually explicit literature in large cities; proportion of public beaches at which full nudity is common; government policy favoring contraceptive education in secondary schools; age at which students receive contraceptive instruction in schools; and minimum legal age for consensual intercourse for girls. They also measured the extent to which countries required parental consent or notification for single women under age 18 to get contraceptives.

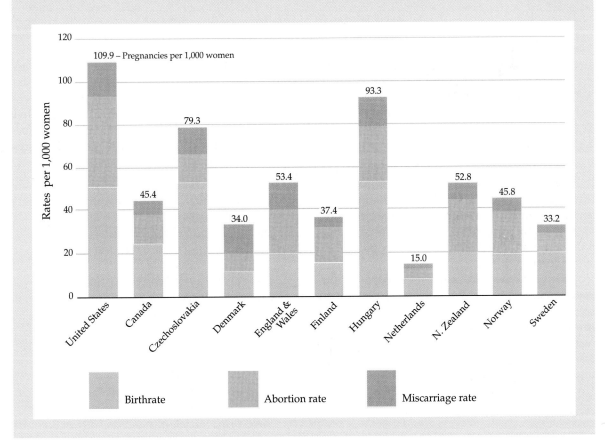

Sweden received the highest rating (16 on a scale that ranged from 1 to 16) regarding openness about sex. If opponents of sex and contraceptive education in the United States are correct in asserting that such education encourages early sexual experimentation and underlies the high levels of unwanted teen pregnancy, then Sweden should have the highest rates of adolescent pregnancy and birth—certainly much higher than that of the United States, which received a 7 on the openness index. In fact, the reverse was true; that is, Swedish teenage birthrates were 11 per 1,000 women compared to 52 per 1,000 in the United States. This discrepancy in birthrates cannot be attributed to a higher abortion rate in Sweden: the rate of abortion per 1,000 women was 18 for Sweden versus 42 per 1,000 for the United States. Moreover, these findings were not peculiar to Sweden but also characterized other European countries with high sexual openness scores, such as Denmark (rating of 14).

Nor do these discrepancies appear to stem from differences in the ages at which Swedish and American women begin to have sexual intercourse. For example, by age 16, 31% of U.S. versus 34% of Swedish women report having had coitus. It is more reasonable to assume that the differential teenage abortion rates and birthrates derive from differences in the two cultures' approaches to sex and contraceptive education. Since 1956, Sweden has mandated such education in the schools for pupils ranging in age from 7 to 19. Further, Swedish birth control clinics operate in close association with the school system, and visiting the birth control clinic is an accepted reason for absence of Swedish adolescents from the classroom.

---

girls become pregnant each year. Thus many girls face the staggering decision of whether to give birth while they are still children themselves. About 10,000 of these girls do give birth, and 17,000 of them obtain abortions. The remaining pregnancies end in miscarriages (Henshaw, 1993; Henshaw & Van Vort, 1989).

What is preventing sexually active adolescents from using reliable contraception, and how can contraceptive use be encouraged among individuals who do not want to conceive? In trying to answer this question, researchers have analyzed the conditions under which people use or avoid contraceptives.

There are four necessary conditions for the use of contraceptives: existence of reliable contraceptives, contraceptive education, easy access to contraceptives, and motivation to employ contraception. In the case of most U.S. teenagers, only one of these conditions—the existence of reliable contraceptives—has been met.

*Contraceptive Education*

Although reliable methods of birth control have been available during the entire lifetime of to-day's adolescents, the lack of contraceptive education remains a major hindrance to contraceptive use. The probable effects of neglecting or providing such education are shown in the cross-national comparison in Box 10.1. About two decades ago, Furstenberg (1976, p. 223) attributed the lack of contraceptive education to a preference in the United States for cure rather than prevention, and to institutional sluggishness:

*The general approach to social problems in American society is reactive rather than preventive. This posture might be understandable if preventive strategies were difficult to devise, but this excuse hardly seems to apply in the case of adolescent parenthood. We possess both the know-how and the techniques to reduce the incidence of early pregnancy and limit the number of adolescent mothers. Family planning programs and abortion counseling, while imperfect strategies, can be effective preventive measures. . . . Despite the fact that a clear majority of Americans favor birth control services for the sexually active teenager and endorse sex education in the schools, some institutional resistance and a great deal of institutional inertia have blocked the development of widespread and intensive sex education and family planning service pro-grams for teenagers. Few populations are as potentially accessible to these services as are school age youth. Yet school systems have been avoided, bypassed, and ignored as sites for pregnancy prevention programs.*

When sex-education courses are offered in the public schools, fewer than 3% of parents refuse to let their children participate, and Gallup polls indicate widespread support among both teachers and the general public for such courses (Marsiglio & Mott, 1986). Although most school districts in large U.S. cities provide information about sex-related topics, either as a separate course or as part of another subject, the quality and comprehensiveness of sex education programs vary widely (Muraskin, 1986) (see Figure 10.4).

Several popular beliefs may account for the reluctance of some authorities, among them school board members and state legislators, to require or at least encourage contraceptive education in the public schools. Many people, for example, believe that if adolescents have accurate information regarding contraception, they will pursue sexual activity. Just how accurate is the belief that contraceptive education encourages premarital and promiscuous sexual expression?

Evidence discussed later in this chapter clearly shows that the proportion of adolescents engaging in premarital sex has risen over the past few decades. The idea that this spurt was caused by the availability of contraceptives rests on the assumption that fear of pregnancy formerly inhibited young people from engaging in nonmarital sex. If this were the case, adolescents today who could not obtain contraceptives would avoid intercourse; only those who had protected themselves from pregnancy with a reliable contraceptive would have intercourse. The soaring teenage pregnancy rates tell us that conditions are, in fact, otherwise.

Statistics on schools that provide sex education and also set up on-site contraceptive clinics suggest that this two-pronged approach may both encourage a delay in first intercourse to later years and reduce the premarital pregnancy rate. For example, an extensive research program was carried out for three years at two junior-high and two senior-high schools in Baltimore, Maryland (Zabin et al., 1986). The experimental group con-

**FIGURE 10.4**
**Reproductive Education**
Many U.S. children receive inadequate education about sexuality and contraception. This pregnant woman, however, is teaching her six-year-old son about contraception and birth. Such open communication may increase his comfort in asking her questions about sexuality as he grows toward adolescence.

sisted of a junior-high school and a senior-high school where students were offered sexuality and contraceptive education, counseling, and services over the three years. The other two schools, which did not render such services, made up the control group. The level of sexual activity among students in all these Baltimore schools was higher than that among students in the nation as a whole. For example, before the program, almost 92% of ninth-grade boys and 54% of ninth-grade girls had had sexual intercourse. But exposure to contraceptive education and services over the three-year period resulted in an increase in the accuracy of students' knowledge about human sexuality, and a delay in the average age of first intercourse.

An even more dramatic demonstration of the effectiveness of the Baltimore sex education program was the finding that the number of 14-year-old girls who became sexually active was reduced by about two-thirds during the first three years of the program's operation. After 28 months, the pregnancy rate had *declined* by 30% in the program schools, whereas it had *increased* by 58% in the two control group schools. Similar increases had occurred in other schools citywide. The findings from these and other studies provide no support for the hypothesis that exposure to sex education and contraceptive information drives up adolescent pregnancy rates (see also Chapter 12).

It is not known just what aspects of such programs are the source of delays in the initiation of sexual activity or of reduced premarital pregnancy rates. Zabin et al. (1986) suggested that the accessibility of the faculty and clinic staff was the major factor. It is possible that simply knowing that contraceptive information, counseling, and services are readily available may encourage teenagers to avail themselves of such programs. In doing so, they raise their awareness of the responsibilities accompanying sexual intimacy, which may lead them to consider their sexual decisions carefully. Clearly, research is needed to identify which aspects of these programs are most closely associated with responsible sexual and contraceptive behavior.

In cases where contraceptive clinics are remote from a public school, adolescents' first visits frequently center on getting pregnancy tests rather than on obtaining contraception. Among women in a national sample, 36% went to a contraceptive clinic only after they suspected pregnancy. Only 14% of teenage women visiting a family planning clinic did so before having sexual intercourse (Alan Guttmacher Institute, 1982). Studies of unmarried women indicate that those with more accurate knowledge about contraception are more likely to use reliable methods consistently than are those with less accurate knowledge (Miller, 1986).

What about the belief that easy access to contraception leads to promiscuity? Evidence from several studies indicates otherwise. In fact, research shows that use of reliable contraceptives is associated with strong commitment to one partner rather than with promiscuous sexual activity involving a number of different partners (Harvey & Scrimshaw, 1988; Miller, 1986). Even

for first intercourse, there is greater use of reliable contraception among couples who are in love or planning to marry than among couples who are less involved with one another. The greater the degree of involvement between a couple the first time they have sex, the more likely they are to use a reliable contraceptive.

## Legal Access to Contraceptives

Access to contraception has become easier for adolescents in recent years. In 1977 the Supreme Court struck down a New York State statute that had prohibited the sale or distribution of nonprescription contraceptives to minors under age 16. This decision, combined with several other rulings, eliminated all legal barriers to the acquisition of contraception by adolescents. By the beginning of the 1980s, however, plans to control adolescents' access to birth control once again emerged. Rules were drafted that would have required contraceptive clinics receiving federal funds to notify parents within 10 days if adolescents under the age of 18 obtained contraception. (Almost all family planning agencies receive some federal funding.)

One of the nation's largest family planning agencies, Planned Parenthood, asserted that if a parental notification law were passed, it would fight the law in the courts rather than comply with it. Planned Parenthood has clinics throughout North America where individuals and couples can obtain medical exams and contraceptives at a nominal price.

## Motivation to Use Contraceptives

Some pregnancies occur despite the conscientious use of reliable contraceptives. Most of the million-plus teenagers who get pregnant each year, however, are not sufficiently motivated to use contraception (Landy et al., 1986).

The accumulated evidence shows that adolescent females who consistently use reliable contraceptives differ from those who do not in background, knowledge, attitudes, and personality. On the basis of research, it is possible to draw a general picture of teenagers from each of these two groups. The socioeconomic status of teenage females who consistently use contraception tends to be higher than that of females who are less conscientious. Moreover, the older, and presumably the more mature, a female is when she first has intercourse, the greater the likelihood that she will use birth control (Chilman, 1980). In addition, the educational and occupational aspirations of teenage females who use contraception are higher than those of teens who do not, and the former are more likely to get a college education (Kantner & Zelnik, 1972).

Although religious affiliation was related to contraceptive use in the past, research suggests that this is no longer the case (McCormick, Izzo, & Folcik, 1985; Tanfer, Grady, Klepinger, & Billy, 1993). Catholics, for example, are now as likely as Protestants to use contraception. On the other hand, frequency of attendance at worship services does appear to be related to the likelihood of contraceptive use. Sexually experienced teenage females regularly attending religious services were less likely to have used an effective method of contraception than were those who rarely attended religious services (Studer & Thornton, 1987).

As we have seen, public education has generally failed to provide birth control information to adolescents. Yet research shows that women who consistently use contraception tend to have more accurate information regarding birth control (Levinson, 1986) than do women who engage in unprotected intercourse. For example, women who use contraception are better informed about the timing of ovulation and the effects of various contraceptives (Kantner & Zelnik, 1972). In addition, adolescent women who take active responsibility for contraception report less fear of parental reaction to their sexual activity than do women who take less responsibility for contraception (Levinson, 1986).

An examination of the relationship of sex education to sexual activity, contraceptive use, and the likelihood of experiencing nonmarital pregnancy led two researchers to this conclusion:

*First, the data seem to provide overwhelming support for the claim that the decision to engage in sexual activity is not influenced by whether or not teenagers have had sex education in school. Second, young women who have had sex education appear less likely than those who have not to become pregnant if they are sexually active. Third, according to the*

*1979 data, young women who have had a course that included discussion of contraceptive methods are more likely to have used a contraceptive at first intercourse. (Zelnik & Kim, 1982, p. 125)*

## Contraception and Sexual Attitudes

Attitudes toward sex are also strongly associated with contraceptive behavior. Consistent use of contraception is more likely among men and women with positive (erotophilic) attitudes and openness toward sex in general and toward their own sexual activity in particular (Fisher et al., 1988; Kelley et al., 1987) (see Figure 10.5). One of our students made a comment that epitomizes

**FIGURE 10.5**
**Erotophilic Approaches to Sex Education**
This teenager appears comfortable in learning about using condoms effectively in a safe-sex education class.

sexual and contraceptive openness. She remarked that she "always carries condoms, just in case the guy doesn't have any." Most people are far less frank about their sexual and contraceptive behavior—and less well prepared. For example, each semester we talk with students who are much less realistic than this young woman. Some who discover that they are pregnant come to us seeking information about various community resources. They cannot deny, of course, that they have been sexually intimate, but many of them describe the occurrence of intercourse as somehow accidental or unintentional, using versions of the claim that "the devil made me do it." They blame arousal ("we got carried away"), intoxication ("I got drunk"), or their partner ("he made me do it"; "she should have stopped me"). People who can not acknowledge that they might be sexually active in some situations are unlikely to employ contraception.

In her questionnaire study of 2,500 women ranging in age from 13 to 26, Lindemann (1975) examined the importance of acknowledging that one is sexually active. She suggested that women who refuse to admit to themselves that they are sexually active avoid making decisions about contraception, and in many cases this avoidance results in pregnancy.

Given the obvious association between sexuality and contraception, it is not surprising that guilt about sex affects attitudes and behavior regarding contraception. In fact, sex guilt may even interfere with a person's ability to learn about contraception. Schwartz (1973) found that when college students heard a lecture containing birth control information that is not commonly known, those who felt guilty about sex received lower scores on a test of their retention of the information than did those who felt less guilty.

If rearing children to feel guilty about their sexual feelings were effective in preventing premarital intercourse, then the negative effect of sex guilt on teenagers' use of contraceptives would not be of great concern. But research involving sexually active college students indicates that sex guilt may be more effective in blocking contraceptive use than in preventing premarital intercourse (Strassberg & Mahoney, 1988). For example, one study showed that college students with high and low levels of guilt about sex did not differ in the ages at which they first had intercourse (Allgeier, Przybyla, & Thompson, 1977). But women with high levels of guilt took an average of 15 months to start using a reliable contraceptive, whereas women who felt less guilt began to use reliable contraceptives within 3½ months of first intercourse.

People who are taught as children to feel guilty about their sexuality may be inhibited from acknowledging to themselves prior to intercourse that they will engage in sexual activity, claiming instead that sex happened spontaneously (see Box 10.2). Not surprisingly, those young women in the Allgeier et al. (1977) study who reported receiving contraceptive help from members of their families showed lower levels of sex guilt. Because both our religious and our legal codes differentiate between intentional and unintentional sins or crimes, adolescents who unintentionally "sin" by getting carried away by their sexual feelings may not feel as responsible as they would if they intentionally engaged in intercourse and planned for it by purchasing contraceptives.

Several other personality variables appear to be related to contraceptive use. The desire to conform to the ideal of the "nice girl" and the fear that their male partners will look down on them if they initiate the use of birth control may inhibit young women from obtaining and using contraception (Fox, G. L., 1977). In fact, at least one study found that men evaluate women who are prepared for birth control more highly than women believe they do. Men's regard for women was unaffected by whether the women planned and initiated the use of contraception (Phillis & Allgeier, 1982).

Presumably, women who are less concerned with conforming to the "nice girl" image are more likely to use contraception. Women who are less traditional in their gender-role identification are more likely to obtain and use reliable contraceptives (Fox, G. L., 1977). In addition, women who believed that what happens to them is a result of their own actions were less likely to have an unplanned pregnancy than were women who perceived their fate as determined by luck or by the choices of others (Steinlauf, 1979).

**Box 10.2**

# Spontaneous Sex: THE BIG LIE

People sometimes object to the notion of using contraception on the grounds that birth-control methods interfere with the spontaneity of sexual intimacy. This reasoning is based on the false assumption that sexual contact occurs without premeditation or forewarning. In truth, although partners may behave spontaneously during a sexual interaction, the decision to become sexually intimate in the first place is not made without at least one partner preparing for intimacy.

Consider the last time that you had a sexual interaction with another person. It may have involved penis-in-vagina, mutual masturbation, or oral-genital contact, or it may have been as simple as a first kiss. The point is that someone, either you or your partner, had to make decisions with the intention of becoming closer sexually. For those sexual contacts involving the risk of conception, a number of acts necessarily precede vaginal penetration: you need to find a private place; there should be agreement between you and your partner that you want to have coitus; and, of course, there is the little matter of removing your clothing so that sexual intercourse can proceed!

Probably the only people who can convincingly claim that at least one of the two participants has spontaneous sex are those who sleep together. For example, married or cohabiting couples may have relatively spontaneous intercourse when one of them awakens feeling desire for the other. Even in this situation, however, a person has to awaken his or her partner to see if he or she is willing to have sex.

In the early stages of a relationship, it is rare that one of the (potential) partners is asleep in the other's company. Except in the case of date rape, both people have probably thought of the possibility of progressing to sexual intimacy—in delightful fantasies, or perhaps with fear. Their fantasies and communication could include erotic contraceptive and prophylactic messages:

*"Oh, honey, I really want to insert your diaphragm so that I can then insert my penis into your vagina . . . would you like me to do that?"*

*"I just woke up from a really horny dream about you; I want us to have oral sex, but after that, I would like you to put your penis inside my vagina. If that is all right with you, I'll go get the condoms from my purse."*

*"You are gorgeous to me. I just had a general screening test for STDs, including AIDS, and I'm negative. But it is important for us to be safe, so I would like for us to play with a condom. Can we roll them on, very, very slowly, over our penises? Your penis is so beautiful and firm, would it be ok if I play with your penis while I put the condom on? Would you play with mine while I roll a condom onto you? Oh, you have gotten even harder—I didn't think that was possible! Ah, sir, would you mind putting your clothed penis into me?"*

Incorporation of methods to reduce the negative consequences of sexuality (unwanted conception, STDs) into our sexual interactions can enhance the pleasure of our sexual lives.

# The Male Role in the Contraceptive Process

Our culture's assumptions about men's and women's differing motivations for intercourse and the possible outcome—pregnancy—have affected the development of contraceptives. The bulk of the blame and responsibility for unwanted pregnancy falls on women. Thus most efforts to increase contraceptive use have targeted women.

Various lines of evidence suggest, however, that men are willing to take contraceptive responsibility, although there is currently only one effective temporary method that men can use: the condom. Yet several cross-cultural studies conducted by the World Health Organization (1980, 1982) indicate that a considerable proportion of men report willingness to use hormonal contraceptives. U.S. studies also indicate that large proportions of men say that they would agree to use a male contraceptive pill if one became available (Gough, 1979; Jaccard et al., 1981). In addition, when teenage couples do employ contraception, half the time they rely on either the condom or withdrawal (the latter method is not notably effective, but it does demonstrate a man's intention to prevent pregnancy). In L. S. Fox's (1983) study of high-school males, 67% reported a preference for taking contraceptive responsibility themselves. In the past few decades, researchers and family planning agencies have shown increased interest in male contraceptive behavior (Marsiglio & Menaghan, 1987; Schinke et al., 1979).

Studies of male contraceptive behavior are generally consistent with studies of female contraceptive behavior. For instance, male college students with positive feelings about sex are more comfortable purchasing condoms from a drugstore than are those with negative attitudes (Fisher, Fisher, & Byrne, 1977). In one study, college men were questioned about their intentions regarding contraceptive use and their feelings about sex. A month later, these men were asked to report whether they had always used contraceptives when having intercourse during the previous month. Reports that they had "always" used contraceptives during the previous month were directly related both to the intentions to use contraceptives and to positive feelings about sex (Fisher, Byrne, & White, 1983). Among married couples with children, egalitarian gender-role attitudes were related to a preference among wives, but not among husbands, for sharing of contraceptive responsibility, but both wives and husbands generally had favorable attitudes toward the development of a male contraceptive pill (Marsiglio & Menaghan, 1987).

Despite men's apparent willingness to use contraceptives, contraceptive use is less likely when a man initiates intercourse than when a woman is the initiator (Harvey & Scrimshaw, 1988). In addition, a couple's failure to anticipate intercourse increases the difficulty of using all methods except the pill, Norplant, and IUD. Strassberg and Mahoney (1988) asked college students to report how long before their last experience of intercourse they knew that they were going to have sex: "a few minutes" was the most common response by both men and women! With so little warning, it would be difficult to obtain even those nonprescription contraceptives that are available at drugstores. Therefore, it is hardly surprising that more than a third of the Strassberg and Mahoney sample reported using no method or an ineffective method such as withdrawal during their most recent intercourse experience.

You may notice that this section on the male role in contraceptive behavior is quite short: there is little research on men's contraceptive attitudes and behaviors. Further studies of the impact of men's attitudes and behaviors on unplanned and unwanted pregnancies are crucial.

## Risks for Women

Although the health risks associated with the use of various contraceptives receive much media publicity, the greatest mortality risk for sexually active women comes from dangers associated with pregnancy and childbirth, which kill 1 in 11,000 women each year. In contrast, the lowest mortality rates are associated with using a barrier method of contraception, such as a diaphragm or a condom, in combination with legal abortion during the first nine weeks if the barrier method fails and a pregnancy occurs: 1 in 400,000 sexually active women dies from this combination of methods (Hatcher et al., 1994). Although some other contraceptive methods are more effective than the barrier methods and thus more likely to eliminate the need for an abortion, they generally pose higher risks of other kinds than the combination of the barrier methods and abortion. For example, 1 in 63,000 nonsmoking oral-contraceptive users dies annually. The use of any contraceptive still poses less risk, however, than unprotected intercourse.

## Methods of Contraception

We now discuss current methods of birth control and their potential advantages and disadvantages, benefits, and impact on sexual response.* Because new information about birth control becomes available each year, it is important to consult a health care provider before making contraceptive choices. In choosing the right method for you, you and your health care provider should take into account your age, lifestyle, personality, and medical history.

## Rhythm

We begin with the so-called *rhythm method*, mainly because the knowledge needed to make this technique effective can be useful in increasing the effectiveness of almost all other birth control methods. The rhythm method was accepted by the Roman Catholic church in 1931 and remains the only birth control method the Church acknowledges besides abstinence. Essentially, it means abstaining from coitus for at least a week around the time of ovulation. The date of ovulation must therefore be determined.

Knowledge of the time of ovulation is useful to women for several reasons. First, pinpointing the date of ovulation and engaging in intercourse at the time can improve the chances of beginning a wanted pregnancy. Second, the timing of intercourse in relation to ovulation is crucial in at least one strategy for attempting to determine the gender of one's child, as described in Chapter 9. Finally, the more women know about the cycles and functioning of their own bodies, the more likely they are to recognize potential medical difficulties. The presently available methods of detecting ovulation involve the use of a calendar, recording one's daily temperature, monitoring cervical mucus, and using ovulation detection kits. About 4% of women report using this

**rhythm method**—a birth control technique based on avoidance of sexual intercourse during a woman's fertile period each month.

---

*Unless otherwise noted, statistics on effectiveness are based on Hatcher et al. (1994).

method as a contraceptive technique (Forrest & Fordyce, 1993).

### The Calendar Method

The calendar method of determining ovulation is essentially based on the law of averages. The average menstrual cycle is about 28 days long, with ovulation occurring on average 14 days *prior* to the onset of the menstrual period. To determine when she ovulates, a woman must be able to predict accurately the day she will begin her next period. Such forecasting can pose a problem because emotional and biological factors such as illness, fatigue, rigorous exercise, and stress can alter the cycle interval. Menstrual regularity is also rare in the first few and last few years of a woman's reproductive span. Further, women occasionally release more than one egg in a particular cycle, which can throw off the timing.

### The Sympto-Thermal Method

To determine the time of ovulation by the *sympto-thermal method*, a woman takes her temperature with a basal-body-temperature thermometer (an ordinary thermometer is not calibrated precisely enough) and examines her cervical mucus. To detect variations in basal body temperature (BBT), a woman must take her temperature each morning before getting out of bed or engaging in any other activity. She then notes her BBT on a chart (see Figure 10.6). Generally low during the first part of the menstrual cycle, the BBT tends to drop slightly on the day of ovulation. As a result of progesterone secretion by the corpus luteum, the BBT then rises on the day after ovulation and remains relatively high through the rest of the cycle. Because the most definite indication of ovulation, the rise in BBT, occurs the day *after* ovulation, successful use of this method depends on a woman keeping track of her cycle for up to six months *and* having a regular cycle. A woman can predict the day she will ovulate only if both conditions are met.

**sympto-thermal method**—a way of determining the date of ovulation based on changes in a woman's basal body temperature and the stretchability of her cervical mucus.

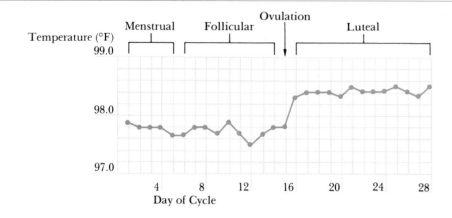

**FIGURE 10.6**
**Basal-Body-Temperature (BBT) Chart**
Note that the temperature pattern for this average woman includes a sharp rise in
BBT on day 17, indicating the point of ovulation as day 16.

The information obtained from the BBT is then confirmed by examining the cervical mucus, because the amount and characteristics of the mucus vary at different points in the menstrual cycle. After menstrual bleeding has stopped, there is generally little or no mucus for a few days. Then a white or cloudy and tacky mucus is discharged. As the mucus increases in amount over the next few days, it gradually becomes clearer and thinner, until there are one or two days during which the mucus is like raw egg white. It is slippery, almost like the lubrication a woman produces when she is sexually aroused. Ovulation occurs within a day of the last of the clear mucus. After ovulation, the mucus becomes cloudy and white again.

During ovulation, the mucus stretches and resembles unbeaten raw egg whites in consistency. To check the extent of stretchiness, a woman first inserts her finger into her vagina to obtain a sample of cervical mucus. After withdrawing her finger, she touches it to her thumb and then slowly pulls her thumb and index finger apart. If ovulation is occurring, she will observe a thin, connecting thread of mucus up to an inch long (see Figure 10.7). During the rest of the menstrual cycle, the mucus does not stretch at all.

Ovulation detection kits are now available in drugstores. This test, which monitors the pres-

ence of an enzyme associated with ovulation, can only confirm, not predict, ovulation (Hatcher et al., 1994). For the purpose of targeting the day of ovulation for conception, the cervical-mucus stretch test is useful. Effective use of the sympto-

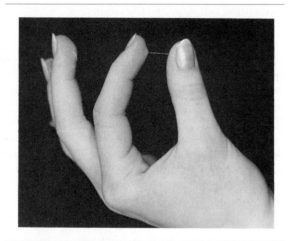

**FIGURE 10.7**
**Stretchability of Cervical Mucus at Ovulation**
At ovulation, a woman's cervical mucus stretches to form a connecting thread up to an inch long, as this photo shows.

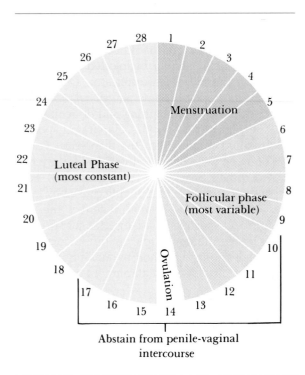

Menstruation

Luteal Phase
(most constant)

Follicular phase
(most variable)

Ovulation

Ovulation

Abstain from penile-vaginal
intercourse

**FIGURE 10.8**
**Hypothetical Menstrual Cycle Illustrating the Use
of the Rhythm Method of Contraception**

thermal method depends on accurately pinpointing the time of ovulation and avoiding unprotected coitus during the fertile period.

After the date of ovulation has been determined using BBT and mucus observation, a woman should avoid coitus for five days prior to ovulation. She should also abstain from coitus for three days following ovulation, because the egg may still be alive. For a graphic representation of the sympto-thermal rhythm method, see Figure 10.8. The effectiveness of the method is greatest when a couple engages in coitus only after ovulation. This practice yields a theoretical failure rate of about 2 pregnancies per 100 women who engage in coitus on a fairly regular basis for a year.

Drawbacks include the fact that accurately determining the date of ovulation takes a minimum of six months. Second, although the sympto-thermal method has no direct physical effect on sexuality, it may have psychological effects for some couples. Depending on the nature

and duration of a couple's relationship, the required periods of abstinence from coitus of one to three weeks out of each cycle depending on the regularity (and thus the predictability) of her menstrual cycle may result in considerable frustration. The temporary ban on coitus need not be a great disadvantage, however, because couples can engage in oral or manual stimulation without fear of conception during those times when a woman is fertile.

The major benefit of the sympto-thermal method is that it does not interfere with the woman's reproductive system in any way; therefore, she need not be concerned about potential side effects. The sympto-thermal method is not as effective as other methods to be described, but it involves far less risk than no method at all.

## Diaphragm and Spermicide

The *diaphragm* is a dome-shaped cap made out of soft rubber that is designed to fit inside the vagina and cover the cervix (see Figure 10.9). It was the first widely available contraceptive for women. Many women abandoned it in favor of the pill during the 1960s, and only about 4% of women currently use it as a contraceptive (Forrest & Fordyce, 1993). All diaphragms should be used with a *spermicide*. Spermicides designed to be used with a diaphragm come in tubes of cream or jelly and are available at drugstores without a prescription.

Diaphragms may be obtained only by prescription from a physician, because they must be fitted to the size of the user. Fitting is done by inserting diaphragms of various sizes lengthwise into the vagina to find the size that fits snugly and comfortably over the cervix and behind the pubic bone.

To use a diaphragm (see Figure 10.10), the user places spermicidal jelly or cream in the center and around the rim of the device. Either the

**diaphragm** (DYE-uh-fram)—a dome-shaped rubber contraceptive device inserted into the vagina to block the cervical opening. The diaphragm should always be used with a spermicide.

**spermicide**—a chemical that kills or immobilizes sperm.

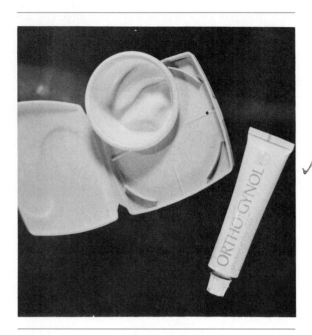

**FIGURE 10.9**
**Diaphragm and Spermicide**

woman or her partner inserts the diaphragm into the vagina with an applicator or with the fingers, positioning the diaphragm so that the side containing the spermicide is next to the cervix. A well-fitted, properly-placed diaphragm is not felt by either man or woman; some women have been known to forget that they are wearing a diaphragm. A diaphragm should be refitted after any changes that might alter vaginal size, such as pregnancy, childbirth, and weight increases or decreases of 10 pounds or more. It should also be inspected regularly for holes or tears. This examination may be done by holding the diaphragm up to a light, or by filling it with water to see whether there are any leaks.

The diaphragm-spermicide method works in two ways. First, the diaphragm provides a physical barrier across the entrance to the uterus, reducing the likelihood that the sperm will reach the egg. Second, the thick spermicide kills or immobilizes the sperm, in addition to providing a physical barrier over the cervix. The diaphragm should be inserted no more than two hours prior to intercourse. It should be left undisturbed for six to eight hours following ejaculation, because

it takes spermicide that long to be effective. If intercourse is desired again within that eight-hour period, the diaphragm should be left in place and more spermicide should be injected into the vagina with the aid of an applicator. During the eight-hour period following ejaculation, the woman should avoid bathing and douching.

The failure rate for the diaphragm-spermicide method ranges from the theoretical yearly rate of 6 per 100 women to the actual failure rate of 18 (Trussell, Strickler, & Vaughan, 1993). Failure of the spermicide is generally caused by leakage. The spermicide is most potent if the diaphragm and spermicide are inserted just prior to penile penetration. A couple can thus increase the effectiveness of the method by making insertion of the spermicide-coated diaphragm part of their lovemaking.

Diaphragm failure is usually associated with the shifting of the device as a result of particularly vigorous intercourse, changes in the size of the vagina during sexual arousal, or use of the woman-above coital position (Hatcher et al., 1994). Therefore, if conception must be avoided, it is wise to use an additional method of contraception, such as a condom, during ovulation.

If the diaphragm is washed and dried gently following removal, sprinkled with cornstarch to keep it soft and dry, and placed in its case when it is not being used, it should remain effective for several years. An additional advantage of the diaphragm-spermicide method is that spermicides kill a number of the organisms that cause STDs (see Chapter 17).

The diaphragm is used only when needed and has no influence on subsequent fertility. In rare cases, an individual may be allergic to the latex in the diaphragm or to the spermicide, but this problem can usually be solved by switching to different brands. The contraceptive effect of the diaphragm is immediately reversible: the couple can simply abandon diaphragm use when they wish to conceive.

The relationship of the diaphragm to sexual response may depend on several factors. Because it must be inserted no more than two hours before coitus, the diaphragm may be an undesirable method for those who value unplanned sex. A couple's response to the spermicide may be positive if they desire more lubrication, but negative

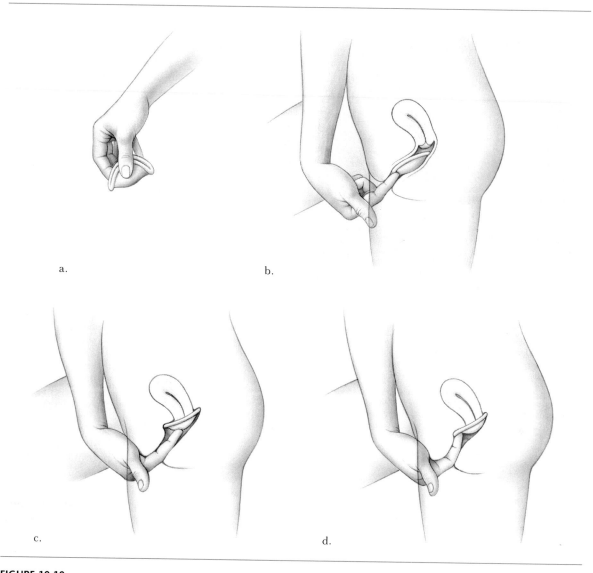

a.

b.

c.

d.

**FIGURE 10.10**

**Effective Use of the Diaphragm-Spermicide Method**

To use this method effectively, a woman should place about a tablespoon of spermicide in the center of the diaphragm and a little spermicide around the rim. The diaphragm is then a) pinched between the thumb and fingers and b) inserted lengthwise into the vagina so that it covers the cervix. The woman should then check to make sure that c) the diaphragm is covering her cervix and d) the edge of the diaphragm closest to the vaginal entrance is lodged behind the pubic bone. To remove the device, she inserts a finger under the rim.

if one or both partners view the spermicide as "messy."

Another potential difficulty with the diaphragm-spermicide method is that it may limit the range of sexual behavior for some couples. For example, the spermicide may inhibit the desire for cunnilingus. Most spermicides are safe and nontoxic, but the odor and the taste of the

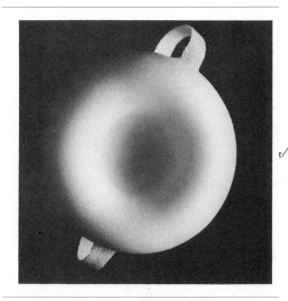

**FIGURE 10.11**

**The Contraceptive Sponge**

The contraceptive sponge is placed against the cervix and contains a spermicide that absorbs and kills sperm. It is effective for approximately 24 hours, at which point it should be removed and discarded.

standard spermicides are not particularly appealing. Tasteless and odorless spermicides are now available, and fruit-flavored spermicides can be purchased in specialty shops or through mail-order catalogues (see Appendix C). An additional potential drawback is that a couple must reapply the spermicide with an applicator after ejaculation if they wish to have intercourse again within the next eight hours.

## Contraceptive Sponge

The *contraceptive sponge* was approved by the FDA in 1983. The sponge is made of polyurethane and contains a spermicide, which the sponge releases gradually. After it has been inserted in the vagina and positioned against the cervix, the sponge absorbs and kills sperm for at least 24 hours. The long period of time during

which each application is effective is a major advantage of this method. Lovemaking is not interrupted because spermicide need not be reapplied before each act of coitus, and the sponge can be inserted well before intercourse. A small loop attached to the sponge makes removal easy (see Figure 10.11).

The failure rate for the sponge ranges from the theoretical yearly rate of 9% to an observed failure rate of 36%, and it is used by about 3% of contracepting women (Forrest & Fordyce, 1993; Trussler et al., 1993). The effectiveness of the contraceptive sponge is lower than that of the diaphragm-spermicide method. Unlike the diaphragm, however, the sponge is available without a prescription.

The contraceptive sponge is associated with a slightly elevated risk of toxic shock syndrome (TSS; see Chapter 14). The risk of TSS can be decreased by removing the sponge within 30 hours after insertion and not using it during menstruation or the postpartum period (Hatcher et al., 1994).

For couples who value uninterrupted lovemaking, and who find jelly or cream spermicides messy or awkward to use, the sponge provides a convenient alternative. Because it is readily available without a prescription, it affords privacy as well as convenience. Harvey, Beckman, and Murray (1989) compared women who used the sponge to women who relied on the pill or diaphragm. They found that sponge users were generally more knowledgeable about contraceptives and reported more consistent use of the sponge than did diaphragm users. The advantages of the sponge over the diaphragm—such as its effectiveness without additional spermicide, even during multiple ejaculations—may contribute to the increased consistency of its use.

## Cervical Cap

The *cervical cap* was invented in the 19th century. Wealthy Victorian women had their physicians insert a cap each month. In current use, it

**contraceptive sponge**—polyurethane vaginal sponge containing spermicide, used for contraception.

**cervical cap**—contraceptive rubber dome that is fitted to a woman's cervix; spermicide is placed inside the cap before it is pressed onto the cervix.

is inserted by the woman or her partner rather than by a physician, and it is removed six or more hours after coitus rather than remaining in place for a month. The cap is a rubber dome that is available in four sizes to fit a woman's cervix (see Figure 10.12). The cervical cap differs from the diaphragm in that it is smaller and can be inserted earlier.

Spermicide is placed inside the cap. With its edges pinched, the cap is then inserted into the vagina and pressed onto the cervix. The woman or her partner should make sure that the cap is snugly fitted against the cervix by putting a finger on the cap and feeling for the cervix through the rubber. The cap may be inserted up to six hours before coitus and, like the diaphragm, should not be removed for at least six hours after ejaculation.

The FDA approved use of the cap in 1988 and concluded that it may remain in place without additional applications of spermicide for 48 hours. The FDA advised that the cap should be prescribed only to women with normal PAP-test results (see Chapter 5) and that users should have a follow-up PAP test three months after beginning use of the device. At a failure rate ranging from 9 to 36 per 100 women, the cap is not quite as effective as the diaphragm (Hatcher et al., 1994). The most frequently cited reason for failure is incorrect or inconsistent use. Reported side effects included unpleasant odor, partner discomfort, and a slightly increased risk of toxic shock syndrome. It is used by less than 1% of contracepting women (Forrest & Fordyce, 1993).

## Condom

The *condom* is the only reliable, temporary method of male contraception now widely available. Condoms can be purchased without a prescription. When unrolled, the rubber or cecum (skin) condom resembles a long, thin balloon. Designed to envelop a man's erect penis, it is put on prior to penetration and intercourse (see Figure

condom—a sheath placed over the erect penis for prevention of pregnancy and protection against disease; usually made of latex.

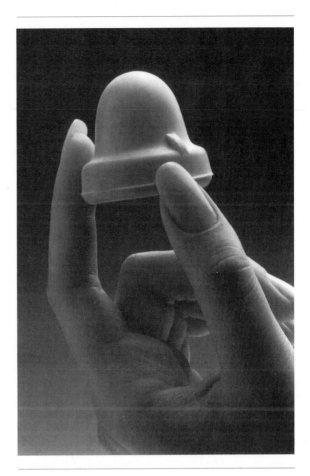

**FIGURE 10.12**
**The Cervical Cap**
The Prentif cavity rim cervical cap is a soft rubber cup that is inserted into the vagina and pressed onto the cervix. Spermicide is used to fill one-third of the dome prior to insertion of the cap.

10.13). About half an inch of space should be left at the condom's tip so that there is room for the ejaculated semen; some condoms come with a protruding tip designed to catch the ejaculate (see Figure 10.14). After intercourse, a man should hold the rim of the condom against the base of his penis as he withdraws from a woman's vagina so that the condom does not come off. After withdrawal, the condom should be taken off and discarded.

Condom use, particularly among young, unmarried men, more than doubled in the decade from 1979 to 1988, with much of the increase in

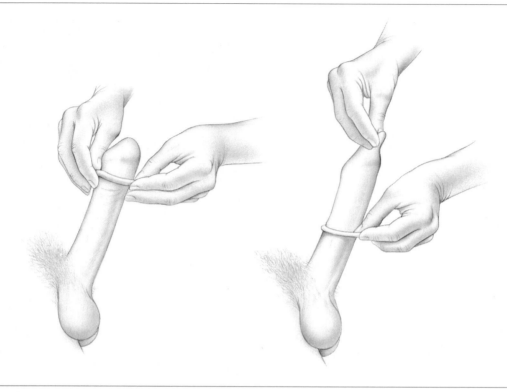

**FIGURE 10.13**
**Putting on the Condom**
The condom is placed over the head of the penis, with a space left at the tip to hold semen. The condom is then rolled all the way down the shaft of the erect penis.

both sales and use occurring since 1986 (Moran et al., 1989; Sonenstein, Pleck, & Ku, 1989). Specifically, in 1979, 21% of men aged 17 to 19 reported having used condoms at last intercourse; in 1988 the comparable figure was 58%. However, a follow-up study of the men in the 1988 study three years later (1991) revealed that as the respondents grew older, the percentage of men who used a condom at last intercourse had dropped to 44% (Pleck, Sonenstein, & Ku, 1993). The researchers stated that this decrease may have stemmed from publicity about AIDS being at a peak during 1988 following the release of the surgeon general's report on AIDS. The men's perception of the risk of contracting AIDS decreased over the next three years (Pleck et al., 1993). These figures are comparable with other research indi-cating that condom use among men declines over time (Tanfer et al., 1993).

The condom works by preventing sperm from entering the vagina. Many condoms come with spermicidal lubricants such as nonoxynol-9 that further boost their effectiveness. The failure rate for condom users ranges between 3% and 12% per year. Because condom manufacture in the United States is supervised by the FDA, breakage is rare. However, improper treatment of the condom by the purchaser can reduce its effectiveness. Condoms should be kept away from heat; for example, a condom should not be kept in a wallet in one's back pocket.

To increase a condom's effectiveness, a man should wear it during any vaginal penetration, and he should hold on to it firmly while with-

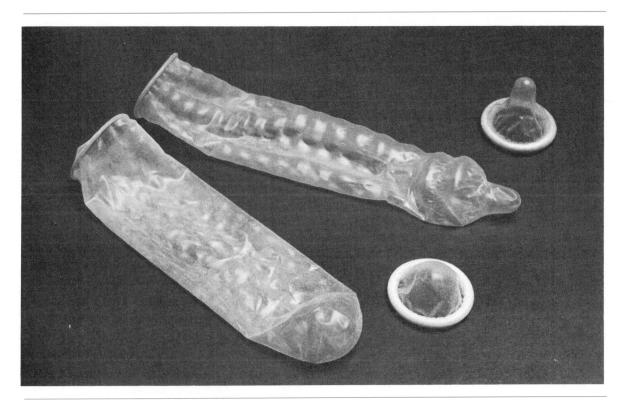

**FIGURE 10.14**
**Examples of Condoms**
The condom on the right has a reservoir at its tip to catch semen upon ejaculation.
A couple relying on a condom without a protruding tip should pinch the bottom
of it when putting it on to leave about an inch of space to catch semen.

drawing. Some men engage in penetration for some time prior to ejaculation and put the condom on only when they intend to ejaculate. This practice raises the failure rate for several reasons. First, the droplet of fluid that appears on a man's penis during arousal but prior to ejaculation sometimes contains sperm (see Chapter 5).

Second, ejaculation may occur before a man can withdraw to put on the condom. Psychological factors may influence the unintentional ejaculation. A man may feel that his "loss of control" is a compliment to his partner. Moreover, a woman may get some pleasure out of encouraging a man to demonstrate his loss of rationality in the heat of passion for her. Whatever psychological satisfactions come into play at the moment of ejaculation, they are quickly replaced by far more negative feelings as the couple anxiously await the arrival of the woman's menstrual period later in the month. Thus a couple relying on the condom should make sure that it is always worn prior to *any* vaginal penetration.

For additional lubrication, a couple can choose lubricated condoms or employ a water-soluble product such as surgical jelly (K-Y jelly, for example) or saliva. Petroleum jelly (such as Vaseline) should be avoided for two reasons: it may damage the condom, and it is not easily discharged from the vagina.

No negative side effects are associated with condom use, and condoms have several advantages. They allow a man to take contraceptive responsibility. Almost 75% of men in a national survey agreed with the statement that using a condom shows that you are a concerned and caring person (Grady, Klepinger, Billy, & Tanfer, 1993). Use of condoms, especially those lubricated with spermicide, has the added advantage of reducing the chances of catching or passing on STDs, including genital herpes (see Chapter 17). Lubricated condoms now come in such flavors as banana, lime, licorice, peppermint, and strawberry. One company markets a condom contained in a plastic cup for women to carry in their purses.

Most men (75%) using condoms report a reduction in sensation to the penis (Grady et al., 1993). According to an old joke, wearing a condom is like taking a shower with a raincoat on. However, a man who ejaculates very quickly may appreciate a slight decrease in sensation, as may his partner, if it prolongs intercourse. About 32% of the men in the Grady et al. study reported that condom use made sex last longer. Latex condoms inhibit the transfer of heat to some degree, whereas the more expensive cecum condom, made from the intestinal tissue of lambs, allows transmission of changes in temperature and results in a more natural sensation for the couple. However, cecum condoms are at least three times more costly, and they provide less protection from sexually transmitted diseases (Cates & Stone, 1992a) (see Chapter 17). In laboratory trials, virus particles pass through cecum condoms because of the size of the pores in the lambskin relative to the size of the viruses.

Some couples may see the act of putting on the condom as an interruption of their sexual expression. Others, however, may incorporate the activity into their pattern of erotic stimulation. In one study, couples who received instructions designed to make condom use more erotic became more positive in their attitudes toward condoms and reported more subjective sexual pleasure in the two-week experiment than did couples who did not receive such instructions (Tanner & Pollack, 1988). Attitudes toward condom use are important. If a couple uses condoms in an erotic fashion (she helps put it on in a sensual way), there tends to be more sexual pleasure (Tanner & Pollack, 1988). Thus the effect of condom use on sexual response depends to some extent on how a couple approaches the method.

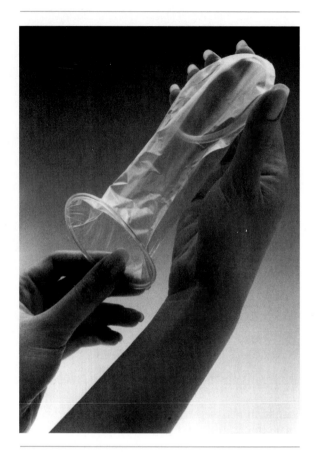

**FIGURE 10.15**
**The Female Condom**
The FDA's approval of the female condom in 1992 gave women an opportunity to use a method that provides a woman with protection from both conception and sexually transmitted diseases.

## Female Condoms

Several intravaginal pouches or "female" condoms have been developed (see Figure 10.15). The *female condom* was approved for use by the FDA in 1992. These pouches are generally made of polyurethane or latex, and line the vagina. In a clinical study of 100 couples, Hatcher (1991)

**female condom**—a pouch placed inside the vagina to line the vaginal walls for prevention of pregnancy and protection against disease.

found that only 1 female condom in 200 broke compared to 1 per 100 for male condoms. The lower breakage rate may stem from the fact that the female condom is almost twice as thick as most male condoms. Female condoms are more expensive and less acceptable to users than are male condoms (Cates & Stone, 1992a). About half of a group of British women who used the female condom for at least three months had a positive attitude toward the method (Ford & Mathie, 1993). Although Hatcher (1991) reported that a number of the couples in his study did not like the device, several women reported having more powerful orgasms than ever, perhaps because of the stimulation of the clitoris exerted by the traction of the device.

## Foams and Suppositories

*Contraceptive foams* and *suppositories* may be purchased without a prescription. These products should be kept cool because heat can decompose them, reducing their effectiveness. Contraceptive foam must be shaken before it is placed in an applicator (see Figure 10.16) and inserted in the vagina before intercourse. It should remain in the vagina for six to eight hours after ejaculation. More foam must be injected before each succeeding ejaculation.

A contraceptive suppository should be placed in the vagina at least 10 minutes and no more than two hours before ejaculation. After insertion, the suppository melts, filling the vagina with a spermicidal foam. Another suppository must be inserted for each subsequent act of intercourse, and a woman should avoid douching or bathing for at least two hours following intercourse.

The chemical components of spermicides kill or immobilize sperm, and their thick consistency provides a physical barrier to the entrance to the cervix. Used alone, they have a relatively high

failure rate of up to 21 per 100 women. Errors in the timing of insertion, as well as coital positions (such as the woman-above position) that allow the foam to move away from the cervix, contribute to the failure rate. Couples can increase the contraceptive effectiveness of spermicides to 95%, however, by using them in combination with a condom (Hatcher et al., 1994). Only 1% to 3% of women use foams or suppositories for contraception (Forrest & Fordyce, 1993).

The relatively high failure rates of foams and suppositories when used alone are one of their disadvantages. In addition, they are irritating to the genital tissues of some people, which is their only physical side effect. They do not interfere with the reproductive system, and their effects are completely and immediately reversible. In combination with barrier methods, they are also effective in reducing the likelihood of contracting STDs (Cates & Stone, 1992a).

Although spermicides have no direct physical effects on sexual response, they may have some psychological disadvantages. Some couples object to the noise produced by the extra liquid during thrusting of the penis into the vagina. Further, some women dislike having to wait several hours after coitus before bathing.

## Oral Contraceptives

When "the pill" was first marketed in the early 1960s, it was the first widely available, coitus-independent method of birth control; that is, for the first time, a couple could reduce their chances of conception without having to remember in the midst of lovemaking to insert a diaphragm and spermicide, put on a condom, and so forth. About 40% of sexually active U.S. women aged 15 to 44 use the pill for contraception (Forrest & Fordyce, 1993). "The pill" actually refers to about 50 different oral contraceptive products available in the United States, all of which contain estrogen and/or progestin. When *oral contraceptives* first received FDA approval in 1960, they contained relatively high doses of progestin (10 mg) and

**contraceptive foam**—a spermicidal foam that is injected into the vagina prior to coitus.

**contraceptive suppository**—a solid contraceptive substance containing a spermicide, inserted in the vagina prior to intercourse.

**oral contraceptives**—pills containing hormones that inhibit ovulation.

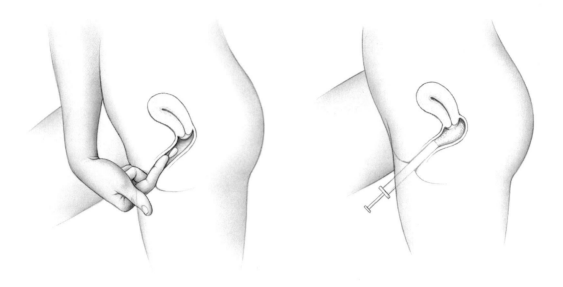

**FIGURE 10.16**
**Vaginal Spermicides**
Suppositories should be inserted deep in the vagina (left), and the timing of intercourse should follow the manufacturer's instructions; the suppositories may take up to 11 minutes to dissolve. Contraceptive foam is inserted with a plastic applicator that must be placed well within the vagina so that the foam covers the cervical opening (right).

estrogen (2 mg). Today the average combination pill contains much lower levels of both progestin (1 mg) and estrogen (½ mg).

Oral contraceptives require a prescription from a physician. To use the pill, a woman takes one each day for 21 days, stops for 7 days to permit menstrual bleeding, and then begins a new cycle. With some brands, the woman takes a pill during the 7 menstrual days as well; however, those 7 pills are placebos and contain no hormones.

Oral contraceptives are highly effective, with a maximum failure rate of 3%. Of all the oral contraceptives, the "combination pill," which acts in several ways, is the most effective. It contains both an estrogen and a progestin.* The estrogen and progestin prevent ovulation. In addition, the progestin appears to interfere with the development of the normal lining of the uterus so that, should ovulation and fertilization occur, implantation is inhibited. The progestin also acts to thicken the cervical mucus, with the result that sperm have a difficult time getting through it.

Another kind of oral contraceptive, the mini-pill, contains very small doses of a potent progestin, which has the effects just described. Although the mini-pill usually does not interfere with ovulation, because it contains no estrogen, it has a very low failure rate, just slightly higher than that of the combination pill. With all these oral contraceptives, a woman should use a back-up method of contraception during the first month she is using the pill.

In contrast, with the *triphasic oral contraceptive*, a woman begins to take the pills on the

---

*There are various terms for the class of synthetic and naturally secreted progestational (pregnancy-supporting) hormones. For simplicity, we use the generic term *progestin* for synthetic progesterone.

**triphasic oral contraceptives**—low-dose birth control pill in which the levels of hormones are varied over the menstrual cycle.

first day of her menstrual cycle and need not use a back-up contraceptive. Like other pills, the triphasic pills contain both estrogen and progestin. The difference between triphasics and other oral contraceptives is that with triphasics, the level of progestin (and in some cases the level of estrogen) varies over the month. This variation permits the use of very low levels of hormones—levels that, we shall see, reduce the risk of negative side effects.

Aside from remembering to take the pill at the same time each day, a woman need do nothing more to increase the effectiveness of the oral contraceptives, provided that she has the correct dosage. Physicians normally attempt to prescribe the lowest possible effective levels of both estrogen and progestin for each woman; sometimes it takes a bit of trial and error to determine the proper dosage.

If a woman forgets to take the pill for one day, she may take two the following day with no measurable rise in the risk of conception. If she forgets the pill for several days, the risk of conception increases. In that case, she should stop taking the pills for seven days and then begin a new pill cycle. In the meantime, she should rely on another method of contraception until she has completed at least seven pills in the new cycle.

Unlike the methods previously described, which block the sperm's access to the uterus, the pill derives its effectiveness from altering the reproductive system (see Figure 10.17). Because hormones in the pill interact with a woman's system, the side effects of pill use are highly individual, depending on a woman's medical history, age, and personal habits. In general, the side effects are minor. They mimic some of the symptoms of early pregnancy, including weight gain, slight breast enlargement and tenderness, reduction in the amount of menstrual discharge during a woman's period, breakthrough bleeding (that is, bleeding not associated with menstruation), emotional depression, and nausea. Headaches, nausea, and dizziness may be a sign that the dosage is too high. Although occasional "spotting" of blood is not unusual, persistent breakthrough bleeding may indicate that the dosage is too low. If any of these conditions arises, a woman should notify her health care provider.

Weight gain and breast enlargement tend to stabilize after a few cycles on the pill. The added

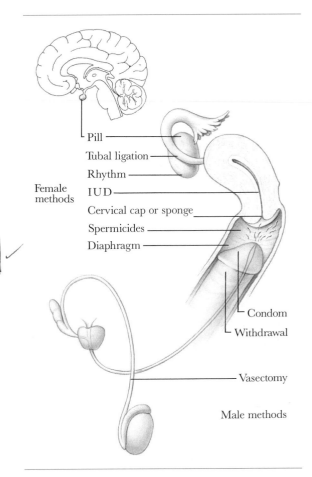

**FIGURE 10.17**
**Location of Contraceptive Effects**
This drawing indicates the sites of effectiveness for male and female contraceptives.

pounds are due to initial increases in appetite and/or fluid and salt retention. The reduction in menstrual discharge tends to continue as long as a woman is taking the pill. Emotional depression, nausea, and breast tenderness, if they occur at all, usually diminish within a few months. Occasionally women on the pill develop brownish spots—chloasma—on their faces. Unless these spots are very noticeable and cosmetically displeasing, they are not a serious problem.

Major side effects from the pill are less common. Involving mainly the cardiovascular (heart

*Pill ↓ cancer risk but breast cancer unclear*

and blood-vessel) system, they include hemorrhaging and blood clotting, which can be fatal. These cardiovascular problems, although rare, have prompted the FDA to urge women to use the lowest-dose pill possible.

The FDA has estimated that from 30% to 40% of the 8 to 10 million women who take the pill smoke. Although the FDA cites 35 as the age beyond which smoking women should not use the pill, Shapiro et al. (1979) found that increased risk was not limited to older women. For women aged 25 to 39 who smoke heavily, for example, the rate of heart disease from clotting was higher among pill users than among women who were not taking the pill. Some of the major hazards associated with pill use, however, are significantly reduced if a woman stops smoking. The health risks of pill use are not simply *added to* but *multiplied by* the health risks from smoking. These risks rise with age and with heavy smoking (15 or more cigarettes a day). Thus, in short, pill users should not smoke cigarettes. Again, it should be emphasized that except for pill users more than 40 years old who also smoke, the use of oral contraceptives is associated with lower mortality rates than is pregnancy (refer to Table 10.2).

A possible association also exists between pill use and cancer. This link, however, has been difficult to evaluate, because carcinogens generally take several decades to produce cancer. Thus it was not until the 1980s that it became possible to compare cancer rates in women who had been taking the pill since the 1960s with cancer rates in women who had not used oral contraceptives. It is ironic that although some women have avoided the pill because of fear of cancer, actuarial data suggest that low-dose contraceptives may actually reduce the likelihood of contracting some forms of cancer and slow the growth of others (Hatcher et al., 1994).

For example, the risk of contracting the most common form of uterine cancer, endometrial cancer, is lower for women who take the pill than for women who do not; taking the pill for just a year appears to be associated with long-term protection. Women who ingest the pill for two years are only 60% as likely to develop endometrial cancer as those who do not, and women who take the pill for four years are only 40% as likely to

develop this form of cancer as those who do not (Schlesselman, 1990). A similar relationship has been found between pill use and ovarian cancer. Women who had used the pill had about a 40% lower risk of ovarian cancer, even if they had quit using the pill 15 years before and had taken it for only three to six months; the protective value increased with the duration of usage. For those who took the pill for 10 or more years, risk dropped by about 80% (Lee, N. C., 1987). In addition, cervical cancer rates among pill users were found to be 0.8 relative to that of nonusers, a fact suggesting that pill users have no increased risk of cervical cancer (Hatcher et al., 1994).

The pill's risks and benefits with regard to breast cancer are less clear. Extensive research by the Centers for Disease Control has indicated that the use of oral contraceptives for a number of years did not increase the risk of breast cancer. But in the late 1980s, researchers were, as Johnson (1989) reported, "jolted by the results of three new analyses of data for premenopausal women, all of which found some connection between the pill and breast cancer" (p. 90). And then in 1992, Rosenberg et al. reported that oral contraceptive use did not raise the risk for breast cancer among Canadian women over age 40. Because the body of evidence on the association between pill use and breast cancer is contradictory, an advisory committee for the FDA met in 1989 to determine whether a change in prescribing practices was warranted. The committee concluded that the findings were not definitive and recommended against passing on any new warnings to users beyond those cautions already given in the package insert (Johnson, 1989). Nevertheless, as with any prescription drug, potential users should obtain the latest information about potential risks from their health care providers.

To investigate the long-term effects of contemporary contraceptives, the Oxford Family Planning Association in Britain began a study of 17,000 women in 1968 (Vessey et al., 1976). Birthrates were analyzed among women who stopped using birth control to become pregnant. Among the women who previously had had children and thus were known to be fertile prior to pill use, some differences in birthrates were found between former pill users and those who had relied on other contraceptives. When the women were studied 30 months after ending pill use, however, those differences had disappeared: all but 8% of both groups had given birth. By 43 months, all but 4% of both groups had given birth. In addition, the Vessey group found no consistent relationship between the method of contraception and a) the incidence of multiple pregnancies, malformations, and stillbirths; b) gender ratio; or c) birth weight.

Conditions that rule out a woman's use of the pill include hepatitis, cystic fibrosis, sickle-cell anemia, diabetes, high blood pressure, varicose veins, phlebitis (vein inflammation), fibroadenomas (fibrous tissue tumors), migraine headaches, and kidney disease. Also, women who suspect that they are pregnant and those who are nursing should use another method of contraception.

The pill appears to be a safe, highly effective contraceptive when used by women who are not susceptible to the hazards described above. Oral contraceptives are not messy and are taken independently of coitus. For women with very heavy or lengthy menstrual periods, the pill has the added advantage of decreasing the menstrual flow. Further, for some women, pill use eliminates, or reduces the severity of, menstrual cramps (Robinson et al., 1992), and consistent pill use almost eliminates unwanted pregnancy.

Comparisons of pill-taking and non-pill-taking women of the same age, race, religion, and education suggest that the pill takers have intercourse more frequently (Bancroft, Sherwin, Alexander, Davidson, & Walker, 1991). It is not clear whether this observed difference stems from the specific hormonal qualities of the pill or users' confidence in its effectiveness and their increased sense of freedom: with the pill, they do not have to put anything on or into the genitals. For couples who place a high premium on unplanned coitus, the pill is a highly desirable method.

## Hormone Implants

In 1990, the FDA approved an implantable slow-release contraceptive for use by U.S. women. Known as *Norplant*, it consists of six thin, flexible

Norplant—a contraceptive implant, inserted into a woman's upper arm, that slowly releases hormones to inhibit ovulation.

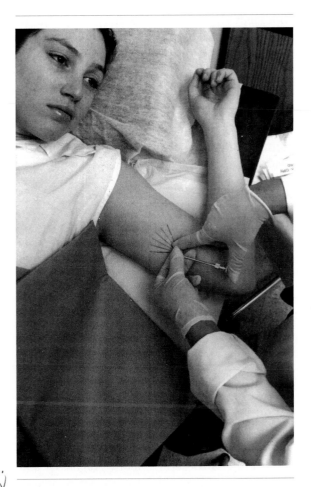

**FIGURE 10.18**
**Contraceptive Implants**
Norplant capsules inserted into a woman's arm provide contraceptive protection by releasing progestin over a five-year period.

capsules, less than 1½ inches long, that are inserted just under the skin of a woman's upper arm (see Figure 10.18). A local anesthetic is administered before insertion of the capsules, so there is usually little or no pain. Over a period of five years these capsules slowly and continuously release levonorgestrel, a synthetic progestin, into the user's bloodstream. The method may be relied on for contraception within 24 hours following insertion.

A variation of the method, Norplant-2, consists of implanting two rods in the upper arm.

Both methods are highly effective, with a failure rate of .09 per 100 women. Although Norplant-2 appears to be slightly more effective during the first two years, its failure rates are higher than those of Norplant during the last three years.

Similar to oral contraceptives, the implants work by suppressing ovulation and thickening cervical mucus, which inhibits the capacity of sperm to enter the uterus. The most common side effects of the method are changes in menstrual symptoms such as irregular bleeding, spotting, and increases and decreases in menstrual flow, especially during the first year (Forrest & Kaeser, 1993). In one study of more than 200 women using Norplant in San Francisco, 82% of the users reported such menstrual changes, but most said that they had expected the changes and were generally not bothered by them (Darney et al., 1990). Other possible side effects include headaches, nervousness, nausea, and dizziness. For women who wish to have Norplant removed, either because of side effects or because they want to become pregnant, removal—accompanied by a local anesthetic—is readily done by a physician.

Of the women in the Darney et al. (1990) study who reported changes in their sex lives after having Norplant inserted (44%), two-thirds reported an improvement, primarily because they were less concerned about pregnancy and thought that sex could be more spontaneous. About 25% of the women reported a decrease in frequency of intercourse either because of menstrual changes or, for a very small number of women, decreased libido.

Medroxyprogesterone acetate (Depo-Provera) is a long-acting progestin that has been approved for contraceptive use in the United States. A single injection is given every three months for contraceptive purposes. The first-year probability of failure is only 0.3% (Hatcher et al., 1994).

## Intrauterine Devices (IUDs)

The *intrauterine device (IUD)* is a small plastic and/or metal device that is placed inside the

**intrauterine device (IUD)**—small plastic device that is inserted into the uterus for contraceptive purposes.

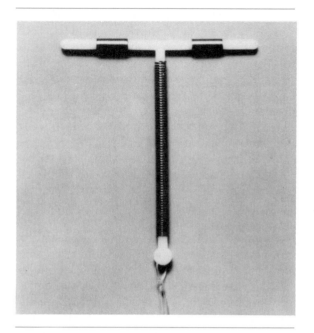

**FIGURE 10.19**
**The Copper T IUD**
These IUDs are a plastic T-shaped device with copper collars on the arms and copper wound around the stem, and Progestasert, which contains progestin. Highly effective, they have an annual failure rate of less than 1 per 100 women.

woman's uterus (see Figure 10.19). The first IUD, the Lippes Loop, was introduced in the United States in the mid-1960s. The IUD must be inserted by a trained physician during or shortly after a menstrual period. An inserter is pushed gently through the cervical opening, and the IUD is released from the inserter into the uterus, where the IUD regains its original shape. The string attached to the IUD hangs from the cervix into the vagina, so that a woman can check it periodically to see that the IUD is still in place. The string also facilitates the removal of the IUD by a physician.

It is not clear precisely how the IUD works, but the low failure rates, ranging from .6 to 2 per 100 women annually, underscore its effectiveness. The mildly irritating effect of the IUD on the uterine wall may stimulate the release of extra amounts of prostaglandins that may in turn trigger spotting or a menstrual period. Thus the IUD may prevent normal development of the uterine lining, so that when a fertilized egg makes its way down the fallopian tube, it cannot implant in the uterus.

Currently, two IUDs are available. Both are medicated, containing either copper (Cu380T-Paragard or Copper T) or progesterone (Progestasert). The Copper-T remains effective for eight years (Forrest & Kaeser, 1993). The hormonal effectiveness of Progestasert lasts a year, after which it must be replaced.

IUD insertion involves varying amounts of discomfort, depending on a woman's history and the diameter of the particular IUD inserter. A woman whose cervix has never been dilated, either medically or during childbirth, may experience considerable pain, but local anesthesia can reduce the discomfort. A rare but potentially fatal risk associated with IUD insertion is perforation or puncturing of the uterus. This risk is lessened when experienced professionals perform the insertion. Other adverse side effects of the IUD include cramping, an increase in the amount and duration of menstrual flow, pelvic inflammatory disease (PID; see Chapter 17), expulsion of the IUD, and ectopic pregnancy (see Chapter 9). These side effects are most pronounced during the initial months of use.

The history of the use of the IUD for birth control provides a classic example of why risks and benefits should be weighed carefully by those making contraceptive choices. In 1965 only 1.3% of all married women using reversible methods of contraception were wearing IUDs. By 1977 this figure had jumped to 15%. But by 1986 all but one IUD (Progestasert) had been withdrawn from the market by their manufacturers. Because the string hanging out of the cervix into the vagina makes it easier for bacteria to travel into the uterus, IUD users were as much as six times more likely to develop PID (and subsequent infertility because of scar tissue in the fallopian tubes) than were women who used other contraceptive methods (Cramer et al., 1985; Daling et al., 1992). The longer these early IUDs were used, the greater the risk of PID and infertility.

The two contemporary IUDs—the Copper T and Progestasert—are highly effective. Providing that users carefully follow instructions regarding safer sex practices, checking to make sure that the IUD is in place, and having regular annual pelvic exams, these two IUDs are relatively free of health risks but are still used by only 1% of sexually active women (Forrest & Fordyce, 1993).

## Relatively Ineffective Methods

The contraceptive methods just described are more effective than is reliance on withdrawal, postcoital douching, or breast-feeding to prevent ovulation. But because millions of people regularly use these three methods, we discuss them briefly.

### Withdrawal

Referred to as coitus interruptus in early sex manuals, *withdrawal* involves removing the penis from the vagina prior to ejaculation. Although the failure rate of this method is as high as 19%, it is still lower than the 85% pregnancy rate of sexually active women who use no method at all.

There are two problems with withdrawal. One arises from the vast difference between intentions and actions. Although a couple may intend to part before the man ejaculates, they may not always achieve this goal for a variety of psychological and physical reasons. The other problem centers on the secretions of the Cowper's glands. When a man becomes aroused, these glands release clear, slippery droplets at the opening of the penis, and sometimes this fluid contains sperm.

### Postcoital Douching

More than a third of U.S. women douche regularly, with 18% doing so at least once a week (Aral, Mosher, & Cates, 1992). Those who did not complete high school were most likely to douche regularly (56%), whereas the least likely were women who had completed college (17%). About 3% of sexually active women may engage in the practice because of the popular—but inaccurate—belief that *postcoital douching* has contraceptive benefits (Forrest & Fordyce, 1993).

---

**withdrawal**—removal of the penis from the vagina before ejaculation.

**postcoital douching** (DOO-shing)—insertion of chemical solutions, some of which can kill sperm, into the vagina after coitus.

*PID—Pelvic Inflammatory Disease)*

Some women use carbonated beverages following coitus in a vain attempt to prevent conception. Such acidic solutions do kill sperm, but they must be in contact with the sperm to do so. Therein lies the problem. Sperm start swimming through the cervix and into the uterus in a matter of seconds after ejaculation. Therefore, even if a woman has an acidic douche ready to insert into her vagina right after ejaculation, many sperm may have already escaped to the safety of her uterus. Further, the carbonation in these drinks may even help push the sperm toward the cervical entrance. Finally, the risk of PID is much greater among women who douche than among those who do not (Scholes et al., 1993).

### Breast-Feeding

Many physicians and laypeople have claimed for years that breast-feeding acts as a natural contraceptive. This claim is based on several observations. First, breast-feeding does appear to delay the return of menstruation following childbirth in some women, although women who rely on the return of menstruation to begin contraceptive use should know that ovulation can occur prior to the resumption of menstruation. Second, cross-cultural comparisons of the interval between one conception and the next in women who breast-feed and those who do not indicate that breast-feeding women take longer to conceive another child (Ellison, 1987; Knodel & Kintner, 1977). It appears that prolactin, a hormone secreted in response to suckling the nipples, is closely related to the mechanism that suppresses ovulation. The frequency of nursing appears to be crucial in delaying ovulation, however. For example, !Kung women, hunter-gatherers in southern Africa, nurse about every 15 minutes during the day and much of the night. In contrast, U.S. women usually nurse about every three or four hours for about 20 minutes each time, and they attempt to eliminate night feedings as soon as possible. In addition, in the absence of a sufficient level of calories (a circumstance more likely in nomadic hunter-gatherer groups than among contemporary North American women), ovulation and menstruation are disrupted.

The reasons for differences in the return of ovulation and menstruation in various popula-

tions are still being investigated. At present, the available data suggest that breast-feeding, in and of itself, is not a reliable form of contraception for North Americans.

## Sterilization

*Sterilization*—the use of surgical procedures to block an egg's passage through the fallopian tube or the sperm's passage through the vas deferens—has been rapidly gaining in worldwide popularity. In 1960 fewer than 6% of American couples relied on sterilization. As recently as 1970, most hospitals used the "rule of 120" in deciding whether to grant a woman's request for sterilization. This rule called for such a request to be denied unless her age multiplied by the number of her children totaled 120 or more. For example, a woman with three children would have to wait until she was 40 before she could be sterilized. After 1970, hospital rules governing sterilization became considerably less restrictive, and it has become the leading method of contraception worldwide. It is estimated that more than 14 million Americans and 100 million couples throughout the world rely on sterilization for birth control (Hatcher et al., 1994).

### Vasectomy

For males, sterilization means a *vasectomy*, a surgical procedure in which the vas deferens is cut. First performed more than 300 years ago, the operation has been carried out routinely since 1925. About half a million vasectomies are performed annually in the United States (Klitsch, 1993). Because the effects of a vasectomy can be permanent, it is important for a man or a couple to consider the decision carefully.

---

**sterilization**—a surgical procedure performed to make an individual incapable of reproduction.

**vasectomy**—male sterilization involving cutting or tying of the vas deferens.

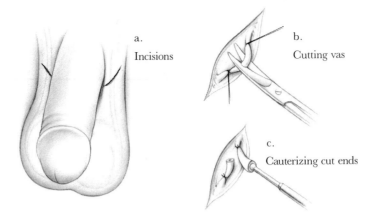

a.
Incisions

b.
Cutting vas

c.
Cauterizing cut ends

**FIGURE 10.20**
**Vasectomy**
A vasectomy prevents sperm from traveling out of the scrotum. Drawing *a* shows the site of the incisions in the scrotum. Drawing *b* illustrates the cutting of the vas deferens with surgical scissors, and *c* shows the blocking of the cut ends of the vas deferens to reduce the chances of their growing back together.

The operation, usually performed on an outpatient basis, requires only a local anesthetic. An incision less than one inch long is made either in the middle or on each side of the scrotum. The vas deferens is cut and blocked, and then the incision is sewn up (see Figure 10.20). Because a vasectomy prevents sperm from traveling beyond the point of incision into the upper part of the vas deferens to join the semen, it is an extremely effective birth control technique, with a failure rate of less than 1%. In rare cases, however, the cut ends of the vas deferens manage to reconnect themselves, and additional surgery is required.

After surgery, another contraceptive should be used until two successive semen analyses have confirmed the absence of sperm. It takes about four to six weeks and 6 to 36 ejaculations to clear remaining sperm from the vas deferens (Olds et al., 1992).

The absorption of sperm into the man's bloodstream when the vas deferens is closed commonly triggers the formation of antibodies. The majority of men who undergo vasectomies apparently manufacture such antibodies during the year following surgery. Thereafter, antibody levels generally decline. The main effect of elevated antibody levels is to increase the effectiveness of the vasectomy as a contraceptive technique, because the antibodies kill sperm. Such antibodies have also been observed among some fertile, nonvasectomized men.

There is a lack of agreement in the results of studies on the relationship between vasectomy and prostate cancer. Studies currently in progress may help to resolve lingering uncertainties about the long-term effects of vasectomy (Klitsch, 1993).

Vasectomized men who change their minds after having a vasectomy may have the procedure reversed through a microsurgery procedure called *vasovasectomy*. Across studies, rates of conception following vasovasectomy have ranged from 16% to 79% (Hatcher et al., 1994). The major factors in the success of vasovasectomy appear to be a relatively short length of time between the vasectomy and the reversal surgery, and the presence of sperm in the vasa deferentia below the point at which the vasectomy

**vasovasectomy**—surgical reversal of vasectomy.

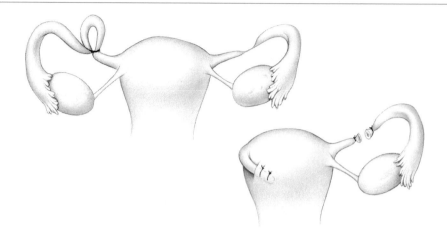

**FIGURE 10.21**
**Tubal Ligation**
In the Pomeroy technique (top drawing), the fallopian tube is grasped by its mid-section and tied to make a loop, which is then cut. The severed ends scar over, leaving a gap of half an inch or more between the ends of the tube. The lower drawing shows the Irving technique, in which the fallopian tubes are cut rather than tied.

was performed (McClure, 1988). Because vaso-vasectomy is not 100% successful, men should not have vasectomies unless they are quite sure that they do not want to father more children. If a man does change his mind after being steril-ized, however, he should undergo vasovasec-tomy as soon as possible.

Before having a vasectomy, a man can place several frozen ejaculates in a sperm bank for use in artificial insemination in the event that he and his partner wish to have children later. Insemi-nation by frozen sperm, however, is not as likely to result in pregnancy as is coitus between a fer-tile man and woman.

The major benefit of a vasectomy is that after all sperm have been eliminated from the ejacu-late, impregnation is impossible. Vasectomy does not alter hormone production or the ability to ejaculate because 95% of the volume of semen is made up of fluids produced by glands located above the point of incision. Moreover, because vasectomy does not influence the production of testosterone or other hormones, no physiologi-cally based effects on sexual desire or respon-siveness would be expected. A wide range of psy-

chological responses may occur, however. Most vasectomized men report either no effect on their sexuality or an improvement in their desire and responsiveness.

## Tubal Ligation

Women are sterilized by cutting and/or tying (li-gating) the fallopian tubes, which effectively blocks the route normally taken by a mature egg to its potential meeting with sperm. *Tubal liga-tion* is considerably more complicated and ex-pensive than vasectomy, generally requiring hos-pitalization, more extensive anesthesia, and a longer recovery period (see Figure 10.21). Still, over half a million U.S. women undergo the pro-cedure annually (Hatcher et al., 1994).

There are a number of variations in female sterilization procedures. One that has been gain-ing in popularity during the last decade is known as the band-aid operation. This method is per-

**tubal ligation** (lye-GAY-shun)—female sterilization involving cutting or tying of the fallopian tubes.

formed with a *laparoscope*, which is inserted into the abdomen through an incision in the well of the navel. A woman is given either a general anesthesia to put her to sleep or a local anesthetic to numb the skin around her navel. A tiny incision is made just below her navel, and carbon dioxide or nitrous oxide is then pumped into the abdominal cavity through a long, hollow needle. The pressure of the gas inflates her abdomen, allowing access to the fallopian tubes. A portion of the tube is grasped and is usually clipped or banded. This procedure is repeated on the other tube, and then the gas is released from the abdomen. Finally, the incision is closed with an absorbable suture and covered with a band-aid, which the woman may remove after eight hours. Complications from female sterilization procedures include bowel perforation, infection, hemorrhage, and adverse effects from anesthesia.

Unlike a vasectomized man, a sterilized woman may engage in coitus without any additional contraception as soon as she wants to, although she may have a day or two of slight discomfort following the procedure. Hormone production and the menstrual cycle are unaffected by tubal ligation, and the operation appears to have no physiological effect on sexual desire or response. Psychological effects range from none to positive, with the latter presumably resulting from the elimination of fears of pregnancy. This confidence is well founded, as the failure rate of tubal ligation is .4 per 100 women (Hatcher et al., 1994), and it is the third most frequently used contraceptive method employed by women (Forrest & Fordyce, 1993).

Just a few years ago, fewer than 25% of women who obtained reversals of tubal ligation were subsequently able to conceive. Recent advances in sophisticated microsurgery techniques have led to much higher rates of success in restoring fertility. The overall rate of live births following reversals now ranges from 40% to 75% (Olds et al., 1992). Like men, however, women should not seek sterilization unless they are quite

sure that they do not want (more) children. Women face higher risks than do men when they undergo sterilization and subsequent reversal surgery.

---

## Contraceptive Techniques of the Future

It should be abundantly clear by now that most of the currently available, effective methods of contraception are designed to be used by women. Moreover, each poses various problems, although any one of them is preferable to unprotected intercourse followed by an unintended pregnancy. We turn now to current research on methods to control male fertility.

### Research on Future Methods of Birth Control for Males

It is unlikely that an effective male method of contraception aside from the condom and sterilization will be available before the year 2000 (Hatcher, et al., 1994). Even after effective methods are found, a number of years will be needed to study the possible long-term side effects before FDA approval can be obtained.

The polyurethane condom should be available by the time this book is published. This condom has been developed to improve sensation and durability because of complaints about interference with sensitivity and pleasure resulting from the use of latex condoms.

There are a number of hormones currently under study. A testosterone derivative suppresses sperm production enough to provide reliable protection (Hatcher et al., 1994). However, because weekly injections of testosterone are required, many men would find this an impractical solution. Hormone delivery systems that can deliver testosterone for two to three months and testosterone-derivative implants that are effective for up to a year are being studied.

The most promising vaccines for men use either follicle stimulating hormone (FSH) or luteinizing hormone releasing factor (LHRH). The FSH

---

**laparoscope** (LAP-ar-oh-SCOPE)—a long, hollow instrument inserted into the abdominal cavity through an incision directly below the navel; used for diagnosis of medical difficulties and for sterilization.

vaccine has eliminated sperm while maintaining normal testosterone levels in monkeys (Hatcher et al., 1994). Alternatively, a vaccine using LHRH shuts down both testosterone and sperm production; to maintain sex drive, men would have to supplement this vaccine with testosterone.

## Research on Future Methods of Birth Control for Females

The vaginal ring, developed by the World Health Organization, is a plastic ring that releases progestin. It is worn around the cervix for three weeks each month and then is removed during menstruation. The vaginal ring appears to have only a 3% failure rate (Hatcher et al., 1994).

Focus on an antipregnancy vaccine for women has involved the hormone human chorionic gonadotropin (HCG). However, because the vaccine also induces abortion, it is unlikely that American companies will pursue this form of birth control within the near future.

Although these birth control methods appear promising, the speed with which they become generally available will be influenced by the amount of money that is devoted to research. An increase in annual expenditures for research and development of new, safe, and effective methods of birth control would accelerate progress. A nationwide survey of American women between the ages of 18 and 44 showed that their main reason for not using available contraceptives—and thus for subjecting themselves to the consequent risk of unintended pregnancy—was fear of side effects. Women under the age of 24 were more fearful than older women and were also less likely to be using any contraceptive method (Forrest & Henshaw, 1983). The cost of raising a baby to adulthood, now estimated to be at least $100,000, should be taken into account as we determine priorities for government spending. Society will pay the costs of raising those babies who are born to economically disadvantaged adolescent mothers who did not intend to become pregnant; thus it is in our best interests to provide as much support as possible for the development of safe, effective, and easily used male and female contraceptives.

## Summary of Major Points _____

1. The development and acceptance of contraceptives.

Although contraceptive techniques have been used throughout history, their use was illegal in the United States well into the 20th century. Legal barriers were slowly eliminated, and in the 1960s the pill and the IUD joined the less reliable barrier methods as popular contraceptives. For various reasons, the focus has been on the development of female rather than male contraceptives. Because the most reliable methods are associated with unwanted side effects for some women, women's groups have called for a greater focus on the development of dependable male methods.

2. The evaluation of contraceptive methods.

The prospective contraceptive user should consider the effectiveness and potential side effects of each method, as well as his or her own habits and preferences. Contraceptive effectiveness and risks depend on the lifestyle and medical history of the user, as well as on the likelihood that a method is employed during every act of coitus. For most women, the greatest risk of illness and death is associated with engaging in unprotected intercourse. In the absence of birth control, 85 out of every 100 sexually active women become pregnant within a year.

3. Barriers to contraceptive use.

Although most people wholeheartedly endorse birth control, adolescents generally engage in sexual intercourse for some time before obtaining reliable contraception. As a result, more than a million single, teenaged females become pregnant each year. Reluctance to obtain and use contraception is associated with certain psychological and social factors. Those young men and women who feel guilty about sexuality and those who are less emotionally committed to their partners are less likely than others to use contraception. Contraceptive knowledge is related to the likelihood of young people's use of birth control, but ready access to contraceptives and emotional factors appear to be more important than information in determining contraceptive use.

4. Temporary methods of contraception.

The safest methods of contraception are the barrier methods: the diaphragm and spermicide, the cervical cap and spermicide, the condom, and spermicidal foams and suppositories. These methods are less effective, however, in preventing conception than are the pill, the IUD, and hormonal implants. Because of the potential risks associated with the pill for some women, a woman's lifestyle and medical history should be carefully evaluated before the pill is prescribed, to verify that she is not in any of the high-risk categories. The main risks imposed by the pill involve the cardiovascular system. Recent research has demonstrated either no relationship between use of the pill and reproductive organ cancers, or a reduced risk of cancer among pill users. Data on the relationship between pill use and breast cancer are contradictory. The effectiveness of the rhythm method may be increased by using several means of determining the date of ovulation. Although withdrawal, postcoital douching, and breast-feeding may reduce the risk of conception slightly, these three attempts at birth control are not notably effective.

5. Permanent methods of contraception.

Sterilization is the most popular method of contraception. Vasectomy, the severing of the two vasa deferentia, is highly effective and entails little risk of side effects for most men. It can be performed at an outpatient clinic, and it does not harm sexual response unless a particular man bases his sense of masculinity on the ability to impregnate. Female sterilization methods are somewhat more complicated than is the vasectomy, because an abdominal incision must be made to expose the fallopian tubes. These methods are highly effective and do not interfere with sexual response. Although physicians report increasing success with sterilization reversals, individuals should not undergo sterilization unless they are certain that they do not wish to conceive.

6. The development and testing of new contraceptives.

Numerous temporary and permanent contraceptive techniques are being developed and tested for the presence of undesirable side effects. Several are designed for male use.

## Review of Key Concepts

1. The number of conceptions that occur when a contraceptive method is used correctly is known as the: a) actual failure rate; b) theoretical failure rate; c) methodological failure rate; d) effective failure rate. (p. 305)

2. Most American adolescents: a) use reliable contraceptive methods; b) remain virgins until around the age of 20; c) become sexually active before age 20; d) use effective contraceptives at the time they become sexually active. (pp. 307–310)

3. Sex education in the schools: a) always contains information on contraception; b) is opposed by most of the general public; c) encourages promiscuity; d) is supported by the majority of the general public. (pp. 310–312)

4. Education about sex and contraception increases adolescent pregnancy rates. True or false, and why? (pp. 310–312)

5. The greatest mortality risk for sexually active women is: a) unprotected sexual intercourse; b) using a barrier method of contraception; c) a first-trimester abortion; d) using birth control pills. (p. 316)

6. Checking the stretchability of cervical mucus is associated with which of the following methods of contraception? a) vaginal suppositories; b) sympto-thermal; c) spermicide; d) diaphragm. (p. 318)

7. The diaphragm should be left in the vagina following male ejaculation for: a) approximately 1 hour; b) 6-8 hours; c) 24 hours; d) none of the above. (p. 320)

8. Some side effects of the pill: a) mimic some of the symptoms of early pregnancy; b) stabilize after a few cycles on the pill; c) occur because the dosage is too high; d) all of the above. (pp. 327–330)

9. The most frequently used birth control method in the world is: a) the pill; b) the diaphragm with spermicide; c) the cervical cap; d) sterilization. (p. 334)

10. Discuss the fallacy that the increase in premarital sex among adolescents over the past few decades is rooted in the easy availability of contraceptives. (pp. 311–314)

11. A married couple, deciding that they want no more children, are considering sterilization. Would you advise a vasectomy for the husband, or a tubal ligation for the wife? Why? (pp. 334–337)

# Resolving Unwanted Pregnancy

*THE four women sat waiting for their turn with the lab technician. Each offered resolutions and bargains.*

JEN: If I'm not pregnant, I'll never forget to take the pill again.

CHRIS: I'll never, ever go to another party without first putting in my diaphragm.

THERESA: How on earth are we going to feed another one? So much for his promises that he'll pull out in time. I'm never going to let him anywhere near me again unless he already has his rubber on!

LUCIA: If only I'm not pregnant, I'll study twice as hard and stay away from men. I faithfully took the pill every day!

After discovering an unwanted pregnancy, a woman has three options: obtaining an *abortion*; continuing the pregnancy, keeping the baby, and rearing it with or without the help of its father; or placing the baby for adoption. In this chapter, we examine the currently available abortion methods and the legal status of this option. We also consider the short-term and long-term effects of choosing this alternative. If an unmarried woman decides against abortion, she is far more likely now than in the past to bring up the baby rather than to place it for adoption. Recent

**abortion**—spontaneous or medical termination of a pregnancy before the fetus can survive outside the uterus.

343

research suggests, however, that without considerable social and economic support, such a mother and her offspring face numerous difficulties. Finally, we discuss the ethical and educational dilemmas of unwanted pregnancy among adolescents.

## Unwanted Pregnancy

Defining the phrase "unwanted and unplanned pregnancy" is tricky. To begin with, the individual words do not necessarily fit together. A conception may be unplanned, but confirmation of the pregnancy may lead a couple to celebrate. Or a pregnancy may be carefully planned but later not wanted for a variety of reasons: the end of a marriage or a relationship, a pregnant woman's exposure to teratogenic drugs or diseases early in pregnancy, or financial setbacks such as loss of a job. Such factors can alter a couple's situation or a woman's situation so drastically that a deliberately conceived fetus can become unwanted. Finally, of course, conception may be both unplanned and unwanted.

It is difficult to obtain an accurate estimate of the annual number of unwanted conceptions. The number of abortions performed annually in the United States—more than 1.5 million—provides a minimum estimate of the number of unwanted pregnancies (Ventura et al., 1992). In addition, well over half a million babies are born annually to unmarried women, only a small percentage of whom wanted to conceive. Thus we might conclude that there are in excess of 2 million unwanted conceptions per year. Two million is also a conservative estimate, however, because this figure does not take into account the number of babies premaritally conceived but not premaritally born, the number of unwanted conceptions leading to birth among married couples, or the number of unwanted pregnancies ending in spontaneous abortion or stillbirth. A third of all U.S. brides, and half of those under 20, are pregnant at their weddings. We discuss the fate of these couples and their offspring later in the chapter. First, we consider the most frequently used method of resolving unwanted pregnancy: abortion.

## Abortion: A Human Dilemma

During the past decade, slightly under one-third of all pregnant American women obtained abortions each year (Ventura et al., 1992). The majority were performed on relatively young, White, unmarried women in the first eight weeks of pregnancy. Nationally, of the 111 pregnancies per 1,000 women aged 15 to 19 that did not end in miscarriage, 59% resulted in birth, and 41% were terminated by abortion (Henshaw, 1993).

Abortion is one of the most controversial moral and legal issues of our time (see Box 11.1). The debate about abortion is complicated by the fact that some methods of contraception can also function as abortives. Both the IUD (see Chapter 10) and RU-486 can be used as methods of early abortion. Most books listing methods of birth control classify these with contraceptives rather than with abortion methods, presumably because any abortions they cause may occur before a woman knows that she is pregnant.

Deliberate abortion is one of the oldest medical procedures known to humans. It has been practiced throughout history since well before the time of Christ, and across Western and non-Western cultures (Bullough, 1994). Attitudes toward the practice have varied greatly. Even the Catholic Church, which currently condemns abortion, has taken an antiabortion stance for only the past century. Until the middle of the 19th century, the Church permitted abortion for the first 40 days following conception because Catholic officials believed that the embryo had no soul until that time (McLaren, 1981). It should be noted that other religions also condemn abortion, but their positions typically do not receive the publicity that papal pronouncements do.

An estimated 36 million to 53 million abortions are performed every year throughout the world. Between 26 million and 31 million of these are legal (Henshaw & Van Vort, 1992). Three-quarters of the world's people live in countries where abortion is legal at least for health reasons, and more than half of these reside in areas where abortion can be obtained on request for *any* reason. Only one nation, Romania, significantly reduced access to legal abortions from 1966 to 1989, as part of its national effort to increase fertility.

**Box 11.1**

## The Legal Status of Abortion in the United States

Laws regulating abortion were nonexistent in the United States at the beginning of the 19th century, but by 1900 abortion was restricted or illegal throughout the nation (D'Emilio & Freedman, 1988). In the past quarter century, however, laws have proliferated liberalizing and then restricting the conditions under which pregnancy could be terminated.

In 1970 the New York State legislature ruled that physicians could provide an abortion for any woman who requested it and who was less than 24 weeks pregnant. The New York law made no restrictions on residence, age, or marital status, nor did it require consent from anyone but the woman (Guttmacher & Kaiser, 1986). Subsequently, thousands of women went to New York to terminate their pregnancies.

### 1. The Supreme Court Decision of 1973

During the next few years following the New York State decision, the U.S. Supreme Court deliberated the issue at length, and in January 1973, seven of the nine justices ruled in *Roe* v. *Wade* to strike down the abortion laws of Texas and Georgia. Essentially, their ruling prohibited states from interfering in decisions reached by a woman and her doctor during the first three months of pregnancy. Their judgment was based on the constitutional guarantee of the right to privacy. Under *Roe*, the right to abortion during the first trimester was deemed fundamental and could not be restricted unless the state could show a compelling reason for doing so. The states' right to regulate abortion to protect the fetus during the last trimester remained intact, except if abortion was necessary to protect a woman's life or health. During the second trimester, states could regulate abortion in ways that are reasonably related to maternal health, by requiring, for example, that an abortion be performed in a hospital.

### 2. The Hyde Amendment

In 1976, antiabortion forces managed to restrict abortion economically with the passage of the Hyde Amendment. This law specified that federal Medicaid money could not be used to pay for abortions except when pregnancy threatened a woman's life or resulted from rape or incest. The law, upheld by the U.S. Supreme Court in 1977, affected one-third of the million women who were eligible to receive Medicaid assistance because of poverty. Denial of Medicaid assistance for abortion meant that these women had either to find funds elsewhere to pay for the procedure or maintain the pregnancy.

In 1981, decisions by the Senate and the Supreme Court further restricted access to abortion. The Senate decided that women who were pregnant as a result of rape or incest could no longer receive Medicaid funds for abortion. In 1993, a strong majority of the House of Representatives voted to retain the Hyde Amendment banning the use of Medicaid funds for abortion but eliminated the ban for women who had become pregnant as a result of rape or incest.

### 3. The Supreme Court Decision of 1983

In 1983, 10 years after the historic *Roe* v. *Wade* decision, the Supreme Court, in a 6–3 decision, essentially reaffirmed a woman's constitutional right to choose whether to maintain or terminate pregnancy. Specifically, the Court ruled against an Akron, Ohio, law requiring that doctors inform abortion patients of potential pain to the fetus as a result of abortion. The Court also ruled that cities cannot impose waiting periods on abortion clients or restrict the location of first- or second-trimester abortions to hospitals. The justices did uphold the right of the states to require that juveniles obtain permission from a parent or judge before undergoing an abortion. In addition, the Court ruled that states may require analysis of fetal tissues, and the presence of a second doctor during an abortion when there is reason to believe that the fetus might survive.

## 4. The Supreme Court Decision of 1989

In a 5–4 decision in 1989, the Supreme Court ruled in favor of Webster in *Webster* v. *Reproductive Health Services*. This ruling narrowed the rights that had been granted by *Roe* v. *Wade*. In *Webster*, the Court upheld the constitutionality of a Missouri law that restricted the availability of public funds for abortion services and required physicians to test for the viability (ability to survive outside the uterus) of a fetus at 20 weeks or more. Although the *Webster* decision has little impact on affluent women, it has had a chilling effect on poor women seeking an abortion. Presumably, the latter would need a significant time span to obtain enough money to pay for an abortion. In the event that they pass the 20-week cutoff in Missouri—or in other states that follow Missouri's lead—the cost of testing for viability (using ultrasonography and amniocentesis) would more than double the cost of terminating the pregnancy.

## 5. The Supreme Court Decisions of 1990–1991

Since 1973, more than half the states have passed parental-notification or consent laws for minors, but the courts have struck down most of these (Worthington, Lawson, & Brubaker et al., 1989). However, in June 1990, the U.S. Supreme Court upheld an Ohio law requiring that a physician personally notify one parent of a minor seeking an abortion. In the event that the minor is unwilling that her parent be notified, she must obtain a judge's permission before obtaining the abortion. This procedure is known as the judicial bypass.

In a 5–4 decision in 1991, the Supreme Court upheld federal regulations enacted in 1988 by the Reagan administration that bar health care professionals in clinics receiving federal funds from discussing abortion with their clients. Known as the "gag rule," this decision affected about 4,000 clinics that annually served about 4.5 million women, most of whom had low incomes. According to provisions of the gag rule, clinic personnel were to respond to questions from clients about abortion by saying that the "clinic does not consider abortion an appropriate method of family planning." (Note that this statement contradicts evidence to be presented later in this chapter under the heading "The Abortion-as-Birth-Control Hypothesis.") The ruling placed physicians and other health care professionals in a difficult ethical and licensing quandary, in that they are expected to obtain informed consent from their patients after describing the range of available options in making medical decisions. Planned Parenthood Federation of America announced that it would "never compromise patient care." The gag rule ended shortly after Clinton was inaugurated in January 1993. One of his first acts as president was to overturn the Reagan administration regulations leading to the gag rule.

## 6. The Supreme Court Decision of 1992

By 1992, 34 states had laws demanding parental consent or notification (or judicial bypass) for minors seeking abortion. By a 5–4 margin, the U.S. Supreme Court reaffirmed the essential features of *Roe* v. *Wade*: that prior to fetal viability, a woman has a constitutional right to obtain an abortion. In *Planned Parenthood of Southeastern Pennsylvania* v. *Casey*, the Court ruled that a state could regulate abortion throughout pregnancy as long as it does not impose an "undue burden" on a woman's right to terminate pregnancy. The Court defined "undue burden" as a regulation that has the purpose or effect of placing a substantial obstacle in the path of a woman seeking an abortion of a nonviable fetus.

The Court upheld several provisions of the Pennsylvania abortion law, including a 24-hour waiting period that follows completion of specific informed-consent requirements, and reporting and record-keeping rules—provisions that the Court had declared unconstitutional just a few years before. The Court also upheld the law's parental consent provision but struck down, as an undue burden, the requirement that a married woman notify her husband of her intent to have an abortion.

If you find the foregoing changes in laws confusing and contradictory, imagine the responses of an underage female experiencing an unwanted pregnancy. People in that position should call their closest Planned Parenthood office to find out the current laws in their state.

These restrictions were enacted during the rule of former dictator Nicolae Ceauşescu. With the overthrow of the Ceauşescu government in 1989, Romania's antiabortion statute was struck down in 1990 (refer to Box 2.2).

The movement toward liberalized abortion laws in many nations has been rooted in three humanitarian principles: 1) the recognition that illegal abortion poses a threat to public health; 2) the belief that social justice requires equal access to abortion for rich and poor alike; and 3) support for a woman's right to control her own body.

## The Moral Debate over Abortion

Attitudes toward abortion vary widely among North Americans (see Figure 11.1). For the past few decades, efforts to make abortion readily available figured prominently in the movement to protect women's rights. In 1978, Mary Clark, coordinator of the California Abortion Rights Action League, described abortion as "the most basic right a woman has. If a woman can't control her body, she has no control over the rest of her life" (*Newsweek*, June 5, 1978, p. 39). The opposite end of the ideological spectrum was reflected in an assertion by the president of March for Life, Nellie Gray: "You are either for killing babies or you're not. You can't be for a little bit of killing babies" (*Newsweek*, June 5, 1978, p. 47).

In support of this latter position, activists have backed various federal antiabortion bills including the Human Life Amendment, which would outlaw almost all abortions by declaring that life begins at conception. Nineteen states have passed resolutions in favor of drafting a constitutional amendment that would ban abortion absolutely, and certain municipalities have passed local ordinances regarding abortion. (During the 1970s, women in Akron, Ohio, were legally required to take their aborted fetuses to a licensed funeral director.) But antiabortion activists have never been more vocal and visible than in the 1990s. Indeed, militant prolife activists, apparently motivated by their belief that abortion is murder, have used arson, fire bombings, and blockades as weapons of intimidation and obstruction. This extreme behavior has inspired various cartoons, among them one in which a prolife speaker is standing in front of a chalkboard on which there appears a list headed by the title "How to Bomb an Abortion Clinic." The speaker asks of the audience, "The question is, if we accidentally kill somebody, do we still value human life?" It should be noted that the major prolife organizations have condemned such violence. However, occasionally individuals associated with these organizations have engaged in violence. For example, in 1993, a physician who performed abortions was shot to death on his arrival at work in Pensacola, Florida, by a participant in a prolife demonstration.

Recent research reveals little support for an absolute ban on abortion. Even among those generally opposed to abortion, there is support for the procedure under some circumstances, such as if the mother's health is endangered or if the pregnancy resulted from rape or incest. Surveys conducted in 1989 revealed that 36% of respondents supported no restrictions on abortion, whereas only 9% wanted abortion banned regardless of the circumstances (Cook, Jelen, & Wilcox, 1993).

**FIGURE 11.1**

**The Abortion Dilemma**

The photo on the left depicts a prochoice demonstration. The strong feelings of the people in this photo are matched by the intensity of feelings of the people in the photo on the right, who hold antiabortion attitudes.

Sociologist Donald Granberg (1981) surveyed the membership of the largest U.S. antiabortion group, the National Right to Life Committee (NRLC), and the largest U.S. prochoice group (favoring legal availability of abortion), the National Abortion Rights Action League (NARAL). The participants' responses to various questions relevant to abortion were then compared with the responses from nationwide samples. As Table 11.1 shows, U.S. attitudes are closer to those held by members of the prochoice group than to those held by members of the antiabortion group.

In addition to the factors listed in Table 11.1, people may consider a woman's sexual behavior in making judgments about the appropriateness of abortion. When asked to evaluate a series of fictitious case histories (see Box 11.2), college students approved of abortion for women who had become pregnant despite the conscientious use of a reliable contraceptive. These students also supported abortion for women who had become pregnant with a steady partner rather than during a casual sexual encounter (Allgeier et al., 1979).

Participants in the study made a number of revealing comments when describing their reasoning. For instance, one person who approved of abortion for "Ruth" said that if Ruth and her boyfriend "are really close, I could see granting

**TABLE 11.1  Abortion Attitudes**

| Question | Percentages of Affirmative Responses | | |
|---|---|---|---|
| | NARAL[a] | U.S. Adults | NRLC[b] |
| Do you think it should be possible for a woman to obtain legal abortion . . . | | | |
| If the woman's own health is seriously endangered by the pregnancy? | 100 | 90 | 15 |
| If she became pregnant as a result of rape? | 100 | 83 | 7 |
| If there is a strong chance of a serious defect in the baby? | 100 | 83 | 4 |
| If the family has a low income and cannot afford any more children? | 98 | 52 | 2 |
| If she is not married and does not want to marry the man? | 98 | 48 | 2 |
| If she is married and does not want to have any more children? | 97 | 47 | 1 |
| If she wants to have an abortion for any reason? | 85 | 41 | 1 |

[a]NARAL: National Abortion Rights Action League.
[b]NRLC: National Right to Life Committee.

Source: Granberg (1981, p. 36). From an article that first appeared in *The Humanist*, 1981. Reprinted by permission.

 **Box 11.2**

## Abortion Case Histories

These are the fictitious descriptions used in the Allgeier et al. studies (1979, 1982) of unmarried women applying for abortion. Volunteers were asked to indicate the extent to which they favored or were against abortion in each case. How do you feel?

**Gloria C.** has been dating a variety of men over the past several years. She has had sexual intercourse with some of them and has always used a diaphragm for contraception. She has become pregnant despite her use of the diaphragm and does not know which man is the father.

**Jill K.** recently discovered that she is pregnant. She has been going with Steve for almost a year. Over the past three months, they have engaged in sexual intercourse about five times. In each instance, they had not planned it, but got carried away and ended up having intercourse without any contraception.

**Sue T.** has had several love affairs in the past two years. She was convinced that premarital pregnancy was something that would never happen to her, so she never worried about birth control. She discovered that she was pregnant several weeks ago but is not sure who the father is.

**Betty P.** has dated a number of different men over the past year and a half. She has had sexual intercourse with some of them, but only during her "safe" time because she wanted to avoid any possibility of getting pregnant. Despite her precautions, she has become pregnant.

**Ruth D.** got a prescription for the pill when she and Greg, her boyfriend for the past year and a half, began having intercourse. Ruth forgot to take her pills with her on a camping trip they went on over a long weekend, and she's now pregnant.

**Debra N.** has no regular boyfriend, but has several friends with whom she occasionally has intercourse. She usually tried to keep track of her menstrual cycle and to avoid having intercourse except when she's safe, but she forgot to write down the date of her last period and recently had intercourse even though she wasn't sure whether she was fertile.

**Kathy B.** usually uses a diaphragm when having sexual intercourse. She went to a party thrown by her cousin, who wanted to fix her up with a friend of hers from work. She didn't have her diaphragm with her, and now she is six weeks pregnant.

it. She did take precautionary measures." This same person denied "Sue's" abortion request, saying, "If Sue had sexual intercourse with other men, I don't think she should be granted an abortion, especially since she doesn't know who the father is." Such reasoning ignores both the argument for fetal rights advanced by the anti-abortion faction and the argument for women's rights offered by the prochoice faction.

The reasoning observed in this study has the effect of rewarding conscientious women by granting them abortions, and "punishing" less responsible women by conferring motherhood on them, or at least full-term pregnancy and birth. Presumably, however, the less responsible women are less desirable candidates for motherhood, at least at this point in their lives, than are the more responsible women. Indeed, Rosen and Martindale's (1978) study of women with problem pregnancies indicated that those who decided to carry and give birth to the child perceived themselves as less competent than those who chose abortion.

Ten years after our series of studies on abortion policies, we were intrigued to learn that a state legislative coordinator for the National Right to Life Committee was quoted as saying that his organization was considering proposals to ban abortions in those cases in which a couple failed to use contraception. Such a law would presumably be difficult to enforce in the absence of witnesses observing the couple at the time of conception!

Attitudes toward abortion vary according to socioeconomic status, race, religious affiliation, and age. Catholics and Mormons hold more negative attitudes toward abortions than do Protestants, agnostics, and atheists (Bowers & Weaver,

1979; Granberg, 1985; Marsiglio & Shehan, 1993). The degree of guilt that a person feels about sex—a factor related to religion—also is associated with abortion attitudes. People with high levels of sex guilt are less accepting of abortions for women who desire them than are those with lower levels of sex guilt (Allgeier et al., 1981, 1982). Blacks feel more negatively about legalized abortion than do Whites (Hall & Ferree, 1986), although race was not a strong predictor among a nationally representative sample of males aged 15 to 19 when other background factors were controlled (Marsiglio & Shehan, 1993). Not surprisingly, unmarried women between menarche and menopause (that is, capable of reproduction) are more supportive of legalized abortion than are other-aged females or males (Betzig & Lombardo, 1992). However, research reviewed and conducted by Marsiglio and Shehan (1993) indicated that North American men under age 30 were less supportive of abortion than were men aged 30 and older. Finally, college-educated Americans, as well as those with higher incomes, are more supportive of legalized abortion than are their less-educated and less-affluent counterparts (Gallup, 1986).

*Reasons for Abortion*

Why do women seek abortions? Women usually cite several concurrent reasons; only 7% of women in a study of 1,900 abortion patients reported that one factor alone influenced their decision (Torres & Forrest, 1988). A further analysis of these data (Russo, Horn, & Schwartz, 1992) is presented in Table 11.2.

More than 75% of unmarried minors reported that they were not mature enough to raise

**TABLE 11.2 Percentages of Five Groups of 1,900 Abortion Patients Giving Various Internal and External Reasons for Abortion: Unmarried Minors and Adult Women by Marital and Parental Status**

| | Unmarried Minors | Unmarried Adults | | Married Adults | |
|---|---|---|---|---|---|
| Reasons | Nonmothers (261) | Mothers (480) | Nonmothers (852) | Mothers (204) | Nonmothers (46) |
| I. Internal reasons | 77.8 | 51.5 | 60.7 | 55.9 | 34.8 |
|   A. Not ready for childrearing | 75.9 | 23.8 | 48.5 | 21.1 | 34.8 |
|     1. Too young/not mature enough to raise a(nother) child | 61.3 | — | 16.1 | — | — |
|     2. Can't take the responsibility | 33.3 | 22.3 | 35.8 | 18.6 | 34.8 |
|   B. Childbearing completed | — | 17.9 | — | 39.7 | — |
|   C. Desire to avoid single parenthood | 5.0 | 18.1 | 21.4 | — | — |
|   D. Health | — | — | — | 10.8 | 6.5 |
|     1. Physical problems | — | — | — | 7.8 | 6.5 |
| II. External reasons | 70.0 | 71.3 | 77.2 | 66.7 | 89.1 |
|   A. General situational factors | 38.3 | 14.8 | 33.6 | 10.3 | 21.7 |
|     1. Education related | 36.8 | 5.2 | 22.7 | — | 13.0 |
|     2. Job related/would interfere with job/career | 8.8 | 7.1 | 15.0 | 6.9 | 13.0 |
|   B. Fetus related | 6.5 | 8.1 | 11.2 | 11.8 | 23.9 |
|     1. Prescription medication | — | — | — | 5.4 | 15.2 |
|     2. Diagnosed fetal defect | — | — | — | — | 6.5 |
|   C. Partner related | 11.9 | 24.0 | 19.0 | 17.2 | 28.3 |
|     1. Partner not ready/wants abortion | 5.0 | — | — | — | 15.2 |
|     2. Relationship may break up/has broken up | — | 7.7 | — | 5.9 | 10.9 |
|   D. Social disapproval of others | 13.8 | — | 9.3 | — | — |
|     1. Doesn't want others to know pregnant | 10.7 | — | 8.5 | — | — |
|   E. Other responsibilities/other children need me | — | 18.5 | — | 17.2 | — |
|   F. Cannot afford to have a baby | 28.4 | 40.0 | 44.2 | 34.3 | 41.3 |

*Note:* From Russo et al. (1992), *Journal of Social Issues.* Analysis based on data set reported in Torres and Forrest (1988). Dashes indicate that subcategory had responses of less than 5%. Married minors (0.7%) and minors who were mothers (3.6%) were not included because there were too few for meaningful comparisons.

a child. Only 5% of this group reported avoiding single parenthood as a reason for abortion. External reasons were also important for minors, with desire to complete education (37%), inability to afford a child (29%), and issues related to social disapproval (14%) and their partner's reaction to the pregnancy (12%) as the most common factors influencing their decision to have an abortion.

Among the four groups of adults in Table 11.2, more than one-third indicated they could not afford to have a baby now. Nonmothers who were unmarried were more likely to say that they were not mature enough to have a child than were women in the other three groups. Married mothers were more likely to give health-related reasons for abortion. Married nonmothers were more concerned with effects of prescription medications, worries having to do with the fetus, and diagnosed fetal defects as reasons for abortion. These results indicate that a woman's reasons for seeking an abortion are multiple and vary according to life circumstances (Russo et al., 1992). They also undermine the simplistic approach to abortion often advocated by antiabortion forces.

### Positions on Abortion

One dictionary defines *murder* as "the unlawful killing of one human being by another, esp. with premeditated malice." Lobbyists for a congressional or constitutional ban on abortion make their case on the grounds that abortion is murder. In contrast, supporters of legalized abortion argue that the practice is not murder because the fetus is not a human being with the legal rights of a person. Actually, both arguments seem faulty to us. If abortion is legal, then pregnancy termination is not unlawful, and there is no evidence to suggest that women seeking abortion feel "premeditated malice" toward the fetus. Biologically, the fetus is clearly alive in the uterus (as were the sperm and egg that contributed to conception), so there is human life. However, the fetus is not viable—capable of survival outside the uterus—until late in the second trimester, and more than 90% of abortions are performed during the first trimester.

In evaluating the issue of legalized abortion, it is important to take the alternatives into account. If legal abortion is unavailable, many women will die from self-administered abortions, from abortions performed by others who lack formal training in abortion procedures, or from the complications of unwanted pregnancy and childbirth. In 1965, eight years before *Roe* v. *Wade*, an estimated 20% of all deaths related to

pregnancy and childbirth were attributable to illegal abortions (Adler et al., 1992). It is estimated that a minimum of 100,000 women's deaths annually are attributable to illegal abortions (Henshaw & Van Vort, 1992). Further, the legalization of abortion has brought about a decrease in the mortality rate of women from pregnancy and childbirth, partly because some women who may be at risk of death from full-term pregnancies are having first-trimester abortions. Maternal mortality is down to an average level of .6 deaths per 100,000 legal abortions worldwide and .4 deaths per 100,000 procedures in the United States (Henshaw & Van Vort, 1992; Koonin et al., 1992).

Participants in the ongoing abortion debate often talk as if there were only two possible positions: proabortion and antiabortion. Yet these two stances represent only the extremes. At one end of the continuum are those who believe that after conception has occurred, a woman should be compelled to give birth, regardless of the woman's life circumstances or the viability of the fetus. Nathanson (1979), a doctor who used to perform abortions, believes that a fetus is entitled to protection from the moment of implantation. Hardin (1974) referred to proponents of this position as advocates of "mandatory motherhood."

At the other extreme are the small minority who favor compulsory abortion. Those who advocate compulsory abortion do so with two different goals in mind: to prevent overpopulation, and to block reproduction by developmentally disabled or emotionally disturbed individuals or those with genetically transmitted diseases. The Chinese, in their program to control the growth of their population, do not physically compel abortion, but they punish couples who already have one child and who refuse to abort subsequent pregnancies (see Figure 11.2). Punishment may include pay cuts or demotions (Mosher, 1983). The Chinese plan to abandon the one-child policy at the end of the century (Greenhalgh & Bongaarts, 1987). In North America there is little support for compulsory abortion.

Between these two extreme positions—compulsory motherhood versus compulsory abortion—there is a third position, maintaining that decisions regarding conception, pregnancy, and birth are best left to the woman or couple involved. Supporters of this stance generally ex-

**FIGURE 11.2**

**Chinese Birth Control Policy**

Chinese couples are strongly encouraged to limit their family size. The posters outside this family planning clinic in Chengdu, China, say, "It is better to have an only child."

press great concern for babies' well-being, arguing that it is wrong to bring unwanted infants into the world, particularly when they are likely to be badly deformed because of prenatal exposure to disease or drugs. In his testimony at a Senate judiciary subcommittee hearing on a "human life" bill that would ban abortion, Dr. George Ryan, then-president of the American College of Obstetricians and Gynecologists, spoke against the bill:

*The same people who want to "save" babies are unwilling to give them food stamps. They don't care if the babies live in roach-infested houses. They don't care if they get adequate schooling. It's a strange contradiction that the people who say they want to save lives have so little compassion for people after they are born.*

Scientists can do little to resolve differences in the moral values of those who disagree over abortion rights. Nathanson (1979) suggested one solution: transplanting an embryo from the uterus of a woman who does not wish to maintain pregnancy to the uterus of a woman desiring a baby. But embryo-transfer procedures are unlikely to eliminate the demand for abortion. For example, in cases in which a pregnant woman's desire for abortion is based on fears that she is carrying a defective embryo, another woman would be unlikely to want the embryo.

*The Abortion-as-Birth-Control Hypothesis*

In 1977 President Jimmy Carter justified his opposition to the federal funding of abortions for poor women on the grounds that such funding might encourage women to use abortion rather than contraception for birth control. How much support exists for this hypothesis? To begin with, there is no 100% effective temporary method of contraception. Although the risk of conception can be dramatically reduced by consistent use of reliable contraceptives, it cannot be totally eliminated by any of the available contraceptive methods. Thus the fact that women get pregnant is not, in and of itself, evidence that they are relying on abortion rather than contraception for birth control. In fact, more than half of all abortion patients in 1987 reported that they had been using contraception during the month in which they conceived (Henshaw & Silverman, 1988).

Second, as we have seen, many adolescents do not use contraceptives. Among adolescents with unintended pregnancies, however, those choosing abortion are more likely to have used contraception than are those opting to maintain the pregnancy (Zelnik & Kantner, 1978).

Third, most investigators of repeat abortion find little evidence that women repeaters fail to use contraception because legal abortion is available (Abrams, 1985). Scientists have compared the contraceptive behavior of women after abortion with that of women after giving birth (Shulman & Merritt, 1976), and with that of women with no prior abortions (Kurstin & Oskamp, 1979). These studies revealed no differences among the groups in contraceptive behavior; in fact, contraceptive usage rates tend to improve following abortion (Miller, 1992).

Despite these data, some would argue that President Carter's point is supported by the abortion recidivism rate (that is, the incidence of a woman having two or more abortions), which is increasing. In 1974 approximately 15% of all legal abortions were repeat abortions. The percentage of repeat abortions climbed to 23% in 1976 and reached 39% in 1983 (Alan Guttmacher Institute, 1986; Henshaw, 1987). But this rise does not necessarily result from the abandonment of contraceptives. Indeed, Tietze (1978) maintained that increasing numbers of repeat abortions would re-

sult from the greater number of women having a *first* abortion. Because undergoing one abortion has no impact on subsequent contraceptive failure, as time goes on, sexually active women risk having a second unwanted pregnancy. In addition, having resolved the first unintended pregnancy through abortion, these women may be more likely than women with no prior abortions to rely again on medical termination of pregnancy when contraception fails.

In light of these and other factors, Tietze concluded that a high repeat-abortion rate is "to be expected without any decline—indeed, even in the face of improvement—in contraceptive practice" (p. 288). Data from nations with a history of legal abortion longer than that of the United States suggest that the percentage of repeat abortions increases for a few years following legalization and then levels off (Tietze & Jain, 1978).

## Abortion: The Process

While the legal and moral debate rages on, more than 1.5 million American women choose to terminate their pregnancies via induced abortion every year. That rate has remained relatively constant for more than 10 years (Russo et al., 1992). One of the following procedures is used.

### Abortion Methods Early in Pregnancy

Three methods exist for women who have engaged in unprotected intercourse and who wish to terminate a potential pregnancy: administration of DES or RU-486, and menstrual extraction. As will be seen, the second method, RU-486, although highly effective, is not available for North American women.

Various hormone preparations are capable of terminating a pregnancy when used within 72 hours after unprotected intercourse. The best known of these drugs—and the only one approved by the FDA—is diethylstilbestrol (DES). Taken in what is popularly called the morning-after pill, DES is a highly potent synthetic estrogen. To end a suspected pregnancy, a woman must begin taking 25 mg of DES twice a day within 72 hours of unprotected intercourse and continue to do so for five days. In general, DES is recommended only in an emergency such as rape. Although it is highly effective in interrupting pregnancy, the side effects (nausea, vomiting, headache, breast tenderness, dizziness, and diarrhea) are quite uncomfortable for many women who use it. DES should not be taken by women for whom estrogen poses a medical hazard.

DES is the least expensive of the early-abortion methods. Its low cost and effectiveness are its main advantages. It is also advantageous for women who wish to avoid knowing whether they are pregnant, because DES is used before a pregnancy is confirmed. Taken later in pregnancy, DES has been associated with genital cancers and other problems in both male and female offspring, as noted in Chapter 2. Used as an abortive, however, DES has not been associated with any long-term side effects. Nonetheless, caution is advised because the hormone has not been used for a long enough period of time for researchers to confirm that effects will not emerge.

Another hormonal abortion procedure, RU-486 (mifepristone), was developed in France and marketed by Roussel-UClaf, the pharmaceutical company from which the *RU* part of its name comes. Taken orally, this drug blocks the action of progesterone, the hormone that prepares the uterine lining for the implantation of a fertilized egg. It can be ingested every month as a contraceptive, but because of uncertainty about its long-term effects, the inventor of the synthetic drug, Etienne Emile Baulieu, does not recommend its use on a regular monthly basis. RU-486 is most effective if taken within 49 days of the last menstrual period. About 3% of women abort within 48 hours of taking the drug. The rest return within 48 hours after taking RU-486 to take a *prostaglandin*, which makes the uterus contract and bleed and is accompanied by mild to severe cramping. This procedure is reportedly 95% to 99% effective in inducing abortion (Henshaw & Van Vort, 1992; Peyron, Aubeny, Targosz, & Silvestre, 1993). The major side effect is prolonged

uterine bleeding, but this usually does not require transfusion or curettage (surgical scraping of the uterus). RU-486 was approved for use in France in 1988 and is being used to perform 25% of the abortions there (Henshaw & Van Vort, 1992). RU-486 is also available in China and Great Britain. Tests of RU-486 began in the United States in the fall of 1994, and it may be available in the next 3 years. Prochoice groups are not the only ones who have protested the banning of RU-486 by the FDA. Because RU-486 holds promise for treating breast cancer, endometriosis (see Chapter 14), Cushing's disease (forms of leukemia, malaria, advanced anemia), other cancers, and perhaps AIDS, groups concerned with the treatment of these conditions have argued for lifting the ban. For example, in testimony before a 1990 congressional subcommittee regarding RU-486, Helen Byrne of the Cancer Patients Action Alliance in New York, a devout Catholic opposed to abortion, stated, "The issue here is not abortion, the issue is the life or death of women with breast cancer." William Regelson, a professor of medicine at the Medical College of Virginia, argued that if RU-486 were not also effective for inducing abortions, it would be considered "a major medical breakthrough."

A third early-abortion method, *menstrual extraction*, involves removal of the menstrual blood and tissue from the uterus with a *cannula* and sometimes a suction machine. This method is generally employed when a woman's period is late by a week or two. A positive pregnancy test is not needed prior to undergoing menstrual extraction; in fact, some women have used the technique simply to shorten the length of their menstrual periods. Casual use of menstrual extraction is not recommended, however, because of the risk of hemorrhage and of introducing bacteria into the uterus. Although at-home menstrual-extraction kits have been manufactured since the early 1970s, with as many as 10,000 extractions

---

**prostaglandins**—hormones that stimulate muscle contractions. They help to regulate ovulation and the release of prolactin from the ovaries.

**menstrual extraction**—removal of menstrual blood and tissue from the uterus.

**cannula** (CAN-u-luh)—a tube inserted into the body through which liquid and/or tissue may be removed.

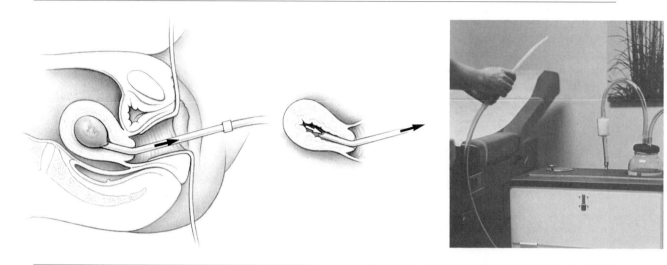

**FIGURE 11.3**
**Vacuum Curette**
In abortion by vacuum aspiration, a vacuum curette that is connected by rubber tubing to a suction machine is inserted through the cervix into the uterus. The vacuum-aspiration machine (right) is used to suction the uterine contents into a jar on top of the machine.

performed in the United States since that time, in 1989 manufacturers discontinued sale of the kits because of the health risks they posed.

The advantages of menstrual extraction are that it is less expensive than a suction abortion (described later) and requires less dilation of the cervix than methods used later in pregnancy. Another advantage of the procedure for some women is that it can be performed before a woman knows whether she is pregnant.

### First-Trimester Abortion Methods

More than 90% of the abortions performed in the United States occur during the first trimester (Henshaw & Van Vort, 1992). Methods include suction abortion and dilation and curettage (D&C).

*Suction abortion*, also called vacuum aspiration, is usually done on an outpatient basis under local anesthesia. It accounts for more than 95% of the first-trimester abortions in most Western countries (Henshaw & Van Vort, 1992). Following urine and blood tests, a woman undergoes a pelvic examination. If the examination indicates that it is safe—that is, early enough in pregnancy—to perform a suction abortion, a local anesthetic is injected into the woman's cervix. The cervix is then dilated, with the extent of the dilation depending on the length of the pregnancy. Next, a cannula is introduced into the uterus through the cervix. The suction machine draws the blood, fetal tissue, and mucus from the uterus and out through the cannula. This part of the procedure generally takes less than five minutes. At this point, a doctor may scrape the uterus with a *curette* to ensure that all fetal material has been removed (see Figure 11.3).

The procedure is then essentially finished, unless a woman has Rh-negative blood, in which

**suction abortion**—removal of the contents of the uterus through use of a suction machine; also called vacuum aspiration.

**curette** (cure-RET)—a scooplike instrument used for scraping bodily tissue.

case she is given a *Rhogam* shot to prevent the formation in subsequent pregnancies of antibodies to fetuses who do not have Rh-negative blood. She rests for a few minutes on the examination table, gets dressed, and then relaxes in the recovery room for 30 minutes or so. Her blood pressure and pulse are checked frequently, and if they are normal, she is released. She is generally advised to have someone else drive her home, and to rest for the remainder of the day. She may return to her normal activities the next day, except for intercourse and douching, which she should avoid for several weeks. Bleeding similar to that experienced during menstruation may continue for several days following a suction abortion. To lessen the chances of infection, a woman should use sanitary napkins rather than tampons to absorb the flow. The majority of women ovulate within three or four weeks following the abortion, and so a couple should resume intercourse only with a reliable contraceptive. Normal menstrual periods typically return within four to eight weeks of the abortion.

Complications of suction abortion may include hemorrhage, uterine perforation, and infection. The most common complication, hemorrhage, afflicts fewer than 1 of every 100 women and is rarely severe enough to require blood transfusions. *Uterine perforation*—the puncturing of the uterine wall with the dilator or curette—is a far more dangerous complication, often requiring repair of the perforation by surgery. In rare cases, a *hysterectomy* may be the only effective method for stopping hemorrhaging from the perforation. The third possible complication, abortion-related infection, is suspected when fever, abdominal pain, or a yellowish vaginal discharge develops; the infection is usually eliminated with antibiotics.

Suction abortion has a number of advantages over the dilation and curettage (D&C) and second-trimester methods described later. The time required for the procedure is shorter, recovery is quicker, and complications are fewer because a woman does not have to recover from the effects of general anesthesia. Suction abortion is also considerably less expensive than a D&C, because for the latter, hospital costs are involved. Further, the risks associated with a suction abortion are fewer than those associated with pregnancy or childbirth.

Many women report little or no pain with suction abortion. A woman who does experience pain either during or following the abortion should not take medications containing aspirin because its anticoagulating effect on blood may increase the risk of hemorrhage. Women who have not previously given birth generally experience more discomfort than do women who have given birth.

The other first-trimester abortion method is *dilation and curettage (D&C)*. D&Cs are also performed for various medical reasons on nonpregnant women. This procedure is similar to the suction abortion, except that a doctor often administers general rather than local anesthesia and uses a curette to scrape out the contents of the uterus instead of suctioning them out. This procedure is still common in developing countries where abortion is legally restricted (Henshaw & Van Vort, 1992).

The D&C is preferable to suction abortion when the pregnancy has progressed to the end of the first trimester. Possible complications from a D&C include those listed for suction abortion (hemorrhage, perforation, and infection), as well as those complications associated with general anesthesia.

## Second-Trimester Abortion Methods

Almost 9% of American women seeking abortions do so after the first trimester of pregnancy (Henshaw & Van Vort, 1992). The maternal mortality rate for abortions performed during the second trimester is much greater than that for abortions performed during the first trimester,

---

**Rhogam** (ROW-gam)—a substance that prevents an Rh-negative woman from developing antibodies to the Rh factor in subsequent embryos.

**uterine perforation**—tearing or puncturing of the uterine wall.

**hysterectomy**—surgical removal of the uterus.

**dilation and curettage (D&C)** (die-LAY-shun and CURE-eh-taj)—dilation of the cervix followed by scraping of the interior of the uterus.

increasing by about 50% for each week beyond the first trimester.

Clearly, the earlier an abortion is obtained, the less risk there is for the woman. However, there are circumstances under which an abortion may not be desired until the second trimester. A woman may be exposed to drugs or to illnesses, such as measles, that can cause deformities in the fetus. Other factors, such as impending divorce or unexpected financial hardship, may also lead to a decision to seek an abortion after the first trimester. Because of the advanced development of the fetus, abortion at this stage is considerably more complicated, both physically and psychologically.

The *dilation and evacuation (D&E)* method, which combines elements of the D&C and vacuum-aspiration methods, is generally used early in the second trimester in a hospital or clinic setting. After administration of local or general anesthesia, the cervix is dilated to a greater extent than with a D&C to allow passage of a larger fetus. Because of fetal skeletal development, special instruments must be used to crush the fetus in the uterus prior to its extraction with a large vacuum curette. The fetal remains are then reassembled to make sure that all the contents of the uterus have been removed. Until the 16th week of pregnancy, the D&E is the safest of the second-trimester methods and takes the shortest time to perform. Starting at the 16th week, it has complication and mortality rates equivalent to those of the other methods. Possible complications include infection, perforation of the uterus, and reactions to the anesthesia.

Abortion by means of an *intra-amniotic injection* is another alternative and accounts for about 1% of all abortions in the United States (Hatcher et al., 1994). With this method, a local anesthetic is first injected into the woman's abdomen. Some amniotic fluid is then withdrawn from the amniotic sac, and it is replaced by about a cup of saline (salt) solution, which causes fetal circulatory arrest. The drug pitocin is also administered to induce labor contractions and expulsion of the fetus and placenta. In some cases, prostaglandins (hormones that cause the smooth muscles to contract) are used instead of the saline solution.

Major complications occur more frequently from intra-amniotic injections than from D&Es. Complications from saline abortions primarily stem from three factors: a) accidental injection into the uterine muscle, blood vessels, or abdominal cavity; b) infection; or c) absorption of some of the saline solution into the bloodstream. Hemorrhage can also occur with saline abortion, but a very small percentage of women hemorrhage seriously enough to require blood transfusions.

When prostaglandins are used instead of a saline solution, complications may include vomiting, nausea, diarrhea, cervical tearing, and asthmalike symptoms. The most common reaction is vomiting, which affects the majority of women. Cervical tearing occurs in about 1 in every 200 women because of the speed with which prostaglandins induce labor. Such tearing is more likely in young women who have not had children than in older women who have given birth. About 2% of women who have a prostaglandin abortion experience an asthmalike condition, apparently from accidental passage of the prostaglandins into the bloodstream. The symptoms include shortness of breath, restlessness, nausea, and vomiting, and sometimes seizures, slowed pulse, and irregular heartbeat. The asthmalike effects pass within 20 minutes because of the rapid metabolization of the prostaglandins, but this method should not be used with asthmatic women.

Abortion via intra-amniotic injection can also be quite painful for some women. As Shapiro (1977, p. 167) put it:

> *The labor is often described by insensitive gynecologists as a "minilabor," slightly more painful than severe menstrual cramps. Nothing could be further from the truth. Despite the small size of the fetus, the labor is often prolonged and very painful, usually requiring liberal amounts of pain medication.*

**dilation and evacuation (D&E)**—an abortion method generally used in the second trimester; the fetus is crushed within the uterus, and the contents of the uterus are then extracted through a vacuum curette.

**intra-amniotic injection** (IN-truh-am-nee-AW-tik)—replacement of amniotic fluid either with prostaglandins or with a salt solution, causing fetal circulatory arrest; used in second-trimester abortions.

The only major advantage of intra-amniotic abortion is that it is preferable to the alternative of giving birth to a fetus that is likely to be deformed or dead. Fewer than 10% of the women who have abortions do so after the first trimester, and many of these women seek abortion only after learning through amniocentesis of major fetal defects.

Another abortion method, *hysterotomy*, is used only when medical conditions contraindicate a D&E or intra-amniotic injection, and when the pregnancy threatens the woman's life. An incision is made in the abdomen through the uterine muscle, and the fetus is removed. Only about 0.1% of abortions require uterine surgery (Tietze, Forrest, & Henshaw, 1988).

## Psychological Responses to Abortion

Numerous studies conducted since the 1970s have examined the reactions of women to their discovery of an unintentional pregnancy and subsequent decision to obtain an abortion. An overview of this research indicates that the greatest distress occurs before the abortion and that severe negative reactions after an abortion are rare (Adler, David, Major, et al., 1990; Adler et al., 1992). For most women, a legal abortion is followed by a mixture of emotions, with positive feelings predominating over negative feelings. This pattern occurs immediately after and up to eight years after abortion. The small minority of women who do report emotional distress within three weeks after abortion are more likely to report: a) that the pregnancy was intended and meaningful; b) that there was lack of support from their parents or partners for the abortion; c) that they felt in conflict and less certain of their decision and coping abilities before the abortion; d) that they blamed themselves for the pregnancy; and e) that they delayed the abortion until the second trimester (Major & Cozzarelli, 1992).

As in other stressful situations, the more support and encouragement that women with unwanted pregnancies receive, the more positive

they are about their ability to cope with an abortion (see Box 11.3). Thus events that impair women's expectations for coping with an abortion, such as receiving counseling that emphasizes the negative effects of abortion or being confronted by individuals picketing abortion clinics, may make it more difficult to adjust to an abortion experience.

Finally, Belenky and Gilligan (1979) found that the abortion dilemma can be an opportunity for personal growth for some women. They investigated the moral reasoning of a group of women who were interviewed before deciding whether to terminate an unwanted pregnancy. The women were interviewed again a year later, and the authors found that

> those who resolved the actual situation at a higher stage of (moral) reasoning . . . were often under high conflict—as they tended to have a difficult time deciding what to do. We called them the Gain group. The women in the Gain group were most likely to emerge from this crisis matured. . . . The pregnancy presented them with contradictions that could not be resolved with their current modes of thought, requiring a reevaluation of their conceptions of self and morality . . . the women in the Gain group were more likely to have achieved improved life circumstances (a year later). . . .
>
> The Stable group . . . tended to show less conflict over their decision than the Gain group. A year later, their stage of moral reasoning and their life circumstances tended to be unchanged.
>
> Those who came to resolve the pregnancy with a lower stage of reasoning . . . —the Loss group—tended to choose a resolution that they themselves had described as inadequate. . .they typically said they would be going through the abortion with blinders on—not thinking, not feeling. (Belenky & Gilligan, 1979, pp. 5–6)

When the researchers interviewed these women again a year later, the only individuals who had a repeat unwanted pregnancy were those in the Loss group.

**hysterotomy** (HIS-ter-AW-tuh-mee)—surgical incision into the uterus; when used for abortion, the fetus is removed through the incision.

**Box 11.3**

## One Woman's Abortion Experience

A year ago my boyfriend and I found out that I was pregnant. We have been dating for almost four years and have been having sex for three of those years. As for birth control, we used the withdrawal method for the first year. We decided that it was too risky, and the fear of pregnancy was there every month. So we both decided to use spermicidal foam. The pill was out of the question for me because there is a history of diabetes in my family.

After about a year of using foam, I became pregnant. We waited for my period to come in October. After a couple weeks, my breasts hurt and I told myself that my period would come soon because my breasts always hurt before my period. A week went by—nothing. My boyfriend decided that I should have a pregnancy test and if it was negative, fine; if it was positive, we would cross that bridge when we came to it.

By this time, all kinds of thoughts were going through my head. I was so nervous and dazed that I couldn't even take my urine sample to the lab. My boyfriend took it for me. We waited for 24 hours to get the results. I prayed that the results would be negative. My boyfriend dialed the number, got off the phone, kissed and hugged me, and then told me that the results were positive. I cried and cried; my boyfriend held me and we cried together. I was totally numb. I couldn't believe it was true. After about an hour we talked and decided that abortion was the only answer. He wanted to finish school and so did I. We also thought about how our families would take the news. My parents would probably disown me, and my boyfriend's mom would probably take it the best, but my boyfriend really wanted to finish his education. So, for those reasons, we called an abortion clinic and made an appointment for the following Tuesday.

During the three-day wait, my boyfriend and I never left each other's sight except for classes. We were determined to go through this together. To this day I don't know how I could have gotten through it without him. We left for the appointment, not saying much on the way. He kept his arm around me the whole way. When we got there, he gave my name to the receptionist and he filled out the forms. I could hardly sign them. After we finished, he was sent to the waiting room, and I was sent to a room with four other women. We were informed that we would be counseled together and we all started talking about how we got pregnant. We all talked and cried together for two hours. The counselor told us exactly what the doctor would do and about the medication we would get before. She also counseled us about birth control and asked if we had any questions. There were many, and after the questions we all went upstairs together. All of us looked after a 16-year-old who got pregnant by her boyfriend who had refused to help her at all, and it helped to comfort her.

We all sat in a room right next to the waiting room where my boyfriend was sitting. It was good to know that he was real close to me. One by one we were called into the room where we would have the abortion, and when someone's name was called we each gave the girl a hug. I hoped it helped them because it sure helped me. When my name was called I went into the room where a nurse was waiting for me. She helped me undress and get onto the table. She talked to me and held my hand. The doctor came in and told me everything he was going to do. By now the medication was taking effect, but I was still shaking. The counselor came in and held my hand and talked with me, which helped immensely. The doctor was great too. He told jokes to help ease the tension. I didn't feel much pain like I thought I would, and when it was over I felt relieved. I was taken to a recovery room that was very pleasant. After I was there a few minutes I started to feel crampy. My counselor asked me if I wanted my boyfriend to come in and sit with me. He came in and I've never seen him look so concerned. He sat with me until I was ready to leave after they had given me the medicine I was to take for a while.

I can't tell you what it meant to have my boyfriend there through the whole thing. He told me afterward on the way back to school that if he could have had the abortion for me, he would have. He said that he knows that he will never really know what I went through.

Now, a year later, I'm a year older and a lot wiser. I have mixed feelings about the abortion now. Sometimes I feel guilty and selfish that I sacrificed a life so that mine would be easier. But we weren't ready to take on the responsibilities of being parents then. I want to work with children and I love being around

them. I know I have to put it in the past, and it has helped to write this experience down. I've gotten out a lot of feelings that I have bottled up. I hope my experience can help someone in the same situation. They need all the support they can get. Compared to many women, I was fortunate. I had the love and support of my boyfriend, and the abortion has made my relationship with my boyfriend (soon my fiancé) a stronger one. Without him, I probably would not have accepted the abortion as I have.

Source: Author's files.

## The Male Role in Abortion

In 1976, the U.S. Supreme Court ruled in *Planned Parenthood* v. *Danforth* that the wife should have the final say when a married couple disagrees about the resolution of a pregnancy. Their ruling was based on the argument that because she is the one who must bear the child and thus is most affected by the pregnancy, she should control the decision regarding abortion. Despite that decision, about 10 states have laws requiring that women notify or have the consent of their husbands before obtaining abortions. However, in 1992, the U.S. Supreme Court ruled (*Planned Parenthood* v. *Casey*) that a Pennsylvania law requiring notification of a husband prior to abortion was unconstitutional.

Research is badly needed on the reactions of male partners before and after decisions about unwanted pregnancy are made. Researchers' neglect of abortion applicants' sexual partners was aptly described two decades ago in terms that remain accurate today:

> *Men are almost ephemeral objects who, once they've done their share in the conception of the fetus, are rarely seen again; or at least they're not very visible in the pages of journal articles on problem pregnancy or on abortion. (Lees, 1975, p. 2)*

Interested in exploring the male role in abortion, Lees interviewed 73 men who accompanied their unmarried partners to a Detroit abortion clinic. He found that the more emotional involvement the men reported with their partners, the greater their anxiety during the pregnancy termination. Lees hypothesized that the higher anxiety of these involved men was probably rooted in empathy and willingness to share the burden of responsibility for the pregnancy and abortion with their partners.

Most college students believe that, in making a decision about an unwanted pregnancy, a woman should consider her partner, although the majority also think that ultimately the decision to terminate or maintain the pregnancy rests with the woman (Rosenwasser, Wright, & Barber, 1987). Shusterman (1979) studied the reactions of male partners via reports that were given by abortion clients. The overwhelming majority of women reported that their partners supported the abortion decision, regardless of the length of the relationship.

It is not known whether men whose partners seek abortions experience guilt over their part in conception, anger, relief that the woman has chosen to abort, or some combination of emotions. Some men believe that their legal exclusion from the decision is unfair and denies them a voice in the choice of deciding whether to become a parent. They are right in feeling that the process is unfair. Biologically, they cannot become pregnant and no amount of legislation can change that fact. However, if a woman is to have control over her body, she must make the final decision about whether to carry a pregnancy to term. Nevertheless, men may not be as powerless as their legal status suggests, for a man's emotional response generally has a substantial impact on his partner. The more involved and supportive the male partner, the greater the self-esteem and self-worth of women who have had an abortion (Majors & Cozzarelli, 1992; Robbins & DeLamater, 1985).

In light of these findings, Lees's recommendation that more research be conducted on pregnant women's partners seems particularly important. He asserted that researchers should

> *not fall into the same trap as we've done before with other subjects, excluding one sex from investigation of the phenomena. Particularly with topics such as problem pregnancy, where each partner's reactions impinge on the other, any such omission will be detrimental to health care and to potential growth. (Lees, 1975, p. 7)*

Further, Lees's point is also relevant to the issue of abortion recidivism—repeat abortion. If, as he recommends, abortion clients' partners are provided with counseling and contraceptive education, couples may be able to work together more effectively to reduce the likelihood of future problem pregnancies.

## Adolescent Parenthood

Our informal contacts with unmarried student couples who are dealing with unplanned pregnancy suggest that young men's reactions to the pregnancy of their lovers vary from strong advocacy of abortion to passionate pleas that the woman maintain the pregnancy. As one young man in the latter group put it, "I don't want her

killing my baby." In this case, however, the young woman chose to abort the fetus after ending the relationship. She said with considerable agitation that it was all well and good for him to lay "guilt trips" on her regarding abortion, but that, because he apparently did not intend to stay around to help with the emotional and physical support of the child for the next 18 years, he could not have any say in the decision.

Just as we have relatively little information about men's roles in, and reactions to, abortion, we have little but anecdotal information about the proportion of men favoring the maintenance of an unplanned pregnancy versus the proportion favoring abortion. We do know that recourse to marriage as a solution is less prevalent than it used to be. The teenage birthrate was higher in 1957 than it was following the legalization of abortion in 1973. With legal abortion unavailable, a pregnant unwed teenager in the 1950s would often acquire a spouse through a "shotgun" wedding, and nearly 25% of 18- and 19-year-old women were married. In the 1950s, about two-thirds of unmarried pregnant women married their partners, whereas only one-third did so following the legalization of abortion (Baldwin, 1976).

## Adolescent Mothers

More than 1 million teenage pregnancies have occurred every year in the United States since 1973 (Henshaw, 1993). As Table 11.3 shows, a greater proportion of women aged 15 to 19 choose to maintain the pregnancy rather than to have an abortion. In 1983 more than half the teenage women who gave birth were unmarried (Alan Guttmacher Institute, 1985). Of those who were married at the time of birth, many had babies who were conceived premaritally. Further, in one study of women who decided to have an abortion, the majority (52%) of married women aged 15 to 17, and most of those aged 18 to 19 (60%), already had children (Powell-Griner, 1987)! Although the birthrate among unmarried teenagers has remained high, at present only about 3% of unmarried mothers elect to place their children for adoption (Sobol & Daly, 1992). The decrease in the popularity of forced marriage and adop-

**TABLE 11.3  Number of Pregnancies, Legal Abortions, and Births for Adolescent Women**[a]

|  | 1975 | 1980 | 1985 | 1988 |
|---|---|---|---|---|
| *Under Age 15* | | | | |
| Pregnancies | 31,950 | 29,080 | 30,930 | 27,720 |
| Legal abortions | 15,260 | 15,340 | 16,970 | 11,461 |
| Births | 12,642 | 10,642 | 10,220 | 13,934 |
| *Age 15 to 19* | | | | |
| Pregnancies | 1,056,120 | 1,151,850 | 1,000,110 | 1,006,010 |
| Legal abortions | 324,930 | 444,780 | 339,200 | 341,218 |
| Births | 582,252 | 552,161 | 467,485 | 473,281 |

[a]*Note:* The total number of abortions and births does not add up to the number of pregnancies because some of the pregnancies end in miscarriages.

Sources: Henshaw and Van Vort (1989); Henshaw (1993).

tion as alternatives for women who maintain pregnancy has resulted in a rise in the number of unmarried mothers (see Figure 11.4).*

In the most extensive longitudinal study of the effects of early motherhood, Frank Furstenberg and his colleagues (Furstenberg, 1976; Furstenberg, Brooks-Gunn, & Morgan, 1987) interviewed 400 women who had experienced unplanned adolescent motherhood. Most were Black and were clients of Baltimore's Adolescent Family Clinic. In the first phase of the study, the mothers were interviewed five years after they had first received services at the clinic. Furstenberg (1976) began this study with the assumption that early parenthood creates many disadvantages for young women and their children, and his data generally supported this assumption.

Some teenage mothers found ways to cope with the problems of early parenthood. But on the whole, these young women consistently experienced greater difficulty in realizing their life plans than did a control group of their nonpregnant classmates. As Furstenberg (1976, p. 219) observed:

*Their prospects of achieving a stable marriage were damaged by the early pregnancy, and they were having great difficulty supporting a family on their own. Poorly educated, unskilled, often burdened by several small children, many of these women at age 20 or 21 had become resigned to a life of economic deprivation.*

Yet 17 years after they had been clients of the clinic, the picture was not as grim for a substantial number of these women. Although 70% of the mothers had received welfare at some time during the 17 years (Furstenberg et al., 1987), two-thirds of them had managed to get off welfare and were employed. Another 9% of the women were actively seeking employment. One-quarter of the women had annual family incomes in excess of $25,000, well above the poverty level at that time. Obviously, adolescent pregnancy

---

*An increasing number of single women seek parenthood through adoption or artificial insemination. These women tend to be older and more capable emotionally and financially of providing for the offspring they choose to have than are young women who do not intend to become pregnant. Here, however, we focus on the large number of adolescent women whose nonmarital pregnancies are accidental.

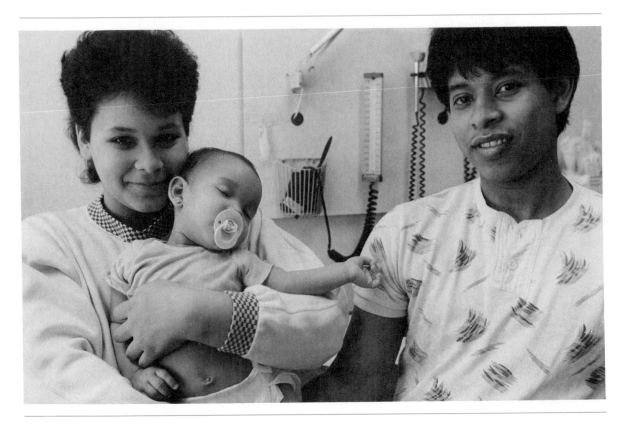

**FIGURE 11.4**
**Adolescent Parenthood**
This 14-year-old mother and 20-year-old boyfriend chose to keep their baby, who
is receiving a pediatric checkup at a hospital in the Bronx.

presents formidable obstacles, and many women in the study remained mired in poverty. But a number rebounded from their adversity and established adequate lives for themselves.

Adolescent mothers who marry are twice as likely to separate or divorce as are married women who have a first child in their 20s. In one study, one-third of the 15- to 19-year-old mothers who had married before giving birth were found to have separated or divorced by the time their children were six years old (Presser, 1980).

What happens to the children of adolescent mothers? When tested at various ages up to their seventh year, the offspring of adolescents were found to be somewhat lower in IQ and cognitive development than the children of older women. Children whose mothers were employed or in school scored higher than those whose mothers were at home full time. Some studies also have shown deficits in the social and emotional development of the children of adolescent mothers, but others have not (Baldwin & Cain, 1980). Many children in the Furstenberg et al. (1987) study appeared destined to experience their own struggles. The children were characterized generally as having high rates of school failure, and adolescent pregnancy by the daughters and juvenile delinquency by the sons were common. Other longitudinal research indicates that the children of adolescent mothers are more likely than the children of older mothers to become adolescent mothers themselves. In fact, the best predictor of whether one becomes an adolescent mother is the age at which one's mother first gave birth. Baldwin and Cain (1980, p. 39) summarized the results of research in this area:

> The effects of adolescent motherhood are observed in their children over many years; such long-term effects are consistent with findings from research on the effects of early childbearing on the teenage mother. These effects are persistent and color the general atmosphere in which a child develops: reduced education and occupational attainment of the mother, increased welfare dependency, higher fertility and marital disruption.

Two variables are strongly associated with the development and life experiences of adolescent mothers and their offspring in the various samples. One of these is the single parent's economic level. The other is the extent of social support received by the single-parent family. The disadvantages experienced by adolescent mothers and their offspring are either reduced or nonexistent when adolescent mothers receive strong social support from older people or have above-average economic resources.

Occasionally, television commentators and print-media columnists blame the welfare system for the illegitimacy rate. Some have even gone so far as to suggest that poor mothers deliberately become pregnant as a way to get more money from federal social-support programs. Cutright (1971) tested this hypothesis several decades ago by examining the relationship between illegitimacy rates and the existence or size of welfare benefits across a large number of countries. He found no relationship between these variables. Studies in the United States also have failed to confirm any relationship between illegitimacy rates and potential welfare benefits (Moore & Caldwell, 1977; Presser, 1974).

Before concluding this description of the experiences of adolescent mothers and their offspring, we consider one other group of women—some of whom were adolescents, and some of whom were older—who experienced unwanted pregnancies. In their cases, requests for abortions were denied because of restrictive abortion legislation in effect in their countries at the time. Reviews of longitudinal research conducted in several European countries compared these mothers and their offspring with matched samples of children of mothers who wanted their pregnancies David, Dytrych, Matejcek, & Schuller, 1988; David, 1992). These children have been studied up through ages 21 to 23. David et al. were careful to note that the fact that the children were unwanted may not be the only factor, or even the major factor, in the deficits observed in these offspring:

> [We] suggest viewing unwantedness in early pregnancy in a global sense; that is, as reflecting and very likely foreshadowing a family atmosphere which in many instances is not conducive to healthy childrearing and likely to impact negatively on the child's subsequent psychosocial development. (p. 123)

Comparisons of the unwanted children with the wanted offspring showed that, as a group, those who were unwanted were less well adjusted at age 9 and at ages 14 to 16 and had greater psychosocial instability at ages 21 to 23. David et al. reported that their adult relationships "with their families of origin, friends, co-workers, supervisors, and especially with their sexual or marital partners are dogged by serious difficulties" (p. 124). Research on the marital partners of unwanted children (now ages 26 to 28) found that they were similar to their spouses. These families have more difficulties or are more problem-prone than families founded by individuals wanted or accepted in early pregnancy (David, 1992). Even so, David et al. (1988) observed that the unwanted offspring were not so much overrepresented on the very negative indicators as they were underrepresented on the positive measures:

> They are rarely observed on any indicator of excellence. . . . Insufficient gratification of basic social and emotional needs (which accompanies many UP [unwanted pregnancy] children from early childhood) tends to create an unfavorable social environment with negative effects in personality development, social relations, and self-realization. Whether or not this tendency will affect the next generation, only time will tell. (p. 124)

These results strongly suggest that in the interests of their children's well-being, prospective parents should delay parenthood until they want to have children.

## Adolescent Fathers

For every adolescent conception that occurs outside of marriage, there is a father as well as a pregnant mother, yet relatively little is known about men who impregnate women to whom they are not married. In an attempt to study these men, Pfuhl (1978, p. 114) wrote the following advertisement:

> FOR RESEARCH PURPOSES: Wish to interview any man who has ever impregnated a woman to whom he was not then married, no matter how the situation was resolved. Information held in strictest confidence.

The major newspapers in Pfuhl's area refused to carry the ad, but a university paper and an underground paper accepted it. The 140 men who volunteered to participate in the study reported involvement in 176 unintended pregnancies.

Most (71%) of the men viewed the conceptions as the result of carelessness or stupidity; only a few (15%) regarded them as moral mistakes. Most men expected to receive negative reactions to the conceptions from their families and others. For example, they anticipated nagging, scolding, parental expressions of profound disappointment, short-term economic sanctions by the family, and temporary expulsion from school or specific school activities. Because of these expected reactions, almost half of the men did not disclose the conceptions to their families. The men who did reveal the unintended conceptions, however, did not experience long-term negative reactions. In fact, one man said:

> I told the debate team and coach that _____ was pregnant. . . . If I'd expected any negative reactions I'd never have told them. But I didn't and I never received any . . . none at all. My friends even made us a poster that read "Better dead than wed" and they all signed it and we still have it. We get a kick out of it. (Pfuhl, 1978, p. 118)

In contrast to the stereotype of men in this situation as heartless sexual exploiters, a large majority of the participants in this study expressed deep care, worry, or concern for the pregnant partner and paid for all or part of the medical expenses of abortion or of pregnancy and birth. In only 5% of the cases did the man report abandoning the woman when she became pregnant. Some who left their partners believed that the woman had become pregnant to maintain a failing relationship, to force marriage, or to escape an unwanted home situation.

Regardless of the good intentions of most of the men in Pfuhl's study, the fate of most adolescent fathers is similar to that of teenage mothers. Generally having come from poor, relatively uneducated backgrounds, they experience serious social and economic disadvantages when compared with young men who postpone fatherhood until a later age (Hardy, Duggan, Masnyk, & Pearson, 1989; Marsiglio, 1987). In one study of young urban fathers, 60% of those not residing with their child and its mother were living with a parent (Hardy et al., 1989). Gradually, many of these fathers decreased their contact with their child. Most of the fathers lacked the necessary skills to provide a stable home environment for their families even if they wanted to do so. In short, poverty is the tie that binds most adolescent fathers and mothers, and although some manage to cope with their situation and succeed, the odds are stacked against them.

## Unwanted Pregnancy in Adolescence: Ethics and Education

On the basis of her extensive review of research, Catherine Chilman (1980) concluded that increases in the number of illegitimate children born to adolescents are probably attributable to liberalized attitudes throughout U.S. society toward both premarital intercourse and illegitimacy. Ironically, the increases may also be partly due to conservatism among such policy-makers as legislators and school-board members.

We might usefully compare our culture's approach to adolescents' sex education with the ways in which we deal with their wishes to learn to drive. Adults might have various responses to young people's desire to drive. They might 1) prohibit adolescents from driving; 2) hand them the car keys with little instruction in safe and responsible driving; 3) wring their hands and mutter "Tsk, tsk" at the incidence of car accidents among untrained and unlicensed drivers; or 4) provide extensive classroom instruction and practical tutoring in driving and encourage en-rollment in these courses by giving course credit, reduced insurance premiums, and the like. In general, our society has taken the fourth of these alternatives regarding driving.

In contrast, we have used all but the fourth alternative to deal with adolescents' capacity for sexual interaction. First, we discourage sexual ex-pression by adolescents. Second, although ado-lescents already have the keys, so to speak, we try to keep them from realizing that they possess those keys rather than showing them how to use them. Thus when they discover the keys anyway, they use them, with minimal instruction on safe and responsible sexual expression. Third, we complain about the incidence of "accidents" (un-intended conceptions) among adolescents un-trained in responsible sexual interactions.

Taking the fourth approach—providing ex-tensive instruction to prospective drivers—does not totally eliminate car accidents, and we cannot expect that offering thorough sex education would eliminate unplanned pregnancies, either. However, following the model used for driver education would be a step in the right direction

when dealing with adolescent sexuality; that is, adolescents could be given extensive classroom instruction on responsible sexual expression. This instruction could include practical tutoring in techniques for inserting diaphragms or putting on condoms (using plastic models of the body), as well as information about obtaining contracep-tion, discussing sexual feelings and responsibili-ties with another person, and recognizing the dif-ference between sexual feelings and sexual actions. Emphasis on the enormous responsibil-ity of child care and on the emotional and finan-cial investment involved in rearing a child for at least two decades could be provided as well. Ex-plicit discussion of these issues in the classroom might furnish a much-needed model for explicit discussion of issues between adolescents when they decide to become sexually involved.

Unfortunately, our society has chosen to avoid discussion of contraceptive use with ado-lescents. Thus it is hardly surprising that the ma-jority of them follow our example and do not dis-cuss the issue among themselves, with fairly predictable results: unintended pregnancies, abortions, and unprepared parenthood.

## Summary of Major Points

1. Unintended and/or unwanted pregnancy.

The number of unintended and unwanted conceptions in the United States has been on the rise, particularly among adolescents. Faced with unwanted conception, more than 1.5 million women a year end their pregnancies through abortion, terminating roughly 30% of all confirmed conceptions. The number of single women who choose to maintain their pregnancies and take on the responsibilities of parent-hood, however, has been increasing dramatically. About 250,000 women do so annually. Few women who now decide to maintain their pregnancies subsequently place their babies for adoption.

2. Access to abortion.

In its historic *Roe* v. *Wade* decision of 1973, the Supreme Court elimi-nated legal barriers to women's right to abortion during the first two trimesters of pregnancy. Citizens have continued to debate the moral-ity of the procedure, however, and those who oppose abortion have succeeded in getting Congress to pass legislation preventing the use of federal funds for abortions. These groups continue to press for a congressional or constitutional ban on abortion. In the 1989 *Webster* decision, the Supreme Court upheld a Missouri law banning the use of public funds for abortion and requiring viability testing for fetuses beyond 20 weeks' gestation. For those women who are able to pay for the procedure, access to abortion remains open. But for poor women, access to safe, legal abortion has been reduced by the *Webster* decision. In 1990 the Supreme Court upheld several state laws requiring notification of one parent of a minor and a 48-hour waiting period before an abortion could take place. Those who favor legal abortion maintain that women should have the sole decision regarding the use of their bodies.

3. Abortion procedures.

Most abortions are performed during the first trimester through either the suction or the D&C method, or a combination of the two. Legal, first-trimester abortions are among the safest of all medical procedures. They take about five minutes and can be done under local anesthesia on an outpatient basis. As long as there are no complications, the patient can return to her normal activities (except for bathing and sexual intercourse) within a day or two. Second-trimester abortions are considerably more complicated and time-consuming. They are performed through injection of saline solution into the amniotic fluid, injection of prostaglandins, or a D&E. The first two methods induce uterine labor contractions and are more uncomfortable than is the D&E, in which the fetus is crushed and extracted from the uterus through a large vacuum tube. Clearly, first-trimester abortion is preferable, but sometimes situations that occur after the first trimester—such as exposure to teratogenic diseases or conditions—prompt women to seek abortion.

4. Emotional responses to abortion.

Relatively little is known about the psychological reactions of women and men in reaching decisions about unwanted pregnancy. However, the vast majority of women who choose abortion report that positive feelings predominate over negative feelings: few experience guilt, sorrow, or severe distress.

5. Abortion as a form of birth control.

The hypothesis that access to abortion reduces the motivation of women to use contraception has been tested in several ways, and there is no evidence to suggest that abortion is replacing contraceptive techniques for the vast majority of women. In fact, among women with an unintended pregnancy, those obtaining abortions are more likely to have used contraception than are those who decide to maintain the pregnancy.

6. Adolescent parenthood.

Compared with women who first give birth in their 20s, teenage mothers (and their offspring) generally suffer a number of long-term disadvantages. Whether particular women and their children experience problems is strongly associated with two factors: financial status and social support. Those adolescent families who have adequate economic resources and those who receive help from older relatives do not have as many difficulties as do adolescent families who receive little economic or social support. Relatively little is known about the men who are faced with an unwanted pregnancy. Most of the men from small, volunteer samples reported feeling concern for the woman and sharing financial responsibility for the resolution of the pregnancy.

## Review of Key Concepts

1. The majority of abortions in the United States are performed on young: a) unmarried White women; b) unmarried Black women; c) married White women; d) married Black women. (p. 344)

2. Research indicates that American attitudes toward abortion are most similar to the positions advanced by: a) NARAL (prochoice); b) NRLC (antiabortion); c) NICK (abortion only when a woman has been raped); d) none of the above. (pp. 348–349)

3. Which of the following groups holds the most negative attitudes toward abortion? a) college-educated people; b) Caucasians; c) Protestants; d) Catholics. (p. 350)

4. DES in the form of the morning-after pill is capable of terminating pregnancy after unprotected intercourse if used within: a) 72 hours; b) one month; c) the first trimester; d) four months. (pp. 354–355)

5. Which of the following is the safest abortion procedure? a) D&C; b) D&E; c) suction abortion; d) intra-amniotic injection. (pp. 356–357)

6. An emergency abortion method in which the fetus is removed through an incision in the abdomen is: a) canalotomy; b) cervectomy; c) D&E; d) hysterotomy. (p. 359)

7. Most women who have had abortions report that they have which of the following feelings about their decision? a) resentment; b) guilt; c) relief; d) giddiness. (p. 359)

8. The more involved and supportive the male partner, the greater the self-esteem and self-worth of a woman who has had an abortion. True or false? (pp. 361–362)

9. The better the welfare benefits in an area, the higher the percentage of illegitimate children. True or false? (p. 365)

10. Discuss the legal status of abortion in the United States.

11. The percentage of abortions that are repeat abortions has steadily increased since the early 1970s. Discuss the possible reasons for this.

12. The authors compare how adolescents learn to drive a car with how they learn about sexuality. Assume that you are a school-board member. How would you alter sex education to attempt to reduce the unwanted pregnancy rate?

# Gender and Sexuality in Childhood and Adolescence

(continued)

$\mathcal{M}$ost people in our culture assume that newborn babies, although created through sexual union, are nonsexual for many years after birth (see Figure 12.1). Infants are the epitome of innocence, and in North America sexuality represents the opposite of innocence. In fact, first coitus is sometimes referred to as the end of innocence.

In this chapter we explore childhood and adolescent sexuality and gender. We begin by considering researchers' persistent difficulties in obtaining information about sexual behavior in childhood and early adolescence—difficulties that are associated with our culture's attitudes toward sexuality. We then examine various theories about the influence of early relationships with family members on personality development. The biological, psychological, and social aspects of gender identity and sexual development are considered, as well as the role of sexual play as a rehearsal for adult interactions and as a source of information about sexuality. Next, we evaluate the quality of sex education both at home and in school and its association with sexual attitudes and knowledge from infancy through adulthood. Then, the process of sexual maturation that marks the end of childhood, and the exploration of sexual behaviors and personal identities through which most adolescents pass, are outlined. Finally, we consider some of the behaviors involved in initial experiences of sexual intimacy with a partner.

## Barriers to Understanding Childhood Sexuality

What is the effect of our cultural assumption that the innocence of infancy is the opposite of sexuality? One effect is that few investigators have dared to delve into sexual feelings and experiences early in the life span because of the taboos that surround childhood eroticism. Even after children reach school age, researchers have difficulty obtaining permission to ask questions

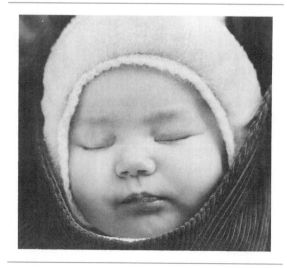

**FIGURE 12.1**
**The Innocent Infant**
Most people make assumptions about infants that influence treatment of and expectations about them.

about what youngsters know about sex, and it is extremely unlikely that researchers would be allowed to ask children what they do sexually.

Just as conducting research on childhood sexuality tends to be forbidden in North American culture, the exploration and expression of childhood sexuality tend to be prohibited or discouraged by parents and other caretakers. In many respects, scientists encounter the same set of problems that children face in their search for sexual information. Children with an active curiosity about sexuality elicit concern, anxiety, and reprimands from parents. Similarly, investigators of childhood sexuality and advocates of sex education are confronted with suspicion and, at times, public attack. Dr. Mary Calderone (see Figure 12.2) was among a group of sex educators and researchers described in a 1981 *Time* magazine article as condoning sexual interactions between children and adults. Calderone clarified her position in a letter quoted in *Sexuality Today* (November 2, 1981):

> *Parents can learn how to socialize their child's sexuality without harming it. They can guide it gently toward maturity by providing adequate and appropriate sexual information at various developmental stages. They can—and should—teach family personal values about all behavior, including sexual, but without fear-inducing guilt about "sin." In this way, I believe that they can keep the talk so ongoing that by adolescence children will still be in communication with their parents, as they are not today. In other words, sexuality, which we all have from birth, is not something nasty, nor does [being sexual] call for instant intercourse or any form of inappropriate genital behavior....*
>
> *I have an uncompromising Quaker— and professional—conscience. I will stubbornly continue, in my conservative, 77-year-old way, to insist until proven wrong by adequate studies that sexual contacts between adults and children are inappropriate and indefensible. And I am on record as holding that same opinion about most teenage sexual intercourse. (p. 3)*

Some of the concern over investigations of sexuality early in the life span stems from worries about the possible effects of sex research on chil-

**FIGURE 12.2**
**Mary Calderone**
Dr. Calderone is a leading proponent of sex education in North America.

dren. Will young people become more curious and experimental about sexuality following questioning about their sexual thoughts or after observations of their sexual behavior? The notion that we do not, or should not, become "sexual" until adulthood has created formidable barriers to learning about our early sexuality.

## Theories About the Development of Gender and Sexuality

When we turn to the issues of sexual preferences, attitudes about masturbation, masturbatory behavior, necking, petting, and stimulation to orgasm, we find not only gender differences but individual variations within the same gender. As with gender-role behaviors, your sexual attitudes and behaviors may seem natural and normal to you. Consider, however, the attitudes and behav-

ior of others whom you know well. It is quite likely that you know of no two people who hold identical points of view. What is the source of these variations? Why do some people find sexual feeling and expression a source of deep pleasure, one of God's great rewards, whereas others feel relatively little interest in this area of life, and still others experience shame, embarrassment, or fear that inhibits their ability to interact sexually with a person whom they love dearly? Such questions have stimulated theorists to devise models of how we acquire variations in our personalities (see Table 12.1). In this section we focus primarily on theorists' attempts to account for the similarities and differences in males' and females' development and expression of sexuality.

As was pointed out in Chapter 3, Sigmund Freud, the founder of psychoanalysis, believed that personality variations result from individuals' experiences as they attempt to cope with sexual energy during successive stages of childhood. We consider three aspects of Freud's model. One is his hypothesis that children compete with the parent of the same gender for a sexual relationship with the parent of the other gender: the *Oedipus complex* and the *Electra complex*. The second involves the ideas that boys relinquish their desire for their mother for fear of losing the penis, and that girls give up desire for their father from an awareness of having already lost the penis: the concepts of *castration anxiety* and *penis envy*. The third aspect of Freud's model of psychosexual development is his belief that after a sexually active first five years, children enter a period of repressed sexual interest and activity, which lasts until about age 11. He called this period *latency*. Freud theorized that if development

**Oedipus complex** (EH-dih-pus)—in Freudian theory, a son's desire for sexual relations with his mother.

**Electra complex**—in Freudian theory, a daughter's desire for sexual relations with her father.

**castration anxiety**—fear of losing the penis, thought by psychoanalysts to result from the child's fear of retaliation for forbidden sexual desire toward a parent.

**penis envy**—in psychoanalytic theory, a woman's wish to possess a penis.

**latency**—in psychoanalytic theory, a stage lasting from about six years of age until puberty, in which there is little observable interest in sexual activity.

TABLE 12.1 **Models of Development and Sexual Capacities**

| Stages | Ages | Freud's Stages | Erikson's Crises | Capacities |
|--------|------|----------------|------------------|------------|
| Infancy | Birth to 18 months | Oral stage | Basic trust vs. mistrust | Sensuality via sucking, touching, holding, bodily contact<br>Genital exploration, erection of penis, lubrication of vagina, and capacity for orgasm |
| Early childhood | 18 months to 3 years | Anal stage | Autonomy vs. doubt, shame | Development of sphincter control; ability in males to produce erections<br>Awareness of nongenital gender differences and gender identity<br>Development of language and potential to begin to acquire sexual vocabulary (names of body parts, processes) |
| Preschool years | 3 to 5 years | Phallic stage (Oedipus/Electra complexes) | Initiative vs. guilt | Deliberate pleasurable self-stimulation<br>Curiosity about sexual and reproductive processes<br>Well-developed gender identity |
| Late childhood | 5 to 11 years | Latency | Industry vs. inferiority | Active sexual exploration with both same- and other-gender friends<br>Active desire for sex information<br>Prepubescent surge in hormones, growth of internal and external sexual organs |
| Adolescence | 12 to 20 years | Genital stage | Identity vs. role confusion | Development of capacities to ejaculate and to menstruate; sexual maturation<br>Increasingly intense romantic attachments<br>Absorption in questions regarding self and identity |

went awry during these early years, psychotherapy could help a person to understand, but not necessarily to eliminate, the effects of destructive early experiences.

Erik Erikson, a psychoanalytic scholar who also proposed that humans go through stages of personality development, was considerably more optimistic than Freud about an individual's

chances of surviving a difficult early childhood if positive experiences followed during later stages. Erikson (1968a, 1968b) saw development as a process in which the person must resolve successive dilemmas. He described eight stages of life, each of which involves a crisis for the individual. In Erikson's view, a crisis is not necessarily a disastrous event. Although it has the potential to overwhelm the individual, it may also be perceived as a challenge, providing the opportunity for growth. Successful resolution of life crises enables us to become healthier, more well-developed, integrated, and mature human beings. Like many other theorists, Erikson perceived the first years of life as extremely important in personality development. Unlike Freud, he thought that, although the development of a trusting nature is crucial for the one-year-old, positive experiences later in life can offset less-than-desirable early life experiences. Similarly, the effect of positive experiences and development during infancy can be overwhelmed by the negative effects of crises arising later in life.

A rather different perspective on the development of sexual behavior and gender differences is held by evolutionary theorists, who view differences between males and females as the result of evolution (Buss, 1994; Buss & Schmitt, 1993; Symons, 1979). Evolutionary theorists assume that gender differences emerged over time and stem from the reproductive success of individuals with adaptive traits. Pointing out that we have been a hunting-and-gathering species for all but a tiny fraction of our history, they argue that those men who had the skills to acquire needed resources (food, shelter) would have been likely to have greater reproductive success than their less skillful counterparts. Selective pressure, then, favored the evolution of such hunting assets as visual and spatial skills, including the ability to calculate distances and directions. Well-developed gross motor skills and aggressiveness in males would also have been valuable.

In contrast, attachment bonds, sociability, and interpersonal sensitivity would have been favored in women because of the usefulness of these traits for the survival and development of children. According to this view, the offspring of women lacking these attributes would have been less likely to survive. Interpersonal sensitivity and the ability to form intense bonds, then, may be part of women's psychobiological structure developed over thousands of years and inherited from our ancestors (see Figure 12.3).

Finally, social learning theorists, as their name implies, attribute similarities and differences in gender roles, sexual attitudes, and sexual behavior to human learning in social contexts. These theorists believe that sexual attitudes and behavior are influenced throughout the life span by rewards, expectations, and punishments associated with sexual activities, as well as by observations of these activities. For example, the first time you heard of deep or "French" kissing, you may have found the concept revolting. Later, in the context of a romantic relationship, you may have responded differently to this behavior. Social learning theorists might attribute your initial attitude to early punishment for sharing food—and thus saliva—with others, and your subsequent reward to your association of deep kissing with pleasurable arousal. Similarly, we learn to exhibit certain traditionally expected behaviors for our gender while visiting an elderly relative, whereas in the company of peers, we often feel freer to behave in a more "unisex" fashion. A social learning theorist would explain these variations in sexual attitudes and gender-role behaviors as stemming from the differential rewards and punishments associated with them at different times and in varying situations.

We examine the process of development primarily through the theoretical framework conceived by Erikson. Other theoretical approaches are discussed when there is information that is relevant to them.

## Infancy: Trust Versus Mistrust

After nine months in the protective uterine environment, an infant emerges into the outside world and is immediately assigned a gender: "It's a girl (boy)!" This assignment is based on the appearance of the baby's external genitals, and most of the time the label fits the infant's genetic gender. New parents describe their infant daughters as smaller, less attentive, softer, and finer-featured than their infant sons (Rubin, Provenzano, & Luria, 1974). It could be argued that parents are simply responding to real differences between the genders. Research shows, however, that the behavior of the adults varies according to whether they believe an infant is male or female regardless of its actual gender (see

**FIGURE 12.3**
**Attachment**
It is clear that mammals become attached to each other relatively easily. Is our capacity for attachment a genetic predisposition?

Figure 12.4). In one study, an infant was introduced as a little girl to one group of mothers and as a little boy to another group of mothers. The mothers were more likely to offer dolls to and to smile at the "female" infant and were more likely to offer trains to the "male" infant (Will, Self, & Datan, 1976). Gender stereotyping of infants is more prevalent among children, adolescents, and young adults than it is among older adults (Stern & Karraker, 1989; Vogel, Lake, Evans, & Karraker, 1991).

In the womb, basic needs are satisfied automatically and continuously through the umbilical cord. After birth, an infant must depend on the responsiveness of adults for its nourishment. Cuddling within the womb is replaced by cuddling with caretakers. Psychologists of all theoretical perspectives agree that if infant needs are satisfied in a loving and consistent way, a trusting stance toward others develops. If, however, caretakers are unloving or react inconsistently to infant needs, the child may form an attitude of generalized mistrust. Without a trusting stance toward life, an optimistic approach toward the future—hope—is unlikely. Instead, according to Erikson, the infant will worry constantly about the satisfaction of current needs and is therefore tied to the present. Thus the quality of the attach-

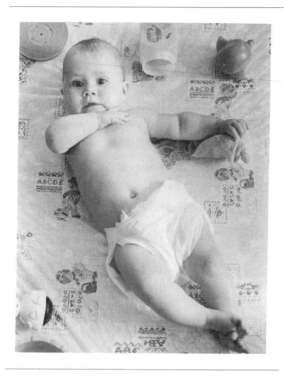

**FIGURE 12.4**
**Describe This Child's Personality**
Adults respond differently to an infant, depending on whether they are told that it is a boy or a girl.

*The new mother touches the baby's fingers and toes with her own fingertips, puts her palm on the baby's torso, and then wraps the baby in her arms. All the while she maintains full eye contact with the infant and her tension mounts until the baby opens its eyes and returns the gaze. Finally, when mothers talk to their babies, they also share a set of actions—wide-open eyes, raised eyebrows, sustained facial expression and baby talk—a shift in speech that elongates the vowels.*

This predisposition among women to form an intense attachment to their young makes evolutionary sense. Humans are much more immature at birth than are infants of other primate species. If they are to survive and prosper, they need prolonged care, which is assured by the intense physical and emotional attachment of the mother to the infant.

## Father-Child Attachment

Until recently, men in almost all cultures contributed little to the direct caregiving of infants (Hoyenga & Hoyenga, 1993a). Now that notions about the natures and roles of males and females have

ment between an infant and its caretakers is important for the infant's development (Belsky, 1991; Shaver & Hazan, 1994).

## Mother-Child Attachment

Women display a number of unlearned responses to their infants that probably enhance the bond between them. An infant's crying stimulates the secretion of oxytocin in its mother, which erects the nipples for nursing and releases the milk. Further, most mothers carry their infants in their left arm without being aware of it while engaging in various chores (Hoyenga & Hoyenga, 1993a; Whiting & Edwards, 1988). In this position, an infant is soothed by the sound of the familiar maternal heartbeat (see Figure 12.5). New mothers also appear to have a relatively predictable sequence of reactions to their babies, as Rossi (1978, p. 75) described:

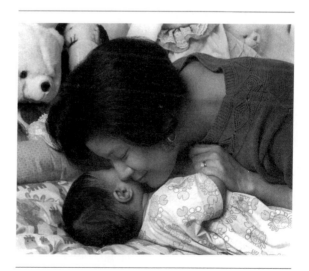

**FIGURE 12.5**
**Mother-Child Bonding**
This mother and baby reflect the beauty of intense bonding.

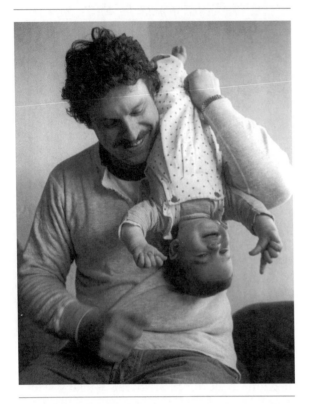

**FIGURE 12.6**
**Father-Child Bonding**
Compared with the contact that mothers have with their children, the contact that fathers have with their children often involves more physical activity.

begun to change in North America, however, many fathers take a much more active role in infant care. Expectant mothers and fathers holding egalitarian views toward women's roles anticipate more father-involvement in infant care than do those holding more traditional perspectives (Fishbein, 1989). Following the birth of a child, fathers who are given the opportunity to have contact with their new babies touch, hold, and kiss them just as much as the infant's mothers do (Parke & O'Leary, 1976). When Parke and Sawin (1976) compared the feeding skills of fathers and mothers, they found both equally adept at responding sensitively to infants' cues.

Regardless of the extent of their contact with their infants, fathers tend to differ from mothers in the kinds of interactions that they have with babies. Initially, the contribution of fathers tends to involve physical assistance: taking care of the infant when the mother is tired, playing with the baby while the mother makes dinner, and taking over some of the routine chores of maintaining the household (Rhoades, 1989). Fathers usually do not become heavily invested in the role of parent until the child begins to walk and talk (Rossi, 1985). Thus mothers are much more involved than fathers in child care during infancy in most cultures (Hoyenga & Hoyenga, 1993b). However, when men assume full responsibility for child care, as in the case of single parenthood, they employ strategies that are considered stereotypically feminine in providing adequate care for their children (Risman, 1989).

Fathers tend to emphasize physical games with their infants (see Figure 12.6), whereas mothers are more likely to engage in verbal games (McDonald & Parke, 1986; Ross & Taylor, 1989). Even among monkeys, physical play is the primary mode of interaction between fathers and their offspring. Possibly because fathers initiate more unusual and physically arousing games, children are more likely to choose their fathers than their mothers as play partners by the time they are 18 months old (Clarke-Stewart, 1978; Whiting & Edwards, 1988). As researchers study the active and close relationships babies can form with their fathers, scholars are beginning to realize fathers' important role in child-rearing.

## Sensuality and Sexuality During Infancy

In discussing early development, we must be careful not to define children's activities by adult standards. For better or worse, by the time we reach adulthood, most of us have learned to differentiate—in fact, to segregate—our sexual feelings and experiences from our other sensations and activities. Young children do not appear to make these distinctions, however. With this in mind, let us consider eroticism during infancy.

### Biosexual Development

Before birth the fetus absorbs hormones secreted by the mother, and their effects do not disappear immediately. Thus, for a brief time after birth, infants show several signs associated with reproductive maturity. The genitals and breasts of baby boys and girls are typically large and prominent. A milky substance is secreted from the tiny nipples of breast-fed infants, who continue to receive some hormones through their mother's milk. Prolactin, responsible for the production of the mother's milk, is found in these infants' urine. Female infants also may have slight vaginal bleeding suggestive of menstruation. All these symptoms gradually fade and have disappeared well before the end of the baby's fourth month.

The ovaries of baby girls have a ribbonlike appearance at birth. They increase quite slowly in size and weight until puberty, when they develop dramatically. Until that time, estrogen secretion is slight and constant; the adrenal glands are thought to be the source of the estrogen. The uterus of a baby girl is tiny, and the fallopian tubes have a convoluted appearance.

The structure of the testes and epididymis of baby boys is established by the middle of the gestation period. Some interstitial cells, which produce testosterone, are present at birth. After some fluctuation in testosterone levels in the first seven months of a male infant's development, testosterone levels remain fairly similar to those in female infants from the third month until the onset of puberty. Adrenal androgen levels, however, rise a few years before puberty begins, in a process called *adrenarche*, which may influence skeletal maturation (Vermeulen, 1986). Like girls, boys experience little development in their sexual and reproductive structures until the onset of puberty.

### Sensual Development

Before a baby begins to acquire language, communication between the infant and the outer world takes place largely through physical sensations. The ways in which adults hold and caress the infant, as well as their responses to the child's discomfort, affect a child's emerging concept of his or her own body and developing sensuality (Hatfield, 1994). It is apparent that human infants are able to decipher body language before they

can understand the content of words. Well-intentioned caretakers who are extremely tense and nervous in their attempts to calm a distressed infant tend to do just the opposite. Conversely, the pleasure and contentment of a nursing mother is mirrored in the pleasure of her infant. A nursing infant sometimes even shows body tension and release similar to that observed during erotic interaction between adults. The important factors in the infant's sensual development are probably the body contact, cuddling, and caressing accompanying feeding rather than the actual source of nourishment (breast or bottle).

From birth on, male babies are capable of erections, and female babies are capable of vaginal lubrication. If erections are not observed during waking hours, they may be seen during the stage of sleep accompanied by rapid eye movement (REM). REM sleep is associated with dream states in children and adults, and erections in males frequently appear during these periods of dreaming.

The signs of infant eroticism—erections and lubrication—are primarily reflexive during the first year of life; that is, touching or brushing the genital area may bring about a "sexual" reflex. The infant does not, as far as we know, fantasize or purposely try to bring about erection or lubrication. Yet there are exceptions. According to one report (Kinsey et al., 1953), six infants under a year of age were observed masturbating. In general, however, genital fondling by infants is not goal-directed, as is adult masturbation. For infants and young children, touching or rubbing the penis or vulva is a generally pleasurable activity like many other sensuous pursuits, such as sucking their fingers and playing with their toes. Only as they mature do children start to masturbate with the intent to have orgasm. Some preliminary reports of children in their first year suggested little or no difference between boys and girls in the frequency of autoerotic play (Roiphe & Galenson, 1981).

### Parental Reactions to Early Sensuality

Our cultural norm of segregating the "sexual" from the rest of our experience begins during infancy. Most parents make a happy fuss over their infants' discovery of their own toes, ears,

---

**adrenarche**—the increase in adrenal androgens several years before puberty in boys.

**FIGURE 12.7**
**Learning to Love**
Cuddling and hugging between adults may have its roots in early contacts between
parents and their babies.

or fingers. But if they make a fuss over the discovery of the penis or the vulva, it is not likely to be a happy or positive fuss. Parents either ignore the discovery, or they actively discourage genital exploration by moving the little fingers or covering the genitals with a diaper. What significance do infants attach to the fact that when they suck on their toes, their parents imitate their behavior and also suck on their infants' toes, but when they pull on the labia or penis, parents do not laughingly join in?

Assumptions that humans naturally differentiate between the genital and nongenital explorations of their infants and naturally avoid any genital contact with infants are not supported by evidence from other cultures (Ford & Beach,

1951). Not only are self-exploration and stimulation accepted in many societies, but in some cultures adults use genital fondling as a method of soothing cranky babies. Mothers in Trinidad, for example, masturbate their babies to calm them and to induce sleep.

Certain learning experiences during infancy may be important for developing the capacity to give and receive erotic pleasure in adulthood. Many expressions of tenderness between parents and their offspring—snuggling, hugging, stroking, and caressing—are similar to intimate behaviors between adults (see Figure 12.7). People who receive little sensual contact during infancy and childhood often have difficulty in accepting and giving tenderness when they grow up. Many of the techniques that are employed by sex therapists can be viewed as attempts to teach inhibited adults how to recapture the pleasure of sensual interaction.

## Early Childhood: Autonomy Versus Shame and Doubt

During the first year of life, children are highly dependent. Others must carry them from one place to another until they are able to crawl and, later, to walk. Others must infer their wants and needs for food, play, and diaper changes, as their cries are still quite undifferentiated. At some point before the end of their first year or shortly into the beginning of their second, however, babies demonstrate rapidly rising levels of physical and verbal competency. In their initial attempts to walk, babies depend on the availability of walls, furniture, and helping hands, but usually within a few months before or after the first birthday, they enter toddlerhood by taking their first unaided, awkward steps.

Erikson (1968a) described the challenge of this second stage as the conflict of autonomy versus shame and doubt. The child's task at this developmental stage is to form a sense of autonomy and a balance between it and feelings of shame and doubt. Children who are encouraged to develop their competencies in a protective environment begin to acquire a sense of autonomy, or the ability to direct and control themselves. This stage can be a trying time for a toddler's parents, particularly in the case of their first child. It is common for parents to feel torn. They may want to let the child explore and try to master the environment—to climb the slide or stairs alone, or to get out of the bathtub unaided instead of being lifted out. Yet they also want to prevent the child from falling or getting hurt. Too much protectiveness and interference thwart the toddler's developing sense of competency; too little protection may cause a toddler to experience the world as a painful and unsafe place. In the first case, Erikson says, the child experiences shame, and in the other, doubt.

## Language, Gender, and Sexuality

Having been told that he is a boy or that she is a girl, a baby quickly acquires a sense of being either male or female. By the time children begin to talk (generally between the first and second year), they can apply the appropriate gender label to themselves. By recognizing basic differences between genders, children begin to grasp the concept of *gender identity*.

Other gender concepts take longer for children to master. For instance, although they can apply the correct gender label to themselves and others at the age of two, they do not necessarily understand the concept of *gender constancy*. A little boy may believe, for example, that at some later point in life he will be a girl.

A female infant assigned a female gender at birth will perceive and describe herself as a female, thereby developing a female gender identity by the time she is two. She learns the behaviors that are expected of females in her culture and incorporates these behaviors into her personality. As she learns about becoming a female, she is learning about *gender roles*. As she gradually assumes the characteristics of this role, she is acquiring a *gender-role identification*.

Instead of relying on a generalized wail when they are hungry or do not wish to do something, during their second year children begin to use short, specific phrases: "Wan banna" (I want a banana) or "No seep" (I don't want to go to sleep). They ask incessantly for labels, saying "Wha zat?" as they point to various objects, including their own body parts.

By this time, children may have already learned, vaguely, by means of their parents'

**gender identity**—the feeling or conviction that one is a male or a female.

**gender constancy**—the concept that gender does not normally change over the life span.

**gender roles**—the traits and behaviors expected of males and of females in a particular culture.

**gender-role identification**—the process by which individuals incorporate behaviors and characteristics of a culturally defined gender role into their own personalities.

behavior, to differentiate between their sexual anatomy and other parts of the body. When such differentiation begins to occur, parents are likely to bolster a child's impression that there is something mysteriously taboo about the genital regions. Children may note that, whereas parents are willing to provide such labels as "nose" and "eyes," they consistently appear reluctant to say "penis" and "vagina." Some parents give minimal information, labeling the entire genital area "your bottom," "your privates," or "down there." Others refuse to provide any label, saying instead, "Never mind" or "Why would you want to know that?"

## Toilet Training and Gender: Differences in Sexual Associations

Within a few months of their second birthday, toddlers begin to demonstrate some rudimentary control of their sphincter muscles, so they are able to deposit their urine and feces in whatever place the culture deems appropriate. Parents employ a variety of toilet-training techniques, but a common theme in parental instruction in our culture is an emphasis on the dirtiness of feces and urine. Thus parents may inadvertently teach an association between the genitals and impurity. Long after children have mastered the lessons regarding appropriate places to eliminate bodily wastes, they may retain the accompanying lesson that the genital area is bad, dirty, and not to be touched for fear of contact with smelly and filthy bodily discharges. This association can be seen in our culture's labeling of sexual stories, allusions, or jokes as "dirty."

This "education" may account for some of the differences between the sexual attitudes and behaviors of boys and girls. Both genders are taught the association between dirt and the genitals, but two factors are likely to make this connection more intense, long-lasting, and sexually inhibiting for women than for men. In general, little boys are dressed in more rugged and easily washed clothing than little girls are, and as they play, little boys are expected to get "dirty" to a greater extent than are little girls. The phrase "dirty little boy" does not have as negative a connotation as the phrase "dirty little girl." Ironically, the association of gender and dirt changes later in the life span; rarely are elderly women referred to as "dirty old women," but a "dirty old man" is someone to avoid.

Although the genitals often are linked with dirtiness for both boys and girls, having the characteristic of "dirtiness" is traditionally a far more serious offense for girls than for boys. The vaginal douche and deodorant industries thrive on the concerns of adolescent and adult women about the cleanliness and odor of their vaginas. In most grocery stores, signs alert customers to the location of the shelves devoted to products for "feminine hygiene." One searches in vain for corresponding "masculine hygiene" sections; there is no parallel marketing of products for hygiene of the penis or scrotum. Thus it would seem that, whereas women need chemical aids to be hygienic and clean, men do not have such problems.

Anatomical differences are another factor leading to differential reactions of males and females to training that the genitals are impure and dirty. Typically, boys are taught to wipe themselves with toilet paper after they defecate but not after they urinate. The fact that a few drops of urine may get on their son's clothing is not a matter of great concern to most parents. In fact, the tolerance of males' urine was immortalized in the old saying

> You can shake it, you can break it,
> you can bang it on the wall,
> but when you put it in your pants,
> that last drop is sure to fall!

Conversely, little girls are taught to wipe themselves no matter what. Because differentiating the urethra from the clitoris and the vagina from the anus is considerably harder than differentiating the penis from the anus, girls may assume that the urethra, clitoris, and vagina are all dirty. When they reach puberty, many girls are taught that menstrual bleeding is unclean, an idea further stamping in the connection between the genitals and dirt for females. The association of dirtiness with the reproductive organs can lead to significant problems with sexual expression later in life.

## Awareness of Gender Differences

The sense of being a male or a female appears to be well developed by the age of two; and by the

**FIGURE 12.8**
**Natural Sex Education**
Some parents insist that their young children are clothed at all times, whereas others consider nudity acceptable under certain conditions. Children such as this four-year-old boy and his one-year-old sister, who have the opportunity to observe their siblings nude, may have healthier and more positive attitudes about the human body.

time children are two and a half, they can correctly apply the label "girl" or "boy" to themselves. During toddlerhood, children can label accurately the gender of others. However, they appear to rely on external appearances based on gender-role norms, such as hairstyles and clothing, rather than on genital anatomy. In their interview study with children, Ronald & Juliette Goldman (1982) found that most children, until they were nine years old, were unable to give an

accurate description of how one could tell whether a newborn baby was a boy or a girl.

These studies notwithstanding, there is considerable difference from one culture to another and from one child to another in awareness of genital differences. This variation suggests that such awareness is at least partially due to differences in the opportunities children have to observe males and females (see Figure 12.8). One little boy we know had apparently been oblivious to any anatomical difference among his sisters, his parents, and himself, despite the fact that he had been taking baths with one or another member of his family since birth. One day shortly before his second birthday, when he and his mother were taking a bath, he began to stare at her vulva. A look of great consternation came over his face, and he asked, "Where *penis?*"

## Preschool Years: Initiative Versus Guilt

The years from ages three to five are filled with opportunities for children to acquire the ability to direct their own activities and affect their environment. According to Erikson, the crisis/opportunity of this stage involves the conflict of initiative versus guilt. Whether children emerge from this stage with their sense of initiative favorably outbalancing their sense of guilt depends largely on how adults respond to the children's self-initiated activities. Ridicule or neglect of the child's budding attempts to interact effectively with the environment inhibits the development of initiative, leading instead to a sense of guilt.

Erikson believed that during this stage children also begin to incorporate criticism and punishment into their self-images, learning to experience not only shame but guilt. Before ages three to five, a child caught by his or her parents doing something that they considered inappropriate would feel ashamed, but the child would likely engage in the same "inappropriate" behavior without any pangs of conscience when a parent or other authority figure were not present. However, both Erikson and Freud believed that from about ages three to five, the child begins to internalize reprimands and prohibitions from authorities. Thus authority figures are no longer necessary to evoke shame over the youngster's wrongdoing. The child's own internal sense of right and wrong becomes important in guiding behavior. It is noteworthy that Freud believed that boys' internalization of parental moral values was more complete than was girls'. He thought that this supposedly greater morality in boys resulted from their higher anxiety, arising

from fear of castration. Girls, in contrast, already punished with castration, had less to fear and developed less of a conscience. As seen throughout this book, however, females appear to be more controlled by societal dictates than do males, a gender difference that social learning theorists attribute to differential socialization rather than to the possession of a penis or a clitoris.

Social learning theorists believe that children continue throughout their development to build up associations of positive and negative consequences with their behavior, thus learning to engage in some acts and to avoid others.

### Gender-Role Socialization

The process of *gender-role socialization* occurs throughout childhood and adolescence as the child is influenced by the family, peer group, and school system. In their classic comparison of a large number of cultures, Barry, Bacon, and Child (1957) found that 82% of the cultures they surveyed encouraged nurturance in girls more than in boys. In contrast, in most societies, achievement (87%) and self-reliance (85%) were emphasized more in the training of boys than in the training of girls.

Both parents usually engage in differentiation based on the gender of their offspring, but distinctions made by fathers are more pronounced than those made by mothers. Fathers rate their sons as being better coordinated, hardier, and stronger than their daughters. In their observations of groups of three-year-old boys and girls and their parents, Jacklin, DiPietro, and Maccoby (1984) found that father-son pairs displayed higher levels of rough-and-tumble play than any other parent-child combination. They concluded that fathers assume more of a role in socializing their children to play according to traditional gender roles than do mothers.

If you have observed parents interacting with their children, you may wonder about the effectiveness of such gender-role training. To the casual observer, some four-year-old girls appear to

**gender-role socialization**—the training of children by parents and other caretakers to behave in ways considered appropriate for their gender.

be quite resistant to parental attempts to encourage them to remain neat and clean, a stereotypically feminine behavior. Similarly, it may seem to you that the crying howl of the frustrated or hurt little boy is so loud that he could not possibly hear his parents' admonition that "big boys don't cry." Nonetheless, such parental efforts to push little boys and girls into gender-stereotypic attitudes and behaviors are not only effective but also begin to show their effects early in life.

The behavior and traits seen as characteristic of masculinity or femininity are culturally defined. In our culture, males have been expected to be active, aggressive, athletic, and unemotional. Females have been expected to be passive, nurturant, yielding, emotional, and gentle. However, the specific traits and behaviors that are expected of males and of females vary from one culture to the next. In New Guinea, for instance, among the Mundugamor, aggressiveness is expected and observed in both men and women. In contrast, the mountain-dwelling Arapesh women and men of New Guinea both behave in ways that are traditionally associated with women in our culture. Among the lake-dwelling Tchambuli of that island, the traditional roles of our culture are reversed, with females being aggressive and males being gentle and nurturant (Mead, 1935).

People vary in the extent to which they incorporate into their own personalities the behaviors expected of males or females in their culture. A particular female may conform to traditional expectations for women, or she may reject them, preferring behavior and characteristics associated with males in her culture. She may also combine both masculine and feminine characteristics in her behavior and personality.

## Gender Similarities and Differences Versus Gender Stereotypes

Some additional concepts are important to understanding gender similarities and differences. A *gender difference* is a reliable difference between the average male and the average female

**gender difference**—a difference in physique, ability, attitude, or behavior found between groups of males and females.

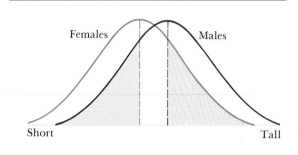

**FIGURE 12.9**
**Overlapping Distributions**
If we plot the heights of males and females, we find that the average male is taller than the average female. Note, however, that there are many females who are taller than the average male (see color shaded area) and many males who are shorter than the average female (see gray shaded area). The distributions of numerous social and physical characteristics of males and females overlap in this way.

that has been scientifically observed when large groups of males and females have been studied. For example, the average male is taller than the average female. It is important to realize, however, that even where gender differences exist, the groups generally overlap. For example, the distribution of height in males overlaps the distribution of height in females: some females are taller than the average male, and some males are shorter than the average female. So knowledge of someone's gender does not allow us to predict his or her height.

Such *overlapping distributions* (see Figure 12.9) characterize almost all aspects of gender, and of sexual behaviors as well, including sexual appetite, speed of arousal and orgasm, frequency of masturbation, and desire for sexual variety. Nonetheless, it is commonly believed that males have larger sexual appetites than do females. Such a belief about the characteristics of a person

**overlapping distribution**—a statistical term describing situations in which the values of a variable for some individual members of two groups are the same, although a difference exists between the overall values of the particular variable for the two groups.

based on his or her gender is a *gender stereotype.* A gender stereotype may be accurate or inaccurate. For example, the stereotype that females are less likely to masturbate than males, or at least to report masturbating, has been supported by research (Kinsey et al., 1953; Leitenberg et al., 1993). In contrast, the gender stereotype that females are less aroused by explicit sexual material has not been supported by contemporary research (Fisher, 1983). Regardless of the accuracy or inaccuracy of a given gender stereotype, we cannot use it as a basis for predicting the behavior of a particular male or female because of the overlapping distribution of gender characteristics and sexual behavior in males and females.

We have devoted considerable space to this discussion of gender similarities and differences versus gender stereotypes because it is important to evaluate when a particular stereotype about gender differences is supported by research and when a stereotype, although commonly believed, does not hold up under the scrutiny of empirical studies. Let us return now to the development of sexual learning during the preschool years.

## Sexual Learning

Just as they display a keen interest in learning about how to be a boy or girl in their culture, most children also reveal a marked curiosity about sexuality during their preschool years. Discouraging and punishing their sexual exploration will lead children to feel guilty about sex. Acknowledging children's curiosity without ridiculing or inhibiting fantasy activity, on the other hand, fosters a sense of competence and encourages assertiveness.

The capacity for self-stimulation and orgasm seems to be potentially available to most children by the age of five. Kinsey and his colleagues (1953) estimated that almost all boys could have orgasm without ejaculation three to five years before reaching puberty, and more than half could reach orgasm by three to four years of age. Equivalent systematic research is lacking for females, but see Box 12.1.

**gender stereotype**—a belief about the characteristics of a person based on gender.

**FIGURE 12.10**
**Childhood Expressions of Affection**
Children begin to hug and cuddle at an early age in imitation of the adults in their environment.

During the preschool years, children's sexuality becomes more social. Children kiss, hug, or hold hands in obvious imitation of adults (see Figure 12.10). Much of their curiosity about sexuality is woven into their play. This play facilitates the intellectual and social development of children, permitting them to explore their environment, to learn about objects, and to solve problems. Through acting out roles in fantasy play, children learn to understand others and to practice roles they will assume as they grow older. They can test without fear the outer limits of what is acceptable. In our culture, much of children's curiosity about their own and others' bodies is expressed through such well-known games as "playing house" and "playing doctor." Interest in these games may be fueled, to some extent, by parents' failure to provide children with explicit information about sexual anatomy and by the absence of opportunities in traditional families for casual observations of parents and siblings when they are nude.

**Box 12.1**

## Mary Steichen's Sex Education

Mary (Steichen) Calderone, M.D., one of the pioneers in education for sexuality, recalls her sexual socialization:

*I have for 70 years known fully and surely that I was female and liked the idea. Although I was a tomboy and had a driving intellect, I enjoyed my own femininity and admired that of others. It was about my eroticism (which emerged so early that I don't even remember being without it) that my mother and I clashed violently for possession and control of what I looked upon as exclusively mine: my body and its pleasure. The fact that from that period on I associated the rage of being forced to go to bed with metal mitts on my hands with sexual arousal and orgasm explains, I believe, some sexual dysfunction from which my adult relationships have suffered. I early sensed that my fath-*

*er's sexuality was intense and that even then in his marriage he behaved with great freedom, as, I have learned since, did most of the artists and many of the elite of those pre–World War I days. I have since concluded that I was a victim of my mother's Puritan anger against her husband. Also in retrospect, I have sensed that she herself was strongly erotic, and this has only served to underline my conviction that in her despair and frustration at what she probably correctly interpreted as her husband's loss of sexual interest in her, she vented her resultant Puritanism in attempts to control what she often openly called my "inherited oversexed tendencies."*

Source: Calderone, 1978, pp. 148–149.

*The Primal Scene: Psychosexual Trauma or Sex Education?*

A child's witnessing of parental lovemaking is referred to as the *primal scene*. Many psychoanalytic therapists believe that this experience can have traumatic effects on a child's psychosexual development. This belief stems, in part, from reports of therapy patients who said that they were shocked and horrified during childhood when they stumbled on their parents having sexual intercourse. Inferences were then made about an association between such exposure and the problems that brought these patients into therapy. However, there is no empirical evidence regarding the effects of accidental observation of parental lovemaking on persons who are not in therapy.

Although they were not directly investigating the impact of the observation of parental lovemaking on offspring, Lewis and Janda (1988)

found that the current sexual adjustment of college students was unrelated to the extent of their childhood memories of parental nudity, exposure to nudity in general, and sleeping in the parents' bed. Greater comfort with present physical contact and affection, as well as more frequent sexual activity, were reported by males and females who had slept in their parents' bed occasionally during childhood. Among males, occasionally sleeping in the parental bed was also related to higher self-esteem and to lower guilt and anxiety.

Given these results, we speculate that the effects of observing parental sexual activity depend on the general family environment. If parents tend to be extremely private about their affection, avoiding any touching, hugging, or kissing except when they are alone; if they avoid any nudity; and if they punish their child's interest in and exploration of his or her own body, the child who observes his or her parents making love witnesses a host of new experiences: nudity and parental contact plus the specific behaviors associated with active intercourse. A child raised in

**primal scene**—a child's observation of parental coitus.

**Box 12.2**

## Children's Sexual Knowledge: An Immoral Research Topic?

Ronald and Juliette Goldman (1982) have described some of the difficulties faced by those who attempt to investigate children's sexuality. The Goldmans interviewed 838 children in Australia, Britain, the United States, Canada, and Sweden, at the ages of 5, 7, 9, 11, 13, and 15. To understand children's thinking about sexuality, they asked each of these children 63 questions.

After examining previous research in the area in the course of designing the study, the Goldmans wrote, "The paucity of published articles reinforced our conviction for the need to undertake what was to prove a difficult and demanding project for the next two years" (1982, pp. xvi–xvii). In selecting the specific topics to be investigated, the Goldmans noted that gathering information on a number of sexual behaviors, including childhood masturbation, would have been

*extremely valuable, but we judged from trial responses that to have included such items would have gone beyond the limits set by social taboos in home, school, and community. . . . Operating within the constraints evident within the public school systems the content had to be adjusted to what was realistically possible and acceptable. The influence of these and other sexual taboos, preventing discussion, exploration or research in certain areas, is in itself an indication of the need for research into sexual thinking. (pp. 62–63)*

The Goldmans carefully designed their interviews to avoid offending school boards and parents, who had to read a description of the research and sign consent forms before children could participate. The researchers experi-

enced no difficulties in obtaining their samples from three of the five countries. The exceptions were the United States and Canada—specifically, the cities of Buffalo and Niagara Falls, New York, and the province of Ontario, Canada:

*On both sides of the Canadian-USA border, despite the continuous efforts of university colleagues to help us make contacts and gain access to schools, we encountered widespread negative attitudes, and considerable opposition. This was so pronounced that after more than a month of fruitless effort, we almost gave up and returned to Britain. However, patient persuasion and persistence succeeded, although the time spent in this process left us less time for the actual interviewing. For this reason the North American sample is the smallest and least satisfactory of the four samples completed.*

*The overall reason for these difficulties would appear to be the direct political control exercised by elected Boards of Education in the USA, to whom area superintendents of schools are responsible. These Boards are usually composed of lay persons who act as watchdogs, if not leaders, of the community. . . . By a misfortune of timing, we were trying to gain entry to schools in New York State only a few weeks before the local Boards of Education elections. Administrators were plainly anxious that our project might provide political ammunition during those elections and leave them exposed to public criticism. . . . One superintendent said to us that he didn't want his home bombed, and another, due to retire shortly, reported that he would not put his pension at risk. (pp. 73–74)*

such a household could have even more difficulty interpreting the primal scene if the parents scold the child and angrily send him or her out of the room, or if they avoid giving any sort of explanation. It would seem reasonable for this

child to have a fearful reaction, perhaps interpreting the event as a violent one in which the parents were hurting each other.

In contrast, a child reared in a generally less restrictive atmosphere would have fewer new experiences to interpret. Upon discovering his or her parents having intercourse, the child might be likely to ask a question already posed in numerous other circumstances: "What're you doing?" If the parents respond with something like, "We're cuddling; do you want to come cuddle for a few minutes before you go back to bed?" the child's reaction will probably not be terribly different from his or her response if the parents were snuggling fully clothed on the couch while watching television when the child wandered in. Parents who opt for this alternative need not worry about the child seeing the father's erection, because loss of erection is notoriously rapid when a man is startled or interrupted. Thus the father's penis would probably be quite flaccid long before the child could climb into bed.

## Children's Sexual Knowledge

A major study by Ronald and Juliette Goldman (1982) yielded some fascinating information about children's developing understanding of sexuality (see Box 12.2). The Goldmans interviewed 838 children in Australia, Britain, Canada, Sweden, and the United States whose ages ranged from 5 to 15 years. Among the 63 questions the Goldmans asked children was, "How can anyone know a newborn baby is a boy or a girl?" They also asked how boys and girls grow differently as they get older. The Goldmans suggested that if Freud's hypotheses are correct regarding the Oedipal conflict, its resolution, and latency (the subsequent period of sexual disinterest and inactivity),

*one would expect many 5-year-olds to be aware of sexual differences and to show relatively little embarrassment when asked the question about newborn babies, and for inhibitions to occur strongly at 7 years with recognition of differences being repressed until about 10 or 11 years of age. A similar observation might be made about castration fears, but there is little evidence for these in the responses of the sample. Only four children, all boys, two at 5 years of age and one at 9 made remarks relating to castration, such as, "We began as girls and a penis grew later" (quite the opposite to castration). The*

*fourth, an Australian boy, aged 11 replied, "If it's a boy it'll have a penis. Girls will have a vagina. . . . It's not sticking out, it's cut, it's right in." This is the only overt reference to "cutting" or castration. There is one further reference, in the answer to pubertal differences about girls, "when they're little they have a dinkle (penis) and when they're older they don't. . . [.] (Q Why?) Because it changes. It goes away" (English boy, 5 years). The strongest evidence expected would be from the responses of girls, but no observations of this kind are made by girls in the entire population sampled. (1982, p. 194)*

To evaluate children's responses to the question of how anyone could know whether a newborn baby was a boy or a girl, the Goldmans devised a scoring system. In their final 3-point system, the following categories were used:

*Score 1: Irrelevant physical factors, authoritarianism, and artificialisms.* This score was given to such responses as "Because mum dressed her in a dress. There's no other way to tell" (Australian girl, 7 years); "Boys and girls are born different. Boys come out a different place [points to navel] and girls here [points to chest]" (North American boy, 7 years).

*Score 2: Semirecognized physicalisms.* This score was given to such responses as "Boys stand up to go to the wee-wee, and girls don't" (English girl, 7 years); "They're different down there . . . some kind of different bottom . . . shapes are different, dunno really" (Australian boy, 9 years); and "Girls don't have dicky birds" (English girl, 7 years).

*Score 3: Physicalisms with named parts.* This score was assigned to such responses as "If it's got a penis or not. If it has it's a boy. Girls have a virginia" (English boy, 11 years) and "Down between your legs, where they go to the locker room. . . . It's embarrassing, but the boy doesn't have a slit down the middle but has a round tube, a penis" (North American boy, 13 years).

Presumably, children who were afraid of being castrated or who believed themselves to be

**FIGURE 12.11**
**Learning to Be "Sexy"**
These little girls have already learned that shapely breasts are part of Western ideas
of female sexual appeal.

already castrated would be aware of the physical differences between males and females. However, at the age of five, the majority of the children in the four English-speaking countries gave responses that demonstrated no awareness of genital differences. Specifically, 88% of the North American children, 80% of the Australian children, and 74% of the English children gave score-1 responses. In contrast to children in the English-speaking countries, only 43% of the Swedish children received a score of 1 at the age of five.

This variation between the English-speaking children and the Swedish children may be due to differences in the educational policies of these cultures. In 1956 Sweden instituted mandatory sex education from kindergarten on and also emphasized gender-role egalitarianism in its educational system. In contrast, almost four decades later, the English-speaking countries are still debating the content of sex-education programs beginning in grade school or junior-high school. Thus it should not be surprising that not until the age of nine have the majority of children advanced beyond a score of 1, except for the majority of North American children, who continue to receive a score of 1 at age nine. These findings do not support Freud's idea that genital anxieties or envies motivate children to identify with their same-gender parents.

One of the most remarkable aspects of this study is the fact that it calls attention to the inability of researchers to test some of Freud's ideas about childhood sexuality and personality development until the latter part of the 20th century. If Freud had not advanced his theories almost a century ago, breaking ground for thinking about sexual development, we might still be unable to inquire about children's sexual thinking.

## Physical Attractiveness

Although preschool children may be unaware of genital differences between males and females, they do appear to notice physical attractiveness. The strong connection in most cultures between physical attractiveness and sexual desirability may have its roots in early childhood. This link, which is exploited in our culture in most communications media and especially in advertising, equates "sex appeal" with our cultural standards of physical attractiveness (see Chapter 16). According to social learning theorists, such learned associations explain the relationship of physical appearance to sexual attraction (see Figure 12.11). In contrast, evolutionary theorists believe that tendencies to evaluate and choose people on the basis of their physical appearance have an evolutionary basis. Specifically, those male ancestors who mated with physically attractive females may have had greater reproductive success than those who chose less attractive partners (Buss, 1994; Symons, 1979). According to this perspective, it is not the attractiveness per se but the association of attractiveness with general physical health and thus greater fitness for reproduction that is significant. This same perspective suggests that females select males on the basis of the ability of the males to protect and provide for them, so size, aggressiveness, and status are more important attributes for males than is physical attractiveness.

Children as young as two months old differentiate between slides of attractive and unattractive female faces (Langlois et al., 1987). These infants spent more time looking at the attractive faces than they did the unattractive faces. Be-

**FIGURE 12.12**
**Adolescent Grooming**
When children are young, their parents often have to nag them about matters of personal hygiene. However, as boys and girls grow into adolescents, they become preoccupied with grooming their personal appearance to make themselves as appealing as possible.

cause these slides were rated as to their attractiveness by college students, it appears that infants and adults use similar standards in evaluating others' attractiveness (see Figure 12.12). Children as young as three to five years old attribute positive qualities and abilities to attractive individuals and negative qualities and abilities to unattractive individuals, just as adults do (Ecker & Weinstein, 1983; Langlois & Roggman, 1990).

Furthermore, the ways in which others treat and respond to children are influenced by the attractiveness of the children. Some research has suggested that children with unattractive body builds or faces may indeed develop the undesirable characteristics attributed to them because of their looks (Langlois & Casey, 1984; Lerner & Lerner, 1977). In other words, these children may learn to behave in a manner that is consistent with others' expectations. As they become older, they may generalize these negative feelings about themselves to include their sexuality. Misled by the cultural myth that only the physically attractive are sexually appealing, they may doubt their desirability as sexual beings.

## Late Childhood: Industry Versus Inferiority

In modern industrialized societies, the child's world expands dramatically with entrance into school. By the sixth year of life, children spend a large portion of their day in the company of peers rather than with family members. In North America, an increasing number of children spend their days with peers in day care long before they enter kindergarten because of the growing number of families in which both parents or the single parent are employed.

The developmental task of this period, according to Erikson, is to strike a balance within the personality by resolving the conflict of industry versus inferiority. For children who are essentially trusting, autonomous, and able to take initiative, there is now the opportunity to take responsibility for schoolwork and other school-related activities. If parents and other caretakers respond positively to the child's work, his or her self-confidence continues to develop. Conversely, sarcastic and derogatory responses undermine the child's sense of industry, leading to a feeling of inferiority instead. If children doubt their skill or status among their peers, they may be discouraged from pursuing further learning.

Freud described the ages of 6 to 11 as a period of latency, a time of disinterest and inactivity regarding sexuality. Let us examine children's behavior during this stage.

## Sexual Rehearsal

Childhood sexual play among many of the primates—the order of mammals that includes lemurs, monkeys, apes, and humans—appears to serve as a rehearsal for adult sexual behavior. Such play has been observed in children in situations where it was not inhibited by adults (Ford & Beach, 1951; Reiss, 1986). The aborigines of Australia's northern coast, for example, had no taboo against infantile sexuality until they came into contact with Western ideas. Aborigine children aged five or six engaged in coital-positioning play, much as rhesus monkeys do. Adults responded to these childhood rehearsals with amusement: "Isn't it cute? They will know how to do it right when they grow up" (Money, 1976, p. 13).

We do not know why some children engage in such rehearsal of adult sexual interaction. Perhaps, as Money suggests, it is a natural developmental stage that all children would act out if not inhibited. Of a small sample of males interviewed before puberty, approximately 70% reported some form of sociosexual play (Kinsey et al., 1948). Of the larger Kinsey sample, 57% of the adult males and 48% of the adult females reported memories of some sex play, mostly between the ages of 8 and 13. As we see from B. F. Skinner's account in Box 12.3, however, our culture has not looked favorably on childhood sexuality.

Most sexual activity in childhood tends to center around discovering and playing with one's body or those of peers. For example, 61% of college students in one study reported that they had had some sexual experience with another child before the age of 13 (Leitenberg, Greenwald, & Tarran, 1989). When these students were compared to students who reported no sexual experience with another child before age 13, there were no differences between the two groups in sexual adjustment during young adulthood. In general, the occurrence or nonoccurrence of sexual activity with another child has little impact on later sexual behavior. Even when the sexual activity involved a sibling, as happened in 17% of the cases, there was no apparent connection to sexual adjustment in young adulthood (Greenwald & Leitenberg, 1989).

**Box 12.3**

## Skinner's Early Experience with Sexuality

Behavioral psychologist B. F. Skinner recalled his childhood experiences with sexuality in the early part of the 20th century. Have things changed that much in the last 70 years?

*One day my mother was entertaining some of her friends on our front porch. A neighbor's property was held in place by a retaining wall, and below the wall, out of sight of their parents but in full view of our porch, their two children, a small boy and girl, were examining each other's private parts. Someone called my mother's attention to this and she sucked in her breath and said, "If I caught my boys doing that, I would skin them alive!"*

*The nearest I came to being caught was when I was perhaps four or five and several boys and I were in the hayloft of a neighbor's barn, examining and talking about our penises. The mother of one of the boys heard us, and when she asked him about it later he confessed. She telephoned my parents, and I was called on the carpet. I lied my way out: I said I had not been doing anything myself, I was merely watching.*

*I must have been punished in some way for very early sex play, perhaps even as a baby, be-*

*cause I was once sent to bed without my supper and felt unjustly treated, and I clearly remember saying to myself, "If they do that, then I'll do this," and I began to play with myself.*

*I learned the technique of masturbation quite by accident, when I was perhaps eleven. Up to that point sexual play had consisted of undirected handling of genitalia. One day another boy and I had gone out of town on our bicycles and walked up a creek, beside which we were later to build a shack. We were sitting in the sun engaged in rather idle sex play when I made several rhythmic strokes which had a highly reinforcing effect. I immediately repeated them with even more reinforcing results. I began a steady movement, making an excited comment to my companion, and then, although I was too young to ejaculate, I had my first orgasm. The only effect was that my penis began to hurt badly. I was panic-stricken: I had broken it! I got up and walked down to the ledge of rocks alongside the creek in despair.*

Source: Skinner, 1976, pp. 64–65.

Perhaps because the threat or use of force was almost nonexistent in the reports of students in this study, negative outcomes were minimal. Other studies have shown similar incidences of preadolescent sexual activity with other children (about 60%) and preadolescent sibling sexual experience (13% to 15%) (Finkelhor, 1980; Sorrenti-Little et al., 1984). Fondling and touching the genitals were the most commonly described activities. In the Finkelhor study, negative reactions to sexual activity with siblings were greater with larger age differences between the siblings, and if force was used to obtain sexual contact. Despite our cultural beliefs about the detrimental effects of such preadolescent contacts, current research indicates little relationship between these expe-

riences and the sexual adjustment of young adults, provided that force is not involved.

### Homosociality

Young people begin to broaden their social contacts as they move into seventh grade and beyond. Cliques—small groups of intimate friends—become important. These tend to be same-gender groups in late childhood and early adolescence, becoming heterosexual in the later stages of adolescence, although many teenagers belong to both kinds of groups. Sharp differentiation of masculine and feminine gender roles, and the development of competence in interpersonal relationships, are facilitated by close

**FIGURE 12.13**
**Homosocial Friendship**
During preadolescence, Western children tend to confine their social relationships
to others of the same gender.

association with same-gender peers. This gender segregation is called *homosociality* (see Figure 12.13). It usually begins around age 8 and peaks at about ages 10 to 13. During this time, children may express considerable distaste for children of the other gender. During the Goldmans' (1982) interviews, children made a number of unsolicited comments such as this one by a boy: "I can't stand the way girls yell and carry on. They're a pain in the neck." A girl commented: "Boys are dirty, messy, noisy creatures. I just don't like them" (p. 187).

**homosociality**—voluntary social segregation in late childhood; a period in which social and personal activities are centered around members of the same gender.

Because children are playing almost exclusively with members of their own gender, it is not surprising to find that homosexual behavior is more common during this period than later in adolescence (Leitenberg, Greenwald, & Tarran, 1989). Homosexual experiences were reported by more than half the boys and more than a third of the girls in Elias and Gebhard's (1969) study of children aged 4 to 14 (see Box 12.4). Generally, these activities involve masturbation, fondling or touching the genitals, and exhibitionism, although occasionally oral and anal contact may occur. Homosexual activities are a common element in sexual development in our culture, and such experiences seldom determine one's preference for sexual partners of the same or other gender in adulthood (Bell et al., 1981; Van Wyk

## Box 12.4

## Sex Education

Two college students described pubertal sexual exploration:

*When we were both about 12, the girl next door and I used to spend a lot of time talking about sex, wondering what you were supposed to do, how it felt, and so forth. Neither of us was yet aware of the potential role to be played by our genitals, nor that men's fingers and penises could be involved. We thought that sex involved a man getting on top of a woman in a bed, and then kissing her fiercely. One afternoon, we decided to try this out to see what it was like. Her parents weren't at home, so we went in and lay down on her bed, and she got on top of me and pressed her closed lips very tightly against mine for a while. I can remember thinking that it was very uncomfortable because she was a lot heavier than I was. Also, it kind of hurt to have her push her mouth against mine so hard. I tried to push her off and we got into rough-housing and giggling. Later,*

*we talked about it and decided that we couldn't see what the big deal about "sex" was all about. It wasn't until years later that I realized that I'd had what is sometimes counted as a "homosexual contact."*

*Two of my friends asked me if I wanted to do the "circle jerk" when I was 12 or 13 years old. They said they did it all the time, but I didn't want to because it seemed wrong; so one said he would do it for me. He masturbated himself and a little bit of semen came out. But he stimulated me orally and used his hand. I didn't ejaculate any semen but I remember getting a feeling sort of like spasms. It was almost painful and I wanted him to stop. I remember pulling away from him and the feeling subsided very fast.*

Source: Authors' files.

---

& Geist, 1984). Fearing this possibility, however, parents who find their children in sexual exploration with other children of the same gender may attach adult meanings to the activity. Inappropriate overreactions by parents may be one of the sources of the widespread antipathy toward same-gender contacts and homosexuality, an attitude known as homophobia ("fear of the same").

Some of this same-gender (and other-gender) sex play stems from an intrinsic curiosity about sexuality. Ironically, the relative paucity of sex education in North America may contribute to such exploration.

## Sex Education

The arguments advanced by those who oppose sex education reflect an unstated assumption: the presupposition that we can choose whether chil-

dren and adolescents receive sex education. It should be amply clear from the evidence that we have discussed so far that children learn about sex from birth on, although the accuracy of their knowledge varies considerably as a function of the source and goals of that education.

## Informal Sex Education

During childhood, some information and many attitudes about sex are acquired in the course of learning sexual slang. Children's informal learning of a sexual vocabulary often takes place without their associating the words with sexual activity. A host of other meanings and associations may be linked to formal sexual terms. Such sexual slang terms as *fuck* and *queer*, for example, are learned and used by children without a sense of their sexual meanings or of the physical activities they entail.

A child's use of these words, however, is charged with emotion, often hostile or aggressive in nature. Slang phrases for such concepts as coitus and fellatio, for example, are frequently used to indicate dislike and verbal hostility. "Screw you!" and "cocksucker," for example, are seldom used publicly as expressions of endearment. The hostile associations with sex words may influence the child's perception of sexuality far into adulthood.

Not surprisingly, it is difficult for many children to make sense of this thing called sexuality, and many kids wonder why it is so important and yet so shrouded in secrecy. Most children hear about sexual intercourse and its connection to pregnancy by the age of eight or nine. However, many of them associate the processes of coitus and birth with the anus. This natural association is reflected in a statement by St. Augustine: *Inter faeces et urinam nascimur* ("We are born between feces and urine"). Children's reaction to coitus as they perceive it may be one of shock, disbelief, and disgust. A friend of ours overheard his son discussing sex and reproduction with another boy, who explained that babies were caused by daddies' sticking their things into mommies' bottoms to plant seed so that a year later "the mommy poops out a baby." Our friend's son's reaction was "Yuck!"

Another idea that children sometimes form about pregnancy is the "digestive fallacy." The Goldmans (1982, p. 49) described it: "Mother eats food and she becomes fat. The food is the baby and it comes out where food normally comes out, through the anus." Such inaccurate explanations were given by the majority of North American children in the Goldmans' study until around the age of 11. At that age, 50% gave realistic descriptions, and at age 13, 79% did so. It is clear from this research that in the absence of information about sex and reproduction, children devise their own explanations.

Even when information is provided, it may take children some time to understand how the process applies to their own parents. One friend of ours had offered her nine-year-old daughter a description of reproduction: "Daddy puts his penis into my vagina, and sperm comes out and it unites with an egg in my uterus." About six months later, our friend told her daughter that she was going to have a baby. Her daughter was pleased with that news but said to her mother

**FIGURE 12.14**
**Sources of Sex Information**
Adolescents receive most of their sexual information from their peers and the media, although some of the information is not particularly accurate.

accusingly, "Why didn't you tell me Daddy was going to put his penis in you?"

Where would you have preferred to receive information about sex? Various studies have shown that the majority of respondents would choose to get their sex education from their parents (Bennett & Dickinson, 1980). But because parents do not provide sufficient details about sex, most young people seek information elsewhere (see Figure 12.14).

Research has shown that when parents accept their children's interest in sex and are willing to discuss sexuality with them, the children tend to delay initial sexual intercourse (Zelnik & Kim, 1982) and to develop sexual attitudes similar to those of their parents (Fisher, 1986). Further, they are more likely to use contraception when they begin sexual activity than are people from families in which sexual discussion is minimal or absent (Fox, 1980; Shah & Zelnik, 1981). When parents and children communicate about sexuality, it appears that attitudes and values are generally conveyed, rather than facts. The sexual knowledge of children who learned about sex at home has not been found to be superior to that of children who learned about sex from other sources (Bennett & Dickinson, 1980; Fisher, 1986).

We might expect physicians to be a potential source of sexual information for their young patients or their patients' parents. However, in a study involving medical students, Fisher, Grenier, Watters, et al. (1988) found that, compared to erotophilic students (see Chapter 6), erotophobic students were less likely to take an elective sexuality course, had less postcourse knowledge about sexuality, and were less willing to treat some kinds of sexual problems. Further, the authors noted troubling gaps in their knowledge: "Many of the students were ignorant of such basic facts as the timing of ovulation, the significance of the clitoris, and the etiology of sexual dysfunction" (Fisher et al., 1988, p. 382). Inaccurate information, as well as the tendency of those medical students with negative attitudes about sex to avoid opportunities to increase their knowledge, may combine to reduce the opportunities for some physicians to provide effective sex education.

## Formal Sex Education

As far as formal instruction is concerned, school districts vary considerably in the kind and amount of information that they provide. In some cases, students receive no more than a couple of hours of instruction, focused almost exclusively on the menstrual cycle. In other instances, students take semester-long courses covering reproduction, contraception, sexually transmitted diseases, and sexual development (Kenney, Guardado, & Brown, 1989). Several studies of the effects of these courses indicate that they improve the accuracy of students' knowledge about sex but do not necessarily produce major changes in sexual attitudes and values (Kirby, 1985, 1989; Parcel, Luttman, & Flaherty-Zonis, 1985). The impact of these programs seems to differ as a function of the messages that are conveyed and the methods used to convey those messages.

Unfortunately, we have little information about the influence of sex education on children because most receive little or no sex education until they are well into adolescence, and in many cases, already sexually experienced. However, we are discussing formal sex education before we describe adolescent development because such education appears to be more effective when it is provided before young people have become sexually experienced.

In the past 15 years, hundreds of sexuality education curricula have been implemented in junior and senior high schools in the United States (Kirby, Barth, Leland, & Fetro, 1991). They can be broadly characterized as employing one of two approaches. One teaches sexual abstinence until marriage and avoids covering methods for responsible nonmarital (or even marital) sexual activity, including contraception for couples who don't wish to conceive and use of condoms to reduce the risk of disease. The other approach emphasizes postponement of early sexual involvement, but provides education for responsible sexual contacts when couples decide they are ready to have sex. Kirby et al. (1991) characterized this approach as

> neither value-free nor moralistic: They do not simply lay out the facts and let the students decide for themselves what is best, nor do they preach that sexual intercourse before marriage is always wrong. Instead, they emphasize that it is a good idea for young people to delay sex and that it is important for all young people to practice effective contraception if they are going to have sex. (p. 254)

This is the first attempt in the United States to provide education that has moved away from the "just say no" approach to deal with factors that need to be considered when one would like to say "yes." Further, it is the first approach to develop programs based on scientific evidence evaluating the outcomes of different sex education strategies. In contrast, however, most school-based sex education programs in the United States have been based more on the values of the school board, community, and teachers than on empirical data, and are known as abstinence-only programs.

### Abstinence-Only Programs

The abstinence-only approach in the United States was favored by the Reagan and Bush administrations for more than a decade, receiving political backing and major funding from the federal government. As will be seen, they are sex-negative, value-laden programs. That is, they do not differentiate between those circumstances that promote pleasuring, bonding, and wanted procreation from those circumstances that expose persons to disease, coercion, and unwanted pregnancy. Also, as we'll see, these sex-negative approaches are demonstrably ineffective. We describe them in some detail because they provide a lesson in how *not* to teach students about the potentially negative outcomes of sexual expression and because these approaches demonstrate serious drawbacks in the "just say no" programs.

Sex education foe Phyllis Schlafly, backed by her Eagle Forum organization, has appeared frequently on television arguing against sex education, claiming that the high levels of unintended adolescent pregnancy in the United States have been *caused* by school-based sex education. Her stance, shared by others who oppose sex and contraceptive education in the schools, represents the classic "Do not confuse me with the facts" position. This stance is clearly contradicted by the Jones et al. (1986) cross-national study (refer to Box 10.1) and the U.S. studies comparing the sexual behaviors and pregnancy rates of adolescents who have and have not received sex and contraceptive education (Howard & McCabe, 1990; Kirby et al., 1991; Zelnik & Kim, 1982).

Ignoring these data, the U.S. government has promoted abstinence to the exclusion of sex and contraceptive education. The Adolescent Family Life Act (AFLA), passed in 1981, permitted the Office of Adolescent Pregnancy Programs to fund projects to promote abstinence from sexual interaction until marriage (Mecklenburg & Thompson, 1983). Since 1987, 22 states have passed laws requiring some type of sex education. Through the AFLA, the Department of Health and Human Services spent millions of dollars annually promoting chastity among U.S. youth (Goodheart, 1992).

One recipient of AFLA support has been the abstinence-only program, "Sex Respect: The Option of True Sexual Freedom." Given its program, the title is reminiscent of George Orwell's notion of "double-speak" in his novel, *1984.* Presumably, "true sexual freedom" would involve the capacity to give responsible informed consent to declining *or having* sexual intimacy with a partner. However, the message promoted in Sex Respect and other similar programs is quite different. Colleen Kelly Mast, the promoter of the

for-profit organization and author of its textbook, has been successful since 1983 in having the program and text accepted in more than 1,800 school districts in all 50 states and in several other countries as well. Hers is one of at least 15 abstinence-only programs currently available (Nazario, 1992).

Her Sex Respect instructor's guide counsels teachers to prohibit discussion of such issues as masturbation, homosexuality, birth control, and abortion (Goodheart, 1992). Mast explains the reason to avoid these issues: "There is a basic sense of modesty and *shame* that comes with discussing intimate sexual topics. . . . *In order to enhance that sense of shame* and not break it down and make sex seem trivial, there are certain things that would be best discussed in the privacy of home" (quoted in Goodheart, 1992, p. 42, emphasis added). Although teachers are trained to avoid discussing contraception in these programs, some teachers do demonstrate condom failure, having students pour water into balloons that have been pricked with pins. As far as it goes, the argument is reasonable. If one poked holes in condoms prior to using them, they would presumably leak. But if condoms are used appropriately (sans pin-pricking) to protect against pregnancy and disease, they are far more effective than unprotected intercourse. Students do not get this information in abstinence-only programs. However, as Reiss put it, the breakage rate of vows of abstinence is far greater than the breakage rate of condoms (Reiss, 1990, p. 125).

Although the AFLA projects were mandated to have an outcome evaluation component, few such evaluation designs have been adequate in providing meaningful data (Hofferth & Hayes, 1987). Specifically, most evaluation efforts lacked appropriate control groups, did not provide adequate evaluation measures relevant to program goals (for example, they measured sexual attitudes, but not self-reported sexual behavior), and relied on inadequate statistical analyses. Regarding the issue of using sexual attitudes as an indication of sexual behavior, Howard and McCabe (1990) found that self-reported attitudes were not good predictors of self-reported sexual behavior.

Only two projects have been published on the outcome of abstinence-only programs during the history of the AFLA (Olson, Wallace, &

Miller, 1984; Vincent, Clearie, & Schluchter, 1987). The Olson et al. study was conducted in high schools in three western states. Students in the program were primarily White, and many were members of the Mormon church. The program emphasized the importance of students' involvement and of discussion of sexual values with their families. This produced short-term increases in parental discussion of sexual values and decreases in self-reported permissive attitudes toward premarital sex. The long-term impact of the program has not been reported, nor has any information been provided on the effect of the program on actual sexual behavior. In another AFLA abstinence-only program, Donahue (1987) found that knowledge increased, but actual sexual behavior did not change. Further, follow-up showed that the program's effects on knowledge had declined three months later.

How effective are abstinence-only programs in affecting actual sexual behavior? Christopher and Roosa (1990) evaluated the outcome of exposure to Lucero and Clark's (1988) AFLA abstinence-only approach, "Success Express Program (SEP)." SEP involved six class sessions provided for children in the sixth and seventh grades. Christopher and Roosa collected pretest data during the first session and posttest data during the final session, both from program participants and from a control group of students who were not enrolled in the SEP. Students came primarily from lower-class families, with 26% of the families below the poverty level. Each student received a questionnaire with a cover letter assuring them that their answers would be kept secret from program leaders and school officials. The SEP was carried out at eight sites, including five schools in which the program was embedded in the health curriculum course. Control group students attended the same schools, but the SEP was not given in their classrooms.

To evaluate the program's effectiveness, Christopher and Roosa (1990) administered measures of self-esteem, family communication, premarital sexual behavior, and premarital sexual attitudes. The only measure that differentiated program participants from control group members in pre- to postprogram responses was lifetime sexual behavior reported at the posttest. Lucero and Clark (1988; the SEP designers) and others who support an abstinence-only approach

must have been shocked at the finding that SEP participants significantly *increased* their mean sexual interaction level between pretest and posttest, whereas control group members did *not*. Examinations of the specific behaviors that increased from pretest to posttest for the participants indicated that SEP males reported increases in touching female breasts, touching female genitals, and genital-to-genital contact. SEP females also reported greater increases in sexual behaviors than did control group females, but the upward shift was not as dramatic as those for SEP males.

In response to the contention (Olson, 1987) that abstinence-only programs may be more effective for virgins than for nonvirgins, Christopher and Roosa (1990) conducted comparisons of SEP students and a control group, excluding those who were not virgins at pretest. Virgin participants reported a significant increase in the lifetime sexual behavior measure, whereas virgin nonparticipants reported no change. Roosa and Christopher (1990) conducted a replication of the study just described and the same general pattern of results emerged with their new sample. Given the results of this abstinence-only evaluation study, it is tempting to speculate that such approaches may stimulate rebellion rather than inspire responsibility. Roosa and Christopher (1990) concluded:

> After almost a decade in which dozens of demonstration abstinence-only programs have been funded under the AFLA legislation, there is no evidence to suggest that this approach will have an impact on adolescent pregnancy rates. [The evaluation studies that have been performed provide] strong arguments for questioning the basic premise that pregnancy prevention programs should be limited to abstinence-only approaches. (p. 366)

### Postponement and Protection Programs

Fortunately, there are other programs that include more thorough sex and contraceptive education. Outcome evaluations of these programs show considerably more promise, without necessarily involving more sessions. For example, Howard and McCabe's (1990) "Postponing

Sexual Involvement Program" involves just five class sessions.

The longitudinal "Reducing the Risk (RTR)" program of Kirby et al. (1991) is among the most well developed of the existing U.S. programs. Kirby et al. had instructors describe social pressures to have sex, describing common "lines" that are used in the attempt to obtain sexual access, and teaching students to develop strategies and skills in response to social pressures to have sex. Students have opportunities to practice talking to one another about abstinence and contraception. The situations they are given to role-play increase in difficulty over the course of the program. The RTR program also gives students practice in obtaining contraceptive information from stores and clinics.

Kirby and his colleagues studied high school students enrolled in 13 California high schools. The majority of the students were in the 10th grade and were assigned to treatment or to control groups. They were surveyed before their exposure to the program, immediately after participation, and then again at 6 and 18 months following participation in the 15-class-period program. The RTR program explicitly stressed that students should avoid unprotected intercourse, either through postponing coitus or engaging only in protected (by contraception) coitus. Students were required to ask their parent(s) about their views on abstinence and contraception. RTR was taught by volunteer high school or middle school instructors who had received a three-day training session, and the program was incorporated into a more comprehensive required health education class.

Among students who were sexually inexperienced at the start of the program, exposure to the RTR program was significantly related to lower likelihood of having experienced coitus 18 months following the program. Specifically, after 18 months, 29% of the treatment group versus 38% of the control group had had coitus. Among all students who had not had coitus at pretest, only 9% of the treatment group had engaged in *unprotected* coitus by 18 months following the program, whereas 16% of the control group had done so, showing an effective 40% reduction in unprotected intercourse.

Another postponement and protection program, "Postponing Sexual Involvement (PSI)," evolved from a curriculum developed in the mid-1970s (Howard & McCabe, 1990). Initial findings from the program were not particularly encouraging, so it was altered in response to findings from studies on the effectiveness of various approaches. First, a number of studies of health-related behaviors found that approaches based on increasing knowledge were not particularly effective in changing young people's behavior regarding drug use, smoking, and early initiation of coitus. A study of 10 knowledge-based sex education programs in the United States indicated that although young people's knowledge increased, they were not more likely to postpone coitus or to use birth control (Ellickson & Robyn, 1987). A further consideration that Howard and McCabe (1990) took into account was the level of cognitive development of adolescents. Until about the age of 16, most adolescents are still using concrete thinking skills and are limited in their ability to recognize the potential ramifications of their choices.

In 1983 the Atlanta schools started a large-scale implementation of the revised PSI program (Howard, Mitchell, & Pollard, 1990). Emphasizing learning experiences rather than lectures, it was designed to encourage students to consider and discuss issues of social and peer pressures to become sexually involved. Students practiced skills at resisting peer pressures to engage in sexual activity. The sessions were led by trained males and females in the 11th or 12th grade. Teen leaders were used because they have been found to produce greater and more lasting effects on teen smoking behavior than have adults (Luepker, Anderson, Murray, & Pachacek, 1983). The five sessions of the experiential portion (that is, the PSI portion) of the program were added to the original five-classroom-session program, producing ten classroom sessions that were presented each year to all eighth grade students in 19 schools, reaching about 4,500 students each year.

The goal of helping young people to postpone sexual involvement was made explicit in the program. A sample of more than 1,000 sexually active girls under the age of 17 indicated that, for 84%, the issue about which they wanted more information was, "How to say 'no' without hurting the other person's feelings" (Howard, 1984). This was clearly a concern for these girls, but it is also presumably of concern to boys. Further, the fact that many of us would like to be skilled at saying no gracefully does not imply that we always want to say no, even to sexual invitations.

Young people are often pressured into doing things they really do not want to do. Pressure to have coitus comes from peers and also from glamorous images presented by the media. Young people need awareness, support, skills, and practice in learning how to resist pressure to become sexually involved. Howard and McCabe (1990) found that "young people respond most favorably to programs promoting postponement of sexual intercourse when the information about how and why to say 'no' comes from peers slightly older than themselves" (p. 22).

The program was evaluated to determine whether adding the PSI component to the existing human sexuality curriculum would reduce the rate of coitus and pregnancy among young people. Members of the sample were interviewed by telephone at the beginning, middle, and end of the eighth grade and at the beginning and end of the ninth grade. Only 1% of the students were not able to get their parents' permission to participate in the interviews. Students were given verbal codes to use so that people within listening distance in their homes would not understand their answers.

For data analyses, students in the PSI program were divided into two groups: those who had not had intercourse before the program, and those who were sexually experienced. These two groups were compared with students in the control group. The proportion of students who reported having had sex by the beginning of the eighth grade was slightly higher in the program schools (25%) than in the control group (23%). Boys in both the experimental and the control groups were much more likely to report having had intercourse (44%) than were girls (9%). For the total group (both experimental and control), preprogram coitus was reported by 25% and no experience was reported by 72%.

The PSI program students who were virgins at the time they enrolled in the program were significantly more likely to postpone sexual intercourse than were the control group students who were virgins at the time of the pretest. Specifically, by the end of the eighth grade, only 4% of PSI students had initiated sex compared to 20% of control group students. PSI students were also significantly less likely to have initiated sex than control group students by the beginning (12% versus 27%) and end (24% versus 39%) of the ninth grade. The differences were particularly striking for girls at each of the three interview periods. For PSI program girls compared to control group girls, 1% versus 15% had initiated sex by the end of the eighth grade; 7% versus 18% by the beginning of the ninth grade; and 17% versus 27% by the end of the ninth grade. The comparable figures for boys at each of the three interview periods were 8% versus 29%, 22% versus 42%, and 39% versus 61%.

These differences were not attributable to opportunities to have sex, that is, whether a student had a boyfriend or a girlfriend. At the beginning of the eighth grade, of PSI program participants who had not had sex, 38% had boyfriends/girlfriends compared to 31% of control group students. By the end of the ninth grade, the comparable figures were 50% and 43%.

Students' evaluation of the usefulness of the program in helping them to postpone sex in the future was overwhelmingly positive: 95% of the students who had not had sex before the program reported that the PSI program would be personally helpful to them to postpone sex in the future. More than 80% described the program as extremely or very helpful.

Contraceptive use was more common among PSI students (nearly 50%) than among control group students (about 33%) among those who had not had sex before the program but did initiate sex at some point after enrollment in the program. Further, 73% of the PSI students who used contraceptives said that they used them because of what they had been taught in the program. Among the control group students, only 38% of contraceptive users reported such use because of what they had learned in school.

In summary, the Howard and McCabe (1990) and Kirby et al. (1991) studies showed an impressive relationship between the provision of sexuality and contraceptive education and the likelihood of engaging in sexual intercourse and of doing so without using contraceptives. *Specifically, those boys and girls who were not yet sexually active at the time that they received such education were more likely to postpone sexual activity than were their counterparts who did not receive such education or who received it after they had already become sexually active.*

Opponents of sex education sometimes cite Freud's latency hypothesis—the idea that late childhood is a time during which sexual interest and activity are repressed, not to emerge again until the onset of puberty. The evidence does not support the latency hypothesis, however. The Goldmans (1982, p. 383) stressed the importance of "emphasizing the latency period as a myth, because latency is an impediment to the early provision of sex education in home and school during the years 5 to 11, the need for which is seen by the children." In fact, the vast majority of children interviewed by the Goldmans believed that sex education should begin in elementary school. Of the 11-year-old English-speaking children, however, fewer than 40% reported having received any sex education in school.

Regardless of their education for handling their emerging sexual feelings as they enter puberty, pubescent development occurs—and along with it, the capacity for procreation. We turn now to this stage in the life cycle.

## Adolescence: Identity Versus Role Confusion

In light of the fact that adolescence (roughly, the years from age 12 to age 20) has been characterized as a time of turbulence, rebelliousness, and stress, the responses of young teenagers to two questions asked by the Goldmans (1982) are somewhat surprising. The Goldmans inquired, "What is the best time to be alive?" and then asked for reasons for the choices. Prior to age 13, children's responses were quite variable, but the majority of 13-year-old respondents chose the teenage years. Some of their reasons: "As a teenager, you're at your physical peak. It's a crucial time which decides what happens [to you] later. You've got your head together more. You know more about life than when you were younger. Your brain works better. You know what to expect" (p. 119).

The responses of these teenagers suggest that they were well on their way to achieving the solid self-concept that Erikson (1968b) proposed is the developmental goal of this period. The challenge of adolescence involves identity versus role confusion, according to Erikson. He noted that the biological events of puberty bring on a physiological revolution, and he pointed out that the adolescent must contend with playing a variety of different roles. One of the most profound is the acquisition of gender-role identification and its interaction with sexual roles.

If you have children or younger brothers and sisters at around puberty, you may remember with amusement one conspicuous aspect of their transition from childhood into adolescence. After years of relative unconcern about appearance, teenagers monopolize bathrooms and mirrors with astounding obsessiveness. Other family members may have difficulty obtaining even a few moments of privacy in the bathroom—let alone the opportunity for a bath, after the adolescent's third shower of the day has used up all the hot water—as the youth tries out the third or fourth change of clothes and hairstyle before leaving for that all-important event, the beginning of another school day.

The adolescent experiments with different roles and fantasies, just as he or she tries out clothing and hairstyles. At this stage, the adolescent runs the risk of developing a fragmented identity. Too much freedom may result in confusion about personal identity. Too little freedom does not permit an exploration of role possibilities and may leave the adolescent ill equipped to deal with adult life. Erikson suggested that moderate levels of freedom, accompanied by structure and advice from parents and other caretakers, can help the adolescent to integrate his or her exploration of various roles into a coherent identity.

In contrast to Erikson, Freud emphasized the biological and genital changes of puberty. Freud called this period—in his framework, the last step in psychosexual development—the genital stage. He hypothesized a resurgence of sexual energy and activity with the onset of puberty. Freud also believed that adolescents experience renewed sexual interest in the parent of the other gender, which generally expresses itself in adolescent crushes on older people.

An emphasis on learned sexual behavior characterizes the approaches taken by such sociological theorists as Gagnon and Simon (1973; Gagnon, 1990). In their view, basic sexual roles and scripts gradually emerge during adolescence. The sexual organs acquire special significance for the individual, providing evidence both of adulthood and of femininity or masculinity. Sexual fantasies develop, serving as rehearsals for eventual interactions and as ways of exploring different sexual scripts. Out of a relatively chaotic approach to sociosexual transactions, complicated sexual scripts emerge. The body parts that can be touched and the circumstances under which they can be caressed, as well as all the subtleties of dating, are incorporated into the adolescent's behavioral repertoire. The diversity and complexity of some of these scripted behavioral sequences are shown later in this chapter. According to the social learning theorists, scripted sexual behavior in adulthood is the outcome of a long and often arduous training period that involves the integration of moral directives, social values, and personal experience.

## Gender-Role Identification

Attitudes and beliefs about appropriate behavior for males and females as a function of gender have changed remarkably in the past few decades, and as we will see, these changes are associated with attitudes about acceptable sexual behavior for men and women. Just three decades ago, behavioral scientists and mental health professionals alike assumed that mentally healthy women were quite different in their personality traits from mentally healthy men (Broverman et al., 1970; Fabrikant, 1974). Many of the most widely used psychological tests measured the extent to which individuals saw themselves as having "masculine" or "feminine" traits. In these tests, either people were asked to indicate their traits, or clinicians evaluated the extent to which various traits were characteristic of them. Take a minute to rank yourself on the scale shown in Table 12.2 to see how gender-role identification was measured.

The developers of these scales made two major assumptions. First, they assumed that the checkmarks of a healthy woman should fall fairly close to the items on the left-hand side of the scales, and those of a healthy adult man close to the right-hand side. Second, they presupposed

---

**TABLE 12.2 Feminine or Masculine?**

To use this scale, place a check mark on each line at the point along the scale that most closely represents your personality.*

| | | |
|---|---|---|
| Passive | ———— | Active |
| Dependent | ———— | Independent |
| Like to take care of others | ———— | Don't like to take care of others |
| Yielding | ———— | Stubborn |
| Nonaggressive | ———— | Aggressive |
| Soft-spoken | ———— | Use harsh language |

*We have placed the so-called masculine traits on one side and feminine traits on the other to make it easy to see the configuration of traits supposedly attributable to the "healthy" man or woman. In practice, the masculine and feminine traits are usually reversed on about half the scales so that they are counterbalanced.

---

that identification with masculine characteristics was the opposite of identification with feminine characteristics; that is, a person was either passive or active, yielding or stubborn. In reality, of course, most of us are yielding under some conditions and stubborn under others.

Armed with these measures, many therapists labeled men "psychologically disturbed" if some of their checkmarks fell to the left-hand side. Similarly, a woman ranking herself as "aggressive," "taking leadership roles," and so forth was considered to be in need of therapy. These people then might have undergone psychotherapy for "gender-role confusion" or "inappropriate gender-role identity." Although use of these labels represented an aesthetic improvement over such phrases as "penis envy" to describe women who felt constrained by traditional gender roles, the concept that men and women are—or should be—distinctly different psychologically was still accepted without question.

In 1973 Anne Constantinople questioned the assumption that masculinity was the opposite of femininity. She suggested that identification with masculine traits might be independent from, rather than the opposite of, identification with feminine traits; that is, one might be active and nurturant, or tender and aggressive, and still be psychologically healthy.

This both/and concept of psychological identification quickly replaced the either/or notion that had dominated earlier personality measures. Sandra Bem developed a gender-identity measure, the Bem Sex Role Inventory (1974), that treated identification with masculine traits as independent of identification with feminine traits. In Bem's scoring system, people who describe themselves as having masculine and feminine traits and behaviors in equal measure are called *androgynous*. Those persons who endorse characteristics traditionally associated with their genetic sex are called *sex-typed* or *gender-typed*.

Bem and others using the scale found that androgynous people, regardless of their gender, responded more flexibly to a variety of situations. They could be nurturant when dealing with people in need but assertive when their rights were in danger of being violated. Sex-typed persons were more limited. Although they could respond readily with behaviors stereotypic of their gender, when a behavior or trait traditionally displayed by the other gender was more appropriate (for instance, nurturance in women, assertiveness in men), they were constrained and uncomfortable (Bem, 1975; Bem & Lenney, 1976; Bem, Martyna, & Watson, 1976).

Although the notion of *androgyny* was obviously a concept whose time had arrived in the 1970s, the idea had been born long before. Carl Jung had written extensively about androgyny decades earlier. He characterized masculine traits and impulses in a woman as her animus, and feminine traits and impulses in a man as his an-

ima. Suggesting that we humans are capable of experiencing and integrating both aspects of ourselves, he too saw adherence to one style and avoidance of the other as limiting human potential. He argued that the central task of our lives during middle age was to integrate our masculine and feminine natures to produce a fully functioning person—as he put it, to achieve "individuation" (Jung, 1946, 1959).

Jung's ideas, although popular with a few psychologists and philosophers, had little impact on most professionals or on the general public until the mid-1970s. It is interesting that in our test-oriented age, it took the development of gender-role identification scales to popularize the idea that psychological health might be more likely among people who have a broad repertoire of traits and behaviors than among those who limit themselves to those characteristics stereotypic of their gender. We will have more to say about gender roles and their relationship to sexual attitudes and behavior as we continue our examination of the development of sexuality across the life span (see Figure 12.15).

## Sexual Exploration in Adolescence

Much has been written, particularly in the popular press, about high levels of sexual permissiveness among contemporary adolescents. The attention is understandable, for research consistently shows that by age 18 the majority of males and females in North America have engaged in coitus and a variety of other sexual activities (Day, 1992; King et al., 1988; Miller & Heaton, 1991).

Although most children stimulate their genitals prior to puberty, the rapid maturation that occurs during puberty tends to be accompanied by an increase in the incidence and frequency of masturbation. Kinsey et al. (1948, 1953) found that 12% of the females and 21% of the males recalled having masturbated to orgasm by the time they were 12. Boys typically learned about masturbation by being told or shown by their peers; in contrast, girls more frequently learned about masturbation through accidental self-discovery.

Data collected by Hunt (1974) indicated that both males and females began masturbating at an earlier age in the 1970s than they did when the

**androgynous** (ann-DRAW-jih-nus)—having both feminine and masculine psychological characteristics.

**sex-typed identification** (also called gender-typed identification)—incorporation into the personality of the behaviors and characteristics expected for one's gender in a particular culture, with avoidance of those characteristics expected of the other gender.

**androgyny** (ann-DRAW-jih-nee)—the ability of a person to express both stereotypically masculine (for example, assertive, athletic) and stereotypically feminine (for example, yielding, nurturing) traits and behaviors; from the Greek *andro,* meaning male, and *gyn,* meaning female.

**FIGURE 12.15**

**Gender and Sexuality over the Life Cycle**

Sexual characteristics such as breasts and beards gradually distinguish males from females as individuals move into their reproductive years, but gender differences diminish as males and females advance into their later years.

Kinsey group did their work. Specifically, 33% of the females in Hunt's sample reported having masturbated to orgasm by age 13, in contrast to 15% of Kinsey's sample. More recently, a survey of New England college students and a cross-sectional sample of Americans found that about 50% of males and 25% of females reported that they had masturbated by age 13 (Janus & Janus, 1993; Leitenberg, Detzer, & Srebnik, 1993). There is also evidence that masturbation is accompanied by less anxiety and guilt now than in the first half of the 20th century. The renowned psychologist B. F. Skinner's account of masturbating as a boy early in the 20th century reflects the fears of his times:

*I worried about the effects of masturbation. . . . Masturbation was supposed to drive boys crazy, and I rather admired a slightly younger boy who told my brother that, whether it did or not, he liked it and was going to go ahead anyway. I once overheard my mother telling my father that a boy down the*

*street masturbated. "It makes a boy so stupid," she said, and my father mumbled some kind of vague agreement, but he knew better, and so did I.*

*I didn't worry about stupidity or insanity, but I did worry about getting caught. . . . [I]n high school . . . I used to drop in to see my grandmother almost every afternoon on my way home from school. We played Pedro, rummy, or dominoes, but I also used to go to the bathroom and masturbate, sitting on the toilet looking at a large plant in a pot of very wet soil which resembled a miniature grove of palm trees in a swamp. Since I did this every day and stayed rather a long time, my grandmother concluded there must be something wrong with my kidneys. She urged my mother to take me to a doctor for an examination. When I heard about it, I no longer had to go to the toilet in the afternoon, and nothing further was done.*

*When I began to play in a dance orchestra, the violinist, considerably older than I, once said that masturbation led to poor eye-sight, and since I wore glasses I was alarmed. Could there be other signs? (1976, pp. 131–132)*

Scientific and societal interpretations of increased adolescent sexual activity vary considerably. Some people consider increases in adolescent sexual expression, including masturbation, to be symptomatic of a decadent society and voice concern that such early "self-indulgence" leads to promiscuity, an inability to form permanent relationships, and soaring divorce rates. Taking a different view, others maintain that, because the onset of sexual maturity (from a biological perspective) occurs in early adolescence, cultural restrictiveness regarding masturbation and nonmarital sexual interaction is unrealistic.

Some scholars, relying on the *secular-decline hypothesis*, have linked the drop in the age at first intercourse to the belief that the age of menarche has declined dramatically over the past 150 years. The secular-decline assumption was based on Tanner's (1962) compilation of available information on the age at menarche in Western Europe. He reported that menarche occurred at the average age of 17 in 1840, and that menarchal age has steadily decreased since then, to its present level of about 12 or 13 (Tanner, 1962; Eveleth & Tanner, 1976). If the age of sexual maturation fell and the age at marriage rose, the present spurt in the incidence of nonmarital adolescent sexual activity and nonmarital pregnancy would be expected. However, historian Vern Bullough (1981) examined information about the samples used by Tanner and noted that only one sample—from a small, isolated Norwegian area—contained women reporting an average age of 17 for menarche. Examination of cross-cultural data showed that the average age of menarche varies between 12.5 and 14.5 for most of the world, about the same range as has been reported throughout most of recorded history. Thus the data do not support the idea that increasing levels of premarital sexual activity in the past few decades stem from decreased age for the onset of puberty.

**secular-decline hypothesis**—the theory that the onset of menstruation has come at an increasingly earlier age over the past century and a half.

How does contemporary adolescent sexual behavior differ from that of previous generations? Is "morality" declining? What are the effects of choosing chastity versus engaging in sexual intimacy during adolescence?

Adolescents are usually anxious and awkward during their initial experiences with sexual and quasi-sexual contact. Many of their early dates may be seen as practice for the more serious pairing that occurs later in adolescence. Concern with kissing and with achieving competence at it is particularly noticeable. Parties often involve kissing games and "making out"; genital fondling is uncommon (DeLamater & MacCorquodale, 1979; Martinson, 1973). Early dating typically starts around the age of 12 or 13, but during early adolescence there appears to be more concern with exchanging rings or trinkets than with exclusive relationships or sexual expression.

## Developing a Sexual Repertoire

As they move into middle adolescence, young males and young females alike begin adding to their sexual repertoire. The role of testosterone in sexual arousal and behavior was examined in a series of studies by Richard Udry and his colleagues (cf. Udry, 1990). Increases in androgenic hormones at puberty were related to measures of sexual motivation (thinking about sex, sexual arousal) and noncoital sexual behavior (for example, masturbation) in both genders. However, initiation of coitus in males was highly hormone dependent and only weakly related to social factors. Among females, the timing of first coitus was strongly related to social factors and was not predicted by identifiable hormone production. For example, virgins whose best boyfriend and best girlfriend had both engaged in sex were six times more likely to engage in coital activity for the first time as were girls who had only one best friend who was sexually experienced. This ratio grew to 20 times as likely when they were compared to girls whose best male and female friend had not engaged in sex.

In one study of more than 1,300 participants, the adolescent sexual experiences and attitudes of college students were compared with those of people of the same age not attending college

TABLE 12.3  Building the Sexual Repertoire: Lifetime Sexual Behavior by Gender and Educational Status

| | Male | | | | Female | | | |
| | Student | | Nonstudent | | Student | | Nonstudent | |
| Behavior | Percent | Age[a] | Percent | Age[a] | Percent | Age[a] | Percent | Age[a] |
| --- | --- | --- | --- | --- | --- | --- | --- | --- |
| Necking | 97 | 14.2 | 98 | 13.9 | 99 | 14.8 | 99 | 14.9 |
| French kissing | 93 | 15.3 | 95 | 15.1 | 95 | 15.8 | 95 | 16.0 |
| Breast fondling | 92 | 15.8 | 92 | 15.5 | 93 | 16.6 | 93 | 16.6 |
| Male fondling of female genitals | 86 | 16.6 | 87 | 16.3 | 82 | 17.2 | 86 | 17.5 |
| Female fondling of male genitals | 82 | 16.8 | 84 | 16.7 | 78 | 17.4 | 81 | 17.8 |
| Genital apposition[b] | 77 | 17.1 | 81 | 16.8 | 72 | 17.6 | 78 | 17.9 |
| Intercourse | 75 | 17.5 | 79 | 17.2 | 60 | 17.9 | 72 | 18.3 |
| Male oral contact with female genitals | 60 | 18.2 | 68 | 17.7 | 59 | 18.1 | 67 | 18.6 |
| Female oral contact with male genitals | 61 | 18.1 | 70 | 17.8 | 54 | 18.1 | 63 | 18.8 |

[a]Includes only those who have engaged in the behavior.

[b]Genital apposition is mutual genital contact without vaginal penetration.

Source: DeLamater & MacCorquodale, *Premarital Sexuality: Attitudes, Relationships, Behavior*, The University of Wisconsin Press. © 1979 by the Board of Regents of the University of Wisconsin System, p. 59.

(DeLamater & MacCorquodale, 1979) (see Table 12.3). Earlier research (Kinsey et al., 1948, 1953) had suggested that educational level was related to kinds of sexual expression, with college-educated people engaging in a greater range of sexual activities and less well-educated people confining their sexual interactions to more conservative activities and positions. DeLamater and MacCorquodale's (1979) data revealed no evidence for this relationship among young people who were or were not attending college. More recent research (Billy et al., 1993) with a national sample of men reinforced Kinsey's findings, although the association between educational level and kinds of sexual activities is becoming less marked.

The National Survey of Family Growth found that increasing proportions of teens are sexually active (Ahlburg & DeVito, 1992). A quarter of 15-year-old females and half of 17-year-old females were sexually active in 1988. These figures represent a 40% to 50% increase over data collected in 1980. DeLamater and MacCorquodale's comparison of attitudes reported in four different studies showed that the majority of men always felt that premarital intercourse was acceptable for them. As shown in Table 12.4, however, an enormous shift has occurred in women's attitudes toward premarital sexual expression.

The *sexual double standard* has a long history. Early studies indicated that both men and women accepted the idea of premarital sexual experience for men but not for women (DeLamater & MacCorquodale, 1979). In a culture that has

**sexual double standard**—the belief that a particular behavior is acceptable for one gender but not for the other.

**TABLE 12.4 Evolving Sexual Attitudes**

### Change in Premarital Standards, 1959–1973

| Standard | Reiss, 1959[a] | | Simon & Gagnon, 1968 | | DeLamater & MacCorquodale, 1973[b] | | | |
|---|---|---|---|---|---|---|---|---|
| | M | F | M | F | SM | NM | SF | NF |
| Abstinence | 28% | 58% | 28% | 55% | 5% | 5% | 11% | 13% |
| Double standard | 30% | 24% | c | c | 0% | 0% | 2% | 1% |
| Permissive with affection (if feel affection, love) | 26% | 16% | 45% | 40% | 55% | 50% | 64% | 54% |
| Permissive without affection (if both want it) | 14% | 2% | 25% | 5% | 40% | 45% | 22% | 31% |
| Number of responses | 386 | 435 | 593 | 584 | 432 | 220 | 429 | 293 |

### Change in Percentage Accepting Premarital Intercourse for Their Own Gender, 1947–1973

| Ehrmann, 1947–1951 | | Reiss, 1959 | | Simon & Gagnon, 1968 | | DeLamater & MacCorquodale, 1973 | |
|---|---|---|---|---|---|---|---|
| M | F | M | F | M | F | M | F |
| 50–75% | 14% | 73% | 17% | 70% | 45% | 95% | 86–87% |

[a]The data presented here are from Reiss (1967, p. 26, Table 2.6). The respondents holding a reverse double standard—that is, coitus accepted for women but not for men—are omitted from this table, as interpretation of this standard and comparison to other studies are not clear-cut.

[b]SM: student males; NM: nonstudent males; SF: student females, NF: nonstudent females.

[c]Respondents were asked for standards only for their own gender.

Source: DeLamater & MacCorquodale, *Premarital Sexuality: Attitudes, Relationships, Behavior*, The University of Wisconsin Press. © 1979 by the Board of Regents of the University of Wisconsin System, p. 228.

traditionally approved of neither homosexuality nor prostitution, such a double standard is puzzling: with whom is it acceptable for men to engage in premarital sex? The answer lies in the distinction that used to be made between "good girls" and "nice girls." A good girl went home after a date and then went to bed. In contrast, a nice girl went to bed and then went home. Men could have sex with nice girls, but marriage proposals were reserved for good girls.

On the basis of their data, DeLamater and MacCorquodale reported: "Our results indicate that, in the strict sense of accepting premarital coitus for men but not for women, the double standard has disappeared" (1979, p. 227). Other evidence suggests, however, that it may be too soon to dismiss the double standard totally. Although it is acceptable for both men and women to engage in premarital intercourse, men and women are stereotypically expected to play dif-

**TABLE 12.5 Strategies for Seeking and Avoiding Sexual Intercourse, Reported by Adolescent Males and Females**

| Strategy | Definition |
| --- | --- |
| Reward | Giving gifts, providing services, and flattering the date in exchange for compliance |
| Coercion | Punishing or threatening to punish noncompliance by withdrawing resources or services or by sharing negative feelings |
| Logic | Using rational, but not moral, arguments to convince the date to have or avoid sexual intercourse |
| Information | Telling the date whether or not sex was desired, in a straightforward or direct manner |
| Manipulation | Hinting at sexual intentions by subtly altering one's appearance, the setting, or the topic of conversation |
| Body language | Using facial expression, posture, physical distance, and relatively subtle gestures to communicate one's sexual intentions |
| Deception | A strategy for having or avoiding sex that relied on giving the date false information |
| Moralizing | Telling the date that it is the influencing agent's legitimate or socially sanctioned right to have or avoid sexual intercourse |
| Relationship conceptualizing | Influencing a date by talking about the relationship and indicating concern for the date's feelings |
| Seduction | A definite step-by-step plan for getting a date to have sexual intercourse, especially a plan that focuses on sexually stimulating the date |

Source: McCormick, N. B. Come-ons and Put-offs: Unmarried students' strategies for having and avoiding intercourse. *Psychology of Women Quarterly*, 4, No. 4, 1979, 194–211. Reprinted by permission of the publisher, Human Sciences Press, New York.

ferent roles in those encounters. Specifically, men are the initiators of sexual interaction, whereas women set limits on the extent of the sexual contact.

McCormick (1979) studied the strategies that men and women use both to initiate and to avoid sexual intimacy. She asked students to imagine that they were alone with an attractive person with whom they had "necked" but not yet had sexual intercourse. The respondents indicated how they might influence that person to have sexual intercourse, as well as what strategies they would use to avoid having sex. A description of the strategies appears in Table 12.5. When Mc-Cormick later presented these same strategies to another group of volunteers, these participants rated the strategies for seeking intercourse as primarily employed by men, and the strategies for avoiding sex as predominantly used by women. These differences appear to be due to different motivational systems. Male motives for sexual intercourse more often include pleasure, fun, and physical reasons, whereas female motives are more often based on love, commitment, and emotions (Buss, 1994; Carroll, Volk, & Hyde, 1985).

Do these beliefs accurately reflect contemporary gender-role behavior in sexual interactions? Research results on this question are mixed, suggesting that we are in a state of transition regarding the influence of traditional gender-role stereotypes in sexual interactions. Men tend to hold more positive attitudes toward the

**FIGURE 12.16**
**Changing Sexual Patterns**
Over the last few decades, gender differences in the type of relationship with the first coital partner have been decreasing. In the past, men were more likely to have first intercourse with a prostitute or casual partner, whereas women engaged in first coitus with a steady partner. Contemporary adolescents, both males and females, generally have first coitus with a partner toward whom they feel an emotional bond.

idea of women's taking the initiative in dating and sexual intimacy than do women. One study showed that initiating sexual activity was becoming more common among college females (Lottes, 1993).

Before they come to the end of adolescence, most people reach the point at which they decide to have sexual intercourse (see Figure 12.16). The majority of contemporary adolescents describe their first sexual partner as someone toward whom they felt emotional attachment or love (Miller, Christopherson, & King, 1993). In contrast, four decades ago men were more likely

than they are currently to have first intercourse with a casual acquaintance or a prostitute. In reviewing research regarding the degree of commitment that people report toward their first sexual partner, DeLamater and MacCorquodale (1979) concluded that women have become more permissive: they engage in intercourse with men toward whom they feel affection rather than waiting until a love relationship develops or until they become engaged. Conversely, men are becoming less permissive: they are more likely than they were formerly to have first intercourse with a person toward whom they feel emotional attachment or love. The net effect of these shifts is a reduction in gender differences regarding the kind of relationship with the first coital partner.

## The Beginnings of Sexual Intimacy with a Partner

The affective responses of women to their first coital experience vary considerably (Schwartz, 1993; Weis, 1983). Although about 64% of the women in Weis's sample reported feeling excited, many also mentioned feeling nervous (76%) or guilty (38%), and fewer than half the women reported feeling pleasure (39%) or satisfaction (25%).

What factors were associated with positive or negative feelings about first intercourse? Weis found that women were more likely to have positive feelings if they described their partner as loving, tender, and considerate than if they did not. That finding is not particularly surprising, but it should be noted that these characteristics of the partner were more important predictors of positive feelings about first coitus than was the official relationship status of the couple (first date, going together, engaged, and so on). Further, women who had had more dating partners and more noncoital sexual experience (necking, petting) prior to first coitus, and those who were

older at first intercourse, were more likely to experience pleasure and less likely to experience anxiety during first coitus than were younger women with fewer dates and less noncoital sexual experience. Finally, there is one other finding from Weis's research that sexually inexperienced males may appreciate: the extent to which women perceived their partners as sexually experienced was *not* related to the women's pleasure, guilt, or anxiety.

Whether they choose to engage in sexual intercourse during adolescence, both males and females exhibit definitive patterns of courtship behavior in approaching and avoiding potential sexual partners. Traditionally, it had been assumed that females have relatively little power or influence over the initiation of courtship. Their primary role has been described as that of a "gatekeeper" who sets limits on the extent of intimacy between the partners. As we described in Chapter 6, however, several recent studies have suggested that females play a more active role in the selection of partners and initiation of courtship than was previously thought. In the next chapter, we consider sexual intimacy during the adult life span, beginning with a discussion of the relationship between sexual and emotional intimacy.

## Summary of Major Points

| | |
|---|---|
| 1. Barriers to knowledge and theoretical perspectives. | Information about sexuality early in the life span has been difficult to obtain, partly because of the belief that children are not sexual and partly because of taboos against asking children about their sexual feelings and behaviors. |
| 2. Infantile sexuality. | Infants are capable of responses that adults label as sexual, including erection and vaginal lubrication. But these responses are primarily reflexive, not intentional. Experiencing cuddling and sensual contact as an infant seems to be important in developing healthy adult sexuality. |
| 3. Early childhood (18 months to 3 years). | Parents convey attitudes about sexuality as they help their offspring develop language skills and bodily control of elimination. Casual genital stimulation occurs among children, but apparently without the goal of reaching orgasm. During early childhood, children learn their own gender and begin to demonstrate some awareness of gender differences, although they use such cues as hair and clothing styles rather than anatomical differences to determine whether others are male or female. |

| | |
|---|---|
| 4. Preschool years (3 years to 5 years). | At this stage, children show increasing independence and self-direction. Although they continue to need protection, their movement toward initiative must also be supported. During this period, children begin to internalize parental and societal expectations about "right" and "wrong" behavior. |
| 5. Gender stereotypes versus gender differences. | Empirical research has demonstrated that males and females are more similar than they are different: most attributes exist on overlapping distributions. Before accepting a cultural belief about a supposed gender difference, it is important to determine whether a) the difference exists, and b) the difference characterizes all males and females or typifies the average male versus the average female. |
| 6. Sexual exploration in childhood. | During early childhood, children actively explore their environment, and their curiosity about sexuality is evident. They play quasi-sexual games and act out adult roles, but the majority do not connect differences in genital anatomy with maleness or femaleness. Variations in physical attractiveness, important in determining adult evaluations of others, begin to influence children in early childhood. During the grade-school years, sexual exploration with others may be stimulated more by curiosity than by arousal. Much of this activity occurs with friends. Friendships at this age are primarily homosocial, and sexual play with children of the same gender is common. Much of the sexual slang learned by children at this age is associated with insults and with dirt. Freud's theory of latency—that children between ages 6 and 11 are uninterested in sex and are sexually inactive—is not supported by research. Instead, children appear to become increasingly interested in and curious about sexuality as they get older. |
| 7. Sex education. | Although children want to obtain information about human sexuality and reproduction, relatively few learn the details of these topics in any formal manner. Most North American children enter puberty with relatively little accurate information about sexuality in general or about the changes occurring in their own bodies. Comparisons of abstinence-only programs with postponement and contraceptive protection programs suggest that the latter are more effective in encouraging young people to postpone sexual activity and to use contraceptives when they do become sexually intimate. |
| 8. Adolescence: identity versus role confusion. | A primary task of adolescence is to begin the development of a coherent identity as a person. One aspect of this developmental stage involves a person's recognition of himself or herself as a male or a female—gender-role identification. In contrast to earlier views, research in the past few decades has suggested that androgyny—the incorporation of characteristics stereotypic of both masculinity and femininity into one's identity—may be beneficial for personality development. |
| 9. Building the sexual repertoire. | Through self-stimulation, experimentation with same-gender friends, behavioral scripts provided by the culture (for example, through peers and the media), and increasingly intimate sexual interactions, adolescents gradually learn to express their sexual feelings. In contrast to earlier generations, by the time they approach the end of adolescence, the majority of Americans have engaged in premarital sex. |

The earlier age of first coitus is not explained by the hypothesis that age of menarche has declined; in fact, the age at menarche has tended to range from 12 to 14 throughout most of recorded history and across most cultures. Male initiation into coitus is strongly related to hormone levels, whereas females' first coitus is more strongly associated with social factors such as peer experience.

10. Initial coital experience. The first occasion of sexual intercourse may be dominated by awkwardness and embarrassment rather than by intimacy and mutual pleasure. Gentleness during first intercourse and greater experience during adolescence with noncoital activities before coitus are associated with more positive feelings about initial intercourse.

## Review of Key Concepts

1. Freud's surveys of childhood sexuality laid the groundwork for the many studies of children that followed. True or false? (pp. 373–374)

2. From birth on: a) males are capable of erection; b) females are capable of vaginal lubrication; c) both males and females are capable of arousal, but cannot have orgasm until puberty; d) both a and b. (p. 379)

3. Erik Erikson maintained that during the second year of life, children face the challenge of: a) industry versus inferiority; b) trust versus mistrust; c) identity versus role confusion; d) autonomy versus shame and doubt. (p. 381)

4. The primal scene refers to: a) a child's witnessing of parental coitus; b) early childhood sex play; c) a child's observation of animal coitus; d) Adam and Eve's first attempt at sexual intercourse. (pp. 387–389)

5. The Goldmans' research on children's sexual knowledge found which group to be most knowledgeable? a) Americans; b) Canadians; c) Swedes; d) Australians. (p. 388)

6. The Goldmans' research supported Freud's theory of a latency period. True or false, and why? (p. 389)

7. The tendency to segregate into same-gender social groups in late childhood and early adolescence is called: a) gender reciprocity; b) homosociality; c) latent homosexuality; d) heterosociality. (pp. 393–394)

8. Comparisons of the effectiveness of abstinence-only sex education programs with postponement and protection sex education programs have found that _____ the onset of sexual activity: a) the former produces delays in; b) neither approach affects; c) the latter produces delays in; d) none of the above; no such comparisons have been made. (pp. 397–402)

9. The association between the dirtiness of human waste products and the genitals may account for some of the differences between the sexual attitudes and behavior of boys and girls. Discuss. (p. 396)

10. Erikson's theory of identity versus role confusion refers to: a) sibling rivalry; b) an adolescent's supposed renewed sexual interest in a parent; c) the incorporation of sexual fantasies into a unified adult pattern of sexual behavior; d) the variety of roles that an adolescent can adopt as a lifestyle. (p. 402)

11. Recent research suggests that: a) boys begin masturbating to orgasm earlier than do girls; b) boys masturbate more frequently than girls; c) both boys and girls begin masturbating at an earlier age than Kinsey reported (1948, 1953); d) all of the above. (p. 405)

12. First coitus by females during adolescence is most strongly associated with: a) an increase in hormones at puberty; b) social factors such as peers' sexual experience; c) their relationship with their father; d) lack of a female role model. (p. 411)

# Gender and Sexuality in Adulthood

THE passage from adolescence to adulthood is often subtle and poorly marked, leaving the adolescent concerned and sometimes confused about his or her identity and proper behavior. In this chapter we examine the phases of exploring sexual behaviors and developing personal identities through which most adults pass. We also look at how sexuality in young adulthood relates to the eventual development of emotional intimacy and to the commitment to a long-term relationship in adulthood. A variety of lifestyle options are available to young adults, including marrying early, postponing marriage, cohabiting, and remaining single. We discuss what is known about the costs and benefits of each of these alternatives. Because most North Americans do marry, the relationship of marriage to the level of sexual activity and satisfaction are also considered. We review research on extramarital affairs and examine how the quality of sexual expression bears on a couple's decision to separate and to divorce. Factors related to postseparation adjustment are also discussed. Finally, we explore the relationship of sexual pleasure to biological, social, and psychological changes among middle-aged and elderly people.

## Young Adulthood

The age at which adolescence ends and adulthood begins is not always clear. Is a 24-year-old graduate student who still depends on his parents for financial support an adult? Is an 18-year-old factory worker who supports herself and has her own apartment an adolescent? Becoming independent of one's parents usually signals the transition from adolescence to adulthood. People achieve such independence at different ages, depending in part on their educational and vocational aspirations.

Regardless of the exact age at which it begins, young adulthood brings new challenges. Erik Erikson described three stages of adulthood (see Table 13.1). Erikson (1968b) proposed that the major task young adults face is developing their capacity to be intimate. Having shaped a firm sense of identity during adolescence, the individual is now able to risk forming close sexual and nonsexual bonds with other people (see Figure 13.1). If a person is unable to develop an intimate relationship, he or she faces the loneliness of isolation. In this section, we examine some of the issues that young adults confront.

The process of getting to know a potential partner for a long-term relationship is variously

**FIGURE 13.1**
**Young Adulthood**
By late adolescence, most people have begun to establish relatively stable, if not necessarily permanent, emotional and sexual relationships.

known as dating, going out, going together, or "seeing" someone. The phenomenon of dating as a means of selecting a marriage partner is a relatively recent (circa 1920) social invention in the United States (Roche, 1986). Current trends in premarital sexual behavior and their related ex-

**TABLE 13.1 Erikson's Stages of Development During Adulthood**

| Age | Crisis or Stage | Sexual Expression and Capacities |
| --- | --- | --- |
| Young adulthood (20–39) | Intimacy versus isolation | Sexual intimacy, capacity for reproduction[a] |
| Middle age (40–64) | Generativity versus stagnation | Parenting, adapting to the aging of the body |
| Old age (65 →) | Ego integrity versus despair | Loss of many attributes considered attractive and sexual |

[a]A person acquires the capacity for reproduction during puberty, but does not generally attain the emotional maturity and economic resources important for the process until young adulthood.

pectations seem to depend on the stage of development in the dating relationship as well as on gender-role stereotypes. Roche (1986) conceptualized the progress of a dating relationship as a progression through the following five stages.

Stage 1: Couple dates without affection.

Stage 2: Couple dates with affection.

Stage 3: Dating individuals consider themselves to be "in love."

Stage 4: Each individual dates the loved person exclusively.

Stage 5: Couple becomes engaged to marry.

Roche asked college students and young adults to indicate what they considered to be proper sexual behavior, ranging from no physical contact to sexual intercourse, during these five stages. During the first three stages, men condoned greater permissiveness and reported that they engaged in significantly more petting than did women. In the last two stages, these gender differences essentially disappeared. Men and women agreed about the appropriateness of light and heavy petting and intercourse during stages 4 and 5, and large numbers of both genders reported engaging in sexual intercourse during those stages. The only gender difference to emerge for later stages involved oral-genital sex, with more men (86%) than women (71%) indicating that oral sex was appropriate at stage 4. It is important to note that both men and women reported greater permissiveness in their actual behavior than in their definitions of proper behavior.

A large majority of the students thought that sexual intercourse was acceptable for a couple who were "in love" and dating each other exclusively. We turn next to a discussion of the association between the level of sexual intimacy between two people and the outcome of their relationship.

## The Relationship Between Sexual Intimacy and Emotional Intimacy

Traditionally, women were taught to use sexual intimacy as a tool for obtaining a marriage proposal. The notion was that men a) would not "respect" women with whom they had had nonmarital coitus, and b) would be less inclined to marry if they were able to get sexual intercourse "free." This idea was based on assumptions that men want sex more than women do and that women want marriage more than men do, conditions requiring a bartering of sex and marriage. It also assumes that the purpose of marriage is to have sex, and that if one can obtain sexual intimacy outside of marriage, there is no particular reason to enter into a marriage contract. To what extent has research supported these assumptions?

Although nonmarital sexual intimacy has become almost universal in North American culture, contemporary attitudes about this practice vary widely. Some individuals believe that early sexual intercourse is an effective and acceptable means by which couples can develop intimacy. Others assert that engaging in intercourse early in a relationship can preclude greater closeness and commitment.

Generally, we lack the longitudinal research needed to answer questions about the role of early emotional and sexual intimacy in relationships. However, one study examined dating couples over a two-year period during their sophomore and junior years of college (Peplau, Rubin, & Hill, 1977). At the beginning of the study, the couples had been dating for an average of about eight months. Few of the 231 couples had made definite plans to marry, although about a fifth of them were living together. On the basis of the couples' responses, three patterns of sexual behavior and emotional intimacy were identified: sexually traditional, sexually moderate, and sexually liberal.

The Peplau group (1977) was interested in the association between the timing of first coitus and the outcome of the relationship. About half the couples reported having had sexual intercourse within a month of their first date (the early-coitus group); the other half reported having been involved for a longer period of time before they had coitus (the later-coitus group). Later-coitus couples reported feeling closer to their partner and knowing him or her better than did the early-coitus couples. A higher proportion of the couples in the later-coitus group reported being in love, and they gave higher estimates of the probability of marrying their partner than did those in the early-coitus group.

Men's reported sexual satisfaction with their partners did not differ as a function of the timing of first coitus together. In contrast, women in the early-coitus group reported greater sexual satisfaction with their partners than did women in the later-coitus group.

Compared with those who were sexually intimate, the couples who abstained from sexual intercourse were less likely to report being in love. A total of 51% of the women and 55% of the men among the abstaining couples reported being in love, compared with 72% of the women and 74% of the men who did have coitus.

Based on what you know so far about the abstaining, early-coitus, and late-coitus couples, which group would you expect to have the highest proportion of weddings, and why? At the end of two years, Peplau et al. were able to obtain information about 221 of the original 231 couples. They found that 20% of them had married, and 34% of them were still dating. The remaining 46% of the couples had broken up. It may surprise you to learn that there was no association between the pattern of their sexual behavior when first contacted (coitus within a month, later coitus, or abstention) and the outcome of their relationship (marriage, dating, or separation) two years later. Peplau et al. found no evidence that sexual intimacy early in a relationship either short-circuits or encourages a long-term commitment. Similarly, abstinence was unrelated to the likelihood of developing a lasting relationship.

As mentioned earlier, the Peplau group had classified their participants as having traditional, moderate, or liberal attitudes. In a 15-year follow-up of these couples, Peplau, Hill, and Rubin (1993) examined the correlation of these attitudes to their participants' relationships. Gender-role attitudes assessed while the volunteers were in college were largely unrelated to general patterns of marriage, childbearing, and employment for either gender. Traditional women were more likely to marry their college sweetheart. The divorce rate among the 73 couples who married their college partner was generally low, and none of the traditional women had divorced.

Peplau et al. measured student attitudes in the 1970s, when the shift toward more liberal sexual attitudes and behavior was at its height. There are indications that contemporary students and adults are somewhat more conservative about sex. In a survey of students enrolled in sex education courses from 1975 through 1984, Story (1985) found increases in conservative sexual attitudes and behaviors. Data presented in the last chapter, and in this one, show that people's attitudes are more conservative than their behavior. Nonetheless, these changes in attitudes suggest concerns about the role of sexuality in nonmarital relationships—concerns perhaps heightened by worries about AIDS and other sexually transmitted diseases.

The trend toward more conservative attitudes about premarital sex does not appear to be reflected in the actual behavior of adolescents. DeBuono, Zinner, Daamen, and McCormack (1990) compared the prevalence of sexual intercourse in college women during 1975, 1986, and 1989. Depending on the year, 87% to 88% of the women had had coitus. Although AIDS has apparently not reduced the likelihood of premarital coitus, condom use, sometimes combined with other contraceptive methods, had increased at each time period: 12% in 1975, 21% in 1986, and 41% in 1989. No differences were found, however, in the number of sexual partners or the likelihood of engaging in fellatio, cunnilingus, or anal sex.

To what extent are shifting norms in other areas relevant to sexuality, relationship and family formation, and other lifestyle issues? We now turn to the available research on these and other questions.

## Lifestyle Choices and Shifting Norms

Young adults face major decisions regarding lifestyles, jobs or careers, and relationships. Their choices can have far-reaching consequences for structuring their lives throughout adulthood and old age.

As is true in all societies that have been studied, more than 90% of Americans marry, and some of those who do not marry form long-lasting intimate bonds in the absence of a marriage license (Buss & Schmitt, 1993). Although long-term relationships, whether between married or unmarried partners, can enrich life and increase the individual's sense of purpose and value, such associations can also be experienced as threatening. A close attachment to another person provides someone with whom to celebrate successes and recover from disappointments. But for some people, the vulnerability that accompanies a close bond is too great a risk; another person can smother you, reject you, or let you down. Finding an optimal level of independence and dependence in a relationship can be emotionally draining and time-consuming. Some individuals deal with the uncertainty by maintaining shallow levels of intimacy, either because they perceive close relationships as a source of entrapment or because they fear loss and rejection. Erikson described these persons as resolving the developmental crisis by maintaining isolation. However, those who resolve the crisis through marriage are not necessarily any happier, as we discuss later.

Until recently, most individuals reaching adulthood perceived their main tasks to be finding gainful employment and selecting a mate with whom to have children. If marriage was postponed, the delay was due more to economic conditions than to personal choice. If one did not take religious vows, he or she was expected to take marital vows, and those who did not were frequently the objects of pity. It was assumed that permanently single people were atypical with respect to physical attractiveness, sexual feeling, and emotional adjustment. Such judgments fell particularly hard on unmarried women, who were commonly thought of as old maids or spinsters.

Choices for contemporary men and women have become considerably more diverse. Instead of the issue of whom to marry, the question centers on whether to marry, and if so, when. Instead of discussing how many children to have, it has become acceptable, at least among some segments of society, to talk about whether to have any children. In addition, most people begin engaging in sexual intercourse before they reach the end of adolescence, and before they marry.

Women have made significant progress toward achieving economic and social equality, but is there any evidence of corresponding changes in women's roles in romantic and marital relationships? If attitudes are changing, what is the

**FIGURE 13.2**
**The Single Lifestyle**
Remaining single is a fulfilling alternative to marriage for many men and women.

influence of new attitudes on contemporary choices regarding lifestyles?

### Single Lifestyles

With the median age at first marriage gradually rising to the mid-20s in the 1990s (26.5 years for men, 24.4 years for women in 1992), more people are single during part or all of their young adulthood (Saluter, 1992) (see Figure 13.2). Even among those who marry, almost 64% return to single status through separation or divorce, and many others return to single status as the result of a spouse's death. When we think of a household, we usually assume that it consists of at least two people. The proportion of households that contain only one person, however, is rising rapidly. Almost 25% of households are composed of a single occupant, as compared to 7% in 1949, a spurt of 40%. The growing incidence of one-person households has stemmed primarily from an increase in the number of never-married persons who either do not intend to marry or are postponing marriage. The rise in the number of one-person households consisting of divorced or separated men under age 35 has been particularly marked. Among women, the number of widows continues to grow, but not so much as the numbers of never-married, divorced, and separated women (U.S. Bureau of the Census, 1993).

Singles, particularly those over 25 years old, are the victims of a number of misconceptions. One of the most common is that they are "swingers." The stereotype of the promiscuous and care-free bedhopper pursuing endless amorous adventures is an enduring fantasy. It is interesting that the alleged swinging lifestyle of an unattached man is often viewed with envy or fascination, whereas single women are often seen as threatening, particularly by their married counterparts. Another misconception about singles is that they are not married because they have been unable to find anyone willing to marry them. Emotional instability, physical unattractiveness, and low intelligence may be attributed to individuals to explain why they are unmarried. The underlying assumption appears to be that all normal people marry. In addition, singles must often endure insinuations that they are homosexuals. Fear of homosexuality is so pervasive in our culture that any deviation from marriage leaves one vulnerable to the charge. The conclusion that an unmarried person must be promiscuous, unattractive, or gay, however, reflects ignorance about single lifestyles.

Although there is no particular type of person who remains single, women with graduate-school training and women with little education (less than five years) contribute disproportionately to the ranks of the never-married (Saluter, 1992). Women with graduate training may perceive marriage as interfering with their career plans. Those with little education may be seen as undesirable partners, especially if their lack of education stems from problems such as low income and mental or physical handicaps.

Being single carries with it the connotation of being sexually available. For some single people, sexual availability can be appealing because of the excitement and variety it affords. A commitment to sexual experimentation may be a primary reason for avoiding marriage. A single lifestyle permits a person to experience a variety of situations and people, offering an opportunity for adventure. Other singles, however, involve themselves with only one partner at a time, sometimes for extended periods. Still others maintain a primary relationship with one person while having secondary sexual relationships with other people.

In departing from the conventional choice of marriage, at least for a period of time, single men and women must develop an alternative network of relationships that provide support and intimacy. Many singles form friendships in the workplace, in school, at parties, and through hobbies and sports. Remaining single has become a workable and satisfying alternative to marriage for many men and women, one that can last for a few years or a lifetime. A form of legal, if not emotional, singleness that has become popular is cohabitation.

### Cohabitation

The practice of sharing a residence with a sexual partner before marriage or instead of marriage—*cohabitation*—has rapidly increased in popularity in the last three decades. In the 1970s, cohabitation among college students attracted the attention of the media. There was an increase in cohabiting among college students, but this reflected a trend already underway among other groups in society. About 25% of college students report having cohabited for some period of time (Newcomb, 1986; Thornton, 1988). In the United States as a whole, the proportion of persons who lived with a partner before marrying for the first time increased from 11% in 1970 to nearly half for recent first marriages (Bumpass, Sweet, & Cherlin, 1991). The actual number of people co-

---

**cohabitation**—an arrangement in which an unmarried couple live together.

habiting is higher because about 20% of cohabitors do not ever expect to marry or marry again.

Is cohabitation just part of a developmental sequence that begins with romantic attraction and proceeds to sexual intimacy, then cohabitation, and finally marriage? Or does the increase in the practice of cohabitation indicate vast changes in our society, from which a new family form is emerging?

Although most cohabitors plan to marry at some point, they do not necessarily intend to marry the person with whom they are living. The majority of cohabiting relationships break up or end in marriage within 18 months (Bumpass et al., 1991). However, about 20% of cohabiting couples have lived together for more than five years. Roughly 40% of cohabiting couples end their relationships before marriage, and marriages that are preceded by cohabitation have higher dissolution rates than marriages without previous cohabitation (DeMaris & Rao, 1992).

The mention of cohabitation usually elicits a stereotyped image of two young people adjusting to living together, but 40% of cohabiting households include children, and 60% of those who remarry report having cohabited, although not necessarily with the person they subsequently married. Most cohabitors report that their lives would be pretty much the same if they were married (Bumpass et al., 1991). So what keeps them from marrying? One factor is education. Cohabitation as a replacement for early marriage is most frequent among those who have not completed high school, leading to a positive correlation between income and expectations of marriage (Bumpass et al., 1991). These people may be waiting to acquire more resources before marrying.

Cohabitors and noncohabitors have been compared on a variety of demographic and personality measures (Blumstein & Schwartz, 1983; Byers & Heinlein, 1989; DeMaris & Rao, 1992). In general, cohabitation is more prevalent in large urban centers. Cohabitors tend to have higher expectations for marriage than do their noncohabiting counterparts. Moreover, cohabitors are more experienced sexually and become intimately involved at younger ages than noncohabitors. Both groups reported similar levels of sex-

ual satisfaction, although cohabiting couples report having sex more frequently than do married couples (Sprecher & McKinney, 1994). Finally, cohabitation for most people appears to be a testing ground for marriage; however, for a smaller number of individuals, it is the preferred family arrangement.

*Relationship Contracts*

Couples who cohabit in part to avoid legal hassles may find some recent court cases sobering. In contrast to laws governing marital relationships, laws concerning cohabitation and the dissolution of cohabiting relationships have not been particularly well defined. As a result, the potential is high for lengthy and expensive legal battles if long-term cohabitants decide to separate. Many attorneys advise a couple intending to cohabit to write up a contract regarding the division of property and income acquired during the relationship to clarify the situation that will arise if or when the individuals decide to separate.

Attempts to design relationship contracts are not recent. According to Caroline Bird (1979, p. 59):

> The earliest was made by Mary Wollstonecraft, author of "A Vindication of the Rights of Women," the document which in 1792 founded women's rights. She and her husband, William Godwin, agreed to keep separate residences so that "the husband only visits his mistress like a lover when each is dressed, rooms are in order, etc." The pioneer of birth control, Margaret Sanger, and her husband, J. Noah H. Slee, had similar arrangements. When Lucy Stone and Henry Blackwell, political activists of their day, were married in 1855, they wrote a declaration of independence from laws that "refuse to recognize the wife as an independent, rational being, while they confer upon the husband an injurious and unnatural superiority."

Whether they want to draw up a contract, all couples who decide to live together—regardless of their marital status—can benefit from considering various material and emotional issues.

Some of the issues that couples may want to discuss are provided in Box 13.1. Therapists working with couples having relationship difficulties often hear such statements as, "Well, I thought I could change him/her" and "I didn't think it was important" in response to questions about whether the client was aware of a particular preference, behavior, or personality characteristics of his or her partner before making a commitment to live with the individual.

If they are able to resolve important differences between them, some cohabiting couples go on to marry one another. Whether they decide to wed the person with whom they have been cohabiting or someone else, the vast majority of people do marry. So we turn now to the topic of matrimony.

## Love and Marriage

Contrary to popular stereotypes, men tend to fall in love more readily than women, and women tend to fall out of love more easily than men. Women are more cautious about entering into a romantic relationship and more likely to weigh a relationship against various alternatives. They are also more likely to end a relationship that seems ill fated.

Clearly, shifting sexual and gender-role norms offer contemporary young adults a broader range of choices than in the past with respect to lifestyle arrangements and the timing of such events as marriage and childbearing. There is less pressure to follow the longstanding

---

### Box 13.1

## Considerations for Couples Planning to Cohabit or Marry

Anyone planning to marry or live with another person should be aware of his or her own feelings and those of the partner. Both participants should be attuned to areas of general agreement and disagreement. Perfect agreement is unlikely and not even necessarily desirable. However, disagreement on many items suggests that a couple may be in for some rough sledding.

You and your partner may wish to respond to these questions independently first, before sharing your responses. On a separate piece of paper, describe your attitude toward each item. Then indicate how important this particular issue is to you by placing a number to the right of the response, using the following scale:

1—not at all important

2—not very important

3—somewhat important

4—important

5—extremely important

1. Who should be responsible for the economic support of the household?

2. Who should be responsible for the physical maintenance of the household (meal preparation, dish and clothes washing, house cleaning, grocery shopping, and so forth)?

3. Who should be responsible for paying bills?

4. How neat and clean do you want the house to be?

5. In general, would you characterize yourself as paying bills and then spending whatever is left as you choose, or spending money as you choose and then paying bills with whatever is left?

6. Do you approve of the use of intoxicants (liquor, nicotine, marijuana, tranquilizers, and so forth)? How do you feel about your partner's using intoxicants?

7. Do you intend to confine sexual intimacy to your partner while you are together?

8. How would you respond to the knowledge that your partner had been sexually intimate with someone else?

9. Do you believe that couples should always inform each other of everything they do, where they go, and whom they see?

10. Do you believe that couples should take vacations together, or do you think that separate vacations are occasionally acceptable?

11. If you and your partner were invited to a party and you did not feel well, would you find it acceptable for your partner to attend the party without you?

12. How do you and your partner feel about having children? If you want children, how many do you want?

13. In the event that you have children, who should take primary care of them?

14. In the event that you do not want children, who would be responsible for birth control?

15. If you and your partner both had rewarding jobs and one of you were offered a pro-motion that required moving to another city, whose job would take precedence, assuming that you wanted to continue to live together?

16. If one of you felt more sexually adventurous (in terms of variations in coital positions or kinds of stimulation, for example) than the other, how would you resolve conflicting desires?

17. Do you believe that holidays should be spent with relatives? If you disagree with your partner on this issue, how would you resolve differences over whether to visit relatives, or whose relatives to visit?

18. How do you feel about your partner's attending conferences, meetings, and conventions without you?

19. How important is religion to you?

20. Do you like to entertain friends at your home?

patterns of marrying in one's early 20s and producing children within the next few years. Although the average age at first marriage has fluctuated considerably over the last half century, it has been rising steadily for the past three decades (see Figure 13.3). Economic factors as well as the tendency of greater numbers of women to seek educational or vocational training appear to have contributed to the shift toward delaying marriage.

In the traditional view of marriage perpetuated in countless movie scripts, marriage is a climactic event, after which a couple live "happily ever after." Many people retain an image of a young couple who, after finishing their educations and spending a period of time engaged to each other, exchange wedding vows in the company of their parents, relatives, and friends. Within a few years, they greet the first of several babies, who are brought up to expect the same idealized future. Television commercials and many situation comedies also still portray this norm. The wife's biggest concerns are removing the rings around her husband's collars and deciding which brand of disposable diapers best protects her baby's bottom.

How accurate is this depiction of families today? Recent census data provide extensive information about the characteristics of contemporary U.S. families. Table 13.2 reveals the contrast between the dream and the reality of U.S. marriages. Some elements of the cultural dream are based on the assumption that there are certain prerequisites for rearing emotionally healthy children. Biases against single-parent families, for example, may rest on the assumption that without both a mother and a father present throughout childhood, an individual will be maladjusted. If that were true, our society would have an enormous number of maladjusted people left over from the 1940s, when large numbers of fathers were killed during World War II or were absent for half a decade. There is no evidence, however, to suggest that the offspring of these men are more maladjusted than are their counterparts from intact families.

contributions by husbands and wives had changed. Women had reduced their meal-preparation time and increased the time they spent with their children. Men's involvement in both meal preparation and child care increased, although these contributions were limited primarily to weekends, regardless of the employment status of their wives.

In sum, most people now have positive attitudes toward women's employment, but working women still carry a disproportionate amount of the responsibility for household tasks, although men's contribution to housework has increased. Nonetheless, the average working woman does two to three times as much family work as does her husband (Major, 1993).

The demands placed on women by having multiple and time-consuming roles can leave little time for leisure or intimacy. Those working couples who desire more time for sexual intimacy could discuss the possibility of the husband expanding his contribution to household chores and the wife reducing the time spent on housework. If each partner assumes responsibility for about half the housework, the couple has additional time to spend on their relationship. For example, in Pleck's (1983) study, there were about 42 hours a week of housework, of which the wife was responsible for 28 hours and the husband for 14 hours. A husband who increases his share to 21 hours could give the couple 7 hours a week to devote to pleasurable pursuits.

### Sex, Time, and Parenthood

High levels of passion are characteristic of the initial stages of a sexual relationship. Research conducted over the past 50 years has consistently shown that married couples engage in sexual intercourse two or three times a week during the early years of marriage, with the frequency of intercourse declining over time. The drop in sexual activity over the duration of a relationship also holds true for couples who cohabit and for gay and lesbian couples (Blumstein & Schwartz, 1989; Sprecher & McKinney, 1994).

Parenthood may be one factor in the reduced frequency of heterosexuals' sexual contact. When they become parents, a couple who formerly made love in the middle of the afternoon regularly find themselves faced with fussing babies and demanding children. By the time the children go to sleep for the night, the ardor that the couple may have felt while making dinner may have faded to a wistful, "Well, honey, maybe tomorrow."

Further, the assumption that there is a tomorrow may decrease a couple's sense of urgency about expressing their sexual feelings immediately. As time goes on, and as a man and a woman grow familiar with each other's responses, there may be a tendency to be somewhat efficient about sex—an inclination that is reinforced by fears that their children will wake up while the couple are making love. In their study of parental status and sexual behavior, Byrne et al. (1977) concluded that couples with large families do not like sex as much as do those with fewer children. In certain cases a decrease in coital activity may be associated with negative sexual attitudes, particularly the belief that the main purpose of sex is to reproduce. For many couples, however, the reduced level of sexual activity may be merely a practical response: the presence of children decreases the opportunity for sexual expression. Some support for this hypothesis was obtained with a small sample of married couples who kept track of their coital rates in diaries. In all cases of couples with children, the arrival of the babies was associated with a reduction in coital frequency (James, 1981).

However, both babies and their parents grow older. In the next section we examine the association of long-term relationships with the quality and frequency of sexual expression.

## Long-Term Relationships

The phrase "until death do us part," included in most marriage vows, had a far more literal meaning for most of human history than it does today. In 19th-century America, marriage lasted an average of only 12 years before one of the partners died. Today, extended human longevity allows for much longer relationships, which may be complicated by the intrusion of some of the problems common to middle and old age. Most of our examination of long-term relationships focuses on marriage because there is little information about extended relationships among unmarried people.

## Sexual Pleasure, Disagreements, and Marital Longevity

Kinsey et al. (1953) noted that a decrease in women's orgasm rates frequently preceded divorce and separation, but the meaning of this change was unclear. Did the marital problems leading to divorce affect wives' sexual responsiveness? Or was it the other way around: did the decline in responsiveness lead to increased marital distance and ultimately divorce? More than a third of the women in Kinsey's sample who described their marriages as unhappy reported having orgasms with their husbands most of the time; paradoxically, more than a third of the women who rarely reached orgasm described their marriages as happy. Several later studies of married couples indicated that happy marriages exist between couples whose sexual encounters are not particularly frequent or earthshaking (Blumstein & Schwartz, 1983; Frank, Anderson, & Rubinstein, 1978). Further, Hunt (1974) found that the most critical factor in sexual satisfaction was the similarity of the couple's sexual desires; that is, if both spouses want sex frequently, or once a month, or not at all, they are happier than if one spouse wants to make love every night and the other would prefer far less frequent sexual intimacy. Sexual incompatibility has been found to be associated with the dissolution of relationships among dating couples, married couples, and homosexual couples (Sprecher & McKinney, 1994).

Contrary to the familiar sentiment "I don't mind fighting because making up is so much fun," the frequency of intercourse may be less important for marital happiness than the relative amounts of time spent making love versus fighting with one another. Wedded happiness is also negatively related to how often a couple argues. But several studies have found that measures of the frequency of sex and of arguments, considered together, are more predictive than the measure of either variable by itself. Specifically, the more often sexual intimacy occurs and the less often arguments occur, the more satisfied couples are with their marriage (Howard & Dawes, 1976; Thornton, 1977).

In summary, although sexual intimacy can be a significant source of marital pleasure, good and frequent sex is not crucial for marital longevity for many couples. In part, this is due to variations in the value placed on sexual attraction versus personal attachment, which changes over the course of a long-term relationship.

## Attraction Versus Attachment in Long-Term Relationships

The decreasing importance of sexuality in a marriage over time, at least in the successful long-term relationships that have been studied, has been examined in terms of sexual attraction and attachment. Troll and Smith (1976) suggested that there is an inverse relationship between these two factors: sexual attraction is high in the beginning of a new relationship, but attachment is low; over the years, sexual attraction diminishes as novelty wanes, but attachment increases. If marital satisfaction or happiness is measured in terms of sexual attraction, a steady decrease over time is inevitable, with perhaps a temporary rise when the children's departure creates a new domestic situation for husband and wife. If marital satisfaction is measured in terms of attachment, security, and loyalty, however, couples' marital happiness tends to increase over time.

As we have seen, the initial phases of most romantic relationships are characterized by passion and sexual intimacy. The experience of being swept away (see Figure 13.4) does not last long, however, as many parents have advised their unheeding offspring over the years. After couples begin to see each other regularly, passion typically lasts approximately 18 months to three years (Fisher, 1992; Tennov, 1979). And after the excitement dies down, couples must deal with various issues that await them as a couple and as individuals. In short, passion and sexual intimacy appear to be more important to loving relationships in early adulthood, whereas tender feelings of affection and loyalty are more

**FIGURE 13.4**
**Attraction in New Relationships**
The beginning of most romantic relationships is characterized by passion and the desire to be close to each other as often as possible.

important to loving relationships in the second half of life (Byrne & Murnen, 1988; Fisher, 1993).

But many people feel some conflict between their needs for security and a stable relationship on the one hand, and a desire for excitement and novelty on the other. The simultaneous yearning for the sexual novelty of a new partner and for the comfort of a steady partner creates a dilemma that many people have difficulty resolving. These reactions to sexual novelty are not confined to humans. The response to a familiar versus a new partner has been reported in a number of mammalian species: a male will readily copulate and ejaculate several times with a sexually receptive

female and then stop. Confronted by a new sexually receptive female, however, the male becomes sexually active again immediately. Such male re-arousal by a new female is called the Coolidge effect, based on this story:

> *One day the President and Mrs. Coolidge were visiting a government farm. Soon after their arrival they were taken off on separate tours. When Mrs. Coolidge passed the chicken pens she paused to ask the man in charge if the rooster copulates more than once each day. "Dozens of times" was the reply. "Please tell that to the President," Mrs. Coolidge requested. When the President passed the pens and was told about the roosters, he asked "Same hen every time?" "Oh no, Mr. President, a different one each time." The President nodded slowly, then said, "Tell that to Mrs. Coolidge." (Bermant, 1976, pp. 76–77)*

Partially because of the inherent tension between the desires for new sexual experiences versus those for continuity and comfort, monogamous relationships are perhaps the most difficult of all human contracts. Additional strain may be added by the fact that such relationships are expected to satisfy so many varied needs for the individuals involved. The needs for passion, security, and play, to name a few, are channeled into monogamous marriages that are typically already strained by concerns about children, vocations, and economics. Slowly and often imperceptibly, these relationships can drift toward dispassionate companionship. As a relationship becomes habitual over time, the partners become limited to a constricted range of experiences because it is difficult to preserve the excitement of a relationship when one is enmeshed in the rituals of security (see Figure 13.5). Some people have attempted to resolve this dilemma by continuing their primary relationship while simultaneously having sexual relations with others outside their marriage.

## Extramarital Sexual Relations

What prompts married people to have sexual relations outside their marriages? Conversely, why do some married people avoid sexual intimacy

**FIGURE 13.5**
**Balancing Stability and Novelty in Long-Term Relationships**
Couples in lengthy relationships can lapse into monotonous, unchanging routines that dull their attraction to one another. However, this sailing couple has discovered the secret to enjoying time engaging in shared activities.

with anyone but their spouses? Finally, what are the effects of extramarital sex on the participating individuals and on the marital relationship?

Extramarital sex can involve either covert or overt activity. Covert activities encompass all extramarital sexual relations that occur without the spouse's knowledge. Overt extramarital sex may take several different forms—open marriage, swinging, mate swapping, and group marriage. In these agreed-upon arrangements, both marital partners engage in extramarital intercourse with others.

Regardless of the form that extramarital sex assumes, a majority of respondents in Western societies disapprove of extramarital relationships (Bringle & Buunk, 1991; Janus & Janus, 1993). This negative attitude is more pronounced in U.S. samples than in those from Western Europe. Attitudes toward extramarital sex may change as a function of marital and social context. For example, most of the respondents in Lawson's (1988) study expected sexual monogamy when they first married but became more tolerant and less insistent on fidelity over the course of the marriage.

The statistics indicating that about three-quarters of those surveyed disapprove of extramarital sex under any conditions are particularly interesting in light of the proportion of the population reporting extramarital sexual activity (Lawson, 1988; Reiss, Anderson, & Sponaugle, 1980). Given reported attitudes, no more than 25% of the population would presumably experience sex with people other than their marital partners. However, it is estimated that at least half of married individuals have had extramarital sexual relations (Blumstein & Schwartz, 1983; Buss & Schmitt, 1993; Thompson, 1983). Evidence that the trend toward extramarital sex has begun to decline, however, has emerged from research conducted in the late 1980s and early 1990s (see Box 13.2). The fear of contracting AIDS may deter some married couples from having sex outside marriage (Billy, Tanfer, Grady, & Klepinger, 1993; Smith, 1991).

### Explaining Extramarital Sex

There is a strong relationship between an individual's sexual attitudes and his or her behavior with respect to premarital sex (Reiss et al., 1980). The more tolerant or permissive one's attitudes toward premarital sex, the more likely it is that one will engage in that activity. For extramarital sex, the relationship between attitudes and behavior may be considerably weaker (Glass & Wright, 1992), in part because of "stronger cultural norms [against extramarital sex] which may not stop the behavior but will produce guilt" (Reiss et al., 1980, p. 398).

The old line "My wife (husband) doesn't understand me" reflects a pervasive cultural belief that a person strays from the marital bed because of marital discontent or dissatisfaction with the

### Box 13.2

## Multiple Sex Partners: A Disappearing Practice?

Studies conducted during the past few decades indicate that sexual experience with multiple partners is common before and during marriage or other relationships involving commitment. But at the beginning of the 1990s, a reversal of this trend was reported based on research conducted by Tom Smith and his colleagues (Greeley, Michael, & Smith, 1990; Smith, 1991).

Researchers have been thwarted in their attempts to obtain funding for studies of the sexual behavior of nationally representative samples of adults, despite the critical need for greater understanding of sexuality to help policy makers find ways of changing behavior to reduce the population's risk of contracting AIDS. But Smith and his colleagues got around the problem by adding a few questions on sexual behavior to the General Social Surveys (GSS), which involve interviews of national samples of U.S. adults. Following the 1988 and 1989 interviews, approximately 1,400 participants responded to a short self-administered questionnaire and then returned it in a sealed envelope. In 1988 the questions centered on the number and gender of sex partners during the past 12 months and their relationship to the respondent. In 1989 questions were added concerning frequency of coitus and the number and gender of sex partners since age 18.

In 1988, 86% of men and 78% of women reported having had only one sexual partner during the previous 12 months. Monogamous behavior increased as a function of age, however: 56% of those aged 18–24 reported only one partner, whereas 95% of sexually active people aged 70 and above reported a sole partner. As might be expected, married people were more monogamous (96%) than were widowed (71%), divorced (62%), separated (78%), and never married people (52%). These

responses applied only to sexual activities during the previous year (Greeley et al., 1990).

Using the same method of appending short self-administered questionnaires to the GSS interviews, Smith (1991) collected additional data in 1989. He found that the average adult had 1.16 sex partners, but this number took into account the 22.1% of the sample who reported abstinence from sexual intercourse. Thus the actual number of sex partners for 78% of the sample approached 1.5 partners; that is, half the sexually active sample had had 2 partners during the previous 12 months.

The distribution of partners and of abstinence across marital status for the year was as follows:

| Marital Status | Average Number of Partners | Percent Abstinent |
|---|---|---|
| Married | .96 | 9.2 |
| Widowed | .21 | 85.9 |
| Divorced | 1.31 | 25.9 |
| Separated | 2.41 | 20.0 |
| Never Married | 1.84 | 24.6 |

In the 12 months preceding the survey, abstinence was highest among the widowed, lowest among the married, and intermediate among the other three groups. Separated respondents reported the most partners. Smith found that in the year prior to the survey, only 1.5% of married people had had a sex partner other than the spouse. Further, men and women did not differ in their reported number of extramarital partners.

When asked about the number of sexual partners they had had since age 18, adults reported an average of 7.15 partners. The distribution of partners since age 18 across current marital status was:

quality of the couple's sex life. In general, the occurrence of extramarital sex has been found to be related to marital unhappiness and dissatisfac-

tion with marital sex (cf. Bringle & Buunk, 1991 for a review of these studies). Summarizing research on national samples of married couples,

| Marital Status | Average Number of Partners |
|----------------|:--------------------------:|
| Married        | 5.72                       |
| Widowed        | 3.01                       |
| Divorced       | 13.30                      |
| Separated      | 11.75                      |
| Never Married  | 8.67                       |

Examining sexual orientation, Smith found that 92.6% of the sample were exclusively heterosexual and that 5.5% comprised homosexuals and bisexuals. The remainder reported no sexual activity. Among those reporting sex with same-gender partners since age 18, 16% were currently abstinent, 22% had same-gender partners at present, and 59% were currently involved in heterosexual relationships. Three percent did not respond to the question.

Smith (1991) concluded that the high fidelity rates indicated that most married people are avoiding exposing themselves or their spouses to AIDS. Further, based on research with the GSS samples, Greeley et al. (1990) found that 11% to 12% of people had reported changing their sexual behavior because of fears of contracting AIDS. The extent to which the recent apparent shift toward greater sexual exclusivity by married people stems from a change in moral views or results from concerns about getting AIDS, however, is not yet known.

Reiss et al. (1980) reported that individuals who rated their marriages as happy were less likely to approve of extramarital sex than were people who rated their marriages as less happy.

Thus the data suggest associations between the likelihood of having affairs and unhappy marriages, but they also indicate that happily married people sometimes have extramarital affairs. In view of the correlational methods used in this research, it is possible that factors other than marital happiness are responsible for the associations found. For example, the belief that one's marriage should fulfill all one's interpersonal needs may be unrealistic. Some people may choose to have extramarital relationships not just because of the sexual variety but because of other shared interests. Friendships between men and women may also provide a strong inducement for extramarital affairs. Anxiety over waning attractiveness, particularly among men, has been implicated as another motivation for extramarital sex, which provides a way for the man to prove to himself that he is still sexually attractive and virile. Like men, women often start affairs in their late 30s or early 40s seeking passion, a reaffirmation of their sexual attractiveness, and the excitement of courtship and love (Bringle & Buunk, 1991; Lawson, 1988). Sexual relationships outside marriage are not limited to middle age, of course.

They can and do occur at any time during a marriage. Teenagers and grandparents have affairs and give a variety of reasons for doing so.

Although husbands are more likely to be involved in extramarital affairs than are wives (Blumstein & Schwartz, 1983; Buss, 1994; Kinsey et al., 1948, 1953), they are also more likely to perceive affairs as destructive—if their wives are "unfaithful"! Kinsey found that twice as many husbands as wives felt that their spouses' extramarital relationships were destructive to the marriage.

Some husbands and wives make it clear to each other that if one spouse ever becomes sexually intimate with another person, the marriage will end. In other marriages, there is an acknowledgment and, at times, an open acceptance of the possibility that one or both spouses may become sexually intimate with someone else. A couple's discussion of the issue might focus on the conditions under which an affair may be mutually acceptable:

"Just make sure I don't know about it!"

"Don't ever expose me to an STD!"

"I don't ever want you to have another man [woman] in our house!"

"What you do out of town is none of my business, but don't get involved with anyone I know, and don't bring pity or embarrassment on me."

"Just keep my feelings in mind. Don't hurt me."

Under what conditions do people perceive extramarital sex as justified? Glass and Wright (1992) distributed questionnaires to adults at an airport and during the lunch hour in downtown Baltimore. Based on the responses of married people in their sample, four factors or reasons emerged, including (a) sexual factors (excitement, enjoyment, curiosity, and novelty); (b) emotional intimacy: (c) extrinsic motivation (career advancement, revenge on spouse); and (d) love. Men were more likely to endorse sex as a justification and women were more likely to see love as a justification for extramarital involvement.

An interesting aspect of Glass and Wright's research is that they went beyond much of the earlier research that defined extramarital involvement as having sexual intercourse. They broadened the definition of extramarital involvement to include sexual involvement without intercourse and/or some type of nonsexual emotional involvement. In their sample, 25% of the women and 44% of the men had experienced extramarital coitus, and the figures rose to 47% of women and 63% of men when sexual involvement without coitus was included.

Sometimes a marital imbalance leads a husband or wife to feel justified in seeking an extramarital relationship. Walster et al. (1978) have distinguished two kinds of imbalance. First, we may feel overbenefited when our marital rewards are greater than our costs. Second, we may experience deprivation when we perceive our investment as greater than our rewards. Finally, *equity* exists when we perceive our rewards as being equal to our investment in the marriage. It is important to note that rewards and investments can be defined in various ways. People bring diverse contributions to a relationship—

**equity**—in reference to a personal relationship, a perceived balance between the benefits the relationship provides and the personal investment it requires.

financial assets, practical know-how, or physical appeal, for example. Walster et al. suggested that spouses who perceive themselves to be either overbenefited or in an equitable relationship would be less likely to involve themselves in extramarital affairs than would spouses who saw themselves as deprived. To test this hypothesis, the researchers used a survey published by *Psychology Today*. To measure perceived equity, they analyzed responses to an item in which the volunteer was asked to describe his or her partner's desirability on a scale ranging from "much more desirable than I" through "as desirable as I" to "much less desirable than I."

Walster et al. believed that spouses would see the relationship as inequitable if they perceived themselves as more desirable than their mates. Consequently, they assumed that these people would engage in affairs earlier in their relationship and with more partners than would those who perceived themselves to be either in an equitable relationship or overbenefited. Their results supported this assumption. Although frequency of extramarital relationships did not vary according to gender or length of the primary relationship, it did vary according to perceptions of the equity of the primary relationship. It was particularly interesting that, among couples who had been together for 15 years or longer, there was little difference between the behavior of deprived men and deprived women. Deprived men reported having had an average of 3.3 partners outside the relationship, as compared with 2.6 partners for deprived women. It is possible, of course, that guilt over these affairs cultivated a tendency in volunteers to deprecate their marital relationships; that is, by lamenting the state of their marriage, they might have been seeking to justify their socially disapproved behavior and thus reduce their guilt.

In a study of married Dutch persons, 30% of whom had been involved in extramarital affairs, Prins, Buunk, and VanYperen (1993) also examined the relationship of equity to the likelihood of such extramarital liaisons. Women who felt deprived *or* advantaged in their marital relationships were more likely to have extramarital relations than were those women who reported equity in their marital relations. In contrast, men's likelihood of engaging in extramarital sex was less related to their relative sense of equity in their marital relationships. Prins et al. also found that although the men reported stronger desires to engage in extramarital sex, there were no differences in the percentage of men and women reporting involvement in such affairs.

### Consensual Extramarital Sex

Some couples reach an agreement that permits each spouse to be sexually active with persons outside their marriage under certain circumstances. Consensual extramarital sex can take various forms. A couple can agree that each partner individually may have intimate relationships with other people. Alternatively, a couple may engage in recreational sex with people who are relative strangers and with whom they tend not to be otherwise involved, an arrangement known as swinging. Or two or more couples may switch partners for purposes of sexual and emotional intercourse, called mate exchange. Finally, in group marriage, couples may share each other's partners, a residence, incomes, child care, and household responsibilities. In group marriage, as in traditional marriage, participants are typically expected to confine their sexual expression to members of the marriage.

Advocates of consensual extramarital sex have argued that the institution of marriage, with its normative requirement of sexual exclusiveness, results in sexual monotony, boredom, and sexual jealousy. They maintain that it is far preferable for a couple to inject variety into their marriage by having extramarital relations openly than to engage in secret and guilt-producing relationships (Gilmartin, 1974; Palson & Palson, 1972). In contrast to these idealistic viewpoints, in a five-year follow-up study of open marriages, Buunk (1991) found a trend for jealousy to increase over this time period. He also reported that over the five years, the quality of the marital relationship deteriorated and sexual satisfaction in the marriage declined. He could not determine whether this was typical of marriages in general or stemmed from the extramarital relationships. Conflicting results were reported from another study in which Rubin and Adams (1986) compared sexually open couples with sexually exclusive couples. They found no difference in marital stability over a five-year period. Obviously, these differing results can be used to support divergent views of the stability of open marriages.

In research on nonswingers' views of swingers (Jenks, 1985), nonswingers judged swingers' attitudes and behavior to be quite different from their own and thus saw practically everything about them as odd or immoral. In fact, however, swingers generally have been found to differ from nonswingers only in the practice of swinging. Brian Gilmartin (1974) conducted one of the more systematic studies of swingers. He compared 100 swinging couples with 100 control-group couples. All participants were legally married, middle-class couples living in suburban residential areas. Compared with nonswingers, swingers reported less gratifying relationships with their parents during childhood and adolescence, viewed their parents and relatives as less important in their lives, and interacted with their parents and relatives less frequently. Gilmartin found many more areas where swingers and nonswingers did not differ, however, and the similarities that he reported are in some ways more interesting than the differences. The two groups did not differ, for example, in reported personal happiness, marital contentment, drinking habits, boredom, or likelihood of seeking therapy.

One additional finding from the Gilmartin study is intriguing. Although the control-group couples were not involved in consensual extramarital sex, 31% of the husbands and 8% of the wives did report having had secret extramarital affairs. In contrast to the earlier hypothesis that extramarital sex occurs because of unhappy marriages, control-group spouses who had had secret affairs perceived their marriages as no less happy than those who reported having been sexually faithful to their spouses. The vast majority of swingers and nonswingers rated their marriages as happy or very happy.

Aside from their sexual behavior, many open couples are conservative in both their political and their social attitudes, and their average educational level is higher than that of the general population (Bell et al., 1975; Gilmartin, 1976;

Jenks, 1985). Research with other samples of swingers, however, has shown them to be liberal and nonreligious (Gilmartin, 1974). Obviously, swingers vary in their political and social attitudes just as people in general do.

## Separation and Divorce

The U.S. divorce rate has been on the rise since the advent of the Industrial Revolution (Fisher, 1992). This increase started to level off in the early 1980s, although 64% of recent first marriages still ended in separation or divorce (Martin & Bumpass, 1989). Most industrialized nations have experienced similar patterns, though divorce is more prevalent in the United States than elsewhere (Ahlburg & DeVita, 1992).

Pessimists point to these statistics as reflections of widespread instability, the decline of the family, and moral decay in contemporary society. This concern about the demise of the family is not new. "The family in its old sense is disappearing from our land, and not only our free institutions are threatened but the very existence of our society is endangered" (Cherlin, 1981, pp. 2–3). This appeared in the Boston *Quarterly Review* in 1859.

On the other hand, optimists take a different view, suggesting that the numbers simply underscore high expectations for the quality of marital relationships. We are, they say, unwilling to settle for the "lives of quiet desperation" that have characterized the many marriages held together for the sake of children or religious or financial considerations. Optimists cite another statistic to buttress their point: 70% of divorced people marry a second partner (Ahlburg & DeVita, 1992; Norton & Moorman, 1987). It seems that these people are rejecting a particular spouse but not the institution of marriage.

How is it that two people can enter marriage full of love, hope, and commitment, only to have the relationship dissolve? Although the causes of divorce are complex and there is not enough evidence to answer this question definitively, certain conditions are associated with the longevity of relationships. Age at marriage and educational level are two of the most consistent (White, 1991). Teenage marriages are more than twice as likely to end than are unions of people in their 20s, with the most stable first marriages occurring among women who wed after the age of 30 (Martin &

Bumpass, 1989; Norton & Moorman, 1987). Divorce peaks between the ages of 20 to 24 for both genders in the United States, which is slightly younger than for other societies for which data are available (Fisher, 1992). The proportion of divorces is highest at around the fourth year of marriage in most of the 24 societies that Fisher studied. In the United States the peak is found somewhat earlier, occurring around the third year of marriage (Fisher, 1992; Kurdek, 1993). Divorce then becomes less and less frequent as marriages ripen.

Individuals with less education are also more likely to divorce. This probably occurs because education is positively related to income and other measures of socioeconomic status that are also negatively related to the likelihood of divorce (White, 1991).

Personal characteristics are also related to divorce. A survey of 160 societies indicated that infidelity, particularly by the wife, was the most common reason given for divorce (Betzig, 1989). Infertility was the next most commonly mentioned reason. Cruelty, especially by the husband, ranked third worldwide among reasons for divorce. Although these reasons are closely related to sex and reproduction, divorce in the contemporary United States seems to be less tied to sex and reproductive reasons. Individuals' accounts of their own divorces implicate such factors as substance abuse, infidelity, personal incompatibility, sexual incompatibility, physical and emotional abuse, financial problems, and gender-role disagreements (White, 1991).

## Adjustment to Separation: Who Suffers Most?

Women are stereotypically portrayed as far more dependent on love and marital relationships than are men, and thus more devastated by separation and divorce. The evidence suggests, however, that the responses of men and women to separation and divorce are somewhat more complicated than usually portrayed.

Men are more likely to experience severe depression, psychopathology, and illnesses requiring hospitalization following divorce than are women. Women's reactions are less severe but more frequent and long-lasting; they include mild depression and anxiety about living alone

*Link to 8's Status*

(Kitson & Morgan, 1991; Riessman & Gerstel, 1985). In addition, divorced women may feel helpless, unattractive, isolated, and concerned about loss of status (Hetherington, Cox, & Cox, 1982). In their review of the literature on gender differences in reactions to divorce, Clarke-Stewart and Bailey (1989) point out that the severe problems men experience actually affect only a minority, whereas the majority of divorced women encounter problems with everyday life adjustment.

These differences may have roots in many factors, including the fact that after divorce, a woman's financial resources are reduced by about 30% (Kitson & Morgan, 1991). Related to their standard of living is the greater difficulty that women may experience in finding employment that provides sufficient income following the loss of the husband's paycheck. In divorce settlements, the custody of children is still generally awarded to women, and the responsibility for rearing children single-handedly may restrict the ability of women to pursue new social relationships.

In research designed to identify variables that correlate with positive adjustment to divorce, Clarke-Stewart and Bailey (1989) interviewed divorced women and men, all of whom had custody of their school-age children. Three years following divorce, the men were generally better adjusted psychologically, had more stable and satisfying jobs, and were more financially successful than were the women. Those women who were better adjusted felt that they had received more social support from their friends and family, were more likely to have moved away following the divorce, and experienced less financial stress.

Other research that has examined the relationship of gender-role attitudes and gender identification to a person's adjustment to divorce has consistently shown more positive adjustment among women with egalitarian gender-role attitudes and with androgynous or masculine identities than among more traditional women. Women with identities that incorporated some typically masculine traits were more likely to see divorce as partly the product of their own needs and behaviors than were more feminine women. As might be expected, divorced women with fewer children, a college degree, a comfortable income, and greater levels of ambition were happier than were divorced women with more children and less money, education, and ambition (Granvold et al., 1979; Hansson et al., 1984; Tcheng-Laroche & Prince, 1979).

In general, postdivorce adjustment is probably less related to gender per se than to the extent to which the divorcing couple want the divorce and have a sense of control over their lives and access to personal, social, and economic resources. Thus as women become more independent and gain greater access to resources and satisfying careers, the gender differences in adjustment to divorce may disappear.

After divorce, men and women usually do not become celibate. Even when concerns about contracting AIDS became widespread, only 20% of the separated and 26% of the divorced people in Smith's (1991) national sample reported abstinence during the previous 12 months. The average number of partners in the previous year was 2.41 for the separated people and 1.31 for the divorced people. Further, the number of partners since age 18 for the currently separated was 11.75 and for the currently divorced was 13.30—higher numbers of partners than for single, married, or widowed people. As might be expected, divorced men were more sexually active than were divorced women, and younger divorced people were more sexually active than were older divorced people (Stack & Gundlach, 1992).

Regardless of marital status, at some point during their 40s or 50s, people begin to assess what they have done with the first half of their lives, as they come to grips with the fact that they no longer have the time—and in some cases, the abilities—that they had as young adults. Contemporary Western values, exalting youth and strength, can make it especially difficult to adjust to aging. In the next section, we consider the impact of aging on sexuality.

## Aging and Sexuality

At what point does a person become middle-aged? If you ask a group of friends and relatives at what age one passes from young adulthood into middle age, you will probably get answers ranging from 35 to 50. It is our impression that the specific age chosen as the beginning of middle age (and, for that matter, old age) increases with the age of the respondent, although we know of no systematic research on the topic. A 16-year-old may regard 30 as middle-aged, but few 30-year-olds feel middle-aged!

As we grow older, we become less alike. On most social, psychological, and biological measures, variations among the test scores of older people are significantly greater than are the ranges among the test scores of younger people. As we age, we integrate an increasing number of experiences and develop a broad range of adaptive responses, so there is a gradual accentuation of individuality and uniqueness.

Preliminary research indicates that this general rule applies to the sexual attitudes and repertoires of middle-aged people. The reason why much of our knowledge about the impact of the aging process on sexual expression is preliminary is that most sex research has focused on individuals in late adolescence or early adulthood. The fact that people beyond early adulthood have received only limited research attention is probably due to several factors, including our species' relative inexperience with aging, traditional beliefs about the purposes of sex, and the greater ease of obtaining samples of college students than of older adults.

For most of human existence, relatively few individuals lived to advanced ages. Even in the United States—which, in terms of human history, has existed for an extremely brief period—it is only recently that living beyond age 40 has become commonplace. When the first U.S. census was taken in 1790, half the people in the nation were under 17 years old. It is expected that half of all Americans will be 35 or older by the year 2000, and within about 30 years from that date, the median age will approach 40. According to the Bureau of the Census (1991), a baby born in 1900 had a life expectancy of 47.3 years (46.3 for males and 48.3 for females). A baby born in 1991, however, has an average life expectancy of 73.2 years if male and 79.4 years if female. So in less than one century, an average of about three decades has been added to the American life span.

The second reason for researchers' limited attention to sexuality and aging—traditional beliefs about the purposes of sex—is related to the first. Because life was short and seldom sweet, it was crucial for our ancestors to reproduce as early and as frequently as possible. The historical equation of reproduction with sexuality, strengthened by thousands of years of struggling to survive as a species, may still affect our vision of sexuality. The identification of sexuality with fertility perpetuates the idea that people beyond their reproductive years are sexless. Decreases in reproductive capacity, however, need not eliminate sexual feelings and responsiveness.

For many nonhuman species, reproductive potential continues until death. Our own species has changed this relationship through a variety of life- and health-maintaining medical and nutritional advances. The extension of our life span beyond the years of fertility has permitted us to experience sexuality for purposes having nothing to do with reproduction. The fact that we now have sizable numbers of people beyond their reproductive years, in turn, allows us to examine the relationship between aging and the capacity for sexual expression.

Nonetheless, in North America, sexuality is generally treated as a quality and activity limited to the young. Many older members of society accept this stereotype, and some of them welcome the release from what they perceive to be a burdensome obligation. Other people, however, find that age brings a different kind of release. As one woman put it,

> The older I get, the more I enjoy sex. When I was in my teens and 20s, I spent a lot of time thinking about how I should act and I felt shy about my body. I know that objectively, I was a lot more attractive then than I am now in my late 40s. But I feel so much freer and prettier now that I don't worry about what I'm supposed to do or how I'm supposed to look. Instead of thinking about what my partner thinks of my body, I'm appreciating my body for the pleasure it gives me. (Authors' files)

## The Double Standard of Aging for Women and Men

In our culture, aging is more of a challenge for women than for men, for two reasons. First, be-

**FIGURE 13.6**
**Sexy Sean**
The actor Sean Connery continues to be a box-office draw despite being in his 60s. In contrast, aging actresses often find leading roles difficult to obtain.

**FIGURE 13.7**
**The Golden Age**
Blanche (Rue McClanahan), a character in the television series "The Golden Girls" and "Golden Palace," is shown in a typical scene entertaining a date. The frank conversations of Blanche, Rose, and Dorothy (not to mention Dorothy's mother) suggest that interest in sexuality does not necessarily evaporate as one ages.

cause female reproductive capacity terminates at menopause, whereas male reproductive capacity wanes gradually, women beyond the age of menopause are more likely to be stereotyped as sexless. (If this stereotype were accurate, there would be little reason to study the sexuality of older women.) Second, the physical characteristics regarded as attractive in females—smooth skin, slim physique, firm breasts—tend to decline earlier than the physical qualities considered sexy in men. A man's gray or white hair is often described as distinguished, and the lines on his face, increasing and becoming more deeply etched with age, as bestowing character (Figure 13.6). His sexual value is defined more by power and status than by physical characteristics. In contrast, a woman's physical appearance has traditionally defined her attractiveness.

The visual media not only perpetuate such stereotypes, but they also help to create unrealistic fantasies. Hollywood generally rejects women of 40 as vital sexual beings but hands many romantic leads to men of that age. Actress Joanne Woodward, in a television interview, compared herself to her husband, actor Paul Newman, as follows: "He gets prettier; I get older." But there are signs that this double standard is gradually changing with the aging of the general population. Television shows such as

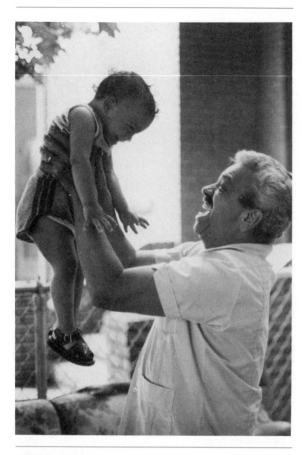

**FIGURE 13.8**
**Generativity Versus Stagnation**
This grandfather's joy in playing with his granddaughter demonstrates a positive resolution of midlife changes. His concern for others helps prevent feelings of stagnation.

"Murphy Brown," starring Candice Bergen in her 40s, "Murder, She Wrote," starring Angela Lansbury in her 60s, and "The Golden Girls," featuring four over-50 women who share a house, are contributing to the portrayal of older women as intelligent, attractive, and sexy (see Figure 13.7).

## Midlife Changes and Assessments

"Midlife crisis" has become a popular phrase. It refers to concern or dissatisfaction in the middle years over one's values and current lifestyle. According to Erikson (1968b), the developmental challenge of this period involves the conflict of generativity versus stagnation. Generativity is expressed not only in involvement with our own children, if we have them, but with children in general: a concern for the future of our species. Successful resolution of this stage requires looking beyond our own goals of personal gratification and yields a sense of intense connection to the well-being of others in our family, community, and nation and to humanity in general (see Figure 13.8). People who do not resolve the crisis of this stage feel little connection with anything beyond their own personal gratification. For such persons, the aging process involves, in Erikson's terminology, stagnation. Failing to form a deep connection with others, these people experience aging simply as an inevitable movement toward loss of physical and personal power and death. Embedded in this period are the biological changes associated with aging.

### Menopause

The average woman experiences *menopause*, the gradual cessation of ovulation and menstruation, at about age 51, although it can occur any time between the ages of 35 and 55. There is usually a seven-year transitional period, known as the perimenopausal stage, characterized by increasing irregularity of menstrual-cycle length and bleeding pattern (Cutler, Garcia, & McCoy, 1987).

One of the most common changes associated with menopause is instability between the cardiovascular and muscle system, which produces fluctuations in the diameter of blood vessels. This fluctuation is the source of the "hot flashes" and sudden sweating that many menopausal women report. Fatigue, depression, and headaches are also common, and some women experience reductions in vaginal lubrication. These symptoms, linked to decreases in estrogen secretion, can persist for several years. The administration of hormone-replacement therapy—usually small doses of estrogen and progesterone—alleviates the unwanted symptoms associated with menopause. Estrogen suppositories or creams placed in the

**menopause**—the cessation of menstruation and the end of a woman's reproductive capacity.

vagina several times a week may also correct estrogen deficiencies. (See Chapter 14 for more information about treatments for negative side effects of menopause.)

Although medical experts once widely agreed that menopausal women experience a declining level of sexual response in correspondence with declining levels of estrogen, more recent studies have found no reduction in arousal during this period (Cutler et al., 1987; Luria & Meade, 1984). Cutler et al. advertised for women to participate in a study of menopause and conducted a series of interviews with the volunteers. To test for levels of estrogen and testosterone secretion, samples of blood plasma were drawn from these women. Participants also kept a prospective diary of the frequency of their sexual activity. (Most research is retrospective—that is, volunteers are asked to remember past events. In prospective measures, participants record events at about the time of their occurrence, and the likelihood of memory errors is lessened.) There was little reduction in vaginal lubrication or sexual arousal for most of the women in the sample, and in general, their sexual arousal patterns were unrelated to their levels of estrogen secretion. Cutler and her colleagues pointed out that the sample comprised relatively well-educated, middle-class women.

The continuance or decline of sexual responsiveness at menopause may be partially a function of a woman's social class. In Hallstrom's (1977) study of 800 women, upper-social-class menopausal women showed less of a decline in sexual interest, capacity for orgasm, and coital frequency than did menopausal women of lower social classes, who revealed age-related deficits in their sexual responses.

In the Cutler et al. (1987) study, although most women's sexuality appeared to be unaffected by menopause and declining levels of estrogen, about 25% of the women had very low estrogen levels, and these individuals were likely to report having sexual activity less than once a week. The design of the Cutler group study does not allow us to determine whether low levels of estrogen cause, or are the result of, low levels of sexual activity, but the findings do suggest that menopause does not bring women's sexual responsiveness to an end.

## Male Menopause?

Questions have arisen regarding whether males experience a menopause in the form of changes in the hormonal relationship between the brain and the gonads, but researchers have drawn no conclusions. A review of the "male menopause" literature found that a significant number of men experience psychological and social difficulties in middle age but these appear to stem from cultural and lifestyle changes rather than from hormonal changes (Fetherstone & Hepworth, 1985).

## Midlife Challenges and Gender Roles

Although many adults experience a time during which they question the value of what they have done and are doing, such soul searching is by no means automatic. The age at onset of such midlife challenges varies, but it tends to occur between 40 and 60. Fear of aging and changes in family relationships as children leave home are associated with the experience of midlife crisis. With the advent of menopause, some women worry that their loss of reproductive capacity renders them useless in a broad range of other areas. People who have perceived themselves as striving toward the future in various realms of their lives may experience some depression as they realize that they have reached a plateau or even the beginnings of decline in job-related activities. Depression may also result from an increase in the frequency of perceived sexual dysfunction, and, as we have seen, some individuals may seek reassurance of their masculinity or femininity through extramarital affairs.

Gender-role inflexibility appears to be associated with difficulties in midlife transitions. The traditional male role requires men to be strong, aggressive, and unemotional—characteristics that are likely to decline during middle age as men experience pronounced changes in themselves and in their families. Rigid adherence to stereotypically masculine characteristics may interfere with midlife adjustment. Men who take on androgynous values and behaviors may find their midlife reassessment easier.

Psychoanalytic theorist Carl Jung (1875–1961) suggested that some characteristics develop in the first half of life at the expense of others that are suppressed. These suppressed characteristics begin to push for expression in middle age. He theorized that as people grow older, former tendencies in their values and even in their bodies are reversed. In fact, there is evidence that gender roles become less important from middle age onward, and that people take on personality attributes traditionally defined as characteristic of the other gender; that is, as men become older, they tend to express their affiliative and nurturant feelings, whereas women become more responsive to and less guilty about their egocentric and assertive impulses (Neugarten & Gutmann, 1968). In traditional societies, women become more assertive as they become older, often becoming more influential in their social groups. Fisher (1992) suggested that biology may play a role. Levels of estrogen decline with menopause, allowing testosterone, which has been linked with assertiveness, to exert greater influence. Psychologically, there is a counterbalancing of personality traits between men and women, and more complex conceptions of what it means to be male and female develop (Sedney, 1985/1986).

This pattern may also hold for sexual motivation. Sprague and Quadagno (1989) found that the proportion of women endorsing physical reasons for coitus increased with age whereas the proportion of men endorsing this motive rose and then declined. The proportion of women reporting a love motive for intercourse declined with age. Thus early gender differences in motives for coitus exhibit some reversals as men and women age.

The physical changes that tend to occur at midlife should affect sexuality, but at present little is known about them. A comparison of Hunt's (1974) and the Kinsey group's (1948, 1953) data suggested that there had been a slight increase in the frequency of reported marital coitus among those between 46 and 60 years of age. Hunt suggested that more liberal attitudes toward sexuality and middle age, as well as a heightened awareness of the variety of coital techniques, was responsible for the increase in marital coitus among the middle-aged. Smith's (1991) data indicated that the average frequency of sexual intercourse during the past year for people aged 40 to 49 was 67 times—that is, more than once a week. From 50 to 59, the average dropped to slightly less than once a week, to 46 acts of coitus

in the previous 12 months. As people advance into old age, the average frequency of intercourse declines further, to 23 times in the past year. However, as seen in the section on old age, there is considerable variation in the sexual practices of elderly people.

## Old Age

When we are less than pleased with something we have done, we typically comfort ourselves with the resolution that we will behave differently in the future. As we enter old age, however, making major changes in personality and lifestyle appears increasingly unrealistic. According to Erikson, the challenge of the last stage of life is to resolve the conflict of integrity versus despair. During self-assessment at this stage, the emphasis is on evaluating the kind of person one has been and the meaning that one's life has had. This evaluative process can produce a sense of satisfaction and integrity. People who have been relatively successful in resolving earlier crises can view their lives as having been purposeful, and the resultant sense of integrity can soften the fear of death. Conversely, the realization that there is not enough time left to try to improve or alter what has been done with one's life may engender a sense of pointlessness and despair. In addition to various psychological changes, aging brings some inevitable physiological changes.

### Physiological Changes in Males

Aging males in species ranging from rodents to humans experience declining levels of testosterone (Hoyenga & Hoyenga, 1993a). With the decline in testosterone secretion, several physiological changes occur. The seminal fluid becomes thinner, and ejaculatory pressure decreases. The prostate gland often enlarges, and its contractions during orgasm weaken. After age 70 the size of the testes begins to decline, as does their firmness, so they do not elevate to the same degree during sexual activity (Handelsman & Staraj, 1985). This decline appears to result from a reduction in the number and size of the interstitial (Leydig) cells, which synthesize and secrete

## Box 13.3

# Aging of the Male Sexual System

1. Males' sexual responsiveness, as measured by ejaculation, masturbation, nocturnal emission, coitus, orgasm, and level of sexual excitement, wanes or declines.

2. Erection of the penis takes longer to occur. The erection can be maintained, however, for extended periods of time without ejaculation.

3. Full erection often does not occur until just before ejaculation.

4. The penis is likely to return to a flaccid state following ejaculation rather than remain erect for a number of minutes.

5. The refractory period between orgasm and subsequent erection and ejaculation increases. After age 60, 12 to 24 hours may

be required before an erection can be attained again.

6. The pleasure associated with ejaculation may decrease because ejaculation may be experienced as seepage rather than forceful expulsion.

7. A single-stage rather than a two-stage ejaculatory response may be experienced.

8. The amount of seminal fluid is markedly reduced.

9. Nipple erection and the sex flush of the skin do not occur as frequently.

10. Secondary erectile dysfunction increases significantly after 50 years of age.

Source: Adapted from Masters & Johnson, 1966.

sex hormones (Schiavi, 1990). The seminiferous tubules, on the other hand, which are the site of sperm production, hold up quite well throughout the aging process. Sperm production is relatively unchanged in older men. There are many cases in which men of advanced age have fathered children. Senator Strom Thurmond of South Carolina, for example, fathered his fourth child at the age of 74.

Changes also occur in the phases of the sexual response cycle (Rowland, Greenleaf, Dorfman, & Davidson, 1993). This is particularly true after the age of 60. Masters and Johnson studied changes in the sexual responses of people from late adolescence to the age of 89. For a summary of their major findings regarding the aging of the male sexual system, see Box 13.3. The changes in response include an increase in the length of time required for erection, penetration, and ejaculation and an extension of the refractory period. An aging male whose penis has been erect for a relatively lengthy period during lovemaking may experience ejaculation as a seeping out of semen rather than a forceful expulsion of seminal fluid.

## Physiological Changes in Females

In women, estrogen production usually begins to decline after age 40, and the decrease continues until about age 60. Women do not appear to experience a reduction in testosterone secretion with aging. With the reduction in estrogen secretion, the vaginal walls of postmenopausal women thin out and no longer have the corrugated appearance of a younger woman's vagina. As the vagina's acidic secretions diminish, the possibility of infection increases. The rate and amount of vaginal lubrication also diminish, although Masters and Johnson (1966) reported exceptions to this rule. Women who were consistently sexually active—having coitus once or twice a week—showed no decline in vaginal lubrication.

Breast tissue atrophies somewhat as the glandular material is slowly replaced by fibrous tissue. Further, the reduced secretion of estrogen after menopause can lead to osteoporosis, or bone deterioration, and many physicians now recommend hormonal-replacement therapy to reduce

### Box 13.4

## Aging of the Female Sexual System

1. The vagina decreases in length and width.

2. The vagina loses some of its elasticity and ability to expand.

3. The vaginal walls become thin and light pinkish in color, in contrast to their earlier thick and reddish appearance.

4. The rate and amount of vaginal lubrication diminishes, sometimes making sexual intercourse painful or difficult.

5. The uterus and cervix shrink in size.

6. Uterine cramping or contractions may make intercourse painful.

7. An urgent need to urinate is frequently experienced after intercourse.

8. Vaginal burning or irritation and pain centered around the pelvis may be experienced in association with sexual activities.

9. Nipple erection during sexual intercourse loses some of its intensity.

10. The sex flush of the skin does not occur as frequently.

11. Vaginal contractions during orgasm last for a shorter period of time.

Source: Adapted from Masters & Johnson, 1966.

the risk of osteoporosis (see Chapter 14). For a summary of other results obtained in Masters and Johnson's observation of the aging process in women, see Box 13.4.

## Social Stereotypes and Self-Image

Social and psychological factors can either diminish or enhance the effects of aging. As noted earlier, our culture widely defines youth as "sexy" and middle age—particularly in women—as "sexless." However, as our elderly population increases, and as we learn more about sexuality among the aged, social recognition and acceptance of the sensual appeal of older people may become more common. In the early 1990s, several groups of older women were featured in talk shows and in live performances around the United States, including the Sensuous Seniors and the Dancing Grannies, who dressed in body suits and performed aerobic dancing to popular music. Ranging in age from their 50s to their 70s, these women appeared to be more agile than many adolescents and young adults. In addition to altering stereotypes about aging women, the vigorous exercise regimen followed by the Dancing Grannies probably has beneficial effects on

their self-esteem and physical health. They were not seeking to portray themselves as young women. Instead, their goal was to demonstrate that elderly women can be sensuous, healthy, and vibrant.

Part of our cultural aversion to perceiving and portraying aging individuals' eroticism may stem from the fact that we identify older people with our parents. Support for the rather Freudian idea that our parents' sexuality may make us uneasy comes from Pocs and Godow's (1976) study of college students' perceptions of the extent of their parents' sexual activity. Because these researchers had no data on the actual sexual activity of the parents of the 646 student participants, they used figures from Kinsey's research. As discussed earlier, contemporary middle-aged and elderly people appear to be more sexually active than were individuals in Kinsey's sample. However, the college students' estimates of their parents' sexual activity were considerably lower than those suggested even by Kinsey's findings. For example, whereas more than half the students thought that their parents engaged in coitus once a month or less, Kinsey found that parents in that age range (41–45 for married women, 45–50 for married men) had coitus about seven times a month. There were even greater discrepancies for such activities as oral-genital stimulation and extramarital sexual relations. Yet the vast majority (90%) of the students thought that their parents were happily married and still in love. They also seemed to believe that their parents' sexual activity played only a minor role in achieving this blissful state.

Hypothesizing that students' low estimates of their parents' sexual activity might be rooted in the failure of many parents to discuss sexuality with their offspring, Murnen and Allgeier (1985) asked students to report how frequently their parents had discussed various aspects of sexuality with them as they were growing up. The more communication about sex that students received from their parents, the higher their estimates of parents' frequency of sexual activity.

In sum, our culture has traditionally propagated stereotypes suggesting that individuals become sexually inactive in their middle and senior years. The persistence of such ideas may make people feel guilt or worry if they continue to have sexual feelings as they advance into and beyond middle age. But just how widespread is termination of sexual expression during old age?

## Aging and Sexual Expression in Both Genders

Older people's sexual activity generally follows the patterns established in younger years. If sex has been a source of caring and comfort, it can provide warmth and security in advanced years. But if sex has caused conflict or pain—or if a person has seldom been interested in or rewarded by sexual activity—old age can represent a welcome opportunity to end sexual relations. Of course, for some elderly people, sexual interactions end because they lack a partner. There is evidence indicating a steady decline in frequency of sexual activity with age (see Table 13.3). However, this pattern varies considerably from one person to the next (Karlen, 1994).

The average man's sexual responsiveness diminishes as he ages. Kinsey et al. (1948) found no other factor for men that affected the frequency of total sexual outlet as much as age. They defined total sexual outlet in terms of six sources of orgasm: masturbation, nocturnal emission, heterosexual petting, heterosexual intercourse, ho-

mosexual relations, and intercourse with other species. The median frequency of orgasm per week from all these sources reached a peak in the late teens and then dropped steadily until age 60. This trend continues into the 70s for sexual intercourse (Smith, 1991).

Perhaps the most noteworthy characteristic of the waning frequency of sexual expression in men is its gradualness. Botwinick (1978) found that, until age 60, the rate of decrease in total sexual outlet from one five-year interval to the next remains the same.

It is more difficult to assess women's sexual expression over the life cycle than men's, for several reasons. First, for unmarried women, societal restrictions tend to inhibit coital activity. Second, for married women, coital activity is likely to be influenced by a husband's sexual inclinations, which show a decline over time. A third complication in measuring female sexuality through the years is that women tend to have orgasm less consistently than do men, who rarely fail to have orgasm during sexual stimulation.

The largest survey to date on sexuality and the elderly relied on responses to a questionnaire appearing in *Consumer Reports* (Brecher, 1984). Although those who could not read or who were sick and disabled were not represented in the sample, the study still provided a wealth of information about the potential for sexuality in later life. Among the many findings was the fact that 59% of the men and 65% of the women 70 years or older still engage in sexual intercourse, and half of them make love at least once a week. Some of the other findings are presented in Table 13.3. It is apparent that many people in this age range remain sexually active, although at a gradually diminishing rate. Sexual activity was not limited to the marital bedroom. Almost 25% of the husbands and 8% of the wives reported that they had engaged in extramarital sex at least once after age 50.

## Decreasing Sexual Activity: Aging or Other Factors?

People tend to assume that aging persons lose their capacity for sexual arousal and response as a result of the physiological changes described earlier. However, given variations in the extent to which sexual expression diminishes or disappears

**TABLE 13.3 Sexual Activity in Those 50 Years of Age and Older**

|  | In Their 50s | 60s | 70 and Over |
|---|---|---|---|
| *Men who masturbate* | 66% | 50% | 43% |
| Frequency of masturbation per week for these men | 1.2 | 0.8 | 0.7 |
| *Husbands who have sex with their wives* | 87% | 78% | 59% |
| Frequency of sex per week for these men | 1.3 | 1.0 | 0.6 |
| *Women who masturbate* | 47% | 37% | 33% |
| Frequency of masturbation per week for these women | 0.7 | 0.6 | 0.7 |
| *Wives who have sex with their husbands* | 88% | 76% | 65% |
| Frequency of sex per week for these women | 1.3 | 1.0 | 0.6 |

Source: Brecher, 1984.

among the aged, researchers have hypothesized that several nonphysiological factors may determine whether sexual expression continues.

One difficulty with research demonstrating a decline in sexual activity over the course of middle and late adulthood is that it is generally cross-sectional; that is, different age groups are surveyed or interviewed at the same point in time. Variations in sexual interest and activity between 30-year-olds and 60-year-olds are then often assumed to be a function of age. These differences, however, may be a function of the time periods during which the groups received their early socialization and value orientations. For example, women growing up in the 1930s were socialized to show little sexual interest or enjoyment, and therefore their frequency of sexual activity may always have been low. In contrast, women reared in the 1960s were exposed to much more permissive attitudes concerning sexuality and may feel freer to respond to their own sexual desires; thus their frequency of sexual activity may be higher. If we were to compare these two groups of women in the 1990s, we might be inclined to attribute their differences in frequency of sexual activity to age rather than to their having been brought up in different historical periods.

The findings of a group of Duke University scientists support the hypothesis that the perceived decline in sexual interest and activity over the second half of life is at least partially a reflection of generational differences rather than an age-related decline. In a longitudinal study of married couples ranging in age from 60 to 94 (George & Weiler, 1981; Newman & Nichols, 1960; Pfeiffer et al., 1968; Verwoerdt et al., 1969), researchers found that patterns of sexual activity remained more stable in middle and later life than was previously thought. Frequency of sexual intercourse for a sample of 278 married couples ranging in age from 46 to 71 years was also studied over a six-year period. The study showed that the frequency of sexual intercourse remained remarkably stable over the six-year period for the group: only about 8% of the men and 15% of the women reported a cessation of sexual activities. In keeping with Kinsey's observation about the frequency of marital intercourse being dependent on men, both men and women in this study attributed the responsibility for ending sexual activity to the male partner.

Although the Duke scientists found a progressive decline in the frequency of sexual expression with advancing age, they also discovered great variations in sexual capacity among their older volunteers. The ability to engage in sexual activity has been reported among 70-, 80-, and 90-year-old people (Brecher, 1984; Karlen, 1994; Weizman & Hart, 1987). After age 80, the most common sexual activity for both men and women was touching and caressing without sexual intercourse, followed by masturbation, and then sexual intercourse (Bretschneider & McCoy, 1988). Sexual activity appears to be associated with two other factors in addition to physiological capability: past sexual activity and opportunity.

The pattern of sexual behavior observed in the Duke group's elderly volunteers appeared to be a continuation of their tendencies toward greater or lesser sexual activity during their younger years. This observation is supported by Masters and Johnson (1966) and Schiavi (1990). The admonition that one should maintain a regular program of physical exercise to be physically fit in later years ("use it or lose it") appears to apply to sexual capacities as well. Volunteers in the Duke studies who engaged in sexual activity relatively frequently during early adulthood and middle age were more sexually active during old age than were volunteers who were less sexually active during their youth and middle age.

Comparisons of married women and single women showed little reported difference in the extent of their sexual interest, but there was more sexual activity among the married women, probably because of the availability of a partner (Pfeiffer et al., 1968; Verwoerdt et al., 1969). Nonavailability of a partner is one of the major obstacles to sexual interaction for heterosexual women during middle and old age (see Figure 13.9). There are almost six times as many widowed women as widowed men in the United States (U.S. Bureau of the Census, 1993). The ratio of unattached older women to unattached older men is further unbalanced by the tendency of men in our society to marry younger women. This may have implications for longevity. Both men and women married to younger spouses tend to live longer than those married to older spouses (Klinger-Vartabedian & Wispe, 1989). It is difficult to determine, however, whether this occurs because healthier or more vigorous older people choose or are chosen by younger people, or because marriage to a younger person is somehow conducive to a longer life. Among couples in which there are age differences, it may be that a sense of one's place in the life cycle is affected by the age of one's spouse. One may feel younger by being married to a younger spouse.

**FIGURE 13.9**
**Lack of Opportunity**
Many older women do not have men their own age with whom to be sexually intimate.

You may have heard people claim that couples who have been married for a long time grow to resemble one another. Zajonc, Adelman, Murphy, & Niedenthal (1987) predicted that spouses develop similar appearances in part because of mimicry; that is, nonverbal expressions of emotions such as smiles, frowns, and grimaces are mimicked or copied by spouses as they relate to others. In long-term relationships, then, partners may grow to look alike as they develop similar smile or frown lines, postures, and movements (see Figure 13.10). If outward appearance is altered through social and biological interplay, it may be that factors influencing aging and mortality can also be affected.

## Retirement

Studies of the effects of retirement on marriage have centered primarily on the division of household tasks and on changes in gender-role differentiation. These studies show a shift toward expressive behavior by both the husband and wife; that is, the husband shifts from the instrumental

**FIGURE 13.10**
**Marriage and Mimicry**
Partners in long-term relationships often begin to resemble one another.

role of provider to what for him is a more expressive role of helping to take care of the house. Traditionally, the wife moves from her formerly instrumental role of homemaker toward the more expressive role of understanding companion. Whether a retired husband who shares in household tasks is comfortable about these activities probably depends on his value system. If a man considers "woman's work" demeaning, then he is unlikely to participate in it. This pattern is already changing as more and more nontraditional people retire.

Retirement erodes one of the key bases for midlife gender typing. For both men and women, retirement can mean a loss of status in the larger society, which values financial independence and personal achievement. Many people view retirement as a threat to their identity. If their sexuality is seen as an extension of this identity, it will probably suffer. Men or women who view their retirement as a loss of power may experience a corresponding loss of sexual appeal.

Retired people have more free time than they did in their work years, and the transition from the structured world of work can be difficult. In a traditional relationship, a husband's retirement can be a mixed blessing for a wife: she may enjoy his companionship but resent his interruption of the household routines that she has established. For couples who continue to be sexually intimate, however, retirement creates the possibility for greater spontaneity in sexual interactions because of the couple's increased leisure time. We can only speculate about how individuals react to this potential because we have little empirical evidence on the relationship between sexuality and retirement.

### Death of One's Mate

The death of a spouse can be devastating for the remaining partner. Interviews conducted with more than 700 widowed Americans revealed that the levels of depression of widowed men were greater than those of widowed women (Umberson, Wortman, & Kessler, 1992). However, the researchers concluded that gender was probably a less important predictor of depression following the death of a spouse than were the different ways in which men and women are affected by widowhood. Specifically, women's depression was primarily associated with financial strain, whereas men's depressiom was related to problems with household management.

Men have an easier time than women in establishing a relationship with a new partner because of the gender differences in mortality rates. In 1991 there were approximately 14 million widowed persons in the United States; 12 million of these were women (U.S. Bureau of the Census, 1993). The median age for widowhood was 49. In view of the preponderance of widows, many elderly women who wish to be sexually active must either have affairs with married men or masturbate if they are unwilling to be a part of a polygynous relationship or unable to change their sexual orientation. Although older women are increasingly open to masturbation as a sexual outlet, masturbation cannot satisfy the need for sexual intimacy in widows who experienced close sexual relations in their marriages (Kansky, 1986). More attention should be devoted to the question of satisfying the needs of the three out of four wives who eventually become widows.

### Institutionalization

Approximately 5% of Americans over 65 are confined to convalescent homes and other institutions (Ahlburg & DeVita, 1992). Until recently, little attention had been paid to their sexual needs. Institutionalized people often encounter regimented environments in which they are assumed to possess the judgment of young children. Institutional design and planning seem to be based on the belief that the institutionalized aged have no interest in sexual activity. Residents who attempt to express sexual needs often are

**FIGURE 13.11**
**Tactile Comfort and Aging**
Touch is as important for the old as for the young.

characterized as "acting out" or suffering from "senile psychosis." However, many residents of convalescent homes retain their interest in intimacy and sexual activity (Bullard-Poe, Powell, & Mulligan, 1994; Mulligan & Palguta, 1991). Typically, staff members have little knowledge of the sexuality of aging, and their ignorance leads to prohibitions or constraints on the most moderate forms of sexual expression. Even tactile comfort is unavailable to many nursing-home residents (see Figure 13.11). Genevay (1975), who observed residents and staff in a nursing home for three months, saw only one incident in which one resident touched another in a sexual way.

The elderly have the right to a living arrangement that allows for the possibility of sexual interaction. Whether an individual chooses to take advantage of the possibility of sexual interaction is, of course, up to him or her. But for those who do, the interaction may be beneficial; one study showed that a gender-integrated living arrangement in a New York City nursing home was associated with increased sexual contacts, a more cheerful atmosphere, and improved self-care (Silverstone & Wynter, 1975).

We hope that, as more attention is focused on meeting the needs of convalescent-home dwellers, administrators will adapt the structures of their institutions to allow for the satisfaction of those needs. Residents whose lives are still enhanced by sexuality should have the opportunity to engage in sexual play in a dignified and private environment. Staff may even find that for some, sexual contact can more effectively treat depression and anxiety than can the drugs so pervasively prescribed in these environments.

More than the sum of biological drives, the erotic impulse is an expression of basic desires for human contact, love, and life itself. The erotic impulse may be a fundamental expression of an appetite for life; starvation of this appetite through premature denial of our continuing erotic impulses may contribute to feelings of isolation and despair. Correlational data support this speculation: older persons who have intimate relationships are more likely than those who do not to enjoy high levels of both objective and self-perceived well-being. These findings suggest that sexual feelings and expression should be nurtured rather than suppressed. Healthful activities during their younger years may help individuals who wish to be sexy, sensuous seniors to increase their likelihood of achieving that goal. In the next chapter, we discuss approaches to enhancing sexual health throughout the life span.

# Summary of Major Points _____

1. **The double standard, sex, and relationship outcomes.**

The sexual double standard—the idea that certain sexual behaviors are more acceptable for one gender than for the other—is showing signs of diminishing. It is now equally acceptable for women and men to engage in sexual intimacy. However, men are still expected to show more initiative in these relationships than are women. Longitudinal research suggests that the point in a relationship at which a couple becomes sexually intimate is unrelated to the likelihood that the relationship will last, at least over a two-year period.

2. **Young adulthood and sexual-lifestyle choices.**

The decision to remain single for varying lengths of time, or permanently, is becoming more acceptable. Choosing singleness does not necessarily mean choosing celibacy. In general, cohabiting individuals do not differ greatly from people who opt to marry before living together. The primary differences appear to be a greater likelihood of flexibility in gender roles and more sexual experience beginning at an earlier age among those who cohabit.

3. **Marriage.**

Contrary to cultural myths regarding the timing of and the roles involved in marriage and parenthood, the majority of contemporary women, regardless of whether they have children, are employed outside the home. The decades since the 1960s have been a period of transition in social attitudes about the tasks and roles of spouses.

4. **Parenthood and sexuality.**

Although children can provide immense satisfaction to a couple, they also appear to have a rather dampening effect on the flexibility of a husband and wife's timing of sexual expression. The presence of children also reduces the frequency of a couple's sexual interaction.

5. **Long-term relationships.**

Sexual satisfaction appears to be less important to perceptions of marital satisfaction as people get older. In general, discord or arguments are not necessarily detrimental to younger couples' marital satisfaction, particularly if couples make love with equal or greater frequency than they fight. Sexual monotony and boredom can be problematic in long-term relationships if couples develop rigid and highly predictable patterns of relating to each other.

6. **Nonmarital relations.**

Disapproval of extramarital sex remains high in the United States. There is evidence, however, that substantial numbers of men and women have been sexually intimate with people other than their spouses. Most married people who have extramarital encounters do so without the agreement, approval, or knowledge of their spouses, but a small number of people engage in consensual extramarital sex, in which both spouses agree to a sexually nonexclusive relationship. Research conducted at the end of the 1980s indicates that Americans have begun to reduce their involvement in extramarital affairs.

7. **Separation and divorce.**

Almost two-thirds of contemporary first marriages end in separation or divorce. A small proportion of divorced men tend to have serious reactions that are more severe than those experienced by women. However, a larger proportion of women than men suffer minor adjustment problems, many linked to access to economic resources and control over their lives. Most men and women are sexually active after divorce, and the majority eventually remarry.

8. **Cultural attitudes toward aging.**

Our society is youth-oriented in its views of what constitutes eroticism, and we tend to equate sexual functioning with reproductive ability, particularly in women. Our perception of sexuality developed in historical periods in which few people reached what we now call middle age. With increased longevity, we must reduce the association of reproductive value with erotic value so that it does not obscure our perception of the pleasure of sexual intimacy during the second half of life. No longer goaded by cultural imperatives to reproduce, mature adults can expand their notions of what it means to be sensuous and erotic. Ironically, at the very age at which we start to experience the beginnings of decline in some of our physiological capacities, an increase in leisure time presents us with the opportunity to become more sensuous and complete beings.

9. **Midlife changes.**

During one's 40s and 50s, physiological changes, which occur more gradually in men than in women, interact with the psychological awareness of being middle-aged. A double standard of aging has led postmenopausal women to be viewed as having lost their erotic appeal, while men continue to be considered sexy as they gain status and power with age.

10. **Sexual expression among the elderly.**

There is considerable variation in the frequency of sexual expression among elderly people. On the basis of cross-sectional data, it has been assumed that the frequency of sexual activity declines steadily with age. Recent longitudinal research, however, indicates that people who enjoy frequent sexual stimulation and interaction during middle age show relatively little decline in sexual expression as they age. There is some reduction in the speed of arousal and orgasmic response, but the frequency of sexual contact among elderly people who choose to remain sexually active is quite stable. Both men and women generally attribute cessation of couples' sexual interaction to a decision made by the man, not by the woman. Correlational data indicate greater health, life satisfaction, and general well-being among elderly people who are sexually active and have intimate relationships than among those who do not engage in sex.

## Review of Key Concepts _____

1. Which of the following stereotypes is not often associated with single lifestyles? a) promiscuous; b) gay; c) attractive; d) emotionally unstable. (pp. 419–420)

2. When compared to noncohabitors, cohabitors generally have been found to: a) be less educated; b) attend church more frequently; c) have longer relationships with their partners; d) both a and b. (p. 421)

3. Research has indicated that employed husbands: a) spend as much time at family work as their wives do if the latter are employed; b) decrease the amount of time they spend at family work if their wives are employed; c) spend more time at family work if their wives are unemployed; d) have begun to increase their contribution to family work. (pp. 424–426)

4. Sexual problems have less impact on the quality of the marital relationship among: a) young couples; b) middle-aged couples; c) older couples; d) none of the above. (pp. 427–428)

5. In some species, a male will copulate with a sexually receptive female and then stop; but if a new receptive female appears, he becomes sexually active again. This phenomenon is known as: a) animal adultery; b) the Coolidge effect; c) satyriasis; d) pan-specific hypersexuality. (p. 428)

6. Most Americans disapprove of extramarital sex. True or false? (p. 429)

7. In general, swingers, when compared to married couples who do not swing: a) report less marital satisfaction; b) use drugs and alcohol more frequently; c) are more similar than dissimilar on most attitudinal and behavioral characteristics; d) are more likely also to engage in covert extramarital affairs. (pp. 433–434)

8. Which of these is related to divorce rates? a) marital age; b) educational level; c) political affiliation; d) both a and b. (pp. 434–435)

9. Women tend to suffer more adjustment difficulties after a relationship ends than do men. True or false, and why? (p. 434)

10. Erikson's developmental crisis of the midlife years involves: a) integrity versus despair; b) sexuality versus money; c) identity versus role confusion; d) generativity versus stagnation. (p. 438)

11. Menopause: a) is the end of a woman's menstrual cycle and reproductive capacity; b) can occur between the ages of 35 and 55 but occurs at age 51 in the average woman; c) is not necessarily accompanied by a reduction in vaginal lubrication or sexual arousal; d) all of the above. (pp. 438–439)

12. Recent longitudinal studies of older married couples suggest that patterns of sexual activity remain more constant than Kinsey et al. found. True or false? (pp. 444–445)

# Enhancing Sexual Health

In their book *Healthy Pleasures* (1989), Robert Ornstein and David Sobel maintained that pleasurable activities are linked to human health and well-being. Ornstein, a psychologist, and Sobel, a physician, have studied particularly healthy and robust people. These individuals tend to ignore standard advice about exercise and diet but have a sense of optimism and an orientation toward pleasure. Ornstein and Sobel emphasized the importance for good health of engaging in enjoyable pursuits such as sex, eating good food, and engaging in playful behavior. They reported that 20 minutes of sexual activity is not only fun but can burn 110 calories!

When Ornstein and Sobel asked sex researchers to explain why sex is good for you, the response was stunned silence. Relatively little research has directly investigated the relationship between sexuality and health. In this chapter, we explore what evidence does exist connecting sexuality to psychological and physical health. Sexual self-esteem and issues related to body image are considered. We describe the effect of impairment, illness, and disease on sexual and reproductive functioning. The role of various substances believed by some to enhance or reduce sexual desire is discussed, as well as the influence of alcohol and drugs on sexual responsiveness. All these factors may interact to affect our sexual well-being and health.

## The Link Between Sexuality and Psychological and Physical Health

People sometimes dichotomize health and speak of an individual as being either healthy or sick. If you reflect on your own experience, however, you are probably aware that at various points you are feeling more or less healthy or ill. In this chapter, we consider human functioning as existing along a continuum. At one end, healthwise, the individual feels utterly on top of the world. At the other end, he or she is totally nonfunctional. Between these two extremes, a person can experience a range of feelings that are a function of the interactions among physiological, psychological, and social factors. For example, at the same time, you may feel physically lethargic because of a flu attack, euphoric over learning that a person to whom you are sexually attracted is attracted to you, and anxious that your parents are irritated by your plans to spend spring break with friends rather than with them.

In more general terms, as we shall see, the potential for a health problem to affect sexuality may also vary as a function of

1. when the problem arises—at birth, during childhood, in adolescence, or during adulthood;

2. whether the health threat is acute or chronic; and

3. what the individual's attitudes about and experiences with sexuality are prior to the onset of a disease or disability.

To use a concrete example, a child growing up in an impoverished area usually has greater exposure to drugs, family disruptions, and street crime, but more limited access to health care and good nutrition than does a child brought up in an affluent area. The accidents of birth that deposit infants into a particular socioeconomic stratum can have an enormous impact on their future physical and mental health and on their attitudes about their sexuality. Similarly, people afflicted with a disease or disability at birth or later in life can experience the world and their own sexuality differently, depending on how they perceive and feel about certain illnesses or medical conditions.

**FIGURE 14.1**

**Self-Esteem and Family Relationships**
President Clinton has talked a number of times about the importance of his mother's emotional support in his achievements. The relationship that they had illustrates the contribution that such support makes in helping us to experience a sense of our own self-esteem.

Our feelings, in turn, may also be affected by the extent to which our social environment is stable and supportive (see Figure 14.1).

### Sexual Self-Esteem

A key ingredient of psychological health is self-esteem—valuing oneself and one's qualities positively. Self-esteem can be high in some areas and low in others. For example, you may feel confident about your interpersonal skills but be less sure of yourself when it comes to speaking publicly or performing in athletic events.

People also vary in their *sexual* self-esteem. More than a decade ago, Hendrick and Hendrick (1983) described the concept of sexual esteem and how it may relate to our general feelings about

**Box 14.1**

## Sexual Self-Esteem

To respond to the short form (Wiederman & Allgeier, 1993) of the Sexuality Scale (Snell & Papini, 1989), place a number corresponding to the following scale in the blank before each number.

Disagree  −2  −1  0  +1  +2  Agree

### Sexual Esteem

____I am a good sexual partner.

____I would rate my sexual skill quite highly.

____I think of myself as a very good sexual partner.

____I would rate myself low as a sexual partner. (R)

____I am confident about myself as a sexual partner.

### Sexual Depression

____I am depressed about the sexual aspects of my life.

____I feel good about my sexuality. (R)

____I am disappointed about the quality of my sex life.

____I feel down about my sex life.

____I feel pleased with my sex life. (R)

### Sexual Preoccupation

____I think about sex all the time.

____I think about sex more than anything else.

____I tend to be preoccupied with sex.

____I am constantly thinking about having sex.

____I think about sex a great deal of the time.

In actual administration of this measure, items for each factor (that is, esteem, depression, and preoccupation) are intermingled. The R next to an item means that it should be reverse-scored. That is, if you gave it a +1, you should give it a −1 in adding up your score.

---

ourselves: "Our personal self-concept is affected by the way we accept the bodily aspect of our sexual nature. Many people comfortably accept sexuality as a part of their nature and like themselves as sexual beings. Such liking in turn feeds into a heightened sense of general self-esteem" (p. 143). Two measures of sexual self-esteem have been developed: the Sexuality Scale (Snell & Papini, 1989) and the Sexual Self-Concept Scale (Winter, 1988). The Sexuality Scale is a 28-item measure evaluating three factors: sexual esteem, sexual depression, and sexual preoccupation (Snell & Papini, 1989, p. 257). Snell and Papini believe that all three of these sexual tendencies (esteem, preoccupation, and depression) are linked to prior learning experiences related to human sexuality. A short form of the Sexuality Scale has been developed (see Box 14.1).

The Sexual Self-Concept Scale measures an individual's evaluation of personal sexual thoughts, feelings, and actions (Winter, 1988). Initially designed to study the relationship between feeling positive about one's sexuality and using contraceptives, this 14-item scale contains such statements as "I consider myself emotionally ready for a sexual relationship" and "I couldn't discuss birth control with my boyfriend/girlfriend without feeling terribly uncomfortable."

Using the Sexuality Scale in research with college students, Snell and Papini (1989) found that for both genders, scores on sexual esteem and sexual depression were negatively correlated; that is, the higher the esteem score, the lower the depression score. However, for women, sexual preoccupation was positively correlated with sexual esteem. In contrast, for men, sexual preoccupation was positively correlated with sexual depression. The authors speculated that these differences may be related to recent trends in thinking about gender and human sexuality. That is, the more comfortable women are with their sexuality—the higher their sexual esteem—the more frequently their thoughts turn to sex. For men, the relationship between sexual depression and sexual preoccupation may stem from an attempt to compensate for feelings of sexual inadequacy: concentrating on their sexuality perhaps allows men to feel better about an unhappy sex life. More recent research with college students indicated that men scored higher than did women on both the sexual esteem and sexual preoccupation scales (Wiederman & Allgeier, 1993).

Winter's (1988) scale has been used in studies of both high school and college students, and Winter found that participants with higher scores were more likely to employ contraception. Age was also linked to a positive sexual self-concept: older students had higher scores than did younger students. This finding supported Winter's expectation that sexual self-esteem increases throughout adolescence.

Research is needed to determine whether sexual self-esteem is related to other healthy sexual practices. For example, we would expect that people with high sexual esteem would be less likely to engage in sexual coercion; more likely to ask for what they want sexually and thus less likely to have dissatisfying and dysfunctional sexual relationships; and less likely to contract sexually transmitted diseases than individuals with low sexual esteem. What other potential benefits of sexual esteem might researchers test?

For many people, self-esteem and a sense of well-being are intimately tied to their physical appearance, particularly their body image, to which we turn now.

## Body Image and Sexuality

Body image refers to the way a person perceives his or her physical appearance. Fisher (1986, 1989) has shown that, like a geographer developing a map of the world, people construct "body maps." The evolution of an individual's body image begins in childhood and is related to the prevailing cultural ethos.

In North American culture, as in many other Western cultures, we experience some discomfort with our body in its natural state. Elaborate rules and conventions dictate how the body is to be decorated, wrapped, or changed to render it socially acceptable. To achieve an ideal body image, a male might, for example, be circumcised and tattooed. He might paint himself or totally cover his body with clothes. Western cultures have a long history of seeing the human body as a disreputable object. This attitude obviously influences the ways in which a child will come to view his or her own body. And intimately related to body image are parallel concerns with those parts of the body that are sexual. As described in Chapter 12, children are subjected to a variety of myths designed to suppress their sexuality. The more destructive of these may lead to serious distortions of body image such as those seen in anorexia nervosa and obesity (Fisher, 1989; Thompson, 1992).

Body image is also affected in our culture by a heavy emphasis on physical attractiveness, particularly during adolescence and young adulthood. In the quest to be sexually appealing, women may enlarge or reduce their breasts, subject themselves to severe diets, suction fat from their stomachs or buttocks, wear restrictive and uncomfortable shoes and clothes, and change their hair color. Many White men and women slather tanning creams on themselves and lie in the sun or in tanning salons to obtain a more desirable skin color, despite the fact that these practices are linked to the subsequent development of skin cancer. Our attempts to "improve" our body image may have implications for sexual behavior. Faith and Schare (1993) found that college students who perceive their bodies in more negative terms describe themselves as less sexually active than do those students with better body images.

As we shall see in Chapter 16, the advertising industry exploits, and to some extent promotes, our cultural preoccupation with physical appearance. Insofar as such concern encourages us to eat a balanced diet, exercise regularly, and incorporate other healthful behaviors into our lifestyles, this emphasis may have positive effects on our general health and, in turn, on our sexual health.

### Exercise, Physical Fitness, and Sexuality

Surprisingly little is known about the relationship between physical fitness and sexuality. It seems logical to assume that the more physically fit your body is, the more responsive to sexual stimulation you become, all other things being equal. For instance, as people age, the body begins to lose its efficiency regarding such vital areas as lung capacity, heart rate, and kidney function. As we saw in Chapter 13, sexual activity also declines with age. Could this decline be offset by diet and exercise? Long-term exercise results in increased blood flow to all organs, including the genitals.

White, Case, McWhirter, and Mattison (1990) assessed the relationship between exercise, physical fitness, and sexuality among middle-aged sedentary men. They compared the effects of nine months of aerobic exercise by these men with a control group of men who participated in organized walking at a moderate pace. The men kept daily diaries during the first and last months of the program. As in previous studies, aerobic exercise increased physical fitness by decreasing coronary heart disease risk factors. Sexual activity such as coitus and masturbation as well as percentage of satisfying orgasms increased more for the exercisers than for the control group. Within the exercising group, moreover, the more physically fit the man, the more sexually responsive he was. Thus it appears that increased physical fitness enhances sexual responsiveness in middle-aged men with a sedentary lifestyle. Obviously, similar research needs to be conducted with women and with other age groups to see if the relationship between fitness and sexual responsiveness holds for them.

### Eating and Sexuality

Our modern culture is especially preoccupied with a rage to be thin, although the ideal of slimness is a relatively recent phenomenon. Freedman (1986) maintained that female beauty as personified by slimness has been an ideal in Western cultures for only 60 of the past 600 years. In contrast, between the years 1400 and 1700 the maternal role was idealized and fat was considered both fashionable and erotic.

How are people of above-average weight affected by the fact that most North Americans associate slimness with physical attractiveness and heaviness with unattractiveness? Do they perceive themselves as unappealing and undesirable? The answer seems to be yes, if we look at the million-plus people who participate in weekly group weight-reduction programs in the United States. Most of these individuals' fear of fat centers on physical appearance, not on health (Cash & Brown, 1989; Ornstein & Sobel, 1989; Rothblum, 1990), and this outlook is more characteristic of women than of men. And women have distorted views of what constitutes ideal weight: even at normal body weight, women are twice as likely as men to regard themselves as overweight (Cash & Hicks, 1990). Rosen and Gross (1987) found that 63% of high school girls were dieting the day they were surveyed, compared with 16% of high school boys. Most of the students in this survey were nonobese by standard measures.

Current societal pressure to be thin evokes a widespread dissatisfaction with body size even among persons (especially women) of average weight. Those who attempt to achieve slimness through dieting and exercise can experience frustration. In a review of the literature, Rothblum (1990) found that dieting and exercise, alone or in combination, usually result in minimal weight loss.

Despite a great deal of speculation and clinical observation, there has been little empirical research on the relationship between obesity and sexuality. For example, observers have variously explained overeating as a substitute for love or an expression of unsatisfied sexual desire, and being overweight as a way to avoid sex and intimacy, a means by which a woman can control her fear of promiscuity, or a substitute for pregnancy (Abramson & Catalano, 1985; Thompson, 1992). Although these may represent some underlying causes of obesity in people undergoing therapy, we have almost no information about the vast majority of obese people who are not in

**FIGURE 14.2**
**Anorexia and Distortions in Body Image**
This painting was done by a woman with anorexia during a severe stage of her illness.

therapy. However, to the extent that physical attractiveness and access to sexual interactions are viewed as the rewards of slimness, obese individuals may feel inadequate.

In its extreme form, concern with—and distortion of—body image is associated with such eating disorders as *anorexia nervosa* and *bulimia*. Anorexia nervosa was described as early as 1873 as "l'anorexie hysterique" ("hysterical anorexia") and was attributed to maladjusted psychosexual development (Coovert, Kinder, &

**anorexia nervosa**—a disorder characterized by weight loss leading to maintenance at less than 85% of expected weight; intense fear of gaining weight; self-concept of being fat, even when emaciated.

**bulimia**—a disorder characterized by uncontrolled binge eating; use of vomiting, laxatives, diuretics, fasting, and exercise to prevent weight gain; over-concern with body shape and weight.

Thompson, 1989). The disorder, which can be life-threatening, is characterized by extreme dieting, resorting to vomiting and purging through laxatives, and reliance on intensive exercise programs—all to the end of reducing body weight. Their perceived need to lose more and more weight reflects a distorted body image of persons with anorexia nervosa, in that they are typically already well under the weight recommended for their height and bone structure (see Figure 14.2).

Bulimia is similar to anorexia nervosa in that bulimic patients are also obsessed with restricting their weight. Bulimics, however, are usually within 10 pounds of their normal weight and engage in a binge-purge cycle to control their weight. That is, they eat to excess on a fairly regular basis and then induce vomiting to eliminate the calories from the ingested food. The repeated induction of vomiting in the purge phase of the cycle can damage the teeth and the esophagus and cause a variety of other problems.

Binge-purge behavior has become a public activity on some college campuses, where "scarf-and-barf" clubs have sprung up. Most "scarf-and-barf" participants, however, probably do not meet the clinical criteria for a diagnosis of bulimia or anorexia. Their behavior differs from the behavior of those with classic eating disorders in that it is more openly acknowledged, social, and temporary. Anorexics and bulimics tend to be secretive about their binge-purge behaviors. It is common for bulimics to have been obese before the onset of the disorder.

Because the onset of anorexia frequently occurs in early adolescence, some experts have suggested that the disorder stems from a desire to avoid sexual and reproductive maturity. In fact, it is common for women with severe cases of anorexia to have amenorrhea (absence of menstrual periods) because of their extremely low weight.

Coovert et al. (1989) reviewed the scientific literature on eating disorders in an attempt to determine the possible role of various sexual factors. Although the authors of individual case reports have claimed that childhood sexual abuse may be more prevalent among anorexics and bulimics, the research does not generally indicate a high prevalence of abuse among those with eating disorders, as compared to members of the population at large.

Another conclusion suggested by the research on eating disorders is that anorexic women tend to be relatively sexually inactive, whereas bulimic women engage in more sexual activity than is typical of anorexic women or of control groups of women without eating disorders (Coovert et al., 1989). Perhaps the anorexic woman is as fearful of sex as she is of food, whereas the bulimic woman may binge on sex in a manner similar to the way in which she binges on food. Further research is needed to explain these differences in the level of sexual activity seen in bulimic and anorexic women.

Because eating disorders are more prevalent among females than males, relatively little research has included male participants. One exception is a study by Herzog, Norman, Gordon, and Pepose (1984) of male anorexics and bulimics. These two groups were less likely to have had sexual relations than a comparison group of females with eating disorders. Herzog et al. also found a high prevalence of homosexuality in the male sample (26%) compared to the female sample (4%). Gay men and heterosexual women may be especially vulnerable to eating disorders because they wish to appear thin (and therefore attractive) to males (Gettelman & Thompson, 1993; Miskin, Striegel-Moore, Timko, & Rodin, 1989).

Significant recovery from anorexia and bulimia can take extended periods of time. Past studies indicate a long-term recovery rate of about 40% and a persistence of the disorder for six or more years in 35% of treated patients (Leon et al., 1987). Leon and her colleagues contacted a group of patients after they had been discharged from the hospital for at least six months and followed them for an average of almost three years. Those patients holding more negative views about sexuality, their body image, and their social skills when they were hospitalized showed a continuation of these feelings and a greater degree of general psychopathology than those patients with less negative views in these realms. The authors suggested that although treatment should focus on stabilizing eating patterns, sexuality and personality issues need to be addressed as well in treating patients with eating disorders.

In summary, a significant number of people in our culture struggle to conform to rigorous cultural standards of physical attractiveness. The fact that the contemporary physical ideal revolves around a trim physique means an unending cycle of dieting for large numbers of North Americans—often even those with little excess weight to lose. Our cultural infatuation with slimness has led to widespread dissatisfaction with and, in some cases, distortion of body image, and researchers have attempted to link these negative feelings to sexual behavior in a variety of ways. Women have been more affected by the cultural obsession with leanness than men because of the greater pressure on women to be sexually attractive. In the next section, we examine a topic that concerns women exclusively: the role of menstruation in health and sexuality over the life span.

## Menstruation and Health

Women experience menarche, on average, at about age 12.5, and menopause sometime between the ages of 48 and 55. During each monthly cycle's premenstrual phase, women have widely been charged with a sort of "menstrual madness," characterized by irrationality and "bitchiness." Ironically, the cessation of menstruation at menopause has also been described as a source of difficulty for women; the comment "She's menopausal" is commonly used to explain why a woman may be irritable or sensitive to criticism. To provide parallel explanations for men's sexual drive or their relatively low threshold for aggression, we might well describe men as "androgenic" or "testosteronal," but such expressions are not part of our cultural vocabulary.

Many cultures have used menstruation itself as a rationale for isolating women or for keeping them away from projects involving the preparation of food and beverages because of fears of contamination by menstrual blood. (Such concerns seem particularly unwarranted in cultures having access to modern methods of absorbing menstrual discharge—see Box 14.2.) In addition, numerous cultures still consider sexual intercourse with a menstruating woman taboo, and many North Americans avoid sexual intimacy with a woman during her menstrual period.

Cultural attitudes about menstruation are also mirrored in the words and phrases by which women commonly refer to their periods: for example, "the curse," "the crud," and being "on the rag." And considerable mythology still swirls around the topic of the impact of menstruation on women's moods and abilities. In essence, some observers have claimed that the hormonal changes that occur four to six days before menstruation cause women physical and emotional problems.

What are the *actual* effects of the hormonal fluctuations of the menstrual cycle on women? There is some support for the hypothesis that there is an association between phases of the menstrual cycle and various bodily and emotional fluctuations.

The days immediately preceding and including ovulation have been associated with a sense of well-being, high energy levels, heightened sexual arousability, and general rises in visual, auditory, and olfactory sensitivity, as well as decreases in sensitivity to pain. However, there is no consistent evidence that sexual arousal and response vary systematically across the phases of the menstrual cycle (Bancroft, 1989; Meuwissen & Over, 1992). The premenstrual phase and the early days of menstruation have been associated with depression, tension, irritability, and lowered self-esteem (Hoyenga & Hoyenga, 1993b; Rossi & Rossi, 1980). Some support for the notion that hormonal fluctuations may be at least partially responsible for these variations comes from several studies in which women using oral contraceptives were compared to women not taking the pill. The pill prevents ovulation and reduces variations in hormone fluctuations; thus it may be significant that women using the pill report fewer mood swings paralleling their menstrual phase than do women not taking oral contraceptives (Caruso & Allgeier, 1987; Rossi & Rossi, 1980). However, systematic differences between women who use the pill and those who do not may be associated with their subjective experiences of the menstrual cycle. For example, women who have positive attitudes about sex and about their own bodies might be more likely to use the pill than might women with more negative attitudes about sex and their bodies (Bancroft et al., 1991). In addition, women on the pill may feel less anxiety about pregnancy during the premenstrual period, and they usually have less menstrual bleeding. It is important to recognize, however, that some women avoid the pill not because of antisex attitudes but because their medical history makes that method inadvisable for them, or they may prefer other contraceptive methods that also protect them from STDs.

Most women do not experience severe premenstrual symptoms. Cox (1983) asked male and female college students to complete a daily checklist of 15 symptoms common to the premenstrual period without telling them that the research focused on menstrual-cycle symptoms. At the premenstrual phase and at midcycle, *none* of the symptoms was more likely to occur in women than in men. On menstrual days, women were more likely than men to report only 3 of the 15 symptoms: bloating, stomach pains, and abdominal cramps. In another study, which examined the moods of married couples, the days of the week were more closely related to mood than was a woman's menstrual cycle phase (Mansfield, Hood, & Henderson, 1989). For example, negative moods were less common on the week-

**Box 14.2**

## Menstruation and the Marketplace

Until the advent of disposable pads and tampons, women used cloth to absorb their menstrual blood. Women welcomed the greater privacy and convenience afforded by disposable pads (sanitary napkins), and the marketing of tampons by Tampax Corporation in the 1930s provided even greater convenience. It was not until the 1960s that other manufacturers entered the multimillion-dollar tampon market. Three-quarters of menstruating U.S. women now use tampons. Competition for their patronage became increasingly fierce after 1972, when the ban on media ads for menstrual products was lifted. The manufacturing giant Procter and Gamble began marketing a tampon called Rely in the mid-1970s. As writer Mary Williams (1980, p. 31) put it,

*The result was a battle of price and technology. Within four years, the plain old cotton tampon had virtually disappeared, replaced by tampons with perfume, tampons made of synthetic fibers, tampons in pink plastic tubes. But as the manufacturers' list of improvements grew, so did the list of health hazards.*

The first report of *toxic shock syndrome* (TSS) appeared in 1978 (Todd et al., 1978), and other cases soon surfaced. Victims suffered from high fever, headache, confusion, rash, edema, hypotension (low blood pressure), sore throat, vomiting, watery diarrhea, and shock, as well as peeling of skin from the palms of the hands and the soles of the feet following an acute episode of the disorder. About 10% of TSS sufferers died.

**toxic shock syndrome**—an illness associated with the bacterium *S. aureus* that is contracted most frequently by menstruating women who use highly absorbent tampons.

A possible link between TSS and menstruation was noted in early 1980. A majority of the victims from whom cultures were obtained had the bacterium *Staphylococcus aureus* in the throat, cervix, vagina, or rectum. The Centers for Disease Control began monitoring the incidence of TSS and studying the phenomenon. Several studies showed a significant correlation between tampon use and the occurrence of TSS. Further, use of the "extra absorbent" Rely tampons was associated with a greater incidence of TSS than was the use of other brands (Centers for Disease Control, 1980).

Tampon use alone does not seem to cause TSS. If women who employ tampons do not have the bacterium *S. aureus* in their bodies, they are not at risk. Further, tampon absorbency is unrelated to the extent to which *S. aureus* will grow when it is present in a woman's body (Schlievert, Blamster, & Kelly, 1984). But the combination of menstruation, the use of highly absorbent tampons, and the presence of *S. aureus* appears to increase the risk of TSS.

By April 1984 a total of 2,509 cases of TSS had been reported, 5% of which were fatal. The proportion of cases resulting in fatality dropped from 10% before 1980 to 2.6% in 1983. The fact that 5% of the cases involved males demonstrates that toxic shock syndrome can occur in the absence of menstruation (Reingold, 1985).

As research on TSS continues, tampon-using women are advised to change tampons frequently and to avoid wearing them continuously. As Williams noted (1980, p. 33):

*In time, medical science may find the cause of toxic shock syndrome. Finding a cure for the profits-before-people syndrome will probably take longer.*

---

end than during the week for these couples, regardless of where the wife was in her menstrual cycle.

Expectations may be important in the experience of menstruation. Women who believe that menstruation is debilitating expect more premenstrual symptoms than do women who perceive menstruation in a more positive way (Brooks et al., 1977). A series of studies with girls from the fifth through the twelfth grade showed that younger girls (fifth and sixth graders) expected less severe menstrual distress than did the older volunteers. This difference was perhaps because the younger girls had had less time to be influenced by cultural expectations than had the older girls (Clarke & Ruble, 1978; Ruble & Brooks, 1977). It is also possible that young girls had not yet experienced any menstrual difficulties, whereas older girls and women had. Finally, women who believe themselves to be in personal control of their lives report shorter menstrual periods than do women who feel less in control of what happens to them (Scott-Palmer & Skevington, 1981).

In her consideration of the cultural aspects of menstrual-cycle experiences, Sherif (1980) made two interesting points. First, she noted the usefulness of menstruation as an excuse for women to avoid work and/or sexual interaction. And the monthly period is still routinely used by some adolescent girls as an excuse to avoid participation in gym classes. The application of this excuse may increase the cultural perception of menstruation as more debilitating than it actually is for many women. In support of this idea, women who, as adolescents, were encouraged to behave as though they were ill when menstruating, or whose mothers provided a model for menstrual distress, were found to report significantly more menstrual symptoms, clinic visits, and disability days for these symptoms as adults than did women whose mothers had not encouraged or modeled such behavior (Whitehead et al., 1986).

Second, in an interesting parallel to Erikson's general definition of crisis as a challenging opportunity rather than a debilitating burden (see Chapter 12), Sherif (1980, p. 265) suggested that menstruation, too, can be seen in this light:

*What constitutes a woman's self is not defined solely by the biological facts of being a woman, including the integral and normal cyclicity that marks her months for three or four decades. It is defined over the years in relation to significant other persons and groups, to activities that she engages in, to the worth attributed to her and to her activities, to her position relative to others, to what she hopes for in the future.*

We have been discussing relatively normal menstrual-cycle fluctuations, but some women experience severe symptoms during part or all six days preceding the onset of each menstrual period. Between 2% and 10% of women experience severe mood changes known as *premenstrual syndrome (PMS)* (Hoyenga & Hoyenga, 1993b). To assist women troubled by PMS, a number of premenstrual-syndrome clinics are now operating in North America. Therapy at one such establishment located in Reading, Massachusetts, includes the elimination of alcohol, salt, and sugar from the diet; administration of B-complex vitamins; a regimen of six small meals a day; exercise; and in some cases, administration of progesterone.

Lawyers in England have successfully used PMS as a defense for young women accused of assault and arson. This legal precedent and the accordance of clinical status to PMS have generated fierce controversy among researchers and feminists alike. Because studies on PMS are quite recent, any conclusions regarding the role of hormone imbalance as a cause of particular behavior in women must be viewed with caution. Feminists fear that using PMS as an excuse for antisocial behavior may aid those who believe that, because of menstrual-cycle fluctuations, women should be prohibited from holding positions of responsibility.

In summary, there is evidence that hormonal fluctuations are associated with mood variations in some women. But women's response to their own cyclicity is also associated with social expectations, as well as with how they have learned to symbolize and label their feelings, as the descriptions of menarche in Box 14.3 illustrate. The fact

**premenstrual syndrome (PMS)**—the depression, irritability, tension, and lowered self-esteem that some women experience prior to and during the early days of the menstrual period.

### Box 14.3

## Meanings of Menarche

*My mother had described menstruation to me and had bought me some sanitary napkins and a belt, and from the time I was about 12, I waited in anticipation for it to appear. Finally, in the middle of my 13th year (I can still remember the exact date), I went to the bathroom and discovered, to my surprise, some blood on the toilet paper. I went racing out of the bathroom, yelling, "I'm a woman, I'm a woman!" at the top of my lungs, only to discover, much to my embarrassment, that my mother had gone out. In response to my father's inquiries, I muttered "Never mind" and waited impatiently for my mother to return so that I could tell her the wonderful news. My irrational sense of pride with myself each month my period began didn't finally diminish until after I'd had several children.*

*I was in the eighth grade when I got my first period. Some of my friends had already started their period, and I was kind of apprehensively awaiting mine. The day it started, my mom was flat on her back with a bad case of the flu, and my dad and brother were avidly watching a football game. After going to the bathroom, I remember wiping myself and knowing something was different because things were slipperier than usual. So when I saw the brown discharge, I didn't know if I should call the doctor or if it was menstrual blood. I wondered if I should use those sanitary napkins that Mom had stored in my closet for the past year "just in case." No one ever told me that menstrual blood could be a brownish color.*

*I can remember trying to figure out how the pad fit on the sanitary napkin belt. I was so scared I almost cried. I wanted to talk to my mom, but I was afraid to because she was sick. So I put on the bulky pad, and I remember being*

*very self-conscious, thinking that everyone noticed. After several checks of the pad, I noticed brown clots building up. I was scared to death, because no one ever told me that happened.*

*Mom asked me the next day if I had my period. She had noticed a napkin as she emptied the trash. She started telling me horror stories of the bad cases of cramps she used to get. I wondered if the dull aches I felt were cramps. I don't think I thought even once that they were cramps before that.*

*I never asked Mom if she told my dad and brother that I had started, but the next day my brother said, "What's the matter, is it that time of the month?" I was really irritable. In fact, my whole family used to be able to tell by my mood if it was "my time."*

*I was bitter for probably about a year because I couldn't understand why women had to go through this torture. I couldn't understand why I had to tell my friends that I couldn't go swimming because I was "ragging it." Finally, I said, "Mom, will you please let me try tampons?" She was a rough case, but I finally convinced her. She thought tampons were nothing but trouble. It turned out that they made all the difference in the world. That dreaded five days was now just like the rest of the month.*

*I was relieved when, after a year, I finally started to have a regular 30-day cycle. Before that it had ranged from 14 to 45 days. I was worried about that, too, but never said anything. Also my flow eventually became red-colored. Boy, was I relieved.*

Source: Authors' files.

that most women do not experience severe symptoms during the premenstrual phase suggests that we need to search for factors in addition to menstrual-cycle phase to account for the high stress experienced by a small percentage of women.

## Menopause

Menopause is also associated with varying levels of symptoms in women. The risks and benefits of *hormone-replacement therapy (HRT)* for post-menopausal women have been debated for some time. The controversy itself is interesting, because if the presence and fluctuation of the hormones during the reproductive years are blamed for women's emotional ups and downs, it would seem that menopause, with its accompanying reductions in the secretion of feminizing hormones, would be characterized by enhanced emotional stability.

Symptoms commonly associated with menopause include nocturnal sweating and daytime or nighttime hot flashes; irritability; fatigue and insomnia; loss of confidence; difficulties with memory, concentration, and decision-making; and reduced vaginal lubrication, in turn causing itching, burning, and dyspareunia (Hoyenga & Hoyenga, 1993b). The range and invasiveness of these side effects vary from one woman to another and interact with social and cultural variables. For example, a woman whose primary sense of usefulness and meaning has been based on the ability to have babies may experience menopause—and the end of the possibility of childbearing—as far more central to her life than a woman who has additional roles for which childbearing is either irrelevant or intrusive. The latter might be more likely to experience menopause as a release from having to worry about contraception or irregular periods.

Small doses of estrogen or a combination of progestins and estrogens given to menopausal and postmenopausal women appear to reduce common menopausal symptoms. Further, HRT can increase vaginal thickness, elasticity, and lubrication. For postmenopausal women who value their sexuality, HRT can help maintain their sense of sexual well-being (Bellerose & Binik, 1993; Darling & McKoy-Smith, 1993; Wall-

---

**hormone-replacement therapy (HRT)**—the use of small doses of estrogen, progesterone, or a combination of the two to counteract the negative side effects of menopause.

---

ing, Anderson, & Johnson, 1990). However, because menopausal symptoms usually disappear on their own within a few years, and because there are concerns that postmenopausal HRT may present certain health risks (see below), some doctors are leery of prescribing HRT.

On the positive side, HRT has been correlated with a reduced risk of serious problems such as heart disease and osteoporosis. Osteoporosis, a metabolic disease resulting in bone loss, is estimated to afflict as many as 20 million Americans, primarily women over age 45. Collapse of the spinal column from a series of small fractures may render a woman with this condition as much as two inches shorter in just a few weeks. Eventually, she develops a "dowager's hump" in the upper back as her spine gives way. Hip fractures are also common in osteoporosis patients, as the condition produces a loss of bone density in the ball-and-socket joint linking the thigh bone to the pelvis.

In 1984 the National Institutes of Health recommended that postmenopausal women take supplementary estrogen. In addition, daily consumption of 1,000 milligrams of calcium—the most common metallic element in human bone—and moderate weight-bearing exercise were recommended to slow the bone-thinning process. Other authorities suggest that women can further reduce the risk of osteoporosis by beginning a regimen of daily calcium and exercise in their early 20s. Glowacki (1988) reported that postmenopausal women who are 25% above their ideal body weight usually manufacture enough estrogen to reduce their risk of osteoporosis.

Estrogen therapy is not without its drawbacks. It appears to increase the risk of endometrial cancer, and it is not advised for women with breast cancer. From a risk-benefit standpoint, however, endometrial cancer is an infrequent cause of death. In addition, women on HRT obtain more frequent checkups than those not on HRT, so that the early detection of problems is likely.

Many medical researchers now believe that the benefits of both short-term and long-term HRT outweigh the risks (Stampfer et al., 1991). Because this medical intervention is relatively new, with research still under way on long-term side effects, menopausal women considering HRT should weigh the delicate balance of risks and benefits.

We have surveyed some of the issues that all women face in dealing with the beginning, duration, and end of their menstrual cycle and how these experiences are related to health and sexuality. In the next section, we examine problems that interfere with the reproductive capacity of both men and women.

## Infertility

As we have seen in previous chapters, one of the driving tenets of evolutionary theory is the production and nurturance of offspring. Reproductive health, signs that a man or woman can procreate, has been given central importance throughout most of human history. Even as technology has produced a cleavage between sex and reproduction, most individuals still see their ability to reproduce as a crucial part of their identity. In this respect, it is interesting to note that "impotence" (a feeling of powerlessness) has often been associated not just with erectile dysfunction but also with the inability to impregnate.

Approximately 15% of people of child-bearing age in the United States experience involuntarily childlessness, or *infertility*, and the incidence is increasing (Leiblum, 1993). A couple is diagnosed as infertile when they have engaged in intercourse without contraception on a regular basis for a year without conceiving a child.

It has been estimated that 20% of all infertility is preventable in that it stems from sexually transmitted diseases, damage to reproductive organs, pelvic inflammatory disease, and environmental hazards to reproductive functioning (Henifin, 1993). About 40% of the time, the woman's reproductive system is the source of the infertility. Infertility is attributed to the man 30%

**infertility**—the inability to conceive, caused by factors in the male, female, or couple that are unrelated to the ability to engage in sexual relations.

of the time; 30% of the time, both partners have conditions that contribute to the problem.

These cold statistics do not reflect the prolonged pain felt by couples who hope for children. In addition to the sadness they feel over their incapacity to conceive, infertile people may fear desertion by their spouses. The spouses may be reluctant to express and thereby resolve their feelings because they don't want to add to the anguish of the infertile mate. Fortunately, great strides have been made in treating and eliminating infertility. Infertility is highest, however, among poor and minority groups, who often have limited access to medical care (Henifin, 1993).

### Sources and Treatment of Female Infertility

Female infertility can result from genetic and chromosomal disorders, hormonal disorders, blockage of the fallopian tubes, problems with implantation of the fertilized egg, and the aging process. When genetic or chromosomal disorders are the root of the problem, little can be done to help a woman conceive. Other causes of female infertility, however, can be treated.

#### Failure to Ovulate

For about 20% of infertile women, failure to ovulate or to ovulate regularly is the source of the problem. Several general conditions, including anemia, vitamin deficiencies, malnutrition, and environmental or psychological stress, are associated with the absence of ovulation (Armstrong, 1986). Correction of these conditions often results in normal menstrual cycles with regular midcycle ovulation. In some women, ovulation is blocked by the presence of a tough membrane around the ovary that keeps eggs from rupturing out of the organ. This condition can be corrected by removing part of the membrane.

Hormonal imbalances can also prevent ovulation. Women with these imbalances may be given a drug such as clomiphene citrate (Clomid) or a hormone such as follicle-stimulating hormone (FSH) to stimulate ovulation. The possibility of multiple births or of side effects such as blood clotting must be considered when these treatments are prescribed. Determining the precise dosage needed for the individual to release just one egg is often difficult. Clomid produces ovulation in about 80% of the women who take it, and about 40% of these women conceive (Olds et al., 1992). The incidence of multiple births—which are almost always twins—is about 5%.

### Blocked Fallopian Tubes

Almost half a million women have fallopian tubes blocked by scar tissue (Andolsek, 1990). The scar tissue can result from various conditions, the most prevalent of which are untreated or late-treated gonorrhea, chlamydia, and pelvic inflammatory disease (see Chapter 17). If the tubes are totally blocked, sperm cannot reach the egg. If the tubes are only partially blocked, sperm may be able to reach the egg, but the fertilized and growing egg may be unable to pass out of the tube into the uterus, resulting in an ectopic pregnancy.

Several procedures can be used to create a pregnancy in cases of blocked fallopian tubes. One of these, known as *in vitro fertilization and embryo transfer (IVF/ET)*, involves removal of ova through small surgical incisions in the abdomen, called *laparoscopy*. After the ova are removed, they are placed in a petri dish where they are fertilized with sperm. The fertilized eggs are then transferred into the uterus of a woman who may or may not be the original donor of the egg. Usually, three or four fertilized eggs are transferred to increase the chances of pregnancy. A couple may have to go through this procedure multiple times before they succeed in conceiving.

The procedure is expensive and usually not covered by medical insurance. It is often not very successful. A survey of U.S. clinics found an average success rate of 11% (Henifin, 1993). The cost-effectiveness of this procedure has been questioned as a technological "fix" that diverts attention away from primary prevention of infertility.

Another procedure used to remedy infertility, called *gamete transfer*, requires at least one intact fallopian tube. In this procedure, a mature egg is taken from a woman's ovary and placed in her fallopian tube, along with a sperm sample. To enhance the likelihood of embryo survival and implantation in the uterus, the woman is given intramuscular doses of progesterone. Approximately 50% of women who become pregnant as a result of gamete transfer have multiple pregnancies, but this rate can be decreased by placing fewer eggs in the fallopian tube. This procedure is less controversial ethically than in vitro fertilization, because conception occurs within the woman's body.

The procedures described above all involve the implantation of a woman's egg into her body. For the estimated 4% of women who have no ovaries, these methods are of no help. In 1986, however, two women without ovaries delivered healthy babies (Navot, Laufer, Kopolovic, et al., 1986) after their husbands' sperm samples were used to fertilize eggs donated by other women. The two infertile women were given estrogen and progesterone to prepare their uterine linings for implantation of the fertilized egg.

### Conditions Related to Aging

Infertility rates increase with age. Many women are now postponing pregnancy until their early 30s or later so they can complete their education, establish a career, or save some money toward financing the rising cost of parenthood. In certain cases, women decide in their 30s that it is time to have a child, only to discover that they cannot become pregnant. For some of these women, infertility factors have always been present. For others, the difficulty in conceiving results from newly emerging medical conditions.

---

**in vitro fertilization and embryo transfer (IVF/ET)** (in VEE-trow)—a procedure in which ova are fertilized in a laboratory and implanted in a woman's uterus.

**laparoscopy** (LAH-par-OS-coe-pee)—surgical incision into the abdomen into which a light and cutting instrument can be introduced.

**gamete transfer**—a procedure in which a mature egg is placed in a woman's fallopian tube, together with a sperm sample, for fertilization.

About 20% of women nearing the age of 30 who have postponed childbearing have difficulty conceiving because of *endometriosis*, a condition in which cells from the endometrium—the lining of the uterus—grow in places other than the uterus (Olds et al., 1992). Symptoms include lower-back pain and severe pain during menstruation or intercourse, but depending on where the cells grow, there may be no symptoms. Endometriosis is treated through surgical removal of the abnormally located cell growths or by administration of danazol, a synthetic hormone. After treatment, many women are able to become pregnant. The cause of endometriosis is unknown, but the disease is less prevalent among women who begin childbearing early in the life cycle.

Until recently it was assumed that the age of a woman was related to birth defects; it was thought that an older woman was more likely to produce a child with moderate to severe health problems. To some extent, the statistical relationship observed among women's age, infertility, and the incidence of birth defects may be *confounded* with the tendency of women in previous generations (when data were collected) to begin having children in their early 20s. This cultural norm left a pool of married women who were childless not by choice but because they were less fertile. If and when those less fertile women did have children, they obviously were older than the average mother. In those cases in which their children were born with birth defects, it was assumed that the mother's age was the cause. But in fact, the birth defects may have been the result of whatever caused the mother's infertility in the first place (hormonal imbalances, for example). If so, the current trend among fertile, career-oriented women toward postponing their first pregnancies could alter the statistical relationship of maternal age to the incidence of infertility, Down's syndrome, and other problems.

**endometriosis** (EN-doe-mee-tree-OH-sis)—a condition in which the cells that form the inner lining of the uterus grow in some place other than the uterus, such as within the pelvic cavity or on the external surface of the ovaries, fallopian tubes, or uterus.

**confound**—a factor other than those under investigation that influences the results of research.

### Other Causes of Female Infertility

The routine use of commercial douches and vaginal deodorants may reduce the chances of conception. Some of these products contain chemicals that inhibit or destroy the motility of sperm. Thick cervical mucus also can inhibit fertility by preventing sperm from entering the uterus. For women with this problem, the use of a mild alkaline douche just before intercourse may be helpful, because it may remove some of this mucus.

## Sources and Treatment of Male Infertility

Little can be done for men whose sterility results from genetic or chromosomal factors. Other sources of infertility in men include undescended testicles, damage to the reproductive organs and ducts, the presence of varicoceles, and the effects of various drugs and environmental pollutants on sperm production.

*Undescended testes* are one cause of male infertility. During prenatal development, the testes are positioned high in the abdominal cavity, but by birth, the testes have normally descended from the abdomen to the scrotum. In about 2% of males, however, one or both of the testes remain inside the abdominal cavity and must be brought down surgically. If this operation is performed before puberty, fertility is generally unimpaired; after puberty, surgical procedures are less effective in producing fertility.

Sperm production takes place only within a limited temperature range. Normal body temperature is too high for the delicate sperm, so when the testes remain within the body, the sperm are destroyed. In fact, when the testes are kept too close to the body by tight clothing, fertility tends to be reduced. Men for whom sterility is a problem are sometimes given the simple but effective advice to wear boxer shorts and looser clothing.

**undescended testes**—a condition in which testes have not dropped down from the abdomen into the scrotum.

Some men develop antibodies to their own sperm for unknown reasons. Witkin and Toth (1983) examined the possibility that genital infections might increase the likelihood that men would manufacture such antibodies. Of 100 men referred for semen analysis for infertility, half of those with genital infections (microorganisms, mycoplasma, chlamydia—see Chapter 17) had antibodies to their own sperm. More research on the relationship of genital infections to the development of sperm antibodies is needed.

Damage to reproductive organs and ducts is another source of male infertility. Mumps, if contracted after puberty, can produce inflammation in the testes. The swelling can compress the delicate seminiferous tubules in which sperm are produced, resulting in the decrease or cessation of sperm production. Some diseases, among them gonorrhea, can produce scar tissue in the vas deferens, interfering with the movement of sperm. As a result, the semen contains either very few sperm or none at all.

A *varicocele* is an enlarged or damaged vein in the testes or vas deferens. The varicocele allows blood to accumulate in the scrotum, increasing its temperature; thus sperm production is impaired. Estimates indicate that as many as 30% of men seen in infertility clinics have some reduction in fertility and some pain from varicoceles, and 30% to 55% of men who undergo corrective treatment are subsequently able to impregnate their wives (Andolsek, 1990).

A review of studies published worldwide from 1940 to 1990 indicated that average sperm density fell by almost 50% (Carlson et al., 1992). The causes of this decrease in sperm count are complicated and not completely understood. They may include nutritional factors, medical conditions, increased drug use, changing patterns of sexual behavior, and elevated stress. Rising levels of environmental pollutants appear to be related to this trend. Such pollutants as PCBs (chemicals used in the manufacture of electrical equipment) and tris (a flame retardant) have been found in higher concentrations in the cells of men with low sperm counts than in those of men with higher sperm counts. The extent to which toxic substances are associated with female infertility is not known.

## Sources of Infertility in a Couple

One cause of infertility in a couple is a woman's production of antibodies that attack the man's sperm cells, causing the cells to clump together and preventing them from getting into the fallopian tubes. In their study of several thousand cases of unexplained infertility, Shulman and his colleagues (1975) found that the incidence of antibody activity against sperm was about 16% in men and about 7% in women.

Some couples are able to overcome this problem if the man uses condoms, and the woman has her blood tested every three months for a year to determine her antibody levels. If the woman is not exposed to sperm, her body will not produce antibodies to them. When testing indicates that the levels of antibodies have decreased significantly, the couple may eliminate the condom and attempt to conceive by having intercourse at ovulation.

Infertility is related to a wide range of negative experiences on those affected. An increase in marital conflict and decreases in sexual self-esteem, satisfaction with one's own sexual performance, and frequency of sexual intercourse have been reported (Andrews, Abbey, & Halman, 1991; Leiblum, 1993). Several decades ago, the psychological problems observed in infertile couples were thought to be a possible cause of their infertility. More recent work, however, has supported the idea that infertility produces the psychological problems (Andrews et al., 1991; Seibel & Taymor, 1982).

## Alternative Avenues to Parenthood

For about half the couples in which one or both spouses have fertility problems, no treatment is available that will permit them to conceive a child together (Andrews et al., 1991). These couples have several alternatives if they continue to desire a child. They may turn to adoption, artificial insemination, or a surrogate mother.

---

**varicoceles** (VARE-uh-coh-SEELZ)—enlarged or damaged veins leading to the testes or vas deferens that can be a cause of male infertility.

About a quarter of infertile couples want to adopt a child. But approximately 2 million couples must compete for the 50,000 American babies placed for adoption each year (Sitomer, 1987). Healthy White infants who can be adopted are scarce, but older children, those with physical and mental handicaps, and members of some racial or ethnic minority groups badly need homes. Couples tend to be reluctant to adopt them, however. Only about 6% of single women who give birth place their children for adoption, and today, most people who adopt are already related in some way to the adopted child. For example, the children of a woman or man who remarries are often adopted by the new spouse (Andolsek, 1990).

When the husband is infertile but the wife is capable of conception and pregnancy, the couple may obtain artificial insemination from a donor (AID). Couples seeking artificial insemination first apply to a clinic offering the service, where they are interviewed to determine the stability of their relationship and the extent to which both spouses freely support conception through this method.

Applicants also receive information about potential donors, including medical history, ethnic background, race, religion, physical characteristics, height, weight, and coloring. If a couple's application is accepted, the woman goes to the clinic at a time when she is ovulating, and "straws" containing frozen sperm samples are placed in her vagina near her cervix. If her husband's fertility problem stems from a low sperm count (but his sperm are highly motile), it is sometimes possible to collect sperm samples from *him*, save them, and then inseminate the woman with her spouse's sperm. This procedure is generally less successful, however, than donor insemination.

An unusual complication has arisen with artificial insemination. Because one man can provide sperm for many women, donor insemination can create many children who are biological half-siblings. In a few cases, weddings between offspring who were conceived with sperm from the same donor have been canceled (Andrews, 1984).

Artificial insemination procedures also can allow a fertile man married to an infertile woman, or to a woman at risk of transmitting a genetic defect, to father children. The man provides sperm for the insemination of a woman other than his wife who volunteers to conceive and give birth to the child. The woman then becomes a surrogate mother, relinquishing the child to the father and his wife after the birth. This procedure is expensive: a couple pay the surrogate mother a fee, plus her medical, travel, and legal expenses.

Surrogate motherhood has created a web of legal and moral controversies. For example, in the event of a birth defect, who is responsible for the physical and financial care of the child? Can a surrogate mother be sued if she engaged in behavior, such as drug use, that harmed the fetus? What happens if one of the participants (the surrogate mother, the father, or his wife) changes his or her mind during the pregnancy? Court cases involving child custody have prompted some states to pass legislation addressing surrogate motherhood, but the issues are by no means resolved.

We have examined some of the causes and treatments of infertility. In the next section, we describe impairments and injuries that affect both reproductive capacity and sexuality.

## Impairments and Injuries

A small minority of individuals enter the world with serious physical or mental conditions that can also restrict or impair their ability to learn about sexuality or to have experiences that can contribute to their sexual functioning later in life. Some of these difficulties can be readily overcome, whereas others burden the person with a permanent challenge to sexual relationships that are satisfying. In a culture that provides less than optimal sex education even for its "normal" people, individuals afflicted with sight or hearing deficits, or with extreme physical or developmental abnormalities or ill health, face a particularly steep uphill climb in trying to attain rewarding sexual relationships. They are not only confronted by ingrained cultural attitudes toward sexuality and toward physically or mentally

**Box 14.4**

## Visual Impairment and Sex Education

Several years ago, two visually impaired students, John and Deb, enrolled in my human sexuality course. Before the semester began, each asked my opinion about options in obtaining notes, studying, and taking exams. I must confess to concern about their ability to do well with some aspects of the course because of my use of audiovisual materials in teaching sexual anatomy and physiology. But several volunteers from the class provided the students with notes and read the text to them, and they answered test items that were given to them orally. They also actively participated in class discussion (and occasionally John's seeing-eye dog did too, with his unexpected barking!). I am happy to report that both students did very well in the course.

John's and Deb's involvement in the course was deeply rewarding and instructive for me, because although I knew that visual cues play a key role in the sexual education and sexual feelings of the sighted, the two students' frank discussions in class and in my office sharpened my awareness of the concrete challenges faced by the visually impaired. John had been totally sightless from birth, whereas Deb's loss of vision resulted from an accident in late childhood. John was not involved in a love relationship at the time, although he had had a couple of romances in the past; Deb currently had a sighted boyfriend.

—E.R.A.

disabled people, but they face especially strong societal taboos against impaired persons who seek an active sex life.

## Sensory Impairments

Given the importance of vision in sex education, interpersonal attraction, signaling of interest, mate selection, and sexual arousal, research on the experiences of people with visual impairments could potentially deepen our understanding of the sexuality of both sighted and visually impaired humans. Unfortunately, there is a relative paucity of research on this topic. The few studies that have been done, however, suggest that, as with various other impairments, the absence of sight interacts with other factors in its impact on human's sexual knowledge and sexual functioning (see Box 14.4). In their review of the research in this area, Gillman and Gordon (1973) noted that gender-role acquisition seems to be relatively unimpeded among blind children, although they may rely heavily on their language skills in developing the traits expected of their gender. Sexual knowledge can be similarly acquired, and the accuracy of what is learned depends on the individual's general intelligence and access to instruction, just as in the case of sighted people. Gillman and Gordon concluded that "when sexual information has been taught from the beginning of school, blind children are as informed as their sighted peers" (1973, p. 59). Some visually impaired people must also contend with other disorders, but it appears to be the other conditions rather than their blindness per se that seriously interfere with their understanding of sexuality.

Because parents are often silent on the topics of sexuality and gender differences in anatomy and functioning, children as a group are usually left to reach their own conclusions (many of them inaccurate). Most young people at least have visual cues to guide them, but those with visual impairment have limited or no access to information about sexuality. Further, the stress placed on physical attributes by many of their peers has little relevance to them and at times seems downright silly (as it often does to some of us who are sighted).

Individuals who are born without the capacity to hear are presumably less affected by parental silence regarding sex education. Nonetheless, the flowering of their capacity to express their sexual feelings may be stunted by rampant prejudice toward the hearing-impaired. For a highly moving, sensitive depiction of the challenges faced by a young deaf woman in attempting to develop her professional skills and personal relationships, we recommend the film *Children of a Lesser God*, which you can rent from video stores.

## Developmental Disabilities

People with IQs below 70 are usually classified as developmentally disabled. Controversy has long surrounded the question of whether the sexual expression of such individuals should be regulated, and few issues related to the treatment of the 6 million Americans who are developmentally impaired have been resolved. If you should ever have a developmentally disabled son or daughter, you will—in addition to helping your child cope with the complexities of modern society, form friendships, find suitable work, and handle the prejudices that such people experience—face a host of challenges as he or she reaches sexual and reproductive maturity. Although developmentally disabled adolescents score below normal on IQ tests, their capacity for sexual intimacy and reproduction may be unimpaired (see Figures 14.3 and 14.4). Moreover, because of a widespread belief that developmentally disabled people are relatively defenseless, they are more susceptible to sexual coercion and exploitation than is the typical adolescent. If the disability is genetically derived, the disabled person's conceiving a child may raise the serious concern that any offspring will inherit the disability. Even if the disability is environmentally rooted, a person with developmental impairments may lack the skills to care for a child without supervision. In such a case, contraceptive protection is especially important, for persons with disabilities do have sexual intercourse.

As the differences between the theoretical and actual failure rates of various contraceptives show, many people in the general population sometimes use birth control methods incorrectly. Teaching the complexities of the use of the pill, diaphragm, or condom to a person with developmental disabilities may be difficult or impossible, depending on the extent of his or her disability. One proposed solution has been to fit

**FIGURE 14.3**
**Getting Ready for a Party**
Anne Marvel helps her friend Caren, age 25, who has Down's syndrome, arrange her hair and make-up before a party.

developmentally disabled women with IUDs, but recent data indicate that IUDs pose grave health risks if one has multiple partners, one of which is heightened susceptibility to serious complications of sexually transmitted diseases (see Chapter 17).

But let us return to the issue of providing birth control to people with developmental disabilities. Some authorities have recommended sterilization for these individuals. Sterilization, however, poses its own problems. First, if a person is truly intellectually impaired, how does one obtain his or her informed consent to proceed with sterilization? Another serious obstacle is the complexity of determining the cause of an

**FIGURE 14.4**
**Caring and Disability**
Human contact is a crucial need for all of us.

apparent disability. For example, an emotional disturbance can be responsible for what appears to be a learning impairment. When the source of the emotional disturbance is removed, individuals formerly labeled as developmentally disabled can have normal learning capacities and can function independently, marry, and rear children. If they are sterilized prior to the change in diagnosis, however, society has inappropriately stripped them of their right to reproduce.

Researchers have recently developed a new approach to teaching persons with developmental disabilities about sexuality and contraceptive responsibility. The method consists of administering hormonal contraceptives along with home-based behavior-modification training. This training, which involves sex education for both patients and their families, aims to reduce the likelihood of sexual abuse, increase the family's understanding of sexual development, and encourage intrafamily communication. The family also receives advice about contraceptive options for the developmentally disabled member, including sterilization (Elkins, Gafford, Wilks, Muram, & Golden, 1986). The search for humane approaches to contraception for people with developmental disabilities is an important one, because no strategy has yet been found that effectively protects these individuals' rights to enjoy intimate relationships while eliminating the po-

tential costs: unwanted births to people who are not developmentally equipped to care adequately for children.

## Physical Disabilities

Although people with such physical disabilities as a missing limb or a malfunctioning organ face prejudice, their disability does not impair their capacity for sexual intimacy. The exceptions are those with certain spinal cord injuries.

As with many other disabilities, the extent and severity of the trauma to the spinal cord directly influence the degree to which physical changes relevant to sexual response occur. Consider Jon Voight's sensitive portrayal of a paraplegic making love with a nonimpaired woman (Jane Fonda) in the movie *Coming Home*, which beautifully demonstrated the fact that sexual and emotional intimacy can flourish even for individuals with massive physical limitations. If you enjoy movies that contain natural rather than contrived depictions of erotic interaction, you may want to rent *Coming Home* from a video store.

The erection and ejaculation reflex centers are located in the lower part of the spinal cord. If these centers have been damaged—as is the case for the paraplegic, who is paralyzed from the waist down, and the quadriplegic, who is paralyzed from the neck down—then the individual is usually incapable of experiencing erection, ejaculation, or orgasm. In the person whose injuries do not involve these centers, sexual response is possible if the genitals are stimulated directly, and a woman with spinal cord damage is still able to conceive and give birth (see Figure 14.5). However, a man's ability to ejaculate is generally lost if communication between the brain and the genitals is interrupted by damage to the spinal cord. In such a case, the spinal cord injury may eliminate the man's natural reproductive capacity (Katz, 1985).

But recently developed laboratory techniques can help the man with spinal cord injuries to impregnate his partner. For example, in electroejaculation-sperm retrieval, ejaculation is electrically stimulated, and the man's sperm are collected for the artificial insemination of his partner. This procedure is now done in spinal cord centers throughout the United States. Thus

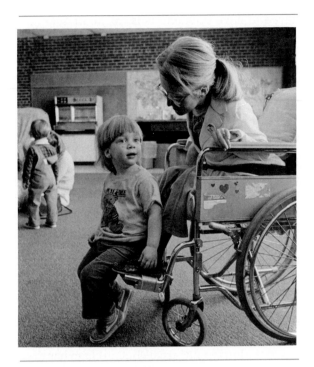

**FIGURE 14.5**

**Quadriplegic Mother and Her Child**
Although spinal cord injuries interfere with many activities, some women with paralyses are still able to reproduce. This mother is shown with her child at nursery school.

conception, pregnancy, and full-term normal births are a realistic expectation for the couple (Cole & Cole, 1990).

Kennedy and Over (1990) examined the relationship between the subjective reactions and the physiological responses of men with spinal cord injuries to erotic films, audiotapes, and fantasies. Before exposure to the erotic media, the men were asked about their erectile capacity. Interestingly, some of those who reported having lost the ability to have an erection had partial or full erections in response to the erotic material; conversely, some who reported having retained their erectile functioning did not become erect while exposed to the erotic stimuli. Furthermore, the men's subjective reports of arousal were not related to their physiological response. That is, the men who did not have erections were no less subjectively aroused by the erotica than were men who experienced erections. This study in-

cluded a control group of men without spinal cord injuries, but their subjective ratings of arousal were no greater than those of the men with such impairments. As Kennedy and Over pointed out, these findings on subjective arousal challenge assertions from some previous literature

> *that emotional responses, including sexual arousal, are lessened by spinal cord injury. . . . [Further], any claim that [spinal-cord-injured] men who gain erections are more "sexual" than [spinal-cord-injured] men who do not is untenable. . . . Sexuality has sensual and romantic dimensions, and not just mechanical and secretory components. (1990, p. 25)*

An interesting interaction between our psyches and our biology is revealed in reports that people with spinal cord injuries can be taught a technique in which they recognize and respond to sexual stimulation from unaffected portions of their bodies, fantasize about genital activity, and experience considerable sexual gratification (Cole, 1979). After becoming adept at this procedure, some men with spinal cord injuries have even reported experiencing multiple orgasmlike feelings and physiological changes, though without ejaculation.

Less is known about the effect of spinal cord injuries on women's sexual response. That women may be able to reestablish satisfying patterns of sexual intimacy with appropriate rehabilitation, however, has been documented by Elle Friedman Becker (1978). Becker experienced spinal cord damage after being thrown from a horse in 1975. In addition to working hard on her rehabilitation both physically and sexually, she conducted a series of interviews with authorities in the field and with 20 other women who also had spinal cord injuries. The book that she wrote based on her research, *Female Sexuality Following Spinal Cord Injury* (1978), provides insights and information that may help others with similar injuries. Another resource for those interested in enhancing the ability of disabled persons to resume satisfying sexual lives is *Who Cares? A Handbook on Sex Education and Counseling for Disabled People* (Cornelius, Chipouras, Makas, & Daniels, 1982).

**FIGURE 14.6**
**The Enduring Capacity for Intimacy**
Paralyzed by a gunshot wound in 1986, police officer Steven McDonald, shown here with his wife, enjoys a loving relationship despite constant physical pain.

Although many disabilities and impairments have profound effects on sexual expression as measured by normative standards, it is apparent that people affected by these conditions do not lose their need for sexual intimacy (Alexander, Sipski, & Findley, 1993); (see Figure 14.6). Growing sensitivity and attention to their needs by the health care community have expanded the sexual horizons of people with impairments and disabilities. As we shall see in the next section, this opening up of opportunity is also true for individuals with an illness or disease that impairs sexual functioning.

## Aphrodisiacs and Anaphrodisiacs

Certain drugs have a reputation for heightening sexual arousal or enhancing the pleasure of sexual stimulation and orgasm. A substance be-

lieved to have such effects is called an *aphrodisiac* (after Aphrodite, the Greek goddess of love). Other substances have the opposite effect attributed to them; that is, they reportedly reduce sexual interest and arousal. These potions are called *anaphrodisiacs.*

### Common Aphrodisiacs

Humans have quested after aphrodisiacs through the ages. The sexual organs of animals, as well as objects that look like sexual organs, have sometimes been used in love potions. Alleged aphrodisiacs favored by various societies have included powdered rhinoceros horn (one of the reasons that the rhinoceros is an endangered species), bees' wings, elephant tusks, oysters, the blood of bats mixed with donkey milk, radishes, elephant sperm, olives, and sheep or bull testes ("Rocky Mountain oysters"). Interestingly, the chemical composition of rhinoceros horn is similar to the human fingernail, but no claim has ever been made that fingernail biting increases sex drive.

Despite longstanding popular beliefs, however, there is not much reliable scientific evidence that such substances can affect sexual functioning. Most information about their effects is based on the retrospective reports of drug users, surveys, anecdotal evidence, or uncontrolled studies. Ideally, research in this area should employ a double-blind design, in which neither the volunteers nor the investigators know who receives the substance under investigation and who gets a placebo instead.

An example of the kind of research needed to refute or substantiate the claim that a food, drug, or treatment alters sexual response may be seen in a study conducted by Herold, Mottin, and Sabry (1979). There is a popular belief that vitamin E positively affects sexual performance. To test this idea, Herold and his colleagues asked volunteer couples to report the frequency of their

**aphrodisiac** (AF-roe-DEE-zee-ak)—a substance that is alleged to arouse sexual desire and increase the capacity for sexual activity.

**anaphrodisiac** (an-AF-roe-DEE-zee-ak)—a substance that is alleged to inhibit sexual desire and activity.

### Box 14.5

### Kegel Exercises

Kegel exercises, named for the physician Arnold Kegel (1952), who devised them, promote healthy muscle tone in the vagina and urethra and can be practiced by both men and women. In addition to increasing your awareness of the location of the pubococcygeal (PC) muscle, which is active during orgasm, exercise for the purpose of toning this muscle may also reduce stress incontinence (involuntary passage of urine upon, for example, sneezing or being tickled), aid women who have recently given birth to restore the vagina to its former tone, and benefit men following surgery for prostate cancer.

You are probably already aware of your PC muscle, although you may not have consciously thought about it. If you have ever urgently needed to urinate or defecate while in the midst of a phone call, you perhaps recall contracting your PC muscle until you could get to a bathroom. The next time you are urinating, you can identify your PC muscle by stopping the flow of urine midstream. The muscle you contracted to halt urination is the PC muscle. Having identified it, you can exercise it in a variety of ways—even in such public situations as sitting in class or waiting in a grocery-store line.

One exercise requires contracting the PC muscle for three seconds, then relaxing it for three seconds, and finally contracting it again. Barbach (1976) suggested doing 10 three-second squeezes at three different times daily. Although the "workout" sounds simple (you can try it as you read this), initially, it may be difficult to hold the contraction for three whole seconds, so you may want to start with one or two seconds and gradually lengthen the contraction time as your PC muscle gets stronger.

Another exercise consists of contracting and releasing the PC muscle as quickly as possible, aiming for a sequence of 10 contraction-release cycles three times a day. A woman may also exercise her PC muscle by pretending that she is trying to pull something into and then push something out of her vagina, again holding each effort for three seconds. Barbach (1976) recommended slowly increasing the number in each series of exercises until you can do 20 repeats of every exercise in succession three times a day. As with any other exercise that you are just beginning, you may feel some tightness or stiffness at first, but with continued practice, the exercise will feel comfortable and can be done with ease.

---

sexual activity and their beliefs regarding the effects of vitamin E. The couples were then randomly assigned to one of two groups. One group received capsules containing vitamin E. The other group received capsules that were identical to the vitamin E capsules in appearance and taste but did not contain the vitamin. Thus the presence or absence of vitamin E was manipulated. The researchers asked the volunteers to complete a questionnaire reporting both their sexual and nonsexual feelings and behavior in the course of taking the capsules.

The random assignment of the couples to the vitamin or nonvitamin group provided a means of controlling the influence of other, irrelevant variables. Participants' descriptions of their sexual outlets during the study indicated that the group taking vitamin E did not differ from the nonvitamin control group in reported levels of sexual activity. The vitamin E group did report a greater number of positive side effects, such as increased energy, than did the nonvitamin group. In the long run, any substance or activity that promotes good health is likely to have a positive impact on sexual functioning—for example, the practice of Kegel exercises (see Box 14.5).

Some drugs may indirectly affect sexual response by generally stimulating physiological or

## Box 14.6

## Aphrodisiacs: Read the Fine Print!

In attempting to understand the decreased sexual interest and erectile dysfunction sometimes experienced by males under treatment for hypertension, or high blood pressure, Stanford University neuroendocrinologist Julian Davidson tested several drugs on rats to alter their sexual response (Clark, Smith, & Davidson, 1984). First injected with a drug commonly prescribed to lower hypertension, the rats displayed no evidence of sexual arousal or motivation to mate. Davidson and his colleagues then administered yohimbine, among other substances, to reverse this effect. Yohimbine eliminated the sexual inhibition produced by the antihypertensive drugs. In addition, a control group of rats given yohimbine without previous administration of antihypertensives became unusually sexually active. Based on further research, Davidson et al. concluded that yohimbine increases arousal in sexually experienced male rats and facilitates copulatory behavior in sexually naive male rats. Their findings were published in *Science* (Clark et al., 1984).

As Levit (1986) later pointed out, the Davidson group had not carried out research on yohimbine's effects on human sexual response, nor had the investigators made any claims about its effects on humans. These facts did not stop national tabloids and mail-order companies from making such claims, however. *Star* described the Davidson research under the headline "'Love Potion' from Tree Works Wonders for Impotent Men, Report Scientists" (January 1, 1985). Stanford University's legal department demanded a retraction of a particular quote attributed to Davidson stating, "We've been having amazing results with our tests on men." One mail-order company has marketed yohimbine-based products as "the cure for sexual impotence." The promotional material includes descriptions of the Davidson group's findings, "but you have to read the fine print underneath the beautiful graphics reproducing our work," said Davidson, "to learn that the 'inexperienced males' are rats, not people" (quoted in Levit, 1986, p. 81).

psychological function. However, many reports of heightened sexual responsiveness following the use of a particular substance may have more to do with a person's beliefs and expectations about the substance than with the substance itself. We will now look at the more common substances that allegedly affect sexual functioning.

Perhaps the best-known reputed aphrodisiac, one that often figures in the fables of sexual conquest by young males, is *cantharides* (Spanish fly). A powder made from dried beetles, this drug inflames and irritates the urinary tract and dilates the genital blood vessels. Spanish fly is a dangerous substance that can cause severe pain and abdominal and urinary tract ulcers; some deaths have even been associated with its use (Goodman & Gilman, 1970).

*Yohimbine*, a drug derived from the bark of the yohimbeca tree, stimulates the nervous system. There have been reports that this alkaline substance intensifies genital sensations and prolongs erection for some men, but more than half the individuals studied have shown little or no benefit from the drug (Rosen & Ashton, 1993). This response rate does not warrant classification of yohimbine as an aphrodisiac. It used to be

**cantharides** (can-THAR-ee-deez)—a powder, popularly called Spanish fly, made from dried beetles; a supposed aphrodisiac that actually causes inflammation and irritation of the urinary tract.

**yohimbine** (YOE-him-bean)—an alleged aphrodisiac derived from the bark of the African yohimbeca tree.

available in a commercial preparation that contained strychnine and testosterone, but this product has been withdrawn from the market. More recently it has appeared as a street drug under the name "yo-yo" (see Box 14.6). The drug is poisonous in large doses.

## Alcohol and Drugs

Alcohol, though a depressant, has a long history of association with enhanced sexual response. Used in moderate amounts, it has a tranquilizing effect, reducing inhibitions that may interfere with sexual enjoyment. In large amounts, however, it impairs all reflexes, including the sexual ones. Heavy alcohol consumption over the long term results in diminished sexual response (Crowe & George, 1989). Indeed, alcoholism is a major cause of erectile failure in men and decreased vaginal lubrication in women. Moreover, some male alcoholics with advanced liver disease show an increased reabsorption of estrogens into the blood, which produces a feminization syndrome that includes erectile failure, atrophy of the testes, and breast enlargement (Segraves, 1988b).

It appears that the erotic effects of moderate amounts of alcohol are due largely to our psychological interpretation of our physical state and to disinhibition (Crowe & George, 1989; Lang, 1985). Both men and women believe that alcohol acts to reduce sexual inhibitions (Brown & Munson, 1987). Further, a drinking woman is perceived by both men and women as more sexually available and more likely to have sex—though less attractive—than a nondrinking woman (George, Gournic, & McAfee, 1988). If we view alcohol as a sexual and social lubricant, we are more likely to engage in sexual behavior when under its influence. Disinhibition of sexual response comes about only because drinking alcohol allows us to attribute our sexual behavior to the effects of alcohol rather than to ourselves—"alcohol made me do it" is the standard excuse. Thus it is the denial of personal responsibility that may prompt us to engage in behaviors that we would enter into more slowly, if at all, under normal conditions (see Figure 14.7).

Research has supported the observation that as a person consumes more than a moderate

**FIGURE 14.7**
**Alcohol, Drugs, and Sexual Inhibitions**
Notice the funnel used by these teenagers to drink beer. The use of alcohol and drugs is likely to reduce sexual inhibitions and to result in decision-making dramatically different from our choices when we are sober.

amount of alcohol, sexual arousal decreases (Rosen, 1991). The sexual response of men and women to erotic films, for example, drops with the consumption of alcohol (Malatesta, Pollack, Wilbanks, & Adams, 1979; Wilson & Lawson, 1978). In one study, male volunteers were given varying amounts of alcohol. They then watched erotic videotapes and were instructed to masturbate. The higher the blood-alcohol concentration, the longer it took the participants to reach orgasm. As the alcohol level in the volunteers' systems increased, arousal, pleasurability, and intensity of orgasm correspondingly decreased.

*Barbiturates* and *sedatives* have an indirect effect on sexual activity similar to that of alcohol. In moderate amounts, these depressants may lower inhibitions and induce a state of relaxation, thus potentially enhancing sexual responsiveness. However, in large doses, they diminish sexual desire and performance. Methaqualone (Quaalude) is a sedative-hypnotic drug that has

barbiturate—a sedative or sleeping pill derived from barbituric acid.

sedative—a substance that eases physical pain and psychological distress.

acquired a reputation as an aphrodisiac. It is commonly prescribed to facilitate sleep and to reduce anxiety. It apparently is more effective in overcoming social inhibitions than in directly stimulating sexual arousal and in this way is similar to alcohol and other central-nervous-system depressants (Rosen, 1991). In high doses, it is associated with loss of erection and inability to have an orgasm.

Various stimulants, too, are widely believed to have aphrodisiac effects. Users of cocaine ("coke" or "snow"), which is extracted from the dried leaf of the South American coca shrub, have reported that the drug increases sexual drive and enhances sexual performance, sometimes producing multiple orgasms, when taken in moderate doses (Rosen, 1991). Because cocaine is also an anesthetic, some users rub it on the head of the penis, or the clitoris, to prolong the pleasures derived from thrusting and clitoral stimulation (Gay, New-Meyer, Perry, Johnson, & Kurland, 1982). Prolonged or heavy use of cocaine often leads to a decline in sexual interest and to sexual dysfunction (Rosen, 1991).

*Amphetamines*, another class of frequently abused stimulants, have varying effects on sexual functioning, depending on the dosage and the individual. Also called "uppers" or "speed," amphetamines energize most users and can increase sexual desire and sexual activity. Prolonged use of amphetamines, however, can inhibit sexual response, cause exhaustion, and induce paranoia. *Amyl nitrate* ("poppers" or "amies") is an amphetamine that dilates the blood vessels. Medically, it is administered to increase blood flow to the heart. Many users report that inhaling it during sexual play or just before orgasm prolongs orgasm and delays ejaculation (Rosen, 1991). Anyone with heart or blood pressure problems should avoid this drug.

Nicotine may have adverse effects on sexual function in some men (Rosen, 1991; White et al., 1990). Most of this evidence has come from men referred for urologic evaluation of erectile dysfunction. Cigarette smoking was more prevalent in this group than in the general population. No studies to date have investigated the relationship of nicotine use to sexual response in women.

Marijuana is reported by more than half its users to enhance sexual pleasure, but most rated its overall effect to be weak (Weller & Halikas, 1984). It is not an aphrodisiac in the sense that it directly stimulates sexual response. Instead, its effects may be similar to those of alcohol, in that it may loosen inhibitions and permit a person to attend to sensual feelings more wholeheartedly than he or she does normally. Devotees also report heightened pleasure in eating and listening to music. Marijuana may, in addition, enhance relaxation in a way that alters sensory experience, allowing one to enjoy any pleasurable activity more intensely than when in a normal state. Some individuals, however, report that marijuana exerts a negative, inhibiting effect on their sexual response (Wolman, 1985). Physiological and psychological reactions to marijuana depend heavily on the user's experience with marijuana, the setting, and his or her attitudes about the drug.

Psychedelic drugs such as LSD and mescaline can alter the sensory experience of sex. Some users report heightened sexual functioning, whereas others see the state induced by these drugs as incompatible with sexual activity (Jarvik & Brecher, 1977). As with other drugs, the response to LSD fluctuates depending on the person ingesting it and on the setting in which it is taken.

*Opiates*, among them heroin, morphine, and their synthetic relatives, such as methadone, depress sexual interest and activity. These drugs can lower testosterone levels in males and inhibit ovulation in females (Wolman, 1985). In the case of opiates, the drug becomes the main focus of

---

**amphetamines**—compounds that stimulate the central nervous system.

**amyl nitrate**—a potentially dangerous drug, usually inhaled, that relaxes muscle spasms and is sometimes used to prolong or intensify the experience of orgasm.

**opiates**—narcotics derived from the opium poppy that tend to induce relaxation or sleep.

interest to addicts, and sex, like most other activities, takes a back seat.

The administration of supplemental testosterone or some other androgen to males with very low levels of testosterone may sharpen sexual response. But giving androgens to individuals with adequate levels of testosterone appears to enhance sexual functioning for only a few hours (Jarvik & Brecher, 1977). Testosterone can also heighten sexual desire in females. It is difficult, however, to find a dosage that will not lead to masculinizing side effects such as beard growth.

Anabolic steroids (AS) are naturally occurring androgens or synthetic derivatives of androgenic compounds sometimes used by body builders (for example, weight lifters) and other athletes to enhance physique and performance. Long-term AS users often show an increase in sexual desire and aggressive behavior (Moss, Panzak, & Tarter, 1993). Although sexual desire appears to be androgen-dependent, erectile function is not (Bancroft, 1989). Thus current AS users experience a greater frequency of erectile dysfunction than athletes who do not use AS (Moss et al., 1993). The increase in sexual desire and aggression without a corresponding increase in erectile functioning may place AS users at greater risk of sexual aggression.

Any prescribed drug that affects the nervous system or blood pressure has the potential to influence sexual behavior. Persons experiencing a change in sexual activity or desire while using a prescribed drug should notify their physician. Antipsychotic drugs such as thorazine tend to decrease sexual desire, sexual excitement, and frequency of orgasm. Drugs used to treat anxiety have effects similar to those of alcohol. Low doses reduce inhibitions and increase sexual excitement and frequency of orgasm, but the muscle-relaxing effects can sometimes inhibit sexual excitement and orgasm. Drugs that lower blood pressure can also depress sexual functioning. More recently developed drugs that reduce elevated blood pressure are less likely to impair men's sexual functioning (Morrissette et al., 1993). Antidepressant medication has been reported to enhance sexual functioning in some people but to impair it in others (Rosen & Ashton, 1993).

Finally, there are a number of drugs, such as Ecstasy, which are reputed to heighten sensory awareness and sexual pleasure. Many of these drugs can have severe side effects.

## Common Anaphrodisiacs

Anaphrodisiacs have been sought at least since the Victorian era to treat sexual offenders and to curb masturbation.

*Saltpeter* (potassium nitrate) has a reputation as a sexual depressant. It was sometimes added to the food of schoolboys and of the inmates of institutions where authorities wanted to inhibit sexual desire and activity. Although saltpeter is a diuretic that increases the voiding of urine, there is no evidence that it inhibits sexual desire or activity. Its reputation may stem from its early use in treating fevers. Indeed, the state of sexual arousal is related to a perceptible rise in body temperature owing to the engorgement of the genitals with blood. To apply slang popular a few years ago, when we are excited we "get hot." People may believe that if saltpeter reduces the body's temperature, it can also extinguish the heat of sexual desire.

Estrogens are highly effective anaphrodisiacs in men because they depress testosterone-related functions. Males who have been given estrogen also experience the feminization of sexual characteristics, such as growth of breasts, rounding of hips, softening of muscle tissue, and decrease in hair and beard growth. Similar effects result from the ingestion of synthetic progestin and antiandrogen drugs such as cyproterone acetate, which have been used to suppress sexual desire in sex offenders (see Chapter 19).

It should be apparent from this discussion that no drug directly determines the course and intensity of sexual response. Rather, drugs only modulate the experience of sexual activity. Human sexual response is a complicated, intricate process that is subject to myriad influences beyond chemicals. Using these drugs, whether to

---

**saltpeter**—a diuretic with an unsupported reputation as an anaphrodisiac.

enhance sexual functioning or to treat a medical condition, can undermine our sexual well-being, as the following discussion illustrates.

## The Interaction of Medical Conditions and Treatments with Sexual Response

Epilepsy provides a good example of the ways in which the sexuality of a person with a physiological problem—in this case, epilepsy—can be affected by that person's emotional concerns, others' reactions and expectations regarding the person's condition, and assumptions made by the providers of treatment programs. Epilepsy is a disorder characterized by seizures and sometimes by a temporary loss of consciousness. The convulsions result from a cerebral dysfunction caused by a lesion or metabolic abnormalities (Jensen, Jensen, & Sorensen, et al., 1990).

Noting that previous research had suggested that 30% to 70% of epileptics have sexual problems, primarily inhibited sexual desire, and that few studies had included epileptic women, Jensen et al. (1990) conducted research to determine the frequency and symptoms of sexual dysfunctions in epileptic men and women. They compared epileptics with diabetics and with a control group of persons who did not have medical problems. In contrast to conclusions from previous research, the frequency and symptoms of sexual dysfunction in people with epilepsy were lower than among diabetics and did not differ from those of the control group of healthy people. As the authors noted, the people with epilepsy were being treated with newer antiepileptic drugs and were free of other medical conditions or psychiatric problems. Is it possible that the conclusions from the earlier studies, suggesting relatively high levels of sexual dysfunction among epileptics, may have been confounded by the medications the participants were taking or the presence of other conditions?

The experience of one of our students suggests how a particular medication or treatment itself might influence sexual functioning. An ep-

ileptic, she has been instructed to take one of the traditional medications for the disorder—phenobarbital—when she feels a seizure coming on. She commented that when she takes the drug, she does not feel like engaging in *any* activity, including sexual interaction. If she were continually on this drug, she would probably be diagnosed as having inhibited sexual desire, which, she assures us, is definitely not the case. The potential for the treatment rather than the medical condition itself to affect sexual responsiveness is supported by Jensen et al.'s (1990) finding that 16% of the people in their sample reported antiepileptic drugs previously prescribed to them had negatively affected their sexual life.

It is also possible that physicians familiar with the findings from previous, less well-controlled studies might tell their epileptic patients to expect difficulties with their sexual functioning. These expectations in turn might prime people with epilepsy to anticipate sexual problems and subsequently to experience them. The Jensen et al. research suggests that not the epilepsy per se but correlates of the epilepsy underlie difficulties in sexual response. Similarly well-controlled studies on other diseases are needed to determine the extent to which factors other than the maladies themselves may impede pleasurable sexual expression.

## A Concluding Note

Our ideas about what it means to be sexual men or women are inextricably tied up with our physical anatomy. Parts of our bodies, particularly those associated with sex, become indices of who we are. When any one of these "sexualized" organs changes with age, accidents, or medical conditions, the individual often feels that his or her masculinity or femininity has been diminished or lost. Such associations of the functioning and appearance of particular parts of our body with our erotic and human value undermine both our emotional health and our sexual well-being. Clearly, some disabilities may negatively affect the ease with which we respond or limit the ways in which we are able to interact, but they need not spell the end of intimate sexual contacts with a loved one. Sexuality, sensuality, and erotic experience are not synonymous with genital response.

The destruction of the stereotype of individuals with diseases or physical impairments as "sexless" would not only help people with disabilities enjoy life; it might also enhance their general health. For example, sexual activity has been associated with reducing insomnia and depression and with relieving arthritis pain by boosting cortisone levels in the blood (Butler & Lewis, 1973).

Regardless of our level of functioning, all of us have a stake in the elimination of useless stereotypes about the relationship of infirmities to sexuality. Any one of us could experience a disabling accident or disease. Out of concern both for ourselves and for those who are currently affected by serious injuries, impairments, or diseases, it behooves us to create an atmosphere supportive of the erotic and sensual needs of all people, regardless of their level of health.

## Summary of Major Points

| | |
|---|---|
| 1. **The construct of healthy functioning and sexual self-esteem.** | Rather than dichotomizing health and illness as either/or conditions, it is more accurate and useful to view health as existing along both psychological and physiological continua. Recently developed measures of sexual self-esteem have found that people high in this attribute are less depressed about their sex lives and more likely to use contraception when appropriate. Preliminary research indicates that sexual self-esteem may manifest itself differently in men than in women, and that positive feelings about our sexual selves appear to increase from the high school years into early adulthood. |
| 2. **Body image and sexuality.** | Body image—our perception of our bodies—is related to prevailing cultural ideals. In contemporary Western cultures, physical attractiveness is seen as connected to slenderness. Thus many people, particularly women, diet rigorously to attain this ideal. Anorexia nervosa and bulimia are conditions characterized by extreme concern with weight reduction. People with anorexia nervosa are relatively inactive sexually, whereas bulimic persons tend to have sex more frequently than is usual for samples drawn from the general population. |
| 3. **Menstruation and health.** | A few women experience severe mood swings and even antisocial behavior during the premenstrual phase, but the "menstrual madness" hypothesis is not supported for the vast majority of women. Although hormonal fluctuations may contribute to the variations in reactions to menstrual-cycle phases seen in some women, religious background and cultural expectations also play a part in these variations. Menopause—the cessation of menstruation, with an accompanying decrease in the secretion of estrogen and progesterone—appears to have a wide range of effects on women's feelings and sexual functioning. For women experiencing uncomfortable side effects, hormone-replacement therapy (HRT) can provide relief and is associated with long-term reductions in the likelihood of other negative effects of aging, such as osteoporosis. |
| 4. **Inability to conceive.** | Many couples have some condition that interferes with fertility. Difficulties with producing sperm or eggs, blockage of ducts (spermatic |

cord, vas deferens, fallopian tubes) and/or allergic reactions to sperm are among the treatable conditions that impair fertility. There is no evidence supporting the stereotype that psychological or emotional problems are a major source of infertility. Artificial insemination, adoption, or a surrogate mother can be solutions for couples unable to obtain infertility treatment.

**5. Impairments and injuries.**    Some people have physical disabilities; others must cope with developmental disabilities. The sexual expression of these people is affected not only by their particular medical condition but also by the attitudes of society and of their caretakers toward the disability or injury. Some loss of sexual capacity may stem from the failure of rehabilitation programs to focus on the sexual needs of their clients and also from the societal assumption that a person with an impairment is no longer a sexual being. The impact of a condition on a person's capacity for sexual relationships varies with the extent of disability, so an individual should never be assumed to be limited to the same degree as the average person in his or her medical category. For example, some persons with spinal cord injuries can experience complete or partial sexual expression or have certain reproductive capacities, depending on the degree and location of their injury.

**6. Aphrodisiacs, alcohol, drugs, and anaphrodisiacs.**    Humans' long quest for chemical substances to increase or decrease sexual desire and performance has generally been fruitless. Some substances may influence sexual response indirectly, either because of beliefs about their powers or because of their effects on psychological feelings. The administration of hormones apparently has little effect on the sexual response of people who secrete normal levels of hormones. The administration of estrogens to men can reduce their sexual response. Caution is advised in taking any so-called aphrodisiacs; some have health-threatening side effects. In small doses, alcohol and some drugs may have indirect effects on sexual expression by reducing inhibitions, but in large doses, or when taken over lengthy periods, these substances usually diminish humans' capacity for satisfying sexual relations.

**7. The interaction of medical conditions and treatments with sexual response.**    Epilepsy is an example of a condition that was assumed to interfere with sexual functioning, but recent well-controlled studies have shown it to be unrelated to a person's ability to have satisfying sexual interactions. Experimenters' traditional neglect of the sexual needs of people with medical conditions or disabilities may have perpetuated the afflicted person's sense of loss. Research is urgently needed on the extent to which various impairments, in and of themselves, contribute to sexual dysfunction. As in the case of epilepsy, researchers may find that medications or expectations, rather than a particular disease or disability itself, are the source of diminished sexual enjoyment.

# Review of Key Concepts

1. Sexual self-esteem and sexual depression are: a) unrelated; b) negatively correlated; c) positively correlated; d) none of the above; no measure of sexual self-esteem yet exists. (pp. 454–456)

2. The current Western obsession with slimness as the ideal in physical attractiveness: a) simply reflects traditional Western values that have idealized slenderness for the past 600 years; b) has resulted in dieting by large numbers of nonobese people; c) has resulted in a reduction in the number of people being treated for eating disorders; d) has increased the general health of Americans. (pp. 456–457)

3. Scientific research has shown that anorexia nervosa is linked to: a) childhood sexual abuse; b) promiscuous sexual behavior; c) unsatisfied sexual desire; d) none of the above. (pp. 458–459)

4. Which of the following hypotheses about menstruation has been confirmed? a) Premenstrual discomfort is caused by hormonal fluctuations. b) Premenstrual syndrome debilitates most women and can cause insanity. c) Premenstrual discomfort results from cultural expectations rather than hormonal influences. d) None of the above hypotheses has been confirmed. (pp. 460–462)

5. Research has demonstrated that the phases of the menstrual cycle: a) are the major determinant of a woman's mood; b) have no effect on a woman's mood; c) can contribute to a woman's mood but are heavily influenced by psychosocial factors; d) negatively affect a woman's partner's mood. (pp. 460–462)

6. Toxic shock syndrome: a) is almost always fatal; b) affects only females; c) is most likely to occur in the use of extra absorbent tampons and the presence of the bacterium *S. aureus*; d) is most likely to occur in sexually active women who use sanitary napkins when menstruating. (p. 461)

7. Studies of hormone-replacement therapy (HRT) for postmenopausal women indicate that: a) moderate amounts of prolactin reduce postmenopausal symptoms; b) small amounts of estrogen and progestins reduce postmenopausal symptoms; c) any HRT increases the risk of cardiovascular disease, osteoporosis, and cervical cancer; d) all of the above. (p. 464)

8. Which of the following is the least likely to result in female infertility? a) genetic and chromosomal disorders; b) hormonal disorders; c) emotional difficulties; d) blockage of the fallopian tubes and problems with implantation of the fertilized egg. (pp. 465–467)

9. Infertility is: a) associated with the woman's production of antibodies that attack the man's sperm cells; b) associated with the couple's emotional resistance to pregnancy and parenthood; c) incurable if it has a physical but not an emotional basis; d) a myth. (pp. 465–468)

10. Discuss the ethical and legal implications of artificial insemination and surrogate motherhood. Should surrogate motherhood be banned? (p. 469)

11. Alcohol is best characterized as: a) a stimulant that increases sexual arousal as larger amounts are consumed; b) a depressant that, when used in large amounts, impairs all reflexes, including sexual ones; c) an aphrodisiac that enhances sexual pleasure; d) a substance that was used in Victorian times as an anaphrodisiac. (p. 477)

12. Opiates such as heroin and morphine: a) like marijuana, are sexually stimulating for some individuals and depressing for others; b) decrease sexual interest and arousal; c) have no effect on sexual arousal; d) increase sexual activity in laboratory rats. (pp. 478–479)

# Sexual Orientation

*W*E each have a sexual orientation. Some of us feel sexual arousal toward individuals of the same gender; others' attraction is directed toward people of the other gender. Some of us find people of both genders sexually appealing.

In this chapter we survey research on human sexual orientation. Most of this research has focused on an attraction to people of the same gender—that is, homosexuality—and our coverage will reflect that bias. Studies of heterosexual orientation have been neglected, perhaps because funding agencies and researchers have perceived heterosexuality as being "natural" or "normal" and thus needing no explanation. We look at homosexuality in other species and cultures, and we also examine the relationship of gender-role identity to sexual orientation. The legal and social treatment of gay people within our culture and the emergence of the gay-liberation movement is considered. We also discuss what is known about the incidence of homosexual behavior and about the characteristics of gay lifestyles. Current explanations of the development of sexual orientation are reviewed. We examine the assumption that people who have an erotic orientation toward others of the same gender are in need of psychotherapy, and we describe attempts to alter sexual orientation. The phenomenon of antigay prejudice, or *homophobia*, has captured the

**homophobia**—fear of and hostility toward homosexuals.

**Box 15.1**

## Variations in Sexual Orientation and Gender Identity

**Heterosexuals.**   People who have sexual relationships primarily or exclusively with members of the other gender.

**Homosexuals.**   People who have sexual relationships primarily or exclusively with members of their own gender.

**Bisexuals.**   People who have sexual relationships with members of either gender, although not necessarily at the same time.

**Transsexuals.**   People who appear biologically to be members of one gender but who feel psychologically as if they were members of the other gender.

**Transvestites.**   People who become sexually aroused when wearing clothing stereotypical of the other gender. (Almost all contemporary transvestites are heterosexual males.)

attention of researchers, and we discuss what their studies have shown about this fear and its consequences. Finally, we consider bisexuals—people for whom gender is not an influence in erotic attraction to others.

## What Is Sexual Orientation?

The phrase "sexual orientation" can be applied to erotic attraction toward people of the same gender (homosexual), the other gender (heterosexual), or both genders (bisexual). Many people confuse gender identity with sexual orientation; that is, they assume that homosexual orientation occurs because of inappropriate gender identification. Consequently, men who prefer male sexual partners are frequently portrayed in the media as highly effeminate—"swishy," in slang parlance. But in fact, the gender-role identities of gay men and lesbians are often consistent with their biological gender. For example, Mary and Susan may both be quite stereotypically feminine in terms of their gender identities, yet they may be involved in a *lesbian* love affair with each

other. There is also a tendency to confuse transvestism and transsexuality with sexual orientation. See Box 15.1 for definitions of some key terms.

Most North Americans reserve the label *heterosexual* for people who have had sexual interactions only with members of the other gender. All others—regardless of how many homosexual or heterosexual interactions they have had—are lumped into the *homosexual* category. How accurate is the common assumption that a heterosexual has sex exclusively with members of the other gender and that a homosexual is anyone who has ever had sex with a person of the same gender? Although we noted in Chapter 2 that the Kinsey group's sample was not representative of the U.S. population, Kinsey et al. (1948) found that 37% of males and 13% of females in their sample had had at least one homosexual encounter. In presenting their findings on the topic, Kinsey and his colleagues (1948) introduced a rating scale that subsequent research has used extensively (see Figure 15.1). Based on their sexual behaviors and erotic feelings, individuals are assigned a place or number on Kinsey's 7-point continuum from exclusive heterosexuality to exclusive homosexuality.

Kinsey's 7-point scale represented an improvement over some of the more simplistic definitions of sexual orientation, but it too has its problems. For instance, it does not establish nu-

**lesbian**—a homosexual female.

| Exclusively heterosexual behavior | Primarily heterosexual, but incidents of homosexual behavior | Primarily heterosexual, but more than incidental homosexual behavior | Equal amounts of heterosexual and homosexual behavior | Primarily homosexual, but more than incidental heterosexual behavior | Primarily homosexual, but incidents of heterosexual behavior | Exclusively homosexual behavior |
|---|---|---|---|---|---|---|
| 0 | 1 | 2 | 3 | 4 | 5 | 6 |

**FIGURE 15.1**

**The Kinsey Continuum**

Rather than treating people as either heterosexual or homosexual, the Kinsey group placed individuals along a continuum divided into 7 categories, as this figure shows.

merical ranges for categorizing sexual orientation. Is a female who has sexual relations with males 65% of the time and with females 35% of the time different from a female whose ratio is 50:50 (bisexual) or 35:65 in the opposite direction, as the Kinsey scale suggests? This question may seem trivial, but it becomes important when individuals are being selected for a research project designed to compare heterosexuals, bisexuals, and homosexuals. Who goes into which group, and why?

Although Kinsey did take psychological reactions to people of the same and other gender into account in classifying sexual orientation—that is, fantasies and feelings about same-gender people by individuals who did not have homosexual contacts—he emphasized behavioral criteria. In contrast, some psychologists, in devising their own definitions of homosexuality, have been relatively unconcerned with whether physical intimacy with a person of the same gender ever occurred. Anna Freud (1953), a noted psychoanalyst and the daughter of Sigmund Freud, maintained that the crucial determinants of homosexuality are one's thoughts and images when masturbating. If fantasies are about members of the same gender, then the person is homosexual. According to her view, a man who becomes sexually aroused by homosexual fantasies while making love to his wife would be classified as a homosexual even if he has never engaged in homosexual behavior. Social scientists such as

Storms (1980, 1981) and Bell et al. (1981) have presented evidence that an individual's erotic fantasies and feelings are indeed central to the development of sexual orientation. These erotic fantasies motivate and give direction to sexual behavior and to the selection of partners. In using the terms *gay*, *homosexual*, and *lesbian* in this chapter, we are referring to an adult who is motivated by a definite erotic desire for members of the same gender and who usually (but not necessarily) engages in overt sexual relations with them.

## Cross-Species Perspectives

Homosexual behavior is fairly common among nonhuman mammals. Mounting of one male by another has been observed among rodents and primates. Male-male mountings are much more likely to occur when one of the males displays feminine behavior, although this feminine behavior is not necessarily a sexual act. For example, among some types of monkeys, a male adopts a "receptive" posture as a gesture of appeasement after an argument with a more dominant male.

Female-female mounting is also common among mammals. Although females of some species also mount males and inanimate objects, mounting by females is most common when the object of their affection is at the peak of her estrous cycle. This appears to be true of chimpanzees, several types of monkeys, cows, lions, and domestic cats.

Hormonal fluctuation associated with the estrous cycle is not the only influence on the homosexual behavior of monkeys, however. Individual characteristics, past experience, level of dominance, sexual stimulation, familiarity, group composition, and affection are other factors that are related to the intensity and duration of the relationship (Srivastava, Borries, & Sommer, 1991).

An explanation of homosexual behavior in other species was proposed by Beach (1976), who asserted that homosexual behavior among primates and mammals is usually an expression of dominance relationships rather than of sexual desire. These animals express their status (dominant or submissive) in a variety of ways. When the expression takes the form of a sexual approach, if one male approaches another male using a dominant style (specifically, mounting and pelvic thrusts), the second male will usually respond with a submissive (receptive) sexual posture. If the same first male approaches the second with submissive sexual behavior, however, the second male will react with dominant sexual behavior.

Beach maintained that the more frequent occurrence of heterosexual behavior than homosexual behavior among mammals stems from differences in male-female gonadal secretion of hormones and in animals' sensitivity to these hormones. Consequently, males are more likely to respond with masculine sexual responses and females with feminine sexual responses, and both genders are more responsive to other-gender patterns of stimulation than to same-gender patterns.

In summary, we can conclude that homosexual interaction is not limited to human beings. It has been observed in most species that researchers have studied (Baum, 1992). Their studies have given us little insight, however, into human homosexual behavior. Therefore, it is advisable to note Beach's (1976, p. 298) warning:

*The fact that some animals engage in homosexual behavior has often been mentioned in discussions of human sexuality, with the implication that the mere existence of the similarity proves something or other about homosexuality in man; e.g., that homosexuality*

*is "biologically normal." The conclusion may or may not be correct but the empirical evidence is irrelevant and neither supports nor denies the deduction.*

## Cross-Cultural Perspectives

It is often notoriously difficult for outsiders to obtain information about a particular culture's sexual patterns. Individuals who engage in homosexual acts in a culture that prohibits this behavior are understandably reluctant to acknowledge their behavior to a visiting scientist. Further, interpreting behavior in a group different from one's own is difficult, given the tendency to see one's own cultural values and beliefs as the best or most natural (see Figure 15.2). It is important to keep these problems in mind as we look at societies that differ from Western industrialized cultures in their responses to homosexual behavior.

Our information about homosexual expression in other cultures is primarily based on anthropologists' observations. In *Patterns of Sexual Behavior* (1951), Ford and Beach reviewed reports of about 190 cultures for which information about sexuality was available. They reported that homosexual behavior was not found to be a predominant sexual activity among adults in any of the societies. In the majority (64%) of the 76 groups for which information on homosexuality was available, same-gender sexual relations were considered to be normal and socially acceptable, at least for certain members of the community; in about a third of the societies, homosexual behavior was reported to be rare, absent, or carried on only in secrecy.

In Chapter 1, we described the Sambia of New Guinea as an example of a culture that prescribes a period of ritualized homosexuality for young males. In fact, about 40 cultures in New Guinea (10% to 20% of the total number of distinct cultures in that region) practice some form of ritualized homosexuality (Herdt, 1984). In these cultures, semen is believed to be a precious resource that must be transferred to a young male to enable him to reach maturity. Techniques for achieving this transfer include oral intercourse, anal intercourse, and masturbation followed by a smearing of semen over the body. North Amer-

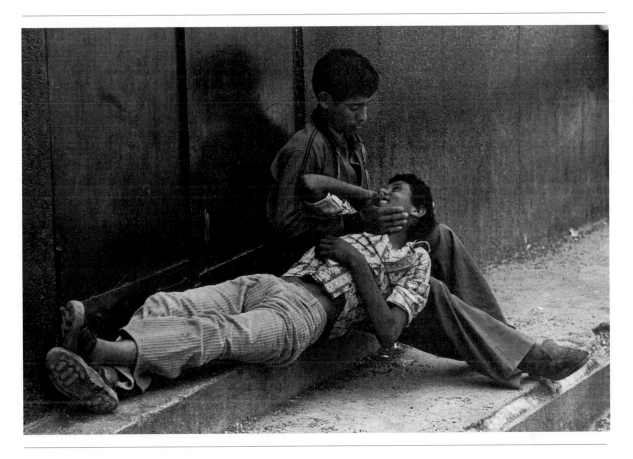

**FIGURE 15.2**
**Behavioral Differences Across Cultures**
The physical affection displayed by these Moroccan males would be unusual among heterosexual men in most of North America. Norms regarding physical contact vary from culture to culture.

icans might view such mandatory universal homosexual behavior among young males as endangering the survival of the group, but contrary to what many people might think, this practice does not lead to permanent homosexuality: most of these young males become exclusively heterosexual, marry, and father children.

Davenport (1965) provided an excellent account of a group of Melanesian people living on a Pacific island, where adult male homosexual relations with adolescents and homosexual relations between two adolescents were completely acceptable and openly discussed. Mutual masturbation and anal intercourse were considered normal within these relationships, although oral-

genital activity was unknown. When a man was about 20, he married a woman, but he could still engage in extramarital homosexual relations. Thus men in this society demonstrated either heterosexual or bisexual behavior. Davenport found no adult males who were exclusively homosexual.

The foregoing groups are examples of societies that have an institutionalized phase of homosexuality for males during their youth. They offer a rather striking contrast to Western expectations regarding adolescent sexuality.

Earlier we mentioned the popular assumption that inappropriate gender-role identification predisposes people to engage in homosexual behavior. The stereotype suggests that homosexuals adopt either male (the butch) or female (the femme) roles. Moreover, a homosexual male who inserts his penis during fellatio or anal intercourse is considered to be active and masculine, whereas a male who receives the penis is seen as passive or feminine. Based on his preference in sexual activities, each "type" supposedly also exhibits stereotypically masculine or feminine attributes in nonsexual areas; however, much of North American and British research does not support this rigid stereotyping. A substantial proportion of male homosexuals show a wide variety of traits associated with both masculine and feminine roles and engage in all forms of, and positions in, homosexual activity. Further, most homosexual men are attracted to masculine rather than to effeminate partners. Similarly, lesbians are attracted to each other on the basis of their femininity (Bell & Weinberg, 1978; Blumstein & Schwartz, 1983; Schreurs, 1993).

As Carrier (1980) pointed out, however, most of this research has focused on middle- and upper-class Western males in developed countries. In contrast to these men, substantial numbers of males in Mexico, Brazil, Greece, and Turkey express a clear preference for playing either the active or the passive role when engaging in homosexual relations. These cultures have rigidly defined gender roles that shape heterosexual as well as homosexual interaction. Apparently, there is little stigma attached to the active, inserter role in homosexual contacts in these groups because this role is considered to be masculine. A man's penetration of another man is viewed as an accomplishment of sorts, like sexual penetration of a woman. But a person who takes the submissive, receptive role is ridiculed and stigmatized as effeminate. In Brazil, for example, the average person does not perceive the man who takes the active sexual role as homosexual (Parker, 1991). When two men engage in sex, only the receptive or feminine man is labeled as homosexual.

It seems, then, that in those cultures or subcultures where rigid gender-role stereotypes prevail, cultural expectations will lead to narrowly prescribed sexual relationships. In predominantly middle- and upper-class North America, where gender roles are more flexible, we find greater variation in sexual expression among both heterosexuals and homosexuals, and less pressure to engage exclusively in sexual activities associated with stereotypically masculine or feminine roles. For example, fellatio appears to be more common among Americans than among, say, Mexicans (Carrier, 1980). Homosexual Mexican males, reflecting their societal values, are expected to achieve sexual satisfaction through anal intercourse rather than fellatio, just as heterosexual Mexicans are expected to prefer sexual intercourse to fellatio. To date, there has been little cross-cultural research on lesbianism. The cross-cultural evidence relevant to homosexuality reflects the powerful influence that cultural expectations regarding gender roles have on sexual interactions.

Reiss (1986) has marshaled evidence indicating that the greater the rigidity in the male gender role in male-dominant societies, the higher the likelihood of male homosexual behavior. Generally in male-dominated societies, not only is a father's involvement in infant care minimal, but a boy often obtains little help from his father in learning how to model normative male behavior. Under these circumstances, narrow and rigid male gender roles and heterosexual roles are more difficult to learn than in a less male-dominant society with less rigid gender roles.

## Legal and Social Status of Homosexuality

Gay people have experienced a long history of oppression. Even in this century, homosexuals have had to deal with the predominant view that they are "sick." Unlike most people with illnesses, however, homosexuals also have had to cope with the knowledge that the behaviors associated with their "illness" were illegal.

It was not until 1974 that members of the American Psychiatric Association (APA) ratified a resolution that "homosexuality per se implies no impairment in judgment, stability, reliability or general social or vocational capabilities," thus removing homosexuality from the list of official mental disorders. However, the APA's most recent classification of mental disorders, the fourth edition of the *Diagnostic and Statistical Manual of the American Psychiatric Association* (*DSM-IV*,

**Box 15.2**

## Alien

In 1952 the U.S. Congress passed the Mc-Carran Act, which, among other provisions, stated that "aliens afflicted with psychopathic personalities are not to be admitted into the United States." As a result of this legislation, homosexual immigrants, who were automatically categorized as psychopathic personalities, were denied entry into the United States. More than a quarter of a century later, sexual orientation was still being used as a basis for barring people from entry, as the following article, which appeared in *The New Republic* on July 21, 1979, reveals.

*DEVIANT CUSTOMS. At two o'clock in the morning on June 26, Karl Kinder, age 32, of Frankfurt, West Germany, arrived at the St. Paul–Minneapolis International Airport on a stopover en route from Germany to Los Angeles. Searching Kinder's luggage, a customs inspector found a copy of* Der Stiefel, *a German gay magazine, and asked, "Are you a homosexual?"*

*"No, I am a bisexual," Kinder says he replied.*

*Immigration officials then informed Kinder that he could not be admitted to the United States, because a section of the 1952 Immigration and Naturalization Act excludes from entry all "aliens afflicted with psychopathic personality, or sexual deviation, or a mental defect." Kinder was offered two options. He could submit to an examination administered by the Public Health Services and a hearing with an immigration judge; or he could return to Germany on the next flight. Kinder chose the latter. He spent the night at the Marriott Inn, escorted by Metropolitan Airport Police, and left the country the next afternoon.*

*If not for a leak to the* Minneapolis Star, *the entire incident would have gone unnoticed. The Immigration and Naturalization Service does not keep a record of aliens it excludes who do not request hearings, so there are no statistics available on how many homosexuals have been turned away. But the National Gay Task Force estimates that a hundred episodes like Kinder's occur each year. A hearing could involve being held in a quarantine or on parole for as long as a month, and—if the ruling is against you—a wait of a year before you can reapply for a visa. So most homosexuals barred at one airport opt to try again at another without making a fuss. (p. 8)*

*Before this 1979 incident, Kinder had made about 20 visits to the United States. Like other foreign homosexuals and bisexuals visiting the United States, he was probably unaware of the U.S. immigration and naturalization policy. The medical "examination" that Kinder would have undergone would have consisted of checking his records in West Germany for homosexual-related crimes and asking him whether or not he was a homosexual. A few months after this incident, the surgeon general, Julius Richmond, directed his staff to cease classifying homosexuality as a mental defect or disease. As a result, the Public Health Service no longer provides medical examinations, but immigration officials still stop people who indicate that they are gay or people whom someone else indicates are gay.*

On July 16, 1982, in the case of *Hill v. Immigration and Naturalization Service*, a federal district court justice in San Francisco issued a permanent injunction banning discrimination against gays and lesbians seeking immigration to the United States. This ruling is only applicable to the judge's northern California district, however.

1994), does include a category called "sexual disorder not otherwise specified," which includes "persistent and marked distress about one's sexual orientation." The removal of homosexuality from the list of mental disorders was due partly to research conducted over the past three decades that failed to establish any direct connection between homosexual orientation and mental or emotional disorders. To some extent, it was also a response to the growing social and political influence of gay people who have fought against psychiatric labeling and criminal prosecution.

### Criminal Law

U.S. criminal law has contributed more than its fair share of discrimination against individuals who engage in homosexual acts. In general, homosexuals have been prosecuted under state *sodomy* laws. These laws generally outlaw "unnatural acts"—nonprocreative activity such as oral sex and anal intercourse. Although many heterosexuals could be prosecuted for breaking these laws, homosexuals traditionally have been singled out for prosecution for these "criminal" activities. Slowly but surely, states have been decriminalizing sodomy. As of 1994, sodomy was no longer considered a crime in more than half the states. The Supreme Court's 1986 decision upholding Georgia's sodomy law (described in Chapter 7) confirmed that any further decriminalization will have to come from state legislatures. In Canada sodomy is known as buggery and includes having sexual relations with animals. An individual can be charged with the offense only if a participant is under age 21, or if the act takes place publicly or involves an animal (*Pocket Criminal Code*, 1987).

### The Gay Liberation Movement

In the United States, the civil rights of homosexuals have been limited by a long tradition of discrimination in such areas as housing, employment, immigration, naturalization, military service, child custody, and marriage (see Box 15.2 on page 491). At the beginning of the 1990s, only the state of Massachusetts had enacted a law prohibiting discrimination against homosexuals in these areas.

The spiraling concerns about homosexual rights in the 1980s and 1990s resulted from gays' efforts to organize and to influence the political process in the time-honored American tradition of participatory democracy. These strategies have

their roots in the older civil-rights movement of the 1950s. The beginning of the gay liberation movement in the United States is usually traced back to an incident on June 27, 1969, when police raided the Stonewall Inn, a gay bar in New York City. The patrons became angry and pelted the officers with bottles and stones until police reinforcements arrived and the crowd dispersed. For the next five nights, crowds of homosexuals, joined by heterosexual sympathizers, gathered in the vicinity of the inn to protest the vice-squad raid and to confront the police. Within a month after the Stonewall riots, the Gay Liberation Front had been organized in New York City. Although groups concerned with gay rights—such as the Mattachine Society; One, Inc.; and Daughters of Bilitis—had existed since the 1950s, it was the Stonewall riots that marked the emergence of homosexuals' political activism. In 1973 the National Gay Task Force (now the National Gay and Lesbian Task Force) was created, and it joined a number of other organizations actively working to end discrimination and to change the negative stereotypes of lesbian women and gay men (see Figure 15.3). Much recent gay activism has been channeled into obtaining increased funding for AIDS research and education, and for providing social support for gay couples who have formed long-term commitments to one another.

The issue of the meanings and definitions of *homosexual, gay,* and *couple* is complex. Definitional difficulties add to the problem of obtaining accurate estimates of the percentage of people who fit into various categories of orientation, and we consider these and other related topics in the next section.

## Homosexual Behavior and Gay Identity

What is the extent of homosexual behavior in our society? The answer depends on how we ask the question. Perhaps the Kinsey group's most frequently quoted finding regarding homosexuality is that, by the age of 45, 37% of the men and 13% of the women in the Kinsey sample had had at least one homosexual encounter leading to orgasm.

---

**sodomy**—"unnatural" sexual acts, which, depending on the jurisdiction, can involve anal sex, oral sex, and/or sex with animals.

**FIGURE 15.3**

**Gay and Lesbian Pride Parade**

Some parents of gay offspring have become members of support groups such as PFLAG (Parents and Friends of Lesbians and Gay Men). Notice the woman to the far right expressing her pride about her straight parents.

Since the Kinsey group's research, there have been a number of attempts to assess sexual orientation in the United States and other countries. Some of these studies have used random probability sampling, tapping a more representative group than did the Kinsey group (Billy et al., 1993; Leigh, Temple, & Trocki, 1993; Smith, 1991). These researchers have come up with markedly lower estimates of the prevalence of homosexuality among Americans.

It is difficult to determine whether the lower numbers reflect more representative sampling techniques or a failure to elicit honest answers from the respondents. Most recent researchers have employed interviewers with only limited training in sexual interviewing, as compared to the extensive experience of the researchers associated with the Kinsey group. For example, in the Smith (1991) study, the interviewers were primarily middle-aged women, most of whom had no college degrees. Gebhard (1993) also pointed out that random probability samples are problematic in trying to determine the incidence of homosexuality:

*Homosexuals migrate from rural communities where it is hard to conceal their orientation, to the anonymity of large cities, so rural samples will be largely devoid of them. In the cities the homosexuals congregate in gay communities. These are usually relatively small and therefore easily missed in random sampling. Worse yet, the custom of interviewing only one member of a household is disastrous in a gay community, where everyone in a household is apt to be homosexual. (p. 64)*

Given all these complications, the best estimate seems to be that about 4% to 6% of men and 2% to 4% of women are predominantly homosexual for a large part of their lives (Diamond, 1993; LeVay, 1993).

What is striking about the variation in the statistics is the substantial number of people who engage in homosexual behavior but do not become exclusively homosexual. The typical male pattern involves homosexual contact during preadolescence and the teens, followed by little or no further homosexual activity. This finding raises an interesting question about sexual orientation: why do a large number of males who engage in youthful homosexual activity eventually indulge primarily in heterosexual relations and presumably maintain a heterosexual identity, whereas others adopt a homosexual identity? On a more concrete level, how do people who have had one or more homosexual contacts know whether they are homosexual or heterosexual? Or, if they have developed a strong emotional attachment to a member of the same gender, how do they decide whether this attachment should be classified as a homosexual orientation or a deep friendship that includes sexual expression? These questions all involve our identities and self-definitions as sexual beings.

## Self-Definition

We humans seem to need to define ourselves. Introverted-extroverted, dominant-submissive, liberal-conservative, graceful-awkward, sophisticated-naive, practical-impractical, generous-stingy, and organized-disorganized are just some of the word pairs with which we try to understand behavior. After we have chosen labels for

ourselves, we tend to behave in accordance with them; that is, we will often ignore or avoid those experiences that do not mesh with the self-identity we have fashioned. You may have experienced a similar phenomenon in reading your horoscope—you accept those descriptions and predictions that fit your expectations and disregard those that do not.

The search for meaning and self-definition is at no time more pressing than during the adolescent struggle to determine a personal and sexual identity. During childhood and adolescence, most people experience a great deal of confusion and ambiguity about sexual thoughts, feelings, and behavior. What is normal and what is deviant or abnormal? What is the appropriate role to choose in relationships with others? In moving awkwardly through this complicated process, a person begins to construct a sexual identity. For most people, one aspect of that identity is heterosexual, but for some it is homosexual or, more rarely, bisexual. The many paths that lead to a homosexual identity are far more difficult to traverse because of the sanctions against homosexual behavior.

Those adults who define themselves as homosexual often experience a sense of being "different" in childhood and adolescence (Bell et al., 1981; Telljohann & Price, 1993; Whitam, 1977). One study of 1,000 gay people indicated that "homosexual feelings" occurred typically at age 14 among males and about age 16 among females. For both males and females, the feelings had arisen at least two years before they ever made genital contact with a person of the same gender (Bell et al., 1981).

Acquiring a gay identity is a gradual process, however. The emergence of homosexual feelings is followed usually by an individual's adoption of the label gay, his or her association with other gay individuals, and a first homosexual love relationship (Harry, 1993; Rust, 1993). There is evidence that young men identify themselves as gay at an earlier age if they are able to meet openly with gay men in a supportive environment where homosexuality is considered normal (Boxer & Cohler, 1989). This sort of environment is most likely to be found in large cities where there are well-developed support systems for gays.

**FIGURE 15.4**
**Public Display of Affection**
Gays who publicly express affection are often criticized for flaunting their homosexuality. It is rare, however, to hear a heterosexual couple walking with their arms around each other condemned for flaunting their sexuality.

After individuals define themselves as gay, the stage is set for a number of other important decisions. Should they remain "in the closet" and keep their sexual orientation as private as possible? If they decide to "come out"—that is, to acknowledge their gay identity to others—how publicly should they express their orientation? Should they tell their family and friends? What about employers and strangers? The coming-out phase is a complex one in the individual's life, during which he or she adopts a gay identity and explores the homosexual community. Most men come out at about age 19 or 20; women, however, tend to come out somewhat later, in their early 20s (Harry, 1993; Rust, 1993).

Although a person's sexual orientation is just one aspect of his or her identity, our society tends to view the sexual orientation of homosexuals as an extremely important, if not the most important, aspect of the individual's identity. Regardless of their occupations, accomplishments, temperaments, and the myriad other factors that make up the complexities of being human, people who choose to express their sexuality with others of the same gender are culturally defined, first and foremost, as homosexuals, a definition that affects the ways in which others interpret all their actions (see Figure 15.4). This drastic oversimplification becomes the interface between conventional heterosexuality and the subculture of homosexuality.

This link between homosexual orientation and other personal characteristics and behaviors is even more problematic when we consider that most homosexuals and heterosexuals cannot easily identify the sexual orientation of other individuals. In one study, students observed videotapes of interviews of heterosexual and homosexual males and females (Berger et. al., 1987). Almost 80% of the students were unable to identify accurately the sexual orientation of those shown in the videotapes beyond chance expectations. The dichotomy so emphasized in our society is not readily apparent to most of us, gay or heterosexual.

Some homosexuals openly exhibit their affection. Faced with the intolerance of conventional heterosexual society, other homosexuals carefully shroud their sexual orientation in secrecy. Most choose a position somewhere between these

**FIGURE 15.5**

**A Married Lesbian Couple**

These two lesbian women have just registered as domestic partners at the Clerk of Courts.

two extremes (Harry, 1993). Homosexuals who tend to be overt about their orientation are most likely to volunteer for research on the topic. Therefore, we know more about the lifestyles of those people than we do about less openly gay persons.

## Gay Lifestyles

Almost all gay men and lesbian women have been involved at some point in a relatively steady relationship with a same-gender partner (McWhirter & Mattison, 1984; Schreurs, 1993). In Bell and Weinberg's (1978) study, more than 50% of the men and approximately 70% of the women were currently involved in a steady relationship (see Figure 15.5).

For those gays who enjoy variety and prefer not to commit themselves to a monogamous relationship, there are a number of ways in which to find like-minded persons. Cruising is one of these, and it has captured the attention of many researchers of homosexuality. Gay bars and nightclubs are the most frequent locales, just as heterosexual dating bars are often the hunting grounds for "straights" looking for a sexual partner. Gay baths, private parties, the streets, public parks, and beaches are other popular locales. Even before the advent of AIDS and concern

about the risks of engaging in sex with anonymous partners, the lowest incidence of cruising occurred in "tearooms" (public restrooms) and movie theaters (Bell & Weinberg, 1978). The interaction between partners in the context of cruising can vary from an impersonal and fleeting encounter in a washroom to the development of a lifelong partnership.

With the growth of gay liberation, a wide variety of support systems for gay individuals has evolved in urban areas. Friends or partners can be found in gay social clubs, churches, political organizations, and discussion groups. Large cities have easily identifiable gay neighborhoods with bookstores, physicians, realtors, clothing stores, lawyers, and many other resources that cater to a gay clientele.

### Sexual Expression

Homosexuals use the same methods of sexual expression as heterosexuals, with the obvious exception of coitus. For lesbians, the most common arousal techniques are cunnilingus, mutual masturbation, and *tribadism*. To perform the last, one woman lies on top of the other and makes rhythmic thrusting movements to stimulate their clitorises. The use of dildoes and the practice of analingus (stimulation of the anal area with the tongue) appear to be relatively rare among lesbians (Schreurs, 1993), despite their popularity in erotic films and books. Gay men most frequently engage in fellatio, mutual masturbation, anal intercourse, and interfemoral intercourse—rubbing the penis between the partner's legs until orgasm (Bell & Weinberg, 1978; Weinrich, 1994).

In their comparison of heterosexual and homosexual physiological responses, Masters and Johnson (1979) found no differences between the two groups in patterns of sexual arousal and orgasm. In other words, a human body responds to sexual stimulation in the same predictable ways whether the arousal comes from males, females, or inanimate objects. The application of sexual stimulation, however, may be somewhat differ-

**tribadism**—sexual activity in which one woman lies on top of another and moves rhythmically for clitoral stimulation.

**FIGURE 15.6**
**Gay Lovemaking**
Research has suggested that gay couples in general may have a more relaxed and less goal-oriented approach to sexual intimacy than do heterosexual couples.

ent in homosexual lovemaking than in heterosexual lovemaking. Masters and Johnson reported that gay people are more relaxed than heterosexuals, tending to adopt a slower and less demanding sexual approach with each other. They seemed to be more wholeheartedly involved in their sexual activity and demonstrated greater communication than the heterosexual couples whom Masters and Johnson studied. The heterosexual couples were described as being more performance-oriented; that is, they spent less time giving sensual pleasure to each other as they pursued orgasm: "At times, they created the impression that the objective of goal attainment was valued almost as much as the subjective experience of orgasmic release" (Masters & Johnson, 1979, p. 65).

Masters and Johnson (1979) attempted to explain these differences by suggesting that it is easier for women to know what pleases women and for men to know what pleases men. Consequently, homosexuals have an intuitive understanding of their partners' sexual wants. Masters and Johnson maintained that a pattern in which partners take turns giving and receiving stimulation reduces fears about sexual performance. They believe that heterosexual interactions in-

volve more dependence on and responsibility for the partner, a pattern that distracts each partner from his or her own subjective experience.

If Masters and Johnson's (1979) findings are generalizable to the larger proportion of sexually proficient and psychologically adjusted homosexuals, then these gay couples may have something to teach heterosexuals about sensuality (see Figure 15.6). The relaxed and less goal-oriented approach of the homosexual couples observed by Masters and Johnson epitomizes the advice that most sex therapists give to both heterosexuals and homosexuals for enhanced sexual enjoyment.

In contrast to Masters and Johnson's conclusions, Jay and Young (1979) reported that 42% of the 1,000 lesbians in their study complained of frequent difficulty in sexual communication with their partners. Further, in Bell and Weinberg's (1978) study, between 43% and 61% of the gay men and women reported that lack of orgasm for themselves or their partner was sometimes a problem.

Research on the values of homosexuals had been negligible until recently. Peplau and Gordon (1983) reported the results of a series of studies comparing the values of gay and heterosexual men and women and found great similarities in the groups' rankings of the values that they considered important in a relationship. Their romantic view of love, degree of commitment, and satisfaction with their relationships were also similar. But gay individuals differed from heterosexuals in that they attached less importance to sexual exclusivity in a relationship. In terms of psychological adjustment and of measures of satisfaction and commitment, there appear to be no differences between monogamous and nonmonogamous gay male couples (Blasband & Peplau, 1985; Kurdek & Schmitt, 1985/1986). Apparently, for gay males, both types of relationships can be satisfying.

Researchers have also found differences between dependent or traditional women involved in lesbian relationships and independent, feminist lesbians (Peplau & Gordon, 1983). Mirroring the tendency of traditional heterosexual women, traditional lesbian women were especially dependent on their partners for fulfilling their needs. In contrast, the independent, feminist lesbians sought satisfaction from professional and community involvement, not just from their love relationships.

### Gender Differences

Surveys of psychological research on homosexuality over the last three decades indicate that the major interest has been in gay men (Watters, 1986). This imbalance in the research has left us with relatively little information about lesbians until quite recently.

Most of the differences that have been found between gay men and lesbian women are those that might be expected from the different socialization experiences of males and females in our culture (Leigh, 1989; Schreurs, 1993). For example, women, regardless of sexual orientation, rank emotional expressiveness and equality in their love relationships as more important than do gay and straight men. And in contrast to many gay male relationships, lesbian love affairs are relatively long-lasting ones in which the couples show a considerable degree of fidelity to each other (Blumstein & Schwartz, 1983; Kurdek & Schmitt, 1987; Peplau & Gordon, 1983; Schreurs, 1993). Perhaps for this reason, public cruising is much less frequent among lesbians than among gay men (Bell & Weinberg, 1978). Only 17% of lesbians, Black and White, had actively sought sexual encounters during the year previous to the research. When the women did cruise, the activity was almost entirely limited to bars and private parties. In contrast, about 85% of Black and White men reported cruising about once a month (Bell & Weinberg, 1978).

One of the most striking differences between homosexual men and women lies in their number of sexual partners. Almost half the White homosexual men in the Bell and Weinberg (1978) study said that they had had at least 50 different sexual partners during their lives, and 28% claimed 1,000 or more partners. In contrast, none of the lesbians in the total sample reported having had this many partners, and more than half had been involved with fewer than 10 sexual partners. One of the unfortunate consequences of the male pattern is that about two out of three reported having had a sexually transmitted disease at one time or another, whereas only one of the 293 women

in this study had ever contracted a sexually transmitted disease from homosexual activity.

Symons (1979) argued that lesbian and gay male sexual behavior represents a pure form of male and female sexuality. Homosexual men, in many respects, show more extremely stereotypical "masculine" sexual behavior than do their heterosexual counterparts; that is, they tend to seek a variety of partners and to engage in impersonal and frequent sexual activity to a greater extent than do heterosexual men. Lesbians tend to form stable, intimate relationships in which sexual relations are generally associated with enduring emotion and a loving partner. According to Masters and Johnson (1979), lesbians show greater consideration for their partners than do gay men. Lesbian relationships are, in these respects, quite similar to heterosexual pairings. Symons suggested that in heterosexual relationships, males and females are forced to compromise their true sexual natures, and if not for the constraints of heterosexual convention, heterosexual men would generally engage in the search for variety and the one-night stands that are characteristic of young gay men. Symons's speculations are supported by empirical observations of gender differences among youthful gays and heterosexuals (Blumstein & Schwartz, 1989). His hypotheses are less compelling when applied to older men and women, regardless of their sexual orientation.

### Aging

There is no particular reason to believe that the biological effects of aging on sexual response are any different for homosexuals than for heterosexuals. Masters and Johnson (1979) have demonstrated that sexual response does not differ according to sexual orientation, and it is difficult to imagine factors that would alter this fact in the second half of life.

In terms of sexual behavior, most studies (Bell & Weinberg, 1978; Kinsey et al., 1948, 1953; McWhirter & Mattison, 1984) suggest that homosexuals experience the same general age-related changes as do their heterosexual counterparts. Wolf (1979) nevertheless found that, although the aging gay people whom she interviewed experienced many of the life changes that are characteristic of our culture at large, their sexual orientation did produce unique challenges as they dealt with the effects of menopause, the changes of midlife, and plans for retirement activities. For gay men, psychological adjustment in later life is associated with a strong commitment to homosexuality, integration into the gay community, low concern with concealment of sexual orientation, and a satisfactory sex life, usually within an exclusive relationship (Berger, 1980).

The stereotype of the aging homosexual as fearful and maladjusted has not been supported by research (Berger, 1980; Kehoe, 1986; Kimmel, 1978). In fact, Weinberg and Williams (1975) found that older respondents tended to have better self-concepts and to be stabler than younger gays. Among the older respondents, more women than men tended to be sexually active, but those men who were still sexually active did not differ from the women in frequency of sexual expression. Women showed more interest than men did in long-term relationships. One difference that emerged from this research was that lesbians were less anxious about growing old than were gay males. The reverse has been found to be true among heterosexuals. Perhaps this is a reflection of the gender of the person one wishes to attract. Because men are attracted to youth and beauty, those people who wish to be sexually attractive to men—heterosexual women and gay men—may become overly concerned about their own youth and beauty, a fact that might make them more vulnerable to eating disorders, for example, in their efforts to remain thin and attractive (Gettelman & Thompson, 1993); (see Chapter 14).

There is some evidence to support the notion that homosexuals do not experience the midlife crisis that many heterosexuals encounter. Relatively early in life, most homosexuals go through a crisis that heterosexuals do not: they must face and manage a conventionally nonaccepted sexual lifestyle. It may be that if this challenge is successfully resolved, the individual's ability to cope with the changes of aging are strengthened (Kelly, 1980). In addition, the majority of homosexuals are not faced with the family responsibilities and changes in family involvement that often confront heterosexuals.

There is little evidence to support the popular myth that gays are considered old at 30 or 40 because they no longer have the fresh look of youth. This myth often embodies the notion that many older gays turn to hustlers, tearoom contacts, and young children for gratification. However, in one study (Harry & DeVall, 1978) of 243 gay men in the Detroit area, those aged 35 years or older reported that they preferred sex with a partner of the same age or only slightly younger than themselves.

Kimmel (1978) pointed out that because of the stigma associated with a homosexual orientation, aging gays are deprived of many of the social supports that benefit their heterosexual age peers. For example, when a heterosexual loses his or her mate through divorce or death, friends and relatives tend to be supportive through a grieving period. But when a homosexual bond ends, friends and relatives may be relieved; when a gay person's mate dies, bereavement may be a solitary experience unless the survivor has a close support network in the gay community.

### Situational Homosexuality

In gender-segregated institutions such as prisons and in some military settings, homosexual relations are fairly common. Homosexual behavior under these conditions is frequently spurred by the lack of opportunity for heterosexual contact and is known as transient or situational homosexuality. In one study of prison life, about 40% of the convict population was found to have engaged in homosexual activity (Clemmer, 1958). Of these, however, only about 10% had engaged in such behavior before they went to jail.

Homosexual interactions in male prisons are often based on the wish to dominate those perceived as weaker or possessing "feminine" characteristics (Long & Sultan, 1987; Prendergast, 1994; Wooden & Parker, 1982). In a situation similar to those reported in the earlier discussion of cross-cultural research on homosexuality, the dominant man does not view himself as a homosexual, and seldom is there reciprocal sex. That is, the dominant man uses the "weaker" man for sexual release but does not in turn provide sexual pleasure for the subordinate man (see Box 18.2 in Chapter 18).

There is little research on sexuality in female prisons (Prendergast, 1994), but about three decades ago, Giallombardo (1966) reported that the majority of women inmates engaged in homosexual behavior. In contrast to male prisoners' interactions, coercion in these contacts was minimal, and affection was common. As might be expected from our earlier discussion of lesbian relationships, women prisoners usually integrated sexuality into an ongoing relationship. Most of the women who engaged in same-gender relations in prison did not think of themselves as homosexuals, and they usually returned to heterosexual behavior when they were released.

In the military, the individual who engages in homosexual behavior because of orientation or the lack of heterosexual opportunity faces grave penalties. He or she is in conflict with Pentagon directive No. 1332.14, which states, "Persons who engage in homosexual conduct" or "demonstrate a propensity" to do so "adversely affect the ability of the armed forces to maintain discipline, good order, and morale." According to Pentagon figures, about 1,400 men and women are discharged annually for violating this directive. The discharges are usually honorable, provided that the offender leaves the service and does not contest the expulsion.

The ban on gays in the military provoked sharp debate in the 1990s (Shilts, 1993). President Clinton initially pledged to end the military's ban on homosexuals, but in the ensuing furor he accepted a compromise proposal: "Don't ask, don't tell, don't pursue." This would allow gays in the military as long as they make no public declarations of their orientation and refrain from homosexual behavior. This approach still does not deal with the basic issue. Until gays are fully accepted in the military, they continue to face stigma and potential extortion.

## Explanations of Sexual Orientation

Historically, most hypotheses that have been advanced to explain sexual orientation have included the notion that people are gay because of defects: inherited disorders, deviant hormonal exposure, harmful family patterns, early sexual experiences, or gender-role nonconformity. If not for negative influences, it was thought, the individual would be heterosexual. We consider this assumption after reviewing the data relevant to each hypothesis.

## Heredity

Historically, scientists have tended to appeal to biological or genetic factors to account for behavioral phenomena that they did not understand, including homosexual behavior. Conclusions based on such influences, even when inaccurate, seem to resolve complex and elusive questions in an orderly way.

Interest in a hereditary basis for homosexuality dates back to the 18th century, when all sexual variations were assumed to be a sign of a degenerate family tree. Not surprisingly, most theorizing regarding homosexuality and heredity has portrayed homosexuality as maladaptive. For example, an early and frequently cited investigator of homosexuality wrote:

> *the urgency of [research] with respect to the genetic aspects of homosexual behavior is underscored by the ominous fact that* **adult homosexuality continues to be an inexhaustible source of unhappiness, discontent, and a distorted sense of human values.** *(Kallmann, 1952, p. 296, emphasis added)*

As this statement demonstrates, Kallmann was not the most objective observer of homosexuality. He conducted an extensive study of sexual orientation in twins, in which he examined *concordance rates*. Kallmann reported that the concordance rate was nearly 100% for monozygotic (genetically identical) twins and about 10% for dizygotic (not genetically identical) twins. Kallmann's work was harshly criticized because many of the men in his study came from prisons and psychiatric institutions, and because there

**concordance rate**—the likelihood that if one person manifests a certain trait, a relative (twin, sibling, uncle, etc.) will manifest that same trait.

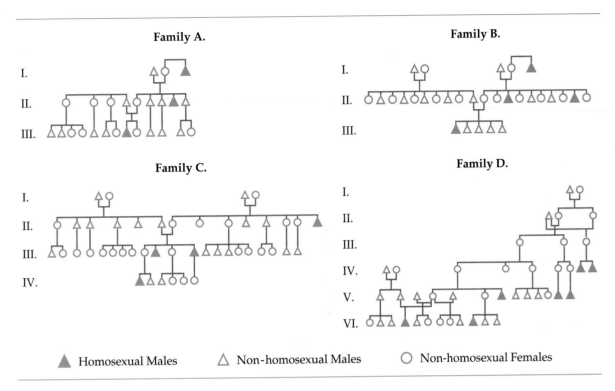

**FIGURE 15.7**

**Family Trees of Families with Homosexual Males**

Samples of homosexual males and their families where asked by Hamer et al. (1993) to identify, if possible, other family members who were/are gay. Families A and B both have a single gay man in each of three maternally related generations. In Family C two gay brothers have a maternally related gay uncle and nephew. Family D, for whom information was obtained about six generations, contains seven (known) gay males. These gay men are all related through the sequential marriage of two sisters to the same husband in generation II. As Hamer et al. (1993) put it, in addition to evidence of transmission of gay male orientation through the maternal line, the striking aspect of these genealogies "is the absence of transmission through the paternal line and the paucity of female homosexuals" (p. 323).

was no information about how Kallmann judged whether the twins were monozygotic (MZ) or dizygotic (DZ).

More recent twin studies have shown concordance rates for homosexual orientation in males to be as high as 66% for MZ twins and 30% for DZ twins (Bailey & Pillard, 1991; Whitam, Diamond, & Martin, 1993). These findings suggest that there may be a genetic contribution to male homosexual orientation. The idea of a genetic or biological basis for some male homosexuals is further reinforced by the report by Hamer, Hu, Magnusen, Hu, and Pattatucci (1993). They

have found a region on the X chromosome that appears to contain a gene or genes for homosexual orientation in 40 pairs of homosexual brothers. Thirty-three of the homosexual brothers had similar genetic markers and appear to have inherited the chromosome responsible for the trait from their mothers. See Figure 15.7 for data from their study showing the relationship of the maternal connection to homosexual orientation in men. For example, in Family A, Generation I, the woman's brother is gay. The woman (let's call her Sally) has one daughter and four sons, one of whom is gay. Sally's daughter then produces a daughter and a son who is gay. It should be noted that Hamer and his colleagues think that homosexuality arises from a variety of causes including both genetic and environmental factors.

There have also been reports (Pillard et al., 1982; Pillard & Weinrich, 1986) that homosexual males are more likely than are heterosexual males to have homosexual brothers. The reasons for the correlation could be genetic, but variables related to prenatal development and/or social development could also contribute to sexual orientation, either alone or in some combination.

In keeping with this emphasis on biology, there have been reports of differences between the brains of homosexual and heterosexual men (LeVay, 1991, 1993; Swaab & Hofman, 1990). A region in the hypothalamus of the brain known as the interstitial nuclei of the anterior hypothalamus (INAH) contains at least four small groups of neurons. The third of these, INAH-3, is generally larger in men than in women, and based on research with animals, the region appears to be involved in male-typical sexual behavior. In an intriguing study, LeVay (1991) hypothesized that the volume of INAH-3 would show a size dimorphism (size difference) not just with biological sex, but with sexual orientation. Specifically, he thought that it would be relatively large in people sexually oriented toward women (heterosexual men and homosexual women) and small in individuals oriented toward men (heterosexual women and homosexual men).

To test this hypothesis, LeVay examined the brain tissues of relatively young deceased people, because alterations in the volume of INAH-3 might differ as a function of the aging process. He compared the INAH regions of the brains of 41 deceased people: 19 homosexual men, 16 heterosexual men, and 6 heterosexual women. The homosexual men all had AIDS. Of the heterosexual men, 6 had AIDS, and the other 10 died of other causes. Of the 6 heterosexual women, 1 had AIDS, and the other 5 died from other causes. LeVay cautioned that the women were "presumably heterosexual" but noted that women's sexual orientation is seldom noted in their medical records. Because he wanted an approximate age-match in the sample, a comparable sample of homosexual women could not be obtained. In comparing INAH-3 regions in the three groups,

LeVay did so without knowledge of the group to which each brain had belonged. Note, however, that because of the absence of homosexual women, he could only test his hypothesis regarding the relationship between the volume of INAH-3 and sexual orientation with men.

LeVay (1991) obtained highly significant differences in the volume of INAH-3 between the three groups. Specifically, as predicted, heterosexual men had a higher volume in that region of the hypothalamus than did homosexual men. Homosexual men were intermediate between heterosexual men and heterosexual women in the INAH-3 volume, with the women having the lowest volume. Had he been able to obtain a sample of lesbian women, it would have been interesting to see if they more closely resembled the heterosexual men than the other two groups. We must emphasize that these results are preliminary and need to be replicated with other larger samples by other researchers. Further, although we have included a description of LeVay's fascinating findings under the heading of heredity, it is possible that environmental factors associated with sexual orientation may alter the volume of this region of the brain.

A number of researchers have suggested that hormones play a role in sexual orientation. We will now examine findings from this area of investigation.

## Hormones

In the 1930s and 1940s, several attempts were made to treat homosexual men with androgens. This approach was based on the idea that gay men were not masculine enough, so they needed a booster of masculinizing hormones. Although the androgen administration usually succeeded in increasing sexual interest and activity, partner orientation remained unchanged. This result is not surprising, considering two facts: heterosexuals do not become homosexuals when androgen levels are decreased through surgical castration or chemical means, and males with sex-hormone deficiencies such as Klinefelter's syndrome (see Chapter 4) do not usually develop a homosexual orientation.

In adult females, androgen excess, which can result from cancer treatments with this hormone or from certain medical syndromes, results in increased sexual interest. Removal of a woman's adrenal gland (the major androgen-producing organ), on the other hand, depresses sexual interest. In both cases, however, sexual orientation remains unaffected.

The vast majority of homosexual males appear to have testosterone levels within the normal range (Gladue, 1987). In evaluating the results of these studies, it is important to remember that testosterone levels fluctuate within each 24-hour period and from one day to the next in the same person (Dabbs, 1990). Plasma and urinary testosterone levels are also sensitive to such factors as general health, diet, drug use, cigarette smoking, sexual activity, use of marijuana, and emotional stress.

Research on sex hormones is even more difficult in females than in males because of the normal fluctuation in women's hormone levels. Past studies indicate that the majority of lesbians appear to have testosterone and estrogen levels within the normal range. About a third of all lesbians studied, however, have shown elevated—but not abnormally high—testosterone levels (Gladue, 1987).

There is growing interest in the possible prenatal hormonal contribution to sexual orientation, but we are probably years away from adequately testing this theoretical link. Even if such a prenatal contribution exists, whether it is overtly expressed would probably depend on a host of other experiential factors.

## Family Influences

Several studies influenced by psychoanalytic theory have explored the role of early family influences in the development of sexual orientation. In one such study, Bieber and his colleagues (1962) described a *triangular system* to account for the development of male homosexuality. This theory suggested that a homosexual was typically the child of an overly intimate, controlling mother and a detached, hostile, rejecting father. Bieber and coworkers based their system on the differences they found between a group of homosexual men and a group of heterosexual men in psychoanalysis. Even so, 38% of the homosexuals did not come from a triangular family system, and 32% of the heterosexuals reported such a family background. At most, the Bieber research suggests that many people in therapy, regardless of their sexual orientation, may be the products of a triangular system. Subsequent research on the issue has been quite contradictory (Milic & Crowne, 1986; Newcomb, 1985; Siegelman, 1987).

Some of the conflicting results emerging from studies of homosexuals' family backgrounds can be attributed to variations in the populations from which the homosexual samples were drawn; in certain studies these populations consisted of patients or prisoners. Siegelman (1972a, 1972b) attempted to reduce the potential bias introduced with such samples by administering questionnaires, including one that measured neuroticism, to groups of "normal" (nonclinical) homosexuals and heterosexuals. When he compared homosexual and heterosexual men who were low in neuroticism, there were no differences in the parental backgrounds of the two groups. The same was true of women who scored low in neuroticism, except that the lesbian women described themselves as less close to their parents and reported less family security and more friction between their parents than did the heterosexual women. Siegelman (1974) noted that this difference could have stemmed from the child rejecting the parent rather than vice versa. Overall, his research supports the idea that parental characteristics may correlate with tendencies toward neuroticism in both homosexuals and heterosexuals but are not related to sexual orientation per se. As Hoffman (1978) noted:

> There is no predictive value of this "typical prehomosexual" family; i.e., if one were to establish that a child was growing up in such a family, one could not reliably predict that the boy would become homosexual. (p. 179)

Therefore, the present evidence on family background and sexual orientation supports the

**triangular system**—a psychoanalytic concept proposing that a male homosexual's parents consist of an intimate, controlling mother and a detached, rejecting father.

position taken by Hooker (1969) about a quarter of a century ago that disturbed parental relations are neither necessary nor sufficient conditions for the development of homosexuality.

## Gender-Role Nonconformity During Childhood

A growing body of evidence indicates that one pathway to becoming a homosexual in adulthood is nonconformity to societal expectations for one's gender in early childhood. Researchers studying homosexual men have reported that "feminine" boys have a much higher probability of becoming adults with a homosexual orientation than do more "masculine" boys (Bailey, Miller, & Willerman, 1993; Bell, Weinberg, & Hammersmith, 1981; Green, 1987; Phillips & Over, 1992). For example, Whitam (1977) found significant differences between adult homosexual and heterosexual men in childhood cross-gender behavior. Homosexual men were more likely to characterize their childhoods as having involved interest in toys stereotypic for girls, cross-dressing, preference for girls' games and activities, preference for the company of women, being regarded as a sissy, and preference for boys in childhood sex play. Practically all homosexuals (97%) in his study reported one or more of these experiences, whereas most heterosexuals (79%) reported none of these experiences.

Adult gay men who have a strong preference for receptive anal intercourse have the strongest recollections of gender-role nonconformity in childhood (Weinrich et al., 1992). If this finding is replicated, it suggests that there may be a distinct subgroup of gay men whose preferred erotic behavior is a continuation of a lifelong gender atypical pattern. Gay men who do not have a strong preference for receptive anal sex have a childhood history that is more conventional regarding gender-role conformity and that has a substantial overlap with the history typical for heterosexual men.

Not all homosexuals display traits or interests atypical of their gender in childhood. About half the homosexual men in the Bell et al. (1981) research appeared to have masculine identities, interests, and activities in childhood, compared to about three-fourths of the heterosexual men. About one-fifth of the lesbian women, compared to one-third of the heterosexual women, reported being highly "feminine" while growing up.

The link between homosexuality and gender nonconformity in childhood has been questioned because of the way in which it was established. In the Bell group's study, individuals were asked to indicate what their childhoods were like. Beyond the usual difficulties associated with remembering events long past, this population may have introduced an additional bias. Having already accepted a gay identity and a set of beliefs about homosexuality, they may have unintentionally edited their memories to make those memories consistent with their current belief systems. Such bias may be particularly problematic when the sample is recruited via the gay-liberation movement.

Green (1987) avoided the problem of inaccurate memories by conducting a longitudinal study in which boys who were effeminate during childhood were compared to a control group of conventional boys. Following these boys into adolescence, he found that the gender nonconformists were more likely to become homosexual than were members of the control group.

Ross (1980) explained the relationship between gender nonconformity and male homosexuality as a self-fulfilling prophecy. Male homosexuals who have internalized the common stereotype of the gay male as effeminate may respond to researchers as they think others expect them to, and in this way they fulfill researchers' expectations. Ross suggested that researchers would find less rigid gender stereotyping in less traditional countries. Studies in Sweden and Australia support his hypothesis. Swedish homosexuals, reared in a society in which adopting nontraditional gender roles is acceptable, recalled less feminine childhood play than did Australian homosexuals, who typically were reared to adopt traditional gender roles. Thus early atypical gender-conforming interests and activities may be related to homosexuality in cultures that emphasize rigid distinctions between masculinity and femininity.

## Early Sexual Experiences

Of the four factors that we have considered thus far, only the last—gender-role nonconformity in childhood—appears to have a fairly solid link to homosexual orientation. Learning through experience appears to be another important factor in adult sexual orientation. In a study of more than 11,000 people, intense sexual experiences and feelings of arousal, pleasure, or discomfort associated with early experiences were the strongest correlates of adult sexual orientation (Van Wyk & Geist, 1984).

Van Wyk and Geist found that at about seven or eight years old, boys and girls became involved in prepubertal sexual play consisting of showing or touching the genitals. For about 4% of the boys and less than 1% of the girls, prepubertal sexual play led to orgasm. In addition, more than 25% of the boys and 10% of the girls masturbated to orgasm before they reached puberty. This greater sexual adventurousness of boys may explain why there are more adult gay men than lesbian women. Males were also more likely than were females to have same-gender sexual contacts during childhood and adolescence. Those boys who learn of masturbation by being masturbated by another male—and, to a lesser extent, those who learn of masturbation by watching other boys masturbate—were more likely to be attracted to men in adulthood than those who learned about masturbation in other ways. The same is true for those whose first orgasm occurred through a homosexual contact (Van Wyk & Geist, 1984).

The picture is somewhat different for girls. When sexual activity goes beyond the showing and touching of genitals, most girls feel concerned, uncomfortable, and pressured rather than pleased and aroused. They may learn to dislike engaging in sexual activity with the kinds of people who pressured or coerced them to do things that made them uncomfortable. Preadolescent girls who engaged in masturbation, oral-genital activity, or coitus with adult males, as well as those whose first sight of a penis occurred during physical contact intense enough to be sexually arousing to them, were more likely than other girls to engage in sexual activity with other females when they became adults.

To summarize: "Those who learn to masturbate by being masturbated by a person of the same sex, those whose first orgasm is in homosexual contact and those who have arousing or uncomfortable sexual experiences seem to develop differently than those who do not have

such experiences" (Van Wyk & Geist, 1984, p. 541). Sexual orientation appears to be fairly well established in males by age 18 and in females by age 21. Masturbatory fantasies may reinforce these sexual orientations through sexual arousal and orgasm (Bell et al., 1981; Storms, 1980, 1981; Van Wyk & Geist, 1984).

Gallup and Suarez (1983) described the development of sexual orientation from an evolutionary viewpoint. They maintained that most young males are motivated primarily by genital sexuality, whereas young females look for lasting and caring relationships. Male homosexuality thus may be a response of young males to limited access to female sexual partners; that is, sexual frustration may leave some males open to homosexual activity as a sexual outlet. The circumstances that may promote a male homosexual orientation are reinforced when we add the complication that young males whose behavior does not conform to traditional gender-role norms may compete less successfully for heterosexual partners.

The evolutionary explanation for the development of homosexual orientation in young women is somewhat different from the explanation for young men. Young women may be put off by early sexual encounters with men and become disenchanted with heterosexual relations. In support of this hypothesis, Bell and Weinberg (1978) reported that approximately 85% of lesbian women—but only about 20% of gay men—engaged in heterosexual intercourse before turning to homosexuality.

Thus Gallup and Suarez see homosexuality as an offshoot of adaptive strategies that are strikingly different for men and women. This evolutionary viewpoint suggests that male homosexuality will continue to be fairly common as long as young males' access to potential heterosexual partners is limited. And as long as young females feel the pressure of male sexual ardor, some will comply by engaging in sexual activity with males, opening a possible path to homosexuality if their heterosexual experience is negative.

The Gallup and Suarez model and the other explanations for homosexual orientation that we have reviewed need to be verified by further empirical research. No one explanation for the development of sexual orientation has been conclusively demonstrated. Further, the bases for the development of heterosexual attraction have been neglected (Storms, 1980, 1981). In summary, there appear to be many different paths to the development of erotic orientation that vary from one culture and historical period to another.

## Sexual Orientation, Adjustment, and Antigay Prejudice

Over the years, homosexuals in North America have been accused of being mentally ill or maladjusted. Mental health professionals have tried to "cure" homosexuals, and researchers have attempted to measure emotional health and adjustment as a function of a person's sexual orientation.

### Adjustment and Sexual Orientation

Early research on the psychological adjustment of homosexuals relied on clinical reports of homosexuals in therapy. The investigators, who were usually therapists, tended to assume that homosexuals were maladjusted; why else would they be in therapy? In another research approach, homosexuals in therapy were compared with control groups of heterosexuals who were usually not in therapy. This design, too, provided evidence that homosexuals were maladjusted. The results of these studies then tended to be generalized to all homosexuals. For an unusual description of this reasoning applied to heterosexuals and violence, see Box 15.3.

Assumptions that homosexuals are maladjusted started changing when researchers began to draw samples from populations of homosexuals who were not in therapy. One strategy used in this kind of research is to administer various psychological tests to see whether there are differences between homosexuals and heterosexuals. Such comparisons should be made, however, only between groups that are matched with respect to criteria such as age, religious beliefs, education, economic level, and relationship status. If such demographic factors are not controlled, it is impossible to know whether it is the influence of these factors or the effect of sexual orientation that is responsible for any differences in psycho-

logical adjustment. Unfortunately, many of these studies did not carefully match heterosexual and homosexual samples and thus yielded inconsistent results. In general, however, there is no evidence of major differences in adjustment between homosexuals and heterosexuals (Gonsiorek, 1991; Siegelman, 1987; Weinrich, 1994).

Some research has indicated that "masculine" homosexual males are better adjusted than are "feminine" homosexual males (Siegelman, 1987). Other studies have suggested that this difference in adjustment also appears to hold true for heterosexual males (Jones et al., 1978). These findings are consistent with research showing that identification with stereotypically masculine personality traits is correlated with a male's self-esteem (Spence & Helmreich, 1978). Psychological identification with stereotypically feminine traits by men may be a better predictor of maladjustment than of sexual orientation. As noted earlier, among cultures with rigid gender-role distinctions, only the male who takes the stereotypically "feminine" role in homosexual activities is stigmatized.

In North American culture, where antigay discrimination and gender-role stereotypes are common, if a homosexual man displays some feminine characteristics, it is often difficult for him to keep his psychological balance. Heterosexuals and homosexuals who display gender-reversed patterns of behavior are both likely to experience adjustment problems. These problems will probably be more severe for the homosexual because she or he violates gender-role norms in a more public and visible way through erotic attachment to persons of the same gender.

Although separating individuals on the basis of sexual orientation is of little predictive value with respect to adjustment, a small proportion of homosexuals have been found to have significant problems with adjustment. For example, Bell and Weinberg (1978) reported that about 12% of the gay men and 5% of the lesbian women in their total sample could be classified as dysfunctional. These individuals experienced numerous problems in their day-to-day lives and appeared to fit society's stereotype of the maladjusted homosexual. What is remarkable, however, is that most gays function as well as their heterosexual counterparts despite society's negative sanctions. Their adjustment in the face of overwhelming so-

**Box 15.3**

## Turning the Tables

The popular press has frequently linked homosexual orientation to various undesirable characteristics. In the following example, the "pathology" associated with heterosexuality is satirically described.

In January 1972, the Los Angeles *Advocate*, the respected nationally distributed gay newspaper, devoted an entire page, including an editorial, to serious questions about the majority culture. The editor asked, "Is *Heterosexuality* an illness?" Most of the page was taken up with abstracts of items—35 of them—found in the pages of the *Los Angeles Times* in the space of five weeks. Here are three of them, and not necessarily the worst.

*CINCINNATI, Jan. 5—Mrs. Eulalia Fuchs, 44, pleaded guilty to manslaughter in the fatal shooting of her husband, Sept. 19, during an argument over whether to watch football on television or listen to music.*

*WASHINGTON, Jan. 6—A 57-year-old woman teacher was shot to death in front of her fifth-grade class after an argument with her estranged husband.*

*GARDEN GROVE, CALIF., Dec. 28—A Stanton man was burned to death early Monday as he was apparently attempting to set fire to the home of his ex-wife and her (new) husband—his brother—police reported.*

The accompanying editorial, "Don't jail heteros; they need help!" read:

*The problem of the violence-prone heterosexual community is alarming to most homosexuals. Some dismiss the problem as an abnormality*
*deeply rooted in heterosexual history; others advocate extreme oppression that has never worked in the past.*

*One gay extremist, for example, regards all heterosexuals as being sick and will have nothing to do with them. He would seize on any pretext he could to put them in jail. He attempted to justify his rigid attitude in a recent interview:*

*"Now someone who's unfortunate enough to be heterosexual and doesn't get into any trouble . . . has nothing to worry about. . . . But the vicious, violent, aggressive, recruiting-type heterosexual is a problem. . . ."*

*We share this individual's concern, but we think that his solution is no solution at all. Jails have been filled with heterosexuals since jails were invented, and heterosexual violence has increased steadily to frightening proportions.*

*So there is overwhelming evidence of a tragic defect in the heterosexual personality. Rather than jail them, however, we think it would be far more valuable to confine heterosexuals to hospitals at some stage in their early development so that those who are most afflicted with the virus of violence can be isolated and treated. Those who are no danger to themselves and others can be released to procreate the nonviolent human beings of the future, while the experts study those who are sick in a serious, all-out attempt to develop a cure.*

*Only when we find such a cure for this heterosexual madness will we achieve that long-sought goal: peace on earth.*

Source: Abbott & Love, 1985, pp. 198–199.

---

cietal burdens is testimony to the adaptiveness and resourcefulness of the human being.

## Therapy

In the past, clinicians treating homosexuals widely assumed that their clients' sexual orientation, rather than the social oppression they experienced because of their orientation, was the crux of their problems. In fact, the psychoanalyst Kenneth Lewes (1988) has outlined how conservative psychoanalytic thought attributed difficulties of both homosexual men and heterosexual women to individual defects rather than to societal expectations. For example, until recently, a woman with young children who went to a psychoanalyst and complained of depression was thought to be maladjusted. Similarly, a homosexual who sought therapy because of feelings of alienation from his family was assumed to be neurotic, with "conversion" to heterosexual orientation the recommended treatment. In contrast with these views, many contemporary therapists explore whether the woman's depression stemmed from feeling trapped all day without adult companionship, and whether the gay man's alienation was rooted in fear of familial rejection if he acknowledges his orientation.

In addition to being ethically questionable, the use of psychoanalysis and behavior therapy to change sexual orientation has been ineffective (Davison, 1991). Most therapists report a "cure" rate ranging from 10% to 30%, depending on the length of client follow-up. An exception is Masters and Johnson's report (1979) that 67% of the gay men and 60% of the gay women in their therapy program had "achieved" heterosexual behavior. All these individuals had applied for therapy because of sexual dissatisfaction. Nearly 25% of the applicants to Masters and Johnson's therapy program were denied admission for a variety of reasons, however, including insufficient motivation. More than half the clients selected were in heterosexual marriages, and only 12 of the 67 men and women were predominantly or exclusively homosexual. Most of the clients fit Kinsey category 3 or 4 (bisexual). Thus reports of Masters and Johnson's success at "changing" homosexuals' orientation should be viewed skeptically.

It is also important to recognize the implicit assumptions about homosexuality made by some clinicians. Bias among therapists is illustrated, for example, by the absence in clinical reports of attempts to change the sexual orientation of dissatisfied heterosexuals to enhance their adjustment. A colleague of ours has expressed the concern that if sexual orientation is discovered to be biologically determined, those who disapprove of homosexuality will try to eliminate that orientation through biological interventions. Such a concern would seem quite unjustified were it not for the work of a contemporary German researcher, Gunter Dörner. He has maintained that homosexuality is the result of abnormal hormonal concentration in the brain during prenatal development that permanently alters certain brain structures. He believed that this condition could be diagnosed during early pregnancy and corrected by prenatal hormone administration. In light of reports that Dörner had put his ideas into practice, the German Society for Sex Research officially criticized his position and questioned his ethics. The society stated that Dörner "openly toys with the idea of endocrinological euthanasia of homosexuality" (Sigusch et al., 1982, p. 448).

Despite some bias among clinicians, many therapists now concentrate on helping their clients to accept their sexual orientation and to develop their potential to survive in an antigay society, rather than on attempting to change their sexual orientation—unless such a change is the client's own goal (Coleman, 1982; Diamant, 1987). In all likelihood the impetus among researchers like Dörner to change or "cure" homosexuals stems from the difficulties of recognizing a difference without labeling it as psychologically abnormal.

## Antigay Prejudice and Discrimination

Although evidence is lacking to support most contemporary U.S. stereotypes about homosexuals, such as the idea that all gays are maladjusted, negative attitudes and discrimination against homosexuals are widespread (Schwanberg, 1993; Weinrich, 1994). For many people, aversion to homosexuals approaches a true phobia—that is, a persistent and irrational fear. The word *homophobia* (Weinberg, 1972) refers to the fear of homosexuals and of any form of same-gender intimacy.

There appears to have been a gradual decrease in antigay prejudice over the past few decades. National surveys measuring attitudes toward homosexual relations between adults found that 81% in 1974, 78% in 1984, and 64% in 1988 believed that such relations were wrong (Davis & Smith, 1984; Herek & Glunt, 1993; Pratte, 1993). In their worst forms, homophobia and antigay discrimination are responsible for the verbal and physical abuse of gays. In recent surveys, as many as 92% of lesbians and gay men reported that they have been verbally abused or threatened because they were gay. As many as 24% report experiencing physical attacks because of their sexual orientation (Herek, 1992). Some commentators speculate that antigay hate crimes are rising as part of the public reaction to the AIDS epidemic. And the response of governments and of public health officials to the AIDS crisis may have lagged because most of the early victims of AIDS in North America were gay men (Shilts, 1987).

Negative attitudes toward homosexuals are more prevalent among males than among females. In addition, compared with people who are tolerant of others' sexual orientation, anti-homosexuals attend church more frequently and are more likely to be affiliated with fundamentalist religions and to come from rural areas. Moreover, they tend to be more authoritarian, feel guiltier about sex, display greater gender-role rigidity, and be more likely to view sex as primarily for procreative purposes than are those who are tolerant of gays (Herek, 1988; Herek & Glunt, 1993; Kurdek, 1988; Long & Sultan, 1987; Page & Yee, 1985). The best predictor of heterosexuals' attitudes toward gay men is personal contact with a gay man or lesbian. Of the respondents in a national survey, 35% of those who had a friend, acquaintance, or relative who was homosexual had more positive attitudes toward gay men than did those who had no such contact (Herek & Glunt, 1993). Thus acknowledging one's homosexual orientation to close associates may lead to more positive attitudes toward homosexuals.

Implicit in many negative attitudes toward gays is the fear that homosexuality is contagious. Perhaps the most damaging myth about homosexuals is that they are abusers of impressionable young children whom they will seduce and lure into a gay lifestyle. Despite the fact that research has not supported it, this belief has caused overwhelming hardships for teachers who are homosexual and for gay parents seeking child custody. Most teenagers have their first homosexual experiences with other adolescents rather than with adults. Furthermore, most child sexual

**FIGURE 15.8**
**Gay Parenting**
A gay father reads his child a bedtime story. There is no evidence that the offspring of gay parents are more likely to become homosexual than are the children of heterosexual parents.

abuse is committed by heterosexual men, not gays.

On a related note, because the vast majority of homosexuals are reared in homes with heterosexual role models, it is unlikely that the offspring of gay parents would become homosexual as a result of the early childhood models they encountered (see Figure 15.8). In fact, research involving lesbian mothers has shown that the mothers' sexual orientation does not produce homosexuality in their children or have damaging consequences for their offspring's development (Coleman, 1990; Green, 1978).

Despite research to the contrary, many people find it difficult to accept the idea that homosexual lifestyles offer legitimate and productive alternatives for some individuals. By treating homosexuals as perverted or diseased, others can

**Box 15.4**

## Education and Homosexuality

*For those of my readers who have really convinced themselves that lesbianism should be legalized and buggery decriminalized, the way ahead is plain and uncomplicated: persuade your state legislators to change existing law. Have them proclaim pederasty perfectly proper, and you'll hear no more from me. But until that happens—and the time it takes should be roughly equivalent to how long it will take before Hell itself freezes over—our course of action is equally clear: don't give criminals teaching credentials and hire them to instruct classes of children. . . .*

*For eight clangorous and combative years, I chaired the statewide credentials commission of the most populous state in the nation. Our job, in large part, was to decide each month whether certain teachers were morally fit to be allowed to teach in California schools. And from the beginning, I do assure you, we took for granted the self-evident proposition that a homosexual in a school job was as preposterously out of the question as a heroin mainliner working in the local drugstore.*

*If it's okay to hire a sex pervert to teach in a public institution and if it's okay to pay a sex pervert with tax money and if it's okay to put a sex pervert in charge of the educational destinies of schoolchildren, then it's just got to be okay to be a sex pervert.*

*This, fellow teachers, we simply cannot have. We cannot have it because the actual survival of our country in the years ahead will depend upon a generation that will grow up straight—in the best sense of that much-abused word—not distorted. Sensible, not absurd.*

*Teachers' colleges should weed out the sexually abnormal before they qualify for the credentials.*

*School principals and superintendents should refuse to rehire probationary teachers who turn out to be abnormal despite the efforts of preliminary screening.*

*And no one who suffers from this kind of abnormality should be recommended for tenure.*

Source: Rafferty, 1977, pp. 91–92.

---

affirm their own normalcy. Thus a sense of "rightness" is maintained by dwelling on the "wrongness" of homosexual lifestyles. The views of California's former superintendent of public instruction, Max Rafferty, reflect this belief system (see Box 15.4). Faced with such discriminatory attitudes and behavior on the part of some public officials, it is not surprising that homosexuals have grown more militant (see Figure 15.9).

We hope that homosexuals will someday be treated as ordinary people and that sexual orientation will become strictly a private issue. Sexual orientation can only be a private issue, however, when society accepts and protects all its variations.

*[handwritten note: Which goes against (or data) all the need for data you presented]*

## Bisexuality

*Bisexuality*, the sexual attraction to both men and women, has received little scientific or social attention in a world polarized into homosexual and heterosexual camps. The homosexual subculture often views the bisexual as someone who is going through a phase of heterosexual encounters because he or she is unwilling to come to

**bisexuality**—the capacity to feel erotic attraction toward or to engage in sexual interaction with both males and females.

**FIGURE 15.9**
**Gay Political Demonstrations**
Earlier movements by gays and others to obtain basic civil rights for homosexuals
are being replaced by attempts to encourage support for education and research
to halt the spread of AIDS.

grips with being homosexual (Coleman, 1987; Rust, 1993). The heterosexual community, meanwhile, tends to lump bisexuals into the general category of homosexuals or view them as mixed-up heterosexuals who need guidance.

Researchers have found, however, that a substantial number of men report bisexual attraction and engage in sex with both men and women during adulthood (Doll et al., 1992; Lever, Kanouse, Rogers, Carson, & Hertz, 1992; Stokes, McKirnan, & Burzette, 1993). In the Stokes et al. (1993) study, more than half the bisexual men remained stable in their rating of their sexual orientation. The remaining men moved toward defining themselves as more attracted to men than to women over a period of a year. Thus bisexu-

ality appears to be predominant pattern for some men, whereas for others, it may be a transitional state on the road to awareness of homosexual orientation. Despite these variations in the permanence of bisexual orientation, bisexuals as a group appear to be as well adjusted psychologically as the heterosexuals and homosexuals who have been studied (Coleman, 1987).

## Incidence

How many people can be classified as bisexuals? As with other classifications, the number depends on the definition of the term. If the criterion is at least one overt sexual experience with a member of each gender, then a third of the

Kinsey group's (1948) males fell into the bisexual category. If the additional 13% who reported having had erotic feelings toward both genders but overt experience with only one of them are added, the total was 46% of the sample. Comparable figures for the Kinsey group's (1953) females are difficult to report, because in presenting their findings the researchers made distinctions based on marital status, age, and other demographic variables. Suffice it to say that about a third as many females as males reported overt experience with both genders, and that about half as many females as males reported erotic responses to both genders. Looking at this question from another standpoint, 52% of the exclusively homosexual and 93% of the predominantly homosexual males in Bell and Weinberg's (1978) study reported that they had engaged in heterosexual coitus at least once. The comparable figures for females were 77% and 93%, respectively.

These statistics indicate that substantial numbers of people who consider themselves to be either heterosexual or homosexual have the capacity to be sexually aroused by and to engage in sexual activity with members of both genders. Many of these individuals engage in same-gender sexual activity only once or a few times, usually in adolescence, and therefore do not really qualify as bisexuals.

## Identity Versus Experience

Many people who have experienced a sexual relationship with both genders do not think of themselves as bisexual. Lever et al. (1992) found that more than two-thirds of bisexually experienced men labeled themselves as heterosexual. One of the most prominent characteristics of whether a bisexually active man identified himself as bisexual was adolescent homosexual experience. The greater the amount of adolescent homosexual experience, the more likely the men were to label themselves as bisexual (Lever et al., 1992). However, many men engage in sexual activities with both genders and continue to consider themselves heterosexuals.

Bisexually experienced men, compared to heterosexual men, report engaging in more high-risk behaviors (multiple partners, anal sex) and are more likely to report having had an STD in the past five years. However, the frequency of these risk characteristics among bisexual men is less than that found among homosexual men (Lever et al., 1992).

## Characteristics

Although we all have the potential to respond erotically to both genders, only some of us do so. What factors lead some people to interact sexually with both men and women?

Answers to that question and many others about bisexuality must be tentative because few studies have investigated people describing themselves as bisexual. In one such study, Blumstein and Schwartz (1976) interviewed 156 bisexuals and found three themes to be particularly prevalent among the respondents. The first of these was sexual experimentation in the context of friendship. Some of the individuals had progressed from intense emotional attachment to sexual involvement with a friend, although they had never previously had an erotic attraction to a person of that gender. The second theme was interaction in group sex. This pathway to bisexuality is quite common for women who are involved in swinging, and who are often encouraged by their husbands or friends to engage in same-gender sexual activity (Dixon, 1984). In this situation, Blumstein and Schwartz's respondents focused on the pleasurable feelings of these encounters rather than on the gender of the person providing the pleasure. The third theme was the presence of a belief system in which bisexuality was seen as a normal state. Some respondents in the study had embraced bisexual identification because they felt that a truly free person should be able to love both genders. Although some respondents had not actually engaged in bisexual relations, many agreed intellectually with Freud's idea of inherent bisexuality.

Comparisons of bisexual men and women who have been heterosexually married show several gender differences. Bisexual women tend to marry at an early age, and they are more likely than bisexual men to become aware of their homosexual feelings after they wed. Bisexual women are also more likely than bisexual men to terminate their marriages early because of conflicts arising from their bisexuality and sexual dissatisfaction (Bell & Weinberg, 1978; Coleman, 1987). The fact that the marriages of bisexual women are shorter than the marriages of bisexual men may stem from the differing socialization of males and females. Like lesbians, bisexual women seem less inclined to engage in multiple sexual relationships than bisexual or homosexual men. The conflict generated by their feelings for a woman in the face of their desire for monogamy may prompt some bisexual women to end their marriages.

Most people who experience erotic feelings toward both genders think of themselves as either homosexual or heterosexual because social and scientific support for the bisexual identity is lacking. Only recently have bisexuals begun to develop social networks. The first international conference was held in Amsterdam in 1991 (Rust, 1993). Perhaps as wider recognition is accorded bisexual orientation, more people will claim this label. It may soften the hard edges of the homosexual and heterosexual categories, which ignore so many people who do not fit neatly into either. If Freud, Kinsey, and the behaviorists are right regarding the human potential for bisexual responses, then recognition of this possibility, whether a person acts on it or not, may be the way out of an illusory heterosexual-homosexual dichotomy.

## Summary of Major Points

1. **Sexual orientation.**

Most individuals confine their sexual interactions to the other gender, although many people who define themselves as heterosexuals have also experienced erotic attraction to members of their own gender. Homosexuals feel attraction toward and interact sexually with people of the same gender. Aside from this sexual orientation toward individuals of the same gender, research has uncovered few systematic differences between heterosexuals and homosexuals.

2. **Gender differences and sexual orientation.**

Gay males tend to seek variety and relatively impersonal sex in a pattern more similar to that of heterosexual males than to that of heterosexual females. Lesbian relationships and values resemble those of heterosexual females. These gender differences are consistent with variations in the ways in which males and females are socialized. It is not known, however, whether socialization is entirely responsible for these differences.

3. **Explanations of sexual orientation.**

The assumption that a homosexual orientation stems either from genetic or hormonal conditions or from a social situation such as a disturbed family relationship dominated early research into the causes of homosexuality. Although there is little evidence to support most of these assumptions, preliminary data suggest a biological contribution to at least some types of homosexuality. Gender-role nonconformity in young boys and sexual experiences in late childhood and adolescence have also been associated with adult homosexual orientation.

4. **Sexual orientation and adjustment.**

Many early studies of the psychological adjustment of homosexuals compared gays in therapy with heterosexuals not in therapy. This research led to the conclusion that gays were maladjusted. More appropriate comparisons have failed to identify reliable differences in people as a function of their sexual orientation.

5. Antigay prejudice and discrimination.

Fear, hatred, and discrimination toward homosexuals characterize the attitudes of many people in our culture. Research on homophobia has been neglected until recently, perhaps because antigay prejudice is so widespread that researchers perceived intense homophobic reactions as "normal." Current and future investigations may increase our understanding of homophobia in particular and prejudice in general.

6. Bisexuality.

Bisexuals are capable of feeling erotic attraction toward and engaging in sexual intimacy with individuals of both genders. They present an interesting question for future research. Why do some people restrict their range of potential partners to one gender (either the same or the other gender), and other people (bisexuals) consider gender unimportant in selecting partners? From this standpoint, exclusive heterosexuals are similar to exclusive homosexuals.

## Review of Key Concepts

1. Homosexual orientation generally results from cross-gender identification in adulthood. True or false, and why? (p. 486)

2. Anna Freud's definition of homosexuality involves: a) the frequency with which an individual engages in same-gender sex; b) the kind of fantasies an individual experiences while engaging in sexual activity; c) the age at which same-gender sexual activity begins; d) the degree of Oedipal repression that an individual has experienced. (p. 487)

3. Homosexual behavior occurs between non-human mammals: a) never; b) occasionally; c) fairly frequently; d) always. (pp. 487–488)

4. In their survey of about 190 cultures, Ford and Beach found that: a) homosexual behavior between adults was predominant in a few cultures; b) homosexual activity was rare or secret in the majority of the cultures studied; c) homosexual relations between male adolescents were socially required in the majority of the cultures; d) same-gender sexual relations were normal and socially acceptable for certain members of the community in the majority of cultures studied. (p. 488)

5. In the United States, the gay-liberation movement is usually dated back to: a) the 1920s; b) the World War II era; c) the late 1960s and early 1970s; d) the onset of the AIDS epidemic in the early 1980s. (p. 492)

6. "Coming out" refers to a homosexual person's: a) first experience of homosexual feelings; b) first homosexual encounter leading to orgasm; c) acknowledgment of his or her gay identity to others; d) withdrawal from active or publicly known homosexual behavior. (p. 495)

7. Gay men and lesbian women differ little in their sexual attitudes and expectations. True or false? (pp. 497–498)

8. The most likely explanation for homosexuality is: a) mutations; b) an excess of testosterone in both male and female homosexuals; c) a family background consisting of an intimate, controlling mother and a detached, rejecting father; d) none of the above. (pp. 500–505)

9. Given the great diversity of cultural attitudes toward homosexuality surveyed in this chapter, as well as the wide variations in homosexual behavior in contemporary Western society, why, in your opinion, are so many societies (including our own) intolerant of same-gender sexuality and prone to stereotype homosexuals?

10. Evaluate Masters and Johnson's assertion that in their lovemaking, gay people are more relaxed and less performance-oriented than are heterosexual couples.

11. Evaluate the evidence for childhood gender-role nonconformity as an explanation for same-gender sexual orientation. Does this explanation suggest that parents can (or should) attempt to control their children's eventual sexual orientation?

12. "Perhaps as wider recognition is accorded bisexual orientation, more people will claim this label. It may soften the hard edges of the homosexual and heterosexual categories, which ignore so many people who do not fit neatly into either." Define bisexuality and evaluate this statement.

# $\mathscr{S}$ex for Profit

$\mathscr{T}$HE next time you watch television or look at a magazine, notice how frequently the commercials or advertisements emphasize sex appeal. Attractive and seductive young models promote everything from mouthwash to cars. The implication of such advertising is that you will be as sexually attractive as the model if you buy product X. In a more direct appeal to sexual response, some films and magazines rely primarily on sexually oriented material to increase marketability. With the growing use of sexual messages in advertising, and the prevalence of graphic depictions of sexuality in films and in print, it is clear that using sex to sell a product makes money.

In this chapter we describe the intersection of sexuality and the profit motive. Much of the controversy about sexual products centers on their possible effect on consumers, particularly those who are young and impressionable. We review what is known about the effects of exposure to various types of erotic media and discuss laws concerning sexually explicit material. In addition to viewing and listening to erotic material, consumers can also buy sexual services from prostitutes. Both women and men sell sexual access to their bodies, but prostitution is primarily a female profession, and most buyers are males. We consider different kinds of prostitutes, legal constraints on prostitution, and the characteristics associated with prostitutes and with those who purchase their services.

## Varieties of Sexual Products

Erotic material may be viewed in magazines, in theaters, at home on television programs and videocassettes; it is found in nightclubs featuring adult entertainment, in adult bookstores, and even in advertisements for products that have no readily apparent connection with sexuality. Before discussing the profits generated by these materials, we need to define a few key terms.

The word *erotica* generally refers to sexually oriented material that is acceptable to the viewer. Sexually oriented material that is not acceptable to the viewer is *pornography*. This term comes from the Greek word *pornographos,* which refers to stories about prostitutes. There are, of course, many definitions of pornography, but they tend to reflect the likes and dislikes of the definer. What one person may find appealing, pleasant, and arousing, another may judge disgusting, unpleasant, and nonarousing. In short, what is erotic to one person may be pornographic to another (Allgeier, Yachanin, Smith, & Myers, 1984).

*Hard-core erotica* or pornography is sexual material that explicitly depicts the genitals or sexual acts. X-rated movies and materials displayed in adult bookstores are usually hard-core. *Soft-core erotica* or pornography is sexual material that is suggestive, but not explicit, in portraying the genitals or sex acts. Magazines that can be purchased from most newsstands, such as *Playboy* and *Penthouse*, are examples of soft-core erotica.

## Magazines and Newspapers

Soft-core erotica made major inroads in the magazine business in 1953, when *Playboy* was launched as a sexually oriented imitator of *Es-*

---

erotica—sexually oriented material that is acceptable to the viewer.

pornography—sexually oriented material that is not acceptable to the viewer.

hard-core erotica—erotica that explicitly depicts the genitals and sexual acts.

soft-core erotica—erotica that is suggestive, but not explicit, in portraying sexual acts.

---

*quire* magazine. *Playboy* was the first widely accepted magazine to display bare breasts and buttocks. In 1970 *Penthouse, Playboy*'s most successful imitator, became the first mass-market magazine to display pubic hair on its models (Mazur, 1986). Other magazines soon followed, and depiction of the genitals became increasingly common. These magazines reached their peak circulation in the 1970s and then began to lose readership, perhaps because they were less explicit than the more "hard-core" magazines (Bogaert, Turkovich, & Hafer, 1993).

Nonetheless, the continuing power of sex in selling magazines is reflected in the sales figures for the swimsuit issue of *Sports Illustrated*. In 1989 *Sports Illustrated* sold 5.5 million copies of its swimsuit issue, almost twice as many copies as are sold of the average issue. Revenue for the issue and tie-ins (videos, calendars) reached about $30 million, which produced quite a profit, given that *Sports Illustrated*'s net income for 1988 was about $90 million. A chain of best-selling British newspapers owned by Rupert Murdoch features a photo of a sexy, partially nude young woman on a daily basis. The publisher of *Rolling Stone* commented that the ideal cover featured "sex, sex, sex, sex. What's new?" (Gross, 1985, p. 52).

## Advertisements

What's new is the extent to which not only the electronic and print media but also advertisers have shown people in various states of undress and intimate poses. Compare the turn-of-the-century French advertisement in Figure 16.1 to the more recent effort of the advertising industry shown in Figure 16.2. These two figures suggest that the use of sexual images has become more overt, and analyses of the content of advertisements during the past two decades support the conclusion that nudity and illusions of intercourse have become increasingly common since the mid-1960s (Soley & Kurzbard, 1986).

This trend may reflect a belief by the advertising industry that sex sells, but does it? Does sexual content in an advertisement enhance the likelihood that consumers will purchase a particular item? The answer appears to be no, unless the product is related to sexuality (Courtney & Whipple, 1983). For products that are unrelated

**FIGURE 16.1**

**Turn-of-the-Century French Advertisement**

This advertisement for *lumières reglées*, or adjustable lights, appeared in 1895. Although the advertisers relied on depictions of scantily dressed women to sell their products, this advertisement is relatively modest by today's standards.

**FIGURE 16.2**

**The Use of Male Nudity to Sell Products**

This French billboard displaying a nude man shows how nudity is used in advertising to promote an underwear product.

to sexuality, research indicates that overt sexual content in ads is less effective than nonsexual content. Although provocative stimuli may grab initial attention, memory of a brand name and comprehension of an ad's message are reduced when there is irrelevant sexual content in the advertisement (Severn, Belch, & Belch, 1990; Soley & Kurzbard, 1986). Despite the absence of evidence for the effectiveness of using sex appeal to sell products, the advertising industry continues to turn out sexually explicit ads. This explicitness brings up the question of what limits, if any, should apply to the advertising industry's at-

tempts to sell products by linking them with sexuality.

In Chapter 6 we described the Sexual Opinion Survey (SOS), responses to which can range from negative (erotophobic) to positive (erotophilic). One survey item reads, "Erotica is obviously filthy, and people should not try to describe it as anything else." An erotophobic person would likely agree with the statement, whereas an erotophilic person would disagree. Not surprisingly, survey data indicate that erotophobic persons report infrequent exposure to erotic material (Fisher et al., 1988). Should erotophobic persons have to tolerate exposure to the sexually suggestive material that permeates contemporary advertising? They can, of course, switch to another television channel if they are offended by a particular advertisement, but it is unlikely that they will find a commercial channel that bans advertisements trying to sell products through sex appeal. They can turn off the television, but this obviously limits their viewing freedom. In buying magazines, papers, and books, erotophobic people can more easily avoid objectionable material, but they still run the risk of unexpectedly encountering erotic items that may offend them.

The overriding question with respect to the use of erotica to sell products is whether there should be some form of censorship in the marketplace. Should the marketplace determine what is acceptable, or should the government decide? Should newspapers and newsmagazines with a general readership contain sexually explicit material? Could it have harmful effects on adults or children? These are the kinds of questions that arise when advertisers depict sexual activity or nudity to sell their wares.

## Television Programs

The use of sex in the electronic and print media is hardly limited to advertisements. One analysis of episodes of 13 daytime network soap operas broadcast during a two-month period—more than 33 hours of programming—showed one scene of petting and three references to intercourse every 2 hours; one scene of coitus every 90 minutes; one instance of prostitution every 4 hours; and one rape every 11 hours. Interestingly, only 3.5% of the sexually active characters were over 40 years old (Greenberg & D'Alessio, 1985).

There has also been a dramatic increase in the depiction of sex on prime-time television since the 1960s (Estep & MacDonald, 1990). As you know from your own viewing experience, one difficulty with television's presentation of sex is that programs depicting sexual encounters rarely deal with the possible consequences of sexual activity. For example, many characters on soap operas have been shown engaging in sex with each other; seldom do the characters discuss potential negative outcomes (unwanted pregnancy, STDs) and what they can do to reduce their risks. The

absence of modeling responsible sexual decision-making may lead viewers into an unrealistic view of the range of consequences for sexual behavior. One study of adolescents found a relationship between the proportion of sexual depictions viewed and their own sexual behavior (Brown & Newcomer, 1991). Nonvirgins were more likely than virgins to watch TV programs that contained sexual content.

Hamburg (1992) and Hechinger (1992) have more globally described television viewing patterns and sexual content. Overall, the average 18-year-old has watched TV for as many as 22,000 hours, compared to 11,000 hours spent in school. U.S. viewers are exposed each year to almost 10,000 scenes of suggested sex or innuendo, and more than 90% of sex portrayals on TV involve people who either are unmarried or are not married to each other!

The tendency to exaggerate the glamour of sexuality has led fundamentalist groups to advocate the censorship of erotic activity on television. Other organizations, including Planned Parenthood, suggest that when sexual activity is portrayed, the possible unwanted consequences should also be presented. Similar advice could be given to the producers of many of the explicit sexual scenes featured in many music videos. The next time you watch a lurid sex scene in a network show or on MTV, think about how you would inject information about responsible sexual behavior into the script. The controversy about the effects of the commercial portrayal of sex intensifies when we turn to films and books that directly aim at evoking sexual arousal.

## Erotic Movies and Videotapes

In the 1970s the market for sexually explicit films flourished. An early sign of growing acceptance of hard-core material was the release in the United States of the Swedish film *I Am Curious (Yellow)* in 1969 (see Figure 16.3). Although tame by today's standards, it was the first X-rated movie to be given wide publicity and shown in regular theaters instead of being restricted to adult cinemas.

The market for cinematic erotica took another turn in the 1980s when the videocassette recorder began to chip into the profits of adult

**FIGURE 16.3**
**I Am Curious (Yellow)**
Actress Lena Nyman is shown in a relatively modest scene in the first X-rated movie
to be shown in regular theaters in the United States in 1969.

theaters and magazines. The steadily climbing sales and rentals of hard-core videocassettes suggest that consumers prefer watching these films in the privacy of the home rather than in a theater (see Box 16.1). The Adult Film and Video Association of America estimated that the number of theaters showing X-rated films dropped from 750 in 1983 to 250 in 1987, and X-rated videos account for an estimated 15% of all video rentals in the United States (Scott, 1990).

Hard-core or X-rated movies probably contain the most explicit depictions of sexuality that North America has produced, but their plots are typically dull and predictable. Sociologist Ira Reiss characterized most X-rated films as having a thin plot and unimpressive acting.

> *The scenes focus upon oral, anal, and coital acts with extensive closeups of that action.*

*The acts are mostly heterosexual, and when they are homosexual, unless the film is made specifically for male homosexuals, the focus is upon lesbian sexual acts. The absence of male homosexuality is due to the strong attempt to appeal to Western heterosexual males' lustful feelings in these films. Little or no physical violence against women occurs in the vast majority of these films. There may be some status differences in the male and female roles portrayed, but physical force rarely enters in obvious ways into the sexual action. I believe that this is the most common form of erotic film today. It is hard-core in that erections and vulvas are shown frequently and usually joined. (1986, pp. 174–175)*

The typical X-rated film is a fantasy about sexually insatiable women who are incapable of

### Box 16.1

## A Cozy Evening at Home

*Every once in awhile, my fiancé and I will rent a couple of sexy movies on a Saturday night to give ourselves a break from the pressures of graduate school. We used to watch the more hard-core X-rated movies, but I think that Scott and I both paid more attention to the woman than the man in those films. It wasn't that I was also turned on by the woman; instead, I felt kind of threatened and afraid that he might compare her to me.*

*We talked about it a couple of months ago and decided that we both preferred R-rated movies. They leave more to the imagination, and we find that more arousing. For example, I really was turned on by parts of* Basic Instinct *and* Indecent Proposal. *We'll put blankets on the floor by the TV, light some candles, and get a nice bottle of wine before we start watching the movie. Usu-*

*ally, at some point during the movie, we'll start playing with each other, which usually means that we end up missing part of the movie. But that's OK, because when we finish making love, we just start watching the movie again.*

*Sometimes, I wonder whether it is the movies that make these times so erotic for us or if it's just that we set aside some time to be with each other without any interruptions. When Scott says to me, "Let's rent a movie tonight," it's like a signal that he wants to make love and I start anticipating being together, and I actually begin to feel turned on even before we watch the movie.*

Source: Authors' files.

---

resisting any type of male sexual advance. In a matter of seconds, regardless of the male's approach, the woman is overcome by her sexual passion and willingly participates in all sorts of sexual activities. In a culture in which males are socialized to be sexual initiators—a role in which they are vulnerable to rejection by females who are not sexually interested in them—it is not difficult to see why the insatiable female fantasy is so popular. Women are depicted as having no negotiating power. As Reiss (1986) pointed out, the situation portrayed in the typical X-rated film is similar to a rape except that in rape the negotiating power is removed by the threat of the male; in the fantasy it is the woman's raging sexual passions that sweep away her negotiating power. Women who view such films may resent the depiction of males as concerned only with having their own sexual interests satisfied and valuing little in their partners beyond sexual access. The female counterpart to this male fantasy can be seen in women's romance novels (see Box 16.2 and Figure 16.4).

Historically, most erotica has been aimed at arousing males. Men's seemingly greater interest in obtaining erotic material probably explains this marketing strategy. In one college sample, men reported viewing erotic material an average of about six hours a month, whereas women reported viewing such material only about two and a half hours a month (Padgett, Brislin-Slutz, & Neal, 1989).

Hard-core and X-rated movies are often the targets of groups that advocate censorship. However, these films generally contain less violence than R-rated films or other movies that children are permitted to see. Robert Rimmer (1984) reported that only about 10% of the 650 X-rated films that he examined contained deviant, sadistic, or violent sex, or sex acts that victimized others. The highest incidence of violence occurs in PG-13 videos, followed by R-rated videos, with X-rated videos trailing far behind (Scott & Cuvelier, 1993). These findings are supported by the following statistics, quoted by Dr. Thomas Radecki, chairperson of the National Coalition on

**Box 16.2**

## Romance Novels: Erotica for Women?

Romance novels have been phenomenally successful in recent years, selling millions of copies and appearing regularly on best-seller lists. They are female fantasies, written mainly by women. The erotic romance generally features a young woman whose innocence is violated by an older man; his repeated assaults result in pregnancy and marriage. The struggle between the two for dominance, the man's eventual triumph, and his ultimate domestication are consistent plot elements. In one study, readers of these novels reported having sexual relations twice as often as nonreaders of romance; in addition, they often used fantasy as a complement to intercourse, whereas nonreaders did so rarely, if at all (Coles & Shamp, 1984). Romance novels are a kind of soft-core erotica that women find socially acceptable.

Reiss (1986) suggested that in one sense female erotic fantasy may be based on the same principle as male erotic fantasy; that is, it is enhanced by removing the negotiating power of one's sexual partner. In romance novels, the male is depicted as obsessed with romance. His intense love for the heroine renders him helpless to resist; he must pursue her and give her what she desires. Feminine gen-

der-role expectations are compatible with this scenario, and a woman can relax her sexual guard and feel safe.

Women are pressured to be both selective and sexually responsive in North American culture. Men are socialized to become sexual initiators, ready to perform at the drop of an eyelash. Is it any wonder that women and men often prefer different types of erotica?

**FIGURE 16.4**
**Romance Novels**
The thriving industry in romance novels, marketed for women, suggests that women's taste in erotica is different from men's, rather than nonexistent.

Television Violence (NCTV): "NCTV has found the 1984 summer Hollywood movies to contain the highest amount of violence ever, 28.5 violent acts per hour, with PG-movies containing some of the highest levels of violence. X-rated movies actually contain far fewer murders and even fewer rapes than PG- or R-rated material" (1984, p. 43).

Further evidence of the general lack of violence in hard-core films emerged from a study in which 150 erotic videos, randomly selected from video outlets in Vancouver, British Columbia, were rated for violence. Fifty-eight of the films were soft-core, and the remainder were hard-

core. The soft-core videos featured significantly more aggressive content than did the hard-core videos, and the number of aggressive scenes was greater in more recent soft-core films (Palys, 1986). The hard-core movies were more likely than the soft-core films to contain sex scenes wherein the participants mutually consented to the activity and engaged in it as equals: 72% of all scenes in the hard-core videos were of this type, as compared to only 49% of all scenes in the soft-core videos.

The consumers of X-rated videos do not fit into any easily identifiable category. Reiss examined six annual surveys of representative groups of Americans 18 and older, conducted between 1973 and 1983 by the National Opinion Research Center (NORC). Approximately 20% of the respondents—25% of the males and 14% of the females—said that they had gone to an X-rated movie during the past year. Almost half of those who had been to an X-rated movie were under age 30, and almost all the others were under 60. The higher the educational attainment, the more likely the person was to have attended an X-rated movie. Of particular relevance to feminists' concerns that X-rated movies may promote gender inequality was Reiss's finding that for each year between 1973 and 1983, people who attended X-rated movies were more, *not less,* egalitarian in their gender-role attitudes than those who did not. Similarly, patrons of an adult movie theater who responded to questionnaires placed on a counter in the theater had more positive attitudes toward women than did college men *and* women (Padgett et al., 1989). Thus research does not support the idea that erotica fosters positive attitudes toward the subordination of women.

## Adult Bookstores

Paralleling the expanding market for sexually explicit films, adult bookstores have also shown growing profits. These bookstores sell hard-core erotica of a sort not readily available at other retail stores. In addition to printed media and videotapes, a range of other products is often available, including such sex toys as vibrators, massage oils, dildos, and other sexual aids. Some stores also offer live sex shows featuring everything from nude dancing to simulated live sexual acts (see Figure 16.5).

A study of 26 adult bookstores in the Philadelphia area found a strong overlap between the stores and such forms of vice as drug distribution, gambling, and prostitution (Potter, 1989). All these establishments had peep-show areas where a customer could enter a booth and insert coins or tokens to watch a film. Twelve had *rap booths* where a viewer could pay for a curtain or blind to be raised. In the rap-booth arrangement, a male or female employee behind a glass partition converses with the customer through a telephone or intercom system. The employee grad-

**FIGURE 16.5**
**Adult Bookstore**
As the window display of this New York City establishment shows, adult bookstores frequently offer a variety of products and services in addition to printed media.

ually undresses and engages in sexual talk with the customer. Eventually, the employee carefully solicits the customer and, for additional payment, goes to the customer's side of the booth (or the two retire to another part of the store) for sex.

*Glory holes* were also provided in 24 of the 26 stores in their peep-show areas (Potter, 1989). The glory hole is a circular opening two to six inches in diameter in the side wall of the booth, through which parts of the anatomy may be inserted. The booths usually feature homosexual themes, and their purpose is to allow two men in adjacent cubicles to engage in manual or oral stimulation. In some of the establishments, prostitution, child pornography, drugs, and gambling were also available on the premises, whereas other stores referred customers to places where they could obtain these services and products.

Thus, in Philadelphia, the retail pornography outlets are intertwined with prostitution and are part of organized criminal networks. FBI investigations have revealed complicated patterns of common ownership of pornography outlets, massage parlors, and after-hours clubs in that city. These patterns are not unique to Philadelphia. Similar arrangements flourish in many cities, contributing to an estimated annual gross income of $2 billion to $9 billion (Potter, 1989).

## Telephone Sex

Those who prefer to obtain sexual stimulation at a distance can dial a 900 telephone number and listen to explicit sexual talk for a price. The so-called dial-a-porn industry allows one to have a conversation with a paid performer at the other end of the line or to listen to a prerecorded message (Glasock & LaRose, 1993). For fees that range from $3 to $12 a minute, a caller can indulge in his or her sexual fantasies with a phone worker who will talk dirty to the caller and charge the episode to that person's monthly telephone bill. Advertisements for such services can be found in the personal ad sections of many newspapers and in sexually oriented magazines.

For this illusion of sexual fulfillment, the caller is often treated to a worker's feigned interest in his or her fantasy. Many calls are forwarded to the worker's home, where he or she may try to titillate the customer while going about such ordinary pursuits as cleaning the kitchen or reading the paper (Borna, Chapman, & Menezes, 1993).

The organizations that provide telephone sex have come under increasing scrutiny by the federal government, and congressional dial-a-porn hearings were held in 1988. The Federal Communications Commission (FCC) fined Audio Enterprises and another company $600,000 each in 1988 for transmitting obscene material across state lines and for not restricting access to their messages by children and nonconsenting adults.

## Computer Sex

The computer combined with modern telephone technology has created a highly efficient means for the transmission of information. Online bulletin boards, known as BBSs, are roughly equivalent to high-tech electronic telephone "party lines." By connecting to a particular BBS, one can use a computer to contact individuals or companies with similar interests in the United States or other places in the world. It should come as no surprise that one of the oldest human drives has hooked up with the latest technology.

Methods of adult-oriented BBSs, with names like ThrobNet and KinkNet, feature libraries of X-rated films and interactive adult games such as "The Interactive Adventures of Seymore Butts." In this game, the wrong answer gets Seymore a refusal or a slap in the face; the right answer lands him in bed, where the viewer gets to see hard-core sex.

Network subscribers can also exchange erotic messages. A couple can meet through the computer, engage in erotic banter, exchange telephone numbers, and arrange a date. Network users usually pay an annual fee ranging from $50 to $100 or an hourly fee ranging from $2 to $5.

## Stripping

Strip-tease dancing has a long history. The gradual shedding of clothes to music has been primarily an entertainment provided by women. Female strippers usually enter the profession to earn a livelihood, and some take in additional money by engaging in prostitution with customers of the club or theater where they perform (Dressel & Peterson, 1982; Thompson & Harred, 1992). In recent times, men have increasingly entered this occupation (see Figure 16.6).

Depending on the locale, strippers may shed all their clothes or strip down to scanty G-strings (the rule in most U.S. cities). Strippers perform in bars, restaurants, theaters, clubs, and private shows. In contrast to most female strippers, male strippers apparently are motivated frequently by the opportunity to meet women (or men) with whom they may subsequently engage in sex— not necessarily for money (Dressel & Peterson,

**FIGURE 16.6**

**Male Stripping: A Relatively Recent Social Phenomenon**

This man retains his G-string (resembling an abbreviated jock strap), the rule in most American cities. However, there are clubs in which both men and women strippers remove all clothing except for garter belts in which audience members can place tips.

1982). Male strip shows often involve costumed individuals or group performances in various scenarios; members of the audience may approach a dancer offering a tip, after which physical contact such as kissing or fondling may occur. In table topping, the disrobing dancers perform on the tables where the customers are seated. Male and female strippers alike believe that society views them in a negative light. Thus they often describe themselves to others as entertainers or dancers in an effort to avoid negative

stereotypes (Dressel & Peterson, 1982; Thompson & Harred, 1992).

## Other Forms of Erotica

Individuals can employ erotica to arouse themselves or a sexual companion. Used with a partner, erotic materials can enhance lovemaking, but some forms can serve as a substitute for those who lack a partner. Consider the following advertisement, typical of those found in contemporary sex-oriented publications.

*PLAYGIRL*

*Lifesize-like in every detail. June is the only human-like action doll available in America. Let her life-like reproduction female qualities astound you as they have others. Her breasts are human-like in every detail, boasting texture and structure right down to the finest point. Her open mouth is an achievement in design; the human-like action, tight flexible cheeks inside the mouth, work on the principle of air suction. Imagine coming home to your own 21st century playgirl, always ready for action. Dress her up in lingerie, bathing suit, dainty underclothes. . . . Think of the fun you'll have dressing June the way you feel a woman should dress.*

More common are the multitudinous products billed as enhancing or increasing sexual proficiency. Vibrators, dildos, creams, pastes, and lubricants are just a few of the items competing for the consumer's business. Individuals or couples may use such sexual aids to heighten their sensations during masturbation or coitus. For example, the Kama Sutra Company manufactures scented lubricants, with one variation aimed at women and the other at men, and notes in its ads that all the products are "designed to bring us closer . . . to encourage us to touch and perceive each other." When one of Kama Sutra's oils is applied to sensitive parts of the body such as the clitoris and labia, it results in a tingling sensation of warmth. Another product, called a pleasure balm, is described as heightening and lengthening sensual pleasure, with a slightly numbing effect. The balm, advertised as tasting like a peppermint stick (this wording suggests the possibility of fellatio), is presumably designed for application to the penis. There is no evidence that these kinds of stimulants are harmful, and they do, in fact, produce the sensations—warmth, numbing—claimed.

Other advertised products are of more dubious quality. Several years ago, we received a promotional piece on a so-called sex pill for men, called NSP-270, that purportedly would compensate for certain male nutritional deficiencies. The four-page brochure claimed that

> *doctors at a famous California Medical School—Board Certified Specialists—experts at helping men with troublesome sex organs—recently announced that rare but reversible sex nutrient depletion can cause a man*
>
> *Loss of Sex Drive!*
>
> *Smaller Than Normal Penis Size!*
>
> *Weak Ejaculation!*
>
> *Sperm That's Only Half Alive!*
>
> *Erections That Can't "Do the Job" with Her!*

The brochure went on to ask, "Is Your Erection Fully Loaded?" and made claims that a "Tennessee Man Doubles the Size of His Penis!"Although the literature contains some remarkable graphs, in which penis-shaped bars indicate the length of a man's penis before and after he has taken NSP-270, readers never learn which famous California medical school has developed this "nutrient." Further, you may have noticed that the advertising blurb confused skilled lovemaking and erectile functioning with unrelated factors such as penis size, strength of ejaculation, and fertility.

Although people widely condemn erotica and sexual aids, the trade would not be flourishing if consumers did not support it with their money. The market for these products may be expected to expand dramatically unless scientists find an immunization or cure for AIDS; that is, many people are likely to prefer self-stimulation through the solitary use of erotica over sex with a partner of unknown background who might transmit AIDS. And even those with a spouse or a regular partner may wish to inject adventure into their sexual relationship by including sexual aids or erotica.

## Erotica and the Law

The word *obscenity* is often used inte bly with the word *pornography*, but *obscenity* also has a legal meaning. In U.S. law, obscenity refers to illegal erotica. In its original sense, obscenity referred to things that should be kept from sight. In drama, for example, certain scenes were implied offstage because they were too personal or too intense for an audience to see. Obscenity had less to do with sex than with such emotions as grief and personal humiliation, which the ancient Greeks banned from the theater. This notion about the privacy of intense emotions almost disappeared with the emergence of television journalism. Daily, we can view others' intense emotion on our news programs. Writings about sex and pictures of sex have also become highly public over the past 30 years. This increased visibility has made it difficult to determine what kinds of erotica, if any, should be considered illegal.

In the United States, laws regulating erotic material date back to the 19th century. The most important one is the Comstock Act, named after its major advocate, Anthony Comstock, the most prominent member of the New York Society for the Suppression of Vice. The Comstock Act, passed in 1873, made mailing obscene, *lascivious*, or *lewd* material a felony. Still in effect, the law is enforced by the Inspection Service of the U.S. Postal Service.

Gradually, however, U.S. courts moved away from the suppression of all depictions of sex-related activities. In a 1933 obscenity trial, federal judge Leonard Woolsey ruled that James Joyce's great novel *Ulysses* was not obscene because the author did not intend the book's "dirty parts" to be sexually arousing; instead, wrote Woolsey, Joyce aimed to portray human consciousness in a new literary mode. When the decision was appealed, Judge Augustus Hand

---

**obscenity**—the legal term for material that is foul, disgusting, lewd, and offensive to accepted standards of decency.

**lascivious**—tending to stimulate sexual desire.

**lewd**—sexually unchaste; inciting lust or debauchery.

proclaimed the doctrine of "dominant effect": obscenity must be evaluated on the basis of the work as a whole. In other words, a little sex can be diluted by a lot of nonsexual content. In a 1936 case, Judge Learned Hand stressed that the positive effects of the context could counterbalance the negative effects of the embedded sexual descriptions.

Enforcement of the law has been uneven because of the difficulty in defining what is obscene. In 1957 the Supreme Court, in *Roth* v. *United States*, attempted to provide a more precise definition of obscenity, and this definition remains the current legal one. In its decision, the Court stated that, for material to be considered obscene, it must meet three essential criteria: 1) it must be offensive to contemporary community standards; 2) the dominant theme of the work must appeal to *prurient* interest in sex; and 3) the work must be devoid of serious literary, artistic, political, or scientific value. Unfortunately, this ruling has not led to a clarification of the legal issues. The meaning of "community standards" is vague. A community can encompass both fundamentalist churches and a university with a liberal faculty; Republicans and Democrats; conservatives and liberals; and elderly, middle-aged, and young persons. How does one arrive at the community standard?

In an attempt to determine whether a homogeneous response to erotic materials could be found, college students at Bowling Green State University participated in a study of "judgments about photographs" (Allgeier et al., 1984). Students at this university are quite conservative, and most regularly attend religious services. They were asked to rate 60 photographs portraying nudity, heterosexual and homosexual activity, group sex, and so on. There was significant variation in the ratings of how arousing, pornographic, and offensive each photo was. As one might expect, the women students were more aroused and less offended by photos of nude males than the men were, with the reverse true of the men. The absence of commonality of responses in this homogeneous group suggests that establishing a community standard would be

even more difficult in a population as diverse as that found in U.S. cities (see Box 16.3).

The Supreme Court attempted to clarify the definition of obscenity in a 1987 decision. The Court ruled six to three that some sexually explicit works may not be obscene even if most people in a city or state think that the works have no serious literary, artistic, political, or scientific value. According to Justice Byron White, "The proper inquiry is not whether an ordinary member of any given community would find literary, artistic, political, or scientific value but whether a reasonable person would find such value in the material taken as a whole." Ambiguity remains, however, about how we define a reasonable person.

Contemporary social pressure to censor erotic depictions comes from two groups, one of which includes mainly political conservatives and religious fundamentalists. This group generally supports strict regulation of sexual behavior and considers use of erotica a pathway to sexual degeneracy. The second group consists of feminists who object to erotica that they consider degrading to women. They see certain forms of erotica as leading to violence against women, a causal relationship expressed most succinctly by Robin Morgan: "Pornography is the theory and rape is the practice" (1980, p. 139) (see Figure 16.7). Many feminists also assert that erotica reinforces traditional gender roles by emphasizing the subordination of women and the power of men in sexual relationships.

In the 1970s some feminists began to distinguish between pornography and erotica. They declared as pornographic those portrayals of women that they felt subordinated or degraded women in sexually explicit situations, and they reserved the term *erotica* for those sexually explicit portrayals that they felt did not abase or demean women (Steinem, 1980). This distinction reflects the difficulty of defining pornography. Essentially, these feminists were saying that pornography was the type of sexual depiction that they found degrading, whereas erotica was the variety that they found interesting. This distinction was recently codified into law in Canada (see Box 16.4). It should be noted, however, that not all feminists support censorship of sexually explicit materials, and some have formed a

*prurient*—provoking lasciviousness.

**Box 16.3**

## Testifying in Toledo

Several years ago, the prosecuting attorney in Toledo, Ohio, directed undercover police to purchase 26 erotic magazines from 11 adult bookstores and then ordered the bookstores closed. The storeowners hired lawyers who had the stores reopened, pending the outcome of a trial to determine whether the magazines were obscene. At that point, I was called by the defense and asked to be an expert witness regarding the obscenity of the magazines. The attorney said that a set of the magazines would be sent to me so that I could make a decision.

I began to go through them on a Friday when our youngest child was at school. The first few were aimed at a heterosexual market, and I felt mildly aroused. As I progressed through the third, fourth, and more of the 26 magazines, those pleasant feelings soon gave way to boredom, followed by irritation, followed by intense boredom.

By the time I had worked (yes, worked!) my way through the pile, I was totally uninterested in anything of a sexual nature. Then I was faced with the problem of where to store the magazines. I finally decided to stash them in the trunk of my car so that our son would not happen upon them, and there they remained for several weeks. Having at one point forgotten about them, I found myself at a loss for words as a grocery-store clerk, helping me load groceries into the trunk, caught sight of the magazines.

The magazines' diverse themes, and the range of fantasies to which they appeared to be directed, surprised me. Each seemed to have a specific target audience in terms of sexual orientation and/or type of sexual activities. Thus, for example, there were entire magazines devoted exclusively to heterosexual oral sex, whereas others focused entirely on anal sex between males. (I was pleased to see that one of the latter recommended that a couple use safer-sex practices during anal sex.) Since that time, I have even seen a magazine containing numerous photos of women in various stages of pregnancy with their legs spread for the camera's benefit. There must be markets for these varying themes: the glossy, full-color magazines are expensive to produce and purchase.

I did agree to testify, although the process and goals were different from those in which I have been trained. Court trials are adversarial processes (who will win?) rather than attempts to obtain accurate information about an issue. The prosecuting attorney asked me several questions before requesting my judgment about the materials. He had one of the magazines in a brown paper bag, and he asked me whether the magazine would appeal to the prurient interest of the average heterosexual man on the street. I could not see which of the magazines he had, and I told the judge that unless I could see it, I would be unable to render a judgment. Everyone laughed, including the judge, who directed the prosecuting attorney to let me examine the magazine. The prosecuting attorney appeared to be quite embarrassed, handing over the bag as if it contained dog excrement. The cover of the magazine in question had several photos of a tanned athletic man holding his penis and was apparently aimed at gay men who enjoy masturbation. I could honestly testify that such a magazine would be unlikely to arouse prurient interest in the average heterosexual man. I was dismissed from the court shortly after that, and the defense won the case.

It should be clear from the foregoing that I did not personally like most of the magazines, but that is not the point. The First Amendment to the Constitution is designed to prevent individuals from imposing their personal tastes on others who have differing opinions. Clearly, some people do enjoy some of these magazines, or the publishers would not be able to stay in business.

Source: E.R.A.

### Box 16.4

## Canada: A Harm-Based Approach to Obscenity

In February 1992, the Supreme Court of Canada ruled that obscenity was to be defined by the harm it does to women's pursuit of equality. In *Butler* v. *Her Majesty the Queen*, the Court unanimously redefined obscenity as sexually explicit material that involves violence or degradation. According to the Canadian Court, violent and degrading sexual material will almost always constitute an undue exploitation of sex and interferes with progress toward gender equality.

The Court's ruling sets out clear guidelines. Adult erotica, no matter how explicit, is not considered obscene. Erotic material that contains violence, degradation, bondage, or children is considered illicit obscenity. In effect, the Court decided that a threat to women's equality is an acceptable ground for some limitation of free speech. As of this writing, Canada is the only nation that has redefined obscenity in terms of harm to women rather than as material that offends moral values.

### FIGURE 16.7
### Violent Pornography and Rape
The relationship between sexual assault and exposure to violent erotica is not completely understood. Research has not demonstrated that viewing violent erotica prompts some men to rape, although such erotica does perpetuate negative attitudes toward women and greater acceptance of rape myths.

lobbying group called "Feminists for Free Expression."

The foregoing definitions have focused on the sentiments of small vocal groups. Seeking to examine the themes that lead to judgments of sexually explicit material as degrading to women, Cowan and Dunn (1994) exposed men and women to clips from X-rated films available from video stores. The clips were selected to represent nine different themes as defined in Table 16.1. Volunteers were asked to rate each clip on scales ranging from 1 (not at all degrading to women) to 14 (extremely degrading to women). Thus means below the midpoint of the 14-point scale (7.5) are on the nondegrading end; those above 7.5 are on the degrading end.

As may be seen in Table 16.1, the entire sample judged the first five themes below the midpoint, whereas the last four themes were judged as degrading to women. However, notice the difference in the ratings by men and women in the last two columns. Across the clips, men were less likely to rate the themes as degrading than were the women. Also, men's judgments were above the midpoint (but just barely) for only two of the nine themes (dominance and objectification), whereas women's judgments were above the midpoint for six of the nine themes. The three themes that they did not rate as degrading were sexually explicit (mutual) behavior, availability, and unreciprocated sex. Cowan and Dunn's (1994) study clearly demonstrated that percep-

**TABLE 16.1 When Does Sexually Explicit Material Degrade Women?**

Presented with video clips containing one of the following nine themes, men and women were asked by Cowan and Dunn (1994) to make judgments on 14-point scales (1 = not at all degrading, 14 = extremely degrading) as to how degrading to women each clip was.

| Theme | | Entire Sample | Women | Men |
|---|---|---|---|---|
| *Sexually explicit behavior* | Sexual activity that is explicit and mutual, without indicating an affectionate personal relationship between the two people. | 4.62 | 5.09 | 4.11 |
| *Unreciprocated sex* | Sexual activity that is one-sided. The woman is used to satisfy the man's needs, but her gratification is not important. | 5.71 | 6.48 | 4.86 |
| *Availability* | Sexual activity showing that the woman is available to anyone who wants her. | 5.97 | 7.02 | 4.84 |
| *Status inequality* | Sexual activity and the accompanying scenario that indicates inequality. The woman appears to have less status than the man; she may be younger, less educated, less intelligent, etc. | 6.99 | 7.90 | 5.98 |
| *Status reduction* | Sexual activity incorporates the idea that a high status woman can be reduced to a purely sexual being. | 7.02 | 7.79 | 6.15 |
| *Submission* | Sexual activity that begins with the woman's unwillingness to participate and ends with her loving it. | 7.40 | 8.13 | 6.62 |
| *Penis/semen worship* | Sexual activity that revolves around worship of the penis. The ejaculate is especially central to the woman's satisfaction. | 8.34 | 9.65 | 6.91 |
| *Dominance* | Sexual activity and the related scenario that explicitly shows that the man is dominant and may command the woman to do what he wishes or insult her without regard for her desires. | 8.87 | 9.91 | 7.68 |
| *Objectification* | Sexual activity that treats the woman as an object or a plaything. | 9.12 | 10.43 | 7.68 |

Adapted from Tables 1 and 3, Cowan and Dunn (1994).

tions of the degradation of women vary as a function of whether the viewers are men or women. Producers of erotic materials might note one other finding from Cowan and Dunn's study: in general, the men and women rated films containing degrading themes as less arousing than films perceived as nondegrading. Thus producers seeking to make films that arouse consumers might do well to strip degrading themes from their movies.

We know of no research exploring judgments of whether certain themes are perceived as degrading to men. In fact, we are not sure how one would construct heterosexual erotica that contained elements that would be judged by women—or men—as degrading to men, short of the rape of men by women, as described in Chapter 18.

Judgments of the themes of sexually explicit material are, of course, a separate issue from judgments about whether such material should be censored. National surveys conducted almost every year from 1973 to 1986 in the United States by the National Opinion Research Center indicated that the majority of respondents in every survey disagreed that the distribution of pornography to adults should be illegal (Smith, 1987). A statewide study in Hawaii also found support for the availability of erotica, although the majority of respondents were relatively conservative on other issues: they favored the death penalty and opposed the legalization of recreational drugs, including marijuana (Diamond & Dannemiller, 1989).

More important than whether people approve of the availability of erotica is whether particular kinds of erotica can be harmful. A choice confronting any society is the degree to which it wants to suppress material that may trigger antisocial behavior in some of its citizens. To protect the First Amendment rights of free expression, the courts have ruled that only those forms of expression that have a "virtual certainty" of producing potential harm can be banned. We now examine what evidence there is on whether certain types of erotica can with "virtual certainty" cause harm.

## The Effects of Erotica

There is intense controversy over the effects of exposure to erotica, particularly violent pornography. We deal with the issue of violent pornography shortly, but in this section our focus is on erotica that portrays consensual sexual activities. Does erotic material containing no aggression against women stimulate people to engage in sexual acts that they would normally avoid? Or does this material provide a sexual outlet for individuals who might use other means to satisfy their

sexual desires if erotica were not available? Is exposure to erotica related to sex crimes and violence? In this discussion we examine what is known about erotica and its effects.

A review of the many experimental studies on exposure to nonaggressive sexual material conducted since 1970 reveals no support for the belief that exposure to nonviolent erotica affects attitudes toward rape or evaluations of rape victims (Davis & Bauserman, 1993; Fisher & Barak, 1991; Linz, 1989). This is true for both short-term (less than an hour) and long-term (anything beyond an hour) exposure to nonviolent erotica. For example, in one study, students were randomly assigned to see either films without erotic or aggressive content (*Cognition and Creativity, The Social Animal*, and *When Will People Help?*) or erotic films without aggressive content (*The Devil and Miss Jones II, Stiff Competition*, and *Pink Lagoon*—the last was edited to remove violent content). These films were shown in five 50-minute sessions on subsequent days. On the last day, students' attitudes toward women were measured, and although women gave more positive scores than did men, attitudes toward women did not differ as a function of whether they spent five hours watching erotic or nonerotic films (Padgett et al., 1989).

One criticism of experimental research, however, is that the behaviors under study are affected by the artificiality of the laboratory setting and may not appear in real-life settings. To avoid such artificiality, Smith and Hand (1987) took advantage of the fact that a sexually explicit movie was screened once each semester at a private southern university. They conducted a field study on the campus to assess the possible links between nonviolent erotica and aggression. In the semester that the researchers carried out the study, the feature movie was *Up and Coming*, which the authors described as a film

> portraying the efforts of a young singer to establish herself in the country and western music industry. Her attempts to reach stardom provided for a number of sexual encounters with and among producers, agents, and fellow performers. In addition to graphic scenes of sexual intercourse, episodes of oral sex, anal sex, lesbianism, and group sex were

*depicted. Though the plot did include a brief scuffle between the singer and a rival female performer, the movie did not portray behavior that could be characterized as overtly sexually violent or coercive. (Smith & Hand, 1987, pp. 391–392)*

On Monday of the week before the film was shown, the authors questioned more than 200 undergraduate women from the campus on whether they had been victims of aggression during the previous weekend. The following Friday night, the film was shown, and the audience included about a third of the undergraduate men at the college. On the next two Mondays following the film's screening, the women were again asked to describe any experiences that they had had with aggression over the previous weekend. There were no significant differences in the percentage of women reporting aggression before the film's showing (20%) versus after its screening (19% and 16%). Furthermore, those women whose male companions attended the movie reported experiencing no more aggression from the men than did the women whose companions had not viewed the film.

While researchers have been attempting to address the issue of the effects of exposure to erotica, governmental bodies have also done so on several occasions, and we turn now to their varying conclusions.

## Public Policy and Erotica

President Lyndon Johnson appointed the U.S. Commission on Obscenity and Pornography in the late 1960s. After funding much research and holding many hearings, the commission released its report in 1970. The commission's efforts were reported in nine technical volumes, two of which were specifically concerned with the effects of erotica. The overall conclusions of the commission (1970) were as follows:

1. Exposure to erotic stimuli produces a substantial degree of sexual arousal in men and women.

2. Depictions of conventional sexual behavior are generally more stimulating than depictions of less conventional sexual activity.

3. Continued or repeated exposure to erotic stimuli over a period of 15 days results in satiation or a marked decrease in sexual arousal and interest in such material.

4. Exposure to erotic material results in an increase in masturbatory and/or coital behaviors among some people, and a decrease in these behaviors among a smaller percentage of people; the majority of individuals report no change in sexual behaviors.

5. Statistical studies of the relationship between the rate of sex crimes and the availability of erotic materials in Denmark found that sex crimes decreased as the availability of erotic material increased.

6. Research indicates that sex offenders have had less adolescent experience with erotica than have other adults.

Essentially, the commission arrived at a "no harm" conclusion, maintaining that, according to the available evidence, exposure to or use of explicit sexual material does not play a significant role in causing crime, delinquency, sexual deviancy, or severe emotional disturbances (Amoroso et al., 1971). Overall, the commission recommended that federal, state, and local legislation should not interfere with the right of adults who wish to read, obtain, or view explicitly sexual materials. And, as was described earlier, recent research with nonviolent erotica offers no reason for challenging the 1970 commission's no harm conclusion.

In 1979 the British government sponsored the Committee on Obscenity and Film Censorship. The committee's conclusions were similar to those of the 1970 U.S. Commission on Pornography and Obscenity. The Canadian government convened a Special Committee on Pornography and Prostitution, which delivered a report in 1985. The Canadian committee found that, although some studies had shown negative correlations with exposure to erotic material, the overall research picture was contradictory and inconclusive and therefore could not be relied

**FIGURE 16.8**

**The Meese Commission Report (1986)**
Edwin Meese III, an attorney general under President Ronald Reagan, holds his pornography panel's controversial report, which recommended a nationwide crackdown on pornography.

upon as a guide for the formation of public policy.

In 1985 the United States Attorney General's Commission on Pornography was formed. Also known as the Meese Commission (for Attorney General Edwin Meese III), it delivered its final report in 1986 after hearing testimony from witnesses around the country and reviewing 2,375 magazines, 725 books, and 2,370 films (see Figure 16.8). The commission claimed to have found a "causal relationship between sexual violence and exposure to erotica that featured children and/or violence." The commission's assertion of this causal link has provoked the most serious criticisms of its conclusions. As described in the next section, a number of studies have examined the correlation between exposure to explicit materials containing sexual violence, and attitudes to-

ward women and assault. However, the design of the studies reviewed by the commission did not permit a determination of the effect of observing sexual violence on subsequent acts of sexually assaultive behavior on adults or children.

Despite the fact that the Meese Commission's conclusions were not warranted by the data its members reviewed, the commission made 92 specific recommendations aimed at halting the spread of erotica. Many of these recommendations related to a more rigorous enforcement of the law with respect to obscene materials.

## Violent Pornography

The research reviewed by the 1970 U.S. Commission on Obscenity and Pornography dealt primarily with themes portraying consensual sexual activities. Thus the committee members could not address the issue of the impact of exposure to violent pornography on viewers' attitudes and behaviors. This is a critical issue to study, especially in light of the increased prevalence of mass-audience feature films that link (female) sexuality and (male) aggression, such as the *Friday the 13th* series.

To examine the effect of exposure to violent pornography, two of the most active researchers on the topic, Malamuth and Donnerstein (1984), exposed men to a series of slides and tapes of women reading stories that included coercive or consensual sexual interaction. These researchers used self-reported arousal as well as genital measures of erection to assess men's responses to these forms of erotica. Before participating in the studies, volunteers were asked to indicate the likelihood that they would commit rape if they could be sure of not getting caught. Those who revealed that they thought they might engage in coercive sexual acts were classified as force-oriented.

Although the designs of these studies varied, the stimuli usually consisted of a story of an attractive woman wandering along a deserted road. A man finds her there, but when he approaches her, she faints. He carries her to his car, and when she awakens they engage in sex. In one version of this basic story, the woman is tied up and forced to have sex in the car. In other variations, she clearly consents to the act. Regardless of which rendition they saw, male volunteers found this story arousing, as indicated both by self-reports and by the extent of their erections. This finding is consistent with others showing that certain rape portrayals elicit relatively high sexual arousal in nonrapists (Malamuth, 1984; Malamuth & Check, 1983).

What about the kind of violent pornography that depicts a positive reaction on the part of the victim? As Donnerstein (1984) pointed out, pornographic media quite often portray victims of assault as responding favorably to a rape. Further, in real life, convicted rapists often fail to perceive their assaults as coercive, believing that their victims desired intercourse and enjoyed their sexual attentions (Gager & Schurr, 1976). Because exposure to violent pornography has been shown to heighten sexual arousal, promote acceptance of rape-supportive attitudes, and foster negative attitudes toward women (Donnerstein & Linz, 1986; Malamuth, 1984), Donnerstein reasoned that such exposure would also increase aggressive behavior against women, particularly when a woman is depicted as having a positive reaction to sexual assault.

To test this hypothesis, each male volunteer was paired with a female confederate, who either angered the man or treated him in a neutral manner. Each man then watched one of four films—a neutral version, a variation that involved consensual interaction, a version in which the victim had a negative reaction to forced sex, or a variation in which the victim's reaction to forced sex was positive. After viewing one of these films, the volunteer was given an opportunity to administer simulated electric shocks to the female confederate. Of the volunteers who had been angered prior to watching the movie, those who had viewed either of the forced-sex films chose to give higher levels of electric shock to the female confederate than did those who viewed either of the other films. Even the nonangered men, however, became more aggressive (as measured by electric-shock level) following exposure to the version of the film showing a positive reaction to forced sex. When a male confederate angered a male volunteer prior to the latter's exposure to

the film, the versions of the film did not affect aggression toward the male confederate (Donnerstein, 1984).

Even a rape portrayal emphasizing the victim's pain and distress may, under certain conditions, stimulate high levels of sexual arousal in viewers. But this effect appears to vary as a function of whether the viewer describes himself as force-oriented (Malamuth, 1981). Force-oriented volunteers reported having more arousal fantasies after exposure to the rape version than after exposure to the mutual-consent version. Non-force-oriented men, however, reported having more arousing fantasies in response to the variations of the story involving mutual consent than in response to the rape variation (see Figure 16.9).

Earlier, in the context of our discussion of nonaggressive erotica, we noted the problem of the artificiality of laboratory settings used in much of the research on the effects of exposure to erotica. Another criticism of laboratory-based

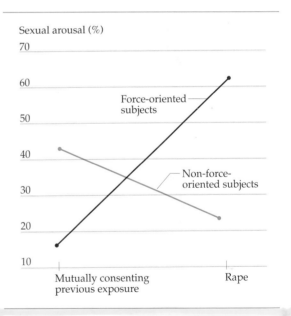

**FIGURE 16.9**

**Violent Pornography and Sexual Arousal**

As this graph illustrates, men who indicate some likelihood that they would commit rape (force-oriented men) are more aroused by violent pornography than are men who indicate that they would not (non-force-oriented).

studies of aggressive behavior in response to portrayals of erotica involves the limited response alternatives that have been provided to respondents (Fisher & Grenier, 1994). To determine if the limited range of responses provided by previous experimenters had affected the findings, Fisher and Grenier provided a broader range of alternatives for volunteers. That is, after being angered by the female confederate and shown sexual material containing violent content, men in Fisher and Grenier's research could select shock, verbal feedback, or the alternative of simply being debriefed, receiving their experimental credit, and terminating their participation in the study. Almost all participants selected the last alternative. Their research is preliminary and needs to be replicated by other researchers to see if their finding holds up, but by providing the option of allowing participants to leave without displaying aggression against the confederate, Fisher and Grenier (1994) provided a more realistic range of responses in the well-controlled environment of the laboratory.

What is the effect of violent pornography on women's arousal? To investigate this question, Stock (1982) presented college women with variations in rape depictions while measuring their genital responses and their subjective reports of arousal. Stock also compared the effect on their arousal levels of highly eroticized versus more realistic rape depictions because Malamuth and Check's depictions had focused on erotic aspects of the interaction rather than on the victims' negative response:

> "Susan was as beautiful as she was intelligent. Her silky blonde hair laid against bare tanned shoulders.... Everything about her appearance was perfect, from her innocent crystal blue eyes to the way her bright yellow halter dress clung to the curves of her body. Her firm breasts bounced slightly beneath her halter as she walked.... He reached around her neck and untied her halter top, baring her large breasts.... He started to moan like a wounded animal as he climaxed into Susan."
> It is possible that such elaborate erotic descriptions, which emphasize the attractiveness of the victim and/or the sexual arousal of the rapist, may have produced an inflated

> positive response to the rape stimuli. This is not an unbiased, neutral description of a rape, but an eroticized, unnecessarily tantalizing description that removes the emphasis from the aggressive nature of the act while dwelling on the sexual elements involved. (Stock, 1982, pp. 2–3)

Accordingly, Stock's volunteers were exposed to either eroticized or realistic rape depictions, as well as to other variations. Based on the women's responses, Stock concluded that "women are not aroused by rape when described in a realistic manner, but only to a distorted misrepresentation of rape in which the victim does not suffer and no harm is done. This is far from the experience of victims of rape" (1982, p. 9).

In their investigations of the effects of violent pornography, it is the romanticized portrayals of rape that concern Malamuth and his colleagues. Stock's finding that women, too, can be aroused by such eroticized rape depictions, but not by realistic rape depictions, also adds to our knowledge about the effects of violent pornography. The belief of some rapists and members of the general public that women secretly enjoy rape is not supported by Stock's conclusions, and her work suggests that society should be concerned about rape representations that lead viewers to perceive sexual assault as an erotic experience. In the context of films and videos portraying sexual assault, how would you work in the message that rape is a frightening and traumatizing experience for its victims?

Further research is needed on the effects of violent pornography—including, for example, the effects on men viewing the variations presented by Stock. Our present knowledge does not permit us to determine whether men who report strong arousal to rape depictions and who are aroused by their own rape fantasies will actually commit rape. On the other hand, Greendlinger and Byrne (1987) found that males with a higher frequency of coercive sexual fantasies reported higher levels of coercive sexual behavior in the past than did males who reported fewer coercive sexual fantasies. These are correlational data, and it is not known whether experience with sexual coercion leads to increased frequency of sexual fantasies, whether frequent coercive fantasies lead to coercive behaviors, or whether additional variables lead to coercive fantasies and behaviors. However, there has been a consistent finding that among college students, sexual arousal in response to coercive sex is associated with a callous attitude toward rape and rape victims, and with a lack of sexual experience (Davis & Bauserman, 1993). Particularly discomforting is the finding that men who find such violent stimuli sexually arousing report higher probabilities that they themselves might engage in rape if they could be sure that they would not be caught (Malamuth & Donnerstein, 1984).

The likelihood of a link between arousal in response to violent pornography and the commission of sexual assault was strengthened by the research of Abel and his colleagues almost two decades ago (Abel et al., 1977, 1978). They found that convicted rapists were as aroused by rape depictions as they were by portrayals of sexual interactions involving mutual consent. Nonrapists, in contrast, were more aroused by portrayals of consensual sex than by portrayals of forced sex.

Violent pornography degrades both women and men because it depicts women as wanting to be attacked, harmed, and assaulted and portrays men as wanting to inflict pain on other human beings. Also, such aggressive depictions are arousing to assaultive men—and to about a third of "normal" men who report that they might rape if they felt certain that they would not get caught. As noted in Chapter 6, however, many men and women report sexual fantasies that involve force, and obviously, most do not carry out their fantasies. In addition, Fisher and Grenier (1994) have provided preliminary evidence that even after having been insulted by a female confederate and exposed to violent sexually explicit material, most men choose to leave the experimental situation rather than to harm the female confederate. Further, there is no definitive evidence indicating that exposure to aggressive pornography causes men to victimize women sexually. Before censorship could be instituted, someone would have to determine what kinds of violent material should be prohibited. Who should make that determination? Another problem is that the effect of censorship in the past has been to increase the profits of the producers of banned material. If violent pornography is found to pose a danger to women, we believe that the withdrawal of consumer support would be far more effective in stopping the production of aggressive pornography than would attempts at censorship.

## Prolonged Exposure

The 1970 Commission on Obscenity and Pornography found that continued or repeated exposure to erotic stimuli resulted in satiation or a marked decrease in sexual arousal and interest in such material. But this conclusion has been challenged by the work of Zillmann and Bryant (1982, 1984, 1987). They concluded that following long-term exposure (4 hours and 48 minutes over a six-week period) to erotica that did not contain overt violence, men and women became more tolerant of bizarre and violent forms of erotica, less supportive of statements about sexual equality, and more lenient in assigning punishment to a rapist whose crime was described in a newspaper account. Prolonged exposure also produced other effects, such as discontent with the physical appearance and sexual performance of an intimate partner and the questioning of the values of marriage. It also deepened men's callousness toward women, as reflected in increased acceptance of such statements as "A woman doesn't mean no until she slaps you" and "If they are old enough to bleed, they are old enough to butcher." The material used by Zillmann and Bryant commonly depicted women as sexually insatiable. Perhaps short-term exposure is not sufficient to provoke attitudinal changes that reflect this unrealistic view of the female sexual appetite. Continued exposure to the portrayal of women as sexually insatiable may have encouraged other related thoughts about female sexual behavior that affected these participants' attitudes. Long-term exposure to erotica, however, did not increase aggressive behaviors.

Other studies of prolonged exposure to nonviolent erotica have reported no change in participants' attitudes toward women, although Kelley and Musialowski (1986) found that viewing erotic movies every day for four days decreased both sexual arousal and desire to see the same films again. Prolonged exposure to pornography that portrays violence against women, however, has consistently been linked to negative effects such as lessened sensitivity toward rape victims and greater acceptance of force in sexual encounters (Davis & Bauserman, 1993; Linz, 1989).

These contradictory findings make it difficult to reach any firm conclusions on the effects of prolonged exposure to nonviolent erotica. Moreover, even in those cases in which negative effects have been found, we do not know how long these effects last, and this is an issue that researchers need to address. For example, it appears that any changes that occur after short-term exposure to erotica are not deeply ingrained, as Malamuth and Check (1984) demonstrated in studies of the effects of debriefing procedures in their experiments. Such debriefings are required by the federal government of agencies that receive federal research funds. All participants are debriefed after completing an experiment to negate any possible effects of the experiment.

In the case of Malamuth and Check's research, the debriefing was designed to counteract the possibility that the films had increased the participants' aggressiveness and negative attitudes toward women. Malamuth and Check used a short procedure for this purpose. They gave subjects a one-page statement informing them that the attitudes of the women they saw in the films were not typical of real women; that is, women are not as sexually receptive as these films suggest, nor do they become aroused when a male attempts to rape them. In addition, the experimenters spoke to the men briefly on the same point. They found that after the simple debriefing, the significant differences between the experimental and control groups in attitudes toward women disappeared completely. In fact, the exposed men were even less callous in their final attitudes than were the men who had not been exposed to any erotica. This kind of study should also be done on the effects of prolonged exposure to erotica to determine whether those effects are as short-lived.

## Cultural Variations

Cultural practices and value systems may temper the influence of viewing erotica. In Japan, for ex-

**FIGURE 16.10**
**Erotic Media in Japan**
This Japanese erotic movie poster appeared in Tokyo's Kagurazaka section, now an after-dark drinking area which formerly contained many geisha houses.

ample, laws still ban the public display of pubic hair and adult genitals (see Figure 16.10). Yet Japanese mass-circulation magazines commonly depict nudity without pubic hair and genitalia, and television shows there are more sexually explicit than those in the United States. Of particular relevance to our discussion is the prominence of bondage and rape themes in both novels and films in Japan. In Japanese films, for example, the plot often involves the rape of a high school girl, a theme that is also evident in cheap erotic novels and sexual cartoons. Abramson and Hayashi (1984) pointed out that one of the best ways to ensure the success of a Japanese adult film is to include the bondage and rape of a young woman.

The popularity of this theme might lead one to suspect that Japan would have a high rate of sexual assault. Yet Japan has one of the lowest reported rates of any industrialized country in the world: only 2.4 reported rapes per 100,000 people, compared to a rate more than 14 times higher in the United States. The assault laws in the two countries are essentially the same, and Japanese women are as reluctant to report assault as are U.S. women. A possible explanation for Japan's low assault rate is that the message expressed in erotica is mediated by cultural values. In Japan, people are socialized to have a strong sense of personal responsibility, respect, and commitment to society, and to experience shame if they behave improperly (Dion & Dion, 1993).

## Children and Pornography

The use of children as models for sexually explicit magazine photos and as stars of erotic movies has become a major concern of many social agencies and citizens' groups. Both houses of Congress held hearings on child erotica in 1977. Witnesses at the hearings estimated that between 300,000 and 600,000 children were involved in the production of erotica, and that more than 260 child-sex publications were being disseminated (Pierce, 1984). After these hearings, the federal government and nearly all state governments enacted laws against the production, distribution, and possession of child erotica.

Involvement in the production of erotica is a form of sexual exploitation that is associated with various adverse emotional, behavioral, and physical reactions in children, as well as in adults who were exploited as children (Finkelhor & Browne, 1985). Evidence of these reactions comes from clinical studies of children who were seeing therapists or other professionals, however, so we need to be careful in generalizing these findings to all children involved in such activity. Furthermore, most children and adolescents lured into making erotica also participated in prostitution or other sexual activities with adults (Burgess et al., 1984), and many came from homes where they experienced neglect and abuse (Silbert & Pines, 1984). It is hard to isolate the effects of their experiences in making erotica from the effects of these other experiences.

Silbert (1986) interviewed hundreds of children, adolescents, and young adults who participated in making erotica and compiled a list of their behavioral traits. Those who were making erotica at the time of the interview were described as uncommunicative, withdrawn, inattentive, and fearful. Retrospective studies of those who had been involved earlier in the production of erotica indicated that as adolescents they tended to be withdrawn, anxious, and paranoid. However, Inciardi (1984) reported that involvement in the production of erotica may not always lead to observable problems. Inciardi interviewed nine girls between the ages of 8 and 12 who had engaged in making erotica and in prostitution and found that the girls showed few overt symptoms. But it is impossible to predict whether they might be affected later when they experience significant life events involving intimacy and sexuality such as dating, marriage, and childbearing, nor is it appropriate to generalize from Inciardi's small sample to the thousands of children and adolescents who participate in producing erotica.

Some people oppose prosecuting those who ensnare children in the manufacture of erotica. Their claim is that viewers experience sexual release from erotica, and that having such an outlet for their sexual tension prevents them from actually seeking out a young person for sexual activities. Current law, however, bars children from participating in the production of erotica because they are incapable of giving informed consent. Those adults who pay, entice, or coerce them to engage in this activity can be prosecuted under child-abuse laws rather than under obscenity laws.

We favor this course of action for three reasons. First, obscenity laws may at times violate First Amendment guarantees of freedom of expression. Second, it is generally accepted that the First Amendment permits the outlawing only of material that is considered offensive to public taste and morality, and, as we have seen, this judgment is often difficult to make. Third, children, whether clothed or nude, are not obscene; it is the exploitation of children that is obscene. Adults who abuse their responsibilities toward children by exploiting them are, therefore, guilty of child abuse. In 1982 the Supreme Court ruled unanimously that states may prosecute publishers and sellers of child erotica without having to prove that the materials showing children engaging in sexual acts are legally obscene, or that they appeal to prurient interests. According to the Court, the simple inclusion of children engaging in sexual acts is enough to justify prosecution.

## Protection from Erotica

Even if it can be demonstrated that certain forms of erotica can lead to undesirable behavior, should the law try to protect consumers from this potential harm? Censorship is certainly one way to attempt to control erotica. Another means might be to provide a warning label similar to that found in cigarette packaging and advertising. The dangers of cigarette smoking are well documented, but the government does not prohibit cigarettes. Rather, it warns the consumer that cigarette smoking is dangerous to one's health. In applying a comparable approach to erotica, however, some questions would arise, as the psychologist Donald Mosher pointed out in his testimony to the Attorney General's Commission on Pornography in 1985: "Is the warning to read 'pornography is dangerous to your morals,' or 'pornography is dangerous to women as a class,' or 'pornography increases your risk of committing a sex offense,' or 'pornography is dangerous to your family,' or 'pornography increases your risk of masturbation'?" (1985, p. 32)

As Mosher pointedly suggested, and as we have emphasized in this chapter, there is no scientific consensus on whether serious harm is likely to result from exposure to erotica. We agree with Donnerstein and Linz (1986) that the basic issue is *violent* images, not *erotic* images. It is interesting that our culture exposes the young to graphic details of violence on television and movie screens and in magazines without the same intense public concern that attends exposure to erotica or pornography.

## Prostitution

We have considered how advertisers use sex to sell products and how materials such as erotic magazines and films, as well as sexual aids, are designed to elicit sexual arousal. In this section, we examine the direct sale of sexual services.

## The Oldest Profession

*Prostitution* appears to have been practiced at least as far back as we have historical records, and hence it is often called the world's oldest profession. The word *prostitute* comes from the Latin *prostituere*, which means "to expose." Under Roman law, prostitution was defined as the sale of one's body indiscriminately and without pleasure.

Prostitution flourished in ancient Rome; street prostitutes offered their services to patrons of the theater, the circus, and gladiator contests. As a prelude to the contests between gladiators, patrons would view shows featuring a variety of sexual acts. After the contest was over, those patrons interested in having sex were taken by the prostitutes to the arches beneath the public buildings, known as the *cellae fornicae*. This practice was so common that the word *fornication* came to mean engaging in nonmarital sexual intercourse (Bullough & Bullough, 1987).

Through recessions and boom times, prostitution remained a means of employment for poverty-stricken females before and after the Roman Empire. Prostitution was widespread in the urban areas of Europe during the Middle Ages. In France, for example, the Paris steam bath, a popular rendezvous spot for prostitutes and customers, was licensed and taxed by the state and closed during Holy Week and Easter. That the prostitutes of Paris had their own patron saint, Mary Magdalene, underscores the Roman Catholic church's tolerance of prostitution during this period. Apparently, the Church had adopted the reasoning of St. Thomas Aquinas, who compared prostitution to sewers in a palace: just as the palace would be polluted by sewage if one removed the sewers, the world would be polluted by lust if society removed the prostitutes.

**prostitution**—the practice of selling sexual stimulation or interaction.

**fornication**—sexual intercourse between people who are not married to each other.

Attitudes toward prostitution shifted in the 1500s. Two factors are related to the decline in the legal toleration of prostitution in the 16th century. First, with the Reformation, Protestant and, later, Catholic authorities came to regard open prostitution as a moral outrage. Second, syphilis began to spread rapidly in Europe after 1500. The disease was thought to have been transmitted to the general population by sailors returning from the New World, and civil and church authorities attempted to limit its spread by imposing tight control over sexual contacts (Bullough & Bullough, 1987).

In the Victorian era in England, a period noted for its supposed purity and prudery, prostitution flourished. Officially, the prostitute was a social outcast, but implicitly she was tolerated. She provided an outlet through which the proper 19th-century husband could satisfy his burdensome passion. Victorian prostitutes were most often women who had been caught in the squalor and degradation of the urban slums that developed around the mining and milling industries. Selling sexual favors was their main hope for survival.

## Prostitution in Contemporary Society

Although there is still a strong relationship between poverty and prostitution, in some ways the nature of prostitution has changed markedly in the 20th century. In the first part of the century, most transactions with prostitutes were conducted in houses where prostitution was the sole business. The employees worked, ate, and slept there. Because small red lights were used to indicate that the houses were open for business, the areas in which they were clustered became known as red-light districts. Houses of prostitution declined in number between the two world wars and almost disappeared after World War II (Winick & Kinsie, 1971). Most contemporary brothels have gone underground and thus are no longer visible to the average citizen. They are more like the speakeasies of Prohibition days, with restricted clientele and police protection. In some nations in northern Europe, as well as in some counties in the state of Nevada, houses of prostitution continue to operate legally. For the

most part, however, prostitutes in contemporary America operate out of a variety of other settings that reflect the economic status of the prostitute.

*Streetwalkers* are on the lowest rung of the ladder in the hierarchy of prostitution. They solicit on the street and often work for, or are attached to, a *pimp*, who usually has more than one woman working for him. He protects them from outside assaults and generally takes care of them, although by the nature of his business, he is also highly manipulative of the women. The pimp usually takes a considerable share of the prostitute's earnings in exchange for his "protection." Some streetwalkers are recruited from among drug abusers and young runaways. However, most pimps are not interested in substance abusers because of economic reasons. Substance abuse is expensive and the addicted prostitute is not a reliable employee (McCormick, 1994).

Streetwalkers have traditionally worked during the night (hence the phrase "ladies of the night"), but daytime solicitation has become common in large cities. Some streetwalkers, for example, solicit by day in X-rated movie houses. After an arrangement has been struck, the streetwalker usually takes her "trick" (customer) to her apartment or to a cheap hotel, where the manager or room clerk typically is fully aware of the situation. A relatively new variation in streetwalking occurs in truckstops and highway rest areas. At truckstops, women known as "commercial beavers" provide sexual services in the drivers' cabs (McCormick, 1994).

Bar and hotel prostitutes are somewhat higher in the hierarchy of prostitutes than are streetwalkers. The bar girl usually enters into an arrangement with the owner or manager of the bar where she works, and may receive a percentage of the drinks that she entices the customer to buy for both of them. More frequently, however, the bar girl is tolerated by the ownership because of the business she attracts. Unlike the streetwalker, the bar girl sometimes finds herself in competition with amateurs and may have to solicit aggressively. The customer may become

**streetwalker**—a prostitute who solicits on the street.

**pimp**—a prostitute's business manager.

### Box 16.5

### Massage-Parlor Employment

*The first ten days in the massage parlor were spent in training, which June described as rigorous and extensive. This training was given by the owner/operator, who gave the girls instructions on how to massage and a list of rules that they were required to follow. These rules were generally aimed at preventing arrest from undercover policemen known to investigate the parlor from time to time. The rules outlined the order in which the girl would dispense her services (massage first, sex later), the amount of time she would spend massaging (no less than 30 minutes), what she would say to the customer (no direct propositions, no mention of extras until the late stages of the massage), and standards of cleanliness. . . . June notes that it was not difficult to convince the customers to ask for extras since after one half hour of rubbing by a nude attendant, the customer was usually sexually aroused. Near the end of the massage, while she was plac-*
*ing her hand near the man's genitals, she would ask the customer if he would like a local (a hand massage). When he agreed to this she would mention that certain gentlemen had given her tips of $20.00 to $30.00 for these extras. At this point the customer would usually proposition her, saying that he would give her money for a hand massage, thus legally clearing her and the parlor. June said that some of the other girls performed more extensive sexual services such as sexual intercourse and fellatio, but she herself preferred to stay with hand jobs. The girls did not receive a salary, obtaining all their income through tips. June said that she was happy with this arrangement, claiming to make about $400.00 to $500.00 per week.*

Source: Prus & Irini, 1980, p. 67.

quite disgruntled if he at first thinks the bar girl is taking an interest in him because of his lovable personality and then discovers that there is a price attached to any sexual activity. The bar girl's fee for sex is generally higher than that charged by the streetwalker.

Because hotel management frowns on open solicitation, hotel prostitutes must be subtle and skilled in sending nonverbal messages to potential clients. After a deal has been made, sexual activity usually takes place in the customer's hotel room or apartment. Many hotel prostitutes work a bar one day and a hotel the next, generally operating without pimps.

One of the more visible forms of prostitution is the storefront variety. In this version, women are employed by massage parlors or thinly disguised business fronts such as escort services to provide sexual services to the customers. Although there are legitimate massage parlors and escort services, many run an operation similar to that described in Box 16.5. Massage and masturbation (M&M) are frequently offered in massage

parlors. For an additional fee, the "hand whores" may provide oral sex or, less frequently, coitus. Many women employed by massage parlors and escort services are amateurs. College students, homemakers, sales clerks, nurses, secretaries, and women in other occupations may supplement their incomes in this manner (McCormick, 1994). Women hired to entertain at conventions through escort services are sometimes prostitutes. They may be asked to service delegates, visitors, and convention personnel, as well as to perform before a limited audience. The performances involve dancing, stripping, and lesbian and heterosexual activities. The convention prostitute may have a pimp who acts as a booking agent.

At the top of the prostitution hierarchy is the *call girl*. She usually works out of a comfortable

**call girl**—a high-priced prostitute whose customers are solicited by telephone or by word-of-mouth references.

apartment, and if she has a pimp, he acts as her business manager. Typically, her prices are high and her clientele is screened, with solicitation generally occurring by telephone. New customers are located through references and word of mouth. The call girl is likely to provide services other than purely sexual ones, such as serving as an attractive date for dinner or a party. It is widely believed that many corporations and government agencies employ call girls to entertain important customers, agents, and dignitaries (see Figure 16.11). Although the use of call girls by government agencies, particularly intelligence agencies, is probably not as great as espionage novels suggest, prostitutes' involvement in espionage has a long history.

*Male Prostitutes*

It should not be surprising that the possibility of earning money for sexual favors has attracted males as well as females. Like their female counterparts, male prostitutes often sell their bodies because they have—or think they have—nothing else salable.

Many heterosexual male prostitutes function in a manner similar to that of call girls. These men may be kept by an older woman, or they may work for an escort service for single, wealthy women. The *gigolo*'s relationship to the client is generally well defined, requiring little or no emotional involvement.

Much more common are males who sell their sexual favors to other men; in fact, most male prostitutes describe themselves as homosexual or bisexual (Earls & David, 1989). The homosexual prostitute is called a hustler or sometimes a boy. Such men usually ply their trade on the street or in gay bars and baths. In the homosexual culture, prostitutes drift in and out of the occupation; homosexual prostitutes are more likely to be part-timers than are heterosexual prostitutes (Luckenbill, 1985).

Male prostitutes tend to be more suspicious, mistrustful, hopeless, lonely, and isolated than are nonprostitute males (Simon, Morse, Osofsky, Balson, & Gaumer, 1992). These characteristics

*gigolo*—a man who is paid to be a woman's escort and to provide her with sexual services; a kept man.

**FIGURE 16.11**
**Hotel Prostitute**
This prostitute sips a drink in a hotel bar while waiting to attract customers.

may be a response to the chaotic and often dangerous environment in which they exist. This environment may intensify the psychological characteristics that led them to "the life" in the first place. More than 80% of the 211 men in Simon et al.'s study used multiple drugs, with alcohol, marijuana, and cocaine being the most common; 28% reported injecting drugs and sharing needles with their customers. This intravenous (IV) drug use is alarming from a public health standpoint because of the possibility of transmitting HIV and other STDs. Condom use was infrequent or never occurred, according to the men and their customers (Morse, Simon, Balson, & Osofsky, 1992). Only one of the 15 male customers interviewed identified himself as homosexual.

## The Trade

Prostitution is a topic that proper society prefers to avoid contemplating. Perhaps because of societal disdain, not only do stereotypes abound but knowledge about prostitution is lacking. It is not uncommon to hear laypersons describe female prostitutes as man-hating lesbians or nymphomaniacs.

The research on female prostitutes indicates that their attitudes toward their clients and toward men in general are varied rather than uniformly negative (Diana, 1985; McCormick, 1994), although adolescent prostitutes tend to have a more negative attitude toward men than do older prostitutes (Gibson-Ainyette, Templer, Brown, & Veaco, 1988). Contrary to the popular belief that prostitutes are sexually unresponsive to their work, a study of 50 streetwalkers in Philadelphia found that 70% of the women reported enjoying intercourse all, most, or some of the time; 83% reported the same degree of pleasure from receiving oral sex; and 63% enjoyed giving oral sex (Savitz & Rosen, 1988). These women reported much more enjoyment in their noncommercial sexual encounters, but the greater the sexual enjoyment in the prostitutes' private sex life, the higher the erotic pleasure reported in their professional realm. Of the 21 women in this sample who always reached orgasm with lovers, 19 reported comparatively high orgasmic frequency (always, usually, sometimes) with clients. In this study, then, the stereotype of the sexually unresponsive prostitute is not supported.

Nor is the other stereotype about female prostitutes—that is, that most are lesbians—supported by research. Most female prostitutes consider themselves heterosexual or bisexual, not homosexual (Diana, 1985; Savitz & Rosen, 1988). Prostitutes sometimes engage in sex with another woman in response to a customer's desires; for example, a male-female couple may hire a prostitute to have sex with one or both of them.

The financial fortune of prostitutes depends on how many tricks they can turn in a working day. (Call girls are typically an exception to this assembly-line approach because they are often hired for an entire evening by a customer.) The more customers a prostitute can bring to orgasm, the more money he or she makes. Thus after a client pays for a particular service, the prostitute generally attempts to bring the customer to orgasm as quickly as possible, usually after two to three minutes of sexual contact. The most frequently reported practice to accomplish this goal is oral sex, as cited by both prostitutes (Diana, 1985; Freund, Leonard, & Lee, 1989) and their customers (Wallace, Beatrice, & Mann, 1988). Most prostitutes prefer oral sex because it takes less effort than coitus, which is the next most common sexual practice. In third place is a half and half: oral stimulation followed by coitus. These kinds of sexual contacts, along with the manual stimulation of customers' genitals, account for almost all sexual transactions between prostitutes and their clients. Vaginal intercourse is more likely to occur if the customer is a regular client, that is, has frequent sexual contacts with the same prostitute over a long period of time—specifically, one to three times a week over one to fourteen years (Freund et al., 1989).

The number of customers that a prostitute services in a working day or night varies greatly, depending on such factors as client availability, the prostitute's mood, and negative characteristics of a potential customer. Published accounts indicate an average of 4 to 12 sexual encounters per workday (Diana, 1985; Freund et al., 1989). The large number of sexual contacts, of course, puts the prostitute (and customer) at an elevated risk of contracting sexually transmitted diseases.

Silbert (1986) reported a growing concern about AIDS among the juvenile prostitutes whom she studied. The specter of a fatal illness has altered the sexual practices of prostitutes, with many now abstaining from high-risk sexual behaviors and regularly employing condoms (Earls & David, 1989; Freund, Leonard, & Lee, 1989). Condom use in sexual encounters has been reported by 38% to 74% of prostitutes, but 45% of the clients of prostitutes report never using condoms (Cohen et al., 1987; Freund et al., 1989; Wallace et al., 1988). More recently, 72% of a sample of 101 male clients of female street prostitutes reported using condoms during vaginal inter-

**Box 16.6**

## What Is Prostitution?

The following observations from former prostitutes illustrate that the distinction between sexual activity for its own sake—and even nonsexual activity—and prostitution is not always easy to make.

*Part of me says there really isn't a line; don't get hung up on thinking a prostitute is the one on the street or the one working out of the house. There are plenty of married women who are having their apartments paid for, they've got food on the table, their kids are being raised, they're living good and they can't stand their husbands; but they go to bed once a week or once a month or whatever because it's the thing to do. That's prostitution, you know she's being kept. Except they have a legal little paper. Part of me says that, and the other part of me goes along with the laws.*

*You keep prostitution to the people who are getting money for it. I mean it's hard. To me they're all into it. But yet I fall into society's bag of what is prostitution and what isn't.*

*I used to refer to waitressing as prostituting my smile. Wherever I waitressed I always made more money than anybody else, even the more experienced girls who had been there longer, and I used to think it was only because I was friendly and smiled. They were paying for someone to be nice to them. But paying for somebody to be nice to you by leaving a big tip for a waitress isn't a hell of a lot different from paying someone to be nice to you sexually.*

Source: Goldstein, 1979, pp. 25–26.

---

course, and 33% reported doing so during oral sex (Freund, Lee, & Leonard, 1991).

### Prostitution and the Law

Prostitution is not an easy activity to define or categorize. For example, if a man or a woman engages in sex with another person to secure a favor, a promotion, or influence, is this prostitution? Consider this account by a former prostitute of her first experience with prostitution:

*It would have been when I was still back in high school, when I screwed my husband-to-be in the back seat of the car. He bought me coke. A Coca-Cola, and popcorn. At the time I didn't consider it [prostitution]. Now I do. At the time I thought I was having fun.* (Goldstein, 1979, p. 23)

Box 16.6 further highlights the difficulty that many people have in distinguishing prostitution from other forms of sexual activity.

Legal definitions of prostitution vary from one time and place to another, but they generally include some notion of indiscriminate sexual activity or promiscuity as well as barter. State legal codes typically forbid making money from the provision of sexual fulfillment. For example, a 1968 ruling of the supreme court of Oregon stated: "The feature which distinguishes a prostitute from other women who engage in illicit intercourse is the indiscrimination with which she offers herself to men for hire" (Rosenbleet & Pariente, 1973, p. 381). Prostitution and commercialized vice include sex offenses such as a) prostitution; b) keeping a *brothel*, or bawdy house, disorderly house, or house of ill fame; c) *pandering*, *procuring*, transporting, or detaining

**brothel**—a house where prostitutes and customers meet for sexual activity.

**pandering**—serving as a go-between in commercial sexual transactions; generally, pimping or procuring.

**procuring**—obtaining customers for a prostitute.

women for immoral purposes; and d) all attempts to commit any of the preceding (Flanagan & Jamieson, 1988).

Every state in the United States has laws regulating prostitution, soliciting for prostitution, or loitering for the purpose of prostitution. Nevada is the only state in which counties are given the option to allow prostitution, and several do. These counties, however, confine prostitution to brothels and have laws against soliciting customers in other vicinities.

The frequency of this "criminal" violation, and the numbers of men and women involved in it, are difficult to estimate. Prostitution is not an offense reported by a victim or complainant, and hence the statistics based on arrests are not a clear reflection of the incidence of this activity. Arrests tend to be sporadic, and differences in the number of arrests from one locality to another may reflect the attitude of local law-enforcement officials rather than the incidence of prostitution.

Prostitution represents the only sexual offense for which women are prosecuted more often than are men. In 1991 there were 94,678 arrests for prostitution and commercialized vice in the United States (Maguire, Pastore, & Flanagan, 1992). The fact that a disproportionate number of Blacks were arrested (46%) probably reflects prostitution's link to economic factors. Those individuals who are arrested for prostitution are usually streetwalkers, who tend to come from the lower socioeconomic strata of our society.

The lure of money for unskilled labor is often difficult to resist. One disturbing statistic is the jump in arrests for prostitution of those under 18 years of age. In 1966 there were 677 arrests in this age group. During the 1980s, the annual arrests for this age group hovered around 2,500, a spurt of almost 400% (Maguire, Pastore, & Flanagan, 1992). In 1982 the U.S. General Accounting Office compiled a report on teenage prostitutes and estimated there were as many as 2.4 million adolescent prostitutes. Many of these children were runaways, some as young as 12 or 13, who were tempted or coerced into prostitution as a means of supporting themselves (see Figure 16.12).

Because of variations in the enforcement of prostitution laws, numerous court challenges have attacked both the laws themselves and the methods of police enforcement. Enforcement

agents often deploy a vice-squad undercover officer to pose as a *john*; the prostitute is arrested when she offers a sexual service for a price. To avoid arrest, the experienced prostitute is careful about how she words her proposition to a potential customer. She may ask him whether he wants a good time or some fun. She also approaches the matter of her fees in a roundabout way. If a prostitute is arrested and convicted, she is usually fined but typically does not spend much time in jail. Either her pimp or a friend usually secures bail money. Fines tend to be minimal, and jail sentences short.

The customer is seldom implicated for his or her contribution to prostitution. Patronizing a prostitute is illegal in some states, but there has been little concerted effort to prosecute customers. In some states, however, the patron of prostitution does face a fine of $500 or more and a year or more in jail. A customer is most likely to be arrested when a female police officer poses as a prostitute and entices him into asking for a sexual service and offering money for it.

The punishment for pimping is much more severe than that for prostitution, although few pimps are arrested. In some states, pimps can receive prison sentences of 10 to 20 years and fines of up to $2,000. Nonetheless, it is the working man or woman in the prostitution network who bears the brunt of legal penalties. To protect themselves, many prostitutes have joined the local and national unions that have emerged in North America and Western Europe.

Two of the most vocal of these groups are COYOTE and Scapegoat. COYOTE ("Call Off Your Old Tired Ethics") was founded in California by Margo St. James (see Figure 16.13) and has chapters nationwide. Scapegoat is a New York City organization. Both groups lobby for the decriminalization of prostitution and offer services to prostitutes. Their members appear in various public forums such as television talk shows.

The decriminalization of prostitution would have a number of advantages for the prostitute and for society. City and state governments spend a great deal of money trying to control prostitution, with little success (Rio, 1991). If prostitution were legalized, pimps would likely

*john*—a slang term for the customer of a prostitute.

# SEX SELLS

Using sexual themes to sell an array of products and entertainments is a common, controversial practice. Everything from books to breath mints, movies to mattresses, and sneakers to sensuous scents has been fair game for marketing mavens. Sex in advertising typically means presenting attractive, sometimes scantily clad models of either gender—first, to catch our attention, and second, to suggest that using a particular product or pursuing a particular activity can endow us with the same sexual aura and appeal.

Many sexually oriented advertisements, including those reproduced here for Guess jeans and Jockey briefs integrate sex into their message. That is, the sexual elements connect with the product's main selling features. But the sexual nature of a promotion does not necessarily relate to a product or its benefits, as the French ad for Gladiator bicycles reveals.

Marketeers have a long history of using sex to sell their wares. The nineteenth century marked a period of rapid expansion in business, and hand in hand with it came a boom in advertising. The rise of the "penny press" in the 1830s; the subsequent flowering of the magazine industry; climbing levels of literacy and education in the Western nations; fattening pay envelopes; and increasing leisure time combined to create a vast consumer market. Advertisers did not hesitate to capitalize on the changes—and to employ appeals to prurient interest along the way.

The first illustration, a woodcut from an American magazine of c. 1880, accompanied a story about infidelity in rural America; the stick-wielding wife is catching her

**American woodcut on rural infidelity, c. 1880**

**Nineteenth-century tradecard for Trix, "Perfume for the Breath"**

Above, **French poster for Gladiator bicycles, c. 1895**

Right, **American circus poster, c. 1920**

**Josephine Baker poster, 1930**

*Vanity Fair* **cover, May 1926**

**Film poster for *The Son of the Sheik*, 1926**

**Film poster for a Mae West movie, 1930s**

I'M OUT FOR A GOOD TIME-AND-A-HALF

A MUTOSCOPE CARD                    PRINTED IN U. S

**Mutoscope card, 1940s**

husband kissing another woman behind a haystack. Tales of illicit love and sex catered to the popular appetite of the times. The trade card for Trix "perfume for the breath" and the sensual French advertisement for "Cycles Gladiator" show the range of items that manufacturers peddled through the use of sexual situations and nudity. Even circus promoters understood the power of sex appeal, as is conveyed by the Ringling Brothers and Barnum & Bailey poster, around 1920, featuring the "dainty" but curvaceous gymnast Miss Leitzel.

The "Jazz Age" of the 1920s, an era when the ideas of Sigmund Freud enjoyed great popularity, brought a new erotic freedom that found expression in lifestyles, literature, and leisure. This 1926 cover from the elite magazine *Vanity Fair* depicts the Three Graces of mythology swaddled in swirling, see-through gossamer. The 1930s poster of the Casino de Paris depicts the sultry American songstress Josephine Baker, the darling of the French night-club circuit, in spare costume and seductive pose. This was also the golden age of the movies, when sexy film idols like Rudolph Valentino (here baring his chest to starlet Vilma Banky in a contemporary movie poster for *The Son of the Sheik*) and Mae West incinerated the silver screen with their blazing sensuality. In the war-torn 1940s, sex sold in simulations of motion pictures marketed to homesick soldiers in the form of "mutoscope" cards like the one here depicting a banana-eating, décolleté beauty. By

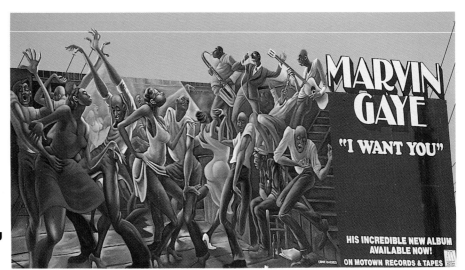

**Billboard promoting a Marvin Gaye record, 1976**

**Ad for Guess jeans for women, 1994**

**Ad for Jockey briefs for men, 1994**

flipping through a series of such images, the observer could escape his troubles in a make-believe moving-picture world.

In the 1970s, the legacy of the permissive sixties was apparent in explicit advertisements featuring cou-

ples in erotic entwinement, such as the 1976 billboard promoting a Marvin Gaye album. The 1980s witnessed advertisers' incorporation of ever-greater degrees of nudity—both male and female—to catch the consumer's eye. The enticing ad for

Guess jeans for women, featuring Drew Barrymore, and the provocative ad for Jockey briefs for men set new standards in the 1990s. What shape the advertising trends of the new century will take is the stuff of fascinating speculation.

**FIGURE 16.12**

**"Tiny Annie" and Her Friends**

These young streetwalkers are seeking customers in Seattle, Washington. Tiny Annie was reported to say, "For a blow-job it would be $30 on up and for a lay it would be $40 on up. Most of these [veteran] ho's charge more than us little kids do."

lose much of their influence on the trade. Prostitutes could be licensed, taxed, and regularly examined for STDs. The civil rights of prostitutes and of their consenting adult clients could be protected.

*Becoming a Prostitute*

A number of studies have attempted to examine the factors or circumstances associated with a female's becoming a prostitute (Boyer & James, 1983; Prus & Irini, 1980; Silbert, 1986). Poverty, disenchantment with life prospects, a tedious job, failure in school, a turbulent home life, and physical and sexual abuse are some of the factors associated with entry into prostitution. Although these background conditions may predispose an individual toward prostitution, they are not sufficient to guarantee entry into the trade. If they were, there would be a lot more prostitutes, given the number of women who come from an impoverished background or who have experienced physical or sexual abuse.

What *is* necessary is contact with someone involved in the world of prostitution—a prostitute or pimp, or a bartender or hotel clerk.

**FIGURE 16.13**
**Margo St. James**
Margo St. James is founder of the California prostitutes' union, COYOTE.

Through these associations, a female learns about the world of prostitution. If she decides to become part of this world, she typically develops a relationship with a pimp. She is taught the tricks of the trade—how to protect herself from disease, dangerous customers, and police officers, and how to do the least amount of work for the most money. Many women enter prostitution as juveniles, often runaways who are recruited by members of the prostitution world (Silbert, 1986). In one study of 200 street prostitutes, almost 80% reported having started prostitution as juveniles. About one-third of these women also reported

having been involved as juveniles in sexually explicit activity that was photographed. Contrary to the popular notion, "once a prostitute, always a prostitute," the average span of a prostitute's career is about five years (Potterat, Woodhouse, Muth, & Muth, 1990).

Like their female counterparts, male prostitutes often come from a background of poverty, strained parental relations, poor education, and little or no work experience (Luckenbill, 1985). If they seek out or are exposed to experienced hustlers or customers, they may choose to enter the trade. Unlike female prostitutes, they usually do not have a pimp, and they are not trained or supervised in the trade. They learn how to hustle by observation and through interaction with other hustlers and customers (Luckenbill, 1985).

### The Prostitute's Clientele

The clients of prostitutes have not been studied thoroughly. Kinsey and his colleagues (1948) found that about 69% of the White men in their sample had had some sexual experience with prostitutes. Many of these men reported only one or two experiences. Hunt's (1974) data indicated that the use of prostitutes' services declined in the under-35 age group. Only 19% of men under 35 with some college education reported having had intercourse with a prostitute.

Using peepholes, one-way mirrors, and other observation posts, Stein (1974) witnessed hundreds of sessions between cooperating prostitutes and their clients. She described the men whom she observed:

> At first I looked for signs of "abnormality" in the clients. I felt that any man who paid for sex must be some kind of "loser." I was disappointed. I saw a few "losers," of course, but most of the clients were agreeable, reasonably attractive, upper-middle-class men, businessmen or professionals. (p. 10)

Studies of massage-parlor patrons on the West Coast (Armstrong, 1978) and in Illinois (Simpson & Schill, 1977) reported that the typical customer appeared to be indistinguishable from the average U.S. male. Interviews with 30 johns who had paid for sex an average of 50 times revealed that almost all were involved in personal relationships that included sexual activity. They purchased sex by choice rather than out of necessity (Holzman & Pines, 1982). In their association with prostitutes, many of these men experienced feelings and displayed behaviors that were typical of regular courtships. For example, before meeting a prostitute, they attempted to make themselves physically appealing by bathing, dressing fashionably, and using cologne. Many were aroused by the potential adventure and danger of associating with a prostitute.

Freund et al.'s (1991) interviewers approached men in their cars, sometimes with introductions by prostitutes, and obtained responses from 101 male clients of prostitutes. These men averaged about 40 years of age (ranging from 21 to 72). Their ethnic background was similar to that of the general population in the area (Camden, New Jersey), and they reported a mean of about five years of using prostitution. Most were regular clients, with 93% reporting visits monthly or more frequently and 63% seeing a prostitute weekly or more frequently. About half had had sex with the same prostitute or the same small group of prostitutes. Only 23 of the men were single; the rest were married (42), widowed (5), or divorced (31).

These studies paint a picture of prostitutes' customers as middle-class men in search of sexual satisfaction and adventure. But prostitutes are undoubtedly used for many different reasons by a wide range of men, including:

1. men with physical or emotional problems that create difficulty in securing a partner;
2. married men in search of novelty without emotional involvement;
3. men whose work involves considerable absence from home;
4. men who seek a type of sex they cannot or will not request from a wife or girlfriend;
5. men who feel that only "bad" girls are truly interested in the pleasures of the flesh.

### A Final Note

Prostitution exists because of the market for it. The same statement applies to erotica and other uses of sex for profit by advertisers and movie and video producers. People are often attracted to erotic or pornographic ventures or to prostitution because these enterprises provide more income than they imagine they might be able to obtain through other employment. Their motivation is, of course, the same one that prompts people to offer any service for which there is a societal demand. Although erotica, sexual themes in advertising, and sexually oriented literature and visual media are likely to continue to thrive, prostitution's popularity may wane as concerns about AIDS grow. Viewing or using erotica or sexual aids by oneself or with a steady partner may continue to flourish because these activities do not expose people to risks to their lives. In contrast, the novelty or adventure associated with buying sexual intimacy from prostitutes will likely be tempered by the possibility of contracting a fatal disease. In the next chapter, appropriately, we turn to a discussion of sexually transmitted diseases, with a large proportion of the analysis devoted to AIDS and its devastating impact.

## Summary of Major Points

| | |
|---|---|
| 1. Soft-core and hard-core erotica. | Materials designed to elicit sexual arousal can be divided into soft-core and hard-core erotica. Soft-core magazines endured substantial losses in readership in the 1980s. Part of this decline is probably attributable to the greater availability of hard-core or X-rated materials and increased sales of sexually explicit videocassette films that consumers can view in the privacy of the home. |
| 2. Sex and the consumer. | Sexuality permeates the U.S. marketplace. It is a staple of U.S. television programming and is endemic to advertising. The images used |

by advertisers and filmmakers glamorize sex without mentioning the possible consequences of sexual activity. Erotic products, advertisements, and services can be found in magazines, newspapers, theaters, and adult bookstores. Consumers can purchase sexual services through telephone sex, strip shows, theaters, or bars.

3. Obscenity.

The United States has moved from banning all depictions of sex-related activities to allowing distribution of material that does not violate the current legal definition of obscenity, which the Supreme Court established in its 1957 decision in *Roth* v. *United States*. For material to be considered obscene, it must meet three essential criteria: 1) it must be offensive to contemporary community standards; 2) its dominant theme must appeal to prurient interest in sex; and 3) the work must be devoid of serious literary, artistic, political, or scientific value. In 1987 the Supreme Court ruled that the proper application of community standards is not whether most people in a locality would find literary, artistic, political, or scientific value in allegedly obscene material but whether a reasonable person would find such value in the material taken as a whole.

4. Effects of erotica.

The available evidence indicates that most forms of erotica do not trigger sexual aggression in or cause harm to observers. Two exceptions may be violent pornography and child pornography.

5. Violent pornography.

Numerous studies have explored the possibility that men's exposure to violent pornography may lead to negative attitudes toward women or to sexually coercive behavior. Researchers have concluded that the majority of college men do not find violent pornography as arousing as depictions of consensual relationships. A sizable minority of men, however, are more aroused by aggressive sexual depictions than by consensual erotica; such responses are characteristic of convicted rapists.

6. Children and pornography.

The Supreme Court ruled in 1982 that states may prosecute the publishers and sellers of child erotica without having to prove that their materials are legally obscene. Because children are not legally capable of informed consent, those adults who pay, entice, or coerce them to engage in sexual activity can be prosecuted under child-abuse laws.

7. Prostitution.

Prostitution has flourished since the beginning of recorded history. Most of its practitioners have come from impoverished backgrounds. Every state in the nation has laws regulating prostitution. Usually, the prostitute is prosecuted rather than the customer. Some prostitutes have organized unions that provide services to improve the working conditions of prostitutes.

# Review of Key Concepts

1. The peak circulation of such magazines as *Playboy* and *Penthouse* came in the: a) 1950s; b) 1960s; c) 1970s; d) 1980s. (p. 518)

2. A major figure contributing to the loosening of government censorship in the United States was: a) Anthony Comstock; b) Leonard Woolsey; c) Hugh Hefner; d) Edwin Meese III. (p. 527)

3. In *Roth* v. *United States*, the U.S. Supreme Court defined as essential criteria for obscenity all of the following *except*: a) it must be offensive to community standards; b) the dominant theme of the work must appeal to prurient interest in sex; c) it must not depict sexually stimulated genitals; d) it must be devoid of serious literary, artistic, political, or scientific value. (p. 528)

4. Among the findings of the U.S. Commission on Obscenity and Pornography (1970) were all of the following *except*: a) depictions of conventional sexual behavior are generally more stimulating than depictions of less conventional sexual activity; b) sex offenders have had more adolescent experience with erotica than have other adults; c) the majority of people report no increase in masturbation or coitus as a result; d) Danish evidence shows that increased availability of erotic material is associated with a decrease in the rate of sex crimes. (p. 533)

5. The overall results of official U.S., British, and Canadian inquiries into the effects of pornography in the 1970s and 1980s was that such material under no circumstances can be considered socially dangerous. True or false? (pp. 533–534)

6. Research in the 1980s by Malamuth and Donnerstein on the connection between erotica and rape suggested that: a) most males would commit rape if they were certain of not getting caught; b) even males who have not just been angered by a woman react pos-

itively to depictions of forced sex in which the female victim seems to enjoy the experience; c) all males report having more arousal fantasies after exposure to a depiction of a rape than before; d) none of the above. (pp. 534–535)

7. Which of the following statements is true? a) We cannot directly test the hypothesis that exposure to pornographic films or stories of coerced sex leads men to rape. b) Exposure to violent erotica increases acceptance of rape myths and reinforces negative attitudes toward women. c) Men who report a greater likelihood to rape in the future if they are sure they would not be caught also report having more rape fantasies. d) all of the above. (pp. 536–537)

8. On the average, X-rated movies depict less violence than PG- or R-rated films. True or false? (pp. 522–523)

9. Why do media depictions of sexual interactions rarely deal with the consequences of this activity? Should anything be done about this situation in your opinion? Why or why not?

10. Distinguish among obscenity, erotica, and pornography. Are these distinctions valid?

11. State the feminist case against pornography. In what ways does it parallel the right-wing and/or fundamentalist case against pornography? How does it differ? Are there circumstances under which you would support the censorship of obscene or pornographic material?

12. State the case for suppressing child pornography. How would you distinguish between the ways in which child pornography and adult pornography should to be handled by the government?

I'd Rather Be 40... Than Pregnant

SAFE SEX TO GO
World's first go-anywhere kit for the sexually active

SAFE SEX TO GO
World's first go-anywhere kit for the sexually active

# Sexually Transmitted Diseases

SEXUAL intimacy can be a source of ecstatic pleasure, but it also carries the risk of exposure to infection from sexually transmitted diseases (STDs). More than 12 million Americans contract an STD each year, many of which result in severe complications including infertility, ectopic pregnancy, morbidity, and death. Two-thirds of STD cases afflict persons under 25 years old, and 3 million teenagers become infected each year with STDs (CDC, 1994; Hatcher et al., 1994). In this chapter we review the common STDs and genital infections. Measures that reduce the risk of contracting or transmitting an STD are discussed. Before we look at the symptoms and treatment of sexually transmitted diseases and infections, we examine how attitudes about sexuality and morality may increase the likelihood of contracting and/or transmitting STDs.

## Attitudes Toward Sexually Transmitted Diseases (STDs)

Some years ago, an anthropologist (Miner, 1956) wrote a description of a people called the Nacirema. These people were notable for their obsessive rituals and their worship at altars made of large white bowls on pedestals of varying heights. Each Nacirema family owned at least three of these bowls, sometimes as many as ten, and they engaged in rituals in front of them half a dozen or more times a day. The cleanliness rituals they performed were thought to bring moral goodness.

*Nacirema* happens to be *American* spelled backward. Indeed, our culture places a high premium on cleanliness, health, and physical beauty. From childhood on, hygiene and health are linked to moral goodness, and dirtiness is linked to sin. We are taught to avoid and fear germs, to bathe or shower daily, and to avoid spreading colds and other infections when we catch them. Although the emphasis on these and other hygienic practices is valuable in reducing sickness and increasing longevity, some negative side effects are associated with our national obsession with cleanliness and health. Among these are the counterproductive personal and societal responses to STDs, which originate in our linking of dirt and disease with sin and sexuality.

Almost half a century ago, the prevalence of sexually transmitted diseases in the United States dropped to a record low. In the apparent belief that the problem had been controlled through the use of penicillin and other antimicrobial agents, the federal government decreased its funding for the containment of STDs. In constant dollars, the government now spends just half of what it did in 1943 to control syphilis.

Current statistics suggest that the belief that STDs were declining as a health problem was overly optimistic. Chlamydia and nongonococcal urethritis (NGU) afflict more than 4 million Americans annually, and it is estimated that more than 30 million have incurable genital herpes (Catotti, Clarke, & Catoe, 1993). The incidence of pelvic inflammatory disease (PID), the product of one or more untreated bacterial STDs, is rising, and it in turn can cause ectopic pregnancies and infertility. Rates of gonorrhea and syphilis fell in most age groups between 1981 and 1991, but they rose or remained steady among Americans younger than 20 (Webster, Berman, & Greenspan, 1993). More than 50% of the cases of syphilis reported in the United States came from California, Florida, and New York (Heimberger et al., 1993).

When a person contracts an STD (formerly called a venereal disease, or VD), the rational response is to have it diagnosed and treated immediately and to notify partners so that they may do the same. The shame and embarrassment associated with STDs, however, inhibit reasonable and healthy responses to dealing with these infections and infestations. To understand the enormity of the STD problem, we must examine the interaction of personal attitudes about sex with the circumstances of the individual who is diagnosed as having an STD. With a few exceptions, the only way to contract an STD is to have intimate physical contact with an infected person. People engaging in the most socially approved sexual relationship—sexual intimacy with only one other person throughout their lives—are extremely unlikely to become infected, as are those without sexual partners. People with STDs, then, come from the portion of the population that is either sexually intimate with more than one person or involved with a nonmonogamous partner.

Many individuals who are diagnosed as having an STD are reluctant to name their partners to physicians or clinic personnel. On one level, it is quite understandable that they would rather deliver the bad news themselves. Instead of doing so, however, these individuals may surreptitiously attempt to discover whether the partner has any symptoms of the particular disease. If the partner appears to be healthy, they may decide to avoid disclosing their own infection, on the assumption that the partner did not catch it. In the case of a marital partner who contracts an STD during extramarital relations, fear of destroying the marriage may dissuade him or her from informing an apparently healthy spouse.

The absence of recognizable symptoms, however, does not provide insurance that the partner does not have the genital infection. Gonorrhea, for example, is notoriously "silent" in women, with an estimated 80% having no recognizable symptoms during the early, and readily treatable, stages of the infection. Many men are also *asymptomatic*. Potterat et al. (1983) examined the partners of a sample of women with gonorrhea. About one-fourth of these males were infected, and of these nearly two-thirds had no symptoms. On the grounds that "men always know when they have gonorrhea," many of the women were reluctant to name their sexual partners. In an unfortunate parallel, when the men were contacted, they were reluctant to seek testing and treatment for gonorrhea because of the same false belief.

## The Relationship of AIDS Knowledge and Attitudes

In recent years, STD research has primarily focused on students' attitudes and knowledge about AIDS. Students from first-year high school students through graduate school are more knowledgable about AIDS than about other STDs (Benton, Mintzes, Kendrick, & Solomon, 1993). Before reading further, you may wish to take the test in Box 17.1 to see how well informed you are. After you have finished reading the chapter, you will be able to score your responses to determine the accuracy of your knowledge.

In a study of high school students in San Francisco, overall awareness that condom use could reduce the risk of transmitting HIV (human immunodeficiency virus, which causes AIDS) was low. Minority students were particularly ill informed about the preventive effectiveness of condom use (DiClemente, Boyer, & Morales, 1988).

Among seventh- and eighth-grade adolescent males, those who were sexually active were less knowledgeable about AIDS, less fearful of contracting HIV, less tolerant of people who have

AIDS, and more likely to engage in risk behaviors than were their peers who were not sexually active (Brown, DiClemente, & Beausoleil, 1992). A similar but less extreme pattern was found among sexually active females of the same ages.

College students are generally knowledgeable about AIDS and HIV, but most report that they take no special precautions against HIV infection (Caron, Davis, Wynn, & Roberts, 1992; DiClemente, Forrest, & Mickler, 1990; Mickler, 1993). The findings that knowledge about AIDS does not correlate consistently with behavior change and the adoption of safer-sex practices indicate that other factors play a role in behavioral change. While these findings do not mean that knowledge and education are unimportant, they do indicate that more effective ways must be sought to educate young people. For example, a short AIDS-prevention curriculum changed AIDS-related knowledge, beliefs, and behaviors among New York City high school students (Walter & Vaughan, 1993). Students who took the course were more likely to have been monogamous and to have used condoms consistently, and they were less likely to have a high-risk partner than were students who did not take the course.

Although these studies imply that knowledge about AIDS is moderate, which is encouraging, other studies (Benton et al., 1993; Carabasi, Green, & Bernt, 1992; Caron et al., 1993) have indicated large gaps in knowledge. In particular, many students are unsure about whether they could contract HIV through casual contact (for example, sharing jacuzzis, using common utensils, eating restaurant food). These studies support the idea that, although students have some knowledge of AIDS, more education is needed, specifically with regard to the modes of HIV transmission.

## Attempts to Reduce STD Transmission

Public health authorities have employed numerous strategies to try to alter sexual practices to reduce the spread of AIDS and other STDs. However, behavior change among sexually active heterosexual adolescents and young adults has been difficult to achieve (Fisher & Fisher, 1992; Melnick et al., 1993). For example, a national survey

---

**asymptomatic** (A-symp-toe-MAH-tik)—without recognizable symptoms.

## Box 17.1

## How Accurate Is Your Knowledge of AIDS?

The following test was adapted from Temoshok, Sweet, and Zich (1987). Those with more accurate scores had less fear of AIDS and were less likely to hold antigay attitudes. In responding to these questions, put a T (true) or F (false) in front of each statement.

_____ 1. AIDS is caused by a virus.

_____ 2. AIDS is caused by inheriting a bad gene or genes.

_____ 3. AIDS is caused by a kind of bacteria.

_____ 4. A person can carry and pass on the virus that causes AIDS without necessarily getting AIDS or looking sick.

_____ 5. HIV can be passed on through semen.

_____ 6. HIV can be passed on through blood or blood products.

_____ 7. You can catch AIDS just as you catch a cold because AIDS can be carried in the air.

_____ 8. AIDS can be passed on by being in the same room as someone with AIDS.

_____ 9. AIDS can be passed on by shaking hands with someone who has AIDS.

_____10. Having a monogamous relationship with an uninfected partner greatly diminishes the risk of HIV infection.

_____11. Using latex condoms properly will reduce the risk of getting AIDS.

_____12. A vaccine for AIDS will be available for the general population within a year.

_____13. Currently, there is no cure for AIDS.

_____14. Fewer than half the people who have gotten AIDS have died.

---

of college students revealed that nearly 50% of the heterosexual respondents reported multiple sexual partners and that approximately 60% used condoms less than half the time when they engage in sexual intercourse (DiClemente et al., 1990).

Surveys of adolescents indicate that they have made few changes in their sexual practices or contraceptives in response to the AIDS epidemic (Kegeles, Adler, & Irwin, 1988; Melnick et al., 1993; Strunin & Hingson, 1987). Minority adolescents appear to be even less likely than their White counterparts to engage in a safer-sex practice such as condom use while having sexual intercourse (Kegeles et al., 1988). When behavior changes are made, the most commonly reported are reducing the number of sex partners and being more careful in partner selection (Melnick et al., 1993).

A survey of adolescents found no relationship between knowledge of AIDS and behavior change, but a perception of susceptibility to HIV infection was strongly associated with a reduction in high-risk behaviors (DiClemente, 1989). Compared to their White counterparts, minority adolescents regarded themselves as less susceptible to AIDS (Mays & Cochran, 1988). In Fisher's (1988) study of potential factors affecting condom use among adolescents, perceived peer-group behavior was the only factor that differentiated adolescents who used condoms from those who did not. Those who viewed their peers as supporting condom use were almost twice as likely to report employing condoms themselves. DiClemente and Houston-Hamilton (1989) found that perceptions of peer-group norms as supporting unprotected sexual intercourse were more prominent among Black than White adolescents.

Joseph, Montgomery, Emmons, et al. (1987) studied the magnitude and predictors of longitudinal behavioral change during 1984–1985 in a sample of 1,000 homosexual men from Chicago, 90% of whom returned completed questionnaires. Self-reports of sexual behavior were obtained at two times, separated by a six-month interval. Although there was considerable variability in the respondents' reported behaviors, average changes were consistently in the direction of safer-sex practices, with clear increases in monogamy, avoidance of anonymous sex partners, and modification of receptive anal sex to include condom use. Joseph et al. found barriers to change stemming from the men's perceived difficulty in controlling their sexual feelings and their continuation of receptive anal sex. Consistent with the findings reported above regarding the importance of adolescents' perception of peer-group norms, the belief that one's friends were adopting recommended behavioral changes was positively and consistently related to adopting safer-sex practices, becoming monogamous, and reducing the number of partners and the frequency of sexual activity. The extent of participation in gay networks was not related to any of the changes. The authors suggested "that it is not participation itself, but the norms shared within a network, that may be the most important in influencing the adoption of behaviors consistent with risk reduction" (Joseph et al., 1987, p. 86).

## Attitudes Toward People with STDs

In addition to dealing with the medical consequences of STDs, infected persons experience adverse psychological reactions. They have lowered self-esteem, feelings of isolation and loss of control, and a negative body image (Catotti et al., 1993; Perlow & Perlow, 1983; Schwab, 1982). There is evidence that sexual attitudes are related to a person's reactions to contracting an STD. For example, emotional stress over having an STD was found to correlate with guilt about masturbation among a group of young women (Houck & Abramson, 1986). Some of the negative psychological reactions and feelings of psychological isolation experienced by infected persons may stem from expectations that others will reject them—a fear that may be realistic. Davis (1983) found that students made more negative attributions about women who were described as having genital herpes than about women whose descriptions were identical except that there was no mention of herpes.

All sexually active people are at risk of contracting STDs, however, and extensive education of the general public and complete reporting by STD patients are important for controlling the spread of STDs. William Darrow, a research sociologist at the Centers for Disease Control (CDC), argued that the medical community must take a more active role in treating and reducing the spread of STDs. In a satirical critique of public and private physicians, he suggested that

> the scene is set for us, with Shepherd tubes and penicillin syringes in hand, to descend from heaven to save humanity from the ravages of the serpentine treponeme, coffee-beaned gonococcus, or some other sexually transmitted pathogen. According to our script, people queue up, drop their drawers and get their butts blessed with a healthy dose of our miracle drugs. Venereal diseases are conquered when, as we say, "we break the chains of infection" that link microbes to men. And when we fail, we say there is something wrong with the sociopolitical setting (e.g., sexual freedom prevails and sexual promiscuity is upon the people); there is something wrong with the microbe (e.g., it is becoming more resistant to our magical potions, so let's double the dose) or there is something wrong with men (i.e., they no longer want to wear the "French cap" and are unwilling to comply with our directives). But we never say, there is something wrong with the way we think, the things we say, or the things we do. (1979, pp. 2–3)

Darrow (1981) believes that physicians should pay closer attention to a) screening people who are susceptible to STDs, b) diagnosing diseases accurately, c) treating each patient adequately, d) completely reporting each case, and e) following up adequately with each patient and his or her partners.

Sexually active people can also take responsibility for controlling STDs by getting themselves screened regularly, becoming more knowledgeable about the most accurate diagnostic methods, and asking their physicians what tests they are using. If a person contracts an STD, the individual has a duty to tell his or her sexual

**TABLE 17.1 Symptoms of Sexually Transmitted Diseases and Genital Infections**

| Bacterial Infections | Symptoms |
|---|---|
| 1. Gonorrhea | *In males:* painful urination; smelly, thick, yellow urethral discharge, appearing two to ten days after sex with infected person.<br>*In females:* vaginal discharge; some pain during urination; mild pelvic discomfort and/or abnormal menstruation (but most women are asymptomatic). |
| 2. Pelvic inflammatory disease (PID) | Intense lower abdominal and/or back pain; tenderness and fever; pain when cervix is moved from side to side. Symptoms usually develop within weeks after the STD that causes PID is contracted. |
| 3. Syphilis | Hard, round, painless sore or chancre with raised edges that appears two weeks to a month after contact. |
| 4. Chlamydia and nongonococcal urethritis (NGU) | *In females:* mild irritation in the genitals; itching and burning during urination; some cervical swelling (but most women are asymptomatic).<br>*In males:* thin, relatively clear, whitish discharge; mild discomfort during urination one to three weeks after contact. |
| 5. Chancroid | Painful, soft genital ulcer developing three to five days after sexual contact with an infected person. Women are frequently asymptomatic. |
| 6. Cystitis | Painful urination; lower back pain; constant urge to urinate. |
| 7. Prostatitis | Groin and lower back pain; fever; burning sensation during and folowing ejaculation; thin mucous discharge from urethra before first morning urination. Prostatitis can be either congestive (from infrequent ejaculation) or infectious (from *E. coli* bacteria). |
| 8. Gardnerella vaginalis | Leukorrhea and unpleasant odor. |
| 9. Shigellosis | Pain; fever; diarrhea; inflammation of the mucous membranes of the large intestines; sometimes vomiting and a burning sensation in the anus. |

partners so that they can be tested and, if necessary, treated. And the patients should have themselves retested after treatment to be sure that they have been cured of those STDs that are curable.

Unfortunately, some STDs are not curable; the most notable contemporary example, of course, is AIDS. The deaths of such public figures as Rock Hudson and Liberace and the spread of AIDS among members of the heterosexual community have done what the deaths of thousands of anonymous AIDS victims were not able to do: spurred governmental and public response to the epidemic (Shilts, 1987). A moving video, "And the Band Played On," based on Randy Shilts's book, was released in 1993, and we highly recommend it for students interested in the competition among public health researchers within the United States and internationally as they attempted to deal with the spread of AIDS. Shilts died of complications from AIDS in 1994.

In the fall of 1986, Surgeon General C. Everett Koop called for thorough sex education, beginning in grade school, to help reduce the spread of AIDS. Education to promote safer-sex practices could help in reducing the transmission not only of AIDS but also of other STDs. We turn now to the symptoms, consequences, and treatment of specific STDs (see Table 17.1), including diseases and infections caused by bacteria, viruses, and parasites.

| *Viral Infections* | **Symptoms** |
|---|---|
| 1. Acquired immunodeficiency syndrome (AIDS) | Swollen lymph nodes; unexplained weight loss; loss of appetite; persistent fevers or night sweats; chronic fatigue; unexplained diarrhea; bloody stools; unexplained bleeding from any body opening; skin rashes; easy bruising; persistent, severe headaches; chronic, dry cough not caused by smoking or a cold; chronic, whitish coating on the tongue or throat. |
| 2. Herpes simplex type II (genital herpes) | Small blisters on the genitals or vulva, developing three to seven days after contact. After tingling, itching, and creating a burning sensation, they break open and spread. |
| 3. Genital warts | Soft, pink, painless single or multiple growths resembling cauliflowers on the genitals or vulva. |
| 4. Hepatitis B | Nausea; vomiting; fatigue; mental depression; jaundice; dark urine. |

| *Parasitic Infections* | **Symptoms** |
|---|---|
| 1. Candidiasis (moniliasis) | Thick, white, cheesy, smelly discharge; inflamed vaginal walls with merging patches of white; swollen labia. |
| 2. Trichomoniasis | Yellow-green or white, smelly discharge that appears four days to a month after contact. |
| 3. Amebiasis (amoebic dysentery) | Constant watery diarrhea. |
| 4. Scabies | Itching and tiny, red, pimplelike skin elevations where eggs are hatched. |
| 5. Pediculosis pubis (crabs) | Skin elevations and itching, usually in pubic hair, produced by the nits of six-legged lice, which mature in two or three weeks and start feeding on blood. |

## Bacterial Infections

STDs caused by bacteria are relatively easy to cure. They include gonorrhea, syphilis, chlamydia and nongonococcal urethritis, cystitis, prostatitis, gardnerella vaginalis, and shigellosis.

### Gonorrhea

*Gonorrhea* infection is caused by gonococcus bacteria (*Neisseria gonorrhoeae*), which thrive on

**gonorrhea**—an STD caused by the bacterium *Neisseria gonorrhoeae*.

mucous membranes in the mouth, vagina, cervix, urethra, and anus. The bacteria can be acquired by kissing or engaging in oral, anal, or vaginal sex with an infected person. There is a popular rumor that gonorrhea can be contracted from toilet seats. In an obvious, if less than delightful, test of this piece of folk wisdom, Gilbaugh and Fuchs (1979) randomly sampled toilet seats in 72 public restrooms and found no gonorrhea bacteria. Although the bacteria from urethral discharge can survive for up to 24 hours on towels and toilet seats and for 3 hours on toilet paper (Neinstein et al., 1984), transmission from these sources has not been demonstrated. The probability of contracting gonorrhea from having intercourse once

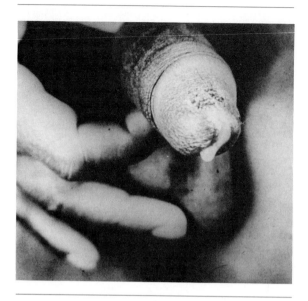

**FIGURE 17.1**

**Gonorrhea Symptoms**

Symptoms of gonorrhea include a yellowish discharge from the urethra and painful urination.

with an infected partner is about 50% for women and 25% for men, and the risk increases with each additional sexual contact (Platt et al., 1983).

Of all age groups, people aged 20 to 24 are at highest risk of contracting gonorrhea. There is little need to worry about the effects of gonorrhea if it is diagnosed and treated quickly. Unfortunately for women, attitudes about STDs in general and the absence of symptoms in the early stages of gonorrhea make early detection difficult. Ironically, sexually active young women routinely have annual PAP smears for cervical cancer but are rarely tested for gonorrhea, although they are considerably less likely to contract cancer than gonorrhea. Sexually active women should request screening for gonorrhea as part of their annual pelvic examinations.

Gonorrhea symptoms usually appear within two to ten days after intimate contact with an infected person. Symptoms in men include painful urination and a smelly urethral discharge that is thick and yellow (see Figure 17.1). Some men experience no symptoms or discomfort, however.

Of women who contract gonorrhea, 80% have mild symptoms or no symptoms at all. Symptoms in the remaining 20% of women include altered vaginal discharge, some pain during urination, mild pelvic discomfort, and/or abnormal menstruation. Yet the presence of these symptoms does not prove that a person has a gonorrhea infection; diagnosis by a physician or clinic is necessary. To test for the presence of gonorrhea, a sample of discharge is obtained by inserting a swab into the urethra or cervix to determine whether the bacteria are present.

Gonorrhea is treated with an injection of procaine penicillin G or with an oral dose of amoxicillin or ampicillin. Although these antibiotic treatments usually kill the bacteria, a follow-up test should be performed to ensure a successful cure. After they have been cured, people are not immune to future infection. Thus another reason why a sexual partner with gonorrhea should be examined and treated is to avoid reinfecting a partner who has been cured. Gonorrhea can also reactivate latent chlamydia (Batteiger et al., 1989). Because of the frequent coexistence of chlamydia (see p. 562) and gonorrhea, the CDC recommends that doctors treating a patient for gonorrhea prescribe additional medication, usually tetracycline, for a week to treat chlamydia.

The usual cure for gonorrhea, procaine penicillin G, is no longer foolproof. The Vietnam War has been held partially responsible for the development of penicillin-resistant strains of gonorrhea. In Southeast Asia during the war, it was possible to get penicillin without a prescription or medical supervision. This widespread, uncontrolled use of penicillin and other antibiotics probably contributed to the development of antibiotic-resistant strains of gonorrhea. The rates of gonorrhea strains that are resistant to antibiotics appear to be increasing and now account for more than 5% of all gonorrhea cases in the United States (Aral & Holmes, 1991; Judson et al., 1991). Further, men engaging in high-risk sexual behaviors were more likely to contract antibiotic-resistant forms of gonorrhea. Some forms of antibiotic-resistant gonorrhea can be treated with an injection of the antibiotic cefataxime.

If not diagnosed and treated within a few weeks, gonorrhea can have serious complica-

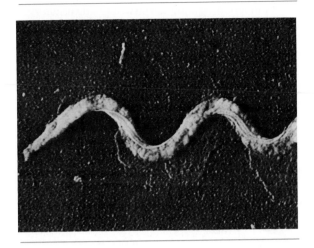

**FIGURE 17.2**
**Syphilis Spirochete**
The spirochete *Treponema pallidum* is the organism that causes syphilis.

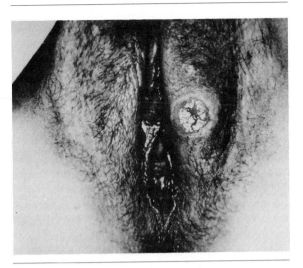

**FIGURE 17.3**
**Syphilis Chancre**
The chancre is a painless sore that appears where the spirochete entered the body.

tions. In males, these may include infection of the prostate, testes, and epididymis, potentially causing sterility. The bladder, kidneys, and rectum of males and females may also be infected with gonorrhea. In females, untreated gonorrhea and other infections may produce pelvic inflammatory disease (see p. 565). Furthermore, women may pass untreated gonorrhea to a baby during childbirth, possibly causing blindness in the infant.

## Syphilis

*Syphilis* is caused by a spirochete, a tiny, corkscrew-shaped bacterium named *Treponema pallidum* (see Figure 17.2). Transmitted through intimate sexual contact with an infected person, syphilis first produces a usually painless *chancre*, a hard, round, dull-red sore or ulcer with raised edges. A chancre can form in the mouth, vagina,

syphilis—a sexually transmitted disease caused by the bacterium *Treponema pallidum*.
chancre (SHANG-ker)—a dull-red, painless, hard, round ulcer with raised edges that forms where the spirochete causing syphilis enters a person's body.

urethra, or rectum, or on the anus, external genitals, or nipples, so almost any act of sexual intimacy with a person who has primary syphilis can allow the microorganism to invade the uninfected person. The probability of infection from one contact with a syphilis carrier is about 30% for women and 20% for men.

Once a major health problem in the United States, syphilis has become somewhat less common, although the incidence rose in the 1980s before dropping in the 1990s. This drop has not been uniform across all groups. Syphilis has been on the rise among adolescents and minority groups.

The chancre typically appears two weeks to a month after exposure to an infectious case of syphilis (see Figure 17.3). Because it is usually painless, a female may not realize that she has the chancre if it breaks out in the vagina, on the cervix, or in the rectum. Similarly, if the chancre erupts within a male's urethra or rectum, he may be unaware of it. After several weeks, the chancre spontaneously disappears, often leaving syphilis patients with the false impression that they have no infection.

Syphilis is usually diagnosed through examination of a blood sample for antibodies. Sometimes a positive result occurs when a person does not currently have syphilis because the antibodies were produced by a related or past infection. If syphilis is present, it is readily treated with benzathine penicillin G, a long-acting penicillin different from the one used to treat gonorrhea. Just as with gonorrhea, exposure to syphilis does not ensure future immunity, so a treated person can be reinfected during subsequent sexual contact with a syphilis carrier.

If not treated, syphilis goes into a second stage, called secondary syphilis, about two weeks to two months after the chancre has healed. Secondary syphilis is characterized by a generalized body rash, sometimes accompanied by headache, fever, indigestion, sore throat, and pains in the joints or muscles. Syphilis is highly contagious during both its primary and secondary stages.

Following the secondary stage, a latent stage begins that can last for 1 to 40 years. It is called latent because no external symptoms are observable, but the spirochetes are nonetheless burrowing their way into internal organs such as the brain, spinal cord, bones, and bodily tissues. After syphilis has been latent for about a year, an untreated person is no longer infectious.

Finally, third-stage, or late, syphilis is reached by about a third to half of all untreated victims. Treatment even at this advanced stage can cure syphilis, but heart failure, loss of muscle control, blindness, deafness, brain damage, and other complications may have already occurred.

In addition to the infected person and his or her sexual partner, untreated syphilis can infect a fetus as well because the spirochetes can cross the placental barrier after the 16th to 18th week of pregnancy. Thus all pregnant women should be tested for syphilis at the time of the first prenatal visit. Congenital syphilis is primarily seen in large cities. Cities in California, Florida, New York, and Texas accounted for 80% of all reported cases in 1985 (Webber & Hauser, 1993). The increase of syphilis in large cities has been linked to crack cocaine use (Ernst & Martin, 1993). Cocaine abusers may offer their sexual services to obtain money to buy the drug or for the drug itself.

Infected pregnant women are administered the same regimen of penicillin (or other antibiotics, if they are allergic to penicillin) as are infected nonpregnant women. After birth, their infants are treated with penicillin. In 90% of the cases in which a pregnant woman's syphilis is not treated during early pregnancy, the fetus is aborted, stillborn, or born with congenital syphilis. The newborn can be treated to prevent further damage, but treatment will not undo the damage that has already been done, which may include partial blindness, deafness, and deformities of the bones and teeth.

## Chlamydia and Nongonococcal Urethritis (NGU)

The STD *chlamydia*, the source of many vaginal and urethral infections in women and men, is caused by *Chlamydia trachomatis* or T-strain *Mycoplasma*, which are both bacterial microorganisms. These bacteria were not isolated until the 1970s. Before that time, infections that did not result from the gonococcus bacterium or other known organisms were diagnosed as *nongonococcal urethritis (NGU)* in men and as vaginitis in women. Chlamydia in men is still frequently referred to as NGU, and about 40% of NGU cases are due to chlamydia infection (CDC, MMWR, August 6, 1993). The incidence of chlamydia has increased markedly since the mid-1970s, and the estimated prevalence among female college students ranges from 6% to 10% (Lee, 1989). With more than 4 million chlamydia infections reported annually, it is the most prevalent bacterial STD in the United States (CDC, MMWR, August 6, 1993). As with gonorrhea and syphilis, the risk for women (40%) is greater than that for men (20%) for acquiring chlamydia from having intercourse once with an infected partner.

---

**chlamydia** (clah-MID-ee-uh)—an STD, frequently asymptomatic in women, caused by the bacterium *Chlamydia trachomatis*.

**nongonococcal urethritis (NGU)** (non-GON-oh-KOK-al yur-ree-THRY-tis)—a term for urethral infections in men that are usually caused by the chlamydia bacterium.

Chlamydia is transmitted primarily through sexual contact, but it can be spread from one body site to another (for example, by touching urethral discharge and then the eyes). It can also be transmitted nonsexually, through contact with the fingers or feces of an infected person. Symptoms generally appear one to three weeks after contact with the infection.

In males, chlamydia symptoms include a thin, relatively clear, whitish discharge. NGU may also trigger inflammation of the urethra and mild discomfort during urination, but approximately 30% of men have no symptoms. Symptoms among the minority of women who have them include mild irritation in the genitals, as well as itching and burning during urination. In addition, cervical edema (swelling) may occur, although most women are unlikely to notice this symptom.

Because most women have no symptoms of chlamydia infection in its early stages, they are unlikely to seek diagnosis and treatment until their reproductive organs have been badly damaged by pelvic inflammatory disease, which can result from a chlamydia infection. Between half and two-thirds of the involuntary infertility stemming from scarring of the fallopian tubes is attributed to untreated chlamydia. For this reason, it is imperative that people who are diagnosed as having chlamydia or NGU inform their sexual partners. Otherwise, the partners may not find out that they have the infection before it has done permanent damage. In one study, more than 1,000 college students were placed into one of three groups: a) those symptomatic for chlamydia, b) those without chlamydia symptoms, and c) those who were asymptomatic but had had recent sexual contact with a partner who was diagnosed with an STD (gonorrhea, chlamydia, or NGU). Almost half the women who had no symptoms but knew that a recent partner had been diagnosed with an STD tested positive for chlamydia, and this was also true of almost a third of men in the group (Lee, 1989). These statistics underscore the importance of routine screening for various STDs including chlamydia among sexually active people.

Chlamydia and NGU can be treated effectively with tetracycline. Pregnant women, however, should be treated with erythromycin instead because of the side effects of tetracycline on fetuses. Penicillin is ineffective in curing this disease.

If left undiagnosed and untreated, both chlamydia and NGU can profoundly affect health and fertility. Infection of the epididymis in men and the fallopian tubes in women can create scar tissue that blocks the passage of sperm or egg, causing permanent sterility. Of infants born to women with untreated chlamydia, 10% to 20% become infected with chlamydia pneumonia, and 20% to 50% develop conjunctivitis, a serious eye infection. In fact, chlamydia is recognized as the greatest cause of preventable blindness in the world (Crum & Ellner, 1985; Rapoza et al., 1986).

## Chancroid

Chancroid is a sexually transmitted disease caused by a short, rod-shaped bacterium called *Hemophilas ducreyi*. In Africa this infection is the most common cause of genital sores and has been strongly linked with prostitution (Aral & Holmes, 1991). In the United States, chancroid was rare until a series of outbreaks in the 1980s among inner-city and migrant labor populations in different parts of the country. The number of reported chancroid cases rose from 665 in 1984 to more than 4,000 in 1992 (CDC, 1993).

About three to five days after contact, a small pimple surrounded by a reddened area appears at the site of infection, usually on the genitals. Within a day or two, it becomes filled with pus and breaks open to form irregular soft ulcerations. The softness of the chancroid sores and their painfulness distinguish them from the hard and painless chancres of syphilis. In more than half of chancroid cases, the lymph nodes on the infected side of the groin become inflamed and swollen. These enlarged lymph nodes, called buboes, can rupture and ooze a thick, creamy pus.

Diagnosis is made through physical examination. Treatment by either erythromycin in pill form or a single injection of ceftriaxone is highly effective unless it is a strain of *H. ducreyi* that is resistant to antibiotics.

## Cystitis

*Cystitis* is sometimes called honeymoon cystitis because it is often brought on by frequent or vigorous intercourse. This condition can occur in both men and women but is more common among women. It is caused by various bacteria, including *Escherichia (E.) coli*, which can be transmitted either nonsexually or sexually. Wiping from the anus toward the urethra (rather than the reverse) may bring *E. coli* from the rectum to the urethral opening. Strenuous intercourse may have the same effect. Within a day or two after bacteria are introduced into the urethra, the person may experience a more or less constant urge to urinate, burning during urination, and pain in the lower back and/or abdomen. Sulfa drugs such as gantrisin are effective in curing the condition, and drinking large quantities of fluids helps to eliminate the infection.

## Prostatitis

*Prostatitis* refers to any infection or inflammation of the prostate gland. Prostatitis affects between 30% and 40% of U.S. men between ages 20 and 40. There are two major types: infectious prostatitis, caused by *E. coli* bacteria, and congestive prostatitis.

Infectious prostatitis can result from the transmission of bacteria during sexual contact. Celibate men can be afflicted with congestive prostatitis (technically not an STD), which may stem from infrequent ejaculation or abstention from sexual activity. Some men are asymptomatic, but when symptoms are present, they include pain in the groin and lower back, fever, and a burning sensation during and following ejaculation. Patients may also notice a thin, watery discharge from the urethra in the morning before they urinate. Infectious prostatitis is commonly treated with antibiotics and the inflammation of the prostate can be reduced by palpating, or manipulating, that organ.

## Other Bacterial Infections

Two other bacterial STDs are *gardnerella vaginalis* and *shigellosis*. Gardnerella vaginalis is caused by the bacterium of the same name. It is sometimes referred to as *vaginitis*; however, this term is misleading. As with some other bacterial infections that are diagnosed as vaginitis, both males and females may contract and transmit gardnerella vaginalis.

Most prevalent among women during their reproductive years, gardnerella vaginalis afflicts an estimated 40% of women seen at STD clinics (Sobel, 1989). In women, this infection results in thin *leukorrhea*, which ranges in color from gray to greenish-yellow and has an unpleasant odor. It is treated by oral administration of the prescription drug Flagyl (metronidazole) to the infected woman and her partner. Flagyl should not be given to pregnant women, particularly in the first trimester; instead, clindamycin is prescribed (CDC, 1985b). Men infected with gardnerella vaginalis are typically asymptomatic, but Watson (1985) concluded that asymptomatic men are the primary source of infection. Some males, however, do develop symptoms, which include urethritis and inflammation of the foreskin or glans.

Shigellosis, caused by the bacterium *Shigella*, is an acute diarrheal disease that can be contracted through sexual contact or contact with feces carrying the bacteria. In the 1990s approximately 17,000 to 24,000 cases of shigellosis were reported annually in the United States (CDC, 1993). Oral stimulation of the anus of an individ-

---

**cystitis** (sis-TYE-tis)—a general term for any inflammation of the urinary bladder marked by pain and frequent urination.

**prostatitis** (praw-stay-TIE-tis)—inflammation of the prostate gland.

**gardnerella vaginalis**—bacterial infection producing a thin, smelly discharge; afflicts both men and women.

**shigellosis** (SHIH-geh-LOW-sis)—a form of dysentery (diarrhea) that can be transmitted by sexual contact, caused by the bacterium *Shigella*.

**vaginitis** (VA-jih-NYE-tis)—a general term for any inflammation of the vagina caused by the gonococcus bacterium or by a fungus.

**leukorrhea** (LOO-kor-REE-ah)—a whitish discharge from the vagina; often caused by a fungus infection.

ual with shigellosis exposes the stimulator to the disease.

Pain, fever, diarrhea, and inflammation of the mucous membranes of the large intestine are among the symptoms of shigellosis. Some people also experience vomiting and a burning sensation in the rectum. Shigellosis is diagnosed by culturing a stool specimen. It can be treated with ampicillin or tetracycline, although *Shigella* bacteria rapidly develop resistance to antibiotics.

## Pelvic Inflammatory Disease (PID)

The most common serious complication of untreated gonorrhea, chlamydia, and other genital infections in females is *pelvic inflammatory disease (PID)*. More than 1 million cases of PID are reported annually in the United States (Rolfs, Galaid, & Zaidi, 1992). In addition to the expense of diagnostic tests, doctor's office visits, medicine, hospitalization, surgical fees, and time lost from work, there are costs to PID sufferers that cannot be measured in dollar amounts. These include pain, anxiety, and the elevated risk of ectopic pregnancy and sterility.

PID develops when chlamydia, gonorrhea, or other infections, among them trichomoniasis (see pp. 559–563), move through the cervix to infect the uterine lining or fallopian tubes. It is estimated that untreated chlamydia causes about half a million cases of PID a year in the United States. Sexually active women who use oral contraceptives are half as likely to be hospitalized for PID as women who do not use contraception (Cates & Stone, 1992b). This protective effect of oral contraceptives was much stronger for chlamydial PID than for gonococcal PID (Wolner-Hanssen et al., 1990). Smoking cigarettes and douching are also associated with an increased risk of contracting PID (Scholes, Daling, & Stergachis, 1992; Scholes et al., 1993).

Some women with acute PID experience intense lower abdominal pain, tenderness, and fever. These women are fortunate because their symptoms at least make it likely that the PID will be discovered and treated before permanent damage is done. Many women with acute PID have less well-defined symptoms and thus may not seek treatment.

PID can develop within weeks after a woman contracts the causative STD. Women with acute PID are sometimes mistakenly diagnosed as having acute appendicitis. When PID is the source of the abdominal pain, movement of the cervix from side to side is painful. In addition, PID pains tend to last considerably longer than appendicitis pains, and the symptoms are more likely to begin within a week of the onset of the menstrual period. The vast majority of patients with acute PID respond quickly to treatment with penicillin, ampicillin, or tetracycline (McCormack, 1994).

The sexually transmitted diseases discussed so far are caused by bacteria and are treated relatively easily. Scientists have not been as successful in finding cures for infections caused by viruses. In the next section we consider AIDS, the most deadly of these viral diseases.

## Acquired Immunodeficiency Syndrome (AIDS)

In the past 15 years, we have witnessed the rapid spread of human immunodeficiency virus (HIV) infection that leads to *acquired immunodeficiency syndrome (AIDS)* throughout the world (see Figure 17.4). AIDS has been devastating not only in terms of its impact on patients and the family members and friends who love them, but also in terms of the increase in antigay discrimination that it has spawned (see Box 17.2). The fact that it first appeared primarily among homosexual men in the United States led some to call AIDS the "gay plague"; however, AIDS is caused by a virus, not by a person's sexual orientation.

AIDS first captured the attention of physicians in 1981, but the syndrome had existed for

---

**pelvic inflammatory disease (PID)**—swelling and inflammation of the uterine tissues, fallopian tubes, and sometimes the ovaries; sometimes results from untreated genital infections.

**acquired immunodeficiency syndrome (AIDS)**—a virally caused condition in which severe suppression of the immune system reduces the body's ability to fight diseases.

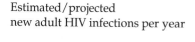

Estimated/projected
new adult HIV infections per year

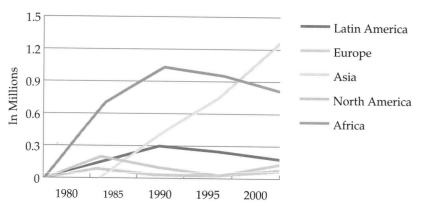

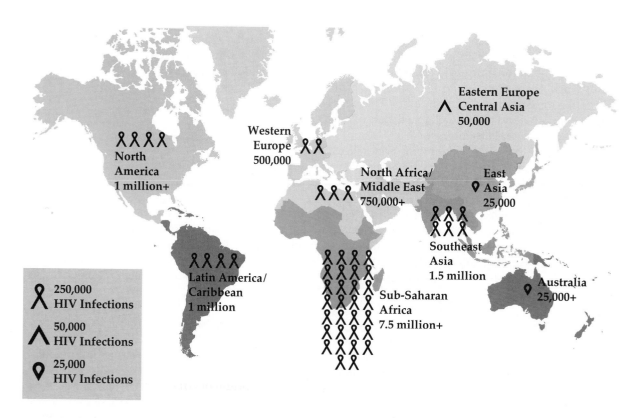

**FIGURE 17.4**

**HIV Infection Now and in the Future**

Throughout the world, more than 14 million people are infected with HIV. The
majority live in Africa, but Asia is estimated to become the next site of widespread
infection.

**Box 17.2**

## An Epidemic of Stigma

As we will see in the next chapter, Sexual Coercion, some of us have a tendency to blame the victim. This victim-blaming phenomenon has been seen in the responses of some people to other members of our society who have contracted HIV. Proposition 64, a referendum to quarantine people found to be HIV+ (positive), was placed on the ballot in the 1986 California election. Voters defeated the proposal, but the fact that many people favored such a quarantine—despite no evidence indicating that AIDS could be spread through casual contact—provides a vivid example of the way in which society sometimes blames the victim.

In an article from which we have taken the title for this box, researchers Herek and Glunt (1988) pointed out that the definition of AIDS as lethal and (initially in the United States, but not elsewhere) most prevalent among gay men and IV-drug users resulted "in a dual stigma: first, from identification of AIDS as a serious illness; second, from the identification of AIDS with persons and groups [gays and IV-drug users] already stigmatized prior to the epidemic" (p. 887). They quoted several instances in which discriminatory behavior appeared to be stimulated by the stigma associated with AIDS.

*In White Plains, New York, a mail carrier refused to deliver mail to an AIDS Task Force office for two weeks because he feared catching the disease* ("Mail Service Ordered to AIDS Center," 1987).

*In Arcadia, Florida, three brothers tested positive for HIV. After word spread of their infection, their barber refused to cut the boys' hair, and the family's minister suggested that they stay away from Sunday church services. Eventually, the family's house was burned down (Robinson, 1987).*

*In 1987, 1,042 incidents of harassment against gay people were reported to the National Gay and Lesbian Task Force (NGLTF) that involved references to AIDS; two-thirds of the local groups who reported incidents to NGLTF expressed the belief that fear and hatred associated with AIDS have fostered antigay violence (NGLTF, 1988).*

*In a 1986 [article] in the* New York Times, *William F. Buckley, Jr., proposed that "everyone detected with AIDS should be tattooed in the upper forearm, to protect common-needle users, and on the buttocks, to prevent the victimization of other homosexuals" (p. A27).*

*In the* American Spectator, *Christopher Monckton (1987) wrote: "Every member of the population should be blood tested every month to detect the presence of antibodies against [AIDS], and all those found to be infected with the virus, even if only as carriers, should be isolated compulsorily, immediately, and permanently" (p. 30).*

After you read the section on AIDS, you may want to return to this box to consider whether the available data on the disease support the attitudes and policies described here.

some time prior to the 1980s. Dr. Grethe Rask is the first westerner known to have died of AIDS. She was a surgeon working in a primitive hospital in Zaire at the time she became sick. She returned in 1977 to her native Denmark, where she died that year at the age of 47 of a puzzling disease, later to be identified as AIDS (Shilts, 1987).

The origin of AIDS has yet to be determined, although most scientists agree that the HIV viruses are basically ape or monkey viruses because of their genetic similarities (Ewald, 1994). Humans have hunted and handled other primates for thousands of years. Anyone who was bitten, scratched, or cut themselves while butchering a primate could have become infected.

Other lines of investigation of the sources of the HIVs have included Africans, Haitians, mosquitoes, and pigs (Biggar, 1986; Norman, 1986). The fact that the vast majority of people who are stricken with AIDS in the United States, Europe, and Africa are in the sexually active age range and/or are the recipients of blood products from other infected people makes mosquitoes an unlikely source. Mosquitoes bite people of all ages, but there are relatively few AIDS patients who are 5 to 13 years old, and those who are within those ages were born to HIV-infected mothers or received HIV-infected blood or plasma. In other words, if mosquitoes were a source, the prevalence of AIDS among children and people of all ages would be much higher. Antibodies to HIV have been found in analyses of blood samples that were collected in the 1960s and 1970s in central and east Africa, lending some support to the hypothesis that AIDS originated there (Epstein et al., 1985; Nahmias et al., 1986). That hypothesis is weakened somewhat by the fact that only since 1980 do African medical records contain descriptions consistent with a diagnosis of AIDS (Biggar, 1986). If the origin of HIV is ultimately determined, that knowledge may contribute to finding a vaccine and a cure.

AIDS patients suffer from severe *immunosuppression*. Normally, our immune systems protect us from various diseases to which we are exposed, but HIV, perhaps in combination with other physiological factors, cripples the immune system. Patients are then vulnerable to numerous opportunistic infections—that is, infections that take hold because the impairment of the body's immune system gives them the opportunity to flourish.

## Prevalence

Before 1981 only 92 people in the United States were diagnosed as having the symptoms later to be called AIDS. From 1981 through 1993, state and territorial health departments reported more than 350,000 cases of AIDS and more than 225,000

**immunosuppression**—the suppression of natural immunologic responses, which produces lowered resistance to disease.

AIDS-related deaths (CDC, February 1994). In 1994 the Centers for Disease Control estimated that about 1 million Americans were HIV-infected. By 1993 AIDS ranked as the leading cause of death among adults 25 to 44 years of age. One reason for the public concern about AIDS is the speed with which it is spreading, as shown by the numbers of new AIDS cases and deaths reported to the CDC each year (see Table 17.2).

Minority group members have been disproportionately represented among U.S. citizens infected with HIV (CDC, 1993). Blacks, who compose 12% of the total U.S. population, and Hispanics, who represent 7%, constitute 32% and 17% of all AIDS cases, respectively. Of HIV-infected children, 79% are Black or Hispanic, as are 74% of all women with AIDS. Intravenous (IV) drug use rather than homosexual activity appears to be the source of most HIV infection among minorities. Nearly half the Black and Hispanic persons with AIDS are heterosexual, compared to fewer than 15% of Whites with AIDS.

AIDS is most prevalent in large urban centers, with three cities (New York, San Francisco, and Los Angeles) accounting for about 60% of all cases. Yet an increasing proportion of all cases is being reported from smaller cities and rural areas (CDC, October 1993). As Figure 17.5 shows, through September 1993, more than half of U.S. AIDS patients were homosexual males, but there is now a higher percentage of HIV-infected heterosexuals than homosexuals. In addition, 24% of AIDS cases occur among those who inject drugs. Figure 17.6 shows the AIDS rates reported state by state from October 1992 through September 1993.

In the United States, a person's risk of contracting AIDS was low if she or he is not a homosexual male or an intravenous drug user. That has been the case in the past, but the number of U.S. heterosexuals with AIDS is clearly increasing, although the overall proportion of heterosexuals with AIDS has remained relatively stable: 5.2% of adult AIDS cases in 1983 versus 5% in the 12 months from October 1992 through September 1993. Further breakdowns of infection rates as a function of gender and age indicate that women, teenagers, and young adults are at higher risk from heterosexual contact than are other groups. Specifically, 37% of U.S. women diagnosed with

TABLE 17.2 Number of Diagnoses of AIDS and Deaths from AIDS in the United States

| Year | Adults and Adolescents | | Children Under 13 Years old | |
|------|-----------|-------------|-----------|--------------|
| | New Cases/Year | Deaths/Year | New Cases/Year | Deaths/Years |
| Before 1981 | 92 | 30 | 6 | 1 |
| 1981 | 306 | 124 | 16 | 8 |
| 1982 | 1,114 | 445 | 29 | 14 |
| 1983 | 2,966 | 1,465 | 74 | 29 |
| 1984 | 5,989 | 3,387 | 113 | 48 |
| 1985 | 11,349 | 6,729 | 227 | 114 |
| 1986 | 18,439 | 11,677 | 327 | 156 |
| 1987 | 27,689 | 15,626 | 475 | 285 |
| 1988 | 34,261 | 20,161 | 596 | 308 |
| 1989 | 40,530 | 26,610 | 685 | 355 |
| 1990 | 44,757 | 29,669 | 734 | 381 |
| 1991 | 53,179 | 33,399 | 682 | 362 |
| 1992 | 62,102 | 34,986 | 702 | 365 |
| 1993 | 53,502 | 33,744 | 568 | 393 |
| Total | 356,275 | 218,052 | 5,234 | 2,819 |

Note: These figures are active AIDS cases, not just HIV-positive test results. They are adapted from the Centers for Disease Control, HIV/AIDS Surveillance Report (1994) and represent U.S. cases reported to the CDC. Figures may be underestimates, as some people with AIDS die of other causes (e.g., car accidents), and some AIDS-related deaths are not reported to the CDC.

AIDS during 1992–1993 became infected through heterosexual contact (versus only 4% of men). Heterosexual contact was the source of transmission among 24% of infected Americans aged 13 to 19 and among 17% of those aged 20 to 24 (CDC, October 1993). Concern is rising about the possibility of transmission by infected prostitutes. In one sample of U.S. AIDS patients, 37% had contracted HIV during heterosexual contact, and almost half these patients reported having had sexual contact with prostitutes (Darrow, 1989).

Data from Haiti and Africa underscore the fact that it is intimate contact with an infected person rather than an individual's sexual orientation that places one at risk of contracting HIV. Research by Johnson (1986) indicated that in 1983, 71% of the cases of AIDS in Haiti involved people in the same groups found to be at high

risk in the United States (homosexual men, intravenous drug users, and so forth), and only 22% involved people outside these groups. By 1985, however, persons with these risks accounted for only 11% of cases, whereas people outside what had been considered the at-risk groups accounted for 72% of cases. The percentage of Haitian women with AIDS jumped from 14% in 1983 to 40% in 1985. Evidence from central and east Africa indicates that heterosexual transmission by prostitutes and their clients may be a major risk in those areas. In various samples of prostitutes, the percentage who had HIV antibodies in their blood ranged from 27% to 88%. HIV antibodies were found more often among African prostitutes of low socioeconomic status than among prostitutes of higher status (de Zalduondo, 1991; Kreiss et al., 1986). In central Africa, AIDS is far more prevalent among hetero-

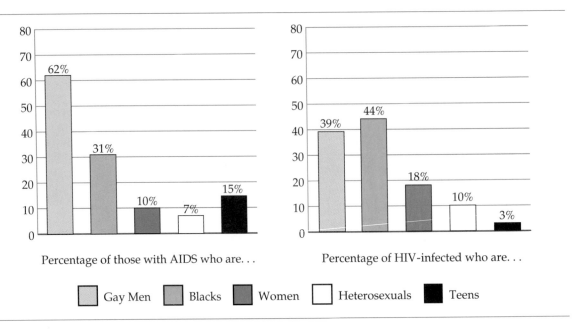

**FIGURE 17.5**

**Aids and HIV Infection Among Americans**

As shown here, the pattern of HIV infection seems to be changing. For example, although 62% of AIDS patients are gay men, only 39% of HIV infected patients are gay men. In contrast, the prevalence of HIV infection among people who have not developed AIDs has increased among Blacks, women, and heterosexuals.

sexuals than among homosexual men, and antibodies to HIV are as common in women as in men (Quinn, Mann, Curran, & Piot, 1986).

It may take 10 years or more for someone infected with HIV to develop AIDS symptoms (Hochhauser & Rothenberger, 1992). The average survival time of an AIDS patient is about 18 to 36 months from initial diagnosis, with only about 3.4% surviving for five years or more (Lemp, Payne, Neal, Temelso, & Rutherford, 1990). Of those diagnosed by 1993, 53% had died (CDC, 1994).

## Causes

The *retrovirus* that causes AIDS was identified in 1983 in France and in 1984 in the United States. The name *human immunodeficiency virus (HIV)*

was accepted by the International Committee for the Taxonomy of Viruses for the AIDS virus. As shown in Box 17.3, the discovery of the cause of AIDS may unfortunately have been delayed by competitiveness and noncooperation among scientists. There are at least five strains of HIV (Science, 1992). The two most prominent are HIV-I, found primarily in the West and responsible for the vast majority of the world's AIDS cases, and HIV-2, most commonly found in Africa.

HIV must make DNA copies of its own RNA structure before it can reproduce itself inside a host cell. It can exist in a dormant DNA state for a long time before it is stimulated by some factor to begin reproducing itself. At that point, the host cell turns into a virus reproducer and dies (Hochhauser & Rothenberger, 1992). HIV destroys the ability of the body's T4 helper cells (T4 helper lymphocytes) to stimulate the immune system to

**retrovirus**—a form of virus that cannot reproduce inside a host cell until it has made DNA copies of its own RNA structure.

**human immunodeficiency virus (HIV)**—the retrovirus that causes AIDS.

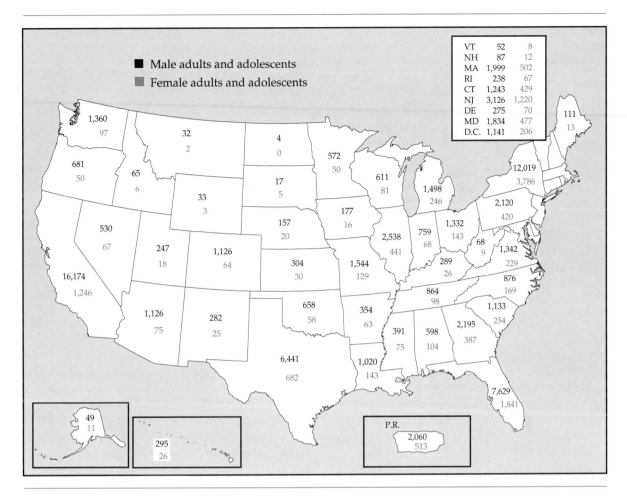

**FIGURE 17.6**
**AIDS Cases Reported October 1992 through September 1993 in the United States**

fight diseases. HIV has been found in blood, semen, vaginal secretions, and breast milk and less frequently in the saliva, tears, and urine of infected individuals (Lifson, 1988). Researchers believe, however, that the risk of contracting AIDS from the saliva, tears, or urine of an infected person is extremely low.

## Risk Factors

The risk of acquiring HIV and developing AIDS appears to be highest among individuals with large numbers of sexual partners and frequent sexual contacts: the more partners a person has, the more likely he or she is to encounter someone carrying the virus. In their review of the research on AIDS in Africa, Quinn et al. (1986) reported

that AIDS patients had had an average of 32 heterosexual partners prior to the diagnosis of AIDS, whereas control groups had had an average of 3 partners.

Engaging in sexual practices with an HIV-infected partner that expose you to blood or semen increases the likelihood of contracting HIV. Those sexual practices that cause fissures or tears in an orifice generate higher risk—by providing HIV with access to the bloodstream—than do practices that are unlikely to damage sensitive bodily tissues. Thus HIV is most prevalent in people who engage in unprotected receptive fisting (insertion of the fist into the anus), receptive anal coitus, receptive fellatio, and analingus.

In an article published in the *Journal of the American Medical Association*, Guinan and Hardy

**Box 17.3**

## Searching for the Cause of AIDS

Investigative reporter Randy Shilts (1987) described the tragic political infighting and societal responses to AIDS in a gripping book, *And the Band Played On*. Fierce competition between public health agencies within the United States, and between the United States and other countries, slowed the search for the cause of AIDS. Further, the U.S. government was reluctant to provide needed funds and staff to further the research. The Centers for Disease Control in particular was seriously understaffed and constrained in its efforts to pinpoint the cause of AIDS. Member of Congress Ted Weiss attempted to remedy the situation in 1983 by holding congressional hearings on AIDS. Shilts wrote:

*Clearly, the administration did not want the story of obstruction and delays to get a messy public airing on Capitol Hill. Still, the administration's stall had been successful in impeding the House of Representatives, dominated by Democrats, from ascertaining the real needs of agencies in time for a concerted AIDS budget plan for fiscal year 1984. . . . The President's budget called for a $300,000 cut in AIDS funding at the Centers for Disease Control for the next year [emphasis added]. . . . There were still no federally funded AIDS-prevention campaigns, and there was nothing resembling a coordinated plan of attack on the disease.*

"*The failure to respond to this epidemic now borders on a national scandal,*" said Dr. Marcus Conant, who led scientific testimony. "*Congress, and indeed the American people, have been misled about the response. We have been led to believe that the response has been timely and that the response has been appropriate, and I would suggest to you that this is not correct*" (Shilts, 1987, p. 359).

Shilts documented the infighting among U.S. public health agencies and the noncooperation between U.S. and French scientists. Scientists, of course, are not immune to rivalry, and any research team assembled to discover the cause of AIDS could expect considerable fame and attention. Shilts reported that requests made by some scientists to other researchers to share information were sometimes ignored. Ironically, French and U.S. scientists announced within months of each other that they had discovered the causative virus, but each group gave it a different name (LAV versus HTLV III). The delays generated by the combination of governmental inertia and domestic and international rivalry in isolating the virus may have, in turn, contributed to the fact that we still have no cure for AIDS.

Our description of Shilts's highly readable book is necessarily brief. We recommend that you read it as a case study of how societies can speed or impede progress in coping with public health threats.

Shilts died of complications from AIDS in 1994.

(1987) concluded, perhaps erroneously, that heterosexual anal intercourse plays little part in the spread of HIV, and an editorial in the same issue of the publication also took that position. However, Voeller (1991) argued that underestimating the incidence and riskiness of heterosexual anal intercourse is dangerous in view of the fact that receptive anal intercourse carries the greatest relative risk of HIV infection for homosexual men. Voeller's review of surveys of sexual practices indicated that more than 10% of U.S. women in the samples engaged in anal intercourse with some regularity. Standard medical or field interviews are unlikely to reveal such activity because of the reluctance of women to admit it except under conditions in which an interviewer is skilled at conveying a nonjudgmental attitude. Voeller concluded that heterosexual anal sex should be carefully monitored by sensitive and skilled researchers who can conduct nonjudgmental interviews. In other countries with high levels of AIDS infection (for example, Brazil), heterosexual anal intercourse—practiced for contraception or for the preservation of virginity—is common (Voeller, 1991).

People with a history of STDs such as gonorrhea and syphilis are also at higher risk of contracting AIDS than are individuals who have never been infected with these agents (Fisher & Fisher, 1992; Hochhauser & Rothenberger, 1992). Scientists do not know the precise reasons for this correlation, but it is possible that a person who has had other STDs has a weakened skin area where the infection occurred, making the area more vulnerable to HIV infection. One possible reason for this relationship is that both treatable STDs and HIV infection are more likely among persons with multiple partners.

Sharing needles during intravenous drug use, too, places people at risk of exposure to HIV-infected blood. In rare cases, individuals have contracted AIDS from contaminated blood products received during medical treatment, but this risk has been greatly reduced with improvements in the screening procedures for HIV infection. About 2% of the U.S. cases of AIDS have resulted from receiving transfusions of contaminated blood (CDC, 1993). There is no risk in *giving* blood, for which sterile, disposable needles are used. AIDS rarely results from casual contact with family members, coworkers, health care personnel, classmates, or others, and then only if contact with the body fluids of infected persons occurs (Hochhauser & Rothenberger, 1992; Rogers, White, Sanders, et al., 1990). Such casual contacts with AIDS patients as shaking hands and hugging do not involve the exchange of body products and thus are not risk factors.

## Symptoms

Acquired immunodeficiency syndrome is called a syndrome because a variety of life-threatening conditions are associated with it. Some of the same symptoms are also associated with other diseases and infections, such as the flu and colds, and with physical and psychological stress. The presence of one of these symptoms, such as swollen lymph nodes, does not necessarily indicate that a person has contracted HIV, particularly if

he or she is not engaging in risky behaviors and is not the partner of someone who is infected with HIV.

Common early signs of AIDS are *lymphadenopathy*, unexplained weight loss, loss of appetite, persistent fevers or night sweats, chronic fatigue, unexplained diarrhea or bloody stools, unexplained bleeding from any body opening, skin rashes, easy bruising, persistent severe headaches, chronic dry cough not caused by smoking or a cold, and a chronic whitish coating on the tongue or throat. All of these symptoms result from the various opportunistic infections to be described.

## Diagnosis

People are diagnosed as having AIDS when they develop one of the opportunistic infections or diseases associated with AIDS and when they receive a positive result from tests for HIV. There may be as long as a six-month period between infection and testing positive for HIV. The opportunistic infections most commonly suffered by AIDS patients are *pneumocystis carinii* pneumonia, Kaposi's sarcoma, and cytomegalovirus infection.

One of the puzzles confronting AIDS researchers and physicians is the meaning of a positive test for HIV antibodies in the absence of these infections. The blood test ELISA (enzyme-linked immunosorbent assay) may indicate that a person has been exposed to HIV, but it does not make entirely clear the risk of subsequent transmission or development of AIDS (see Box 17.4). Although the CDC concluded that the currently available blood tests for HIV antibodies are highly accurate, the ELISA test is not perfect. That is, occasionally a person receives a false-positive result (erroneously indicating HIV antibodies when there are none) or a false-negative result (incorrectly indicating no HIV antibodies when they are in fact present).

Because it can take 10 years or longer for HIV to damage the immune system, it is not yet

---

**lymphadenopathy**—condition involving enlarged swollen lymph nodes in the neck, armpits, and/or groin.

known what percentage of people who have HIV antibodies will develop AIDS. A study of homosexual men in Denmark begun in 1981 by Melbye et al. (1986) showed that a large percentage of those with HIV antibodies eventually experienced symptoms of AIDS. In 1981 all the people with HIV antibodies were healthy. Within three and a half years, 92% of them showed marked decreases in the number of T4 helper cells.

## Treatment

There may never be a cure for AIDS, but there are treatments for some of the opportunistic infections that attack people with impaired immune systems, and certain experimental drugs

have been found to slow the effects of the AIDS virus to some extent. One of the most promising is AZT (zidovudine). AZT has proved to be more effective than placebos in extending the lives of AIDS patients and was licensed by the Food and Drug Administration in 1987. Despite AZT's effectiveness in reducing the severity of illness and extending the lives of AIDS patients, the drug has potential side effects. Anemia often develops, and low numbers of white blood cells and platelets have also been observed in some patients. AZT's apparent toxicity to bone marrow is responsible for these conditions, and the suppression of bone marrow is a major reason for drug failure (CDC, MMWR, 1/26/90; Yarchoan, Mitsuya, & Broder, 1988). Another problem with

---

### Bob 17.4

## Being Tested for HIV Antibodies

As I sit here dispassionately describing the testing process for HIV antibodies, I vividly remember my own motives for, and experience of, being tested. I was aware that, although the exact incubation period for AIDS is not known, AIDS can take many years to develop. When I learned of the extent of AIDS in east and central Africa, I realized that the hepatitis that my husband and I had contracted while in Africa is one of the infections associated with AIDS. Shortly after I made this connection, a local hospital initiated a free and anonymous AIDS testing program, and one of my students asked whether I thought it really was confidential. He is gay, and he was afraid that if he were tested, his parents, potential employers, and others might find out. I was willing to be tested with him because I thought that it might be beneficial to find out firsthand about the procedures and the extent of anonymity. We called to make appointments, and on a snowy Monday evening we drove to the hospital to have the ELISA test done.

When we arrived at the hospital's testing site, the receptionist gave us each a slip with a four-digit number on it and told us to have a seat. Soon a volunteer counselor came out and called my number. He gave me a short ques-

tionnaire to fill out anonymously, on which I was to indicate such details as my age, gender, sexual orientation, marital status, number of sexual partners in the recent past, and drug-use patterns. When I returned the questionnaire, he read it over and asked why I wanted to be tested because I did not seem to fit any of the high-risk groups. I explained about Africa and related my other reasons. He then competently obtained my informed consent (see Chapter 2) regarding the blood test and the hospital's procedures to guarantee anonymity. He also told me that the results would be available in a week and that the test was not always completely accurate.

I was shown an informational videotape reviewing much of the same material that the counselor had presented. A nurse took a sample of my blood, wrote my number on the vial, and directed me back to the receptionist, who scheduled my appointment for the following week. I found my friend, and we drove home, comparing notes on the way. He was worried, and we talked about his potential risk. After I dropped him at his dorm, I began to feel anxious about my own test results. I talked with Rick about it, and during the next week I thought a great deal about what I might do if the test result were positive. Would that mean I could no longer have sex? What effect would that have on our marriage? If I had AIDS, could I have already transmitted it to my husband, or, alternatively, had he given it to me? If I was infected, I was pretty sure that it would have been in Africa, and our youngest child was born after that. Would that mean that our son might have AIDS as well? Although I knew rationally that my chances of having AIDS were extremely low, I was also aware that the scientific community believes HIV carriers can transmit the virus to others. During that week my friend, who was more at risk, came to my office several times, feeling scared and shaky.

Monday finally arrived, and we drove to the hospital. The hospital staff had said that under no circumstances would they give the results over the phone or to anyone who did not present a numbered slip. This policy was intended to ensure anonymity and to provide a program of counseling and medical follow-up for individuals who received positive test results. I was amazed at how relieved I was to be told that my test was negative, and I was delighted to see the huge grin on my friend's face when he returned to the waiting room. On the drive home, we talked about our anxiety during the past week, which was nothing compared to the fear, anguish, and eventual physical pain of those who get positive test results and go on to develop AIDS.

—E.R.A.

---

AZT is that HIV can become resistant to the drug with long-term treatment. Thus researchers are seeking alternative treatments for AIDS patients.

Scientists are also working on vaccines for HIV. In 1987 the first AIDS vaccine entered clinical trials in the United States (Hochhauser & Rothenberger, 1992). At this point, the results of research with this vaccine are ambiguous. Other experimental vaccines have emerged since 1987, but scientists have encountered major problems in trying to develop an HIV vaccine. No animal model for the disease exists to assist researchers in formulating vaccines. Therefore, research must be conducted with humans, and that raises controversial ethical problems. Furthermore, there are many strains of HIV, and the virus is constantly mutating.

## Opportunistic Infections That Attack AIDS Patients

*Pneumocystis carinii pneumonia (PCP)* was a rare parasitic infection of the lungs usually observed only in cancer patients who were undergoing chemotherapy or in organ-transplant patients who were given drugs to suppress their immune systems. PCP is now the most common opportunistic disease associated with AIDS. The drugs used to treat PCP can prevent PCP if given early enough in the course of the HIV infection (Redfield & Burke, 1988). Approximately 60% of AIDS patients experience serious side effects from these drugs, however, and researchers are therefore testing other medications in the ongoing search for more effective and less dangerous treatments.

*Kaposi's sarcoma (KS)* is a rare form of cancer of the skin and connective tissues (bones, fats, and muscles), which in the past mainly affected elderly men in western societies. In some parts of Africa, KS accounts for 9% of all cancers detected in men. Some KS patients develop lesions on their palate (roof of the mouth), face, arms, and other locations on their skin (see Figure 17.7). By 1989, 15% of all U.S. adults with AIDS had

**pneumocystis carinii pneumonia (PCP)** (NEW-moh-SIS-tis kah-RYE-nee-EYE)—a form of pneumonia that commonly appears in persons whose immune systems are highly suppressed.

**Kaposi's sarcoma (KS)** (KAP-uh-seez sar-KOE-mah)—formerly, a rare type of cancer of the skin and connective tissue. It is now more common as one of the opportunistic infections that attacks AIDS patients and appears as lesions on the skin.

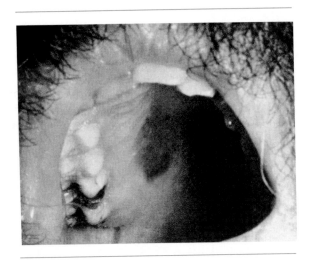

**FIGURE 17.7**

**Kaposi's Sarcoma (KS)**

Kaposi's sarcoma was once a rare form of cancer. A virulent variety of the disease afflicts some AIDS patients, often appearing first as a lesion on the palate.

developed KS, with a higher rate observed among homosexual or bisexual men (21%) than among other adults (3%) (Lifson et al., 1990).

In Africa, KS is not always associated with AIDS-related damage to the immune system (Biggar, 1986). Moreover, the appearance of KS in an American or a European is only one diagnostic indicator of AIDS. Thus the onset of KS is not necessarily related to AIDS. AIDS-related KS is usually rapidly fatal, as the cancer spreads through the lymph nodes, internal organs, trunk, and face. Men who develop KS have a shorter interval from the time they are diagnosed with HIV to the development of AIDS than do men without KS (Lifson et al., 1990). In contrast, non-AIDS-related KS (also called classical KS) progresses slowly, first appearing in the form of lesions on the limbs.

*Cytomegalovirus (CMV)* infections, which are caused by a group of herpes viruses, result in enlargement of the cells in various parts of the body, including the lungs, intestines, and central nervous system. CMV symptoms include fever, blindness, pneumonia, colitis, and low blood-cell counts. There are now two treatments that halt the progression of CMV-induced blindness (Redfield & Burke, 1988). Other opportunistic infections attacking AIDS patients without KS or PCP account for only a small proportion of cases.

AIDS patients are understandably deeply depressed when their disease is diagnosed. In some cases, however, the depression may be a response to the impact of HIV on the spinal cord and brain, which can produce neurological deficits called *AIDS dementia complex*. Brains of infected persons decrease in size through the atrophy (wasting away) of some nerve cells, some of their neurons stop functioning, and small amounts of myelin (protective fatty material encasing some nerve fibers) are lost from nerve-cell sheaths. In the early stages of AIDS dementia, patients may experience forgetfulness, withdrawal, and difficulty concentrating. Then problems with walking and talking develop, and response time in visual and motor tasks becomes impaired. Later, AIDS dementia patients experience seizures and spasms (Hall, 1988).

## Children with AIDS

HIV can pass from an infected mother to her fetus during pregnancy and to a baby through breast milk. About a third of all babies born to mothers with HIV become infected with the virus. However, research results from several studies reported by Hatcher (1994) indicate that the rate of HIV-infected babies was only about 8% if their HIV-infected mothers were being treated with AZT during their pregnancies. Children born before their mothers contract HIV, however, appear not to be at risk of developing HIV (Brooks-Gunn, Boyer, & Hein, 1988). Among children diagnosed as having AIDS, 88% had at least one parent with AIDS or with increased risk of de-

---

**cytomegalovirus (CMV)** (sye-toe-MEG-uh-low-VYE-ruhs)—one of a group of viruses causing cell enlargement in various internal organs.

**AIDS dementia complex**—infection of the brain by HIV, resulting in the deterioration and loss of nerve cells and subsequent deficiencies in visual, mental, and motor abilities.

veloping AIDS. Another 7% had contracted AIDS during blood transfusions (CDC, 1993).

## Protection Against AIDS

Unless a person is celibate or involved with an uninfected partner in a monogamous relationship, he or she should take direct steps to reduce the risk of HIV infection. Methods of lowering one's risk of contracting STDs in general are described at the end of this chapter in the section on safer-sex practices. Many of these techniques are directly applicable to AIDS. Even those that are not still reduce one's overall risk of developing AIDS because of the association between a history of other STDs and the risk of contracting AIDS.

The relationship between getting AIDS and having a history of other STDs provides an excellent example of a case in which it is important to distinguish between causal and correlational relationships, as discussed in Chapter 2. The AIDS-STD correlation may simply be evidence of the fact that people with AIDS and those with the other STDs share certain risk factors, such as having unprotected sex with a large number of partners, not using a barrier contraceptive method, and engaging in sexual practices that increase the likelihood that one will become infected if one has sex with an infected partner. If AIDS and other STDs simply have risk factors in common, then "Jane," with a history of other STDs, is at no greater risk of contracting AIDS than is "Joan," with no previous STDs, provided that both women now practice safer sex. If her history of other STDs increases Jane's vulnerability to contracting AIDS when she is exposed to HIV, however, Jane has reason to be more concerned than Joan. It is possible that elevated vulnerability to AIDS could result from changes in body cells or a weakening of the immune system brought about by infection with STDs, particularly viral STDs that produce genital ulcers (Quinn et al., 1986). If further research supports these or other relationships, then the inference that a history of STDs causes a heightened vulnerability to HIV would be appropriate. At this point, however, all we know is that there is a correlation between having a history of STDs and contracting HIV.

Popular awareness of AIDS may be having some impact on contemporary sexual practices. Almost 50% of young male and female respondents reported having made at least one change in their sexual behavior in response to the AIDS epidemic. The most commonly reported behavior changes were reducing the number of sex partners and being more careful in partner selection (Melnick et al., 1993). In several studies involving hundreds of men, the average number of sexual partners that they reported decreased, the proportion of men reporting only a single sexual partner doubled, and the number of men abstaining from sex increased. The proportion of people engaging in such risky behaviors as unprotected anal intercourse, fellatio, and fisting is also on the decline; these practices are being replaced by mutual masturbation or masturbation in the presence of one's partner (Coates, Stall, & Hoff, 1990; Juran, 1989). Interviews conducted with asymptomatic gay and bisexual men in New York City found that 84% of the men had modified their sexual behavior since the outbreak of the AIDS epidemic (Siegel, Bauman, Christ, & Krown, 1988). These men had reduced their total number of partners and their number of anonymous partners, although 70% of them reported a continuation of sexual behaviors that exposed them to HIV infection. In fact, for every two men who shifted from risky to safer-sex practices between the first and second interviews, one respondent shifted from safer to riskier sexual behavior.

Although these alterations in sexual practices in the gay community are not as extensive as hoped for, modifications toward safer-sex practices may be more prevalent among homosexual than heterosexual couples (Juran, 1989). Even in the early years of the epidemic, Judson (1983) compared the rates of gonorrhea between 1982 and 1983 and found a 39% reduction in the number of cases in homosexual men. Similar decreases did not appear for heterosexual men and women, probably because of the mistaken and dangerous belief that AIDS is caused by homosexual practices, when in fact it is caused by a virus. One of the reasons why AIDS initially may have been more prevalent among homosexuals than among U.S. heterosexuals is that homosexuals do not use contraceptives. Barrier methods

## Living with AIDS

Fear. Anger. Hopelessness. Ostracism. Isolation. These shattering feelings are daily fare for many of the more than 350,000 U.S. residents and the estimated 17 million people worldwide with confirmed cases of AIDS as of 1994. A bleak future looms for those like the Ugandan mother and child with AIDS—for whom even minimal health care is a faint hope—and the Florida family in which three young hemophiliac brothers are HIV-positive as a result of contaminated blood transfusions. But many people with AIDS have found not only comfort, but also a purpose for living, in touching other people's lives. Among those who have vigorously embraced life are AIDS patient David Hefner (shown at far right with his bride), who did not allow the disease to disrupt his marriage plans; and Belgian-born Niro Asistent, a long-term survivor who now heads a therapy program called Self-Healing AIDS-Related Experiment (SHARE). Others, like the men with AIDS participating in a Washington, D.C., march, work tirelessly to promote funding for research that promises a vaccine or even a cure for the very disease that has stricken them.

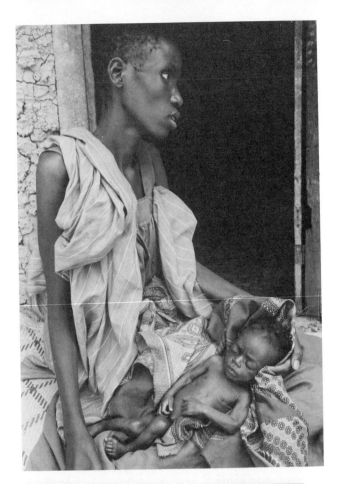

Top, **Ugandan mother and child AIDS patients**
Above, **Niro Asistent**

Above, **David Hefner and bride**

Left, **Florida family. The three sons have AIDS.**
Below, **AIDS march in Washington, D.C.**

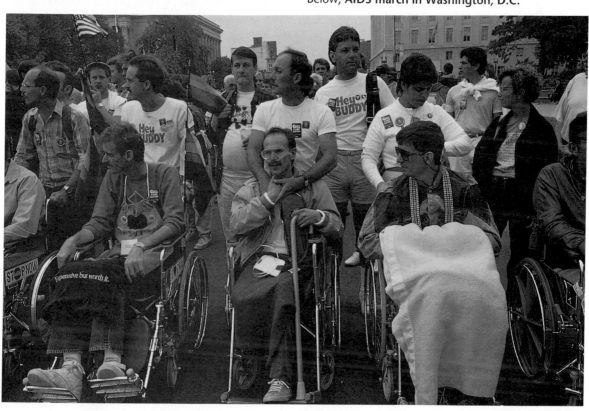

579

of contraception (the condom, the diaphragm, and the female condom) reduce the risk of HIV transmission when used properly. The protective effect of barrier methods of contraception is further supported by the fact that AIDS is as prevalent among females as males in some African populations, most of whom do not use these contraceptives. As William Darrow (1989) of the CDC put it, "A properly used condom will give the user at least 0.03 mm of protection, and that could be the difference between life and death" (p. 159). Asking about the health and sexual risk-taking behaviors of potential partners is crucial in slowing the spread of AIDS, but it is also important in reducing the incidence of other viral STDs, a topic to which we turn now.

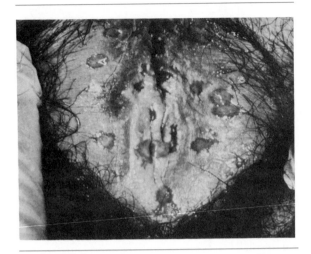

**FIGURE 17.8**
**Herpes II Sores**
Herpes II patients experience periodic outbreaks of these sores.

## Other Viral STDs

Like AIDS, the other sexually transmitted viruses are incurable at present. That is, although they can be treated, no methods are yet available to purge the causative virus from the body to prevent recurrent episodes of these diseases. These virally produced STDs include genital herpes, genital warts, and hepatitis B.

### Herpes Simplex Type II

Many people have experienced the episodic, mildly painful, and unsightly fever blisters or cold sores of herpes simplex type I. The initial tingling on or near the lip signaling the onset of an active attack of this virus is easily recognizable. After the virus has been contracted, it remains dormant most of the time, erupting on the skin often at times of physical or psychological stress. Although most people do not welcome the irritating sores, herpes I is not worrisome once the lesions have healed.

A related virus, *herpes simplex type II* (called herpes II or genital herpes), should be regarded

with considerably more concern, particularly by women who wish to have children. Herpes II causes most genital herpes infections, although herpes I may also appear on the genitals if they are orally stimulated by a partner with an active outbreak of herpes I around the mouth. Conversely, herpes II may develop in the mouth if an individual orally stimulates the genitals of a partner who has an active infection of herpes II.

The CDC estimates that there are about half a million new cases of herpes II each year, with several million people experiencing recurrent episodes annually. About 30 million Americans are now believed to have this incurable disease (Catotti et al., 1993).

Genital herpes is most often contracted through physical contact with the open herpes II sores of an infected person. In its dormant phase, the disease is less contagious. The symptoms, which include small blisters similar to those created by herpes I, generally appear at the site of the infection three to seven days after infection (see Figure 17.8). They may tingle and itch, or they may produce a painful burning sensation. When the blisters break open, the infection can spread to other parts of the body. The open wounds are also susceptible to secondary infec-

**herpes simplex type II**—a viral infection contracted through physical contact with an infected person during an active outbreak of the sores.

tions from skin bacteria. Other symptoms of genital herpes include fever and swollen lymph glands. In women, herpes II blisters commonly break out on the outer and inner lips of the vagina, the clitoral hood, and the cervix. In men, the blisters tend to erupt on the glans or foreskin of the penis.

The first outbreak of genital herpes typically brings considerable pain at the site of the sores, accompanied by more generalized flulike symptoms. Primary herpes infections characteristically produce open sores that last for an average of 16 to 21 days in men and 10 to 16 days in women. In general, symptoms and complications of recurrent outbreaks are milder than those associated with the primary outbreak of herpes (Catotti et al., 1993).

The intense pain experienced by most new patients with genital herpes alerts them to the fact that they have a serious infection and may increase the likelihood that they will visit a physician or clinic for diagnosis and treatment. Research suggests, however, that there is considerable variation in the extent of the symptoms experienced by patients with primary genital herpes. For some, the symptoms may be so mild as to be misdiagnosed or undetected (Catotti et al., 1993). Patients with mild symptoms may be more likely to transmit herpes to others because they do not realize that they have the virus.

Laboratory studies reveal that some contraceptives are effective in reducing the risk of transmitting or of contracting herpes II. Spermicides containing nonoxynol-9 have been shown to deactivate the herpes virus on contact (Catotti et al., 1993). Condoms also block the passage of the virus in laboratory tests. Although sexual contact should be avoided during active herpes II outbreaks, laboratory studies suggest that sexual intercourse is probably safe during remission of herpes II provided that a couple uses condoms with liberal amounts of spermicide.

Accurate diagnosis of genital herpes is enhanced by obtaining samples of the infected tissue early in the infection and subjecting them to laboratory analysis. There is no cure for herpes infections, but the drug acyclovir may shorten the time required for the healing of herpes lesions in persons experiencing their initial episode. Insofar as it reduces the amount of virus exuded from the lesions, acyclovir in ointment form (Zovirax) may lower contagion. This drug diminishes pain for men, but not for women. Another medication, foscarnet cream, may reduce herpes II healing time in men and lessen swelling, blisters, and ulcers in both men and women (Wallin et al., 1985).

If the only effects of the virus were the irritating, periodic outbreaks of blisters, herpes II would be of minor significance. Herpes II poses a triple threat, however: it can affect the offspring of women afflicted with it, it is linked to cancer, and so far it is incurable. Pregnant women with herpes II may pass the virus on to a fetus through the placenta. Should the fetus escape infection before birth, it may become infected in its passage through the cervix and vagina during birth if the virus is active. Pregnant women in high-risk groups are generally tested at the onset of labor. If herpes II is active when the woman is in labor, the baby is delivered by Cesarean section (Catotti et al., 1993).

Primary herpes infections can cause fetal malformation, abortion, and premature labor. Neonatal herpes can result in death or severe neurologic and ocular (eye-related) difficulties. Although transmission of herpes to the fetus through the placenta or to the infant during birth can have severe, even fatal, consequences for the infant, recent research suggests that antiviral chemotherapy can reduce the negative effects as well as the mortality rate (Catotti et al., 1993).

Although researchers are working on a cure, current treatments only reduce the discomfort of the symptoms; they do not eliminate the virus. In some patients, however, the disease appears to go into remission, with no further outbreaks of the symptoms for years after the initial episodes.

Given these consequences, many people naturally experience intense emotional reactions when they are initially diagnosed as having genital herpes. Women with genital herpes report significantly more emotional stress than do women with curable STDs (Catotti et al., 1993). Therefore, it is important that herpes patients receive counseling about ways of reducing or avoiding stressful factors in their lives and of coping with recurrent outbreaks of herpes. Herpes II patients have banded together to form an organization called the Herpes Resource Center, which disseminates information about recent

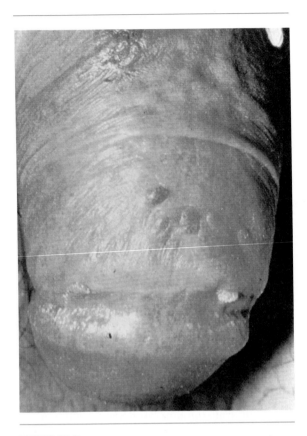

**FIGURE 17.9**
**Genital Warts**
The common genital wart is a soft, velvety lesion that can be sexually transmitted.

research and on sources of emotional support for those with herpes II. (Consult Appendix C for further information.)

## Genital Warts

*Genital warts* are also known as venereal warts or condyloma acuminata. Caused by the human papilloma virus (HPV), they are soft, pink, painless, single or multiple growths resembling a small cauliflower (see Figure 17.9). The virus is transmitted through direct contact with the warts

during vaginal, oral, or anal intercourse, but it may also be contracted through nonsexual contact. The warts are highly contagious. However, if they are on the penis or in the vagina, abstinence from intercourse or the use of a condom until the warts have been removed can lessen the likelihood of transmitting the virus.

More than a million cases of genital warts requiring treatment have been reported each year in the United States (Amschler, 1991). Most male partners of women with genital warts or HPV have no visible genital warts, and at present there is no screening test for the presence of the HPV in men without visible warts. The warts begin to appear one to three months after contact and are diagnosed visually. They may be removed by freezing (cryotherapy), burning, dehydration with an electrical needle, or surgery. If the warts are atypical or persistent, they should be biopsied to determine whether they are precancerous. Approximately 60 HPV types have been identified so far, and a number of these have been linked to cancer of the genital tract, particularly cervical cancer (Koutsky et al., 1992; Olds et al., 1992).

Although genital warts sometimes regress without treatment, they may spread and grow to the point where they block the vaginal or rectal opening. Further, the virus can be transmitted to a baby during vaginal delivery if the warts are located on the cervix or in the vagina.

## Hepatitis B

There are different types of hepatitis, each of which is thought to be caused by a different virus (Stevens et al., 1990). In all forms of hepatitis, the virus attacks the liver. Our main concern here is with *hepatitis B* because it can be transmitted through exposure to the blood, saliva, or semen of infectious carriers, although saliva and semen tend to have lower concentrations of the virus than does blood. The causative agent is called the hepatitis B virus (HBV). Approximately 300,000 people, most of them young adults, are infected each year (Aral & Holmes, 1991). About 10,000 require hospitalization, and about 250 of the pa-

---

**genital warts**—warts on the genitals that are caused by a virus and spread by physical contact with an infected person.

**hepatitis B**—a virus that attacks the liver; often sexually transmitted.

tients die annually. Up to 10% of young adults with HBV infections become carriers, and the United States has an estimated pool of half a million to 1 million carriers.

HBV infection usually begins within 30 to 120 days after exposure to an infectious carrier. The most common symptoms include mild fever, fatigue, sore muscles, headache, upset stomach, skin rash, joint pains, and dark urine. The characteristic external sign is a yellowing of the whites of the eyes. The skin may also become yellow, or jaundiced. The disease is diagnosed by a specific blood test, the hepatitis B surface-antigen test.

We are happy to end this depressing section on the effects of sexually transmitted viral infections by reporting that an effective vaccine against HBV was licensed in 1981, making hepatitis B the one viral STD that can be prevented by a vaccine. The CDC (1985a, p. 319) reported that protection against HBV "is virtually complete for persons who develop adequate antibody levels after vaccination." Members of high-risk groups listed earlier should definitely consider getting the hepatitis B vaccine.

## Parasitic Infections

We now turn to some of the sexually transmitted infections caused by parasites, fungi, and yeasts. These include candidiasis, trichomoniasis, amebiasis, scabies, and pediculosis pubis.

## Candidiasis

The yeastlike fungus *Candida albicans* (also known as moniliasis, and commonly called a yeast infection) normally lives in the mouth, the digestive tract, and the vagina. Growth of the fungus is usually restricted by the presence of harmless bacteria. When these controlling bacteria are reduced in number by antibiotics, frequent douching, pregnancy, diabetes, or other conditions such as oral contraceptive use that increase the alkalinity of the vaginal environment, the unrestricted growth of the fungus in the vagina can result in infection.

*Candidiasis* produces a thick, white vaginal discharge resembling the curd of cottage cheese, an unpleasant yeasty odor, and severe itching. The vaginal walls may be inflamed, the labia sometimes swell, and intercourse may be painful. Candidiasis is diagnosed by visually examining a fresh specimen of discharge or by growing the fungus in a culture. It is treated with antibiotic-antifungal compounds in suppositories or ointments, many of which are available without a prescription. During treatment, couples should abstain from coitus or use a condom to avoid infection or reinfection of the partners.

## Trichomoniasis

*Trichomoniasis* is a parasitic infection that prompts an estimated 1 million women and 40,000 men annually to see their physicians (Thomason & Gelbart, 1989). Trichomoniasis is caused by a parasite called *Trichomonas vaginalis*. It can be transmitted through sexual interaction, but infection can also result from contact with infected wet towels and wet bathing suits.

The incubation period ranges from four days to a month. A minority of women with this infection produce a frothy yellow-green or white vaginal discharge with a strong odor, and some men have an inflamed urethra (urethritis). The majority of people with trichomoniasis, however, are asymptomatic. Women infected with trichomoniasis are almost twice as likely as other women to develop tubal adhesions leading to infertility (Grodstein, Goldman, & Cramer, 1993).

A diagnosis is made by examining a sample of the discharge for trichomonads under a microscope. Both the person who has been diagnosed as having trichomoniasis and his or her partner(s) are given metronidazole (Flagyl) to eliminate the infection. This drug, which must not be taken in combination with alcohol, is risky for

candidiasis (KAN-dih-DYE-ah-sis)—an infection of the vulva and vagina caused by the excess growth of a fungus that occurs normally in the body.

trichomoniasis (TRIK-uh-muh-NYE-ah-sis)—an inflammation of the vagina characterized by a whitish discharge, caused by a parasite.

pregnant women during the first trimester. For women with severe symptoms after the first trimester, a single dose of 2 gm of metronidazole by mouth is prescribed.

## Other Parasitic Infections

*Amebiasis*, also known as amebic dysentery, is caused by a one-celled animal, *Entamoeba histolytica*. Amebiasis is transmitted through both sexual contact and exposure to contaminated water and food. Analingus and fellatio following anal sex can transmit the parasite. Amebic infection is treated by a variety of medications, including Flagyl.

*Scabies* is a highly contagious infestation by tiny, eight-legged parasitic mites called *Sarcoptes scabiei*. These creatures travel quickly and can be transmitted both sexually and nonsexually. When the eggs deposited by the mites hatch, they cause red, itchy, pimplelike bumps on the skin. Scabies can be diagnosed through microscopic inspection of infected skin and treated with the nonprescription compound gamma benzene hexachloride (Kwell in the United States; Kwellada in Canada), which is applied as a shampoo from the neck down. In addition, scabies sufferers must wash all bedding and clothing to get rid of the eggs.

*Pediculosis pubis*, or crabs, is an infestation of six-legged lice about the size of a pinhead. They inhabit hairy areas of the pubic region, anus, underarms, and eyelashes. Eggs, or nits, are laid by the female. These nits mature in two or three weeks and begin feeding on blood, producing inflammation of the skin and itching. They may be transmitted sexually, or nonsexually through contact with infected bedding, towels, or clothing. Like scabies, crabs can be eliminated by shampooing the infected areas with gamma ben-

zene hexachloride (Kwell or Kwellada). Crabs can also be eliminated with piperonyl butoxide A-200 (Pyrinate R). These and other preparations can be purchased over the counter in most states.

## Safer-Sex Practices: Reducing the Risk of Contracting STDs

A good friend called recently to say that she had separated from her husband. We discussed the possibility of her forming a bond with someone else. Her response was that becoming sexually intimate is not easy these days, considering the spread of AIDS and other STDs.

There has been a lot of discussion about "safe sex" in the media, but you may have noticed that we have consistently used the phrase "safer sex" in this text. The reason is that, from the standpoint of wanting to avoid an STD (or, for that matter, an unwanted pregnancy), there is no such thing as safe sex if genital contact is involved. However, there are practices that reduce the risk of exposure to negative consequences of engaging in genital sex with a partner. These include abstinence, avoiding anonymous "one-night stands," communicating clearly about your sexual policies with a person prior to deciding whether to become sexually intimate with him or her, limiting sexual activities to contacts that do not involve bodily penetration, and using condoms during any sexual intimacy.

For many couples, one of the most difficult steps involved in making a decision about whether to become more sexually intimate and in engaging in safer-sex practices is discussing the matter with each other. But frank and open dialogue is absolutely essential if you are to make wise decisions about developing a relationship that may affect your physical and psychological well-being for the rest of your life. To make sexual decisions in the dark, so to speak, is like driving with your eyes closed. In the remainder of this chapter, we describe the formation of sexual policies, relationship negotiation, and some of the other practices listed above. In the event that you do choose to become more emotionally and sexually involved with another person, the dis-

**amebiasis** (AM-uh-BYE-uh-sis)—a parasitic infection of the colon that results in frequent diarrhea.

**scabies**—a contagious skin condition caused by an insect that burrows under the skin.

**pediculosis pubis** (pe-DIK-you-LOW-sis PYOU-bis)—lice infestation of the pubic hair; commonly referred to as crabs.

cussions that you have prior to making that decision ultimately enhance your emotional and physical intimacy as a couple.

## Relationship Negotiation

Most of us are sexually attracted to many different people in our lives, but we generally go through a screening process (although we may not think of it that way) as we try to decide whether to act on our attractions. Some people choose not to act on their attraction to an individual because they wish to wait until they are in a relationship involving serious commitment, engagement, or marriage before becoming sexually intimate. Others may avoid acting on sexual attraction because they are already in a monogamous relationship with another person. And people who are unattached or who are not in a monogamous relationship may feel attracted to someone on the basis of his or her looks, but after a few conversations, they may realize that the person's physical appearance is all that they find attractive.

Assuming that you are a terrific human being with a wide range of attractive and valuable attributes, you can afford to be selective about your choice of sexual partners and practices. Being selective requires that you devote some time to deciding your sexual policies. ''Sexual policies'' and ''selective'' may sound abstract and vague, but determining sexual policies so that one can be selective involves a series of concrete steps.

1. *Determine your own sexual policies.* You should make decisions about sexual policies when you are calm and able to think clearly, not when you are sexually aroused and have to make a decision about a particular person. As you may know, it is difficult to think about policies when you are feeling passionate. In forming your policies, it is useful to ask yourself questions about the conditions under which you wish to become physically and emotionally intimate with another person.

   a. Do I want a potential sexual partner to be someone with whom I also feel mutual friendship?

   b. Do I want a relationship in which mutual trust can develop?

   c. Do I want to select partners who are capable of valuing others as much as they value themselves?

   d. What kind of relationship am I seeking, with what level of mutual commitment?

   We know two students—one a heterosexual woman and the other a gay man—who, for different reasons, plan to avoid serious commitments for a couple of years. Neither of them is averse to casual relationships, but both make it clear to potential partners that they are not emotionally available for any intense or long-term relationship. Neither of them is sexually active often, but when they are, they rely on the safer-sex practices described here.

2. *Communicate your policies to a potential partner.* After you become aware that you and another person are interested in each other, it is important to spend some time getting to know one another before deciding to become sexually intimate. Your prospective partner may appear to meet the criteria that you established in your sexual policies, but first impressions are not always accurate. In addition, there is a tendency to ascribe motives and characteristics to another person whom we find attractive without explicitly verbalizing our own motives and policies or asking the other person about his or hers.

3. *Identify the extent to which your own past sexual behaviors pose a potential risk to the person in whom you are interested.* If you have been sexually active with others, have you been tested for STDs to make sure that you will not transmit an STD to this new person? You should be able to give this new person that information. You need not deliver a litany of names and specific episodes, but if, for example, you were sexually involved with someone and broke off the relationship because you discovered that your former partner was also having sex with someone else, then you are at risk of having contracted an STD. Until you have been tested and found to be free of any STDs, you risk transmitting an STD to a new sexual partner.

4. *Ask about your potential partner's risk of having contracted an STD.* If that person cares about you, she or he should willingly provide you with the same information. If the individual

refuses to tell you about the frequency of his or her past sexual experiences with different partners, then perhaps your criteria for an intimate sexual relationship have not been met. Remember that some people who are currently healthy may be engaging in sexual practices that put them at risk of transmitting an STD. For example, we know a woman who was approached for a sexual encounter by a man whom she liked very much. She was aware, however—and he frankly acknowledged—that he frequently engaged in group sex. She conceded her fondness and attraction for him but told him that, although she accepted his sexual lifestyle, it involved more risk than she was willing to take. He accepted her rejection of a sexual relationship gracefully, and they remained good friends.

5. *Postpone physical intimacy involving the exchange of body fluids until laboratory tests have verified that you are both free of STDs.* You may perceive our emphasis on getting oneself tested before entering a new relationship as an expensive practice that kills sexual spontaneity. But keep in mind that it is not nearly so expensive as contracting an STD, particularly one of the incurable viral diseases. In addition, a clinic in your area may provide testing services free or on a sliding scale based on income.

   If, after considering your own values and establishing open communication, you and the other person decide that you feel sufficiently committed to each other to make love, both of you can reduce the risk of infection by incorporating safer-sex practices into your lovemaking. If a couple approaches the situation with some imagination and perhaps humor, these practices can be both erotic and romantic as well as safety-enhancing. They need not resemble a medical examination or a police body search. But remember that, if you care enough about your partner to want to be sexually intimate with him or her, you should also want to protect the person—as well as yourself–against possible disease.

6. *Shower or bathe together before becoming sexually intimate.* Washing yourselves and each other can be highly erotic (see Figure 17.10). It also gives you both the opportunity to observe each other's bodies.

7. *Learn about each other's bodies.* You may want to invest in some pink light bulbs for your bedroom (or wherever you choose to make love). If you notice any unusual characteristics (for example, bumps or discharge), you should ask about them. If you suspect that one of you has developed symptoms of an STD, you should delay further physical intimacy.

8. *Use condoms during all sexual acts.* If you find that the standard latex condoms reduce the amount of stimulation that you experience, you may want to purchase cecum condoms (described in Chapter 10). Because they are more porous, however, they are not as effective in preventing pregnancy or transmission of STDs. If you find the usual spermicides less than aesthetically pleasing, you may want to obtain one of the flavored spermicides. As we have seen, if used together, condoms and spermicides can be highly effective in reducing the likelihood of transmitting most STDs.

   In the event that you and your partner decide to make a long-term, monogamous commitment to one another and neither of you is infected, condom and spermicide use can be abandoned (and will have to be if your long-term commitment includes plans for children!). Provided that neither of you engages in injection drug use and that you maintain a monogamous relationship, you have little risk of contracting an STD.

## Other Practices That Reduce Risk

Our intention in providing the following list of practices is not to be moralistic but to help you avoid contracting AIDS or any of the other STDs.

1. Do not use intravenous drugs, iso-butyl, or poppers (amyl nitrate) (see Chapter 14).

2. Do not share needles or any other IV-drug equipment.

3. Do not use the belongings of others that contain any of their body fluids (blood, saliva, urine, semen, and so forth).

**FIGURE 17.10**
**Bathing Together**
By bathing or showering together, you can enjoy erotic play and have an opportunity to see each other's bodies.

4. Avoid unprotected sexual intimacy with IV-drug users. It is estimated that many of the new AIDS cases will result from people who inject drugs or have had unprotected sexual contact with IV-drug users.

5. Finally, remain abstinent until you are confident that sexual activity between you and a desired partner will not pose health risks for either of you.

If you are sexually active and nonmonogamous, following these safer-sex and general health practices is extremely important. You may also want to amend your present sexual lifestyle until vaccines against the viral STDs become available. Our capacities to provide one another with sexual pleasure—not to mention our lives—can be seriously jeopardized by AIDS or other STDs. If one does not practice abstinence, there is no absolute guarantee that a sexual contact will not result in an STD. Although those who wish to remain sexually active and healthy may not be thrilled about altering their sexual practices to avoid disease, for most people, survival is more important than high-risk sexual encounters with a variety of partners about whom you know relatively little.

## Summary of Major Points

1. Diagnosis of sexually transmitted diseases.

It is important for sexually active people to obtain diagnosis and treatment of any suspicious symptoms because most of the STDs are readily cured in their early stages. Further, the partners of a person with an STD must be informed that they have been exposed because as many as 80% of women and many men may be asymptomatic with some of the STDs. Failure to obtain early diagnosis and treatment can lead to various medical problems, including sterility and even death. Because of the high proportion of asymptomatic infections, sexually active people should be tested for STDs during their annual pelvic (female) or urologic (male) examinations.

2. Categories of STDs.

The STDs can be classified into three major categories: bacterial infections, viral diseases, and parasitic infestations. Except for the viral STDs, these can be readily cured in their early stages. However, contracting an STD in the past may increase one's chances of contracting HIV; thus sexually active people should take preventive measures to avoid any STD.

3. STDs caused by bacteria.

The bacterial infections include gonorrhea, syphilis, chlamydia, nongonococcal urethritis (NGU), cystitis, prostatitis, gardnerella vaginalis, and shigellosis. The most common serious complication of untreated bacterial genital infections in women is pelvic inflammatory disease (PID). A variety of medications are successful in treating these conditions, particularly if they are used in the early stages of the infection.

4. STDs caused by viruses.

The viral STDs include AIDS, herpes II, genital warts, and hepatitis B. Although there are treatments for the symptoms and for some complications of these diseases, none can be cured. There is a vaccine for hepatitis B, however, and people at risk of contracting it should be vaccinated.

5. STDs caused by parasites.

Infections caused by parasites, fungi, and yeasts include candidiasis, trichomoniasis, amebiasis, scabies, and pediculosis pubis. Antibiotic and antifungal compounds are generally effective in treating these infections.

6. Safer-sex practices.

Except for celibacy, there is no way to eliminate the risk of contracting STDs. But sexually active people can sharply reduce the likelihood of contracting AIDS and other STDs by refraining from IV-drug use, avoiding contact with others' body fluids (including blood and semen), and adopting safer-sex practices. Reducing exposure to STDs involves careful selection of partners and the correct and consistent use of latex condoms and ample amounts of spermicide. Condoms reduce the likelihood of transmitting or contracting most STDs, and spermicides are effective in killing many of the organisms that cause STDs, including herpes.

**Note:** AIDS information is available from the following sources. *United States:* For a tape recording of the latest information, call, toll-free, 1-800-342-AIDS. AIDS information is available (although not always toll-free) from the Department of Health in each state and the District of Columbia; to inquire about a toll-free number in your locale, call 1-800-555-1212.

*Canada:* National AIDS Centre, Ottawa, 1-613-957-1772. Toronto Area Gay Hotline, 1-416-964-6600.

## Review of Key Concepts

1. It is estimated that of today's adolescents, _____will have contracted an STD by the time they are 25 years old. a) one-tenth; b) one-fourth; c) one-third; d) one-half. (p. 553)

2. STDs caused by bacteria are relatively easy to cure. True or false? (p. 591)

3. Which of the following statements about gonorrhea is not true? a) It is frequently asymptomatic in infected women. b) It is transmissible by kissing as well as by sexual intercourse. c) It is always curable by procaine penicillin G. d) Reported incidence has increased since the 1970s. (pp. 559–560)

4. Pelvic inflammatory disease (PID) is: a) the most common serious complication of untreated gonorrhea, chlamydia, and other genital infections in females; b) a cause of ectopic pregnancy and sterility; c) sometimes mistaken for appendicitis; d) all of the above. (p. 565)

5. Gardnerella and candidiasis are relatively rare infections that can be contracted only by women. True or false? (p. 564)

6. HIV is: a) the antibody whose presence in a person's blood shows infection with AIDS; b) an acronym for the two groups most at risk for contracting AIDS: homosexuals and intravenous drug users; c) the retrovirus that causes AIDS; d) a drug that slows the course of AIDS infection. (pp. 567–570)

7. Which of the following statements about the spread of HIV is *not* true? a) It is more likely to occur among people with a history of other STDs. b) The risk of contracting HIV rises dramatically with the number of sexual partners one has. c) The disease is sometimes contracted in the process of donating blood. d) Pregnant women can transmit the virus to their fetuses. (pp. 571–573)

8. Symptoms of AIDS can resemble those of the flu, colds, and physical and psychological stress. True or false? (p. 573)

9. The blood test for HIV known as ELISA can determine with 100% accuracy whether an individual is HIV-positive. True or false? (p. 573)

10. The safer-sex practices that reduce the risk of contracting HIV or other STDs include all of the following *except*: a) using male condoms; b) using female condoms; c) limiting the number of sexual contacts; d) douching. (pp. 577–580)

11. Chlamydia is: a) caused by a relatively minor virus; b) an infection affecting only women; c) transmissible only by sexual contact; d) none of the above. (pp. 562–563)

12. Describe the precautions you can take to reduce the risk that you and your sexual partner(s) will contract an STD.

# Sexual Coercion

THE ways in which human beings relate to one another sexually reflect the complexity of human emotions and motivations. Sexual activity can be a medium for expressing the deepest and most pleasurable feelings we have, or a vehicle for the degradation and abuse of another. In this chapter we discuss sexual interactions that are marked by various forms of coercion. First, we consider sexual assault, in which one person is forced by physical or psychological means into sexual activity by one or more other people. Second, we examine sexual harassment, in which economic, evaluative, or psychological power is used to pressure a person with less power into sexual relations. Finally, we discuss the sexual abuse of children by adults.

## Sexual Assault

*Sexual assault* is one of the most exploitive forms of sexual encounter. Often including *rape*, it is an expression of aggression through sex. In this section, we look at some of the myths that surround rape and sexual assault. We consider both the

**sexual assault**—forcing another person to have sexual contact.
**rape**—sexual intercourse that occurs without consent under actual or threatened force.

victims of sexual assault and the various types of sexual assault. Then we survey the characteristics of sexual aggressors and victims and the factors associated with sexual assault. Finally, we look at the consequences of sexual assault for the victim, and the responses by police and the courts to the offense.

## The Magnitude of the Problem

How long will it take you to read this chapter? Assuming that you are interrupted a couple of times, it may take you three hours. During that time, there will be more than 37 rapes reported to authorities in the United States. In 1992 (the latest year for which statistics are available) more than 109,000 rapes were reported, and these resulted in about 39,000 arrests (Uniform Crime Reports, 1993).

The number of sexual assaults reported annually to criminal justice authorities is a vast underestimate of the actual number of assaults committed each year because most assault victims do not report the crime (Allgeier, 1987; Koss, 1992; McCormick, 1994). Until recently, most research on sexual assault was conducted with those victims who reported the assault to authorities and with convicted rapists. Not only do most victims fail to report the attack, but even when they do, police may dismiss the report as unfounded—that is, they do not believe that a sexual assault really occurred. Therefore, most of our prior knowledge about sexual assault was limited to victims who reported and assailants who were convicted.

More recent research involving surveys of nonreporting victims and nonidentified rapists has greatly expanded our understanding of sexual assault. The results of these studies have also challenged a number of common myths about sexual assault.

## Rape Myths

There are many myths about sexual assault. Some of these are supported by evidence; others are utterly false. Before reading further, you might want to take the sexual-assault stereotypes test in Box 18.1.

One of the most common myths about rape is that it occurs because women tempt men be-

yond males' capacity to control themselves. At least two beliefs are reflected in this myth. One is that the victim is at least partially responsible for the attack. This idea is called victim precipitation. It has its historical roots in the ancient notion that women are dangerous seductresses and that men must be wary of women's power to excite them into a state of uncontrollable lust.

This conviction is closely related to the second idea: that after lust has been triggered, people are powerless to prevent themselves from sexually attacking the person who elicited the lust. To evaluate the accuracy of these beliefs, we need to review what is known about the victims of rape, the perpetrators of the crime, and the circumstances under which rape occurs.

## The Sexual-Assault Offender

Until recently, information about the characteristics of sexual-assault offenders was limited to those who had been arrested for an assault. Sample bias is even greater in research on rapists than in research on their victims. About a third of reported sexual assaults in 1992 resulted in the arrest of alleged assailants (Uniform Crime Reports, 1993). In the remaining cases reported to authorities, the assailants could not be found, there was not enough evidence to proceed legally, or police did not believe that a rape had occurred.

Further, recent research suggests that it is inappropriate to generalize from small samples of convicted rapists to the total population of those who coerce others into sexual contact. Hence we differentiate between *convicted* rapists and *unidentified* rapists, the latter being persons who admit anonymously that they have forced others to have sexual contact but whose victims did not report them to authorities, or who were reported but not caught, arrested, or convicted.

Although the ages of those arrested for sexual assault range from 10 to 65, men aged 18 to 24 account for most arrests (Uniform Crime Reports, 1993). The majority of convicted rapists use weapons to coerce their victims, and in three-quarters of the cases, physical force is also employed. The majority of offenders are either drinking or drunk at the time of the sexual assault (Abbey, Ross, & McDuffie, 1993; Barbaree, Hudson, & Seto, 1993; Schram, 1978). Although

**Box 18.1**

## Sexual-Assault Stereotypes

Lightly pencil in your answers to each of the following statements so that you can change those that are incorrect after you have finished reading the chapter. Which statements are true?

### The Rapist

1. Only a male can be a rapist.
2. Men rape because they are unable to obtain sexual release in any other way.
3. Men rape because of hormonally caused excessive sex drives.
4. Castration of the testes prevents rapists from attacking more victims.
5. After a man reaches a certain level of sexual arousal, he is unable to control his impulse to engage in intercourse.
6. Pornographic material containing rape scenes provokes men to commit sexual assault.
7. The majority of rapes occur when the assailant has been drinking.
8. The vast majority of men rape women whom they have never met.
9. The average convicted rapist spends at least 10 years in prison.
10. The majority of men who are brought to trial for rape are convicted of that charge.

### The Victim

1. The majority of raped women secretly want to be forced to have sex.
2. A woman cannot be raped against her will.
3. A man cannot be raped by a woman.
4. A man cannot be raped by another man.
5. The majority of women who charge rape actually consent to the act and change their minds later.
6. The majority of women who are raped by acquaintances consent to the act and then charge rape when the relationship breaks up.
7. A married woman cannot be raped by her husband.
8. The majority of rape victims are highly attractive women who are assaulted while walking alone at night.
9. A brutal, violent sexual attack is much more traumatic for the victim than a sexual attack not involving physical violence.
10. Attack by a stranger is more traumatic than attack by an acquaintance.

---

most convicted rapists are heterosexual men in their late adolescence or early 20s, women, gay males, and young boys have also been convicted of rape.

In contrast to convicted rapists, unidentified rapists rarely use weapons; instead, they rely on verbal coercion, threats, and physical restraint. The deliberate attempt to intoxicate their victims with alcohol or other drugs appears to be a common coercive strategy that is used by both con-

victed and unidentified assailants (Abbey et al., 1993; Barbaree et al., 1993; Kanin, 1985; Koss & Dinero, 1988).

*Socialization Experiences of Sex Offenders*

Examination of the childhood and adolescence of convicted sex offenders and unidentified assailants has yielded both similarities and differences in the two groups.

**Convicted Assailants**    First, as noted by William Prendergast (1987), a psychologist who worked with convicted male rapists in a prison environment for more than 25 years, many of these men lack self-confidence from an early age. They may compensate for their general sense of inadequacy with exaggerated demonstrations of masculinity, which include assault.

Second, an unusually high proportion of convicted rapists were themselves victims of violent sexual abuse, physical assault, and/or neglect during their preschool, childhood, and adolescent years (McCormick, 1994; Sack & Mason, 1980).

Third, it is perhaps not surprising, given the first two findings, that many adult sex offenders report a pattern of having sexually victimized others during their childhood and adolescence. Half of adult sexual offenders reported that they had also committed sex crimes during adolescence (Barbaree et al., 1993).

**Unidentified Assailants**    In the case of unidentified offenders, the individuals' backgrounds may be more representative of the general population than are those of convicted rapists. Smithyman (1979) obtained a sample of 50 unidentified rapists by soliciting research participants through advertisements. (This method of obtaining the sample limits generalizability to those men who would be willing to participate in such a study, of course.) Of the men who responded, 72% had never been arrested for any crime, and only 6% had been arrested for sexual offenses; 84% had high school diplomas and 58% had entered college; 42% held white-collar jobs; and 26% were married. Similarly, other research comparing unidentified assailants and nonassailants has found no differences in race, social class, or place of residence between the two groups, a finding consistent with those in other self-report studies of unidentified assailants (Ageton, 1983; Polk et al., 1981).

The socialization experiences of unidentified assailants, however, do appear to differ from those of nonassailants. Ageton's (1983) data from unidentified adolescent offenders showed a pattern of estrangement from the values of families and teachers. These boys engaged in various delinquent activities and identified with delinquent peer groups. Compared with their nonassaultive

peers, they expected to receive more negative labeling from both their parents and their teachers. In Ageton's five-year longitudinal study, these differences in assaultive and nonassaultive males were found before as well as after they had coerced females to have sex.

Similarly, Kanin's (1985) data indicated that college males who engaged in sexually coercive behavior said that their best friends would "definitely approve" of forcing particular types of women to have sex with them. If the males perceived their potential victims to be "loose," "teasers," "pick-ups," or "economic exploiters," then coercion was justified in their own eyes, and they expected that their peers would approve of their behavior. In the opinion of the men in Kanin's sample, if these women would not consent to sexual contact, then they "deserved" to be forced because they had violated sexual expectations that they raised by "flaunting, advertising, and promising sexual accessibility" (p. 225). Alder (1985) found the same general pattern of attitudes in a sample of adult men. The assaultive men were more likely than the nonassaultive men to have sexually aggressive male friends, to have served in Vietnam, and to see women as legitimate victims of sexual assault.

Finally, almost 3,000 men responded to the questionnaires administered by Koss and her colleagues, and of these, 600 admitted perpetrating some act of aggression since age 14. Behaviors that met the legal definition of rape were reported by 131 men. The more assaultive men differed from the less assaultive and nonassaultive men in several socialization characteristics, and in fact, early experiences appeared to be the best predictor of assaultive behavior (Koss & Dinero, 1988). For example, the assaultive men had greater exposure to family violence, were more likely to experience childhood sexual abuse, and began having sex—both consensual and forced—at earlier ages. Consistent with Kanin's findings, the assaultive men were more likely to report involvement with peer groups that reinforced highly sexualized views of women.

A general portrait emerges from these studies comparing unidentified assailants with nonassailants. The offender tends to be relatively alienated from his family and school-system values, and to have experienced family violence and childhood sexual abuse. Moreover, he identifies with a rape-supportive peer group and a value system that supports his belief that the coercion of some women is justified by the women's behavior, even though they have not consented to sexual contact.

## Attitudes and Personality Traits of Assailants

Psychological tests of convicted rapists do not paint a uniform picture. There is some evidence that many rapists may be guilt-ridden individuals who attempt to inhibit expressions of aggression (Levin & Stava, 1987). Obviously, these attempts at inhibition are not always successful. Some authorities have suggested that rapists are mentally deficient, but the IQs of convicted rapists do not generally differ from those of men convicted of nonsexual crimes (Vera et al., 1979; Wolfe & Baker, 1980).

Studies in which the personality and attitudes of unidentified rapists were compared with those of nonassaultive men have revealed no single factor related to high levels of sexual aggression. With a sample of men ranging in age from 18 to 47, Malamuth (1986) found that hostility toward women, acceptance of interpersonal violence, and dominance as a sexual motive were positively related to self-reported sexual aggression. In Rapaport and Burkhart's (1984) research, the more coercion the unidentified assailants reported, the lower their scores on measures of responsibility and positive socialization. The assailants in Rapaport and Burkhart's research also saw sexual aggression as more acceptable than did the nonassailants. Further, when exposed to videotaped rape depictions, unidentified assaultive men show fewer negative emotional reactions than do nonrapists. Specifically, rapists report less disgust, anger, fear, distress, shame, contempt, and guilt than do nonrapists in response to depictions of rape (Mosher & Anderson, 1986).

In an intriguing study of college students, Mahoney, Shively, and Traw (1986) obtained self-reports of coercive behavior and measures of *hypermasculinity*. A man's rating on the hyper-

hypermasculinity—exaggeration of male dominance through an emphasis on male virility, strength, and aggression.

masculinity scale (Mosher & Sirkin, 1984) is determined by asking him to indicate which of two statements best describes him. The following are four examples from the 30 pairs:

1. a. I like fast cars and fast women.
   b. I like dependable cars and faithful women.
2. a. It's natural for men to get into fights.
   b. Physical violence never solves an issue.
3. a. You have to screw some women before they know who is boss.
   b. You have to love some women before they know you don't want to be boss.
4. a. I like wild, uninhibited parties.
   b. I like quiet parties with good conversations.

Those who tended to endorse the "a" alternatives as self-descriptive—the hypermasculine men—reported having engaged in more sexually coercive behaviors than did those males endorsing the "b" alternatives. In light of the Mahoney group's (1986) findings and Kanin's (1985) conclusion that assailants and their peers perceived some types of women as legitimate targets of coercion, it is tempting to speculate that hypermasculine males are most attracted to the very kind of women that they perceive as deserving of assault.

Other researchers have hypothesized that traditional gender-role identification and gender-role attitudes are related to the likelihood of engaging in sexual coercion. Among both males and females, traditional attitudes toward gender roles are correlated with a belief in rape myths, although the relationship is stronger for males than for females (Costin, 1985). Similarly, traditional males are more likely than androgynous or egalitarian males to report that they would engage in rape if they could be sure of not being caught (Check & Malamuth, 1983; Tieger, 1981). But researchers have not found a *consistent* relationship between traditional gender-role beliefs and anonymous self-reporting of sexual assault by males. Ageton (1983), for example, found no difference between assailants and nonassailants in gender-role attitudes, and Rapaport and Burkhart (1984) discovered no relationship between degree of involvement in sexually coercive behavior and measures of gender-role attitudes or identification. Traditional views are probably not by themselves predictors of sexual assault, but in combination with factors such as hostility toward women, hypermasculinity, irresponsibility, and the absence of disgust and guilt about assault, they may reduce inhibitions against engaging in coercion.

## Sexual Characteristics of Assailants

It is common to think of rapists as sexually pre-occupied people with high sex drives. A rather different picture emerged from the work of Groth and Burgess (1977), who conducted clinical interviews with 170 men convicted of sexual assault. The researchers also examined almost 100 women who were victims of sexual assault and studied the victims' descriptions of the assault to the police. Only a quarter of the convicted rapists had no problems with erection or ejaculation during the assault. About one-third of the men showed clear evidence of sexual dysfunction of some type. The proportion of men experiencing retarded ejaculation (15%) was far higher than that generally found in other samples. For example, Masters and Johnson (1970) estimated that only about 1 in 700 men (0.14%) experiences retarded ejaculation.

Taken as a whole, Groth and Burgess's (1977) data (see Table 18.1) suggest quite a high rate of sexual dysfunction among rapists. Ironically, practically none of the convicted rapists reported similar dysfunctions in their sexual relations with *consenting* partners. Rather, their dysfunctions appeared to be specific to the context of rape. In support of these findings, Selkin (1975) found that vaginal intercourse occurred in less than half the rape cases investigated. These observations are consistent with the notion that rape is not primarily sexually motivated but instead is an attempt to dominate and subjugate another person. There remains the larger question, however, of why the anger, resentment, and need to control are expressed sexually.

Studies of unidentified rapists are more supportive of the notion that rapists have strong sexual appetites. Compared with nonrapists, the unidentified rapists in Kanin's (1985) sample had had a greater number of sexual partners, as well as considerably more sexual outlets: the average number of orgasms per month from coitus, fel-

### TABLE 18.1  Sexual Dysfunction During Rape

|  | Number | Percent |
|---|---|---|
| Sexual dysfunction | | |
| Erectile dysfunction | 27 | 16 |
| Retarded ejaculation | 26 | 15 |
| Premature ejaculation | 5 | 3 |
| No dysfunction | 43 | 25 |
| No attempt at penetration | 16 | 9 |
| Assault interrupted | 10 | 6 |
| Victim resisted successfully | 8 | 5 |
| No data available | 35 | 21 |

Note: These data indicate that 25 percent of the convicted rapists in this sample were able to complete an act of intercourse during rape. Among the remaining 75 percent, intercourse was not completed because of dysfunction, victim's resistance, and so forth.

Source: Adapted from Groth and Burgess, 1977, p. 765. By permission of the *New England Journal of Medicine* (297, 764–766, 1977).

latio, and masturbation was 6, compared to 0.8 for the nonassailants. The unidentified rapists were also more persistent in their quest for sexual contact and used more exploitative strategies to obtain sex. When asked how often they attempted to seduce a new date, 62% of the unidentified rapists responded "most of the time," compared to 19% of the nonrapists.

Consistent with Kanin's data, Mahoney et al. (1986) found that the greater the number of sexually coercive experiences the college males in their sample reported, the more their coital experience, lifetime number of intercourse partners, years of sexual activity, and number of coital partners per year. In fact, the strongest predictor of coercive behaviors for these men was their lifetime number of intercourse partners. Similarly, Byers and Lewis (1988) found that more sexually experienced college males reported more disagreements with their dates about desired levels of sexual intimacy (he wanted more, she wanted less) than did less sexually experienced college males, with 16% of the men in the former group attempting to continue the unwanted advances (usually toward coitus) after their dates had refused to consent.

Part of the discrepancy between results of studies of convicted rapists and those of studies of unidentified rapists regarding aggressive versus sexual motivations may stem from the level of relationship between the rapist and the victim. Women who are raped by strangers are far more likely to report the assault (McCormick, 1994), a situation resulting in an overrepresentation of stranger assaults among convicted rapists. It may be that convicted males who rape strangers are using sex to express aggressive, hostile motives, whereas males who rape acquaintances are using aggressiveness to achieve sexual goals, a notion to which we will return when we examine hypotheses about the causes of rape. Before turning to that topic, we consider victims of sexual coercion.

## Victims of Sexual Coercion

Victims of sexual assault come from all walks of life. In trying to describe the typical victim of sexual coercion, we face some of the same generalization problems that have plagued research on rapists. We will distinguish among those victims who report their assaults to authorities; those victims who do not report their assaults but who anonymously acknowledge during victimization surveys that they have been assaulted; and those victims who do neither and about whom we know nothing.

Many people think of the typical sexual assault as the rape of a young woman by someone whom she does not know. However, between a third and a half of sexual assaults reported to authorities involve people who know each other, and among unidentified victims, the overwhelming majority know their assailants. Sometimes they have just met, sometimes they have been casually dating for a while, and sometimes they are married to each other. Many sexual assaults involve more than one assailant. Further, some of the victims of sexual assault by individuals or gangs are male. Although the sexual assault of males is less prevalent than the sexual assault of females, we begin with the coercion of males, for the reasons outlined by Cherry.

### Male Victims of Assault

Psychologist Frances Cherry has written:

> When I have introduced the topic of rape in my classes, students often snicker when I raise the possibility that a man can be raped by a woman. Some of the men have sat back in their desks, opened their arms, and sighed "rape me." When I further suggest we consider that men are raped by men, the men's chortles and sighs abruptly turn to nervous laughter, downward turning of the head and closing of the legs and arms. (1983, p. 247)

Cherry noted that this approach to discussing rape is useful for two reasons:

> First, [students] begin to examine their commonly held belief that rape is primarily sexual. They begin to look at the intent of the rapist not to seduce but to overpower and physically assault another person. Second, as the life-threatening aspects of rape become more real, students begin to question their acceptance of the idea that women are responsible for rape and are legitimate victims of rape. (p. 247)

Even when we consider men as rape victims, we think of them as being at risk of sexual assault only when they are in prison, and only by male assailants. Few people feel sympathetic to the fate of imprisoned men. But reports of male victims from rape-crisis centers and the data from several recent studies document the fact that noncriminal men can also be sexually assaulted by women (Struckman-Johnson & Struckman-Johnson, 1994). In fact, each year more than 9,000 men report having been sexually assaulted (U.S. Department of Justice, 1990). Because assaulted men (like women) are reluctant to report sexual assaults, the incidence is probably far higher than the Justice Department statistics indicate. A victimization survey of a representative sample of Los Angeles households conducted by Sorenson, Stein, Siegel, Golding, and Burnam (1987) indicated that of the 1,480 men interviewed, 7.2% reported having been pressured or forced into sexual contact. Among the White college-educated 18- to 39-year-old members of the sample, the rate was 16%. The majority of the unwanted

## Box 18.2

## Male Rape

This account was sent to us by a young convict after he took a human sexuality course in prison:

*It was the policy for inmates to shower—all at once—in a large shower room. While showering, I was aware of a hand brushing against my genitals. As I turned and looked around, I observed a young male on his hands and knees as a much larger youth began raping him anally. The cries were loud and scary as the incident continued. I pretended not to notice as another man stepped in front of the youth and began to force his penis into the youth's mouth. I stood there in sheer disbelief as the youth became a sexual "sandwich" for the two larger youths. After they had both ejaculated, they punched and kicked the smaller man until he lay still on the floor—blood and semen running from his anus. . . . It was not a pretty sight. It is a memory which is deeply imbedded in my mind—as vivid as though it was yesterday. Whatever happened to the young man who was victimized? He committed suicide three days later.*

contacts had been by female acquaintances. Although the form of coercion usually involved verbal pressure, in about 10% of the cases, physical harm or threats had been used. For 39% of the assaulted men, some form (vaginal, oral, or anal) of intercourse occurred.

Results of research by Groth and Burgess (1980) focusing on convicted male rapists showed that three-quarters of their male victims were total strangers to them. Groth and Burgess identified three styles of attack, which they labeled entrapment, intimidation, and physical force. Like victimized women, men who are raped find the event traumatic and the reporting of it difficult (see Box 18.2). Later in the chapter, we describe the after-effects of rape on women; following rape, many men experience the same sorts of disruptions in eating, sleeping, sexual relationships, social relationships, and psychological functioning as women report (Struckman-Johnson, 1991).

Many states still define rape as an act by a man against a woman. If a male is raped, the crime is usually charged under sodomy laws. According to most sodomy laws, however, both participants are guilty of an "unnatural act" or a "crime against nature." Further, although new federal guidelines prohibit introducing a female's sexual history in a rape case, the sexual history of male victims can be used as a defense.

Perhaps because of the traditional definition of rape as an act committed by a male against a female, most researchers studying acquaintance assault have constructed their measures on the assumption that males are perpetrators and females are victims. As Struckman-Johnson (1988) pointed out, however, this may represent an experimental bias, for as we have seen, males can also be rape victims. Further, females can be perpetrators (Aizenman & Kelley, 1988; Muehlenhard & Cook, 1988). Struckman-Johnson (1988) administered a survey to college students that allowed them—regardless of their gender—to respond as assailants, victims, or both. In her sample, 22% of the women and 16% of the men reported that they had experienced at least one forced-sex episode. Among the 800 students queried by Aizenman and Kelley (1988), 25% of the women and 7% of the men reported experiencing sexual violence in dating relationships. As might be expected, the strategies used to obtain sex by males and females differed. In Struckman-Johnson's study, sexual coercion through physical restraint was reported by 53% of the female victims, compared to 9% of the male victims. In contrast, male victims were more likely to report the use of psychological force (48%) than were female victims (16%).

Struckman-Johnson (1988) asked her respondents to write descriptions of the forced-sex episodes. Those provided by men may sound quite familiar to women who have experienced sexual coercion through psychological strategies:

> *I was at a formal, my date pressured me into having sex even after I said no. . . . She told me that she wanted sex but I refused then. She kept persisting, so I gave in.*

> *She said I didn't like her if I didn't want to. Massive guilt trip. I didn't want to.*

> *She was drunk and said if I didn't that she would break up with me.*

> *She layed on top of me when I was drunk and took my clothing off and went to work.*

> *I was invited over for a party, unaware that it was a date. As the evening wore on, I got the message that the girl was my date. I didn't have to make a move on her because she was all over me. She wouldn't take no for an answer. Usually I like to get to know the person. I felt I was forced into sex. After, I felt terrible and used. (pp. 238–239)*

Two of the men in Struckman-Johnson's sample reported being coerced into sex because the women threatened to expose negative information about them to their parents or an employer. The long-term correlates reported by men of being coerced by female acquaintances, however, were less severe than those reported by coerced women.

Subsequent research with a sample of more than 200 college men indicated that about a third had been the recipients of coercive sexual contact, and the contact resulted in forced intercourse for 22% of the men (Struckman-Johnson & Struckman-Johnson, 1994). For 12% of the incidents, the force used included physical restraint, physical intimidation, threat of harm, or harm. Of the total sample, 24% of the men had been coerced by women, 4% by men, and 6% by both genders. The self-reported negative emotional impact was less when the coercion was from female than

from male perpetrators. In addition to the fear, anger, and self-blame that is commonly felt by women who have experienced coercion, the men coerced by women felt that their masculinity had been threatened; those heterosexual men coerced by men were concerned about perceptions of their sexual orientation, as shown by one man's interview responses:

> *I cannot handle another man being physically attracted to me. I can't get over it . . . it's almost like I don't deserve to be a man because I'm attracting other men. A woman attracts a man. So its like I'm in limbo. I'm an in-between. I'm not gay. I know I'm not gay, but then again, I can't establish my manhood.*

### Female Victims of Assault

The incidence of the sexual assault of women is difficult to estimate because the relevant statistics are compiled in different ways by different sources. For 1992, 109,000 U.S. women reported being sexually assaulted. Thus 78 of every 100,000 females reported to police an assault that ultimately found its way into reports provided by police to the FBI for 1992 (Uniform Crime Reports, 1993). This rate was 7% higher than that for 1984. For reasons we will discuss, the police decide that some cases are unfounded; the FBI statistics therefore provide an estimate of the prevalence of reports that are believed by the police.

To grasp how rates can vary depending on the source, it is useful to compare rates of assault perpetrated on females by adolescent males according to three different sources in 1978: FBI statistics, the National Crime Survey (NCS), and the Sexual Assault Project (SAP) (Ageton, 1983):

*FBI:* 50 males aged 12 to 19 per 100,000 males (based on arrests made)

*NCS:* 120 males per 100,000 males (based on female victims' reports to surveyors)

*SAP:* 5,000 to 16,000 males aged 13 to 19 per 100,000 males

At first glance, this enormous variation seems to serve as a classic case of "you can prove anything with statistics." The range in the SAP estimates results from the fact that the figures are based on reports given by a nationally representative sample of adolescent males and females. Ageton (1983) concluded that the upper estimate (16,000) was probably the most accurate because of the problem of underreporting.

Studies of adolescents are particularly important because of the consistent finding (both among victims who report to authorities and among those who report only anonymously on victimization surveys) that females in their adolescence and early 20s are at the greatest risk of sexual assault. In the McCahill group's (1979) study, two-thirds of the females who reported to hospital emergency rooms after being assaulted were under the age of 21. Other studies have revealed the same general relationship between age and risk of assault among both victims who report to authorities and victims who do not report (Ageton, 1983; McCormick, 1994).

Although research on victims who report the assault to authorities has suggested that they come predominantly from lower socioeconomic classes (McCahill et al., 1979), such studies may overrepresent the poor because victims who can afford to do so may seek treatment from private sources to avoid having to deal with the police and the media. Findings based on representative samples show that a woman's risk of sexual assault is unrelated to her social class (Ageton, 1983).

The popular perceptions (and FBI statistics) notwithstanding, the overwhelming majority of female victims know their assailants. The level of relationship varies considerably across studies; assailants range from casual acquaintances of the victims to friends, teachers, neighbors, classmates, dates, lovers, fiancés, and spouses. In Russell's (1984) study of women in San Francisco, 91% of the victims knew their assailants. Among samples of college students, between 86% and 98% of the victims knew their attackers (Koss, Dinero, Seibel, & Cox, 1988; Mynatt & Allgeier, 1990; Parcell & Kanin, 1976). This consistent finding does not mean that the FBI statistics are wrong; instead, as noted earlier, because the victims of acquaintances rarely report the assaults to authorities, rapes by strangers are overrepresented in the FBI files (Allgeier, 1987).

Acquaintance assault (sometimes called date rape) first received attention when Kirkpatrick

and Kanin (1957) surveyed college women regarding their experience with offensive sexual aggression. Sixty-two percent of these women reported experiencing at least one episode of offensive force in the year before they entered college. At least one incident of offensive sexual aggression during the previous year in college was also reported by 56% of these women.

Perhaps the most startling statistics, however, emerged from a study of the responses of a random sample of 400 college men to a questionnaire containing inquiries about the use of offensive sexual aggression (Kanin, 1969). Specifically, the men were asked whether they had personally attempted to have sexual intercourse with a woman by using force that was disagreeable and offensive to her. About 22% of these men admitted to the use of force in 181 such attempts. Most studies have shown that anywhere from 40% to 80% of various samples of college women report being victims of sexual aggression (Craig, 1990; Kanin & Parcell, 1977; Mynatt & Allgeier, 1990). An exceptionally low rate of reported victimization of females emerged from the Koss and Dinero (1988) study of 32 colleges: 28%. Some of the variations in reported rapes may stem from the means of data collection. For example, in the Koss research program, students were asked to complete questionnaires containing 330 items while they were in classrooms. Most other studies of this sort provide settings with more privacy or ask participants to complete the measures at home and later return them. The latter approach would be likely to yield a more accurate report of assault experiences.

The form and the extent of force experienced by female victims seem to vary as a function of whether the assailant is a stranger or an acquaintance, and whether the sample of victims is drawn from those who report to authorities or those who report anonymously on questionnaires. As we might expect, acquaintance assaults are less likely to involve either a weapon or physical injury to the victim than are assaults by strangers (Koss et al., 1988). Of the victims in the McCahill group's (1979) study of women seen in emergency rooms, 64% reported being pushed or held during the assault. Slapping (17%), brutal beatings (22%), and/or choking (20%) were also reported by victims. Among nonreporting victims of assault by acquaintances, however, verbal threats and coercion and the use of physical restraint were found to be more common (Allgeier, 1987; Koss et al., 1988). Among college students, the pattern of assaults sometimes involves a man's attempt to engage in a particular sexual activity with little or no prior sexual play. As Parcell and Kanin (1976) noted:

*These episodes usually consist of males going for the "whole scene" in one relatively simultaneous maneuver, rather than proceeding along some sequential seductive order. In other words, the abrupt aggressive act may include some combination of efforts at kissing, fondling, attempting to remove clothing, maneuvering the female into a coitally advantageous position, male exposure, and so on. (pp. 19–20)*

The behavioral and emotional reactions of female victims of sexual aggression during the assault demonstrate the offensive nature of these attacks. The typical victim puts up some kind of resistance, including arguing, fighting, pleading, crying, screaming, and preventive maneuvering or flight (Parcell & Kanin, 1976; Koss et al., 1988).

The majority of assaulted women feel extremely hostile following the attack, with about a third reporting anger and/or disgust. Other emotional reactions include fear, guilt, and emotional pain. Women with relatively assertive personalities, however, make fewer internal attributions of responsibility; that is, they engage in less self-blame for the assault than do women who are relatively nonassertive (Mynatt & Allgeier, 1990). An interesting finding emerged from Parcell's (1980) study, in which he asked a random sample of senior college women about their experience with male sexual aggression (see Table 18.2). After responding to a question about whether a man had attempted to force them to have sex against their will, women were asked to indicate whether they would consider such an act rape. Only 11% of the women who had encountered such force considered this action to be rape. The other 89% appeared to accept attempts at forced sexual intercourse as an expected part of male-female relationships.

Similarly, 73% of the women categorized as rape victims in the Koss et al. (1988) study did not define their experience as "rape." These women apparently did not recognize that their self-reported experience met the legal criteria for sexual assault. Further clouding our interpretations of rape, 42% of women categorized as rape victims in Koss's study later had consensual sex with the man who had allegedly raped them earlier (Gilbert, 1992).

One of the questions used to define rape in this study was, "Have you ever had sexual intercourse when you didn't want to because a man gave alcohol or drugs?" As Roiphe (1993) pointed out, the odd wording of this question raises the issue of responsibility. A man may give a woman alcohol or drugs, but she chooses whether to consume them (unless they are slipped into a supposedly nonalcoholic punch). This demonstrates—as do other issues—that some "rapes" are not easily defined.

As with acquaintance rape, sex forced upon women by their husbands is seldom defined by the women as rape or sexual assault and is almost never reported to authorities (Russell, 1982). Among the college-student sample studied by Koss et al. (1988), 351 of the women (11%) were

**TABLE 18.2 Parcell's College-Dating Study**

| Item | Percent Responding Yes |
|---|---|
| 1. Since entering college, has a male ever attempted to force you to have sexual intercourse against your will? | 37 |
| 2. Would you consider this attempted rape or rape? | 11 |
| 3. Since entering college, has a male ever attempted to force you to have oral contact with his genitals against your will? | 21 |
| 4. Since entering college, has a male ever attempted to force you to have anal intercourse against your will? | 9 |

Note: A random sample of graduating college women were contacted and asked to respond to a dating questionnaire. Of these 300 women, 78 percent responded.

married. Of these, 13% reported having been raped by spouses or family members.

Until recently, a sexually victimized wife could not charge her spouse with sexual assault. Traditionally, state laws defined sexual assault as involving a male assailant not married to his female victim. The first state to eliminate the use of marriage or cohabitation as a defense against the charge of rape was Oregon, in the late 1970s. By the mid-1990s, the majority of states had eliminated the spousal exception clause.

## What Provokes Sexual Assault?

Among the current hypotheses used to explain rape are victim precipitation, uncontrollable lust, uncontrollable aggression, exaggerated gender-role identity, and exposure to violent pornography. We dealt in Chapter 16 with the relationship between exposure to violent pornography and subsequent sexual aggression. Essentially, the research indicates that males who are angered by female confederates in experiments conducted in laboratory settings are more aggressive toward those females after seeing sexually explicit materials depicting violence against women. In addition, exposure to violent pornography has been shown to increase acceptance of rape myths and negative attitudes toward women. We do not know whether exposure to violent pornography sufficiently lowers inhibitions against aggression in the real world to the point that a man who is irritated by a woman and then sees violent pornography would actually seek out that woman to rape her. We now turn to the hypothesis that has received the least support: the notion that victims cause assailants to rape them.

### Victim Precipitation

The majority of adults—both men and women—blame the victims of sexual assault for provocative behaviors before, during, and after they have been forced to engage in sex. Almost all research on victim-blaming for sexual assault has focused on attitudes toward female victims. It might be illuminating to study attitudes toward male victims to see whether the same pattern of belief in

*victim precipitation* exists when the victim is a man. Discussing the blaming of female victims, Parcell and Kanin observed that

> *it is very curious how some males can define a female's style of dress, her vocabulary, her accepting a drink, a dance, or a ride home, or her participation in any form of sexual activity as signifying complete sexual accessibility. (1976, pp. 5–6)*

The belief that a victim precipitates assault by her behavior comes in a number of guises. About two-thirds of a sample of U.S. citizens agreed that "women provoke rape by their appearance or behavior" (Feild & Bienen, 1980). Teenagers—males and females alike—are less likely to perceive the wearing of an open shirt, tight pants, or a tight bathing suit as a signal of sexual interest or availability by a man than by a woman (Zellman & Goodchilds, 1983). In addition to being held responsible for assaults because of the way they dress, women, according to various surveys, are also held accountable if they hitchhike or enter a man's apartment (Burt, 1980).

Another common assumption is that women may actively participate in, or even initiate, sexual activity but "cry rape" later. A few researchers have even concluded that some victims provoke their own assaults. For example, sociologist Menachem Amir (1971) concluded that 19% of assaulted women prompted their own rapes. Amir defined a rape as involving victim precipitation under certain conditions, including: a) instances in which "the victim actually, or so it was deemed, agreed to sexual relations but retracted before the actual act *or did not react strongly enough when the suggestion was made by the offender(s)*" (p. 266, emphasis added); b) cases involving risky situations, particularly if the woman used behavior that "could be interpreted as indecency in language and gestures, or constituted what could be taken as an invitation to sexual relations" (p. 266); c) incidents about which the police report contained such judgmental statements as

***victim precipitation***—the notion that the victim of an attack is at least partially responsible for the attack.

"she behaved provocatively," "seems she was seductive," "she was irresponsible and endangered herself," "known as a prostitute," or "known in the neighborhood as a bad character" (p. 266). Amir concluded that "if penal justice is to be fair it must be attentive to these problems of degrees of victim responsibility for her own victimization" (p. 276). Amir's bases for concluding victim precipitation have been strongly challenged (McCormick, 1994).

At odds with the stereotypes of victims provoking their own assaults were the results of a study sponsored by the Federal Commission on Crimes of Violence, which concluded that only 4% to 6% of rape charges involve victim precipitation (Curtis, 1974). That study was conducted more than two decades ago; the assault rate has risen since that time, but there is reason to believe that low rates of victim precipitation still exist. However, research is needed to address that question.

Another mistaken belief that contributes to the tendency to blame victims for sexual assault is the idea that a woman cannot be raped against her will. Therefore, if she was raped, she must have wanted the assault, at least unconsciously. Again, as popular awareness of the victimization of males increases, it would be interesting to see whether the public believes that a man cannot be raped against his will.

Individual differences have also been identified in people's tendency to attribute responsibility for rape to victims. As might be expected, people who endorse traditional roles for women, who have greater acceptance of rape myths, and who perceive rape as motivated by sexual rather than aggressive motives are more likely to blame victims for assault than are those who endorse egalitarian gender roles, are less supportive of rape myths, and believe rape stems from aggression rather than sexual urges (Crawford & McCaul, 1987; Feild, 1978; Weidner & Griffitt, 1983).

*Uncontrolled Lust*
*or Uncontrolled Aggression?*

Belief in victim precipitation may stem in part from the assumption that a rapist attacks a victim out of an intense, overpowering sexual drive unleashed by a sexually provocative woman. During one rape trial observed by the McCahill (1979) group,

> *the defense argued to the jury that the victim "really isn't very pretty. I'll bet she invented the story of rape to attract attention to herself, or perhaps she even consented out of loneliness." Then dropping his voice and speaking specifically to the men in the jury, he added, "I'm sure you've all heard women lie through their teeth when they're lonely." In the same case, as further proof the defense asked the wife of the defendant, a very attractive young woman, to parade before the jury, while he commented, "She is really more attractive than the complaining witness. Why would he need to rape this homely girl anyway with a wife like this?" (p. 188)*

As Feild and Bienen (1980) pointed out, if a relatively unattractive victim charges rape, she may be perceived as lying—"No one would be turned on by her," the thinking would go. However, if the victim is attractive, some observers would maintain that the rapist was so overcome with passion that he could not help himself. Clearly, both approaches imply that the rapist's motivation is sexual rather than assaultive. Despite this common belief, most experts have concluded that sexual attraction and arousal have little to do with rape. (See Ellis, 1993, for another point of view.)

These conclusions are based on several different lines of evidence. First, let us examine the idea that sexual arousal can lead to sexual assault. Almost half the citizens in Feild and Bienen's (1980) research thought that most rapists commit rape out of a desire for sex. The vast majority believed that rape is a sex crime, and that it is committed by sexually frustrated individuals. If this were true, the incidence of rape would presumably be lower in permissive societies that provide acceptable sources of sexual release. This belief has in fact led, at times, to advocacy of legalized prostitution. Access to prostitutes, however, does not appear to reduce the incidence of rape. Rape is as prevalent where prostitutes are readily available as it is where prostitution is forbidden (Rio, 1991).

The hypothesis that rape is solely a product of sexual frustration is further weakened by the fact that most rapists have other sources of sexual release. Some are married, some live with partners, and some have consensual sex with their girlfriends. Even for the intensely sexually aroused man who lacks a sexual partner, there is always masturbation. If sexual release were the only motive for rape, most men would probably be reluctant to attack unwilling victims.

What about the idea that sexual assault stems from aggression and frustration? It is true that sexual assaults commonly increase during times of societal upheaval, war, and economic instability, all major sources of frustration and powerlessness. For example, with the massive influx of refugees into the Miami area in the early 1980s, the rate of sexual assault in that area doubled. Based on a major study of sexual assault in five U.S. cities, Schram (1978) observed:

> The sexual act or acts performed are often intended to humiliate and degrade . . . bottles, gun barrels and sticks may be thrust into [the victim's] vagina or anus; she may be compelled to swallow urine or perform fellatio with such force that she thinks she might strangle or suffocate; her breasts may be bitten or burned with cigarettes. (p. 53)

Such cruel violence plainly indicates extreme anger and aggression.

The conclusion that aggressive rather than sexual goals motivate the rapist is based on studies of convicted rapists, most of whom have attacked strangers. There is some evidence that unidentified males who rape acquaintances may have both aggressive and sexual motives. For example, Kanin (1985) found that the male assailants in his sample perceived themselves to be sexually deprived. Although the average number of monthly sexual outlets they reported far exceeded the number reported by nonassailants in his sample (6 versus less than 1), the number of sexual outlets they desired was 4.5 orgasms per week, compared to 2.8 for the control group. Kanin argued that assailants are therefore experiencing a sense of relative sexual deprivation. The flaw in this argument is that the nonassailants

also report a desire for greater sexual contact than they are having, but apparently they do not feel compelled to force women to engage in nonconsensual sex. Assailants reported receiving considerably more pressure from their peers to engage in sexual activity than did nonassailants. This finding provides some support for the idea that exaggerated gender-role norms and identification may underlie the perpetration of sexual assault, a hypothesis to which we now turn.

### Exaggerated Gender-Role Identity

Exaggerated adherence by both men and women to traditional gender-role norms may contribute to the occurrence of sexual assault. Specifically, the traditional socialization of men and women may set the stage for conflict and for sexual assault. Men are trained to believe that a truly masculine man is aggressive and has intense sexual needs. In fact, many men have felt pressured to engage in sexual activities when they did not wish to do so because of concerns about perceptions of their masculinity (Muehlenhard & Cook, 1988; O'Sullivan & Byers, 1993; Struckman-Johnson & Struckman-Johnson, 1994).

Traditional socialization also propagates the belief that women are not particularly interested in sex but that, with enough persuasion and seductive power, they can be "awakened" sexually. Accordingly, some rapists believe that even though their victims struggled, the women secretly enjoyed their rapist's sexual prowess. In other words, the assumption is that just because a woman *says* no it does not necessarily signify that she *means* no. Further, even if she means no initially, the sexual episode will lead her to change her mind.

For women, traditional feminine socialization only increases the barriers to communication between men and women. Women are encouraged to give conflicting messages. They are taught that the attention of men is extremely important and that the best way to obtain such attention is to be sexually attractive and desirable. According to the conventional wisdom, however, a "good" woman does not agree to sexual relations readily; even when she is sexually interested in her partner, she is supposed to maintain a facade of passive disinclination. If she appears to be too interested in having sex, she risks being labeled as "easy." As described in Chapter 6, some women have reported using the token no when they desired closer sexual intimacy to avoid assignment of such negative labels (Muehlenhard, 1988). Men are expected to push the issue of sex, and women are expected to resist. Both men and women learn about these gender-role expectations at an early age, which may impede rather than enhance heterosexual communication. Further, some acquaintance assaults may result from the confusing communication with which young people must cope when they are attempting to decipher others' desires.

Several other aspects of the relationship between traditional gender-role norms and rape should be mentioned. First, people who view women in traditional roles are likely to see rape as being the woman's fault and as being motivated by a man's need for sex. They also tend to believe that punishment for rape should be harsh because they perceive a raped woman as having lost something valuable (Feild & Bienen, 1980). Second, individuals who hold traditional gender-role attitudes are equally aroused by erotic stories of coercive and consenting sexual interactions, whereas people with more egalitarian attitudes are more aroused by stories of consenting than of coercive sex (Check & Malamuth, 1983). Third, those with traditional gender-role attitudes perceive rape victims as responding more favorably to coerced sex than do those holding more egalitarian gender-role attitudes. Traditional men also report a greater likelihood of committing assault (if assured that they would not be caught) than do more egalitarian men (Check & Malamuth, 1983). In addition, males who indicate some likelihood of committing rape if they could be sure of not getting caught are more aroused by rape depictions than are men who indicate no likelihood of raping someone (Malamuth, 1981). Finally, rapists themselves tend to be strong believers in the double standard, and so, ironically, they place great value on a woman's virginity (McCormick, 1994).

The belief that men ought to—or at least inevitably do—push for sexual intimacy and that women must therefore set limits is deeply ingrained in both Eastern and Western cultural traditions. Thus, as noted in Chapter 6, it is im-

portant that parents and others who help to shape young people's outlook and behavior take responsibility for teaching youths to communicate what they do and do not want in their interpersonal interactions, so that they may reduce the potential conflict arising from traditional male and female roles. Children and adolescents need to understand that violence is not a solution to anything, and that it is possible to clarify their present interest or lack of interest in sexual intimacy by discussing sexual feelings honestly and directly with potential partners.

We hope that research over the next few years will yield more information relevant to these hypotheses about the causes of sexual assault. In the meantime, both research and the efforts of various women's groups have done a great deal to reduce the pain associated with the aftermath of rape.

## The Aftermath of Sexual Assault

The anguish wrought by sexual assault often extends far beyond the actual experience (see Figure 18.1). For many victims, the rape episode itself is only the preface to a series of traumatic events that can go on for years. Further, the common belief that rape by a stranger is more traumatic than rape by a boyfriend or husband is not supported by research on assault (Kilpatrick, Best, Saunders, & Veronen, 1988; McCahill et al., 1979). The Kilpatrick group's study found that women assaulted by spouses or dates were as likely as those attacked by strangers to be "depressed, fearful, obsessive-compulsive, and sexually dysfunctional years after the assault" (p. 343). Table 18.3 highlights some of the difficulties experienced by assault victims during just the first year following the assault.

On the basis of their research with victims of rape seen at Boston City Hospital, Burgess and Holmstrom (1974) described a rape-trauma syndrome. The *rape-trauma syndrome* consists of two phases. The acute phase, which can last for several weeks after the rape, generally includes

rape-trauma syndrome—emotional and behavioral consequences that a victim experiences after being raped.

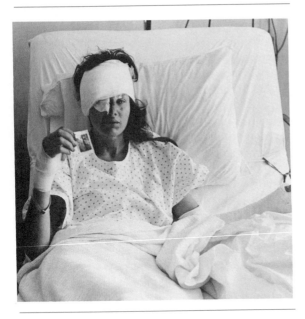

**FIGURE 18.1**
**The Assault Victim**
A typical assault victim experiences heightened fears and insecurities, troubled relationships, and changes in eating and sleeping patterns for at least a year following the incident. This rape victim, who escaped her assailant by leaping from a car, holds a picture of the scene of the assault.

**FIGURE 18.2**
**Counseling Following a Sexual Assault**
After a sexual assault, it is important that victims receive counseling and support to help reduce their fears and alleviate inappropriate feelings of guilt over the attack.

one of two basic reactions. With an expressive reaction, the victim cries frequently and expresses feelings of fear, anxiety, tension, and anger. With a controlled reaction, the woman is composed, calm, and subdued.

Following the acute phase, women go through a long-term reorganization phase. During this period, which can last more than a year, women experience a variety of reactions. Some move repeatedly and switch jobs or stop going to work. Fears of any situation resembling that in which the rape occurred are common. In addition, women experience many of the adjustment problems noted among the victims studied by the McCahill group (1979).

Finally, some women have a silent rape reaction (Burgess & Holmstrom, 1974). These women experience the kinds of reactions described above but they do not tell anyone about the assault. They are thereby deprived of the op-

portunity to obtain the support and counseling that may help them to resolve their fears and their undeserved feelings of guilt (see Figure 18.2).

The stress response patterns of victims of sexual coercion are consistent with the diagnostic criteria for post-traumatic stress disorder (PTSD), described in the fourth edition of the *Diagnostic and Statistical Manual (DSM-IV)* within the category of anxiety disorders (Burgess & Holmstrom, 1985). This diagnosis is often applied to Vietnam veterans, but Burgess and Holmstrom maintain that rape victims commonly experience similar anxiety problems. The principal characteristics of

**TABLE 18.3 Post-Assault Adjustment Problems**

| Adjustment Problem | Immediately After the Rape | 1 Year After the Rape |
|---|---|---|
| Increased fear of streets | 65.9% | 54.1% |
| Increased negative feelings toward unknown men | 57.5 | 50.7 |
| Decreased social activities | 50.3 | 53.6 |
| Change in sleeping patterns | 49.9 | 43.0 |
| Change in eating habits | 47.3 | 43.0 |
| Worsened sexual relations with partner[a] | 46.6 | 39.1 |
| Increased fear of being home alone | 43.2 | 24.8 |
| Worsened heterosexual relationships | 40.2 | 26.2 |
| Increased negative feelings toward known men | 36.6 | 29.3 |
| Increased nightmares | 31.1 | 20.7 |
| Worsened relations with husband or boyfriend[a] | 26.9 | 26.0 |
| Increased insecurities concerning sexual attractiveness | 18.7 | 15.7 |
| Worsened relations with family | 17.0 | 15.2 |

[a]Computed only for appropriate age groupings.

Source: McCahill et al., 1979, p. 74. Lexington Books, copyright 1979, D. C. Heath and Co. Preprinted by permission of the publisher.

individuals diagnosed as having PTSD are the experience of a major source of stress, intrusive imagery, numbing, and the development of two or more of the following symptoms that were not present before the stressing experience (Burgess & Holmstrom, 1985):

1. an exaggerated startle response, or hyperalertness;

2. disturbance in sleep patterns;

3. guilt about surviving or about behavior employed during the episode;

4. impairment of memory and/or power of concentration;

5. avoidance of activities that arouse recollection;

6. symptoms that symbolize or resemble the event, including anniversary anxiety reactions on the day or time of the month that the event occurred. If the stressor was a rape, the victim may experience disruptions in consensual sexual relationships; avoidance of sexual activities that he or she formerly enjoyed; or disturbances related to specific activities that took place during the event, such as swallowing if the assault involved forced oral penetration.

An event (in this case, rape) is defined as a major stressor if it is of significant magnitude to produce distinguishable symptoms in almost everyone experiencing it. "Intrusive imagery" refers to recurrent and intrusive memories, mental images, and/or nightmares related to the event; for example, rape victims say, "It is the first thing I think of when I wake up in the morning," or "I see his face on every man." One woman reported that she panicked when two people who were acting suspiciously came into the store where she worked (Burgess & Holmstrom, 1985, p. 50). "Numbing" refers to the experience of reduced responsiveness or reduced involvement with the environment. Victims may refer to being in a state of shock, or they may say that their assault experience does not seem real or that they cannot believe that it happened. One husband, commenting on the change in his wife's behavior

**Box 18.3**

## Was He Asking for It?

John Jones walks six blocks from his office to the subway every day after work. Occasionally, he gives some coins to some of the beggars who solicit money along his route.

One evening, he stayed at work later than usual because he had been invited to a dinner party and needed to change his clothes. He brought a nice shirt and sports coat with him to work and changed in the restroom. It was dark and rainy when he left the office. The other office workers had left for home earlier, and the street was deserted. About halfway to the subway, John noticed one of the beggars to whom he had occasionally given spare change approaching him. The man held out his hand, but John smiled and said, "Sorry, but I'm afraid I don't have any extra today," and continued on his way. He thought that the beggar was following him, so with some apprehension, he began walking more quickly. The next thing he knew, he had been tackled to the ground, and the beggar told him to give him his wallet or "I'll cut you up good!" It had gotten quite dark, so John could not see if the man had a knife or some other weapon; he decided that maybe it would be best if he just gave up the wallet. The beggar grabbed it and ran off.

John staggered home to call the police. When he got home, he still felt upset, so he fixed a drink, took a shower, and changed into dry clothes to try to calm down before making the call. He was told to come to the station to file a report.

Throughout his dealings with the police, and later, in court, John was exposed continuously to statements and questioning that sug-

gested that he had not really been robbed or that he had provoked the beggar into the assault.

1. It is six blocks between your office and the subway, so why didn't you take a cab? Aren't you asking for it when you parade the street every night?

2. Have you ever given away money to anyone before?

3. Did you ever give money to the person you *claim* mugged you?

4. You don't look like you've been hurt; how do we know that a mugging occurred?

5. Can you prove your wallet was taken?

6. Why were you so dressed up? Wasn't that just inviting the assault?

7. You've given him a dollar or two before and now you claim he took your wallet containing $50, but in giving him some money, weren't you in effect consenting to give him all your money?

8. You didn't resist the mugger; therefore, you must have really wanted to give him your wallet.

9. You said that he threatened you, but you didn't see the knife, and in fact, you handed over your wallet to him, so it doesn't sound like a mugging at all.

10. If you really were mugged, why did you wait two hours before calling? Maybe you really wanted to give the man your money at the time but then changed your mind later.

after she had been raped, said that "she used to be the spark plug in the family" (Burgess & Holmstrom, 1985, p. 50).

It should be clear from what you have already read that Burgess and Holmstrom are cor-

rect in saying that many victims of rape experience the criteria associated with the diagnosis of post-traumatic stress disorder. In addition to their personal reactions, many assault victims have to contend with a series of painful and humiliating episodes in police stations and in the courts, as Box 18.3 reveals. The aftermath of the mugging described in Box 18.3 seems ridiculously farfetched. It is not so farfetched, however, when the crime is sexual assault. In fact, by substituting the idea of sex for the idea of money in these questions, you can obtain a fairly realistic picture of the kind of interrogation that many victims of sexual assault have endured.

In response to the U.S. law-enforcement and judicial systems' inhumane treatment of many assault victims in the past, the burdens of rape victims have been lightened in recent years. The advent of rape-crisis centers, human-relations training programs for police, and reforms in most states' sexual-assault laws has broken a previously persistent pattern of institutionalized punishment of sexual-assault victims.

## What Should Assault Victims Do?

A victim of sexual assault should call the nearest rape-crisis center for help before changing clothes, bathing, or doing anything else. Many crisis centers provide a volunteer to accompany the victim during everything from initial medical treatment to final court appearances. Some centers also offer group-counseling sessions to help victims cope with the immediate and long-term effects of the attack. There are many of these centers throughout North America.

In the course of the medical examination and treatment administered after an assault, a victim usually receives a physical examination and an inspection of the genitals or other areas violated during the assault. A sperm sample is collected if possible and other evidence of assault is documented. Many states have recently passed laws requiring the county or state to pay the cost of such medical examinations. Nevada's law is quite comprehensive, taking financial responsibility not only for the medical treatment and counseling of the victim but also for the counseling of the victim's spouse (Feild & Bienen, 1980).

After undergoing a medical examination and treatment, the victim should report the assault to the police. The majority of victims, however, do not do so. Many are reluctant because they feel guilty and responsible for the assault. Further, some victims fear rejection by their mates, family members, and friends in the event that the assault becomes public knowledge. The small proportion of victims who overcome their fears and inhibitions enough to report the assault have no guarantee that the police will record the charge or that the rapist will be convicted.

## Sexual Assault and the Criminal Justice System

Police may determine that an assault charge is unfounded for many reasons (Burgess & Holmstrom, 1974; McCahill et al., 1979). If there are obvious discrepancies in the victim's story, or if the police conclude from their investigation that no offense occurred or was attempted, they will declare the charge unfounded. The McCahill group (1979) suggested that these may be legitimate reasons for making such a judgment. They note, however, that the police often use three other illegitimate reasons (but see Box 18.4).

The first of these is a prejudice against a specific victim and/or against the social class to which he or she belongs. Men and women who are poor, members of minority groups, prostitutes, or drug or alcohol abusers are likely to be objects of this kind of discrimination.

Second, if police believe that the victim in some way provoked the attack through dress or behavior, they may declare a case unfounded, regardless of the criminality of the episode itself. Feild and Bienen (1980) found that 78% of the 254 patrol officers whom they studied believed that women provoke rape by their appearance or by their behavior.

Third, even if police believe that an assault occurred, they may declare a case unfounded if the defendant seems unlikely to be convicted in court. For example, women who consume alcohol are often perceived as partially responsible for their assaults (Abbey et al., 1993). Police may feel that such women will be unable to withstand the courtroom tactics of defendants, so they do not file charges. If some rapists, in fact, select women who consume alcohol, the failure of police to record these assaults suggests that they are unintentionally aiding the rapists rather than the victims.

When a case is determined to be unfounded, it is not included in the crime statistics, and the

## Box 18.4

## False Rape Allegations

Just as there are many factors that lead authorities to declare a case unfounded when a rape actually occurred, there are a number of variables that contribute to false allegations of rape. Kanin (1994) studied the forcible rape cases over a nine-year period in a small city in a midwestern state. Of the 109 rapes reported, 41% of these were subsequently discovered to be false. These false allegations appeared to serve three major functions for the complainants (persons making charges).

1. *Alibi.* The need to provide a plausible explanation for some unfortunate or unforeseen consequence of a consensual sexual encounter. For example:

    *An unmarried 16-year-old female had sex with her boyfriend and later became concerned that she might be pregnant. She said she had been raped by an unknown assailant in the hopes that the hospital would give her something to abort the possible pregnancy. (p. 85)*

2. *Revenge.* Retaliation against a rejecting male. For example:

    *A 17-year-old female came to headquarters and said that she had been raped by a house parent*

*in the group home in which she lived. A female house parent accompanied her to the station and told the police she did not believe that a rape had occurred. The complainant failed the polygraph examination and then admitted that she liked the house parent, and when he refused her advances, she reported the rape to "get even with him." (p. 87)*

3. *Attention Seeking.* Fabrication where no one is usually identified as the rapist. For example:

    *An unmarried female, age 17, had been having violent quarrels with her mother, who was critical of her laziness and style of life. She reported that she was raped so that her mother would "get off my back and give me a little sympathy." (p. 87)*

Thus although rape charges are sometimes wrongly declared to be unfounded, sometimes a person is wrongly accused of rape. This situation illustrates the importance of following "due process" procedures to protect the rights of both the complainant and the alleged perpetrator.

---

authorities do not deal with it in any way. Under these conditions, victims may find themselves in the unexpected and bewildering predicament of having come to the police for aid (depicted by the media as the courageous and correct course to take), only to have the door slammed in their faces.

The assistance of a female crisis center volunteer is potentially useful in reducing the likelihood that the police will judge an assault charge unfounded. Moreover, the McCahill group's (1979) study of rape reports in Philadelphia showed that the presence of another woman during the report—whether she was the police officer taking the report or the secretary taking notes during the interview—was associated with a re-

duced proportion of rape charges that are declared unfounded.

About half of all complaints that are declared founded do *not* result in an arrest. Moreover, of those arrested, only 58% are prosecuted, and of those prosecuted, 46% are acquitted or have their cases dismissed. Based on these figures, a rapist's chances of being convicted for assault are only 4 in 100 (Feild & Bienen, 1980). Most of us would be willing to bet quite a bit of money if the probability of losing were only 4%.

### State Laws on Sexual Assault

In an effort to improve these rather grim statistics, dramatic changes are being made in the legal

**FIGURE 18.3**

**Political Activism and Rape-Reform Laws**
The fact that all 50 states have introduced reforms in their assault laws presumably is partially due to the efforts of demonstrators to call attention to sexual violence in our society. Take Back the Night marches, such as this one in New York City, have become common in many U.S. communities.

definition of assault and the treatment of the victim whose case does reach the courtroom. When victims, aided by crisis center volunteers, report assaults to the police and tell their stories in court, they not only diminish their own feelings of helplessness but also have the satisfaction of reducing the likelihood that the rapist will be able to attack others in the future.

Although every state in the United States has a law against rape or sexual assault, the specific definition of the crime has varied from state to state. In 1974 Michigan became the first state to enact a rape-reform law intended to end millennia of myths and legal traditions regarding rape. Since that time, all 50 states have made some

modifications in their sexual-assault laws. The reforms have included one or more of the following goals: a) to increase the likelihood of reporting assault, as well as the arrest and conviction rates; b) to make the legal standards for sexual assault consistent with those for other crimes; c) to increase victims' control over decisions made in the criminal-justice system; d) to limit cross-examination so as to protect victims from demeaning treatment during rape trials; and e) to sensitize and educate society about the status and rights of women (see Figure 18.3) (Marsh, 1988).

Many states no longer employ the term *rape* because of its connotation of forced penile-vaginal penetration. The broader phrase "sexual assault,'' which implies coercive sexual contact that does not necessarily involve penile-vaginal intercourse, has become more common. Also, many states have rewritten their laws in gender-neutral terms so that the victim and the offender can be either male or female. Finally, as noted earlier, more than half the states have eliminated marital status as a defense against sexual assault.

## What Constitutes Consent Versus Nonconsent?

The issue of consent remains a crucial one in the definition of sexual assault. In the hypothetical story presented in Box 18.3, it was implied that the mugged man consented to the mugging because he had earlier given away money to many people, including the mugger. That is, of course, patently absurd. However, the same logic has prevailed both in societal attitudes toward rape victims and in the arguments of attorneys defending alleged rapists; that is, if a victim, in the past, had consented to sex with anyone, or if she and the offender had ever engaged in a sexual interaction—even kissing—then the traditional view was that she must have consented to whatever sexual acts her assailant desired. In response to objections that such assumptions essentially put the victim rather than the assailant on trial, the U.S. Congress passed a law in 1979 known as the Rape Victim's Privacy Act. This law limited the extent to which evidence of the victim's previous sexual experience with people other than the defendant could be introduced. As President Jimmy Carter observed when he signed the bill:

*Too often rape trials have been as humiliating as the sexual assault itself. By restricting testimony on the victim's prior sexual behavior to that genuinely relevant to the defense, the Rape Victim's Act will prevent a defendant from making the victim's past the issue in the trials.*

This legislation may counteract the influence of a bias documented by Williams and Jacoby (1989) in laboratory research. They found that sexually experienced women are evaluated more negatively than are inexperienced women.

Another major change in some states' sexual assault laws is the elimination of the requirement that, to prove a sexual assault, the victim must have resisted. Under some circumstances, passive submission may be the victim's best strategy. Some victims who adopt passivity, however, have defense attorneys later describe them as having consented to the sexual contact. To prove nonconsent, the victims had to have done everything in their power to resist the assault, even if their actions might have exposed them to further brutality and injury. In part because of the work of rape-crisis centers throughout the country, lawmakers and judges are beginning to realize that a woman need not have the kind of injuries shown in Figure 18.2 to be a nonconsenting victim of sexual assault.

Steven Box (1983) pointed out the difficulty of establishing what is meant by the absence of consent. He observed that

*by making lack of consent the distinguishing feature of rape, the law misses an obvious point. It is not so much the absence of consent, although that has to exist, but the presence of coercion which makes rape fundamentally different from normal acts of intercourse. In a situation where the female's choice is severely restricted by the male being able to impose sanctions for refusal, the question of her consent should become secondary to his ability to coerce. (p. 123)*

Arguing that individuals should not be required to risk serious injury or even death to prove a charge of sexual assault later, legal reformers are working toward changing legislation in those states where a victim's resistance is still an issue, so that victims need prove only that the attacker threatened, and might have used, physical force.

Clearly, the victims of sexual coercion face ongoing difficulties long after they experience an episode of sexual assault. It would be desirable to find a means of preventing all sexual coercion, but at this point that objective appears to be impossible. We cannot imprison all males because some men force other persons to have sex, or, for that matter, all females because a small percentage of women compel others to have sex. Further, no infallible methods exist to predict which individuals will become rapists. Despite these obstacles, accumulated evidence has begun to suggest that there are some steps that an individual can take to reduce the risk of becoming a victim of sexual coercion.

## Factors Associated with Being Sexually Assaulted

In this section we review research that has compared sexual-coercion victims with nonvictims. Because there is no way to eliminate the risk that someone will *attempt* to coerce you, we also examine strategies that women have employed to escape assault. Although parallel data for male victims and nonvictims are lacking, much of the following discussion also applies to potential male victims.

At the outset, we must acknowledge that a discussion of risk-reduction strategies may be perceived by some as a demonstration that victims of assault secretly desire rape or bring on their assaults by taking risky or foolish chances. By way of analogy, consider another common crime, burglary. Providing information about the relative effectiveness of various burglary-prevention strategies that families might take does not imply that families victimized by thieves *want* to be burglarized. Nor should a family be blamed for provoking a burglary if they suspend delivery of their newspaper and mail while vacationing but fail to install timers that automatically turn the lights on at dusk.

Similarly, none of us is free of the risk of sexual coercion, and assault victims should not be blamed for attacks they suffer. There are strategies, however, that can be used to reduce the likelihood of an assault or to fend off an assault attempt. Of course, some victim-risk factors, such as age, are beyond the control of potential victims, but a few other factors have been identified that can be affected by choice.

As reviewed earlier, women in their adolescence and early 20s are at greater risk of an assault attempt than are older women. Marital status is also correlated with risk of assault, with single women being at greatest risk, followed by divorced or separated women; married women are at least risk (McCahill et al., 1979; Russell, 1984). Studies of reported assaults have shown an overrepresentation of poor and/or non-White women. But this difference may stem from the fact that these women have less access to non-public sources of support following assault than do their more affluent, White counterparts. Representative samples of unidentified victims indicate that social class and race are not accurate predictors of sexual assault. In any event, it is difficult or impossible to alter factors such as age, marital status, or socioeconomic status to try to reduce the risk of assault.

Other risk factors have been identified that are somewhat more controllable. The chances of victimization increase as women lead "riskier" (less protected or less "traditional") lives—for example, by being sexually active, living apart from parents and (if in college) outside a dorm, lacking a visible male partner, experimenting with drugs, or having alcohol-abuse problems (Abbey et al., 1993; Koss, 1985; Mynatt & Allgeier, 1990). Among adolescent women, those who are alienated from their parents and teachers, identify with a delinquent peer group, and engage in delinquent acts themselves are more likely to become victims of sexual assault than are their non-alienated counterparts (Ageton, 1983).

The general sexual climate within the peer groups of victims differs from that within the peer groups of nonvictims. Of those females aged 14 to 17 in Hall and Flannery's (1985) study who said that none of the five girls whom they knew best had had sex, 6% had been raped. Of those who said that three to five of their girlfriends had had sex, 22% had been raped. Hall and Flannery hypothesized that if a young woman is part of a peer group known to be sexually active and is sexually active herself, the man who rapes her may perceive her as being interested in sex and as having led him on.

In addition, the consensual sexual experience of sexual-assault victims is greater than that of nonvictims (Koss, 1985; Koss & Dinero, 1988; Mynatt & Allgeier, 1990). In Koss's research, victims reported an average of 12 sexual partners, whereas nonvictims reported an average of 4 partners. Compared with nonvictims, those women experiencing rape were more likely to have had as their first sexual partners strangers, casual dates, or married men, and were less likely to have had as their first sexual partners steady boyfriends or fiancés. Motives for having first intercourse also varied between the two groups. Victims were more likely to report that they felt pressured or obligated or that there was nothing that they could do about it. In contrast, nonvictims engaged in first intercourse because of their own desire or a desire to please their partners. Victims in the Koss study were also less likely than nonvictims to report that they believed that their first intercourse experience would lead to marriage.

### Reducing Your Risk of Sexual Assault

Many of these steps are more applicable to acquaintance assault than to assault by strangers, but, as we have seen, most assaults involve acquaintances.

1. *Determine your sexual policies.* What are the conditions under which you would find sexual intimacy acceptable? If you have not thought about what you need in a relationship before you would feel comfortable with or desirous of sexual contact, you may communicate considerable ambivalence about your wishes to a partner, who may interpret your ambiguity as a desire for him to "persuade" you. Thus it may be helpful to make a list of your general sexual policies. What kind of person would you find acceptable as a potential sexual partner? How well would you want to know this person prior to physical intimacy? How much commitment would you need before you found sexual relations acceptable? Where and when would sexual contact be comfortable for you? Add any other factors that you consider important in making a decision about having a sexual relationship. People sometimes alter their policies, but it is advantageous for you to clarify in your own mind the general conditions under which sexual intimacy is acceptable to you.

2. *Discuss your policies regarding sexual activities.* We commonly negotiate such nonsexual activities as where to eat dinner and what movie to see; why not explicitly negotiate the acceptability and timing of sexual activities as well? Although evidence directly demonstrates that such negotiations do *not* eliminate the risk of

assault attempts, the directness and firmness with which a woman communicates her nonconsent to sexual intercourse are positively related to successfully resisting an attempt at forced sexual contact (Bart & O'Brien, 1985; Byers & Lewis, 1988; Quinsey & Upfold, 1985).

3. *Negotiate in public, and avoid being alone with a person until you believe that you can trust him or her.* An individual's perpetration of an assault on another person is more difficult if other people are present than if the couple are alone in an apartment or an isolated car. Quinsey and Upfold's (1985) analysis of attempted versus completed rapes indicated that rapists were least likely to be deterred when the attempt was made inside a building or car and against someone whom they knew.

4. *Avoid becoming intoxicated if you are with a person with whom you do not wish to become intimate.* Use of alcohol or drugs by assailants and victims is common at the time of a sexual assault (Barbaree et al., 1993; Koss et al., 1988). Intoxication lowers the inhibitions of a potential assailant; it may also impede the ability of a potential victim to escape an assault attempt.

5. *Make your feelings known both verbally and nonverbally.* In the event that someone does try to force you to have sex, communicate in every way possible that you do not want sexual contact (see Figure 18.4).

In their victimization survey of 60,000 U.S. households, the Bureau of Justice Statistics (1986) found that potential sexual-assault victims were able to fight off the assailant 51% of the time when he carried a gun, 58% of the time when he carried a knife, and 72% of the time when he was unarmed. Bart (1981) compared the experiences of a sample of women who had successfully resisted assault on one occasion and had been raped on another occasion. On the occasions when they were raped, talking was the main strategy they used to try to thwart the rape; on the occasions when they successfully resisted the assault attempt, they employed several strategies, including struggling, screaming, and talking. Victim resistance of any kind tends to deter assault, but screaming is a particularly strong deterrent (Quinsey & Upfold, 1985). Most males interpret screaming as strong evidence of noncon-

**FIGURE 18.4**

**Self-Defense Against Sexual Assault**

Self-defense classes may help women to reduce their vulnerability to sexual assault
in two ways: by providing specific techniques with which to confront an assailant
and by increasing the ability to escape assault situations.

sent (Byers & Lewis, 1988). The fact that a scream
is more likely to be effective if someone can hear
it is another reason to avoid being alone with a
person until you believe that you can trust him
or her.

Males have cited victim resistance as the primary reason for the failure of an assault attempt.
The only other reason for "failure" reported by
the males was their own guilt or fright (Ageton,
1983). Some self-identified rapists in Kanin's
(1985) sample reported surprise that their victims
had been so easily intimidated; the assailants described other occasions of (unsuccessful) assault
attempts on dates that clearly had been rebuffed.

One important qualification should be added
here. Although the vast majority of assaults are
carried out by acquaintances and do not involve
the threat of lethal weapons, if someone attempts

to assault you using a weapon as the means of
coercion, resistance may be ill advised.

In summary, take as much active control of
your environment as you can. Remember, however, that following all these steps will not eliminate the possibility of being sexually assaulted
or seriously injured during an assault. There are
no absolute rules for dealing with all assaults; ultimately, you must decide which strategy seems
most likely to get you out of the particular assault
situation with the least amount of harm. We live
in a society in which violence is commonplace,
and hostility and aggression are often expressed
against inappropriate targets. Changes in societal
attitudes will come slowly. In the meantime, we
hope that the information provided in this chapter will help you reduce your risk of being sexually assaulted. In the next section we consider

another form of coercion that some of the preceding steps may be useful in combating: sexual harassment.

## Sexual Harassment

People can be coerced into sexual contacts through means other than those described in the preceding overview. In this section we discuss the abuse of power to coerce others into sexual relations. *Sexual harassment* appears in diverse guises and in many different environments. For example, an employer may use the power to hire, promote, and fire to force an employee into having sexual relations (see Figure 18.5). An instructor may use the power to grade to coerce sexual intimacy. Harassment can also take place in the context of the relationship between doctors—either physicians or psychotherapists—and their patients or clients, and between clergy and parishioners. All these situations involve interactions between two people who are not equal in power, and the individual with greater economic, evaluative, or psychological power may employ that advantage to obtain sexual gratification from an individual who is in a subordinate position.

Sexual harassment is quite common. An overview of studies on sexual harassment in a variety of settings suggests that female workers or students have at least a 40% chance of encountering sexual harassment in their place of work or study (Barak, Fisher, & Houston, 1992).

### Sexual Harassment in Occupational Settings

Sexual harassment was not clearly perceived as a social problem before the mid-1970s (Brewer & Berk, 1982). Initially, the law defined sexual harassment rather narrowly as constituting the re-

**FIGURE 18.5**
**Sexual Harassment at Work**
Sexual harassment may involve physical force, or it may occur in more subtle ways, as this photograph shows. The man's body position makes it difficult for the woman to avoid his advances. If he is her employer, she may be afraid to tell him to move away out of fear that he will use his power as her boss to retaliate with negative evaluations or termination of her job.

quirement that sexual relations be part of getting or keeping a job. Equal Employment Opportunity Commission (EEOC) rulings on sexual harassment in 1980 expanded the definition to encompass *any* unwanted verbal or nonverbal sexual behavior in the workplace. The EEOC ruled that unwelcome sexual advances, requests for sexual favors, and other verbal or physical contact of a sexual nature constitute sexual harassment when a) submission to such conduct is made either explicitly or implicitly a term or condition of an individual's employment; b) submission to or rejection of such conduct by an individual is used as the basis for employment decisions affecting the individual; or c) such conduct has the purpose or effect of unreasonably interfering with an individual's work performance or creating an intimidating, hostile, or offensive working environment.

Early research on harassment relied on self-selected respondents such as women attending a meeting on the topic of harassment, the vast ma-

**sexual harassment**—the use of status and/or power to coerce or attempt to coerce a person into having sex; also, suggestive or lewd comments directed at a person in occupational, educational, or therapeutic settings.

**Box 18.5**

## Research Findings on Sexual Harassment

1. About a third to half of working women have suffered some negative consequences from sexual harassment, whereas few men report problems in this area.

2. When asked whether they had ever quit a job because of sexual harassment, 10% to 15% of working women say yes.

3. Married women are less likely to report having been victimized by harassment than are single, divorced, or cohabiting women.

4. Men are more flattered by sexual overtures from women at work than are women by such overtures from men.

5. About half of male initiators are supervisors, and the more severe the harassment, the more likely the initiator is to be a supervisor rather than a coworker.

6. Men who rate high on a measure of likelihood to harass sexually hold adversarial sexual beliefs, have difficulty assuming others' perspectives, endorse traditional male gender-role stereotypes, are high in authoritarianism, and report a higher likelihood of raping if assured of not being caught.

Sources: Bingham & Scherer, 1993; Gutek, 1985; Loy & Stewart, 1984; Pryor, 1994; Tangri, Burt, & Johnson, 1982.

jority of whom had experienced on-the-job harassment (Silverman, 1976). Later studies employing random samples of workers probably provide a more accurate estimate of the extent of harassment in the United States; some of the findings from these studies are presented in Box 18.5. Grieco (1987) mailed questionnaires to all nurses in Boone County, Missouri, inquiring about their experiences with harassment during their careers. Grieco ranked the 496 nurses who responded according to the most severe form of harassment that they had experienced:

0 = no harassment (18%)

1 = suggestive stares, comments, whistles, or other behaviors (13%)

2 = lewd comments (13%)

3 = grossly inappropriate sexual comment or brief, minor touching (35%)

4 = grossly inappropriate touching (e.g., breast fondling, mauling) (20%)

5 = attempted or actual rape (1%)

A greater proportion of female nurses (82%) than male nurses (67%) reported having been harassed. The fact that the majority of both males

and females reported harassment suggests that the phenomenon is common.

Bullough's (1990) historical review of sexual harassment in the nursing profession suggests that this trend is not recent. In fact, he suggests that the famous nurse Florence Nightingale took steps in her training of nurses to prevent them from being harassed by establishing separate residence areas for nurses and writing regularly to hospital authorities about her concerns:

> In fact, the danger of dark stairwells is a reoccurring theme in her letters. She was also concerned with the treatment of nurses by male physicians and surgeons and mentioned some of the worst offenders by name. Somehow nurses needed to be protected from this. (p. 6)

A telephone survey indicated that the greater the organizational power of the harasser over the harassed, the greater the seriousness of the harassment (Loy & Stewart, 1984). Other research has revealed that, although supervisors are more likely to harass subordinates than are other coworkers, victims are also harassed by customers, clients, and other people with whom they must cooperate, such as a partner in a police car (Benson & Thomson, 1982). For example, although harassment levels of 3 or above on Grieco's (1987) scale were more likely from doctors (31%) than coworkers (22%), the greatest proportion of harassers were patients (54%).

Harassment victims report various reactions to the unwanted approaches, including nervousness, loss of motivation, sleeplessness, uncontrolled anger or crying, and weight loss. The women in Loy and Stewart's (1984) sample reacted to their harassment with responses ranging from ignoring the harassment (32%) to saying something to the harasser (39%) to quitting their jobs or seeking a transfer (17%). Fewer than 2% of the women sought legal help, and only 3% approached a grievance committee, perhaps because such committees are a relatively new phenomenon in workplaces. Harassment victims in Gutek's (1985) random sample of workers in the Los Angeles area were also unlikely to report the episode(s) to authorities. Awareness of the problem has increased recently, however, with the rise in demonstrations by women's groups to call attention to the issue, and because of some well-publicized lawsuits.

Like perpetrators of sexual assault, those who sexually harass their employees or coworkers appear to have a strong need for dominance and power (Gutek & Nakamura, 1983). As is the case with sexual assault, some observers blame the victim for "inviting" sexual harassment. During her testimony before a Senate subcommittee reviewing federal guidelines aimed at eliminating harassment, antifeminist Phyllis Schlafly suggested that victims ask for their harassment:

> Sexual harassment on the job is not a problem for the virtuous woman, except in the rarest of cases. . . . Men hardly ever ask sexual favors of women from whom the certain answer is no. . . . Virtuous women are seldom accosted by unwelcome sexual propositions or familiarities. (Committee on Labor and Human Resources, 1981, p. 400)

Schlafly provided no data to support her assertions. Generalizing from the research conducted on victim precipitation in cases of sexual assault, however, the actual situation is probably the reverse of that described by Schlafly. That is, except in the rarest cases, it is most likely that sexual harassment victims do not cause their own victimization.

Not all sexual intimacy between coworkers constitutes harassment. As Gutek and Nakamura (1983) pointed out, mutual attraction and flirtation commonly occur in the workplace, and men and women alike sometimes seek, and find, marriage partners at work. Mutually consenting adult sexual relations are difficult to attain, however, when there is an imbalance of power between partners in work or educational settings, the topic to which we turn now.

## Sexual Harassment in Educational Settings

Sexual harassment in college settings differs in several respects from sexual harassment in the workplace. Although students are highly dependent on faculty members for grades, letters of recommendation, and research opportunities, they may have more options than employees for finding other faculty members with whom they can work if a particular faculty member attempts to harass them. Furthermore, students are in school for only a specific period of time, whereas employees may feel pressured to put up with harassment because of the need to keep a job or preserve seniority. On the other hand, students tend to be more vulnerable and naive about harassment than employees. Students who are in their late teens or early 20s may be flattered by the attention of a professor of whom they are in awe, and they may not understand the inappropriateness of having sexual relations with a powerful person who is in a position to provide or withhold aid that is important for the student's future career. Some students do feel coerced, however (see Box 18.6).

Harassment in educational settings is quite prevalent at both the undergraduate and the graduate-school levels. In their review of studies conducted at 11 different universities, Allen and Okawa (1987) found that, in response to anonymous questionnaires, between 13% and 33% of students reported experiencing harassment, which ranged from instructors' leering and patting in an offensive manner to threats or bribery to gain sexual intimacy. Although you may think

**Box 18.6**

## Student-Instructor Sexual Relations: Sexual Harassment?

In a random sample of undergraduate and graduate-student males and females, Allgeier, Travis, Zeller, and Royster (1990) asked students about their experiences with sexual invitations or relationships with their instructors. Instructors who have such relationships with students in their classes may have a conflict of interest between their personal feelings and their professional responsibilities. We did not use the phrase "sexual harassment" in the study. We found that, although some students were distressed by the invitation, others reported having a positive experience with the instructor. Men were as likely to report having (hetero)sexual affairs with their instructors as were women, but men were less likely to be disturbed by an instructor's advances than women were. Here are a few abridged versions of their experiences.

The first case exemplifies classic sexual harassment. This 23-year-old woman in a master's program was approached half a dozen times by a faculty member whom she had considered her mentor. She no longer has a mentor and now would not consider working with a male professor.

*The [first] approach took place in the professor's office during a scheduled review of an assignment (all students in the class had these reviews done). I was asking a question when he came to my chair, and brought me into his arms, saying, "I need a hug." I was so ignorant it never entered my mind that a professor would put the moves on one of his students. He kissed me on the mouth, which shocked me and frightened me a bit. He said: "I want to have you in my life forever, not for just a little while." He even had tears in his eyes. Through the assignments that were done, this man gained access to personal information about his students which I believe he used to choose whom to pursue. There were more contacts . . . , including his coming to my home, professing undying love. I am thankful that I never went to bed with the man. I later discovered that there were six or seven students he had pursued.*

*Of the other women I spoke to, I was the only one willing to confront him. I met with him and told him all that I had found out. He denied all of it, including his encounters with me, and said that I must have imagined it. The next week, he took some key people in my professional and personal life out to lunch and informed them that I was mentally impaired. He told them that I was a dependent personality and that I had pursued him sexually. He said he had rebuffed me, after much patient endurance, and that now I was trying to ruin him by spreading rumors about him pursuing me.*

On the other hand, there are instances in which students perceive sexual liaisons as completely acceptable if they are by mutual consent. The majority of students experiencing such relationships did not feel harmed or put at a disadvantage by having sex with their instructors. An undergraduate woman reported a romantic relationship with a male teaching assistant, asserting that they kept their educational association separate from their personal relationship. "I'm very glad our relationship occurred. He's one of the best friends I've met here," she wrote. Students feeling this way are unlikely to be swayed by university policies prohibiting instructor-student affairs.

Even so, given the potential for abuse by the instructor or by the student, as the following description shows, an instructor is wise to postpone a sexual liaison with a student until the end of the educational connection, with its various sources of impact on the student (grades, assistantships, letters of recommendation), and sometimes on the instructor. This was the experience of an 18-year-old male who was approached by a female graduate student instructor.

*She told me that she was very lonely and that she found me attractive. She asked me to come over to her place, and at first I was hesitant, but then she told me I would get an A! I really didn't get an educational experience. I was given an A for satisfying her sexually. I still feel hurt and used because I came here to get an education. Also I feel resentful and am very wary of female teachers. It ended because she said she was moving on to another student in her class this semester. I told her if she doesn't give me money, I'll tell. I think it is very wrong, a blatant disregard of the purposes of an education.*

that these students are imagining that their instructors' interest in them is not just academic, Fitzgerald and her colleagues (1988) administered an anonymous survey to male faculty, and 25% of them reported having had sexual encounters with students. It is interesting that only one faculty member described the relationship as harassment.

Somers (1982) found that 6% of the females in her sample had experienced subtle pressure to engage in sexual activity in return for a grade, a job, or a promotion on campus, and 11% had been subjected to offensive touching, patting, or pinching by their instructors. In Somers's sample, 8% of the women reported that either they themselves or others whom they knew had dropped a class or avoided a particular instructor or teaching assistant because of his embarrassing sexual language or advances. You may have had a similar experience, or you may know of other students who have avoided a class because of the reputation of the professor or teaching assistant. You may have simply accepted it as part of life, but it is sad to have the potential resources available to you as a college student reduced by the specter of harassment.

As with sexual assault, the reporting of harassment to academic authorities is uncommon. For example, in Allen and Okawa's (1987) study, although 81% of harassed students at the University of Illinois knew that campus policy prohibited sexual harassment, only 5% of those who had experienced harassment reported it to any university office or official. This low rate of reporting may stem from students' reporting experiences that objectively constitute sexual harassment on anonymous surveys, but rarely perceiving themselves as having been sexually harassed (Barak et al., 1992).

Inappropriate sexual contact also occurs between graduate students and their professors.

Several surveys have been conducted to determine the prevalence of sexual contact between female psychologists and their professors during graduate-school training. Between 14% and 25% of the women in these samples reported such intimacy, and almost half reported having been the target of sexual advances by one or more of their professors. Inappropriate sexual contacts with their professors are more likely among younger than older female graduate students, and more likely among those who were divorcing or separating during training (34%) than among women who were single or married (22%) (Glaser & Thorpe, 1986; Pope, Levenson, & Schover, 1979; Robinson & Reid, 1985). The problem with such student-teacher relationships, of course, is that the students have less power than professors and thus cannot freely give informed consent. The vulnerability of students to advances by their professors is underscored by findings from Glaser and Thorpe's (1986) survey of female psychologists. Those who had been approached sexually by, and/or had sex with, their professors reported that as students they had at the time perceived the advances as less coercive, unethical, and disruptive of their educational relationships with their professors than they now perceived them to be.

Some universities have taken forceful steps to counteract this threat to educational freedom. In 1986, for example, the University of Iowa adopted a policy prohibiting any form of sexual advances, requests for sexual favors, or other verbal or physical conduct of a sexual nature toward students by faculty members. The policy also bars faculty members from having romantic relationships with students enrolled in their classes or with students whose academic work they are supervising.

If you are sexually harassed by an instructor, you should contact authorities on your campus about the incident. Seek out another professor whom you trust or the chairperson of the department. If these people are not supportive, talk with someone at the campus affirmative-action or civil-rights office. Sometimes students are reluctant to report such incidents for fear that the instructor in question will give them failing grades or will be fired. Current affirmative-action regulations protect people who file harassment complaints from grade discrimination. If you believe that the instructor who has made advances toward you is not approaching other students, and if there have been no other reports of harassment, the instructor generally is put on probation and watched closely. Assuming that there are no further reports of harassment, no career damage occurs. It is common for instructors who engage in such behavior to do so with many students, however; thus those who are reluctant to report an incident should consider the welfare of their fellow students, who could also become targets, rather than that of the harassing instructor.

## Sexual Harassment in Therapeutic Settings

The issue of power difference is particularly stark in the case of the sexual harassment of a patient or client by a physician or psychotherapist. Physicians and psychologists are highly trained, powerful members of society. They usually have more status than the patients or clients who, because of illness or psychological difficulties, seek their help. For the patient or client, compounding the problem of dealing with sexual harassment is the fact that a client's charge of abuse may be ascribed by the therapist or physician to the client's mental instability (similar to the situation faced by the student described in Box 18.6).

Occasionally, one-sided or mutual attraction may develop between the professional and the patient: 87% of the 575 psychotherapists surveyed by Pope, Keith-Spiegel, and Tabachnick (1986) reported feeling sexual attraction toward certain clients. As noted in Chapter 8, such feelings are normal, but professionals who act on their erotic feelings with people who come to them for help are not serving their clients' best interests. Nonetheless, studies with different

samples indicate that 5% to 10% of therapists become sexually intimate with their clients (Pope et al., 1986). Further, about three-quarters of therapists who have sex with their clients do so with numerous clients; Pope and Bouhoutsos (1987) reported that one therapist had been involved in sexual relations with more than 100 clients.

Such therapist-client sexual contacts accounted for 56% of the disciplinary actions taken by the licensing board for psychologists in California (Vinson, 1984). Cases involving physicians and their patients have also been reported (Dale, 1986; Plaut & Foster, 1986). The long-term correlates of such contact for the clients or patients are almost always negative, ranging from hesitation about seeking further professional help to depression, hospitalization, and suicide (Bouhoutsos et al., 1983; Grunebaum, 1986; Sonne et al., 1985; Zelen, 1985).

In addition to the problems attending sexual relationships between people unequal in status, problems arise from the fact that professionals' and clients' motives for sexual intimacy are likely to be quite different. Professionals may perceive themselves as offering therapeutic contact for a brief period of time, but clients, generally dependent while seeking therapeutic or medical help, may believe that they are in love and that their sexual contact is part of a long-term primary relationship, perhaps leading to marriage.

## Sexual Abuse of Children

We turn now to the phenomenon of adult-child sexual relations, the variations in the self-reported consequences for children, and possible reasons for the sexual victimization of children. We also discuss incestuous relationships, with an emphasis on adult-child sexual relations.

Adult-child sexual interactions by definition involve coercion because children are not legally capable of giving informed consent to sexual activity. An individual who provides informed consent understands both the meaning and the possible consequences of an action, but children and young adolescents do not have a clear understanding of sexuality. One of the main reasons adults are severely punished for sexual activities with children is that they take advantage of a child's naiveté. Because a minor cannot give informed consent, sexual relations with a minor are punishable under *statutory rape* laws, even if the minor cooperated willingly.

When a sexual relationship involves two people who are related to each other, it is called *incest*. In general, incest refers to any sexual interaction between individuals who are so closely related that marriage between them would be illegal. The word *incest* comes from Latin and means ''impure'' or ''soiled.'' Although incest can occur between two people of any age, it most frequently involves a child and an adult family member or sibling. Of the thousands of cultures about which we have information, only a few have not held rigidly to a taboo against incest within the immediate family. Such findings have led some to claim that the taboo against incest is universal. This conclusion needs to be qualified, however, by the fact that the definition of incest varies from one time and place to another.

In the United States, the definition of a child or minor varies from one state to another, but the age of consent usually ranges from 16 to 18. Sexual activity between a child—however defined—and an adult is a crime in every state. Doctors, psychologists, teachers, and health professionals who work with children are legally required to report to legal authorities all suspected cases of the sexual abuse of children. By law, authorities must investigate these reports, and district attorneys must prosecute the cases.

## Prevalence of Sexual Abuse of Children

Although some cultures permit adult-child sexual contact, they are the exception rather than the rule (Reiss, 1986). Media attention to the sexual abuse of children has been particularly widespread in North America, but the phenomenon exists internationally. In Sweden, for example, research with a sample of 1,000 adults indicated that 9% of the women and 3% of the men reported having been sexually abused before they were 18 years old (Reiss, 1986).

In attempting to determine the prevalence of any phenomenon in a nation, it is useful to have a nationally representative sample, but until Finkelhor, Hotaling, Lewis, and Smith (1990) reported the results of a telephone poll of more than 2,600 U.S. adults, no such data were available on the prevalence of the sexual abuse of children. Because we refer often to their findings in the remainder of this chapter, we will describe their procedures.

Random-digit dialing allowed the researchers to tap both listed and unlisted telephone numbers. This approach has the additional advantage of preventing identification of respondents by either name or address, thus increasing anonymity. However, generalizations from the findings of Finkelhor and his colleagues are limited by several factors, including the difficulty of recalling past events (see Chapter 2) and a 24% refusal rate. Still, the demographics of their sample conformed with those of U.S. citizens as a whole. The researchers asked respondents four screening questions about past experiences (occurring at age 18 or under) with what they might now consider to be sexual abuse. These included attempts by others to touch them sexually, to initiate sexual acts including intercourse, to photograph them in the nude, to exhibit themselves, or to perform sex acts in their presence (p. 20).

Of the respondents, 27% of the women and 16% of the men answered yes to one of the questions, and detailed follow-up questions were then posed to probe their experience further. For a breakdown of these experiences, see Table 18.4. A remarkably similar proportion (25%) of women in the Kinsey group's (1953) sample reported having been sexually approached in childhood by adults.

Other contemporary estimates, based on random samples of adults, indicate rates of unwanted sexual contact during childhood ranging from 6% to 62% for females and from 3% to 6% for males (Beitchman et al., 1992; Hrabowy & All-

---

**statutory rape**—sexual intercourse with a person who is under the legal age of consent.

**incest**—sexual activity between family members who are too closely related to be able to marry legally.

**TABLE 18.4 Sexual-Abuse Experiences of a Representative American Sample**

Participants in a telephone survey were asked, with respect to each of the following experiences, if they could remember having had any of those experiences "that you would now consider sexual abuse" prior to age 19. Here are their responses.

| Experiences | Men (N = 1145) Percentage Responding Yes | Women (N = 1481) Percentage Responding Yes |
|---|---|---|
| 1. Being the target of attempted or completed sexual intercourse | 9.5 | 14.6 |
| 2. Being touched, grabbed, kissed, or having your body rubbed by someone else's body | 4.5 | 19.6 |
| 3. Being photographed nude | — | 0.1 |
| 4. Having someone exhibit their body parts | 1.0 | 3.2 |
| 5. Having sex acts performed in your presence | 0.3 | 0.3 |
| 6. Having oral sex or sodomy | 0.4 | 0.1 |

Source: Adapted from Finkelhor et al., 1990, p. 21.

geier, 1987; Kilpatrick, 1992). These figures vary to some extent as a function of the population being sampled, the definition of sexual abuse (whether the word *unwanted* is included), and the cut-off age employed (for example, whether respondents are asked about unwanted sexual contacts before the age of 14, 16, or 18).

In the Finkelhor et al. (1990) national sample, 9% of the males and 22% of the females who reported being victims of attempted or completed sexual relations during childhood had experienced them with relatives—aunts or uncles, siblings, parents, or stepparents. An additional 5% of males and 5% of females had been involved in attempted or completed sexual contacts with cousins, but such relations are not illegal in some states. Reports of sexual contact with mothers were extremely rare: only 1 person (a female) in almost 800 college students in Finkelhor's (1979) survey reported an incestuous experience with a mother.

In another survey, Nelson (1986) studied the experiences of 100 individuals who answered the following ad, which she placed in several national newspapers and magazines.

*Research Project: Looking for people who have had incest experience (good or bad) for questionnaire and/or interview. Write P.O. Box _____ .*

Her ad yielded 100 participants, who reported a total of 137 episodes of incest. Seventy-six percent of the contacts occurred when the respondents were children. Of the 137 incidents, 67 were father-child incest, 58 were sibling contacts, 9 involved adult relative-child contacts, and only 3 involved mother-son incest. One man reported that as an adult, he had had coitus with his adult sister, his mother, and his grandmother! The experience was described as positive by more than 75% of the men versus only 25% of the women. As would be expected, those who saw themselves as consenting partners were three times more likely to have positive feelings about the experience than were those who perceived themselves as perpetrators or victims. Only one of the episodes was reported to the police. The majority of respondents (58%) felt that the laws should be changed to allow consensual (presumably adult-adult) incest relationships (see Box 18.7).

In the United States, the number of cases of child abuse* reported annually to the American Humane Association's national data-collection system leaped from 1,975 to 22,918 from 1976 to 1982. This huge jump in reported child sexual abuse probably resulted from increased media attention and the enforcement of state laws requiring health professionals to report suspected cases of sexual abuse, rather than from a sudden epidemic in the incidence of the sexual abuse of children. Support for the conclusion that the actual incidence of child abuse is not showing systematic marked increases comes from examination of data from different *cohorts* in Finkelhor et al.'s (1990) sample. Specifically, the sexual abuse rates for older women—with the exception of those aged 60 and above at the time of the survey—were quite similar:

Ages 18–29: 30%

Ages 30–39: 31%

Ages 40–49: 37%

Ages 50–59: 29%

Ages 60 and above: 19%

Rates for males, although showing a lower range of 11% to 19%, have the same general, nonsystematic fluctuations as are found among females. A national survey in Canada found no cohort effects, although there was an elevated rate of experience with sexual abuse during childhood among women aged 18 to 20 at the time of the survey (Badgley et al., 1984). However, there does not appear to be an increasing epidemic of sexual abuse of children. Instead, particular conditions—more or less prominent at various

cohort—a group from a particular generation; for example, those born from 1960 to 1969 are members of a different cohort than those born from 1970 to 1979.

---

*We occasionally use the phrase "child abuse" synonymously with the phrase "sexual abuse of children". The kind of child abuse that involves the neglect of children or the nonsexual physical beatings and other abuse of children has not disappeared, but as Okami (1990) pointed out, such destructive behavior has taken a back seat to the sexual abuse of children in the concerns of our society, funding agencies, and researchers; it is also beyond the scope of this book.

points in the past few generations—may increase the likelihood of child abuse (and other forms of abuse and violence, such as sexual assault). We look at these next.

## Risk Factors for Sexual Abuse During Childhood

Based on their nationally representative study of adults, Finkelhor et al. (1990) identified two risk factors for males and four primary risk factors for females for sexual abuse during childhood. For males, the risk factors were living with their mothers alone or living with two nonbiological parents. For females, the risk factors included having an unhappy family life, living without a biological parent, having an inadequate sex education, and region of residence. Separation from a biological parent during a major portion of childhood was also a risk factor in a survey by Bagley and Ramsey (1986).

Based on his earlier sample of college students, Finkelhor (1984) identified some of these factors plus some additional risk variables. Notably, having a stepfather was associated with having been sexually abused, although not necessarily by the stepfather. Also, being reared by a sex-punitive mother was correlated with experiencing sexual abuse. By "sex-punitive mother," Finkelhor meant a mother who warned, scolded, and punished her children for asking questions about sexuality, for masturbating, and for looking at sexually suggestive or explicit pictures. Finkelhor found that girls with sex-punitive mothers were 75% more vulnerable to sexual victimization than was the typical girl in the sample, and having a sex-punitive mother was the second most powerful predictor of victimization after having a stepfather. Finkelhor (1984) suggested that

*if mothers have repressed all the healthier ways of satisfying sexual curiosity, these daughters may be more vulnerable to an adult or authority figure who appears to give them permission and opportunity to explore sex, albeit in the process of being exploited. ... Whatever the precise mechanism, it is clear from this finding that it is not sexually*

**Box 18.7**

## Incest Between Adults

In this chapter we have concentrated on incestuous relationships involving children because we have been concerned here with the topic of sexual coercion. Incestuous relationships between adults, however, need not involve coercion: both participants can freely choose to become sexually involved with one another. Such associations between adults, although not necessarily coercive, are illegal in our culture. Do you think that they should be? Why or why not?

It has been claimed that incestuous relationships lead to genetic inbreeding, and that the incest taboos arose because of fears that incestuous mating would cause a deterioration of genetic quality and a rise in sickliness, degeneracy, idiocy, and sterility. Research on the inbreeding of animals and studies of children born of incestuous relationships do not support this claim. Inbreeding intensifies the inheritance of traits, both adaptive and maladaptive, but the risk that offspring will suffer from recessive hereditary disorders is negligible if the defect has not previously manifested itself in the family.

A much more plausible explanation of the origin of the incest taboo is that it arose to preserve the family unit and to promote the development of larger social units through the ties of kinship. The theory of alliance, advocated by the French anthropologist Claude Levi-Strauss, posits that women are exchanged between groups to form alliances and promote harmony. Such unions freed early human societies from exclusive reliance on their own limited materials and products. Incest taboos discouraged social and economic inbreeding that would work against the alliances. As high-density technology developed, fewer and fewer people needed to be involved in trade, and as a result the incest taboo weakened, affecting fewer and fewer people outside the nuclear family (Cohen, 1978).

Today the incest taboo functions to maintain the integrity of the family unit. Sexual competition within the family can be a source of disruption and instability, as we have seen in documented cases of incest.

On the basis of the foregoing information on incest, some people have suggested that sex, marriage, and reproduction between *adult* family members—a brother and sister or two cousins, for example—who are living on their own should be a matter of personal choice rather than a legal issue.

In May 1979 Victoria Pittorino, 24, married David Goddu, 22. Although they are brother and sister, they were separated as infants by adoption. When they met as adults, according to Victoria, it was love at first sight. Shortly after their wedding, Massachusetts authorities charged them with incest. The newlyweds were found guilty and put on probation with the stipulation that they not live together as husband and wife. Do you agree with the Massachusetts ruling, or do you believe that the couple should be free to marry?

---

*lax, but sexually severe, families that foster a high risk for sexual exploitation. (p. 27)*

In general, it appears that children in disrupted, isolated, and economically poor families are at higher risk of sexual abuse than youngsters in more stable and middle class families, although child abuse occurs in all social strata (Finkelhor et al., 1990; Kinsey et al., 1953).

## Characteristics of Adult-Child Sexual Contacts

A review of the research that has focused on children who have been sexually abused, or on adults who remember having been sexually abused as children, indicates that heterosexual men are the perpetrators in 95% of the cases of sexual abuse of girls and 80% of the cases of sexual abuse of boys (Finkelhor & Russell, 1984). Second, sexual abusers are not generally violent (Okami & Goldberg, 1992): in a national sample, physical force was used in only 19% of incidents involving girls and in 15% of episodes involving boys (Finkelhor et al., 1990). Third, children, like women, are more likely to be sexually abused by acquaintances—relatives, siblings, family friends, and neighbors—than by strangers (Finkelhor et al., 1990; Russell, 1984). In the Finkelhor et al. (1990) research, a stranger was the perpetrator in 21% of the cases involving girls and in 40% of the cases involving boys. Sexual advances frequently occur in the child's home or in the residence of the perpetrator rather than in alleys or woods.

## Long-Term Correlates of Sexual Abuse

Although most people vehemently condemn adult-child sexual contacts and claim that such associations have dire effects on the child that last into adulthood, a few defend such relationships. In 1984 the Dutch psychologist Theodorus Sandfort published a report of his research with 25 boys, aged 10 to 16, who were involved in pedophilic relationships with adult males. The boys were located through their adult partners and interviewed. Most of the boys described their pedophilic relationships as predominantly positive and did not perceive them as representing abuse of authority by adults. Most researchers and clinicians, however, would argue that the boys, particularly the younger ones, are not old enough to make that kind of judgment or to give informed consent to such relationships. Concluding that the sexual interactions were unrelated to the boys' sense of general well-being, Sandfort asserted that "in my opinion, provisions which provide extra protection to children should not interfere with their rights of sexual self-determination, and this should include the right to accept as well as to refuse the sexual initiative of an adult" (p. 141).

Similar views have been voiced in North America as well. There is a small group in the United States called the Rene Guyon Society that advocates both child-child and child-adult sex. This group claims that sex at an early age prevents divorce and delinquency. In the 1930s Rene Guyon, for whom the society was named, wrote *Ethics of Sexual Acts*, in which he presented children's sexual relations with others as examples of sexual freedom.

Does sex during childhood reduce the likelihood of divorce and delinquency, or does it lead to maladjustment and prostitution, as others have claimed? Although a great deal has been written about the "effects" that sexual relations with adults may have on children, most of the literature is either speculative or based on biased samples from which little can be concluded. For example, because psychotherapists often uncover child-adult sexual incidents in the backgrounds of their clients, they have sometimes concluded that these experiences underlie the problems that led the person to seek therapy. Similarly, because substantial numbers of prostitutes have backgrounds that include sexual contact with adults during their childhoods, some observers have assumed that early sexual experience leads to prostitution. A number of clinicians have concluded that sexual abuse during one's childhood leaves deep emotional scars that contribute to adult psychopathology and difficulties with sex and relationships (de Young, 1982; Fritz, Stoll, & Wagner, 1981). However, the samples on which these conclusions are based have come from court referrals or psychotherapy clients, and generalizations from such biased samples should be made very cautiously.

A review of studies on the long-term correlates of childhood sexual abuse indicated that compared to women with no history of childhood sexual abuse, those women who did report such a history were more likely to experience depression, sexual dysfunction, anxiety or fear, homosexual experience, and revictimization experiences (Beitchman et al., 1992). Revictimization—also known as victim recidivism—refers to findings that adults who report unwanted childhood sexual experiences are also more likely than adults who do not report such experiences in childhood to report unwanted sexual experiences in adulthood (Possage & Allgeier, 1993; Stevenson & Gajarsky, 1991).

Systematic surveys of normal populations suggest that child-adult sexual contacts per se do not inevitably lead to long-term problems in adult functioning (Kilpatrick, 1992). In a survey of 501 predominantly middle-class women, the majority (55%) reported having had some sexual experience with peers or adults during childhood (Kilpatrick, 1986). The presence or absence of sexual contact during childhood, however, was unrelated to stressful family relations, depression, marital satisfaction, sexual satisfaction, or self-esteem in adulthood.

We might expect that children's sexual experience with a relative—particularly a parent—would have more damaging consequences than sexual abuse by a nonrelative because incest would presumably disrupt the child's sense of stability within the family. In support of this hypothesis, Kilpatrick (1986) found that adults whose childhood sexual experiences involved a parent or other relative who used pressure, force, or guilt to obtain the sexual contact did show somewhat more impairment in their adult functioning in all of the areas measured except sexual satisfaction. In terms of its impact on adult functioning, however, the crucial issue appears to be the use of invasive force and coercion by a relative during childhood rather than sexual contact per se. Another study of a random sample of more than 1,000 female college students also indicated that the majority of respondents had unwanted sexual contacts during childhood; consistent with Kilpatrick's findings, their experiences were unrelated to the women's current psychological adjustment, self-esteem, assertiveness, or trust (Hrabowy & Allgeier, 1987). But among the women who had unwanted childhood sexual experiences, the more invasive the act, the more currently troubled the women were by it. Even so, the level of invasiveness was not related to the general measures of psychological adjustment.

Many mental health professionals believe that the reactions of parents, relatives, and adult authorities to sexual incidents are the key factors in determining the effect of these events on children. Young children have little understanding of what is sexual. Therefore, they have difficulty in labeling the incident, if they seek to label it at all. Older children are more aware of sex and thus, depending on what they have learned about sexuality, are more likely to react to abusive incidents with vague feelings of wrongdoing or guilt over their participation, even if they were

coerced. Their feelings of guilt can be either reduced or increased by adults' reactions (see Figure 18.6).

If adults overreact to incidents of child sexual abuse, the young victims may feel that they are guilty of some unspeakable act and may blame themselves for what occurred. However, if adults act reasonably, attributing responsibility to the offending adult, where it belongs, children can come away from the experience with minimal distress. It is also important that parents not focus on the sexual nature of the incident. Finkelhor (1979) found that sexual activity per se, whether it involved exhibitionism, fondling of the genitals, or sexual intercourse, had no relationship to the degree of trauma experienced by children. The two factors that contributed the most to a traumatic or negative reaction in a child were the use of force and a large age difference between the offending adult and the child. The more force and the greater the difference in age, the more negative the children's reaction.

Results of another study, involving students who in their childhood had sexual contact with adults, led to a different conclusion, however. Those women who reported having succumbed to sexual activity during childhood without being physically forced indicated that the absence of physical coercion intensified the trauma (Fritz et al., 1981). It was not as easy for these women to forgive themselves for participation as it was for women who had been verbally or physically threatened or attacked. Results of the McCahill group's study of rape victims led to similar conclusions. That is, strong force is traumatizing because of the fear it evokes, but no force at all may heighten the victim's guilt.

Fear is a child's most common reaction to a forced sexual interaction with an adult; 58% of the girls in the Finkelhor (1979) study reported having been fearful. Fear may also be the primary reason why children avoid telling anyone about an incident of abuse by an adult. Only 37% of the girls and 27% of the boys reported an incident of sexual contact to their parents or other adults (Finkelhor, 1979).

When a child does report a pedophilic contact to an elder person, the adult may, for various reasons, cover it up rather than report it. First, he or she may not believe the child. Such

**FIGURE 18.6**
**Counseling a Sexually Abused Child**
The post-abuse adjustment of children can be hindered or helped by the responses
of adults to the abuse episode. The youngsters need to be reassured that the abuse
was not their fault.

nonrecognition of the sexual contact may be the response that is most damaging to the child's self-concept. Even when an adult believes a child, the adult may avoid reporting the incident for fear of entanglement with legal or social-welfare authorities. In their survey of almost 200 parents with children ranging in age from 5 to 18, Gaines and Allgeier (1993) gave the parents hypothetical descriptions of a child-abuse situation in which the perpetrator was a family member, a family friend, or a stranger. Parents indicated that they would be significantly less likely to report the abuse to authorities if the perpetrator was a family member rather than a friend, and, in turn, less likely to report the abuse if the perpetrator was a friend rather than a stranger. If the offender is a family member or close friend, a parent or adult who learns of the incident may worry that the

child or the adult offender will be removed from the home. This concern is a relatively realistic one: many of our legal and social policies regarding the sexual abuse of children have had the unintended side effect of further disrupting the family rather than aiding the adjustment of children, particularly when the adult-child contact involves relatives (Denton, 1987).

However, if a young person is able to talk with a supportive person—whether a family member or a counselor—about an abusive sexual interaction, residual feelings of shame or fear may subside. It is important for the child or adolescent to vent the emotions and concerns that may stem from such contacts. An anxious overreaction on the part of family members, friends, or therapists may communicate to a child or adolescent that there is something wrong with him or her. Instead, a supportive person should discuss the situation with the adolescent or child in a matter-of-fact way and use the following guidelines in the conversation.

1. Sexual feelings and the desire for sexual attention are perfectly normal.
2. It is considered inappropriate for adults to interact sexually with children.
3. Sex is not evil, nor are all adults bad. In fact, the adult with whom the child had sexual contact is not necessarily a "bad" person. The behavior of the adult under these conditions, however, was inappropriate.

It is crucial to stress that the child is not responsible and should not feel guilty. Clearly, the use of children by adults to meet their own needs is exploitive.

## Prevention of Childhood Sexual Abuse

Childhood sexual abuse prevention (CSAP) programs have proliferated in the past two decades, with millions of children in North America taking part in them. Viewed as a first line of defense against child sexual abuse, these programs are designed to enable children to identify and avoid sexual abuse, but can create undesirable side effects. Psychologist James Krivacska (1991) has identified two cornerstones of the CSAP philosophy: the touch continuum and empowerment.

The touch continuum defines what is good touch (touch that feels good and is good for the child), bad touch (touch that the child wishes to avoid such as unwanted hugs or touch that hurts), and confusing touch (touch that may start out feeling good, but ends up being bad touch). Contact with the genitals is often described as bad touch, although the genitals in these programs are often referred to vaguely as "parts covered by a bathing suit" or "private parts." A child's initial introduction to an adult talking about human genitals may convey the idea that touching the genitals is bad (Krivacska, 1990, 1991).

The second major cornerstone of CSAP programs is the concept of empowerment. This refers to individuals' playing a role in avoiding sexual abuse. It assumes that children can take responsibility for themselves and make choices about how they lead their lives. This assumption is problematic when applied to young children, who do not have an adequate understanding of complex sociosexual interactions. Thus, as Krivacska (1991) noted, children may be placed in a guilt-producing double-bind:

> . . . the programs deny that children are at all responsible or to blame for sexual abuse, yet they teach them that they are responsible for preventing the abuse. This is clearly unreasonable. In their attempts to reduce children's guilt in having been sexually abused, most CSAP programs also unintentionally increase children's feelings of guilt when they find themselves in situations where they are unable to prevent the abuse from happening again after they have been exposed to the program. (p. 4)

It is ironic that school systems that have so persistently avoided sex education at the elementary school level often feel no qualms about exposing children to CSAP programs. Thus a child's first encounter with a formal presentation about sexuality is in terms of abuse. The implications of this approach will probably be seen in the sexual attitudes of future generations.

We agree with Krivacska that sexual abuse prevention programs need to be included in a larger program of sexuality education for primary school children. This sexuality education needs to be geared toward activity promoting and encouraging the age-appropriate development of their sexuality. For example, Wurtele (1993) reported that a CSAP program for Head Start preschoolers that included teaching children the correct names for their genitals as well as emphasizing that it was acceptable to touch their own genitals in private appeared to affect positively the preschoolers' attitudes toward their own sexuality.

Before ending this section, it may be helpful to put the phenomenon of child sexual abuse into perspective by examining rates of other forms of victimization of children. David Finkelhor, one of the foremost authorities on the topic of sexual abuse, has provided rates of childhood victimization ranging from the least common to the most common per 1,000 U.S. children (Finkelhor

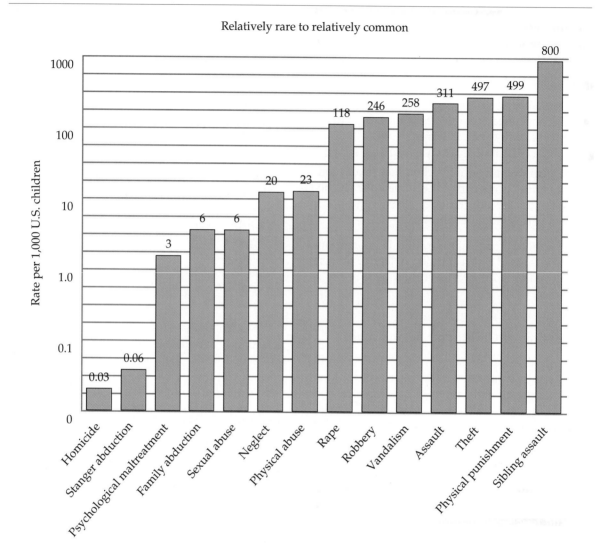

Relatively rare to relatively common

Source: Adapted from information in Finkelhor and Dziuba-Leatherman, 1994.

**FIGURE 18.7**

**Forms of Child Victimization**

These rates of various forms of victimization of children demonstrate that many potentially harmful behaviors are far more common than the highly publicized crime of child sexual abuse.

& Dziuba-Leatherman, 1994). As may be seen by inspection of Figure 18.7, of the 14 forms of victimization, assault by siblings ranks first, childhood sexual abuse ranks tenth, and homicide ranks fourteenth. It is curious that the more prevalent forms of childhood victimization have received far less publicity than childhood sexual abuse.

## Gender Differences in Sexually Coercive Behavior

We conclude by examining in detail a finding that has cropped up throughout this chapter: most victims of rape, harassment, pedophilia, and incest are females, and most perpetrators are males. Some people might use this finding to buttress an argument that males are innately dominating and aggressive and that females are destined to be victims, submissive and masochistic. But for various reasons, this simplistic explanation is unconvincing. First, in all coercive episodes, there are instances in which males are the victims and females the perpetrators. Second, many—probably most—males do not coerce sexually, and many females experience a lifetime free of sexual victimization. Third, research on cross-cultural differences in the incidence of rape, discussed earlier, suggests that rape and other forms of sexual coercion may result from social factors.

One key to reducing the occurrence of sexual coercion of children might be to determine why the overwhelming majority of assailants are males and victims are females. Finkelhor and Russell (1984) have described concisely most of the proposed hypotheses about these gender differences. We present these and review the evidence relevant to each.

1. *The "limp penis" theory.* According to this notion, because males cannot be forced to make their penises erect, potential female perpetrators cannot gain sexual satisfaction from unwilling males and therefore do not even try. There are several flaws embedded in this idea. First, of course, is the fact that erections are not always relevant in the sexual satisfaction of most females, as noted in Chapter 7. In addition, as discussed earlier, males can be physically manipulated to erection even when they do not desire sex (Sarrel & Masters, 1982; Struckman-Johnson, 1991). Also, some men report engaging in sex when they do not want to because they feel psychologically coerced by women (Muehlenhard & Cook, 1988). Further, in the sexual abuse of children, many perpetrators trick or bribe their victims into sexual contact or engage in genital manipulation aimed at arousing them, and women can presumably perform such tasks at least as seductively as men (Finkelhor & Russell, 1984). Thus the "limp penis" theory does not account for gender differences in the likelihood of being a perpetrator or victim.

2. *Differential socialization to be caretakers.* Our culture gives females far more training than males in nurturant behavior. Such socialization would presumably sensitize women to children's welfare and reduce the likelihood that they would attempt to fulfill sexual desires at children's expense (Herman, 1981). Moreover, women typically have more opportunity than men to interact with children, a circumstance strengthening their bond with and sense of protectiveness toward children. It is possible that differential socialization and child-care responsibilities of males and females would dispose women to be less likely than men to sexually abuse children, but this argument is weakened by the fact that women are more likely to abuse their children physically than are men (Maden & Wrench, 1977).

3. *Differential sexual preferences.* Our informal language is replete with phrases that suggest pedophilia. Rarely does one hear references to a romantic or erotic relationship between a woman and her "boy," but it is difficult to listen to a popular music station for long without hearing an adult male singing about his "girl" or "baby." The common pairing of "man" with "girl," strictly speaking, refers to a pedophilic relationship, although we may not think of it in that way unless sensitized to the issue. Women in most cultures involve themselves with men who are older and larger than they are, whereas men generally select partners who are younger and smaller (Buss, 1994). Thus erotic arousal in response to children would presumably require less of an alteration of culturally sanctioned sexual preferences for males than for females.

4. *Differential roles in sexual relations.* Women are traditionally socialized to expect men to initiate sexual contact, whereas males learn to take the initiative in sexual relations and to overcome any (anticipated) female resistance.

This cultural pattern may make males more likely than females to initiate sexual contacts with children.

5. *Differential perceptions of sexual content in interactions.* Women are less likely than men to perceive social interactions as having sexual content (Abbey, 1987; Shea, 1993) and thus may be less likely to perceive affectionate contacts with children as indicating sexual availability.

6. *Differential reactions to loss of sexual outlets.* In the absence of sexual partners, men seem to suffer more of a loss of self-esteem than do women (Buss, 1994). Under these conditions, men may be more likely to use children sexually to regain their self-esteem.

7. *Differential identification with sexual victimization.* Females are more frequently the recipients of sexual coercion than are males. As a result, they may be more likely to empathize with feelings of exploitation and thus be less likely to express their sexual feelings toward children.

8. *Differential social supports for coercive behavior.* Earlier, we reviewed Kanin's (1985) findings that assaultive males receive far more approval from their peers for having sex and for sexually coercing females than do nonassaultive males. Although we are unaware of any research that has examined peer supports for sex and sexual coercion among females, in general females receive less support for displaying strong sexual appetites; in fact, they are likely to be called "loose" or "sluts" when they have multiple partners. In addition, throughout most of history, women and children have been viewed as the property of men. Father-initiated sexual activity within the family often has been seen as a right and thus, although not approved of, has usually not been punished. Wives, who have been seen as the property of their husbands, have had few rights, sexual or otherwise.

If differential socialization and differential expectations of men and women contribute to the phenomenon of sexual coercion, then certain trends in North American society may help to reduce the incidence of all forms of coercion. Specifically, as more egalitarian and less possessive sexual relationships become the norm, the equation of sexuality with dominance and aggression may be lessened.

# Summary of Major Points

1. **Varieties of sexual assault.** The word *rape* tends to elicit images of attack by a stranger lurking in the bushes, but a large majority of sexual assaults are carried out by people who are acquainted casually or intimately with the victim. Date rape is prevalent in our culture, and about one-quarter of the college men in one sample reported that they had attempted to force sexual relations. Many college women anonymously report that men have forced or attempted to force them to have sex. Males and spouses also experience sexual coercion. Although the majority of rapists and victims are in their adolescence or early 20s, sexual assault may occur from prepubescence to old age.

2. **Characteristics of sexual assailants.** Convicted sex offenders tend to be aggressive and lacking in self-esteem. Many report having been sexually and/or physically abused during childhood and adolescence. Moreover, the stereotype of the assailant as a sexually driven male without access to willing partners is not supported by research: many offenders are in fact involved in relationships with consenting sexual partners—wives or girlfriends—at the time of the assault. Further, their rate of sexual dysfunction is higher when they use force than when they engage in sex with a consenting partner, and much higher than that of men in general. Unidentified assailants tend to be alienated from their families and supported by peers who encourage and approve both of sexual exploits and of the victimization of particular categories of women.

3. **Sexual assault stereotypes.** Three major hypotheses have been advanced as possible explanations of sexual assault. These include victim precipitation, uncontrolled lust or uncontrolled aggression, and exaggerated gender-role identity. The notion that victims precipitate sexual assault is completely unsubstantiated in about 95% of the cases. There is some support for the theory that offenders are motivated by aggression and general feelings of inadequacy, but little evidence exists in favor of the uncontrolled-lust hypothesis.

4. **Reducing vulnerability to sexual assault.** Ways that potential victims may reduce their chances of being sexually assaulted include knowing one's own sexual policies, avoiding being alone or intoxicated with a person one does not know well, and communicating one's disinterest in having sex in a clear and straightforward manner. In the event that a potential assailant persists, multiple strategies (talking, screaming, running away, and so forth) are more effective in dissuading the attack than are single strategies.

5. **Sexual harassment.** Harassment of subordinates by employers and of students by teachers appears to be relatively common. More than 10% of women in a random sample said that they had quit a job because of sexual harassment, and 25% of female graduate students report having been sexually intimate with professors. In addition, sexual harassment occasionally occurs between therapists and clients, with a number of reported negative side effects for the clients. Recently passed legislation protects employees from unwanted sexual approaches.

6. The sexual coercion of children.

Although a small minority in the United States support the idea that adult-child sexual interaction may benefit the child, most people vehemently reject the notion. Because children do not understand the nature and potential consequences of sexual activity, they are unable to give informed consent to such interaction. The long-term correlates of sexual contacts vary considerably as a function of the age difference between the child and the perpetrator, the degree of force, and the level of invasiveness. Despite some psychologists' claims, based on their clinical cases, that such experiences *cause* adult maladjustment, studies of normal samples indicate no differences in measures of psychological adjustment as a function of having had unwanted sexual experiences during childhood. The responses of other adults in the child's environment to the sexual episode may be related to the extent to which the child can cope with the experience. A child who reports having been sexually victimized by an adult should receive support and counseling to reduce his or her feelings of guilt and responsibility.

7. Incestuous relationships.

The long-term correlates of incest involving adult-child contacts are similar to those cited above regarding the sexual abuse of children. Although many participants in incestuous relationships (particularly child-adult incest episodes) perceive the experience negatively, some participants have positive reactions to interactions perceived as involving mutual consent. Children, of course, cannot give informed consent because of their inability to understand all the potential ramifications of sexual contacts.

8. Gender differences in sexual coercion.

Males are far more likely to use sexual coercion than are females, and females are far more likely to be sexually coerced than are males. Several theories attempt to explain the reasons for these gender differences. To the extent that differences in the sexual socialization of men and women contribute to the problem, the growing support in recent years for gender equality in personal, educational, and occupational environments may gradually reduce the prevalence of all forms of sexual coercion.

## Review of Key Concepts

1. All the following statements are false rape myths *except*:  a) The majority of rape victims are attractive women who are attacked while walking alone at night.  b) The majority of rapists have other means of sexual release.  c) The majority of women who charge rape actually consent to the act and then change their minds later.  d) Most rapists are men whose hormones trigger an excessive sex drive. (p. 593)

2. In males, a consistent relationship has been established between holding traditional gender-role beliefs and self-reported sexual assault. True or false? (p. 595)

3. Sexual assaults are more likely to be reported to authorities when the assailant is:  a) a stranger;  b) a casual acquaintance;  c) a steady date;  d) a spouse. (pp. 597–600)

4. Outside prisons, the rape of men is practically nonexistent. True or false? (pp. 597–599)

5. Reactions characteristic of post-traumatic stress disorder (PTSD) include all the following *except*:  a) cardiovascular impairment;  b) disturbance in sleep pattern;  c) an impairment of memory and/or power of concentration;  d) exaggerated startle response. (pp. 605–607)

6. A rapist's chances of being arrested, charged, and convicted are approximately:  a) 4 in 100; b) 1 in 10;  c) 1 in 5;  d) 2 in 3. (p. 610)

7. A woman's chances of suffering sexual assault appear to increase sharply if she is single, sexually active, or identified with a delinquent group. True or false, and why? (pp. 613–614)

8. Rapists typically report that victim resistance does not affect their willingness to proceed with the assault. True or false? (pp. 614–615)

9. Discuss the phenomenon of acquaintance assault. Include the issues of its prevalence and methods of attempting to prevent it. In your answer, consider the personality traits and gender-role expectations of both victim and assailant.

10. What evidence is there that rapists' primary motives are domination and the desire to control and humiliate rather than an overpowering sexual desire? To what extent does this evidence undermine conventional rape myths?

11. Sexual harassment was not clearly perceived as a social problem before the:  a) 1920s; b) 1940s;  c) 1960s;  d) 1970s. (p. 616)

12. Describe the steps that a student should take to avoid and, if necessary, deal with sexual harassment by an instructor.

13. During the past four decades, the reports of sexual abuse of children:  a) have increased dramatically;  b) have dropped dramatically; c) have shown few systematic fluctuations; d) none of the above. (p. 624)

# Atypical Sexual Activity

*You* *pervert!*
High school students commonly use this epithet, usually jokingly, to label someone who engages in a quasi-sexual behavior deviating slightly from the norm. What does the word *perversion* mean? One dictionary defines *perversion* as a maladjustment involving aberrant or deviant ways of seeking sexual satisfaction. A problem with this label and other similar terms, such as *deviation*, is that what is considered aberrant or deviant at one time and place might be considered normal at other times and places (Simon, 1994).

In this chapter we examine atypical sexual expression and the characteristics and possible motivations of those who engage in uncommon practices, including people who are sexually attracted to children. We also review what is known about transvestism and other paraphilias. The various treatments given to those who have strayed from what North American culture considers normal sexual behavior are examined. Some of these behaviors, although atypical, do not involve or victimize others and so are considered to be more curious or annoying than dangerous. Other paraphilias are invasive of others' rights and thus can be seen as part of the continuum of coercive sexual behavior. In considering societal responses to paraphilias, it is important

**perversion**—deviance from the normal in sexual activities or desires.

to differentiate between those that are simply variations from normal or typical behavior and those that infringe on the lives of other people.

## The Paraphilias

Because beliefs change with respect to what sexual activities are normal, many clinicians prefer to avoid the term *perversion* or the phrase "sexual deviance." Someone who practices an atypical sexual activity is not necessarily dangerous or in need of therapy. *Paraphilia* (the love of the unusual, or atypical, sexual activity) is the term now used for a restricted group of sexual behaviors that are considered unusual for the person performing them or for his or her society.

The current view of paraphilias differs from earlier definitions of sexual deviance. For example, the second edition of the *Diagnostic and Statistical Manual of the American Psychiatric Association* (*DSM-II*, 1968) classified sexual behavior as abnormal if it "deviated from a defined norm of heterosexual coitus between adults under nonbizarre circumstances." According to this definition, homosexuality was automatically classified as a deviation. More recently, clinicians have labeled an atypical pattern of sexual behavior as a variation rather than a deviation, and this approach "implies neither health nor illness, goodness nor badness, usefulness nor uselessness" (Stoller, 1977, p. 192). Such labeling describes rather than evaluates the behavior. Although many experts find descriptive labeling a useful approach to discussing the paraphilias, some people have difficulty separating description from evaluation.

Because of social and legal restrictions, reliable data on the frequency of paraphilic behaviors are limited. Most of our information about the paraphilias comes from people who have been arrested or who are in therapy. The likelihood that the majority of people who engage in paraphilias do not fall into either of these two categories limits our ability to generalize most research findings.

One solidly supported generalization about paraphilias, however, does appear to be appropriate. Males are far more likely to engage in paraphilias than are females. In 1991, for example, more than 90% of the more than 100,000 people who were arrested for sexual offenses other than rape and prostitution in the United States were males (Uniform Crime Reports, 1992).

Atypical sexual patterns can coexist with emotional disorders. People who confine their sexual outlets to strange and occasionally bizarre activities sometimes have trouble relating to other adults in a meaningful way. Yet many individuals who engage in paraphilic acts are able to take part in "normal" sexual behavior with adult partners without relying on paraphilic fantasies or behaviors to generate sexual excitement (Abel et al., 1987; Brame, Brame, & Jacobs, 1993).

Some paraphilias (for example, voyeurism, exhibitionism) invade the rights of other people. Other paraphilias (for example, fetishes, crossdressing, transsexuality) involve no offenses against other people but simply represent individual differences. We examine first the noninvasive paraphilias.

## The Noninvasive Consensual Paraphilias

Many types of atypical sexual behavior involve consensual adults who mutually agree to observe, participate in, or just put up with the behavior in question. No one's rights are violated and the vast majority of society's members are unaware that the behaviors even exist, except for those who watch sensation-seeking talk shows such as *Donahue* or *Sally Jesse Raphael*.

### Fetishes

The term *fetish* is derived from the Portuguese word *fetico*, meaning "charmed" or "obsessive

**paraphilia** (par-rah-FILL-ee-ah)—love of the unusual; the term now used to describe sexual activities that were formerly labeled deviant (*para:* beside or amiss; *philia:* love).

fascination." In current clinical terms, *fetishism* refers to the use of nonliving objects as a preferred or exclusive means of inducing sexual arousal. Thus some object comes to symbolize or embody the sexual arousal value usually reserved for human beings. To some extent, we are all fetishists, in that various objects can sexually arouse us. We may associate items of clothing with particular body parts or with a particular person. Bras, underpants, and jock straps have definite associations with specific body parts and may acquire the capacity to arouse us sexually by themselves. Similarly, cars, perfumes, or hairstyles that we associate with a loved one can arouse us.

Fetishism is thought to be primarily a male characteristic. There have been very few documented cases of female fetishism (Arndt, 1991). There is also little information about the prevalence of fetishism in the general population. Most frequently, fetish objects are used in connection with fantasy and masturbation. Sometimes they are employed to build arousal during sexual intercourse or in combination with other forms of sexual expression. For example, a masochist may prefer to be whipped by a woman dressed in leather boots.

Some people seek partners for fetishistic sexual acts by advertising in underground newspapers. Prostitutes commonly consider fetishists good customers, and many specialize in fulfilling unusual sexual preferences.

Although the list of possible fetish objects is inexhaustible, certain items are more likely than others to be associated with sexual arousal, perhaps because they are more similar in texture or appearance to the genitals. Shoes, boots, and undergarments are frequent objects of fetishistic interest. In addition, items made of leather, rubber, fur, or silk seem to be particularly popular fetishes in our culture.

Feet and their coverings have been used as symbols for sex in many cultures throughout history, and the foot has been one of the most common phallic symbols. In Slovene, a language spoken in Eastern Europe, the penis is called *tretja noga*, or "third foot." On the feast day of St. Cosimo in the area around Naples, Italy, a large phallic object called "the big toe of St. Cosimo" is offered to the saint (Rossi, 1976). The practice of binding the feet of young Chinese girls persisted for more than 1,000 years because small feet were considered erotic. Known as the lotus or lily foot, the bound foot came to have almost as much erogenous importance as the vagina itself. And as Rossi (1976, p. 15) noted:

> The romantic and sexual magic of the shoe flourishes in many forms. In Sicily, young women sleep with a shoe under their pillow to improve their chances of getting a husband. In rural Greece, the woman believes that a lost lover can be retrieved by burning an old shoe. In Spain and Mexico, admiring women toss a slipper into the bullring to applaud the matador. He picks up the shoes gently as kittens, kisses them, and tosses them back into the crowd.

In North American culture, the erotic symbolism of the foot is much more subtle. Shoes are still tied to the back of the car of a newly married couple, however. Perhaps the foot has been erotically significant because it is one of the body's most sensitive tactile organs, possessing a heavy concentration of nerve endings. The feet also participate reflexively during orgasm in what are called carpopedal spasms. Whatever the reasons for eroticizing feet, since ancient times there has been a nearly universal relationship between the foot as a male sexual symbol and the shoe as a female sexual symbol.

Shoes are generally made of leather, which is animal skin. Perhaps it is this juxtaposition of skin against skin that gives objects like shoes their erotic appeal. Aromas are also an important source of arousal for many people, and leather certainly has a distinctive odor. Thus the shoe or leather fetishist may be only carrying to an extreme a general human attraction toward these objects.

Freud believed that in childhood, fetishists develop the idea that their mother possesses a penis, and then in adulthood they persist in

---

**fetishism**—obtaining sexual excitement primarily or exclusively from an inanimate object or a particular part of the body.

believing that their mother has some kind of mysterious penis for which the fetish object is a substitute. A typical psychoanalytic case study involved a shoe fetishist who became fixated after seeing his governess expose her foot when he was a young boy (Fenichel, 1945). The psychoanalytic view holds that the boy equated the foot with the penis, and so the boy concluded, "My governess has a penis." The shoe supposedly stimulated sexual arousal because viewing it quieted the boy's castration anxiety. The Freudian theorist Otto Fenichel imagined the reasoning process to be something like the following: the idea that there are human beings without a penis and that I might myself be one of them makes it difficult for me to become sexually aroused. But now I see a symbol of a penis in a woman; that helps me quiet my fear, and I can allow myself to be sexually aroused (Fenichel, 1945).

Behavioral approaches also stress the association between the fetishistic object and sexual arousal. Sexual arousal and orgasm, which are both reflexive responses, may be accidentally elicited by a strong emotional experience involving some particular object or body part.

This initial conditioning experience may be strengthened through the reinforcement of masturbation and orgasm. The potential for an object to acquire sexual meaning was demonstrated in the conditioning experiment described in Chapter 3, in which Rachman (1966) evoked a sexual response to boots. Fetishism is probably learned early in life. In one study of 100 people with rubber fetishes, the average age at which they first experienced attraction toward rubber objects or material was just under 11 (Gosselin, 1978).

## Transvestism

A man who has strong urges to dress in women's clothing and who becomes sexually aroused while wearing feminine apparel is called a *transvestite*, or TV. For the most part, a transvestite's cross-dressing is not an attempt to reject his biological gender. There is some overlap between

transvestism and transsexualism, in that some transsexuals report that cross-dressing was sexually arousing to them prior to gender-reassignment surgery, and some transvestites report that they have considered undergoing sex-reassignment surgery (Buhrich & Beaumont, 1981; Blanchard, 1989). Although transvestism can be seen as a mild expression of discontent with one's biological sex and gender roles, it seldom entails the extreme rejection of one's biological sex seen in transsexualism. Gays sometimes cross-dress to attract a partner, but wearing clothes of the other gender does not in and of itself sexually arouse most homosexuals.

There is a subgroup of transvestites who desire at least partial physical feminization through hormones or surgery. Buhrich and McConaghy (1985) classified these individuals as marginal transvestites and referred to the transvestites who do not want physical feminization as nuclear transvestites. Marginal transvestites report significantly more feminine behavior during childhood and adolescence than do nuclear transvestites, and both groups report more feminine behavior than do "normal" males (Buhrich & McConaghy, 1985).

A further distinction has been made with heterosexual men who regularly fantasize about themselves as women but do not cross-dress (Blanchard, 1992). These men are sexually aroused by imagining themselves as women but do not act on their fantasies.

Cross-dressing has been reported in Greek legend and among Roman emperors. It existed during the Middle Ages, and it is recognized and accepted today in many cultures (Bullough & Bullough, 1993). One of the major charges against Joan of Arc in her trial for heresy was her preference for male hairstyles and attire (see Figure 19.1).

Although in both industrialized and nonindustrialized cultures it is usually males who practice transvestism, Bullough and Bullough (1993) noted that during the Middle Ages there were more reports of female than of male transvestites. Until the late 1960s, most of our information about transvestites came from the reports of clinicians working with men who wished to be rid of their desire to cross-dress. Since that time, several research teams have sampled groups of

transvestite—a person sexually stimulated or gratified by wearing the clothes of the other gender.

**FIGURE 19.1**
**Joan of Arc**
In the heresy trial of Joan of Arc, one charge against her was her preference for male hairstyles and attire.

transvestites from the general population in order to survey a nonclinical sample.

## Nonclinical Samples of Transvestites

Researchers have primarily used two strategies to obtain information from the nonclinical population of transvestites. They have recruited participants from the subscribers to such magazines as *Transvestia* and from members of social clubs in the United States and Australia (Buhrich & Beaumont, 1981; Buhrich & McConaghy, 1977; Bullough, Bullough, & Smith, 1983; Docter, 1988;

Prince & Bentler, 1972). Results from some of these studies are shown in Table 19.1.

Another example involves research with members of a club begun in Australia in 1971. The club's founder had placed an ad in an Australian newspaper seeking a response from "TV enthusiasts who would like to meet and discuss more on the subject." Not surprisingly, most of the replies came from people who were television fans. However, the few people who understood that "TV" stood for transvestite did meet and formed the Seahorse Club, named for a graceful creature that demonstrates a "combination at times of both gender roles" (Buhrich, 1976, p. 331).

Several aspects of research on nonclinical samples tend to contradict commonly held stereotypes about transvestites. For example, most (72% to 90%) respondents described themselves as heterosexual, and only a small percentage considered themselves exclusively homosexual. Most reported having been treated as boys—not as girls—during childhood, and very few reported being cross-dressed by their parents. Most began cross-dressing between the ages of 8 to 11.

In addition to employing questionnaires, some researchers also administered various personality measures to nonclinical samples of transvestites and to control groups, and then compared the results. In general, transvestites tended to score higher on scales of femininity and lower on scales of masculinity than did control groups. Transvestites also revealed more inhibition in interpersonal relations, less involvement with other individuals, and more independence when compared to a control group of middle managers taking a sensitivity-training course (Bentler & Prince, 1970). Most studies yielded no evidence that transvestism is associated with any major psychiatric symptoms (Beatrice, 1985; Bentler, Sherman, & Prince, 1970).

Cross-dressing is usually done at periodic intervals. Buhrich and McConaghy (1977) reported that the majority of their sample cross-dressed a little more than once a month. Masturbation may take place during the cross-dressing episode, but often the cross-dressing itself produces orgasm. Although most of the transvestites reported that they felt like women when cross-dressed, they said that they felt like men when nude, as well

**TABLE 19.1 Comparisons Across Studies of Male Transvestites**

|  | Prince & Bentler | Buhrich & McConaghy | Buhrich & Beaumont | Buhrich & Beaumont | Bullough et al. | Docter |
|---|---|---|---|---|---|---|
| Heterosexual (%) | 89 | 83 | 72 | 87 | 97 | — |
| Exclusively homosexual (%) | 9 | 3 | 5 | 6 | — | — |
| Some homosexual (%) | 28 | 17 | 44 | 48 | 18 | 28 |
| Ever married (%) | 78 | 80 | 88 | 83 | — | 82 |
| Median age | 30s | 39 | 39 | 47 | 43 | — |
| Ever on hormones (%) | 5 | 17 | 12 | 10 | 25 | — |
| Considered sex change (%) | — | 25 | 69 | 60 | — | — |
| Any psychotherapy (%) | 26 | — | — | — | 54 | — |
| Median age at first cross-dress | 10 | — | 11 | 11 | 8 | 9 |
| Two-parent homes (%) | 82 | — | — | — | 85 | 80 |
| Cross-dressed by parents (%) | 4–6 | 4 | — | — | — | — |
| Date published | 1972 | 1977 | 1981 | 1981 | 1983 | 1988 |
| Sample size | 504 | 35 | 86 | 126 | 65 | 110 |
| Place | U.S. | Aust. | Aust. | U.S. | U.S. | U.S. |

Source: Adapted from Docter, R. F. (1988) *Transvestites and transsexuals: Toward a theory of cross-dressing behavior.* New York: Plenum Press.

as when dressed in their usual attire. When they were exposed to motion pictures of nudes, their erotic responses, as measured by penile volume, fell within the normal range for heterosexual males (Buhrich & McConaghy, 1977; Buhrich et al., 1979).

As might be expected, given the strength of attitudes in our own culture regarding gender roles, the transvestites' desire to cross-dress introduces some novel problems into their relationships. Most (78% to 88%) either had been or still were married. The majority of the transvestites in Buhrich's (1976) sample thought that their desire to cross-dress would disappear with marriage, so they did not tell their wives about it before marriage. Some wives were unaware of their husbands' cross-dressing, even after they had been married for years. When wives did find out that their husbands were transvestites, their responses ran the gamut from complete disapproval and antagonism to full acceptance and cooperation, the latter to the point of the wives'

lending their husbands their own clothing (see Figure 19.2). Wives sometimes accompany their husbands when they appear in public in feminine attire (Brown & Collier, 1989; Buhrich, 1976). And many wives even report having sex with their husbands when their husband is cross-dressed (Bullough & Weinberg, 1988). Some transvestites are pressured by their wives to seek therapy, but transvestites "are ambivalent about being 'cured.' The suggestion to wear feminine-looking shirts or 'unisex' clothes holds no interest for them. To satisfy his urge, the transvestite must fully and without compromise be dressed as a woman" (Buhrich, 1976, p. 334).

Most children of transvestites who have been told about their fathers' cross-dressing are either indifferent about it or are accepting. The response has apparently depended on the preexisting relationship between the father and his children, but the fear that peers might tease them about their fathers seemed to be the children's main concern (Buhrich, 1976).

**FIGURE 19.2**
**Davida and Corrine**
Davida enjoys having his mate Corrine dress him up in some of her clothes, and he feels that he can express his emotions more freely when he is dressed as Davida.

## Explanations of Transvestism

At this point, we have no conclusive explanation of the urge to cross-dress. Male hormone deficiency has been suggested as one cause, and there have been attempts to measure the plasma testosterone levels of transvestites. Buhrich and his associates (1979) compared the levels of plasma testosterone and other sex hormones of 26 trans-vestites with those of 22 nontransvestite males and found that the two groups did not differ in their levels of sex hormones.

One particularly puzzling aspect of transvestism is its apparent absence among contemporary Western females. On the basis of their observations of 20th-century Western societies, some writers have argued that female transvestism is rare because norms with respect to what one may wear are far less restrictive for females than they are for males. For example, if you caught your aunt foraging in the kitchen for a midnight snack dressed in your uncle's pajama top, you might think she looked cute. Your reaction would probably be quite different, however, if you were to find your uncle rummaging through the refrigerator with your aunt's negligee on.

Although it is true that our norms regarding clothing styles are far more restrictive for males than for females, several factors argue against this difference in restrictiveness as the cause of the extreme gender difference in the incidence of transvestism. First, there have been few reports of female arousal as a function of wearing, say, men's jeans and work shirts. So it is not just that females can "get away with" cross-dressing without having a transvestite label attached to them. Most females who wear men's garb do not appear to derive the sexual satisfaction that males experience when they cross-dress. Second, Buhrich's (1976) research suggested that transvestites' urge to cross-dress is not satisfied by wearing ambiguous or unisex attire. Instead, they tend to desire apparel that is exclusively for females—for example, lacy bras, slips, and garter belts. (Similar behavior on the part of a female might be to don a pair of jockey shorts.) Third, transvestism most frequently appears in those cultures with relaxed rather than restrictive gender-role norms. In all probability, then, the restrictiveness of norms for male clothing styles is not responsible for the incidence of male transvestism and the absence of female transvestism in the 20th century.

The anthropologist Robert Munroe (1981) and his colleagues (Munroe & Munroe, 1977, 1980; Munroe, Whiting, & Hally, 1969) have suggested possible explanations. They reviewed cross-cultural research on transvestism to explore whether any social or economic factors were associated with the practice. Almost all societies that had been studied had only a few transvestites, but transvestism was most likely to be prevalent in cultures having two characteristics: relaxed gender-role norms and greater pressure on the male than on the female to ensure the family's economic survival. It is tempting to speculate that transvestism appears in those cultures because of the attractiveness of the female role. In contrast to cultures with rigid gender-role norms and a lower status for women, cultures with relaxed norms grant women many of the privileges accorded to men. At the same time, women in most cultures do not have as much pressure and responsibility for economic survival placed on them as men do. Men's economic burdens may perhaps lead some males to take a "vacation" by temporarily abandoning their role as provider and symbolically adopting women's roles, behaviors, and attire. Even if this speculation is eventually supported by further evidence, it still leaves many questions unanswered, including why the urge to cross-dress begins so early in life and why it is associated with arousal.

Whatever the explanation of the desire to cross-dress, it is clear that transvestites are not rejecting their biological sex. Instead, they find pleasure in occasionally donning the intimate attire typically worn by members of the other gender in their society. In contrast, transsexuals dislike the anatomical attributes of their biological sex, and many of them seek the anatomical characteristics of the other gender. We turn now to that phenomenon.

## Transsexuality

As members of a culture that is fascinated by sexual symbols of manhood (for example, penis size and functioning) and of womanhood (such as breast size), many of us cannot comprehend the feelings of a person consumed with an ardent desire to be rid of the physical attributes of his or her gender. Indeed, most people in our culture who are dissatisfied with their sexual organs seek to enhance rather than to eliminate them.

But for some men, their own male organs and functions violate their feminine psychological identity. These men are male-to-female (M-F) transsexuals. Similarly, for the female-to-male (F-M) transsexual, the physical symbols of the female biological sex conflict with an intense identification with maleness and the masculine role.

### Definition and Incidence

A *transsexual* is a biologically normal male or female who feels that he or she is a member of the other gender. Because psychological gender identity seems to be a more important determinant of self-concept than genetic, hormonal, or genital gender, we will use the pronoun *she* when referring to genetic males who hold feminine gender identities, and the pronoun *he* when discussing genetic females whose gender identity is masculine.

The term *transsexualism* was first used in 1910 by Magnus Hirschfeld and later by David O. Cauldwell (1949) in his diagnosis of psychopathia transsexualism for a genetic female who believed himself to be a male. A few years later, in 1953, Harry Benjamin described the syndrome more fully (Bullough & Bullough, 1993). Although transsexualism has only recently been defined, historical records describe a number of individuals who managed to live as members of the other gender (Bullough & Bullough, 1993). Classical mythology also contains repeated references to people who wished they were of the other gender.

It is easy to become confused if you try to categorize a transsexual's sexual orientation. From a genetic standpoint, we could conclude that many transsexuals have homosexual orientations because they are genetic males who are attracted to men or genetic females who are attracted to women. On the other hand, from a psychological standpoint, most M-F transsexuals feel as if they are really women and perceive their attraction to men as demonstrating heterosexual orientation. Among M-F transsexuals, only about 20% to 30% report having erotic experience primarily or only with women, and erotic experience with men is even less common among F-M transsexuals. Some F-M transsexuals who report sexual experience with women indicate that

---

**transsexual**—a person whose gender identity is different from his or her anatomical sex.

dressing in women's apparel is sexually arousing. In various studies of transsexuals, up to a third of transsexuals reported little or no sexual activity before surgery and were classified as asexual (Bentler, 1976; Blanchard, 1989; Freund, Steiner, & Chan, 1982).

It is estimated that one in every 50,000 individuals over the age of 15 is likely to be transsexual. In most cultures, it appears that transsexualism is distributed evenly among males and females (Pauly, 1990).

### M-F Transsexualism

Although not the first to seek and obtain surgery, George Jorgensen was the first American whose sex reassignment was widely publicized. His childhood and adolescence were similar in many ways to those of other transsexuals. At an early age, he identified more strongly with characteristics associated with girls than with those linked to boys. He remembered wishing for a pretty doll with long golden hair for Christmas when he was five years old; he was disappointed to get a red model train instead (Jorgensen, 1967). He avoided rough-and-tumble games and fistfights and described himself as having been frail and introverted as a child. At the age of 19, he was drafted into the service. At that point he weighed 98 pounds and had underdeveloped genitals and almost no beard.

He experienced emotional feelings for several men but did not view these attachments as homosexual. He felt himself to be a woman. He wanted to relate to men and to the world at large as a woman, and he read everything that he could find about sex hormones. He moved to Copenhagen, Denmark, in 1950 after hearing that surgery for his condition might be available. In 1952, after taking estrogen on a regular basis, he underwent a series of three operations. Two months later, at the age of 26, she returned to the United States as Christine Jorgensen.

Jorgensen's parents were unaware of her decision to seek gender reassignment until after the surgery was performed. They initially reacted with anguish but later accepted the decision. Jorgensen never regretted her decision, and she felt that if she had not been able to get the surgery, she might not have survived. Christine Jorgensen

**FIGURE 19.3**
**Karen Ullane**
Ullane lost her pilot's job at Eastern Airlines in 1984 after undergoing sex-reassignment surgery. She was rehired after winning her case in court.

never married but was engaged twice and reported having been in love with several men. She died in 1989.

Subsequent research involving transsexuals who have undergone gender reassignment in the United States over the past few decades suggests that Jorgensen's feelings are quite representative (see Figure 19.3). The results of physical examinations and of chromosome and hormone tests of presurgical transsexuals are generally in the normal range for males. Yet M-F transsexuals are repelled by their sexual organs. Some transsexuals, lacking access to sex-reassignment surgery, have been so desperate that they have attempted self-castration.

**Behavioral Characteristics**   For most M-F transsexuals, identification with females and a preference for girl's clothing, or cross-dressing, begin at an early age. On psychological inventories, the scores of feminine boys are very similar to those of girls of the same age (Bullough & Bullough, 1993). In adolescence and adulthood, some transsexuals engage in what is described as "hyperfeminine" behavior, characterized by "an overwhelming aroma of perfume, seductive behavior, and attire which is inappropriate to the occasion" (Pauly, 1974b, p. 510). Researchers have also noted tendencies among transsexuals to give responses on psychological inventories that are more stereotypically feminine than those given by control groups of women (McCauley & Ehrhardt, 1977).

In a study of behavioral differences between M-F transsexuals and women, Barlow et al. (1980) pointed out that typical men and women differ in the way they sit, stand, and walk. For example, women generally sit with their buttocks against the back of the chair, whereas men sit with their buttocks away from the chair back. Women tend to stand as if keeping their feet on a line, whereas men stand as if straddling a line. Observing these and other behaviors in a sample of presurgical transsexuals, Barlow found that they engaged in significantly more stereotypically feminine behaviors than did a control group of women who had been selected because of their highly stereotypical feminine appearance. In their desire for a feminine identity, then, some transsexuals may overdo the associated behaviors.

The sexual practices of those who believe that their biological gender is the wrong one reflect their convictions about their true identities. M-F transsexuals who marry women tend to visualize themselves as women during coitus with their wives. Some are able to have intercourse only by imagining that they have a vagina that is being penetrated by their wife's imaginary penis (Money & Primrose, 1968). Those M-F transsexuals most dissatisfied with their gender report high sexual arousal to images of themselves as nude women (Blanchard, 1993). Transsexuals who have anal intercourse with men do not view the act as homosexual because they believe themselves to be female regardless of whether they have undergone surgery.

For people who experience no conflict between their anatomy and their gender identity, the desire for sex-reassignment surgery may be the most difficult aspect of transsexualism to comprehend. For many transsexuals, however, the elimination of the penis as well as other reminders of their genetic gender provide a welcome relief.

**M-F Sex Reassignment**   More than 40 hospitals and clinics in North America have provided transsexuals with therapy and surgery since the first sex-reassignment operation was performed at the Johns Hopkins University Hospital in Baltimore in 1966 (Pauly & Edgerton, 1986). Those seeking surgery undergo several years of treatment, and the costs of surgery are currently about $15,000 (Lief & Hubschman, 1993). Applicants are first evaluated psychologically; individuals who appear to be suffering from disturbances other than a conflict of gender identity are not accepted for surgery. The psychological screening can test the skill of the most experienced clinician, because many of the applicants have read the research literature on transsexualism and seem to know the answers before the clinician has asked the questions.

Those transsexuals whose main problem appears to be the incongruence of their psychological and biological gender identities are instructed to live as women by adopting women's clothing and a feminine lifestyle for three months to a year or longer. If they successfully accommodate to this lifestyle, they are given an estrogenic compound to increase the softness of their skin, the size of their breasts, and the fat deposits on their hips. The growth of facial and body hair is reduced by this hormone, and pubic hair begins to grow in a typically female pattern. Muscle strength and libido diminish, and a gradual reduction takes place in the frequency of erection and ejaculation and the amount of semen. The estrogen treatment does not alter voice pitch, so M-F transsexuals often take lessons to change their voice. The hormonal therapy has little effect on penis length but does reduce the size of the testicles. These effects can be accentuated by administration of antiandrogenic drugs that lower testosterone levels (Asscheman & Gooren, 1992).

If, after a year or more, a transsexual still wishes sex-reassignment surgery, a series of op-

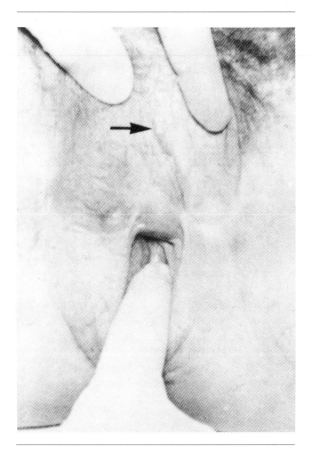

**FIGURE 19.4**
**Male-to-Female Sex-Reassignment Surgery**
The arrow indicates the new clitoris, and the index finger is within the vaginal canal. Labia have been created from the original scrotum.

erations is performed. The testes and penis are removed, and silicone may be implanted in the breasts. Labia and a facsimile of a vagina are constructed (see Figure 19.4). The skin of the penis, with its sensitive nerve endings, is laid inside the vagina, and a form is placed within the vagina for several hours each day to keep the grafted skin from growing together. Body and facial hair may be removed by electrolysis, and plastic surgery may be performed to feminize the person's appearance. With the removal of the testes, the source of sperm and of most of the masculinizing hormones is eliminated, and sterility results.

M-F transsexuals may engage in sexual intercourse, however, and many report erotic feelings and orgasm after their operations (Lief & Hubschman, 1993).

### F-M Transsexualism

Although there are some similarities between male and female transsexuals, several studies also suggest certain intriguing differences in both overt behavior and aspects of sex-reassignment surgery.

**Behavioral Characteristics**    Most F-M transsexuals report having thought of themselves as boys for as long as they can remember, with cross-identification first occurring at about three or four years of age (Pauly, 1985). Cross-dressing, a preference for boys instead of girls as close friends, and a dislike for dolls and other stereotypically feminine toys during childhood are typical of girls who become transsexuals. If they play house, these girls volunteer for the father role, and their interest in parenthood is confined to fantasies of being a husband and father. In general, they report no interest in handling babies (Ehrhardt et al., 1979).

Most young girls with no gender-identity conflicts go through normal transitory periods wherein they express the desire to be a boy and so may be labeled tomboys. Parents therefore need not necessarily be concerned if their daughters engage in tomboyish behavior. For F-M transsexuals, however, the preference for masculine activities and attire persists for years and is coupled with a strong rejection of the feminine role. Further, their sense of being male despite having anatomical and assigned roles as females is a source of pain and confusion for them (Bullough & Bullough, 1993).

Puberty is an especially difficult time for female transsexuals. Although many girls express fear or disgust upon first experiencing menstruation—particularly when sex education is inadequate—menarche is usually a source of pleasure for them as a symbol of their emerging womanhood. However, F-M transsexuals feel intense revulsion toward menarche and other aspects of female development. Moreover, although girls in our culture commonly exaggerate their developing breasts with the aid of tissues, wadded-up stockings, and the like—understandable behavior, given our society's obsessive interest in breasts—transsexuals commonly report having hidden or bound their developing breasts (Ehrhardt et al., 1979; Steiner, 1985).

Many F-M transsexuals report an awareness of having been attracted to females during early adolescence, but they generally do not begin having sexual relations with women until about five years later, at about the age of 18. Their sexual partners are often markedly feminine, heterosexual women, although some report relationships with gay men (Devor, 1993). During sexual relations, many F-M transsexuals do not allow their partners to see them nude, penetrate their vaginas, or touch their breasts and other parts of their bodies (McCauley & Ehrhardt, 1980). Of those who do permit touching, most limit the contact to clitoral stimulation. Transsexuals whose clitorises have been enlarged through androgenic compounds often imagine their clitorises to be penises. In the discussion of M-F transsexuality, we noted that several researchers have found that some males take the stereotypically feminine role to such an extreme that they fashion themselves into caricatures of women. Pauly's (1985) research suggested that F-M transsexuals take on the masculine role more believably than their M-F counterparts take on the feminine role. The scores of female transsexuals on psychological inventories are either slightly more feminine than, or comparable to, those of normal men (Money & Brennan, 1968). The responses of most F-M transsexuals on diagnostic inventories indicate no severe psychological disturbance other than gender-identity conflict (Coleman, Bockting, & Gooeren, 1993; Strassberg et al., 1979).

**F-M Gender Reassignment**    After psychological screening, applicants for F-M sex-reassignment surgery are asked to live as males for three months to a year or more. If they are successful in this adaptation, they are given androgenic compounds. These masculinizing compounds stimulate the growth of facial and body hair, slightly decrease breast size, and increase the size of the clitoris. The androgenic compounds also suppress menstruation and deepen the voice (Asscheman & Gooren, 1992).

If the person still desires surgery after having lived as a male for a year or so, a series of operations is performed. As it is easier to remove than to add body parts, sex-reassignment surgery is more complex and expensive—about $50,000 (Lief & Hubschman, 1993). It is also frequently less successful for F-M transsexuals than for their M-F counterparts.

For some F-M transsexuals, the lack of success with constructing an artificial penis leads them to avoid this surgery, as shown in this excerpt from Brame et al. (1993, p. 424):

> *If you have the female-to-male surgery and get a constructed penis, they take out all the internals, the uterus and ovaries, and they close up the vagina, and they reroute the urethra, which can cause problems later. There's a lot of reconstruction. The male-to-female stuff is peanuts by comparison. Female-to-male is also more expensive than the male-to-female. I was quoted a cost [of] around $60,000. There are other things I can think of to buy with $60,000 than a dick that doesn't work.  —Kelly T.*

For those who choose to have this surgery, skin from the labia and abdomen is used to fashion a penis and scrotum. An artificial testis may be placed in each side of the scrotum. The penis looks quite realistic (see Figure 19.5), but no surgical procedure at present can create a penis that becomes erect in response to sexual stimulation. Several techniques are available for providing a rigid penis for purposes of sexual penetration. One of these involves making a skin tube on the underside of the penis into which a rigid silicone rod may be inserted. Alternatively, inflatable devices that produce erection may be provided. Although the artificial penis does not respond to physical stimulation, erotic feelings and orgasm remain if the clitoris has been left embedded at the base of the penis (see Chapter 8). Additional surgery can involve removing the breasts, uterus, and ovaries and sealing off the vagina. Excision of the ovaries eliminates eggs and the primary source of estrogen, so, like the M-F transsexual, the F-M transsexual can no longer reproduce.

Ideally, a postsurgical transsexual continues to receive medical follow-up and counseling. Such therapy can also be beneficial to a transsex-

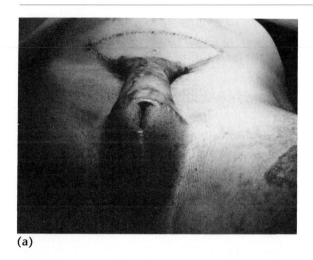

(a)

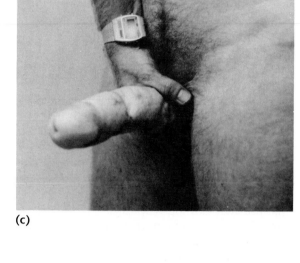

(c)

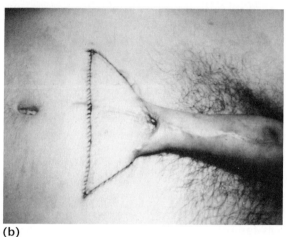

(b)

**FIGURE 19.5**
**Female-to-Male Sex-Reassignment Surgery**
In female-to-male sex-reassignment surgery, an artificial penis is created. Artificial means of producing an erection are available if an erect penis is desired.

ual's family and lover. Unfortunately, these postoperative practices are not always followed.

*Controversies About Transsexualism*

The causes and definition of transsexualism, and especially the drastic surgical treatment of it, are all subjects of heated debate among professionals. Many professionals have questioned the automatic application of the term *transsexual* to anyone who requests sex-reassignment surgery,

because such a request can stem from a variety of motives (Bullough & Bullough, 1993). Some individuals function in a psychologically healthy fashion except for a deeply felt conflict between anatomical features and psychological gender identity, and for them, the use of the term *transsexual* may be appropriate. Other persons, however, may be generally maladjusted and may blame their inability to deal effectively with various life crises on a gender-identity conflict. Lothstein suggested, for example, that disturbed aging people with gender-identity conflicts sometimes may "believe it is possible to cheat death by changing sex" (1979, p. 433). Further, researchers' estimates (Pauly & Edgerton, 1986) indicate that about a third of applicants for sex-reassignment surgery are homosexuals who cannot accept their sexual orientation and apply for reassignment surgery mainly in the hope of bringing their practices into compliance with a heterosexually oriented society. Still other people may view the painful surgery as a method of punishing themselves for real or imagined "sins." None of these individuals fits the definition of a transsexual.

Accordingly, Meyer (1974) recommended use of the phrase "gender dysphoria syndrome," coined by Fisk (1973), to refer to the following conditions: a sense of inappropriateness or incapacity in the biological gender role; a sense that improvement will occur with role reversal; sexual attraction to persons of the same biological gender; and an active desire for reassignment surgery. The term *transsexual*, however, is the one that most frequently appears in the research and medical literature.

**Explanations of Transsexualism**   There is no agreement as to why some people feel an intense conflict over gender identity. Transsexuality is definitely not a form of hermaphroditism, nor is there any evidence that it is associated with pre-natal exposure to high levels of inappropriate hormones. However, a third of a sample of 22 F-M transsexuals were found to have abnormal brain-wave patterns, and Pauly (1974) speculated that prenatal hormone exposure might have dis-turbed areas of the brain that affect stereotypical masculine and feminine behavior. Other studies have reported similar percentages of abnormal brain-wave patterns in transsexuals, but the sig-nificance of these findings is still not known (Hoenig, 1985). Postmortem study of the brains of transsexuals has not shown differences be-tween them and "normal" brains (Emory, Wil-liams, Cole, Amparo, & Meyer, 1991).

Hormonal explanations of transsexualism have fared no better. Most adult transsexuals have hormone levels that fall within the normal range for their genetic gender (Jones, 1974; Good-man et al., 1985).

In another attempt to understand the causes of transsexualism, early family experiences were examined to determine whether parents modeled or encouraged cross-gender identification. Be-cause gender identity is learned very early in life, and most transsexuals report cross-identification well before puberty, it is possible that dynamics within the family might be linked to the devel-opment of transsexuality. However, no system-atic patterns have emerged with respect to par-ents. Most of the genetic females with a gender-identity conflict in research by Ehrhardt et al. (1979) had been raised by both parents dur-ing childhood and adolescence. Some indicated a preference for their mothers, and some for their fathers. The remainder indicated that they cared equally for both parents.

In summary, until further research has been done focusing on large samples of transsexuals, the most honest answer we can give to the ques-tion of what causes transsexualism is that we do not know.

**Treatment: Surgery or Psychotherapy?** The is-sue of the clinical treatment for transsexuals has sparked fiery controversy among professionals. Until the 1960s, the U.S. medical profession was generally opposed to sex-reassignment surgery, defining the problem of transsexualism as psy-chological rather than medical in nature. Since 1966, however, when gynecologist Howard Jones, plastic surgeon Milton T. Edgerton, and psychologist John Money initiated the first sex-reassignment surgery and therapy in the United States, the frequency of such surgery has in-creased (Money, 1988).

Faced with a desperate plea for surgery on the part of a transsexual whose conflict is a source of great pain and who may have contemplated or even attempted suicide (Lothstein, 1979), phy-sicians obviously have a difficult choice. If they could look into a crystal ball and clearly see that the individual's postsurgical life would be a vast improvement over his or her years of presurgical anguish, many would probably support the use of sex-reassignment surgery. The "crystal ball" that would help scientists is a large, well-con-trolled study comparing the well-being of trans-sexuals before and after surgery, and the well-being of transsexuals who do and do not receive reassignment surgery. But several factors have made obtaining reliable information on postsur-gical adjustment difficult (Hunt & Hampson, 1980). First, the samples available in any one gen-der-identity clinic are typically quite small. For example, 65 sex-reassignment surgeries have been performed at Pennsylvania Hospital in Phil-adelphia since the hospital began the procedure in 1968, fewer than 3 a year (Lief & Hubschman, 1993). Second, long-term access to transsexuals who have undergone reassignment surgery is difficult. Many wish to avoid reminders of their former gender, and some resent the intrusion of researchers.

Most transsexuals claim to be happier follow-ing surgery than prior to it and report that they would go through the procedure again (Green & Fleming, 1990; Lief & Hubschman, 1993). There appear to be gender differences in postsurgical adjustment, however. F-M transsexuals more often have stable relationships with a partner and appear more socially adjusted than M-F transsexuals do (Kockott & Fahrner, 1988; Verschoor & Poortinga, 1988).

One study suggests that surgery is not necessarily essential to a transsexual's psychosocial adjustment. A comparison of the social and psychological adjustment of 34 postsurgical transsexuals with that of 66 transsexuals who did not receive surgery revealed improvements in both groups (Meyer & Reter, 1979). For example, both experienced a 70% decrease in the number of visits to psychiatrists over a six-year period. This research suggests that the drastic sex-reassignment surgery provided no greater overall psychosocial adjustment than the simple passage of time combined with limited support from clinical personnel. To some extent, people's attitudes regarding the appropriateness of surgery depend on what they view as the source of the problem. Virginia Prince (1977) has suggested that surgical solutions to conflicts of gender identity represent a confusion between biology and psychology. In her succinctly stated opinion, surgery "is only a painful, expensive, dangerous and misguided attempt to achieve between the legs what must eventually and inevitably be achieved between the ears."

On the other hand, psychological adjustment was found to be greater in postsurgical transsexuals than in presurgical transsexuals, and the quality of the surgery also may affect postsurgical adjustment (Fleming et al., 1981; Pfäfflin, 1992; Ross & Need, 1989). Obviously, there is a need for further research to determine whether the operation makes enough of a difference to justify the pain, expense, and drastic anatomical and hormonal alterations. The evidence does clearly suggest, however, that sex-reassignment surgery can alleviate the emotional distress associated with feeling that one is of a different gender than one's anatomy indicates (Green & Fleming, 1990; Pfäfflin, 1992).

Research on transsexualism holds the promise of helping us to unfold the mysteries surrounding gender development and identity. As Stoller (1975) pointed out, transsexual surgery is an experiment that researchers would never dare to perform on those with consistent biological and psychological gender identities.

Earlier, we alluded to hypotheses that some individuals seeking reassignment surgery may be motivated by the desire to punish themselves for real or imagined "sins." Such a connection between sexuality and the infliction of real or symbolic pain is a theme for those engaging in sadomasochistic activities, a topic to which we turn now.

## Sexual Sadism and Sexual Masochism

*Sexual sadism* refers to the infliction of physical or psychological pain on another living creature to produce sexual excitement. In this section our consideration is limited to consenting partners, for sadism performed on an unwilling victim is sexual assault.

Only those pain-inflicting acts that sexually excite the inflictor can be classified as sadistic. In mild forms of sadism, the administering of pain can be primarily symbolic, such as beating someone with a soft object that is designed to resemble a hard club. In these cases, the partner just pretends to be in pain (Stoller, 1977). At the other end of the continuum is the sadist who can become aroused only if the partner is savagely attacked or even murdered. In this case, it is not the dead body that excites the sadist but the victim's suffering and dying. Sadism has traditionally been associated exclusively with men, although as we shall see, that stereotype is not supported by the data.

*Sexual masochism* refers to experiencing sexual arousal by suffering physical or psychological pain that is produced in specific ways. The individual may be aroused by being whipped, cut, pricked, bound, spanked, or verbally humiliated. A masochist responds sexually only to particular sorts of pain. A masochist who becomes sexually aroused while being whipped, for example, does not respond with erection or vaginal lubrication if a car door is slammed on his or her finger. The

**sexual sadism**—the intentional infliction of pain or humiliation on another person for sexual excitement.

**sexual masochism**—sexual gratification through experiencing pain and humiliation.

### Box 19.1

## Pain and Sexual Arousal

One of the unusual relationships that can exist between the perception of pain and sexual arousal is illustrated in the following excerpt from Brame, Brame, and Jacob's (1993) book, *Different Loving: An Exploration of the World of Sexual Dominance and Submission:*

*The real nature of S&M was driven home to me about 15 years ago. I was doing a movie called* House of Sin. *There was an S&M scene [with] a mistress and her slave, who were, in real life, living together. She had him on the floor, with his hands tied behind him. She had a dog chain wrapped around his cock and balls and was lifting him off the floor by his cock and balls and*

*smacking him across the nuts, hard enough so that every guy in the room had his legs crossed. Two things stuck in my mind: First, that while this was happening, this guy had an incredible erection, and two, as soon as I yelled, "Cut!" he immediately started to bitch and moan about the fact that he was lying on a hardwood floor and didn't have a pillow behind his head. At that moment I realized that what she was doing to his genitals was not painful; the little bit of pressure on the back of his head, that's what his brain was interpreting as pain. But the hard pressure of her hand coming in contact with his nuts was erotically stimulating. I realized that in S&M, if it's painful, you're doing it wrong. (pp. 42–43)*

masochist usually has specific requirements with respect to the manner in which pain is inflicted, the area of the body assaulted, and the person who inflicts the pain (see Box 19.1). If the pattern is not followed, then the pain will lose its arousal power.

In Western cultures, although women commonly indulge in masochistic fantasies, they rarely experience sexual excitement that is specifically provoked by physical pain. When women report enjoying masochism, questioning often reveals that the source of excitement was the concentration of feeling and attention directed at them by the person inflicting the pain rather than the pain itself (Stoller, 1977).

Most current information about sadism and masochism comes from clinical case reports, but another source is several questionnaire studies that have been conducted with individuals located through sadomasochistic magazines and clubs (Breslow, Evans, & Langley, 1985; Spengler, 1977). More than half the respondents indicated that they played both dominant and submissive roles within the sadomasochistic context. This finding suggests that individuals who participate in sexual activities involving the intentional in-

fliction of pain are more accurately described by the compound term *sadomasochist* than by the word *sadist* or *masochist*. In one study, 25% of respondents were women who were not prostitutes (Breslow et al., 1985). This percentage is surprising in light of an earlier research conclusion that most women who participate in sadomasochism are prostitutes doing so for financial reasons (Spengler, 1977).

Male respondents indicated that they first became aware of their sadomasochistic interests at around age 15 years, whereas females reported that they became interested in sadomasochism at about age 22. Men seemed to discover sadomasochism on their own, whereas women tended to be introduced to it by a sexual partner. Both men and women viewed sadomasochism as primarily sexual foreplay. Perhaps because there appear to be more men than women involved in the sadomasochistic subculture, female respondents had sadomasochistic sex more often and with more different partners than did males. Table 19.2 shows the respondents' behavioral preferences. The more extreme forms of sexual activity associated with sadomasochism, such as torture and use of excrement, were relatively rare.

## Table 19.2 Sadomasochistic Sexual Interests: A Comparison of the Sadomasochistic Sexual Preferences of Females and Males

| Interest | Male (%) | Female (%) |
| --- | --- | --- |
| Spanking | 79 | 80 |
| Master-slave relationships | 79 | 76 |
| Oral sex | 77 | 90 |
| Masturbation | 70 | 73 |
| Bondage | 67 | 88 |
| Humiliation | 65 | 61 |
| Erotic lingerie | 63 | 88 |
| Restraint | 60 | 83 |
| Anal sex | 58 | 51 |
| Pain | 51 | 34 |
| Whipping | 47 | 39 |
| Rubber/leather | 42 | 42 |
| Boots/shoes | 40 | 49 |
| Verbal abuse | 40 | 51 |
| Stringent bondage | 39 | 54 |
| Enemas | 33 | 22 |
| Torture | 32 | 32 |
| Golden showers | 30 | 37 |
| Transvestism | 28 | 20 |
| Petticoat punishment | 25 | 20 |
| Toilet activities | 19 | 12 |

Source: Based on responses to questionnaires completed by individuals located through sadomasochistic magazines and clubs, by N. Breslow, L. Evans, J. Langley, 1985. *Archives of Sexual Behavior 14*, p. 315. Copyright 1985 by Plenum Publishing Company. Reprinted by permission.

The most popular sadomasochistic sexual activities, which include spanking and master-slave relationships, are featured in sadomasochistic magazines and movies. Sadomasochists may belong to special clubs, or they may visit prostitutes who indulge their fantasies. For many years, Monique von Cleef operated a "House of Torture" in a luxurious 16-room home in Newark, New Jersey. She specialized in sadomasochistic services for males with a sexual affinity for leather. Her employees, whom she called "leather social workers," wore knee-high or hip-high leather boots and leather clothing. When the police raided her establishment, they found card files on more than 15,000 patrons.

Sadomasochistic sexual practices may also include what is called bondage and discipline (B&D), a pattern in which a sexual partner is tied up and then sexually stimulated. The exchange may involve dog collars, leashes, and chains but usually follows predetermined patterns and stops short of physical harm (see Figure 19.6).

What seems to be central to sadomasochistic activities is a master-slave relationship. The partner playing the master can, for a time, exercise complete control over the other person, and the partner playing the slave can give up all personal responsibility. Sexual expression is controlled and predictable in these carefully structured situations (Brame, Brame, & Jacobs, 1993; Weinberg, 1987), and it is common for couples to engage in elaborate negotiations about their specific roles before beginning sadomasochistic play. Again, we emphasize the difference between consensual sadomasochistic activities versus invasive sadism in which one person attempts to, or does, exert complete control over another person against that person's will.

### Sadomasochism and Beliefs About Gender Differences

Richard von Krafft-Ebing, the 19th-century chronicler of atypical sexuality (see Chapter 3), believed that sadism was a pathological exaggeration of the normal psychology of men and that masochism was a distorted extension of normal female sexual inclinations. He saw sadism as an essentially masculine disorder, and masochism as a feminine disorder. Krafft-Ebing was apparently unconcerned that the Austrian novelist after whom he named the syndrome of masochism, Leopold von Sacher-Masoch, was a man. Sadism takes its name from the 18th-century French writer, the Marquis de Sade.

Like Krafft-Ebing, some psychoanalytic authors also stressed a gender difference in sadomasochism. For example, psychoanalyst Helene Deutsch, in her book *The Psychology of Women* (1944), advanced the belief that species survival depended to some extent on females' associating pain with pleasure. She devoted an entire chapter to the topic. However, men and women *both* engage in sadism, and their masochistic partners are both men and women.

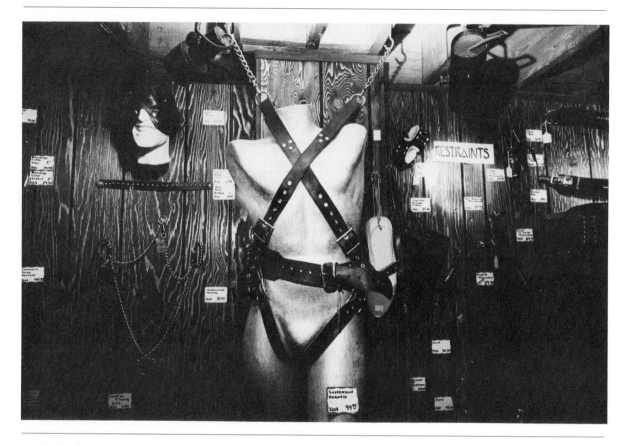

**FIGURE 19.6**
**Tools of Bondage and Discipline**
The bondage apparel displayed in this sex-specialty shop in San Francisco is
designed for sadomasochistic activities.

Research on normal populations suggests that there is a *slight* difference in the proportion of males and females who enjoy sadomasochism in some form. For example, Kinsey et al. (1953) found that 22% of males and 12% of females reported some sexual arousal from sadistic stories. A large number of women and men also reported erotic responses to being bitten, as Table 19.3 shows. Of those who enjoyed being bitten, a little more than half reported that biting frequently accompanied their sexual activities.

Other research indicates that males are slightly more inclined to inflict pain and females are more likely to receive pain during erotic activities (Hunt, 1974). Among the unmarried volunteers in Hunt's survey, 10% of the women and 6% of the men reported obtaining sexual pleasure from enduring pain, although Hunt's respondents also reported activities in which they inflicted pain, such as beating, hitting, scratching, and pinching. These small differences between men and women do not support the concept that women are inclined toward masochism and men toward sadism.

There appear to be gender differences, however, in how males and females approach masochism. Male masochism appears to be an escape strategy from the traditional male role (Baumeister, 1988a). Being humiliated and degraded, and sacrificing or postponing one's own sexual pleasure, contradict the masculine archetype. This escape from self may reduce high levels of self-

**TABLE 19.3  Normal Sadomasochism**

| Erotic Responses to Being Bitten | By Females (%) | By Males (%) |
|---|---|---|
| Definite and/or frequent | 26 | 26 |
| Some response | 29 | 24 |
| Never | 45 | 50 |
| Number of people interviewed | 2,200 | 567 |
| **Erotic Arousal from Sadomasochistic Stories** | **By Females (%)** | **By Males (%)** |
| Definite and/or frequent | 3 | 10 |
| Some response | 9 | 12 |
| Never | 88 | 78 |
| Number of people interviewed | 2,800 | 1,016 |

Source: Adapted from Kinsey, A.C., Pomeroy, W., Martin, C., Gebhard, P. *Sexual Behavior in the Human Female*, pp. 677–678. Philadelphia: Saunders, 1953. By permission of the Kinsey Institute for Research in Sex, Gender, and Reproduction, Inc.

awareness and intensify a focus on the immediate present and on bodily sensations. Female masochism follows a different route in escaping from one's everyday self by exaggerating the female stereotype. The woman devotes herself to her partner's pleasure, and her role is transformed to "remove responsibility, insecurity, and sexual inhibition" (Baumeister, 1988b, p. 497).

## The Invasive Paraphilias

Invasive paraphilias involve behaviors that violate other people's personal space. That is, few people would consent to unexpectedly encountering someone exposing his genitalia to them. Similarly, while undressing or making love in the bedroom, most of us would not welcome the idea that someone was observing us with binoculars from behind a tree in our backyard.

John Money (1988) claims to have identified about 40 paraphilias. Many individuals who are arrested for invasive paraphilic behaviors do not qualify for a clinical label because they do not have recurrent intense sexual urges and sexually arousing fantasies of the paraphilic behavior. They may resort to the paraphilia for lack of a socially appropriate sex partner, because of an unusual opportunity, or out of a desire to experiment. As we consider the major paraphilias, it is also important to remember that personal or subjective considerations often play a greater role in labeling a person as sexually atypical than do objective, scientific facts (Levine & Troiden, 1988). In this section, we describe those paraphilias that intrude on other people's rights.

## Voyeurism

*Voyeurism* refers to obtaining sexual gratification by observing others who are undressing, naked, or participating in sexual activity. Many people enjoy observing nudity and sexual activity, as the

**voyeurism** (VOY-yer-ism)—obtaining sexual arousal by observing people without their consent when they are undressed or occupied in sexual activity.

**FIGURE 19.7**
**A Life-Drawing Class**
This artist would not be considered a voyeur, nor the model an exhibitionist, because both are consenting to the activity.

popularity of erotic literature and X-rated movies and tapes demonstrates. You may therefore wonder where the dividing line is between "normal" looking and voyeurism (see Figure 19.7). After all, in our culture, watching women has been as accepted a male pastime as watching the Super Bowl, and it is certainly a component of courtship behavior.* Viewing scantily attired or nude females is also acceptable in many circumstances in our culture. Beauty contestants, models in men's magazines, scantily attired cheerleaders, waitresses in topless-bottomless bars, and bikini-clad women at a pool or beach are all objects of culturally sanctioned gazing.

Although women traditionally have been assumed to possess little interest in the uncovered bodies of men, the popularity of male strip shows, male go-go dancers, and photos of men in women's magazines such as *Cosmopolitan* is evidence to the contrary. Like girl-watching, women's interest in these phenomena is considered normal rather than voyeuristic.

Looking becomes voyeurism, a criminal offense, when the voyeur observes people who are unaware that they are being watched or who are unwilling to be observed. Because only a few states prohibit voyeurism, voyeurs are often prosecuted under antiloitering and disorderly conduct laws. For the voyeur, the viewing of strangers without consent is the primary or preferred sexual activity.

Convicted voyeurs are almost always male. Many women enjoy observing nude males; indeed, when shown pictures or films of nude males, women report as much sexual arousal as men do when shown pictures or films of nude females (Fisher, 1983). But women seldom invest the energy required to seek out unsuspecting men for observation.

This gender difference may stem from cultural constraints against women's actively seeking out sexual stimuli. Alternatively, the difference may be due to men's greater receptivity or sensitivity to visual sexual stimuli. One hypothesis holds that men's keener interest in visual sexual stimuli is rooted in our evolutionary past. That is, women's physical attractiveness may have symbolized general health and therefore reproductive fitness (Buss, 1994; Fisher, 1992). Male sexual arousal at the sight of nude or partially nude females was therefore a critical part of the process leading to reproduction.

Ford and Beach's (1951) review of cross-cultural studies showed that no group in the sample allowed women to expose their genitals except under restricted circumstances. This prohibition may prevent accidental exposure under conditions that might provoke unwanted sexual advances by men toward women, thus preserving women's opportunity to choose a mate with qualities of reproductive fitness. Margaret Mead (1967) pointed out that in all societies, girls are permanently clothed before boys are. She maintained that because older boys and men find young girls attractive, the bodies of young girls as well as of their older sisters and mothers must be guarded from the male eye.

---

*By describing these or other behaviors, we do not advocate them. We are simply attempting to describe behaviors generally accepted as normal in Western culture.

It is also possible, however, that there are more female voyeurs than arrest and conviction records indicate. A man out for a walk who stops to view a nude woman in a window may be arrested for voyeurism. But if a man undresses in front of a window and a woman stops to look, the man may be as likely to be arrested for exhibitionism as the woman for voyeurism. Police and court records may reflect this bias.

### Characteristics of Voyeurs

Voyeurs tend to be young and male, with the average age at first conviction being 24 (Gebhard et al., 1965). Gebhard and his associates found that few voyeurs had serious mental disorders, and alcohol or drugs were seldom involved in their "peeping." Some voyeurs resemble other sex offenders in displaying deficient sexual relationships, but others are able to interact sexually with consenting partners with no evidence of dysfunction.

The voyeur derives sexual arousal from the notion that he is violating the privacy of his victims. Like practitioners of other criminal sexual variations, the "peeping tom" may be stimulated by the danger of apprehension. The willingness to run risks is what distinguishes the voyeur from the average woman watcher. The desire for this element of risk-taking may explain why voyeurs do not overflow nudist camps, strip shows, or other places where observing nude bodies is considered acceptable. The voyeur may scale high fences, bore holes in bedroom walls, risk injury from watchdogs, and endure terrible weather conditions to observe what excites him. The act of looking is usually accompanied by sexual excitement, and frequently by orgasm. Sometimes the voyeur masturbates while he is gazing at unsuspecting targets, or he may do so later when reliving the situation in fantasy.

As with other paraphilias, the cause of voyeurism is not known. Behaviorists emphasize that the association of sexual arousal with peeping may be accidental. If a male masturbates while peeping or later while recalling the act in fantasy, the association is further strengthened. Repeated incidents can lead to reliance on peeping as the main source of sexual arousal.

Some psychoanalysts trace the disorder back to childhood episodes in which the individual witnessed his parents having intercourse. For persons who have poorly developed social and sexual skills, voyeurism provides a means of sexual gratification that avoids the potential threat of sexual interaction. Taking the risk of being caught may bolster the voyeur's often deficient sense of masculinity, just as it does for the exhibitionist.

## Exhibitionism

*Exhibitionism* refers to obtaining erotic gratification from displaying one's genitals. The public display of the genitals, or indecent exposure, is illegal in every state. Exposing one's genitals to another person in private is, of course, a normal part of sexual interaction. It is only when this activity becomes the primary or preferred source of sexual gratification and involves unwilling or unsuspecting victims that it becomes problematic (see Figure 19.8).

As with most other paraphilias, exhibitionism is almost exclusively a male activity. There are only three published cases of exhibitionism in women who were not retarded, epileptic, or schizophrenic (Arndt, 1991; Freund & Blanchard, 1986). Whereas exhibitionism by a man is seen as threatening, a woman's partial or full exposure of her breasts and/or genitals is usually perceived as seductive, even though it is technically criminal if done publicly. Because stripteasers and nude models—both male and female—shed their clothes primarily for economic gain rather than for sexual pleasure, they are not considered exhibitionists.

Exhibitionism is the most common sexual offense, accounting for about a third of all sex-crime arrests (Arndt, 1991). Exhibitionism almost always violates indecent-exposure laws. Generally, indecent exposure is a misdemeanor unless it is committed under "aggravating" circumstances, which include having minors as victims or having a number of previous convictions for indecent exposure. When it is a misdemeanor, penalties range from a small fine to a jail term of up to one year. Exhibitionism occurs primarily during warm weather (May to September), in the

**exhibitionism**—the act of exposing one's genitals to an unwilling observer to obtain sexual gratification.

**FIGURE 19.8**
**Public Nudity**
Some individuals display their unclothed bodies at parties or festivals. This behavior
is not considered to be exhibitionism from a clinical viewpoint.

middle of the week, between 3:00 P.M. and 6:00 P.M., and in public settings (Arndt, 1991; MacDonald, 1973). The key to arrest, of course, is the fact that the exhibitionist exposes himself to an unwilling or unsuspecting viewer. Contrary to the *DSM-IV*'s definition of exhibitionism as involving the baring of the genitals to strangers, a study of college women found that 36% of the reported exposure episodes involved men known by the victims (Cox, 1988). This suggests that a change in the *DSM-IV*'s definition of exhibitionism would be appropriate.

The exhibitionist apparently derives gratification from the startled or frightened response of his target. If a woman pays no attention to him or calmly tells him that he is foolish or disturbed, the exhibitionist gets little pleasure from the episode. In most instances, when a woman has approached rather than fled from an exhibitionist,

he has rapidly retreated. It is common for the exhibitionist to have an erection when he exposes himself. About half of one sample of 130 exhibitionists reported always or almost always having erections when exhibiting (Langevin et al., 1979). Almost half this group reported masturbating when exposing themselves.

Many exhibitionists use the episode as a source of fantasy for later masturbation. There is evidence to suggest that indulging in such fantasies during masturbation may be critical in the development and maintenance of exhibitionist behavior (Blair & Lanyon, 1981).

*Characteristics of Exhibitionists*

Exhibitionistic men are typically in their 20s the first time they expose themselves (Arndt, 1991). The most frequent targets of these displays are

16- to 30-year-old women (Langevin et al., 1979). A substantial number of men in the Langevin et al. (1979) study wanted the women to whom they exposed themselves to be impressed by the size of their penises. They described the desire for sexual relationships with their victims as a secondary motivation.

Exhibitionists generally score in the normal range on measures of intelligence, personality, and psychological adjustment (Arndt, 1991; Levin & Stava, 1987). Although no difference in testosterone levels has been found between exhibitionists and other men, certain biological conditions may contribute to exhibitionism. Some developmentally disabled individuals may not be fully aware of the social disapproval associated with the exposure of their genitals at inappropriate times and places. Likewise, older men may suffer from senile brain deterioration that can lead to decreased self-control.

All definitions of exhibitionism include the association of exposure with sexual excitement. The sexual arousal may be generated by the response of the woman to whom men expose themselves. However, nearly half the 130 exhibitionists in the Langevin et al. (1979) study reported that they exposed themselves without physical gratification. These men may be as motivated by the thrill-seeking aspect of exhibitionism as they are by its overt sexual aspects. The exhibitionist is more likely to be apprehended than is any other type of sexual offender. Perhaps the tension and thrill of potential arrest are attractive to the exhibitionist. For many exhibitionists, self-exposure may be a way of compensating for timidity and lack of assertiveness. The exhibitionistic act may make them feel like powerful men, and the danger of being apprehended and prosecuted as criminals may contribute to this feeling. The psychoanalytic view of exhibitionism fits with this general picture: it is thought that by displaying the penis, exhibitionists seek to prove to the world and, most important, to adult women that they are indeed men.

The association of masculinity with exposing must be extremely powerful, because being convicted of a sex offense can result in social and professional ruin. Once ruined, many exhibitionists have little to deter them from subsequent "flashing." One-third of the convicted offenders in a study by the Kinsey group had four to six previous convictions, and another 10% had been convicted seven times or more (Gebhard et al., 1965). This recidivism rate may reflect the fact that many exhibitionists display themselves repeatedly in the same place and at the same time of day with seeming disregard of the danger of being caught again.

Some authorities believe that narcissism, an extreme form of self-admiration, plays a role in exhibitionism. Many exhibitionists expose themselves even when they have opportunities for sexual contact. A wife or lover can admire an exhibitionist's penis for only so long. Perhaps "the exhibitionist may be like an actor on the stage who wants an audience but does not want it to participate in his act" (Langevin et al., 1979, p. 328).

Although most experts consider exhibitionism and voyeurism to be distinct syndromes, many individuals indulge in both activities. For example, some exhibitionists may peep when exposing is not possible or is too risky. Almost half the exhibitionists in the Langevin et al. (1979) study reported having peeped at least once. Interestingly, just under a third of the men in the control groups also admitted to having peeped at least once. Of a group of more than 600 men referred to a clinic for sexual offenses, all those who had engaged in voyeurism also had committed other sexual offenses (Langevin, Paitich, & Russon, 1985). Because voyeurism is almost always related to other paraphilias, one could argue that "pure" voyeurism is a rarity.

### Obscene Telephone Calls

People who describe sexual activities to a listener over the telephone can be thought of as exhibitionists. They are "exhibiting" verbally. Like the man who exposes his genitals, the obscene caller enjoys the frightened or startled response of the victim. Masturbation during or shortly after the call is common, and almost all obscene calls are made by men rather than women. In one study, 61% of the women had received obscene phone calls (Herold, Mantle, & Zemitis, 1979).

The recipient of such telephone calls can be unnerved if the calls are made repeatedly by someone who breathes heavily or describes sexual acts. However, a person who receives an obscene phone call should try to react in the same calm manner advocated for the target of an exhibitionist. Shock or fright is usually what the caller wishes to provoke, presumably because this response is sexually exciting. After the nature of an obscene phone call becomes apparent, it is appropriate either to hang up without saying anything or to say something like "Sorry, I don't have the time for this nonsense" or "Why don't you get yourself to a mental health center?" and then hang up. Still another alternative is to blow a whistle into the receiver and then hang up. A man recently called our house purportedly wanting to do a survey on female lingerie, and he has called many of our women students with the same ploy. When I (E.R.A.) answered the phone and heard his pitch, I said, "Certainly, just let me turn on the speaker phone so that my husband can hear." The caller immediately hung up. If you are the recipient of such repeated calls, you should report the calls to the telephone company and to the police. Persistent obscene calls can sometimes be traced.

## Frotteurism

*Frotteurism* is characterized by touching or rubbing one's body against a nonconsenting person, usually a woman. The frotteur usually rubs his penis, usually covered, against a woman to achieve sexual arousal and/or orgasm. Subways, buses, and other crowded situations provide opportunities for such gratification, which typically elicits either little notice or only minor annoyance from the target. Frotteurism often occurs in conjunction with other paraphilias. In one study, almost 70% of males referred for frotteurism were found to have been involved in either voyeurism, exhibitionism, or rape (Freund & Blanchard, 1986). Thus it appears that many men arrested for one of the invasive paraphilias also practice others. For example, the paraphilias that we have just described—voyeurism, exhibitionism, and frotteurism—are behaviors that may be practiced by people who are sexually attracted to children: pedophiles.

**frotteurism**—obtaining sexual arousal by touching or rubbing one's body against the body of an unsuspecting or nonconsenting person.

## Pedophilia

The term *pedophilia* has its origin in Greek and literally means "love of children." The pedophile, or sexual abuser of children, is usually envisioned as a "dirty old man" who lures an innocent young girl into a dark alley or the woods, where he rapes her. As such, child molesters are regarded with even more disgust and rage than are rapists. In prisons, the sexual abuser of a child tends to be the prisoner most despised by guards and other inmates alike. How accurate is this stereotype of pedophiles? At the outset, we should note that people who approach children sexually (primarily men) are usually either related to, or acquaintances of, the youngsters.

Those convicted of sexual offenses against minors tend to be older than other convicted sex offenders. Their average age at conviction is 35, and about a quarter are over 45 (Arndt, 1991; Gebhard et al., 1965). In contrast to the past clinical and survey literature that described the pedophile as conservative, socially inadequate, psychosexually immature, and psychologically disturbed, Okami and Goldberg (1992) found no evidence to support these assumptions in their review of the literature. Even if we just consider convicted child sex offenders, clear-cut psychiatric disturbance is not generally apparent, although many child offenders tend toward shyness, loneliness, low self-esteem, isolation, and sensitivity to the evaluations of others (Okami & Goldberg, 1992). In general, the younger the victim, the more likely that the sexual offender exhibits psychopathology (Kalichman, 1991). Similar to sexually coercive college males, convicted offenders of sexual crimes against children do not appear to lack appropriate social skills (Koralewski & Conger, 1992; Okami & Goldberg, 1992).

Many offenders against children also engage in a full range of sexual activities with adult women, frequently including oral and vaginal sex. This pattern is also followed when they victimize adolescents (Finkelhor et al., 1990; Okami, 1991). There is some evidence, however, that "child sex offenders" adjust their sexual behaviors to the age level of their partner or victim

**pedophilia** (PEH-doe-FILL-ee-ah)—sexual contact between an adult and a child.

(Okami & Goldberg, 1992). That is, they will engage in the early stages of a normal courtship sequence—looking and touching—but they generally avoid more intimate forms of sexual contact. In only 4% of cases studied by Finkelhor (1979) did the prepubescent girls report that coitus had occurred between them and the offender. The contact was confined to exhibitionism in 20% of the episodes and to touching and fondling of the genitals in another 38% of child-adult sexual interactions.

A primary and relatively permanent sexual interest in children (true pedophilia) actually characterizes only a quarter to a third of imprisoned child molesters. The rest of those convicted of the offense appear to have made advances to a child for situational reasons. That is, the contact occurred during periods of stress, frustration, or lack of other sexual outlets, or during an unusual opportunity (Arndt, 1991; Gebhard et al., 1965). The conclusions of Gebhard et al. (1965) and others, based on research with *convicted* offenders, suggest that sexual interest in children is a specific deviant psychological state afflicting a small group of men who have had traumatizing developmental experiences, including having been sexually abused as children themselves. As Finkelhor (1984) pointed out, however, the convicted sex offenders are the ones who are most compulsive, repetitive, blatant, and extreme in their abusive behavior. Generalization from convicted to undetected child abusers may be inappropriate, as undetected offenders are probably people with much less conspicuous psychological abnormality.

If a person develops a sexual interest in children, how is this interest translated into behavior? From time to time, all of us experience arousal under inappropriate conditions or toward inappropriate people, and we choose not to act on our arousal. You may feel attracted to your best friend's partner, or you may get inexplicably "turned on" while sitting in class one day, but you inhibit your feelings to avoid hurting your friends or embarrassing yourself. The sexual abuser, however, may be uninhibited as a result of various factors, a major one being alcohol and alcoholism (Arndt, 1991).

Another factor implicated in the dynamics of offending are cognitions or ideas that are used to define, evaluate, and justify the inappropriate sexual behavior. These cognitive distortions are thought to allow the person to bypass his normal inhibitions. In a study of 101 child sex offenders undergoing treatment, the following cognitive distortions were the most frequently mentioned when the men were asked to report what they were thinking at the time of the offense (Neidigh & Krop, 1992, p. 212):

"She enjoyed it."

"This won't hurt her or affect her in any way."

"This is not so bad, it's not really wrong."

"I was high on alcohol or drugs at the time."

"I wasn't thinking at all or I wouldn't have done it."

"No one will ever find out so I won't get caught."

"She is flirting and teasing me, she wants me to do it."

It has also been suggested that the exposure of pedophiles to child pornography may incite them to act on their sexual fantasies about children (Densen-Gerber, 1983; Russell, 1984). Experimental research relevant to this hypothesis is not available because no one has yet been able to design ethically acceptable research to test it. It is apparent that we know very little about pedophilia beyond clinical observations. We hope that knowledge about this disorder will change in the near future.

## Zoophilia

A human's sexual interaction with a member of another species—a dog, horse, or sheep, for example—is known as *zoophilia* or bestiality. The use of animals as the preferred or exclusive means of obtaining erotic pleasure is relatively rare; most often an animal is employed sexually because the person lacks a human partner.

References to sexual contact between animals and humans appear throughout recorded

**zoophilia** (ZOO-oh-FILL-ee-ah)—sexual activity with animals; also known as bestiality.

**FIGURE 19.9**

**Picasso's Etching of the Centaur and a Woman**
Sexual contacts between humans and animals have been depicted in both art and mythology throughout history.

history. Such contact is depicted often in ancient mythology and classical art. Greek mythology abounds with tales of human and animal sexual unions. The more familiar offspring of these unions were centaurs, who were part horse (see Figure 19.9); minotaurs, who were part bull; and satyrs, who were part goat. Some modern pornography also contains depictions of sexual relations between humans (usually women) and animals. It has been suggested that a devotee of this kind of pornography is excited by the degradation of the woman rather than by the sexual activity itself.

*Incidence and Characteristics*

About 8% of the males and 4% of the females in the Kinsey group's (1948) sample reported having had sexual experience with animals, but rates among boys raised on farms were considerably higher. About 17% of farm boys experienced sexual arousal to the point of orgasm as a result of contact with animals (Kinsey et al., 1948). The same percentage of boys had animal contacts that did not result in orgasm. Coitus with animals such as calves and sheep was the most common form of sexual interaction reported by the Kinsey

group's adolescent male volunteers. In another common pattern, reported especially among residents of urban areas, household pets—most often dogs and sometimes cats—stimulated their owners' genitals. Hunt (1974) found similar animal categories but a decrease of about 5% of males and 2% of females reporting such contacts.

The great majority of animal contacts reported by the Kinsey group's male volunteers occurred during adolescence, prior to the beginning of extensive sexual relations with women. By adulthood, most of the men had abandoned their sexual contacts with animals. The majority of the animal interactions reported by Kinsey would not conform to the diagnosis of zoophilia. That is, the animal was used because no human partner was available, and the animal was not the preferred means of sexual gratification.

It appears that substantial numbers of people find observation of animals in coitus to be sexually arousing (see Table 19.4). Almost a third of the males and 16% of the females in the Kinsey (1953) group reported that they had experienced an erotic response when observing copulating animals.

In addition to arguing that sexual contact with animals per se was not aberrant, Kinsey expressed concern over the fact that the laws in most states treat bestiality (zoophilia) as a crime and punish it with stiff prison terms. He considered the laws unrealistic, given the relatively frequent occurrence of animal contacts in the general farm population. Kinsey suggested that the incidence of sex with animals closely paralleled that of prostitution and homosexuality, and thus he questioned whether zoophilia should even be classified as a paraphilia.

## Necrophilia and Miscellaneous "Philias"

In Box 19.2, we list some of the more unusual paraphilias. We describe a few of these here.

Having sexual relations with a corpse is called *necrophilia*. Clinically, necrophilia differs from extreme sadism in that the source of sexual excitement appears to have nothing to do with

**necrophilia**—sexual arousal and/or activity with a corpse.

**TABLE 19.4 Erotic Responses to Observing Animals in Coitus**

| Erotic Response | By Females (%) | By Males (%) |
|---|---|---|
| Definite and/or frequent | 5 | 11 |
| Some response | 11 | 21 |
| Never | 84 | 68 |
| Number of people interviewed | 5,250 | 4,082 |

Source: Adapted from Kinsey, A.C., Pomeroy, W., Martin, C., Gebhard, P. *Sexual Behavior in the Human Female*, p. 663. Philadelphia: Saunders, 1953. By permission of the Kinsey Institute for Research in Sex, Gender, and Reproduction, Inc.

the pain or death of the sex object. Instead, the excitement is associated with the dead body.

Beit-Hallahmi (1985) described a clinical case of necrophiliac behavior by a convicted murderer of a woman. Apparently the murderer believed in *vagina dentata*, the myth (described in Chapter 1) that the vagina has dangerous teeth. He also believed that men could encounter other sharp objects in the vagina and thus had been afraid to have intercourse with his eventual victim while she was alive. Even after killing her, he found it necessary to mutilate her vagina before copulating with her.

Despite jokes about morticians who enjoy sex with corpses, necrophilia appears to be extremely rare. Those few persons who have reported necrophilic behavior typically have had severe emotional problems. We personally have had contact with only one person who claimed to have had intercourse with a corpse. At the time we had contact with him, he was incarcerated in a maximum security hospital for the criminally insane.

One of the more bizarre "philias" involves using a rope, belt, or the like to apply pressure to one's neck to decrease oxygen supply to the brain and to elevate the carbon-dioxide level in the blood. This produces a state of euphoria that enhances the pleasure derived from masturbation to orgasm. Tragically, this practice, called *asphyxiophilia*, often leads to death by hanging even though the victim may have tried to use safety mechanisms to avoid death. Little is known about the practice, but investigations of asphyxiophilia deaths indicate that most practitioners

were apparently in good mental health with no overt signs of depression or death wishes (Innala & Ernulf, 1989). It has been estimated that between 250 and 1,000 deaths occur yearly in the United States as a result of asphyxiophilia (Hazelwood, Dietz, & Burgess, 1983).

## Compulsive Sexual Behavior

Many individuals who engage in paraphilic behaviors would be described by the psychologist Patrick Carnes (1983, 1990, 1991) as "sexual addicts." Just as alcoholism or drug dependency involves a pathological relationship with a mood-altering chemical, so "sexual addiction" involves a pathological relationship with mood-altering sexual experiences. According to Carnes, who has developed a treatment program for sexual addiction, addiction progresses through a four-step cycle that intensifies with each repetition:

1. *Preoccupation*—a trancelike engrossment in thoughts of sex, which creates a compulsive search for sexual stimulation.

2. *Ritualization*—special routines that precede sexual behavior and intensify sexual arousal and excitement.

3. *Compulsive sexual behavior*—the sexual act itself, which addicts are unable to control or stop.

4. *Despair*—the feeling of utter hopelessness that addicts of every kind have about their behavior.

**Box 19.2**

## Unusual Paraphilias

In addition to the paraphilias that we have already described in some detail, some people are aroused by other objects that most people do not find sexually stimulating. *Partialism* refers to an exclusive focus on a particular part of the body for arousal. *Coprophilia* is arousal associated with feces, either depositing them on the partner or having them deposited on oneself. *Urophilia* is similar, except that the arousal stems from urine instead of feces. *Klismaphilia* refers to arousal from receiving enemas.

A person occasionally experiencing arousal from one of these sources might not be diagnosed as having a paraphilia needing treatment unless the person is very distressed by it. The *DSM-IV* differentiates between persons with mild (has fantasies or urges but has never acted on them), moderate (has occasionally acted on them), and severe (has repeatedly acted on them) paraphilic urges.

Although little research has been conducted on the idea of sexual addiction, some aspects of Carnes's framework mesh well with what is known about other addictions. Sexual addicts are able to alter their mood by entering into an obsessive trance wherein they are preoccupied by thoughts of sex. According to Carnes, the addict is trying to recapture the intoxication of young love.

As we shall see in Chapter 20, trancelike states are often a part of intense sexual encounters in normal relationships. In the addict's case, however, the individual is preoccupied with sex and intensifies his or her preoccupation through rituals. For example, the exhibitionist may develop a number of regular routes that he ritualistically follows at certain times when he wants to expose himself. Eventually, the compulsive sexual behavior begins to be noticed because the addict can no longer control it. The despair that the addict experiences after the sexual act can be numbed or alleviated by sexual preoccupation, which begins the addiction cycle anew. Carnes advocates treatment based on family therapy and the 12-step treatment model used in the Alcoholics Anonymous program. At present, adequate information is lacking about the effectiveness of this approach for reducing compulsive sexual behavior.

The concept of sexual addiction or compulsion is highly controversial (Coleman, 1991; Levine & Troiden, 1988; Money, 1988). As Money (1988) has suggested, the notion of addiction to

sex is not logical. In the context of sexual arousal, there can only be addiction to some*thing* or some*one*. Pointing out that an alcoholic is not addicted to thirst but to alcohol, Money fears that the logical treatment outcome for sexual addiction would be sexual abstinence. For their part, Levine and Troiden (1988) expressed concern about the invention of a new "disease" that would threaten the liberties of sexually variant people. They noted that rather than pertaining to an actual clinical entity, the concept of sexual addiction refers to learned patterns of behavior that are stigmatized by the value judgments of health professionals. These criticisms of the notion of sexual addiction are especially revealing when we consider that the medical establishment defined masturbation, oral sex, homosexuality, and high levels of sexual activity ("promiscuity") as forms of mental illness in the first edition of the *DSM* in 1952. The fact that these behaviors are no longer considered pathological reflects altered social values rather than advances in clinical research.

## Treatment of the Invasive Paraphilias

Paraphiliacs are often the objects of greater outrage than are rapists, even when the former use little or no force against the victim. The public's widespread sense of moral outrage is reflected in many of the painful and dubious treatments administered to individuals who engage in paraphilias. Electroconvulsive therapy (ECT) or shock treatment, castration, and mood-altering drugs have all been used at one time or another to treat sexual offenders. These methods supposedly aim not to punish such individuals but to cure them of their paraphilic preferences.

## Psychotherapy

Conventional counseling or psychotherapy has not been very effective in modifying paraphiliacs' behavior. Success rates in this area compare with those of standard psychotherapy treating drug addiction or alcoholism. The reasons for the poor track record of traditional treatments are unclear. Some researchers have speculated that the unusual behavior is crucial for paraphiliacs' mental stability (Stoller, 1977). According to this view, without their paraphilia, patients would undergo severe mental deterioration. More recent cognitive-behavioral therapies have been shown to be very effective in treating paraphilias (Abel, Osborn, Anthony, & Gardos, 1992; Pithers, 1993).

Although people are punished for sexual deviance, they also experience rewards. For example, paraphiliacs whose activities make them liable to arrest, such as exhibitionists, voyeurs, and pedophiliacs, seem to have a strong need to run great risks. The constant danger of arrest becomes as arousing as the sexual activity itself. As far as we know, no one has tried to modify paraphiliacs' behavior by substituting more socially acceptable forms of risk-taking, such as skydiving or motorcycle stunt driving, that might satisfy paraphiliacs' apparent need to tempt fate. This approach, in combination with therapy for the sexual element of the problem, would at least be less painful than some of the past treatment techniques.

The difficulties encountered in treating paraphiliacs may be related to the restrictive and often emotionally impoverished environments that many of them experienced as children and adolescents. It is difficult to undo the effects of years of conditioning in one or two hours a week of therapy. Like rapists, convicted sex offenders report more physical and sexual abuse in their childhood than do those convicted of nonsexual crimes (Barbaree et al., 1993; Dwyer & Amberson, 1989; Sack & Mason, 1980). The odds of being convicted of a sex crime were eight times greater for those who reported physical abuse as a child than for those who did not.

The development of a specific paraphilia is probably due more to accidental conditioning than to anything else. All present explanations of the paraphilias are still speculative. Attempts to treat these problems, however, have not been deterred by the scarcity of information about them.

## Surgical Castration

"It is evident that castration turns the clock back to medieval times, when amputation of the hands was practiced as a means of curing thievery" (Heim & Hursch, 1979, p. 303). In the past, castration was used for many reasons: to prevent procreation by those who were judged undesirable, to punish certain crimes, and, more recently, to treat violent sexual offenders. Castration was recommended as a treatment for "sexual overexcitement" in the late 18th century and was first used as a therapy in 1889 (Karpman, 1954). Castration can involve excision of the testes or removal of the entire external genital system, including the penis. Castration for "therapeutic" purposes involves removal of the testes only (orchiectomy).

Although the surgical castration of incarcerated sexual offenders is not unknown in North America, it has been practiced on a much wider scale in some northern European countries. In the Zurich region of Switzerland alone, more than 10,000 patients have been castrated for various psychiatric reasons since 1910 (Heim, 1981). The appeal of castration as a treatment for sexual offenders lies in the inaccurate belief that testosterone, produced by the testes, is necessary for sexual behavior.

This reasoning has a straightforward appeal, but we hope by now you are convinced that the causes of sexual behavior are far more complicated than this surgical treatment suggests. Reducing the amount of testosterone in the blood system does not always change sexual behavior. Contrary to the prevalent myth that the sex offender has an abnormally strong sex drive, many sex offenders have little sexual desire or are sexually dysfunctional (Gebhard et al., 1965; Groth & Burgess, 1977). Presumably, castration would not have a marked effect on the behavior of an offender who already had a weak sex drive.

In his review of the effects of castration after puberty on a variety of animals, Rogers (1976) concluded that in many species, the operation had little influence on sexual performance. He suggested that the heightened secretion of sex hormones that begins in puberty is necessary for the initial development of the capacity for sexual behavior. Once established, however, the pattern of sexual behavior becomes, to a large extent, independent of hormonal control.

There is substantial evidence that the effect of castration on male sex drive is strongly influenced by an individual's psychological attitude toward castration. As Ford and Beach (1951, p. 232) stated:

> We consider it more probable that some men, being convinced in advance that the operation will deprive them of potency, actually experience a lessening of sexual ability. Other individuals unprejudiced by such anticipatory effects are able to copulate frequently despite loss of hormonal support.

This reasoning is further supported by follow-up research with castrated sex offenders in West Germany (Heim, 1981). Questionnaires were mailed to a group of sex criminals who had been castrated before release from prison. These individuals had been out of jail for periods ranging from 4 months to 13 years. They reported sharp reductions in the frequency of coitus, masturbation, sexual thoughts, sex drive, and sexual arousability. Almost a third of the men, however, could still have sexual intercourse.

### Chemical Treatment

Certain treatments involve the administration of chemicals to inhibit desire in sex offenders. Chemical treatment has the same goal as surgical castration, but with a major advantage for the offender: he keeps his testes.

Estrogens have been found to reduce sex drive in paraphilic men, but they are no longer used because they can have feminizing effects on the male physique, including enlargement of the breasts (Bradford, 1993). In contrast, there are antiandrogenic drugs that interfere with the action of testosterone but do not feminize the body. Medroxyprogesterone (MPA; trade name, Depo-Provera) and cyproterone acetate (CPA) are the most commonly used antiandrogens in North America. They block the effects of testosterone on the target organs. This treatment does not affect the direction of sexual behavior, but it does reduce or inhibit sexual response. Clinical studies indicate that these antiandrogens are fairly effective in suppressing sexual fantasy, desire, and arousal in men (Bradford & Pawlak, 1993; Cooper, 1986; Money, 1988). When used in conjunction with counseling, they benefit some sex offenders. The best candidates for this treatment are self-referred, highly motivated men with good social support (Cooper, 1986).

Adequate empirical studies of the effects of these chemicals on sexual behavior are still needed, and side effects and short- and long-term behavior changes need to be assessed. At present, they offer considerable promise in the treatment of sex offenders.

### Psychosurgery

*Psychosurgery*—brain surgery to control or eliminate sexual behavior—is relatively rare in North America. In West Germany, Rieber and Sigusch (1979) reported that about 70 men had undergone psychosurgery since 1962. The typical operation involved the destruction of a part of the hypothalamus, although other brain regions are sometimes eliminated also. The area of the hypothalamus destroyed corresponds to a "mating" center in certain animals, including rats.

Rieber and Sigusch (1979) stressed that the assumption that such surgery can affect sexual behavior in humans is highly debatable. The surgery has been performed on aggressive sex offenders, exhibitionists, "hypersexual" men, and homosexuals. Reports on the effects of the operation have been vague, although occasionally "dizzy spells, feelings of ravenous hunger, increase in weight, and a tendency to verbal ag-

---

**psychosurgery**—surgical procedures to change or alter psychological functioning and behavior.

gression" (Rieber & Sigusch, 1979, p. 525) have been mentioned as side effects. We agree with Rieber and Sigusch that all such surgery should be discontinued until there is more information about its effects. Pertinent data may be obtainable through observation of individuals who have suffered brain injury as a result of accidents or medical treatments.

## Cognitive-Behavior Therapies

Cognitive-behavior therapists teach techniques to decrease or control paraphiliac sexual motivation and behavior. The cognitive component involves modifying distorted ideas or cognitions that paraphiliacs use to justify their behavior. Most comprehensive cognitive-behavior therapy programs generally include the following components:

1. behavior therapy to reduce inappropriate sexual arousal and to enhance or maintain appropriate sexual arousal;

2. training to develop or to enhance prosocial skills;

3. modification of distorted cognitions and development of victim empathy; and

4. relapse prevention to enhance maintenance of treatment gains (Abel et al., 1992, p. 256).

An example of a comprehensive cognitive-behavior approach to the treatment of exhibitionism was reported by Marshall, Eccles, and Barbaree (1991). They instructed exhibitionists to carry smelling salts (which have an unpleasant odor) to inhale whenever they felt the urge to expose themselves. This helped the offender to develop control over his thoughts by associating aversive smell with deviant fantasies. Another facet of their approach was *covert sensitization.* The client carries cards that contain descriptions of various circumstances that lead to exposing the genitals. On the reverse side of the card are a series of descriptions of the terrible effects of ex-

hibiting. The exhibitionist is told to read the cards at least three times a day and whenever he feels a strong urge to expose himself. Additional aspects of this program include training in assertion and stress management, changing cognitive distortions through role-playing, and training in relationship skills.

## Other Approaches

In addition to the organic and cognitive-behavior therapies, a wide range of other therapeutic techniques can help clients to develop more socially approved sexual-arousal patterns and skills. For example, in directed masturbation therapy, the client is instructed to masturbate to socially acceptable sexual fantasies and to cease masturbating to paraphilic themes (Laws & Marshall, 1991). As the client learns that he can successfully masturbate to nondeviant themes, he gradually changes his self-definition from sexually deviant to normal. Other approaches include family or systems psychotherapy, group therapy, psychoanalysis, and systematic desensitization.

Researchers have begun to demonstrate the effectiveness of cognitive-behavior therapies in reducing recidivism rates (Abel et al., 1992; Pithers, 1993). A factor complicating the effective treatment of convicted sex offenders is the reality that therapy typically is conducted while the offenders are incarcerated, either in psychiatric hospitals or in prison environments. Prisons tend to have small numbers of therapists, and, given their caseloads, they often can offer only perfunctory treatment. Despite these problems, cognitive-behavior therapies and pharmacological approaches appear to be effective in treating sex offenders. The question facing society is whether to opt for rehabilitation/treatment or to incarcerate offenders without therapy. The latter option is the one most commonly adopted, and it is associated with recidivism and, eventually, more victims.

## Summary of Major Points _____

| | |
|---|---|
| 1. Fetishism. | Strictly speaking, a person is a fetishist when he or she requires the presence of an inanimate object in order to become sexually aroused. To the extent to which we learn to associate inanimate objects such as clothing with arousal, we all have minor fetishes. |
| 2. Transvestism. | Often confused with homosexuality and/or transsexuality, transvestism, or cross-dressing, usually is practiced by individuals who are biologically and psychologically masculine but who derive erotic pleasure from wearing stereotypically feminine attire. |
| 3. Transsexualism. | Some people whose genetic, gonadal, hormonal, and genital gender development all coincide nevertheless believe themselves to be members of the other gender. Although the causes of this phenomenon are unknown, many transsexuals who undergo surgical sex reassignment report greater happiness and adjustment in their new status. But surgery does not improve adjustment for all transsexuals. Given the drastic nature of sex-reassignment surgery, some scientists have called for a halt to transsexual surgery until we have a better understanding of transsexual identity. |
| 4. Sadomasochism. | Sadists are aroused by inflicting pain on others, and masochists are erotically stimulated by receiving pain. Sadomasochism is distinguished from sexual assault in that both participants consent to the activity. A variant of this fetish, bondage and discipline, involves symbolic dominance and submission more than it involves physical pain. Some early theorists assumed that males took the role of sadists and inflicted pain on female masochists. Recent data, however, do not provide support for clear-cut gender differences in preference for one role or the other. |
| 5. Voyeurism and exhibitionism. | Voyeurism involves observing others who are nude and/or sexually involved without their consent, and exhibitionism is showing others one's genitals without being invited to do so. As far as is known, voyeurs and exhibitionists are almost exclusively male. Victims of voyeurs and exhibitionists may be startled and/or frightened by the intrusion, but a calm response is generally most effective in discouraging the behavior and is least likely to reward the perpetrator. |
| 6. Pedophilia. | Adults convicted of sexual contacts with children resemble convicted rapists with respect to feelings of inadequacy, although they do not appear to be as aggressive as rapists. Factors that impair judgment, such as alcohol and emotional disturbance, are quite common among those convicted of sexual relations with children. |
| 7. Zoophilia. | This paraphilia refers to sexual activity with animals. Most individuals who report engaging in sex with animals do not describe it as a preferred or exclusive mode of sexual interaction. When zoophilia occurs, it usually takes place during adolescence and is abandoned in adulthood. |

8. Compulsive sexual behavior.

Many paraphilias seem similar to addictions to alcohol or drugs. The individual engages in the behavior to alter his or her mood and seems unable to control the behavior.

9. Treatment of the invasive paraphilias.

Numerous approaches are used to treat paraphiliacs. Many early treatments resembled punishments more than effective therapies. Cognitive-behavior therapies and pharmacological treatments appear to be highly effective in treating paraphilias. Whether these treatments are employed depends on whether society emphasizes rehabilitation and treatment or incarceration and punishment.

## Review of Key Concepts

1. Fetishism is as common among women as it is among men. True or false? (p. 639)

2. Transvestism is a: a) symptom of homosexual tendencies; b) symptom of schizophrenia; c) behavior that some heterosexuals enjoy; d) consequence of being raised in a household where there was no strong father figure. (pp. 640–642)

3. A transsexual is: a) an androgynous person; b) a person of either gender who enjoys dressing as a member of the other gender but is not homosexual; c) a person who is sexually attracted to either gender; d) a biologically normal male or female who believes that he or she is a member of the other gender. (p. 644)

4. Transsexualism: a) is caused by prenatal exposure to high levels of inappropriate hormones; b) results from unusual bonding patterns between parents and children; c) probably results from abnormal genetic inheritance; d) is caused by unknown factors. (p. 650)

5. Sex-reassignment surgery is: a) still illegal in the United States and is limited to Scandinavian countries and Japan; b) now performed in the United States at a rate of about 5,000 operations per year; c) recommended by physicians for all persons who are uncomfortable with their gender identity; d) none of the above. (pp. 650–651)

6. Compared to other sex offenders, pedophiles are typically: a) younger; b) older; c) more violent; d) more assertive. (p. 660)

7. Zoophilia involves: a) enjoying viewing monkeys and other captive animals engaging in sexual activity; b) taking a young child to a zoo with the idea of later persuading the child to have sex; c) human-animal sexual contact; d) none of the above. (pp. 661–662)

8. Masochists are always sexually aroused by the infliction of pain. True or false, and why? (pp. 651–652)

9. Most sadomasochists are: a) dangerous psychopaths; b) males or females who are sexually aroused by ritualized pain and/or degradation; c) persons who enjoy receiving and/or inflicting actual pain; d) none of the above. (pp. 651–653)

10. In the treatment of paraphilias, the most effective procedure appears to be: a) family therapy; b) brain surgery; c) chemical treatment; d) psychoanalysis. (pp. 665–667)

11. Discuss Patrick Carnes's description of paraphilic behaviors as forms of sexual addiction and the controversy over the use of this term.

12. Explain cognitive-behavior therapy and how it is used to treat sex offenders.

# $\mathcal{L}$oving Sexual Interactions

$\mathcal{S}$EX , as we have seen, can be used for the domination and exploitation of others, but it can also be fun, relaxing, and physically rewarding. And sexual interactions, in the context of strong attachment, mutual respect, and concern for a partner's feelings and well-being, can allow us to realize our potential to take part in one of the most remarkable experiences available to human beings. A loving sexual relationship can provide what Abraham Maslow (1962) called a *peak experience*. How we develop the capacity to participate in a loving sexual relationship is the topic of this final chapter. First, we look at the relationship between being loved during infancy and childhood and the capacity to love others during adulthood. We then examine models of the development of love relationships. Finally, we turn to some of the problems that couples need to resolve in order to develop enduring relationships characterized by loving sexual expression.

What is love? It can be a momentary feeling or attitude that results in a loving act, such as helping a hurt person. It can be a more enduring feeling or attitude directed toward a specific person over a long period of time. Love can take a variety of forms, which we consider later in the chapter. For now, we rely on science-fiction

**peak experience**—Maslow's term for a personal experience that generates feelings of ecstasy, peace, and unity with the universe.

writer Robert Heinlein's (1961) definition: love is the feeling that someone else's needs and well-being are as important to you as your own. A more formal statement of the same idea is that love is a cognitive merging of self and other so that other's outcomes, resources, and so on, are perceived as one's own (Aron, Aron, Tuder, & Nelson, 1991).

## Being Loved

### Early Experience

What does a child need to grow into a mature, loving person? We cannot systematically vary the environment in which children are raised in order to examine, experimentally, the effects of different kinds of child rearing on personality development. However, observations of abused and neglected children, experimental research with primates, and cross-cultural correlational studies offer clues to the importance of early experience in creating our capacity to grow physically and emotionally, to love ourselves, and to form loving bonds with others. Physical and/or emotional abuse or neglect during infancy and childhood are associated with personal, social, and sexual maladjustment in adulthood.

*The Primate Studies*

Erik Erikson's contention that consistent loving care during infancy and childhood is necessary for the development of basic trust is supported by experimental research with primates (Harlow & Mears, 1979). Young monkeys undergo a relatively lengthy period of dependence on adult care that is somewhat similar to that of human children. Rhesus monkey mothers are protective and typically nurse their infants for a year or more. The kind of care that the monkey receives profoundly affects its later behavior, as does its contact with other infant and juvenile monkeys.

In one famous study, monkeys were separated from their mothers shortly after birth and reared in a laboratory. The infants were put into cages with one or two surrogate mothers. One surrogate was a plain wire-mesh cylinder, and

**FIGURE 20.1**
**Contact Comfort**
That infant monkeys need contact comfort is revealed in their choosing a cloth-covered surrogate more frequently than a wire surrogate that provides milk.

the other was a terrycloth-covered form. The monkeys were fed from bottles connected to these surrogates. When the monkeys were allowed to choose between the two surrogate mothers, even those who got their milk from the wire mother spent more time clinging to the cloth mother (see Figure 20.1). Neither group of monkeys grew up normally, and as adults all were unable to mate in the usual fashion (Harlow & Harlow, 1962).

In another series of studies, young rhesus monkeys were brought up in either total or partial isolation. Total isolation was attained by placing each monkey in a stainless-steel chamber right after birth. Lighting, temperature, cage cleaning, food, and water were provided by remote control, and the totally isolated monkeys saw no living beings. Those reared in partial isolation were placed alone in wire cages, from which they could see and hear other young monkeys, although they could not physically interact with them.

The longer the monkeys were isolated, the more abnormal and maladjusted they became. Monkeys reared in isolation for six months were described as social misfits; monkeys isolated for the first year of life appeared to be little more than "semi-animated vegetables" (Suomi & Harlow, 1971). As they advanced into childhood and adolescence, these monkeys were still social misfits compared with those who were reared with their mothers and peers. The monkeys who had been isolated for six months had biologically normal reproductive systems but were sexually incompetent:

> Their gymnastic qualifications are only quaint and cursory as compared with sexual achievement customary at these ages. Isolates may grasp other monkeys of either sex by the head and throat aimlessly, a semi-erotic exercise without amorous achievements. . . . the exercise leaves the totally isolated monkey working at cross purposes with reality. (Harlow & Novak, 1973, p. 468)

Those monkeys isolated for a year did not even approximate the botched sexual behavior of the six-month isolates; they attempted no sexual contact at all. The lack of successful mating on the part of these isolates may have been fortunate, for isolated females who had been impregnated accidentally or artificially were generally rejecting or incompetent mothers. Early deprivation thus has devastating effects on monkeys' sexual behavior in adolescence and adulthood.

An intriguing series of studies has demonstrated, however, that these maladjustments may not be permanent or irreversible. In a kind of sex-therapy procedure, isolated monkeys were paired with younger normal monkeys for specific periods of time, such as two hours a day for three days a week. The individual therapy sessions were augmented with group therapy involving two isolates and two "therapists" (normal monkeys). After six months of therapy, the isolates showed remarkable improvement in their behavior. By adolescence, the isolates' sexual behavior was normal for their age (Novak & Harlow, 1975; Suomi et al., 1972).

Harlow postulated that if the infant experiences a severe lack or loss of contact comfort from the parents, normal body contact will be extremely difficult to accept when the time arrives for social play and peer love:

> It is this knowledge of learning what the body as a whole can do, in air and sea, on land and snow, that reinforces the first pleasure in mastery and also gives the first confidence in self. . . . The basis for self-esteem is a prerequisite for the love of living and loving, no matter what love at what age or stage. (Harlow & Mears, 1979, p. 170)

### Deprivation or Enhancement?

Human infants reared in an orphanage or an institution where they receive only rudimentary care come closest to experiencing the deprivation encountered by the monkeys in the Harlow studies. In the past, institutionalized babies were traditionally kept in individual cubicles separated from other infants, and their adult contact was brief and hurried. For example, in one case, eight infants had to share one nurse (Spitz, 1947). These children were thus deprived of the range of sensory stimulation that a child normally receives from being picked up, cuddled, talked to, played with, and rocked. An impoverished environment of this kind was associated with major disturbances in interpersonal relationships and with emotional problems during childhood and adolescence (Casler, 1968).

Some people who are deprived of human contact and affection during childhood seem unable to form meaningful social relationships in adulthood. Others have been characterized as having insatiable needs for attention and affection. Although the consequences of such early deprivation on later love relationships and sexual interactions have not been directly assessed among humans, early deprivation is not likely to produce a trusting, loving person.

Because of the remarkable similarities between human infants and other primate infants, Bowlby (1979) hypothesized that the attachment between infant and caregiver forms the basis for later attachments in adulthood. Attachment theory postulates that the original function of this early affectional bonding in humans was to protect infants from predators and other threats to survival (Ainsworth, Blehar, Waters, & Wall, 1978; Bowlby, 1973; Shaver, Hazan, & Bradshaw, 1988). Bowlby (1973) believed that infants and children construct mental models of themselves and their caretakers, and that these models and the behavior patterns influenced by them affect their relationships throughout the life span.

A major contribution to understanding how differences in early caregiving are related to personality differences in young children was made by Mary Ainsworth and her colleagues (Ainsworth et al., 1978). They observed mother-infant dyads at home and in a laboratory situation called the Strange Situation. They were interested in seeing how infants would react to novel toys, an unfamiliar adult, and a brief separation from their mother. Ainsworth et al. reported three major kinds of dyads: secure, anxious-ambivalent, and avoidant.

The psychologist Robert Hatfield (1994) provided an overview of the differences that were found:

> . . . In secure parent-child attachments, the parent was a good "student." These parents usually noticed, understood, and responded appropriately to the "lessons" offered by the infant or toddler. Almost all the infants' lessons involved touch. They signal to their parents to "pick me up, hold me, feed me, burp me, soothe me, stimulate me, change me, and make the pain or discomfort go away." Of course, occasionally the signal was, "I'm overstimulated, so please leave me alone for a few minutes." These healthy "parent students" and "child teachers" are synchronized to each other, communicating and learning in a rhythm of increasing complexity.
>
> It was found that, for the . . . [avoidant] parent and child, there is a great deal of obvious neglect of the offspring by the parent. The parent "students" usually are uninterested in the lessons offered by their . . . [offspring] and generally ignore the signals of

the child. When the infant "teacher" tries even harder to interest these parents, the mother or father usually responds with even more neglect or with verbal or physical abuse. These infants rapidly become impatient teachers and the home "classroom" is filled with the turmoil of rapidly escalating frustration of teacher and student. Within the first year or two, these children eventually give up most efforts to "teach," learn to suppress their signals for attention, and are likely to become sullen, chronically miserable, or ill. Whichever child responses occur, the outcome is commonly devastating on many levels for the child, the parent-child attachment, and subsequent relationships as the child grows to adulthood. . . .

> Ainsworth's . . . category of the . . . ["anxious ambivalent"] child is not a median category somewhere between the . . . ["secure" and "avoidant"] attachment classifications. The parent of the . . . [anxious ambivalent] child may sometimes appear to be a "supermom" or "superdad," in that they tend to hold and give just as much, or more, attention to their child than do the parents of the healthy attachment children. The primary difference is that these, like the . . . [avoidant] parents, are also very poor parent "students." They and their child are, more often than not, out of synchronization with one another. This frequently "overinvolved" parent is not actually responding to the signals of the child, but instead responds to his or her own personal needs and desires. Because these parents are busily working at trying to care for the child, the toss of the dice says that the parent and child will occasionally be in synch and the child's needs will be met. When this occurs, it confuses the child into believing that the parent is finally "getting it," only to be followed by the majority of situations in which the child's signals are unanswered (or incorrectly answered). The randomly reinforced and anxiously attached child usually does not give up, even though it may be in her or his best interest. In a frustrated and disconsolate manner, the child continues to try to get through to the unreceptive parent and will likely continue these

**Box 20.1**

## Attachment Styles and Adult Relationships

Attachment styles are associated with many behaviors exhibited by individuals with their romantic partners.

People with secure attachment

seldom worry about being abandoned by their partner

believe other people are well-intentioned

view their relationship as a trusting partnership

place highest value and derive most pleasure from relationships rather than from work

People with anxious-ambivalent attachment

often worry that their partners do not love them or will leave them

would like others to be closer to them

feel it is easy to fall in love

experience high degrees of sexual attraction and jealousy

report frequent emotional ups and downs

more frequently experience obsessive love

worry about love interfering with work

People with avoidant attachment

are uncomfortable being close to others

tend to fear intimacy

are afraid of becoming dependent on another

expect that love relationships are destined to fail

report emotional ups and downs

experience high degrees of jealousy

tend to prefer work over love relationships

Because of the absence of longitudinal research or of studies of attempts of people to change their attachment styles, we do not know the extent to which individuals can alter attachment styles developed during infancy. However, evidence is accumulating in support of the basic tenets of attachment theory, and research is needed on the possibility of altering one's attachment style in adulthood.

Sources: Feeney and Noller, 1990, 1991; Hazan and Shaver, 1990, 1993; Shaver et al., 1988.

*patterns into adulthood with poor choices of enabling relationships.**

This classic study has been replicated and extended by many other researchers (Elicker, Englund, & Sroufe, 1992). Secure children are more socially competent, have higher self-esteem, and have more satisfying relationships than do avoidant and anxious-ambivalent children. Attachment behaviors that are assessed at age one appear to be good predictors of later childhood social behaviors.

*Source: Robert Hatfield (1994). Touch and Sexuality. In Vern Bullough and Bonnie Bullough (Eds.), *Human Sexuality: An Encyclopedia* (pp. 582–583). New York: Garland.

Attachment styles have also been found to be related to romantic relationships in adults (Feeney & Noller, 1990, 1991; Hazan & Shaver, 1993; Shaver et al., 1998). A summary of these findings is presented in Box 20.1. Although there has been no longitudinal research tracing attachment styles from infancy through adulthood, evidence is accumulating to support the hypothesis that early attachment between infants and their caretakers plays an important role in the infants' later relationships.

In Chapter 18 we reviewed numerous studies that examined the childhood experiences of adults who sexually assault others. These studies indicate that a high proportion of sexually violent adults were themselves physically and sexually

**FIGURE 20.2**
**A Child Who Is Loved Becomes a Loving Child**
Infants who are hugged and caressed are more likely to become trusting and affectionate adults.

**FIGURE 20.3**
**Parent-Child Affection**
This little girl lovingly expresses her affection toward her father.

abused during childhood. Just as abuse breeds violence, caring breeds love. At first the child is a passive recipient of the care and affection of its parents, but before long, a loved child becomes a loving child (see Figures 20.2 and 20.3). From a very early age, loved children derive a great deal of pleasure from displaying affection for their parents and others.

Freud contended that this love contains a sexual component. Children's love clearly includes the sensual pleasure derived from intimate body contact with members of the family (see Figure 20.4). The supposition that the child desires sexual intercourse, however, depends on whether the child can conceptualize this activity. At this point we have no evidence that young children have such a concept, and the Goldmans' (1982) research strongly suggests that they do not. In fact, many preadolescent children, upon hearing about the activity leading to conception, express revulsion. Children's occasional expression of the desire to marry one or both of their parents probably stems from their love of their

parents, their observation of the pleasure that their parents take in their marriage, and a desire to maintain ongoing connection with their parents, rather than from copulatory urges.

### Cross-Cultural Observations

In some cultures, infants and children are given minimal physical affection and body contact in the belief that the withholding of physical intimacy makes them grow up to be independent and self-reliant. In other cultures, however, adults take great pleasure in holding, caressing, stroking, and playing with babies (Hatfield, 1994; Thayer, 1987). Prescott (1975) examined the relationship between the treatment of infants and the level of adult violence in 49 cultures. Those cultures in which infants are reared with a great deal of physical affection tend to display little

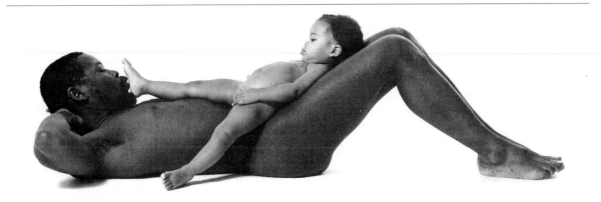

**FIGURE 20.4**
**Physical Intimacy**
Children take a great deal of pleasure in physical intimacy without thinking of it as "sexual."

physical violence; conversely, those cultures in which infants are deprived of physical affection display high levels of physical violence among adults.

On the basis of these observations, Prescott suggested that affection and aggression are, to some extent, mutually exclusive. That is, children reared with physical affection are likely to be affectionate and nonviolent as adults. Prescott (1975) believed that in the absence of physical affection during infancy and childhood, brain development is restricted, with the result that adult aggressiveness becomes more likely. Social learning theorists suggest a modeling effect: children learn affectionate or aggressive behavior from affectionate or aggressive parents and peers. Whether the mechanisms producing affectionate or aggressive adults are due to structural alterations in the brain and/or to social learning experiences, it is clear that children who receive love and physical affection are more likely to give love and respect themselves.

## Self-Love

Most of us have heard exhortations against selfishness from our parents, religious leaders, and teachers all our lives. In stressing that one of the factors most consistently associated with healthy psychological functioning and adjustment is self-esteem, are we advocating selfishness? Not at all; there is a world of difference between self-esteem, or self-love, and selfishness.

### Self-Love Versus Selfishness

Answering the following questions illuminates the enormous gulf between self-love and selfishness.

1. When was the last time you felt unhappy with yourself (insecure, hassled, irritable)?

2. When did you last feel very happy with yourself (proud of yourself, pleased with some of your personal qualities)?

3. How did you behave toward others on those two occasions? On which occasion were you most kind, generous, sensitive to others' feelings, and willing to go out of your way to help other people?

In all probability, you were more selfish when you were unhappy with yourself. When we dislike ourselves, our energies are directed toward protecting and helping ourselves, not toward protecting and helping others. It is when we love ourselves that we are most capable of giving to and loving others. Similarly, when we are insecure and ashamed of our bodies, our energies are concentrated on hiding and protecting ourselves. It is difficult to make love to another person when we are ashamed or embarrassed about our own feelings and our own bodies.

Love for oneself, then, is intricately connected with love for any other being. According to Erich Fromm,

> The affirmation of one's own life, happiness, growth, freedom is rooted in one's capacity to love.... If an individual is able to love productively, he loves himself too; if he can love only others, he cannot love at all. (1956, p. 60)

## Loving Others

Writers have tried throughout history to describe love's elusive qualities:

> Love is patient and kind; love is not jealous or boastful;
> It is not arrogant or rude. Love does not insist on its own way; it is not irritable or resentful;
> It does not rejoice at wrong, but rejoices in the right.
> Love bears all things, believes all things, hopes all things, endures all things.

> (St. Paul, I Corinthians 13: 4–7)

> Tell me whom you love and I will tell you who you are, and more especially, who you want to be.

> (Reik, 1949, p. 46)

> The supreme happiness of life is the conviction of being loved for yourself, or, more correctly, in spite of yourself.

> (Victor Hugo)

> All the fearful counterfeits of love—possessiveness, lust, vanity, jealousy—are closer to hate; they concentrate on the object, guard it, suck it dry. The counterfeit lover is suspicious of other people, resentful of the outside activities of the "loved one," seeking continually to remake the object into its own image. ...A person who does not become pleasanter to the world when he or she falls "in love" is not really in love. Love is not a trance but a transformation; not merely a focusing but a

fanning-out; not a barrier that divides the lovers from the world but a bridge that unites them to it.

> (Sidney Harris, 1981, p. 1)

> Love is aim-inhibited sexuality.

> (Sigmund Freud, 1955, p. 142)

> Death and delight, anguish and joy, anxiety and the wonder of birth—these are the warp and woof of which the fabric of human love is woven.

> (Rollo May, 1969, p. 100)

Although love has fascinated philosophers, theologians, writers, poets, and artists for ages, only recently have scientists attempted to describe and measure it.

## Constructions of Love

The scientific investigation of love has increased markedly in the past three decades. Many recent studies have focused on romantic love, at least in part owing to researchers' reliance on college students as volunteers. Although romantic love is thought to be in full bloom during late adolescence, it remains to be seen whether the results obtained from this age group are characteristic of other points in the life span. Researchers have explored the relationship between love and friendship (Hendrick & Hendrick, 1992; Sternberg, 1991), passionate and companionate love (Hatfield & Rapson, 1993), and attachment and love (Shaver & Hazan, 1993). The components and forms of love have also been probed (Hendrick & Hendrick, 1993; Sternberg, 1991).

Many scales employed to measure love reflect a stereotypically feminine perspective that emphasizes emotional expression and shared feelings. These measures have resulted in what Cancian (1986) has called the feminization of love and may yield an incomplete conception of it. For example, in one study, some of the behaviors described as love were "communicating without words," "sharing someone's feelings," and "letting someone know all about you" (Foa et al., 1987). Generally, these are the expressive aspects of love, and women tend to have more expressive skill than do men. Instrumental behaviors, more stereotypical of men than of women, are usually neglected in measures of love. Practical help, shared physical activities, and emphasis on physical sex are some of the characteristics associated with men. Because many of our measures of love reflect the stereotypically feminine ideal, it is not surprising that women emerge as more capable of love than do men. For example, a woman would be perceived as showing love if, at the end of a long day, she shares her feelings about a hassle at work or asks about her partner's feelings (expressive behaviors). If, on that same evening, her partner noticed that her tire was flat and decided to change it for her (an instrumental behavior), this would not necessarily be perceived as showing love.

Rather than trying to make men become more "loving" by becoming more stereotypically feminine, Cancian (1986) argued for a more androgynous conception of love that is both expressive and instrumental. As she put it:

> *Who is more loving: a couple who confide most of their experiences to each other but rarely cooperate or give each other practical help, or a couple who help each other through many crises and cooperate in running a household but rarely discuss their personal experiences? Both relationships are limited. Most people would probably choose a combination: A relationship that integrates both feminine and masculine styles of loving, an androgynous love. (p. 709)*

Given the foregoing analysis, and in light of gender differences in attitudes about sex described throughout this book, it should come as no surprise that there are also gender differences in attitudes about love. Men tend to differentiate love and sex more strongly than do women (Hendrick & Hendrick, 1993). Gender differences in attitudes about love are strongest for homosexuals, less strong for single heterosexuals, and least strong for married heterosexuals. This pattern of results is also found in Sweden, although the differences are not as pronounced, indicating a greater likelihood of fusing sex and love in that culture. There is also evidence that the tendency to differentiate between love and sex decreases as people grow older (Foa et al., 1987; Sprague & Quadagno, 1989).

Men are more likely than women to view love as a game to be played out with a number of partners (Hendrick & Hendrick, 1993; Sawrer, Kalichman, Johnson, Early, & Ali, 1993). This orientation can lead to the manipulation of others and sexual aggression, and men who perceive love as a game may be wary of emotional investment. Women are more likely to merge love and friendship than are men. Perhaps because women have been socialized to view sex as a precious commodity that must be guarded, they are also more pragmatic about love than are males. That is, they emphasize "love planning" based on the potential of a lover to meet particular criteria.

## Forms of Love

Psychologist Robert J. Sternberg (1986, 1991) devised a theoretical framework to account for the various forms that loving can take. We use this model because of its usefulness in shedding light on different kinds of love, although there is some question as to how distinct from one another some of these variants are (Hendrick & Hendrick, 1992). Sternberg maintained that love could be understood in terms of three components: 1) intimacy, which includes the feelings of closeness and connectedness that one experiences in loving relationships; 2) passion, which refers to the drives that lead to romance, physical attraction, and sexual interaction in a loving relationship; and 3) decision and commitment, which encompass (in the short run) the decision that one loves another and (in the long run) the commitment to maintain the love.

Intimacy, according to Sternberg, is the *emotional* component of love. It grows steadily in the early phases of a relationship but later tends to level off. It is the major component of most loving relationships that we have with family, friends, and lovers.

Passion is the *motivational* component of love. Passion develops quickly in relationships but then typically levels off. It involves a high degree of physiological arousal and an intense desire to be united with the loved one. In its purest form, it can be seen in the experience of "love at first sight."

Decision and commitment are the *cognitive* components of love. Commitment increases gradually at first and then grows more rapidly as a relationship develops. The love of a parent for a child is often distinguished by a high level of commitment.

Although these three components are all important parts of loving relationships, their strength may differ from one relationship to another and may change over time within the same relationship. The amount of love that one experiences depends on the absolute strengths of these three components, and the kind of love one experiences depends on their relative strengths. Sternberg represents the various possible relationships as triangles (see Figure 20.5). The absence of all three components is nonlove (see part *a* of Figure 20.5), which describes the majority of our relationships—those with casual acquaintances. When all three components of Sternberg's love triangle are present in a relationship, there exists what he calls consummate or complete love (see part *h* of Figure 20.5). According to Sternberg, that is the kind of love that people strive for but find difficult to sustain. It is possible only in very special relationships.

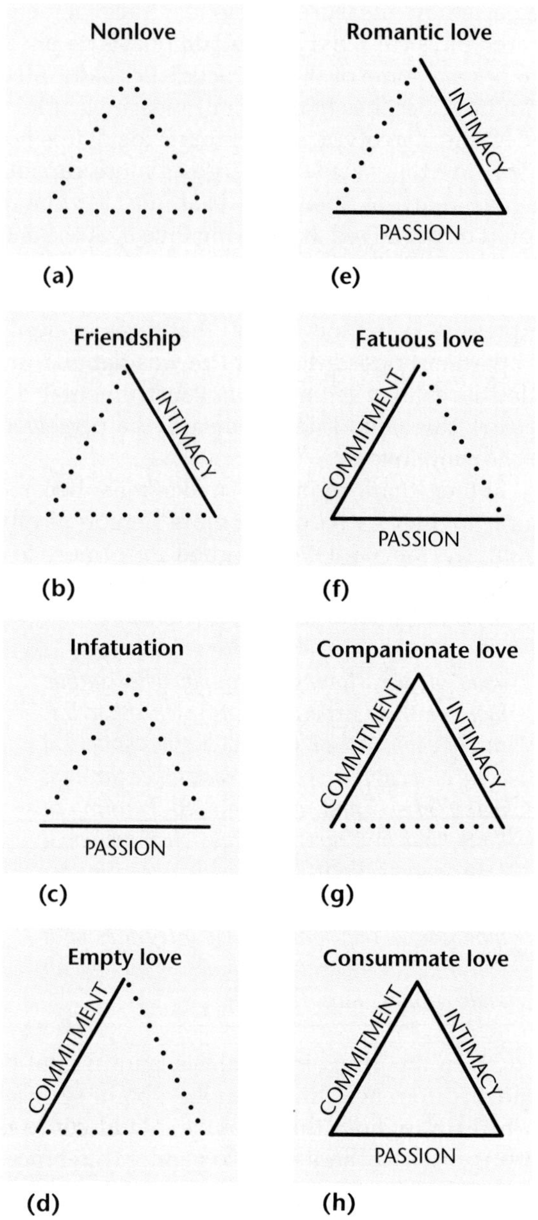

### Friendship

The first type of love that most of us experience outside our families is a close friendship with a person of the same gender. Friendship, or liking, is reserved for close friends; passing acquaintances do not inspire it. According to Sternberg, a friendship occurs when one experiences the intimacy component of love without passion and decision/commitment (see part *b* of Figure 20.5). Also known as *philia* and *platonic love*, friendship is a form of love in which we are as concerned with the well-being of our friend as we are with our own well-being. It is possible for friendships to evolve into relationships characterized by passionate arousal and long-term com-

**philia**—love involving concern with the well-being of a friend.

**platonic love**—nonsexual love for another person, often referred to as spiritual love.

**FIGURE 20.5**
**The Forms of Love**

mitment, but when this occurs, the friendship goes beyond liking and becomes another form of love.

Most people view friendship as a relationship between equals that is characterized by shar-

**FIGURE 20.6**
**Female Friendship**
Here two friends share some time outside of the fine-arts library at UCLA. Friendships between people of the same gender are still seen as more readily achieved than those between males and females.

ing and caring (Blieszner & Adams, 1992). It is interesting that throughout most of history, the experience of this kind of love between a man and a woman was seen as unlikely or impossible. Among the early Greeks, the deepest love was believed to exist in the friendship of two males who might also be involved in an erotic love relationship.

With the movement toward equality for men and women in the 20th century, intense friendship is no longer confined to partners of the same gender. Nonetheless, 75% of the respondents in a magazine survey (*Psychology Today*, 1979) saw same-gender friendships as different from other-gender friendships (see Figure 20.6). Friendships between men and women were seen as more difficult and complicated because of potential sex-

ual tensions, the lack of social support for male-female friendships, and the belief that men and women have less in common than do friends of the same gender. Evidence that these beliefs may be changing comes from a more recent study, in which more than a quarter of the respondents listed a member of the other gender as their best friend, and about half the sample claimed at least one person of the other gender as a close friend (Davis, 1985).

### Infatuation

One dictionary defines *infatuate* as "to inspire with a foolish or extravagant love or admiration." In Sternberg's framework, *infatuation* involves passionate arousal without the intimacy and decision/commitment components of love (see part *c* of Figure 20.5). Infatuated love is "love at first sight." It is essentially the same kind of love that Tennov called *limerence*—a love characterized by preoccupation, acute longing, exaggeration of the other's good qualities, seesawing emotion, and aching in the chest. These characteristics can be experienced as either intensely pleasurable or painful, depending on the response of the loved one, or "limerent object."

Unlike other forms of love, limerence is an all-or-nothing state that men and women experience in similar ways. Based on several hundred descriptions of limerence obtained through personal interviews, Tennov (1979) outlined a number of traits that a person in this state may exhibit:

1. *Preoccupation with the limerent object.* You are unable to think about anything else but the object of your affection. Everything you do is calculated in terms of how the limerent object would respond—whether he or she would like or dislike it. You may feel happy or sad depending on the degree of attention you get from your limerent object.

2. *Intrusive or unintentional thinking about the limerent object.* In addition to spending a great

**infatuation**—foolish and irrational love.

**limerence** (LIH-mer-ence)—love marked by obsession and preoccupation with the loved one.

deal of time intentionally fantasizing about the limerent object, you find that thoughts about your beloved intrude and interfere with other mental activity in an apparently involuntary way. You may be working on a paper or performing some task at work when thoughts and fantasies of the love object come to the fore.

3. *Desire for exclusivity with the limerent object.* You crave the limerent object and no one else. You want commitment to ensure exclusivity even when it is premature or inappropriate. This can lead you to smother the object of your affection with attention and pressure rather than allowing the relationship to develop gradually.

Tennov proposed that limerence develops in stages, the first being admiration for another person who possesses valued qualities and for whom one feels a basic liking. This stage is followed by an awareness of sexual attraction. Once admiration and sexual attraction are present, the next step is to undergo an experience that raises the probability that these feelings might be reciprocated. This experience could be something as simple as observing a look or gesture or being asked to go to dinner or a party.

At this point in the development of limerence, the first "crystalization" occurs: one begins to focus on the good qualities of the limerent object and to disregard his or her bad qualities. After the first crystalization, if the two people develop a mutual attraction, the intensity of the romantic involvement is relatively mild. Doubt about the limerent object's commitment, however, can evoke extreme, or "crazy," limerence. The interaction between hopefulness and uncertainty leads to the second crystalization, which results in feeling an intense attraction to the other person. For the individual who is not so infatuated, the developmental process just described stops early, and the intensity of full-fledged limerence is never felt. Nonlimerents are generally more practical about their romantic involvements.

Limerence is a tantalizing state that promises great things that never can be fully realized. In the beginning it can also be devastating, especially if the limerent object is lost abruptly. Tennov outlines three ways in which limerent at-

traction can end. The first is through the development of a deeper relationship, which evolves if one is able to withstand the major disappointments and emptiness of fading limerence. The second is through abandonment owing to a lack of reciprocity on the part of the limerent object. The third is through the transfer of attention to another limerent object—a continuation of the limerent state. Tennov maintains that full-blown limerence cannot develop without an element of uncertainty.

### Romantic Love

The deeper relationship that may blossom out of limerent love, or infatuation, is characterized by romantic love. Romantic love comprises intimacy as well as passion (see part *e* of Figure 20.5). It is the "Romeo and Juliet" type of love—liking with the added excitement of physical attraction and arousal, but without commitment.

Humans' first experience of romantic love can occur during infancy and childhood. Infants normally display a passionate attachment to their parents (Shaver et al., 1988). Much like adolescent and young adult lovers, they get intense pleasure in parental attention and approval, and they express distress when separated and affection when reunited. Five-year-olds often display passionate love for others by reporting that there is another child they cannot stop thinking about, whom they want to be near, and whom they would like to touch and be touched by (Carlson & Hatfield, 1992). The Greeks called this form of love *eros*. Romantic love was idealized by the late philosopher Alan Watts (1970), who suggested that our relationship to the loved one reflects our relationship to life itself. If we try to control or possess it, we are doomed to disappointment, for even under the best of circumstances, life and love can be influenced but not controlled. Romantic love can be one of the most intense and dramatic ways in which a human being comes into union and conscious relationship with another person.

Many people wonder whether it is possible to have a romantic love relationship with more

**eros**—erotic love.

than one person in a lifetime. When an intense romantic relationship ends, it is common to feel that you will never again experience romantic love. Yet as people who find another mate after separation, divorce, or the death of a beloved partner discover, it is possible to form a romantic bond with more than one person.

Unlike Tennov and Sternberg, some researchers maintain that romantic love does not differ from infatuation. For example, Berscheid and Walster (1981) contended that defining our feelings as love depends on a two-stage process: first, we become physiologically aroused; and second, cognitive labeling takes place.

Prior to the development of Berscheid and Walster's model, many researchers assumed that loving was an intense form of liking, governed by the same principles. Voluminous research by Byrne (1971) and others had indicated that we like those who share our values and attitudes and who evaluate us positively. We find associating with someone who shares our beliefs and attitudes rewarding, because he or she affirms our perceptions of the world. And obviously, we find compliments or positive evaluations rewarding.

Berscheid and Walster conceded that we are more disposed to like those who reward us than those who do not, but they point to the fact that people have been known to become highly infatuated with a person whom others perceive as not rewarding or even as punishing; from this phenomenon comes the axiom, ''Love is blind.'' For example, you may have known someone who was kind and considerate and who wanted very much to have a close relationship with you. Although you may have respected and cared about the person and even felt a platonic love for him or her, somehow the passionate feelings that you associate with being in love were missing. And perhaps there was another person—sometimes warm and loving, other times inconsiderate and callous—for whom you felt an overwhelming attraction, obsessional thoughts, and seesaw emotions that you defined as love.

Berscheid and Walster cited two other reasons for their rejection of the idea that loving is simply a more intense form of liking, explained by the same principles: unrequited love and jealousy. In unrequited love you feel and/or express intense feelings for another person, but the object of your desire behaves as if you do not exist or, worse, appears to be repelled by you. Jealousy is not an emotion that most of us find rewarding, and yet many of us have experienced heightened feelings of desire for a person after thinking that he or she was attracted to someone else.

Based on these and other similar observations, Berscheid and Walster proposed that we are more likely to label our feelings toward someone as love when we are physiologically aroused. An obvious source of physiological arousal, of course, is sexual arousal. But as we noted in Chapter 6 in the discussion of their experiment involving two bridges, Berscheid and Walster argue that *any* source of physiological arousal—for example, fear, euphoria, or anxiety—can increase the likelihood of our defining our feeling as love.

The second step, cognitive labeling, occurs because we seek an explanation for our feelings. Most of us are conditioned over a long period to associate feelings of arousal with romantic attraction. Berscheid and Walster's two-stage theory of love (or infatuation) helps to explain why we may perceive punishing sources of arousal such as jealousy and anxiety as indicators of the strength of our feelings for others.

## Empty Love

Sternberg describes empty love as commitment without intimacy or passion (see part *d* of Figure 20.5). It can be the kind of love, for example, that is seen in a 25-year-old marriage that has become stagnant. Intimacy and passion have died out, and all that remains is commitment. Although North Americans may associate this type of love with the final stages of a long-term relationship, in other societies it may be the starting point of a relationship. For example, in cultures in which marriages are arranged, a couple may begin a relationship with little beyond a commitment to try to love each other.

## Fatuous Love

Fatuous love involves passion and commitment but no intimacy (see part *f* of Figure 20.5). Sternberg (1991) described it as the form of love that we associate with whirlwind courtships. Girl meets boy; the next week they are engaged; a

**FIGURE 20.7**
**Companionate Love**
Long-term relationships tend to be characterized by intimacy and commitment, even for people who experience passion with less frequency than they earlier felt.

month later they are married. This type of love is fatuous, or foolish, because a commitment is made based only on the heady chemistry of passion without the stabilizing effect of intimacy. Fatuous love is unlikely to sustain a long-term relationship.

### Companionate Love

Companionate love involves intimacy and commitment but no passion (see part *g* of Figure 20.5). It is essentially a long-term friendship such as often develops in marriage after a couple's passion has died down (see Figure 20.7).

Strongly connected couples beyond the surging emotions of passion usually develop a system of shared values. The extent of support and interplay is often unspoken and habitual, and only upon death or divorce do they become aware of how much they have lost. Having been concerned with what was not working well, they may have failed to realize fully how many of their joint pursuits did work (Carlson & Hatfield, 1992).

### Consummate Love

As mentioned earlier, consummate love is the combination of all three components of Sternberg's triangle. Although it is most often associated with romantic relationships, it can occur in other contexts. One can experience a love for one's child, for example, that has the deep emotional involvement of the intimacy component, the satisfaction of motivational needs (such as nurturance and self-esteem) of the passion component, and the dedication of the decision/commitment component. Achieving consummate love, according to Sternberg, is like losing weight: difficult but not impossible. After the goal has been reached, maintaining it becomes the problem—whether keeping the weight off or keeping the consummate love alive.

## Love Versus Lust

One dictionary defines *lust* as "an intense longing" and "sexual desire often to an intense or unrestrained degree." In Sternberg's (1986) theory, lust is the passionate component of love. Lust or passion can be so strong as to elicit the feelings and behaviors often associated with emotional disturbance. Infatuated people may be distracted by obsessional thoughts about the object of their affection. Normally poised and well coordinated, they may find themselves speechless and clumsy in the presence of the person to whom they are attracted. Mood shifts from euphoria to depression are common, and a person's priorities may be drastically altered, at least temporarily. For some people, the experience of falling in love bears a striking resemblance to temporary insanity. Perhaps this similarity underlies the expression, "I'm crazy about you."

### Feelings Versus Behaviors

Like fear, hunger, happiness, and anxiety, lust is a human feeling. You cannot choose to experience or to avoid feelings, but you can control your responses to them. If you are dieting, you may choose to have just one egg at breakfast

**lust**—a strong sexual desire or need.

rather than two, even though you may still be hungry after eating the single egg. If you experience irritation with your partner while at a party, you may choose to scream and yell publicly or you may opt to postpone the "scene" until the two of you are alone. Similarly, if you are feeling lust, you may deal with it in various ways, including having sex with the nearest willing person, masturbating, running a mile, or taking a cold shower. We are responsible for the specific acts and behaviors we choose, but because we do not choose the specific feelings we have, guilt (or pride) over our feelings is inappropriate. Feelings are neither good nor bad, moral nor immoral, although some feelings are more pleasant than others.

## Confusing Lust and Love

Lust is a normal, healthy human emotion that can be very pleasurable for two people when they both desire sexual expression with one another. It is reasonable for two adults who are sexually attracted to each other to choose to express their lust by becoming sexually intimate. If the two people do not deal honestly with their feelings prior to engaging in sexual activity, however, these feelings can lead to considerable pain and guilt. As Erich Fromm (1956, pp. 54–55) put it,

> Sexual desire can be stimulated by the anxiety of aloneness, by the wish to conquer or be conquered, by vanity, by the wish to hurt and even to destroy, as much as it can be stimulated by love. It seems that sexual desire can easily blend with and be stimulated by any strong emotion, of which love is only one. Because sexual desire is in the minds of most people coupled with the idea of love, they are easily misled to conclude that they love each other when they want each other physically. . . . If the desire for physical union is not stimulated by love, . . . it never leads to union in more than an orgiastic, transitory sense. Sexual attraction creates, for the moment, the illusion of "union," yet without love this union leaves strangers as far apart as they were before—sometimes it makes them ashamed of each other, or even makes them hate each other, because when the illu-

sion has gone they feel their estrangement even more markedly than before.

Differences in the sexual socialization of males and females in North American culture contribute to the difficulties that adolescents in particular have in communicating their feelings. Specifically, females are traditionally taught to look for a partner for an enduring romantic relationship, whereas males are culturally conditioned to seek sexual experience per se. Feeling lust (but not love), a young man may attempt sexual activity with a young woman. She may interpret his sexual attentions as love, and indeed he may say "I love you" to persuade her to agree to sexual intimacy. If his acts are based primarily on feelings of lust, he attains his goal when he has an orgasm. The young woman's objectives and expectations may be quite different. For her, sexual intimacy may be a means to the goal of an enduring relationship rather than an end in itself. There is no reason why a young man and woman (or any other couple, for that matter) should not have sexual relations that are based on lust; but honest communication and agreement about expectations must occur prior to sexual intimacy if people are to avoid using others or feeling used. In the absence of honest disclosure of feelings and goals, prospective sex partners may exploit one another.

As noted earlier, there is an old cliché suggesting that men use love to get sex and women use sex to get love. With North American culture's progress toward gender equality in recent decades, some men complain that women exploit them sexually, and women may protest that "just because I went to bed with him, he thinks he owns me." There is evidence to suggest, however, that young women are still more likely than young men to find sex acceptable only in a love relationship (Buss, 1994; Roche, 1986).

A striking example of this difference is reflected in two studies by Clark and Hatfield (1989). In these experiments, male and female confederates of average attractiveness approached students on a college campus and said, "I have been noticing you around campus. I find you to be very attractive." The confederate then asked the students one of three questions: 1) Would you go out with me tonight? 2) Would you come over to my apartment tonight? or 3) Would you go to bed with me tonight? None of the women who were approached agreed to go to bed with the male confederate, whereas more than two-thirds of the males agreed to such a proposal. These studies were done before the threat of AIDS was well known—the data were collected in 1978 and 1982—and men since may have become more hesitant to agree to a sexual encounter with a woman whom they do not know. Future research should investigate this possibility. In any event, these studies illustrate the pronounced difference between men and women in willingness to engage in sexual intimacy outside the context of a committed or loving relationship. People may also differ in the meanings that they attach to the word *love*, and we turn now to this issue.

---

## Love as Dependency, Jealousy, and Other Unlovely Feelings

Even when two people sincerely believe that they love each other, problems may arise because of differences in their interpretations of the word *love*. As we have seen, love can take many different forms. The word *love* may connote both passion and a commitment so strong that a temporary absence of sexual pleasure is cheerfully accepted. It may carry the message that "I will sacrifice for you" and "you should sacrifice for me." It may mean "I have the right to influence what you do," or it may sometimes be used to express a state of tension. At other times, *love* can communicate a sense of peacefulness.

### Dependency and Control

The first love that most humans experience is the parental love received during infancy, a time when we are highly dependent. It has been proposed that humans have a fundamental need for social attachment that is conditioned in particular ways by specific cultures (Shaver et al., 1988). One way that North American adolescents and adults satisfy this need is through romantic love. Dependency has been seen as a central component of romantic love by a number of researchers

(Dion & Dion, 1988). Those people who view the events that affect them (including love) as being largely under their own control, called internals, are less likely to report that they have been in love than are externals. Externals see most of their personal experiences as the products of powerful external sources beyond their control—God, astrology, or luck, for example. Externals tend to report their experience of romantic love as more volatile and mysterious than do internals.

North Americans tend to prepare their offspring to seek security through emotional attachment to other people. In its extreme form, the association of security with attachment can lead to exaggerated expectations about what another person in a relationship can provide. Some people seek security and self-gratification through one other person, who provides a buffer against an often tumultuous and threatening world. Just as people can become addicted to drugs, to work, or (as we saw in Chapter 19) to atypical sexual practices, so can they become desperately attached to another person. Such an attachment may lead to what Peele and Brodsky (1975) call interpersonal addiction (see Box 20.2), the classic syndrome involving both tolerance and withdrawal.

You are probably familiar with the concepts of tolerance and withdrawal as applied to substance abuse. As people's dependency on a particular drug grows, they acquire a tolerance for it and their bodies require more and more of the substance to provide a reassuring "high." Over time, most addicted people become increasingly unable to cope with the problems and uncertainties that attracted them to the drug. They cannot envision everyday life without the drug and feel unable to free themselves from its grip. When the drug is not available, their bodies react to withdrawal with fever, sweating, shivering, and alternating patterns of insomnia and drowsiness. Addicts even experience anxiety over the *potential* unavailability of the drug, the use of which constitutes a major ritual in their lives. As Peele (1988) pointed out, drugs can give life structure and provide security against the anxiety associated with novelty and challenge.

Just as drug addicts seek security in chemicals, some individuals seek comfort and security in an emotional attachment to another person.

**Box 20.2**

## Love Junkies?

Although people often speak of the "chemistry of love," little is known about chemical states associated with love. Dr. Michael R. Liebowitz (1983) has suggested that a brain chemical, like phenylethylamine (PEA), may be involved in the more extreme cases of "love sickness." PEA is a chemical compound similar to amphetamine. According to Dr. Liebowitz, love brings on a giddy response similar to an amphetamine high. If a romance abruptly ends, the distressed lover experiences a depression similar to amphetamine withdrawal. The similarity between the feelings experienced in amphetamine withdrawal and the crash of a romance is due to the brain manufacturing PEA in response to love and shutting down production in response to the dissolution of a relationship. While studying a group of women who exhibited a history of disastrous love relationships, Liebowitz noticed that many of these women were attractive and competent, but their ability to function well at work or in social situations depended on their love situation. Liebowitz suggested that the women's level of PEA fluctuated wildly because of an "unstable control mechanism" that might be acquired or inherited.

The women were treated by a combination of psychotherapy and medication to relieve the compulsion to find a new "fix" in another lover. Drugs that inhibit the breakdown of PEA, such as the antidepressant medications known as monoamine oxidase inhibitors, are effective in elevating the spirits of these women. Psychotherapy is helpful in revealing their self-defeating patterns of choosing inappropriate lovers and in teaching them better coping skills.

Sources: Fisher, 1992; Liebowitz, 1983.

They can become so addicted to another that they let go of all other interests and activities (see Figure 20.8). According to Peele and Brodsky (1974, p. 25),

> As an addictive relationship unfolds, the lovers may seem to be seeing each other for the pleasure and excitement of it, but this doesn't last. After a while, the lovers are just there for each other, not for mutual growth or self-expression, but for comfort and familiarity. They reach a tolerance for each other. As for withdrawal, we have all seen the emotional and physical havoc that follows in the wake of some breakups, and the desperate ploys a jilted lover will try in order to get another "shot" of his or her beloved.

It is not unusual to see two adolescents or young adults make their relationship the focal point of their lives. Nothing will satisfy them but to be with the other person constantly. All other persons and activities recede into the background, and each lover acts as if his or her partner might disappear from the face of the earth if not in his or her company. The lovers fill the empty spaces in their lives with one another. Possessiveness and jealousy encircle the relationship. Any attempt by either partner to gain some independence is viewed by the other as a threat, but their stifling of each other's personal growth ultimately destroys the relationship.

It is when such a relationship breaks up that the lovers' addiction is most noticeable. The two people who have been so totally "in love" may suddenly hate each other. Their callous disregard for each other's feelings may indicate that they have always been thinking more of themselves than of each other. The case history in Box 20.3 illustrates this pattern.

Lovers sometimes talk as if their love were unconditional. This outlook is reinforced in traditional North American marriage vows, by which the couple pledge to love one another in sickness and in health, for richer or for poorer,

**FIGURE 20.8**
**Dependency or Love?**
Some people become so dependent on a partner that they drop other relationships and interests, clinging so fiercely that one or the other person may begin to feel smothered.

and so forth. Certainly a marital commitment should not be severed because of changes in a partner's health or wealth. The concept of unconditional love applied to a relationship between adults, however, often masks dependency. Adults who value themselves do not unconditionally accept a relationship with a partner who abuses them. For example, an unhappy woman who puts up with a continued pattern of physical or emotional abuse from her partner remains in the relationship out of dependency, not love. The husband who fails to assert his rights as an adult to determine his own activities and time schedules does so not from love but from the inability or unwillingness to function as an independent adult.

Just as we may confuse love with dependency, we may define an emotion as love when

it is actually jealousy. Of all the feelings we experience, jealousy is among the most unpleasant. In the grip of this painful emotion, the most poised, self-confident, attractive person can disintegrate into a frightened, hostile, suspicious, defensive, complaining being.

## Jealousy

One of the potential drawbacks of becoming attached to another person is that the bond can make us vulnerable to jealousy. Feelings of jealousy can be so intense and unpleasant as to provoke us to attempt to control and possess the sexual thoughts, feelings, and expression of the person to whom we are attached. There is evidence that men and women differ in their perceptions of the behaviors that indicate infidelity and that elicit jealousy (see Box 20.4).

Because jealousy, or at least competition for mates, is apparent among mammals, Kinsey, as well as many contemporary evolutionary theorists (Buss, 1994; Fisher, 1992; Symons, 1979), considered jealousy and competition to be a part of our evolutionary inheritance. Male jealousy is a major motive for spousal homicide in North America (Buss, 1994; Fisher, 1992). Reiss (1986) also believed jealousy to be a universal emotion, but he did not link it to our genetic heritage. Instead, he maintained that all societies set boundaries for important relationships, particularly marriages. When the boundaries of a relationship are violated, jealousy arises. The observation that *not* everyone experiences jealousy upon learning of a mate's sexual interaction with another person suggests, however, that the capacity for jealousy can be affected by psychological and social experiences. That is, in cultures that permit polygamous marriages, husbands and wives do not associate outside sexual activity with anger and with fear of rejection and loss to the same degree that North Americans do (Allgeier, 1992).

Some researchers have concluded that the extent to which jealousy dominates and overwhelms an individual's sense of well-being is related to such characteristics as insecurity, inadequacy, and dependency (Buss, 1994; Fisher, 1992). Women are more likely to experience jealousy when they are feeling inadequate. On the basis of his longitudinal research, White (1981;

**Box 20.3**

## "Love" as Dependence

Don and Pam met while she was a junior in high school. He worked in a bank and attended college part time for two years after graduating from high school. Don's mother died when he was nine years old, and his father never remarried. The relationship between Don and his father was quite distant; he saw his father only a few times a year, although they lived in the same city. Don had few friends and was unsure about what he wanted to do with his life. When he met Pam, he was uncertain about remaining at the bank and could not decide on his college major.

Pam and her family constantly bickered. Her father often beat her for minor transgressions while her mother stood passively by. In addition, she was continually the target of verbal criticism from her parents, who vented on her their feelings of dissatisfaction with their relationship. She was trying to find a way out of an intolerable situation when she met Don. It was close to love at first sight when they met at a dance. They began dating and spending as much time together as they could. He drove her to school before he went to work, and after school she waited at a nearby diner for him to get off work. Their lives were rapidly consumed by each other. He dropped out of school to have more time to spend with her, and Pam's friends seldom saw her after she met Don. Six months after they met, Pam became pregnant, and they were married shortly thereafter. She skipped her senior year, and Don continued to work at the bank. For the next two years, they continued to make up the total fabric of each other's lives. Their daughter was important but peripheral to their passion for each other.

Slowly, however, things unraveled. Pam felt isolated at home with the child and worried incessantly about Don if he did not call her from work at least once a day. She began having episodic depressions, thinking about finishing high school and getting a job to break the isolation. Don could not understand her need to get out of the house. Weren't their love and their child enough for her? He became obsessed with the idea that she should not finish her education or start a job until their daughter reached school age. He began calling home four or five times a day to make sure that she was not going out. He became enraged if his telephone calls were not answered immediately.

Finally, Pam took their daughter and went to stay with an aunt to escape Don's possessiveness. He called constantly, imploring her to come back and accusing her of seeing someone else. He began to threaten her, and when that did not work, he talked of suicide. Don was experiencing withdrawal. He had difficulty sleeping; he was obsessed with thoughts of his wife. He lost his appetite and experienced attacks of nausea, heart palpitations, perspiration, and feelings of dread.

Pam tired of staying with her aunt. She saw no future there, and she was pleased in a way she could not fully understand with Don's demonstrations of undying love. She felt adrift, going nowhere, and she decided to reunite with Don.

Their relationship for the past five years has shifted between separation and reunion. Neither can break the dependence on the other. Don's possessiveness is best summed up by his own words when he reacted to the threat of another separation from Pam: "I love you so much I could kill you." Both partners have lost their capacity for independent living. They are threatened by any change or growth in each other. They try to blot out the emptiness of their lives with pledges of undying love. They have become less and less able to cope with the outside world.

Source: Authors' files.

## Box 20.4

## Dating Infidelity

Before a serious commitment exists between two people, it is common for each of them to go out with other people. Difficulties can arise, of course, if one member of a couple believes that they are at a later stage in the dating relationship than the other partner does, or if they have different values about the extent of dating and sexual exclusivity that should exist between them at a specific dating stage. To examine a phenomenon that they labeled dating infidelity, Roscoe, Cavanaugh, and Kennedy (1988) gathered the responses of 247 unmarried college students to the following questions:

(1) What behaviors do you think constitute being ''unfaithful'' to a dating partner provided the couple is in a serious dating relationship (in other words, they have assumed that they are to date only each other)?

(2) What are some reasons a person in a serious dating relationship would be ''unfaithful'' to a dating partner?

(3) What would you do if you learned that your dating partner was ''unfaithful'' to you? (p. 37)

If you are currently in what you consider to be a serious dating relationship, you and your partner might want to discuss these questions with one another. In general, students in the Roscoe et al. study described three major behaviors as constituting infidelity if done with someone else: dating or spending time; having sexual intercourse; and engaging in other sexual interactions, such as flirting, kissing, neck-

ing, and petting. Men and women differed in their views of infidelity, however, with more women than men listing dating or spending time with another and keeping secrets from the primary partner. In contrast, men were more likely than women to state that having sexual interactions with another person constituted unfaithfulness.

The top three reasons why students thought infidelity would occur were dissatisfaction with the relationship, boredom, and revenge, anger, or jealousy. More women than men listed relationship dissatisfaction as a reason, and more men than women listed sexual incompatibility and lack of communication or understanding as a potential cause for infidelity. If they learned that their dating partner had been unfaithful, 44% of the students said that they would terminate the relationship, with women more likely than men to indicate that they would first discuss the situation with the partner.

A final interesting set of findings from Roscoe et al.'s (1988) research concerned their examination of students' attitudes as a function of whether they reported always having been faithful. A slight majority of both men and women stated that they had not always been faithful in a dating relationship. Those who had engaged in dating infidelity at some time, compared to those who had always been faithful, were more likely to give the following reasons for a person's dating infidelity: dissatisfaction with the relationship, sexual incompatibility, and being insecure or unsure about the relationship.

White & Helbick, 1988) concluded that the feelings of inadequacy evoke the jealousy. In men, he believed, the relationship is reversed; men become aware of jealousy and then begin to feel inadequate.

There is evidence that some people deliberately provoke jealousy in their partners. Women

are more likely than men to report this behavior. The most common method of piquing jealousy reported by White's respondents was talking to the mate about how appealing someone else was, and the most common motive was to get more attention from the mate. Other methods included flirting, dating others, pretending to be attached to someone else, and talking about a former partner.

We know a woman who has had a number of extramarital affairs and characterizes them all as a form of revenge. That is, whenever she learned of another of her husband's affairs, she sought an extramarital relationship to even the score. Women's general response to jealousy, however, is to increase efforts to make themselves attractive to the primary partner. In contrast, men seek outside relationships for solace and retribution. Jealousy is more common among younger than older people and among less educated than more educated people, and it is more intense in new relationships than in those of longer duration. Finally, people who report overall dissatisfaction with their lives have more frequent bouts of jealousy than do happier people (Wiederman & Allgeier, 1993).

Although there are a number of utopian societies in North America that have restricted their members' sexual interactions and structured family life in such a way as to minimize jealousy, jealousy is a fact of life for most Americans. Some researchers maintain that in the context of Western norms that revere pairing, family orientation, ownership, private property, competition, and the ideal of the perfect relationship, jealousy is inevitable (Reiss, 1986; Wiederman & Allgeier, 1993).

How can one cope with the painful feelings of jealousy and minimize the destructive behaviors that those feelings sometimes elicit? Persons who feel threatened by jealousy in a relationship commonly withdraw from their partner or go on the attack. Either response can stimulate a similar reaction—withdrawal or counterattack—in the partner. These responses may be perceived by the jealous partner as further evidence that his or her fears are justified. An alternative reaction to feelings of jealousy is to *acknowledge* one's feelings and to describe their source: "Mike, I'm feeling jealous and afraid that you've lost interest in me because of the time you spent talking with Jen at the party." Because no attack or withdrawal is involved in this reaction, Mike may be more disposed to provide reassurance and a hug than he would be if his partner stomped angrily into the bedroom, muttering, "Well, you certainly have the hots for Jen, don't you?" If one partner continually punishes the other partner by attacking

or withdrawing when there has been no real violation of their relationship agreement, the accusations may produce the violation that the jealous partner fears.

There are instances in which, because one partner *has* violated the agreement between the couple, the other partner's jealousy and anger are justified. In that case, too, successful resolution is more likely if the partner presents an honest, direct description of his or her feelings about the other person's behavior.

Finally, some couples have problems in negotiating their differences because of the intensity of their desire for intimate contact. In an intriguing article called "Intimate Terrorism," Miller (1977, p. 79) eloquently described some of the difficulties inherent in intimate relationships after they have progressed beyond initial infatuation:

> Intimacy is as much about power as it is about love. The power struggle is rarely explicit at first, because infatuation and courtship are so satisfying, but it begins to surface when the relationship becomes a matter of daily living.

Miller's work with couples experiencing this kind of contention is described in Box 20.5.

## Loving Sexual Interactions

Earlier we described Peele and Brodsky's (1975) concept of addiction. By way of contrast, they also described some of the characteristics of mature love, and the following five questions are based on their work. If you are part of a loving sexual relationship, you and your partner might want to answer these questions individually and then discuss your responses.

1. Have you continued to maintain individual interests, including meaningful personal relationships with people other than your partner?

2. Are you and your lover friends? If your erotic involvement ended, would you continue to see one another as friends?

3. Have you maintained a secure belief in your own value as an independent person?

**Box 20.5**

## Intimate Terrorism

Gestalt psychotherapist Michael Vincent Miller has described the process of "intimate terrorism" between partners. He suggests that we spend much of our lives

*caught in the tension between the push of personal identity and the pull of intimacy. We want to be independent and self-reliant, but at the same time deeply attached to someone else. The needs for identity and intimacy seem to be at odds and yet they are really inseparable aspects of each other. (1977, p. 80).*

Miller asserted that in healthy relationships, the partners make use of their personality differences by learning from one another, so that each partner's repertoire is expanded. In contrast, Miller observed a polarization in many of the troubled couples with whom he has worked: each partner takes the opposite approach with respect to rationality and emotionality, for example:

*In one couple I know, the wife attacks the husband with her energy and a steady diet of confrontation. She surrounds him with declarations of "I feel this," and "I want this," and then pro-*

*ceeds to attack his noncommittal responses as a sign of his inability to feel anything toward her or respond to her demands. These attacks lead him to barricade his emotions even more.*

*He, in turn, sabotages her by discounting her feelings with his calm rational approach to life. This exaggerated reasonableness is little more than evasion and delay, but it succeeds in making her over emotional and a little crazy. (pp. 80, 82)*

Miller saw the fears of abandonment and of engulfment among some of the couples whom he treated as having originated in early childhood. He suggested that some parents may use childhood fears of abandonment and loss of love to control their children's behavior. Through this kind of experience, the child learns to perceive love as hard to get, something that must be earned and, once acquired, held onto tightly. Parents who smother a child with too much intimacy and attention can threaten the child's identity as a separate being. For people to make good contact, Miller says, a delicate balance is needed between sharing and privacy.

---

4. Is your relationship integrated with the rest of your life rather than set off or isolated from your other activities?

5. Finally, do you feel improved by the relationship? Have you become stronger, more attractive, more accomplished, and more sensitive since becoming involved with your partner?

Few of us can give an unqualified and enthusiastic "yes" in response to all five questions. In any case, relationships—especially good ones—are always changing, and thus your answers may differ from one month or year to the next. If either you or your partner feels, however, that the answer to two or more of these questions is a sad "no," you may want to discuss the possibility of making some changes in your relationship.

The quality of a relationship is not appropriately measured by its complete absence of problems. There is no such thing as a perfect relationship that is always problem-free. Instead, the qualities that are important in a loving sexual (or, for that matter, nonsexual) relationship are honesty, integrity, and concern for resolving problems in such a way as to best meet the needs of *both* partners.

A couple can have a richly satisfying relationship without seeing eye to eye on everything. In fact, if they are both healthy, independent adults, differences of opinion are inevitable. Disagreements about fundamental aspects of the relationship, however, may make the couple's long-term investment in the union inadvisable. For example, before making a long-term commitment, a couple should discuss their feelings regarding whether they should be sexually exclusive or free to have other sexual relationships, whether they want children, and whether their relationship will be characterized by highly traditional or egalitarian roles. There are many other areas in which agreement is not at all necessary. For example, whereas a woman who believes that a couple should share all activities may feel deserted as a result of her mate's solo interest in gardening or golf, people with well-developed avocations may welcome the fact that their spouses also have independent interests and hobbies. In fact, the combination of taking part in some activities independently of one another and cultivating common interests is related to the satisfaction of partners in a long-term relationship.

## Vitality in Long-Term Relationships

At the beginning of a relationship, there is a great deal of arousal that is not purely sexual. Uncertainty about how the relationship will turn out generates its own excitement or arousal. Not knowing how the other person feels, and wondering about our own attractiveness and sexual performance, lend a dimension of vulnerability and risk to initial involvement with another person.

After a relationship has existed for a while, the sexual arousal may be as strong as it was initially, but if the relationship is characterized by mutual trust and commitment, the other contributions to the feelings of arousal may fade. In any good ongoing relationship—whether with parents, children, siblings, roommates, or coworkers—there are cycles. Different points in the cycle are characterized by periods of intense connection, irritation, indifference, and dislike. In some couples, the individuals fall into rigid ways of relating to each other socially and sexually. Reliance on inflexible and highly predictable schedules, social activities, and patterns of sexual interaction can deaden the sense of passion and excitement in the relationship and lead to automatic rather than spontaneous interaction.

Even among couples who have relatively flexible relationships, expectations based on the dizzying feelings that occur during courtship can cause difficulties. We have some recently married friends who are now going through the normal adjustment process associated with marriage. At times during their premarital affair, they would ignore work or other obligations in favor of romantic time alone together. Now they have integrated their relationship into the rest of their activities, but in their busy lives, time for sex no longer "spontaneously" occurs. Of course, it never did. It is simply the case that earlier, the couple gave sexual intimacy the highest priority in their hierarchy of activities, whereas now it has taken place as one of numerous other important commitments. For them and for all of us who value the pleasure and intimacy shared during loving sexual interactions, it is essential to set aside periods of leisure time for emotional and sexual bonding.

Another trap that busy people should avoid is viewing sex as one more task in the roster of daily chores. People who typically view participation in sexual interaction with their partner as just another of their many duties are more likely to develop sexual problems in response to stresses from work or other sources. A sexual relationship that is vulnerable to stress often follows a conventional but unrealistic script in which the partners feel compelled to play their respective roles. Heavy breathing, erections, lubrication, and orgasm are the criteria. It is the type of sex you have to be up for, and the kind of sex you avoid if you have a headache rather than the kind that relieves headaches; the kind that risks coronaries rather than the kind that relaxes; the kind that is just another duty rather than the kind that is a break from daily responsibilities.

In contrast, sexual intimacy can be viewed as a relief from life's chores and responsibilities. The partners involve themselves sexually for reassurance and support rather than to try to live out some rare media depiction. They can be genuinely irresponsible. Free to express insecurities, worries, and doubts, they can obtain relief from such feelings, with orgasms being a secondary goal. Individuals who view their sexual relationship in this way are less likely to develop sexual problems when they are under stress, depressed, or suffering from midlife crisis or physical pain.

People who like themselves and take pleasure in life are exciting to be around. Thus it is important for each of us to do things that enhance both our self-regard and our daily pleasure if we wish to have vital and loving sexual interactions with our partners.

In addition, it is essential that we give ourselves the time and leisure to share feelings about our experiences and about each other. At times, engaging in honest sharing can be painful and exhausting, and leaving ourselves vulnerable can be threatening. If we develop our own capacities to love and if we choose our partner wisely, however, we can share our vulnerability with another independent adult. Making the commitment to nourish our relationships with mutual giving and receiving can provide us with one of life's greatest rewards: loving sexual interactions.

## Summary of Major Points

| | |
|---|---|
| 1. **Early experiences and the capacity to love.** | Experimental studies with primates, correlational research on a number of cultures, and observations of the development of neglected and abused children all suggest that the young need physical and emotional affection to become well-adjusted adults. |
| 2. **Self-love versus selfishness.** | Although sometimes confused, these two characteristics have different sources and consequences. When we feel competent and pleased with ourselves, we are far kinder to others than when the reverse is true. At those times when we do not love and respect ourselves, we withdraw and act selfishly. Self-love and appreciation, then, are related to loving and appreciating others. |
| 3. **Three forms of love.** | The different forms that love can take may be understood in terms of three components: intimacy, passion, and decision/commitment. Romantic love, for example, includes intimacy and passion but not decision/commitment. Whereas infatuation involves only passionate arousal, romantic love is liking with the added excitement of physical attraction and arousal. Other types of love are friendship, empty love, fatuous love, companionate love, and consummate love. |
| 4. **Love versus lust.** | Initially, erotic lovers typically feel enormous arousal from a number of sources, including sexual desire and anxiety over rejection. Whether they are experiencing lust, infatuation, or the beginning stages of an enduring romantic love, an obsessional preoccupation with the other person is common. A mutual lustful attraction can be highly, if briefly, pleasurable to some couples, but difficulties can arise if one partner is motivated by lust and the other by a commitment to developing an enduring romantic bond. The sharing of feelings and intentions by both partners can minimize the feelings of guilt and exploitation that can arise when two people have conflicting perceptions of a relationship. |
| 5. **Dependency and jealousy.** | These two arousal-laden emotions are frequently confused with the arousal associated with erotic love. Dependency and jealousy are more commonly and intensely experienced by people who lack self-confidence and self-esteem, and both can result in manipulative, exploitive, and nonloving behavior. Most of us fall prey to these painful emotions at one time or another. Communicating feelings instead of accusing and attacking one's partner reduces the destructive effects of dependency and jealousy. |

6. Loving sexual interactions.

Independent, mature, self-confident adults have the greatest capacity for healthy, mutually enhancing, loving sexual interactions. When two such adults form an erotic bond, they can enjoy their similarities and yet be comfortable with their differences. Making another person the exclusive focus of one's life can reduce the vitality of a relationship. If, instead, each partner develops his or her own potential, each is better able to contribute his or her unique qualities to a mutually satisfying and stimulating relationship. This ideal cannot be easily attained or constantly maintained, but striving toward it contributes to the hope, pride, and pleasure that characterize enduring and loving sexual interactions.

## Review of Key Concepts

1. Harlow's experiments with primates established that: a) monkeys raised in isolation for at least six months irreversibly become adult social and sexual misfits; b) monkeys' and humans' need for nurturing as infants are fundamentally different; c) controlled interactions with younger "normal" monkeys can restore isolated monkeys' ability to function sexually and socially; d) none of the above. (p. 672–673)

2. Although both social learning theorists and Prescott agree that children reared in violent cultures are more likely than others to be violent adults, they disagree as to the explanation. True or false? (pp. 676–677)

3. In Sternberg's formulation, romantic love means: a) passion alone; b) passion and intimacy but not commitment; c) passion, intimacy, and commitment together; d) commitment and passion but not intimacy. (pp. 679–683)

4. Sternberg believes that "consummate" or "complete" love is: a) often striven for but rarely attained; b) attained early in a relationship but often diminished over time; c) generally attained after long intimacy; d) impossible for normal human beings. (pp. 680–684)

5. Friendship, according to Sternberg, is fundamentally different from all the forms of love he analyzes. True or false, and why? (pp. 680–681)

6. "Limerence," or infatuation, has no place in Sternberg's model of love. True or false, and why? (pp. 681–682)

7. Feelings of jealousy are probably: a) similar in all cultures; b) similar in Western men and women; c) associated with feelings of inadequacy; d) none of the above. (pp. 688–691)

8. Discuss the importance of experiencing love and trust in childhood as a prerequisite for developing an adult personality capable of giving and receiving love. Draw upon your understanding of primate studies and the experiences of children reared in institutions or in cultures that encourage interpersonal violence, as well as upon what you have learned in earlier chapters about sexual assault and the sexual abuse of children.

9. "The person who truly loves, cares for another person more than himself or herself." Discuss.

10. In what ways may understanding the distinction between love and lust be important to our capacity for successful interactions with potential and actual sexual partners?

11. "Men use love to get sex and women use sex to get love." Comment.

12. Discuss the extent to which feelings of dependency can either enhance or cripple a loving relationship.

# Appendix A

***Answer Key:*** **Sexual Knowledge Survey**

T = True, F = False

| | | | | |
|---|---|---|---|---|
| 1. T | 13. F | 25. F | 37. T | 49. F |
| 2. F | 14. T | 26. T | 38. F | 50. T |
| 3. T | 15. F | 27. T | 39. T | 51. F |
| 4. F | 16. F | 28. T | 40. F | 52. T |
| 5. T | 17. F | 29. F | 41. T | 53. T |
| 6. F | 18. F | 30. F | 42. F | 54. F |
| 7. T | 19. T | 31. F | 43. T | 55. F |
| 8. F | 20. F | 32. F | 44. T | 56. T |
| 9. F | 21. F | 33. T | 45. T | 57. F |
| 10. T | 22. F | 34. F | 46. T | 58. T |
| 11. T | 23. F | 35. T | 47. T | 59. F |
| 12. T | 24. T | 36. T | 48. F | 60. T |

In a few instances, authorities may differ on the answers. All these questions and the controversies surrounding them are dealt with in this book.

# Appendix B

## Sources of Information About Sexuality

Former students frequently approach us for current information about some of the topics we had covered in class. Some students are also interested in further training in human sexuality or in joining professional organizations devoted to furthering research, therapy, and education about human sexuality. Other students are faced with writing term papers in other courses about issues raised in the human sexuality class, and they request names of journals and important books relevant to their topic. Accordingly, we recommend the following sources of information.

## Professional Organizations

American Association of Sex Educators, Counselors, and Therapists (AASECT)
    Executive Director, AASECT
    435 N. Michigan Ave., Suite 1717
    Chicago, IL 60611-4067

Association of Gay and Lesbian Psychiatrists
    1439 Pineville Rd.
    New Hope, PA 18938

Coalition on Sexuality and Disability
    132 Holbrook Rd.
    Holbrook, NY 11741

Feminist Alliance Against Rape
    P.O. Box 21033
    Washington, DC 20009

Harry Benjamin International Gender Dysphoria Association
    18333 Egret Bay Blvd., Suite 560
    Houston, TX 77058

National Council on Family Relations
    3989 Central Ave. N.E., Suite 550
    Minneapolis, MN 55421

National Gay Task Force Fund for Human Dignity
    80 Fifth Ave., #1601
    New York, NY 10011

Planned Parenthood Federation of America
    810 Seventh Ave.
    New York, NY 10019

Sex Information and Education Council of Canada (SIECAN)
    Executive Director, SIECAN
    850 Coxwell
    East York, Ontario M4C 5R1

Sexuality Information and Education Council of the United States (SIECUS)
    Executive Director, SIECUS
    130 W. 42nd St.
    New York, NY 10036

The Society for the Scientific Study of Sex (SSSS)
    Executive Director, SSSS
    P.O. Box 208
    Mt. Vernon, IA 52314

Society for Sex Therapy and Research (SSTAR)
    Stanley Althoff, Secretary
    University Hospital of Cleveland
    2074 Abington Rd.
    Cleveland, OH 44106

The World Association of Sexology (WAS)
    c/o Eli Coleman
    1300 So. 2nd St., Suite 180
    Minneapolis, MN 55454-1015

American Board of Sexology
1929 18th St. NW, Suite 1166
Washington, DC 20009

## Journals Publishing Sexuality Research Reports

Research on sexuality is published in numerous journals, so our list is necessarily selective. To track down journals that publish research on your topic, check the text references on the subject and look at recent issues of the journals listed there. For example, if you are interested in the phenomenon of sexual assault, read that chapter in the text (Chapter 18), list the authors cited and the journals in which they have published, and go to the library for the most current information. You will find the journals listed below in many university libraries.

*AIDS Education and Prevention*   As implied by its name, contains research reports relevant to evaluations of programs aimed at reducing the risk of contracting HIV.

*Archives of Sexual Behavior*   Publishes articles on all sexuality topics, but tends to emphasize research on variations in sexual orientation and gender-role identification.

*Family Planning Perspectives*   Published by the Alan Guttmacher Institute, the research wing of Planned Parenthood. Focuses on research on reproductive decision making and methods of birth control.

*Journal of Divorce*   As implied by its name, publishes research on correlates of relationship termination.

*Journal of the History of Sexuality*   Publishes historical analyses across topics relevant to sexuality.

*Journal of Homosexuality*   Contains research on the development and correlates of particular sexual orientations.

*Journal of Marriage and the Family*   Features research on variables associated with the quality of marital and family functioning.

*Journal of Psychology and Human Sexuality*   Focuses on psychological variables and their relationship to a wide range of sexual issues.

*Journal of Sex and Marital Therapy*   Reports on the effectiveness of different therapeutic techniques for individuals with sexual or marital difficulties.

*Journal of Sex Education and Therapy*   Publishes research on correlates of sexual knowledge and research that evaluates interventions for providing sex education and therapy.

*The Journal of Sex Research*   The oldest journal that focuses exclusively on research across the spectrum of human sexual experience.

*Lifestyles*   Publishes articles relevant to cohabitation, aging and sexuality, and lifestyle variations.

*Personal Relationships*   Focuses on research on romantic attraction, intimacy, and attachment.

*Sex Over Forty*   Publishes information and research on sexuality and aging.

*Sex Roles: A Journal of Research*   Focuses on all aspects of gender roles and norms, including their interaction with sexual relationships.

*Sexual Well-Being*   Newsletter devoted to sexuality and health.

*Sexuality and Disability*   Contains information relevant to the sexual expression of persons with disabilities.

*SIECUS Reports*   Published by the Sex Education and Information Council of the United States. Emphasizes topics relevant to sex education but also publishes articles on all topics in the human sexuality field, as well as reviews of contemporary books and audiovisual materials.

## Books on Sexuality

Barbach, L. G., & Levine, L. (1980). *Shared intimacies: Women's sexual experiences.* New York: Anchor Press.

Barbach and Levine describe a range of women's sexual fantasies. Readers may find some of these erotically appealing and others interesting in terms of the variety of human sexual experiences that can have arousal value to others.

Beere, C. A. (1990). *Sex and gender issues: A handbook of tests and measures.* New York: Greenwood Press.

For students interested in conducting research on sexual topics, this handbook will help them locate appropriate measures with known psycho-metric properties.

Bell, A. R., Weinberg, M. S., & Hammersmith, S. K. (1981). *Sexual preference: Its development in men and women.* Bloomington, IN: Indiana University Press.

This work is based on extensive interviews concerning the childhood experiences of a large sample of heterosexual and homosexual people. The authors learned that some homosexuals engaged in gender-role nonconforming behavior during childhood, but found little else that systematically distinguished heterosexual and homosexual people.

Boston Women's Health Book Collective (1992). *The new our bodies, ourselves.* New York: Simon & Schuster.

A practical and reliable guide to women's health, with an emphasis on self-reliance.

Boswell, J. (1980). *Christianity, social tolerance, and homosexuality.* Chicago, IL: University of Chicago Press.

This controversial book examines the reactions of the Church to homosexual relations from the time of Christ to the 14th century. Boswell concluded that Christian intolerance of homosexuality is not an essential feature of Christianity but emerged after a thousand years of Church history.

Bullough, V. L., & Bullough, B. (Eds.) (1994). *Human sexuality: An encyclopedia.* New York: Garland.

This encyclopedia contains entries from many experts in the field on topics ranging from abortion to virility.

Buss, D. M. (1994). *The evolution of desire: Strategies of human mating.* New York: Basic Books.

In this evolutionary analysis of human mating strategies that raises important questions about fidelity, jealousy, and sexual harmony, Buss makes a strong argument for coming to grips with the selfish side of human nature if we are to control our destiny.

Calderone, M. S., & Johnson, E. W. (1989). *The Family Book About Sexuality.* New York: Harper & Row.

This useful book is highly recommended for families in which parents have had minimal exposure to sex education.

Calderone, M. S., & Ramey, J. W. (1982). *Talking with your child about sex.* New York: Random House.

This book is divided by developmental stage, beginning with the newborn and the first 18 months and ending with ages 10–12. An excellent present for first-time parents who want to provide accurate information and encourage open communication about sexual topics.

Cassell, C. (1984). *Swept Away.* New York: Simon & Schuster.

This book sensitizes the reader to the maladaptive ways in which young women are typically socialized to handle their sexuality. Cassell's title refers to women's tendency to rely on the feeling of being swept off their feet by "love" instead of making rational sexual decisions. This is essentially an essay aimed at helping women to increase their assertiveness, and therefore freedom of choice, about the person with whom and the conditions under which they become sexually intimate.

Davis, C. M., Yarber, W. L., & Davis, S. L. (Eds.) (1988). *Sexuality-related measures: A compendium.* Lake Mills, IA: Graphics Publishing Company.

For students interested in conducting a study of human sexual attitudes and behaviors, this compendium provides the first collection of pencil-paper measures of many different aspects of sexuality. It may be obtained by writing to Dr. William Yarber, Health Education, HPER Building, Bloomington, IN 47405.

Denes, M. (1976). *In necessity and sorrow: Life and death in an abortion hospital.* New York: Basic Books.

This is an eloquent and unusually well-balanced discussion of the abortion dilemma. Denes presents the reality of the procedures of second trimester abortion in graphic detail, but also considers the life circumstances of women who seek pregnancy termination at this stage. An important book for those interested in the pro-choice, pro-life debate.

Fisher, H. (1994). *The anatomy of love*. New York: Ballantine Books.

Fisher challenges many current beliefs about sexual love, adultery, and coercion. She argues that current sexual practices can only be fully understood by examining our evolutionary past.

Frayser, S. G., & Whitby, T. J. (1987). *Studies in human sexuality: A selected guide*. Littleton, CO: Libraries Unlimited.

This is an annotated bibliography of more than 600 books and monographs relevant to human sexuality. The authors review previous works done on topics that will be of interest to students developing research proposals.

Gilligan, C. (1982). *In a different voice: Psychological theory and women's development*. Cambridge, MA: Harvard University Press.

Based on research by Gilligan and others, the author suggests that females' moral perspectives differ from those of males, but that these differences don't necessarily imply that one gender is more highly developed morally.

Goldman, R., & Goldman, J. (1982). *Children's sexual thinking: A comparative study of children aged 5 to 15 years in Australia, North America, Britain, and Sweden*. London: Routledge & Kegan Paul.

The Goldmans' book is a unique contribution to our understanding of the development of children's ideas about sexuality, reproduction, gender, and gender roles. The book is extremely interesting to read and is particularly useful for students planning to work with children in educational or therapeutic settings and for those who intend to become parents.

Grauerholz, E., & Koralewski, M. (Eds.) (1990). *Sexual coercion: Its nature, causes, and prevention*. Lexington, MA: Lexington Books.

Composed of original essays by sexual assault researchers written for advanced undergraduates and graduate students, this book provides a broad overview of contemporary knowledge about assault and methods that may be used to reduce its occurrence.

Green, R. (1987). *The "sissy boy syndrome" and the development of homosexuality: A 15-year prospective study*. New Haven, CT: Yale University Press.

Green reports the results of longitudinal research on a sample of boys in therapy for engaging in extensive cross-gender behavior and dressing compared with a sample of similar boys who did not receive such therapy.

Gregor, T. (1985). *Anxious pleasures: The sexual lives of an Amazonian people*. Chicago, IL: University of Chicago Press.

This is a fascinating account of the sexual beliefs and behaviors of the Mehinaku, a contemporary tribe living in Brazil. The title derives from Gregor's conclusion that although the males enjoy sexual interaction, they also experience considerable anxiety because of their perception of women's reproductive power.

Grosskurth, P. (1980). *Havelock Ellis: A biography*. New York: Knopf.

This description of Ellis's personal and professional life provides a view of Western attitudes toward sexual expression and variation at the turn of the century. Ellis's relationship with birth control pioneer Margaret Sanger is also discussed. An enjoyable book about two pioneers who tried to further our understanding of human sexuality.

Hatcher, R. A., et al. (1994). *Contraceptive technology* (16th Ed.). New York: Irvington.

This "bible" of contraceptive knowledge is the most reliable guide for engaging in responsible sexual behavior.

Heiman, J. R., & LoPiccolo, J. (1988). *Becoming orgasmic: A sexual and personal growth program for women* (revised and expanded edition). New York: Prentice-Hall.

This book gives practical step-by-step suggestions for helping women to increase their ability to respond sexually with greater freedom.

Herdt, G. H. (1981). *Guardians of the flutes: Idioms of masculinity*. New York: McGraw-Hill.

Herdt lived for two years with the Sambia, a fictitious name for a tribe living in the Highlands of New Guinea. The Sambia are similar to the Mehinaku (see the description of Gregor, above) in their concern about female power over reproduction. Herdt's research challenges many contemporary assumptions about the fixed nature of sexual orientation.

Hrdy, S. B. (1981). *The woman that never evolved.* Cambridge, MA: Harvard University Press.

In her attempt to understand why males have been dominant over females, Hrdy reviews the literature on animals, particularly focusing on the sexual and reproductive behavior of primates. Her study contributes to a greater understanding of socio-biological perspectives.

Jones, J. H. (1993). *The Tuskegee syphilis experiment: A tragedy of race and medicine revisited.* New York: The Free Press.

This book provides an extremely good example of the importance of adhering to ethical guidelines in conducting research. It is a shocking chronicle of the observation of the long-term correlates of syphilis infection among poor, uneducated Black Southerners. Even after an effective cure for the disease had been found, the research team continued to study these syphilis victims without informing them of possible treatment.

Malamuth, N. M., & Donnerstein, E. (Eds.) (1984). *Pornography and sexual aggression.* Orlando, FL: Academic Press.

This is a useful resource book for students interested in the relationship between exposure to violent erotica and subsequent aggressiveness.

McCormick, N. B. (1994). *Sexual salvation.* New York: Greenwood Press.

A remarkably balanced book that examines sexual politics relevant to issues of feminism, coercion, orientation, prostitution, pornography, and other contemporary controversies.

McWhirter, D. P., & Mattison, A. M. (1984). *The male couple: How relationships develop.* Englewood Cliffs, NJ: Prentice-Hall.

A refreshing book by psychiatrist McWhirter and psychologist Mattison, themselves a male couple, that reports results of interviews with male couples. They describe the stages these couples go through, from the relationship's initial formation to renewal experienced over two decades. It may be particularly helpful for young men and women who are erotically attracted to others of the same gender and who lack models for forming an enduring and committed relationship.

Ogden, G. (1994). *Women who love sex.* New York: Pocket Books.

Based on interviews with hundreds of women who describe their sources of sexual pleasure, this book may be helpful to both men and women in opening communication between them.

Olds, S. W. (1985). *The eternal garden: Seasons of our sexuality.* New York: Times Books.

Sally Olds interviews people in the various stages of adult life and explores a variety of consensual sexual lifestyles ranging from celibacy to swinging. Olds is a fine writer, and this is a good book for students interested in the range of sexual expression.

Perper, T. (1985). *Sexual signals: The biology of love.* Philadelphia, PA: ISI Press.

Perper reports the results of his extensive observations of heterosexual flirting in dating bars, parties, and other places where singles meet, challenging the contemporary assumption that women are passive participants in the courtship process.

Pope, K. S., Sonne, J. L., & Holroyd, J. (1993). *Sexual feelings in psychotherapy: Explorations for therapists and therapists-in-training.* Washington, DC: American Psychological Association.

Important reading for anyone planning a career in the helping professions, this book will increase their awareness of the potential impact of sexual feelings with clients while providing practical suggestions for dealing with these feelings constructively.

Prentky, R. A., & Quinsey, V. L. (Eds.) (1988). *Human sexual aggression: Current perspectives.* New York: New York Academy of Sciences.

Providing an overview of empirical research on sexual aggression, this book's six parts cover psychological and typological issues, biological issues, treatment and prevention, victim issues, and social policy.

Reed, J. (1984). *The birth control movement and American society: From private vice to public virtue.* Princeton, NJ: Princeton University Press.

This is a fascinating and readable account of the scientific and political obstacles confronting early developers of oral contraceptives.

Reiss, I. L. (1990). *An end to shame: Shaping our next sexual revolution.* Buffalo, NY: Prometheus Books.

Reiss challenges the social policies that have been developed to cope with teenage pregnancy, rape, STDs, and other sexual problems. Noting the ineffectiveness of contemporary programs, he calls for a more rational examination of American thinking about sexuality.

Shilts, R. (1987). *And the band played on: People, politics, and the AIDS epidemic.* New York: St. Martin's Press.

This extraordinary book reads like a suspense novel. You promise yourself that you will read just one more chapter before going to sleep, and half a dozen chapters later, you are still reading. Randy Shilts, who was an investigative reporter for the *San Francisco Chronicle,* chronicles the resistance of the Reagan administration to respond to the impending epidemic; the absence of funds seriously hampered the Centers for Disease Control in its attempt to discover the cause(s) of AIDS. Inter-agency and cross-national competition are also described. Shilts succumbed to AIDS-related pneumonia in 1994.

Suggs, D. N., & Miracle, A. W. (Eds.) (1993). *Culture and human sexuality: A reader.* Pacific Grove, CA: Brooks Cole.

This edited book contains articles on the diversity of sexual practices in cultures throughout the world.

Symons, D. (1979). *The evolution of human sexuality.* New York: Oxford University Press.

Using an evolutionary perspective, Symons speculates about the possible causes of contemporary gender differences in sexual interests and behaviors. A highly provocative and readable book, we recommend it as a very broad attempt to understand our species' sexual behavior.

Szasz, T. (1990). *Sex by prescription.* New York: Penguin Books.

This short book takes on the sex therapy industry and is critical of many of the assumptions that guide the practices of many sex therapists.

Whipple, B., & Ogden, G. (1989). *Safe encounters: How women can say yes to pleasure and no to unsafe sex.* New York: McGraw-Hill.

The authors offer practical information on safer-sex practices that need to be considered by women and men alike in making sexual decisions to reduce their risks of contracting AIDS and other STDs.

Zilbergeld, B. (1992). *The new male sexuality.* New York: Bantam Books.

A sex therapist, Zilbergeld presents an overview of male sexuality written for men, but his book may also be useful reading for women.

# Appendix C

## Self-Help Organizations

In many cases, you can find the service or information you are seeking by consulting either the white or yellow pages in your local telephone book. If there is a crisis center in your area, its staff can also provide referrals. In the event that the information or service that you want is not locally available, the following sources can be helpful.

## Contraception

The Planned Parenthood Federation of America, (800) 829-7732, can provide referrals to the nearest Planned Parenthood clinics or other contraception clinics to those seeking information, contraceptives, and checkups. These services may also be offered by the student health service at your college or university, or by the local public health department.

## Erotic Products

Eve's Garden, 119 West 57th St., New York, NY 10019, (800) 848-3837, offers a variety of products from books about sexuality to sexual toys, vibrators, massage creams, and erotic contraceptives. You may write to Eve's Garden for a catalog of mail-order products.

## Gay and Lesbian Issues

Parents and Friends of Lesbians and Gays (PFLAG), P.O. Box 27605, Central Station, Washington, DC 20038, (202) 638-4200. The goal of this volunteer peer group is to help parents to accept and understand their gay offspring.

Association of Gay and Lesbian Psychiatrists, 1439 Pineville Rd., New Hope, PA 12938. Contacting this organization may be useful for gay individuals or couples seeking a therapist who will not operate on the assumption that their problems stem from their sexual orientation.

The National Gay and Lesbian Task Force in Washington, DC, has a hotline for reporting violence against gays. Call (202) 332-6483. The Hate Crimes hotline may also be called: (800) 347-4283.

## Sexual Dysfunctions

The American Association for Sex Educators, Counselors, and Therapists, (312) 644-0828, can provide the names of people in your area whom the organization has certified as sex therapists. Your county or state mental health board can also give the names of licensed therapists in your area.

For those who would like information on erectile dysfunctions, the following organizations may be contacted: Impotence Information Center, Department USA, P.O. Box 9, Minneapolis, MN 55440, (800) 843-4315, or Impotents Anonymous, 119 S. Ruth St., Maryville, TN 37801, (615) 983-6092.

## Sexual Information

The Sex Information and Education Council of the United States (SIECUS). SIECUS appears under Professional Organizations in Appendix B, but individuals with personal questions or concerns can call SIECUS for information about sexuality at (212) 206-7798.

## Sexually Transmitted Diseases

The Public Health Service offers several AIDS Hotlines. Call (800) 342-AIDS. This telephone number is staffed 24 hours a day, 7 days a week. Spanish speakers may call (800) 344-7432, daily from 8 A.M. to 2 A.M., EST. There is a TTY number for the hearing impaired: (800) 243-7889, Monday through Friday from 10 A.M. to 10 P.M. EST.

The Herpes Resource Center, 260 Sheridan Ave., Palo Alto, CA 94306, (919) 361-2120.

The STD National Hotline can be consulted for information about sexually transmitted diseases and referrals to STD clinics. Call (800) 227-8922.

# Glossary

**abortion**—spontaneous or medical termination of a pregnancy before the fetus can survive outside the uterus.

**acquired immunodeficiency syndrome (AIDS)**—a virally caused condition in which severe suppression of the immune system reduces the body's ability to fight diseases.

**actual failure rate**—the failure rate of a contraceptive method that takes into account both failure of the method and human failure to use it correctly.

**adrenarche**—the increase in adrenal androgens several years before puberty in boys.

**adultery**—in contemporary Western legal terms, a married person's having sexual relations with someone other than the spouse.

**AIDS dementia complex**—infection of the brain by HIV, resulting in the deterioration and loss of nerve cells and subsequent deficiencies in visual, mental, and motor abilities.

**alkaline**—having the power to neutralize acids.

**alveoli** (AL-vee-OH-lee)—milk-secreting cells in the breast.

**amebiasis** (AM-uh-BYE-uh-sis)—a parasitic infection of the colon that results in frequent diarrhea.

**amenorrhea** (a-MEN-or-REE-ah)—abnormal absence of menstruation.

**amniocentesis**—a diagnostic procedure in which amniotic fluid is extracted from the uterus and fetal cells are analyzed for chromosome defects.

**amniotic fluid**—the watery liquid that surrounds a developing fetus in the uterus.

**amniotic sac**—the pouch containing amniotic fluid that envelops a developing fetus in the uterus.

**amphetamines**—compounds that stimulate the central nervous system.

**amygdala**—brain center involved in the regulation of sexual motivation.

**amyl nitrate**—a potentially dangerous drug, usually inhaled, that relaxes muscle spasms and is sometimes used to prolong or intensify the experience of orgasm.

**analingus** (A-nul-LING-gus)—oral stimulation of the anus.

**anaphrodisiac** (an-AF-roe-DEE-zee-ak)—a substance that is alleged to inhibit sexual desire and activity.

**androgens**—generic term for hormones that promote development and functioning of the male reproductive system.

**androgyny** (an-DRAW-jih-nee)—possessing both masculine and feminine personality characteristics.

**anorexia nervosa**—an eating disorder characterized by an obsession with being extremely thin.

**aphrodisiac** (AF-roe-DEE-zee-ak)—a substance that is alleged to arouse sexual desire and increase the capacity for sexual activity.

**areola** (AIR-ee-OH-lah)—the darkened skin surrounding the nipples, containing oil-secreting glands.

**artificiality**—the extent to which a research setting differs from one's normal living environment.

**asceticism** (uh-SET-ih-SIH-zum)—the practice of extreme self-denial, especially for religious reasons.

**asexual**—without sexual feelings or qualities.

**asymptomatic** (A-sym-toe-MAH-tik)—without recognizable symptoms.

**autonomic nervous system**—the system of nerve cells and fibers that regulates involuntary actions such as smooth-muscle and glandular activity.

**autosomes**—the 22 pairs of chromosomes that are involved in general body development in humans.

**barbiturate**—a sedative or sleeping pill derived from barbituric acid.

**Barr body**—condensed, inactive X chromosome that distinguishes female cells from male cells. It appears as a dense clump when stained and examined under a microscope.

**behaviorism**—a theoretical approach that emphasizes the importance of studying observable activity.

**bias**—an attitude for or against a particular theory or hypothesis that influences one's judgment.

**biopsy**—surgical removal of tissue for diagnostic purposes.

**birth control**—the regulation of conception, pregnancy, or birth by preventive devices or methods.

**bisexuality**—the capacity to feel erotic attraction toward or to engage in sexual interaction with both males and females.

**body cells**—all the cells in the body except germ cells.

**Braxton-Hicks contractions**—irregular contractions of the uterus that are often mistaken for the onset of labor.

**breech presentation**—a birth position in which the baby's buttocks appear first.

**brothel**—a house where prostitutes and customers meet for sexual activity.

**bulimia**—an eating disorder characterized by uncontrolled binge eating followed by purging—vomiting, fasting, exercising.

**call girl**—a high-priced prostitute whose customers are solicited by telephone or by word-of-mouth references.

**candidiasis** (KAN-dih-DYE-ah-sis)—an infection of the vulva and vagina caused by the excess growth of a fungus that occurs normally in the body.

**cannula** (CAN-u-luh)—a tube inserted into the body through which liquid and/or tissue may be removed.

**cantharides** (kan-THAR-ih-deez)—a powder, popularly called Spanish fly, made from dried beetles; a supposed aphrodisiac that causes inflammation and irritation of the urinary tract.

**castration**—the surgical removal of the testes or ovaries.

**castration anxiety**—fear of losing the penis, thought by psychoanalysts to result from the child's fear of retaliation for forbidden sexual desire toward a parent.

**celibacy**—abstention from sexual intercourse.

**central nervous system (CNS)**—the part of the nervous system that consists of the brain and spinal cord.

**cerebrum**—the surface layer of cell bodies that constitutes the bulk of the brain in humans.

**cervical cap**—contraceptive rubber dome that is fitted to a woman's cervix; spermicide is placed inside the cap before it is pressed onto the cervix.

**cervix**—the lower end of the uterus, where it opens into the vagina.

**chancre** (SHANG-ker)—a dull red, painless, hard, round ulcer with raised edges that forms where the spirochete causing syphilis enters a person's body.

**chastity**—sexual abstinence.

**chemotherapy**—treatment of an illness through the use of chemicals.

**chlamydia** (clah-MID-ee-uh)—an STD, frequently asymptomatic in women, caused by the bacterium *Chlamydia trachomatis*.

**chorionic-villi sampling**—a procedure in which embryonic cells are removed from the tissue surrounding the embryo and then analyzed for evidence of genetic defects.

**chromatin** (CROW-mah-tin)—the substance in the nucleus of a cell from which chromosomes form during mitosis.

**chromosomes**—the strands of deoxyribonucleic acid and protein in the nucleus of each cell.

**circumcision**—the surgical removal of parts of the genitals, including the foreskin from the penis of a male or the hood from the clitoris of a female. In some cultures, the labia and/or clitoris are removed.

**clitoris** (CLIH-tor-is)—the small, highly sensitive erectile tissue located just below the point where the minor lips converge at the top of the vulva; its only known function is to provide female sexual pleasure.

**cognitive** (KOG-nih-tiv)—related to the act or process of engaging in mental activity.

**cohabitation**—an arrangement in which an unmarried couple live together.

**cohort**—a group from a particular generation; for example, those born from 1960 to 1969 are members of a different cohort than those born from 1970 to 1979.

**coitus**—penetration of the vagina by the penis, also called sexual intercourse.

**colostrum** (cuh-LAWS-trum)—a thin, yellowish fluid, high in proteins and antibodies, secreted from the nipples before and around the time of birth.

**concordance rate**—the likelihood that if one person manifests a certain trait, a relative (twin, sibling, uncle, et cetera) will manifest that same trait.

**conditioned response (CR)**—an acquired response to a stimulus that did not originally evoke such a response.

**conditioned stimulus (CS)**—in classical conditioning, a stimulus that is paired with an unconditioned stimulus until it evokes a response that was previously associated with the unconditioned stimulus.

**condom**—a sheath placed over the erect penis for prevention of pregnancy and protection against disease; usually made of latex.

**confound**—a factor other than those under investigation that influences the results of research.

**contraceptive**—any technique, drug, or device that prevents conception.

**contraceptive foam**—a spermicidal foam that is injected into the vagina prior to coitus.

**contraceptive sponge**—polyurethane vaginal sponge containing spermicide, used for contraception.

**contraceptive suppository**—a solid contraceptive substance containing a spermicide, inserted in the vagina prior to intercourse.

**control variable**—a variable that is held constant or controlled to reduce its influence on the dependent variable.

**copulation** (kop-you-LAY-shun)—sexual intercourse involving insertion of the penis into the vagina.

**corona** (cor-OH-nah)—the sensitive rim of the glans.

**corpora cavernosa** (COR-por-ah kah-ver-NOH-sa)—two columns within the penis that contain small cavities capable of filling with blood to produce erection.

**corpus luteum** (COR-pus LOO-tee-um)—the cell mass that remains after a follicle has released an egg; it secretes progesterone and estrogen.

**corpus spongiosum** (COR-pus spun-gee-OH-sum)—a column of spongy tissue within the penis that surrounds the urethra and is capable of blood engorgement during sexual arousal.

**correlational methods**—research methods involving the measurement of two or more variables to determine the extent of their relationship.

**courtly love**—a form of intense love not to be contaminated by lust or coitus.

**Cowper's glands** (COW-perz)—two small glands that secrete a clear, alkaline fluid into the urethra during sexual arousal.

**cremaster muscle** (CRE-mah-ster)—the muscle that runs from the testes into the spermatic cord and controls the proximity of the testes to the body.

**cross-sectional research**—comparisons of distinct but similar groups over the same time period.

**cunnilingus** (KUN-nih-LING-gus)—oral stimulation of the female genitals.

**curette** (cure-RET)—a scooplike instrument used for scraping bodily tissue.

**cystitis** (sis-TYE-tis)—a general term for any inflammation of the urinary bladder marked by pain and frequent urination.

**cytomegalovirus (CMV)** (sye-toe-MEG-uh-low-VYE-rus)—one of a group of viruses causing cell enlargement in various internal organs.

**deoxyribonucleic acid (DNA)** (dee-OX-see-RYE-boh-new-KLAY-ik)—a chemically complex nucleic acid that is a principal element of genes.

**dependent variable**—a variable that is measured or observed.

**diaphragm** (DYE-uh-fram)—a dome-shaped rubber contraceptive device inserted into the vagina to block the cervical opening. The diaphragm should always be used with a spermicide.

**dihydrotestosterone (DHT)**—a hormone produced from testosterone that is responsible for the development of the external genitals of the male fetus.

**dilation** (dye-LAY-shun)—expansion or opening up of the cervix prior to birth.

**dilation and curettage (D&C)** (CURE-eh-taj)—dilation of the cervix followed by scraping of the interior of the uterus.

**dilation and evacuation (D&E)**—an abortion method generally used in the second trimester; the fetus is crushed within the uterus, and the contents of the uterus are then extracted through a vacuum curette.

**dyspareunia** (DIS-par-OO-nee-ah)—painful intercourse.

**eclampsia**—a severe state of toxemia that can occur in late pregnancy, leading to convulsions and coma in the pregnant woman.

**ectopic pregnancy**—a pregnancy that occurs when a fertilized egg implants itself somewhere outside the uterus. In most cases, the site of implantation is a fallopian tube, in which case the condition is known as tubal pregnancy.

**effacement**—flattening and thinning of the cervix that occurs before and during childbirth.

**effleurage**—a Lamaze massage technique involving light circular stroking of the abdomen with the fingertips.

**ego**—in psychoanalysis, the rational level of personality.

**ejaculation**—expulsion of seminal fluid out of the urethra during orgasm.

**ejaculatory duct** (ee-JAK-u-la-TOR-ee)—the tubelike passageway that carries semen from the prostate gland to the urethra.

**Electra complex**—in Freudian theory, a daughter's desire for sexual relations with her father.

**embryo**—the unborn organism from the second to about the eighth week of pregnancy.

**emission**—propulsion of sperm and fluid to the base of the urethra during orgasm.

**endocrine gland** (EN-doe-crin)—a ductless gland that discharges its products directly into the bloodstream.

**endometriosis** (EN-doe-mee-tree-OH-sis)—a condition in which the cells that form the inner lining of the uterus grow in some place other than the uterus, such as within the pelvic cavity or on the external surface of the ovaries, fallopian tubes, or uterus.

**endometrium** (en-doe-MEE-tree-um)—the lining of the uterus, part of which is shed during menstruation.

**engagement**—movement of the fetus into a lower position in the mother's abdominal cavity, with its head past her pelvic bone structure.

**epididymis** (ep-ih-DIH-dih-mis)—tightly coiled tubules, located at the top of the testes, in which sperm are stored.

**epinephrine**—secreted by the adrenal gland, a hormone that is involved in emotional excitement; sometimes called adrenaline.

**episiotomy** (eh-PEE-zee-AW-taw-mee)—an incision made from the bottom of the entrance to the vagina down toward the anus to prevent vaginal and anal tissues from injury during childbirth.

**equity**—in reference to a personal relationship, a perceived balance between the benefits the relationship provides and the personal investment it requires.

**erectile dysfunction**—recurrent and persistent inability to attain or maintain a firm erection, despite adequate stimulation.

**erogenous zones**—areas of the body that are erotically sensitive to tactile stimulation.

**eros**—erotic love.

**erotica**—sexually oriented material that is acceptable to the viewer.

**erotophilic**—having a positive emotional response to sexual feelings and experiences.

**erotophobic**—having a negative emotional response to sexual feelings and experiences.

**estradiol**—the major natural estrogen, secreted by the ovaries, testes, and placenta.

**estrogens**—generic term for hormones that stimulate maturation and functioning of the female reproductive system.

**estrus**—in many nonhuman species, a peaking of the sexual cycle that signals ovulation; "in heat."

**exhibitionism**—the act of exposing one's genitals to an unwilling observer to obtain sexual gratification.

**experimental methods**—research methods involving the manipulation of one or more independent variables to determine their influence on dependent variables.

**fallopian tubes** (fah-LOW-pee-un)—the tubes through which eggs, or ova, are transported from the ovaries to the uterus; fertilization normally takes place within these tubes.

**fantasy**—a usually pleasant mental image unrestrained by the realities of the external world.

**fellatio** (fell-LAY-shee-oh)—oral stimulation of the male genitals.

**female condom**—a pouch placed inside the vagina to line the vaginal walls for prevention of pregnancy and protection against disease.

**fetal alcohol syndrome (FAS)**—a disorder found in the offspring of problem drinkers. FAS causes a group of specific symptoms, including mental retardation.

**fetishism**—obtaining sexual excitement primarily or exclusively from an inanimate object or a particular part of the body.

**fetus**—the unborn organism from the ninth week up until birth.

**fitness**—a measure of one's success in transmitting genes to the next generation (reproductive success).

**follicle** (FAHL-lih-kul)—in the ovary, the sac of estrogen-secreting cells that contains an egg.

**follicle-stimulating hormone (FSH)**—a gonadotropin that induces the maturation of the ovarian follicles in females and sperm production in males.

**follicular phase**—menstrual-cycle stage during which FSH stimulates the growth of the ovarian follicles.

**fornication**—sexual intercourse between people who are not married to each other.

**freedom from coercion**—an ethical principle requiring that potential volunteers be free to accept or decline participation in research without penalty.

**frenulum** (FREN-you-lum)—a small piece of skin on the underside of the male glans where the glans meets the body of the penis.

**frotteurism**—obtaining sexual arousal by touching or rubbing one's body against the body of an unsuspecting or nonconsenting person.

**gamete transfer**—a procedure in which a mature egg is placed in a woman's fallopian tube, together with a sperm sample, for fertilization.

**gardnerella vaginalis**—bacterial infection producing a thin, smelly discharge; afflicts both men and women.

**gender** (JEN-der)—the characteristics associated with being a male or a female in a particular culture.

**gender constancy**—the concept that gender does not normally change over the life span.

**gender difference**—a difference in physique, ability, attitude, or behavior found between groups of males and females.

**gender identity**—the feeling or conviction that one is a male or a female.

**gender-role identification**—the process by which individuals incorporate behaviors and characteristics of a culturally defined gender role into their own personalities.

**gender roles**—the traits and behaviors expected of males and of females in a particular culture.

**gender-role socialization**—the training of children by parents and other caretakers to behave in ways considered appropriate for their gender.

**gender stereotype**—a belief about the characteristics of a person based on gender.

**generalizability**—the extent to which the results of a study conducted with a particular sample represent the population from which the sample was drawn.

**genes**—part of DNA molecules found in chromosomes of cells that are responsible for the transmission of hereditary material from parents to offspring.

**genital tubercle**—a small protruding bud of fetal tissue that develops into either a penis or a clitoris.

**genital warts**—warts on the genitals that are caused by a virus and spread by physical contact with an infected person.

**germ cells**—sperm or egg cells.

**gestation**—the entire period of prenatal development from conception to birth.

**gigolo**—a man who is paid to be a woman's escort and to provide her with sexual services; a kept man.

**glans** (glanz)—the sensitive tip of the penis or clitoris.

**gonadotropins** (goe-NAH-doe-TROE-pinz)—chemicals produced by the pituitary gland that stimulate the gonads.

**gonorrhea**—an STD caused by the bacterium *Neisseria gonorrhoeae*.

**Gräfenberg spot** (GRAY-fen-berg)—also known as G spot; an area of sensitivity accessed through the upper wall of the vagina, usually within two inches of the vaginal entrance.

**hard-core erotica**—erotica that explicitly depicts the genitals and sexual acts.

**hepatitis B**—a virus that attacks the liver; often sexually transmitted.

**hermaphroditism**—condition in which a person is born with both male and female characteristics, such as an ovary on one side and a testis on the other.

**herpes simplex type II**—a viral infection contracted through physical contact with an infected person during an active outbreak of the sores.

**hominid**—humanlike creature.

**homophobia**—obsessive fear of and hostility toward homosexuals.

**Homo sapiens**—the modern human being.

**homosociality**—voluntary social segregation in late childhood; a period in which social and personal activities are centered around members of the same gender.

**hormone-replacement therapy (HRT)**—the use of small doses of estrogen, progesterone, or a combination of the two to counteract the hormonal effects of menopause.

**hormones** (HOR-mohnz)—the internal secretions of the endocrine glands that are distributed via the bloodstream.

**human chorionic gonadotropin (HCG)** (CORE-ee-ON-ik goe-NAH-doe-TROE-pin)—a hormone produced by the placenta.

**human immunodeficiency virus (HIV)**—the retrovirus that causes AIDS.

**hymen** (HYE-men)—a layer of tissue that partially covers the vaginal entrance of most females at birth.

**hypermasculinity**—exaggeration of male dominance through an emphasis on male virility, strength, and aggression.

**hypoactive sexual desire**—lack of interest in sexual expression with anyone.

**hypothalamus**—a marble-size structure at the base of the brain that regulates emotional and motivational aspects of behavior.

**hypothesis** (hy-PAW-theh-sis)—statement of a specific relationship between two or more variables.

**hysterectomy**—surgical removal of the uterus.

**hysterotomy** (HIS-ter-AW-tuh-mee)—surgical incision into the uterus; when used for abortion, the fetus is removed through the incision.

**id**—in psychoanalysis, the source of psychic energy derived from instinctive drives.

**immunosuppression**—the suppression of natural immunologic responses, which produces lowered resistance to disease.

**incest**—sexual activity between family members who are too closely related to be able to marry legally.

**inclusive fitness**—a measure of the total contribution of genes to the next generation by oneself and those with whom one shares genes, such as siblings and cousins.

**independent variable**—a variable that is manipulated or varied by the experimenter.

**infanticide**—killing of a baby.

**infatuation**—foolish and irrational love.

**infertility**—the inability to conceive, caused by factors in the male, female, or couple that are unrelated to the ability to engage in sexual relations.

**inhibited orgasm**—persistent difficulty in having orgasm or inability to have orgasm; in males, also called ejaculatory incompetence or retarded ejaculation.

**inner lips or labia minora** (LAY-bee-ah mih-NOR-ah)—the hairless lips between the outer lips that enclose the clitoris and the vaginal opening.

**instinct**—as Freud used this term, biological excitation that leads to mental activity.

**interstitial cells**—cells in the spaces between the seminiferous tubules that secrete hormones; also known as Leydig cells.

**intra-amniotic injection** (IN-truh-am-nee-AW-tik)—replacement of amniotic fluid either with prostaglandins or with a salt solution, causing fetal circulatory arrest; used in second-trimester abortions.

**intrauterine device (IUD)**—small plastic or metal device that is inserted into the uterus for contraceptive purposes.

**intromission**—insertion of the penis into the vagina.

**in vitro fertilization** (in VEE-trow)—a procedure in which a woman's egg is removed from her body, fertilized in a laboratory, and then implanted in her uterus.

**john**—a slang term for the customer of a prostitute.

**Kaposi's sarcoma (KS)** (KAP-uh-seez sar-KOE-mah)—formerly, a rare type of cancer of the skin and connective tissue. It is now common as one of the opportunistic infections that attacks AIDS patients, and appears as lesions on the skin.

**kinship**—a social relationship defined either by descent ties, such as those to parents, children, and siblings, or by ties to in-laws via marriage.

**labioscrotal swelling**—the fetal tissue that develops into either the scrotum in a male or the two outer vaginal lips in a female.

**labor**—the process of childbirth, consisting of contractions, thinning out and expansion of the cervix, delivery of the baby, and expulsion of the placenta.

**lanugo** (lah-NEW-goe)—fine hair that appears on the developing fetus during the fifth or sixth month.

**laparoscope** (LAP-ar-o-SCOPE)—a long, hollow instrument inserted into the abdominal cavity through an incision directly below the navel; used for diagnosis of medical difficulties and for sterilization.

**laparoscopy** (LAH-par-OS-coe-pee)—surgical incision into the abdomen into which a light and cutting instrument can be introduced.

**lascivious**—tending to stimulate sexual desire.

**latency**—in psychoanalytic theory, a stage lasting from about six years of age until puberty, in which there is little observable interest in sexual activity.

**lesbian**—a homosexual female.

**leukorrhea** (LOO-kor-REE-ah)—a whitish discharge from the vagina; often caused by a fungus infection.

**lewd**—sexually unchaste; inciting lust or debauchery.

**libido** (lih-BEE-doe)—psychoanalytic term for sexual energy or drive.

**limbic system**—the set of structures around the midbrain involved in regulating emotional and motivational behaviors.

**limerence** (LIH-mer-ence)—love marked by obsession and preoccupation with the loved one.

**lochia** (LOH-kee-ah)—dark-colored vaginal discharge that follows childbirth for several weeks.

**longitudinal research**—comparisons of the same group over different time periods.

**lubricant**—a shiny, slippery fluid secreted through the walls of the vagina during sexual arousal.

**lumpectomy**—surgical procedure in which a malignant breast tumor and surrounding tissue are removed while the rest of the breast is left intact.

**lust**—a strong sexual desire or need.

**luteal phase**—menstrual-cycle stage following ovulation during which growth of the uterine lining is stimulated by the secretion of progesterone from the corpus luteum.

**luteinizing hormone (LH)**—a gonadotropin that stimulates female ovulation and male androgen secretion.

**lymphadenopathy**—condition involving enlarged swollen lymph nodes in the neck, armpits, and/or groin.

**malignancy**—a cancerous growth.

**mammography** (mam-MAW-graf-ee)—a technique for X-raying the breasts to detect the presence or absence of a tumor.

**mastectomy**—surgery involving removal of a breast.

**masturbation**—self-stimulation of the genitals.

**meiosis** (my-O-sis)—cell division leading to the formation of gametes, in which the number of chromosomes is reduced by half.

**menarche** (MEN-ark)—the first menstrual period.

**menopause**—the cessation of menstruation and the end of a woman's reproductive capacity.

**menstrual extraction**—removal of menstrual blood and tissue from the uterus.

**menstruation**—the sloughing of the uterus's endometrial lining, which is discharged through the vaginal opening.

**midwife**—a person who has received special training as a birth attendant.

**mitosis** (my-TOE-sis)—a form of cell division in which the nucleus divides into two daughter cells, each of which receives one nucleus and is an exact duplicate of the parent cell.

**modeling**—learning through the observation of others.

**monogamy** (muh-NAW-guh-mee)—a marital form in which a person mates with just one other person.

**mons pubis**—a cushion of fatty tissue above a woman's labia that is covered by pubic hair.

**motile**—exhibiting or demonstrating the power of motion.

**Müllerian-duct system**—fetal tissue that develops into the internal female reproductive structures if the fetus is genetically female.

**Müllerian-inhibiting substance (MIS)**—a hormone secreted by the fetal testes that inhibits the growth and development of the Müllerian-duct system.

**myometrium** (my-o-MEE-tree-um)—the smooth muscle layer of the uterine wall.

**myotonia** (MY-o-TONE-ee-ah)—involuntary contractions of the muscles during the sexual response cycle.

**natural selection**—the process whereby species evolve genetically as a result of variations in the reproductive success of their ancestors.

**necrophilia**—sexual arousal and/or activity with a corpse.

**neurogenic**—caused by a problem in the nervous system.

**neuroticism**—an emotional disturbance in which the individual is unable to cope with his or her anxieties and conflicts.

**neurotransmitter**—one of many different body chemicals released by brain and nerve cells that carry messages between cells.

**nocturnal emission**—ejaculation of semen during sleep.

**nocturnal orgasm**—orgasm that occurs when a person is asleep.

**nongonococcal urethritis** (non-GON-oh-KOK-al yur-ree-THRY-tis)—a term for urethral infections in men that are usually caused by the chlamydia bacterium.

**normative**—the average response of members of a sample.

**Norplant**—a contraceptive implant, inserted into a woman's upper arm, that slowly releases hormones to inhibit ovulation.

**nymphomania**—excessive and uncontrollable sexual desire in women.

**obscenity**—the legal term for material that is foul, disgusting, lewd, and offensive to accepted standards of decency.

**obsessive-compulsive reaction**—a condition in which a person engages in compulsive behaviors in reaction to persistent or obsessive thoughts.

**Oedipus complex** (EH-dih-pus)—in Freudian theory, a son's desire for sexual relations with his mother.

**ontogeny** (on-TOJ-en-ee)—the history of the development of an individual organism.

**operational definition**—description of a variable in such a way that it can be measured.

**opiates**—narcotics derived from the opium poppy that tend to induce relaxation or sleep.

**oral contraceptives**—pills containing hormones that inhibit ovulation.

**outer lips or labia majora** (LAY-bee-ah ma-JOR-ah)—the hair-covered lips that enfold the inner lips, the clitoris, and the vaginal entrance.

**ovaries** (O-vah-rees)—two small organs that produce eggs and hormones; located above and to each side of the uterus.

**ovotestes**—gonads that do not develop into ovaries or testes.

**ovulation**—the release of a mature egg from an ovary.

**pandering**—serving as a go-between in commercial sexual transactions; generally, pimping or procuring.

**paraphilia** (par-rah-FILL-ee-ah)—love of the unusual; the term now used to describe sexual activities that were formerly labeled deviant (*para*: beside or amiss; *philia*: love).

**parasympathetic nervous system**—the part of the autonomic nervous system that is active in relaxed or quiescent states of the body.

**participant observation**—conducting research while simultaneously engaging in the behavior with the group being studied.

**passive immunity**—immunity to certain diseases or conditions acquired by a baby when it receives its mother's antibodies through her breast milk.

**patriarchy** (PAY-tree-ar-kee)—a society in which men have supremacy over women, who are legally and socially dependent on them.

**peak experience**—Maslow's term for a personal experience that generates feelings of ecstasy, peace, and unity with the universe.

**pederasty** (PEH-dur-AS-tee)—sex between an adult and a child, usually an adult male and child.

**pediculosis pubis** (pe-DIK-you-LOW-sis PYOU-bis)—lice infestation of the pubic hair; commonly referred to as crabs.

**pedophilia** (PEH-doe-FIL-ee-ah)—a sexual variation characterized by adult sexual attraction to prepubescent children.

**pelvic inflammatory disease (PID)**—swelling and inflammation of the uterine tissues, fallopian tubes, and sometimes the ovaries.

**pelvic nerve**—the parasympathetic nerve involved in involuntary sexual responses of the genital organs.

**penis** (PEE-nis)—the male sexual organ.

**penis envy**—in psychoanalytic theory, a woman's wish to possess a penis.

**perimetrium** (peh-rih-MEE-tree-um)—the thin connective-tissue membrane covering the outside of the uterus.

**peripheral nervous system**—the part of the nervous system outside the brain and spinal cord.

**perversion**—deviance from the normal in sexual activities or desires.

**phallus**—the penis.

**pheromones** (FARE-oh-mohnz)—externally secreted chemical substances to which other members of a common species respond.

**philia**—love involving concern with the well-being of a friend.

**phobic**—irrationally fearful.

**phylogeny** (fy-LOJ-en-ee)—the evolutionary history of a species or group.

**pimp**—a prostitute's business manager.

**placebo** (pluh-SEE-bow)—an inert substance used in place of an active drug; usually given to the control group in an experiment.

**placenta**—the organ formed by the joining of the tissue of the uterine wall with that of the developing fetus; a major source of hormones during pregnancy.

**platonic love**—nonsexual love for another person, often referred to as spiritual love.

**pneumocystis carinii pneumonia (PCP)** (NEW-moh-SIS-tis kah-RYE-nee-EYE)—a form of pneumonia that commonly appears in persons whose immune systems are highly suppressed.

**pornography**—sexually oriented material that is not acceptable to the viewer.

**postcoital douching** (DOO-shing)—insertion of chemical solutions, some of which can kill sperm, into the vagina after coitus.

**postpartum** (post-PAR-tum)—relating to the time immediately following birth.

**postpartum depression**—sadness or general letdown experienced by some women following childbirth.

**pre-eclampsia**—a maternal condition that may occur in the last trimester of pregnancy; symptoms include swelling, high blood pressure, and retention of toxic body wastes (hence the more general term toxemia).

**premature ejaculation**—unintentional ejaculation prior to or shortly following insertion of the penis in the vagina.

**premenstrual phase**—the six days prior to menstruation when the corpus luteum begins to disintegrate if the egg has not been fertilized.

**premenstrual syndrome (PMS)**—the depression, irritability, tension, and lowered self-esteem that some women experience prior to and during the early days of the menstrual period.

**priapism** (PRE-uh-PIZ-um)—prolonged erection that is not linked to sexual arousal.

**primal scene**—a child's observation of parental coitus.

**proceptivity**—the initiation and escalation of a sexual interaction with another person.

**procuring**—obtaining customers for a prostitute.

**progestins**—generic term for hormones that prepare the female reproductive system for pregnancy.

**prostaglandins**—hormones that stimulate muscle contraction.

**prostate gland**—gland located at the base of the male urinary bladder that supplies most of the seminal fluid.

**prostatic acid phosphatase (PAP)**—a fluid secreted by the prostate gland.

**prostatitis** (praw-stay-TIH-tis)—inflammation of the prostate gland.

**prosthesis**—artificial replacement for a body part.

**prostitution**—the practice of selling sexual stimulation or interaction.

**proximate cause**—explanations of behavior that focus on the immediate sources (how a particular behavior came to exist).

**prurient**—provoking lasciviousness.

**psychosurgery**—surgical procedures to change or alter psychological functioning and behavior.

**pubococcygeus muscle** (PC muscle) (pew-bow-cawk-SEE-gee-us)—the muscle that surrounds the vaginal entrance and walls.

**pudendal nerve**—the nerve that passes from the external genitals through spinal cord segments S2 through S4, transmitting sensations from the genitals.

**purdah**—the practice of secluding women from men.

**quickening**—the first fetal movements felt by the mother.

**radiation**—treatment of an illness by directing X-rays at a malignancy to kill cancer cells.

**rape**—sexual intercourse that occurs without consent under actual or threatened force.

**rape-trauma syndrome**—emotional and behavioral consequences that a victim experiences after being raped.

**reactivity**—the tendency of a measurement instrument (or observer) to influence the behavior under observation.

**reductionism**—explaining complex processes in terms of basic physical/chemical activities (for example, explaining human sexual desire just in terms of hormonal activity).

**refractory period**—the period immediately following ejaculation, during which further arousal is not possible; not present in the female's sexual response cycle.

**reliability**—the extent to which a measure elicits the same response at different times.

**replication**—the practice of repeating a study with a different group of research participants to determine whether the results of previous research are reliable.

**reproductive bias**—the belief that procreation is the sole purpose for sexual contact.

**reproductive success**—the extent to which organisms are able to produce offspring who survive long enough to pass on their genes to successive generations.

**reticular activating system (RAS)**—the system of nerve paths within the brain that is involved in arousal.

**retrograde ejaculation**—a condition in which the neck of the bladder does not contract during ejaculation, resulting in semen discharging into the man's bladder.

**retrovirus**—a virus that reverses the normal genetic process causing the host cell to replicate the virus instead of itself.

**Rhogam** (ROW-gam)—a substance that prevents an Rh-negative woman from developing antibodies to the Rh factor in subsequent embryos.

**rhythm method**—a birth control technique based on avoidance of sexual intercourse during a woman's fertile period each month.

**saltpeter**—a diuretic with an unsupported reputation as an anaphrodisiac.

**sampling**—the process of selecting a representative part of a population.

**satyriasis** (SAH-ter-RYE-uh-sis)—excessive and uncontrollable sexual desire in men.

**scabies**—a contagious skin condition caused by an insect that burrows under the skin.

**scripts**—largely unconscious, culturally determined mental plans that individuals use to organize and guide their behavior.

**scrotum** (SCROH-tum)—the sac that contains the testes.

**sedative**—a substance that eases physical pain and psychological distress.

**self-report bias**—bias introduced into the results of a study stemming either from participants' desire to appear "normal" or from memory lapses.

**semen** (SEE-men)—the milky-white alkaline fluid containing sperm; a product of fluids from the epididymis, seminal vesicles, prostate, and Cowper's glands, combined with sperm cells from the testes.

**seminiferous tubules** (se-me-NIF-er-us)—long, thin, tightly coiled tubes, located in the testes, that produce sperm.

**sensate focus**—an exercise involving concentration on sensations produced by touching.

**serial monogamy**—a marital form in which a person mates with just one other person at a time but may end that relationship and form another.

**sex chromosomes**—the pair of chromosomes that determines whether an individual is female or male.

**sex guilt**—sense of guilt resulting from the violation of personal standards of proper sexual behavior.

**sex linkage**—the connection between the sex chromosomes and the genes one inherits. When a person inherits a sex chromosome, he or she also inherits the genes it carries.

**sex-typed identification** (also called gender-typed identification)—incorporation into the personality of the behaviors and characteristics expected for one's gender in a particular culture with avoidance of those characteristics expected of the other gender.

**sexual arousal disorder**—failure to obtain or maintain erection or vaginal lubrication and swelling, despite adequate stimulation.

**sexual assault**—coercion of a nonconsenting person to have sexual contact.

**sexual aversion disorder**—a dysfunction characterized by extreme dislike and avoidance of genital contact with a partner.

**sexual double standard**—the belief that a particular behavior is acceptable for one gender but not for the other.

**sexual harassment**—the use of status and/or power to coerce or attempt to coerce a person into having sex; also, suggestive or lewd comments directed at a person in occupational, educational, or therapeutic settings.

**sexual masochism**—sexual gratification through the experiencing of pain and humiliation.

**sexual sadism**—the intentional infliction of pain or humiliation on another person for sexual excitement.

**sexual surrogate**—a member of a sex therapy team whose role is to have sexual interactions with a client as part of the therapy.

**shigellosis** (SHIH-geh-LOW-sis)—a form of dysentery (diarrhea) that can be transmitted by sexual contact, caused by the bacterium *Shigella*.

**socialization**—the process of developing the skills needed to interact with others in one's culture.

**sodomy**—"unnatural" sexual acts which, depending on the jurisdiction, can involve anal sex, oral sex, and/or sex with animals.

**soft-core erotica**—erotica that is suggestive, but not explicit, in portraying sexual acts.

**soixante-neuf** (SWAH-sahnt-nuff) (French, meaning *sixty-nine*)—simultaneous oral stimulation by both partners of one another's genitals.

**spectating**—evaluating and observing one's sexual activity rather than becoming immersed in the sexual experience.

**spermarche**—the beginning of sperm emission in adolescent boys.

**spermatic cord** (spur-MAH-tik)—the cord that suspends the testes and contains the vas deferens, blood vessels, nerves, and the cremaster muscle.

**spermicide**—a chemical that kills or immobilizes sperm.

**sperm-separation method**—a method of gender selection in which X-bearing and Y-bearing sperm are separated and the woman is artificially inseminated with Y-bearing sperm.

**squeeze technique**—a treatment for premature ejaculation in which a man signals his partner to apply manual pressure to his penis to avert ejaculation.

**statutory rape**—sexual intercourse with a person who is under the legal age of consent.

**sterilization**—a surgical procedure performed to make an individual incapable of reproduction.

**stimulus** (STIM-you-lus)—any objectively describable situation or event that produces a response in an organism.

**streetwalker**—a prostitute who solicits on the street.

**stress**—physical, emotional, or mental strain or tension.

**suction abortion**—removal of the fetus from the uterus through use of a suction machine; also called vacuum aspiration.

**superego**—in psychoanalysis, the level of personality corresponding to the conscience.

**sympathetic nervous system**—the part of the autonomic nervous system that is active in emotional or physical excitement and stress.

**sympto-thermal method**—a way of determining the date of ovulation based on changes in a woman's basal body temperature and the stretchability of her cervical mucus.

**syphilis**—a sexually transmitted disease caused by the bacterium *Treponema pallidum*.

**systematic desensitization**—a behavior therapy in which deep relaxation is used to reduce anxiety associated with certain situations.

**teratogenic**—causing birth defects.

**testes** (TES-tees)—two small, oval organs, located in the scrotum, that produce mature sperm and sex hormones.

**testosterone**—the major natural androgen.

**thalamus**—the major brain center involved in the transmission of sensory impulses to the cerebral cortex.

**theoretical failure rate**—the failure rate of a contraceptive method when it is used correctly.

**transition**—a short period of intense and very frequent contractions that complete dilation of the cervix to 10 cm.

**transsexual**—a person whose gender identity is different from his or her anatomical sex.

**transverse presentation**—a birth position in which the baby's side appears first.

**transvestite**—a person sexually stimulated or gratified by wearing the clothes of the other gender.

**triangular system**—a psychoanalytic concept proposing that a male homosexual's parents consist of an intimate, controlling mother and a detached, rejecting father.

**tribadism**—sexual activity in which one woman lies on top of another and moves rhythmically for clitoral stimulation.

**trichomoniasis** (TRIK-uh-muh-NYE-ah-sis)—an inflammation of the vagina characterized by a whitish discharge, caused by a parasite.

**triphasic oral contraceptives**—low-dose birth control pill in which the levels of hormones are varied over the menstrual cycle.

**tubal ligation** (lye-GAY-shun)—female sterilization involving cutting or tying of the fallopian tubes.

**tubal pregnancy**—an ectopic pregnancy in which the embryo is implanted in the woman's fallopian tube.

**ultimate cause**—explanations of behavior that focus on why a particular behavior increased reproductive success during the process of evolution.

**ultrasonography**—a procedure in which sound waves and a computer are used to create a visual representation of the fetus.

**umbilical cord**—the connection of the fetus to the placenta, through which the fetus is nourished.

**unconditioned response (UCR)**—a stimulus-evoked response that is not dependent on experience or learning.

**unconditioned stimulus (UCS)**—a stimulus that evokes a response that is not dependent on prior learning.

**undescended testes**—a condition in which testes have not dropped down from the abdomen into the scrotum.

**urethra** (yur-REE-thrah)—the duct or tube through which urine and ejaculate leave the body.

**urogenital folds**—folds or strips of skin on each side of the genital tubercle of the fetus that fuse to form the urethral tube in a male or the inner vaginal lips in a female.

**uterine perforation**—tearing or puncturing of the uterine wall.

**uterus**—the site of implantation of the fertilized cell mass, where the fetus develops during gestation; also called the womb.

**vagina** (vah-JYE-nah)—the portion of the female sexual system that extends from the uterus to the vulva.

**vaginismus** (VAH-jih-NIS-mus)—involuntary spasms of the pelvic musculature surrounding the outer third of the vagina.

**vaginitis** (VA-jih-NYE-tis)—a general term for any inflammation of the vagina caused by the gonococcus bacterium or by a fungus.

**validity**—the extent to which a measure accurately reflects what it is designed to measure.

**variable**—any situation or behavior capable of change or variation.

**varicoceles** (VARE-uh-coh-SEELZ)—enlarged or damaged veins leading to the testes or vas deferens that can be a cause of male infertility.

**vascular**—pertaining to the vessels that transport body liquids such as blood and lymph.

**vas deferens** (vas DEH-fur-renz)—the slender duct through which sperm are transported from each testis to the ejaculatory duct at the base of the urethra.

**vasectomy**—male sterilization involving cutting or tying of the vas deferens.

**vasocongestion** (VAY-soh-con-JES-tion)—the process that results in an increase of blood in the genital organs of either males or females or in breasts of females during sexual arousal.

**vasovasectomy**—surgical reversal of vasectomy.

**vernix caseosa** (VUR-nix kah-see-OH-sah)—a greasy substance that protects the skin of the fetus.

**victim precipitation**—the notion that the victim of an attack is at least partially responsible for the attack.

**volunteer bias**—bias introduced into the results of a study stemming from systematic differences between those who volunteer for research and those who avoid participation.

**voyeurism** (VOY-yer-izm)—obtaining sexual arousal by observing people without their consent when they are undressed or occupied in sexual activity.

**vulva** (VULL-vah)—the external female genitals, including the mons pubis, the outer and inner lips, the clitoris, and the vaginal opening.

**withdrawal**—removal of the penis from the vagina before ejaculation.

**Wolffian-duct system**—fetal tissue that develops into the internal male reproductive structures if the fetus is genetically male.

**yohimbine** (YO-him-bean)—an alleged aphrodisiac derived from the bark of the African yohimbé tree.

**zoophilia** (ZOO-oh-FIL-ee-ah)—sexual activity with animals; also known as bestiality.

**zygote** (ZYE-goat)—the developing organism from fertilization to implantation.

# References

Abbey, A. (1982). Sex differences in attributions for friendly behavior: Do males misperceive females' friendliness? *Journal of Personality and Social Psychology, 42,* 830–838.

Abbey, A. (1987). Misperceptions of friendly behavior as sexual interest: A survey of naturally occurring incidents. *Psychology of Women Quarterly, 11,* 173–194.

Abbey, A., Ross, L. T., & McDuffie, D. (1993). Alcohol's role in sexual assault. In R. R. Watson (Ed.), *Drug and alcohol abuse reviews,* Vol. 5: *Addictive behaviors in women* (pp. 1–27). Totawa, NJ: Humana Press, Inc.

Abbott, S., & Love, B. (1985). *Sappho was a right-on woman: A liberated view of lesbianism.* New York: Stein and Day.

Abel, G. G., Barlow, D. H., Blanchard, E., & Guild, D. (1977). The components of rapists' sexual arousal. *Archives of General Psychiatry, 34,* 895–903.

Abel, G. G., Becker, J. V., Mittelman, M., Cunningham-Rathner, J., Rouleau, J. L., & Murphy, W. D. (1987). Self-reported sex crimes of non-incarcerated paraphiliacs. *Journal of Interpersonal Violence, 2,* 3–25.

Abel, G. G., Becker, J. V., Kunningham-Rathner, J., Nittleman, M., & Primack, M. (1982). Differential diagnosis in diabetic: Validity of sexual symptomology. *Neurobiological Urodynamics, 1,* 57.

Abel, G. G., Becker, J., Murphy, W. D., & Flanagan, B. (1981). Identifying dangerous child molesters. In R. B. Stuart (Ed.), *Violent behavior* (pp. 116–137). New York: Brunner/Mazel.

Abel, G. G., Blanchard, E. B., Becker, J. V., & Djenderedjian, A. (1978). Differentiating sexual aggressiveness with penile measures. *Criminal Justice and Behavior, 5,* 315–332.

Abel, G. G., Osborn, C. A., Anthony, D., & Gardos, P. (1992). Current treatments of paraphiliacs. In J. Bancroft, C. M. Davis, & H. J. Ruppel, Jr. (Eds.). *Annual Review of Sex Research,* Vol. III (pp. 255–290). Lake Mills, IA: The Society for the Scientific Study of Sex.

Abel, G. G., Osborn, C. A., & Twigg, D. A. (1993). Sexual assault through the life span: Adult offenders with juvenile histories. In H. E. Barbaree, W. L. Marshall, & S. M. Hudson (Eds.), *The juvenile sex offender* (pp. 104–117). New York: Guilford Press.

Abelson, R. (1981). Psychological status of the script concept. *American Psychologist, 36,* 715–729.

Abramson, E. E., & Catalano, S. (1985). Weight loss and sexual behavior. *The Journal of Obesity and Weight Regulation, 4,* 268–273.

Abramson, P. R., & Hayashi, H. (1984). Pornography in Japan: Cross-cultural and theoretical considerations. In N. M. Malamuth & E. Donnerstein (Eds.), *Pornography and sexual aggression* (pp. 173–183). Orlando, FL: Academic Press.

Adams, H. E., Motsinger, P., McAnulty, R. D., & Moore, A. L. (1992). Voluntary control of penile tumescence among homosexual and heterosexual subjects. *Archives of Sexual Behavior, 21,* 17–31.

Addiego, F., Belzer, E., Comolli, J., Moger, W., Perry, J., & Whipple, B. (1981). Female ejaculation: A case study. *The Journal of Sex Research, 17,* 13–21.

Adler, N. E., David, H. P., Major, B. N., Roth, S. H., Russo, N. F., & Wyatt, G. E. (1990). Psychological responses after abortion. *Science, 248,* 41–44.

Adler, N. E., David, H. P., Major, B. N., Roth, S. H., Russo, N. F., & Wyatt, G. E. (1992). Psychological factors in abortion: A review. *American Psychologist, 47,* 1194–1204.

Ageton, S. S. (1983). *Sexual assault among adolescents.* Lexington, MA: Lexington Books.

Ahlburg, D. A., & DeVita, C. J. (1992). New realities of the American family. *Population Bulletin, 47* (2), 1–42.

Ainsworth, M. D. S., Blehar, M. C., Waters, E., & Wall, S. (1978). *Patterns of attachment: A psychological study of the strange situation.* Hillsdale, NJ: Lawrence Erlbaum Associates.

Aizenman, M., & Kelley, G. (1988). The incidence of violence and acquaintance rape in dating relationships among college men and women. *Journal of College Student Development, 29,* 305–311.

Alan Guttmacher Institute (1981). *Teenage pregnancy: The problem that hasn't gone away.* New York: Alan Guttmacher Institute.

Alan Guttmacher Institute (1982). Family planning and teenagers: The facts. *Public Policy: Issues in Brief, 2* (1), 1–2.

Alder, C. (1985). An exploration of self-reported sexually aggressive behavior. *Crime and Delinquency, 31,* 306–331.

Alexander, C. J., Sipski, M. L., & Findley, T. W. (1993).

Sexual activities, desire, and satisfaction in males pre- and post-spinal cord injury. *Archives of Sexual Behavior, 22,* 217–228.

Alfonso, V. C., Allison, D. B., & Dunn, G. M. (1992). Sexual fantasy and satisfaction: A multidimensional analysis of gender differences. *Journal of Psychology and Human Sexuality, 5,* 19–37.

Allen, D., & Okawa, J. B. (1987). A counseling center looks at sexual harassment. *Journal of NAWDAC, 50,* 9–15.

Allgeier, A. R. (1983). Informational barriers to contraception. In D. Byrne & W. Fisher (Eds.), *Adolescents, sex, and contraception* (pp. 143–169). Hillsdale, NJ: Lawrence Erlbaum Associates.

Allgeier, A. R. (1994a). Nymphomania. In V. Bullough & B. Bullough (Eds.), *Human sexuality: An encyclopedia* (p. 422). New York: Garland Publishing.

Allgeier, A. R. (1994b). Sociobiology. In V. Bullough & B. Bullough (Eds.), *Human sexuality: An encyclopedia* (pp. 561–564). New York: Garland Publishing.

Allgeier, A. R., Allgeier, E. R., & Rywick, T. (1981). Orientations toward abortion: Guilt or knowledge? *Adolescence, 16,* 273–280.

Allgeier, A. R., Allgeier, E. R., & Rywick, T. (1982). Response to requests for abortion: The influence of guilt and knowledge. *Journal of Applied Social Psychology, 12,* 282–292.

Allgeier, E. R. (1984). The personal perils of sex researchers: Vern Bullough and William Masters. *SIECUS Reports, 12* (4), 16–19.

Allgeier, E. R. (1986, July). *Cross-cultural views on sexuality.* Invited Lecture, 1986 Kinsey Summer Institute, Bloomington, IN. (a)

Allgeier, E. R. (1986). Ethical guidelines for ethics committees. *SIECUS Reports, 14* (4),11–13. (b)

Allgeier, E. R. (1987). Coercive versus consensual sexual interactions. *G. Stanley Hall Lecture Series,* Vol. 7 (pp. 7–63). Washington, D.C.: American Psychological Association.

Allgeier, E. R. (1989, November). *Pleasures and dangers in sexual relationships: Risks in taking positions about sexual issues.* Plenary presentation at the Annual Meeting of The Society for the Scientific Study of Sex, Toronto, Canada.

Allgeier, E. R. (1992). So-so sexuality: Field research on gender roles with a preliterate polygynous tribe. In G. G. Brannigan & M. R. Merrens (Eds.), *The undaunted psychologist: Adventures in research* (pp. 218–234). New York: McGraw Hill.

Allgeier, E. R., Allgeier, A. R., & Rywick, T. (1979). Abortion: Reward for conscientious contraceptive use? *The Journal of Sex Research, 15,* 64–75.

Allgeier, E. R., & Fogel, A. F. (1978). Coital position and sex roles: Responses to cross-sex behavior in bed. *Journal of Consulting and Clinical Psychology, 46,* 588–589.

Allgeier, E. R., Przybyla, D. P, & Thompson, M. E. (1977, November). *Planned sin: Sex guilt and contraception.* Paper presented at the meeting of the Psychonomic Society, Washington, D.C.

Allgeier, E. R., & Royster, B. J. T. (1991). New approaches to dating and sexuality. In E. Grauerholz & M. Koralewski (Eds.), *Sexual coercion: Its nature, causes and prevention* (pp. 133–147). Lexington, MA: Lexington Books.

Allgeier, E. R., Travis, S. K., Zeller, R., & Royster, B. J. T. (1990). *Constructions of consensual versus coercive sex: A survey of student-instructor sexual contacts.* Paper presented at the Western Region meeting of The Society for the Scientific Study of Sex, San Francisco, CA.

Allgeier, E. R., Yachanin, S. A., Smith, K. H., & Myers, J. G. (1984, May). *Are erotic photographs pornographic, offensive, and/or arousing? Correlations among judgments.* Paper presented at the meeting of the Midwestern Psychological Association, Chicago, IL.

American Cancer Society (1993). *Cancer facts and figures—1993.* Atlanta, GA: American Cancer Society, Inc.

American Psychiatric Association (1987). *Diagnostic and statistical manual of mental disorders* (3rd ed., revised). Washington, D.C.: American Psychiatric Association.

American Psychiatric Association (1994). *Diagnostic and statistical manual of mental disorders* (4th ed.). Washington, D. C.: American Psychiatric Association.

Amir, M. (1971). *Patterns in forcible rape.* Chicago, IL: University of Chicago Press.

Amoroso, D. M., Brown, M., Pruesse, M., Ware, E. E., & Pithey, D. W. (1971). An investigation of behavioral, psychological, and physical reactions to pornographic stimuli. In *Technical Report of the Commission on Obscenity and Pornography* Vol. 8 (pp. 1–40). Washington, D.C.: U.S. Government Printing Office.

Amschler, D. H. (1991). The rising incidence of HPV infection and its implications for reproductive health. *Journal of Sex Education and Therapy, 17,* 244–250.

Andolsek, K. M. (1990). *Obstetric care: Standards of prenatal, intrapartum, and postpartum management.* Philadelphia, PA: Lea & Febiger.

Andrews, F. M., Abbey, A., & Halman, L. J. (1991). Stress from infertility, marriage factors, and subjective well-being of wives and husbands. *Journal of Health and Social Behavior, 32,* 238–253.

Andrews, L. B. (1984). Yours, mine, and theirs. *Psychology Today,* December, 20–29.

Apfelbaum, B. (1989). Retarded ejaculation: A much-misunderstood syndrome. In S. R. Leiblum & R. C. Rosen (Eds.), *Principles and practices of sex therapy* (2nd Ed.) (pp. 168–206). New York: Guilford Press.

Aral, S. O., & Holmes, K. K. (1991). Sexually transmitted diseases in the AIDS era. *Scientific American, 264*, 62–69.

Aral, S. O., Mosher, W. D., & Cates, W., Jr., (1992). Vaginal douching among women of reproductive age in the United States: 1988. *American Journal of Public Health, 82*, 210–214.

Araoz, D. (1985). *The new hypnosis.* New York: Brunner/Mazel.

Armstrong, D. T. (1986). Environmental stress and ovarian function. *Biology of Reproduction, 34*, 29–39.

Armstrong, E. G. (1978). Massage parlors and their customers. *Archives of Sexual Behavior, 7*, 117–125.

Arndt, W. B. (1991). *Gender disorders and the paraphilias.* Madison, CT: International Universities Press, Inc.

Arndt, W. B., Foehl, J. C., & Good, F. E. (1985). Specific sexual fantasy themes: A multidimensional study. *Journal of Personality and Social Psychology, 48*, 472–480.

Aron, A., Aron, E. N., Tudor, M., & Nelson, G. (1991). Close relationships as including other in the self. *Journal of Personality and Social Psychology, 60*, 241–253.

Asayama, S. (1976). Sexual behavior in Japanese students: Comparisons of 1974, 1960, and 1952. *Archives of Sexual Behavior, 5*, 371–390.

Asscheman, H., & Gooren, L. J. G. (1992). Hormone treatment in transsexuals. *Journal of Psychology and Human Sexuality, 5* (4), 39–54.

Badgley, F., Allard, H., McCormick, N. et al. (1984). *Sexual offences against children* (Vol. 1). Ottawa, Canada: Canadian Government Publishing Centre.

Bagley, C., & Ramsey, R. (1986). Sexual abuse in childhood: Psychosocial outcomes and implications for social work practice. *Journal of Social Work and Human Sexuality, 4*, 33–47.

Bailey, J. M., Miller, J. S., & Willerman, L. (1993). Maternally related childhood gender nonconformity in homosexuals and heterosexuals. *Archives of Sexual Behavior, 22*, 461–469.

Bailey, J. M., & Pillard, R. C. (1991). A genetic study of male sexual orientation. *Archives of General Psychiatry, 48*, 1089–1096.

Baldwin, W. (1976). *Adolescent pregnancy and childbearing: Growing concerns for Americans.* Washington, D.C.: Population Reference Bureau.

Baldwin, W. & Cain, V. S. (1980). The children of teenage parents. *Family Planning Perspectives, 12*, 34–39, 42–43.

Bancroft, J. (1989). *Human sexuality and its problems* (2nd Ed.). Edinburgh, Scotland: Churchill-Livingston.

Bancroft, J., Sherwin, B. B., Alexander, G. M., Davidson, D. W., & Walker, A. (1991). Oral contraceptives, androgens, and the sexuality of young women: I. A comparison of sexual experience, sexual attitudes, and gender role in oral contraceptive users and non-users. *Archives of Sexual Behavior, 20*, 105–120.

Bandura, A. (1986). *Social foundations of thought and action.* Englewood Cliffs, NJ: Prentice-Hall.

Bandura, A. (1989). Human agency in social cognitive theory. *American Psychologist, 44*, 1175–1184.

Barak, A., Fisher, W. A., & Houston, S. (1992). Individual difference correlates of the experience of sexual harassment among female university students. *Journal of Applied Social Psychology, 22*, 17–37.

Barbach, L. G. (1976). *For yourself: The fulfillment of female sexuality.* New York: Anchor/Doubleday.

Barbach, L. G. (1980). Group treatment of anorgasmic women. In S. R. Leiblum & L. A. Pervin (Eds.), *Principles and practice of sex therapy* (pp. 107–146). New York: Guilford Press.

Barbach, L. G., & Levine, L. (1980). *Shared intimacies: Women's sexual experiences.* New York: Anchor Press.

Barbaree, H. E., Hudson, S. M., & Seto, M. C. (1993). Sexual assault in society: The role of the juvenile offender. In H. E. Barbaree, W. L. Marshall, & S. M. Hudson, (Eds.), *The juvenile sex offender* (pp. 1–24). New York: Guilford Press.

Barkow, J. H., Cosmides, L., & Tooby, J. (Eds.) (1992). *The adapted mind: Evolutionary psychology and the generation of culture.* New York: Oxford University Press.

Barlow, D. (1986). Causes of sexual dysfunction: The role of anxiety and cognitive interference. *Journal of Consulting and Clinical Psychology, 54*, 140–148.

Barnard, K. E., & Brazelton, T. B. (Eds.) (1990). *Touch: The foundation of experience.* Madison, CT: International Universities Press.

Barry, H., III, Bacon, M. K., & Child, I. L. (1957). A cross-cultural survey of some sex differences in socialization. *Journal of Abnormal and Social Psychology, 55*, 327–332.

Bart, P. B. (1981). A study of women who both were raped and avoided rape. *Journal of Social Issues, 37* (4), 123–137.

Bart, P. B., & O'Brien, P. H. (1985). *Stopping rape: Successful survival strategies.* New York: Pergamon.

Bartell, G. D. (1970). Group sex among the mid-Americans. *The Journal of Sex Research, 6*, 113–130.

Batra, A. K., & Lue, T. F. (1990). Physiology and pathology of penile erection. In J. Bancroft, C. M. Davis, & D. Weinstein (Eds.), *Annual Review of Sex Research,*

Vol. 1 (pp. 251–263). Lake Mills, IA: The Society for the Scientific Study of Sex.

Batteiger, B. E., Fraiz, J., Newhall, W. J., Katz, B. P., & Jones, R. B. (1989). Association of recurrent chlamydial infection with gonorrhea. *The Journal of Infectious Diseases, 159,* 661–669.

Baum, M. J. (1992). Neuroendocrinology of sexual behavior in the male. In J. B. Barker, S. M. Breedlove, and D. Crews (Eds.), *Behavioral endocrinology* (pp. 97–130). Cambridge, MA: The MIT Press.

Baumeister, R. F. (1988a). Masochism as escape from self. *The Journal of Sex Research, 25,* 28–59.

Baumeister, R. F. (1988b). Gender differences in masochistic scripts. *The Journal of Sex Research, 25,* 478–499.

Beach, F. A. (Ed.) (1976). *Human sexuality in four perspectives.* Baltimore, MD: Johns Hopkins University Press.

Beach, F. A. (1979). Animal modes and psychological inference. In H. A. Katchadourian (Ed.), *Human sexuality: A comparative and developmental perspective* (pp. 98–112). Berkeley, CA: University of California Press.

Beatrice, J. (1985). A psychological comparison of heterosexuals, transvestites, preoperative transsexuals, and postoperative transsexuals. *Journal of Nervous and Mental Disease, 173,* 358–365.

Beck, J. G. (1993). Vaginismus. In W. O'Donahue & J. H. Geer (Eds.), *Handbook of sexual dysfunctions: Assessment and treatment* (pp. 381–397). Boston, MA: Allyn and Bacon.

Becker, E. F. (1978). *Female sexuality following spinal cord injury.* Bloomington, IL: Accent Special Publications.

Beere, C. A. (1990). *Sex and gender issues: A handbook of tests and measures.* New York: Greenwood Press.

Beigel, H. G. (1953). The meaning of coital postures. *International Journal of Sexology, 4,* 136–143.

Beitchman, J. H., Zucker, K. J., Hood, J. E., DaCosta, G. A., Akman, D., & Cassavia, E. (1992). A review of the long-term effects of child sexual abuse. *Child Abuse and Neglect, 16,* 101–118.

Beit-Hallahmi, B. (1985). Dangers of the vagina. *British Journal of Medical Psychology, 58,* 351–356.

Belenky, M. F., & Gilligan, C. (1979, September). *Impact of abortion decisions on moral development and life circumstance.* Paper presented at the meeting of the American Psychological Association, New York.

Bell, A. R., & Weinberg, M. S. (1978). *Homosexualities.* New York: Simon & Schuster.

Bell, A. R., Weinberg, M. S., & Hammersmith, S. K. (1981). *Sexual preference: Its development in men and women.* Bloomington, IN: Indiana University Press.

Bell, R. R., Turner, S., & Rosen, L. A. (1975). A multivariate analysis of female extramarital coitus. *Journal of Marriage and the Family, 37,* 375–384.

Bellerose, S. B., & Binik, Y. M. (1993). Body image and sexuality in oophorectomized women. *Archives of Sexual Behavior, 22,* 435–459.

Belsky, J. (1991). Parental and nonparental child care and children's socioemotional development. In A. Booth (Ed.), *Contemporary families: Looking forward, looking back* (pp. 122–140). Minneapolis, MN: National Council on Family Relations.

Belzer, E. G. (1981). Orgasmic expulsions of women: A review and heuristic inquiry. *The Journal of Sex Research, 17,* 1–12.

Belzer, E. G., Whipple, B., & Moger, W. (1984). On female ejaculation. *The Journal of Sex Research, 20,* 403–406.

Bem, S. L. (1974). The measurement of psychological androgyny. *Journal of Consulting and Clinical Psychology, 42,* 155–162.

Bem, S. L. (1975). Sex-role adaptability: One consequence of psychological androgyny. *Journal of Personality and Social Psychology, 31,* 634–643.

Bem, S. L., & Lenney, E. (1976). Sex typing and avoidance of cross-sex behavior. *Journal of Personality and Social Psychology, 3,* 48–54.

Bem, S. L., Martyna, W., & Watson, C. (1976). Sex typing and androgyny: Further exploration of the expressive domain. *Journal of Personality and Social Psychology, 34,* 1016–1023.

Benedek, T. (1959). Sexual functions in women and their disturbance. In S. Arieti (Ed.), *American handbook of psychiatry,* Vol. 1 (pp. 727–748). New York: Basic Books.

Bennett, S. M., & Dickinson, W. B. (1980). Student-parent rapport and parent involvement in sex, birth control, and venereal disease education. *The Journal of Sex Research, 16,* 114–130.

Benson, D. J., & Thomson, G. (1982). Sexual harassment on a university campus: The confluence of authority relations, sexual interest, and gender stratification. *Social Problems, 29,* 236–251.

Bentler, P. M., & Peeler, W. H. (1979). Models of female orgasm. *Archives of Sexual Behavior, 8,* 405–424.

Bentler, P. M., & Prince, C. (1969). Personality characteristics of male transvestites: III. *Journal of Abnormal Psychology, 74,* 140–143.

Bentler, P. M., Sherman, R. W., & Prince, V. (1970). Personality characteristics of male transvestites. *Journal of Clinical Psychology, 26,* 287–291.

Benton, J. M., Mintzes, J. L., Kendrick, A. F., & Soloman, R. D. (1993). Alternative conceptions in sexually transmitted diseases: A cross-age study. *Journal of Sex Education and Therapy, 19,* 165–182.

Berger, G., Hank, L., Rauzi, T., & Simkins, L. (1987).

Detection of sexual orientation by heterosexuals and homosexuals. *Journal of Homosexuality, 13,* 83–100.

Berger, R. (1980). Psychological adaptation of the older homosexual male. *Journal of Homosexuality, 5,* 161–175.

Bermant, G. (1976). Sexual behavior: Hard times with the Coolidge Effect. In M. H. Siegel & H. P. Zeigler (Eds.), *Psychological research: The inside story* (pp. 76–103). New York: Harper & Row.

Berscheid, E. (1983). Emotion. In H. H. Kelley et al. (Eds.), *Close relationships* (pp. 110–168). New York: W. H. Freeman and Co.

Berscheid, E., & Walster, E. (1974). Physical attractiveness. In L. Berkowitz (Ed.), *Advances in experimental social psychology* (pp. 157–215). New York: Academic Press.

Berscheid, E., Walster, E., & Bohrnstedt, G. (1972). Body image. *Psychology Today, 6,* 57–66.

Berscheid, E., Walster, E., & Bohrnstedt, G. (1973). The body image report. *Psychology Today, 7,* 119–131.

Bersoff, D. N., & Ogden, D. W. (1991). APA amicus curiae briefs: Furthering lesbian and gay male civil rights. *American Psychologist, 46,* 950–956.

Betzig, L. (1989). Causes of conjugal dissolution: A cross-cultural study. *Current Anthropology, 30,* 654–676.

Betzig, L. (1992). Roman polygyny. *Ethology and Sociobiology, 13,* 309–349.

Betzig, L., & Lombardo, L. H. (1992). Who's pro-choice and why. *Ethology and Sociobiology, 13,* 49–71.

Bieber, I., Dain, H. J., & Dince, P. R. (1962). *Homosexuality: A psychoanalytic study.* New York: Basic Books.

Biggar, R. J. (1986). The AIDS problem in Africa. *The Lancet,* January 11, 79–83.

Billy, J. O. G., Tanfer, K., Grady, W. R., & Klepinger, D. H. (1993). The sexual behavior of men in the United States. *Family Planning Perspectives, 25,* 52–60.

Bingham, S. G., & Scherer, L. L. (1993). Factors associated with responses to sexual harassment and satisfaction with outcome. *Sex Roles, 29,* 239–269.

Bird, C. (1979). *The two-paycheck marriage.* New York: Rawson, Wade.

Bixler, R. H. (1982). Sibling incest in the royal families of Egypt, Peru, and Hawaii. *The Journal of Sex Research, 18,* 264–281.

Blair, C. D., & Lanyon, R. (1981). Exhibitionism: Etiology and treatment. *Psychological Bulletin, 89,* 439–463.

Blanchard, R. (1989). The classification and labeling of nonhomosexual gender dsyphorias. *Archives of Sexual Behavior, 18,* 315–334.

Blanchard, R. (1992). Nonmonotonic relation of autogynephilia and heterosexual attraction. *Journal of Abnormal Psychology, 101,* 271–276.

Blanchard, R. (1993). Varieties of autogynephilia and their relationship to gender dysphoria. *Archives of Sexual Behavior, 22,* 241–251.

Blasband, M. A., & Peplau, L. A. (1985). Sexual exclusivity versus openness in gay male couples. *Archives of Sexual Behavior, 14,* 395–412.

Blieszner, R., & Adams, R. G. (1992). *Adult friendship.* Newbury Park, CA: Sage.

Blumstein, P. W., & Schwartz, P. (1976). Bisexuality in men. *Urban Life, 5,* 339–359.

Blumstein, P. W., & Schwartz, P. (1983). *American couples.* New York: William Morrow.

Blumstein, P. W., & Schwartz, P. (1989). Intimate relationships and the creation of sexuality. In B. J. Risman & P. Schwartz, (Eds.), *Gender in intimate relationships* (pp. 120–129). Belmont, CA: Wadsworth Publishing.

Bogaert, A. F., Turkovich, D. A., & Hafer, C. L. (1993). A content analysis of *Playboy* centrefolds from 1953–1990: Changes in explicitness, objectification, and model's age. *The Journal of Sex Research, 30,* 135–139.

Bongaarts, J. (1984). Building a family: Unplanned events. *Studies in Family Planning, 15* (1), 14–19.

Bohlen, J. G., Held, J. P., & Sanderson, M. O. (1980). The male orgasm: Pelvic contractions measured by anal probe. *Archives of Sexual Behavior, 9,* 503–521.

Booth, W. (1989). WHO seeks global data on sexual practices. *Science, 244,* 418–419.

Borna, S., Chapman, J., & Menezes, D. (1993). Deceptive nature of dial-a-porn commercials and public policy alternatives. *Journal of Business Ethics, 12,* 503–509.

Boswell, J. (1980). *Christianity, social tolerance, and homosexuality.* Chicago, IL: University of Chicago Press.

Botwinick, J. (1978). Sexuality and sexual relations. In J. Botwinick (Ed.), *Aging and behavior* (pp. 42–58). New York: Springer.

Bouhoutsos, J. C. (1985). Therapist-client sexual involvement: A challenge for mental health professionals and educators. *American Journal of Orthopsychiatry, 55,* 177–182.

Bouhoutsos, J. C., Holroyd, J., Lerman, H., Forer, B., & Greenberg, M. (1983). Sexual intimacy between psychotherapists and patients. *Professional Psychology, 14,* 185–196.

Bourgue, L. B. (1989). *Defining rape.* Durham, NC: Duke University Press.

Bowen, D. J., Urban, N., Carrell, D., & Kinne, S. (1993). Comparison of strategies to prevent breast cancer mortality. *Journal of Social Issues, 49* (2), 35–66.

Bowers, J. K., & Weaver, H. B. (1979). Development of a dual-form abortion scale. *The Journal of Sex Research, 15,* 158–165.

Bowlby, J. (1973). *Attachment and Loss:* Vol. 2. *Separation, anxiety and anger*. New York: Basic Books.

Box, S. (1983). *Power, crime, and mystification*. London: Tavistock Publications Ltd.

Boxer, A. M., & Cohler, B. J. (1989). The life course of gay and lesbian youth: An immodest proposal for the study of lives. *Journal of Homosexuality, 17,* 315–355.

Boyer, D. K., & James, J. (1983). Prostitutes vs. victims. In D. MacNamara & A. Karmen (Eds.), *Deviants: Victims or victimizers?* (pp. 109–146). Beverly Hills, CA: Sage.

Bradford, J. M. W. (1993). The pharmacological treatment of the adolescent sex offender. In H. E. Barbaree, W. L. Marshall, & S. M. Hudson (Eds.), *The juvenile sex offender* (pp. 278–288). New York: Guilford Press.

Bradford, J. M. W., & Pawlak, A. (1993). Double-blind placebo crossover study of cyproterone acetate in the treatment of the paraphilias. *Archives of Sexual Behavior, 22,* 383–402.

Brame, G. G., Brame, W. D., & Jacobs, J. (1993). *Different loving: An exploration of the world of sexual dominance and submission*. New York: Villard Books.

Breakwell, G. M., & Fife-Schaw, C. (1992). Sexual activities and preferences in a United Kingdom sample of 16-to-20 year olds. *Archives of Sexual Behavior, 21,* 271–293.

Brecher, E. M., & the Editors of Consumer Reports Books (1984). *Love, sex, and aging*. Boston, MA: Little, Brown.

Breslow, N., Evans, L., & Langley, J. (1985). On the prevalence and roles of females in the sadomasochistic subculture: Report on an empirical study. *Archives of Sexual Behavior, 14,* 303–317.

Bretschneider, J. G., & McCoy, N. L. (1988). Sexual interest and behavior in 80- to 102-year-olds. *Archives of Sexual Behavior, 17,* 109–129.

Brewer, M. B., & Berk, R. A. (1982). Beyond nine to five: Introduction. *Journal of Social Issues, 38,* 1–4.

Bringle, R. G., & Buunk, B. P. (1991). Extradyadic relationships and sexual jealousy. In K. McKinney & S. Sprecher (Eds.), *Sexuality in close relationships* (pp. 135–153). Hillsdale, NJ: Lawrence Erlbaum Associates.

Brooks, J., Ruble, D. N., & Clarke, A. E. (1977). College women's attitudes and expectations concerning menstrual-related changes. *Psychosomatic Medicine, 39,* 288–298.

Brooks-Gunn, J., Boyer, C. B., & Hein, K. (1988). Preventing HIV infection and AIDS in children and adolescents. *American Psychologist, 43,* 958–964.

Broverman, I. K., Broverman, D. M., Clarkson, F. E., Rosenkrantz, P., & Vogel, S. R. (1970). Sex-role stereotypes and clinical judgments of mental health. *Journal of Consulting Psychology, 34,* 1–7.

Brown, G. R., & Collier, Z. (1989). Transvestites' women revisited: A nonpatient sample. *Archives of Sexual Behavior, 18,* 73–83.

Brown, J. D., & Newcomer, S. F. (1991). Television viewing and adolescents' sexual behavior. *Journal of Homosexuality, 21,* 77–91.

Brown, L. K., DiClemente, R. J., & Beausoleil, N. I. (1992). Comparison of Human Immunodeficiency Virus related knowledge, attitudes, and behaviors among sexually active and abstinent young adolescents. *Journal of Adolescent Health, 13,* 140–149.

Brown, S. A., & Munson, E. (1987). Extroversion, anxiety and the perceived effects of alcohol. *Journal of Studies on Alcohol, 48,* 272–276.

Buhrich, N. A., (1976). A heterosexual transvestite club: Psychiatric aspects. *Australian and New Zealand Journal of Psychiatry, 10,* 331–335.

Buhrich, N. A. (1977). Transvestism in history. *Journal of Nervous and Mental Disorders, 165,* 65–67.

Buhrich, N. A., & Beaumont, T. (1981). Comparison of transvestism in Australia and America. *Archives of Sexual Behavior, 10,* 269–279.

Buhrich, N. A., & McConaghy, N. (1977). The discrete syndromes of transvestism and transsexualism. *Archives of Sexual Behavior, 6,* 483–496.

Buhrich, N. A., & McConaghy, N. (1979). Three clinically discrete categories of fetishistic transvestism. *Archives of Sexual Behavior, 8,* 151–157.

Buhrich, N. A., & McConaghy, N. (1985). Preadult feminine behaviors of male transvestites. *Archives of Sexual Behavior, 14,* 413–420.

Buhrich, N. A., Theile, H., Yaw, A., & Crawford, A. (1979). Plasma testosterone, serum FSH, and serum LH levels in transvestites. *Archives of Sexual Behavior, 8,* 49–53.

Bullard-Poe, L., Powell, C., & Mulligan, T. (1994). The importance of intimacy to men living in a nursing home. *Archives of Sexual Behavior, 23,* 231–236.

Bullough, B. (1994). Abortion. In V. Bullough & B. Bullough (Eds.), *Human sexuality: An encyclopedia* (pp. 3–8). New York: Garland Publishing.

Bullough, V. (1980). *Sexual variance in society and history*. Chicago, IL: University of Chicago Press.

Bullough, V. (1981). Age at menarche: A misunderstanding. *Science, 213,* 365–366.

Bullough, V. (1983, November). *Presidential Address: The problems of doing research in a delicate field*. Presented at the annual meeting of The Society for the Scientific Study of Sex, Chicago, IL.

Bullough, V. L. (1990). History and the understanding of human sexuality. In J. Bancroft, C. M. Davis, & D. Weinstein (Eds.), *Annual Review of Sex Research*, Vol.

1 (pp. 75–92). Lake Mills, IA: The Society for the Scientific Study of Sex.

Bullough, V. (1990). Nightingale, nursing and harassment. *Image: Journal of Nursing Scholarship, 22,* 4–7.

Bullough, V. L., & Bullough, B. (1977). *Sin, sickness, and sanity.* New York: New American Library.

Bullough, V. L., & Bullough, B. (1987). *Women and prostitution: A social history.* Buffalo, NY: Prometheus Books.

Bullough, V. L., & Bullough, B. (1993). *Cross dressing, sex, and gender.* Philadelphia, PA: University of Pennsylvania.

Bullough, V. L., Bullough, B., & Smith, R. (1983). A comparative study of male transvestites, male-to-female transsexuals and male homosexuals. *The Journal of Sex Research, 19,* 238–257.

Bullough, V. L., Shelton, B., & Slavin, S. (1988). *The subordinated sex: A history of attitudes toward women.* Athens, GA: University of Georgia Press.

Bullough, V. L., & Weinberg, J. S. (1988). Women married to transvestites: Problems and adjustments. *Journal of Psychology and Human Sexuality, 1,* 83–104.

Bumpass, L. L., Sweet, J. A., & Cherlin, A. (1991). The role of cohabitation in declining rates of marriage. *Journal of Marriage and the Family, 53,* 913–927.

Burg, B. R. (1988). Nocturnal emission and masturbatory frequency relationships: A 19th century account. *The Journal of Sex Research, 24,* 216–220.

Burgess, A. W., Hartman, C. R., MacCausland, M. P., & Powers, P. (1984). Response patterns in children and adolescents exploited through sex rings and pornography. *American Journal of Psychiatry, 141,* 656–662.

Burgess, A. W., & Holmstrom, L. L. (1974). *Rape: Victims of crisis.* Bowie, MD: Robert J. Brady Co.

Burgess, A. W., & Holmstrom, L. L. (1985). Rape trauma syndrome and post traumatic stress disorder. In A. W. Burgess (Ed.), *Rape and sexual assault: A research handbook* (pp. 46–60). New York: Garland Publishing.

Burt, M. R. (1980). Cultural myths and supports for rape. *Journal of Personality and Social Psychology, 38,* 217–230.

Buss, D. M. (1989). Sex differences in human mate preferences: Evolutionary hypotheses tested in 37 cultures. *Behavioral and Brain Sciences, 12,* 1–49.

Buss, D. M. (1991). Evolutionary personality psychology. *Annual Review of Psychology, 42,* 459–491.

Buss, D. M. (1992). Mate preference mechanisms: Consequences for partner choice and intrasexual competition. In J. H. Barkow, L. Cosmides, & J. Tooby (Eds.), *The adapted mind: Evolutionary psychology and the generation of culture* (pp. 249–266). New York: Oxford University Press.

Buss, D. M. (1994). *The evolution of desire: Strategies of human mating.* New York: Basic Books.

Buss, D. M., Larsen, R. J., Western, D., & Semmelroth, J. (1992). Sex differences in jealousy: Evolution, physiology, and psychology. *Psychological Science, 3,* 251–255.

Buss, D. M., & Schmitt, D. P. (1993). Sexual strategies theory: A contextual evolutionary analysis of human mating. *Psychological Review, 100,* 204–232.

Butler, C. A. (1976). New data about female sexual response. *Journal of Sex and Marital Therapy, 2,* 40–46.

Butler, R. N., & Lewis, M. I. (1973). *Aging and mental health.* St. Louis, MO: C. V. Mosby.

Buunk, B. P. (1991). Jealousy in close relationships: An exchange-theoretical perspective. In P. Palovy (Ed.), *The psychology of jealousy and envy* (pp. 148–177). New York: Guilford Press.

Byers, E. S., & Heinlein, L. (1989). Predicting initiation and refusals of sexual activities in married and cohabiting couples. *The Journal of Sex Research, 26,* 210–231.

Byers, E. S., & Lewis, K. (1988). Dating couples' disagreements over the desired level of sexual intimacy. *The Journal of Sex Research, 24,* 15–29.

Byrne, D. (1971). *The attraction paradigm.* New York: Academic Press.

Byrne, D. (1977). Social psychology and the study of sexual behavior. *Personality and Social Psychology Bulletin, 3,* 3–30.

Byrne, D., & Fisher, W. A. (Eds.) (1983). *Adolescents, sex, and contraception.* Hillsdale, NJ: Lawrence Erlbaum Associates.

Byrne, D., Fisher, W. A., Lamberth, J., & Mitchell, H. E. (1974). Evaluations of erotica: Facts or feelings? *Journal of Personality and Social Psychology, 79,* 111–116.

Byrne, D., Jazwinski, C., DeNinno, J. A., & Fisher, W. A. (1977). Negative sexual attitudes and contraception. In D. Byrne & L. Byrne (Eds.), *Exploring human sexuality* (pp. 331–342). New York: Crowell.

Byrne, D., & Lamberth, J. (1971). The effect of erotic stimuli on sex arousal, evaluative responses, and subsequent behavior. *Technical reports of the Commission on Obscenity and Pornography,* Vol. 8 (pp. 41–67). Washington, D. C.: U.S. Government Printing Office.

Byrne, D., & Murnen, S. K. (1988). Maintaining loving relationships. In R. J. Sternberg & M. L. Barnes (Eds.), *The psychology of love* (pp. 293–310). New Haven, CT: Yale University Press.

Byrne, D., & Schulte, L. (1990). Personality dispositions as mediators of sexual responses. In J. Bancroft, C. M. Davis, & D. Weinstein (Eds.), *Annual Review of Sex Research,* Vol. 1 (pp. 93–117). Lake Mills, IA: The Society for the Scientific Study of Sex.

Cadman, D., Gafini, A., & McNamee, J. (1984). Newborn circumcision: An economic perspective. *Canadian Medical Association Journal, 131*, 1353–1355.

Cado, S., & Leitenberg, H. (1990). Guilt reactions to sexual fantasies during intercourse. *Archives of Sexual Behavior, 19*, 49–63.

Caird, W. K., & Wincze, J. P. (1977). *Sex therapy: A behavioral approach*. New York: Harper & Row.

Calderone, M. S. (1978). Is sex education preventative? In C. P. Qualls, J. P. Wincze, & D. H. Barlow (Eds.), *The prevention of sexual disorders: Issues and approaches* (pp. 139–155). New York: Plenum.

Campbell, M. K., Waller, L., Andolsek, K. M., Huff, P., & Bucci, K. (1990). Infant feeding and nutrition. In K. M. Andolsek (Ed.), *Obstetric care: Standards of prenatal, peripartum and postpartum management* (pp. 206–221). Philadelphia, PA: Lea & Febiger.

Cancian, F. M. (1986). The feminization of love. *Signs: Journal of Women in Culture and Society, 11*, 692–709.

Cannon, D. (1987, November). *Twenty years of sex guilt: Construct validation of the concept*. Paper presented at the Annual Meeting of The Society for the Scientific Study of Sex, Atlanta, GA.

Carabasi, J. M., Greene, W. H., & Bernt, F. M. (1992). Preliminary findings from the survey about AIDS for seventh and eighth graders. *AIDS Education and Prevention, 4*, 240–250.

Carballo, M., Cleland, J., Carael, M., & Albrecht, G. (1989). A cross national study of patterns of sexual behavior. *The Journal of Sex Research, 26*, 287–299.

Carlier, J. G., & Steeno, O. P. (1985). Olgarche: The age of first ejaculation. *Andrologica, 17*, 104–106.

Carlson, E., Ginerman, A., Keiding, N., & Skakkebaek, N. E. (1992). Evidence for decreasing quality of sperm during past 30 years. *British Medical Journal, 305, 609*, 613.

Carlson, J., & Hatfield, E. (1992). *The psychology of emotion*. Fort Worth, TX: Holt, Rinehart, & Winston.

Carmichael, M. S., Warburton, V. L., Dixen, J., & Davidson, J. M. (1994). Relationships among cardiovascular, muscular and oxytocin responses during human sexual activity. *Archives of Sexual Behavior, 23*, 59–79.

Carnes, P. (1983). *The sexual addiction*. Minneapolis, MN: CompCare.

Carnes, P. (1990). Sexual addiction: Progress, criticism, challenges. *American Journal of Preventive Psychiatry and Neurology, 2*, 1–8.

Carnes, P. (1991). *Don't call it love: Recovering from sexual addiction*. New York: Bantam.

Caron, S. L., Davis, C. M., Halteman, W. A., & Stickle, M. (1993). Predictors of condom-related behavior among first-year college students. *The Journal of Sex Research, 30*, 252—259.

Caron, S. L., Davis, C. M., Wynn, R. L., & Roberts, W. (1992). "America responds to AIDS," but did college students? Differences between March, 1987 and September, 1988. *AIDS Education and Prevention, 4*, 18–28.

Carrier, J. M. (1980). Homosexual behavior in cross-cultural perspective. In J. Marmor (Ed.), *Homosexual behavior* (pp. 100–122). New York: Basic Books.

Carroll, J. L., Volk, K. D., & Hyde, J. S. (1985). Differences between males and females in motives for engaging in sexual intercourse. *Archives of Sexual Behavior, 14*, 131–139.

Carter, C. S. (1992). Hormonal influences on human sexual behavior. In J. B. Becker, S. M. Breedlove, & D. Crews (Eds.), *Behavioral endocrinology* (pp. 131–142). Cambridge, MA: The MIT Press.

Caruso, S. M., & Allgeier, E. R. (1987, May). *The Premenstrual Assessment Form: Scoring methods, reliability, and behavioral correlates*. Paper presented at the meeting of the Midwestern Psychological Association, Chicago, IL.

Cash, T. F., & Brown, T. A. (1989). Gender and body images: Stereotypes and realities. *Sex Roles, 21*, 361–373.

Cash, T. F., & Hicks, K. L. (1990). Being fat versus thinking fat: Relationship with body image, eating behaviors and well-being. *Cognitive Therapy and Research, 14*, 327–341.

Casler, L. (1968). Perceptual deprivation in institutional settings. In G. Newton & S. Levine (Eds.), *Early experience and behavior* (pp. 573–626). New York: Springer.

Cassell, C. (1984). *Swept away*. New York: Simon & Schuster.

Catania, A. C. (1992). Reinforcement. In L. R. Squire (Ed.), *Encyclopedia of learning and memory* (pp. 558–562). New York: MacMillan.

Cates, W. C., Jr., & Stone, K. M. (1992a). Family planning, sexually transmitted diseases, and contraceptive choice: A literature update—Part I. *Family Planning Perspectives, 24*, 75–84.

Cates, W. C., Jr., & Stone, K. M. (1992b). Family planning, sexually transmitted diseases, and contraceptive choice: A literature update—Part II. *Family Planning Perspectives, 24*, 122–128.

Catotti, D. N., Clarke, P., & Catoe, K. E. (1993). Herpes revisited. *Sexually Transmitted Diseases, 20*, 77–80.

Centers for Disease Control (1980, September 19). Follow-up on toxic-shock syndrome. *Morbidity and Mortality Weekly Report*. Atlanta, GA: Centers for Disease Control.

Centers for Disease Control (1985a). Recommendations for protection against viral hepatitis. *Morbidity and Mortality Weekly Report, 34*, 313–335.

Centers for Disease Control (1985b). STD treatment guidelines. *Morbidity and Mortality Weekly Report Supplement, 34,* 45.

Centers for Disease Control (1985c). Summary—Cases of specified, notifiable diseases, United States. *Morbidity and Mortality Weekly Report, 34,* 756.

Centers for Disease Control (1993, August 6). Recommendations for the prevention and management of chlamydia trachomatis infections. *Morbidity and Mortality Weekly Report, 42,* RR–12.

Centers for Disease Control (1994, February). *HIV/AIDS surveillance report.* Atlanta, GA: Centers for Disease Control.

Check, J. V. P., & Malamuth, N. M. (1983). Sex-role stereotyping and reactions to depictions of stranger versus acquaintance rape. *Journal of Personality and Social Psychology, 45,* 344–356.

Cherry, F. (1983). Gender roles and sexual violence. In E. R. Allgeier & N. B. McCormick (Eds.), *Changing boundaries: Gender roles and sexual behavior* (pp. 245–260). Palo Alto, CA: Mayfield.

Chick, D., & Gold, S. R. (1987–1988). A review of influences on sexual fantasy: Attitudes, experience, guilt, and gender. *Imagination, Cognition, and Personality, 7,* 61–76.

Chilman, C. S. (1980). *Adolescent sexuality in a changing American society: Social and psychological perspectives.* Washington, D.C.: U.S. Government Printing Office.

Chodorow, N. (1978). *The reproduction of mothering.* Berkeley, CA: University of California Press.

Christopher, F. S., Johnson, D. C., & Roosa, M. W. (1993). Family, individual, and social correlates of early Hispanic adolescent sexual expression. *The Journal of Sex Research, 30,* 54–61.

Christopher, F. S., & Roosa, M. W. (1990). An evaluation of an adolescent pregnancy prevention program: Is "Just say no" enough? *Family Relations, 39,* 68–72.

Clark, R. D. & Hatfield, E. (1989). Gender differences in receptivity to sexual offers. *Journal of Psychology and Human Sexuality, 2,* 39–55.

Clark, J. T., Smith, E. R., & Davidson, J. M. (1984). Enhancement of sexual motivation in male rats by yohimbine. *Science, 225,* 847–849.

Clark, M. (1986, July 14). Women and AIDS. *Newsweek,* 60–61.

Clarke, A. E., & Ruble, D. N. (1978). Young adolescents' beliefs concerning menstruation. *Child Development, 49,* 231–234.

Clarke-Stewart, K. A. (1978). And Daddy makes three. *Child Development, 49,* 466–478.

Clarke-Stewart, K. A., & Bailey, B. L. (1989). Adjusting to divorce: Why do men have it easier? *Journal of Divorce, 13,* 75–94.

Clement, U. (1990). Surveys of heterosexual behavior. In J. Bancroft, C. M. Davis, & D. Weinstein (Eds.), *Annual Review of Sex Research,* Vol. 1. (pp. 45–74). Lake Mills, IA: The Society for the Scientific Study of Sex.

Clement, U., & Friedemann, P. (1980). Changes in personality scores among couples subsequent to sex therapy. *Archives of Sexual Behavior, 9,* 235–244.

Clement, U., Schmidt, G., & Kruse, M. (1984). Changes in sex differences in sexual behavior: A replication of a study on West German students (1966–1981). *Archives of Sexual Behavior, 13,* 99–120.

Clemmer, D. (1958). *Some aspects of sexual behavior in the prison community.* Proceedings of the Eighty-Eighth Annual Congress of Corrections of the American Correctional Institution (p. 383). Detroit, MI.

Clifford, R. E. (1978). Subjective sexual experience in college women. *Archives of Sexual Behavior, 7,* 183–197.

Coates, T. J., Stall, R. D., & Hoff, C. C. (1990). Changes in sexual behavior among gay and bisexual men since the beginning of the AIDS epidemic. In I. L. Temoshok & A. Baum (Eds.), *Psychological perspectives on AIDS: Etiology, prevention, and treatment* (pp. 103–138). Hillsdale, NJ: Lawrence Erlbaum Associates.

Cohen, J. (1979). Male roles in mid-life. *Family Coordinator, 28,* 465–471.

Cohen, J. B., Hauer, L. B., Poole, L. E., & Wofsy, C. B. (1987). *Sexual and other practices and risk of HIV infection in a cohort of 450 sexually active women in San Francisco.* Paper presented at the Third International Conference on AIDS.

Cohen, Y. (1978). The disappearance of the incest taboo. *Human Nature, 1,* 72–78.

Cole, T. M. (1979). Sex and patients with spinal cord injuries. *Western Journal of Medicine, 131,* 131–132.

Cole, T. M., & Cole, S. S. (1990). Rehabilitation of problems of sexuality in physical disability. In F. Kohke & J. Lehmann (Eds.), *Krusen's handbook of physical medicine and rehabilitation* (4th Ed.). Philadephia, PA: Saunders.

Coleman, E. (1982). Changing approaches to the treatment of homosexuality: A review. In W. Paul, J. D. Weinrich, J. C. Gonsiorek, & M. E. Hotvedt (Eds.), *Homosexuality: Social, Psychological, and Biological Issues* (pp. 81–88). Beverly Hills, CA: Sage.

Coleman, E. (1986). Sexual compulsion vs. sexual addiction: The debate continues. *SIECUS Reports, 14,* 7–10.

Coleman, E. (1987). Bisexuality: Challenging our understanding of sexual orientation. *Sexuality and Medicine, 1,* 225–242.

Coleman, E. (1990). The married lesbian. *Marriage and Family Review, 13,* 119–135.

Coleman, E. (1991). Compulsive sexual behavior: New concepts and treatments. *Journal of Psychology and Human Sexuality, 4* (2), 37–52.

Coleman, E., Bockting, W. O., & Gooren, L. (1993). Homosexual and bisexual identity in sex-reassigned female-to-male transsexuals. *Archives of Sexual Behavior, 22,* 37–50.

Coleman, E., Cesnik, J., Moore, A., & Dwyer, S. M. (1992). An exploratory study of the role of psychotropic medications in the treatment of sexual offenders. *Journal of Offender Rehabilitation, 18,* 75–88.

Coles, C. D., & Shamp, M. J. (1984). Some sexual, personality, and demographic characteristics of women readers of erotic romances. *Archives of Sexual Behavior, 13,* 187–209.

Colton, T., Greenberg, E. R., Noller, K., Resseguie, L., Heeren, T., & Zhang, Y. (1993). Breast cancer in mothers prescribed diethylstilbestrol in pregnancy. *Journal of the American Medical Association, 269,* 2096–2100.

Committee on Labor and Human Resources (1981). Sex discrimination in the workplace. *Hearings before the Committee on Labor and Human Resources, United States Senate, Ninety-seventh Congress.* First session on Examination of Issues Affecting Women in Our Nation's Labor Force, January 28 & April 21, 1981. Washington, D.C.: U.S. Government Printing Office.

Connors, M. E., & Morse, W. (1993). Sexual abuse and eating disorders: A review. *International Journal of Eating Disorders, 13* (1), 1–11.

Constantine, L. E., & Martinson, F. M. (1981). Child sexuality: Here there be dragons. In L. E. Constantine & F. M. Martinson (Eds.), *Children and sex: New findings, new perspectives* (pp. 3–8). Boston, MA: Little, Brown.

Constantinople, A. (1973). Masculinity-femininity: An exception to a famous dictum? *Psychological Bulletin, 80,* 389–407.

Cook, E. A., Jelen, T. J., & Wilcox, C. (1993). Measuring public attitudes on abortion: Methodological and substantive considerations. *Family Planning Perspectives, 25,* 118–121, 145.

Coontz, S. (1992). *The way we never were: American families and the nostalgia trap.* New York: Basic Books.

Cooper, A. J. (1986). Progestogens in the treatment of male sex offenders: A review. *Canadian Journal of Psychiatry, 31,* 73–79.

Coovert, D. L., Kinder, B. N., & Thompson, J. K. (1989). The psychosexual aspects of anorexia nervosa and bulimia: A review of the literature. *Clinical Psychology Review, 9,* 169–180.

Cornelius, D. A., Chipouras, S., Makas, E., & Daniels, S. M. (1982). *Who cares: A handbook on sex education and counseling services for disabled people.* Baltimore, MD: University Park.

Costin, F. (1985). Beliefs about rape and women's social roles. *Archives of Sexual Behavior, 14,* 319–325.

Courtney, A. E., & Whipple, T. W. (1983). *Sex stereotyping in advertising.* Lexington, MA: D. C. Heath.

Cowan, G., & Dunn, K. F. (1994). What themes in pornography lead to perceptions of the degradation of women? *The Journal of Sex Research, 31,* 11–22.

Cox, D. J. (1980). Exhibitionism: An overview. In D. J. Cox & R. J. Daitzman (Eds.), *Exhibitionism: Description, assessment and treatment* (pp. 3–10). New York: Garland Publishing.

Cox, D. J. (1983). Menstrual symptoms in college students: A controlled study. *Journal of Behavioral Medicine, 6,* 335–338.

Cox, D. J. (1988). Incidence and nature of male genital exposure behavior as reported by college women. *The Journal of Sex Research, 24,* 227–234.

Craig, M. E. (1990). Coercive sexuality in dating relationships. *Clinical Psychology Review, 10,* 395–423.

Cramer, D. W., Schiff, I., Schoenbaum, S. C., Gibson, M., Belisle, S., Albrecht, B., Stillman, R. J., Berger, M. J., Wilson, E., & Stadel, B. V. (1985). Tubal infertility and the intrauterine device. *The New England Journal of Medicine, 312,* 941–947.

Cranston-Cuebas, M. A., & Barlow, D. H. (1990). Cognitive and affective contributions to sexual functioning. In J. Bancroft, C. M. Davis, & D. Weinstein (Eds.), *Annual Review of Sex Research,* Vol. I. Lake Mills, IA: The Society for the Scientific Study of Sex.

Crawford, J. J., & McCaul, K. D. (1987, May). *Explaining gender differences in attributions of blame to rape victims.* Paper presented at the meeting of the Midwestern Psychological Association, Chicago, IL.

Crenshaw, T. L., Goldberg, J. P., & Stein, W. C. (1987). Pharmacologic modification of psychosexual dysfunction. *Journal of Sex and Marital Therapy, 13,* 239–250.

Crepault, C., Abraham, G., Porto, R., & Couture, M. (1977). Erotic imagery in women. In R. Gemme & C. C. Wheeler (Eds.), *Progress in sexology* (pp. 267–283). New York: Plenum.

Crowe, L. C., & George, W. H. (1989). Alcohol and human sexuality: Review and integration. *Psychological Bulletin, 102,* 374–386.

Crum, C., & Ellner, P. D. (1985). Chlamydial infestations: Making the diagnosis. *Contemporary Obstetrics and Gynecology, 25,* 153–159, 163, 165, 168.

Curtis, L. (1974). Victim precipitation and violent crime. *Social Problems, 21,* 594–605.

Cutler, W. B., Garcia, C. R., & McCoy, N. (1987). Perimenopausal sexuality. *Archives of Sexual Behavior, 16,* 225–234.

Cutright, P. (1971). Illegitimacy: Myths, causes and cures. *Family Planning Perspectives, 3,* 26–48.

Dabbs, J. M., Jr. (1990). Salivary testosterone measurements: Reliability across hours, days, and weeks. *Physiology and Behavior, 48,* 83–86.

Dale, J. (1986). The rape crisis center view. In A. W. Burgess & C. R. Hartman (Eds.), *Sexual exploitation of patients by health professionals* (pp. 84–96). New York: Praeger.

Daling, J. R., Weiss, N. B., Voight, L. F., McKnight, B., & Moore, D. E. (1992). The intrauterine device and primary tubal infertility. *New England Journal of Medicine, 326,* 203–204.

Daly, M., & Wilson, M. (1978). *Sex, evolution, and behavior.* Belmont, CA: Wadsworth.

Daly, M., & Wilson, M. (1989). Homicide and cultural evolution. *Ethology and Sociobiology, 10,* 99–110.

Darling, C. A., & Davidson, J. K., Sr. (1986). Enhancing relationships: Understanding the feminine mystique of pretending orgasm. *Journal of Sex and Marital Therapy, 12,* 182–196.

Darling, C. A., Davidson, J. K., Sr., & Cox, R. P. (1991). Female sexual response and the timing of partner orgasm. *Journal of Sex and Marital Therapy, 17,* 3–20.

Darling, C. A., Davidson, J. K., Sr., & Jennings, D. A. (1991). The female sexual response revisited: Understanding the multiorgasmic response in women. *Archives of Sexual Behavior, 20,* 527–540.

Darling, C. A., Kallen, D. J., & VanDusen, J. E. (1984). Sex in transition, 1900–1980. *Journal of Youth and Adolescence, 13,* 385–389.

Darling, C. A., & McKoy-Smith, Y. M. (1993). Understanding hysterectomies: Sexual satisfaction and quality of life. *The Journal of Sex Research, 30,* 324–335.

Darney, P. D., Atkinson, E., Tanner, S., MacPherson, S., Hellerstein, S., & Alvarado, A. (1990). Acceptance and perceptions of NORPLANT among users in San Francisco, USA. *Studies in Family Planning, 21,* 152–160.

Darrow, W. W. (1979, November). *Social and psychological aspects of the sexually transmitted diseases: A different view.* Paper presented at the New York City Health Department Seminar on Sexually Transmitted Diseases.

Darrow, W. W. (1981). Social and psychologic aspects of the sexually transmitted diseases: A different view. *Cutis, 27,* 307–316.

Darrow, W. W. (1989). Condom use and use-effectiveness in a high-risk population. *Sexually Transmitted Diseases, 16,* 157–160.

Davenport, W. H. (1965). Sexual patterns and their regulation in a society of the Southwest Pacific. In F. A. Beach (Ed.), *Sex and behavior* (pp. 164–207). New York: Wiley.

Davenport, W. H. (1978). Sex in cross-cultural perspective. In F. A. Beach (Ed.), *Human sexuality in four perspectives* (pp. 115–163). Baltimore, MD: Johns Hopkins University Press.

David, H. P. (1992). Born unwanted: Long-term developmental effects of denied abortion. *Journal of Social Issues, 48* (3), 163–181.

David, H. P., Dytrych, Z., Matejcek, Z., & Schuller, V. (Eds.) (1988). *Born unwanted: Developmental effects of denied abortion.* New York: Springer.

Davidson, J. K., Sr., & Darling, C. A. (1989). Perceived differences in the female orgasmic response: New meanings for sexual satisfaction. *Family Practice Research Journal, 8,* 75–84.

Davidson, J. K., Sr., & Hoffman, L. E. (1986). Sexual fantasies and sexual satisfaction: An empirical analysis of erotic thought. *The Journal of Sex Research, 22,* 184–205.

Davidson, J. K., Sr., Darling, C., & Conway-Welch, C. (1989). The role of the Gräfenberg spot and female ejaculation in the female orgasmic response: An empirical analysis. *Journal of Sex and Marital Therapy, 15,* 102–119.

Davis, C. M. (1983). *Judgments of women with genital herpes.* Paper presented at the Annual Meeting of The Society for the Scientific Study of Sex, Chicago, IL.

Davis, C. M., & Bauserman, R. (1993). Exposure to sexually explicit materials: An attitude change perspective. In J. Bancroft, C. M. Davis, & H. J. Ruppel, Jr. (Eds.), *Annual Review of Sex Research,* Vol. IV (pp. 121–209). Mt. Vernon, IA: The Society for the Scientific Study of Sex.

Davis, C. M., Yarber, W. L., & Davis, S. L. (Eds.) (1988). *Sexuality measures: A compendium.* Lake Mills, IA: Graphic.

Davis, J. A., & Smith, T. (1984). *General social surveys, 1972–1984: Cumulative data.* New Haven, CT: Yale University, Roper Center for Public Opinion Research.

Davis, K. E. (1985). Near and dear: Friendship and love compared. *Psychology Today, 19* (12), 22–30.

Davison, G. C. (1991). Constructionism and morality in therapy for homosexuality. In J. C. Gonsiorek & J. D. Weinrich (Eds.), *Homosexuality: Research implications for public policy* (pp. 137–148). Newbury Park, CA: Sage.

Dawson, D. A. (1986). The effects of sex education on adolescent behavior. *Family Planning Perspectives, 18,* 162–170.

Day, R. D. (1992). The transition to first intercourse

among racially and culturally diverse youth. *Journal of Marriage and the Family, 54,* 749–762.

DeBuono, B. A., Zinner, S. H., Daamen, M., & McCormack, W. M. (1990). Sexual behavior of college women in 1975, 1986, and 1989. *New England Journal of Medicine, 322,* 821–825.

de Carvalho, M., Robertson, S., & Klaus, M. H. (1984). Does the duration and frequency of early breast feeding affect nipple pain? *Birth, 11,* 81–84.

Degler, C. (1980). *At odds: Women and the family in America from the revolution to the present.* Oxford, England: Oxford University Press.

Dekker, J. (1993). Inhibited male orgasm. In W. O'Donahue & J. H. Geer (Eds.), *Handbook of sexual dysfunctions: Assessment and treatment* (pp. 279–301). Boston, MA: Allyn and Bacon.

DeLamater, J. D., & MacCorquodale, P. (1979). *Premarital sexuality: Attitudes, relationships, behavior.* Madison, WI: University of Wisconsin Press.

DeMaris, A., & Rao, K.V. (1992). Premarital cohabitation and subsequent marital stability in the United States: A reassessment. *Journal of Marriage and the Family, 54,* 178–190.

D'Emilio, J., & Freedman, E. B. (1988). *Intimate matters: A history of sexuality in America.* New York: Harper & Row.

Denton, L. (1987). Child abuse reporting laws: Are they a barrier to helping troubled families? *The APA Monitor, 18* (6), 1, 22–23.

Derogatis, L. (1981). Psychopathology in individuals with sexual dysfunction. *American Journal of Psychiatry, 138,* 757–763.

Derogatis, L., & Meyer, J. K. A. (1979). A psychological profile of the sexual dysfunctions. *Archives of Sexual Behavior, 8,* 201–224.

de Sade, Donatien, the Marquis. *Justine* (R. Seaver & A. Wainhouse, Trans.) (1965). New York: Grove Press.

de Sade, Donatien, the Marquis. *Juliette* (A. Wainhouse, Trans.) (1968). New York: Grove Press.

Deutsch, H. (1944). *The psychology of women: A psychoanalytic interpretation,* Vol. 1. New York: Grune & Stratton.

Devor, Holly (1993). Sexual orientation identities, attractions, and practices of female-to-male transsexuals. *The Journal of Sex Research, 30,* 303–315.

de Young, M. (1982). *The sexual victimization of children.* Jefferson, NC: McFarland & Company.

de Zalduondo, B. D. (1991). Prostitution viewed cross-culturally: Toward recontextualizing sex work in AIDS intervention research. *The Journal of Sex Research, 28,* 223–248.

Diamond, M. (1993). Homosexuality and bisexuality in different populations. *Archives of Sexual Behavior, 22,* 291–310.

Diamond, M., & Dannemiller, J. E. (1989). Pornography and community standards in Hawaii: Comparisons with other states. *Archives of Sexual Behavior, 18,* 475–495.

Diamant, L. (1987). The therapies. In L. Diamant (Ed.), *Male and female homosexuality: Psychological approaches* (pp. 199–217). Washington, D.C.: Hemisphere.

Diana, L. (1985). *The prostitute and her clients.* Springfield, IL: Charles C Thomas.

Dick-Read, G. (1932/1959). *Childbirth without fear* (2nd Rev. Ed.) New York: Harper & Row.

DiClemente, R. J. (1989). Adolescents and AIDS: An update. *Multicultural Inquiry and Research on AIDS, 3* (1), 3–4, 7.

DiClemente, R. J., Boyer, C. B., & Morales, E. (1988). Minorities and AIDS: Knowledge, attitudes, and misconceptions among Black and Latino adolescents. *American Journal of Public Health, 1,* 55–57.

DiClemente, R. J., Forrest, K., & Mickler, S. E. (1990). College students' knowledge and attitudes about HIV and changes in HIV-preventive behaviors. *AIDS Education and Prevention, 2,* 201–212.

DiClemente, R. J., & Houston-Hamilton, A. (1989). Health promotion strategies for prevention of Human Immunodeficiency Virus infection among minority adolescents. *Health Education, 20* (5), 39–43.

Dion, K. L., & Dion, K. K. (1988). Romantic love: Individual and cultural perspectives. In R. J. Sternberg & M. L. Barnes (Eds.), *The psychology of love* (pp. 264–289). New Haven, CT: Yale University Press.

Dion, K. K., & Dion, K. L. (1993). Individualistic and collectivistic perspectives on gender and the cultural context of love and intimacy. *Journal of Social Issues, 49* (3), 53–69.

Dixon, J. K. (1984). The commencement of bisexual activity in swinging married women over age 30. *The Journal of Sex Research, 20,* 71–90.

Docter, R. F. (1988). *Transvestites and transsexuals: Towards a theory of gender behavior.* New York: Plenum Press.

Dodson, B. (1987). *Sex for one: The joy of self-loving.* New York: Harmony Books.

Doll, L. S., Peterson, L. R., White, C. R., Johnson, E. S., Ward, J. W., & the Blood Donor Study Group (1992). Homosexually and non-homosexually identified men who have sex with men: A behavioral comparison. *The Journal of Sex Research, 29,* 1–14.

Donahue, M. J. (1987, September). *Promoting abstinence: Is it viable?* Paper presented at an Office of Adolescent Pregnancy Programs technical workshop, Washington, D.C.

Donnelly, D. A. (1993). Sexually inactive marriages. *The Journal of Sex Research, 30,* 171–179.

Donnerstein, E. (1984). Pornography: Its effect on violence against women. In N. M. Malamuth & E. Donnerstein (Eds.), *Pornography and sexual aggression* (pp. 53–81). Orlando, FL: Academic Press.

Donnerstein, E., & Linz, D. (1986). Mass media, sexual violence, and media violence. *American Behavioral Scientist, 29*, 601–618.

Dornan, W. A., & Malsbury, C. W. (1989). Neuropeptides and male sexual behavior. *Neuroscience and Biobehavioral Reviews, 13*, 1–15.

Douthitt, R. A. (1989). The division of labor within the home: Have gender roles changed? *Sex Roles, 20*, 693–704.

Dover, K. J. (1978). *Greek homosexuality.* Cambridge, MA: Harvard University Press.

Dressel, P. L., & Petersen, D. M. (1982). Becoming a male stripper: Recruitment, socialization, and ideological development. *Work and Occupations, 9*, 387–406.

Dunn, M. E., & Trost, J. E. (1989). Male multiple orgasms: A descriptive study. *Archives of Sexual Behavior, 18*, 377–399.

Dutton, D. G., & Aron, A. P. (1974). Some evidence for heightened sexual attraction under conditions of high anxiety. *Journal of Personality and Social Psychology, 30*, 510–517.

Dwyer, S. M., & Amberson, J. I. (1989). Behavioral patterns and personality characteristics of 56 sex offenders: A preliminary study. *Journal of Psychology and Human Sexuality, 2*, 105–118.

Eakins, P. S. (1989). Free standing birth centers in California. *Journal of Reproductive Medicine, 34*, 960–970.

Earls, C. M., & David, H. (1989). A psychosocial study of male prostitution. *Archives of Sexual Behavior, 18*, 401–419.

Ecker, N., & Weinstein, S. (1983, April). *The relationship between attributes of sexual competency, physical appearance, and narcissism.* Paper presented at the conference of the Eastern Region of The Society for the Scientific Study of Sex, Philadelphia, PA.

Ehrhardt, A. A. (1975). Prenatal hormone exposure and psychosexual differentiation. In E. J. Sacher (Ed.), *Topics in psychoendocrinology* (pp. 67–82). New York: Grune & Stratton.

Ehrhardt, A. A., & Meyer-Bahlburg, H. F. L. (1981). Effects of prenatal sex hormones on gender-related behavior. *Science, 211*, 1312–1318.

Ehrhardt, A. A., Meyer-Bahlburg, H. F. L., Feldman, J. L., & Ince, S. (1984). Sex-dimorphic behavior in childhood subsequent to prenatal exposure to exogenous progesterones and estrogens. *Archives of Sexual Behavior, 13*, 457–477.

Elias, J., & Gebhard, P. (1969). Sexuality and sexual learning in childhood. *Phi Delta Kappan, 50*, 401–405.

Elicker, J. M., Englund, M., & Sroufe, L. A. (1992). Predicting peer competence and peer relationships in childhood from early parent-child relationships. In R. Parke & G. Ladd (Eds.), *Family-peer relations: Modes of linkage* (pp. 77–106). Hillsdale, NJ: Lawrence Erlbaum Associates.

Elkins, T., Gafford, L., Wilks, C., Muram, D., & Golden, G. (1986). A model clinical approach to the reproductive health concerns of the mentally handicapped. *Obstetrics and Gynecology, 68*, 185–188.

Ellickson, P., & Robyn, A. (1987). Toward more effective drug prevention programs. *The Rand Publication Series.* Santa Monica, CA: The Rand Corporation.

Ellis, B. J., & Symons, D. (1990). Sex differences in sexual fantasy: An evolutionary psychological approach. *The Journal of Sex Research, 27*, 527–555.

Ellis, H. H. (1933). *Psychology of sex: A manual for students.* New York: Long & Smith.

Ellis, H. H. (1942). *Studies in the psychology of sex* (2 Vols.). New York: Random House. (Originally published in 7 volumes, 1896–1928).

Ellis, L. (1991). A biosocial theory of social stratification derived from the concepts of pro/antisociality and r/K selection. *Politics and the Life Sciences, 10*, 5–44.

Ellis, L. (1993). Rape as a biosocial phenomenon. In G. C. N. Hall, R. Hirschman, J. R. Graham, & M. Z. Zaragoza (Eds.), *Sexual aggression: Issues in etiology, assessments, and treatment* (pp. 17–41). Washington, D.C.: Taylor and Francis.

Ellis, L., & Ames, M. A. (1987). Neurohormonal functioning and sexual orientation: A theory of homosexuality-heterosexuality. *Psychological Bulletin, 101*, 233–258.

Emory, L. E., Williams, D. H., Cole, C. M., Amparo, E. G., & Meyer, W. J. (1991). Anatomic variation of the corpus callosum in persons with gender dysphoria. *Archives of Sexual Behavior, 20*, 409–417.

Emster, V. L. (1975). American menstrual expressions. *Sex Roles, 1*, 3–13.

Epstein, J. S., Moffitt, A. L., Mayner, R. E. et al. (1985, September). *Antibodies reactive with HTLV-III found in freezer-banked sera from children in West Africa* (abstract 217). Twenty-fifth Interscience Conference on Anti-microbial Agents and Chemotherapy, Minneapolis, MN.

Epstein, L. M. (1967). *Sex, laws and customs in Judaism.* New York: KTAV Publishing House.

Erikson, E. H. (1968a). *Childhood and society* (Rev. Ed.). New York: Norton.

Erikson, E. H. (1968b). *Identity, youth, and crisis.* New York: Norton.

Ernst, A. A., & Martin, D. H. (1993). High syphilis rates among cocaine abusers identified in an emergency department. *Sexually Transmitted Diseases, 20,* 66–69.

Estep, R., & MacDonald, P. T. (1990, March). *Prime time television's depiction of sex: The sixties vs. the eighties.* Paper presented at the Annual Western Region Meeting of The Society for the Scientific Study of Sex, San Francisco, CA.

Ewald, P. W. (1994). *Evolution of infectious disease.* New York: Oxford University Press.

Eveleth, P. B., & Tanner, J. M. (1976). *Worldwide variation in human growth.* Cambridge, England: Cambridge University Press.

Fabrikant, B. (1974). The psychotherapist and the female patient: Perceptions, misperceptions, and change. In V. Franks & V. Burtle (Eds.), *Women in therapy* (pp. 83–109). New York: Bruner/Mazel.

Faderman, L. (1992). The return of butch and femme: A phenomenon in lesbian sexuality of the 1980s and 1990s. *Journal of the History of Sexuality, 4,* 578–596.

Fairchild, H. H. (1991). Scientific racism: The cloak of objectivity. *Journal of Social Issues, 47* (3), 101–115.

Faith, M. S., & Schare, M. L. (1993). The role of body image in sexually avoidant behavior. *Archives of Sexual Behavior, 22,* 345–356.

Fausto-Sterling, A. (1992). Why do we know so little about human sex? *Discover, 13* (6), 28–30.

Feeney, J. A., & Noller, P. (1990). Attachment style as a predictor of adult romantic relationships. *Journal of Personality and Social Psychology, 58,* 281–291.

Feeney, J. A., & Noller, P. (1991). Attachment style and verbal descriptions of romantic partners. *Journal of Social and Personal Relationships, 8,* 187–215.

Feild, H. S. (1978). Attitudes toward rape: A comparative analysis of police, rapists, crisis counselors, and citizens. *Journal of Personality and Social Psychology, 36,* 156–179.

Feild, H. S., & Bienen, L. B. (1980). *Jurors and rape.* Lexington, MA: D. C. Heath.

Felton, G., & Segelman, F. (1978). Lamaze childbirth training and changes in belief about personality. *Birth and the Family Journal, 5,* 141–150.

Fenichel, O. (1945). *The psychoanalytic theory of neurosis.* New York: Norton.

Fetherstone, M., & Hepworth, M. (1985). The male menopause: Lifestyle and sexuality. *Maturitas, 7,* 235–246.

Finkelhor, D. (1979). *Sexually victimized children.* New York: Free Press.

Finkelhor, D. (1980). Sex among siblings: A survey on prevalence, variety, and effects. *Archives of Sexual Behavior, 9,* 171–197.

Finkelhor, D. (1984). *Child sexual abuse: New theory & research.* New York: Free Press.

Finkelhor, D., & Browne, A. (1985). The traumatic impact of child sexual abuse. *American Journal of Orthopsychiatry, 55,* 530–541.

Finkelhor, D., & Dziuba-Leatherman, J. (1994). Victimization of children. *American Psychologist, 49,* 173–183.

Finkelhor, D., Hotaling, G., Lewis, I. A., & Smith, C. (1990). Sexual abuse in a national survey of adult men and women: Prevalence, characteristics, and risk factors. *Child Abuse & Neglect, 14,* 19–28.

Finkelhor, D., & Russell, D. E. H. (1984). The gender gap among perpetrators of child sexual abuse. In D. E. H. Russell, *Sexual exploitation: Rape, child sexual abuse, and workplace harassment* (pp. 215–231). Beverly Hills, CA: Sage.

Fishbein, E. G. (1989). Predicting paternal involvement with a newborn by attitude toward women's roles. In P. N. Stern (Ed.), *Pregnancy and parenting* (pp. 91–97). New York: Hemisphere.

Fisher, H. (1992). *The anatomy of love.* New York: Norton.

Fisher, J. D. (1988). Possible effects of reference group–based social influence on AIDS-risk prevention. *American Psychologist, 43,* 914–920.

Fisher, J. D., & Fisher, W. A. (1992). Changing AIDS-risk behavior. *Psychological Bulletin, 117,* 455–474.

Fisher, S. (1973). *The female orgasm.* New York: Basic Books.

Fisher, S. (1986). *Development and structure of the body image* (Vols. 1 & 2). Hillsdale, NJ: Lawrence Erlbaum Associates.

Fisher, S. (1989). *Sexual images of the self: The psychology of erotic sensation.* Hillsdale, NJ: Lawrence Erlbaum Associates.

Fisher, T. D. (1986a). Parent-child communication about sex and young adolescents' sexual knowledge and attitudes. *Adolescence, 21,* 517–527.

Fisher, T. D. (1986b). An exploratory study of parent-child communication about sex and the sexual attitudes of early, middle, and late adolescents. *Journal of Genetic Psychology, 147,* 543–557.

Fisher, T. D. (1987). Family communication and the sexual behavior and attitudes of college students. *Journal of Youth and Adolescence, 16,* 481–495.

Fisher, T. D. (1988). The relationship between parent-child communication about sexuality and college students' sexual behavior and attitudes as a function of parental proximity. *The Journal of Sex Research, 24,* 305–311.

Fisher, T. D. (1989a). An extension of the findings of Moore, Peterson, and Furstenberg (1986) regarding family sexual communication and adolescent sexual behavior. *Journal of Marriage and the Family, 51,* 637–639.

Fisher, T. D. (1989b). Confessions of a closet sex researcher. *The Journal of Sex Research, 26,* 144–147.

Fisher, T. D. (1993). A comparison of various measures of family sexual communication: Psychometric properties, validity, and behavioral correlates. *The Journal of Sex Research, 30,* 229–238.

Fisher, T. D., & Hall, R. G. (1988). A scale for the comparison of the sexual attitudes of adolescents and their parents. *The Journal of Sex Research, 24,* 90–100.

Fisher, W. A. (1983). Gender, gender role identification, and response to erotica. In E. R. Allgeier & N. B. McCormick (Eds.), *Changing boundaries: Gender roles and sexual behavior* (pp. 261–284). Palo Alto, CA: Mayfield.

Fisher, W. A. (1984). Predicting contraceptive behavior among university men: The roles of emotions and behavioral intentions. *Journal of Applied Social Psychology, 14,* 104–123.

Fisher, W. A., & Barak, A. (1991). Pornography, erotica, and behavior: More questions than answers. *International Journal of Law and Psychiatry, 14,* 65–83.

Fisher, W. A., Branscombe, N. R., & Lemery, C. R. (1983). The bigger the better? Arousal and attributional responses to erotic stimuli that depict different-size penises. *The Journal of Sex Research, 19,* 377–396.

Fisher, W. A., Byrne, D., & White, L. A. (1983). Emotional barriers to contraception. In D. Byrne & W. A. Fisher (Eds.), *Adolescents, sex, and contraception* (pp. 207–239). Hillsdale, NJ: Lawrence Erlbaum Associates.

Fisher, W. A., Byrne, D., White, L. A., & Kelley, K. (1988). Erotophobia-erotophilia as a dimension of personality. *The Journal of Sex Research, 25,* 123–151.

Fisher, W. A., Fisher, J. D., & Byrne, D. (1977). Consumer reactions to contraceptive purchasing. *Personality and Social Psychology Bulletin, 3,* 293–296.

Fisher, W. A., & Grenier, G. (1994). Violent pornography, antiwoman thoughts, and antiwoman acts: In search of reliable effects. *The Journal of Sex Research, 31,* 23–38.

Fisher, W. A., Grenier, G., Watters, W. W., Lamont, J., Cohen, M., & Askwith, J. (1988). Students' sexual knowledge, attitudes toward sex, and willingness to treat sexual concerns. *Journal of Medical Education, 63,* 379–385.

Fisk, N. (1973, February). *Gender dysphoria syndrome— The how, why, and what of a condition.* Interdisciplinary Symposium on Transsexualism. Stanford University School of Medicine, Palo Alto, CA.

Fitzgerald, L. F., Weitzman, L. M., Gold, Y., & Ormerod, M. (1988). Academic harassment: Sex and denial in scholarly garb. *Psychology of Women Quarterly, 12,* 329–340.

Flandrin, J. L. (1977). Repression and change in the sexual life of young people in medieval and early modern times. *Journal of Family History, 2,* 196–210.

Flandrin, J. L. (1991). *Sex in the western world: The development of attitudes and behavior* (S. Collins, Trans.). Chur, Switzerland: Harwood Academic.

Fleming, M., Cohen, D., Salt, P., James, D., & Jenkins, S. (1981). A study of pre- and postsurgical transsexuals: MMPI characteristics. *Archives of Sexual Behavior, 19,* 161–170.

Foa, U. G., Anderson, B., Converse, J., Jr., Urbansky, W. A., Cowley III, M. J., Muhlhausen, S. M., & Tornbloom, K. Y. (1987). Gender-related sexual attitudes: Some crosscultural similarities and differences. *Sex Roles, 16,* 511–519.

Ford, B. (1980). *Patterns of sex.* New York: St. Martin's Press.

Ford, C. S., & Beach, F. A. (1951). *Patterns of sexual behavior.* New York: Harper & Row.

Ford, N., & Mathie, E. (1993). The acceptability and experience of the female condom, Femidom®, among family planning clinic attenders. *British Journal of Family Planning, 19,* 187–192.

Forrest, J. D., & Fordyce, R. R. (1993). Women's contraceptive attitudes and use in 1992. *Family Planning Perspectives, 25,* 175–179.

Forrest, J. D., & Henshaw, S. K. (1983). What U.S. women think and do about contraception. *Family Planning Perspectives, 15,* 157–158, 160–166.

Forrest, J. D., & Kaeser, L. (1993). Questions of balance: Issues emerging from the introduction of the hormonal implant. *Family Planning Perspectives, 25,* 127–132.

Fox, C. A. (1977). Orgasm and fertility. In R. Gemme & C. Wheeler (Eds.), *Progress in Sexology* (pp. 351–355). New York: Plenum.

Fox, G. L. (1977). "Nice girl": Social control of women through a value construct. *Signs, 2,* 805–817.

Fox, G. L. (1980). The mother–adolescent daughter relationship as a sexual socialization structure: A research review. *Family Relations, 29,* 21–28.

Fox, L. S. (1983). Adolescent male reproductive responsibility in a white, middle-class sample. *Social Work in Education, 6,* 32–43.

Frank, E., Anderson, C., & Rubinstein, D. (1978). Frequency of sexual dysfunction in "normal" couples. *New England Journal of Medicine, 299,* 111–115.

Franzoi, S. L., & Herzog, M. E. (1987). Judging physical attractiveness: What body aspects do we use? *Personality and Social Psychology Bulletin, 13,* 19–33.

Frayser, S. G., & Whitby, T. J. (1987). *Studies in human sexuality: A selected guide.* Littleton, CO: Libraries Unlimited, Inc.

Freed, R. S., & Freed, S. A. (1989). Beliefs and practices

resulting in female deaths and fewer females than males in India. *Population and Environment, 10,* 144–161.

Freedman, R. (1986). *Beauty bound.* Lexington, MA: D. C. Heath.

Freud, A. (1953). *The ego and mechanisms of defense.* New York: International Universities Press. (Originally published, 1936.)

Freud, S. (1955). *Beyond the pleasure principle, group psychology and other works,* Vol. 18. London, England: Hogarth.

Freud, S. (1963). *Three essays on the theory of sexuality* (U. Strachey, Ed. and Trans.). New York: Basic Books. (Originally published, 1905.)

Freund, K. (1985). Cross-gender identity in a broader context. In B. W. Steiner (Ed.), *Gender dysphoria: Development, research, management* (pp. 259–324). New York: Plenum.

Freund, K., & Blanchard, R. (1986). The concept of courtship disorder. *Journal of Sex and Marital Therapy, 12,* 79–92.

Freund, K., & Langevin, R. (1976). Bisexuality in homosexual pedophilia. *Archives of Sexual Behavior, 5,* 415–423.

Freund, K., Scher, H., & Hucher, S. (1983). The courtship disorders. *Archives of Sexual Behavior, 12,* 369–379.

Freund, K., Scher, H, Racansky, I. G., Campbell, K., & Heasman, J. (1986). Males disposed to rape. *Archives of Sexual Behavior, 15,* 23–35.

Freund, K., Steiner, B. W., & Chan, S. (1982). Two types of cross-gender identity. *Archives of Sexual Behavior, 11,* 49–63.

Freund, M., Lee, N., & Leonard, T. (1991). Sexual behavior of clients with street prostitutes in Camden, NJ. *The Journal of Sex Research, 28,* 579–591.

Freund, M., Leonard, T. I., & Lee, N. (1989). Sexual behavior of resident street prostitutes with their clients in Camden, New Jersey. *The Journal of Sex Research, 26,* 460–478.

Fritz, G. S., Stoll, K., & Wagner, N. A. (1981). A comparison of males and females who were sexually molested as children. *Journal of Sex and Marital Therapy, 7,* 54–59.

Fromm, E. (1956). *The art of loving.* New York: Harper & Row.

Fromm, E. (1973). *The anatomy of human destructiveness.* New York: Holt, Rinehart & Winston.

Furstenberg, F. F. (1976). *Unplanned parenthood: The social consequences of teenage childbearing.* New York: Free Press.

Furstenberg, F. F., Brooks-Gunn, J., & Morgan, S. P. (1987). *Adolescent mothers in later life.* New York: Cambridge University Press.

Fyke, F. E., Kazmier, S. J., & Harms, R. W. (1985). Venous air embolism: Life-threatening complications of orogenital sex during pregnancy. *The American Journal of Medicine, 78,* 333–336.

Gager, H., & Schurr, C. (1976). *Sexual assault: Confronting rape in America.* New York: Grosset & Dunlap.

Gagnon, J. H. (1965). Female child victims of sex offenses. *Social Problems, 13,* 179–192.

Gagnon, J. H. (1977). *Human sexualities.* Glenview, IL: Scott, Foresman.

Gagnon, J. H. (1985). Attitudes and responses of parents to preadolescent masturbation. *Archives of Sexual Behavior, 14,* 451–466.

Gagnon, J. H. (1990). The explicit and implicit use of the scripting perspective in sex research. In J. Bancroft, C. M. Davis, & D. Weinstein (Eds.), *Annual Review of Sex Research,* Vol. 1 (pp. 1–43). Lake Mills, IA: The Society for the Scientific Study of Sex.

Gagnon, J. H., & Simon, W. (1973). *Sexual conduct: The social sources of human sexuality.* Chicago, IL: Aldine.

Gagnon, J. H., & Simon, W. (1987). The sexual scripting of oral genital contacts. *Archives of Sexual Behavior, 16,* 1–25.

Gaines, M. E., & Allgeier, E. R. (1993, May). *Parents' knowledge, attitudes, and responses to child sexual abuse.* Paper presented at the Annual Meeting of the Midcontinent Region of The Society for the Scientific Study of Sex, Cincinnatti, OH.

Gallo, P. G., & Viviani, F. (1992). The origin of infibulation in Somalia: An ethological hypothesis. *Ethology and Sociobiology, 13,* 253–265.

Gallup, G. G., & Suarez, S. D. (1983). Homosexuality as a by-product of selection for optimal heterosexual strategies. *Perspectives in Biology and Medicine, 26,* 315–322.

Gallup, G. H. (1987). More today than in 1985 thought that premarital sex was wrong. *The Gallup Report, 263,* 20.

Gandhy, S. (1988). Crimes against women in India. *Philosophy and Social Action, 14* (4), 22–30.

Gao, J., Shen, H., Zheng, S., Fan, H. M., Wu, M. H., Hani, L. H., & Yao, G. Z. (1986). A randomized comparative clinical evaluation of the steel ring, the VCu 200, and the TCu220c IUDS. *Contraception, 33,* 443–454.

Garnets, L., Hancock, K. A., Cochran, S. D., Goodchilds, J., & Peplau, L. A. (1991). Issues in psychotherapy with lesbians and gay men: A survey of psychologists. *American Psychologist, 46,* 964–972.

Gates, C. C. (1988). The "most-significant-other" in the care of breast cancer patient. *Ca—A Cancer Journal for Clinicians, 38,* 146–153.

Gaulier, B., & Allgeier, E. R. (1988, April). *Male versus*

*female perceptions of sexual intent in a dyadic interaction.* Paper presented at the Midwestern Psychological Association, Chicago, IL.

Gaulier, B., Travis, S. K., & Allgeier, E. R. (1986, June). *Proceptive behavior and the use of behavioral cues in heterosexual courtship.* Presented at the Annual Meeting of the Midcontinent Region of The Society for the Scientific Study of Sex, Madison, WI.

Gay, G. R., New-Meyer, J. D., Perry, M., Johnson, G., & Kurland, M. (1982). Love and haight: The sensuous hippie revisited. Drug/sex practices in San Francisco, 1980–1981. *Journal of Psychoactive Drugs, 14,* 111–123.

Gay, P. (1984). *The bourgeois experience: Victoria to Freud. Education of the senses,* Vol. I. New York: Oxford University Press.

Gay, P. (1988). *Freud: A life for our time.* New York: Norton.

Gebhard, P. H. (1977). The acquisition of basic sex information. *The Journal of Sex Research, 13,* 148–169.

Gebhard, P. H. (1987, April). *Fireside chat.* Presentation at the annual meeting of the Midcontinent Region of The Society for the Scientific Study of Sex, Bloomington, IN.

Gebhard, P. H. (1993). Kinsey's famous figures. *Indiana Alumni Magazine,* 64.

Gebhard, P. H., Gagnon, J. H., Pomeroy, W. B., & Christenson, C. V. (1965). *Sex offenders.* New York: Harper & Row.

Gecas, V., & Schwalbe, M. L. (1986). Parental behavior and adolescent self-esteem. *Journal of Marriage and the Family, 48,* 37–46.

Genevay, B. (1975). Age is killing us softly . . . when we deny the part of us which is sexual. In L. M. Burnside (Ed.), *Sexuality and aging* (pp. 67–75). Los Angeles, CA: University of Southern California Press.

Gentry, C. (1991). *J. Edgar Hoover: The man, the secrets.* New York: Norton.

George, L. K., & Weiler, S. J. (1981). Sexuality in middle and late life: The effects of age, cohort and gender. *Archives of General Psychiatry, 38,* 919–923.

George, W. H., Gournic, S. J., & McAfee, M. R. (1988). Perceptions of postdrinking female sexuality: Effects of gender, beverage choice, and drink payment. *Journal of Applied Social Psychology, 18,* 1295–1317.

Gerrard, M. (1987). Sex, sex guilt, and contraceptive use revisited: The 1980s. *Journal of Personality and Social Psychology, 53,* 975–980.

Gerrard, M., & Gibbons, F. X. (1982). Sexual experience, sex guilt, and sexual moral reasoning. *Journal of Personality, 50,* 345–359.

Gettelman, T. E., & Thompson, J. K. (1993). Actual differences and stereotypical perceptions in body image and eating disturbance: A comparison of male and female heterosexual and homosexual samples. *Sex Roles, 29,* 545–562.

Giallombardo, R. (1966). *Society of women.* New York: Wiley.

Gibson-Ainyette, I., Templer, D. I., Brown, R., & Veaco, L. (1988). Adolescent female prostitutes. *Archives of Sexual Behavior, 17,* 431–438.

Gigy, L., & Kelly, J. B. (1992). Reasons for divorce: Perspectives of divorcing men and women. *Journal of Divorce and Remarriage, 18,* 169–187.

Gilbaugh, J., & Fuchs, P. (1979). The gonococcus and the toilet seat. *New England Journal of Medicine, 301,* 91–93.

Gilbert, N. (1992). Realities and mythologies of rape. *Society, 29,* 4–10.

Gilligan, C. (1982). *In a different voice: Psychological theory and women's development.* Cambridge, MA: Harvard University Press.

Gillman, A. E., & Gordon, A. R. (1973). Sexual behavior in the blind. *Medical Aspects of Human Sexuality, 7* (6), 48–60.

Gilmartin, B. G. (1974). Sexual deviance and social networks: A study of social, family, and marital interaction patterns among comarital sex participants. In J. R. Smith & L. C. Smith (Eds.), *Beyond monogamy: Recent studies of sexual alternatives in marriage* (pp. 291–323). Baltimore, MD: Johns Hopkins University Press.

Gilmartin, B. G. (1976). Jealousy among the swingers. In G. Clanton & L. Smith (Eds.), *Jealousy* (pp. 152–158). Englewood Cliffs, NJ: Prentice-Hall.

Gilroy, F., & Steinbacher, R. (1983). Preselection of child's sex: Technological utilization and feminism. *Psychological Reports, 53,* 671–676.

Gladue, B. A. (1987). Psychobiological contributions. In L. Diamant (Ed.), *Male and female homosexuality: Psychological approaches* (pp. 129–153). Washington, D.C.: Hemisphere.

Glaser, R. D., & Thorpe, J. S. (1986). Unethical intimacy: A survey of sexual contact and advances between psychology educators and female graduate students. *American Psychologist, 41,* 43–51.

Glasock, J., & LaRose, R. (1993). Dial-a-porn recordings: The role of the female participant in male sexual fantasies. *Journal of Broadcaster and Electronic Media, 39,* 313–324.

Glass, R., & Ericsson, R. (1982). *Getting pregnant in the 1980s.* Berkeley, CA: University of California Press.

Glass, S. P., & Wright, T. L. (1992). Justifications for extramarital relationships: The association between attitudes, behaviors, and gender. *The Journal of Sex Research, 29,* 361–387.

Glick, P. C. (1984). Marriage, divorce, and living arrangements: Prospective changes. *Journal of Family Issues, 5,* 7–26.

Glowacki, G. A. (1988). A new look at osteoporosis and estrogen replacement therapy. *Comprehensive Therapy, 14* (2), 49–53.

Godlewski, J. (1988). Transsexualism and anatomic sex ratio reversal in Poland. *Archives of Sexual Behavior, 17,* 547–548.

Gold, S. R. (1991). History of child sexual abuse and adult sexual fantasies. *Violence and Victims, 6,* 75–82.

Gold, S. R., Balzano, B. F., & Stamey, R. (1991). Two studies of females' sexual force fantasies. *Journal of Sex Education and Therapy, 17,* 15–26.

Gold, S. R., & Gold, R. G. (1991). Gender differences in first sexual fantasies. *Journal of Sex Education and Therapy, 17,* 207–216.

Gold, S. R., & Gold, R. G. (1993). Sexual aversions: A hidden disorder. In W. O'Donahue & J. H. Geer (Eds.), *Handbook of sexual dysfunctions: Assessment and treatment* (pp. 83–102). Boston, MA: Allyn and Bacon.

Goldfarb, L., Gerrard, M., Gibbons, F. X., & Plante, T. (1988). Attitudes toward sex, arousal, and the retention of contraceptive information. *Journal of Personality and Social Psychology, 55,* 634–641.

Goldman, R., & Goldman, J. (1982). *Children's sexual thinking: A comparative study of children aged 5 to 15 years in Australia, North America, Britain, and Sweden.* London, England: Routledge & Kegan Paul.

Goldstein, B. (1976). *Introduction to human sexuality.* New York: McGraw-Hill.

Goldstein, M. (1986). The future of male birth control. *Planned Parenthood Review, 6* (3), 11–12.

Goldstein, P. J. (1979). *Prostitution and drugs.* Lexington, MA: Lexington Books.

Gonsiorek, J. C. (1991). The empirical basis for the demise of the illness model of homosexuality. In J. C. Gonsiorek & J. D. Weinrich (Eds.), *Homosexuality: Research implications for public policy* (pp. 115–136). Newbury Park, CA: Sage.

Goodall, J. (1971). *Tiwi wives.* Seattle, WA: University of Washington Press.

Goodheart, A. (1992). Abstinence Ed.: How everything you need to know about sex you won't be allowed to ask. *Playboy, 39,* 42–44.

Goodman, L. S., & Gilman, A. (Eds.) (1970). *The pharmacological basis of therapeutics.* London, England: MacMillan.

Goodman, R. E., Anderson, D. C., Bu'lock, D. E., Sheffield, B., Lynch, S. S., & Butt, W. R. (1985). Study of the effect of estradiol on gonadotropin levels in untreated male-to-female transsexuals. *Archives of Sexual Behavior, 14,* 141–146.

Gorski, R. A. (1987). Sex differences in the rodent brain:

Their nature and origin. In J. M. Reinisch, L. A. Rosenbloom, & S. A. Sanders (Eds.), *Masculinity/femininity: Basic perspectives* (pp. 37–67). New York: Oxford University Press.

Gosselin, C. (1978). Personality attributes of the average rubber fetishist. In M. Cook & G. D. Wilson (Eds.), *Love and attraction* (pp. 395–399). Oxford, England: Pergamon.

Gough, H. G. (1979). Some factors related to men's stated willingness to use a male contraceptive pill. *The Journal of Sex Research, 15,* 27–37.

Goy, R. W., & Phoenix, C. H. (1971). The effects of testosterone propionate administered before birth on the development of behavior in genetic female rhesus monkeys. In C. Sawyer & R. A. Gorski (Eds.), *Steroid hormones and brain function* (pp. 193–213). Berkeley, CA: University of California Press.

Graber, B. (1993). Medical aspects of sexual arousal disorders. In W. O'Donohue & J. H. Geer (Eds.), *Handbook of sexual dysfunctions: Assessment and treatment* (pp. 103–156). Boston, MA: Allyn and Bacon.

Grady, W. R., Hayward, M. D., & Yagi, J. (1986). Contraceptive failure in the United States: Estimates from the 1982 national survey of family growth. *Family Planning Perspectives, 18,* 200–209.

Grady, W. R., Klepinger, D. H., Billy, J. O. G., & Tanfer, K. (1993). Condom characteristics: The perceptions and preferences of men in the United States. *Family Planning Perspectives, 25,* 67–73.

Gräfenberg, E. (1950). The role of the urethra in female orgasm. *The International Journal of Sexology, 3,* 145–148.

Granberg, D. (1981). The abortion controversy: An overview. *The Humanist, 41,* 28–38.

Granberg, D. (1985). The United States Senate votes to uphold Roe versus Wade. *Population Research and Policy Review, 4,* 115–131.

Granvold, D. K., Pedler, L. M., & Schellie, S. G. (1979). A study of sex role expectancy and female postdivorce adjustment. *Journal of Divorce, 2,* 383–393.

Greeley, A. M., Michael, R. T., & Smith, T. W. (1989). *A most monogamous people: Americans and their sexual partners.* GSS Topical Report No. 17, Chicago, IL, National Opinion Research Center.

Green, R. (1974). *Sexual identity conflict in children and adults.* New York: Basic Books.

Green, R. (1978). Sexual identity of 37 children raised by homosexual or transsexual parents. *American Journal of Psychiatry, 135,* 692–697.

Green, R. (1979). Childhood cross-gender behavior and subsequent sexual preference. *American Journal of Psychiatry, 136,* 106–108.

Green, R. (1987). *The "sissy boy syndrome" and the de-*

*velopment of homosexuality: A 15-year prospective study.* New Haven, CT: Yale University Press.

Green, R., & Fleming, D. T. (1990). Transsexual surgery follow-up: Status in the 1990s. In J. Bancroft, C. M. Davis, & D. Weinstein (Eds.), *Annual Review of Sex Research,* Vol. 1 (pp. 163–174). Lake Mills, IA: The Society for the Scientific Study of Sex.

Greenberg, B. S., & D'Alessio, D. D. (1985). Quantity and quality of sex in the soaps. *Broadcasting and Electronic Media, 29,* 309–321.

Greenberg, D. F. (1988). *The construction of homosexuality.* Chicago, IL: University of Chicago Press.

Greendlinger, V., & Byrne, D. (1987). Coercive sexual fantasies of college men as predictors of self-reported likelihood to rape and overt sexual aggression. *The Journal of Sex Research, 23,* 1–11.

Greenhalgh, S., & Bongaarts, J. (1987). Fertility policy in China: Future options. *Science, 235,* 1167–1172.

Greenwald, E., & Leitenberg, H. (1989). Long-term effects of sexual experiences with siblings and non-siblings during childhood. *Archives of Sexual Behavior, 18,* 389–399.

Gregor, T. (1985). *Anxious pleasures: The sexual lives of an Amazonian people.* Chicago, IL: University of Chicago Press.

Grieco, A. (1987). Scope and nature of sexual harassment in nursing. *The Journal of Sex Research, 23,* 261–266.

Grodstein, F., Goldman, M. B., & Cramer, D. W. (1993). Relation of tubal infertility to history of sexually transmitted diseases. *American Journal of Epidemiology, 137,* 577–584.

Gross, J. (1990). Be all that you can be. *Toledo Blade.* Toledo, OH, April 15, Section F, p. 3.

Gross, M. (1985, July/August). Sex sells. *Saturday Review,* 50–52, 91.

Grosskurth, P. (1980). *Havelock Ellis: A biography.* New York: Knopf.

Groth, A. N. (1978). Guidelines for the assessment and management of the offender. In A. W. Burgess, A. N. Groth, L. L. Holmstrom, & S. M. Sgroi (Eds.), *Sexual assault of children and adolescents* (pp. 25–42). Lexington, MA: Lexington Books.

Groth, A. N. (1979). *Men who rape: The psychology of the offender.* New York: Plenum.

Groth, A. N., & Burgess, A. W. (1977). Sexual dysfunction during rape. *New England Journal of Medicine, 297,* 764–766.

Groth, A. N., & Burgess, A. W. (1980). Male rape: Offenders and victims. *American Journal of Psychiatry, 137,* 806–810.

Grunebaum, H. (1986). Harmful psychotherapy experiences. *American Journal of Psychotherapy, 40,* 165–176.

Guinan, M. E., & Hardy, A. (1987). Epidemiology of AIDS in women in the United States: 1981 through 1986. *Journal of the American Medical Association, 257,* 2039–2042.

Gunzenhauser, N. (Ed.) (1990). *Advances in touch: New implications in human development.* Skillman, NJ: Johnson & Johnson.

Gutek, B. A. (1985). *Sex and the workplace.* San Francisco, CA: Jossey-Bass.

Gutek, B. A., & Nakamura, C. Y. (1983). Gender role and sexuality in the world of work. In E. R. Allgeier & N. B. McCormick (Eds.), *Changing boundaries: Gender roles and sexual behavior* (pp. 182–201). Palo Alto, CA: Mayfield.

Guttmacher, A. F., & Kaiser, I. H. (1986). The genesis of liberalized abortion in New York: A personal insight. In J. D. Butler & D. F. Walbert (Eds.), *Abortion, medicine, and the law* (3rd Ed.) (pp. 229–246). New York: Facts on File Publications.

Halderman, B. L., & Zelhart, P. F. (1985). A study of fantasy: Determinants of fantasy, function, and content. *Journal of Clinical Psychology, 41,* 325–330.

Hall, E. J., & Ferree, M. M. (1986). Race differences in abortion attitudes. *Public Opinion Quarterly, 50,* 193–207.

Hall, E. R., & Flannery, P. J. (1985). Prevalence and correlates of sexual assault experiences in adolescents. *Victimology: An International Journal, 9,* 398–406.

Hall, N. R. S. (1988). The virology of AIDS. *American Psychologist, 43,* 907–913.

Hallstrom, T. (1977). Sexuality in the climacteric. *Clinical Obstetrics and Gynecology, 4,* 227–239.

Halpern, C. T., Udry, J. R., & Suchindran, C. (1994). Effects of repeated questionnaire administration in longitudinal studies of adolescent males' sexual behavior. *Archives of Sexual Behavior, 23,* 41–57.

Hamburg, D. A. (1992). *Today's children: Creating a future for a generation in crisis.* New York: Times Books.

Hamer, D. H., Hu, S., Magnuson, V. L., Hu, N., & Pattatucci, A. M. L. (1993). A linkage between DNA markers on the X chromosome and male sexual orientation. *Science, 261,* 321–327.

Handelsman, D. J., & Staraj, S. (1985). Testicular size: The effects of aging, malnutrition, and illness. *Journal of Andrology, 6,* 144–151.

Hansson, R. O., Knopf, M. F., Downs, E. A., Monroe, P. R., Stegman, S. E., & Wadley, D. S. (1984). Femininity, masculinity, and adjustment to divorce among women. *Psychology of Women Quarterly, 8,* 248–260.

Hardin, G. (1974). *Mandatory motherhood: The true meaning of ''right to life.''* Boston, MA: Beacon Press.

Hardy, J. B., Duggan, A. K., Masnyk, K., & Pearson, C. (1989). Fathers of children born to young urban mothers. *Family Planning Perspectives, 21,* 159–163, 187.

Hariton, B. E., & Singer, J. L. (1974). Women's fantasies during sexual intercourse: Normative and theoretical implications. *Journal of Consulting and Clinical Psychology, 42,* 313–322.

Harkin, A. M., & Hurley, M. (1988). National survey on public knowledge of AIDS in Ireland. *Health Education Research, 3* (1), 25–29.

Harlow, H. F., & Harlow, M. K. (1962). The effect of rearing conditions on behavior. *Bulletin of the Meninger Clinic, 26,* 213–224.

Harlow, H. F., & Mears, C. (1979). *The human model: Primate perspectives.* Washington, D.C.: V. H. Winston.

Harlow, H. F., & Novak, M. A. (1973). Psychopathological perspectives. *Perspectives in Biology and Medicine, 16,* 461–478.

Harris, S. (1981, October 20). Strictly personal. *Toledo Blade,* Toledo, OH, p. 1.

Harry, J. (1982). *Gay children grow up.* New York: Praeger.

Harry, J. (1984/1985). Sexual orientation as testing. *Journal of Homosexuality, 10,* 111–123.

Harry, J. (1993). Being out: A general model. *Journal of Homosexuality, 26,* 25–40.

Harry, J., & DeVall, W. B. (1978). *The social organization of gay males.* New York: Praeger.

Hart, J., Cohen, E., Gingold, A., & Homburg, R. (1991). Sexual behavior in pregnancy: A study of 219 women. *Journal of Sex Education and Therapy, 17,* 86–90.

Hartman, W. E., & Fithian, M. A. (1984). *Any man can.* New York: St. Martin's.

Harvey, S. M., Beckman, L. J., & Murray, J. (1989). Factors associated with use of the contraceptive sponge. *Family Planning Perspectives, 21,* 179.

Harvey, S. M., & Scrimshaw, S. C. M. (1988). Coitus-dependent contraceptives: Factors associated with effective use. *The Journal of Sex Research, 25,* 364–378.

Hatcher, R. A., Trussell, J., Stewart, F., Stewart, G. K., Kowal, D., Guest, F., Cates, W., & Policar, M. S. (1994). *Contraceptive technology 1992–1994* (16th Rev. Ed.). New York: Irvington.

Hatfield, E., & Rapson, R. L. (1993). *Love, sex, and intimacy: Their psychology, biology, and history.* New York: HarperCollins.

Hatfield, R. W. (1994). Touch and sexuality. In V. L. Bullough & B. Bullough (Eds.), *Human sexuality: An encyclopedia* (pp. 581–587). New York: Garland Publishing.

Haub, C. (1992). New U.N. projections show uncertainty of future world. *Population Today, 20,* 6.

Hawton, K. (1992). Sex therapy research: Has it withered on the vine? In J. Bancroft, C. M. Davis, & H. J. Ruppel, Jr. (Eds.), *Annual Review of Sex Research,* Vol. III (pp. 49–72). Lake Mills, IA: The Society for the Scientific Study of Sex.

Hayes, C. D. (Ed.) (1987). *Risking the future: Adolescent sexuality, pregnancy, and childbearing,* Vol. 1. Washington, D.C.: National Academy Press.

Haynes, J. D. (1994). Pheromones. In V. L. Bullough & B. Bullough (Eds.), *Human sexuality: An encyclopedia* (pp. 441–442). New York: Garland Publishing.

Hazan, C., & Shaver, P. R. (1990). Love and work: An attachment-theoretical perspective. *Journal of Personality and Social Psychology, 52,* 511–524.

Hazelwood, R. R., Dietz, P. E., & Burgess, A. W. (1983). *Autoerotic fatalities.* Lexington, MA: D. C. Heath.

Hechinger, F. M. (1992). *Fateful choices: Healthy youth for the 21st century.* New York: Hill and Wang.

Heim, N. (1981). Sexual behavior of castrated sex offenders. *Archives of Sexual Behavior, 10,* 11–19.

Heim, N., & Hursch, C. J. (1979). Castration for sex offenders: Treatment or punishment? A review and critique of recent European literature. *Archives of Sexual Behavior, 8,* 281–304.

Heiman, J. R. (1975). The physiology of erotica: Women's sexual arousal. *Psychology Today, 8,* 90–94.

Heiman, J. R. (1977). A psychophysiological exploration of sexual arousal patterns in females and males. *Psychophysiology, 14,* 266–274.

Heiman, J. R., Gladue, B. A., Roberts, C. W., & LoPiccolo, J. (1986). Historical and current factors discriminating sexually functional from sexually dysfunctional married couples. *Journal of Marital and Family Therapy, 12,* 163–174.

Heiman, J. R., & LoPiccolo, J. (1988). *Becoming orgasmic.* Englewood Cliffs, NJ: Prentice-Hall.

Heimberger, T. S., Chang, H. H., Birkhead, G. S., DeFerdinando, G. O., Greenberg, A. J., Gunn, R., & Morse, D. L. (1993). High prevalence of syphilis detected through a jail screening program. *Archives of Internal Medicine, 153,* 1799–1804.

Heinlein, R. (1961). *Stranger in a strange land.* New York: Putnam.

Hellerstein, H. K., & Friedman, E. H. (1970). Sexual activity and the postcoronary patient. *Archives of Internal Medicine, 125,* 987–999.

The Helper (1986, Spring). *Preventing transmission of genital herpes: Some guidelines.* 1–4.

Henderson, J. S. (1983). Effects of a prenatal teaching program on postpartum regeneration of the pubococcygeal muscle. *Journal of Obstetrics, Gynecology, and Neonatal Nursing, 12,* 403–408.

Hendrick, C., & Hendrick, S. S. (1983) Liking, loving and relating. Monterey, CA: Brooks/Cole.

Hendrick, C., & Hendrick, S. S. (1993). *Romantic love.* Newbury Park, CA: Sage.

Hendrick, S. S., & Hendrick, C. (1992). *Liking, loving, and relating*. Pacific Grove, CA: Brooks/Cole.

Henifin, M. S. (1993). New reproductive technologies: Equity and access to reproductive health care. *Journal of Social Issues, 49* (2), 61–74.

Henshaw, S. K. (1987). Characteristics of U.S. women having abortions, 1982–1983. *Family Planning Perspectives, 19*, 5–9.

Henshaw, S. K. (1993). Teenage abortion, birth and pregnancy statistics by state, 1988. *Family Planning Perspectives, 25*, 122–126.

Henshaw, S. K., & Silverman, J. (1988). The characteristics and prior contraceptive use of U.S. abortion patients. *Family Planning Perspectives, 20*, 158–168.

Henshaw, S. K., & Van Vort, J. (1989). Patterns and trends in teenage abortion and pregnancy. In S. K. Henshaw, A. M. Kenney, D. Somberg, & J. Van Vort (Eds.), *Teenage pregnancy in the United States* (pp. 1–44). New York: Alan Guttmacher Institute.

Henshaw, S. K., & Van Vort, J. (1992). *Abortion factbook, 1992 edition: Readings, trends, and state and local data to 1988*. New York: Alan Guttmacher Institute.

Herbst, A. L., Cole, P., Colton, T., Robboy, S. J., & Scully, R. E. (1977). Age-incidence and risk of diethylstilbestrol-related clear-cell adenocarcinoma of the vagina and cervix. *American Journal of Obstetrics and Gynecology, 128*, 43–50.

Herdt, G. H. (1981). *Guardians of the flutes: Idioms of masculinity*. New York: McGraw-Hill.

Herdt, G. H. (Ed.) (1984). *Ritualized homosexuality in Melanesia*. Berkeley, CA: University of California Press.

Herdt, G. H. (1990). Developmental discontinuities and sexual orientation across cultures. In D. P. McWhirter, S. A. Sanders, & J. M. Reinisch (Eds.), *Concepts of sexual orientation* (pp. 208–236). New York: Oxford University Press.

Herdt, G. H., & Davidson, J. (1988). The Sambia "Turnim Man": Sociocultural and clinical aspects of gender formation in male pseudohermaphrodites with 5-alpha reductase-defiency in Papua New Guinea. *Archives of Sexual Behavior, 17*, 33–56.

Herek, G. M. (1988). Heterosexuals' attitudes toward lesbians and gay men: Correlates and gender differences. *The Journal of Sex Research, 25*, 451–477.

Herek, G. M. (1989). Hate crimes against lesbians and gay men: Issues for research and policy. *American Psychologist, 44*, 948–955.

Herek, G. M. (1992). The social context of hate crimes: Notes on cultural heterosexism. In G. M. Herek & K. T. Berrill (Eds.), *Hate crimes: Confronting violence against lesbians and gay men* (pp. 89–104). Newbury Park, CA: Sage.

Herek, G. M., & Glunt, E. K. (1988). An epidemic of stigma: Public reactions to AIDS. *American Psychologist, 43*, 886–891.

Herek, G. M., & Glunt, E. K. (1993). Interpersonal contact and heterosexuals' attitudes toward gay men: Results from a national survey. *The Journal of Sex Research, 30*, 239–244.

Herek, G. M., Kimmel, D. C., Amaro, H., & Melton, G. B. (1991). Avoiding heterosexist bias in psychological research. *American Psychologist, 46*, 957–963.

Herman, J. (1981). *Father-daughter incest*. Cambridge, MA: Harvard University Press.

Herold, E. E., Mantle, D., & Zemitis, O. (1979). A study of sexual offenses against females. *Adolescence, 14*, 65–72.

Herold, E., Mottin, J., & Sabry, Z. (1979). The effect of vitamin E on human sexuality. *Archives of Sexual Behavior, 8*, 397–403.

Herzog, D. B., Norman, D. K., Gordon, C., & Pepose, M. (1984). Sexual conflict and eating disorders in 27 males. *American Journal of Psychiatry, 141*, 989–990.

Hetherington, E. M., Cox, M., & Cox, R. (1982). Effects of divorce on parents and children. In M. E. Lamb (Ed.), *Nontraditional families: Parenting and child development* (pp. 233–288). Hillsdale, NJ: Lawrence Erlbaum Associates.

Hirsch, M., Zunenfield, B., Moden, M., Ovadia, J., & Shemesh, J. (1985). Spermarche: The age of onset of sperm emission. *Journal of Adolescent Health Care, 6*, 35–39.

Hill, D. J., & Shugg, D. (1989). Breast self-examination practices and attitudes among breast cancer, benign breast disease and general practice patients. *Health Education Research, 4*, 193–203.

Hite, S. (1976). *The Hite report*. New York: Macmillan.

Hite, S. (1981). *The Hite report on male sexuality*. New York: Macmillan.

Hochhauser, M., & Rothenberger III, J. H. (1992). *AIDS Education*. Dubuque, IA: William C. Brown.

Hoenig, J. (1985). Etiology of transsexualism. In B. W. Steiner (Ed.), *Gender dysphoria: Development, research, and management* (pp. 11–32). New York: Plenum.

Hofferth, S. L., & Hayes, C. D. (Eds.) (1987). *Risking the future: Adolescent sexuality, pregnancy, and childbearing*, Vol. 2. Washington, D.C.: National Academy Press.

Hoffman, M. (1978). Homosexuality. In F. A. Beach (Ed.), *Human sexuality in four perspectives* (pp. 164–189). Baltimore, MD: Johns Hopkins University Press.

Holzman, H. R., & Pines, S. (1982). Buying sex: The phenomenology of being a john. *Deviant Behavior: An Interdisciplinary Journal, 4*, 89–116.

Hooker, E. (1969). Parental relations and male homosexuality in patient and nonpatient samples. *Journal of Consulting and Clinical Psychology, 33*, 140–142.

Hoon, P. W., Wincze, J. P., & Hoon, E. F. (1976). Physiological assessment of sexual arousal in women. *Psychophysiology, 13*, 196–204.

Hopkins, D. R. (1987). AIDS in minority populations in the United States. *Public Health Reports, 102*, 620–681.

Horney, K. (1933). The denial of the vagina. *International Journal of Psychoanalysis, 14*, 57–70.

Houck, E. L., & Abramson, P. R. (1986). Masturbatory guilt and the psychological consequences of sexually transmitted diseases among women. *Journal of Research in Personality, 20*, 267–275.

Howard, J. W., & Dawes, R. M. (1976). Linear prediction of marital happiness. *Personality and Social Psychology Bulletin, 2*, 478–480.

Howard, M. (1984). Unpublished data. Atlanta, GA: Grady Memorial Hospital.

Howard, M., & McCabe, J. B. (1990). Helping teenagers postpone sexual involvement. *Family Planning Perspectives, 22*, 21–26.

Howard, M., Mitchell, M., & Pollard, B. (1990, Revised). *Postponing sexual involvement: An educational series for young teens.* Atlanta, GA: Grady Memorial Hospital.

Hoyenga, K. B., & Hoyenga, K. T. (1993a). *A manual to accompany Gender-related differences: Origins and outcomes.* Boston, MA: Allyn and Bacon.

Hoyenga, K. B., & Hoyenga, K. T. (1993b). *Gender-related differences: Origins and outcomes.* Boston, MA: Allyn and Bacon.

Hrabowy, I., & Allgeier, E. R. (1987, May). *Relationship of level of sexual invasiveness of child abuse to psychological functioning among adult women.* Paper presented at the Midwestern Psychological Association meeting, Chicago, IL.

Huff, P., & Bucci, K. (1990). Breast-feeding and the excretion of drugs in breast milk. In K. M. Andolsek (Ed.), *Obstetric care: Standards of prenatal peripartum and postpartum management* (pp. 222–236). Philadelphia, PA: Lea & Febiger.

Hulka, B. (1987). Replacement estrogens and risk of gynecologic cancer and breast cancer. *Cancer, 60*, 1960–1964.

Humphreys, L. (1975). *Tearoom trade: Impersonal sex in public places* (Rev. Ed.). Chicago, IL: Aldine.

Hunt, D. D., & Hampson, J. L. (1980). Transsexualism: A standardized psychosocial rating format for the evaluation of results of sex reassignment surgery. *Archives of Sexual Behavior, 9*, 255–263.

Hunt, M. (1974). *Sexual behavior in the 1970s.* Chicago, IL: Playboy Press.

Hupka, R. B. (1981). Cultural determinants of jealousy. *Alternative Lifestyles, 4*, 310–356.

Hurlbert, D. F., & Whittaker, K. E. (1991). The role of masturbation in marital and sexual satisfaction: A comparative study of female masturbators and non-masturbators. *Journal of Sex Education and Therapy, 17*, 272–282.

Hurtig, A. L., & Rosenthal, I. M. (1987). Psychological functioning in early treated cases of female pseudohermaphroditism caused by virilizing congenital adrenal hyperplasia. *Archives of Sexual Behavior, 16*, 209–222.

Imperato-McGinley, J., Guerrero, L., Gautier, T., & Peterson, R. (1974). Steroid 5 α reductase deficiency in man: An inherited form of male pseudohermaphroditism. *Science, 186*, 1213–1215.

Imperato-McGinley, J., Peterson, R. E., Gautier, T., Looper, G., Danner, R., Arthur, A., Morris, P. L., Sweeney, W. J., & Schackleton, C. (1982). Hormonal evaluation of a large kindred with complete androgen insensitivity: Evidence for secondary 5-alpha-reductase deficiency. *Journal of Clinical Endocrinology Metabolism, 54*, 15–22.

Inciardi, J. A. (1984). Little girls and sex: A glimpse at the world of the ''baby pro.'' *Deviant Behavior, 4*, 71–78.

Innala, S. M. & Ernulf, K. E. (1989). Asphyxiophilia in Scandinavia. *Archives of Sexual Behavior, 18*, 181–189.

Isis (1976, October). *Excision in Africa*, 12–15.

Jaccard, J., Hand, D., Ku, L., Richardson, K., & Abella, R. (1981). Attitudes toward male oral contraceptives: Implications for models of the relationship between beliefs and attitudes. *Journal of Applied Social Psychology, 11*, 181–191.

Jacklin, C. N., DiPietro, J. A., & Maccoby, E. E. (1984). Sex-typing behavior and sex-typing pressure in child-parent interaction. *Archives of Sexual Behavior, 13*, 413–425.

Jacobs, P. A., Brunton, M., Melville, M. M., Britain, R. P., & McClemont, W. F. (1965). Aggressive behavior, mental subnormality, and the XYY male. *Nature, 208*, 1351–1352.

James, W. H. (1981). The honeymoon effect on marital coitus. *The Journal of Sex Research, 17*, 114–123.

Jamison, P. L., & Gebhard, P. H. (1988). Penis size increase between flaccid and erect states: An analysis of the Kinsey data. *The Journal of Sex Research, 24*, 177–183.

Janus, S. S., & Janus, C. L. (1993). *The Janus report on sexual behavior.* New York: John Wiley.

Jarvik, M. E., & Beecher, E. M. (1977). Drugs and sex: Inhibition and enhancement effects. In J. Money & H. Musaph (Eds.), *Handbook of sexology* (pp. 1095–1106). Amsterdam, Holland: Elsevier/North Holland Biomedical Press.

Jay, K., & Young, A. (1979). *The gay report.* New York: Summit Books.

Jemail, J. A., & Geer, J. H. (1977). Sexual scripts. In R. Gemme & C. Wheeler (Eds.), *Progress in sexology* (pp. 513–522). New York: Plenum.

Jenks, R. J. (1985). Swinging: A replication and test of a theory. *The Journal of Sex Research, 21,* 199–205.

Jensen, P., Jensen, S. B., Sørensen, P. S., Bjerre, B. D., Rizzi, D. A., Sørensen, A. S., Klysner, R., Brinch, K., Jespersen, B., & Neilsen, H. (1990). Sexual dysfunction in male and female patients with epilepsy: A study of 86 outpatients. *Archives of Sexual Behavior, 19,* 1–14.

Johnson, J. H. (1989). Weighing the evidence on the pill and breast cancer. *Family Planning Perspectives, 21,* 89–92.

Jones, E. F., Forrest, J. D., Goldman, N., Henshaw, S., Lincoln, R., Rosoff, J. I., Westoff, C. F., & Wulf, D. (1986). *Teenage pregnancy in industrialized countries.* New Haven, CT: Yale University Press.

Jones, E. F., Forrest, J. D., Silverman, J., & Torres, A. (1988). Unintended pregnancy, contraceptive practice, and family planning services in developed countries. *Family Planning Perspectives, 20* (2), 53–55, 58–67.

Jones, J. H. (1981). *Bad blood: The Tuskegee syphilis experiment.* New York: Free Press.

Jones, J. R. (1974). Plasma testosterone concentrations in female transsexuals. In D. R. Laub & P. Gandy (Eds.), *Proceedings of the Second Interdisciplinary Symposium on the Gender Dysphoria Syndrome.* Ann Arbor, MI: Edward Brothers.

Jones, W. H., Chernovetz, M. E., & Hansson, R. O. (1978). The enigma of androgyny: Differential implications for males and females? *Journal of Consulting and Clinical Psychology, 46,* 298–313.

Jorgensen, C. (1967). *Christine Jorgensen: Personal biography.* New York: Ericksson.

Joseph, J. G., Montgomery, S. B., Emmons, C. et al. (1987). Magnitude and determinants of behavioral risk reduction: Longitudinal analysis of a cohort at risk for AIDS. *Psychology and Health, 1* (1), 73–95.

Judson, F. N. (1983). Fear of AIDS and gonorrhea rates in homosexual men. *Lancet, 2,* 159–160.

Judson, F. N., Eron, L. J., Lutz, B., Rand, K. H., Tennican, P. O., & Magabgab, N. J. (1991). Multicenter study of a single 500-mg. dose of cefotaxime for treatment of uncomplicated gonorrhea. *Sexually Transmitted Diseases, 18,* 41–43.

Jung, C. G. (1946). *Psychological types.* New York: Harcourt Brace.

Jung, C. G. (1959). The archetypes and the collective unconscious. In H. Read, M. Fordham, & G. Adler (Eds.), *The collected works of C. G. Jung,* Vol. 9. New York: Pantheon.

Juran, S. (1989). Sexual behavior changes as a result of a concern about AIDS: Gays, straights, females and males. *Journal of Psychology and Human Sexuality, 2,* 61–77.

Kallmann, F. J. A. (1952). A comparative twin study on the genetic aspects of male homosexuality. *Journal of Nervous and Mental Disease, 115,* 283–298.

Kagan, J., & Snidman, N. (1991). Temperamental factors in human development. *American Psychologist, 46,* 856–872.

Kalichman, S. C. (1991). Psychopathology and personality characteristics of criminal sexual offenders as a function of victim age. *Archives of Sexual Behavior, 20,* 187–197.

Kanin, E. J. (1969). Selected dyadic aspects of male sex aggression. *The Journal of Sex Research, 5,* 12–28.

Kanin, E. J. (1985). Date rapists: Differential sexual socialization and relative deprivation. *Archives of Sexual Behavior, 14,* 219–231.

Kanin, E. J. (1994). False rape allegations. *Archives of Sexual Behavior, 23,* 81–92.

Kanin, E. J., & Parcell, S. R. (1977). Sexual aggression: A second look at the offended female. *Archives of Sexual Behavior, 6,* 67–76.

Kansky, J. (1986). Sexuality of widows: A study of the sexual practices of widows during the first fourteen months of bereavement. *Journal of Sex and Marital Therapy, 12,* 307–321.

Kantner, J. F., & Zelnik, M. (1972). Sexual experience of young unmarried women in the United States. *Family Planning Perspectives, 4,* 9–18.

Kaplan, E. H. (1988). Crisis? A brief critique of Masters, Johnson, and Kolodny. *The Journal of Sex Research, 25,* 317–322.

Kaplan, H. S. (1974). *The new sex therapy.* New York: Bruner/Mazel.

Kaplan, H. S. (1979). *Disorders of sexual desire.* New York: Bruner/Mazel.

Karlen, A. (1971). *Sexuality and homosexuality.* New York: Norton.

Karlen, A. (1994). Aging and sexuality. In V. L. Bullough & B. Bullough (Eds.), *Human sexuality: An encyclopedia* (pp. 12–15). New York: Garland Publishing.

Karpman, B. (1954). *The sexual offender and his offenses.* New York: Julian Press.

Katz, R. I. (1985). Neurologic disease and sexual dysfunction. In M. Farber (Ed.), *Human sexuality: Psychosocial effects of disease* (pp. 264–273). New York: Macmillan.

Kegel, A. M. (1952). Sexual functions of the pubococcygeus muscle. *Western Journal of Surgery, Obstetrics, and Gynecology, 60,* 521–524.

Kegeles, S. M., Adler, N. E., & Irwin, C. E. (1988). Sexually active adolescents and condoms: Changes over the year in knowledge, attitudes and use. *American Journal of Public Health, 78,* 460–461.

Kehoe, M. (1986). Lesbians over 65: A tripling invisible minority. *Journal of Homosexuality, 12,* 139–152.

Kelley, K., & Musialowski, D. (1986). Repeated exposure to sexually explicit stimuli: Novelty, sex, and sexual attitudes. *Archives of Sexual Behavior, 15,* 487–498.

Kelley, K., Smeaton, G., Byrne, D., Przybyla, D. P. J., & Fisher, W. A. (1987). Predicting sexual attitudes and contraception across five college samples. *Human Relations, 40,* 237–254.

Kelly, J. (1980). Homosexuality and aging. In J. L. Marmor (Ed.), *Homosexual behavior* (pp. 176–193). New York: Basic Books.

Kelly, M. P., Strassberg, D. S., & Kircher, J. R. (1990). Attitudinal and experiential correlates of anorgasmia. *Archives of Sexual Behavior, 19,* 165–177.

Kennedy, S., & Over, R. (1990). Psychophysiological assessment of male sexual arousal following spinal cord injury. *Archives of Sexual Behavior, 19,* 15–27.

Kenney, A. M., Guardado, S., & Brown, L. (1989). Sex education and AIDS education in the schools: What states and large school districts are doing. *Family Planning Perspectives, 21,* 56–64.

Kenrick, D. T., & Keefe, D. C. (1992). Age preference in mates reflect sex differences in human reproductive strategies. *Behavioral and Brain Sciences, 15,* 75–133.

Kephart, W. M. (1967). Some correlates of romantic love. *Journal of Marriage and the Family, 29,* 470–474.

Kilpatrick, A. C. (1986). Some correlates of women's childhood sexual experiences: A retrospective study. *The Journal of Sex Research, 22,* 221–242.

Kilpatrick, A. C. (1992). *Long-range effects of childhood and adolescent sexual experiences: Myths, mores, and menaces.* Hillsdale, NJ: Lawrence Erlbaum Associates.

Kilpatrick, D. G., Best, C. L., Saunders, B. E., & Veronen, L. J. (1988). Rape in marriage and in dating relationships: How bad is it for mental health? In R. A. Prentky & V. L. Quinsey (Eds.), *Human sexual aggression: Current perspectives* (pp. 335–344). New York: New York Academy of Sciences.

Kimmel, D. (1978). Adult development and aging: A gay perspective. *Journal of Social Issues, 34* (3), 113–130.

King, A. J. C., Beazley, R. P., Warren, W. K., Hankins, C A., Robertson, A. S., & Radford, J. L. (1988). *Canada youth & AIDS study.* Ottawa, Canada: Federal Centre for AIDS Health Protection Branch, Health and Welfare Canada.

Kinsey, A. C., Pomeroy, W., & Martin, C. (1948). *Sexual behavior in the human male.* Philadelphia, PA: Saunders.

Kinsey, A. C., Pomeroy, W., Martin, C., & Gebhard, P. (1953). *Sexual behavior in the human female.* Philadelphia, PA: Saunders.

Kirby, D. (1985). The effects of selected sexuality education programs: Toward a more realistic goal. *Journal of Sex Education and Therapy, 11,* 28–37.

Kirby, D., Barth, R. P., Leland, N., & Fetro, J. V. (1991). Reducing the risk: Impact of a new curriculum on sexual risk-taking. *Family Planning Perspectives, 23,* 253–263.

Kirkpatrick, C., & Kanin, E. (1957). Male sex aggression on a university campus. *American Sociological Review, 22,* 52–58.

Kitson, G. C., & Morgan, L. A. (1991). The multiple consequences of divorce. In A. Booth (Ed.), *Contemporary families: Looking forward, looking backward* (pp. 150–161). Minneapolis, MN: National Council on Family Relations.

Klassen, A. D., & Wilsnack, S. C. (1986). Sexual experience and drinking among women in a U.S. national survey. *Archives of Sexual Behavior, 15,* 363–392.

Klein, F. (1993). *The bisexual option* (2nd Ed.). Binghamton, NY: Haworth Press.

Klinger-Vartabedian, L., & Wispe, L. (1989). Age differences in marriage and female longevity. *Journal of Marriage and the Family, 51,* 195–202.

Klitsch, M. (1988). FDA approval ends cervical cap's marathon. *Family Planning Perspectives, 20,* 137–138.

Klitsch, M. (1993). Vasectomy and prostate cancer: More questions than answers. *Family Planning Perspectives, 25,* 133–135.

Knightly, P., Evans, H., Potter, E., & Wallace, M. (1979). *Suffer the children.* New York: Viking.

Knodel, J., & Kintner, H. (1977). The impact of breast-feeding patterns on the biometric analysis of infant mortality. *Demography, 14,* 391–409.

Knoth, R., Boyd, K., & Singer, B. (1988). Empirical tests of sexual selection theory: Prediction of onset, intensity, and time course of sexual arousal. *The Journal of Sex Research, 24,* 73–89.

Kockott, G., & Fahrner, E. M. (1988). Male-to-female and female-to-male transsexuals: A comparison. *Archives of Sexual Behavior, 17,* 539–546.

Kolodny, R. C. (1981). Evaluating sex therapy: Process and outcome at the Masters and Johnson Institute. *The Journal of Sex Research, 17,* 301–318.

Kolodny, R. C., Masters, W. H., Kolodny, R. M., & Toro, G. (1974). Depression of plasma testosterone levels after chronic intensive marijuana use. *New England Journal of Medicine, 290,* 872–874.

Koonin, L. M., Smith, J. C., Ramick, M., & Lawson, H. (1992). Abortion surveillance—United States. *Morbidity and Mortality Weekly Report, 41,* Special Supplement 5.

Koop, C. E. (1987). *Surgeon General's report on Acquired*

*Immune Deficiency Syndrome.* Washington, D.C.: U.S. Dept. of Health and Human Services, Public Health Services.

Koralewski, M. K., & Conger, J. C. (1992). The assessment of social skills among sexually coercive college males. *The Journal of Sex Research, 29,* 169–188.

Koss, M. P. (1985). The hidden rape victim: Personality, attitudinal, and situational characteristics. *Psychology of Women Quarterly, 9,* 193–212.

Koss, M. P. (1987). Hidden rape: Incidence, prevalence, and descriptive characteristics of sexual aggression and victimization in a national sample of college students. In A. W. Burgess (Ed.), *Sexual assault,* Vol. 3. New York: Garland Publishing.

Koss, M. P. (1992). The underdetection of rape: Methodological choices influence incidence estimates. *Journal of Social Issues, 48* (1), 61–76.

Koss, M. P., & Dinero, T. E. (1988). Predictors of sexual aggression among a national sample of male college students. In R. A. Prentky & V. L. Quinsey (Eds.), *Human sexual aggression: Current perspectives* (pp. 133–147). New York: Annals of the New York Academy of Sciences.

Koss, M. P., & Dinero, T. E. (1989). Discriminant analysis of risk factors for sexual victimization among a national sample of college women. *Journal of Consulting and Clinical Psychology, 57,* 242–250.

Koss, M. P., Dinero, T. E., Seibel, C. A. & Cox, S. L. (1988). Stranger and acquaintance rape: Are there differences in the victim's experience? *Psychology of Women Quarterly, 12,* 1–24.

Koutsky, L. A., Holmes, K. K., Critchlow, C. W., Stevens, C. E., Paavonen, J., Beckman, A. M., DeRouen, T. A., Galloway, D. A., Vernon, D., & Kiviat, N. B. (1992). A cohort study of the risk of cervical intra-epithelial neoplasia grade 2 or 3 in relation to papilloma virus infection. *New England Journal of Medicine, 327,* 1272–1278.

Krall, V., Feinstein, S., & Kennedy, D. (1980). Birth weight and measures of development, object constancy, and attachment in multiple birth infants: A brief report. *The International Journal of Behavioral Development, 3,* 501–505.

Kraemer, G. N. (1992). A psychobiological theory of attachment. *Behavioral and Brain Sciences, 15,* 493–541.

Krane, R. J. (1986). Surgical implants for impotence: Indications and procedures. In R. J. Santen & K. S. Swerdloff (Eds.), *Male reproductive dysfunction* (pp. 563–576). New York: Marcel Dekker.

Kreiss, J. K., Koech, D., Plummer, F. A. et al. (1986). AIDS virus infection in Nairobi prostitutes: Spread of the epidemic to East Africa. *New England Journal of Medicine, 314,* 414–418.

Krivacska, J. J. (1990). Child sexual abuse and its prevention. In M. E. Perry (Ed.), *Handbook of sexology: Childhood and adolescent sexology,* Vol. 7 (pp. 395–426). Amsterdam, Holland: Elsevier Science Publishers.

Krivacska, J. J. (1992). Child sexual abuse prevention programs: The need for childhood sexuality education. *SIECUS Reports, 19,* 1–7.

Kurdek, L. A. (1988). Correlates of negative attitudes toward homosexuals in heterosexual college students. *Sex Roles, 18,* 727–738.

Kurdek, L. A. (1993). Predicting marital dissolution: A 5-year prospective longitudinal study of newlywed couples. *Journal of Personality and Social Psychology, 64,* 221–242.

Kurdek, L. A., & Schmitt, J. P. (1985/1986). Relationship quality of gay men in closed or open relationships. *Journal of Homosexuality, 12,* 85–99.

Kurdek, L. A., & Schmitt, J. P. (1987). Partner homogamy in married, heterosexual cohabiting, gay, and lesbian couples. *The Journal of Sex Research, 23,* 212–232.

Kurstin, C., & Oskamp, S. (1979, September). *Contraceptive behavior after abortion.* Paper presented at the American Psychological Association convention, New York.

Ladas, A. K., Whipple, B., & Perry, J. D. (1982). *The G spot and other recent discoveries about human sexuality.* New York: Holt, Rinehart & Winston.

Lamont, J. (1977). Vaginismus. In R. Gemme & C. Wheeler (Eds.), *Progress in sexology* (pp. 185–195). New York: Plenum.

Landy, E., Bertrand, J. T., Cherry, F., & Rice, J. (1986). Teen pregnancy in New Orleans: Factors that differentiate teens who deliver, abort, and successfully contracept. *Journal of Youth and Adolescence, 15,* 259–274.

Lang, A. R. (1985). The social psychology of drinking and human sexuality. *Journal of Drug Issues, 15,* 273–289.

Langevin, R., Paitich, D. P., Ramsay, G., Anderson, C., Kamrad, J., Pope, S., Geller, G., Pearl, L., & Newman, S. (1979). Experimental studies of the etiology of genital exhibitionism. *Archives of Sexual Behavior, 8,* 307–331.

Langevin, R., Paitich, D. P., & Russon, A. E. (1985). Voyeurism: Does it predict sexual aggression or violence in general? In R. Langevin (Ed.), *Erotic preference, gender identity, and aggression in men* (pp. 77–98). Hillsdale, NJ: Lawrence Erlbaum Associates.

Langevin, R., Paitich, D. P., & Steiner, B. W. (1977). The clinical profile of male transsexuals living as females vs. those living as males. *Archives of Sexual Behavior, 6,* 143–154.

Langlois, J. H., & Casey, R. J. (1984, April). *Baby beautiful: The relationship between infant physical attractive-*

*ness and maternal behavior.* Paper presented at the 4th biennial International Conference on Infant Studies, New York.

Langlois, J. H., & Roggman, L. A. (1990). Attractive faces are only average. *Psychological Science, 1*, 115–121.

Langlois, J. H., Roggman, L. A., Casey, R. J. et al. (1987). Infant preferences for attractive faces: Rudiments of a stereotype? *Developmental Psychology, 23*, 363–369.

Laumann, E. O., Gagnon, J. H., & Michael, R. T. (1993, November). A sociological perspective on sexual action. Plenary Address presented at the Annual Meeting of The Society for the Scientific Study of Sex, Chicago, IL.

Laughlin, C. D., Jr., & Allgeier, E. R. (1979). *Ethnography of the So of northeastern Uganda.* New Haven, CT: Human Relations Area Files, Inc.

Lawrence, D. H. (1930). *Lady Chatterley's lover.* New York: W. Faro.

Laws, D. R., & Marshall, W. L. (1991). Masturbatory reconditioning with sexual deviates: An evaluative review. *Advances in Behavior, Research, and Therapy, 13*, 13–25.

Lawson, A. (1988). *Adultery: An analysis of love and betrayal.* New York: Basic Books.

Lazarus, A. A. (1989). Dyspareunia: A multimodel psychotherapeutic perspective. In S. R. Leiblum & R. C. Rosen (Eds.), *Principles and practices of sex therapy* (2nd Ed.) (pp. 89–112). New York: Guilford Press.

Lee, H. (1989). Genital chlamydial infection in female and male college students. *Journal of American College Health, 37*, 288–291.

Lee, N. C. (1987). Combination oral contraceptive use and the risk of endometrial cancer. *Journal of the American Medical Association, 257*, 796–800.

Lees, R. B. (1975, March). *Men and abortion: Anxiety and social supports.* Paper presented at the conference on New Research on Women and Sex Roles, Ann Arbor, MI.

Legros, J. J., Mormont, C., & Servais, J. (1978). A psycho-neuroendocrinological study of erectile psychogenic impotence: A comparison between normal patients and patients with abnormal reactions to glucose tolerance test. In L. Corenza, P. Pancheri, & L. Zichella (Eds.), *Clinical psychoneuroendocrinology in reproduction* (pp. 301–319). New York: Academic Press.

Leiblum, S. R. (1993). The impact of fertility on sexual and marital satisfaction. In J. Bancroft, C. M. Davis, & H. J. Ruppel, Jr., (Eds.), *Annual Review of Sex Research* Vol. IV (pp. 99–120). Mt. Vernon, IA: The Society for the Scientific Study of Sex.

Leiblum, S. R., Pervin, L. A., & Campbell, E. H. (1989). The treatment of vaginismus: Success and failure. In S. R. Leiblum & R. C. Rosen (Eds.), *Principles and*

*practice of sex therapy* (2nd Ed.) (pp. 113–138). New York: Guilford Press.

Leiblum, S. R., & Rosen, R. C. (1988). Introduction: Changing perspectives on sexual desire. In S. R. Leiblum & R. C. Rosen (Eds.), *Sexual desire disorders* (pp. 1–16). New York: Guilford Press.

Leiblum, S. R., & Rosen, R. C. (1989). Introduction: Sex therapy in the age of AIDS. In S. R. Leiblum & R. C. Rosen (Eds.), *Principles and practice of sex therapy* (2nd Ed.) (pp. 1–16). New York: Guilford Press.

Leigh, B. C. (1989). Reasons for having and avoiding sex: Gender, sexual orientation, and relationship to sexual behavior. *The Journal of Sex Research, 26*, 199–209.

Leigh, B. C., Temple, M. T., & Trocki, K. F. (1993). The sexual behavior of U.S. adults: Results from a national survey. *American Journal of Public Health, 83*, 1400–1408.

Leitenberg, H., Detzer, M. J., & Srebnik, D. (1993). Gender differences in masturbation and the relationship of masturbation experience in preadolescence and/or early adolescence in sexual behavior and sexual adjustment in young adulthood. *Archives of Sexual Behavior, 22*, 87–98.

Leitenberg, H., Greenwald, E., & Tarran, M. (1989). The relationship between sexual activity among children during preadolescence and/or early adolescence and sexual behavior and sexual adjustment in young adulthood. *Archives of Sexual Behavior, 18*, 299–313.

Lemp, G. F., Payne, S. F., Neal, D., Temelso, T., & Rutherford, G. W. (1990). Survival trends for patients with AIDS. *Journal of the American Medical Association, 263*, 402–406.

Leon, G. R., Lucas, A. R., Ferdinand, R. F., Mangelsdorf, C., & Colligan, R. C. (1987). Attitudes about sexuality and other psychological characteristics as predictors of follow-up status in anorexia nervosa. *International Journal of Eating Disorders, 6*, 477–484.

Lerner, R. M., & Lerner, J. (1977). Effects of age, sex, and physical attractiveness on child-peer relations, academic performance, and elementary school adjustment. *Developmental Psychology, 13*, 585–590.

Letourneau, E., & O'Donohue, W. (1993). Sexual desire disorders. In W. O'Donohue & J. H. Geer (Eds.), *Handbook of sexual dysfunctions: Assessment and treatment* (pp. 53–81). Boston, MA: Allyn and Bacon.

LeVay, S. (1991). A difference in hypothalmic structure between heterosexual and homosexual men. *Science, 253*, 1034–1037.

LeVay, S. (1993). *The sexual brain.* Cambridge, MA: The MIT Press.

Lever, J., Kanouse, D. E., Rogers, W. H., Carson, S., & Hertz, R. (1992). Behavior patterns and sexual identity of gay males. *The Journal of Sex Research, 29,* 141–167.

Levin, R. J. (1992). The mechanisms of human female sexual arousal. In J. Bancroft, C. M. Davis, & H. J. Ruppel, Jr. (Eds.), *Annual Review of Sex Research,* Vol. 3. Lake Mills, IA: The Society for the Scientific Study of Sex.

Levin, M. P., & Troiden, R. R. (1988). The myth of sexual compulsivity. *The Journal of Sex Research, 25,* 347–363.

Levin, S. M., & Stava, L. (1987). Personality characteristics of sex offenders: A review. *Archives of Sexual Behavior, 16,* 57–79.

Levinson, R. A. (1986). Contraceptive self-efficacy: A perspective on teenage girls' contraceptive behavior. *The Journal of Sex Research, 22,* 347–369.

Levit, S. (1986, January/February). Caro Professors Aphrodisiaco. *Science, 86,* 80–81.

Levitan, M. (1988). *Textbook of human genetics.* New York: Oxford University Press.

Lev-Ran, A. (1977). Sex reversal as related to clinical syndromes in human beings. In J. Money & H. Musaph (Eds.), *Handbook of sexology,* Vol. 2. New York: Elsevier/North Holland.

Lewes, K. (1988). *The psychoanalytic theory of male homosexuality.* New York: Simon & Schuster.

Lewis, R. J., & Janda, L. H. (1988). The relationship between adult sexual adjustment and childhood experiences regarding nudity, sleeping in parental bed, and parental attitudes toward sexuality. *Archives of Sexual Behavior, 17,* 349–362.

Liebowitz, M. R. (1983). *The chemistry of love.* Boston, MA: Little, Brown.

Lief, H. I., & Hubschman, L. (1993). Orgasm in the postoperative transsexual. *Archives of Sexual Behavior, 22,* 145–155.

Lifson, A. R. (1988). Do alternate modes for transmission of human immunodeficiency virus exist? *Journal of the American Medical Association, 259,* 1353–1356.

Lifson, A. R., Darrow, W. W., Hessol, N. A., O'Malley, P. M., Barnhart, J. L., Jaffer, H. W., & Rutherford, G. W. (1990). Kaposi's Sarcoma in a cohort of homosexual and bisexual men. *American Journal of Epidemiology, 131,* 221–231.

Lightfoot-Klein, H. (1989). The sexual experience and marital adjustment of genitally circumcized and infibulated females in the Sudan. *The Journal of Sex Research, 26,* 375–392.

Lindemann, C. (1975). *Birth control and unmarried young women.* New York: Springer.

Linz, D. (1989). Exposure to sexually explicit materials and attitudes toward rape: A comparison of study results. *The Journal of Sex Research, 26,* 50–84.

Lish, J. D., Meyer-Bahlburg, H. F. L., Ehrhardt, A. A.,

Travis, B. G., & Veridian, N. P. (1992). Prenatal exposure to diethylstilbestrol (DES): Childhood play behavior and adult gender-role behavior in women. *Archives of Sexual Behavior, 21,* 423–441.

Long, G. T., & Sultan, F. E. (1987). Contributions from social psychology. In L. Diamant (Ed.), *Male and female homosexuality: Psychological approaches* (pp. 221–236). Washington, D. C.: Hemisphere.

LoPiccolo, J., & Friedman, J. M. (1988). Broad spectrum treatment of low sexual desire: Integration of cognitive, behavioral, and systemic therapy. In S. R. Leiblum & R. C. Rosen (Eds.), *Sexual desire disorders* (pp. 107–144). New York: Guilford Press.

LoPiccolo, J., Heiman, J. R., Hogan, D. R., & Roberts, C. W. (1985). Effectiveness of single therapists versus cotherapy teams in sex therapy. *Journal of Consulting and Clinical Psychology, 53,* 287–294.

LoPiccolo, J., & Lobitz, C. (1972). The role of masturbation in the treatment of orgasmic dysfunction. *Archives of Sexual Behavior, 2,* 163–171.

LoPiccolo, J., & Stock, W. E. (1986). Treatment of sexual dysfunction. *Journal of Consulting and Clinical Psychology, 54,* 158–167.

Lothstein, L. M. (1979). The aging gender dysphoria (transsexual) patient. *Archives of Sexual Behavior, 8,* 431–444.

Lottes, I. L. (1993). Nontraditional gender roles and the sexual experience of heterosexual college students. *Sex Roles, 29,* 645–669.

Loy, P. H., & Stewart, L. P. (1984). The extent and effects of the sexual harassment of working women. *Sociological Focus, 17,* 31–43.

Lucero, E., & Clark, T. (1988). *The Success express curriculum.* Unpublished manuscript. Maricopa County YWCA, Phoenix, AZ.

Luckenbill, D. F. (1985). Entering male prostitution. *Urban Life, 14,* 131–153.

Luepker, R. V., Johnson, C. A., Murray, D. M., & Pechacek, T. F. (1983). *Journal of Behavioral Medicine, 6,* 53–62.

Lukusa, T., Fryns, J. P., & Van Den Berghe, T. (1992). The role of the Y-chromosome in sex determination. *Genetic Counseling, 3,* 1–11.

Lunde, I., Larsen, K. L., Fog, E., & Garde, K. (1991). Sexual desire, orgasm, and fantasies: A study of 625 Danish women born in 1910, 1936, and 1958. *Journal of Sex Education and Therapy, 17,* 111–115.

Luria, Z., & Meade, R. G. (1984). Sexuality and the middle-aged woman. In G. Baruch & J. Brooks-Gunn (Eds.), *Women in midlife* (pp. 391–397). New York: Plenum.

Lykken, D., McGue, A., Tellegen, A., & Bouchard, T. A., Jr. (1992). Emergenesis: Genetic traits that may not run in families. *American Psychologist, 47,* 1565–1577.

Lyon, M. F. (1962). Sex chromatin and gene action in the mammalian X-chromosome. *American Journal of Human Genetics, 14,* 135–148.

MacDonald, J. M. (1973). *Indecent exposure.* Springfield, IL: Charles C Thomas.

MacLusky, N. J., & Naftolin, F. (1981). Sexual differentiation of the central nervous system. *Science, 211,* 1294–1303.

Maden, M., & Wrench, D. (1977). Significant findings in child abuse research. *Victimology, 2,* 196–224.

Magoun, H. W. (1981). John B. Watson and the study of human sexual behavior. *The Journal of Sex Research, 17,* 368–378.

Maguire, K., Pastore, A. L., & Flanagan, T. J. (1992). *Sourcebook of criminal justice statistics—1992.* Washington, D.C.: U.S. Government Printing Office.

Mahoney, E. R., Shively, M. D., & Traw, M. (1986). Sexual coercion and assault: Male socialization and female risk. *Sexual Coercion and Assault, 1,* 2–8.

Major, B. (1993). Gender, entitlement, and the distribution of family labor. *Journal of Social Issues, 49* (3), 141–159.

Major, B., & Cozzarelli, C. (1992). Psychosocial predictors of adjustment to abortion. *Journal of Social Issues, 48* (3), 121–142.

Malamuth, N. M. (1981). Rape proclivity among males. *Journal of Social Issues, 37* (4), 138–157.

Malamuth, N. M. (1984). Aggression against women: Cultural and individual causes. In N. M. Malamuth & E. Donnerstein (Eds.), *Pornography and sexual aggression* (pp. 19–52). Orlando, FL: Academic Press.

Malamuth, N. M. (1986). Predictors of naturalistic sexual aggression. *Journal of Personality and Social Psychology, 50,* 953–962.

Malamuth, N. M., & Check, J. V. P. (1983). Sexual arousal to rape depictions: Individual differences. *Journal of Abnormal Psychology, 92,* 55–67.

Malamuth, N. M., & Check, J. V. P. (1984). Debriefing effectiveness following exposure to pornographic rape depictions. *The Journal of Sex Research, 20,* 1–13.

Malamuth, N. M., & Donnerstein, E. (1984). *Pornography and sexual aggression.* Orlando, FL: Academic Press.

Malatesta, V. J., Pollack, R. H., Wilbanks, W. A., & Adams, H. E. (1979). Alcohol effects on the orgasmic-ejaculatory response of human males. *The Journal of Sex Research, 15,* 101–107.

Mann, J. (1977). Retarded ejaculation and treatment. In R. Gemme & C. Wheeler (Eds.), *Progress in sexology* (pp. 197–204). New York: Plenum.

Mansfield, P. K., Hood, K. E., & Henderson, J. (1989). Women and their husbands: Mood and arousal fluctuations across the menstrual cycle and day of the week. *Psychosomatic Medicine, 51,* 66–80.

Marieskind, H. I. (1989). Cesarean section in the United States: Has it changed since 1979? *Birth, 16,* 196–202.

Markman, H. J., & Hahlweg, K. (1993). The prediction and prevention of marital distress. *Clinical Psychology Review, 13,* 29–43.

Marmor, J. L. (1954). Some considerations concerning orgasm in the female. *Psychosomatic Medicine, 16,* 240–245.

Marsh, J. C. (1988). What have we learned about legislative remedies for rape? In R. A. Prentky & V. L. Quinsey (Eds.), *Human sexual aggression: Current perspectives* (pp. 388–399). New York: New York Academy of Sciences.

Marshall, D. (1971). Sexual behavior on Mangaia. In D. Marshall & R. Suggs (Eds.), *Human sexual behavior: Variations in the ethnographic spectrum* (pp. 103–162). Englewood Cliffs, NJ: Prentice-Hall.

Marshall, W. L., Eccles, A., & Barbaree, H. E. (1991). The treatment of exhibitionists: A focus on sexual deviance versus cognitive and relationship features. *Behavior Research and Therapy, 29,* 129–135.

Marsiglio, W. (1987). Adolescent fathers in the United States: Their initial living arrangements, marital experience and educational outcomes. *Family Planning Perspectives, 19,* 240–251.

Marsiglio, W., & Menaghan, E. G. (1987). Couples and the male birth control pill: A future alternative in contraceptive selection. *The Journal of Sex Research, 23,* 34–49.

Marsiglio, W., & Mott, F. L. (1986). The impact of sex education on sexual activity, contraceptive use, and premarital pregnancy among American teenagers. *Family Planning Perspectives, 18,* 151–162.

Marsiglio, W., & Shehan, C. L. (1993). Adolescent males' abortion attitudes: Data from a national survey. *Family Planning Perspectives, 25,* 162–169.

Martin, T. C., & Bumpass, L. L. (1989). Recent trends in marital disruption. *Demography, 26,* 37–51.

Martinson, F. M. (1973). *Infant and child sexuality: A sociological perspective.* St. Peter, MN: The Book Mark, GAC.

Martinson, F. M. (1981). Eroticism in infancy and childhood. In L. L. Constantine & F. M. Martinson (Eds.), *Children and sex: New findings, new perspectives* (pp. 23–35). Boston, MA: Little, Brown.

Marx, J. L. (1989a). Grass-roots drug testing. *Science, 244,* 917.

Marx, J. L. (1989b). AIDS drugs—Coming but not here. *Science, 244,* 287.

Maslow, A. H. (1962). *Toward a psychology of being.* Princeton, NJ: Van Nostrand.

Masters, W. H., & Johnson, V. E. (1966). *Human sexual response.* Boston, MA: Little, Brown.

Masters, W. H., & Johnson, V. E. (1970). *Human sexual inadequacy.* Boston, MA: Little, Brown.

Masters, W. H., & Johnson, V. E. (1979). *Homosexuality in perspective.* Boston, MA: Little, Brown.

Masters, W. H., Johnson, V. E., & Kolodny, R. (1988). *CRISIS: Heterosexual behavior in the age of AIDS.* New York: Grove Press.

Mattson, S., & Smith, J. E. (1993). *Core curriculum for maternal-newborn nursing.* Philadelphia, PA: Saunders.

May, R. (1969). *Love and will.* New York: Norton.

Mays, V. M. & Cochran, S. D. (1988). Issues in the perception of AIDS risk and risk reduction activities by Black and Hispanic/Latino women. *American Psychologist, 43,* 949–957.

Mazur, A. (1986). U. S. trends in feminine beauty, and overadaptation. *The Journal of Sex Research, 22,* 281–303.

McCabe, M. P., & Delaney, S. M. (1992). An evaluation of therapeutic programs for the treatment of secondary inorgasmia in women. *Archives of Sexual Behavior, 21,* 69–89.

McCahill, T. W., Meyer, L. C., & Fischman, A. M. (1979). *The aftermath of rape.* Lexington, MA: Lexington Books.

McCarthy, B. W. (1993). Relapse prevention strategies and techniques in sex therapy. *Journal of Sex and Marital Therapy, 19,* 142–146.

McCarthy, J., & McMillan, S. (1990). Patient/partner satisfaction with penile implant surgery. *Journal of Sex Education and Therapy, 16,* 25–37.

McCauley, E. A., & Ehrhardt, A. A. (1976). Female sexual response: Hormonal and behavioral interactions. *Primary Care, 3,* 455–476.

McCauley, E. A., & Ehrhardt, A. A. (1977). Role expectations and definitions: A comparison of female transsexuals and lesbians. *Journal of Homosexuality, 3,* 137–147.

McCauley, E. A., & Ehrhardt, A. A. (1980). Sexual behavior in female transsexuals and lesbians. *The Journal of Sex Research, 16,* 202–211.

McClintock, M. K. (1971). Menstrual synchrony and suppression. *Nature, 299,* 244–245.

McClure, R. D. (1988). Male reproductive microsurgery. In E. A. Tanagho, T. F. Lue, & R. D. McClure (Eds.), *Contemporary management of impotence and infertility* (pp. 323–334). Baltimore, MD: William Wilkins.

McCormack, W. M. (1994). Pelvic inflammatory disease. *New England Journal of Medicine, 333* (2), 115–119.

McCormick, N. B. (1979). Come-ons and put-offs: Unmarried students' strategies for having and avoiding sexual intercourse. *Psychology of Women Quarterly, 4,* 194–211.

McCormick, N. B. (1994). *Sexual salvation.* Westport, CT: Greenwood.

McCormick, N. B., Izzo, A., & Folcik, J. (1985). Adolescents, values, sexuality, and contraception in a rural New York county. *Adolescence, 10,* 385–395.

McCormick, N. B., & Jones, A. J. (1989). Gender differences in nonverbal flirtation. *Journal of Sex Education and Therapy, 15,* 271–282.

McDonald, K., & Parke, R. D. (1986). Parent-child physical play: The effects of sex and age of children and parents. *Sex Roles, 15,* 367–378.

McKusick, V. A. (1992). *Mendelian inheritance in man: Catalogs of autosomal dominant, autosomal recessive, and X-linked phenotypes* (10th Ed.). Baltimore, MD: Johns Hopkins University Press.

McKusick, V. A., & Amberger, J. A. (1993). The morbid anatomy of the human genome: Chromosomal location of the mutations causing disease. *Journal of Medical Genetics, 30,* 1–26.

McLaren, A. (1981). ''Barrenness against nature'': Recourse to abortion in preindustrial England. *The Journal of Sex Research, 17,* 224–237.

McWhirter, D. P, & Mattison, A. M. (1984). *The male couple: How relationships develop.* Englewood Cliffs, NJ: Prentice-Hall.

Mead, M. (1935). *Sex and temperament in three primitive societies.* New York: William Morrow.

Mead, M. (1967). *Male and female: A study of sexes in a changing world.* New York: William Morrow.

Mecklenburg, M. E., & Thompson, P. G. (1983). The adolescent family life program as a preventative measure. *Public Health Reports, 98,* 21–27.

Meinardus, 0. (1967). Mythological, historical, and sociological aspects of the practice of female circumcision among the Egyptians. *Acta Ethnographics Academicae Scientarum Hungaricae,* 387–397.

Melbye, M., Biggar, R. J., Ebbesen, P., Neuland, C., Goedert, J. J., Faber, V., Lorenzen, I., Shinhoj, P., Gallo, R. C., & Blattner, W. A. (1986). Long-term seropositivity for human T-lymphotropic virus type III in homosexual men without the acquired immunodeficiency syndrome: Development of immunologic and clinical abnormalities. *Annals of Internal Medicine, 104,* 496–500.

Melnick, S. L., Jeffrey, W. R., Burke, G. L., Gilbertson, D. T., Perkins, L. L., Sidney, S., McCreath, H. E., Wagenknecht, L. E., & Hulley, S. B. (1993). Changes in sexual behavior by young urban heterosexual adults in response to the AIDS epidemic. *Public Health Reports, 108,* 582–588.

Meuwissen, I., & Over, R. (1992). Sexual arousal across phases of the human menstrual cycle. *Archives of Sexual Behavior, 21,* 101–119.

Meyer, J. K. (1974). Clinical variants among applicants

for sex reassignment. *Archives of Sexual Behavior, 3,* 527–558.

Meyer, J. K., & Reter, D. J. (1979). Sex reassignment. *Archives of General Psychiatry, 36,* 1010–1015.

Meyer III, W. J., Finkelstein, J. W., Stuart, C. A. et al. (1981). Physical and hormonal evaluation of transsexual patients during hormonal therapy. *Archives of Sexual Behavior, 10,* 347–356.

Meyer-Bahlburg, H. F. L. (1979). Sex hormones and female homosexuality: A critical examination. *Archives of Sexual Behavior, 8,* 101–119.

Meyer-Bahlburg, H. F. L. (1984). Psychoendocrine research on sexual orientation. Current status and future options. *Progress in Brain Research, 61,* 367–390.

Mezey, G. C., & King, M. B. (Eds.) (1992). *Male victims of sexual assault.* New York: Oxford University Press.

Mickler, S. E. (1993). Perceptions of vulnerability: Impact on AIDS-preventive behavior among college adolescents. *AIDS Education and Prevention, 5,* 43–53.

Milic, J. H., & Crowne, D. P. (1986). Recalled parent-child relations and need for approval of homosexual and heterosexual men. *Archives of Sexual Behavior, 15,* 239–246.

Miller, B. C., Christopherson, C. R., & King, P. K. (1993). Sexual behavior in adolescence. In T. S. Gullotta, G. R. Adams, & R. Montemayor (Eds.), *Adolescent sexuality* (pp. 57–76). Newbury Park, CA: Sage.

Miller, B. C., & Heaton, J. B. (1991). Age at first sexual intercourse and the timing of marriage and childbirth. *Journal of Marriage and the Family, 53,* 719–732.

Miller, M. V. (1977). Intimate terrorism. *Psychology Today, 10,* 79–80, 82.

Miller, W. B. (1986). Why some women fail to use their contraceptive method: A psychological investigation. *Family Planning Perspectives, 18,* 27–32.

Miller, W. B. (1992). An empirical study of the psychological antecedents and consequences of induced abortion. *Journal of Social Issues, 48* (3), 67–93.

Miner, H. (1956). Body ritual among the Nacirema. *American Anthropologist, 58,* 503–507.

Minton, H. L. (Ed.) (1993). *Gay and lesbian studies: The emergence of a discipline.* Binghamton, NY: Haworth Press.

Mittwoch, U. (1990). Sex differences in mammals and tempo of growth and probabilities vs. switches. *Journal of Theoretical Biology, 137,* 445–455.

Monckton, C. (1987, January). AIDS: A British view. *American Spectator,* 29–32.

Money, J. (1976). Childhood: The last frontier in sex research. *The Sciences, 16,* 12–27.

Money, J. (1980). *Love and lovesickness.* Baltimore, MD: Johns Hopkins University Press.

Money, J. (1983). *The destroying angel.* Buffalo, NY: Prometheus Books.

Money, J. (1988). *Gay, straight, and in-between: The sexology of erotic orientation.* New York: Oxford University Press.

Money, J. (1991). *Genes, genitals, hormones, and gender: Selected readings in sexology.* Amsterdam, Holland: Global Academic Publishers.

Money, J., & Brennan, J. J. (1968). Sexual dimorphism in the psychology of female transsexuals. *Journal of Nervous and Mental Disease, 147,* 487–499.

Money, J., & Ehrhardt, A. A. (1972). *Man & woman, boy & girl.* Baltimore, MD: Johns Hopkins University Press.

Money, J., Ehrhardt, A. A., & Masica, D. N. (1968). Fetal reminization induced by androgen insensitivity in the testicular reminizing syndrome: Effect on marriage and maternalism. *Johns Hopkins Medical Journal, 123,* 105–114.

Money, J., & Primrose, C. (1968). Sexual dimorphism and dissociation in the psychology of male transsexuals. *Journal of Nervous and Mental Disease, 147,* 472–486.

Money, J., & Walker, P. A. (1977). Counseling the transsexual. In J. Money & H. Musaph (Eds.), *Handbook of sexology* (pp. 1289–1301). Amsterdam, Holland: Elsevier/North Holland Biomedical Press.

Montagu, A. (1969). *Sex, man, and society.* New York: Tower Publications.

Moore, K., & Caldwell, S. B. (1977). *Out-of-wedlock childbearing.* Washington, D.C.: Urban Institute.

Moore, K. A., Peterson, J. L, & Furstenberg, F. F. (1986). Parental attitudes and the occurrence of early sexual activity. *Journal of Marriage and the Family, 48,* 777–782.

Moore, K. L. (1988). *The developing human: Clinically oriented embryology* (4th Ed.). Philadelphia, PA: Saunders.

Moore, K. L. (1989). *Before we are born* (3rd Ed.). Philadelphia, PA: Saunders.

Moore, M. M. (1985). Nonverbal courtship patterns in women: Context and consequences. *Ethology and Sociobiology, 6,* 201–212.

Moore, M. M. (1993, November). *Courtship signaling and adolescents: Girls just wanna have fun.* Paper presented at the Annual Meeting of The Society for the Scientific Study of Sex, Chicago, IL.

Moran, J. S., Janes, H. R., Peterman, T. A., & Stone, K. M. (1990). Increase in condom sales following AIDS education and publicity, United States. *American Journal of Public Health, 80,* 607–608.

Morbidity and Monthly Weekly Report (MMWR) (1993). Rates of cesarean delivery—United States, 1991. *MMWR, 42,* 285–289.

Morgan, R. (1980). Theory and practice: Pornography and rape. In L. Lederer (Ed.), *Take back the night: Women on pornography* (pp. 134–140). New York: William Morrow.

Morgan, S. (1982). *Coping with hysterectomy.* New York: Dial.

Morokoff, P. J. (1986). Volunteer bias in the psychophysiological study of female sexuality. *The Journal of Sex Research, 22,* 35–51.

Morokoff, P. J., & Gilliland, R. (1993). Stress, sexual functioning, and marital satisfaction. *The Journal of Sex Research, 30,* 43–53.

Morris, N. M., & Udry, J. R. (1978). Pheromonal influences on human sexual behavior: An experiential search. *Journal of Biosocial Science, 10,* 147–159.

Morrissette, D. L., Skinner, M. H., Hoffman, B. B., Levine, R. E., & Davidson, J. M. (1993). Effects of antihypertensive drugs atenolol and nifedipine on sexual function in older men: A placebo-controlled, cross-over study. *Archives of Sexual Behavior, 22,* 99–109.

Morse, E. V., Simon, P. M., Balson, P. M., & Osofsky, H. J. (1992). Sexual behavior patterns of customers of male street prostitutes. *Archives of Sexual Behavior, 21,* 347–357.

Mosher, D. L. (1966). The development and multitrait-multimethod matrix analysis of three measures of three aspects of guilt. *Journal of Consulting and Clinical Psychology, 30,* 25–29.

Mosher, D. L. (1980). Three dimensions of depth and involvement in human sexual response. *The Journal of Sex Research, 16,* 1–42.

Mosher, D. L. (1985, September). *Freedom of inquiry and scientific consensus on pornography.* Testimony in hearings before the Attorney General's Commission on Pornography, Houston, TX.

Mosher, D. L. (1988a). Balancing the rights of subjects, scientists, and society: 10 principles for human subject committees. *The Journal of Sex Research, 24,* 378–385.

Mosher, D. L. (1988b). Revised Mosher guilt inventory. In C. M. Davis, W. L. Yarber, & S. Davis (Eds.), *Sexuality-related measures: A compendium* (pp. 152–155). Lake Mills, IA: The Society for the Scientific Study of Sex.

Mosher, D. L., & Anderson, R. D. (1986). Macho personality, sexual aggression, and reactions to guided imagery of realistic rape. *Journal of Research in Personality, 20,* 77–94.

Mosher, D. L., & Sirkin, M. (1984). Measuring a macho personality constellation. *Journal of Research in Personality, 18,* 150–163.

Mosher, S. W. (1983). *Broken earth: The rural Chinese.* New York: Free Press.

Moss, H. B., Panzak, G. L., & Tarter, R. E. (1993). Sexual functioning of male anabolic steroid abusers. *Archives of Sexual Behavior, 22,* 1–12.

Mott, F. L. (1978). *Women, work, and the family.* Lexington, MA: D. C. Heath.

Muehlenhard, C. L. (1988). "Nice women" don't say yes and "real men" don't say no: How miscommunication and the double standard can cause sexual problems. *Women and Therapy, 7* (2/3), 95–108.

Muehlenhard, C. L., & Cook, S. W. (1988). Men's self-reports of unwanted sexual activity. *The Journal of Sex Research, 24,* 58–72.

Muehlenhard, C. L., & Felts, A. S. (1987). *An analysis of causal factors for men's attitudes about the justifiability of date rape.* Unpublished raw data.

Muehlenhard, C. L., & Hollabaugh, L. C. (1988). Do women sometimes say no when they mean yes? The prevalence and correlates of women's token resistance to sex. *Journal of Personality and Social Psychology, 54,* 872–879.

Mulligan, T., & Palguta, R. F. (1991). Sexual interest, activity, and satisfaction among male nursing home residents. *Archives of Sexual Behavior, 20,* 199–204.

Mumford, K. J. (1992). "Lost manhood" found: Male sexual impotence and Victorian culture in the United States. *Journal of the History of Sexuality, 3,* 33–57.

Munroe, R. L., & Munroe, R. H. (1977). Male transvestism and subsistence economy. *The Journal of Social Psychology, 103,* 307–308.

Munroe, R. L., Whiting, J. W. M., & Haley, D. J. (1969). Institutionalized male transvestism and sex distinctions. *American Anthropologist, 71,* 87–91.

Muraskin, L. D. (1986). Sex education mandates: Are they the answer? *Family Planning Perspectives, 18,* 171–174.

Murnen, S. K., & Allgeier, E. R. (1985, May). *Estimations of parental sexual frequency and parent-child communication.* Paper presented at the meeting of the Midwestern Psychological Association, Chicago, IL.

Murstein, B. (1974). *Love, sex, and marriage through the ages.* New York: Springer.

Mynatt, C. R., & Allgeier, E. R. (1990). Risk factors, self-attributions and adjustment problems among victims of sexual coercion. *Journal of Applied Social Psychology, 20,* 130–153.

Nadler, R. D. (1990). Homosexual behavior in nonhuman primates. In D. P. McWhirter, S. A. Sanders, & J. M. Reinisch (Eds.), *Homosexuality/heterosexuality: Concepts of sexual orientation* (pp. 138–170). New York: Oxford University Press.

Naeye, R. L. (1979). Coitus and associated amniotic-fluid infections. *New England Journal of Medicine, 301,* 1198–1200.

Nahmias, J., Weis, J., Yao, X., Lee, F., Kodsi, R., Schanfield, M., Matthews, T., Bolognesi, D., Durack, D., Motulsky, A., Kanki, P., & Essex, M. (1986). Evidence for human infection with an HTLV III/LAV-like virus in Central Africa, 1959. *Lancet, 1,* 1279–1280.

Nahmias, S. (1989). A model of HIV diffusion from a single source. *The Journal of Sex Research, 26,* 15–25.

Nathanson, B. N. (1979). *Aborting America.* New York: Doubleday.

National Gay and Lesbian Task Force (1988). *Anti-gay violence, victimization, and defamation in 1987.* Washington, D.C.: National Gay and Lesbian Task Force.

National Institutes of Health Consensus Statement (1984). *Diagnostic ultrasound imaging in pregnancy.* Washington, D.C.: U.S. Department of Health and Human Services.

Navot, D., Laufer, N., Kopolovic, J., Rabinowitz, R., Birkenfeld, A., Lewin, A., Granat, M., Margalioth, E. J., & Schenker, J. G. (1986). Artificially induced endometrial cycles and establishment of pregnancies in absence of ovaries. *New England Journal of Medicine, 314,* 806–811.

Nazario, S. L. (1992, February 20). Schools teach the virtue of virginity. *The Wall Street Journal,* B1, B5.

Neidigh, L., & Krop, H. (1992). Cognitive distortions among child sexual offenders. *Journal of Sex Education and Therapy, 18,* 208–215.

Neinstein, L., Goldering, J., & Carpenter, F. (1984). Nonsexual transmission of sexually transmitted diseases: An infrequent occurrence. *Pediatrics, 74,* 67–76.

Nelson, J. A. (1981). The impact of incest: Factors in self-evaluation. In L. L. Constantine & E M. Martinson (Eds.), *Children and sex: New findings, new perspectives* (pp. 163–174). Boston, MA: Little, Brown.

Nelson, J. A. (1986). Incest: Self-report findings from a nonclinical sample. *The Journal of Sex Research, 22,* 463–477.

Newcomb, M. D. (1985). The role of perceived relative parent personality in the development of heterosexuals, homosexuals and transvestites. *Archives of Sexual Behavior, 14,* 147–164.

Newcomb, M. D. (1986). Sexual behavior of cohabitors: A comparison of three independent samples. *The Journal of Sex Research, 22,* 492–513.

Newman, G., & Nichols, C. R. (1960). Sexual activities and attitudes in older persons. *Journal of the American Medical Association, 173,* 33–35.

Niemela, P. (1982). Overemphasis of mother role and the development of the child. In I. Gross, J. Downing, & A. D'Heurle (Eds.), *Sex-role attitudes and cultural change* (pp. 157–162). Dordrecht, Holland: Reidel.

Norman, C. (1986). Sex and needles, not insects and pigs, spread AIDS in Florida town. *Science, 234,* 415–417.

Norton, A. J., & Moorman, J. E. (1987). Current trends in marriage and divorce among American women. *Journal of Marriage and the Family, 49,* 3–14.

Novak, M. A., & Harlow, H. F. (1975). Social recovery of monkeys isolated for the first year of life. *Developmental Psychology, 11,* 453–465.

O'Donohue, W., & Geer, J. H. (Eds.) (1992a). *The sexual abuse of children,* Vol. I: *Theory and research.* Hillsdale, NJ: Lawrence Erlbaum Associates.

O'Donohue, W., & Geer, J. H. (Eds.) (1992b). *The sexual abuse of children,* Vol. II: *Clinical issues.* Hillsdale, NJ: Lawrence Erlbaum Associates.

Offir, J. T., Fisher, J. D., Williams, S. S., & Fisher, W. A. (1993). Reasons for inconsistent AIDS-preventive behaviors among gay men. *The Journal of Sex Research, 30,* 62–69.

Okami, P. (1990). Sociopolitical biases in the contemporary scientific literature on adult human sexual behavior with children and adolescents. In J. Feierman (Ed.), *Pedophilia: Bio-social dimensions* (pp. 91–121). New York: Springer-Verlag.

Okami, P. (1991). Self-reports of "positive" childhood and adolescent sexual contacts with older persons: An exploratory study. *Archives of Sexual Behavior, 20,* 437–457.

Okami, P., & Goldberg, A. (1992). Personality correlates of pedophilia: Are they reliable indicators? *The Journal of Sex Research, 29,* 297–328.

Olds, J., & Milner, P. M. (1954). Positive reinforcement produced by electrical stimulation of the septal area and other regions of the rat brain. *Journal of Comparative and Physiological Psychology, 47,* 419–427.

Olds, S. B., London, M. L., & Ladewig, P. W. (1992). *Maternal-newborn nursing* (4th Ed.). Redwood City, CA: Addison-Wesley Nursing.

Oliver, M. B., & Hyde, J. S. (1993). Gender differences in sexuality: A meta-analysis. *Psychological Bulletin, 114,* 29–51.

Olson, T. D. (1987, September). *Adolescent pregnancy and abstinence: How far have we come?* Paper presented at an Office of Adolescent Pregnancy Programs technical workshop, Washington, D.C.

Olson, T. D., Wallace, D. M., & Miller, B. C. (1984). Primary prevention of adolescent pregnancy: Promoting family involvement through a school curriculum. *Journal of Primary Prevention, 5,* 75–91.

Ornstein, R. & Sobel, D. (1989). *Healthy pleasures.* Reading, MA: Addison-Wesley.

O'Sullivan, L. F., & Allgeier, E. R. (1994). Dissembling a stereotype: Gender differences in the use of token resistance. *Journal of Applied Social Psychology. 24,* 1035–1055.

O'Sullivan, L. F., & Byers, E. S. (1992). Incorporating the roles of initiation and restriction in sexual dating interactions. *The Journal of Sex Research, 29,* 435–446.

O'Sullivan, L. F., & Byers, E. S. (1993). Eroding stereotypes: College women's attempts to influence reluctant male sexual partners. *The Journal of Sex Research, 30*, 270–282.

Overstreet, J. W. (1986). Human sperm function: Acquisition in the male and expression in the female. In R. J. Santen & R. S. Swerdloff (Eds.), *Male reproductive dysfunction* (pp. 29–47). New York: Marcel Dekker.

Oyama, S. (1991). Bodies and minds: Dualism in evolutionary theory. *Journal of Social Issues, 47* (3), 27–42.

Padgett, V. R., Brislin-Slutz, J. A., & Neal, J. A. (1989). Pornography, erotica, and attitudes toward women: The effects of repeated exposure. *The Journal of Sex Research, 26*, 479–491.

Page, S., & Yee, M. (1985). Conception of male and female homosexual stereotypes among university undergraduates. *Journal of Homosexuality, 12*, 109–118.

Paige, K. E. (1978). The ritual of circumcision. *Human Nature, 1*, 40–48.

Palson, C., & Palson, R. (1972). Swinging in wedlock. *Transaction (formerly Society), 9*, 28–37.

Palys, T. S. (1986). Testing the common wisdom: The social content of video pornography. *Canadian Psychology, 27* (1), 22–35.

Papadopoulos, C. (1989). *Sexual aspects of cardiovascular disease.* New York: Praeger.

Parcel, G. S., Luttman, D., & Flaberty-Zonis, C. (1985). Development and evaluation of sexuality education curriculum for young adolescents. *Journal of Sex Education and Therapy, 11*, 38–45.

Parcell, S. R., & Kanin, E. J. (1976, September). *Male sex aggression: A survey of victimized college women.* Paper presented at the Second International Symposium on Victimology, Boston, MA.

Parke, R. D., & O'Leary, S. E. (1976). Father-mother-infant interaction in the newborn period: Some findings, some observations, and some unresolved issues. In K. Riegel & J. Meachem (Eds.), *The developing individual in a changing world: Social and environmental issues,* Vol. 2 (pp. 653–663). The Hague, Holland: Mouton.

Parke, R. D., & Sawin, D. (1976). The father's role in infancy: A re-evaluation. *Family Coordinator, 25*, 356–372.

Parker, R. (1991). *Bodies, pleasures, and passions: Sexual culture in contemporary Brazil.* Boston, MA: Beacon Press.

Parrot, A. (1985). *Sexual assertiveness dramatization.* Ithaca, NY: Cornell University.

Pauly, I. B. (1974). Female transsexualism: Part II. *Archives of Sexual Behavior, 3*, 509–526.

Pauly, I. B. (1985). Gender identity disorders. In M. Farber (Ed.), *Human sexuality: Psychosexual effects of disease* (pp. 295–316). New York: Macmillan.

Pauly, I. B. (1990). Gender identity disorders: Evaluation and treatment. *Journal of Sex Education and Therapy, 16*, 2–24.

Pauly, I. B., & Edgerton, M. T. (1986). The gender identity movement: A growing surgical-psychiatric liaison. *Archives of Sexual Behavior, 15*, 315–330.

Peckham, C. H., & King, R. W. (1963). A study of intercurrent conditions observed during pregnancy. *American Journal of Obstetrics and Gynecology, 83*, 609–624.

Peele, S. (1988). Fools for love. In R. J. Sternberg & M. L. Barnes (Eds.), *The psychology of love* (pp. 159–188). New Haven, CT: Yale University Press.

Peele, S., & Brodsky, A. (1974). Love can be an addiction. *Psychology Today, 8*, 22–26.

Peele, S., & Brodsky, A. (1975). *Love and addiction.* New York: Maplinger.

Pelletier, L. A., & Herold, E. S. (1988). The relationship of age, sex guilt and sexual experience with female sexual fantasies. *The Journal of Sex Research, 24*, 250–256.

Penfield, W. (1975). *The mystery of the mind: A critical study of consciousness and the human brain.* Princeton, NJ: Princeton University Press.

Peplau, L. A. (1979). Power in dating relationships. In J. Freeman (Ed.), *Women: A feminist perspective* (2nd Ed.) (pp. 100–112). Palo Alto, CA: Mayfield.

Peplau, L. A., & Cochran, S. D. (1981). Value orientations in the intimate relationships of gay men. *Journal of Homosexuality, 6*, 1–19.

Peplau, L. A., & Gordon, S. L. (1983). The intimate relationships of lesbians and gay men. In E. R. Allgeier & N. B. McCormick (Eds.), *Changing boundaries: Gender roles and sexual behavior* (pp. 226–244). Palo Alto, CA: Mayfield.

Peplau, L. A., Hill, C. T., & Rubin, Z. (1993). Sex role attitudes in dating and marriage: A 15-year follow-up of the Boston couples study. *Journal of Social Issues, 49* (3), 31–52.

Peplau, L. A., Rubin, Z., & Hill, C. T. (1977). Sexual intimacy in dating relationships. *Journal of Social Issues, 33*, 86–109.

Perlow, D. L., & Perlow, J. S. (1983). *Herpes: Coping with the new epidemic.* Englewood Cliffs, NJ: Prentice-Hall.

Perper, T. (1985). *Sex signals: The biology of love.* Philadelphia, PA: ISI Press.

Perry, J. D., & Whipple, B. (1981). Pelvic muscle strength of female ejaculators: Evidence in support of a new theory of orgasm. *The Journal of Sex Research, 17*, 22–39.

Perry, J. D., & Whipple, B. (1982). Multiple components of female orgasm. In B. Graber (Ed.), *Circumvaginal musculature and sexual function* (pp. 101–114). New York: S. Karger.

Perry, M. E. (Ed.) (1990). *Handbook of sexology: Childhood and adolescent sexology*, Vol. VII. Amsterdam, Holland: Elsevier.

Persky, H., Strauss, D., Lief, H. I., Miller, W. R., & O'Brien, C. P. (1981). Effect of the research process on human sexual behavior. *Psychiatric Research, 16*, 41–52.

Peyron, R., Aubeny, E., Targosz, V., & Silvestre, L. (1993). Early termination of pregnancy with Mifepriston (RU 486) and the orally active prostaglandin misoprostol. *New England Journal of Medicine, 328*, 1509–1513.

Pfäfflin, F. (1992). Regrets after sex reassignment surgery. *Journal of Psychology and Human Sexuality, 5* (4), 69–85.

Pfeiffer, E., Verwoerdt, A., & Wang, H. (1968). Sexual behavior in aged men and women. *Archives of General Psychiatry, 19*, 756–758.

Pfuhl, E. H., Jr. (1978). The unwed father: A "non-deviant" rule breaker. *The Sociological Quarterly, 19*, 113–128.

Phillips, G., & Over, R. (1992). Adult sexual orientation in relation to memories of childhood gender conforming and gender nonconforming behaviors. *Archives of Sexual Behavior, 21*, 543–558.

Phillis, D. E., & Allgeier, E. R. (1982, August). *Taking the initiative: A green light for contraceptive responsibility?* Paper presented at the meeting of the American Psychological Association, Washington, D.C.

Pierce, R. L. (1984). Child pornography: A hidden dimension of child abuse. *Child Abuse and Neglect, 8*, 483–493.

Pillard, R. C., Poumadere, J., & Carretta, R. A. (1982). A family study of sexual orientation. *Archives of Sexual Behavior, 11*, 511–520.

Pillard, R. C., & Weinrich, J. D. (1986). Evidence of familial nature of male homosexuality. *Archives of General Psychiatry, 43*, 808–812.

Pithers, W. D. (1993). Treatment of rapists: Reinterpretation of early outcome data and exploratory constructs to chance therapeutic efficacy. In G. C. Hall, R. Hirschman, J. R. Graham, & M. S. Zaragosa (Eds.), *Sexual aggression: Issues in etiology, assessment, and treatment* (pp. 167–196). Bristol, PA: Taylor and Francis.

Platt, R., Rice, P., & McCormack, W. (1983). Risk of acquiring gonorrhea and prevalence of abnormal adnexal findings among women recently exposed to gonorrhea. *Journal of the American Medical Association, 250*, 3205–3209.

Plaut, S. M., & Foster, B. H. (1986). Roles of the health professional in cases involving sexual exploitation of patients. In A. W. Burgess & C. R. Hartman (Eds.), *Sexual exploitation of patients by health professionals* (pp. 5–25). New York: Praeger.

Pleck, J. (1983). Husband's paid work and family roles. In H. Lopata & J. Pleck (Eds.), *Research in the interweave of social roles*, Vol. 3: *Families and jobs* (pp. 251–333). Greenwich, CT: JAI Press.

Pleck, J. H., Sonenstein, F. L., & Ku, L. (1993). Changes in adolescent males' use of and attitudes toward condoms, 1988–1991. *Family Planning Perspectives, 25*, 106–110, 117.

Pocket Criminal Code (1987). Toronto, Canada: Carswell.

Pocs, O., & Godow, A. (1976). Can students view parents as sexual beings? *The Family Coordinator, 26*, 31–36.

Polk, K., Adler, C., Bazemore, G. et al. (1981). Becoming adult: An analysis of maturational development from age 16 to 30 of a cohort of young men. *Final report of the Marion county youth survey*. Eugene, OR: University of Oregon.

Pomeroy, W. B. (1975). The diagnosis and treatment of transvestites and transsexuals. *Journal of Sex and Marital Therapy, 1*, 215–224.

Pope, K. S., & Bouhoutsos, J. C. (1987). *Sexual intimacy between therapists and patients*. New York: Praeger.

Pope, K. S., Keith-Spiegel, P., & Tabachnick, B. G. (1986). Sexual attraction to clients: The human therapist and the (sometimes) inhuman training system. *American Psychologist, 41*, 147–158.

Pope, K. S., Levenson, H., & Schover, L. R. (1979). Sexual intimacy in psychology training: Results and implications of a national survey. *American Psychologist, 34*, 682–689.

Pope, K. S., Sonne, J. L., & Holroyd, J. (1993). *Sexual feelings in psychotherapy: Explorations for therapists and therapists-in-training*. Washington, D.C.: American Psychological Association.

Pope, K. S., Tabachnick, B. G., & Keith-Spiegel, P. (1987). Ethics of practice: The beliefs and behaviors of psychologists as therapists. *American Psychologist, 42*, 993–1006.

Potter, G. (1989). The retail pornography industry and the organization of vice. *Deviant Behavior, 10*, 233–251.

Potterat, J. J., Woodhouse, D. E., Muth, J. B., & Muth, S. Q. (1990). Estimating the prevalence and career longevity of prostitute women. *The Journal of Sex Research, 27*, 233–243.

Potterat, J. J., Woodhouse, D. E., Pratts, C. I., Markewic, G. S., & Fogle, J. S. (1983). Women contacts of men with gonorrhea: Case finding yields. *Sexually Transmitted Diseases, 10*, 29–32.

Powell-Griner, E. (1987). Induced terminations of pregnancy: Reporting states, 1984. *Monthly Vital Statistics Report, 36* (5), Supplement (2).

Prasad, S. (1993, February 25). India asks moms to abandon babies, not kill them. *Bowling Green Sentinel-Tribune*, p. 10.

Pratte, T. (1993). A comparative study of attitudes toward homosexuality: 1986–1991. *Journal of Homosexuality, 26*, 77–83.

Prendergast, W. E. (1987). Delayed reactions to childhood sexual molestation. *The Journal of Clinical Practice in Sexuality.*

Prendergast, W. E. (1994). Prisons: Sex in prison. In V. L. Bullough & B. Bullough (Eds.), *Human sexuality: An encyclopedia* (pp. 488–493). New York: Garland Publishing.

Prescott, J. W. (1975, April). Body pleasure and the origins of violence. *The Futurist*, 64–74.

Presser, H. B. (1974). Early motherhood: Ignorance or bliss? *Family Planning Perspectives, 6*, 8–14.

Presser, H. B. (1980). *The social and demographic consequences of teenage childbearing for urban women.* (Final report to NICHD.) Washington, D.C.: National Technical Information Service.

Preti, G., Cutler, W. B., Garcia, C. R., Huggins, G. R., & Lawley, H. J. (1986). Human axillary secretions influence women's menstual cycles: The role of donor extracts in females. *Hormones and Behavior, 20*, 474–482.

Prince, V. (1977, September). *Sexual identity versus general identity: The real confusion.* Paper presented at the meeting of the American Psychological Association, Toronto, Canada.

Prince, V., & Bentler, P. M. (1972). Survey of 504 cases of transvestism. *Psychological Reports, 31*, 903–917.

Prins, K. S., Buunk, B. P., & VanYperen, N. W. (1993). Equity, normative disapproval and extramarital relationships. *Journal of Social and Personal Relationships, 10*, 39–53.

Pritchard, J. A., MacDonald, D., & Gant, N. (1985). *Williams obstetrics* (17th Ed.). Norwalk, CT: Appleton-Century-Crofts.

Prus, R., & Irini, S. (1980). *Hookers, rounders, and desk clerks.* Toronto, Canada: Gage.

Pryor, J. B. (1994). Sexual cognition processes in men high in the likelihood to sexually harass. *Personality and Social Psychology Bulletin, 20*, 163–169.

Przybyla, D. P. J., Byrne, D., & Allgeier, E. R. (1988). Sexual attitudes as correlates of sexual details in human figure drawing. *Archives of Sexual Behavior, 17*, 99–105.

Purifoy, F. E., Grodsky, A., & Giambra, L. M. (1992). The relationship of sexual daydreaming to sexual activity, sexual drive, and sexual attitudes for women across the life-span. *Archives of Sexual Behavior, 21*, 369–385.

Quevillon, R. P. (1993). Dyspareunia. In W. O'Donohue & J. H. Geer (Eds.), *Handbook of sexual dysfunctions:* *Assessment and treatment* (pp. 367–380). Boston, MA: Allyn and Bacon.

Quinn, T. C., Mann, J. M., Curran, J. W., & Piot, P. (1986). AIDS in Africa: An epidemiologic paradigm. *Science, 234*, 951–963.

Quinsey, V. L., & Upfold, D. (1985). Rape completion and victim injury as a function of female resistance strategy. *Canadian Journal of Behavioural Science, 17*, 40–50.

Rachman, S. (1966). Sexual fetishism: An experimental analogue. *Psychological Record, 16*, 293–295.

Radecki, T. (1984). Midsection: Sex & censorship. *Film Comment, 20* (60), 43–44.

Rafferty, M. (1977). Should gays teach school? *Phi Delta Kappan, 59*, 91–92.

Rainwater, L., & Weinstein, K. (1960). *And the poor get children.* Chicago, IL: Quadrangle Books.

Rapaport, K., & Burkhart, B. R. (1984). Personality and attitudinal correlates of sexually coercive college males. *Journal of Abnormal Personality, 93*, 216–221.

Rapoza, P. A., Quinn, T. C., Kiessling, L. A., Green, W. R., & Taylor, H. R. (1986). Assessment of neonatal conjunctivitis with a direct immunofluorescent monoclonal antibody stain for chlamydia. *Journal of the American Medical Association, 256*, 3369–3373.

Read, J. S., & Klebanoff, M. A. for the Vaginal Infections and Prematurity Study Group (1993). Sexual intercourse during pregnancy and preterm delivery: Effects of vaginal microorganisms. *American Journal of Obstetrics and Gynecology, 168*, 514–519.

Reamy, K., & White, S. E. (1985). Sexuality in pregnancy and the puerperium: A review. *Obstetrical and Gynecological Survey, 40*, 8–13.

Reamy, K. J., & White, S. E. (1987). Sexuality in the puerperium: A review. *Archives of Sexual Behavior, 16*, 165–186.

Redfield, R. R. & Burke, D. S. (1988). HIV infection: The clinical picture. *Scientific American, 259* (4), 90–98.

Reed, J. (1984). *From private vice to public virtue.* New York: Basic Books.

Reich, W. (1942). *The function of the orgasm.* New York: Orgone Institute Press.

Reik, T. (1949). *Of love and lust: On the psychoanalysis of romantic and sexual emotions.* New York: Farrar, Straus & Giroux.

Reingold, A. L. (1985). Epidemiology of toxic shock syndrome, United States 1980–1984. *Centers for Disease Control MMWR, 33* (335),1955–2255.

Reinisch, J. M., Ziemba-Davis, M., & Sanders, S. (1991). Hormonal contributions to sexually dimorphic behavioral development in humans. *Psychoneuroendocrinology, 16*, 213–278.

Reiss, I. L. (1986). *Journey into sexuality: An exploratory voyage.* Englewood Cliffs, NJ: Prentice-Hall.

Reiss, I. L. (1990). *An end to shame: Shaping our next sexual revolution*. Buffalo, NY: Prometheus.

Reiss, I. L., Anderson, R. E., & Sponaugle, G. C. (1980). A multivariate model of the determinants of extramarital sexual permissiveness. *Journal of Marriage and the Family, 42*, 395–411.

Rhoades, J. M. (1989). Social support and the transition to the maternal role. In P. N. Stern (Ed.), *Pregnancy and parenting* (pp. 131–141). New York: Hemisphere.

Riddle, J. M., Estes, J. W., & Russell, J. C. (1994). Ever since Eve . . . Birth control in the ancient world. *Archaeology, 47* (2), 29–35.

Rieber, I., & Sigusch, V. (1979). Psychosurgery on sex offenders and sexual deviants in West Germany. *Archives of Sexual Behavior, 8*, 523–527.

Riessman, C. K., & Gerstel, N. (1985). Marital dissolution and health: Do males or females have greater risk? *Social Science & Medicine, 20*, 617–635.

Rimmer, R. H. (1984). *The X-rated violence videotape guide*. New York: Arlington House.

Rio, L. M. (1991). Psychological and sociological research and decriminalization or legalization of prostitution. *Archives of Sexual Behavior, 20*, 205–218.

Risman, B. J. (1989). Can men "mother"? Life as a single father. In B. J. Risman & P. Schwartz (Eds.), *Gender in intimate relationships* (pp. 155–164). Belmont, CA: Wadsworth.

Risman, B. J., Hill, C., Rubin, Z., & Peplau, L. A. (1981). Living together in college: Implications for courtship. *Journal of Marriage and the Family, 43*, 77–83.

Robbins, J. M., & DeLamater, J. D. (1985). Support from significant others and loneliness following induced abortion. *Social Psychiatry, 20*, 92–99.

Robbins, M. B., & Jensen, G. G. (1978). Multiple orgasm in males. *The Journal of Sex Research, 14*, 21–26.

Robinson, J. (1987, September 12). Senators told of family's plight with AIDS. *Boston Globe*, p. 1.

Robinson, M. (1959). *The power of sexual surrender*. Garden City, NY: Doubleday.

Robinson, P. A. (1976). *The modernization of sex*. New York: Harper & Row.

Robinson, W. L., & Reid, P. T. (1985). Sexual intimacies in psychology revisited. *Professional Psychology: Research and Practice, 16*, 512–550.

Robson, W. L. M., & Leung, A. K. C. (1992). The circumcision question. *Postgraduate Medicine, 91*, 237–242, 244.

Roche, J. P. (1986). Premarital sex: Attitudes and behavior by dating stage. *Adolescence, 21*, 107–121.

Rogers, L. (1976). Male hormones and behavior. In B. Lloyd & J. Archer (Eds.), *Exploring sex differences* (pp. 157–184). London, England: Academic Press.

Rogers, M. F., White, C. R., Sanders, R., Schable, C.,

Ksell, T. E., Wasserman, R. L., Bellanti, J. A., Peters, S. M., & Wray, B. B. (1990). Lack of transmission of human immunodeficiency virus from infected children to their household contacts. *Pediatrics, 85*, 210–214.

Roiphe, H., & Galenson, E. (1981). *Infantile origins of sexual identity*. New York: International Universities Press.

Roiphe, K. (1993). *The morning after: Sex, fear, and feminism on campus*. Boston, MA: Little, Brown.

Rolfs, R. T., Galaid, E. I., & Zaidi, A. A. (1992). Pelvic inflammatory disease: Trends in hospitalizations and office visits, 1979 through 1988. *American Journal of Obstetrics and Gynecology, 166*, 983–991.

Rollins, B. (1976). *First you cry*. Philadelphia, PA: Lippincott.

Rooks, J. P., Weatherby, N. L., Ernst, E. K. M., Stapleton, S., Rosen, D., & Rosenfield, A. (1989). Outcomes of care in birth centers. *New England Journal of Medicine, 321*, 1804–1811.

Roose, M. W., & Christopher, F. S. (1990). Evaluation of an abstinence-only adolescent pregnancy prevention program: A replication. *Family Relations, 39*, 363–367.

Rorvik, D. M., & Shettles, L. B. (1977). *Choose your baby's sex*. New York: Dodd, Mead.

Rosen, J. C., & Gross, J. (1987). Prevalence of weight reducing and weight gaining in adolescent girls and boys. *Health Psychology, 6*, 131–147.

Rosen, R. C. (1991). Alcohol and drug effects on sexual response: Human experimental and clinical studies. In J. Bancroft, C. M. Davis, & H. J. Ruppel, Jr. (Eds.), *Annual Review of Sex Research*, Vol. II (pp. 119–179). Lake Mills, IA: The Society for the Scientific Study of Sex.

Rosen, R. C., & Ashton, A. K. (1993). Prosocial drugs: Empirical status of the "new aphrodisiacs." *Archives of Sexual Behavior, 22*, 521–543.

Rosen, R. C. & Beck, J. G. (1988). *Patterns of sexual arousal*. New York: Guilford.

Rosen, R. H., & Martindale, I. J. (1978). Sex role perceptions and the abortion decision. *The Journal of Sex Research, 14*, 231–245.

Rosenberg, L., Palmer, J. R., Clarke, E. A., & Shapiro, S. (1992). A case-control study of the risk of breast cancer in relation to oral contraceptive use. *American Journal of Epidemiology, 13*, 1437–1444.

Rosenbleet, C., & Pariente, B. (1973). The prostitution of the criminal law. *American Criminal Law Review, 11*, 373–427.

Rosenwasser, S. M., Wright, L. S., & Barber, R. B. (1987). The rights and responsibilities of men in abortion situations. *The Journal of Sex Research, 23*, 97–105.

Ross, H., & Taylor, H. (1989). Do boys prefer daddy or his physical style of play? *Sex Roles, 20*, 23–33.

Ross, M. W. (1980). Retrospective distortion in homosexual research. *Archives of Sexual Behavior, 9,* 523–531.

Ross, M. W., & Need, J. A. (1989). Effects of adequacy of gender reassignment surgery on psychological adjustment: A follow-up of fourteen male-to-female patients. *Archives of Sexual Behavior, 18,* 145–153.

Rossi, A. S. (1978). The biosocial side of parenthood. *Human Nature, 1,* 72–79.

Rossi, A. S. (1985). Gender and parenthood. In A. S. Rossi (Ed.), *Gender and the life course* (pp. 161–191). Hawthorne, NY: Aldine.

Rossi, A. S., & Rossi, P. E. (1980). Body time and social time: Mood patterns by menstrual cycle phase and day of week. In J. E. Parsons (Ed.), *The psychobiology of sex differences and sex roles* (pp. 269–304). New York: McGraw-Hill.

Rossi, W. (1976). *The sex life of the foot and shoe.* New York: Dutton.

Rothblum, E. D. (1990). Women and weight: Fad and fiction. *The Journal of Psychology, 124,* 5–24.

Rotheram-Borus, M. J., Koopman, C., & Ehrhardt, A. A. (1991). Homeless youths and HIV infection. *American Psychologist, 46,* 1188–1197.

Rowland, D. L., Greenleaf, W. J., Dorfman, L. J., & Davidson, J. M. (1993). Aging and sexual function in men. *Archives of Sexual Behavior, 22,* 545–557.

Rubin, A. M., & Adams, J. R. (1986). Outcomes of sexually open marriages. *The Journal of Sex Research, 22,* 311–319.

Rubin, J. Z., Provenzano, F., & Luria, Z. (1974). The eye of the beholder: Parents' view of the sex of newborns. *American Journal of Orthopsychiatry, 44,* 512–519.

Ruble, D. N., & Brooks, J. (1977, March). *Adolescents' attitudes about menstruation.* Paper presented at the biennial meeting of the Society for Research in Child Development, New Orleans, LA.

Russell, D. E. H. (1990). *Rape in marriage* (Expanded and Revised Edition). Bloomington, IN: Indiana University Press.

Russell, D. E. H. (1984). *Sexual exploitation: Rape, child sexual abuse, and workplace harassment.* Beverly Hills, CA: Sage.

Russell, M. J., Switz, G. M., & Thompson, K. T. (1980). Olfactory influences on the human menstrual cycle. *Pharmacology Biochemistry and Behavior, 13,* 737, 738.

Russo, N. F., Horn, J. D., & Schwartz, R. (1992). U.S. abortion in context: Selected characteristics and motivations of women seeking abortions. *Journal of Social Issues, 48* (3), 183–202.

Rust, P. C. (1993a). 'Coming out' in the age of social constructionism: Sexual identity formation among lesbian and bisexual women. *Gender and Society, 7,* 50–77.

Rust, P. C. (1993b). Neutralizing the political threat of the marginal woman: Lesbians' beliefs about bisexual women. *The Journal of Sex Research, 30,* 214–228.

Saal, F. E., Johnson, C. B., & Weber, N. (1989). Friendly or sexy? It may depend on whom you ask. *Psychology of Women Quarterly, 13,* 263–276.

Sack, W. H., & Mason, R. (1980). Child abuse and conviction of sexual crimes: A preliminary finding. *Law and Human Behavior, 4,* 211–215.

Salisbury, J. E. (Ed.) (1991). *Sex in the middle ages: A book of essays.* New York: Garland Publishing.

Saluter, A. F. (1992). Marital status and living arrangements: March, 1992. *Current Population Reports,* Series P20-468.

Sanders, S. A., & Reinisch, J. M. (1990). Biological and social influences on the endocrinology of puberty: Some additional considerations. In J. Bancroft & J. M. Reinisch (Eds.), *Adolescence and puberty* (pp. 50–62). New York: Oxford University Press.

Sandfort, T. G. M. (1984). Sex in pedophiliac relationships: An empirical investigation among a non-representative group of boys. *The Journal of Sex Research, 20,* 123–142.

Sarrel, P. M., & Masters, W. (1982). Sexual molestation of men by women. *Archives of Sexual Behavior, 11,* 117–132.

Saunders, D. M., Fisher, W. A., Hewitt, E. C., & Clayton, J. P. (1985). A method for empirically assessing volunteer selection effects: Recruitment procedures and responses to erotica. *Journal of Personality and Social Psychology, 49,* 1703–1712.

Saunders, E. J. (1988). Physical and psychological problems associated with exposure to diethylstilbestrol (DES). *Hospital and Community Psychiatry, 39,* 73–77.

Savitz, L., & Rosen, L. (1988). The sexuality of prostitutes: Sexual enjoyment reported by "streetwalkers." *The Journal of Sex Research, 24,* 200–208.

Sawrer, D. B., Kalichman, S. C., Johnson, J. R., Early, J., & Ali, S. (1993). Sexual aggression and love styles: An exploratory study. *Archives of Sexual Behavior, 22,* 265–275.

Scheer, R. (1976). Jimmy, we hardly knew y'all. *Playboy, 23* (11), 91–92.

Schiavi, R. C. (1990). Sexuality and aging in men. In J. Bancroft, C. M. Davis, & D. Weinstein (Eds.), *Annual Review of Sex Research,* Vol. 1 (pp. 227–246). Lake Mills, IA: The Society for the Scientific Study of Sex.

Schinke, S. P., Gilchrist, L. D., & Small, R. W. (1979). Preventing unwanted adolescent pregnancy: A cognitive-behavioral approach. *American Journal of Orthopsychiatry, 49,* 81–88.

Schlesselman, J. J. (1990). Oral contraception and breast cancer. *American Journal of Obstetrics and Gynecology, 163,* 1379–1387.

Schlievert, P. M., Blamster, D. A., & Kelly, J. A. (1984). Toxic shock syndrome: Staphylococcus aureus: Effect of tampons on toxic shock syndrome toxin 1 production. *Obstetrics and Gynecology, 64,* 666–671.

Schoen, E. J., Anderson, G., Bohon, C., Hinman, F., Poland, R., & Wakeman, E. M. (1989). Report of the AAP Task Force on Circumcision. *Pediatrics, 84,* 388–391.

Scholes, D., Daling, J. R., & Stergachis, A. S. (1992). Current cigarette smoking and risk of acute pelvic inflammatory disease. *American Journal of Public Health, 82,* 1352–1356.

Scholes, D., Daling, J. R., Stergachis, A. S., Weiss, N. S., Wang, S. P., & Grayston, J. T. (1993). Vaginal douching as a risk factor for acute pelvic inflammatory disease. *Obstetrics and Gynecology, 81,* 601–606.

Schover, L., & Jenson, S. B. (1988). *Sexuality and chronic illness: A comprehensive approach.* New York: Guilford Press.

Schram, D. D. (1978). Rape. In J. R. Chapman & M. Gates (Eds.), *The victimization of women* (pp. 53–79). Beverly Hills, CA: Sage.

Schreiner-Engel, P., & Schiavi, R. C. (1986). Lifetime psychopathology in individuals with low sexual desire. *The Journal of Nervous and Mental Disease, 174,* 646–651.

Schreiner-Engel, P., Schiavi, R., Vietorisz, D., & Smith, H. (1987). The differential impact of diabetes type on female sexuality. *Journal of Psychosomatic Research, 31,* 22–33.

Schreurs, K. M. G. (1993). Sexuality in lesbian couples: The importance of gender. In J. Bancroft, C. M. Davis, & H. J. Ruppel, Jr. (Eds.), *Annual review of sex research,* Vol. IV (pp. 49–66). Mt. Vernon, IA: The Society for the Scientific Study of Sex.

Schultz, W. C. M. W., Van De Wiel, H. B. M., Hahn, D. E. E., & Van Driel, M. F. (1992). Sexuality and cancer in women. In J. Bancroft, C. M. Davis, & H. J. Ruppel, Jr. (Eds.), *Annual Review of Sex Research,* Vol. III (pp. 151–200). Lake Mills, IA: The Society for the Scientific Study of Sex.

Schumacher, S., & Lloyd, C. W. (1981). Physiological and psychological factors in impotence. *The Journal of Sex Research, 17,* 40–53.

Schwab, J. J. (1982). Psychiatric aspects of infectious diseases. *Current Psychiatric Therapies, 21,* 225–239.

Schwanberg, S. L. (1993). Attitudes towards gay and lesbian women: Instrumentation issues. *Journal of Homosexuality, 26,* 99–136.

Schwartz, I. M. (1993). Affective reactions of American and Swedish women to their first premarital coitus: A cross-cultural comparison. *The Journal of Sex Research, 30,* 18–26.

Schwartz, S. (1973). Effects of sex guilt and sexual arousal on the retention of birth control information. *Journal of Consulting and Clinical Psychology, 41,* 61–64.

Science (1992). HIV comes in five family groups. *Science, 256,* 966.

Scott, J. E. (1990, April). *Regulation of sexual materials: Where do we draw the line?* Colloquium presented at Bowling Green State University, Bowling Green, OH.

Scott, J. E., & Cuvelier, S. J. (1993). Violence and sexual violence in pornography: Is it really increasing? *Archives of Sexual Behavior, 22,* 357–371.

Scott-Palmer, J., & Skevington, S. M. (1981). Pain during childbirth and menstruation: A study of locus of control. *Journal of Psychosomatic Research, 25,* 151–155.

Sedney, M. A. (1985/1986). Growing more complex: Conceptions of sex roles across adulthood. *International Journal of Aging and Human Development, 22,* 15–29.

Segraves, K. A., Segraves, R. T., & Schoenberg, H. W. (1987). Use of sexual history to differentiate organic from psychogenic impotence. *Archives of Sexual Behavior, 16,* 125–137.

Segraves, K. B., & Segraves, R. T. (1991). Multiple phase sexual dysfunction. *Journal of Sex Education and Therapy, 17,* 153–156.

Segraves, R. T. (1988a). Drugs and desire. In S. R. Leiblum & R. C. Rosen (Eds.), *Sexual desire disorders* (pp. 313–347). New York: Guilford Press.

Segraves, R. T. (1988b). Hormones and libido. In S. R. Leiblum & R. C. Rosen (Eds.), *Sexual desire disorders* (pp. 271–312). New York: Guilford Press.

Seibel, M. M., & Taymor, M. L. (1982). Emotional aspects of infertility. *Fertility and Sterility, 37,* 137–145.

Selkin, J. (1975). Rape. *Psychology Today, 8* (8), 70–76.

Sem-Jacobsen, C. W. (1968). *Depth-electrographic stimulation of the human brain and behaviour.* Springfield, MA: Charles C Thomas.

Sevely, J. L., & Bennett, J. W. (1978). Concerning female ejaculation and the female prostate. *The Journal of Sex Research, 14,* 1–20.

Severn, J., Belch, G. E., & Belch, M. A. (1990). The effects of sexual and non-sexual advertising appeals and information level on cognitive processing and communication effectiveness. *Journal of Advertising, 19,* 14–22.

Shah, E., & Zelnik, M. (1981). Parent and peer influence on sexual behavior, contraceptive use, and pregnancy experience of young women. *Journal of Marriage and the Family, 43,* 339–348.

Shannon, T. W. (1913). *Self-knowledge and guide to sex instruction: Vital facts of life for all ages.* Marietta, OH: S. A. Multikin.

Shapiro, H. I. (1977). *The birth control book.* New York: St. Martin's.

Shapiro, S., Sloan, D., Rosenberg, L., Kaufman, D. W., Stolley, P. D., & Miettinen, O. S. (1979). Oral contraceptive use in relation to myocardial infarction. *Lancet, 1*, 743–747.

Shaver, P. R., & Hazan, C. (1993). Adult attachment: Theory and research. In W. Jones and D. Perlman (Eds.), *Advances in personal relationships*, Vol. 4 (pp. 29–70). London, England: Jessica Kingsley.

Shaver, P. R., & Hazan, C. (1994). Attachment. In A. L. Weber & J. H. Harvey (Eds.), *Perspectives on close relationships* (pp. 110–130). Boston, MA: Allyn and Bacon.

Shaver, P. R., Hazan, C., & Bradshaw, D. (1988). Love as attachment. In R. J. Sternberg & M. L. Barnes (Eds.), *The psychology of love* (pp. 68–99). New Haven, CT: Yale University Press.

Shea, M. E. (1993). The effects of selective evaluation on the perception of female cues in sexually coercive and noncoercive males. *Archives of Sexual Behavior, 22*, 415–433.

Sherfey, J. (1972). *The nature and evolution of female sexuality.* New York: Random House.

Sherif, C. W. (1980). A social psychological perspective on the menstrual cycle. In J. E. Parsons (Ed.), *The psychobiology of sex differences and sex roles* (pp. 245–268). New York: McGraw-Hill.

Sherwin, B. B. (1991). The psychoendrocrinology of aging and female sexuality. In J. Bancroft, C. M. Davis, & H. J. Ruppel, Jr. (Eds.), *Annual Review of Sex Research*, Vol. II (pp. 181–198). Lake Mills, IA: The Society for the Scientific Study of Sex.

Shettles, L. B. (1972, June). Predetermining children's sex. *Medical Aspects of Human Sexuality, 6* (6), 172.

Shilts, R. (1987). *And the band played on: Politics, people, and the AIDS epidemic.* New York: St. Martin's.

Shilts, R. (1993). *Conduct unbecoming: Lesbians and gays in the military, Vietnam to the Persian Gulf.* New York: St. Martin's.

Shulman, J. J., & Merritt, C. G. (1976). Postpartum contraception: Subsequent pregnancy, delivery, and abortion rates. *Fertility and Sterility, 27*, 97–103.

Shulman, S., Jackson, H., & Stone, M. L. (1975). Antibodies to spermatozoa. *American Journal of Obstetrics and Gynecology, 123*, 139–144.

Shusterman, L. R. (1979). Predicting the psychological consequences of abortion. *Social Science and Medicine, 13*, 683–689.

Siegel, K., Bauman, L. J., Christ, G. H., & Krown, S. (1988). Patterns of change in sexual behavior among gay men in New York City. *Archives of Sexual Behavior, 17*, 481–497.

Siegelman, M. (1972a). Adjustment of homosexual and heterosexual women. *British Journal of Psychiatry, 120*, 477–481.

Siegelman, M. (1972b). Adjustment of homosexuals and heterosexuals. *Archives of Sexual Behavior, 2*, 9–25.

Siegelman, M. (1974). Parental background of male homosexuals and heterosexuals. *Archives of Sexual Behavior, 3*, 13–18.

Siegelman, M. (1987). Empirical input. In L. Diamant (Ed.), *Male and female homosexuality: Psychological approaches* (pp. 33–79). Washington, D.C.: Hemisphere.

Sigusch, V., Schorsch, E., Dannecker, M., & Schmidt, G. (1982). Guest editorial: Official statement by the German Society for Sex Research on the research of Prof. Dr. Gunter Dörner on the subject of homosexuality. *Archives of Sexual Behavior, 11*, 445–449.

Silberstein, L. R., Mishkind, M. E., Striegel-Moore, R. H., Timko, C., & Rodin, J. (1989). Men and their bodies: A comparison of homosexual and heterosexual men. *Psychosomatic Medicine, 51*, 337–346.

Silbert, M. H. (1986, June). *The effects on juveniles of being used for prostitution and pornography.* Paper presented at the Surgeon General's Workshop on Pornography and Public Health, Arlington, VA.

Silbert, M. H., & Pines, A. (1984). Pornography and sexual abuse of women. *Sex Roles, 10*, 857–868.

Silverman, D. (1976). Sexual harassment: Working women's dilemma. *Quest, 3*, 15–24.

Silverstone, B., & Wynter, L. (1975). The effect of introducing a heterosexual living space. *The Gerontologist, 15*, 83–87.

Simcock, B. (1985). Sons and daughters—a sex preselection study. *Medical Journal of Australia, 142*, 541–542.

Simon, W. (1994). Deviance as history: The future of perversion. *Archives of Sexual Behavior, 23*, 1–20.

Simon, P. M., Morse, E. V., Osofsky, J., Balson, P. M., & Gaumer, R. (1992). Psychological characteristics of a sample of male street prostitutes. *Archives of Sexual Behavior, 21*, 33–44.

Simpson, J. A., Campbell, B., & Berscheid, E. (1986). The association between romantic love and marriage: Kephart (1967) twice revisited. *Personality and Social Psychology Bulletin, 12*, 363–372.

Simpson, M., & Schill, T. (1977). Patrons of massage parlors: Some facts and figures. *Archives of Sexual Behavior, 6*, 521–525.

Singer, J., & Singer, I. (1978). Types of female orgasm. In J. LoPiccolo & L. LoPiccolo (Eds.), *Handbook of sex therapy* (pp. 175–186). New York: Plenum.

Sitomer, C. J. (1987, May 27). Adopting today: More options, more debate. *Christian Science Monitor*, p. 14.

Sivin, I. (1988). International experience with NORPLANT and NORPLANT 2 contraceptives. *Studies in Family Planning, 19*, 81–94.

Skinner, B. F. (1976). *Particulars of my life*. New York: Knopf.

Skinner, B. F. (1981). Notebooks. *Psychology Today, 15,* 63–70. (Excerpted from Epstein, R., *Notebooks, B. F. Skinner*. Englewood Cliffs, NJ: Prentice-Hall, 1980).

Slag, M. F., Morley, J. E., Elson, M. K., Trence, D. L., Nelson, C. J., Nelson, A. E., Kinlaw, W. B., Beyer, H. S., Nuttall, F. Q., & Shafer, R. B. (1983). Impotence in medical clinic outpatients. *Journal of the American Medical Association, 249,* 1736–1740.

Smith, M. D., & Hand, C. (1987). The pornography/aggression linkage: Results from a field study. *Deviant Behavior, 8,* 389–399.

Smith, T. (1990, February). *Adult sexual behavior in 1989: Number of partners, frequency and risk*. Paper presented at the American Association for the Advancement of Science, New Orleans, LA.

Smith, T. W. (1987). The polls—a review: The use of public opinion data by the attorney general's commission on pornography. *Public Opinion Quarterly, 51,* 249–267.

Smith, T. W. (1991). Adult sexual behavior in 1989: Number of partners, frequency of intercourse, and risk of AIDS. *Family Planning Perspectives, 23,* 102–107.

Smithyman, S. D. (1979). Characteristics of "undetected" rapists. In W. H. Parsonage (Ed.), *Perspectives on victimology* (pp. 99–120). Beverly Hills, CA: Sage.

Snell, W. E., Fisher, T. D., & Schuh, T. (1992). Reliability and validity of the Sexuality Scale: A measure of sexual-esteem, sexual-depression, and sexual-preoccupation. *The Journal of Sex Research, 29,* 261–273.

Snell, W. E., Jr., & Papini, D. R. (1989). The Sexuality Scale: An instrument to measure sexual-esteem, sexual-depression, and sexual-preoccupation. *The Journal of Sex Research, 26,* 256–263.

Snyder, P. (1974). Prostitution in Asia. *The Journal of Sex Research, 10,* 119–127.

Sobel, J. D. (1989). Bacterial vaginosis—An ecological mystery. *Annals of Internal Medicine, 111,* 551–555.

Sobol, M. P., & Daly, K. J. (1992). The adoption alternative for pregnant adolescents: Decision making, consequences, and policy implications. *Journal of Social Issues, 48* (3), 143–161.

Soley, L. C., & Kurzbard, G. (1986). Sex in advertising: A comparison of 1964 and 1984 magazine advertisements. *Journal of Advertising, 15,* 46–54.

Somers, A. (1982). Sexual harassment in academe: Legal issues and definitions. *Journal of Social Issues, 38* (4), 23–32.

Sonenstein, F. L., Pleck, J. H., & Ku, L. C. (1989). Sexual activity, condom use and AIDS awareness among adolescent males. *Family Planning Perspectives, 21,* 152–158.

Sonne, J., Meyer, C. B., Borys, D., & Marshall, Y. (1985). Clients' reactions to sexual intimacy in therapy. *American Journal of Orthopsychiatry, 55,* 183–189.

Sontag, L. (1966). Implications of fetal behavior and environment for adult personalities. *Annals of the New York Academy of Science, 134,* 782–786.

Sorenson, S. B., Stein, J. A., Siegel, J. M., Golding, J. M., & Burnam, M. A. (1987). The prevalence of adult sexual assault: The Los Angeles Epidemiologic Catchment Area Project. *American Journal of Epidemiology, 126,* 1154–1164.

Sorrenti-Little, L., Bagley, C., & Robertson, S. (1984). An operational definition of the long-term harmfulness of sexual relations with peers and adults by young children. *Canadian Child, 9,* 46–57.

Spector, I. P., & Carey, M. P. (1990). Incidence and prevalence of sexual dysfunctions: A critical review of the empirical literature. *Archives of Sexual Behavior, 19,* 389–408.

Spence, J. T., & Helmreich, R. L. (1978). *Masculinity and femininity*. Austin, TX: University of Texas Press.

Spengler, A. (1977). Manifest sadomasochism of males: Results of an empirical study. *Archives of Sexual Behavior, 6,* 441–456.

Spitz, R. A. (1947). Hospitalism: A follow-up report. In D. Fenichel, P. Greenacre, & A. Freud (Eds.), *Psychoanalytic studies of the child*, Vol. 2 (pp. 113–117). New York: International Universities Press.

Sprague, J., & Quadagno, D. (1989). Gender and sexual motivation: An exploration of two assumptions. *Journal of Psychology and Human Sexuality, 2,* 57–76.

Sprecher, S., & McKinney, K. (1994). Sexuality in close relationships. In A. L. Weber & J. H. Harvey (Eds.), *Perspectives on close relationships* (pp. 193–216). Boston, MA: Allyn and Bacon.

Srivastava, A., Borries, C., & Sommer, V. (1991). Homosexual mounting in free-ranging female hanuman langurs (presbytis entellus). *Archives of Sexual Behavior, 20,* 487–512.

Stack, S., & Gundlach, J. H. (1992). Divorce and sex. *Archives of Sexual Behavior, 21,* 359–367.

Stake, J. E., & Oliver, J. (1991). Sexual contact and touching between therapist and client: A survey of psychologists' attitudes and behavior. *Professional Psychology: Research and Practice, 22,* 297–307.

Stampfer, M., Colditz, G. A., Willett, W. C., Manson, J. E., Rosher, B., Speizer, F. E., & Hennekens, C. H. (1991). Postmenopausal estrogen therapy and cardiovascular disease—ten-year follow-up from the Nurses Health Study. *New England Journal of Medicine, 325,* 756–762.

Stein, M. L. (1974). *Lovers, friends, slaves . . . : The nine male sexual types, their psycho-sexual transactions with call girls*. New York: Berkley.

Steinbacher, R. (1980). Preselection of sex: The social consequences of choice. *The Sciences, 20,* 6–9, 28.

Steinbacher, R., & Gilroy, F. D. (1986). Preference for sex of child among primiparous women. *The Journal of Psychology, 119,* 541–547.

Steinbacher, R., & Gilroy, F. D. (1990). Sex selection technology: A prediction of its use and effect. *The Journal of Psychology, 124,* 283–288.

Steinem, G. (1980). Erotica and pornography. In L. Lederer (Ed.), *Take back the night: Women on pornography.* New York: Morrow.

Steiner, B. W. (1985). The management of patients with gender disorders. In B. W. Steiner (Ed.), *Gender dysphoria: Development, research, management* (pp. 325–350). New York: Plenum.

Steinlauf, B. (1979). Problem solving skills, locus of control, and the contraceptive effectiveness of young women. *Child Development, 50,* 268–271.

Stern, M., & Karraker, K. H. (1989). Sex stereotyping in infants: A review of gender labeling. *Sex Roles, 20,* 501–522.

Sternberg, R. J. (with C. Whitney) (1991). *Love the way you want it: Using your head in matters of the heart.*

Stevens, C. E., Taylor, P. E., Pindyck, J. et al. (1990). Epidemiology of hepatitis C virus: A preliminary study in volunteer blood donors. *Journal of the American Medical Association, 263* (1), 49–53.

Stevenson, M. R., & Gajarsky, W. M. (1991). Unwanted childhood sexual experiences relate to later revictimization and male perpetration. *Journal of Psychology and Human Sexuality, 4* (4), 57–70.

Stock, W. E. (1982, November). *The effect of violent pornography on women.* Paper presented at the national meeting of The Society for the Scientific Study of Sex, San Francisco, CA.

Stock, W. E. (1993). Inhibited female orgasm. In W. O'Donohue & J. H. Geer (Eds.), *Handbook of sexual dysfunctions: Assessment and treatment* (pp. 253–277). Boston, MA: Allyn and Bacon.

Stokes, J. P., McKirnan, D. J., & Burzette, R. G. (1993). Sexual behavior, condom use, and stability of sexual orientation in bisexual men. *The Journal of Sex Research, 30,* 203–213.

Stoller, R. J. (1972). Male transsexualism: Uneasiness. *Danish Medical Bulletin, 19,* 301–316.

Stoller, R. J. (1975). *Sex and gender: The transsexual experiment,* Vol. 2. London, England: Hogarth Press.

Stoller, R. J. (1977). Sexual deviations. In F. A. Beach (Ed.), *Human sexuality in four perspectives* (pp. 190–214). Baltimore, MD: Johns Hopkins University Press.

Stoller, R. J. (1982). Transvestism in women. *Archives of Sexual Behavior, 11,* 99–115.

Stoller, R. J. (1991). *Porn: Myths for the twentieth century.* New Haven, CT: Yale University Press.

Stone, L. (1977). *The family, sex, and marriage in England: 1500–1800.* New York: Harper & Row.

Storms, M. D. (1980). Theories of sexual orientation. *Journal of Personality and Social Psychology, 38,* 783–792.

Storms, M. D. (1981). A theory of erotic orientation development. *Psychological Review, 88,* 340–353.

Story, M. D. (1985). A comparison of university student experience with various sexual outlets in 1974 and 1984. *Journal of Sex Education and Therapy, 11* (2), 35–41.

Story, M. D. (1993). Personal and professional perspectives on social nudism: Should you be personally involved in your research? *The Journal of Sex Research, 30,* 111–114.

Strassberg, D. S., Kelly, M. P., Carroll, C., & Kircher, J. C. (1987). The psychophysiological nature of premature ejaculation. *Archives of Sexual Behavior, 16,* 327–336.

Strassberg, D. S., & Mahoney, J. M. (1988). Correlates of the contraceptive behavior of adolescents/young adults. *The Journal of Sex Research, 25,* 531–536.

Strassberg, D. S., Mahoney, J. M., Schangaard, M., & Hale, V. E. (1990). The role of anxiety in premature ejaculation: A psychophysiological model. *Archives of Sexual Behavior, 19,* 251–257.

Strassberg, D. S., Roback, H., Cunningham, J., McKee, E., & Larson, P. (1979). Psychopathology in self-identified female-to-male transsexuals, homosexuals, and heterosexuals. *Archives of Sexual Behavior, 8,* 419–496.

Struckman-Johnson, C. (1988). Forced sex on dates: It happens to men, too. *The Journal of Sex Research, 24,* 234–241.

Struckman-Johnson, C. (1991). Male victims of acquaintance rape. In A. Parrot and L. Bechhover (Eds.), *Acquaintance rape—the hidden crime* (pp. 192–214). New York: Wiley.

Struckman-Johnson, C., & Struckman-Johnson, D. (1994). Men pressured and forced into sexual experience. *Archives of Sexual Behavior, 23,* 93–114.

Strum, S. C. (1975). New insights into baboon behavior: Life with the pumphouse gang. *National Geographic, 147,* 627–691.

Stuart, F. M., Hammond, D. C., & Pett, M. A. (1987). Psychological characteristics of women with inhibited sexual desire. *Journal of Sex and Marital Therapy, 12,* 108–115.

Studer, M., & Thornton, A. (1987). Adolescent religiosity and contraceptive usage. *Journal of Marriage and the Family, 49,* 117–128.

Sue, D. (1979). Erotic fantasies of college students during coitus. *The Journal of Sex Research, 15,* 299–305.

Suomi, S. J., & Harlow, H. F. (1971). Abnormal social behavior in young monkeys. In J. Hellmuth (Ed.),

*Exceptional infant: Studies in abnormality*, Vol. 2 (pp. 483–529). New York: Brunner/Mazel.

Suomi, S. J., Harlow, H. F., & McKinney, W. T. (1972). Monkey psychiatrists. *American Journal of Psychiatry*, *128*, 41–46.

Swaab, D. F., & Hofman, M. A. (1990). An enlarged suprachiasmatic nucleus in homosexual men. *Brain Research*, *537*, 141.

Symons, D. (1979). *The evolution of human sexuality.* New York: Oxford University Press.

Szasz, T. (1970). *The manufacture of madness.* New York: Harper & Row.

Szasz, T. (1990). *Sex by prescription.* Syracuse, NY: Syracuse University Press.

Talbot, R. M. R., Beech, H. R., & Vaughan, M. (1980). A normative appraisal of erotic fantasies in women. *British Journal of Social and Clinical Psychology*, *19*, 81–83.

Tamsen, L., & Eneroth, P. (1986). Serum levels of pregnancy-specific Bi-glycoprotein (SP1) and human chorionic gonadotropin (B-hCG) in women using an intrauterine device. *Contraception*, *33*, 497–501.

Tanfer, K., Grady, W. R., Klepinger, D. H., & Billy, J. O. G. (1993). Condom use among U.S. men, 1991. *Family Planning Perspectives*, *25*, 61–66.

Tangri, S. S., Burt, M. R., & Johnson, L. B. (1982). Sexual harassment at work: Three explanatory models. *Journal of Social Issues*, *38* (4), 33–54.

Tanner, J. M. (1962). *Growth at adolescence* (2nd Ed.). Oxford, England: Blackwell.

Tanner, W. M., & Pollack, R. H. (1988). The effect of condom use and erotic instructions on attitudes toward condoms. *The Journal of Sex Research*, *25*, 537–541.

Tcheng-Laroche, F., & Prince, R. H. (1979). Middle-income, divorced female heads of families: Their lifestyles, health, and stress levels. *Canadian Journal of Psychiatry*, *24*, 35–42.

Telljohann, S. K., & Price, J. H. (1993). A qualitative examination of adolescent homosexuals' life experiences: Ramification for secondary school personnel. *Journal of Homosexuality*, *26*, 41–56.

Temoshok, L., Sweet, D. M., & Zich, J. (1987). A three city comparison of the public's knowledge and attitudes about AIDS. *Psychology and Health*, *1*, 43–60.

Tennov, D. (1979). *Love and limerence.* New York: Stein & Day.

Terman, L. M. (1938). *Psychological factors in marital happiness.* New York: McGraw-Hill.

Thacker, T. B., & Banta, H. D. (1983). Benefits and risks of episiotomy: Interpretative review of the English literature, 1960–1980. *Obstetrical and Gynecological Survey*, *38*, 322–338.

Thayer, S. (1987). History and strategies of research on social touch. *Journal of Nonverbal Behavior*, *11*, 12–28.

Thomason, J. L., & Gelbart, S. M. (1989). Trichomonas vaginalis. *Obstetrics and Gynecology*, *74*, 536–541.

Thompson, A. P. (1983). Extramarital sex: A review of the research literature. *The Journal of Sex Research*, *19*, 1–22.

Thompson, J. K. (1992). Body image: Extent of disturbance, associated features, assessment methodologies, intervention strategies, and a proposal for a new DSM-IV diagnostic category—Body Image Disorder. In M. Herson, R. M. Eisler, & P. M. Miller (Eds.), *Progress in behavior modification* (pp. 000–000). Sycamore, IL: Sycamore Publishing.

Thornhill, R., & Thornhill, N. W. (1992). The evolutionary psychology of men's coercive sexuality. *Behavioral and Brain Sciences*, *15*, 363–421.

Thornton, A. (1988). Cohabitation and marriage in the 1980s. *Demography*, *25*, 497.

Thornton, B. (1977). Toward a linear prediction model of marital happiness. *Personality and Social Psychology Bulletin*, *3*, 674–676.

Tiefer, L. (1978). The kiss. *Human Nature*, *1*, 28, 30–37.

Tiefer, L., & Melman, A. (1989). Comprehensive evaluation of erectile dysfunction and medical treatments. In S. R. Leiblum & R. C. Rosen (Eds.), *Principles and practices of sex therapy* (2nd Ed.) (pp. 207–236). New York: Guilford Press.

Tieger, T. (1981). Self-rated likelihood of raping and the social perception of rape. *Journal of Research in Personality*, *15*, 147–158.

Tietze, C. (1978). Repeat abortions—why more? *Family Planning Perspectives*, *10*, 286–288.

Tietze, C., & Henshaw, S. (1986). *Induced abortion: A world review.* New York: Alan Guttmacher Institute.

Tietze, C., & Jain, A. (1978). The mathematics of repeat abortion: Explaining the increase. *Studies in Family Planning*, *9*, 294–299.

Tietze, C., & Lewit, S. (1979). Life risks associated with reversible methods of fertility regulation. *International Journal of Gynecology and Obstetrics*, *16*, 456–459.

Tims, A. R., & Masland, J. L. (1985). Measurement of family communication patterns. *Communication Research*, *12*, 35–57.

Todd, J., Fishaut, M., Kapral, F., & Welch, J. (1978). Toxic-shock syndrome associated with phase-group-I staphylococci. *Lancet*, *2*, 1116–1118.

Tollison, C. D., & Adams, H. E. (1979). *Sexual disorders: Treatment, theory, research.* New York: Gardner.

Tooby, J., & Cosmides, L. (1990). On the universality of human nature and the uniqueness of the individual: The role of genetics and adaptation. *Journal of Personality*, *58*, 17–68.

Tooby, J., & Cosmides, L. (1992). The psychological foundations of culture. In J. Barkow, L. Cosmides, & J. Tooby (Eds.), *The adapted mind: Evolutionary psychology and the generation of culture* (pp. 19–136). New York: Oxford University Press.

Trivers, R. E. (1972). Parental investment and sexual selection. In B. Campbell (Ed.), *Sexual selection and the descent of man* (pp. 136–179). Chicago, IL: Aldine.

Troiden, R. R. (1988). *Gay and lesbian identity formation: A sociological analysis.* Dix Hills, NY: General Hall, Inc.

Troll, L. E., & Smith, J. (1976). Attachment through the life span: Some questions about dyadic bonds among adults. *Human Development, 19,* 135–182.

Trudgill, E. (1976). *Madonnas and Magdalens: The origins and development of Victorian sexual attitudes.* New York: Holmes & Meier.

Trussell, J., Strickler, J., & Vaughn, B. (1993). Contraceptive efficacy of the diaphragm, the sponge, and the cervical cap. *Family Planning Perspectives, 25,* 100–105, 135.

Turner, L. A., Froman, S. L., Althof, S. E., Levine, S. B., Tobias, J. R., Kursh, E. D., Bodner, D. R., & Resnick, M. I. (1990). Intracavernous injections in the management of diabetic impotence. *Journal of Sex Education and Therapy, 16,* 126–136.

Twain, M. (1976). *Some remarks on the science of onanism.* In the Mammath Cod Address to the Stomach Club with an Introduction by G. Legman, Waukesha, WI: Maladicta Press. (Original remarks delivered in 1879.)

Udry, J. R. (1990). Hormonal and social determinants of adolescent sexual initiation. In J. Bancroft & J. M. Reinisch (Eds.), *Adolescence and puberty* (pp. 70–87). New York: Oxford University Press.

Udry, J. R. (1993). The politics of sex research. *The Journal of Sex Research, 30,* 103–110.

Ulibarri, C. M., & Yahr, P. (1993). Ontogeny of the sexually dimorphic area of the gerbil hypothalamus. *Developmental Brain Research, 74,* 14–24.

Umberson, D., Wortman, C. B., & Kessler, R. C. (1992). Widowhood and depression: Explaining long-term gender differences in vulnerability. *Journal of Health and Social Behavior, 33,* 10–24.

Uniform Crime Reports (1989). *Federal Bureau of Investigation.* Washington D.C.: U.S. Justice Department.

Uniform Crime Reports (1992). *Federal Bureau of Investigation.* Washington, D.C.: U.S. Justice Department.

Uniform Crime Reports for the United States, 1992 (1993). *Federal Bureau of Investigation.* Washington, D.C.: U.S. Government Printing Office.

U.S. Attorney General's Commission on Pornography (1986). *Final report of the Attorney General's Commission on Pornography.* Washington, D.C.: U.S. Justice Department.

U.S. Bureau of the Census (1985). *Fertility of American women: June, 1985.* (Current Population Reports, Series P-20, No. 401.) Washington, D.C.: U.S. Government Printing Office.

U.S. Bureau of the Census (1986). *Marital status and living arrangements: March 1986 Advance Report.* (Current Population Reports, Series P-20, No. 403.) Washington, D.C.: U.S. Government Printing Office.

U.S. Bureau of the Census (1989a). *Changes in American family life.* (Current Population Reports, Series P-23, No. 163.) Washington, D.C.: U.S. Government Printing Office.

U.S. Bureau of the Census (1989b). *Studies in marriage and the family.* (Current Population Reports, Series P-23, No. 162.) Washington, D.C.: U.S. Government Printing Office.

U.S. Bureau of the Census (1990). *Statistical abstract of the United States, 1990* (110th Ed.). Washington, D.C.: U. S. Government Printing Office.

U.S. Bureau of the Census (1991). *Statistical Abstract of the United States, 1991* (111th ed.). Washington, D.C.: U.S. Government Printing Office.

U.S. Commission on Obscenity and Pornography (1970). *The report of the Commission on Obscenity and Pornography.* Washington, D.C.: U.S. Government Printing Office.

U.S. Department of Justice, Bureau of Justice Statistics (1990). *Sourcebook of criminal justice statistics—1989.* Washington, D.C.: U.S. Government Printing Office.

Valenstein, E. (1973). *Brain control: A critical examination of brain stimulation and psychosurgery.* New York: Wiley.

Vance, E. B., & Wagner, N. N. (1976). Written descriptions of orgasm: A study of sex differences. *Archives of Sexual Behavior, 5,* 87–98.

van de Velde, T. H. (1930). *Ideal marriage: Its physiology and technique.* New York: Covici-Friede.

Vanggaard, T. (1972). *Phallos: A symbol of its history in the male world.* New York: International Universities Press.

Van Wyk, P. H., & Geist, C. S. (1984). Psychosocial development of heterosexual, bisexual, and homosexual behavior. *Archives of Sexual Behavior, 13,* 505–544.

Ventura, S. J. et al. (1992). Trends in pregnancy and pregnancy rates, United States, 1980–1988. *Monthly Vital Statistics, 41* (6). Supplement.

Vera, H., Barnard, G. W., & Holzer, C. (1979). The intelligence of rapists: New data. *Archives of Sexual Behavior, 8,* 375–378.

Verma, R. S. (1990). *The genome.* New York: VCH Publishers.

Vermeulen, A. (1986). Leydig cell physiology. In R. J.

Santen & R. S. Swerdloff (Eds.), *Male reproductive dysfunction* (pp. 49–76). New York: Marcel Dekker.

Verschoor, A. M., & Poortinga, J. (1988). Psychosocial differences between Dutch male and female transsexuals. *Archives of Sexual Behavior, 17,* 173–178.

Verwoerdt, A., Pfeiffer, E., & Wang, H. S. (1969). Sexual behavior in senescence: Patterns of sexual activity and interest. *Geriatrics, 24,* 137–144.

Vessey, M., Doll, R., Peto, R., Johnson, B., & Wiggins, P. A. (1976). A long-term follow-up study of women using different methods of contraception: An interim report. *Journal of Biosocial Science, 8,* 373–427.

Vessey, M., McPherson, K., Lawless, M., & Yeates, D. (1985). Oral contraception and serious psychiatric illness: Absence of an association. *British Journal of Psychiatry, 146,* 45–49.

Vidal, G. (1979). Sex is politics. *Playboy, 26,* 174, 346.

Vincent, M. L., Clearie, A. F., & Schluchter, M. D. (1987). Reducing adolescent pregnancy through school and community based education. *Journal of the American Medical Association, 257,* 3382–3386.

Vinson, J. S. (1984). *Sexual contact with psychotherapists: A study of client reactions and complaint procedures.* Unpublished doctoral dissertation. California School of Professional Psychology, Berkeley, CA.

Voeller, B. (1991). AIDS and heterosexual anal intercourse. *Archives of Sexual Behavior, 20,* 233–276.

Vogel, D. A., Lake, M. A., Evans, S., & Karraker, K. H. (1991). Children's and adults' sex-stereotyped perceptions of infants. *Sex Roles, 24,* 605–616.

Wabrek, A. J., & Burchell, R. C. (1980). Male sexual dysfunction associated with coronary heart disease. *Archives of Sexual Behavior, 9,* 69–75.

Wagner, G., & Kaplan, H. S. (1993). *The new injection treatment for impotence.* New York: Brunner/Mazel.

Wallin, J., Lernestedt, J. O., Ogenstad, S., & Lycke, F. (1985). Topical treatment of recurrent genital herpes infections with foscarnet. *Scandinavian Journal of Infectious Diseases, 17,* 165–172.

Walling, M., Anderson, B. L. & Johnson, S. R. (1990). Hormonal replacement theory for women: A review of sexual outcomes and related gynecological effects. *Archives of Sexual Behavior, 19,* 119–137.

Walling, W. H. (1904). *Sexology.* Philadelphia, PA: Puritan.

Walster, E., Walster, G. W., & Berscheid, E. (1978). *Equity: Theory and research.* Boston, MA: Allyn and Bacon.

Walter, H. J., & Vaughan, R. D. (1993). AIDS risk reduction among a multiethnic sample of urban high school students. *Journal of the American Medical Association, 270,* 725–730.

Watson, R. (1985). Gardnerella vaginalis: Genitourinary passage in men. *Urology, 25,* 217–222.

Watters, A. T. (1986). Heterosexual bias in psychological research on lesbianism and male homosexuality (1979–1983), utilizing the bibliographic and taxonomic system of Morin. *Journal of Homosexuality, 13,* 35–48.

Watts, A. (1970). *Nature, man and woman.* New York: Vintage.

Webber, M. P., & Hauser, W. A. (1993). Secular trends in New York City hospital discharge diagnoses of congenital syphilis and cocaine dependence, 1982–88. *Public Health Reports, 108,* 279–284.

Webster, L. A., Berman, S. M., & Greenspan, J. R. (1993). Surveillance for gonorrhea and primary and secondary syphilis among adolescents, United States—1981–1991. *Morbidity and Mortality Weekly Report,* Supplement, Vol. 42, No. SS-3, 1–11.

Weidner, G., & Griffitt, W. (1983). Rape: A sexual stigma? *Journal of Personality, 51,* 152–166.

Weinberg, G. (1972). *Society and the healthy homosexual.* New York: St. Martin's.

Weinberg, M. S., & Williams, C. J. (1975). *Male homosexuals: Their problems and adaptations.* New York: Penguin.

Weinberg, T. S. (1987). Sadomasochism in the United States: A review of recent sociological literature. *The Journal of Sex Research, 23,* 50–69.

Weinrich, J. D. (1987). *Sexual landscapes.* New York: Scribner.

Weinrich, J. D. (1994). Homosexuality. In V. L. Bullough & B. Bullough (Eds.), *Human sexuality: An encyclopedia* (pp. 277–283). New York: Garland Publishing.

Weinrich, J. D., Grant, I., Jacobson, D. L., Robinson, S. R., McCutchan, J. A., and the HNRC Group (1992). Effects of recalled childhood gender nonconformity on adult genitoerotic role and AIDS exposure. *Archives of Sexual Behavior, 21,* 559–585.

Weis, D. L. (1983). Affective reactions of women to their initial experience of coitus. *The Journal of Sex Research, 19,* 209–237.

Weizman, R., & Hart, J. (1987). Sexual behavior in healthy married elderly men. *Archives of Sexual Behavior, 16,* 39–44.

Welch, M. R., & Kartub, P. (1978). Socio-cultural correlates of incidence of impotence: A cross-cultural study. *The Journal of Sex Research, 14,* 218–230.

Welham, C. J. (1990). Incest: An evolutionary model. *Ethology and Sociobiology, 11,* 97–111.

Weller, R. A., & Halika, J. (1984). Marijuana use and sexual behavior. *The Journal of Sex Research, 20,* 186–193.

Wells, B. (1986). Predictors of female nocturnal orgasm. *The Journal of Sex Research, 23,* 421–437.

West, D. J. (1993). *Male prostitution.* Binghamton, NY: Haworth Press.

Whipple, B., Ogden, G., & Komisaruk, B. R. (1992). Physiological correlates of imagery-induced orgasm in women. *Archives of Sexual Behavior, 21,* 121–133.

Whitam, F. L. (1977). Childhood indicators of male homosexuality. *Archives of Sexual Behavior, 6,* 89–96.

Whitam, F. L., Diamond, M., & Martin, J. (1993). Homosexual orientation in twins: A report on 61 pairs and three triplet sets. *Archives of Sexual Behavior, 22,* 187–206.

Whitam, F. L., & Mathy, R. M. (1986). *Male homosexuality in four societies: Brazil, Guatemala, the Philippines, and the United States.* New York: Praeger.

White, G. L. (1981). Relative involvement, inadequacy, and jealousy: A test of a causal model. *Alternative Lifestyles, 4,* 291–309.

White, G. L., & Helbick, R. M. (1988). Understanding and treating jealousy. In R. A. Brown & J. F. Fields (Eds.), *Treatment of sexual problems in individuals and couples therapy* (pp. 245–265). Boston, MA: PMA Publishing.

White, G. L., & Kight, T. D. (1984). Misattribution of arousal and attraction: Effects of salience of explanations for arousal. *Journal of Experimental Social Psychology, 20,* 55–64.

White, J. R., Case, D. A., McWhirter, D., & Mattison, A. M. (1990). Enhanced sexual behavior in exercising men. *Archives of Sexual Behavior, 19,* 193–209.

White, L. K. (1991). Determinants of divorce: A review of research in the eighties. In A. Booth (Ed.), *Contemporary families: Looking forward, looking back* (pp. 141–149). Minneapolis, MN: National Council on Family Relations.

Whitehead, W. E., Busch, C. M., Heller, B. R., & Costa, P. J. (1986). Social learning influences on menstrual symptoms and illness behavior. *Health Psychology, 5,* 13–23.

Whiting, B., & Edwards, C. P. (1988). *Children of different worlds.* Cambridge, MA: Harvard University Press.

Whitley, B. E., Jr. (1989). Correlates of oral genital experience among college students. *Journal of Psychology and Human Sexuality, 2,* 151–163.

Wiederman, M. W. (1993). Demographic and sexual characteristics of nonresponders to sexual experience items in a national survey. *The Journal of Sex Research, 30,* 27–35.

Wiederman, M. W., & Allgeier, E. R. (1992). Gender differences in mate selection criteria: Sociobiological or socioeconomic explanation? *Ethology and Sociobiology, 13,* 115–124.

Wiederman, M. W., & Allgeier, E. R. (1994). Mate selection. In V. L. Bullough & B. Bullough (Eds.), *Human sexuality: An encyclopedia* (pp. 386–390). New York: Garland Publishing.

Wiederman, M. W., & Allgeier, E. R. (1993a). Gender differences in sexual jealousy: Adaptionist or social learning explanation. *Ethology and Sociobiology, 14,* 115–140.

Wiederman, M. W., & Allgeier, E. R. (1993b). The measurement of sexual esteem: Investigation of Snell and Papini's (1989) Sexuality Scale. *Journal of Research in Personality, 27,* 88–102.

Wiederman, M. W., Allgeier, E. R., & Weiner, A. (1992, June). *People's perceptions of vocalizations made during sexual intercourse.* Paper presentation at the Midcontinent Region meeting of The Society for the Scientific Study of Sex, Big Rapids, MI.

Wiederman, M. W., Weis, D. L., & Allgeier, E. R. (1994). The effect of question preface on response rates to a telephone survey of sexual experience. *Archives of Sexual Behavior, 23,* 203–215.

Will, J. A., Self, P. A., & Datan, N. (1976). Maternal behavior and perceived sex of infant. *American Journal of Orthopsychiatry, 49,* 135–139.

Williams, G. C. (1966). *Adaptation and natural selection: A critique of some current evolutionary thought.* Princeton, NJ: Princeton University Press.

Williams, J. D., & Jacoby, A. R. (1989). The effects of premarital and homosexual experience on dating and marriage desirability. *Journal of Marriage and the Family, 51,* 489–497.

Williams, M. (1980). Toxic-shock syndrome: The disease in the tampon industry. *The Progressive, 44,* 30–33.

Williams, M. H. (1992). Exploitation and inference: Mapping the damage from therapist-patient sexual involvement. *American Psychologist, 47,* 412–421.

Williams, W. L. (1993). Being gay and doing research on homosexuality in non-western cultures. *The Journal of Sex Research, 30,* 115–120.

Williamson, N. E. (1978). Boys or girls? Parents' preferences and sex control. *Population Bulletin, 33,* 3–35.

Wilson, E. O. (1978). *On human nature.* Cambridge, MA: Harvard University Press.

Wilson, G. T., & Lawson, D. M. (1978). Expectancies, alcohol, and sexual arousal in women. *Journal of Abnormal Psychology, 87,* 358–367.

Wincze, J. P., Albert, A., & Bansal, S. (1993). Sexual arousal in diabetic females: Physiological and self-report measures. *Archives of Sexual Behavior, 22,* 587–601.

Winick, C. (1991). Are pictures more valid than words in conveying the content of sex in the media? Studies in North Carolina and New York state. *Archives of Sexual Behavior, 20,* 345–357.

Winick, C., & Kinsie, P. (1971). *The lively commerce: Prostitution in the United States.* Chicago, IL: Quadrangle Books.

Winter, L. (1988). The role of sexual self-concept in the use of contraceptives. *Family Planning Perspectives, 20*, 123–127.

Witkin, H., Mednick, S., Schulsinger, F., Bakkestrom, E., Christiansen, K. O., Goodenough, D. R., Hirschhorn, K., Lundsteen, C., Owen, D. R., Philip, J., Rubin, D. B., & Stocking, M. (1976). Criminality in XYY and XXY men. *Science, 193*, 147–155.

Witkin, M. H. (1975). Sex therapy and mastectomy. *Journal of Sex and Marital Therapy, 1*, 290–304.

Witkin, S., & Toth, A. (1983). Relationship between genital tract infections, sperm antibodies in seminal fluid, and infertility. *Fertility and Sterility, 40*, 805–808.

Wolbarst, A. L. (1932). Circumcision and penile cancer. *Lancet, 1*, 150–153.

Wolchik, S. A., Braver, S. L., & Jensen, K. (1985). Volunteer bias in erotica research: Effects of intrusiveness of measure of sexual background. *Archives of Sexual Behavior, 14*, 93–107.

Wolf, D. G. (1979). *The lesbian community*. Berkeley, CA: University of California Press.

Wolfe, J., & Baker, V. (1980). Characteristics of imprisoned rapists and circumstances of the rape. In C. G. Warner (Ed.), *Rape and sexual assault* (pp. 265–278). Germantown, MD: Aspen Systems Co.

Wolman, T. (1985). Drug addiction. In M. Farber (Ed.), *Human sexuality* (pp. 277–285). New York: Macmillan.

Wolner-Hanssen, P., Eschenbach, D. A., Paavonen, J., Kiviat, N., & Stevens, C. E. (1990). Decreased risk of symptomatic chlamydial pelvic inflammatory disease associated with oral contraceptive use. *Journal of the American Medical Association, 263* (1), 54–59.

Wolpe, J. (1958). *Psychotherapy by reciprocal inhibition*. Stanford, CA: Stanford University Press.

Wooden, W., & Parker, J. (1982). *Men behind bars: Sexual exploitation in prison*. New York: Plenum.

World Health Organization Task Force on Psychological Research in Family Planning (1980). Acceptability of drugs for male fertility regulation: A prospectus and some preliminary data. *Contraception, 21*, 121–134.

World Health Organization Task Force on Psychological Research on Family Planning (1982). Hormonal contraception for men: Acceptability and effects on sexuality. *Studies in Family Planning, 13*, 328–342.

Worthington, E. L., Jr., Larson, D. B., Brubaker, M. W., Colecchi, C., Berry, J. T., & Morrow, D. (1989). The benefits of legislation requiring parental involvement prior to adolescent abortion. *American Psychologist, 44*, 1542–1545.

Wurtele, S. K. (1993). Enhancing children's sexual development through child sexual abuse programs. *Journal of Sex Education and Therapy, 19*, 37–46.

Yarchoan, R., Mitsuya, H., & Broder, S. (1988). AIDS therapies. *Scientific American, 259* (4), 110–119.

Yarris, E., & Allgeier, E. R. (1988). Sexual socialization for therapists: Applications for the counseling/psychotherapy of women. In E. Cole & E. D. Rothblum (Eds.), *Women and sex therapy: Closing the circle of sexual knowledge* (pp. 57–75). Binghamton, NY: Haworth Press.

Young, M. (1989). Self-esteem and sexual behavior among early adolescents. *FLEducator*, 16–19.

Zajonc, R., Adelman, P. K., Murphy, S. T., & Niedenthal, P. M. (1987). Convergence in the physical appearance of spouses. *Motivation and Emotion, 2*, 335–346.

Zaviacic, M., & Whipple, B. (1993). Update on the female prostate and the phenomenon of female ejaculation. *The Journal of Sex Research, 30*, 148–151.

Zax, M., Sameroff, A., & Farnum, J. (1975). Childbirth education, maternal attitude and delivery. *American Journal of Obstetrics and Gynecology, 123*, 185–190.

Zelen, S. L. (1985). Sexualization of therapeutic relationships: The dual vulnerability of patient and therapist. *Psychotherapy, 22*, 178–185.

Zellman, G. L., & Goodchilds, J. D. (1983). Becoming sexual in adolescence. In E. R. Allgeier & N. B. McCormick (Eds.), *Changing boundaries: Gender roles and sexual behavior* (pp. 49–63). Palo Alto, CA: Mayfield.

Zelnik, M., & Kantner, J. F. (1978). Contraceptive patterns and premarital pregnancy among women aged 15–19 in 1976. *Family Planning Perspectives, 10*, 135–142.

Zelnik, M., & Kim, Y. J. (1982). Sex education and its association with teenage sexual activity, pregnancy, and contraceptive use. *Family Planning Perspectives, 14*, 117–119, 123–126.

Zilbergeld, B., & Evans, M. (1980). The inadequacy of Masters and Johnson. *Psychology Today, 14*, 29–43.

Zilbergeld, B., & Hammond, D. C. (1988). The use of hypnosis in treating desire disorders. In S. R. Leiblum & R. C. Rosen (Eds.), *Sexual desire disorders* (pp. 192–225). New York: Guilford Press.

Zillmann, D., & Bryant, J. (1982). Pornography, sexual callousness, and the trivialization of rape. *Journal of Communication, 32* (4), 10–21.

Zillmann, D., & Bryant, J. (1984). Effects of massive exposure to pornography. In N. M. Malamuth & E. Donnerstein (Eds.), *Pornography and sexual aggression* (pp. 115–138). Orlando, FL: Academic Press.

Zillmann, D., & Bryant, J. (1988). Pornography's impact on sexual satisfaction. *Journal of Applied Social Psychology, 18*, 438–453.

Zuckerman, M., & Miyake, K. (1993). The attractive voice: What makes it so? *Journal of Nonverbal Behavior, 7*, 119–135.

# Credits

## Excerpts

Whipple, pp. 132–133. From Whipple, B., *How to Find the Gräfenberg Spot.* Cherry Hill, NJ: Beverly Whipple, 1981.

Barbach and Levine, pp. 172, 195–196. Excerpt from *Shared Intimacies: Women's Sexual Experiences* by Lonnie Barbach and Linda Levine, pp. 11, 85–86, 91–92. Copyright © 1980 by Lonnie Barbach and Linda Levine. Reprinted by permission of Doubleday, a division of Bantam, Doubleday, Dell Publishing Group, Inc.

Goldman and Goldman, p. 388. Excerpt from *Children's Sexual Thinking* by Ronald and Juliette Goldman. Copyright © 1982. Reprinted with permission of Routledge, Kegan Paul, Ltd.

Skinner, pp. 393, 405. From *Particulars Of My Life* by B. F. Skinner, pp. 64–65, 131–132. Copyright © 1976 by B. F. Skinner. Reprinted by permission of Alfred A. Knopf, Inc.

*The New Republic,* p. 491. From *The New Republic,* July 21, 1976, p. 8. Excerpted by permission of *The New Republic,* © 1990, The New Republic, Inc.

Hatfield, p. 675. Adapted from "Touch and Sexuality" by Robert Hatfield in Vern Alboa, ed. *Human Sexuality: An Encyclopedia* pp. 582–583 © 1994 Garland Publishing, Inc. Reprinted with the permission of Garland Publishing, Inc.

## Illustrations

**2:** The Granger Collection. **3:** The Granger Collection. **5:** *Adam and Eve,* 1504 by Albrecht Dürer. Minneapolis Institute of Arts, The Christine N. and Swan J. Turnblad Memorial Fund, 1958. **6:** Erich Lessing/ Art Resource, NY. **9:** The Bettmann Archive. **10:** Bildarchiv Preussischer Kulturbesitz. **11:** (left) The Bettmann Archive. **11:** (right) Culver Pictures, Inc. **13:** Scala/Art Resource, NY. **17:** Rare Book Department, Countway Medical Library, Harvard University. **20:** The Bettmann Archive. **21:** Megdalione di Tazza Attica. Alinari/Art Resource, NY. **25:** UPI/ Bettmann Newsphoto. **27:** Christine Spengler/ Sygma. **30:** © Andrew Brilliant/Carol Palmer. **31:** © Andrew Brilliant/Carol Palmer. **32:** National Library of Medicine, Bethesda, MD. **33:** (left) Countway Medical Library, Harvard University. **33:** (right) The

Bettmann Archive. **36:** Reproduced by permission of The Kinsey Institute for Research in Sex, Gender and Reproduction, Inc. **37:** Ira Wyman/Sygma. **45:** Reuters/Bettmann Newsphoto. **47:** © Andrew Brilliant/ Carol Palmer. **48:** © Andrew Brilliant/Carol Palmer. **53:** Frank Siteman/The Picture Cube. **56:** © The National Geographic Society. Photo by Timothy Ransom. **58:** (top) Farrell Instruments, Inc., Grand Island, Nebraska. **58:** (bottom) Courtesy Perry Meter Systems/Biotechnologies. **64:** Barbara Rios/Photo Researchers. **65:** Barbara Rios/Photo Researchers. **67:** (top) National Portrait Gallery, London. **67:** (bottom) Stewart Halperin/Animals, Animals. **69:** © Joel Gordon. **71:** Carol Palmer/The Picture Cube. **74:** Mary Evans Picture Library/Sigmund Freud Copyrights. **77:** © Joel Gordon. **82:** Courtesy Ira Reiss. **84:** Barbara Alper/Stock, Boston. **90:** Barbara Campbell/Liaison. **91:** Barbara Campbell/Liaison. **94:** (top) Dr. E. S. E. Hafez/C. S. Mott Center for Human Growth and Development. **94:** (bottom) D. W. Fawcett/Photo Researchers. **95:** Leonard Lessin/ Photo Researchers. **96:** Courtesy of Uta Francke, M.D., Department of Human Genetics, Yale University. **100:** (left) © Petit Format/Nestle/Photo Researchers. **100:** (right) Lennart Nilsson photograph from *A Child Is Born,* Albert Bonniers Forlag AB, Stockholm, Delacorte Press, NY. **101:** James Stevenson/Science Source/Photo Researchers. **114:** *Sex Errors of the Body,* by John Money, 2nd Edition. Baltimore, Brookes Publishing, 1994. **116:** *Sex Errors of the Body,* by John Money, 2nd Edition. Baltimore, Brookes Publishing, 1994. **122:** Jan Cobb/The Image Bank. **123:** Jan Cobb/The Image Bank. **152:** Greg Smith/Picture Group. **160:** Bob Daemmrich/The Image Works. **161:** Bob Daemmrich/The Image Works. **162:** Author's photo. **163:** © Andrew Brilliant/Carol Palmer. **166:** Spencer Grant/Stock, Boston. **178:** Robert V. Eckert, Jr./The Picture Cube. **194:** Nancy Durell McKenna from *Woman's Experience of Sex,* Sheila Kitzinger; published by Dorling Kindersley, UK/Photo Researchers. **195:** Nancy Durell McKenna from *Woman's Experience of Sex,* Sheila Kitzinger; published by Dorling Kindersley, UK/ Photo Researchers. **203:** © Tequila Minsky. **207:** Johnny Crawford/Gamma Liaison. **230:** © Mark

*Area* by Charles E. Horton, M.D. © J. B. Lippincott Company. **649:** Courtesy, David W. Foerster, M.D. and Charles L. Reynolds, M.D. **654:** Robert V. Eckert/Stock, Boston. **656:** Jeff Albertson/Stock, Boston. **658:** Timothy Healy/Design Conceptions. **662:** *Sculptor with Centaur and Women* by Pablo Picasso, Sotheby Parke Bernet/Art Resource, NY. **670:** Nancy Durrell McKenna/Photo Researchers. **671:** Nancy Durrell McKenna/Photo Researchers. **672:** Harry F. Harlow, University of Wisconsin Priate Laboratory. **676:** (left) Bruce Byers/FPG. **676:** (right) © Joel Gordon. **677:** Barbara Jaffe. **681:** Spencer Grant/The Picture Cube. **684:** Boston Globe photo by John Tlumacki. **688:** Susan Lapides/Design Conceptions.

## Color Inserts

*Beauty and Sexuality*

**Page 1:**  (top) Photographed by V. Lefteroff/The Bettmann Archive; (bottom) Nimatallah/Art Resource, NY.

**Page 2:**  (top left) The Bettmann Archive; (top right) Scala/Art Resource, NY; (bottom left) Giraudon/Art Resource, NY; (bottom right) Tate Gallery, London/Art Resource, NY.

**Page 3:**  (top) Shooting Star International; (bottom left) Kobal Collection/SuperStock International, Inc.; (bottom right) Sygma Newsphotos.

**Page 4:**  (top left) Jim Olive/Click/Chicago; (top right) Alan Tannenbaum/Sygma; (bottom left) Eric Robert/Sygma; (bottom right) Kip Rano/Gamma-Liaison.

*Sex Sells*

**Page 1:**  (top) The Bettmann Archive; (bottom) The Bettmann Archive.

**Page 2:**  (top left) The Granger Collection; (top right) The Granger Collection; (bottom left) The Granger Collection; (bottom right) Art Resource, NY.

**Page 3:**  (top left) The Granger Collection; (top right) The Granger Collection; (bottom) Archiv fur Kunst und Geschichte.

**Page 4:**  (top) Craig Aurness/West Light; (bottom left) Courtesy Guess?Jeans; (bottom right) JOCKEY and JOCKEY Figure Design are trademarks of and used with permission of Jockey International, Inc.

# Index of Names

# Index of Subjects